OFFICIAL
FOOTBALL
YEARBOOK 2010-2011
OF THE ENGLISH AND SCOTTISH LEAGUES

Forewords by **Sir Bobby Charlton** and **Craig Levein**

IN PARTNERSHIP WITH

DESIGN AND PRODUCTION: Richard Mulligan, Simon Plunkett (Press Association Sport)
HEAD OF CONTENT: Peter Marshall
EDITOR: Andrew McDermott
HEAD OF PRODUCTION: Chris Wiltshire

CONTRIBUTORS: Alaric Beaumont-Baker, Duncan Bech, Mark Bowering, Roddy Brooks, Andrew Carless, Eleanor Crooks, Adrian Curtis, John Curtis, Chris Devine, Ronnie Esplin, Wayne Gardiner, Jamie Gardner, Ken Gaunt, Lisa Gray, Andy Hampson, Ross Heppenstall, Paul Hirst, Gareth Jones, Frank Malley, Carl Markham, Lynne Maxwell, Gavin McCafferty, Robert Meaden, Phil Medlicott, Maurice Parker, Simon Peach, Dominic Picksley, Tom Rostance, Ben Rumsby, Andy Sims, Damian Spellman, Simon Stone, Mark Tattersall, Sean Taylor, Pete Thompson, Jon Veal, Joseph Verney, Mark Walker, Stuart Walker, Nigel Whiteley, Jim Van Wijk, Drew Williams. (Press Association Sport)

Cover and inside photography © Press Association Photos

First published 2010 by
A&C Black Publishers Ltd
36 Soho Square, London W1D 3QY
www.acblack.com

Copyright © Press Association Sport 2010

ISBN 978-1-408-12915-9

A CIP catalogue record for this book is available from the British Library.

Designed and typeset in Expert Sans by Press Association Sport, Bridgegate, Howden,
East Yorkshire, DN14 7AE
Printed and Bound in the UK by Martins the Printers

This book is produced using paper that is made from wood grown in managed, sustainable forests. It is natural, renewable and recyclable. The logging and manufacturing processes conform to the environmental regulations of the country of origin.

**PRESS
ASSOCIATION**
Sport
www.pa-sport.com

CONTENTS

SIR BOBBY CHARLTON

I T WILL take something pretty special to top the 2009/10 campaign for excitement and drama at all levels of English football. It has been one of those extraordinary, magical seasons. From the title race in the Barclays Premier League to the battle to retain Football League status, there have been so many twists and turns along the way. I'm sure the public and the media must have loved it.

The old adage that a domestic campaign is a marathon not a sprint certainly proved to be the case in the Barclays Premier League. To win the title you need patience, to steer clear of injuries and suspensions and definitely some luck along the way. My club, Manchester United, were found wanting a little bit at the end so credit must go to Chelsea, who showed themselves to be a very capable outfit and deserved champions. To secure a Barclays Premier League and FA Cup double in Carlo Ancelotti's first season in England speaks volumes of his quality as a manager.

Harry Redknapp and Roy Hodgson are two other managers who deserve plenty of praise. Exciting times lie ahead for Tottenham, and clinching UEFA Champions League football for the first time is a marvellous achievement by Harry. I think Spurs will acquit themselves well in Europe.

Unfortunately, it was not to be for Fulham in the Europa League final, but obviously they have got a really marvellous manager in Roy and they will be a threat again in the coming season, along with the likes of Everton and Aston Villa.

I have no doubt that Manchester City will also be in the hunt for a top-four finish in 2010/11, having narrowly missed out to Spurs this year. Liverpool, with their reputation and stature in the game, should also be back challenging for honours.

It is pleasing to see a big, well-supported club like Newcastle return to the top flight so quickly, after they clinched the Coca-Cola Championship title, and it adds great colour to the Barclays Premier League to have Blackpool in there as well for the first time following their play-off heroics.

Leeds will have grand designs on securing back-to-back promotions following their elevation from Coca-Cola League 1, along with champions Norwich, and with a fair

'The old adage that a domestic campaign is a marathon not a sprint certainly proved to be the case in the Barclays Premier League'

wind and a couple of decent signings the Yorkshire side could do exactly that. The manner in which Leeds beat Manchester United in the FA Cup particularly impressed me. We will just have to wait and see what the future holds for them.

If the new Notts County owners put a few pounds into the kitty at Meadow Lane following their success in winning Coca-Cola League 2, then there is no reason why they should not progress further and perhaps even go as high as the Barclays Premier League. It is really not that long ago since

the Magpies were in the old First Division. Rochdale and Bournemouth will join them in the third tier next season. My uncle Stan used to play for Rochdale, so I always look out for the club's results, and to be promoted for the first time since 1969 is something to be cherished.

Sir Bobby Charlton
1966 World Cup winner

CRAIG LEVEIN

IT HAS been another exciting season in Scotland.

There was a great finale to the Clydesdale Bank Premier League campaign, and it is testament to the fantastic job done by Walter Smith that Rangers retained the title with several games to spare. The biggest compliment I can pay Walter, who was unable to buy any players, is that no other manager would have been able to deal with the off-the-field problems he has had. I know the difficulties of being a club manager and trying to keep moving forward; the slightest thing can upset the rhythm of the team. To keep focused while he and Ally McCoist were working without contracts is an achievement that deserves enormous credit.

Celtic had a great finish to the season, but there was a spell when Hibernian were in a fairly good position in the SPL and Dundee United were getting reasonably close to the Old Firm. However, it is very difficult to maintain that consistency. It is difficult to challenge on a regular basis as teams tend to lose their best players following a successful year. But if my old club, Dundee United, can keep their team together then I feel they can improve, even after winning the Active Nation Scottish Cup, as they have a lot of good, young players.

I was disappointed to see Falkirk relegated. I'm a big admirer of Steven Pressley and he is the right man to get the club straight back up, just like Inverness have done.

Dundee spent a lot in the Irn-Bru First Division, but events in that League proved that it is not all about money. It is about building a team and trusting your manager to get over the line. All credit to Terry Butcher and Maurice Malpas at Inverness – they found their form at the right time and some of their football was great to watch.

My former Hearts teammate Allan Moore did a fantastic job in leading Stirling Albion to the Irn-Bru Second Division title. It's no coincidence that the guys who are getting success have been allowed time to mould things as they want them.

I was delighted that Livingston got promoted from the Irn-Bru Third Division having been demoted two divisions last year, because their problems were nothing to do with the people currently in charge. Gordon McDougall was the chairman at Cowdenbeath when I was there. He was a fantastic guy to work for, and all credit to manager Gary Bollan.

I love to see Scottish teams doing well in Europe. It was not long ago that we had three teams still in the European competitions beyond Christmas. A lot depends on how our teams cope early on against opponents who have played a couple of qualifying rounds or are in the middle of their season.

The national team have four European Championship qualifiers coming up early on in the new season and I have high hopes. I was encouraged by what I saw in our win against the Czech Republic, and also going to watch a lot of games in England – the Scottish players have invariably been the best on the park. We have a lot of players in the Barclays Premier League and that is a good gauge of how well Scottish football is doing.

'I know the difficulties of being a club manager and trying to keep moving forward; the slightest thing can upset the rhythm of the team'

Craig Levein
Scotland national team coach

FOOTBALL REMEMBERS SOME OF ITS TRUE GREATS

FOOTBALL united in 2009/10 to mourn the death of Sir Bobby Robson. Robson lost his courageous and lengthy battle against cancer in July when he passed away at his family home aged 76. A host of high-profile sporting figures were among the 1,000-strong congregation who gathered at Durham Cathedral to pay their respects to the former England, Ipswich, Newcastle and Barcelona manager, who spent his final years raising more than £1 million for charity in the fight against cancer.

During his astonishing 54 years in football, Robson guided Ipswich to FA Cup and UEFA Cup success, won domestic titles in both Portugal and Holland, claimed the European Cup Winners' Cup with Barcelona and took England to the quarter-finals and semi-finals of the 1986 and 1990 World Cup respectively.

Gary Lineker led the tributes, saying: 'Bobby was not just a brilliant leader of men that brought the absolute best out of his players, but he was without question the single most enthusiastic and passionate man in football. He made you feel good about yourself and good about the game. He loved the game and the game loved him. He was a lion of a man; no, make that three lions.'

Sir Alex Ferguson added: 'Friends have said to me you should never finish a eulogy with a cliché such as "we'll never see his like again" ... but we won't.'

On the announcement of Sir Bobby's death, both Ipswich's Portman Road and Newcastle's St James' Park were turned into shrines, with flowers, banners and messages showing what he meant to his former clubs.

A little more than a month after his death the two sides met at Portman Road in a Coca-Cola Championship game at which Newcastle and Ipswich fans joined together in a moving minute's applause. Lady Elsie Robson and 40 Ipswich stars led the tribute at half-time in a truly emotional ceremony.

Ipswich also chose the day to announce the naming of a stand in honour of their former manager.

This season started and ended in sombre fashion as 2009/10 also marked the 25th anniversary of the Bradford City fire, which claimed the lives of 56 football fans on 11th May 1985. Around 2,000 people stood in silence at a ceremony to remember the occasion and Bradford's Centenary Square was a mass of claret and amber scarves.

Some notable greats of the game also passed away this season. Burnley fans mourned the loss of a trio of club legends in Tommy Cummings, Adam Blacklaw and Billy Ingham. Blacklaw and Cummings, a former chairman of the Professional Footballers' Association, both formed part of the Burnley side crowned champions of England in 1959/60 and were beaten in the FA Cup final by Tottenham in 1962. The duo played a combined total of more than 850 games for the Clarets during the 1950s and 1960s, while Ingham – who was affectionately nicknamed the 'Ginger Pele' – made his debut for the club in 1972 before later joining Bradford. Cummings was 80, Blacklaw was 72 and Ingham was 57.

Fond farewell

Keith Alexander was 53 when he died suddenly in March, and his loss was felt at clubs throughout England. Alexander became the first full-time black manager in the Football League when he took charge at Lincoln in 1993.

He guided the Imps into the play-offs in four successive seasons during his second spell at Sincil Bank and also helped Macclesfield stave off the threat of relegation in 2008.

The three Merseyside clubs bade a fond farewell to Alan A'Court, Ray Lambert, Alex Parker and Percy Steele.

A'Court made over 350 appearances for Liverpool and scored the first competitive

CLOCKWISE FROM LEFT: Sir Bobby Robson; Terry Venables, Sir Alex Ferguson, Paul Gascoigne, Brendan Foster, Gary Lineker and Bryan Robson at the thanksgiving service; Lineker gives the eulogy; Sir Bobby's widow, Lady Elsie, views tributes at St James' Park

goal of Bill Shankly's tenure as manager. He also represented England at the 1958 World Cup. The former winger ended his playing days with Tranmere before embarking on a coaching career. He was 75 when he lost his battle with cancer in December.

Lambert, a former Anfield teammate of A'Court, also passed away this season, while Tranmere fans mourned Steele, who played over 300 games for the club.

Former Everton, Falkirk and Scotland defender Parker died in January aged 74 following a heart attack. Like A'Court, he featured at the World Cup in Sweden, and he also helped the Toffees to win the First Division title in 1962/63.

Albert Scanlon, one of the famous Busby Babes, died in December. Scanlon overcame the broken leg and fractured skull that he sustained in the Munich air disaster in 1958

to represent Manchester United, Newcastle, Lincoln and Mansfield.

Former Chelsea duo of Bobby Campbell and Petar Borota passed away in May and February respectively, while the death of Dumbarton captain Gordon Lennon at the age of 26 in June stunned Scottish football. Lennon had skippered the Sons to the Irn-Bru Third Division title in 2008/09.

Swansea were also left in a state of shock following the death of Austrian striker Besian Idrizaj aged just 22.

Ipswich stalwarts Bill Baxter and John Elsworthy passed away within four months of each other. They helped steer the club to both the Second Division title in 1960/61 and the First Division crown the following season. They both made more than 400 appearances for the Suffolk club.

Terry Bly died following a heart attack in September. Bly was part of the Norwich side that famously knocked Manchester United out of the FA Cup in 1958/59 before the Canaries lost to Luton in the semi-finals.

The game also lost another prolific former striker in Blackpool legend Ray Charnley, while ex-Sheffield Wednesday and Northampton defender Paul Shirtliff and Hibs stalwart Bobby Smith were among the other names mourned by the world of football.

FROM LEFT: Macclesfield manager Keith Alexander; goalkeeper Joe Hart with a wreath in memory of his Birmingham and England predecessor Gil Merrick; Liverpool and England winger Alan A'Court; a young fan lays flowers at the Valley Parade memorial

THE 2009/10 season will be remembered for shock results and the end of the monopoly of the 'big four' in the Barclays Premier League. For the first time since the 2004/05 campaign, one of the illustrious quartet dropped out and that was, surprisingly, my old club, Liverpool. Harry Redknapp's Tottenham took full advantage of Rafael Benitez's team's poor form as the 2008/09 runners-up lost a staggering 11 games.

Chelsea ended Manchester United's three-year reign as Barclays Premier League champions with the race going down to the final day of the campaign. An 8–0 drubbing of Wigan followed by a 1–0 win in the FA Cup final meant that Carlo Ancelotti not only won the 'double' in his first season, but his side did it in style.

The Italian saw his team become the first top division side to score more than 100 goals in a season since Spurs back in 1963. Main man Didier Drogba played his part as he recaptured his best form with 29 League goals winning him the Golden Boot. After the season the Stamford Bridge club had, they can certainly no longer be tagged as 'boring'.

As per usual there were a high number of managerial casualties with Mark Hughes, who left Manchester City, the biggest name among the list. Birmingham were arguably the surprise team of the season as Alex McLeish's men finished ninth in their first season back in the top flight.

In Europe, the Barclays Premier League teams failed to dominate as they have in recent seasons, with all four clubs knocked out before the semi-final stage of the UEFA Champions League. However, Roy Hodgson, voted Manager of the Year by his peers, took Fulham to the Europa League final. Roy's team could not complete the fairytale ending in the final but the veteran boss has transformed the club since taking over, turning the Cottagers from relegation candidates into a respected European side. He has done a simply sensational job.

Newcastle bounced straight back up from the Coca-Cola Championship at the first attempt, which is great news for the Barclays Premier League as the Magpies are far too big a club to be out of the top division.

Similarly, Leeds finally won promotion from Coca-Cola League 1 at the third time of asking. It certainly was a memorable season for Simon Grayson's team who produced the FA Cup shock of the season by beating Manchester United at Old Trafford.

Notts County were the main story of Coca-Cola League 2 as they were tipped to embark on a Real Madrid-style spending spree after the arrival of Sven-Goran Eriksson and Sol Campbell. However, despite failing to either splash the cash or keep that pair at the club, the Magpies still managed to win the title.

In Scotland, Rangers retained the Clydesdale Bank Premier League title as Celtic ended the season trophyless for the first time in seven years. A poor season for the Bhoys culminated in a shock 2–0 Scottish Cup semi-final defeat to Ross County, who then lost in the final to Dundee United. The team from Tannadice ended their centenary season by picking up the Scottish Cup for only the second time in their history.

The events of the 2009/10 season will never be forgotten ... roll on 2010/11!

Alan Hansen
Pundit with The New Football Pools

IT HAS BEEN another fantastic season for domestic football this year, with high drama stealing centre stage at both ends of the tables, and twists and turns on and off the pitch.

The season also proved to be an eventful one for The New Football Pools, from battling the big freeze in January to our biggest ever top-prize payout in March – it has certainly been an exciting few months!

January saw the Pools Panel's busiest Saturday for more than 25 years when England World Cup winners Gordon Banks and Roger Hunt and former Scotland international Tony Green deliberated over the outcome of 40 postponed games. Not since the early 1980s have so many games been postponed over one weekend.

2009/10 was a record season for us; our biggest ever top-prize payout of £4million was shared during one weekend in March. The 15 winners, including a Stoke City fan who scooped £1million, gathered at Goodison Park at our special celebratory event to receive their winning cheques from Roger Hunt and Alan Hansen.

It's also been a busy year for our support of football in the community. During the season we began funding a number of social inclusion programmes across health, employment, youth development and pan-disability football provision. The £5.9million donated by The New Football Pools across the Barclays Premier League and Coca-Cola Football League clubs, as well as clubs in Scotland, will have a positive impact on the lives and welfare of the fans of over 100 football clubs involved over the next two to three years.

In a World Cup year, we are also delighted to be supporting the Blind World Championships 2010. The tournament, held in August, will see 10 nations, including England, compete for automatic qualification for the 2012 Para-Olympics.

We look forward to the 2010/11 season, as we bring more exciting prediction games to fans across the UK who want to get in on the action, putting their skills to the test to win big cash prizes. Log onto www.footballpools.com to play and you could be our next big winner!

Ian Penrose – CEO, Sportech PLC
(owner of The New Football Pools)

CLOCKWISE FROM LEFT: Mark Halsey is welcomed back as he takes charge of his first game after overcoming cancer, Rotherham against Port Vale at the Don Valley Stadium in April; the events leave his wife Michelle emotional; Mike Riley enjoys himself during 2009/10

'It has been a great year, and referees have played their part in that. The challenge now is to keep things improving year on year'

FOOTBALL is an emotional game and it is a referee's lot that, in making decisions, you will not please everyone all of the time.

Matches are passionate and in the heat of battle you are always going to get strong emotions, but when you actually step away from the matchday environment and reflect on incidents of contention, you see a very healthy and respectful dialogue between the referees and the managers and players. You can question individual decisions but, on the whole, all competitions are thriving and I think referees are thriving along with them.

The 2009/10 Barclays Premier League title race went down to the last day and the final fixtures also decided issues of European placings, relegation and promotion right through the Leagues in England and Scotland, so it has been a great year, and referees have played their part in that. The challenge now is to keep things improving year on year.

Ahead of the 2010/11 campaign we have a number of meetings with the League Managers' Association, the Professional Footballers' Association and various other groups, including supporter associations, where we will sit down and reflect on the issues that we think have arisen from the season and look at how we might work together to combat them.

As well as that, we still have the 'Respect' campaign and the 'Get On With The Game' programme, which have both been very successful since their inception. One of the primary concerns was that, after the initial fanfare of the launches, things could revert to how they were before, but I think it is a credit to the players and to the managers that it has not been the case, and both campaigns continue to challenge the players to take more responsibility for their actions on the pitch – and they have responded.

Amy Fearn made history during 2009/10 in becoming the first female to take charge of a Coca-Cola Championship match when she took over from Tony Bates during the game between Coventry and Nottingham Forest in February. She was widely praised by the players afterwards for her handling of the game, but that was no surprise to us.

Equally significant has been Mark Halsey's return to the game after suffering from cancer. If you think where he was at Christmas, it is testament to his determination and motivation that he has put himself through hours and hours of training to make his way back to refereeing. And that is not only due to Mark himself, but the support that he has had from his family as well. The really nice thing from a refereeing point of view was the warmth of the reception awarded to him from the whole of football on his return. It was very special for him, but it also shows what a great community spirit and relationship there is between referees and the rest of the game.

Mike Riley
General manager, Professional Game Match Officials Board

BRITISH LEAGUES SITTING AT THE TOP OF THE WORLD

BRITISH football is renowned throughout the world as a melting pot of nationalities, sporting cultures and tactical ideals, and the country's key role in the global game has been evident at the 2010 FIFA World Cup finals in South Africa.

As well as cheering on England's heroes, football fans back in the UK also spent their summer following the progress of some of the familiar overseas players who ply their trade in the Barclays Premier League, the Clydesdale Bank Premier League or in the Football League.

At the last World Cup in Germany in 2006, more than 80 players from the Barclays Premier League represented the competing nations. In 2010, that figure is likely to have increased, as more than 300 players from over 65 countries were registered with English top-flight clubs at the start of the 2009/10 domestic campaign.

Internationals from all four corners of the globe who play their club football in Britain have long had their sights set on the event in South Africa. From the Barclays Premier League, England's homegrown stars will share the headlines with the likes of Fernando Torres (Liverpool and Spain), Carlos Tevez (Manchester City and Argentina), Nicolas Anelka (Chelsea and

The strength of the English and Scottish Leagues was proven at the 2010 World Cup

France) and Ji-Sung Park (Manchester United and South Korea).

In addition, Jay DeMerit (Watford and USA), Georgios Samaras (Celtic and Greece) and Marek Cech (West Brom and Slovakia) are among a large group of players highlighting the increasingly cosmopolitan make-up of our domestic game.

It is clear that British football has never been so attractive to players from all over the world, and it has also never been more popular among the fans. More than 200 countries now receive regular live broadcasts of British football matches, with the appetite for the game among overseas supporters continuing to grow year on year.

In 2008/09 the Barclays Premier League carried out its 'Fan Survey', which estimated that the global reach of the English top flight now extends to a staggering cumulative audience of 2.65 billion. Against such a backdrop it is not hard to see why clubs like Manchester United and Chelsea are among the best supported and most financially powerful in the world.

Sir Alex Ferguson has taken his side to Africa, Asia and the Americas numerous times for matches in recent years and in 2009 his side played pre-season preparation games in China, South Korea, Malaysia and Indonesia.

Wider audience

It is not merely in the Far East where the export of British football has proved so popular either. Last summer, Chelsea toured the USA and Arsenal hosted a pre-season tournament involving teams from Spain, France and Scotland.

Clever marketing has taken the national sport to a new and wider audience – Sheffield United, for example, have an innovative link-up with Chinese side Chengdu Blades as well as similar

FROM TOP: Manchester United's South Korean midfielder Ji-Sung Park; New Zealand ace Michael McGlinchey was on loan at Motherwell; Newcastle's Argentinian winger Jonas Gutierrez is challenged by West Brom's Chilean defender Gonzalo Jara

CLOCKWISE FROM ABOVE: Some of Chelsea's international stars John Terry (England), Didier Drogba (Ivory Coast), Ashley Cole (England) and Florent Malouda (France) celebrate a goal; Rangers' USA star DaMarcus Beasley

'British football has never been so attractive to players from all over the world, and it has also never been more popular among the fans'

arrangements with Australian A-League outfit Central Coast Mariners and Hungary's Ferencvaros, all of which have contributed to boosting the Blades' profile.

But all that is nothing without on-field entertainment, and in England and Scotland this year the action on the pitch has once again confirmed the real reason why our domestic game is so popular.

Chelsea's Barclays Premier League title success on the final day of the season was just one of a number of thrilling stories and memorable matches throughout the divisions both north and south of the border, as the Blues' Barclays Premier League and FA Cup double brought to a successful conclusion a superb debut campaign for their Italian manager Carlo Ancelotti.

While, undoubtedly, the Barclays Premier League appeals across the globe, it must be pointed out that huge crowds and television audiences are also pulled in by England's lower leagues and in Scotland.

The npower Championship is, according to recent statistics, the fourth most popular league in Europe, beating Italy's Serie A and Ligue 1 in France in terms of total attendance. Likewise in Scotland, where regular attendance figures at Celtic Park and Ibrox pit the Old Firm giants among the top 15 clubs in Europe, while Football League teams such as Newcastle, Derby, Sheffield United, Leeds and Norwich attracted larger audiences in 2009/10 than many of their top-flight counterparts in some of the major continental leagues.

Barclays Manager of the Month
Harry Redknapp (Tottenham)
Barclays Player of the Month
Jermain Defoe (Tottenham)
Top: Chelsea (12) **Bottom:** Portsmouth (0)
Top scorers: Defoe (Tottenham), Rooney (Man Utd).....4

Coca-Cola Manager of the Month
Chris Hughton (Newcastle)
Coca-Cola Player of the Month
Shola Ameobi (Newcastle)
Top: Newcastle (13) **Bottom:** Barnsley (1)
Top scorer: Chopra (Cardiff)..........................7

Coca-Cola Manager of the Month
Phil Parkinson (Charlton)
Coca-Cola Player of the Month
Lloyd Sam (Charlton)
Top: Charlton (15) **Bottom:** Southampton (-7)
Top scorer: Beckford (Leeds) 5

Coca-Cola Manager of the Month
John Still (Dagenham)
Coca-Cola Player of the Month
Ismail Yakubu (Barnet)
Top: Dagenham (12) **Bottom:** Darlington (1)
Top scorer: Benson (Dagenham) 5

Clydesdale Bank Manager of the Month
Tony Mowbray (Celtic)
Clydesdale Bank Player of the Month
Danny Cadamarteri (Dundee Utd)
Clydesdale Bank Young Player of the Month
Ross Forbes (Motherwell)
Top: Rangers (9) **Bottom:** Hamilton (0)
Top scorers: Boyd (Rangers), Cadamarteri (Dundee
Utd), McGinn (St Mirren)............................4

Irn-Bru Phenomenal Manager of the Month
First Division
Gordon Chisholm (Queen of the South)
Top: Raith (8) **Bottom:** Ayr (2)
Second Division
Allan Maitland (Alloa)
Top: Alloa (10) **Bottom:** Dumbarton (1)
Third Division
Dick Campbell (Forfar)
Top: Forfar (10) **Bottom:** Montrose (1)
Irn-Bru Phenomenal Player of the Month
Gary Harkins (Dundee)
Irn-Bru Phenomenal Young Player of the Month
Iain Vigurs (Ross County)

CHELSEA and Manchester United kicked off the campaign with the traditional curtain raiser at Wembley: the Charity Shield.

It was a first taste of English football for the Blues' new manager, Carlo Ancelotti, and it proved to be a successful debut as the Italian's side won a tense penalty shoot-out, with Salomon Kalou netting the decisive spot-kick for the 2009 FA Cup holders.

The action on the pitch was a welcome breather from a hectic summer that, in the absence of a major international tournament, was dominated by transfer activity.

Manchester City boss Mark Hughes led the way, taking the club's total outlay to in excess of £100million with the eventual signing of Joleon Lescott and deals for Gareth Barry, Carlos Tevez, Emmanuel Adebayor, Kolo Toure and Roque Santa Cruz. Everton used part of the £24million fee they received for Lescott to sign Sylvain Distin from Portsmouth, as well as Russian winger Diniyar Bilyaletdinov.

Pompey were the Barclays Premier League's biggest selling club as Peter Crouch, Niko Kranjcar and Jermain Defoe all left for Tottenham, Glen Johnson headed to Liverpool for £18million and Sol Campbell signed for Coca-Cola League Two side Notts County, who had already appointed Sven-Goran Eriksson as director of football.

Manchester United allowed Cristiano Ronaldo to leave for Real Madrid in a world-record £80million deal, offsetting that loss at a fraction of the cost with the arrivals of Antonio Valencia, Gabriel Obertan and Michael Owen – who opened his account in a 5–0 rout of Wigan later in the month.

Liverpool's main movement was in replacing Xabi Alonso – who also left for Real – with Italian midfielder Alberto Aquilani. Chelsea signed Yuri Zhirkov and Daniel Sturridge, while Aston Villa bought British

Massimo Donati scored for Celtic against Arsenal in the Champions League, but the Bhoys were eliminated

Kalou hands Chelsea the first trophy of the campaign as Hughes spends big at Eastlands

with Fabian Delph, Stewart Downing and Stephen Warnock joining Irish arrival Richard Dunne.

In the Coca-Cola Championship, recently-relegated Middlesbrough sold both Tuncay and Robert Huth to Stoke for a combined £9million and Ipswich made nine signings as Roy Keane oversaw a summer of transformation. Nottingham Forest manager Billy Davies also had a busy pre-season, spending a total of £5.2million on eight players.

In Scotland, newly-appointed Celtic boss Tony Mowbray started his reign favouring evolution over revolution as Marc-Antoine Fortune and Daniel Fox arrived, while Paul Hartley and Jan Vennegoor of Hesselink departed. Old Firm rivals Rangers allowed Barry Ferguson and Charlie Adam to head for England.

Memorable start
The new Barclays Premier League season kicked off at Stamford Bridge, where Ancelotti's men got the ball rolling with a last-gasp 2–1 win over Hull. The Blues ended the month with a perfect record, alongside Spurs and Manchester City.

Elsewhere, Arsenal thrashed Everton 6–1 at Goodison Park to provide the main talking point of the opening weekend, while reigning champions Manchester United followed up an unconvincing win over newly-promoted Birmingham with the shock result of the month as they lost 1–0 to new boys Burnley. It proved to be a memorable start for Owen Coyle's men as they also claimed the scalp of Everton.

By the end of the month in the Championship, only Cardiff separated the sides relegated from the Barclays Premier League in the top four places as Newcastle, West Brom and Middlesbrough each enjoyed solid starts.

The first managerial casualty of the season came in Coca-Cola League 1, as Norwich's Bryan Gunn was sacked shortly after the opening-day 7–1 defeat to local rivals Colchester. He

CLOCKWISE FROM ABOVE: Mark Hughes welcomes new signings Sylvinho and Joleon Lescott to Manchester City; Sven-Goran Eriksson receives a warm reception at Notts County; Michael Owen scores his first Manchester United goal at Wigan

was replaced by the man who masterminded that win, U's boss Paul Lambert.

Leeds looked in determined mood as they began another season in England's third tier with five straight wins, as did League 1 newcomers Charlton.

In Coca-Cola League 2, Eriksson's Notts County failed to follow up a 5–0 victory over Bradford as they suffered two defeats in their next four games. That left them trailing behind Dagenham & Redbridge, Rotherham and surprise package Bournemouth, who all

shared top spot with 12 points from the first possible 15.

The Old Firm duo enjoyed comfortable opening wins in the Clydesdale Bank Premier League, while Raith, Alloa and Forfar topped Irn-Bru Divisions One, Two and Three respectively.

Celtic and Arsenal went head to head for a place in the UEFA Champions League group stages in the final qualifying round and Arsène Wenger's side dominated the two-legged tie, winning 5–1 on aggregate. That result saw the Scottish side drop down

into UEFA's newest competition, the Europa League, alongside Fulham and Everton, although Villa failed to qualify after losing on away goals to Rapid Vienna. Hearts, Aberdeen, Motherwell and Falkirk had already suffered similar disappointments in the earlier qualifying rounds.

The Champions League draw was made towards the end of the month and Rangers were placed in a tough group alongside Sevilla and Stuttgart, although they avoided the English representatives, Manchester United, Chelsea, Liverpool and Arsenal.

SEPTEMBER

Barclays Manager of the Month
Sir Alex Ferguson (Manchester Utd)
Barclays Player of the Month
Fernando Torres (Liverpool)
Top: Manchester Utd (18) **Bottom:** Portsmouth (0)
Top scorer: Torres (Liverpool)..........................5

Coca-Cola Manager of the Month
Chris Hughton (Newcastle)
Player of the Month
Leon Best (Coventry)
Top: Newcastle (23) **Bottom:** Ipswich (5)
Top scorers: Fryatt (Leicester), Best (Coventry)...........5

Coca-Cola Manager of the Month
Paul Trollope (Bristol Rovers)
Player of the Month
Nicky Forster (Brighton)
Top: Leeds (26) **Bottom:** Southampton (-1)
Top scorer: Forster (Brighton)..........................5

Coca-Cola Manager of the Month
Keith Hill (Rochdale)
Player of the Month
Brett Pitman (Bournemouth)
Top: Bournemouth (24) **Bottom:** Darlington (2)
Top scorers: Pitman (Bournemouth), Hughes (Notts C) .5

Clydesdale Bank Manager of the Month
John Hughes (Hibernian)
Clydesdale Bank Player of the Month
Derek Riordan (Hibernian)
Clydesdale Bank Young Player of the Month
Craig Thomson (Hearts)
Top: Celtic (16) **Bottom:** St Johnstone (3)
Top scorers: Stokes, Riordan (Hibernian),
Santana (Hearts) 2

Irn-Bru Phenomenal Manager of the Month
First Division
Jocky Scott (Dundee)
Top: Queen of the South (14) **Bottom:** Airdrie (4)
Second Division
Allan Moore (Stirling)
Top: Stirling (16) **Bottom:** Clyde (4)
Third Division
Jim McInally (East Stirling)
Top: Berwick (16) **Bottom:** Montrose (2)
Irn-Bru Phenomenal Player of the Month
Derek Gaston (Albion)
Irn-Bru Phenomenal Young Player of the Month
Leigh Griffiths (Dundee)

SEPTEMBER began with transfer deadline day, but uncharacteristically that provided few shocks or surprises. Everton, fresh from the sale of Joleon Lescott in August, brought in Johnny Heitinga from Atletico Madrid while James Collins swapped West Ham for Aston Villa.

Arguably the biggest transfer story to emerge from the month was the two-year ban imposed by FIFA on Chelsea for their part in signing French prospect Gael Kakuta from Lens in 2007. The Stamford Bridge club were found guilty of inducing the youngster to break his contract as a 16-year-old, but their transfer ban was later lifted following an appeal to the Court of Arbitration for Sport.

On the pitch, domestic football temporarily took a back seat as qualifying for the 2010 World Cup finals occupied the home nations. England secured their passage to South Africa thanks to two goals apiece from Frank Lampard and Steven Gerrard and a strike from Wayne Rooney in a 5–1 victory over Croatia at Wembley. That made it eight wins from eight qualifying games for Fabio Capello's team.

Scotland missed out on a place after a 1–0 defeat to Holland at Hampden Park. Combined with Norway's 2–1 win at home to Macedonia, the result left them third in the final Group Nine standings.

Northern Ireland also suffered a setback with a 2–0 defeat at home to Slovakia, while Wales lost 3–1 to Russia to see their hopes of making the finals mathematically ended.

The action in the Barclays Premier League continued at a frenzied pace, and Manchester United began the month with a 3–1 win at Tottenham, despite having Paul Scholes sent off.

Carlo Ancelotti's positive start as Chelsea boss

Joy for Capello and England as they reach World Cup, but heartache for Scotland

continued, making the Blues the team to catch at the top of the table. They set the pace as a late Florent Malouda strike secured them a battling 2–1 win at Stoke.

In the Coca-Cola Championship, Ipswich remained winless under manager Roy Keane following three draws and two defeats in the month, while at the top, the relegated duo of Newcastle and West Brom made light of their struggles of the previous season as they continued to dominate in their new surroundings.

It was a similar story in Coca-Cola League 1, where Charlton pushed Leeds all the way for the top spot, although Bristol Rovers and Colchester kept up the pressure behind them. At the bottom, Tranmere continued to struggle, although John Barnes' side did end a run of seven League games without a win when they beat Wycombe 1–0 on September 29.

Managerial merry-go-round
In Coca-Cola League 2, Notts County were rocked by the sudden departure of Sol Campbell, who left having played just one game for the club. It was a busy period of change for managers as Lincoln replaced Peter Jackson with former Blackburn and Chelsea striker Chris Sutton, Mark Robins swapped Rotherham for Barnsley and was duly replaced at Millmoor by the returning Ronnie Moore, and Colin Todd and Stuart Gray were sacked from their positions at Darlington and Northampton respectively.

It was a barren month for Rangers fans as Walter Smith's side struggled to three goalless draws, handing the initiative in the Clydesdale Bank Premier League to Glasgow rivals Celtic. The Bhoys went four

Sol Campbell's Notts County career lasted just one match before he quit the club

CLOCKWISE FROM ABOVE: Ipswich fans pay tribute to Sir Bobby Robson following their former manager's death from cancer; Darren Fletcher looks dejected after Scotland failed to qualify for the World Cup finals; England celebrate after booking their trip to South Africa

points clear at the top of the table by the end of September with back-to-back wins over Hearts and St Mirren.

Outside of the SPL, East Stirlingshire continued their solid progress of recent seasons with three wins from four League games to move into third place in the Irn-Bru Third Division behind Livingston and Berwick. In Division One, it was a poor month for Dunfermline, who managed just one goal in three straight defeats.

Amid the frantic action on the pitch, the football world took a step back to pay tribute to a passing legend, Sir Bobby Robson. The former Ipswich, Barcelona, PSV Eindhoven, Newcastle and England manager had died at his home in County Durham in July at the age of 76 following a long fight against cancer. The great and the good of the game assembled for an emotional thanksgiving service held at Durham Cathedral on 21 September where Sir Alex Ferguson and Gary Lineker led the tributes. The Manchester United manager said: 'It's been one of the privileges of my life to have met him and been enthused by him. He

influenced me then and will always influence me.'

Former England international Lineker, who played under Robson as England made the semi-finals of the 1990 World Cup, said of his former manager: 'He was everything that was good about the game. He loved the game and the game loved him. He was a lion of a man. No, make that three lions. Sir Bobby Robson, we will miss you, but we will never, ever forget you.'

It was a sad end to the month as football remembered a true great.

Barclays Manager of the Month
Roy Hodgson (Fulham)
Barclays Player of the Month
Robin van Persie (Arsenal)
Top: Chelsea (27) Bottom: Portsmouth (7)
Top scorer: Van Persie (Arsenal).....................5

Coca-Cola Manager of the Month
David Jones (Cardiff)
Coca-Cola Player of the Month
Peter Whittingham (Cardiff)
Top: West Brom (28) Bottom: Ipswich (11)
Top scorer: Whittingham (Cardiff) 7

Coca-Cola Manager of the Month
Kenny Jackett (Millwall)
Coca-Cola Player of the Month
Grant Holt (Norwich)
Top: Leeds (36) Bottom: Wycombe (8)
Top scorers: Barnard (Southend), Holt (Norwich),
Lambert (Southampton) 5

Coca-Cola Manager of the Month
John Sheridan (Chesterfield)
Coca-Cola Player of the Month
Kasper Schmeichel (Notts County)
Top: Bournemouth (31) Bottom: Darlington (5)
Top scorer: Zola (Crewe) 5

Clydesdale Bank Manager of the Month
Jim Gannon (Motherwell)
Clydesdale Bank Player of the Month
Liam Miller (Hibernian)
Clydesdale Bank Young Player of the Month
Lukas Jutkiewicz (Motherwell)
Top: Celtic (23) Bottom: Falkirk (4)
Top scorer: Jutkiewicz (Motherwell) 3

Irn-Bru Phenomenal Manager of the Month
First Division
Dick Campbell (Partick)
Top: Queen of the South (23) Bottom: Ayr (7)
Second Division
Allan Maitland (Alloa)
Top: Stirling (24) Bottom: Arbroath (11)
Third Division
Gerry McCabe (Dumbarton)
Top: Livingston (22) Bottom: Montrose (3)
Irn-Bru Phenomenal Player of the Month
Paul Sheerin (St Johnstone)
Irn-Bru Phenomenal Young Player of the Month
Craig O'Reilly (East Fife)

LIVERPOOL'S indifferent start to the season extended into October as the Anfield club endured their worst run of defeats for 22 years. Goals from Nicolas Anelka and Florent Malouda saw the Reds suffer a 2–0 reverse against Chelsea at Stamford Bridge in one of four successive losses for Rafael Benitez's side in all competitions.

Controversy reigned during the following game when Darren Bent's shot beat goalkeeper Jose Reina via a deflection off a Liverpool-branded beach ball thrown from the crowd at the Stadium of Light, and Sunderland went on to claim a 1–0 victory.

A deserved 2–0 success over 10-man Manchester United eased the pressure on the Reds briefly before two defeats in the space of three days saw them knocked out of the Carling Cup by Arsenal and then finish with nine men in a 3–1 loss at an increasingly impressive Fulham, with the Reds' Philipp Degen and Jamie Carragher both sent off at Craven Cottage.

In addition to beating Liverpool, Chelsea scored 17 goals without reply over the course of four games against Atletico Madrid, Blackburn and Bolton (twice) in all competitions having bounced back from a 2–1 defeat at Aston Villa.

The return of England midfielder Joe Cole following 10 months out with a knee ligament injury also provided a timely lift for the Blues, who were boosted further when Barclays Premier League title rivals Manchester United were held to a 2–2 draw by Sunderland at Old Trafford.

There was heartache for the Black Cats in the Carling Cup, though, as Aston Villa goalkeeper Brad Guzan saved three spot-kicks in a thrilling penalty shoot-out at the Stadium of Light after their fourth-round tie had ended goalless.

Thanks to Guzan's match-winning heroics, Villa joined the likes of Manchester United, Blackburn, Portsmouth and Tottenham in the

Jimmy Bullard was back in a Hull shirt after returning from a long-term knee injury

Liverpool continue to struggle, while Hearts snatch a shock CIS Cup win at Celtic Park

quarter-finals, while Chelsea and Manchester City brushed aside Bolton and Scunthorpe respectively.

The first Old Firm derby of the season proved eventful in Scotland – Kenny Miller scoring twice in the opening 16 minutes for hosts Rangers before Celtic winger Aiden McGeady pulled a goal back from the penalty spot.

But disappointment followed for the Gers in the form of a second successive 4–1 home defeat in the UEFA Champions League – this time against Romanian side Unirea Urziceni – while Celtic fared little better in the UEFA Europa League before being knocked out of the Co-operative Insurance Cup by Hearts. Michael Stewart held his nerve to score the only goal against the holders at Celtic Park.

There was also something of a shock result at McDiarmid Park as St Johnstone beat Dundee United 2–1, while there were wins for St Mirren and Rangers over Motherwell and Dundee respectively. The Well, though, did manage to go through October unbeaten in the Clydesdale Bank Premier League.

Dundee had a month to savour in the Irn-Bru First Division with three wins and two draws, while Cowdenbeath's 5–0 victory over Peterhead kept up their charge in the Second Division.

Livingston proved to be the team to watch in the fourth tier of Scottish football as they embarked on a 10-game unbeaten streak in all competitions that lasted until mid-December.

Message of intent
October saw a number of managerial changes in the Coca-Cola Football League. Gareth Southgate was sacked by Middlesbrough, despite the club being just one point off the top of the Championship. He was replaced by Gordon Strachan.

Tranmere also parted company with John Barnes and his assistant Jason McAteer in League 1, while Ian McParland left Notts County four days before what would have been

CLOCKWISE FROM ABOVE: Jamie Carragher is sent off on a miserable day for Liverpool at Fulham; Cardiff's Peter Whittingham (left) celebrates one of seven League goals during October; Gareth Southgate gets his coat as he is sacked by Middlesbrough; Michael Stewart scores in Hearts' Co-operative Insurance Cup defeat of Celtic

WHAT THEY SAID

'Thank heavens Argentina don't watch him – he'd walk into their team. Whenever they ask for a video of him, I'll just send them ones of him making gaffes from about 10 years ago!'
Crystal Palace boss Neil Warnock is hopeful Argentina will continue to ignore the exploits of Julian Speroni

'Little things are going in my favour – hitting one off the top of a balloon and it goes in the corner – but I'll take it.'
Sunderland striker Darren Bent was not complaining about his freak winner against Liverpool

'I just said: "It wasn't me". The referee asked: "Who was it?" – and no one volunteered.'
Fulham defender Brede Hangeland on the refereeing mix-up that nearly saw him wrongly red-carded in the Europa League against Roma

'It was an emotional night for me. You think people have forgotten you so to come out there and hear them singing my name, it's just brilliant. This is my club.'
Joe Cole on his return against QPR in the Carling Cup after eight months out with an injury

his second anniversary in charge of the League 2 club. Newcastle, still riding high at the summit of the Championship table, named Chris Hughton as their permanent manager and also announced that the club had been taken off the market by owner Mike Ashley.

Leeds edged out fellow League 1 high-flyers Norwich 2–1 at Elland Road courtesy of Jermaine Beckford's last-gasp winning goal, and Rochdale sent out a clear message of intent to the rest of League 2 by beating Bournemouth 4–0 at Dean Court.

The Johnstone's Paint Trophy served up plenty of excitement as Southampton, Swindon, Chesterfield and Hereford beat Torquay, Exeter, Huddersfield and Aldershot respectively on penalties.

Elsewhere, Jimmy Bullard made his first appearance for Hull since suffering a serious knee injury on his debut in January, Avram Grant was appointed as the new director of football at Portsmouth and Hong Kong businessman Carson Yeung completed his takeover of Birmingham. The Football Association rejected Sheffield United

goalkeeper Paddy Kenny's appeal against a nine-month suspension for failing a drugs test and Fulham boss Roy Hodgson revealed he had turned down offers from both Sweden and Norway to become their national-team manager.

England completed their successful World Cup qualifying campaign with a 3–0 win over Belarus courtesy of goals from Peter Crouch (two) and Shaun Wright-Phillips, while the Republic of Ireland were left facing the prospect of a play-off against France to reach South Africa.

Barclays Manager of the Month
Carlo Ancelotti (Chelsea)
Barclays Player of the Month
Jimmy Bullard (Hull)
Top: Chelsea (36) **Bottom:** Portsmouth (7)
Top scorer: Defoe (Tottenham).........................5

Coca-Cola Manager of the Month
Chris Hughton (Newcastle)
Coca-Cola Player of the Month
Darren Ambrose (Crystal Palace)
Top: Newcastle (39) **Bottom:** Peterborough (12)
Top scorer: Henderson (Sheffield Utd) 5

Coca-Cola Manager of the Month
Lee Clark (Huddersfield)
Coca-Cola Player of the Month
Robbie Williams (Huddersfield)
Top: Leeds (42) **Bottom:** Tranmere (13)
Top scorers: Hughes, Lines (Bristol R), Hoolahan
(Norwich), Lallana (Southampton), Platt (Colchester)... 3

Coca-Cola Manager of the Month
Ronnie Moore (Rotherham)
Coca-Cola Player of the Month
Lawrence Wilson (Morecambe)
Top: Bournemouth (36) **Bottom:** Darlington (8)
Top scorers: Le Fondre (Rotherham), Morrell (Bury),
Pitman (Bournemouth).................................3

Clydesdale Bank Manager of the Month
Craig Levein (Dundee Utd)
Clydesdale Bank Player of the Month
Andy Webster (Dundee Utd)
Clydesdale Bank Young Player of the Month
Peter Pawlett (Aberdeen)
Top: Celtic (27) **Bottom:** Falkirk (8)
Top scorer: McDonald (Celtic) 4

Irn-Bru Phenomenal Manager of the Month
First Division
Jim McIntyre (Dunfermline)
Top: Queen of the South (27) **Bottom:** Airdrie (7)
Second Division
Danny Lennon (Cowdenbeath)
Top: Cowdenbeath (28) **Bottom:** Clyde (12)
Third Division
Gary Bollan (Livingston)
Top: Livingston (31) **Bottom:** Montrose (5)
Irn-Bru Phenomenal Player of the Month
Jonathan Hayes (Inverness)
Irn-Bru Phenomenal Young Player of the Month
Keaghan Jacobs (Livingston)

NOVEMBER was dominated by the Republic of Ireland's bid to reach the World Cup – both on the pitch and off it.

Giovanni Trapattoni's men were paired with France in the qualifying play-offs and faced an uphill task in the second leg after Nicolas Anelka had given Les Bleus a 1–0 lead to take back with them to Paris.

The tie was put in the balance when Robbie Keane levelled matters to set up extra-time, before Thierry Henry clearly handled the ball to set up William Gallas for France's controversial winner.

The Football Association of Ireland (FAI) lodged a formal complaint with FIFA and chief executive John Delaney demanded that the game be replayed, which Henry himself conceded would be 'the fairest solution'. That request was turned down, as was the plea for the Republic of Ireland to play in the World Cup as the 33rd nation in South Africa.

During the same international window, England lost their friendly against Brazil in Doha 1–0 and Scotland suffered a 3–0 loss in Wales, which prompted the sacking of manager George Burley.

In the UEFA Champions League, Manchester United, Chelsea and Arsenal all won their groups but Liverpool crashed out despite a 1–0 win away to Debrecen as Group E rivals Fiorentina beat Lyon by the same scoreline. Rangers lost 2–0 at home to Stuttgart to leave them without the consolation of a UEFA Europa League spot.

In that competition, Fulham took the lead at Roma but ended with nine men and a 2–1 defeat, while Celtic's goalless draw at Hamburg did little to boost their hopes of progressing and Everton were beaten 2–0 by Benfica.

As well as their success in Europe, the month also proved to be a good one domestically for Chelsea, who won all three of their Barclays Premier League games without conceding. John Terry grabbed the only goal to edge out Manchester United at Stamford Bridge and the 4–0 triumph over Wolves saw the Blues set a new club record of 12 straight home

Henry ends Ireland's World Cup dream, while Liverpool bow out of the Champions League

wins. A 3–0 success at Arsenal further boosted their title hopes.

Jermain Defoe became only the third player to score five times in a Premier League match as Tottenham beat Wigan 9–1 at White Hart Lane. His former club Portsmouth confirmed Avram Grant as their new manager but Wayne Rooney's hat-trick ensured the Israeli began his reign with a 4–1 defeat against Manchester United.

Newcastle continued to lead the way in the Coca-Cola Championship as they won all four of their matches during the month, while at the foot of the table Peterborough appointed former Kettering boss Mark Cooper as Darren Ferguson's successor.

In Coca-Cola League 1, former Chelsea midfielder Gus Poyet replaced Russell Slade as Brighton manager. On the pitch, free-scoring Huddersfield surged into the play-off places, helped by a 6–0 win over Wycombe, while Leeds remained clear at the top of the table. Rotherham and Morecambe enjoyed 100 per cent records over the course of the month in Coca-Cola League 2.

Biggest shock
The FA Cup got into full swing, with rounds one and two both taking place in November as the lower league clubs battled it out for a potentially lucrative third-round place.

The biggest shock of the first round was Charlton's 1–0 defeat at non-League side Northwich Victoria, while York, Staines, Luton, Bath City and Kettering also knocked out Football League opposition. Kettering were rewarded with a home tie against Leeds. Simon Grayson's men were on course for a defeat against the minnows in that fixture before they equalised to set up a replay at Elland Road. The return game saw Leeds pushed all the way to extra-time before a late

Gus Poyet took over as Brighton manager

CLOCKWISE FROM ABOVE: Dundee celebrate winning the ALBA Cup; Thierry Henry consoles Richard Dunne after the Frenchman's handball helped to end Ireland's hopes of making the World Cup; Tottenham's players enjoy another goal in the thrashing of Wigan

TOTTENHAM	9
WIGAN	1

flurry of goals ensured a flattering 5–1 scoreline. Staines also went into the hat for the third round having held Millwall to a 1–1 draw, but a 4–0 defeat in the rematch denied them a home clash with Derby.

An almost flawless month for Leeds saw them reach the Northern Area semi-finals of the Johnstone's Paint Trophy with a 3–1 win at home to Grimsby. Carlisle, Accrington and Bradford also progressed.

In the Southern section, Hereford and Norwich both held their nerve in penalty shoot-outs at the expense of Leyton Orient

and Swindon respectively. They were joined in the semi-finals by MK Dons and Southampton.

Dundee claimed the first silverware of the season in Scotland after coming from 2–0 down to beat Inverness Caledonian Thistle 3–2 in the final of the ALBA Challenge Cup at McDiarmid Park. Teenager Craig Forsyth, whose father Stewart was part of the last Dundee team to win the competition 19 years earlier, struck the winner.

It was also a good month for city rivals Dundee United in the Clydesdale Bank

Premier League, as their first victory over Celtic in 10 years helped them to claim seven points from three games and finish November just four points behind the leaders with a game in hand.

The cold weather affected the schedule in Scotland but Dunfermline won both their Irn-Bru First Division games, including a 2–1 victory at Raith in the Fife derby.

Cowdenbeath took over at the top of the Irn-Bru Second Division after beating Clyde, while Livingston continued to lead the way in the Irn-Bru Third Division.

Barclays Manager of the Month
Alex McLeish (Birmingham)
Barclays Player of the Month
Carlos Tevez (Manchester City)
Top: Chelsea (45) **Bottom:** Portsmouth (14)
Top scorer: Tevez (Manchester City)..............................7

Coca-Cola Manager of the Month
Billy Davies (Nottingham Forest)
Coca-Cola Player of the Month
Lee Camp (Nottingham Forest)
Top: Newcastle (51) **Bottom:** Peterborough (18)
Top scorers: Eastwood (Coventry), Sharp (Doncaster), Earnshaw (Nottingham Forest)..........................4

Coca-Cola Manager of the Month
Paul Lambert (Norwich)
Coca-Cola Player of the Month
Jermaine Beckford (Leeds)
Top: Leeds (56) **Bottom:** Stockport (14)
Top scorer: Morison (Millwall)..........................6

Coca-Cola Manager of the Month
Keith Hill (Rochdale)
Coca-Cola Player of the Month
Craig Dawson (Rochdale)
Top: Rochdale (51) **Bottom:** Darlington (8)
Top scorer: Hughes (Notts County)..........................6

Clydesdale Bank Manager of the Month
Walter Smith (Rangers)
Clydesdale Bank Player of the Month
Kris Boyd (Rangers)
Clydesdale Bank Young Player of the Month
Anthony Stokes (Hibernian)
Top: Rangers (43) **Bottom:** Falkirk (12)
Top scorer: Boyd (Rangers)..........................11

Irn-Bru Phenomenal Manager of the Month
First Division
Jocky Scott (Dundee)
Top: Dundee (40) **Bottom:** Airdrie (8)
Second Division
Allan Maitland (Alloa)
Top: Cowdenbeath (34) **Bottom:** Clyde (15)
Third Division
Jim McInally (East Stirling)
Top: Livingston (34) **Bottom:** Montrose (6)
Irn-Bru Phenomenal Player of the Month
Gary Harkins (Dundee)
Irn-Bru Phenomenal Young Player of the Month
Andrew Halliday (Livingston)

THE decade ended with a new man installed at the top of Scottish football, with Craig Levein installed as the new national coach. Levein called time on his three-year tenure at Dundee United to succeed George Burley.

The 45-year-old, who was capped 16 times by his country in the 1990s, admitted it was a 'dream come true' to be handed the job.

Peter Houston took over on a temporary basis at Tannadice, but was powerless to prevent United suffering a 7–1 defeat at Rangers in their final game of December.

The events at Manchester City and Bolton also provided plenty of talking points. The Eastlands club started the month by progressing to the Ca rling Cup semi-finals at the expense of Arsenal and beating Barclays Premier League leaders Chelsea 2–1. They finished it with a new manager.

Mark Hughes was sacked after 18 months in charge directly after the 4–3 win over Sunderland in the Barclays Premier League. A run of two wins from 11 Barclays Premier League games ultimately sealed the Welshman's fate and the club's owners immediately replaced him with former Inter Milan boss Roberto Mancini.

There was little seasonal cheer for Gary Megson as he was dismissed as Bolton manager following 26 months in the hotseat, while Fulham boss Roy Hodgson was rewarded with a 12-month rolling contract after guiding the Cottagers into the knockout stages of the UEFA Europa League with wins over CSKA Sofia and FC Basle.

Clydesdale Bank Premier League club Motherwell also parted company with Jim Gannon, paving the way for Craig Brown to make a return to Scottish football, and Jim Magilton left QPR by mutual consent.

Stewart Downing scored on his first start for Aston Villa as they beat Portsmouth 4–2 to join Manchester

Craig Levein is revealed as Scotland's new coach

Levein replaces Burley in Scotland hotseat, while both Hughes and Megson are sacked

City in the last four of the Carling Cup alongside Blackburn – who knocked out Chelsea 4–3 on penalties – and holders Manchester United.

Darron Gibson was the quarter-final hero for United, scoring twice against Tottenham at Old Trafford. Blackburn's win over Chelsea came 24 hours before boss Sam Allardyce declared himself 'fit and well' after undergoing heart surgery.

For Chelsea, their spot-kick setback at Ewood Park was one of a handful of disappointing results at the end of 2009. As well having lost on the road at City – when Frank Lampard had a penalty saved by Shay Given – the Blues dropped points at home for the first time in the season following a 3–3 draw with Everton.

Draws at West Ham and in-form Birmingham – who were unbeaten in December – followed to blow the title race wide open, but nearest rivals United were left to rue defeats against Fulham and Villa. Gabriel Agbonlahor headed the only goal of the game as Villa celebrated their first victory at Old Trafford since 1983.

Michael Owen's hat-trick against Wolfsburg in the UEFA Champions League at least gave the Red Devils something to savour, as did Ryan Giggs beating bookies' favourite Jenson Button to claim the BBC Sports Personality of the Year award.

Prolific start
Unlike United, Arsenal, Liverpool and Rangers all finished their Champions League group campaigns with defeats.

Kris Boyd continued his prolific start to the campaign and in the process eclipsed Henrik Larsson's all-time scoring record in the Clydesdale Bank Premier League.

Boyd's five-goal haul in Rangers' thrashing of

CLOCKWISE FROM ABOVE:
Mark Hughes was sacked by Manchester City; Gabriel Agbonlahor heads Aston Villa to victory at Old Trafford for the first time since 1983; Ryan Giggs was a worthy winner of the BBC Sports Personality Award

Dundee United took him to 160 in the Scottish top flight – two ahead of the Swede.

There were also goals aplenty in the Active Nation Scottish Cup as Livingston thrashed Clyde 7–1 in their third-round replay. Stenhousemuir also beat Cove Rangers 5–0, Raith Rovers triumphed 4–1 at Peterhead and Brechin ran out 4–2 victors over Wick Academy.

Leeds and Carlisle reached the Northern Area final of the Johnstone's Paint Trophy after getting the better of Accrington and Bradford respectively, with MK Dons and Southampton doing likewise in the Southern Area having seen off the challenge of Hereford and Norwich.

Four goals in 11 minutes late on at Elland Road extinguished Kettering's FA Cup dreams after the minnows forced extra-time against Leeds in their second-round replay before losing 5–1, while Luton and Barrow ousted Rotherham and Oxford respectively.

Ross County and Airdrie United shared an eight-goal thriller at Victoria Park as the home side triumphed 5–3 in the Irn-Bru First Division and Dundee ended the month undefeated, with midfielder Gary Harkins on target in four successive wins.

The cold snap decimated the fixture list lower down the leagues in Scotland, meaning only 12 games in the Irn-Bru Second Division could take place in December, with the same number of fixtures going ahead in the Irn-Bru Third Division.

Elsewhere, the World Cup draw pitted England in Group C along with the United States, Algeria and Slovenia, while injury problems forced former West Ham striker Dean Ashton to retire.

Barclays Manager of the Month
David Moyes (Everton)
Barclays Player of the Month
Wayne Rooney (Manchester Utd)
Top: Chelsea (54) **Bottom:** Portsmouth (15)
Top scorer: Rooney (Man Utd) 6

Coca-Cola Manager of the Month
Alan Irvine (Sheffield W)
Coca-Cola Player of the Month
Charlie Adam (Blackpool)
Top: Newcastle (56) **Bottom:** Peterborough (18)
Top scorer: Adam (Blackpool) 4

Coca-Cola Manager of the Month
Paul Lambert (Norwich)
Coca-Cola Player of the Month
Billy Paynter (Swindon)
Top: Norwich (63) **Bottom:** Stockport (16)
Top scorers: Martin (Norwich), Paynter (Swindon) 5

Coca-Cola Manager of the Month
Ian Sampson (Northampton)
Coca-Cola Player of the Month
Ryan Lowe (Bury)
Top: Rochdale (56) **Bottom:** Darlington (11)
Top scorers: Richards (Port V), Hibbert (Shrewsbury),
Harrad (Burton) O'Grady (Rochdale) 3

Clydesdale Bank Manager of the Month
Craig Brown (Motherwell)
Clydesdale Bank Player of the Month
Steven Davis (Rangers)
Clydesdale Bank Young Player of the Month
Fraser Fyvie (Aberdeen)
Top: Rangers (54) **Bottom:** Falkirk (14)
Top scorer: Daly (Dundee Utd) 5

Irn-Bru Phenomenal Manager of the Month
First Division
Derek Adams (Ross County)
Top: Dundee (44) **Bottom:** Airdrie Utd (11)
Second Division
Allan Maitland (Alloa)
Top: Cowdenbeath (35) **Bottom:** Clyde (15)
Third Division
Gardner Speirs (Queen's Park)
Top: Livingston (38) **Bottom:** Montrose (9)
Irn-Bru Phenomenal Player of the Month
Paul Lawson (Ross County)
Irn-Bru Phenomenal Young Player of the Month
Barry Douglas (Queen's Park)

THE ARRIVAL of 2010 brought with it age-old problems for football's administrators as the worst winter for 25 years caused havoc with the January fixture list. Matches at all levels were hit hard and the freezing conditions saw 52 games across England and Scotland postponed on the weekend of January 9–10 alone. However, when games were able to kick-off, some thrilling cup action more than made up for any delays.

January was a month of giantkillings as the FA Cup delivered a series of dramatic ties in which underdogs rose to the fore. Coca-Cola Championship side Reading started things off in the third round with an impressive 1–1 home draw against seven-time winners Liverpool to earn a replay, which they went on to win 2–1 after extra-time at Anfield 11 days later.

The biggest shock took place at Old Trafford, where Manchester United fell at the third-round stage for the first time under Sir Alex Ferguson. Leeds secured a memorable 1–0 win courtesy of Jermaine Beckford's strike.

In the next round, Arsenal were the third of the Barclays Premier League title contenders to see their ambitions in the Cup halted as they lost 3–1 to a determined Stoke side at the Britannia Stadium, while Burnley were beaten by Reading and Everton slipped up at home to Birmingham. Leeds again made headlines by holding Tottenham to a replay.

In Scotland it was a similar story as Rangers were held to a 3–3 draw against Hamilton in the fourth round of the Active Nation Scottish Cup, although Walter Smith's men triumphed 2–0 in the replay at Ibrox.

A two-legged semi-final in the Carling Cup meant Manchester City's new boss, Roberto Mancini, faced Manchester United

Sol Campbell made a shock return to Arsenal

Leeds stun Old Trafford with a shock FA Cup win, while it's all quiet on the transfer front

for the first time. The Italian gained the upper hand when the first leg finished 2–1 to his side thanks to two goals from ex-United striker Carlos Tevez. But when the teams met again at Old Trafford, United got the better of their near-neighbours as goals from Paul Scholes, Michael Carrick and Wayne Rooney sealed a 4–3 aggregate win.

Their reward was a day out at Wembley to face Aston Villa, who booked their passage to the final with a high-scoring success over fellow Barclays Premier League side Blackburn. The first clash at Ewood Park ended 1–0 to Martin O'Neill's men before the return leg burst into life, with Villa going through 7–4 on aggregate.

Despite their cup joy, it was a tough month overall for Villa as their hopes of finishing in the top four in the Barclays Premier League suffered a blow. They claimed just one League win in their three matches during the month, while Chelsea maintained their status as Barclays Premier League leaders with three wins from three, despite the absence of several key players at the African Cup of Nations in Angola.

Arsenal lost to Manchester United and, at the bottom, Sunderland's slump in form continued with a second successive month without a League win. Elsewhere, Bolton gained a victory for newly-appointed manager Owen Coyle against his former club Burnley.

While the flurry of managerial changes slowed a little in January, Paul Hart was sacked from his post at QPR after just 28 days and Darren Ferguson made a return to management at Preston.

Familiar faces
In the Clydesdale Bank Premier League, Jim Jefferies left his post at Kilmarnock by mutual consent, but he soon returned to the dugout when he was appointed at Hearts. Killie, meanwhile, turned to another experienced manager in Jimmy Calderwood.

The promotion race started to take shape in the Championship as Newcastle, Nottingham Forest and West Brom all continued to push

CLOCKWISE FROM ABOVE: Rangers' Steven Davis is named SPL player of the month; Paul Hart was sacked by QPR after less than a month; Jermaine Beckford fires the only goal of the game as the League 1 side shocks Manchester United in the FA Cup third round

for the two automatic places. In League 1, Norwich maintained their run of form with six wins to end the month three points clear at the top of table, while Northampton went five games unbeaten in League 2.

Rangers built up a 10-point lead in the SPL with victories over Hamilton, St Mirren and Falkirk, while lower down it was a good month for Alloa in the Irn-Bru Second Division and Queen's Park in the Irn-Bru Third Division.

It was a surprisingly quiet month in the transfer market as the speculated big spending of Chelsea, Arsenal, Birmingham and Manchester City failed to materialise, although the mid-season window did see the return of some familiar faces.

Sol Campbell rejoined Arsenal, just a few months after leaving League 2 side Notts County, and another Arsenal old boy, Patrick Vieira, arrived back in the Barclays Premier League at Manchester City. City also signed Adam Johnson from Middlesbrough for an undisclosed fee.

Birmingham spent a combined fee in the region of £6million to bring in Michel and Craig Gardner, although one of the most expensive transfers of the window was actually agreed for the summer as Manchester United struck a deal with Fulham to sign defender Chris Smalling for a fee believed to be around £7million at the end of the 2009/10 season.

In the Championship, Middlesbrough signed five players from Celtic as new Riverside boss Gordon Strachan turned to some familiar faces, while his replacement as Bhoys manager, Tony Mowbray, brought in five players of his own.

Barclays Manager of the Month
Roy Hodgson (Fulham)
Barclays Player of the Month
Mark Schwarzer (Fulham)
Top: Chelsea (61) **Bottom:** Portsmouth (19)
Top scorer: Drogba (Chelsea) 5

Coca-Cola Manager of the Month
Nigel Pearson (Leicester)
Coca-Cola Player of the Month
Paul Gallagher (Leicester)
Top: Newcastle (69) **Bottom:** Peterborough (24)
Top scorer: Carroll (Newcastle)........................ 5

Coca-Cola Manager of the Month
Lee Clark (Huddersfield)
Coca-Cola Player of the Month
Neil Harris (Millwall)
Top: Norwich (72) **Bottom:** Stockport (23)
Top scorers: Becchio (Leeds), Harris (Millwall),
Paynter (Swindon) 5

Coca-Cola Manager of the Month
John Sheridan (Chesterfield)
Coca-Cola Player of the Month
Wayne Brown (Bury)
Top: Rochdale (65) **Bottom:** Darlington (15)
Top scorer: Le Fondre (Rotherham) 5

Clydesdale Bank Manager of the Month
Craig Brown (Motherwell)
Clydesdale Bank Player of the Month
David Weir (Rangers)
Clydesdale Bank Young Player of the Month
Chris Maguire (Kilmarnock)
Top: Rangers (61) **Bottom:** Falkirk (20)
Top scorers: Craig (St Johnstone), Maguire (Kilmarnock),
MacLean (Aberdeen), Stokes (Hibs) 4

Irn-Bru Phenomenal Manager of the Month
First Division
John McGlynn (Raith)
Top: Dundee (47) **Bottom:** Airdrie (11)
Second Division
Jim Weir (Arbroath)
Top: Alloa (44) **Bottom:** Clyde (15)
Third Division
Dick Campbell (Forfar)
Top: Livingston (51) **Bottom:** Montrose (9)
Irn-Bru Phenomenal Player of the Month
Stuart Noble (Alloa)
Irn-Bru Phenomenal Young Player of the Month
Callum Booth (Arbroath)

MANCHESTER UNITED secured the first major piece of silverware of the season in England after coming from behind to beat Aston Villa at Wembley and retain the Carling Cup.

Villa had made a dream start as they took the lead in only the fifth minute when Nemanja Vidic brought down Gabriel Agbonlahor in the box, but escaped further punishment, and James Milner converted the penalty. United needed just seven minutes to level when Dimitar Berbatov set up Michael Owen, and the comeback was complete in the 74th minute when Wayne Rooney headed in Antonio Valencia's cross from the right to earn the club's third success in the competition in five years.

It was also a great month for Fulham as they continued to cope impressively with the demands of both European and domestic football. In the Barclays Premier League they were unbeaten in February as three home wins and two draws on their travels saw them climb to ninth, with goalkeeper Mark Schwarzer conceding just one goal in that time. Added to that, the Cottagers' 1–1 second-leg draw in Ukraine was enough to knock UEFA Cup holders Shakhtar Donetsk out of the UEFA Europa League and set up a mouth-watering tie with Juventus in the last 16.

Liverpool also progressed after overcoming Unirea 4–1 on aggregate, but their Merseyside rivals, Everton, were well beaten by Sporting Lisbon despite a 1–0 win against the Portuguese side in the first leg at Goodison Park.

In the UEFA Champions League, Chelsea lost 2–1 at Jose Mourinho's Inter Milan in the first leg of their last-16 tie and Arsenal went down by the same scoreline against Porto. Manchester United looked on course to progress, though, as Rooney's double helped earn a 3–2 win at AC Milan.

It was a month of mixed emotions for Portsmouth. Off the pitch they went into administration

Goalkeeper Mark Schwarzer was in great form with Fulham

Rooney and Owen star in cup final victory, while Fulham progress at home and abroad

and were left facing almost certain relegation, but a 4–1 victory at rivals Southampton secured local bragging rights and a place in the last eight of the FA Cup.

Earlier in the month, Leeds' run was finally ended with a 3–1 fourth-round replay defeat to Tottenham, with Harry Redknapp's men also needing a second meeting to get past fellow Premier League side Bolton in the fifth round.

Despite seeing Sven-Goran Eriksson quit his role as director of football during February, Notts County stunned Premier League opponents Wigan with a 2–0 win in their fourth-round replay. However, the Coca-Cola League 2 outfit could not reproduce their heroics in the last 16 as they lost 4–0 to Fulham. With the Magpies out, Reading became the only Football League side to progress to the quarter-finals as they won 3–2 at Coca-Cola Championship rivals West Bromwich Albion.

Failure to take advantage
Chelsea, who had their transfer embargo lifted by the Court of Arbitration for Sport, were one point clear at the top of the Barclays Premier League at the end of February. The Blues beat title rivals Arsenal 2–0 at Stamford Bridge, but could only manage a 1–1 draw at relegation-threatened Hull and suffered defeats to Everton and Manchester City.

Manchester United failed to take advantage as they also lost at Everton and drew with Aston Villa, while 10-man Liverpool beat Everton 1–0 in the 213th Merseyside derby.

Leicester got their promotion bid back on track in the Championship with an unbeaten run in February that included a win over Midlands rivals Nottingham Forest, but Newcastle and West Brom continued to occupy the automatic promotion places.

In Coca-Cola League 1, Leeds' unbeaten home record was ended by Walsall as Norwich moved five points clear at the top. The Elland Road club also suffered

CLOCKWISE FROM ABOVE: Manchester United's Patrice Evra lifts the Carling Cup trophy; Robbie Keane makes his Celtic debut at Kilmarnock; Paul Gallagher smashes home a goal in Leicester's win against Nottingham Forest; Chesterfield enjoy a victory over Bury

disappointment in the Johnstone's Paint Trophy after losing on penalties to Carlisle in the Northern Area final following a 3–2 win at Brunton Park. Southampton were the Southern Area winners after beating MK Dons 3–1 in the home leg to earn a 4–1 aggregate success and a trip to Wembley.

Chesterfield enjoyed a run of five straight wins during the month in League 2, while Bury beat leaders Rochdale to strengthen their bid for automatic promotion.

In Scotland, Celtic fans greeted Tottenham striker Robbie Keane at Parkhead after his loan move on deadline day. He made his debut less than 48 hours later, but could not prevent a 1–0 defeat to Kilmarnock in the Clydesdale Bank Premier League, while a 1–0 defeat in the Old Firm match at Ibrox left leaders Rangers 10 points clear with a game in hand.

Rangers also reached the final of the Co-operative Insurance Cup following a 2–0 victory over St Johnstone, with St Mirren edging out Hearts 1–0 in the other semi-final. Having set up a meeting at Hampden, Rangers also faced St Mirren in the Active Nation Scottish Cup and needed a replay before progressing 1–0. Ross County were the big winners in the fifth round with a 9–0 rout of Stirling Albion and Raith Rovers caused an upset, beating Aberdeen 1–0 in a replay at Pittodrie.

Dundee remained top of the Irn-Bru First Division and leaders Alloa achieved three wins and a draw in the Irn-Bru Second Division thanks to five goals from Stuart Noble. Forfar and Livingston enjoyed a good month in the Irn-Bru Third Division, with the latter ending the month on top of the table.

Barclays Manager of the Month
David Moyes (Everton)
Barclays Player of the Month
Florent Malouda (Chelsea)
Top: Man Utd (72) **Bottom:** Portsmouth (13)
Top scorer: Bent (Sunderland) 5

Coca-Cola Manager of the Month
Brian McDermott (Reading)
Coca-Cola Player of the Month
Gylfi Sigurdsson (Reading)
Top: Newcastle (83) **Bottom:** Peterborough (30)
Top scorers: Carroll, Lovenkrands (Newcastle) 4

Coca-Cola Manager of the Month
Kenny Jackett (Millwall)
Coca-Cola Player of the Month
Steve Morison (Millwall)
Top: Norwich (82) **Bottom:** Stockport (24)
Top scorer: Morison (Millwall)........................... 5

Coca-Cola Manager of the Month
Steve Cotterill (Notts County)
Coca-Cola Player of the Month
Neal Bishop (Notts County)
Top: Rochdale (78) **Bottom:** Darlington (19)
Top scorers: Donaldson (Crewe), Richards (Port Vale),
Somma (Lincoln)... 4

Clydesdale Bank Manager of the Month
Peter Houston (Dundee Utd)
Clydesdale Bank Player of the Month
Robbie Keane (Celtic)
Clydesdale Bank Young Player of the Month
Anthony Stokes (Hibernian)
Top: Rangers (70) **Bottom:** Falkirk (22)
Top scorer: Keane (Celtic) 3

Irn-Bru Phenomenal Manager of the Month
First Division
Terry Butcher (Inverness)
Top: Inverness (55) **Bottom:** Airdrie (19)
Second Division
Danny Lennon (Cowdenbeath)
Top: Alloa (56) **Bottom:** Clyde (21)
Third Division
Steven Tweed (Montrose)
Top: Livingston (64) **Bottom:** Elgin (22)
Irn-Bru Phenomenal Player of the Month
Adam Rooney (Inverness)
Irn-Bru Phenomenal Young Player of the Month
Michael Tidser (Morton)

SOUTHAMPTON'S 34-year wait for silverware came to an emphatic end in the final of the Johnstone's Paint Trophy. A crowd of more than 73,000 descended on Wembley as the Saints ran out 4–1 winners over Carlisle. Rickie Lambert, Adam Lallana, Papa Waigo and Michail Antonio were all on target for Alan Pardew's side inside the opening hour before Gary Madine headed a consolation goal for the Cumbrians.

Another team on the trophy trail were Rangers, who won the Co-operative Insurance Cup despite being reduced to nine men in the final against St Mirren at Hampden. Kevin Thomson and Danny Wilson were both shown red cards before Kenny Miller scored the only goal of the game late on when he rose to head home a Steven Naismith cross. That was enough to give Rangers a record 26th triumph in the competition. However, the Gers were quickly brought back down to earth three days later when they exited the Active Nation Scottish Cup. A last-gasp winner from Dundee United's David Robertson edged out Walter Smith's men in the quarter-final replay at Tannadice following a 3–3 draw in the first encounter.

Another late goal, this time from Scott Boyd, helped Ross County progress into the semi-finals of the Scottish Cup at the expense of Hibernian, while Raith Rovers beat Dundee 2–1 and Celtic were 3–0 winners at Kilmarnock thanks to a second-half hat-trick from Robbie Keane.

The Hoops ended March with a new manager. Tony Mowbray was sacked following the 4–0 loss at St Mirren and Neil Lennon replaced him on a temporary basis.

Hull placed Phil Brown on gardening leave in the aftermath of the 2–1 defeat against Arsenal that left the club in the bottom three of the Barclays Premier League with nine games remaining. Iain Dowie, the former Crystal Palace and QPR boss, took charge.

Meanwhile, QPR unveiled Neil Warnock as their new manager having agreed

Tim Cahill scored in the win at Manchester City during a good month for Everton

It's Cup final glory for Southampton and Rangers, while Dowie replaces Brown at Hull

a compensation package with Crystal Palace.

Greg Clarke was appointed Football League chairman while, over at the FA, Ian Watmore resigned from his role as chief executive.

José Mourinho returned to haunt Chelsea when Inter Milan claimed a 3–1 aggregate victory in their Champions League last-16 tie, while Arsenal and Manchester United were more ruthless in front of goal. Wayne Rooney scored four times for United in the 7–2 aggregate win over AC Milan and the England striker was also on target during his side's 2–1 first-leg defeat at Bayern Munich in the quarter-finals. Nicklas Bendtner netted a hat-trick as Arsenal beat Porto 6–2 on aggregate. The Gunners then battled back from two goals down to draw 2–2 against Barcelona in the first leg of their quarter-final.

Another remarkable European comeback saw Fulham beat Juventus 5–4 on aggregate to go through to the last eight of the Europa League. The Cottagers had trailed 4–1 on aggregate at one stage before a Zoltan Gera brace and further strikes from Clint Dempsey and Bobby Zamora put them through.

Maximum points
Everton were the form team in the Barclays Premier League as they went through the month unbeaten, and Wolves significantly boosted their survival hopes with wins at fellow strugglers West Ham and Burnley.

At the opposite end of the table, the title race intensified. Manchester United fell behind to an early Fernando Torres header before beating Liverpool 2–1 at Old Trafford, and Chelsea netted seven goals at home for the second time in the season as Frank Lampard's

CLOCKWISE FROM ABOVE: Alan Pardew lifts the Johnstone's Paint Trophy; José Mourinho is surrounded by photographers at Stamford Bridge; Millwall's prolific Steve Morison scores in the Lions' win against Leeds

four-goal haul paved the way for a 7–1 victory over Aston Villa. Arsenal kept in touch with the top two, having taken maximum points off Burnley, Hull and West Ham.

Manchester City finished the month in fifth place with a 3–0 win over 10-man Wigan as Carlos Tevez scored a hat-trick, while Portsmouth's nine-point deduction for entering administration was confirmed.

Reading's FA Cup run ended in the quarter-finals when Aston Villa battled from two goals down to triumph 4–2 at the Madejski Stadium thanks to a second-half

treble from John Carew. Holders Chelsea joined Villa in the final four along with Portsmouth and Tottenham. Not even an FA Cup exit could take the gloss off a productive month for Reading, whose revival in the Coca-Cola Championship under Brian McDermott continued with four wins and two draws.

Millwall's push for automatic promotion from Coca-Cola League 1 also gathered pace with successive victories over Carlisle, Charlton, Leeds and Stockport, while Steve Cotterill got off to a flying start in charge of

Notts County by collecting 17 points from a possible 21 in March.

Adam Rooney's five goals in seven games helped Inverness to establish a four-point lead at the summit of the Irn-Bru First Division. Cowdenbeath kept their promotion hopes alive in the Irn-Bru Second Division with a 6–2 success over East Fife that was followed by further triumphs against Arbroath and Clyde.

Montrose finally ended their wait for a first home win of the Irn-Bru Third Division season with a 4–0 victory over Forfar.

Barclays Manager of the Month
Martin O'Neill (Aston Villa)
Barclays Player of the Month
Gareth Bale (Tottenham)
Top: Chelsea (80) **Bottom:** Portsmouth (20)
Top scorers: Adebayor (Man City), Bent (Sunderland) 4

Coca-Cola Manager of the Month
Chris Hughton (Newcastle)
Coca-Cola Player of the Month
Kevin Nolan (Newcastle)
Top: Newcastle (99) **Bottom:** Peterborough (31)
Top scorer: Hooper (Scunthorpe) 7

Coca-Cola Manager of the Month
Lee Clark (Huddersfield)
Coca-Cola Player of the Month
Michael Nelson (Norwich)
Top: Norwich (92) **Bottom:** Stockport (25)
Top scorer: O'Donovan (Hartlepool)................................ 6

Coca-Cola Manager of the Month
Steve Cotterill (Notts County)
Coca-Cola Player of the Month
Neal Bishop (Notts County)
Top: Notts County (89) **Bottom:** Darlington (27)
Top scorer: Pitman (Bournemouth) 6

Clydesdale Bank Manager of the Month
Billy Reid (Hamilton)
Clydesdale Bank Player of the Month
Kenny Miller (Rangers)
Clydesdale Bank Young Player of the Month
Graham Carey (St Mirren)
Top: Rangers (83) **Bottom:** Falkirk (28)
Top scorers: Daly (Dundee Utd), Dorman (St Mirren), Keane (Celtic), Lafferty (Rangers), Sutton (Motherwell), Thomas (Hamilton) 3

Irn-Bru Phenomenal Manager of the Month
First Division
Kenny Black (Airdrie)
Top: Inverness (70) **Bottom:** Ayr (31)
Second Division
Allan Moore (Stirling)
Top: Stirling (64) **Bottom:** Clyde (28)
Third Division
Dick Campbell (Forfar)
Top: Livingston (78) **Bottom:** Montrose (24)
Irn-Bru Phenomenal Player of the Month
Jonathan Hayes (Inverness)
Irn-Bru Phenomenal Young Player of the Month
Connor Stevenson (Clyde)

RANGERS celebrated success in April as they wrapped up the Clydesdale Bank Premier League title with three games to spare. Walter Smith's side confirmed their second successive triumph as Kyle Lafferty's goal at Easter Road handed them a decisive 1–0 win over Hibernian.

It was a testing month for archrivals Celtic, who not only had to look on as their Old Firm counterparts won the title, but were also dumped out of the Active Nation Scottish Cup. Neil Lennon's side suffered a surprise 2–0 semi-final defeat at the hands of Irn-Bru First Division outfit Ross County. Derek Adams' men were rewarded with a date against SPL side Dundee United for the final at Hampden after the Tangerines beat Raith in the second semi-final.

Elsewhere in Scotland, Livingston sealed the Irn-Bru Third Division title at the first attempt to leapfrog Clyde, whose relegation from the Irn-Bru Second Division was confirmed, while former Rangers and England captain Terry Butcher led Inverness Caledonian Thistle to the First Division championship.

In England, the race for fourth place dominated much of the attention in the top flight. Teenage midfielder Danny Rose announced his arrival on the Barclays Premier League stage with a dream debut, as his stunning left-footed volley helped Tottenham to a derby win over Arsenal. That was part of a memorable week for Harry Redknapp's side, who also overcame Chelsea at White Hart Lane courtesy of a Jermain Defoe penalty and Gareth Bale's goal. The 2–1 defeat was a rare reverse for Carlo Ancelotti's men, who won their other three Barclays Premier League games in the month, including a 2–1 triumph at Manchester United that saw them overtake their title rivals at the top of the table.

Chelsea also beat Aston Villa in the FA Cup to set up a Wembley final against Portsmouth, who edged past Tottenham 2–0 after extra-time in the

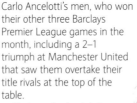

Danny Rose marked his Tottenham debut with a stunning goal against Arsenal

Rangers make sure of the SPL title, while Celtic are the subject of a major Cup shock

other semi-final. That was a rare moment of light relief for the Pompey faithful, as their side's relegation from the top flight was confirmed following West Ham's win over Sunderland. Burnley followed them in dropping down a division after a 4–0 defeat at home to Liverpool.

Manchester City stumbled a little as wins over Birmingham and Burnley were followed by a draw with Arsenal and a defeat to rivals United courtesy of an injury-time Paul Scholes goal.

In the Coca-Cola Championship, Roberto Di Matteo's West Brom booked an immediate return to the Barclays Premier League alongside Newcastle, who secured the title with a 2–0 win at Plymouth that simultaneously condemned Argyle to relegation.

Peterborough also went down, while the battle to avoid the final relegation place turned into a two-horse race between Crystal Palace and Sheffield Wednesday. Blackpool picked up four wins from five games to move into the top six at the expense of Swansea.

Mixed success
In Coca-Cola League 1, Norwich's run under Paul Lambert led to promotion, which was confirmed following a 1–0 win at Charlton. However, the race for second place continued to surprise and Leeds, Millwall and Charlton all suffered an indifferent run of results.

Geraint Williams left his post as Leyton Orient manager, but he was not the only boss to be shown the door in April as Ian Hendon and Paul Simpson also departed Barnet and Shrewsbury respectively in Coca-Cola League 2.

Darlington's fate was sealed as they dropped out of the Football League. Their 5–0 home

CLOCKWISE FROM ABOVE:
Kyle Lafferty's goal sealed a
second successive title for
Rangers; Didier Drogba fires in
a crucial winner for Chelsea at
Old Trafford; Norwich's win at
Charlton seals promotion

defeat to Notts County also saw the
Magpies clinch the title. Steve Cotterill's
men, who enjoyed a run of seven straight
wins in the League, went up alongside
Bournemouth and Rochdale, the latter
securing a first promotion in 41 years.

In Europe, England's five-year run of
providing at least one finalist in the UEFA
Champions League came to an end.
Arsenal's bid was halted in the quarter-finals
by Barcelona, while Manchester United fell
to an away-goals defeat against German
giants Bayern Munich.

It was a different story in the Europa
League, though, as Fulham and Liverpool
progressed to the semi-finals courtesy of
impressive wins over Wolfsburg and Benfica
respectively. Those victories set up a last-
four tie for Roy Hodgson's side against
another German outfit, Hamburg, while the
Reds were handed a meeting with Atlético
Madrid. Playing without the sidelined
Fernando Torres, and having had to travel by
land due to the airflight ban imposed due to
the Icelandic volcano ash, Rafael Benitez's
men suffered a 1–0 defeat in Spain and,

although they wiped out the deficit in the
return leg, a crucial extra-time goal at
Anfield sent Atlético through on the away-
goals rule.

Fulham did progress, but made life hard
for themselves once again. The Cottagers
held out for a goalless draw in Germany
before going a goal down at Craven Cottage
in the return leg. However, that sparked yet
another comeback, as goals from Simon
Davies and Zoltan Gera sealed a win and
ensured that Fulham's European adventure,
which began in July, lasted until May.

Winners Chelsea
Champions League qualifiers Chelsea, Manchester United, Arsenal, Tottenham
Europa League qualifiers Manchester City, Aston Villa, Liverpool
Relegated Burnley, Hull, Portsmouth

Winners Newcastle
Promoted West Brom, Blackpool
Play-offs: Nottingham Forest, Leicester, Cardiff, Blackpool
Relegated: Sheffield Wednesday, Plymouth, Peterborough

Winners Norwich
Promoted Leeds, Millwall
Play-offs: Millwall, Charlton, Swindon, Huddersfield
Relegated: Gillingham, Wycombe, Southend, Stockport

Winners Notts County
Promoted Bournemouth, Rochdale, Dagenham & Redbridge
Play-offs: Morecambe, Rotherham, Aldershot Town, Dagenham & Redbridge
Relegated: Grimsby, Darlington

Winners Rangers
Champions League qualifiers Rangers, Celtic
Europa League qualifiers Dundee United, Hibernian, Motherwell
Relegated: Falkirk

FIRST DIVISION
Winners Inverness
Relegated Airdrie (play-off), Ayr
SECOND DIVISION
Winners Stirling Albion
Promoted Cowdenbeath (play-off)
Play-offs Alloa, Brechin
Relegated Arbroath (play-off), Clyde
THIRD DIVISION
Winners Livingston
Promoted Forfar (play-off)
Play-offs East Stirling, Queen's Park

CHELSEA, Tottenham, Blackpool, Millwall, Dundee United and Dagenham were among those who etched their names into the history books as the 2009/10 season came to an eventful conclusion.

Carlo Ancelotti put the seal on a memorable first year in English football by guiding Chelsea to the club's first Barclays Premier League and FA Cup double.

An 8–0 final-day victory over Wigan proved to be enough to end Manchester United's domestic dominance and ensured that the Blues were crowned Barclays Premier League champions for the third time in the last six seasons.

Didier Drogba scored a second-half hat-trick against the Latics, and his 29-goal haul for the season saw him beat Wayne Rooney to the Golden Boot award. Drogba's treble also helped Chelsea to set a new Barclays Premier League goalscoring record in a single season with a return of 103 goals from 38 games. United ended their campaign with a 4–0 defeat of Stoke.

With the title back in the Stamford Bridge trophy cabinet, Ancelotti then inspired a 1–0 FA Cup final success over Portsmouth. Drogba's second-half free-kick separated the sides and maintained the Ivory Coast striker's impressive run of scoring in all six competitive games he has played at the new Wembley.

Missed penalties from Kevin-Prince Boateng and Frank Lampard added to the drama, while Chelsea were thwarted by the woodwork five times. Avram Grant resigned as Pompey manager five days after the FA Cup final following a six-month spell in charge of the club.

Elsewhere, Peter Crouch celebrated arguably the most important goal of his career in the 1–0 success at Manchester City during the penultimate game of the Barclays Premier League season to ensure Tottenham edged out the Eastlands side, Aston Villa and Liverpool in the race for fourth place and UEFA Champions League qualification.

Jon Nurse celebrates Dagenham's play-off final victory

Chelsea clinch the double, while Spurs win the race for the Champions League

Hull's relegation from the top flight was confirmed following a 2–2 draw with Wigan, while West Ham sacked manager Gianfranco Zola and Coventry parted company with Chris Coleman and placed Aidy Boothroyd in charge.

Fulham lost the Europa League final 2–1 in Hamburg when Diego Forlan netted an extra-time goal for Atlético Madrid. Simon Davies had cancelled out Forlan's opener, only for the Uruguay striker to net a 116th-minute winner for the Spanish side.

Fairytale victory
Brett Ormerod's goal ensured a fairytale victory for Blackpool in the Coca-Cola Championship play-off final. Cardiff had twice taken the lead at Wembley through Michael Chopra and Joe Ledley, only for Blackpool to hit back courtesy of Charlie Adam and Gary Taylor-Fletcher. Ormerod netted the winner on the stroke of half-time to send the Lancashire club up to the Barclays Premier League for the first time.

The Seasiders, who have been out of the top flight since 1971, had beaten Nottingham Forest 6–4 on aggregate to progress to the final, while Cardiff goalkeeper David Marshall saved twice in his side's play-off semi-final penalty shoot-out against Leicester.

The final day of the Football League campaign also provided plenty of drama. Leeds claimed automatic promotion from Coca-Cola League 1 the hard way having gone a goal down against Bristol Rovers and been reduced to 10 men before mounting a comeback. At the opposite end of the table, Gillingham suffered relegation after a 3–0 loss at Wycombe, while Grimsby dropped out of Coca-Cola League 2. Swindon and Millwall met for the League 1 play-off

CLOCKWISE FROM ABOVE: Dundee United manager Peter Houston, left, chairman Stephen Thompson, centre, and Andy Webster celebrate with the Scottish Cup; Gianfranco Zola was dismissed as West Ham boss; Chelsea are crowned Barclays Premier League champions; Blackpool's Brett Ormerod hoists aloft the Coca-Cola Championship play-off trophy at Wembley

final after they had despatched of Charlton and Huddersfield, and it was the Lions who triumphed at Wembley through a Paul Robinson goal.

Dagenham and Redbridge met Rotherham in the League 2 play-off final, where Ryan Taylor's brace for the Millers was cancelled out by strikes from Paul Benson, man of the match Danny Green and Jon Nurse as the Daggers secured promotion into England's third tier for the first time.

Celtic came out on top in the final Old Firm derby of the season, beating Rangers 2–1 at Celtic Park, and Kilmarnock retained their Clydesdale Bank Premier League status at the expense of Falkirk, who were relegated after the two sides had battled out a goalless draw on the final day.

Fir Park hosted a 12-goal thriller when Motherwell came from 6–2 down to draw 6–6 against Hibernian in the highest-scoring game ever played in the Clydesdale Bank Premier League.

However, Hibs had the last word when they beat Motherwell to fourth place to secure European football thanks to a 2–0 win over Dundee United. United enjoyed a memorable May and won the Active Nation Scottish Cup final by beating Ross County 3–0 at Hampden. Craig Conway's late brace dashed County's hopes as United won the competition for the first time since 1994.

Stirling clinched the Irn-Bru Second Division title on goal difference ahead of Alloa, who lost in the play-off semi-finals to eventual winners Cowdenbeath.

Dick Campbell led 10-man Forfar to promotion from the Irn-Bru Third Division with a 2–0 win over Arbroath in the play-offs.

CONTINUING OUR SUPPORT OF GOOD CAUSES

DURING the last 12 months, The New Football Pools has been funding a number of community-related schemes linked to clubs in the Barclays Premier League and The Football League.

The New Football Pools has donated some £5.9million over three years to support a series of community initiatives which will have a positive impact on the lives and welfare of the fans of more than 100 football clubs.

The Pools has contributed more than £1.1 billion to the arts, sporting and good causes since 1923, with almost £530million given to British football alone. Whilst in the past we have invested in infrastructure, ground safety, and bricks and mortar, currently we are heavily focused on community programmes and the many social aspects in and around football.

Nigel Clough was among those at the launch of the Every Player Counts scheme

PREMIER LEAGUE INTO WORK

As an Official Licensee of the Premier League, following our donation of £1.63million to fund the Premier League Health project last season, The New Football Pools has donated a further £206,400 to trial the new Premier League into Work scheme. Working with four Barclays Premier League clubs during the 2009/10 season – Chelsea, Everton, Portsmouth and Sunderland – the programme aims to use the power of football to assist unemployed people back into work, training or education.

EVERY PLAYER COUNTS

In August 2009, we joined forces with The Football League Trust to launch Every Player Counts, a scheme to improve the provision of disability football across the communities of 42 Football League clubs over the next three years.

The scheme officially launched at Derby County's Pride Park, with guests including outgoing Football League chairman Lord Mawhinney, Gerry Sutcliffe MP and Derby County manager Nigel Clough.

This unprecedented new partnership, that will increase disability football provision across England and Wales, received a donation of £2.59million from The New Football Pools.

Premier League into Work has been rolled out at four clubs, including Chelsea

Alan Hansen and Roger Hunt help celebrate our biggest-ever Pools payout

THE NEW FOOTBALL POOLS PLAYER OF THE SEASON

What a fantastic football season we have had this year, with some outstanding team and individual performances across all 92 English League clubs. The New Football Pools panel of football experts and pundits has once again analysed individual player performances across the leagues to produce its definitive 2009/10 'Player of the Season' in The Official Football Yearbook.

From assists to saves, and goals to the number of games played, the panel looked at all the criteria that depict a great performance, to cherry pick those players who made the biggest impact during the exhilarating 2009/10 campaign.

We would like to congratulate each and every winner of this terrific accolade. Read on to see whether your favourite player matches the verdict of our panel.

Pienaar (Everton)

Harte (Carlisle)

ALBION IN THE COMMUNITY

Albion in the Community is the charitable arm of Brighton & Hove Albion, one of the 42 clubs involved in the Every Player Counts scheme. In 2010 its work with disabled people in Sussex was judged the country's Best Community Project by the Football League.

The project uses football and sport as an incentive and motivator to do things that most of us take for granted, and makes a positive impact in the lives of people who want to be viewed in terms of their ability, rather than their disability.

One of its participants, Spencer Radley-Martin, is a shining example of how, through the power of football, a young man has achieved as a player, inspired as a volunteer coach, recognised his potential as a future employee, begun to fulfil his dreams as a person and made everyone who knows him so proud.

Spencer joined Brighton & Hove Albion's Seagulls Specials (one of the football clubs for disabled children and adults) as a child 11 years ago and since then has grown into the most remarkable young man.

Now involved in the Every Player Counts scheme, his commitment and dedication to football and the club are second to none.

Spencer is a very focused young man and works hard to fulfil his dreams. He has given hundreds of hours of his time to volunteer in the junior section of the club and is a

Spencer Radley-Martin has benefitted from Albion in the Community

fantastic role model for the younger players and is able to give something to the club that the coaches are not able to.

He is an inspiration and a true ambassador for the Every Player Counts programme.

It is for this reason that Spencer was the ideal winner of the Every Player Counts Player of the Year 2010.

RECORD BREAKERS

2009/10 was a record season for The New Football Pools; our biggest ever top prize payout of £4million was shared during one weekend in March.

One of the winners, John Proudlove, who is a lifelong Stoke City supporter, turned his 71p stake into a £1million win and met World Cup winner and Potters legend Gordon Banks to celebrate the huge payout.

John joined the 14 other winners from all corners of the UK, who shared the remaining £3million, at a special celebratory event. They were handed their winning cheques by 1966 World Cup winner Roger Hunt and Match of the Day pundit and former Liverpool captain Alan Hansen.

BARCLAYS PREMIER LEAGUE STATISTICS 2009/10

PLAYER OF THE SEASON
Wayne Rooney (Manchester United)

MANAGER OF THE SEASON
Harry Redknapp (Tottenham)

THE PLAYER WITH THE MOST...

GOALS Didier Drogba (Chelsea)	**29**
SHOTS ON TARGET Wayne Rooney (Man Utd)	**94**
SHOTS OFF TARGET Didier Drogba (Chelsea)	**71**
SHOTS WITHOUT SCORING Stiliyan Petrov (Aston Villa)	**34**
SHOTS PER GOAL Jordi Gomez (Wigan)	**40**
ASSISTS Frank Lampard (Chelsea)	**17**
OFFSIDES Darren Bent (Sunderland)	**56**
FOULS Kevin Davies (Bolton)	**103**
FREE-KICKS WON Steven Pienaar (Everton)	**91**
PENALTIES SCORED Frank Lampard (Chelsea)	**10**
GOALS SCORED DIRECT FROM FREE-KICKS Drogba (Chelsea), Larsson (Birmingham)	**3**
SAVES MADE Brian Jensen (Burnley)	**244**
DEFENSIVE CLEARANCES Roger Johnson (Birmingham)	**98**
DEFENSIVE BLOCKS James Collins (Aston Villa)	**44**

THE TEAM WITH THE MOST...

GOALS	Chelsea	103
SHOTS ON TARGET	Chelsea	397
SHOTS OFF TARGET	Chelsea	310
CORNERS	Man Utd	295
FOULS	Blackburn	528
WOODWORK STRIKES	Liverpool	16
OFFSIDES	Blackburn, Man City	119
PENALTIES CONCEDED	Burnley, Portsmouth, Tottenham	9
PENALTIES AWARDED	Chelsea	12
PENALTIES SCORED	Portsmouth	11
YELLOW CARDS	Sunderland	82
RED CARDS	Sunderland	9

TOTALS 2009/10

GOALS

Total	1053
Home	645
Away	408

CARDS

Yellow	1242
Average per game	3.27
Reds	68
Average per game	0.18

ATTENDANCES

Total	12,977,252

HAS the greatest prize in English football ever been won in such an emphatic manner?

On the final day of the 2009/10 Barclays Premier League season, Chelsea beat Wigan 8–0 at Stamford Bridge. That result brought the Blues' total number of League goals to 103, a new Premier League record, making them the first team to top the century-mark in the top flight since Tottenham scored 111 in 1962/63.

It also saw Chelsea record 86 points to beat Manchester United, for whom Wayne Rooney was at his sublime best in scoring 26 League goals, into second place by a single point. Most importantly, though, it saw Chelsea deliver their third Barclays Premier League title under the ownership of Roman Abramovich and prompted manager Carlo Ancelotti, after his first season in charge, to predict that the future is blue.

'We had a fantastic season, not only by winning the Premier League, but because we showed a good style on the pitch,' said Ancelotti, who was indebted to the goals of Didier Drogba more than anybody – with the Ivory Coast striker picking up the Golden Boot for his 29 in the Barclays Premier League.

'I hope to stay here a long time and win a lot of titles,' the Italian added.

If the final day carried a sense of the routine, then the previous 10 months could not have been more unpredictable.

Once-mighty Liverpool failed to qualify for the Champions League, languishing in seventh place with the club up for sale and manager Rafael Benitez departed by mutual consent at the end of the season.

Portsmouth were docked nine points for going into administration with debts in excess of £130million and they were subsequently relegated.

Burnley made a sparkling return to the big time with home wins over Manchester United and Everton to occupy 10th place in the table at the end of October, only to then fall like a stone when manager Owen Coyle opted to leave Turf Moor and take over at Bolton. The Clarets were joined in making their exit to the Coca-Cola Championship by Hull, another club who switched managers during the campaign, in their case by their own choosing, with Phil Brown sent on gardening leave to be replaced by Iain Dowie.

The struggle at the bottom was as frantic as usual with West Ham surviving by the slenderest of margins, while Wolves

While Chelsea stormed to the title, there was also excitement in the race for fourth and the battle to avoid the drop

found some grit in the latter half of the season and Wigan maintained their top-flight status with a spectacular 3–2 win over Arsenal at the DW Stadium, their three goals all coming in the last 11 minutes after they had gone 2–0 down.

In many ways, Wigan typified the competitiveness and unpredictable nature of the Barclays Premier League. They suffered the biggest defeat of the season, crashing 9–1 to Tottenham at White Hart Lane as well as their 8–0 drubbing at Stamford Bridge, but they also recorded home victories against Chelsea, Liverpool and Arsenal.

Sunderland had a campaign of consolidation under Steve Bruce marred by a winless run of 14 games over the New Year period, while Birmingham were the season's overachievers, finishing ninth under the meticulous leadership of Alex McLeish.

Fulham boss Roy Hodgson deserves a special mention for the way in which he successfully delivered a mid-table finish while juggling a run to the FA Cup quarter-finals and a place in the Europa League final.

Stirring win

The chase for fourth spot and that final Champions League qualifying place was arguably as interesting as the battle for the title itself. It saw Aston Villa fall short for yet another season while Manchester City, having spent the most under Sheikh Mansour, finished fifth after jettisoning manager Mark Hughes in mid-season and replacing him with Italian Roberto Mancini.

In the end, it was Tottenham who earned that place in the preliminary round of the UEFA Champions League with a stirring win against City at Eastlands. Their strength in depth, their attacking options, their desire to entertain and the inspirational touch of manager Harry Redknapp proved particularly impressive.

But they were just one of the many highlights in what was another memorable Barclays Premier League campaign.

FINAL BARCLAYS PREMIER LEAGUE TABLE

Pos	Team	P	HOME					AWAY					GD	Pts
			W	D	L	F	A	W	D	L	F	A		
1	Chelsea	38	17	1	1	68	14	10	4	5	35	18	71	86
2	Man Utd	38	16	1	2	52	12	11	3	5	34	16	58	85
3	Arsenal	38	15	2	2	48	15	8	4	7	35	26	42	75
4	Tottenham	38	14	2	3	40	12	7	5	7	27	29	26	70
5	Man City	38	12	4	3	41	14	6	9	4	32	25	28	67
6	Aston Villa	38	8	8	3	29	16	9	5	5	23	23	13	64
7	Liverpool	38	13	3	3	43	15	5	6	8	18	20	26	63
8	Everton	38	11	6	2	35	21	5	7	7	25	28	11	61
9	Birmingham	38	8	9	2	19	13	5	2	12	19	34	-9	50
10	Blackburn	38	10	6	3	28	18	3	5	11	13	37	-14	50
11	Stoke	38	7	6	6	24	21	4	8	7	10	27	-14	47
12	Fulham	38	11	3	5	27	15	1	7	11	12	31	-7	46
13	Sunderland	38	9	7	3	32	19	2	4	13	16	37	-8	44
14	Bolton	38	6	6	7	26	31	4	3	12	16	36	-25	39
15	Wolves	38	5	6	8	13	22	4	5	10	19	34	-24	38
16	Wigan	38	6	7	6	19	24	3	2	14	18	55	-42	36
17	West Ham	38	7	5	7	30	29	1	6	12	17	37	-19	35
18	Burnley	38	7	5	7	25	30	1	1	17	17	52	-40	30
19	Hull	38	6	6	7	22	29	0	6	13	12	46	-41	30
20	Portsmouth*	38	5	3	11	24	32	2	4	13	10	34	-32	19

*9 points deducted

Tom Huddlestone and Gareth Bale rejoice as Tottenham qualify for the UEFA Champions League

Chelsea celebrate winning the Barclays Premier League after pipping Manchester United to the title

BARCLAYS PREMIER LEAGUE

BARCLAYS PREMIER LEAGUE RESULTS

HOME \ AWAY	ARSENAL	ASTON VILLA	BIRMINGHAM	BLACKBURN	BOLTON	BURNLEY	CHELSEA	EVERTON	FULHAM	HULL	LIVERPOOL	MAN CITY	MAN UTD	PORTSMOUTH	STOKE	SUNDERLAND	TOTTENHAM	WEST HAM	WIGAN	WOLVES
ARSENAL	–	3-0	3-1	6-2	4-2	3-1	0-3	2-2	4-0	3-0	1-0	0-0	1-3	4-1	2-0	2-0	3-0	2-0	4-0	1-0
ASTON VILLA	0-0	–	1-0	0-1	5-1	5-2	2-1	2-2	2-0	3-0	0-1	1-1	1-1	2-0	1-0	1-1	1-1	0-0	0-2	2-2
BIRMINGHAM	1-1	0-1	–	2-1	1-2	2-1	0-0	2-2	1-0	0-0	1-1	0-0	1-1	1-0	0-0	2-1	1-1	1-0	1-0	2-1
BLACKBURN	2-1	2-1	2-1	–	3-0	3-2	1-1	2-3	2-0	1-0	0-0	0-2	0-0	3-1	0-0	2-2	0-2	0-0	2-1	3-1
BOLTON	0-2	0-1	2-1	0-2	–	1-0	0-4	3-2	0-0	2-2	2-3	3-3	0-4	2-2	1-1	0-1	2-2	3-1	4-0	1-0
BURNLEY	1-1	1-1	2-1	0-1	1-1	–	1-2	1-0	1-1	2-0	0-4	1-6	1-0	1-2	1-1	3-1	4-2	2-1	1-3	1-2
CHELSEA	2-0	7-1	3-0	5-0	1-0	3-0	–	3-3	2-1	2-1	2-0	2-4	1-0	2-1	7-0	7-2	3-0	4-1	8-0	4-0
EVERTON	1-6	1-1	1-1	3-0	2-0	2-0	2-1	–	2-1	5-1	0-2	2-0	3-1	1-0	1-1	2-0	2-2	2-2	2-1	1-1
FULHAM	0-1	0-2	2-1	3-0	1-1	3-0	0-2	2-1	–	2-0	3-1	1-2	3-0	1-0	0-1	1-0	0-0	3-2	2-1	0-0
HULL	1-2	0-2	0-1	0-0	1-0	1-4	1-1	3-2	2-0	–	0-0	2-1	1-3	0-0	2-1	0-1	1-5	3-3	2-1	2-2
LIVERPOOL	1-2	1-3	2-2	2-1	2-0	4-0	0-2	1-0	0-0	6-1	–	2-2	2-0	4-1	4-0	3-0	2-0	3-0	2-1	2-0
MAN CITY	4-2	3-1	5-1	4-1	2-0	3-3	2-1	0-2	2-2	1-1	0-0	–	0-1	2-0	2-0	4-3	0-1	3-1	3-0	1-0
MAN UTD	2-1	0-1	1-0	2-0	2-1	3-0	1-0	3-0	3-0	4-0	2-1	4-3	–	5-0	4-0	2-2	3-1	3-0	5-0	3-0
PORTSMOUTH	1-4	1-2	1-2	0-0	2-3	2-0	0-5	0-1	0-1	3-2	2-0	0-1	1-4	–	1-2	1-1	1-2	1-1	1-1	3-1
STOKE	1-3	0-0	0-1	3-0	1-2	2-0	1-2	0-0	3-2	2-0	1-1	1-1	0-2	1-0	–	1-0	1-2	2-1	2-2	2-2
SUNDERLAND	1-0	0-2	3-1	2-1	4-0	2-1	1-3	1-1	0-0	4-1	1-0	1-1	0-1	1-1	0-0	–	3-1	2-2	1-1	5-2
TOTTENHAM	2-1	0-0	2-1	3-1	1-0	5-0	2-1	2-1	2-0	0-0	2-1	3-0	1-3	2-0	0-1	2-0	–	2-0	9-1	0-1
WEST HAM	2-2	2-1	2-0	0-0	1-2	5-3	1-1	1-2	2-2	3-0	2-3	1-1	0-4	2-0	0-1	1-0	1-2	–	3-2	1-3
WIGAN	3-2	1-2	2-3	1-1	0-0	1-0	3-1	0-1	1-1	2-2	1-0	1-1	0-5	0-0	1-1	1-0	0-3	1-0	–	0-1
WOLVES	1-4	1-1	0-1	1-1	2-1	2-0	0-2	0-0	2-1	1-1	0-0	0-3	0-1	0-1	0-0	2-1	1-0	0-2	0-2	–

Didier Drogba (Chelsea)

TEAM DISCIPLINE

TEAM	Y	R
Sunderland	82	9
Bolton	75	5
Portsmouth	71	5
Hull	67	6
Stoke	66	5
Birmingham	75	1
Wolves	65	4
West Ham	65	3
Wigan	64	3
Chelsea	57	5
Liverpool	56	5
Aston Villa	60	2
Blackburn	59	2
Man Utd	52	4
Everton	58	2
Burnley	57	2
Tottenham	58	1
Arsenal	56	1
Man City	52	2
Fulham	46	1

Petr Cech (Chelsea)

LEADING SCORERS

PLAYER	TEAM	GLS
Didier Drogba	Chelsea	29
Wayne Rooney	Man Utd	26
Darren Bent	Sunderland	24
Carlos Tevez	Man City	23
Frank Lampard	Chelsea	22
Fernando Torres	Liverpool	18
Jermain Defoe	Tottenham	18
Cesc Fabregas	Arsenal	15
Emmanuel Adebayor	Man City	14
Gabriel Agbonlahor	Aston Villa	13

LEADING GOALKEEPERS

PLAYER	TEAM	CLEAN SHEET
Petr Cech	Chelsea	17
Jose Reina	Liverpool	17
Brad Friedel	Aston Villa	15
Mark Schwarzer	Fulham	12
Edwin Van der Sar	Man Utd	12
Paul Robinson	Blackburn	12
Heurelho Gomes	Tottenham	12
Thomas Sorensen	Stoke	11
Tim Howard	Everton	11
Manuel Almunia	Arsenal	10

BARCLAYS PREMIER LEAGUE TABLES

HOME TABLE

	P	W	D	L	F	A	GD	PTS
Chelsea	19	17	1	1	68	14	54	52
Man Utd	19	16	1	2	52	12	40	49
Arsenal	19	15	2	2	48	15	33	47
Tottenham	19	14	2	3	40	12	28	44
Liverpool	19	13	3	3	43	15	28	42
Man City	19	12	4	3	41	20	21	40
Everton	19	11	6	2	35	21	14	39
Fulham	19	11	3	5	27	15	12	36
Blackburn	19	10	6	3	28	18	10	36
Sunderland	19	9	7	3	32	19	13	34
Birmingham	19	8	9	2	19	13	6	33
Aston Villa	19	8	8	3	29	16	13	32
Stoke	19	7	6	6	24	21	3	27
West Ham	19	7	5	7	30	29	1	26
Burnley	19	7	5	7	25	30	-5	26
Wigan	19	6	7	6	19	24	-5	25
Bolton	19	6	6	7	26	31	-5	24
Hull	19	6	6	7	22	29	-7	24
Wolves	19	5	6	8	13	22	-9	21
Portsmouth	19	5	3	11	24	32	-8	18

AWAY TABLE

	P	W	D	L	F	A	GD	PTS
Man Utd	19	11	3	5	34	16	18	36
Chelsea	19	10	4	5	35	18	17	34
Aston Villa	19	9	5	5	23	23	0	32
Arsenal	19	8	4	7	35	26	9	28
Man City	19	6	9	4	32	25	7	27
Tottenham	19	7	5	7	27	29	-2	26
Everton	19	5	7	7	25	28	-3	22
Liverpool	19	5	6	8	18	20	-2	21
Stoke	19	4	8	7	10	27	-17	20
Birmingham	19	5	2	12	19	34	-15	17
Wolves	19	4	5	10	19	34	-15	17
Bolton	19	4	3	12	16	36	-20	15
Blackburn	19	3	5	11	13	37	-24	14
Wigan	19	3	2	14	18	55	-37	11
Fulham	19	1	7	11	12	31	-19	10
Sunderland	19	2	4	13	16	37	-21	10
Portsmouth	19	2	4	13	10	34	-24	10
West Ham	19	1	6	12	17	37	-20	9
Hull	19	0	6	13	12	46	-34	6
Burnley	19	1	1	17	17	52	-35	4

FIRST-HALF TABLE

	P	W	D	L	F	A	GD	PTS
Chelsea	38	21	12	5	43	17	26	75
Arsenal	38	18	13	7	37	20	17	67
Tottenham	38	18	12	8	28	14	14	66
Man City	38	16	14	8	37	21	16	62
Man Utd	38	15	16	7	28	13	15	61
Liverpool	38	12	19	7	26	16	10	55
Everton	38	13	16	9	24	23	1	55
Aston Villa	38	12	18	8	27	19	8	54
Sunderland	38	14	11	13	25	26	-1	53
Stoke	38	9	22	7	18	16	2	49
Bolton	38	13	9	16	23	25	-2	48
Birmingham	38	10	16	12	17	20	-3	46
Blackburn	38	11	13	14	19	23	-4	46
West Ham	38	10	14	14	22	27	-5	44
Wolves	38	10	11	17	13	26	-13	41
Wigan	38	8	16	14	14	24	-10	40
Fulham	38	9	13	16	12	24	-12	40
Hull	38	6	15	17	20	31	-11	33
Portsmouth	38	6	13	19	14	36	-22	31
Burnley	38	6	13	19	15	41	-26	31

SECOND-HALF TABLE

	P	W	D	L	F	A	GD	PTS
Man Utd	38	25	8	5	58	15	43	83
Chelsea	38	24	8	6	60	15	45	80
Arsenal	38	22	9	7	46	21	25	75
Liverpool	38	16	15	7	35	19	16	63
Man City	38	15	16	7	36	24	12	61
Aston Villa	38	16	13	9	25	20	5	61
Tottenham	38	15	13	10	39	27	12	58
Everton	38	14	15	9	36	26	10	57
Fulham	38	13	14	11	27	22	5	53
Portsmouth	38	11	14	13	20	30	-10	47
Burnley	38	11	11	16	27	41	-14	44
Blackburn	38	9	15	14	22	32	-10	42
Stoke	38	9	14	15	16	32	-16	41
Birmingham	38	7	18	13	21	27	-6	39
Wolves	38	7	17	14	19	30	-11	38
Wigan	38	9	11	18	23	55	-32	38
West Ham	38	9	10	19	25	39	-14	37
Sunderland	38	7	15	16	23	30	-7	36
Bolton	38	4	16	18	19	42	-23	28
Hull	38	6	10	22	14	44	-30	28

STADIUM STATISTICS

GROUND	TEAM	M	GLS	GLS/M
Stamford Bridge	Chelsea	19	82	4.32
Old Trafford	Man Utd	19	64	3.37
Emirates Stadium	Arsenal	19	63	3.32
City of Manchester	Man City	19	61	3.21
Upton Park	West Ham	19	59	3.11
Anfield	Liverpool	19	58	3.05
Reebok Stadium	Bolton	19	57	3.00
Fratton Park	Portsmouth	19	56	2.95
Goodison Park	Everton	19	56	2.95
Turf Moor	Burnley	19	55	2.89

GROUND	TEAM	M	GLS	GLS/M
White Hart Lane	Tottenham	19	52	2.74
KC Stadium	Hull	19	51	2.68
Stadium of Light	Sunderland	19	51	2.68
Ewood Park	Blackburn	19	46	2.42
Britannia Stadium	Stoke	19	45	2.37
Villa Park	Aston Villa	19	45	2.37
DW Stadium	Wigan	19	43	2.26
Craven Cottage	Fulham	19	42	2.21
Molineux	Wolves	19	35	1.84
St Andrews	Birmingham	19	32	1.68

PENALTIES

TOTAL AWARDED	111
SCORED	86
SAVED	23
MISSED	2

EARLIEST STRIKE

DARREN BENT

(SUNDERLAND v Tottenham) 0:36

LATEST STRIKE

WADE ELLIOTT

(Hull v BURNLEY) 95:48

EARLIEST CARD

KEVIN DAVIES

(Fulham v BOLTON) 2.30

Kevin Davies (Bolton)

SEQUENCES

Wins	Chelsea 6
15/08/2009–20/09/2009	
Losses	Portsmouth 7
15/08/2009–26/09/2009	
Draws	Man City 7
05/10/2009–28/11/2009	
Undefeated	Birmingham 12
24/10/2009–09/01/2010	
Without win	Sunderland 14
28/11/2009–28/02/2010	
Undefeated home	Birmingham 15
24/10/2009–01/05/2010	
Undefeated away	Man City 7
16/02/2010–09/05/2010	
Without scoring	Bolton 5
30/01/2010–21/02/2010	
Without conceding	Tottenham 5
16/12/2009–16/01/2010	
Scoring	Chelsea 18
15/08/2009–20/12/2009	
Conceding	Bolton 20
15/08/2009–20/01/2010	

BARCLAYS PREMIER LEAGUE

BARCLAYS PREMIER LEAGUE GAMES SINCE...

	a win	a home win	an away win	a defeat	a home defeat	an away defeat	a score draw	a no-score draw	conceding a goal	scoring a goal	conceding more than one	scoring more than one	keeping a clean sheet	failing to score	winning consecutive games	losing consecutive games	gaining a point	losing a point	win by more than one	loss by more than one
Arsenal	0	0	4	1	7	0	6	2	1	0	1	0	0	2	7	3	0	1	0	13
Aston Villa	2	1	1	0	0	0	5	11	0	1	1	3	2	0	2	0	2	0	3	1
Birmingham	1	0	5	0	15	0	5	3	0	0	0	1	3	2	10	7	1	0	43	4
Blackburn	0	0	0	3	1	4	2	4	1	0	3	1	0	4	0	9	0	2	11	9
Bolton	0	0	1	1	2	0	2	13	0	0	2	0	8	1	10	4	0	1	8	6
Burnley	0	0	2	1	1	0	9	66	0	0	0	0	27	2	35	1	0	1	0	2
Chelsea	0	0	0	3	5	1	8	19	3	0	3	0	0	19	0	152	0	3	0	10
Everton	0	0	1	11	12	6	4	1	2	0	3	2	0	1	2	24	0	1	7	24
Fulham	2	1	18	0	0	0	22	4	0	2	0	2	4	0	11	0	2	0	12	0
Hull	7	4	24	2	1	2	1	0	1	1	1	1	0	0	67	2	0	0	7	3
Liverpool	2	1	1	1	0	3	5	0	1	2	1	2	0	0	2	29	0	0	2	1
Man City	2	1	2	1	0	7	0	3	0	0	8	2	3	1	5	39	0	0	2	8
Man Utd	0	0	0	5	2	5	12	4	2	0	5	0	0	4	0	47	0	4	0	11
Portsmouth	1	0	5	0	1	0	2	4	0	1	2	1	4	0	69	6	1	0	1	6
Stoke	1	2	1	0	1	0	10	2	0	1	0	6	1	0	6	3	1	0	6	0
Sunderland	2	1	1	0	0	0	7	11	0	0	0	3	2	1	2	0	2	0	5	6
Tottenham	1	0	1	0	11	0	14	13	0	0	0	0	1	12	1	27	1	0	7	0
West Ham	2	1	18	1	3	0	0	15	0	0	1	1	4	3	12	6	0	0	12	3
Wigan	3	1	8	0	4	0	1	4	0	1	0	1	4	0	37	5	1	0	18	0
Wolves	0	0	3	1	4	0	2	3	0	0	1	0	3	3	22	10	0	1	7	1

GOALS SCORED/CONCEDED
PER FIVE-MINUTE INTERVALS

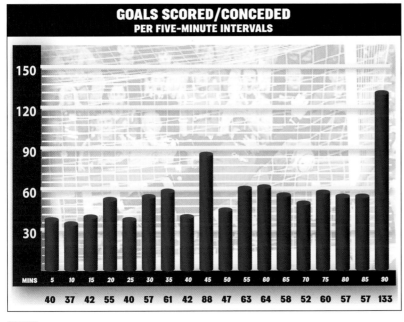

MINS	5	10	15	20	25	30	35	40	45	50	55	60	65	70	75	80	85	90
	40	37	42	55	40	57	61	42	88	47	63	64	58	52	60	57	57	133

LATE GOALS
IN THE LAST 10 MINUTES OF MATCHES

TEAM	F	A
Arsenal	20	8
Aston Villa	7	11
Birmingham	6	14
Blackburn	5	11
Bolton	7	10
Burnley	9	13
Chelsea	19	4
Everton	18	6
Fulham	4	7
Hull	2	19
Liverpool	9	6
Man City	11	9
Man Utd	19	3
Portsmouth	9	10
Stoke	5	14
Sunderland	6	9
Tottenham	13	10
West Ham	9	6
Wigan	8	13
Wolves	4	7

DISCIPLINARY RECORDS (All domestic competitions)

Y=1PT/R=2PT

ARSENAL	FOULS	Y	R
Alex Song	58	12	0
Cesc Fabregas	30	5	0
Thomas Vermaelen	26	3	1
Gael Clichy	21	4	0
Emmanuel Eboue	16	4	0
Bacary Sagna	24	3	0

ASTON VILLA	FOULS	Y	R
Stiliyan Petrov	51	11	0
Carlos Cuellar	31	7	1
Richard Dunne	36	7	0
Ashley Young	49	6	0
Gabriel Agbonlahor	56	5	0
James Milner	42	5	0

BIRMINGHAM	FOULS	Y	R
Barry Ferguson	40	10	1
Stephen Carr	41	10	0
Lee Bowyer	45	8	0
Roger Johnson	23	8	0
James McFadden	45	6	0
Cameron Jerome	40	5	0

BLACKBURN	FOULS	Y	R
Christopher Samba	50	5	2
Steven Nzonzi	58	7	0
David Dunn	34	7	0
Morten Gamst Pedersen	42	5	0
Michel Salgado	32	5	0
Gael Givet	21	5	0

BOLTON	FOULS	Y	R
Fabrice Muamba	63	11	0
Kevin Davies	103	9	0
Tamir Cohen	50	7	1
Paul Robinson	32	7	0
Gretar Rafn Steinsson	19	4	1
Jlloyd Samuel	12	4	1

BURNLEY	FOULS	Y	R
Tyrone Mears	40	7	0
Clarke Carlisle	25	7	0
Michael Duff	15	6	0
Wade Elliott	65	5	0
Andre Bikey	55	5	0
Kevin McDonald	20	5	0

CHELSEA	FOULS	Y	R
John Terry	32	9	1
Didier Drogba	59	7	0
Branislav Ivanovic	37	6	0
Florent Malouda	26	4	1
Ricardo Carvalho	22	5	0
Deco	21	5	0

EVERTON	FOULS	Y	R
Steven Pienaar	40	9	1
Tim Cahill	84	10	0
Johnny Heitinga	48	9	0
Marouane Fellaini	61	7	0
Leon Osman	28	4	0
Jack Rodwell	16	4	0

FULHAM	FOULS	Y	R
Danny Murphy	32	5	0
Jonathan Greening	31	5	0
John Pantsil	21	5	0
Chris Baird	28	4	0
Kagisho Dikgacoi	10	2	1
Bobby Zamora	57	3	0

HULL	FOULS	Y	R
Craig Fagan	56	7	1
Bernard Mendy	22	6	1
George Boateng	55	4	2
Andy Dawson	30	7	0
Deiberson Geovanni	27	4	1
Jozy Altidore	25	4	1

LIVERPOOL	FOULS	Y	R
Javier Mascherano	67	10	2
Leiva Lucas	57	9	0
Jamie Carragher	24	7	1
Steven Gerrard	28	6	0
Fernando Torres	34	5	0
Martin Skrtel	18	5	0

MAN CITY	FOULS	Y	R
Pablo Zabaleta	46	12	1
Nigel De Jong	48	9	0
Craig Bellamy	24	5	1
Carlos Tevez	36	6	0
Gareth Barry	57	4	0
Micah Richards	39	4	0

MAN UTD	FOULS	Y	R
Paul Scholes	32	10	1
Nemanja Vidic	31	9	1
Darren Fletcher	35	5	1
Patrice Evra	41	6	0
Wayne Rooney	24	6	0
Gary Neville	19	3	1

PORTSMOUTH	FOULS	Y	R
Kevin-Prince Boateng	50	8	0
Jamie O'Hara	29	8	0
Aruna Dindane	39	7	0
Aaron Mokoena	35	7	0
Michael Brown	43	5	1
Richard Hughes	16	5	0

STOKE	FOULS	Y	R
Ricardo Fuller	58	10	0
Dean Whitehead	47	8	1
Ryan Shawcross	31	8	1
Glenn Whelan	32	9	0
Andy Wilkinson	28	7	1
Abdoulaye Faye	23	5	2

SUNDERLAND	FOULS	Y	R
Lorik Cana	59	11	1
Michael Turner	35	8	2
Kieran Richardson	49	8	1
Lee Cattermole	37	8	1
Phillip Bardsley	36	8	0
David Meyler	19	4	1

TOTTENHAM	FOULS	Y	R
Wilson Palacios	69	10	0
Tom Huddlestone	57	10	0
Jermaine Jenas	11	6	0
Jermain Defoe	34	4	1
Benoit Assou-Ekotto	26	5	0
Sebastien Bassong	22	4	0

WEST HAM	FOULS	Y	R
Scott Parker	32	9	1
Radoslav Kovac	34	8	1
Mark Noble	36	6	1
Julien Faubert	27	6	0
Alessandro Diamanti	43	5	0
Guillermo Franco	29	5	0

WIGAN	FOULS	Y	R
Titus Bramble	27	10	0
Hendry Thomas	64	8	1
Charles N'Zogbia	53	7	0
Maynor Figueroa	38	7	0
Gary Caldwell	17	3	2
Hugo Rodallega	46	6	0

WOLVES	FOULS	Y	R
Karl Henry	60	6	1
Richard Stearman	15	5	1
Christophe Berra	45	6	0
Michael Mancienne	26	6	0
Stephen Ward	18	3	1
Kevin Doyle	44	4	0

REFEREE STATISTICS

	GAMES	Y	R	AVE
Mark Halsey	1	0	0	0.00
Anthony Taylor	2	5	0	2.50
Peter Walton	27	67	4	2.63
Chris Foy	26	69	2	2.73
Mark Clattenburg	31	84	5	2.87
Lee Mason	22	60	6	3.00
Phil Dowd	29	88	5	3.21
Michael Jones	20	64	1	3.25
Alan Wiley	26	81	5	3.31

	GAMES	Y	R	AVE
Kevin Friend	13	41	4	3.46
Lee Probert	22	75	6	3.68
Howard Webb	28	101	3	3.71
Andre Marriner	28	97	9	3.79
Steve Bennett	29	109	5	3.93
Stuart Attwell	15	58	2	4.00
Mike Dean	30	116	6	4.06
Martin Atkinson	31	127	5	4.26

MOST CARDS IN A SINGLE MATCH

REFEREE	MATCH	DATE	Y	R	TOT
Howard Webb	Wolves v Wigan	16/01/2010	7	2	9
Lee Probert	Birmingham v Wolves	07/02/2010	9	0	9
Mike Dean	Man Utd v Arsenal	29/08/2009	9	0	9
Stuart Attwell	Sunderland v Wigan	06/02/2010	9	0	9
Andre Marriner	Everton v Tottenham	06/12/2009	8	0	8
Martin Atkinson	Liverpool v Everton	06/02/2010	6	2	8
Phil Dowd	Portsmouth v Tottenham	17/10/2009	6	2	8

Martin Atkinson

FRANK LAMPARD'S stunning end-of-season form not only paved the way for Chelsea to win their first Barclays Premier League title in four years, but it also helped the England midfielder to claim top spot in the 2009/10 Actim Index.

Lampard scored 10 goals in the final 10 games as the Blues lifted the crown. Coupled with a season's tally of 17 assists, that was enough to see him surge up the Index to finish at the summit with 776 points.

Lampard finished the campaign with 22 Barclays Premier League goals, although it was his teammate Didier Drogba who won the Golden Boot with an impressive 29. The Ivory Coast international's haul came from 87 shots on target and earned him a second-place finish, 73 points behind Lampard.

Carlos Tevez's move across Manchester proved a success as the City striker finished third on 673 points, while the 2008/09 champion, Nicolas Anelka, posted a fourth-place finish.

For a long time it looked as though Arsenal's Cesc Fabregas would take the Index title. He led the rankings for much of the season, but then had his campaign ended by injury in March and he slipped down to fifth. Manchester United's failure to retain their title was highlighted by the appearance of only three of their players in the top 20, with Wayne Rooney finishing seventh, Patrice Evra 10th and Antonio Valencia 13th.

Everton goalkeeper Tim Howard spent more time than anyone on the pitch, racking up an impressive 3680 minutes of playing time, but he was not the busiest of all the keepers as Burnley's Brian Jensen made the most saves, keeping out 241 efforts.

Lampard and Tottenham's Jermain Defoe shared the highest individual match score, with both recording 87-point hauls. Lampard's came in the 7–1 rout of Aston Villa, while Defoe's tally was down to his five goals in the 9–1 win over Wigan.

ACTIM PLAYER RANKINGS FOR THE 2009/2010 BARCLAYS PREMIER LEAGUE SEASON

	NAME	TEAM	INDEX SCORE		NAME	TEAM	INDEX SCORE		NAME	TEAM	INDEX SCORE
1	Frank Lampard	Chelsea	776	34	Fernando Torres	Liverpool	425	67	Stephen Warnock	Aston Villa	369
2	Didier Drogba	Chelsea	703	35	Tim Cahill	Everton	423	68	Nemanja Vidic	Man Utd	369
3	Carlos Tevez	Man City	673	36	Bacary Sagna	Arsenal	422	69	Branislav Ivanovic	Chelsea	368
4	Nicolas Anelka	Chelsea	658	37	James Collins	Aston Villa	420	70	Nani	Man Utd	367
5	Cesc Fabregas	Arsenal	636	38	Jody Craddock	Wolves	418	71	Liam Ridgewell	Birmingham	366
6	Gabriel Agbonlahor	Aston Villa	621	39	Jamie Carragher	Liverpool	417	72	Aaron Hughes	Fulham	365
7	Wayne Rooney	Man Utd	585	40	Heurelho Gomes	Tottenham	415	73	Charles N'Zogbia	Wigan	365
8	Darren Bent	Sunderland	581	41	Andrey Arshavin	Arsenal	413	74	Brian Jensen	Burnley	364
9	Florent Malouda	Chelsea	578	42	Roger Johnson	Birmingham	407	75	Jussi Jaaskelainen	Bolton	363
10	Patrice Evra	Man Utd	574	43	Shay Given	Man City	404	76	William Gallas	Arsenal	362
11	James Milner	Aston Villa	560	44	Mark Schwarzer	Fulham	403	77	John Carew	Aston Villa	362
12	Richard Dunne	Aston Villa	551	45	Ryan Giggs	Man Utd	402	78	Gael Givet	Blackburn	359
13	Antonio Valencia	Man Utd	544	46	Matthew Etherington	Stoke	400	79	Ryan Shawcross	Stoke	353
14	Carlos Cuellar	Aston Villa	538	47	Steven Pienaar	Everton	397	80	Robert Green	West Ham	352
15	Ashley Young	Aston Villa	523	48	Vedran Corluka	Tottenham	395	81	Aaron Lennon	Tottenham	352
16	Jermain Defoe	Tottenham	523	49	Damien Duff	Fulham	394	82	Thomas Sorensen	Stoke	350
17	Petr Cech	Chelsea	518	50	Benoit Assou-Ekotto	Tottenham	392	83	Brede Hangeland	Fulham	345
18	Emmanuel Adebayor	Man City	505	51	Manuel Almunia	Arsenal	386	84	Andy Dawson	Hull	343
19	Leighton Baines	Everton	504	52	Stephen Carr	Birmingham	384	85	Tyrone Mears	Burnley	342
20	Craig Bellamy	Man City	499	53	Kolo Toure	Man City	383	86	Kenwyne Jones	Sunderland	341
21	Dirk Kuyt	Liverpool	494	54	Titus Bramble	Wigan	382	87	Matthew Upson	West Ham	340
22	John Terry	Chelsea	488	55	Cameron Jerome	Birmingham	382	88	Barry Ferguson	Birmingham	340
23	Brad Friedel	Aston Villa	481	56	Lee Bowyer	Birmingham	381	89	Peter Crouch	Tottenham	337
24	Jose Reina	Liverpool	473	57	Wade Elliott	Burnley	378	90	Yossi Benayoun	Liverpool	335
25	Steven Gerrard	Liverpool	471	58	Stephen Hunt	Hull	376	91	Graham Alexander	Burnley	333
26	Thomas Vermaelen	Arsenal	465	59	Glen Johnson	Liverpool	376	92	Bobby Zamora	Fulham	332
27	Dimitar Berbatov	Man Utd	460	60	Paul Robinson	Blackburn	375	93	Johnny Heitinga	Everton	332
28	Darren Fletcher	Man Utd	445	61	Ryan Nelsen	Blackburn	374	94	Michael Turner	Sunderland	331
29	Gareth Barry	Man City	432	62	Michael Dawson	Tottenham	373	95	Matthew Jarvis	Wolves	329
30	Abou Diaby	Arsenal	432	63	Michael Ballack	Chelsea	372	96	Christopher Samba	Blackburn	323
31	Joe Hart	Birmingham	430	64	Sylvain Distin	Everton	372	97	Scott Parker	West Ham	323
32	Ashley Cole	Chelsea	429	65	Emiliano Insua	Liverpool	371	98	Sebastian Larsson	Birmingham	323
33	Tim Howard	Everton	429	66	Stiliyan Petrov	Aston Villa	370	99	Scott Dann	Birmingham	323
								100	James McFadden	Birmingham	320

LEADING PLAYERS IN THE ACTIM INDEX BY POSITION

TOP 5 GOALKEEPERS

Name	Index Score	Overall Index Rank	Team
Petr Cech	518	17	Chelsea
Brad Friedel	481	23	Aston Villa
Jose Reina	473	24	Liverpool
Joe Hart	430	31	Birmingham
Tim Howard	429	33	Everton

TOP 5 MIDFIELDERS

Name	Index Score	Overall Index Rank	Team
Frank Lampard	776	1	Chelsea
Cesc Fabregas	636	5	Arsenal
Florent Malouda	578	9	Chelsea
James Milner	560	11	Aston Villa
Antonio Valencia	544	13	Man Utd

TOP 5 DEFENDERS

Name	Index Score	Overall Index Rank	Team
Patrice Evra	574	10	Man Utd
Richard Dunne	551	12	Aston Villa
Carlos Cuellar	538	14	Aston Villa
Leighton Baines	504	19	Everton
John Terry	488	22	Chelsea

TOP 5 STRIKERS

Name	Index Score	Overall Index Rank	Team
Didier Drogba	703	2	Chelsea
Carlos Tevez	673	3	Man City
Nicolas Anelka	658	4	Chelsea
Gabriel Agbonlahor	621	6	Aston Villa
Wayne Rooney	585	7	Man Utd

Patrice Evra (Manchester Utd)

BEST INDIVIDUAL MATCH SCORES

Player	Team	Score
Frank Lampard	Chelsea	87
27/03/2010: Chelsea 7–1 Aston Villa		
Jermain Defoe	Tottenham	87
22/11/2009: Tottenham 9–1 Wigan		
Robbie Keane	Tottenham	80
26/09/2009: Tottenham 5–0 Burnley		
Yossi Benayoun	Liverpool	74
12/09/2009: Liverpool 4–0 Burnley		
Salomon Kalou	Chelsea	70
25/04/2010: Chelsea 7–0 Stoke		
Cesc Fabregas	Arsenal	68
04/10/2009: Arsenal 6–2 Blackburn		
Carlos Tevez	Man City	67
29/03/2010: Man City 3–0 Wigan		
Frank Lampard	Chelsea	64
25/04/2010: Chelsea 7–0 Stoke		
Aruna Dindane	Portsmouth	64
31/10/2009: Portsmouth 4–0 Wigan		
Cesc Fabregas	Arsenal	63
15/08/2009: Everton 1–6 Arsenal		
Wayne Rooney	Man Utd	63
23/01/2010: Man Utd 4–0 Hull		
Fernando Torres	Liverpool	63
15/03/2010: Liverpool 4–1 Portsmouth		
Emmanuel Adebayor	Man City	61
03/04/2010: Burnley 1–6 Man City		
Carlos Tevez	Man City	60
11/01/2010: Man City 4–1 Blackburn		
Aaron Lennon	Tottenham	60
22/11/2009: Tottenham 9–1 Wigan		
Antonio Valencia	Man Utd	59
30/12/2009: Man Utd 5–0 Wigan		

ACTIM INDEX TEAM OF THE SEASON

PATRICE EVRA (574) Man Utd

FLORENT MALOUDA (578) Chelsea

JOHN TERRY (488) Chelsea

FRANK LAMPARD (776) Chelsea

CARLOS TEVEZ (673) Man City

PETR CECH (518) Chelsea

CESC FABREGAS (636) Arsenal

DIDIER DROGBA (703) Chelsea

RICHARD DUNNE (551) Aston Villa

CARLOS CUELLAR (538) Aston Villa

JAMES MILNER (560) Aston Villa

BY TEAM

	Score	Rank
ARSENAL		
Cesc Fabregas	636	5
ASTON VILLA		
Gabriel Agbonlahor	621	6
BIRMINGHAM		
Joe Hart	430	31
BLACKBURN		
Paul Robinson	375	60
BOLTON		
Jussi Jaaskelainen	363	75
BURNLEY		
Wade Elliott	378	57
CHELSEA		
Frank Lampard	776	1
EVERTON		
Leighton Baines	504	19
FULHAM		
Mark Schwarzer	403	44
HULL		
Stephen Hunt	376	58
LIVERPOOL		
Dirk Kuyt	494	21
MAN CITY		
Carlos Tevez	673	3
MAN UTD		
Wayne Rooney	585	7
PORTSMOUTH		
Aruna Dindane	226	184
STOKE		
Matthew Etherington	400	46
SUNDERLAND		
Darren Bent	581	8
TOTTENHAM		
Jermain Defoe	523	16
WEST HAM		
Robert Green	352	80
WIGAN		
Titus Bramble	382	54
WOLVES		
Jody Craddock	418	38

ARSENAL

CLUB SUMMARY

FORMED	1886
MANAGER	Arsène Wenger
GROUND	Emirates Stadium
CAPACITY	60,000
NICKNAME	The Gunners
WEBSITE	www.arsenal.com

The New Football Pools PLAYER OF THE SEASON

Cesc Fabregas

OVERALL

P	W	D	L	F	A	GD
55	33	8	14	116	63	53

BARCLAYS PREMIER LEAGUE

Pos	P	W	D	L	F	A	GD	Pts
3	38	23	6	9	83	41	42	75

HOME

Pos	P	W	D	L	F	A	GD	Pts
3	19	15	2	2	48	15	33	47

AWAY

Pos	P	W	D	L	F	A	GD	Pts
4	19	8	4	7	35	26	9	28

CUP PROGRESS DETAILS

Competition	Round reached	Knocked out by
Champions League	QF	Barcelona
FA Cup	R4	Stoke
Carling Cup	QF	Man City

BIGGEST WIN (ALL COMPS)

15/08/09 6–1 v Everton

BIGGEST DEFEAT (ALL COMPS)

06/04/10 1–4 v Barcelona

THE PLAYER WITH THE MOST

GOALS SCORED	Cesc Fabregas	**15**
SHOTS ON TARGET	Andrey Arshavin	**46**
SHOTS OFF TARGET	Cesc Fabregas	**28**
SHOTS WITHOUT SCORING	Gael Clichy	**8**
ASSISTS	Cesc Fabregas	**15**
OFFSIDES	Andrey Arshavin	**22**
FOULS	Alex Song	**54**
FOULS WITHOUT A CARD	Aaron Ramsey	**9**
FREE-KICKS WON	Cesc Fabregas	**56**
DEFENSIVE CLEARANCES	William Gallas	**28**

 actim INDEX FOR THE 2009/10 BARCLAYS PREMIER LEAGUE SEASON

RANK	PLAYER	PTS
5	Cesc Fabregas	636
26	Thomas Vermaelen	465
30	Abou Diaby	432

ATTENDANCE RECORD

HIGH	AVERAGE	LOW
60,103	59,927	59,084
v Tottenham (31/10/2009)		v Bolton (20/01/2010)

CLOCKWISE FROM ABOVE: Cesc Fabregas scores in the opening-day thrashing of Everton; Arsenal defenders watch on in horror as Manuel Almunia palms home an own goal against Manchester United; Thomas Vermaelen celebrates with Gael Clichy; Robin van Persie's injury, while on international duty, was a serious blow

AT TIMES during the 2009/10 season, it looked like Arsenal would sweep all before them. However, once again Arsène Wenger's young Gunners failed to deliver when it mattered most.

Before the campaign started it was Arsenal, rather than Liverpool, who the pundits all tipped to face a struggle to hold onto their coveted top-four place. However, Wenger's squad rose to the challenge in the early part of the campaign. An emphatic 6–1 thrashing of Everton on the opening day of the season and safe progress past Celtic into the group stages of the UEFA Champions League proved that summer departures Emmanuel Adebayor and Kolo Toure would not be missed too much.

Back-to-back defeats at both Manchester clubs led to questions again being raised, but the Gunners responded with six wins from seven League matches.

Disaster struck in the November international break when Holland forward Robin van Persie suffered a serious ankle injury and was ruled out for five months. There is no doubt that the loss of the skilful Dutchman was a major blow and was possibly fatal to the Gunners' Barclays Premier League title hopes.

Defeat at Sunderland was swiftly followed by a 3–0 home reverse against Chelsea on 29th November, as Didier Drogba again proved too hot for the Arsenal defence to handle. Arsenal were seemingly cast adrift with an 11-point deficit. Wenger, though,

Arsenal maintained their title hopes until the final weeks of the season, but again had to settle for a year without silverware

begged to differ, defiantly claiming both Chelsea and United would drop points. As it transpired, Wenger was correct, and Arsenal were able to claw back points on Chelsea and Manchester United in one of the most unpredictable seasons in the League history.

Hopes of Carling Cup success for Wenger's youngsters ended in a 3–0 quarter-final loss at Manchester City yet, despite going out of the FA Cup at Stoke with a much-changed side, Arsenal returned, albeit briefly, to the top of the table when they beat Bolton 4–2 at the Emirates Stadium on 20th January.

Back-to-back defeats – against United at home and away at Chelsea – seemed to have again put paid to any realistic hopes of a first title since 2003/4. However, six straight victories – including a last-gasp strike by fit-again Nicklas Bendtner at Hull – saw Arsenal once more in with a shout of title glory as they prepared for a mouth-watering Champions League quarter-final against Barcelona.

That, though, was as good as it got. Both William Gallas and, crucially, captain Cesc Fabregas suffered season-ending injuries in the first leg against the Catalans, which finished 2–2 at the Emirates Stadium after

the Gunners came back from two goals down. They headed to the Nou Camp severely weakened and, while they took an early lead, that only served to fire up Lionel Messi to score four mesmerising goals in a 4–1 home win. It was a defeat from which Arsenal never recovered.

Wenger's young team, given added experience by the signing of Sol Campbell in January, could not find the maturity to deliver as they lost to arch-rivals Tottenham, now chasing down fourth spot. Even the return of Van Persie could not bring a grand finale.

Arsenal threw away a 2–0 lead in the final 10 minutes at Wigan to lose 3–2, which finally shut the door on their title hopes. The Gunners were left needing a result against Europa League finalists Fulham on the last day to make sure of third place, and with it direct qualification to the group stages of the Champions League. While a routine 4–0 victory over the much-changed Cottagers produced the minimum requirement from the season, Wenger knows 2010/11 must be different.

'I felt this year I must win a trophy and we were very close. It will be a decisive year next year for this team, that is for sure,' he said. 'The future of our team lies in how well we can respond to big disappointments.'

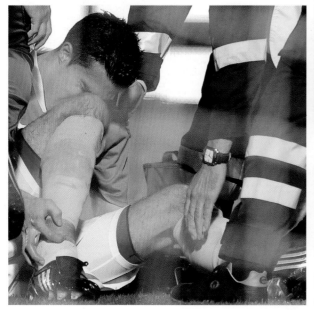

ARSENAL

AUGUST

15th ● Everton A W 1–6 **Att:** 39,309. **Ref:** M Halsey – (4-3-3): Almunia, Sagna, Gallas¹, Vermaelen¹, Clichy, Fabregas² (Ramsey 72), Song, Denilson¹, Bendtner (Eboue 63), van Persie (Eduardo¹ 72), Arshavin. **Subs not used:** Mannone, Silvestre, Gibbs, Merida.

18th ● Celtic A W 0–2 **Att:** 58,000. **Ref:** M Busacca – (4-3-2-1): Almunia, Sagna, Vermaelen, Gallas¹, Clichy, Song, Fabregas, Denilson, van Persie, Arshavin (Diaby 69), Bendtner. **Subs not used:** Mannone, Eduardo, Ramsey, Silvestre, Eboue, Gibbs. Caldwell OG.

22nd ● Portsmouth H W 4–1 **Att:** 60,049. **Ref:** S Bennett – (4-4-2): Almunia, Eboue, Gallas¹, Vermaelen, Gibbs, Diaby¹², Fabregas (Ramsey¹ 46), Denilson, Arshavin (Merida 71), van Persie, Eduardo (Bendtner 71). **Subs not used:** Sagna, Mannone, Song, Clichy.

26th ● Celtic H W 3–1 **Att:** 59,962. **Ref:** M Mejuto Gonzalez – (4-4-2): Almunia, Sagna, Gallas, Vermaelen, Clichy, Eboue▮ (Wilshere 72), Song, Denilson▮, Diaby (Ramsey 61), Eduardo¹ (Arshavin¹ 71), Bendtner. **Subs not used:** Mannone, van Persie, Silvestre, Traore. Agg: 5–1.

29th ● Man Utd A L 2–1 **Att:** 75,095. **Ref:** M Dean – (4-5-1): Almunia▮, Sagna▮, Gallas▮, Vermaelen, Clichy, Eboue▮ (Bendtner 71), Denilson (Eduardo 79), Song▮, Diaby, Arshavin¹ (Ramsey 81), van Persie▮. **Subs not used:** Mannone, Silvestre, Wilshere, Gibbs.

SEPTEMBER

12th ● Man City A L 4–2 **Att:** 47,339. **Ref:** M Clattenburg – (4-5-1): Almunia, Sagna▮ (Eboue 77), Vermaelen, Gallas, Clichy, Bendtner, Song▮ (Eduardo 77), Fabregas, Denilson (Rosicky¹ 52), Diaby, van Persie¹. **Subs not used:** Mannone, Ramsey, Silvestre, Gibbs.

16th ● Standard Liège A W 2–3 **Att:** 58,100. **Ref:** E Iturralde Gonzalez – (4-5-1): Mannone, Eboue (Sagna 80), Gallas, Vermaelen¹, Clichy▮, Diaby, Fabregas, Song (Wilshere 80), Rosicky (Ramsey 70), Eduardo¹ (Wilshere 86), Bendtner¹. **Subs not used:** Szczesny, Silvestre, Gibbs, Watt.

19th ● Wigan H W 4–0 **Att:** 59,103. **Ref:** M Jones – (4-3-3): Mannone, Sagna, Gallas, Vermaelen², Clichy, Eboue▮ (Rosicky 73), Song▮, Fabregas¹, Diaby (Ramsey 66), Eduardo¹ (Bendtner 73), van Persie. **Subs not used:** Szczesny, Silvestre, Merida, Gibbs.

22nd ● West Brom H W 2–0 **Att:** 56,592. **Ref:** L Mason – (4-4-2): Szczesny, Gilbert, Senderos▮, Silvestre, Traore (Barazite 69), Wilshere, Coquelin (Randall 58), Ramsey▮, Gibbs, Sunu (Vela¹ 58), Watt¹. **Subs not used:** Shea, Bartley, Eastmond, Frimpong.

26th ● Fulham A W 0–1 **Att:** 25,700. **Ref:** M Atkinson – (4-2-3-1): Mannone, Sagna, Gallas, Vermaelen, Clichy, Song, Diaby, Bendtner, Fabregas, Arshavin (Rosicky 68), van Persie¹ (Eboue 83). **Subs not used:** Szczesny, Vela, Ramsey, Silvestre, Gibbs.

29th ● Olympiacos H W 2–0 **Att:** 59,884. **Ref:** S Lannoy – (4-1-4-1): Mannone, Sagna, Gallas, Vermaelen, Clichy, Song, Rosicky (Eduardo 66), Fabregas▮, Diaby (Vela 78), Arshavin¹, van Persie▮ (Ramsey 85). **Subs not used:** Szczesny, Sagna, Senderos, Gibbs.

OCTOBER

4th ● Blackburn H W 6–2 **Att:** 59,431. **Ref:** P Walton – (4-3-3): Mannone, Sagna, Gallas, Vermaelen¹, Clichy, Fabregas¹ (Ramsey 76), Song, Diaby, Rosicky (Walcott¹ 69), van Persie▮, Arshavin¹ (Bendtner¹ 76). **Subs not used:** Szczesny, Silvestre, Eboue, Gibbs.

17th ● Birmingham H W 3–1 **Att:** 60,082. **Ref:** L Probert – (4-3-3): Mannone, Eboue (Wilshere 90), Gallas, Vermaelen¹, Gibbs, Fabregas, Song▮, Diaby¹, Walcott (Arshavin¹ 33), van Persie¹, Rosicky (Sagna 72). **Subs not used:** Almunia, Ramsey, Silvestre, Traore.

20th ● AZ A D 1–1 **Att:** 16,000. **Ref:** M Hansson – (4-1-4-1): Mannone, Sagna, Gallas, Vermaelen, Clichy▮, Song, Eboue (Ramsey 82), Fabregas¹, Diaby, Arshavin, van Persie▮ (Vela¹ 75). **Subs not used:** Almunia, Silvestre, Wilshere, Gibbs, Merida.

25th ● West Ham A D 2–2 **Att:** 34,442. **Ref:** C Foy – (4-5-1): Mannone¹, Sagna, Vermaelen, Clichy, Eboue▮ (Bendtner 82), Song, Fabregas, Diaby (Eduardo 88), Arshavin, van Persie¹. **Subs not used:** Almunia¹, Nasri, Ramsey, Silvestre, Gibbs.

28th ● Liverpool H W 2–1 **Att:** 60,004. **Ref:** A Wiley – (4-1-4-1): Fabianski, Gilbert, Senderos, Silvestre, Gibbs, Eastmond (Randall 75), Bendtner¹ (Watt 76), Nasri, Ramsey, Merida¹ (Coquelin 87), Eduardo. **Subs not used:** Szczesny, Bartley, Frimpong, Sunu.

31st ● Tottenham H W 3–0 **Att:** 60,103. **Ref:** M Clattenburg – (4-3-3): Almunia, Sagna, Gallas, Vermaelen▮, Clichy, Fabregas¹, Song, Diaby, Bendtner (Eduardo 37), van Persie² (Ramsey 86), Arshavin (Eboue 78). **Subs not used:** Mannone, Senderos, Nasri, Gibbs.

NOVEMBER

4th ● AZ H W 4–1 **Att:** 59,345. **Ref:** A Hamer – (4-4-1-1): Almunia, Eboue, Gallas, Vermaelen, Gibbs, Song, Diaby¹, Fabregas² (Ramsey 66), Nasri¹, van Persie (Eduardo 67), Arshavin (Rosicky 74). **Subs not used:** Mannone, Sagna, Senderos, Silvestre.

7th ● Wolverhampton A W 1–4 **Att:** 28,937. **Ref:** S Bennett – (4-2-3-1): Almunia, Sagna, Gallas▮, Vermaelen, Gibbs▮, Ramsey, Diaby (Song 24), Arshavin▮¹ (Nasri 74), Fabregas¹, Eduardo (Rosicky 70), van Persie. **Subs not used:** Mannone, Senderos, Silvestre, Eboue. Zubar OG, Craddock OG.

21st ● Sunderland A L 1–0 **Att:** 44,918. **Ref:** A Wiley – (4-3-3): Almunia, Sagna, Vermaelen, Gallas, Traore▮, Song, Ramsey (Arshavin 60), Fabregas, Rosicky (Walcott 72), Eduardo (Vela 72), Nasri. **Subs not used:** Mannone, Denilson, Silvestre, Eboue.

24th ● Standard Liège H W 2–0 **Att:** 59,941. **Ref:** K Plautz – (4-3-2-1): Almunia, Eboue, Gallas (Silvestre 46), Vermaelen, Gibbs, Fabregas▮, Song, Denilson¹ (Rosicky 66), Nasri¹ (Walcott 60), Arshavin, Vela. **Subs not used:** Mannone, Sagna, Eduardo, Traore.

29th ● Chelsea H L 0–3 **Att:** 60,067. **Ref:** A Marriner – (4-3-3): Almunia, Sagna, Gallas, Vermaelen, Traore▮, Fabregas▮, Song (Walcott 46), Denilson, Nasri (Rosicky 65), Eduardo (Vela 57), Arshavin. **Subs not used:** Fabianski, Ramsey, Silvestre, Eboue.

DECEMBER

2nd ● Man City A L 3–0 **Att:** 46,015. **Ref:** C Foy – (4-3-3): Fabianski, Eboue, Song▮, Silvestre▮, Traore▮, Eastmond▮ (Watt 68), Merida, Ramsey▮, Rosicky, Wilshere▮, Vela. **Subs not used:** Mannone, Bartley, Coquelin, Frimpong, Gilbert, Randall.

5th ● Stoke H W 2–0 **Att:** 60,048. **Ref:** M Clattenburg – (4-3-3): Almunia, Sagna, Gallas, Vermaelen, Traore (Silvestre 88), Eboue (Ramsey¹ 54), Fabregas, Denilson, Nasri, Rosicky (Vela 46), Arshavin¹. **Subs not used:** Fabianski, Senderos, Wilshere, Merida.

9th ● Olympiacos A L 1–0 **Att:** 30,000. **Ref:** L Cortez Batista – (4-3-2-1): Fabianski, Gilbert, Bartley, Silvestre, Cruise, Ramsey, Song, Merida▮, Walcott, Wilshere (Sunu 77), Vela. **Subs not used:** Mannone, Coquelin, Eastmond, Ayling, Randall.

13th ● Liverpool H W 1–2 **Att:** 43,853. **Ref:** H Webb – (4-3-3): Almunia, Sagna, Gallas, Vermaelen, Traore (Silvestre 87), Fabregas▮, Song, Denilson▮, Walcott (Diaby 70), Arshavin▮¹ (Ramsey 90), Nasri. **Subs not used:** Fabianski, Eduardo, Vela, Wilshere. Johnson OG.

16th ● Burnley A D 1–1 **Att:** 21,309. **Ref:** M Dean – (4-5-1): Almunia, Sagna, Vermaelen, Gallas, Silvestre, Walcott (Eduardo 63), Fabregas¹ (Ramsey 43), Song, Diaby, Nasri, Arshavin. **Subs not used:** Fabianski, Vela, Wilshere, Eboue, Emmanuel–Thomas.

19th ● Hull H W 3–0 **Att:** 60,006. **Ref:** S Bennett – (4-2-3-1): Almunia, Sagna, Vermaelen, Gallas, Silvestre, Song, Denilson¹, Nasri▮ (Ramsey 68), Diaby¹, Eduardo¹ (Walcott 75), Arshavin (Vela 83). **Subs not used:** Fabianski, Sagna, Wilshere, Emmanuel–Thomas.

27th ● Aston Villa H W 3–0 **Att:** 60,056. **Ref:** P Dowd – (4-2-3-1): Almunia, Sagna, Gallas, Vermaelen, Traore, Song▮, Denilson (Fabregas² 57 (Ramsey 84)), Nasri, Diaby¹, Eduardo (Walcott 63), Arshavin. **Subs not used:** Fabianski, Vela, Silvestre, Eboue.

30th ● Portsmouth A W 1–4 **Att:** 20,404. **Ref:** A Wiley – (4-3-3): Almunia, Sagna, Gallas, Vermaelen, Traore, Ramsey¹, Song¹, Diaby, Nasri¹ (Eastmond 85), Eduardo (Rosicky 71), Arshavin (Vela 82). **Subs not used:** Fabianski, Silvestre, Wilshere, Merida. Kaboul OG.

● Barclays Premier League ● FA Cup ● Carling Cup ● UEFA Champions League ● Europa League ● FA Community Shield ▮ Yellow Card ▮ Red Card

RESULTS 2009/10

JANUARY

3rd	● West Ham	A	W 1–2	**Att:** 25,549. **Ref:** M Clattenburg – (4-3-3): Fabianski, Sagna, Vermaelen, Gallas, Silvestre, Song▌, Ramsey▌, Merida (Diaby 65), Wilshere (Nasri 65), Vela, Eduardo¹. **Subs not used:** Mannone, Traore, Eastmond, Emmanuel–Thomas, Gilbert.
9th	● Everton	H	D 2–2	**Att:** 60,053. **Ref:** P Walton – (4-3-3): Almunia, Sagna, Gallas, Vermaelen, Traore, Denilson (Merida 84), Diaby, Ramsey (Rosicky¹ 65), Nasri, Eduardo (Vela 74), Arshavin. **Subs not used:** Fabianski, Silvestre, Eastmond, Emmanuel–Thomas. Osman OG.
17th	● Bolton	A	W 0–2	**Att:** 23,893. **Ref:** P Dowd – (4-3-2-1): Almunia, Sagna, Gallas, Vermaelen▌, Traore, Fabregas¹, Eastmond (Merida¹ 63), Diaby, Rosicky¹ (Clichy 74), Eduardo (Vela 84), Arshavin. **Subs not used:** Fabianski, Silvestre, Coquelin, Emmanuel–Thomas.
20th	● Bolton	H	W 4–2	**Att:** 59,084. **Ref:** A Wiley – (4-3-3): Almunia, Sagna, Gallas, Vermaelen¹, Clichy, Fabregas¹, Denilson, Diaby (Eastmond 76), Rosicky¹ (Vela 88), Arshavin¹, Eduardo (Walcott 90). **Subs not used:** Fabianski, Silvestre, Traore, Emmanuel–Thomas.
24th	● Stoke	A	L 3–1	**Att:** 19,735. **Ref:** M Atkinson – (4-3-3): Fabianski, Coquelin (Ramsey 67), Campbell, Silvestre, Traore, Eastmond, Denilson¹, Fabregas, Walcott (Eduardo 67), Emmanuel-Thomas (Arshavin 67), Vela. **Subs not used:** Mannone, Rosicky, Bartley, Frimpong.
27th	● Aston Villa	A	D 0–0	**Att:** 39,601. **Ref:** L Probert – (4-3-3): Almunia, Sagna, Gallas, Vermaelen▌ (Campbell 35), Clichy▌, Denilson, Fabregas, Ramsey, Rosicky (Nasri 79), Eduardo (Bendtner 62), Arshavin. **Subs not used:** Fabianski, Walcott, Traore, Eastmond.
31st	● Man Utd	H	L 1–3	**Att:** 60,091. **Ref:** C Foy – (4-3-3): Almunia, Sagna (Bendtner 72), Gallas, Vermaelen▌, Clichy, Fabregas, Song▌, Denilson (Walcott 61), Nasri, Arshavin, Rosicky (Eboue 71). **Subs not used:** Fabianski, Ramsey, Silvestre, Traore.

FEBRUARY

7th	● Chelsea	A	L 2–0	**Att:** 41,794. **Ref:** M Dean – (4-3-3): Almunia, Sagna (Eboue 74), Vermaelen, Gallas, Clichy, Diaby (Rosicky 74), Song▌, Fabregas▌, Nasri, Walcott (Bendtner 64), Arshavin. **Subs not used:** Fabianski, Denilson, Ramsey, Campbell.
10th	● Liverpool	H	W 1–0	**Att:** 60,045. **Ref:** H Webb – (4-3-3): Almunia, Eboue, Gallas, Vermaelen, Clichy▌, Fabregas▌, Song, Diaby¹, Nasri (Rosicky 33), Bendtner▌ (Sagna 81), Arshavin (Walcott 67). **Subs not used:** Fabianski, Denilson, Traore, Campbell.
17th	◉ FC Porto	A	L 2–1	**Att:** 45,600. **Ref:** M Hansson – (4-3-3): Fabianski, Sagna, Campbell¹, Vermaelen, Clichy, Diaby▌, Denilson, Fabregas, Rosicky (Walcott 68), Nasri (Eboue 88). **Subs not used:** Mannone, Ramsey, Silvestre, Traore.
20th	● Sunderland	H	W 2–0	**Att:** 60,083. **Ref:** S Bennett – (4-1-4-1): Almunia, Eboue (Denilson 89), Silvestre, Vermaelen, Clichy, Song, Walcott (Sagna 78), Fabregas▌¹, Ramsey, Nasri (Rosicky 72), Bendtner¹. **Subs not used:** Fabianski, Vela, Traore, Campbell.
27th	● Stoke	A	W 1–3	**Att:** 27,011. **Ref:** P Walton – (4-5-1): Almunia, Sagna, Vermaelen¹, Campbell, Clichy, Eboue (Walcott 75), Fabregas¹, Song▌, Ramsey (Rosicky 69), Nasri (Eduardo 83), Bendtner¹. **Subs not used:** Fabianski, Vela, Silvestre, Traore.

MARCH

6th	● Burnley	H	W 3–1	**Att:** 60,043. **Ref:** C Foy – (4-5-1): Almunia, Eboue, Silvestre, Vermaelen, Clichy, Walcott¹, Rosicky (Arshavin¹ 61), Denilson, Fabregas¹ (Diaby 39), Nasri, Bendtner (Eduardo 73). **Subs not used:** Fabianski, Sagna, Traore, Eastmond.
9th	◉ FC Porto	H	W 5–0	**Att:** 59,661. **Ref:** F De Bleeckere – (4-3-3): Almunia, Sagna, Campbell, Vermaelen▌, Clichy, Nasri¹ (Denilson 72), Song, Diaby, Rosicky (Eboue¹ 57), Bendtner¹³, Arshavin (Walcott 76). **Subs not used:** Fabianski, Eduardo, Silvestre, Traore. Agg: 6–2.
13th	● Hull	A	W 1–2	**Att:** 25,023. **Ref:** A Marriner – (4-2-3-1): Almunia, Sagna, Campbell▌, Vermaelen, Clichy, Denilson, Diaby, Eboue (Walcott 65), Nasri (Eduardo 76), Arshavin¹, Bendtner¹. **Subs not used:** Fabianski, Silvestre, Traore, Merida, Eastmond.
20th	● West Ham	H	W 2–0	**Att:** 60,077. **Ref:** M Atkinson – (4-3-3): Almunia, Eboue, Campbell▌, Vermaelen▌, Clichy, Fabregas¹, Song, Denilson¹, Nasri (Sagna 74), Bendtner (Diaby 58), Arshavin (Eduardo 84). **Subs not used:** Fabianski, Rosicky, Walcott, Silvestre.
27th	● Birmingham	A	D 1–1	**Att:** 27,039. **Ref:** H Webb – (4-2-3-1): Almunia, Sagna, Campbell, Diaby, Clichy▌, Denilson, Song▌, Walcott (Nasri¹ 68), Fabregas, Rosicky (Arshavin 68), Bendtner. **Subs not used:** Fabianski, Eduardo, Vela, Eboue, Traore.
31st	● Barcelona	H	D 2–2	**Att:** 59,572. **Ref:** M Busacca – (4-3-3): Almunia, Sagna (Walcott¹ 66), Gallas (Denilson 44), Vermaelen, Clichy, Fabregas¹▌, Song▌, Diaby▌, Nasri, Bendtner, Arshavin▌ (Eboue¹ 27). **Subs not used:** Fabianski, Rosicky, Eduardo, Campbell.

APRIL

3rd	● Wolverhampton	H	W 1–0	**Att:** 60,067. **Ref:** A Marriner – (4-3-3): Almunia, Sagna, Campbell, Vermaelen, Silvestre, Eboue (Bendtner¹ 64), Song (Nasri 71), Denilson, Walcott, Eduardo (Vela 79), Rosicky. **Subs not used:** Fabianski, Diaby, Clichy, Eastmond.
6th	● Barcelona	A	L 4–1	**Att:** 95,000. **Ref:** W Stark – (4-2-3-1): Almunia, Sagna, Vermaelen, Silvestre (Eboue 63), Clichy, Denilson▌, Diaby, Walcott, Nasri, Rosicky▌ (Eduardo 73), Bendtner¹. **Subs not used:** Fabianski, Traore, Campbell, Merida, Eastmond. Agg: 6–3.
14th	● Tottenham	A	L 2–1	**Att:** 36,041. **Ref:** M Clattenburg – (4-3-3): Almunia, Sagna (Walcott 52), Campbell, Vermaelen (Silvestre 20), Clichy, Eboue, Diaby, Denilson▌ (van Persie 68), Rosicky, Bendtner¹, Nasri. **Subs not used:** Fabianski, Eduardo, Merida, Eastmond.
18th	● Wigan	A	L 3–2	**Att:** 22,113. **Ref:** L Mason – (4-4-1-1): Fabianski, Sagna, Campbell, Silvestre¹, Clichy, Walcott¹ (Eboue 81), Eastmond (van Persie 90), Diaby, Nasri▌, Rosicky (Merida 81), Bendtner. **Subs not used:** Mannone, Vela, Traore, Henderson.
24th	● Man City	H	D 0–0	**Att:** 60,086. **Ref:** M Dean – (4-2-3-1): Fabianski, Sagna, Campbell, Silvestre▌, Clichy, Song▌, Diaby▌, Walcott (Bendtner 68), Nasri, Rosicky (Eboue 68), van Persie▌. **Subs not used:** Mannone, Eduardo, Vela, Traore, Eastmond.

MAY

3rd	● Blackburn	A	L 2–1	**Att:** 26,138. **Ref:** 275441 – (4-3-3): Fabianski, Sagna, Campbell▌, Silvestre▌, Traore, Eboue (Eduardo 77), Diaby, Walcott, Nasri, Vela (Arshavin 67), van Persie¹. **Subs not used:** Mannone, Djourou, Gibbs, Eastmond, Henderson.
9th	● Fulham	H	W 4–0	**Att:** 60,039. **Ref:** M Jones – (4-2-3-1): Fabianski▌, Sagna, Campbell, Silvestre (Djourou 62), Clichy, Eboue▌, Diaby, Walcott (Lansbury 77), Nasri, Arshavin¹ (Vela¹ 77), van Persie¹. **Subs not used:** Mannone, Gibbs, Merida, Eastmond. Baird OG.

● Barclays Premier League ● FA Cup ◉ Carling Cup ● UEFA Champions League ● Europa League ● FA Community Shield ▌ Yellow Card ▌ Red Card

OFFICIAL FOOTBALL YEARBOOK OF THE ENGLISH & SCOTTISH LEAGUES 2010-2011 **45**

ARSENAL

BARCLAYS PREMIER LEAGUE GOALKEEPER STATS

Player	Minutes on pitch	Appearances	Match starts	Completed matches	Sub appearances	Subbed off	Saved with feet	Punched	Parried	Tipped over	Fumbled	Tipped round	Caught	Blocked	Clean sheets	Goals conceded	Save %	Saved	Resulting in goals	Opposition miss	Fouls committed	Free-kicks won	Yellow cards	Red cards
Manuel Almunia	2799	29	29	29	0	0	0	19	8	1	3	4	88	5	10	31	80.13	2	4	0	1	7	1	0
Lukasz Fabianski	386	4	4	4	0	0	0	3	1	2	0	0	12	0	2	5	78.26	0	0	0	0	2	1	0
Vito Mannone	484	5	5	5	0	0	0	2	11	0	0	2	9	0	2	5	82.76	0	1	0	0	2	1	0

BARCLAYS PREMIER LEAGUE OUTFIELD PLAYER STATS

Player	Minutes on pitch	Appearances	Match starts	Completed matches	Substitute appearances	Subbed off	Goals scored	Assists	Shots on target	Shots off target	Crosses	Tackles made	Defensive clearances	Defensive blocks	Fouls committed	Free-kicks won	Caught offside	Yellow cards	Red cards
Andrey Arshavin	2395	30	25	13	5	12	10	2	46	25	33	12	0	1	38	30	22	2	0
Nicklas Bendtner	1337	23	13	8	10	5	6	6	23	24	7	5	8	0	10	13	9	2	0
Sol Campbell	1028	11	10	10	1	0	0	0	2	3	0	17	6	9	9	5	0	3	0
Gael Clichy	2246	24	23	23	1	0	0	1	5	3	24	29	6	3	21	25	1	4	0
Neves Denilson	1666	20	19	13	1	6	3	3	14	6	5	15	7	2	29	38	0	2	0
Abou Diaby	2483	29	26	21	3	5	6	3	22	10	2	31	18	4	49	44	4	2	0
Johan Djourou	32	1	0	0	1	0	0	0	0	0	0	0	0	0	1	3	0	0	0
Craig Eastmond	184	4	2	0	2	2	0	0	2	0	0	8	2	0	3	4	0	0	0
Emmanuel Eboue	1597	25	17	7	8	10	1	4	4	9	15	18	4	2	16	42	5	4	0
Eduardo Da Silva	1195	24	13	0	11	13	2	6	19	17	8	5	0	1	9	9	9	0	0
Cesc Fabregas	2329	27	26	20	1	6	15	15	41	28	61	23	3	3	30	56	2	5	0
William Gallas	2509	26	26	26	0	0	3	0	7	7	0	19	28	13	12	12	6	2	0
Kieran Gibbs	287	3	3	3	0	0	0	0	1	0	1	3	2	0	2	1	1	1	0
Henri Lansbury	17	1	0	0	1	0	0	0	1	0	0	0	0	0	0	0	1	0	0
Fran Merida	80	4	0	0	4	0	1	0	1	0	0	1	0	0	2	3	0	0	0
Samir Nasri	2003	26	22	14	4	8	2	5	24	9	30	12	1	1	12	19	6	2	0
Aaron Ramsey	854	18	7	4	11	3	3	3	7	9	4	3	1	0	9	13	0	0	0
Tomas Rosicky	1387	25	14	2	11	12	3	4	20	15	12	10	1	0	11	32	2	1	0
Bacary Sagna	2961	35	31	27	4	4	0	5	2	6	70	31	12	8	24	38	0	3	0
Mikael Silvestre	929	12	9	8	3	1	1	0	2	2	4	9	2	3	12	5	0	2	0
Alex Song	2394	26	25	22	1	3	1	1	5	7	2	26	10	5	54	38	0	10	0
Armand Traore	850	9	9	7	0	2	0	0	0	0	9	9	9	1	5	6	0	2	0
Carlos Vela	278	11	1	1	10	1	1	0	2	2	1	1	0	0	6	7	2	0	0
Thomas Vermaelen	2999	33	33	30	0	2	7	1	19	15	0	31	15	13	26	26	3	3	1
Theo Walcott	1210	23	12	3	11	9	3	2	18	11	37	9	1	0	7	15	5	0	0
Jack Wilshere	4	1	0	0	1	0	0	0	0	0	0	0	0	0	0	0	0	0	0
Robin van Persie	1339	16	14	11	2	3	9	7	41	25	19	2	7	0	23	26	19	3	0

actim

BARCLAYS PREMIER LEAGUE

SEASON TOTALS

Goals scored	83
Goals conceded	41
Clean sheets	14
Shots on target	328
Shots off target	233
Shots per goal	6.76
Pens awarded	4
Pens scored	3
Pens conceded	7
Offsides	97
Corners	258
Crosses	345
Players used	30
Fouls committed	421
Free-kicks won	521

CARDS RECEIVED

56   1

SEQUENCES

Wins	6
(10/02/10–20/03/10)	
Losses	2
(on four occasions)	
Draws	–
(–)	
Undefeated	10
(05/12/09–27/01/10)	
Without win	4
(14/04/10–03/05/10)	
Undefeated home	7
(10/02/10–09/05/10)	
Undefeated away	5
(13/12/09–27/01/10)	
Without scoring	2
(21/11/09–29/11/09)	
Without conceding	2
(on three occasions)	
Scoring	11
(15/08/09–07/11/09)	
Conceding	4
(15/08/09–12/09/09)	

LEAGUE POSITION AT THE END OF EACH MONTH

AUG	SEP	OCT	NOV	DEC	JAN	FEB	MAR	APR	MAY
6	6	3	4	3	3	3	3	3	3

SEASON INFORMATION

Highest position: 1
Lowest position: 9
Average goals scored per game: 2.18
Average goals conceded per game: 1.08

MATCH RECORDS

Goals scored per match

		W	D	L	Pts
Failed to score	5	0	2	3	2
Scored 1 goal	9	3	2	4	11
Scored 2 goals	10	6	2	2	20
Scored 3 goals	6	6	0	0	18
Scored 4+ goals	8	8	0	0	24

Goals conceded per match

		W	D	L	Pts
Clean sheet	14	12	2	0	38
Conceded 1 goal	12	9	2	1	29
Conceded 2 goals	8	2	2	4	8
Conceded 3 goals	3	0	0	3	0
Conceded 4+ goals	1	0	0	1	0

EARLIEST STRIKE

NEVES DENILSON
(v West Ham) 4:28

LATEST STRIKE

NICKLAS BENDTNER
(v Wolves) 93:55

Theo Walcott

GOAL DETAILS

How the goals were struck

SCORED		CONCEDED
48	Right foot	19
20	Left foot	9
12	Header	11
3	Other	2

How the goals were struck

SCORED		CONCEDED
60	Open play	25
5	Cross	2
5	Corner	4
3	Penalty	5
3	Direct from free-kick	1
3	Free-kick	1
4	Own goal	3

Distance from goal

SCORED		CONCEDED
27	6YDS	14
40	18YDS	24
16	18+YDS	3

GOALS SCORED/CONCEDED PER FIVE-MINUTE INTERVALS

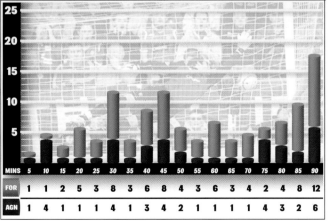

MINS	5	10	15	20	25	30	35	40	45	50	55	60	65	70	75	80	85	90
FOR	1	1	2	5	3	8	3	6	8	4	3	6	3	4	2	4	8	12
AGN	1	4	1	1	1	4	1	3	4	2	1	1	1	1	4	3	2	6

ASTON VILLA

CLUB SUMMARY

FORMED	1874
MANAGER	Martin O'Neill
GROUND	Villa Park
CAPACITY	42,584
NICKNAME	The Villans
WEBSITE	www.avfc.co.uk

The New Football Pools PLAYER OF THE SEASON — James Milner

OVERALL
P	W	D	L	F	A	GD
52	26	15	11	82	60	22

BARCLAYS PREMIER LEAGUE
Pos	P	W	D	L	F	A	GD	Pts
6	38	17	13	8	52	39	13	64

HOME
Pos	P	W	D	L	F	A	GD	Pts
12	19	8	8	3	29	16	13	32

AWAY
Pos	P	W	D	L	F	A	GD	Pts
3	19	9	5	5	23	23	0	32

CUP PROGRESS DETAILS
Competition	Round reached	Knocked out by
Europa League	R2	Rapid Vienna
FA Cup	SF	Chelsea
Carling Cup	R-UP	Man Utd

BIGGEST WIN (ALL COMPS)
07/11/09 5–1 v Bolton

BIGGEST DEFEAT (ALL COMPS)
27/03/10 1–7 v Chelsea

THE PLAYER WITH THE MOST
GOALS SCORED	Gabriel Agbonlahor	**13**
SHOTS ON TARGET	Gabriel Agbonlahor	**50**
SHOTS OFF TARGET	Ashley Young	**26**
SHOTS WITHOUT SCORING	Stiliyan Petrov	**34**
ASSISTS	James Milner	**12**
OFFSIDES	Gabriel Agbonlahor	**38**
FOULS	John Carew	**61**
FOULS WITHOUT A CARD	Stewart Downing	**7**
FREE-KICKS WON	Stiliyan Petrov	**77**
DEFENSIVE CLEARANCES	Richard Dunne	**74**

actim INDEX FOR THE 2009/10 BARCLAYS PREMIER LEAGUE SEASON

RANK	PLAYER	PTS
6	Gabriel Agbonlahor	621
11	James Milner	560
12	Richard Dunne	551

ATTENDANCE RECORD
HIGH	AVERAGE	LOW
42,788	38,573	32,917
v Liverpool (29/12/2009)		v Fulham (30/08/2009)

ASTON VILLA were left to reflect on what might have been after coming close to achieving a domestic Cup double and narrowly missing out on a UEFA Champions League spot so coveted by manager Martin O'Neill.

O'Neill may have subsequently pointed to a couple of contentious refereeing decisions as having a significant bearing on Villa's failure to collect their first major silverware for 14 years, but the club ultimately again paid the price for running out of steam in the final part of the season when a top-four spot looked up for grabs.

This time around their downfall was a series of draws rather than a run of defeats – apart from a humiliating 7–1 loss at Chelsea – which had been the case 12 months earlier. Being held at home by Wolves and then Sunderland before that heavy setback at Stamford Bridge in the space of eight days at the end of March proved to be pivotal in the final outcome. Villa were always playing catch-up on the likes of Tottenham and Manchester City after that, although qualifying for the Europa League for a third successive season is no mean feat.

O'Neill had offset the loss of captain Gareth Barry to Manchester City for £12million by splashing out nearly £40million in the summer of 2009 on Stewart Downing, Stephen Warnock, Richard Dunne, James Collins, Fabian Delph and Habib Beye. Crucially, he was not able to bring in additional quality during the winter transfer window that might have given Villa a fresh injection of impetus. O'Neill eventually conceded that he had to adapt a 'sell to buy' policy in January if he was to add to his squad.

In February, Villa reached the Carling Cup final – their first domestic Cup final appearance for a decade – only to lose 2–1 to Manchester United, despite going ahead through an early James Milner penalty. In the League, their top-four challenge subsequently fizzled out, while they returned to Wembley for an FA Cup semi-final against Chelsea but were swept aside 3–0 with all three goals coming in the last 25 minutes.

They at least had the consolation of enjoying bragging rights over city rivals Birmingham, with a 1–0 win at St Andrew's in September being followed up by the same scoreline at Villa Park in the penultimate home game of the season.

O'Neill often spoke of the need to rotate because progress in both Cup competitions meant that his side found themselves with a demanding League schedule – one spell in March consisted of five games in 15 days. But instead he preferred to keep faith with his tried-and-tested group of 13 to 14 players, even when the likes of Dunne, Warnock and inspirational captain Stiliyan Petrov were not 100 per cent fit.

The major plus point of the season was the form of Milner, whom O'Neill successfully converted from a wide player into a central midfielder. Milner revelled in the role with his vision and ceaseless energy and he also reached double figures for goals and impressed England manager Fabio Capello. His form led to the two big-spending Manchester clubs, City and United, being linked with a move for the former Leeds and Newcastle player, although O'Neill has stressed the need for Villa to keep hold of their best players if they are to make further progress.

Ashley Young again impressed on the right flank with his skill and accuracy from crosses and at dead-ball situations. Up front, John Carew, after an injury-hit start to the season, and Gabriel Agbonlahor managed 30-plus goals between them in all competitions but Emile Heskey became a marginal figure at a time when he was looking to impress Capello in the battle for a World Cup spot.

Petrov successfully filled the role of captain vacated by Barry after his move to Eastlands and Dunne and Collins formed a solid centre-back pairing.

O'Neill will certainly want to bolster his ranks ahead of 2010/11, but Villa may well have already made their most important signing when the Northern Irishman made public his desire to stay with the club following rumours that he was about to quit in the summer.

> Martin O'Neill's Villa battled for most of the season on three fronts, but ultimately came up short in the League and both Cups

CLOCKWISE FROM ABOVE: Ashley Young smashes home a penalty as Aston Villa beat Liverpool 3–1 at Anfield in the second fixture of the season; Martin O'Neill and James Collins look on as Manchester United lift the Carling Cup trophy following a 2–1 final defeat at Wembley; James Milner and Gabriel Agbonlahor celebrate a December win over Sunderland

ASTON VILLA

AUGUST

15th ● Wigan   H   L 0–2   **Att:** 35,578. **Ref:** M Clattenburg – (4-4-2): Friedel, Beye (Albrighton 68), Cuellar, Davies, Shorey, Milner, Delph▮ (Sidwell 61), Petrov, A Young▮, Agbonlahor (Delfouneso 77), Heskey. **Subs not used:** Guzan, Reo-Coker, Gardner, Clark.

20th ● Rapid Vienna   A   L 1–0   **Att:** 17,800. **Ref:** A Tudor – (4-5-1): Guzan, Shorey, Davies (Lowry 80), Cuellar, Beye, A Young, Sidwell▮, Reo-Coker, Gardner (Agbonlahor 55), Milner, Heskey. **Subs not used:** Friedel, Albrighton, Delfouneso, Delph, Petrov.

24th ● Liverpool   A   W 1–3   **Att:** 43,667. **Ref:** M Atkinson – (4-5-1): Friedel, Beye, Davies▮, Cuellar, Shorey, Milner, Sidwell, Petrov, Reo-Coker▮, A Young▮ (Heskey 80), Agbonlahor. **Subs not used:** Guzan, Albrighton, Delfouneso, Delph, Gardner, Lowry. Lucas OG.

27th ● Rapid Vienna   H   W 2–1   **Att:** 22,563. **Ref:** C Velasco Carballo – (4-4-2): Guzan, Beye, Cuellar▮, Davies (Lowry 83), Shorey, Milner▮, Petrov, Delph (Albrighton 86), A Young▮, Heskey (Agbonlahor 82), Carew▮. **Subs not used:** Friedel, Sidwell, Reo-Coker, Gardner. Agg: 2-2; Rapid Vienna win on away goals rule.

30th ● Fulham   H   W 2–0   **Att:** 32,917. **Ref:** S Bennett – (4-5-1): Friedel, Beye, Cuellar, Clark, Shorey, Petrov, Milner, Sidwell▮, Reo-Coker (Carew 72), A Young, Agbonlahor▮. **Subs not used:** Guzan, Albrighton, Delph, Heskey, Warnock, Gardner. Pantsil OG.

SEPTEMBER

13th ● Birmingham   A   W 0–1   **Att:** 25,196. **Ref:** H Webb – (4-4-2): Friedel, Cuellar, Dunne, Collins, Warnock, Milner, Sidwell▮, Reo-Coker (Carew 71), Petrov, A Young, Agbonlahor▮▮. **Subs not used:** Guzan, Delph, Heskey, Shorey, Beye, Gardner.

19th ● Portsmouth   H   W 2–0   **Att:** 35,979. **Ref:** S Attwell – (4-1-3-2): Friedel, Cuellar▮, Dunne, Collins, Warnock, Petrov, Milner▮, Sidwell, A Young, Agbonlahor▮▮, Carew (Heskey 65 (Delph 80)). **Subs not used:** Guzan, Delfouneso, Shorey, Beye, Gardner.

23rd ● Cardiff   H   W 1–0   **Att:** 22,527. **Ref:** A Taylor – (4-4-2): Guzan, Beye▮, Cuellar, Collins, Shorey, Milner, Delph▮, Petrov, Gardner (Albrighton 79), Agbonlahor▮, Carew. **Subs not used:** Friedel, Sidwell, Dunne, Delfouneso, Warnock, Clark.

26th ● Blackburn   A   L 2–1   **Att:** 25,172. **Ref:** M Clattenburg – (4-4-2): Friedel, Cuellar, Dunne, Collins, Warnock, Milner, Delph▮ (Heskey 57), Petrov▮, A Young, Carew, Agbonlahor▮. **Subs not used:** Guzan, Delfouneso, Reo-Coker, Shorey, Beye, Gardner.

OCTOBER

5th ● Man City   H   D 1–1   **Att:** 37,924. **Ref:** M Dean – (4-1-3-2): Friedel, Cuellar, Dunne▮, Collins, Warnock, Milner, Petrov▮, Sidwell, A Young (Reo-Coker 81), Agbonlahor, Carew (Heskey 69). **Subs not used:** Guzan, Delph, Shorey, Beye, Gardner.

17th ● Chelsea   H   W 2–1   **Att:** 39,047. **Ref:** K Friend – (4-1-3-2): Friedel, Cuellar, Collins▮, Dunne▮, Warnock, Petrov, Milner▮, Sidwell, A Young, Carew (Heskey 82), Agbonlahor▮. **Subs not used:** Guzan, Delph, Reo-Coker, Shorey, Beye, Gardner.

24th ● Wolverhampton   A   D 1–1   **Att:** 28,734. **Ref:** P Walton – (4-4-2): Friedel, Cuellar, Collins, Dunne, Warnock▮, Milner, Petrov, Sidwell, A Young, Carew▮ (Heskey 71), Agbonlahor▮. **Subs not used:** Guzan, L Young, Delph, Reo-Coker, Gardner, Clark.

27th ● Sunderland   A   D 0–0   **Att:** 27,666. **Ref:** P Dowd – (4-4-2): Guzan, Cuellar, Dunne, Collins▮, Warnock▮, Milner, Reo-Coker (Delph 91), Petrov▮ (Sidwell 115), A Young, Agbonlahor, Heskey (Carew 77). **Subs not used:** Friedel, L Young, Shorey, Beye. AET – Score after 90 mins 0–0. Aston Villa win 3–1 on penalties.

31st ● Everton   A   D 1–1   **Att:** 36,648. **Ref:** L Probert – (4-4-2): Friedel, Cuellar▮▮, Dunne, Collins, Warnock▮, Milner (Carew▮▮ 46), Petrov (Reo-Coker 90), Sidwell, A Young, Heskey, Agbonlahor. **Subs not used:** Guzan, L Young, Delph, Shorey, Beye.

NOVEMBER

4th ● West Ham   A   L 2–1   **Att:** 30,024. **Ref:** S Bennett – (4-4-2): Friedel, Beye▮▮, Dunne, Collins▮, Warnock, Agbonlahor, Petrov▮, Sidwell, A Young▮▮, Heskey (Reo-Coker 46), Carew (L Young 86). **Subs not used:** Guzan, Albrighton, Delfouneso, Delph, Shorey.

7th ● Bolton   H   W 5–1   **Att:** 38,101. **Ref:** M Clattenburg – (4-4-2): Friedel, L Young▮, Cuellar▮, Dunne, Warnock, Milner▮ (Delfouneso 82), Reo-Coker (Delph 86), Sidwell (Gardner▮ 86), A Young, Carew▮, Agbonlahor▮. **Subs not used:** Guzan, Albrighton, Shorey, Clark.

21st ● Burnley   A   D 1–1   **Att:** 21,178. **Ref:** H Webb – (4-4-2): Friedel, L Young (Heskey▮ 80), Cuellar▮, Dunne▮, Warnock, Milner, Petrov, Sidwell▮ (Downing 70), A Young, Carew, Agbonlahor. **Subs not used:** Guzan, Delph, Reo-Coker, Shorey, Beye.

28th ● Tottenham   H   D 1–1   **Att:** 39,866. **Ref:** P Dowd – (4-4-2): Friedel, L Young, Beye, Cuellar, Dunne, Milner, Petrov, Reo-Coker (Sidwell 71), A Young, Agbonlahor▮, Carew (Heskey 75). **Subs not used:** Guzan, Downing, Delph, Gardner, Clark.

DECEMBER

1st ● Portsmouth   A   W 2–4   **Att:** 17,034. **Ref:** L Mason – (4-3-3): Guzan, L Young▮, Dunne, Cuellar, Warnock, Milner▮▮, Petrov, Downing▮, Agbonlahor▮▮, Heskey▮ (Delfouneso 90), A Young. **Subs not used:** Friedel, Delph, Reo-Coker, Beye, Gardner, Clark.

5th ● Hull   H   W 3–0   **Att:** 39,748. **Ref:** S Attwell – (4-4-2): Friedel, L Young▮▮, Dunne▮, Cuellar▮, Warnock, A Young, Milner▮, Petrov▮, Downing, Agbonlahor, Heskey (Carew▮ 78). **Subs not used:** Guzan, Sidwell, Delph, Reo-Coker, Beye, Collins.

12th ● Man Utd   A   W 0–1   **Att:** 75,130. **Ref:** M Atkinson – (4-4-2): Friedel, L Young▮, Dunne, Cuellar, Warnock (Collins 62), A Young, Milner, Petrov, Downing (Reo-Coker 81), Agbonlahor▮, Heskey (Carew 74). **Subs not used:** Guzan, Sidwell, Delph, Beye.

15th ● Sunderland   A   W 0–2   **Att:** 34,821. **Ref:** K Friend – (4-4-2): Friedel, L Young▮, Cuellar, Dunne, Warnock, A Young, Petrov, Milner▮▮, Downing, Heskey▮, Agbonlahor (Sidwell 90). **Subs not used:** Guzan, Carew, Delph, Reo-Coker, Beye, Collins.

19th ● Stoke   H   W 1–0   **Att:** 35,852. **Ref:** L Probert – (4-4-2): Friedel, L Young, Cuellar, Dunne, Warnock, A Young, Milner, Petrov, Downing (Sidwell 81), Agbonlahor, Heskey (Carew▮ 23). **Subs not used:** Guzan, Delph, Reo-Coker, Beye, Collins.

27th ● Arsenal   A   L 3–0   **Att:** 60,056. **Ref:** P Dowd – (4-4-2): Friedel, L Young▮ (Delph▮ 76), Dunne, Cuellar▮, Warnock, A Young, Petrov, Milner, Downing, Agbonlahor, Heskey (Carew 63). **Subs not used:** Guzan, Sidwell, Reo-Coker, Beye, Collins.

29th ● Liverpool   H   L 0–1   **Att:** 42,788. **Ref:** L Probert – (4-4-2): Friedel, L Young, Cuellar, Dunne▮, Warnock, Reo-Coker (Albrighton 72), Milner, Petrov, Downing (Sidwell 79), Agbonlahor, Carew. **Subs not used:** Guzan, Delfouneso, Delph, Beye, Collins.

JANUARY

2nd ● Blackburn   H   W 3–1   **Att:** 25,453. **Ref:** H Webb – (4-4-2): Guzan, Beye, Cuellar▮, Collins, Warnock, A Young, Reo-Coker▮, Delph (Sidwell 46), Downing, Delfouneso▮ (Carew▮ 75), Heskey. **Subs not used:** Friedel, L Young, Dunne, Albrighton, Petrov.

14th ● Blackburn   A   W 0–1   **Att:** 18,595. **Ref:** M Clattenburg – (4-4-2): Guzan, Collins, Dunne, Cuellar, Warnock, A Young, Milner▮, Petrov, Downing, Heskey (Sidwell 71), Agbonlahor▮. **Subs not used:** Friedel, L Young, Carew, Delph, Reo-Coker, Beye.

17th ● West Ham   H   D 0–0   **Att:** 35,646. **Ref:** M Jones – (4-1-3-2): Friedel, Cuellar, Collins, Dunne, Petrov▮, A Young, Milner, Downing, Agbonlahor, Heskey (Carew 57). **Subs not used:** Guzan, L Young, Sidwell, Delfouneso, Delph, Beye.

20th ● Blackburn   H   W 6–4   **Att:** 40,406. **Ref:** M Atkinson – (4-1-3-2): Guzan, Cuellar, Dunne, Collins, Warnock▮, Petrov, Milner▮▮, Downing (Sidwell 86), A Young▮, Agbonlahor▮, Heskey▮▮▮. **Subs not used:** Friedel, L Young, Albrighton, Delfouneso, Delph, Beye. Nzonzi OG. Agg: 7–4.

● Barclays Premier League ● FA Cup ● Carling Cup ● UEFA Champions League ● Europa League ● FA Community Shield   ▮ Yellow Card ▮ Red Card

RESULTS 2009/10

23rd	● Brighton	H	W 3–2	**Att:** 39,725. **Ref:** A Taylor – (4-5-1): Guzan, L Young[1], Beye, Collins▮, Warnock (C Davies 50), Albrighton (Milner 13), Sidwell, Downing, Delph[1], A Young (Lowry 86), Delfouneso[1]. **Subs not used:** Friedel, Agbonlahor, Petrov, Clark.
27th	● Arsenal	H	D 0–0	**Att:** 39,601. **Ref:** L Probert – (4-4-2): Friedel, Cuellar, Collins, Dunne▮, L Young, A Young, Milner, Petrov, Downing, Agbonlahor, Heskey▮ (Delph 78). **Subs not used:** Guzan, Sidwell, Delfouneso, Davies, Shorey, Beye.
30th	● Fulham	A	W 0–2	**Att:** 25,408. **Ref:** L Mason – (4-4-2): Friedel, Cuellar, Collins, Dunne, L Young▮, Downing, Milner, Petrov, A Young, Heskey▮, Agbonlahor[2]. **Subs not used:** Guzan, Sidwell, Delfouneso, C Davies, Delph, Shorey, Beye.

FEBRUARY

6th	● Tottenham	A	D 0–0	**Att:** 35,899. **Ref:** C Foy – (4-4-2): Friedel, Cuellar, Collins, Dunne, L Young, A Young, Milner, Petrov, Downing (Sidwell 88), Heskey (Carew 21), Agbonlahor. **Subs not used:** Guzan, Delfouneso, Davies, Delph, Beye.
10th	● Man Utd	H	D 1–1	**Att:** 42,788. **Ref:** P Walton – (4-1-4-1): Friedel, Cuellar[1], Collins, Dunne, L Young, Petrov (Sidwell 64), A Young, Milner, Delph (Carew 58), Downing, Agbonlahor. **Subs not used:** Guzan, Delfouneso, Davies, Salifou, Beye.
14th	● Crystal Palace	A	D 2–2	**Att:** 20,486. **Ref:** K Friend – (4-5-1): Friedel, L Young, Dunne, Collins[1], Warnock, A Young, Milner, Delph▮ (Delfouneso 75), Petrov[1], Downing, Heskey (Carew 46). **Subs not used:** Guzan, Sidwell, Davies, Beye, Cuellar.
21st	● Burnley	H	W 5–2	**Att:** 38,709. **Ref:** S Attwell – (4-4-2): Friedel, Cuellar, Dunne, Collins, Warnock, A Young[1] (Sidwell 82), Milner, Petrov, Downing[2], Agbonlahor[1] (Carew 71), Heskey▮ (Delfouneso 76). **Subs not used:** Guzan, L Young, Delph, Beye.
24th	● Crystal Palace	H	W 3–1	**Att:** 31,874. **Ref:** M Atkinson – (4-4-2): Guzan, L Young, Cuellar, Dunne, Warnock, A Young, Milner, Delph (Sidwell 76), Downing, Carew[2], Agbonlahor[1]. **Subs not used:** Friedel, Delfouneso, Davies, Heskey, Beye, Collins.
28th	◎ Man Utd	N	L 1–2	**Att:** 88,596. **Ref:** P Dowd – (4-4-2): Friedel, Cuellar (Carew 80), Collins▮, Dunne, Warnock, A Young, Milner[1], Petrov, Downing▮, Heskey, Agbonlahor. **Subs not used:** Guzan, L Young, Sidwell, Delfouneso, Delph, Beye.

MARCH

7th	● Reading	A	W 2–4	**Att:** 23,175. **Ref:** M Dean – (4-4-2): Friedel, Cuellar, Dunne▮, Collins▮, Warnock, Downing (Sidwell 90), Milner▮, Petrov, A Young[1], Carew[3], Heskey. **Subs not used:** Guzan, L Young, Albrighton, Delfouneso, Delph, Beye.
13th	● Stoke	A	D 0–0	**Att:** 27,598. **Ref:** K Friend – (4-4-2): Friedel, Cuellar▮, Dunne▮, Collins, Warnock▮, Downing, Milner▮, Petrov, A Young, Heskey, Carew (Agbonlahor 77). **Subs not used:** Guzan, L Young, Sidwell, Delfouneso, Delph, Beye.
16th	● Wigan	A	W 1–2	**Att:** 16,186. **Ref:** S Bennett – (4-4-2): Friedel, Cuellar, Dunne▮, Collins, Warnock, Downing, Milner[1], Petrov, A Young, Agbonlahor (Sidwell 81), Carew (Heskey 81). **Subs not used:** Guzan, L Young, Delfouneso, Delph, Beye. McCarthy OG.
20th	● Wolverhampton	H	D 2–2	**Att:** 37,562. **Ref:** M Clattenburg – (4-4-2): Friedel, Cuellar, Collins, Dunne (Albrighton 72), Warnock, A Young, Milner, Petrov▮, Downing (Sidwell 77), Carew[2], Heskey. **Subs not used:** Guzan, L Young, Delfouneso, Beye, Clark.
24th	● Sunderland	H	D 1–1	**Att:** 37,473. **Ref:** M Dean – (4-4-2): Friedel, Cuellar, Collins, Dunne, Warnock, A Young, Milner (Sidwell 77), Petrov, Downing, Carew[1], Heskey (Delfouneso 14). **Subs not used:** Guzan, L Young, Albrighton, Salifou, Beye.
27th	● Chelsea	A	L 7–1	**Att:** 41,825. **Ref:** P Walton – (4-4-2): Friedel, L Young, Collins, Dunne▮, Warnock, Milner, Petrov▮ (Downing 63), Sidwell, A Young, Carew[1] (Delfouneso 63), Agbonlahor (Beye 71). **Subs not used:** Guzan, Davies, Salifou, Cuellar.

APRIL

3rd	● Bolton	A	W 0–1	**Att:** 21,111. **Ref:** M Jones – (4-4-2): Friedel, Cuellar, Dunne, Collins, Warnock, A Young[1], Petrov, Delph (Sidwell 75), Downing, Carew (Heskey 70), Agbonlahor. **Subs not used:** Guzan, L Young, Milner, Delfouneso, Beye.
10th	● Chelsea	N	L 0–3	**Att:** 85,472. **Ref:** H Webb – (4-4-2): Friedel, Cuellar, Dunne, Collins, Warnock, A Young, Milner, Petrov, Downing, Agbonlahor, Carew (Heskey 82). **Subs not used:** Guzan, L Young, Sidwell, Delfouneso, Delph, Beye.
14th	● Everton	H	D 2–2	**Att:** 38,729. **Ref:** M Atkinson – (4-1-3-2): Friedel, Cuellar, Collins, Dunne, Warnock (Delfouneso 77), Petrov▮, A Young, Milner▮, Downing, Agbonlahor[1], Carew. **Subs not used:** Guzan, L Young, Sidwell, Delph, Heskey, Beye. Jagielka OG.
18th	● Portsmouth	A	W 1–2	**Att:** 16,523. **Ref:** L Probert – (4-4-2): Friedel, Cuellar, Dunne, Collins, Warnock, A Young, Milner, Petrov, Downing, Carew[1] (Heskey 72), Agbonlahor (Delfouneso[1] 80). **Subs not used:** Guzan, Sidwell, Reo-Coker, Beye, Clark.
21st	● Hull	A	W 0–2	**Att:** 23,842. **Ref:** M Dean – (4-4-2): Friedel, Cuellar, Collins, Dunne, Warnock, Downing, Milner▮▮, Petrov▮ (Sidwell 84), A Young, Agbonlahor[1], Carew (Heskey 90). **Subs not used:** Guzan, L Young, Delfouneso, Reo-Coker, Beye.
25th	● Birmingham	H	W 1–0	**Att:** 42,788. **Ref:** M Atkinson – (4-4-2): Friedel, Cuellar▮, Collins, Dunne, Warnock, Downing, Petrov, Milner[1], A Young, Agbonlahor, Carew (Heskey 70). **Subs not used:** Guzan, L Young, Sidwell, Delfouneso, Reo-Coker, Beye.

MAY

1st	● Man City	A	L 3–1	**Att:** 47,102. **Ref:** M Clattenburg – (4-4-2): Friedel, Cuellar, Collins▮, Dunne, Warnock (Heskey 74), Downing, Petrov▮, Milner, A Young, Carew[1] (Delfouneso 74), Agbonlahor. **Subs not used:** Guzan, L Young, Sidwell, Reo-Coker, Beye.
9th	● Blackburn	H	L 0–1	**Att:** 41,799. **Ref:** S Bennett – (4-4-2): Friedel, Cuellar, Collins, Dunne▮, Warnock (L Young▮ 41), A Young, Milner, Petrov, Downing, Carew (Heskey 75), Agbonlahor (Delfouneso 78). **Subs not used:** Guzan, Sidwell, Reo-Coker, Beye.

● Barclays Premier League ● FA Cup ● Carling Cup ● UEFA Champions League ● Europa League ● FA Community Shield ▮ Yellow Card ▮ Red Card

ASTON VILLA

BARCLAYS PREMIER LEAGUE GOALKEEPER STATS

Player	Minutes on pitch	Appearances	Match starts	Completed matches	Sub appearances	Subbed off	Saved with feet	Punched	Parried	Tipped over	Fumbled	Tipped round	Caught	Blocked	Clean sheets	Goals conceded	Save %	Saved	Resulting in goals	Opposition miss	Fouls committed	Free-kicks won	Yellow cards	Red cards
Brad Friedel	3638	38	38	38	0	0	1	27	37	10	0	11	96	8	15	39	82.97	0	6	0	0	5	0	0

BARCLAYS PREMIER LEAGUE OUTFIELD PLAYER STATS

Player	Minutes on pitch	Appearances	Match starts	Completed matches	Substitute appearances	Subbed off	Goals scored	Assists	Shots on target	Shots off target	Crosses	Tackles made	Defensive clearances	Defensive blocks	Fouls committed	Free-kicks won	Caught offside	Yellow cards	Red cards
Gabriel Agbonlahor	3259	36	35	28	1	7	13	5	50	13	32	17	4	3	47	56	38	3	0
Marc Albrighton	72	3	0	0	3	0	0	0	0	0	4	0	0	1	1	0	0	0	0
Habib Beye	465	6	5	3	1	1	0	0	0	0	1	4	4	3	3	1	1	1	1
John Carew	2213	33	22	7	11	15	10	5	29	22	9	4	25	4	61	16	20	2	0
Ciaran Clark	94	1	1	1	0	0	0	0	0	1	0	0	1	0	0	1	0	0	0
James Collins	2524	27	26	26	1	0	1	0	13	12	0	44	41	38	29	11	0	2	0
Carlos Cuellar	3439	36	36	35	0	0	2	3	7	5	20	57	51	30	31	12	0	7	1
Curtis Davies	192	2	2	2	0	0	1	0	2	0	0	3	8	0	3	1	0	0	0
Nathan Delfouneso	223	9	0	0	9	0	1	0	4	1	4	0	0	0	2	2	1	0	0
Fabian Delph	311	8	4	0	4	4	0	0	2	1	2	2	0	1	6	5	0	3	0
Stewart Downing	2191	25	23	18	2	5	2	1	29	16	67	19	4	3	7	12	3	0	0
Richard Dunne	3329	35	35	34	0	1	3	0	8	10	0	61	74	41	36	18	1	7	0
Craig Gardner	7	1	0	0	1	0	0	0	0	0	0	0	0	0	1	0	0	1	0
Emile Heskey	1401	31	16	5	15	11	3	2	15	2	2	13	12	1	29	31	5	2	0
James Milner	3366	36	36	33	0	3	7	12	31	24	93	64	6	9	42	54	2	5	0
Stiliyan Petrov	3459	37	37	33	0	4	0	2	16	18	11	63	24	17	45	77	1	10	0
Nigel Reo-Coker	551	10	6	1	4	5	0	1	2	2	0	7	1	1	8	6	1	1	0
Nicky Shorey	286	3	3	3	0	0	0	1	1	0	6	3	0	0	1	0	0	0	0
Steve Sidwell	1337	25	12	10	13	2	0	2	9	17	4	17	7	5	24	8	2	3	0
Stephen Warnock	2753	30	30	26	0	4	0	3	2	6	40	53	14	13	20	23	1	3	0
Luke Young	1364	16	14	12	2	2	0	0	4	1	11	20	13	4	16	6	1	4	0
Ashley Young	3499	37	37	34	0	3	5	10	24	26	178	40	2	1	49	75	8	6	0

actim

BARCLAYS PREMIER LEAGUE

SEASON TOTALS

Goals scored	52
Goals conceded	39
Clean sheets	15
Shots on target	239
Shots off target	190
Shots per goal	8.25
Pens awarded	8
Pens scored	5
Pens conceded	6
Offsides	85
Corners	241
Crosses	484
Players used	23
Fouls committed	461
Free-kicks won	420

CARDS RECEIVED

60 **2**

SEQUENCES

Wins	4
(on two occasions)	
Losses	2
(on two occasions)	
Draws	2
(on five occasions)	
Undefeated	10
(17/01/10–24/03/10)	
Without win	4
(27/12/09–27/01/10)	
Undefeated home	8
(on two occasions)	
Undefeated away	4
(30/01/10–16/03/10)	
Without scoring	4
(27/12/09–27/01/10)	
Without conceding	4
(on two occasions)	
Scoring	17
(24/08/09–19/12/09)	
Conceding	9
(26/09/09–28/11/09)	

League position chart

AUG SEP OCT NOV DEC JAN FEB MAR APR MAY

LEAGUE POSITION AT THE END OF EACH MONTH

8 7 7 6 6 7 7 7 5 6

SEASON INFORMATION

Highest position: 3
Lowest position: 17
Average goals scored per game: 1.37
Average goals conceded per game: 1.03

MATCH RECORDS

Goals scored per match

		W	D	L	Pts
Failed to score	8	0	4	4	4
Scored 1 goal	16	5	7	4	22
Scored 2 goals	10	8	2	0	26
Scored 3 goals	2	2	0	0	6
Scored 4+ goals	2	2	0	0	6

Goals conceded per match

		W	D	L	Pts
Clean sheet	15	11	4	0	37
Conceded 1 goal	14	5	7	2	22
Conceded 2 goals	6	1	2	3	5
Conceded 3 goals	2	0	0	2	0
Conceded 4+ goals	1	0	0	1	0

GOALS SCORED/CONCEDED PER FIVE-MINUTE INTERVALS

MINS	5	10	15	20	25	30	35	40	45	50	55	60	65	70	75	80	85	90
FOR	3	1	4	4	3	3	4	1	4	1	3	3	4	1	4	2	4	3
AGN	0	3	2	0	5	1	1	1	6	0	0	2	2	2	2	1	4	7

EARLIEST STRIKE

GABRIEL AGBONLAHOR
(v Blackburn) 2:19

LATEST STRIKE

JOHN CAREW
(v Hull) 87:23

John Carew

GOAL DETAILS

How the goals were struck

SCORED		CONCEDED
25	Right foot	29
11	Left foot	5
16	Header	5
0	Other	0

How the goals were struck

SCORED		CONCEDED
30	Open play	21
10	Cross	3
3	Corner	1
5	Penalty	6
0	Direct from free-kick	1
0	Free-kick	4
4	Own goal	3

Distance from goal

SCORED		CONCEDED
19	6YDS	13
26	18YDS	22
7	18+YDS	4

BIRMINGHAM CITY

CLUB SUMMARY

FORMED	1875
MANAGER	Alex McLeish
GROUND	St Andrew's
CAPACITY	30,079
NICKNAME	The Blues
WEBSITE	www.bcfc.com

The New
Football Pools
PLAYER OF THE SEASON

Joe Hart

OVERALL

P	W	D	L	F	A	GD
45	17	12	16	45	54	-9

BARCLAYS PREMIER LEAGUE

Pos	P	W	D	L	F	A	GD	Pts
9	38	13	11	14	38	47	-9	50

HOME

Pos	P	W	D	L	F	A	GD	Pts
11	19	8	9	2	19	13	6	33

AWAY

Pos	P	W	D	L	F	A	GD	Pts
10	19	5	2	12	19	34	-15	17

CUP PROGRESS DETAILS

Competition	Round reached	Knocked out by
FA Cup	QF	Portsmouth
Carling Cup	R3	Sunderland

BIGGEST WIN (ALL COMPS)
05/12/09 3–2 v Wigan

BIGGEST DEFEAT (ALL COMPS)
11/04/10 1–5 v Man City

THE PLAYER WITH THE MOST

GOALS SCORED Cameron Jerome		**11**
SHOTS ON TARGET Cameron Jerome		**40**
SHOTS OFF TARGET Cameron Jerome		**26**
SHOTS WITHOUT SCORING Keith Fahey		**19**
ASSISTS Christian Benitez		**5**
OFFSIDES Christian Benitez		**40**
FOULS Lee Bowyer, James McFadden		**45**
FOULS WITHOUT A CARD Kevin Phillips		**4**
FREE-KICKS WON Lee Bowyer		**71**
DEFENSIVE CLEARANCES Roger Johnson		**98**

actim INDEX FOR THE 2009/10 BARCLAYS PREMIER LEAGUE SEASON

RANK	PLAYER	PTS
31	Joe Hart	430
42	Roger Johnson	407
52	Stephen Carr	384

ATTENDANCE RECORD

HIGH	AVERAGE	LOW
28,958	25,246	19,922
v Chelsea (26/12/2009)		v Portsmouth (19/08/2009)

CLOCKWISE FROM ABOVE: On-loan goalkeeper Joe Hart makes a great save in a narrow defeat at Arsenal; Cameron Jerome scores the first of two goals against Portsmouth in March; Alex McLeish looks on during his side's 11-match unbeaten run; Lee Bowyer gets lifted up following his winning goal against West Ham

BIRMINGHAM confounded the pre-season predictions of many by holding down a top-10 position in the Barclays Premier League for the majority of the 2009/10 campaign and eventually finishing in ninth place.

Alex McLeish's side had been tipped to make a swift return to the Coca-Cola Championship after finishing runners-up to Wolves but McLeish brought together a mixture of youth and experience to ensure City remained in the top flight, having previously yo-yoed between the two divisions.

Carson Yeung's takeover of the club, following 16 years under the stewardship of David Sullivan and David Gold, was confirmed in October, with the Hong Kong businessman promising to invest major funds in the team to build on the successes of 2009/10.

It was Birmingham's home form that provided the bedrock for their success as they remained unbeaten in front of their own fans following a defeat to Bolton in late September. The Blues also achieved the not inconsiderable feat of taking a point off each of the so-called 'big four' of Manchester United, Chelsea, Arsenal and Liverpool, in addition to UEFA Champions League hopefuls Tottenham and Manchester City.

McLeish spent only around £10million net in the summer before Gold and Sullivan departed to take over at West Ham. But the former Rangers and Scotland manager used his limited funds wisely on two vastly experienced midfielders in Lee Bowyer and Barry Ferguson, as well as defenders Roger Johnson and Scott Dann.

Bowyer had already proved his worth during the second half of the promotion season on loan from West Ham and he chipped in with some crucial goals after making his move permanent. Ferguson also arrived from Rangers following a turbulent few months and fitted effortlessly into a deeper midfield role.

However, it was at the back that former Scotland defender McLeish really showed his worth. In the centre of defence, Johnson and Dann made the step up from Cardiff and Coventry respectively and their resolute performances typified the spirit engendered in the City side by McLeish.

The Blues boss was also inspired as he took a chance on a loanee goalkeeper, a once-retired right-back and converted a central defender into a left-back.

Joe Hart was a revelation in goal during a season-long loan from Manchester City, and ultimately did enough to make the England squad for the World Cup.

Stephen Carr had been persuaded to come out of retirement by McLeish midway through the previous campaign and the former Newcastle and Ireland player proved to be a solid performer on the right flank and took over the captain's armband from Lee Carsley.

At left-back, former central defender Liam Ridgewell performed well enough to keep out more orthodox wide men Gregory Vignal and Franck Queudrue and also weighed in with some priceless goals from deep against Tottenham and Liverpool.

City struggled for goals up front but Cameron Jerome confirmed his promise by achieving double figures and Kevin Phillips proved that he can still make an impact in the twilight of his career from the substitutes' bench.

McLeish is keen on bringing in a proven striker, as he proved in trying to sign Kenwyne Jones and Roman Pavlyuchenko during the January transfer window from Sunderland and Tottenham respectively. He will also expect January signing Michel, from Sporting Gijón, to make his mark in midfield in the coming season having taken time to adjust.

The acid test for the Blues will come when opponents no longer regard them as a surprise commodity and the likes of Johnson and Dann will have to prove they are not one-season wonders, with top-flight strikers sure to have a better understanding of their strengths and weaknesses.

McLeish has shown himself to be ahead of the game so far in terms of assembling a squad with the qualities needed to remain among the elite and now he must look to establish the Blues in the Barclays Premier League.

Birmingham made the step up to the top flight look easy, with Alex McLeish making the most of the players at his disposal

BIRMINGHAM CITY

RESULTS 2009/10

AUGUST

16th	● Man Utd	A	L 1-0	**Att:** 75,062. **Ref:** L Mason – (4-5-1): Hart, Carr, R Johnson, Queudrue, Vignal▌, Larsson (O'Shea 81), Ferguson, Carsley (Benitez 74), Fahey, McFadden, Jerome (O'Connor 65). **Subs not used:** M Taylor, Phillips, McSheffrey, Parnaby.
19th	● Portsmouth	H	W 1-0	**Att:** 19,922. **Ref:** L Probert – (4-4-2): Hart, Carr, R Johnson, Queudrue, Vignal (Parnaby 49), Larsson, Ferguson, Fahey, McFadden▌, O'Connor (Benitez 81), Jerome (Phillips 54). **Subs not used:** M Taylor, Carsley McSheffrey, O'Shea.
22nd	● Stoke	H	D 0-0	**Att:** 21,694. **Ref:** C Foy – (4-4-2): Hart, Parnaby, Queudrue, R Johnson, Carr, Bowyer (Larsson 61), Ferguson, Fahey, McFadden, O'Connor, Phillips (Benitez 53). **Subs not used:** M Taylor, Espinoza, McSheffrey, O'Shea, Carsley.
25th	● Southampton	A	W 1-2	**Att:** 11,753. **Ref:** P Crossley – (4-5-1): M Taylor, Parnaby, Espinoza▌, Queudrue, Carr, O'Shea (McFadden 46), Larsson (O'Connor 61), Carsley▌, Bowyer▌, McSheffrey, Benitez. **Subs not used:** Hart, R Johnson, Ferguson.
29th	● Tottenham	A	L 2-1	**Att:** 35,318. **Ref:** P Walton – (4-5-1): Hart, Parnaby, R Johnson, Queudrue, Carr▌, Larsson (McSheffrey 90), Ferguson, Carsley (Benitez 73), Bowyer▌, McFadden, O'Connor▌. **Subs not used:** M Taylor, Phillips, Espinoza, O'Shea.

SEPTEMBER

13th	● Aston Villa	H	L 0-1	**Att:** 25,196. **Ref:** H Webb – (4-5-1): Hart, Tainio, R Johnson, Queudrue, Parnaby▌, Larsson, Bowyer, Ferguson, McFadden (Carsley 46 (Phillips 86)), Fahey, O'Connor (Benitez 79). **Subs not used:** M Taylor, Espinoza, McSheffrey, D Johnson.
19th	● Hull	A	W 0-1	**Att:** 23,759. **Ref:** P Dowd – (4-5-1): Hart, Parnaby, Dann, R Johnson, Carr▌, McSheffrey (O'Connor▌ 62), Bowyer, Tainio, Ferguson, Fahey, Benitez. **Subs not used:** M Taylor, Phillips, Espinoza, O'Shea, Sammons.
22nd	● Sunderland	A	L 2-0	**Att:** 20,576. **Ref:** M Dean – (4-4-2): M Taylor, Espinoza▌, Ridgewell, Dann, Parnaby (Preston▌ 79), O'Connor, Sammons, Ferguson (Fahey 63), McSheffrey, O'Shea (Bowyer 63), Phillips. **Subs not used:** Doyle, Benitez, R Johnson.
26th	● Bolton	H	L 1-2	**Att:** 28,671. **Ref:** S Bennett – (4-5-1): Hart, Carr▌, R Johnson▌, Dann, Vignal (Phillips▌ 76), Larsson, Bowyer, Tainio (O'Connor 61), Ferguson, Fahey, Benitez. **Subs not used:** M Taylor, Ridgewell, Espinoza, McSheffrey, Carsley.

OCTOBER

3rd	● Burnley	A	L 2-1	**Att:** 20,102. **Ref:** K Friend – (4-4-1-1): Hart, Carr▌, R Johnson, Dann▌, Queudrue (Ridgewell 46), Fahey (Larsson[1] 46), Ferguson▌, Tainio (Phillips 67), McFadden, Bowyer, O'Connor. **Subs not used:** M Taylor, McSheffrey, O'Shea, Carsley.
17th	● Arsenal	A	L 3-1	**Att:** 60,082. **Ref:** L Probert – (4-5-1): Hart▌, Carr, R Johnson, Dann, Ridgewell▌, Larsson, Ferguson, Bowyer▌, Carsley (Phillips 79), McFadden (McSheffrey 70), Jerome (O'Connor 61). **Subs not used:** M Taylor, D Johnson, Bent, O'Shea.
24th	● Sunderland	H	W 2-1	**Att:** 21,723. **Ref:** M Atkinson – (4-4-2): Hart, Carr, R Johnson▌, Dann, Ridgewell[1], Larsson (Carsley 84), Ferguson▌, Bowyer, McFadden[1] (O'Connor 76), Jerome (McSheffrey▌ 76), Benitez. **Subs not used:** M Taylor, Phillips, Queudrue, Parnaby.

NOVEMBER

1st	● Man City	H	D 0-0	**Att:** 21,462. **Ref:** M Dean – (4-4-2): M Taylor, Carr, R Johnson, Dann▌, Ridgewell, Larsson, Ferguson▌▌, Bowyer, McFadden▌ (Fahey 61), Jerome (Phillips 88), Benitez. **Subs not used:** Doyle, McSheffrey, Parnaby, Carsley, Vignal.
9th	● Liverpool	A	D 2-2	**Att:** 42,560. **Ref:** P Walton – (4-4-1-1): Hart, Carr, R Johnson, Dann, Ridgewell, Larsson, Bowyer, Tainio (Carsley▌ 15), McFadden▌ (Vignal 67), Benitez[1] (McSheffrey 86), Jerome[1]. **Subs not used:** M Taylor, Phillips, Espinoza, Queudrue.
21st	● Fulham	H	W 1-0	**Att:** 23,659. **Ref:** C Foy – (4-4-2): Hart, Carr, R Johnson, Dann, Ridgewell, Larsson, Ferguson, Bowyer▌▌, McFadden, Jerome, Benitez (Fahey 71). **Subs not used:** M Taylor, Phillips, McSheffrey, Carsley, Vignal, Mutch.
29th	● Wolverhampton	A	W 0-1	**Att:** 26,668. **Ref:** M Clattenburg – (4-4-2): Hart, Carr, R Johnson, Dann, Ridgewell, Larsson, Ferguson, Bowyer[1], McFadden, Jerome▌, Benitez (Fahey 87). **Subs not used:** M Taylor, McSheffrey, Queudrue, O'Shea, Carsley, Vignal.

DECEMBER

5th	● Wigan	A	W 2-3	**Att:** 18,797. **Ref:** L Probert – (4-4-2): Hart, Carr, Dann, R Johnson, Ridgewell, Larsson[2], Ferguson, Bowyer, McFadden, Benitez[1], Jerome (Fahey 81). **Subs not used:** M Taylor, McSheffrey, Queudrue, O'Shea, Carsley, Vignal.
12th	● West Ham	H	W 1-0	**Att:** 28,203. **Ref:** L Mason – (4-4-2): Hart, Carr, R Johnson, Dann, Ridgewell, Larsson, Ferguson▌, Bowyer[1], McFadden (Phillips 90), Jerome, Benitez (Fahey 90). **Subs not used:** M Taylor, McSheffrey, Queudrue, O'Shea, Carsley, Vignal.
15th	● Blackburn	H	W 2-1	**Att:** 23,187. **Ref:** M Jones – (4-4-2): Hart, Carr, R Johnson, Dann, Ridgewell, Larsson, Ferguson▌, Bowyer, McFadden (Fahey 82), Jerome▌ (Phillips 90), Benitez. **Subs not used:** M Taylor, Vignal, McSheffrey, O'Shea, Carsley, Phillips.
20th	● Everton	A	D 1-1	**Att:** 33,660. **Ref:** S Attwell – (4-4-2): Hart▌, Carr, R Johnson, Dann, Ridgewell, Larsson▌[1], Bowyer, Ferguson, McFadden (Fahey 69), Jerome, Benitez (Vignal 82). **Subs not used:** M Taylor, Phillips, McSheffrey, D Johnson, Carsley.
26th	● Chelsea	H	D 0-0	**Att:** 28,958. **Ref:** P Walton – (4-4-2): Hart, Carr, R Johnson, Dann, Ridgewell, Larsson (D Johnson 88), Ferguson, Bowyer▌, McFadden (Fahey 77), Jerome, Benitez. **Subs not used:** M Taylor, Phillips, McSheffrey, Carsley, Vignal.
28th	● Stoke	A	W 0-1	**Att:** 27,211. **Ref:** M Atkinson – (4-4-2): Hart, Carr▌, R Johnson, Dann, Ridgewell, Larsson (Fahey 77), Ferguson, Bowyer▌, McFadden, Jerome▌▌, Benitez. **Subs not used:** M Taylor, Phillips, McSheffrey, D Johnson, Carsley, Vignal.

JANUARY

2nd	● Nottm Forest	A	D 0-0	**Att:** 20,975. **Ref:** S Bennett – (4-4-2): Hart▌, Parnaby (McSheffrey 21), Ridgewell, R Johnson, Vignal, D Johnson, Ferguson, Carsley (Bowyer 39), Fahey, Phillips (Benitez 85), Jerome. **Subs not used:** Doyle, Martin Taylor, McFadden, Queudrue.
9th	● Man Utd	H	D 1-1	**Att:** 28,907. **Ref:** M Clattenburg – (4-4-2): Hart, Carr▌, R Johnson, Dann, Ridgewell, Larsson▌ (Fahey 83), Ferguson, Bowyer, McFadden, Jerome[1], Benitez. **Subs not used:** M Taylor, Martin Taylor, Phillips, McSheffrey, Queudrue, Parnaby.
12th	● Nottm Forest	H	W 1-0	**Att:** 9,399. **Ref:** K Friend – (4-4-2): Hart, Carr, R Johnson, Dann, Ridgewell, Larsson, Ferguson▌[1], Bowyer▌ (Fahey 64), McFadden (D Johnson 76), Jerome, Benitez (Phillips 68). **Subs not used:** M Taylor, Martin Taylor, McSheffrey, Queudrue.
23rd	● Everton	H	W 1-2	**Att:** 30,875. **Ref:** H Webb – (4-4-1-1): Hart, Carr, R Johnson, Dann, Ridgewell, Larsson, Bowyer, Ferguson[1], Fahey, McFadden (McSheffrey 89), Benitez[1] (Jervis 79). **Subs not used:** M Taylor, Marcos Madera, Queudrue, D Johnson, Vignal.
27th	● Chelsea	A	L 3-0	**Att:** 41,293. **Ref:** S Bennett – (4-4-2): Hart, Carr, R Johnson, Dann, Ridgewell, Larsson, Bowyer, Ferguson, McFadden▌ (Marcos Madera 72), Jerome (Fahey 56), Benitez. **Subs not used:** M Taylor, McSheffrey, Queudrue, D Johnson, Vignal.
30th	● Tottenham	H	D 1-1	**Att:** 27,238. **Ref:** S Attwell – (4-4-2): Hart, Carr▌, R Johnson▌, Dann, Ridgewell[1], Larsson (Fahey 58), Bowyer▌ (Marcos Madera 65), Ferguson, McFadden▌, Benitez, Jerome. **Subs not used:** M Taylor, Queudrue, D Johnson, Vignal, Gardner.

● Barclays Premier League ● FA Cup ● Carling Cup ● UEFA Champions League ● Europa League ● FA Community Shield ▌ Yellow Card ▌ Red Card

RESULTS 2009/10

FEBRUARY

7th	● Wolverhampton	H	W 2–1	**Att:** 24,165. **Ref:** L Probert – (4-4-2): Hart▌, Carr, R Johnson▌, Dann▌, Ridgewell, Larsson (Gardner 68), Ferguson▌, Bowyer▌, McFadden (Fahey 74), Jerome, Benitez (Phillips[2] 63). **Subs not used:** M Taylor, Michel, Vignal, Jervis.
10th	● West Ham	A	L 2–0	**Att:** 34,458. **Ref:** M Dean – (4-4-2): Hart, Carr, R Johnson, Dann▌, Ridgewell, Gardner, Ferguson, Bowyer▌ (Michel 77), Fahey (McFadden 66), Phillips, Jerome. **Subs not used:** M Taylor, Larsson, Parnaby, Vignal, Jervis.
13th	● Derby	A	W 1–2	**Att:** 21,043. **Ref:** M Atkinson – (4-4-2): Hart, Carr, R Johnson, Dann[1], Ridgewell[1], Larsson (Fahey 64), Bowyer, Ferguson, McFadden (Gardner[1] 82), Jerome, Benitez (Phillips 65). **Subs not used:** M Taylor, Madera, Parnaby, Vignal.
21st	● Fulham	A	L 2–1	**Att:** 21,758. **Ref:** P Dowd – (4-4-2): Hart, Carr, Dann, R Johnson, Ridgewell, Fahey, Bowyer, Ferguson (Michel 90), Larsson (Gardner 68), McFadden▌, Jerome (Phillips 77). **Subs not used:** M Taylor, Benitez, Parnaby, Vignal. Baird OG.
27th	● Wigan	H	W 1–0	**Att:** 25,921. **Ref:** A Taylor – (4-4-2): Hart, Carr (Gardner 84), R Johnson, Dann, Ridgewell▌, Larsson, Ferguson, Bowyer, Fahey, Jerome (Michel 90), McFadden[1] (Phillips 64). **Subs not used:** M Taylor, Benitez, Parnaby, Vignal.

MARCH

6th	● Portsmouth	A	L 2–0	**Att:** 20,456. **Ref:** S Bennett – (4-4-2): Hart, Carr, R Johnson, Dann, Ridgewell, Larsson (Gardner 84), Bowyer, Ferguson▌, Fahey (Phillips 72), McFadden (Benitez 75), Jerome. **Subs not used:** M Taylor, Murphy, Michel, Parnaby.
9th	● Portsmouth	A	W 1–2	**Att:** 18,465. **Ref:** M Jones – (4-4-2): Hart, Parnaby (Tainio 52), R Johnson, Dann, Ridgewell, Gardner, Ferguson, Michel▌ (Larsson 77), Fahey, Jerome[2], Benitez▌ (McFadden 80). **Subs not used:** M Taylor, Murphy, Queudrue, Jervis.
13th	● Everton	H	D 2–2	**Att:** 24,579. **Ref:** L Probert – (4-4-2): Hart, Carr, R Johnson, Dann, Ridgewell, Gardner[1] (Larsson 59), Ferguson, Bowyer▌, Fahey, Jerome[1], Benitez (McFadden 72). **Subs not used:** M Taylor, Phillips, Michel, Queudrue, Tainio.
20th	● Sunderland	A	L 3–1	**Att:** 37,962. **Ref:** P Walton – (4-4-2): Hart, Carr, Dann, R Johnson, Ridgewell, Gardner▌, Michel (Bowyer 72), Ferguson, Fahey (McFadden 59), Jerome[1], Benitez (Phillips 60). **Subs not used:** M Taylor, Larsson, Parnaby, Vignal.
24th	● Blackburn	A	L 2–1	**Att:** 23,856. **Ref:** M Clattenburg – (4-4-1-1): Hart, Carr▌, R Johnson, Dann, Ridgewell, Gardner (Larsson 74), Bowyer, Ferguson, Fahey (Phillips 79), McFadden▌, Jerome (Benitez 73). **Subs not used:** M Taylor, Michel, Parnaby, Vignal.
27th	● Arsenal	H	D 1–1	**Att:** 27,039. **Ref:** H Webb – (4-4-2): Hart, Carr▌, R Johnson, Dann, Ridgewell, Gardner▌, Ferguson▌, Bowyer▌, Fahey (Phillips[1] 83), Jerome, McFadden (Benitez 76). **Subs not used:** M Taylor, Larsson, Michel, Parnaby, Vignal.

APRIL

4th	● Liverpool	H	D 1–1	**Att:** 27,909. **Ref:** M Atkinson – (4-4-2): Hart, Carr, R Johnson, Dann, Ridgewell▌, Gardner▌, Ferguson, Bowyer, Fahey▌, Jerome, McFadden (Phillips 78). **Subs not used:** M Taylor, Larsson, Benitez, Michel, Parnaby, Vignal.
11th	● Man City	A	L 5–1	**Att:** 45,209. **Ref:** P Dowd – (4-4-2): M Taylor, Carr (Larsson 57), R Johnson, Dann, Ridgewell, Gardner, Bowyer, Ferguson, Fahey▌ (Phillips 66), Jerome▌ (Benitez 72), McFadden. **Subs not used:** Doyle, Michel, Parnaby, Vignal.
17th	● Hull	H	D 0–0	**Att:** 26,669. **Ref:** M Clattenburg – (4-4-2): Hart, Carr, R Johnson, Dann, Ridgewell, Gardner, Ferguson, Bowyer, Fahey (Larsson 63), Jerome, McFadden (Phillips 60). **Subs not used:** M Taylor, Benitez, Michel, Parnaby, Vignal.
25th	● Aston Villa	A	L 1–0	**Att:** 42,788. **Ref:** M Atkinson – (4-5-1): Hart, Carr▌, R Johnson▌, Ridgewell, Vignal▌ (Parnaby 75), Larsson (Fahey 75), Gardner (Phillips 85), Bowyer, Ferguson▌, McFadden, Jerome. **Subs not used:** M Taylor, Benitez, Michel, Tainio.

MAY

1st	● Burnley	H	W 2–1	**Att:** 24,578. **Ref:** P Walton – (4-4-2): Hart, Parnaby▌ (Fahey 79), R Johnson, Ridgewell, Vignal▌, Larsson, Bowyer, Ferguson, McFadden (Michel 66), Jerome[1] (Carsley 90), Benitez[1]. **Subs not used:** M Taylor, Murphy, Tainio, Redmond.
9th	● Bolton	A	L 2–1	**Att:** 22,863. **Ref:** K Friend – (4-4-1-1): Hart, Carr, Ridgewell▌, R Johnson▌, Vignal, Larsson▌ (Benitez 65), Bowyer▌, Ferguson, McFadden▌[1], Michel (Fahey 74), Jerome. **Subs not used:** M Taylor, Murphy, Parnaby, Carsley, Mutch.

● Barclays Premier League ● FA Cup ● Carling Cup ● UEFA Champions League ● Europa League ● FA Community Shield   ▌Yellow Card ▌Red Card

Roger Johnson holds off Wolves' Sylvan Ebanks-Blake as Lee Bowyer watches on. Johnson, signed from Cardiff, was a key figure in Birmingham's defence during 2009/10

BIRMINGHAM CITY

BARCLAYS PREMIER LEAGUE GOALKEEPER STATS

Player	Minutes on pitch	Appearances	Match starts	Completed matches	Sub appearances	Subbed off	Saved with feet	Punched	Parried	Tipped over	Fumbled	Tipped round	Caught	Blocked	Clean sheets	Goals conceded	Save %	Saved	Resulting in goals	Opposition miss	Fouls committed	Free-kicks won	Yellow cards	Red cards
Joe Hart	3451	36	36	36	0	0	0	21	26	9	1	10	161	5	10	42	84.67	0	2	0	1	6	3	0
Maik Taylor	194	2	2	2	0	0	0	0	1	1	1	1	6	0	1	5	64.29	0	1	0	0	0	0	0

BARCLAYS PREMIER LEAGUE OUTFIELD PLAYER STATS

Player	Minutes on pitch	Appearances	Match starts	Completed matches	Substitute appearances	Subbed off	Goals scored	Assists	Shots on target	Shots off target	Crosses	Tackles made	Defensive clearances	Defensive blocks	Fouls committed	Free-kicks won	Caught offside	Yellow cards	Red cards
Christian Benitez	2057	30	21	12	9	9	3	5	31	11	7	4	1	1	18	36	40	1	0
Lee Bowyer	3205	35	34	31	1	3	5	3	25	20	16	62	12	10	45	71	2	8	0
Stephen Carr	3308	35	35	33	0	2	0	2	3	1	37	45	33	17	41	23	0	10	0
Lee Carsley	366	7	3	0	4	4	0	0	1	2	0	4	12	6	4	2	0	1	0
Scott Dann	2880	30	30	30	0	0	0	2	2	9	2	46	63	24	25	18	1	4	0
Keith Fahey	1844	34	18	11	16	7	0	3	11	8	23	32	5	4	8	25	0	2	0
Barry Ferguson	3543	37	37	35	0	1	0	0	7	8	13	46	29	17	35	44	1	8	1
Craig Gardner	954	13	10	7	3	3	1	2	10	5	18	25	7	3	22	11	1	3	0
Cameron Jerome	2819	32	32	20	0	12	11	4	40	26	16	13	16	0	40	40	19	5	0
Roger Johnson	3645	38	38	38	0	0	0	1	6	9	4	45	98	31	23	68	5	8	0
Damien Johnson	8	1	0	0	1	0	0	0	0	1	1	0	0	0	0	0	0	0	0
Sebastian Larsson	2510	33	26	15	7	11	4	3	23	15	72	36	11	5	35	20	3	3	0
James McFadden	2777	36	32	16	4	16	5	3	28	17	77	39	9	3	45	48	10	6	0
Gary McSheffrey	122	5	1	0	4	1	0	0	1	1	5	0	1	0	4	3	0	1	0
Michel	343	9	3	0	6	3	0	1	1	2	2	11	5	0	10	6	0	1	0
Garry O'Connor	593	10	5	3	5	2	1	0	9	5	1	2	2	0	4	5	8	2	0
James O'Shea	12	1	0	0	1	0	0	0	0	0	0	1	0	0	0	0	0	0	0
Stuart Parnaby	581	8	6	4	2	2	0	0	2	2	5	6	3	1	5	3	0	2	0
Kevin Phillips	505	19	2	1	17	1	4	0	12	3	0	2	0	0	4	7	5	0	0
Franck Queudrue	521	6	6	5	0	1	0	0	2	0	1	18	13	4	4	9	0	0	0
Liam Ridgewell	2931	31	30	30	1	0	3	1	7	5	27	51	36	15	21	29	5	4	0
Teemu Tainio	378	6	5	2	1	3	0	0	0	2	3	6	5	1	3	6	0	0	0
Gregory Vignal	529	8	6	3	2	3	0	0	1	1	14	13	9	3	10	12	0	3	0

actim

BARCLAYS PREMIER LEAGUE

SEASON TOTALS

Goals scored	38
Goals conceded	47
Clean sheets	11
Shots on target	222
Shots off target	153
Shots per goal	9.87
Pens awarded	4
Pens scored	2
Pens conceded	3
Offsides	100
Corners	188
Crosses	345
Players used	25
Fouls committed	407
Free-kicks won	492

CARDS RECEIVED

75 1

SEQUENCES

Wins	5
(21/11/09–15/12/09)	
Losses	3
(26/09/09–17/10/09)	
Draws	2
(on three occasions)	
Undefeated	12
(24/10/09–09/01/10)	
Without win	8
(13/03/10–25/04/10)	
Undefeated home	15
(24/10/09–01/05/10)	
Undefeated away	5
(09/11/09–28/12/09)	
Without scoring	2
(17/04/10–25/04/10)	
Without conceding	2
(on three occasions)	
Scoring	9
(21/02/10–11/04/10)	
Conceding	7
(09/03/10–11/04/10)	

LEAGUE POSITION AT THE END OF EACH MONTH

AUG	SEP	OCT	NOV	DEC	JAN	FEB	MAR	APR	MAY
12	14	15	11	8	8	8	9	9	9

SEASON INFORMATION
Highest position: 3
Lowest position: 17
Average goals scored per game: 1.00
Average goals conceded per game: 1.24

MATCH RECORDS

Goals scored per match

		W	D	L	Pts
Failed to score	9	0	4	5	4
Scored 1 goal	21	7	5	9	26
Scored 2 goals	7	5	2	0	17
Scored 3 goals	1	1	0	0	3
Scored 4+ goals	0	0	0	0	0

Goals conceded per match

		W	D	L	Pts
Clean sheet	11	7	4	0	25
Conceded 1 goal	13	5	5	3	20
Conceded 2 goals	10	1	2	7	5
Conceded 3 goals	3	0	0	3	0
Conceded 4+ goals	1	0	0	1	0

GOALS SCORED/CONCEDED
PER FIVE-MINUTE INTERVALS

MINS	5	10	15	20	25	30	35	40	45	50	55	60	65	70	75	80	85	90
FOR	2	0	1	2	1	3	0	3	5	3	3	2	1	1	3	2	2	4
AGN	4	1	2	3	1	0	4	2	3	1	1	2	2	4	3	0	5	9

EARLIEST STRIKE
LEE BOWYER
(v Wolves) 2:02

LATEST STRIKE
SEBASTIAN LARSSON
(v Burnley) 94:41

Barry Ferguson

GOAL DETAILS

How the goals were struck

SCORED		CONCEDED
23	Right foot	18
6	Left foot	20
4	Header	9
5	Other	0

How the goals were struck

SCORED		CONCEDED
20	Open play	31
4	Cross	3
3	Corner	2
2	Penalty	3
4	Direct from free-kick	3
3	Free-kick	4
2	Own goal	1

Distance from goal

SCORED		CONCEDED
16	6YDS	19
14	18YDS	21
8	18+YDS	7

BLACKBURN ROVERS

CLUB SUMMARY

FORMED	1875
MANAGER	Sam Allardyce
GROUND	Ewood Park
CAPACITY	31,367
NICKNAME	Rovers
WEBSITE	www.rovers.co.uk

The New Football Pools PLAYER OF THE SEASON — David Dunn

OVERALL
P	W	D	L	F	A	GD
45	16	12	17	58	71	-13

BARCLAYS PREMIER LEAGUE
Pos	P	W	D	L	F	A	GD	Pts
10	38	13	11	14	41	55	-14	50

HOME
Pos	P	W	D	L	F	A	GD	Pts
9	19	10	6	3	28	18	10	36

AWAY
Pos	P	W	D	L	F	A	GD	Pts
13	19	3	5	11	13	37	-24	14

CUP PROGRESS DETAILS
Competition	Round reached	Knocked out by
FA Cup	R3	Aston Villa
Carling Cup	SF	Aston Villa

BIGGEST WIN (ALL COMPS)
27/10/09 5–2 v Peterborough

BIGGEST DEFEAT (ALL COMPS)
24/10/09 0–5 v Chelsea

THE PLAYER WITH THE MOST
GOALS SCORED David Dunn	**9**
SHOTS ON TARGET Morten Gamst Pedersen	**30**
SHOTS OFF TARGET Morten Gamst Pedersen	**26**
SHOTS WITHOUT SCORING David Hoilett	**23**
ASSISTS Morten Gamst Pedersen	**6**
OFFSIDES Jason Roberts, Franco Di Santo	**20**
FOULS Steven Nzonzi	**55**
FOULS WITHOUT A CARD David Hoilett	**20**
FREE-KICKS WON Jason Roberts	**50**
DEFENSIVE CLEARANCES Christopher Samba	**65**

actim INDEX FOR THE 2009/10 BARCLAYS PREMIER LEAGUE SEASON

RANK	PLAYER	PTS
60	Paul Robinson	375
61	Ryan Nelsen	374
78	Gael Givet	359

ATTENDANCE RECORD
HIGH	AVERAGE	LOW
29,912	25,428	21,287
v Man Utd (11/04/2010)		v Fulham (17/01/2010)

CLOCKWISE FROM ABOVE: Paul Robinson watches James Milner's effort roll over the line during the Carling Cup semi-final; Jason Roberts celebrates scoring in a 3–0 win against Bolton; Chris Samba helps Rovers to a victory over Arsenal; David Dunn is jubilant after scoring the winner against rivals Burnley at Turf Moor

SAM ALLARDYCE knows what he does best and he stuck to it resolutely at Blackburn during the 2009/10 season. The former Bolton and Newcastle manager has shaped a squad made up primarily of grafters, but featuring touches of flair, into a side that enjoyed a season of relative stability in the Barclays Premier League.

Much like the sides he oversaw during an eight-year spell at Bolton, Allardyce's Rovers played football which was often attritional but generally effective. A top-10 finish, a run to the Carling Cup semi-finals and the emergence of a promising crop of youngsters all demonstrate progress after the previous season's flirtation with relegation.

Allardyce has overcome various obstacles to turn the club around since his appointment as Paul Ince's successor in December 2008 and his first full campaign in charge at Ewood Park should be viewed as a job well done.

Things looked ominous when Rovers – who had sold key players in Roque Santa Cruz and Stephen Warnock over the summer and seen another key man, Tugay, retire – failed to record a win in their opening three League fixtures. But September concluded with victory over Aston Villa and the next home game saw Blackburn take the all-important scalp of local rivals Burnley in an exhilarating 3–2 triumph.

Rovers began to reap the rewards of Sam Allardyce's organisational talents as they secured a top-10 League position

The derby success was sandwiched between two heavy away defeats, a 6–2 reverse at Arsenal and then a 5–0 loss at Chelsea, indicating the frailty of Allardyce's team on the road. However, it subsequently came to light that Blackburn had considered requesting the Stamford Bridge fixture be postponed after the squad, and Allardyce himself, was hit by an outbreak of swine flu.

Worse was to come for the manager, who had to miss four games after tests revealed in November that he required heart surgery. Allardyce's players performed admirably in his absence, however. By the time he returned to work Blackburn had consolidated their mid-table position under the guidance of assistant manager Neil McDonald and beaten Chelsea on a penalty shoot-out, following a dramatic 3–3 draw, to set up a clash with Aston Villa in the last four of the Carling Cup. The semi-final was arguably even more thrilling but ended in heartbreak as Rovers, narrowly defeated 1–0 at home in the first leg, scored four times at Villa Park – only to concede six at the other end.

The Wembley dream was over but Blackburn finished the campaign strongly, having their say at both ends of the table.

Rovers delighted in deepening Burnley's relegation fears by completing the double over their neighbours with a 1–0 win at Turf Moor and, either side of that, they held Chelsea and Manchester United to draws at Ewood Park, which appeared to dent both sides' title challenges at the time.

Blackburn lost only once in their final nine Barclays Premier League games, concluding the campaign with a 2–1 victory over Arsenal at home and a final-day 1–0 win at Villa to secure an impressive 10th-placed finish.

Chelsea manager Carlo Ancelotti and Liverpool's Rafael Benitez were among those to criticise Blackburn's direct approach during the course of the campaign but, while several teams attempting a more flowing style scrambled at the bottom, Allardyce's tactics kept his side well away from trouble.

The bedrock of Blackburn's season was their solid record at home, where they lost only three times in the League, and the return to form of midfielder David Dunn, who finished as their top goalscorer.

Rookies Phil Jones, Nikola Kalinic, Martin Olsson and Steven Nzonzi also made notable contributions and, if Rovers can improve on the road and find a reliable striker, the future looks bright.

BLACKBURN ROVERS

RESULTS 2009/10

AUGUST

15th ● Man City H L 0–2 **Att:** 29,584. **Ref:** M Dean – (4-4-2): Robinson, Jacobsen, Samba, Givet, Warnock▮, Diouf (Hoilett 86), Andrews (Gallagher▮ 75), Nzonzi, Pedersen, Roberts (Di Santo 65), McCarthy. **Subs not used:** Brown, Grella, Khizanishvili, Olsson.

22nd ● Sunderland A L 2–1 **Att:** 37,106. **Ref:** A Wiley – (4-4-2): Robinson, Jacobsen, Samba, Nelsen (Olsson 46), Givet▮, Diouf (McCarthy▮ 71), Andrews, Nzonzi, Pedersen, Roberts, Di Santo (Kalinic 14). **Subs not used:** Brown, Emerton, Grella, Hoilett.

25th ● Gillingham A W 1–3 **Att:** 7,293. **Ref:** K Friend – (4-4-2): Brown▮, Reid▮ (Grella 46), Khizanishvili, Givet, Olsson▮, Dunn[1] (Van Heerden 59), Andrews, Pedersen[1], Nzonzi, Hoilett[1], Kalinic▮ (Roberts 46). **Subs not used:** Fielding, Jacobsen, Warnock, Jones.

29th ● West Ham H D 0–0 **Att:** 23,421. **Ref:** P Dowd – (4-2-3-1): Robinson, Jacobsen, Samba, Givet, Chimbonda, Grella, Nzonzi (Hoilett 60), Andrews, Dunn, Pedersen, Roberts (Kalinic 75). **Subs not used:** Brown, Emerton, Khizanishvili, Olsson, Salgado.

SEPTEMBER

12th ● Wolverhampton H W 3–1 **Att:** 24,845. **Ref:** S Bennett – (4-2-3-1): Robinson, Jacobsen (Salgado 85), Samba (Nelsen 75), Givet, Chimbonda, Andrews▮, Grella, Diouf[1], Dunn[1], Pedersen (Emerton 73), Roberts[1]. **Subs not used:** Brown, Kalinic, Di Santo, Hoilett.

20th ● Everton A L 3–0 **Att:** 35,546. **Ref:** L Mason – (4-2-3-1): Robinson, Salgado (Kalinic 62), Samba, Givet (Nelsen 46), Chimbonda, Andrews, Grella, Diouf▮, Dunn▮, Pedersen (Hoilett 51), Roberts. **Subs not used:** Brown, Emerton, McCarthy, Nzonzi.

22nd ● Nottm Forest A W 0–1 **Att:** 11,553. **Ref:** M Oliver – (4-4-2): Brown, Salgado▮ (Jacobsen 61), Nelsen, Jones, Olsson, Emerton, Nzonzi, Reid (Andrews 75), Hoilett, McCarthy[1] (Chimbonda 90), Kalinic. **Subs not used:** Fielding, Doran, Van Heerden, Gunning.

26th ● Aston Villa H W 2–1 **Att:** 25,172. **Ref:** M Clattenburg – (4-2-3-1): Robinson, Jacobsen, Samba[1] (Salgado 90), Nelsen, Chimbonda, Nzonzi, Grella▮, Diouf (Andrews 71), Dunn[1], Pedersen (Emerton 56), Di Santo. **Subs not used:** Brown, McCarthy, Kalinic, Hoilett.

OCTOBER

4th ● Arsenal A L 6–2 **Att:** 59,431. **Ref:** P Walton – (4-4-1-1): Robinson, Jacobsen, Givet, Chimbonda, Olsson, Emerton (Pedersen 55), Andrews, Nzonzi[1], Diouf, Dunn[1] (McCarthy 61) (Hoilett 70), Di Santo▮. **Subs not used:** Brown, Kalinic, Salgado, Jones.

18th ● Burnley H W 3–2 **Att:** 26,689. **Ref:** C Foy – (4-2-3-1): Robinson, Jacobsen, Samba▮, Nelsen, Chimbonda[1] (Givet 87), Nzonzi▮, Andrews, Diouf (Emerton 81), Dunn[1], Pedersen, Di Santo[1] (Roberts 75). **Subs not used:** Brown, McCarthy, Hoilett, Salgado.

24th ● Chelsea A L 5–0 **Att:** 40,836. **Ref:** A Wiley – (4-4-1-1): Robinson, Jacobsen (Salgado 60), Olsson, Nelsen, Givet, Andrews, Nzonzi, Pedersen▮ (Hoilett 69), Emerton, Diouf, Roberts (Kalinic 53). **Subs not used:** Brown, McCarthy, Reid, Jones.

27th ● Peterborough H W 5–2 **Att:** 8,419. **Ref:** A Taylor – (4-4-2): Brown, Salgado[1], Jones, Givet▮ (Nelsen 59), Olsson, Hoilett, Reid[1] (Dunn 70), Emerton (Andrews 77), Pedersen[1], McCarthy[1], Kalinic[1]. **Subs not used:** Robinson, Jacobsen, Roberts, Van Heerden.

31st ● Man Utd A L 2–0 **Att:** 74,658. **Ref:** P Dowd – (4-1-4-1): Robinson, Chimbonda▮, Samba, Nelsen, Givet, Nzonzi, Emerton▮, Dunn (McCarthy 83), Andrews (Pedersen 57), Diouf, Di Santo (Kalinic 76). **Subs not used:** Brown, Grella, Hoilett, Salgado.

NOVEMBER

7th ● Portsmouth H W 3–1 **Att:** 23,110. **Ref:** A Marriner – (4-4-1-1): Robinson, Chimbonda▮, Samba, Nelsen[1]▮, Givet▮, Diouf (McCarthy 46), Nzonzi, Emerton, Pedersen (Roberts[2] 46), Dunn, Di Santo (Andrews 84). **Subs not used:** Brown, Kalinic, Hoilett, Salgado.

22nd ● Bolton A W 0–2 **Att:** 21,777. **Ref:** M Dean – (4-3-1-2): Robinson, Chimbonda, Samba, Nelsen, Givet (Jacobsen 35), Dunn[1] (Grella 84), Nzonzi, Emerton, Diouf, Di Santo (McCarthy 71), Roberts. **Subs not used:** Brown, Andrews, Kalinic, Salgado. Ricketts OG.

25th ● Fulham A L 3–0 **Att:** 21,414. **Ref:** S Attwell – (4-4-2): Robinson, Jacobsen, Samba, Nelsen, Chimbonda, Andrews, Dunn, Grella, Diouf, Di Santo (Kalinic 66), Roberts (McCarthy 66). **Subs not used:** Brown, Pedersen, Nzonzi, Hoilett, Salgado.

28th ● Stoke H D 0–0 **Att:** 25,143. **Ref:** H Webb – (4-4-1-1): Robinson, Chimbonda, Samba, Nelsen, Givet, Emerton, Nzonzi, Andrews (Grella 46), Diouf (Pedersen 67), Dunn (Roberts 32), Di Santo▮. **Subs not used:** Brown, McCarthy, Kalinic, Salgado.

DECEMBER

2nd ● Chelsea H D 3–3 **Att:** 18,136. **Ref:** A Wiley – (4-3-1-2): Robinson, Salgado, Samba, Nelsen, Chimbonda, Emerton[1], Nzonzi (Van Heerden 91), Pedersen (Grella▮ 62), McCarthy[1], Roberts (Hoilett 70), Kalinic[1]. **Subs not used:** Brown, Givet, Diouf, Jones. AET – Score after 90 mins 2–2. Blackburn win 4–3 on penalties.

5th ● Liverpool H D 0–0 **Att:** 29,660. **Ref:** M Atkinson – (4-4-1-1): Robinson, Chimbonda, Samba, Nelsen, Givet, Emerton, Nzonzi, Grella, Diouf▮ (Hoilett 72), McCarthy (Kalinic 77), Di Santo (Andrews 85). **Subs not used:** Brown, Roberts, Pedersen, Salgado.

12th ● Hull H D 0–0 **Att:** 24,124. **Ref:** C Foy – (4-4-1-1): Robinson, Chimbonda, Samba▮, Nelsen, Givet, Hoilett, Nzonzi, Grella (Andrews 40), Emerton, McCarthy (Kalinic▮ 59), Di Santo (Roberts 76). **Subs not used:** Brown, Pedersen, Diouf, Salgado.

15th ● Birmingham A L 2–1 **Att:** 23,187. **Ref:** M Jones – (4-4-2): Robinson, Chimbonda, Samba, Nelsen▮, Givet, Diouf (Hoilett 53), Emerton (Andrews 22), Nzonzi▮, Pedersen, Roberts (McCarthy 71), Kalinic. **Subs not used:** Brown, Salgado, Jacobsen, Di Santo.

19th ● Tottenham H L 0–2 **Att:** 26,490. **Ref:** P Walton – (4-4-2): Robinson, Jacobsen, Nelsen, Givet, Chimbonda, Salgado (Pedersen 64), Nzonzi, Grella, Hoilett (Roberts 81), McCarthy, Di Santo (Kalinic 72). **Subs not used:** Brown, Andrews, Diouf, Jones.

26th ● Wigan A D 1–1 **Att:** 20,243. **Ref:** M Clattenburg – (4-4-1-1): Robinson, Chimbonda▮ (Jacobsen 67), Samba, Nelsen, Givet▮, Salgado▮ (Pedersen 76), Nzonzi▮, Andrews, Hoilett, McCarthy[1], Di Santo (Roberts 72). **Subs not used:** Brown, Diouf, Kalinic, Jones.

28th ● Sunderland H D 2–2 **Att:** 25,656. **Ref:** M Dean – (4-4-2): Robinson, Chimbonda, Samba, Nelsen, Givet, Hoilett (Diouf[1] 74), Andrews, Nzonzi, Pedersen[1], Roberts (Kalinic 73), McCarthy▮ (Di Santo 73). **Subs not used:** Brown, Jacobsen, Olsson, Salgado.

JANUARY

2nd ● Aston Villa A L 3–1 **Att:** 25,453. **Ref:** H Webb – (4-4-2): Brown, Chimbonda, Givet, Jones, Olsson, Salgado▮ (Rigters 76), Dunn (Khizanishvili 54), Reid, Diouf▮, Di Santo (Pedersen 45), Kalinic[1]. **Subs not used:** Robinson, Doran, Hoilett, Gunning.

11th ● Man City A L 4–1 **Att:** 40,292. **Ref:** C Foy – (4-4-1-1): Robinson, Jacobsen, Samba, Nelsen, Givet, Emerton, Andrews (Hoilett 46), Nzonzi, Pedersen▮, Dunn (Olsson 66), Di Santo (Kalinic 46). **Subs not used:** Brown, Reid, Salgado, Chimbonda.

14th ● Aston Villa A L 0–1 **Att:** 18,595. **Ref:** M Atkinson – (4-4-1-1): Robinson, Jacobsen (Olsson 46), Samba, Nelsen, Chimbonda, Salgado (Reid 71), Emerton, Nzonzi, Pedersen (McCarthy▮ 75), Dunn, Kalinic. **Subs not used:** Brown, Hoilett, Di Santo, Jones.

17th ● Fulham H W 2–0 **Att:** 21,287. **Ref:** K Friend – (4-4-2): Robinson, Chimbonda, Samba[1]▮, Nelsen[1], Givet (Hoilett 58), Emerton (Salgado 83), Nzonzi, Reid (Andrews 70), Olsson, Kalinic, McCarthy. **Subs not used:** Brown, Di Santo, Dunn, Rigters.

20th ● Aston Villa A L 6–4 **Att:** 40,406. **Ref:** M Atkinson – (4-4-1-1): Robinson, Chimbonda, Samba▮, Nelsen, Givet▮, Emerton[1], Nzonzi▮ (Reid 61), Pedersen, Olsson[1], Dunn (McCarthy 56), Kalinic[2] (Di Santo 72). **Subs not used:** Brown, Andrews, Hoilett, Salgado. Agg: 7–4.

● Barclays Premier League ● FA Cup ● Carling Cup ● UEFA Champions League ● Europa League ● FA Community Shield   ▮ Yellow Card ▮ Red Card

RESULTS 2009/10

| 27th | ● Wigan | H | W 2–1 | Att: 22,190. Ref: L Mason – (4-2-3-1): Robinson▌, Chimbonda, Nelsen, Givet, Olsson, Emerton, Nzonzi▌, Hoilett (Reid▌ 54), Pedersen¹, Diouf (Di Santo 77), Kalinic¹ (Roberts 77). Subs not used: Brown, Andrews, Salgado, Jones. |
| 30th | ● West Ham | A | D 0–0 | Att: 33,093. Ref: P Walton – (4-5-1): Robinson, Chimbonda, Samba, Nelsen, Olsson, Diouf (Hoilett 83), Emerton▌ (Andrews 58), Givet, Nzonzi, Pedersen, Kalinic (Roberts 71). Subs not used: Brown, Reid, Di Santo, Salgado. |

FEBRUARY

6th	● Stoke	A	L 3–0	Att: 27,386. Ref: S Bennett – (4-5-1): Robinson, Chimbonda (Salgado 65), Nelsen, Samba▌, Givet, Di Santo (Andrews¹ 60), Emerton, Nzonzi (Reid 73), Pedersen, Olsson, Kalinic. Subs not used: Brown, Roberts, Diouf, Hoilett.
10th	● Hull	H	W 1–0	Att: 23,518. Ref: L Probert – (4-5-1): Robinson, Salgado, Nelsen▌, Givet, Olsson¹, Andrews, Nzonzi, Emerton (Roberts 70), Pedersen, Diouf, Kalinic (Reid 90). Subs not used: Brown, Hoilett, Di Santo, Jones, Chimbonda.
21st	● Bolton	H	W 3–0	Att: 23,888. Ref: C Foy – (4-2-3-1): Robinson, Salgado, Nelsen (Grella 38), Givet¹, Olsson, Andrews, Nzonzi, Hoilett (Roberts¹ 60), Pedersen, Diouf, Kalinic¹ (Dunn 87). Subs not used: Brown, Reid, Di Santo, Chimbonda.
28th	● Liverpool	A	L 2–1	Att: 42,795. Ref: A Wiley – (4-4-1-1): Robinson, Salgado, Samba, Givet, Olsson▌ (Chimbonda 51), Hoilett (Roberts 64) Nzonzi▌ (Grella 60), Andrews¹, Pedersen, Diouf▌, Kalinic▌. Subs not used: Brown, Emerton, Dunn, Di Santo.

MARCH

13th	● Tottenham	A	L 3–1	Att: 35,474. Ref: H Webb – (4-4-1-1): Robinson (Brown 25), Salgado, Samba¹, Givet (Di Santo 74), Chimbonda, Emerton (Andrews 62), Nzonzi, Pedersen, Olsson, Dunn, Kalinic. Subs not used: Roberts, Diouf, Basturk, Hoilett.
21st	● Chelsea	H	D 1–1	Att: 25,554. Ref: S Bennett – (4-2-3-1): Brown, Salgado, Samba, Jones, Olsson, Andrews, Nzonzi (Hoilett 90), Dunn (Emerton 56), Pedersen, Diouf▌, Kalinic (Roberts 63). Subs not used: Bunn, Jacobsen, Linganzi, Chimbonda.
24th	● Birmingham	H	W 2–1	Att: 23,856. Ref: M Clattenburg – (4-2-3-1): Brown, Salgado, Samba, Jones, Olsson, Nzonzi, Andrews▌, Pedersen, Dunn▌² (Emerton 87), Diouf (Hoilett 69), Kalinic (Roberts 46). Subs not used: Bunn, Nelsen, Di Santo, Chimbonda.
28th	● Burnley	A	W 0–1	Att: 21,546. Ref: M Dean – (4-3-3): Brown, Salgado (Chimbonda 84), Jones, Samba▌, Givet▌, Dunn¹, Nzonzi, Olsson, Diouf (Emerton 65), Roberts (Di Santo 74), Pedersen. Subs not used: Bunn, Grella, Kalinic, Hoilett.

APRIL

3rd	● Portsmouth	A	D 0–0	Att: 16,207. Ref: S Bennett – (4-4-1-1): Robinson, Salgado, Samba, Jones, Givet, Diouf (Hoilett 76), Nzonzi (Grella 64), Pedersen, Olsson, Dunn▌ (Kalinic 80), Roberts. Subs not used: Brown, Emerton, Linganzi, Di Santo.
11th	● Man Utd	H	D 0–0	Att: 29,912. Ref: P Walton – (4-2-3-1): Robinson, Salgado▌, Samba (Nelsen 33), Jones, Givet, Nzonzi, Grella, Emerton (Dunn 46), Pedersen, Olsson (Diouf 70), Kalinic. Subs not used: Brown, Roberts, Andrews, Di Santo.
17th	● Everton	H	L 2–3	Att: 27,022. Ref: A Marriner – (4-2-3-1): Robinson, Salgado, Nelsen, Jones, Givet, Andrews▌ (Hoilett 71), Nzonzi¹, Dunn, Pedersen▌ (Roberts▌ 64), Olsson (Di Santo 90), Kalinic. Subs not used: Brown, Grella, Basturk, Chimbonda.
24th	● Wolverhampton	A	D 1–1	Att: 28,967. Ref: M Clattenburg – (3-5-2): Robinson, Nelsen¹, Jones, Givet, Salgado, Basturk (Dunn 46), Nzonzi, Pedersen▌, Olsson, Kalinic (Andrews 57), Roberts (Di Santo 85). Subs not used: Brown, Jacobsen, Linganzi, Hoilett.

MAY

| 3rd | ● Arsenal | H | W 2–1 | Att: 26,138. Ref: 275441 – (4-4-2): Robinson, Salgado, Samba¹, Nelsen, Givet, Andrews, Grella▌ (Hoilett 57), Dunn¹ (Jones 85), Pedersen▌, Olsson, Roberts. Subs not used: Brown, Jacobsen, Emerton, Basturk, Di Santo. |
| 9th | ● Aston Villa | A | W 0–1 | Att: 41,799. Ref: S Bennett – (4-5-1): Robinson, Salgado, Samba, Hanley, Givet (Jones 63), Hoilett, Linganzi (Pedersen 46), Andrews, Dunn▌, Olsson, Roberts (Emerton 86). Subs not used: Brown, Jacobsen, Grella, Kalinic. Dunne OG. |

● Barclays Premier League ● FA Cup ● Carling Cup ● UEFA Champions League ● Europa League ● FA Community Shield   ▌Yellow Card ▌Red Card

Sam Allardyce celebrates Rovers' win at rivals Burnley in March

BLACKBURN ROVERS

BARCLAYS PREMIER LEAGUE GOALKEEPER STATS

Player	Minutes on pitch	Appearances	Match starts	Completed matches	Sub appearances	Subbed off	Saved with feet	Punched	Parried	Tipped over	Fumbled	Tipped round	Caught	Blocked	Clean sheets	Goals conceded	Save %	Saved	Resulting in goals	Opposition miss	Fouls committed	Free-kicks won	Yellow cards	Red cards
Jason Brown	361	4	3	3	1	0	0	1	5	0	1	0	8	0	1	5	73.68	0	0	0	0	0	0	0
Paul Robinson	3275	35	35	34	0	1	2	18	28	9	4	9	88	6	12	50	76.19	0	2	0	0	3	1	0

BARCLAYS PREMIER LEAGUE OUTFIELD PLAYER STATS

Player	Minutes on pitch	Appearances	Match starts	Completed matches	Substitute appearances	Subbed off	Goals scored	Assists	Shots on target	Shots off target	Crosses	Tackles made	Defensive clearances	Defensive blocks	Fouls committed	Free-kicks won	Caught offside	Yellow cards	Red cards
Keith Andrews	2256	32	22	17	10	5	1	0	17	14	13	23	26	8	37	18	0	4	0
Yildiray Basturk	45	1	1	0	0	1	0	0	0	0	0	1	0	0	1	0	0	0	0
Pascal Chimbonda	2090	24	22	19	2	3	1	2	4	3	11	24	22	6	10	31	1	3	0
Franco Di Santo	1215	22	15	3	7	12	1	2	13	5	8	5	0	1	35	17	20	3	0
El-Hadji Diouf	2029	26	24	11	2	13	3	2	10	7	60	18	4	5	30	38	9	3	0
David Dunn	1802	23	20	11	3	9	9	2	23	12	31	17	4	3	34	39	13	7	0
Brett Emerton	1506	24	17	10	7	7	0	2	11	8	31	19	4	0	19	8	4	2	0
Paul Gallagher	19	1	0	0	0	0	0	0	0	0	0	0	0	0	0	0	0	1	0
Gael Givet	2964	34	33	28	1	5	2	2	5	4	6	47	42	18	19	21	0	3	0
Vincenzo Grella	1010	15	10	7	5	2	0	0	1	5	10	14	1	0	19	12	0	2	1
Grant Hanley	96	1	1	1	0	0	0	0	0	1	0	0	4	1	2	2	0	0	0
David Hoilett	1023	23	8	3	15	5	0	0	14	9	19	11	2	0	20	13	2	0	0
Lars Jacobsen	1101	13	11	9	2	2	0	0	1	0	10	12	7	2	1	5	0	0	0
Phil Jones	712	9	7	7	2	0	0	0	2	2	1	17	15	3	4	7	0	0	0
Nikola Kalinic	1545	26	14	7	12	7	2	1	10	18	2	8	1	1	41	31	19	2	0
Amine Linganzi	45	1	1	0	0	1	0	0	0	0	0	2	0	0	0	0	0	0	0
Benedict McCarthy	758	14	7	3	7	4	1	3	14	12	21	5	2	1	11	13	10	2	0
Ryan Nelsen	2408	28	25	23	3	2	4	2	11	3	4	34	54	21	31	18	1	3	0
Steven Nzonzi	3038	33	33	28	0	5	2	0	12	19	4	45	16	7	55	20	2	6	0
Martin Olsson	1828	21	19	16	2	3	1	2	15	13	23	27	9	6	11	37	7	1	0
Morten Gamst Pedersen	2576	33	27	21	6	6	3	6	30	26	110	35	10	2	42	35	9	5	0
Steven Reid	140	4	1	0	3	1	0	0	0	1	0	3	0	0	3	2	0	1	0
Jason Roberts	1654	29	15	6	14	9	5	3	20	10	6	9	1	2	34	50	20	1	0
Michel Salgado	1530	21	16	12	5	4	0	1	2	4	11	33	9	7	22	11	0	3	0
Christopher Samba	2748	30	30	26	0	3	4	0	24	20	3	37	65	21	44	17	2	5	1
Stephen Warnock	96	1	1	1	0	0	0	0	0	0	0	3	1	0	1	1	0	0	0

actim | BARCLAYS PREMIER LEAGUE

SEASON TOTALS

Goals scored	41
Goals conceded	55
Clean sheets	13
Shots on target	239
Shots off target	196
Shots per goal	10.61
Pens awarded	3
Pens scored	3
Pens conceded	2
Offsides	119
Corners	182
Crosses	385
Players used	28
Fouls committed	528
Free-kicks won	449

CARDS RECEIVED

59 **2**

SEQUENCES

Wins	2
(on five occasions)	
Losses	2
(on four occasions)	
Draws	3
(28/11/09–12/12/09)	
Undefeated	5
(21/03/10–11/04/10)	
Without win	9
(25/11/09–11/01/10)	
Undefeated home	8
(28/12/09–11/04/10)	
Undefeated away	4
(28/03/10–09/05/10)	
Without scoring	4
(25/11/09–12/12/09)	
Without conceding	3
(on two occasions)	
Scoring	7
(10/02/10–28/03/10)	
Conceding	8
(12/09/09–07/11/09)	

SEASON INFORMATION

Highest position: 4
Lowest position: 20
Average goals scored per game: 1.08
Average goals conceded per game: 1.45

LEAGUE POSITION AT THE END OF EACH MONTH

AUG	SEP	OCT	NOV	DEC	JAN	FEB	MAR	APR	MAY
18	15	17	13	13	10	12	10	11	10

MATCH RECORDS

Goals scored per match

		W	D	L	Pts
Failed to score	14	0	7	7	7
Scored 1 goal	11	3	3	5	12
Scored 2 goals	9	6	1	2	19
Scored 3 goals	4	4	0	0	12
Scored 4+ goals	0	0	0	0	0

Goals conceded per match

		W	D	L	Pts
Clean sheet	13	6	7	0	25
Conceded 1 goal	9	6	3	0	21
Conceded 2 goals	8	1	1	6	4
Conceded 3 goals	5	0	0	5	0
Conceded 4+ goals	3	0	0	3	0

GOALS SCORED/CONCEDED
PER FIVE-MINUTE INTERVALS

MINS	5	10	15	20	25	30	35	40	45	50	55	60	65	70	75	80	85	90
FOR	2	1	0	4	4	3	1	1	3	0	3	1	1	5	4	3	2	2
AGN	4	3	3	3	1	0	0	2	2	5	3	8	4	2	2	1	1	3	8

EARLIEST STRIKE
STEVEN NZONZI
(v Arsenal) 3:38

LATEST STRIKE
DAVID DUNN
(v Aston Villa) 88:01

Michel Salgado

GOAL DETAILS

How the goals were struck

SCORED		CONCEDED
19	Right foot	33
7	Left foot	13
13	Header	9
2	Other	0

How the goals were struck

SCORED		CONCEDED
20	Open play	36
4	Cross	7
8	Corner	7
3	Penalty	2
0	Direct from free-kick	1
3	Free-kick	1
3	Own goal	1

Distance from goal

SCORED		CONCEDED
20	6YDS	22
14	18YDS	24
7	18+YDS	9

BOLTON WANDERERS

CLUB SUMMARY

FORMED	1874
MANAGER	Owen Coyle
GROUND	Reebok Stadium
CAPACITY	27,879
NICKNAME	The Trotters
WEBSITE	www.bwfc.co.uk

The New Football Pools PLAYER OF THE SEASON — Lee Chung-Yong

OVERALL
P	W	D	L	F	A	GD
45	14	10	21	53	77	-24

BARCLAYS PREMIER LEAGUE
Pos	P	W	D	L	F	A	GD	Pts
14	38	10	9	19	42	67	-25	39

HOME
Pos	P	W	D	L	F	A	GD	Pts
17	19	6	6	7	26	31	-5	24

AWAY
Pos	P	W	D	L	F	A	GD	Pts
12	19	4	3	12	16	36	-20	15

CUP PROGRESS DETAILS
Competition	Round reached	Knocked out by
FA Cup	R5	Tottenham
Carling Cup	R4	Chelsea

BIGGEST WIN (ALL COMPS)
4–0 on 2 occasions

BIGGEST DEFEAT (ALL COMPS)
07/11/09 1–5 v Aston Villa

THE PLAYER WITH THE MOST
GOALS SCORED	Matthew Taylor, Ivan Klasnic	**8**
SHOTS ON TARGET	Matthew Taylor	**55**
SHOTS OFF TARGET	Matthew Taylor	**40**
SHOTS WITHOUT SCORING	Gretar Rafn Steinsson	**9**
ASSISTS	Kevin Davies	**8**
OFFSIDES	Kevin Davies	**23**
FOULS	Kevin Davies	**103**
FOULS WITHOUT A CARD	Andrew O'Brien	**15**
FREE-KICKS WON	Kevin Davies	**88**
DEFENSIVE CLEARANCES	Zat Knight	**72**

actim INDEX — FOR THE 2009/10 BARCLAYS PREMIER LEAGUE SEASON

RANK	PLAYER	PTS
75	Jussi Jaaskelainen	363
101	Gary Cahill	319
106	Zat Knight	314

ATTENDANCE RECORD
HIGH	AVERAGE	LOW
25,370	21,881	17,849
v Man Utd (27/03/2010)		v West Ham (15/12/2009)

BOLTON secured their position in the Barclays Premier League for a 10th successive season, an achievement that chairman Phil Gartside believes should not be overlooked after a turbulent nine months at the Reebok Stadium.

Survival looked a distant prospect when Owen Coyle replaced Gary Megson as Wanderers' manager in January. The Trotters were in the relegation zone when Coyle swapped Burnley for their local rivals but by the time the season had finished, the Scot had led them up to 14th place in the Barclays Premier League table.

Gartside insists that revival is enough to see the campaign marked down as a success. He said: 'We have had our ups and downs but to be taking our place again in the top flight of English football is a considerable achievement.'

He is right. This, after all, is a small-town club with a limited fanbase and limited resources. Owner Eddie Davies and Gartside are both ambitious but they know their financial limitations in a rich marketplace. They are also not afraid to make difficult decisions.

Megson departed at the turn of the year following a poor home draw against Hull, a result that left Bolton in the Barclays Premier League's bottom three and fearing for their future. The former West Brom boss never won over a section of the club's supporters but he can take credit for bringing in two key players of the 2009/10 campaign in South Korea winger Lee Chung-Yong, from FC Seoul, and Ivan Klasnic, on loan from French club Nantes. Lee, 21, won a string of club awards in his debut season while Klasnic was consistently a handful for opposition defences.

The arrival of a new manager marked the second time in three years that Bolton had made a change in mid-season, with Megson himself having replaced Sammy Lee in 2007.

Coyle was greeted like a long-lost son, and in a way he was. A former striker for the club in the 1990s when they enjoyed several exciting Cup runs and first reached the Premier League, he returned to Bolton in early 2010 and was given a hero's welcome. The Scot's exit from Burnley was clearly a difficult decision given that he had led them from Coca-Cola Championship strugglers to promotion but he was keen to emphasise that the move was down to his old allegiance to the Trotters and the club's

The arrival of Owen Coyle helped Bolton maintain their top-flight status, while also pleasing the club's supporters

ambition and exisiting infrastructure, rather than for any mercenary reasons. Ultimately, Coyle seems to have made the right decision for himself as his new club stayed up while his former employers went straight back down.

The Glasgow-born boss quickly recognised what was needed to revive an ailing side. He promised a more expansive game and brought in young playmaker Jack Wilshere from Arsenal and winger Vladimir Weiss from Manchester City, both on loan.

At just 18, Wilshere displayed remarkable maturity and the dynamic at Bolton changed both on the pitch and in the stands.

While four successive defeats through March and April left the club looking anxiously over their shoulders, crucially the crowd stayed with Coyle and his players. They were rewarded with a 2–1 victory against Stoke at the Britannia Stadium thanks to a brace from Matthew Taylor, which helped ease the nerves and all but secured their top-flight status.

Bolton eventually amassed 39 points, thanks to a home win against Birmingham on the final day of the campaign. That was enough to put them nine points clear of the third-bottom club, Burnley.

Coyle, though, knows that there is still plenty of work to do to shape a side in his image, and he would like Wilshere and Weiss to return in the 2010/11 season. He also sees Klasnic as part of his plans but accepts that there needs to be some hard financial bargaining on that front.

However, Gartside has promised Coyle funds to strengthen his squad. The chairman explained: 'We have always backed the boss in the transfer windows and it will be no different this time. We will work hard to bring success back to the club and with Owen at the helm, we have someone committed to the Wanderers.'

CLOCKWISE FROM ABOVE: Kevin Davies scores a penalty in the vital 4–0 win against Wigan; Jack Wilshere joined Wanderers on loan from Arsenal; Owen Coyle was a popular appointment after replacing Gary Megson in January; Fabrice Muamba and Jlloyd Samuel show their frustration as Bolton fall to a second 4–0 defeat to Chelsea in four days in October

BOLTON WANDERERS

AUGUST

15th ● Sunderland — H — L 0–1 — **Att:** 22,247. **Ref:** A Marriner – (4-4-1-1): Jaaskelainen, Ricketts, Cahill, Knight, Robinson, McCann (Lee 68), Davis▮, Muamba, Taylor, Elmander (Ward 83), K Davies. **Subs not used:** Al Habsi, Samuel, M Davies, Cohen, O'Brien.

22nd ● Hull — A — L 1–0 — **Att:** 22,999. **Ref:** M Jones – (4-5-1): Jaaskelainen, Ricketts, Cahill, Knight, Robinson (Samuel 78), Davis▮, M Davies (Ward 81), Muamba, K Davies, Taylor, Elmander▮ (Lee 71). **Subs not used:** Al Habsi, Steinsson, McCann, Shittu.

25th ● Tranmere — A — W 0–1 — **Att:** 5,381. **Ref:** N Miller – (4-5-1): Jaaskelainen, Ricketts, Samuel, Cahill, Knight, K Davies¹, M Davies (Lee 64), Davis, Muamba (McCann 80), Taylor, Elmander. **Subs not used:** Al Habsi, Steinsson, Robinson, O'Brien, Ward.

29th ● Liverpool — H — L 2–3 — **Att:** 23,284. **Ref:** A Wiley – (4-5-1): Jaaskelainen, Ricketts, Cahill▮, Knight, Samuel, Elmander (Basham 59), Muamba▮, Riga 90), Davis▮, Cohen¹ (Steinsson 78), Taylor, K Davies¹. **Subs not used:** Al Habsi, Robinson, Lee, O'Brien.

SEPTEMBER

12th ● Portsmouth — A — W 2–3 — **Att:** 17,564. **Ref:** C Foy – (4-5-1): Jaaskelainen, Ricketts (Klasnic 71), Knight, Cahill▮, Samuel, Steinsson, Cohen¹ (McCann 77), M Davies (Basham 71), Muamba, Taylor▮, K Davies. **Subs not used:** Al Habsi, Robinson, Lee, O'Brien.

19th ● Stoke — H — D 1–1 — **Att:** 20,265. **Ref:** M Clattenburg – (4-5-1): Jaaskelainen, Ricketts, Cahill, Knight, Samuel▮, Steinsson (Klasnic 46), McCann, Muamba (Gardner 46), Cohen, Taylor¹, K Davies▮. **Subs not used:** Al Habsi, Elmander, Davis, Lee, O'Brien.

22nd ● West Ham — H — W 3–1 — **Att:** 8,050. **Ref:** H Webb – (4-4-2): Jaaskelainen, Ricketts, Cahill¹, Knight, Samuel, Taylor, Muamba, McCann (Cohen 82), Gardner (Lee 69), K Davies¹, Klasnic (Elmander¹ 77). **Subs not used:** Al Habsi, Steinsson, M Davies, O'Brien. AET – Score after 90 mins 1–1.

26th ● Birmingham — A — W 1–2 — **Att:** 28,671. **Ref:** S Bennett – (4-5-1): Jaaskelainen, Ricketts, Knight, Cahill, Samuel▮, Cohen¹, Muamba, Taylor, K Davies, Gardner (McCann 71), Klasnic (Lee¹ 54). **Subs not used:** Al Habsi, Elmander, Steinsson, M Davies, O'Brien.

OCTOBER

3rd ● Tottenham — H — D 2–2 — **Att:** 21,305. **Ref:** M Jones – (4-3-3): Jaaskelainen, Ricketts, Cahill, Knight, Samuel, Gardner¹, Muamba▮ (McCann 74), Cohen▮, Lee (Klasnic 87), K Davies¹, Taylor (M Davies 81). **Subs not used:** Al Habsi, Robinson, Steinsson, Shittu.

17th ● Man Utd — A — L 2–1 — **Att:** 75,103. **Ref:** M Clattenburg – (4-5-1): Jaaskelainen, Ricketts, Knight, Cahill, Samuel, Lee (Klasnic 53), Cohen (M Davies 63), Muamba (Basham 77), Gardner, Taylor▮, K Davies. **Subs not used:** Al Habsi, Robinson, Steinsson, McCann.

25th ● Everton — H — W 3–2 — **Att:** 21,547. **Ref:** P Dowd – (4-1-4-1): Jaaskelainen, Ricketts, Cahill¹▮, Knight, Samuel▮, Muamba, Lee¹ (Basham 88), Cohen, Gardner (Klasnic¹ 64), Taylor, K Davies▮. **Subs not used:** Al Habsi, Steinsson, M Davies, O'Brien, Robinson.

28th ● Chelsea — A — L 4–0 — **Att:** 41,538. **Ref:** A Marriner – (4-1-4-1): Al Habsi, Ricketts, Knight, Cahill, Samuel, Muamba, Steinsson (Elmander 46), M Davies, Gardner, Taylor (Basham 64), Klasnic. **Subs not used:** Jaaskelainen, Robinson, Cohen, Lee, O'Brien.

31st ● Chelsea — H — L 0–4 — **Att:** 22,680. **Ref:** P Walton – (4-1-2-1-2): Jaaskelainen, Ricketts, Cahill, Knight, Samuel▮, Muamba (M Davies 65), Basham (Robinson▮ 46), Cohen, Lee (Gardner 46), K Davies, Elmander. **Subs not used:** Al Habsi, O'Brien, Taylor, Steinsson.

NOVEMBER

7th ● Aston Villa — A — L 5–1 — **Att:** 38,101. **Ref:** M Clattenburg – (4-5-1): Jaaskelainen, Ricketts (Steinsson 69), Cahill▮, Knight, Robinson▮, Lee, Muamba, Cohen▮ (Elmander¹ 29), Taylor, Gardner, K Davies▮. **Subs not used:** Al Habsi, M Davies, Klasnic, Basham, O'Brien.

22nd ● Blackburn — H — L 0–2 — **Att:** 21,777. **Ref:** M Dean – (4-4-2): Jaaskelainen, Ricketts, Cahill, O'Brien, Samuel, Taylor▮, Muamba▮, McCann (M Davies 69), Gardner (Lee 69), Elmander (Klasnic 66), K Davies. **Subs not used:** Al Habsi, Knight, Steinsson, Basham.

28th ● Fulham — A — D 1–1 — **Att:** 23,554. **Ref:** S Bennett – (4-3-3): Jaaskelainen▮, Steinsson▮, O'Brien, Cahill, Samuel▮, Cohen (M Davies 78), Gardner▮, McCann▮, Taylor, K Davies, Klasnic¹ (Muamba 60). **Subs not used:** Al Habsi, Elmander, Knight, Ricketts, Lee.

DECEMBER

5th ● Wolverhampton — A — L 2–1 — **Att:** 27,362. **Ref:** C Foy – (4-5-1): Jaaskelainen, Steinsson, Cahill, O'Brien, Samuel (Elmander¹ 71), Lee, Gardner, McCann▮, Cohen, Taylor, Klasnic. **Subs not used:** Al Habsi, Muamba, Knight, M Davies, Ricketts, Obadeyi.

12th ● Man City — H — D 3–3 — **Att:** 22,735. **Ref:** M Clattenburg – (4-4-2): Jaaskelainen, Steinsson, Cahill¹, Knight, Robinson, Lee, Muamba (M Davies▮ 80), Cohen▮, Taylor, K Davies, Klasnic▮² (Elmander 72). **Subs not used:** Al Habsi, Samuel, Ricketts, Basham, O'Brien.

15th ● West Ham — H — W 3–1 — **Att:** 17,849. **Ref:** A Marriner – (4-4-2): Jaaskelainen, Steinsson, Cahill¹, Knight, Robinson, Lee¹, Muamba▮, Cohen▮, Taylor (Gardner 76), K Davies, Klasnic▮ (Basham 82). **Subs not used:** Al Habsi, Samuel, Elmander, Ricketts, O'Brien.

26th ● Burnley — A — D 1–1 — **Att:** 21,761. **Ref:** C Foy – (4-4-2): Jaaskelainen, Steinsson, Cahill, Knight, Robinson, Lee (Gardner 73), Basham, Cohen, Taylor¹, K Davies, Klasnic (M Davies 67). **Subs not used:** Al Habsi, Samuel, Elmander, Ricketts, O'Brien.

29th ● Hull — H — D 2–2 — **Att:** 20,696. **Ref:** P Dowd – (4-4-2): Jaaskelainen, Steinsson, Cahill, Knight, Robinson, Lee, Muamba, Cohen, Taylor, K Davies¹, Klasnic¹ (McCann▮ 75). **Subs not used:** Al Habsi, Elmander, Gardner, M Davies, Ricketts, O'Brien.

JANUARY

2nd ● Lincoln City — H — W 4–0 — **Att:** 11,193. **Ref:** M Oliver – (4-4-2): Al Habsi, Steinsson, Cahill¹, O'Brien, Robinson, Lee¹ (Cohen 80), Muamba (M Davies¹ 46), Gardner, Taylor, K Davies, Klasnic (Elmander 58). **Subs not used:** Bogdan, Knight, Samuel, Ricketts. Swaibu OG.

17th ● Arsenal — H — L 0–2 — **Att:** 23,893. **Ref:** P Dowd – (4-4-2): Jaaskelainen, Steinsson, Cahill, Knight, Robinson▮, Lee, Muamba (McCann 61), Cohen (Gardner 80), Taylor, Klasnic (Elmander 80), K Davies. **Subs not used:** Al Habsi, M Davies, Ricketts, O'Brien.

20th ● Arsenal — A — L 4–2 — **Att:** 59,084. **Ref:** A Wiley – (4-5-1): Jaaskelainen, Steinsson, Cahill¹, Knight, Robinson (Ricketts 90), Lee (Klasnic 81), M Davies (McCann▮ 56), Muamba▮, Cohen, Taylor¹, K Davies. **Subs not used:** Al Habsi, Samuel, Elmander, O'Brien.

23rd ● Sheff Utd — H — W 2–0 — **Att:** 14,572. **Ref:** A Marriner – (4-4-2): Jaaskelainen, Steinsson¹, Cahill, Knight, Samuel (Basham 85), Lee, Ricketts, Muamba, Cohen, K Davies (Riga 88), Klasnic (Elmander¹ 76). **Subs not used:** Al Habsi, Robinson, O'Brien, Vaz Te.

26th ● Burnley — H — W 1–0 — **Att:** 23,986. **Ref:** M Atkinson – (4-4-2): Jaaskelainen, Steinsson, Cahill, Knight, Ricketts, Lee¹ (Weiss 90), Muamba, Cohen▮, Taylor (Gardner 77), Klasnic (Elmander 52), K Davies▮. **Subs not used:** Al Habsi, Samuel, Robinson, O'Brien.

30th ● Liverpool — A — L 2–0 — **Att:** 43,413. **Ref:** S Bennett – (4-5-1): Jaaskelainen, Steinsson, Cahill, Knight▮, Ricketts, Lee▮, Muamba (Elmander 78), M Davies▮, Cohen (Gardner 60), Taylor (Weiss 65), K Davies. **Subs not used:** Al Habsi, Robinson, O'Brien, Wilshere.

FEBRUARY

6th ● Fulham — H — D 0–0 — **Att:** 22,289. **Ref:** M Clattenburg – (4-5-1): Jaaskelainen, Robinson, O'Brien (Basham 63), Knight, Ricketts, Lee, M Davies (Elmander 57), Muamba, Cohen, Taylor (Weiss 71), K Davies. **Subs not used:** Al Habsi, Samuel, Gardner, Wilshere.

● Barclays Premier League ● FA Cup ● Carling Cup ● UEFA Champions League ● Europa League ● FA Community Shield   ▮ Yellow Card ▮ Red Card

RESULTS 2009/10

9th	● Man City	A	L 2-0	**Att:** 42,016. **Ref:** M Jones – (4-5-1): Jaaskelainen, Steinsson, Knight, Ricketts, Robinson▌, K Davies, Cohen (M Davies 74), Muamba▌, Wilshere, Lee, Elmander. **Subs not used:** Al Habsi, Samuel, Gardner, Basham, O'Brien.
14th	● Tottenham	H	D 1-1	**Att:** 13,596. **Ref:** P Dowd – (4-4-2): Jaaskelainen, Steinsson, Ricketts, Knight▌ (O'Brien 63), Robinson, Lee (M Davies¹ 74), Muamba, Gardner, Taylor¹ (Cohen 88), K Davies, Elmander. **Subs not used:** Al Habsi, Samuel, Riga, Holden.
17th	● Wigan	A	D 0-0	**Att:** 18,089. **Ref:** H Webb – (4-4-2): Jaaskelainen, Steinsson, Ricketts, Knight, Robinson, Lee (Weiss 70), Muamba▌, Gardner (Cohen 84), Taylor (Wilshere 87), Elmander, K Davies. **Subs not used:** Al Habsi, Samuel, M Davies, O'Brien.
21st	● Blackburn	A	L 3-0	**Att:** 23,888. **Ref:** C Foy – (4-4-2): Jaaskelainen, Steinsson, Ricketts, Knight, Robinson, Lee, Muamba (M Davies 59), Gardner, Taylor (Weiss 59), Elmander (Klasnic 69), K Davies. **Subs not used:** Al Habsi, Cohen, O'Brien, Wilshere.
24th	● Tottenham	A	L 4-0	**Att:** 31,436. **Ref:** P Walton – (4-5-1): Jaaskelainen, Ricketts, Knight, O'Brien, Samuel, Holden, Cohen, Muamba, Gardner (Lee 79), Taylor (Riga 56), Klasnic. **Subs not used:** Al Habsi, Robinson, K Davies, Shittu.
27th	● Wolverhampton	H	W 1-0	**Att:** 21,261. **Ref:** A Marriner – (4-1-3-2): Jaaskelainen, Steinsson, Ricketts, Knight¹, Robinson, Muamba, Lee (Weiss 90), Wilshere (Taylor 81), Holden, Elmander (Klasnic 64), K Davies. **Subs not used:** Al Habsi, Riga, Cohen, O'Brien.

MARCH

6th	● West Ham	A	W 1-2	**Att:** 33,824. **Ref:** L Probert – (4-4-2): Jaaskelainen▌, Steinsson, Knight, Ricketts, Robinson▌, Lee, Cohen▌, Muamba▌, Wilshere▌ (Taylor 78), Elmander (Gardner 74), K Davies¹. **Subs not used:** Al Habsi, Riga, Klasnic, O'Brien, Weiss.
9th	● Sunderland	A	L 4-0	**Att:** 36,087. **Ref:** S Bennett – (4-4-2): Jaaskelainen, Steinsson, Robinson, Ricketts▌, Knight, Steinsson, Gardner (Taylor 73), Wilshere, Muamba (Weiss 57), Lee▌, K Davies, Elmander (Klasnic 65). **Subs not used:** Al Habsi, Samuel, Riga, O'Brien.
13th	● Wigan	H	W 4-0	**Att:** 20,053. **Ref:** M Dean – (4-4-1-1): Jaaskelainen, Steinsson, O'Brien, Knight, Robinson, Lee (Weiss 72), Muamba¹, Cohen▌, Wilshere (Taylor¹ 67), K Davies¹ (Klasnic 76), Elmander¹. **Subs not used:** Al Habsi, Riga, Gardner, Shittu.
20th	● Everton	A	L 2-0	**Att:** 36,503. **Ref:** A Wiley – (4-4-2): Jaaskelainen, Steinsson▌, O'Brien, Knight, Robinson, Lee▌, Muamba, Cohen (M Davies 84), Wilshere (Taylor 81), K Davies, Elmander (Ricketts 71). **Subs not used:** Al Habsi, Cahill, Riga, Weiss.
27th	● Man Utd	H	L 0-4	**Att:** 25,370. **Ref:** M Atkinson – (4-1-3-2): Jaaskelainen, Ricketts, Cahill, Knight, Samuel, Muamba, Lee, Cohen (Taylor 73), Wilshere, Elmander (Klasnic 73), K Davies. **Subs not used:** Al Habsi, Riga, M Davies, O'Brien, Weiss.

APRIL

3rd	● Aston Villa	H	L 0-1	**Att:** 21,111. **Ref:** M Jones – (4-4-2): Jaaskelainen▌, Ricketts▌, Cahill, Knight, Robinson, Lee (Taylor 78), Muamba, Cohen (Weiss 66), Wilshere, K Davies, Elmander (Klasnic 57). **Subs not used:** Al Habsi, Samuel, Steinsson, O'Brien.
13th	● Chelsea	A	L 1-0	**Att:** 40,539. **Ref:** L Probert – (4-1-4-1): Jaaskelainen, Steinsson, Cahill, Knight, Robinson, Lee (Klasnic 82), Muamba, Ricketts, Taylor, Wilshere (Elmander▌ 82), K Davies▌. **Subs not used:** Al Habsi, Samuel, M Davies, Cohen, Weiss.
17th	● Stoke	A	W 1-2	**Att:** 27,250. **Ref:** S Attwell – (4-5-1): Jaaskelainen, Steinsson, Cahill, Knight, Robinson, Lee (Weiss 71), Ricketts (Klasnic 46), Muamba (M Davies 82), Wilshere▌, Taylor², K Davies. **Subs not used:** Al Habsi, Samuel, Elmander, Cohen.
24th	● Portsmouth	H	D 2-2	**Att:** 20,526. **Ref:** H Webb – (4-4-2): Jaaskelainen, Steinsson, Cahill, Knight, Robinson, Weiss (Lee 70), Muamba▌, Wilshere (M Davies¹ 81), Taylor, Klasnic¹ (Elmander 75), K Davies. **Subs not used:** Al Habsi, Samuel, Ricketts, Cohen.

MAY

1st	● Tottenham	A	L 1-0	**Att:** 35,852. **Ref:** C Foy – (4-4-2): Jaaskelainen, Steinsson, Cahill, Knight, Robinson▌, Weiss (Lee 61), Muamba (Gardner 78), Wilshere▌, Taylor▌, K Davies, Klasnic (Elmander 60). **Subs not used:** Al Habsi, Samuel, M Davies, Ricketts.
9th	● Birmingham	H	W 2-1	**Att:** 22,863. **Ref:** K Friend – (4-4-2): Jaaskelainen, Steinsson, Cahill, Knight, Robinson, Weiss (Lee 65), Muamba, Wilshere (Gardner 90), Taylor (Holden 66), Klasnic¹▌, K Davies¹. **Subs not used:** Al Habsi, Samuel, M Davies, Ricketts.

● Barclays Premier League ● FA Cup ● Carling Cup ● UEFA Champions League ● Europa League ● FA Community Shield ▌Yellow Card ▌Red Card

Matthew Taylor scores in the win at Stoke in April that virtually assured Bolton's survival in the top flight

BOLTON WANDERERS

BARCLAYS PREMIER LEAGUE GOALKEEPER STATS

Player	Minutes on pitch	Appearances	Match starts	Completed matches	Sub appearances	Subbed off	SAVES BREAKDOWN								Clean sheets	Goals conceded	Save %	PENALTIES			Fouls committed	Free-kicks won	Yellow cards	Red cards
							Saved with feet	Punched	Parried	Tipped over	Fumbled	Tipped round	Caught	Blocked				Saved	Resulting in goals	Opposition miss				
Jussi Jaaskelainen	3654	38	38	38	0	0	3	17	38	6	1	12	127	8	5	67	75.90	2	3	0	1	4	3	0

BARCLAYS PREMIER LEAGUE OUTFIELD PLAYER STATS

Player	Minutes on pitch	Appearances	Match starts	Completed matches	Substitute appearances	Subbed off	Goals scored	Assists	Shots on target	Shots off target	Crosses	Tackles made	Defensive clearances	Defensive blocks	Fouls committed	Free-kicks won	Caught offside	Yellow cards	Red cards
Chris Basham	267	8	2	1	6	0	0	1	2	2	1	3	4	2	3	1	0	0	0
Gary Cahill	2789	29	29	29	0	0	5	1	17	16	0	66	55	24	24	35	0	3	0
Tamir Cohen	2202	27	26	14	1	11	3	5	22	25	4	52	16	10	50	22	0	7	1
Mark Davies	610	17	5	1	12	4	0	0	6	3	3	45	4	1	12	13	1	1	0
Kevin Davies	3542	37	37	36	0	1	7	8	31	28	22	55	15	1	103	88	23	9	0
Sean Davis	247	3	3	2	0	0	0	0	2	0	9	26	0	0	11	4	0	3	1
Johan Elmander	1438	25	15	4	10	11	3	1	23	15	6	31	15	2	29	20	6	2	0
Ricardo Gardner	1182	21	11	6	10	5	1	1	6	7	13	25	7	2	13	16	4	1	0
Stuart Holden	124	2	1	1	1	0	0	0	1	2	2	1	2	0	4	1	0	0	0
Ivan Klasnic	1300	27	12	2	15	10	8	1	32	20	2	7	3	2	18	10	12	4	0
Zat Knight	3366	35	35	35	0	0	1	0	4	12	4	74	72	25	20	24	0	1	0
Lee Chung-Yong	2552	34	27	14	7	13	4	6	11	13	50	48	4	1	19	39	5	4	0
Gavin McCann	581	11	5	3	6	2	0	0	2	1	6	9	4	1	11	3	1	4	0
Fabrice Muamba	3111	36	35	23	1	12	1	0	16	16	2	115	8	4	63	17	1	11	0
Andrew O'Brien	545	6	6	5	0	1	0	0	0	0	0	4	15	7	15	5	0	0	0
Samuel Ricketts	2314	27	25	21	2	3	0	2	3	3	40	69	29	15	16	19	1	2	1
Mustapha Riga	4	1	0	0	1	0	0	0	0	0	0	0	0	0	0	0	0	0	0
Paul Robinson	2335	25	24	22	1	2	0	2	0	0	33	73	22	7	32	27	0	7	0
Jlloyd Samuel	1095	13	12	10	1	1	0	0	0	0	10	32	14	9	12	12	1	4	0
Gretar Rafn Steinsson	2368	27	25	23	2	1	0	2	3	6	24	53	19	11	19	16	0	4	0
Matthew Taylor	2754	37	29	21	8	8	8	3	55	40	94	41	19	8	22	29	2	2	0
Daniel Ward	25	2	0	0	2	0	0	0	0	0	0	8	0	0	0	0	0	0	0
Vladimir Weiss	434	13	3	0	10	3	0	0	3	3	1	12	6	0	0	3	14	0	0
Jack Wilshere	1138	14	13	5	1	8	1	1	7	7	20	17	0	1	23	32	0	3	0

BARCLAYS PREMIER LEAGUE

SEASON TOTALS

Goals scored	42
Goals conceded	67
Clean sheets	5
Shots on target	247
Shots off target	214
Shots per goal	10.98
Pens awarded	4
Pens scored	4
Pens conceded	5
Offsides	58
Corners	192
Crosses	357
Players used	25
Fouls committed	521
Free-kicks won	454

CARDS RECEIVED

75 5

SEQUENCES

Wins	2
(27/02/10–06/03/10)	
Losses	4
(20/03/10–13/04/10)	
Draws	2
(26/12/09–29/12/09)	
Undefeated	4
(on two occasions)	
Without win	6
(31/10/09–12/12/09)	
Undefeated home	4
(26/01/10–13/03/10)	
Undefeated away	2
(12/09/09–26/09/09)	
Without scoring	5
(30/01/10–21/02/10)	
Without conceding	–
(–)	
Scoring	7
(29/08/09–25/10/09)	
Conceding	20
(15/08/09–20/01/10)	

LEAGUE POSITION AT THE END OF EACH MONTH

AUG	SEP	OCT	NOV	DEC	JAN	FEB	MAR	APR	MAY
19	13	14	18	18	16	15	15	14	14

SEASON INFORMATION

Highest position: 11
Lowest position: 19
Average goals scored per game: 1.11
Average goals conceded per game: 1.76

MATCH RECORDS

Goals scored per match

		W	D	L	Pts
Failed to score	16	0	2	14	2
Scored 1 goal	8	2	3	3	9
Scored 2 goals	9	4	3	2	15
Scored 3 goals	4	3	1	0	10
Scored 4+ goals	1	1	0	0	3

Goals conceded per match

		W	D	L	Pts
Clean sheet	5	3	2	0	11
Conceded 1 goal	13	5	3	5	18
Conceded 2 goals	12	2	3	7	9
Conceded 3 goals	3	0	1	2	1
Conceded 4+ goals	5	0	0	5	0

GOALS SCORED/CONCEDED PER FIVE-MINUTE INTERVALS

MINS	5	10	15	20	25	30	35	40	45	50	55	60	65	70	75	80	85	90
FOR	1	4	2	3	0	5	4	0	4	2	2	1	2	2	1	2	1	6
AGN	5	0	2	0	1	2	5	3	7	0	5	2	6	4	10	5	6	4

EARLIEST STRIKE

RICARDO GARDNER
(v Tottenham) 3:10

LATEST STRIKE

GARY CAHILL
(v Portsmouth) 88:29

Gary Cahill

GOAL DETAILS

How the goals were struck

SCORED		CONCEDED
8	Right foot	44
24	Left foot	12
10	Header	9
0	Other	2

How the goals were struck

SCORED		CONCEDED
27	Open play	46
5	Cross	6
2	Corner	4
4	Penalty	3
2	Direct from free-kick	1
2	Free-kick	3
0	Own goal	4

Distance from goal

SCORED		CONCEDED
17	6YDS	22
21	18YDS	37
4	18+YDS	8

CLUB SUMMARY

FORMED	1882
MANAGER	Brian Laws
GROUND	Turf Moor
CAPACITY	22,619
NICKNAME	The Clarets
WEBSITE	www.burnleyfootballclub.com

The New Football Pools PLAYER OF THE SEASON — *Steven Fletcher*

OVERALL

P	W	D	L	F	A	GD
42	10	6	26	48	88	-40

BARCLAYS PREMIER LEAGUE

Pos	P	W	D	L	F	A	GD	Pts
18	38	8	6	24	42	82	-40	30

HOME

Pos	P	W	D	L	F	A	GD	Pts
15	19	7	5	7	25	30	-5	26

AWAY

Pos	P	W	D	L	F	A	GD	Pts
20	19	1	1	17	17	52	-35	4

CUP PROGRESS DETAILS

Competition	Round reached	Knocked out by
FA Cup	R4	Reading
Carling Cup	R3	Barnsley

BIGGEST WIN (ALL COMPS)
10/04/10 4–1 v Hull

BIGGEST DEFEAT (ALL COMPS)
03/04/10 1–6 v Man City

THE PLAYER WITH THE MOST

GOALS SCORED	Steven Fletcher	**8**
SHOTS ON TARGET	Chris Eagles	**35**
SHOTS OFF TARGET	Steven Fletcher	**37**
SHOTS WITHOUT SCORING	Tyrone Mears	**18**
ASSISTS	Tyrone Mears	**6**
OFFSIDES	Steven Fletcher	**26**
FOULS	Wade Elliott	**65**
FOULS WITHOUT A CARD	David Nugent	**21**
FREE-KICKS WON	Steven Fletcher	**59**
DEFENSIVE CLEARANCES	Clarke Carlisle	**58**

actim INDEX — FOR THE 2009/10 BARCLAYS PREMIER LEAGUE SEASON

RANK	PLAYER	PTS
57	Wade Elliott	378
74	Brian Jensen	364
85	Tyrone Mears	342

ATTENDANCE RECORD

HIGH	AVERAGE	LOW
21,761	20,654	18,397
v Bolton (26/12/2009)		v Fulham (12/12/2009)

CLOCKWISE FROM ABOVE: Steven Fletcher fires home the first goal in a 2–1 win over Birmingham; Martin Paterson applauds the fans after home defeat to Liverpool means relegation is assured; Brian Laws oversees his first game as Burnley manager – a 3–0 defeat at Old Trafford; Brian Jensen picks the ball out of the net for a fifth time during a heavy defeat at Aston Villa

BURNLEY'S return to the top flight for the first time in 33 years was not only a season of two halves but it was effectively a tale of two managers. Owen Coyle was the man who got the Clarets promoted on a shoestring budget and he made a good start in his bid to keep them up. When he left to join former club Bolton in January he was replaced by Brian Laws, who found his Barclays Premier League managerial debut difficult having been plunged straight into a relegation battle.

It was a fight that he ultimately failed to win as Burnley's early-season promise evaporated during a harsh late winter and spring as the club returned to the npower Championship after the briefest of stays.

Laws won just three and drew one of his 18 League matches after taking over in mid-January. Although Coyle's record of five wins and five draws does not look that much different, had Laws matched it then the Clarets would have finished just below mid-table.

What was particularly disappointing for all those in east Lancashire was that the campaign – the Clarets' first in the top flight since 1975/76 – had promised to be so much better. Hopes and expectations were raised, perhaps somewhat unrealistically, by a victory over defending champions Manchester United in Turf Moor's first Barclays Premier League match.

Burnley were on cloud nine when that was followed up by a second home win against an injury-hit Everton side, with Wade Elliott – the man whose Wembley strike helped the Clarets reach the Barclays Premier League – on goalscoring duties in another 1–0 win. However, even at that early stage Coyle warned against getting carried away, stressing that the club's safety-first target was paramount.

What Burnley had going for them in abundance was the belief surging through their squad, with the team playing above themselves for their manager. It was a sense of unity that carried the Clarets through the first few months of the season as they capitalised on the feel-good factor at Turf Moor, where they were backed by vociferous capacity crowds.

Away from home it was a different matter, and their failure to pick up points on the road became an increasing source of concern. The longer their run went on, the more of an issue it became, and it was those difficulties that ultimately led to relegation.

There were a few highlights along the way but what Burnley really needed was consistency. Turf Moor's first match back in the top division of English football against United was a game few fans will ever forget. Goalkeeper Brian Jensen saved Michael Carrick's penalty before Robbie Blake smashed in one of the club's goals of the season – a stunning angled volley – to defeat Sir Alex Ferguson's side, which featured Wayne Rooney, Michael Owen and Ryan Giggs. The 19th-minute goal shook the old ground to its very foundations, bringing cheers not seen since the glory days of the post-War period.

A first home defeat was something of a surprise when it came, as it was to Wigan, themselves inconsistent performers for much of the campaign. But it did not burst the Turf Moor bubble as the Clarets remained unbeaten in home games against Hull, Aston Villa, Fulham, Arsenal and Bolton, accruing a win and four draws.

Unfortunately, their away record gradually became a burden and their first point on the road came from a creditable 3–3 draw at UEFA Champions League hopefuls Manchester City in early November. However, far from being the turning point, the problems on their travels continued.

Coyle's departure to former club Bolton was a major blow and Laws' attempts to patch things up and revive the players' belief proved fruitless. By the latter stages of the season, displays at home were proving just as frustrating for the Clarets fans as their continuing away misery. The low point was a 6–1 defeat to Manchester City at Turf Moor, in which they were 4–0 down within the first 20 minutes.

Such performances did little to endear Laws to the supporters, but chairman Barry Kilby gave the manager his backing in the summer.

The Clarets paid the price for their poor away form and the loss of Owen Coyle as they made a quick return to the Championship

BURNLEY

RESULTS 2009/10

AUGUST

15th ● Stoke A L 2-0 **Att:** 27,385. **Ref:** S Bennett – (4-1-4-1): Jensen, Mears, Carlisle, Jordan▌, Kalvenes, Alexander▌ (Thompson 82), Paterson (Eagles 72), Elliott, McCann, Blake (Guerrero 72), Fletcher. **Subs not used:** Penny, McDonald, Gudjonsson, Eckersley.

19th ● Man Utd H W 1-0 **Att:** 20,872. **Ref:** A Wiley – (4-1-4-2): Jensen, Mears, Bikey, Carlisle, Jordan, Blake▌, McCann, Alexander (Gudjonsson 73), Elliott, Fletcher (Thompson 81), Paterson (Eagles 73). **Subs not used:** Penny, Kalvenes, McDonald, Guerrero.

23rd ● Everton H W 1-0 **Att:** 19,983. **Ref:** P Dowd – (4-1-4-1): Jensen, Mears, Carlisle, Bikey, Jordan, Alexander, Fletcher (Thompson 86), Elliott▌, McCann, Blake (Guerrero 84), Paterson (Eagles 79). **Subs not used:** Penny, Kalvenes, McDonald, Gudjonsson.

25th ● Hartlepool A W 1-2 **Att:** 3,501. **Ref:** J Moss – (4-4-2): Penny, Eckersley▌, Edgar, Bikey, Easton▌, Eagles (Blake 65), Gudjonsson, McDonald, Guerrero, Rodriguez▌ (Fletcher[2] 61), Thompson (Paterson 61). **Subs not used:** Jensen, Elliott, Alexander, Jordan. AET – Score after 90 mins 1-1.

29th ● Chelsea A L 3-0 **Att:** 40,906. **Ref:** M Clattenburg – (4-1-4-1): Jensen, Mears▌, Carlisle, Bikey, Jordan, Alexander (McDonald 74), Blake (Guerrero 78), Elliott, McCann, Paterson (Gudjonsson 58), Fletcher. **Subs not used:** Penny, Kalvenes, Thompson, Eagles.

SEPTEMBER

12th ● Liverpool A L 4-0 **Att:** 43,817. **Ref:** L Mason – (4-1-4-1): Jensen, Mears, Carlisle, Bikey, Jordan▌, Alexander (Gudjonsson 75), Blake (Eagles▌ 58), McCann, Elliott, Fletcher, Paterson (Nugent 70). **Subs not used:** Penny, McDonald, Thompson, Guerrero.

19th ● Sunderland H W 3-1 **Att:** 20,196. **Ref:** C Foy – (4-4-2): Jensen, Mears, Carlisle, Bikey, Jordan, Elliott, Alexander[1], McCann (Gudjonsson 28), Blake, Fletcher (Eagles 64), Paterson (Nugent[2] 57). **Subs not used:** Penny, McDonald, Thompson, Guerrero.

22nd ● Barnsley A L 3-2 **Att:** 6,270. **Ref:** M Clattenburg – (4-4-2): Jensen (Penny 34), Eckersley▌ (Duff▌ 46), Carlisle, Bikey, Kalvenes, Eagles[1], McDonald, Gudjonsson, Guerrero, Fletcher[1], Paterson (Rodriguez 15). **Subs not used:** Elliott, Edgar, Blake, Easton.

26th ● Tottenham A L 5-0 **Att:** 35,462. **Ref:** M Dean – (4-1-4-1): Jensen, Mears, Carlisle, Bikey▌, Jordan, Alexander, Fletcher (Thompson 72), Elliott, Gudjonsson, Blake (Guerrero 81), Nugent (Eagles 63). **Subs not used:** Penny, Duff, Caldwell, McDonald.

OCTOBER

3rd ● Birmingham H W 2-1 **Att:** 20,102. **Ref:** K Friend – (4-1-4-1): Jensen, Mears, Carlisle, Caldwell, Jordan, Alexander, Fletcher[1] (Eagles 72), Elliott, Bikey[1], Blake (Kalvenes 90), Nugent (Thompson 86). **Subs not used:** Penny, Duff, McDonald, Gudjonsson.

18th ● Blackburn A L 3-2 **Att:** 26,689. **Ref:** C Foy – (4-4-2): Jensen▌, Mears▌, Carlisle, Caldwell, Jordan, Elliott, Alexander, Bikey (McDonald 78), Blake[1], Nugent (Thompson 72), Fletcher (Eagles[1] 59). **Subs not used:** Penny, Kalvenes, Duff, Gudjonsson.

24th ● Wigan A L 1-3 **Att:** 19,430. **Ref:** L Mason – (4-4-2): Jensen (Penny 15), Mears, Carlisle▌, Caldwell, Jordan, Eagles, Bikey (McDonald 82), Alexander▌, Elliott, Blake (Nugent 67), Fletcher[1]. **Subs not used:** Duff, Gudjonsson, Thompson, Guerrero.

31st ● Hull H W 2-0 **Att:** 20,219. **Ref:** M Jones – (4-5-1): Jensen, Mears, Carlisle, Caldwell, Jordan, Eagles (Guerrero 85), Bikey, Alexander[2], Elliott▌, Blake (McDonald 72), Fletcher (Nugent 78). **Subs not used:** Penny, Duff, Gudjonsson, Thompson.

NOVEMBER

7th ● Man City A D 3-3 **Att:** 47,205. **Ref:** S Attwell – (4-2-3-1): Jensen, Mears▌, Carlisle, Caldwell, Jordan, Alexander[1], Bikey▌ (McDonald[1] 61), Eagles (Nugent 71), Elliott, Blake (Gudjonsson 62), Fletcher[1]. **Subs not used:** Penny, Duff, Thompson, Guerrero.

21st ● Aston Villa H D 1-1 **Att:** 21,178. **Ref:** H Webb – (4-2-3-1): Jensen, Mears, Carlisle, Caldwell[1], Jordan, Alexander, Bikey, Eagles (McDonald 69), Elliott, Blake (Gudjonsson 81), Fletcher (Nugent 74). **Subs not used:** Penny, Duff, Thompson, Guerrero.

28th ● West Ham A L 5-3 **Att:** 34,003. **Ref:** C Foy – (4-4-1-1): Jensen▌, Mears, Carlisle, Caldwell▌, Jordan (Kalvenes 55), Eagles[1], Alexander (McDonald 70), Bikey, Blake (Nugent 55), Elliott, Fletcher[2]. **Subs not used:** Penny, Duff, Gudjonsson, Thompson.

DECEMBER

5th ● Portsmouth A L 2-0 **Att:** 17,822. **Ref:** P Dowd – (4-4-2): Jensen, Mears▌, Carlisle, Bikey▌, Jordan, Elliott, Alexander, McDonald, Eagles (Guerrero 73), Fletcher, Blake (Thompson 68). **Subs not used:** Penny, Kalvenes, Duff, Gudjonsson, Easton.

12th ● Fulham H D 1-1 **Att:** 18,397. **Ref:** M Jones – (4-5-1): Jensen, Mears, Carlisle, Caldwell, Jordan, Eagles (Guerrero 86), Alexander, Bikey (McDonald 77), Elliott[1], Blake (Nugent 56), Fletcher. **Subs not used:** Penny, Kalvenes, Gudjonsson, Thompson.

16th ● Arsenal H D 1-1 **Att:** 21,309. **Ref:** M Dean – (4-5-1): Jensen, Mears, Caldwell▌, Carlisle, Jordan, Eagles▌ (Blake 83), Elliott, Alexander[1], Bikey (Gudjonsson 70), McDonald, Fletcher (Nugent 83). **Subs not used:** Penny, Kalvenes, Thompson, Guerrero.

20th ● Wolverhampton A L 2-0 **Att:** 27,410. **Ref:** M Atkinson – (4-1-4-1): Jensen, Mears, Carlisle (Duff 34), Caldwell (Gudjonsson▌ 67), Jordan, Alexander, Elliott, McDonald, Bikey (Nugent 52), Eagles, Fletcher. **Subs not used:** Penny, Blake, Thompson, Guerrero.

26th ● Bolton H D 1-1 **Att:** 21,761. **Ref:** C Foy – (4-4-2): Jensen, Mears, Duff, Bikey, Jordan, Elliott, McDonald, Alexander, Eagles, Nugent[1], Fletcher (Blake 80). **Subs not used:** Penny, Kalvenes, Gudjonsson, Edgar, Thompson, Guerrero.

28th ● Everton A L 2-0 **Att:** 39,419. **Ref:** H Webb – (4-1-4-1): Jensen, Mears▌, Duff▌, Bikey▌, Jordan▌, Alexander, Eagles, Elliott▌ (Blake 85), McDonald, Fletcher (Thompson 81), Nugent (Kalvenes 63). **Subs not used:** Penny, Gudjonsson, Edgar, Guerrero.

JANUARY

2nd ● Milton Keynes Dons A W 1-2 **Att:** 11,816. **Ref:** T Bates – (4-4-2): Jensen, Eckersley, Duff, Bikey, Kalvenes, Elliott, Alexander[1], McDonald (Gudjonsson 71), Eagles, Blake, Fletcher[1] (Thompson 88). **Subs not used:** Penny, Edgar, Easton, Guerrero, Harvey.

16th ● Man Utd A L 3-0 **Att:** 75,120. **Ref:** L Probert – (4-2-3-1): Jensen, Mears, Edgar, Duff, Jordan, Alexander, McDonald (Gudjonsson 73), Eagles (Blake 83), Elliott, Nugent, Fletcher (Thompson 36). **Subs not used:** Penny, Kalvenes, Eckersley, Guerrero.

23rd ● Reading A L 1-0 **Att:** 12,910. **Ref:** A D'Urso – (4-5-1): Jensen, Mears, Edgar, Duff, McCann▌, Eagles▌, McDonald, Alexander, Gudjonsson (Blake 85), Elliott, Thompson (Paterson 46). **Subs not used:** Penny, Carlisle, Rodriguez, Easton, Guerrero.

26th ● Bolton A L 1-0 **Att:** 23,986. **Ref:** M Atkinson – (4-3-3): Jensen, Mears, Duff, Carlisle, Kalvenes, Elliott▌, Alexander (Paterson 16), McCann (McDonald▌ 12), Nugent, Fletcher, Eagles (Nimani N'galou 65). **Subs not used:** Penny, Edgar, Blake, Thompson.

30th ● Chelsea H L 1-2 **Att:** 21,131. **Ref:** P Dowd – (4-4-1-1): Jensen, Mears, Cort, Carlisle, Kalvenes (Edgar 35), Elliott, Bikey▌, McDonald (Paterson 60), Eagles, Blake (Thompson 72), Fletcher[1]. **Subs not used:** Weaver, Duff, Gudjonsson, Nimani N'galou.

FEBRUARY

6th ● West Ham H W 2-1 **Att:** 21,001. **Ref:** H Webb – (4-4-2): Jensen, Mears, Cort, Carlisle, Fox▌▌ (Edgar 86), Elliott, Bikey, McDonald▌, Blake (Paterson 72), Nugent[1] (Thompson 88), Fletcher. **Subs not used:** Weaver, Duff, Eagles, Cork.

● Barclays Premier League ● FA Cup ● Carling Cup ● UEFA Champions League ● Europa League ● FA Community Shield ▌ Yellow Card ▌ Red Card

RESULTS 2009/10

9th	● Fulham	A	L 3–0	**Att:** 23,005. **Ref:** C Foy – (4-4-2): Jensen, Mears, Carlisle, Cort (Eagles 32), Edgar, Elliott (Cork 56), Bikey, McDonald, Fox, Fletcher, Nugent (Paterson 76). **Subs not used:** Weaver, Duff, Blake, Thompson.
21st	● Aston Villa	A	L 5–2	**Att:** 38,709. **Ref:** S Attwell – (4-4-2): Jensen, Mears, Carlisle, Cort, Fox, Eagles, Cork, Bikey, McDonald (Elliott 64), Nugent (Nimani N'galou‖ 70), Fletcher‖ (Paterson[1] 82). **Subs not used:** Weaver, Duff, Blake, Thompson.
27th	● Portsmouth	H	L 1–2	**Att:** 19,714. **Ref:** M Clattenburg – (4-4-2): Jensen, Mears, Carlisle‖, Cort, Fox, Elliott (Eagles 63), McDonald, Bikey (Cork 63), Blake (Thompson 80), Fletcher, Paterson[1]. **Subs not used:** Weaver, Duff, Edgar, Jordan.

MARCH

6th	● Arsenal	A	L 3–1	**Att:** 60,043. **Ref:** C Foy – (4-5-1): Jensen, Mears, Carlisle‖, Cort, Fox, Paterson‖ (Thompson 73), Alexander (Bikey 65), McDonald‖ (Elliott‖ 53), Cork, Eagles, Nugent[1]. **Subs not used:** Weaver, Duff, Blake, Jordan.
10th	● Stoke	H	D 1–1	**Att:** 20,323. **Ref:** H Webb – (4-4-2): Jensen, Mears, Carlisle‖, Cort, Fox (Jordan 77), Paterson, Alexander, Cork (McDonald 46), Eagles, Nugent[1], Thompson (Elliott 71). **Subs not used:** Weaver, Duff, Blake, Bikey.
13th	● Wolverhampton	H	L 1–2	**Att:** 21,217. **Ref:** S Bennett – (4-4-2): Jensen‖, Mears, Carlisle, Cort, Fox (Jordan 39), Elliott, Alexander, Bikey (Blake 54), Eagles (Thompson[1] 54), Paterson, Nugent. **Subs not used:** Weaver, Duff, Edgar, Rodriguez.
20th	● Wigan	A	L 1–0	**Att:** 18,498. **Ref:** M Jones – (4-1-3-2): Jensen, Mears‖, Duff‖, Cort, Jordan, Alexander, Elliott, McDonald‖, Paterson (Eagles 82), Fletcher (Blake 68), Nugent. **Subs not used:** Weaver, Edgar, Bikey, Thompson, Cork.
28th	● Blackburn	H	L 0–1	**Att:** 21,546. **Ref:** M Dean – (4-3-3): Jensen, Mears, Duff‖, Cort, Jordan (Fox‖ 43), Alexander‖ (Eagles 71), Elliott, McDonald, Paterson (Blake 59), Fletcher, Nugent. **Subs not used:** Weaver, Carlisle, Thompson, Cork.

APRIL

3rd	● Man City	H	L 1–6	**Att:** 21,330. **Ref:** A Wiley – (4-2-3-1): Jensen, Mears, Duff, Cort, Fox, McDonald (Cork 46), Alexander, Nugent, Blake (Elliott 46), Eagles, Fletcher[1] (Paterson 80). **Subs not used:** Weaver, Carlisle, Bikey, Thompson.
10th	● Hull	A	W 1–4	**Att:** 24,369. **Ref:** M Atkinson – (4-1-4-1): Jensen, Mears‖, Duff (Caldwell 85), Cort, Fox, Alexander[2], Paterson[1], Cork, Elliott[1], Nugent (Thompson 90), Fletcher (Bikey 86). **Subs not used:** Weaver, Carlisle, Blake, Eagles.
17th	● Sunderland	A	L 2–1	**Att:** 41,341. **Ref:** H Webb – (4-5-1): Jensen, Mears, Cort, Duff‖, Fox, Paterson (Thompson‖ 46), Elliott, Alexander, Cork (Blake 81), Eagles, Fletcher. **Subs not used:** Weaver, Carlisle, Caldwell, Bikey, Jordan.
25th	● Liverpool	H	L 0–4	**Att:** 21,553. **Ref:** P Dowd – (4-3-3): Jensen, Mears, Duff‖, Cort, Fox, Cork‖, Alexander (Blake 63), Elliott, Paterson (Eagles 71), Fletcher, Nugent (Thompson 77). **Subs not used:** Weaver, Caldwell, Rodriguez, Bikey.

MAY

| 1st | ● Birmingham | A | L 2–1 | **Att:** 24,578. **Ref:** P Walton – (4-3-3): Jensen, Mears, Cort, Caldwell, Fox‖, Cork, Alexander (McDonald 86), Nugent (Blake 65), Fletcher (Thompson[1] 68), Paterson, Elliott. **Subs not used:** Weaver, Duff, Rodriguez, Bikey. |
| 9th | ● Tottenham | H | W 4–2 | **Att:** 21,161. **Ref:** M Dean – (4-1-4-1): Jensen, Mears, Caldwell, Bikey, Fox, Alexander, Paterson[1] (Eagles 90), Elliott, Cork[1], Nugent (Blake 79), Fletcher (Thompson[1] 86). **Subs not used:** Weaver, Duff, Jordan, McDonald. |

● Barclays Premier League ● FA Cup ● Carling Cup ● UEFA Champions League ● Europa League ● FA Community Shield ‖ Yellow Card ▮ Red Card

Robbie Blake celebrates his match-winning goal against Manchester United in Burnley's first home game of the season

BURNLEY

BARCLAYS PREMIER LEAGUE GOALKEEPER STATS

Player	Minutes on pitch	Appearances	Match starts	Completed matches	Sub appearances	Subbed off	Saved with feet	Punched	Parried	Tipped over	Fumbled	Tipped round	Caught	Blocked	Clean sheets	Goals conceded	Save %	Saved	Resulting in goals	Opposition miss	Fouls committed	Free-kicks won	Yellow cards	Red cards
Brian Jensen	3555	38	38	37	0	1	3	17	32	6	1	17	166	2	3	79	75.47	3	5	1	4	6	3	0
Diego Penny	86	1	0	0	1	0	0	0	0	0	0	0	1	0	0	3	25.00	0	0	0	0	0	0	0

BARCLAYS PREMIER LEAGUE OUTFIELD PLAYER STATS

Player	Minutes on pitch	Appearances	Match starts	Completed matches	Substitute appearances	Subbed off	Goals scored	Assists	Shots on target	Shots off target	Crosses	Tackles made	Defensive clearances	Defensive blocks	Fouls committed	Free-kicks won	Caught offside	Yellow cards	Red cards
Graham Alexander	2882	33	33	23	0	10	7	1	14	6	28	33	23	7	24	32	0	3	0
Andre Bikey	2307	28	26	18	2	8	1	1	13	17	0	39	23	11	55	27	0	5	0
Robbie Blake	1735	31	20	3	11	17	2	4	20	9	50	18	1	2	5	31	2	1	0
Steven Caldwell	1134	13	12	10	1	1	1	0	2	4	0	15	12	10	14	12	0	1	1
Clarke Carlisle	2526	27	27	26	0	1	0	0	4	6	1	46	58	20	25	25	1	7	0
Jack Cork	820	11	8	6	3	2	1	3	6	1	3	9	1	2	6	11	0	1	0
Leon Cort	1378	15	15	14	0	1	0	1	3	2	0	29	22	17	6	9	0	0	0
Michael Duff	1012	11	10	9	1	1	0	0	1	4	1	17	16	6	12	11	0	5	0
Chris Eagles	2109	34	20	11	14	9	2	3	35	19	57	24	0	0	9	35	2	2	0
David Edgar	261	4	2	2	2	0	0	0	0	0	0	8	1	1	7	2	0	0	0
Wade Elliott	3320	38	34	31	4	3	4	5	23	11	61	41	12	6	65	34	1	5	0
Steven Fletcher	2986	35	35	17	0	18	8	5	34	37	18	27	5	2	41	59	26	1	0
Daniel Fox	1217	14	13	10	1	3	1	1	5	8	23	29	12	5	9	7	0	3	0
Joey Gudjonsson	350	10	1	1	9	0	0	0	0	3	1	2	4	1	3	4	1	1	0
Fernando Guerrero	97	7	0	0	7	0	0	0	1	1	1	2	0	0	0	3	0	0	0
Stephen Jordan	2150	25	23	20	2	2	0	1	2	0	21	33	12	9	26	16	0	3	0
Christian Kalvenes	302	6	3	2	3	1	0	0	1	1	0	2	1	2	4	1	0	0	0
Chris McCann	514	7	7	5	0	2	0	0	2	1	9	3	0	1	2	5	0	0	0
Kevin McDonald	1570	26	15	10	11	5	1	1	7	6	12	31	3	6	20	11	2	5	0
Tyrone Mears	3642	38	38	38	0	0	0	6	9	9	52	71	19	19	40	44	2	7	0
Frederic Nimani N'galou	53	2	0	0	2	0	0	0	0	0	0	0	0	0	1	0	1	0	0
David Nugent	1980	30	20	9	10	11	6	3	23	14	10	12	7	1	21	28	18	0	0
Martin Paterson	1503	23	17	5	6	12	4	2	19	12	44	20	1	2	20	24	9	2	0
Steven Thompson	471	20	1	0	19	1	4	0	4	7	3	7	2	3	15	5	2	0	0

actim

SEASON TOTALS

Goals scored	42
Goals conceded	82
Clean sheets	3
Shots on target	228
Shots off target	178
Shots per goal	9.67
Pens awarded	6
Pens scored	6
Pens conceded	9
Offsides	67
Corners	180
Crosses	395
Players used	26
Fouls committed	434
Free-kicks won	442

SEASON INFORMATION

Highest position: 7
Lowest position: 20
Average goals scored per game: 1.11
Average goals conceded per game: 2.16

LEAGUE POSITION AT THE END OF EACH MONTH

AUG	SEP	OCT	NOV	DEC	JAN	FEB	MAR	APR	MAY
10	11	10	12	14	18	19	19	19	18

CARDS RECEIVED

57 **2**

SEQUENCES

Wins	2
(19/08/09–23/08/09)	
Losses	4
(on three occasions)	
Draws	2
(on two occasions)	
Undefeated	3
(31/10/09–21/11/09)	
Without win	12
(07/11/09–30/01/10)	
Undefeated home	5
(31/10/09–26/12/09)	
Undefeated away	–
(–)	
Without scoring	3
(28/12/09–26/01/10)	
Without conceding	2
(19/08/09–23/08/09)	
Scoring	7
(03/10/09–28/11/09)	
Conceding	7
(29/08/09–24/10/09)	

MATCH RECORDS

Goals scored per match

		W	D	L	Pts
Failed to score	13	0	0	13	0
Scored 1 goal	15	2	5	8	11
Scored 2 goals	5	3	0	2	9
Scored 3 goals	3	1	1	1	4
Scored 4+ goals	2	2	0	0	6

Goals conceded per match

		W	D	L	Pts
Clean sheet	3	3	0	0	9
Conceded 1 goal	12	4	5	3	17
Conceded 2 goals	10	1	0	9	3
Conceded 3 goals	7	0	1	6	1
Conceded 4+ goals	6	0	0	6	0

GOALS SCORED/CONCEDED PER FIVE-MINUTE INTERVALS

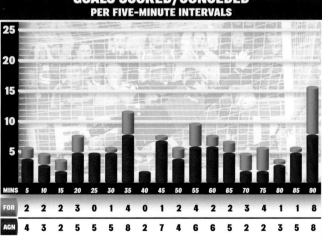

MINS	5	10	15	20	25	30	35	40	45	50	55	60	65	70	75	80	85	90
FOR	2	2	2	3	0	1	4	0	1	2	4	2	2	3	4	1	1	8
AGN	4	3	2	5	5	5	8	2	7	4	6	6	5	2	2	3	5	8

EARLIEST STRIKE

STEVEN FLETCHER
(v Wigan) 3:44

LATEST STRIKE

WADE ELLIOTT
(v Hull) 95:48

Graham Alexander

GOAL DETAILS

How the goals were struck

SCORED		CONCEDED
25	Right foot	38
11	Left foot	27
6	Header	14
0	Other	3

How the goals were struck

SCORED		CONCEDED
26	Open play	54
7	Cross	8
0	Corner	5
6	Penalty	5
2	Direct from free-kick	3
1	Free-kick	4
0	Own goal	3

Distance from goal

SCORED		CONCEDED
13	6YDS	32
24	18YDS	42
5	18+YDS	8

CHELSEA

CLUB SUMMARY

FORMED	1905
MANAGER	Carlo Ancelotti
GROUND	Stamford Bridge
CAPACITY	42,420
NICKNAME	The Blues
WEBSITE	www.chelseafc.com

The New Football Pools PLAYER OF THE SEASON — Florent Malouda

OVERALL

P	W	D	L	F	A	GD
56	39	9	8	142	45	97

BARCLAYS PREMIER LEAGUE

Pos	P	W	D	L	F	A	GD	Pts
1	38	27	5	6	103	32	71	86

HOME

Pos	P	W	D	L	F	A	GD	Pts
1	19	17	1	1	68	14	54	52

AWAY

Pos	P	W	D	L	F	A	GD	Pts
2	19	10	4	5	35	18	17	34

CUP PROGRESS DETAILS

Competition	Round reached	Knocked out by
Champions League	KOR1	Inter Milan
FA Cup	WON	
Carling Cup	QF	Blackburn

BIGGEST WIN (ALL COMPS)
09/05/10 8-0 v Wigan

BIGGEST DEFEAT (ALL COMPS)
27/02/10 2-4 v Man City

THE PLAYER WITH THE MOST

GOALS SCORED Didier Drogba	**29**
SHOTS ON TARGET Didier Drogba	**87**
SHOTS OFF TARGET Didier Drogba	**71**
SHOTS WITHOUT SCORING Mikel	**9**
ASSISTS Frank Lampard	**17**
OFFSIDES Didier Drogba	**33**
FOULS Didier Drogba	**59**
FOULS WITHOUT A CARD Frank Lampard	**23**
FREE-KICKS WON Didier Drogba	**57**
DEFENSIVE CLEARANCES John Terry	**62**

actim INDEX FOR THE 2009/10 BARCLAYS PREMIER LEAGUE SEASON

RANK	PLAYER	PTS
1	Frank Lampard	776
2	Didier Drogba	703
4	Nicolas Anelka	658

ATTENDANCE RECORD

HIGH	AVERAGE	LOW
41,836	41,423	40,137
v Man Utd (08/11/2009)		v Portsmouth (16/12/2009)

CLOCKWISE FROM ABOVE: Frank Lampard celebrates his goal in the win at Liverpool in May; Chelsea's stars lift the Barclays Premier League trophy; Carlo Ancelotti lines up alongside José Mourinho as the Inter Milan coach returned to Stamford Bridge with Inter; Joe Cole enjoys his goal against Manchester United

CARLO ANCELOTTI finally exorcised the ghost of José Mourinho as he guided Chelsea to a historic Barclays Premier League and FA Cup double.

The amiable Italian, who arrived from AC Milan last summer, had to do it the hard way, with injuries robbing him of several key players and off-the-field issues threatening to disrupt the campaign.

The season began with a penalty shoot-out victory over Manchester United at Wembley in the Community Shield and when the Barclays Premier League campaign got under way, Chelsea went unbeaten until they travelled to Wigan at the end of September. Hull, Sunderland, Fulham, Burnley, Stoke and Tottenham were all despatched, with Didier Drogba scoring five goals during those games.

Initially, Frank Lampard found it hard to adjust to Ancelotti's new 'Christmas Tree' formation and he struggled to find the net, but he went on to score 26 times as Chelsea eventually lifted the Barclays Premier League trophy with a record haul of 103 goals.

Lampard's change in fortune arrived when he was returned to a more central position in a 4-3-3 formation as Chelsea went on the rampage, scoring 17 goals without reply in four consecutive games in October. The following month proved to be a key one for Ancelotti's side, with John Terry's header giving them a home win over Manchester

Chelsea just could not stop scoring as they recorded a League and FA Cup double for the first time

United before a 3–0 victory at Arsenal put them 11 points clear at the top of the table.

Drogba went on to finish the season with 29 League goals to claim the Golden Boot, but Chelsea's first major blip was about to halt their progress. A weakened side crashed out of the Carling Cup on penalties to Blackburn and then December draws – at home to Everton and away at Birmingham and West Ham – put the brakes on their title challenge. They ended the year with a 2–1 win over Fulham but by that stage they had lost Michael Essien with a hamstring injury. Worse news followed when the Ghana international hurt his knee in the African Nations Cup and he did not play for the Blues again before the end of the season.

Chelsea also lost Drogba and Salomon Kalou to African Nations Cup duty but, while they were away, the rest of Ancelotti's side shrugged off any doubts that they would cope. They hammered Watford 5–0 in the FA Cup and then sent Sunderland packing 7–2 at Stamford Bridge. A 2–0 home win over Arsenal in February made Chelsea look unstoppable, but then stories relating to off-the-field matters threatened to hamper their challenge. Terry was stripped of the England

captaincy following newspaper allegations about his private life and two uncharacteristic errors from the big defender gave Everton a 2–1 victory at Goodison Park. That was followed by a 2–1 defeat against Mourinho's Inter Milan in the UEFA Champions League and a 4–2 home loss to Manchester City.

Ancelotti managed to steady the ship briefly, but Inter completed their European job at Stamford Bridge and then Chelsea drew at Blackburn to leave them trailing United at the top of the League.

A clear-the-air meeting between the management and the players after the Blackburn draw proved to be pivotal as Chelsea bounced back in style. They hit Portsmouth for five, Aston Villa for seven and came away from Manchester United with a 2–1 win. The League was now Chelsea's to lose, but they kept their nerve.

The Blues did suffer a 2–1 setback at Tottenham but a 7–0 win over Stoke, a 2–0 victory at Liverpool and a last-day 8–0 win over Wigan sealed the title. And just a week later, Drogba's stunning free-kick was enough to see off Portsmouth in the FA Cup final as Chelsea captured both major domestic trophies in the same season for the first time in their history.

CHELSEA

RESULTS 2009/10

AUGUST

9th ● Man Utd — N — D 2-2 — **Att:** 85,896. **Ref:** C Foy – (4-1-3-2): Cech, Ivanovic (Bosingwa 46), Terry, Carvalho[1], A Cole, Mikel (Ballack 65), Essien, Lampard[1], Malouda (Deco 77), Drogba, Anelka (Kalou 83). **Subs not used:** Hilario, Alex, Belletti. Chelsea win 4-1 on penalties.

15th ● Hull — H — W 2-1 — **Att:** 41,597. **Ref:** A Wiley – (4-4-2): Cech, Bosingwa, Carvalho, Terry, A Cole, Mikel (Ballack 46), Essien, Malouda (Deco 69), Lampard, Anelka (Kalou 79), Drogba[2]. **Subs not used:** Turnbull, Ivanovic, Sturridge, Hutchinson.

18th ● Sunderland — A — W 1-3 — **Att:** 41,179. **Ref:** S Bennett – (4-3-3): Cech, Bosingwa, Ivanovic, Terry, A Cole, Essien, Ballack, Lampard[1], Kalou (Malouda 76), Drogba (Sturridge 84), Deco[1] (Shevchenko 86). **Subs not used:** Hilario, Carvalho, Mikel, Anelka.

23rd ● Fulham — A — W 0-2 — **Att:** 25,404. **Ref:** A Marriner – (4-1-2-1-2): Cech, Bosingwa (Hutchinson 86), Carvalho, Terry, A Cole, Mikel, Ballack, Malouda, Lampard (Deco 81), Drogba[1], Anelka[1]. **Subs not used:** Turnbull, Ivanovic, Essien, Kalou, Sturridge.

29th ● Burnley — H — W 3-0 — **Att:** 40,906. **Ref:** M Clattenburg – (4-1-2-1-2): Cech, Bosingwa (Belletti 66), Carvalho, Terry, A Cole[1], Essien, Ballack[1] (Mikel 83), Deco, Lampard, Anelka[1], Drogba (Kalou 75). **Subs not used:** Hilario, Ivanovic, Malouda, Sturridge.

SEPTEMBER

12th ● Stoke — A — W 1-2 — **Att:** 27,440. **Ref:** M Dean – (4-1-2-1-2): Cech, Bosingwa, Ivanovic, Terry, A Cole, Mikel (Belletti 83), Ballack (Essien 66), Malouda[1], Lampard, Kalou (Anelka 64), Drogba[1]. **Subs not used:** Hilario, Carvalho, Sturridge, Hutchinson.

15th ● FC Porto — H — W 1-0 — **Att:** 39,436. **Ref:** K Plautz – (4-5-1): Cech, A Cole, Terry, Carvalho, Ivanovic, Malouda[1], Lampard, Essien, Ballack, Kalou (Belletti 77), Anelka[1]. **Subs not used:** Turnbull, J Cole, Sturridge, Hutchinson, Bruma, Borini.

20th ● Tottenham — H — W 3-0 — **Att:** 41,623. **Ref:** H Webb – (4-4-2): Cech, Bosingwa, Carvalho, Terry, A Cole[1], Ballack[1] (Mikel 62), Essien, Lampard, Malouda, Anelka (Borini 89), Drogba[1] (Kalou 85). **Subs not used:** Hilario, Carvalho, Mikel, Hutchinson.

23rd ● QPR — H — W 1-0 — **Att:** 37,781. **Ref:** M Jones – (4-4-2): Hilario, Ivanovic, Ferreira, Hutchinson (Terry 77), Belletti, Malouda (Lampard 46), Zhirkov (A Cole 69), Mikel, J Cole, Borini, Kalou[1]. **Subs not used:** Turnbull, Essien, Matic, Bruma.

26th ● Wigan — A — L 3-1 — **Att:** 18,542. **Ref:** P Dowd – (4-1-3-2): Cech, Bosingwa (Kalou 68), Carvalho, Terry, A Cole, Essien, Mikel (Belletti 46), Malouda (Hilario 52), Lampard, Ballack, Anelka. **Subs not used:** Ivanovic, Zhirkov, Ferreira, Borini.

30th ● Apoel Nicosia — A — W 0-1 — **Att:** 20,000. **Ref:** B Layec – (4-3-3): Cech, Ivanovic, Carvalho, Terry, A Cole, Belletti (Deco 68), Essien, Lampard, Kalou (J Cole 80), Anelka[1], Malouda. **Subs not used:** Hilario, Zhirkov, Sturridge, Hutchinson, Bruma.

OCTOBER

4th ● Liverpool — H — W 2-0 — **Att:** 41,732. **Ref:** M Atkinson – (4-3-2-1): Hilario, Ivanovic, Carvalho, Terry, A Cole, Ballack, Essien, Lampard, Anelka[1], Deco (Malouda 76), Drogba. **Subs not used:** Turnbull, J Cole, Zhirkov, Kalou, Sturridge, Belletti.

17th ● Aston Villa — A — L 2-1 — **Att:** 39,047. **Ref:** K Friend – (4-1-2-1-2): Cech, Bosingwa (Ivanovic 69), Carvalho, Terry, A Cole, Essien, Malouda (J Cole 85), Lampard, Deco, Anelka, Drogba[1]. **Subs not used:** Hilario, Zhirkov, Kalou, Sturridge, Belletti.

21st ● Atletico Madrid — H — W 4-0 — **Att:** 39,997. **Ref:** F Meyer – (4-1-2-1-2): Cech, Belletti, Ivanovic, Terry, A Cole (Malouda 75), Essien, Ballack, Lampard[1], Deco, Kalou[1] (Zhirkov 73), Anelka (Sturridge 78). **Subs not used:** Hilario, Carvalho, J Cole, Bruma. Perea OG.

24th ● Blackburn — H — W 5-0 — **Att:** 40,836. **Ref:** A Wiley – (4-4-2): Cech, Ivanovic, Carvalho (Bruma 67), Terry, Belletti (Ferreira 61), Essien[1], Ballack, Lampard[2], J Cole (Sturridge 77), Anelka, Drogba[1]. **Subs not used:** Hilario, Malouda, Deco, Kalou. Givet OG.

28th ● Bolton — H — W 4-0 — **Att:** 41,538. **Ref:** A Marriner – (4-1-2-1-2): Hilario (Turnbull 23), Belletti, Ivanovic, Alex, Ferreira, Deco[1], Ballack, Malouda[1], J Cole, Kalou[1] (Essien 46), Sturridge (Drogba[1] 62). **Subs not used:** Lampard, Matic, Bruma, Borini.

31st ● Bolton — A — W 0-4 — **Att:** 22,680. **Ref:** P Walton – (4-1-2-1-2): Cech, Ivanovic, Carvalho, Terry, Ferreira, Essien, Ballack, Lampard[1], Deco[1], Anelka, Drogba[1]. **Subs not used:** Turnbull, J Cole, Malouda, Sturridge, Alex, Belletti, Borini. Knight OG.

NOVEMBER

3rd ● Atletico Madrid — A — D 2-2 — **Att:** 45,000. **Ref:** B Kuipers – (4-4-2): Cech, Belletti, Alex, Terry, A Cole, Malouda, Essien (Ballack 59), J Cole (Deco 70), Lampard, Drogba[2], Kalou (Anelka 70). **Subs not used:** Hilario, Ivanovic, Carvalho, Sturridge.

8th ● Man Utd — H — W 1-0 — **Att:** 41,836. **Ref:** M Atkinson – (4-4-2): Cech, Ivanovic, Carvalho, Terry[1], A Cole, Essien, Lampard, Ballack, Deco (J Cole 63), Drogba (Kalou 83), Anelka (Alex 90). **Subs not used:** Hilario, Mikel, Malouda, Ferreira.

21st ● Wolverhampton — H — W 4-0 — **Att:** 41,786. **Ref:** L Mason – (4-1-2-1-2): Cech, Belletti, Alex, Terry, A Cole[1], Essien[2], Mikel, J Cole, Malouda[1] (Matic 69), Anelka (Kakuta 59), Kalou (Borini 78). **Subs not used:** Hilario, Ivanovic, Zhirkov, Ferreira.

25th ● FC Porto — A — W 0-1 — **Att:** 35,000. **Ref:** J Eriksson – (4-1-2-1-2): Cech, Ivanovic, Carvalho, Terry, Zhirkov, Mikel, Ballack (Essien 68), Malouda, Deco (J Cole 76), Anelka[1], Drogba. **Subs not used:** Turnbull, A Cole, Kalou, Alex, Belletti.

29th ● Arsenal — A — W 0-3 — **Att:** 60,067. **Ref:** A Marriner – (4-1-2-1-2): Cech, Ivanovic, Carvalho, Terry, A Cole (Ferreira 72), Mikel, Essien, Lampard, J Cole (Deco 68), Anelka, Drogba[2] (Malouda 87). **Subs not used:** Hilario, Ballack, Zhirkov, Kalou. Vermaelen OG.

DECEMBER

2nd ● Blackburn — A — D 3-3 — **Att:** 18,136. **Ref:** A Wiley – (4-1-2-1-2): Hilario, Belletti (Bruma 46), Ivanovic, Ferreira[1], Zhirkov, Mikel, Ballack, Deco (Drogba[1] 46), J Cole (Kakuta 46), Kalou[1], Malouda. **Subs not used:** Turnbull, Matic, Hutchinson, Borini. AET – Score after 90 mins 2-2. Blackburn win 4-3 on penalties.

5th ● Man City — A — L 2-1 — **Att:** 47,348. **Ref:** H Webb – (4-4-2): Cech, Ivanovic (Belletti 63), Terry (Malouda 88), A Cole, Essien, Ballack (Mikel 64), Lampard, Deco, Drogba, Anelka. **Subs not used:** Hilario, J Cole, Zhirkov, Ferreira. Adebayor OG.

8th ● Apoel Nicosia — H — D 2-2 — **Att:** 40,917. **Ref:** M Trefoloni – (4-2-3-1): Turnbull, Belletti, Terry, Carvalho, Zhirkov, Mikel, Essien[1] (Lampard 26), J Cole, Kakuta (Borini 73), Malouda, Drogba[1]. **Subs not used:** Hilario, Ivanovic, Anelka, Bruma, Philliskirk.

12th ● Everton — H — D 3-3 — **Att:** 41,579. **Ref:** P Dowd – (4-4-2): Cech, Ivanovic, Carvalho (Belletti 85), Terry, A Cole, Mikel (Borini 88), Ballack, Lampard, J Cole (Malouda 76), Anelka[1], Drogba[2]. **Subs not used:** Hilario, Ferreira, Matic.

16th ● Portsmouth — H — W 2-1 — **Att:** 40,137. **Ref:** M Clattenburg – (4-1-2-1-2): Cech, Ivanovic, Alex, Terry, A Cole, Mikel (Malouda 64), Ballack, Lampard[1], Deco (J Cole 58), Anelka[1], Kalou (Borini 72). **Subs not used:** Hilario, Carvalho, Zhirkov, Ferreira.

20th ● West Ham — A — D 1-1 — **Att:** 33,388. **Ref:** M Dean – (4-3-1-2): Cech, Ivanovic, Carvalho, Terry, A Cole, Ballack, Lampard[1], Malouda (Mikel 46), J Cole (Zhirkov 75), Drogba, Kalou (Sturridge 46). **Subs not used:** Hilario, Ferreira, Alex, Belletti.

26th ● Birmingham — A — D 0-0 — **Att:** 28,958. **Ref:** P Walton – (4-3-1-2): Cech, Ivanovic, Terry, Alex, A Cole, Belletti, Mikel (Ballack 85), Malouda, Lampard (J Cole 79), Drogba, Sturridge (Kalou 67). **Subs not used:** Hilario, Carvalho, Zhirkov, Ferreira.

● Barclays Premier League ● FA Cup ● Carling Cup ● UEFA Champions League ● Europa League ● FA Community Shield   ▌ Yellow Card ▐ Red Card

RESULTS 2009/10

28th ● Fulham   H   W 2-1   **Att:** 41,805. **Ref:** A Marriner – (4-4-2): Cech, Ferreira (Ivanovic 64), Carvalho, Terry, Zhirkov (A Cole 84), Mikel (Sturridge 70), Ballack, Lampard, J Cole, Drogba[1], Kalou. **Subs not used:** Hilario, Alex, Belletti, Kakuta. Smalling OG.

JANUARY

3rd ● Watford   H   W 5-0   **Att:** 40,912. **Ref:** K Friend – (4-3-2-1): Hilario, Ivanovic, Alex, Terry, A Cole (Kakuta 74), Lampard[1], Belletti (Matic 65), Zhirkov, J Cole, Malouda[1], Sturridge[2] (Borini 70). **Subs not used:** Turnbull, Carvalho, Ballack, Ferreira. Eustace OG.

16th ● Sunderland   H   W 7-2   **Att:** 41,776. **Ref:** C Foy – (4-4-2): Cech, Ivanovic, Carvalho, Terry (Alex 46), A Cole[1] (Zhirkov 46), Ballack[1], Belletti, Lampard[2], J Cole, Anelka[2], Malouda[1]. **Subs not used:** Hilario, Ferreira, Sturridge, Matic, Borini.

23rd ● Preston   A   W 0-2   **Att:** 23,119. **Ref:** M Dean – (4-4-2): Hilario, Ferreira, Alex, Terry, Zhirkov, Belletti (Malouda 19), Ballack, Lampard (J Cole 66), Deco, Anelka[1], Sturridge[1]. **Subs not used:** Turnbull, Ivanovic, Matic, Borini, Van Aanholt.

27th ● Birmingham   H   W 3-0   **Att:** 41,293. **Ref:** S Bennett – (4-1-2-1-2): Cech, Ivanovic, Terry, Carvalho, A Cole, Ballack, Lampard[2], Deco, Malouda[1], J Cole (Zhirkov 81), Anelka (Sturridge 88). **Subs not used:** Turnbull, Ferreira, Matic, Alex, Borini.

30th ● Burnley   A   W 1-2   **Att:** 21,131. **Ref:** P Dowd – (4-3-2-1): Cech, Ivanovic, Alex, Terry[1], A Cole (Deco 76), Ballack, Zhirkov, Lampard, J Cole (Sturridge 72), Malouda, Anelka[1]. **Subs not used:** Turnbull, Carvalho, Ferreira, Matic, Borini.

FEBRUARY

2nd ● Hull   A   D 1-1   **Att:** 24,957. **Ref:** M Clattenburg – (4-3-2-1): Cech, Ivanovic[1], Carvalho, Terry[1], Zhirkov (A Cole 81), Ballack (J Cole 71), Deco, Lampard, Anelka (Sturridge 81), Malouda, Drogba[1]. **Subs not used:** Turnbull, Ferreira, Kalou, Alex.

7th ● Arsenal   H   W 2-0   **Att:** 41,794. **Ref:** M Dean – (4-3-3): Cech, Ivanovic, Carvalho, Terry, A Cole[1], Mikel, Ballack (Zhirkov 81), Lampard, Malouda, Drogba[2] (Kalou 90), Anelka (J Cole 87). **Subs not used:** Hilario, Ferreira, Deco, Alex.

10th ● Everton   A   L 2-1   **Att:** 36,411. **Ref:** A Wiley – (4-3-3): Cech, Ivanovic, Carvalho, Terry, A Cole (Ballack 56), Lampard, Mikel[1] (Sturridge 76), Zhirkov, Anelka (Kalou 69), Drogba, Malouda[1]. **Subs not used:** Hilario, Ferreira, Matic, Bruma.

13th ● Cardiff   H   W 4-1   **Att:** 40,827. **Ref:** A Marriner – (4-4-2): Hilario, Ferreira, Alex[1], Carvalho[1], Zhirkov, Ballack[1], Mikel, Lampard, J Cole (Kalou[1] 46), Drogba (Borini 88), Sturridge[1] (Malouda 78). **Subs not used:** Turnbull, Ivanovic, Bruma, Matic.

20th ● Wolverhampton   A   W 0-2   **Att:** 28,978. **Ref:** K Friend – (4-3-3): Cech, Ferreira, Ivanovic, Terry, Zhirkov (Bruma 56), J Cole, Mikel, Ballack[1], Anelka, Drogba[2], Malouda. **Subs not used:** Hilario, Kalou, Sturridge, Matic, Kakuta, Borini.

24th ◐ Inter Milan   A   L 2-1   **Att:** 84,638. **Ref:** M Mejuto Gonzalez – (4-3-3): Cech (Hilario 61), Ivanovic, Carvalho, Terry, Malouda, Ballack, Mikel, Lampard, Anelka, Drogba, Kalou[1] (Sturridge 78). **Subs not used:** J Cole, Alex, Belletti, Bruma, Borini.

27th ● Man City   H   L 2-4   **Att:** 41,814. **Ref:** M Dean – (4-3-3): Hilario, Ivanovic[1], Carvalho (Kalou 69), Terry[1], Malouda, Ballack[1] (Belletti[1] 60), Mikel, Lampard[2], Anelka, Drogba, J Cole (Sturridge 60). **Subs not used:** Turnbull, Ferreira, Matic, Alex.

MARCH

7th ● Stoke   H   W 2-0   **Att:** 41,322. **Ref:** M Atkinson – (4-3-3): Hilario, Ivanovic, Alex, Terry[1], Ferreira, Malouda, Mikel, Lampard[1], Anelka, Drogba, Kalou. **Subs not used:** Turnbull, J Cole, Deco, Sturridge, Matic, Kakuta, Van Aanholt.

13th ● West Ham   H   W 4-1   **Att:** 41,755. **Ref:** M Clattenburg – (4-3-3): Turnbull, Ivanovic (Zhirkov 80), Alex[1], Terry, Ferreira, Ballack, Mikel, Lampard, Anelka (J Cole 66), Drogba[2], Malouda[1] (Kalou 87). **Subs not used:** Taylor, Deco, Sturridge, Bruma.

16th ◐ Inter Milan   H   L 0-1   **Att:** 38,107. **Ref:** W Stark – (4-3-3): Turnbull, Ivanovic, Alex, Terry[1], Zhirkov (Kalou 73), Ballack (J Cole 62), Mikel, Lampard, Anelka, Drogba[1], Malouda[1]. **Subs not used:** R Taylor, Carvalho, Sturridge, Belletti, Bruma. Agg: 1-3.

21st ● Blackburn   A   D 1-1   **Att:** 25,554. **Ref:** S Bennett – (4-1-2-1-2): Turnbull, Ivanovic (Zhirkov 45), Alex, Terry, Ferreira, Mikel, Kalou (Deco 74), Malouda, Lampard, Anelka (Sturridge 90), Drogba[1]. **Subs not used:** Sebek, J Cole, Matic, Bruma.

24th ● Portsmouth   A   W 0-5   **Att:** 18,753. **Ref:** L Mason – (4-3-3): Cech, Ferreira, Carvalho (Alex 37), Terry, Zhirkov (Van Aanholt 71), Lampard[1], Mikel[1], Deco, Sturridge (J Cole 55), Drogba[2], Malouda[2]. **Subs not used:** Turnbull, Kalou, Anelka, Bruma.

27th ● Aston Villa   H   W 7-1   **Att:** 41,825. **Ref:** P Walton – (4-3-3): Cech, Ferreira[1], Alex, Terry, Zhirkov[1] (Van Aanholt 76), Deco[1] (Ballack 72), Mikel, Lampard[4], J Cole (Kalou[1] 76), Anelka, Malouda[2]. **Subs not used:** Turnbull, Drogba, Sturridge, Bruma.

APRIL

3rd ● Man Utd   A   W 1-2   **Att:** 75,217. **Ref:** M Dean – (4-5-1): Cech, Ferreira, Alex, Terry, Zhirkov, J Cole[1] (Kalou 73), Deco[1] (Ballack 82), Lampard, Mikel, Malouda, Anelka (Drogba[1] 69). **Subs not used:** Turnbull, Sturridge, Belletti, Bruma.

10th ● Aston Villa   N   W 0-3   **Att:** 85,472. **Ref:** H Webb – (4-3-3): Cech, Ferreira, Terry[1], Alex, Zhirkov, Deco[1] (Ballack 76), Mikel[1], Lampard[1], J Cole (Kalou 65), Drogba[1] (Anelka 80), Malouda[1]. **Subs not used:** Hilario, Ivanovic, Sturridge, Belletti.

13th ● Bolton   H   W 1-0   **Att:** 40,539. **Ref:** L Probert – (4-3-3): Cech, Ferreira, Alex[1], Terry, Zhirkov, Ballack, Mikel, Lampard, Kalou (J Cole 77), Drogba, Anelka[1] (Malouda 67). **Subs not used:** Hilario, Deco, Sturridge, Bruma, Van Aanholt.

17th ● Tottenham   A   L 2-1   **Att:** 35,814. **Ref:** P Dowd – (4-3-3): Cech, Ferreira (Ivanovic 46), Alex[1], Terry[1], Zhirkov[1], Deco[1], Mikel (Ballack 33), Lampard[1], J Cole (Anelka 46), Drogba, Malouda. **Subs not used:** Hilario, A Cole, Kalou, Sturridge.

25th ● Stoke   H   W 7-0   **Att:** 41,013. **Ref:** S Bennett – (4-3-3): Cech, Ferreira (Hutchinson 73), Ivanovic, Alex, A Cole, Lampard[2], Ballack, Malouda[1], Kalou[3] (J Cole 71), Drogba, Anelka (Sturridge[1] 79). **Subs not used:** Hilario, Zhirkov, Belletti, Van Aanholt.

MAY

2nd ● Liverpool   A   W 0-2   **Att:** 44,375. **Ref:** A Wiley – (4-3-3): Cech, Ivanovic, Terry, Alex, A Cole, Lampard[1], Ballack[1], Malouda[1], Kalou (Zhirkov 88), Drogba[1], Anelka (J Cole 90). **Subs not used:** Hilario, Ferreira, Deco, Sturridge, Belletti.

9th ● Wigan   H   W 8-0   **Att:** 41,383. **Ref:** M Atkinson – (4-3-3): Cech, Ivanovic (Belletti 58), Alex, Terry, A Cole[1], Lampard[1], Ballack (Matic 70), Malouda, Kalou[1] (J Cole 58), Drogba[3], Anelka[2]. **Subs not used:** Hilario, Zhirkov, Ferreira, Sturridge.

15th ● Portsmouth   N   W 1-0   **Att:** 88,335. **Ref:** C Foy – (4-3-3): Cech, Ivanovic, Alex, Terry, A Cole, Lampard, Ballack (Belletti 44), Malouda, Anelka (Sturridge 90), Drogba[1], Kalou (J Cole 71). **Subs not used:** Hilario, Zhirkov, Ferreira, Matic.

● Barclays Premier League ● FA Cup ◐ Carling Cup ◐ UEFA Champions League ● Europa League ◐ FA Community Shield   ▌Yellow Card ▌Red Card

CHELSEA

BARCLAYS PREMIER LEAGUE GOALKEEPER STATS

Player	Minutes on pitch	Appearances	Match starts	Completed matches	Sub appearances	Subbed off	Saved with feet	Punched	Parried	Tipped over	Fumbled	Tipped round	Caught	Blocked	Clean sheets	Goals conceded	Save %	Saved	Resulting in goals	Opposition miss	Fouls committed	Free-kicks won	Yellow cards	Red cards
Petr Cech	3238	34	34	33	0	0	1	17	13	7	1	6	117	3	17	23	87.70	1	2	0	1	3	0	1
Henrique Hilario	237	3	2	2	1	0	0	2	1	0	0	1	6	0	1	7	58.82	0	2	0	0	1	0	0
Ross Turnbull	192	2	2	2	0	0	0	1	1	0	0	0	4	0	0	2	75.00	0	0	0	0	0	0	0

BARCLAYS PREMIER LEAGUE OUTFIELD PLAYER STATS

Player	Minutes on pitch	Appearances	Match starts	Completed matches	Substitute appearances	Subbed off	Goals scored	Assists	Shots on target	Shots off target	Crosses	Tackles made	Defensive clearances	Defensive blocks	Fouls committed	Free-kicks won	Caught offside	Yellow cards	Red cards
Alex	1364	16	13	13	3	0	1	0	14	9	0	24	23	7	15	1	0	2	0
Nicolas Anelka	2842	33	31	17	2	14	11	10	58	22	58	11	2	0	22	33	26	0	0
Michael Ballack	2523	32	26	18	6	7	4	5	22	23	27	28	13	4	50	40	3	3	1
Juliano Belletti	528	11	4	2	7	1	0	1	1	5	7	3	1	1	8	6	0	1	1
Fabio Borini	51	4	0	0	4	0	0	0	2	1	0	0	0	0	1	2	0	0	0
Jose Bosingwa	689	8	8	4	0	4	0	1	3	2	23	5	1	0	14	9	2	0	0
Jeffrey Bruma	64	2	0	0	2	0	0	0	0	0	0	0	0	1	1	0	0	0	0
Ricardo Carvalho	1974	22	22	17	0	5	0	1	4	4	9	19	23	8	20	6	0	4	0
Joe Cole	1365	26	14	4	12	10	2	6	18	17	29	10	1	0	17	9	3	2	0
Ashley Cole	2307	27	25	21	2	4	4	4	10	3	34	51	10	2	13	42	5	4	0
Deco	1319	19	14	8	5	6	2	2	9	7	17	15	3	0	13	20	0	4	0
Didier Drogba	2962	32	31	25	1	6	29	13	87	71	52	14	24	0	59	57	33	7	0
Michael Essien	1284	14	13	13	1	0	3	0	18	16	6	10	9	3	13	28	0	2	0
Paulo Ferreira	1017	13	11	8	2	3	0	0	1	1	19	17	6	4	8	10	0	2	0
Sam Hutchinson	27	2	0	0	2	0	0	1	0	1	2	4	0	0	1	0	0	0	0
Branislav Ivanovic	2418	28	25	22	3	3	1	6	10	12	46	43	25	4	37	31	0	6	0
Gael Kakuta	34	1	0	0	1	0	0	0	0	2	1	0	0	0	0	2	0	0	0
Salomon Kalou	1044	23	11	1	12	10	5	4	14	20	14	15	2	0	15	11	9	2	0
Frank Lampard	3452	36	36	34	0	2	22	17	66	53	54	51	24	5	23	29	4	0	0
Florent Malouda	2466	33	26	19	7	6	12	9	30	18	68	11	7	2	26	38	6	4	1
Nemanja Matic	46	2	0	0	2	0	0	0	0	1	0	1	1	0	1	0	0	0	0
Mikel	1850	25	21	11	4	10	0	1	2	7	3	14	6	3	35	29	0	3	0
Andriy Shevchenko	6	1	0	0	1	0	0	0	0	0	0	0	1	0	0	1	0	0	0
Daniel Sturridge	335	13	0	0	11	2	1	2	9	5	7	3	0	1	3	6	0	0	0
John Terry	3481	37	37	34	0	2	2	2	9	9	3	50	62	10	29	25	0	7	1
Patrick Van Aanholt	41	2	0	0	2	0	0	0	0	0	2	0	1	0	1	0	0	0	0
Yuri Zhirkov	1019	17	10	5	7	5	0	4	1	1	29	13	14	1	16	16	0	4	0

actim

BARCLAYS PREMIER LEAGUE

SEASON TOTALS

Goals scored	103
Goals conceded	32
Clean sheets	18
Shots on target	386
Shots off target	311
Shots per goal	6.77
Pens awarded	12
Pens scored	11
Pens conceded	5
Offsides	91
Corners	287
Crosses	511
Players used	30
Fouls committed	442
Free-kicks won	455

CARDS RECEIVED

57 **5**

SEQUENCES

Wins	6
(15/08/09–20/09/09)	
Losses	–
(–)	
Draws	2
(20/12/09–26/12/09)	
Undefeated	10
(12/12/09–07/02/10)	
Without win	2
(on two occasions)	
Undefeated home	13
(15/08/09–07/02/10)	
Undefeated away	4
(on two occasions)	
Without scoring	–
(–)	
Without conceding	5
(24/10/09–29/11/09)	
Scoring	18
(15/08/09–20/12/09)	
Conceding	4
(05/12/09–20/12/09)	

AUG	SEP	OCT	NOV	DEC	JAN	FEB	MAR	APR	MAY
1	2	1	1	1	1	1	2	1	1

LEAGUE POSITION AT THE END OF EACH MONTH

SEASON INFORMATION
Highest position: 1
Lowest position: 7
Average goals scored per game: 2.71
Average goals conceded per game: 0.84

MATCH RECORDS

Goals scored per match

		W	D	L	Pts
Failed to score	1	0	1	0	1
Scored 1 goal	10	2	3	5	9
Scored 2 goals	12	11	0	1	33
Scored 3 goals	6	5	1	0	16
Scored 4+ goals	9	9	0	0	27

Goals conceded per match

		W	D	L	Pts
Clean sheet	18	17	1	0	52
Conceded 1 goal	12	9	3	0	30
Conceded 2 goals	5	1	0	4	3
Conceded 3 goals	2	0	1	1	1
Conceded 4+ goals	1	0	0	1	0

EARLIEST STRIKE
FLORENT MALOUDA
(v Wolves) 4:21

LATEST STRIKE
FLORENT MALOUDA
(v Stoke) 93:33

Florent Malouda

GOAL DETAILS

How the goals were struck

SCORED		CONCEDED
60	Right foot	13
25	Left foot	9
16	Header	8
2	Other	2

How the goals were struck

SCORED		CONCEDED
58	Open play	17
21	Cross	3
3	Corner	5
11	Penalty	4
3	Direct from free-kick	1
3	Free-kick	1
4	Own goal	1

Distance from goal

SCORED		CONCEDED
48	6YDS	15
46	18YDS	13
9	18+YDS	4

GOALS SCORED/CONCEDED
PER FIVE-MINUTE INTERVALS

MINS	5	10	15	20	25	30	35	40	45	50	55	60	65	70	75	80	85	90
FOR	2	5	3	6	6	1	7	3	10	4	6	9	8	5	2	7	4	15
AGN	1	0	2	2	0	4	3	1	4	1	4	2	1	1	1	1	1	3

EVERTON

EVERTON fell just short in their late charge for a European place after an outstanding finish to their Barclays Premier League campaign.

David Moyes' men hit form from December and lost just two of their last 24 games following a disappointing, injury-ravaged start. Their final position of eighth was just two points below that of seventh-placed Liverpool, the last of the Europa League qualifiers, and left Moyes to wonder what might have been had the season started differently.

Hopes were high at Goodison Park at the start of August after they had finished fifth and reached the FA Cup final in 2008/09. Attention was diverted, however, by the acrimonious sale of England defender Joleon Lescott to Manchester City and a 6–1 thrashing by Arsenal on the opening day was a severe setback.

Promoted Burnley compounded their misery in the second game and the absence of several key players was keenly felt as the team struggled to build momentum. Mikel Arteta, Phil Jagielka and Victor Anichebe all missed the first half of the season with long-term injuries and captain Phil Neville, Joseph Yobo, Leon Osman and Steven Pienaar were also out for lengthy spells.

The Europa League provided an early diversion but, having progressed comfortably through the opening games, a 5–0 defeat by Benfica in Lisbon in October did little for confidence. However, the nadir came just over a month later as the Toffees went 3–0 down inside 28 minutes at struggling Hull. Coming on the same day as plans for a new stadium at Kirkby were knocked back, the mood at the club was at a low.

Arch-rivals Liverpool, naturally, took delight in rubbing salt into the wounds with a derby victory at Goodison Park but Everton's season began to turn in their next home game against Tottenham in early December. Another bad result seemed likely as Spurs opened up a 2–0 lead but substitute Seamus Coleman, who ended the season on loan at Blackpool in a bid to gather further experience, was outstanding on his home debut and led a superb fightback. Tim Cahill and Louis Saha scored to level inside the last 12 minutes but the truly pivotal moment came in injury time. Everton's good work

A fabulous second half of the season saw a resurgent Toffees side come close to securing a European spot

could have been undone as Tony Hibbert conceded a late penalty but Tim Howard saved from Jermain Defoe in front of a raucous crowd and the revival began in earnest.

Everton went on a nine-game unbeaten run and spirits were not even dampened when that sequence was ended by Liverpool in a game that saw Pienaar sent off and Marouane Fellaini suffer a season-ending injury. Eventual champions Chelsea were beaten on a pulsating night at Goodison and title challengers Manchester United went the same way little more than a week later.

The Europa League campaign ended with defeat to Sporting Lisbon at the last-32 stage, but hopes of qualifying for the competition again no longer seemed fanciful. Everton strung together seven successive home League wins – their best run for 20 years – and the top teams came into sight. Defeat at Tottenham in late February proved to be the only other serious blemish in a strong run-in.

A handful of draws, however, just kept the likes of Liverpool and Aston Villa out of reach. Birmingham, Wolves, West Ham, Villa and Stoke all frustrated the Toffees, although there was a hugely satisfying win at Manchester City and exhilarating last-gasp wins against Blackburn, Fulham and – on the final day – Portsmouth.

Eighth position may be a disappointment given pre-season expectations but it was ultimately satisfying bearing in mind the club had slipped to 16th in November. A number of players ended the campaign with their reputations enhanced, including Howard, Pienaar, Saha, Leighton Baines and John Heitinga. Another key man was the Russian import Diniyar Bilyaletdinov, who scored nine goals from midfield following his move from Lokomotiv Moscow in August 2009.

CLOCKWISE FROM ABOVE: Everton launched what proved to be a disappointing Europa League campaign with a 4-0 thrashing of AEK Athens at Goodison Park; Tim Cahill displays his usual celebratory routine after scoring the only goal in an away win at Wigan; David Moyes shows his delight after his side overcame high-flying Manchester City in a 2-0 victory at Eastlands

EVERTON

RESULTS 2009/10

AUGUST

15th ● Arsenal H L 1–6 **Att:** 39,309. **Ref:** M Halsey – (4-4-1-1): Howard, Hibbert (Gosling 58), Yobo, Lescott, Baines, Osman (Saha¹ 58), Neville, Cahill, Pienaar, Fellaini, Jo (Rodwell 58). **Subs not used:** Nash, Vaughan, Duffy, Baxter.

20th ◉ Sigma Olomouc H W 4–0 **Att:** 27,433. **Ref:** L Cortez Batista – (4-5-1): Howard, Hibbert, Neville, Yobo, Baines, Osman, Fellaini, Rodwell² (Gosling 77), Cahill, Pienaar (Vaughan 82), Saha² (Jo 79). **Subs not used:** Nash, Duffy, Baxter, Wallace.

23rd ● Burnley A L 1–0 **Att:** 19,983. **Ref:** P Dowd – (4-5-1): Howard, Hibbert, Yobo, Neville, Baines, Osman, Rodwell, Fellaini (Jo 65), Cahill, Pienaar, Saha. **Subs not used:** Nash, Vaughan, Gosling, Duffy, Baxter, Wallace.

27th ◉ Sigma Olomouc A D 1–1 **Att:** 10,212. **Ref:** F Fautrel – (4-5-1): Howard, Hibbert█, Neville, Yobo, Baines, Osman (Baxter 66), Rodwell, Pienaar¹ (Wallace 66), Fellaini, Gosling█, Jo (Yakubu 76). **Subs not used:** Nash, Saha, Cahill, Duffy. Agg: 1-5.

30th ● Wigan H W 2–1 **Att:** 35,122. **Ref:** L Probert – (4-4-1-1): Howard, Hibbert, Yobo, Distin, Baines¹, Osman█ (Fellaini 70), Neville, Rodwell, Pienaar (Bilyaletdinov 89), Cahill, Saha¹ (Jo 76). **Subs not used:** Nash, Gosling, Duffy, Agard.

SEPTEMBER

13th ● Fulham A L 2–1 **Att:** 24,191. **Ref:** P Walton – (4-4-1-1): Howard, Hibbert, Yobo, Distin, Baines█, Osman (Yakubu 81), Neville (Heitinga 65), Rodwell, Pienaar, Cahill¹, Jo (Fellaini 69). **Subs not used:** Nash, Bilyaletdinov, Vaughan, Gosling.

17th ◉ AEK Athens H W 4–0 **Att:** 26,747. **Ref:** R Malek – (4-5-1): Howard, Gosling, Yobo¹, Distin¹, Baines, Pienaar¹ (Saha█ 67), Cahill█ (Osman 46), Rodwell, Fellaini, Bilyaletdinov (Yakubu 52), Jo¹. **Subs not used:** Nash, Baxter, Wallace, Mustafi.

20th ● Blackburn H W 3–0 **Att:** 35,546. **Ref:** L Mason – (4-4-1-1): Howard, Heitinga█, Yobo¹, Distin, Baines, Osman (Gosling 82), Rodwell, Cahill (Hibbert 77), Pienaar, Fellaini, Saha² (Jo 73). **Subs not used:** Nash, Yakubu, Agard, Wallace.

23rd ◉ Hull A W 0–4 **Att:** 13,558. **Ref:** S Bennett – (4-4-2): Howard, Hibbert, Heitinga, Distin, Baines (Neill 62), Osman¹, Gosling¹, Rodwell, Bilyaletdinov (Agard 84), Jo¹, Yakubu¹ (Fellaini 46). **Subs not used:** Nash, Saha, Cahill, Duffy.

26th ● Portsmouth A W 0–1 **Att:** 18,116. **Ref:** A Wiley – (4-4-1-1): Howard, Heitinga, Yobo█, Distin, Baines, Osman (Hibbert 74), Fellaini█, Rodwell, Pienaar (Bilyaletdinov 60), Cahill, Saha¹ (Jo 90). **Subs not used:** Nash, Gosling, Yakubu, Neill.

OCTOBER

1st ◉ BATE A W 1–2 **Att:** 23,000. **Ref:** P Balaj – (4-4-1-1): Howard, Gosling, Hibbert, Distin, Baines, Osman█, Cahill¹, Fellaini█, Bilyaletdinov (Baxter 90), Jo, Yakubu (Agard█ 79). **Subs not used:** Nash, Duffy, Wallace, Mustafi, Akpan.

4th ● Stoke H D 1–1 **Att:** 36,753. **Ref:** A Marriner – (4-4-1-1): Howard, Hibbert, Heitinga, Distin, Baines, Osman¹ (Yakubu 76), Rodwell, Cahill, Bilyaletdinov (Jo 75), Fellaini█, Saha. **Subs not used:** Nash, Gosling, Neill, Agard, Baxter.

17th ● Wolverhampton H D 1–1 **Att:** 39,319. **Ref:** S Attwell – (4-4-1-1): Howard█, Hibbert (Yakubu 46), Yobo, Distin, Baines, Osman (Fellaini 77), Rodwell, Heitinga, Bilyaletdinov¹, Cahill, Saha (Jo 73). **Subs not used:** Nash, Gosling, Neill, Coleman.

22nd ◉ Benfica A L 5–0 **Att:** 44,534. **Ref:** N Ivanov – (4-4-2): Howard, Gosling█, Hibbert, Distin, Coleman, Fellaini, Cahill, Rodwell, Bilyaletdinov (Saha█ 60), Jo, Yakubu (Baxter 71). **Subs not used:** Nash, Duffy, Agard, Wallace, Akpan.

25th ● Bolton A L 3–2 **Att:** 21,547. **Ref:** P Dowd – (4-4-2): Howard, Hibbert, Heitinga (Coleman 80), Distin, Neill, Gosling, Rodwell, Cahill, Jo, Saha¹, Fellaini¹█. **Subs not used:** Nash, Duffy, Agard, Baxter, Wallace, Akpan.

27th ◉ Tottenham A L 2–0 **Att:** 35,843. **Ref:** L Mason – (4-4-2): Howard, Hibbert, Heitinga█, Distin, Neill, Cahill█, Gosling, Rodwell, Fellaini, Saha (Jo 46), Yakubu. **Subs not used:** Nash, Coleman, Duffy, Agard, Baxter, Wallace.

31st ● Aston Villa H D 1–1 **Att:** 36,648. **Ref:** L Probert – (4-4-1-1): Howard, Neill, Yobo, Distin, Baines, Cahill█, Rodwell, Heitinga, Bilyaletdinov¹█, Fellaini (Saha 72), Yakubu (Jo 90). **Subs not used:** Nash, Gosling, Coleman, Duffy, Agard.

NOVEMBER

5th ◉ Benfica H L 0–2 **Att:** 30,790. **Ref:** S Ennjimi – (4-4-1-1): Howard, Hibbert█, Yobo, Distin, Baines, Gosling (Jo 69), Fellaini, Rodwell█, Bilyaletdinov, Cahill, Yakubu█ (Agard 81). **Subs not used:** Nash, Coleman, Duffy, Baxter, Wallace.

8th ● West Ham A W 1–2 **Att:** 32,466. **Ref:** A Wiley – (4-5-1): Howard, Hibbert█, Yobo█, Distin, Baines, Heitinga█, Gosling¹ (Neill 76), Fellaini█, Rodwell, Cahill, Saha¹ (Yakubu 57). **Subs not used:** Nash, Coleman, Wallace, Agard, Baxter.

21st ● Man Utd A L 3–0 **Att:** 75,169. **Ref:** A Wiley – (4-4-1-1): Howard, Neill, Yobo, Distin, Baines, Gosling (Yakubu 46), Rodwell, Heitinga, Cahill█ (Jo 82), Fellaini█, Saha (Hibbert 83). **Subs not used:** Nash, Coleman, Duffy, Baxter.

25th ● Hull L 3–2 **Att:** 24,685. **Ref:** M Atkinson – (4-4-2): Howard, Neill█, Yobo, Distin, Baines, Cahill█, Rodwell (Jo 60), Heitinga█, Pienaar¹, Saha¹, Yakubu (Gosling 46). **Subs not used:** Nash, Hibbert, Coleman, Duffy, Baxter. Zayatte OG.

29th ● Liverpool H L 0–2 **Att:** 39,652. **Ref:** A Wiley – (4-4-1-1): Howard, Hibbert, Yobo (Neill 86), Distin, Baines, Pienaar, Heitinga█, Fellaini, Bilyaletdinov, Cahill (Yakubu 82), Jo (Saha 66). **Subs not used:** Nash, Gosling, Coleman, Baxter.

DECEMBER

2nd ◉ AEK Athens A W 0–1 **Att:** 15,000. **Ref:** C Circhetta – (4-4-2): Howard█, Gosling (Baxter 10), Hibbert█, Distin (Duffy 18), Baines, Pienaar, Coleman, Fellaini, Bilyaletdinov¹█, Cahill█, Jo (Yakubu 73). **Subs not used:** Nash, Saha, Agard, Mustafi.

6th ● Tottenham H D 2–2 **Att:** 34,003. **Ref:** A Marriner – (4-4-1-1): Howard, Neill, Hibbert, Yobo (Coleman 15), Baines█, Pienaar, Rodwell█ (Yakubu 62), Fellaini█, Bilyaletdinov, Cahill█, Jo (Saha¹ 62). **Subs not used:** Nash, Duffy, Agard, Baxter.

12th ● Chelsea A D 3–3 **Att:** 41,579. **Ref:** P Dowd – (4-3-3): Howard, Hibbert, Neill, Heitinga█, Baines, Rodwell, Fellaini, Bilyaletdinov, Jo (Yakubu¹ 45), Saha¹ (Agard 90), Pienaar. **Subs not used:** Nash, Coleman, Duffy, Akpan, Mustafi. Cech OG.

17th ◉ BATE H L 0–1 **Att:** 18,242. **Ref:** S Dereli – (4-4-2): Nash, Coleman, Hibbert (Mustafi 76), Duffy█, Bidwell, Osman (Craig 81), Forshaw, Rodwell (Akpan 8), Baxter, Agard, Yakubu. **Subs not used:** Howard, Garbutt, McAleny, Nsiala.

20th ● Birmingham H D 1–1 **Att:** 33,660. **Ref:** S Attwell – (4-4-1-1): Howard, Neill█, Hibbert█, Yobo, Baines, Pienaar, Osman (Vaughan 90), Cahill, Bilyaletdinov¹ (Yakubu 70), Fellaini, Saha. **Subs not used:** Nash, Coleman, Duffy, Agard, Baxter.

26th ◉ Sunderland A D 1–1 **Att:** 46,990. **Ref:** M Atkinson – (4-4-2): Howard, Baines, Heitinga, Neill, Hibbert, Pienaar, Osman (Yakubu 69), Fellaini¹, Bilyaletdinov█, Saha█ (Vaughan 87), Cahill█. **Subs not used:** Nash, Neville, Coleman, Duffy, Baxter.

28th ● Burnley H W 2–0 **Att:** 39,419. **Ref:** H Webb – (4-4-1-1): Howard, Hibbert, Heitinga, Neill, Baines, Bilyaletdinov (Vaughan¹ 81), Osman, Fellaini, Pienaar¹█, Cahill (Neville 60), Yakubu. **Subs not used:** Nash, Coleman, Duffy, Agard, Baxter.

JANUARY

● Barclays Premier League ● FA Cup ◉ Carling Cup ◉ UEFA Champions League ◉ Europa League ● FA Community Shield   █ Yellow Card █ Red Card

RESULTS 2009/10

2nd	● Carlisle	H	W 3–1	**Att:** 31,196. **Ref:** J Moss – (4-5-1): Howard, Hibbert (Coleman 80), Heitinga, Neill, Baines¹, Pienaar, Neville▌, Cahill¹, Fellaini▌, Bilyaletdinov, Vaughan¹ (Agard 86). **Subs not used:** Nash, Duffy, Forshaw, Baxter, Mustafi.
9th	● Arsenal	A	D 2–2	**Att:** 60,053. **Ref:** P Walton – (4-4-1-1): Howard, Neville, Neill, Heitinga, Baines, Osman¹, Cahill, Fellaini, Pienaar▌, Donovan (Bilyaletdinov 68), Saha (Vaughan 74). **Subs not used:** Nash, Coleman, Duffy, Baxter, Mustafi.
16th	● Man City	H	W 2–0	**Att:** 37,378. **Ref:** A Marriner – (4-4-1-1): Howard, Neville, Heitinga, Distin (Coleman 70), Baines, Donovan (Baxter 90), Fellaini, Pienaar¹, Bilyaletdinov, Cahill, Saha¹ (Vaughan 84). **Subs not used:** Nash, Forshaw, Mustafi.
23rd	● Birmingham	H	L 1–2	**Att:** 30,875. **Ref:** H Webb – (4-4-1-1): Howard, Neville, Distin, Heitinga, Baines, Pienaar, Cahill▌, Fellaini, Bilyaletdinov (Osman▌ 46), Donovan (Arteta 76), Saha (Vaughan 69). **Subs not used:** Nash, Coleman, Duffy, Baxter.
27th	● Sunderland	H	W 2–0	**Att:** 32,163. **Ref:** P Dowd – (4-4-1-1): Howard, Neville, Heitinga, Distin, Baines, Donovan¹ (Arteta 75), Fellaini, Osman, Pienaar (Anichebe 90), Cahill▌, Saha (Vaughan 77). **Subs not used:** Nash, Bilyaletdinov, Senderos, Coleman.
30th	● Wigan	A	W 0–1	**Att:** 16,869. **Ref:** L Probert – (4-4-1-1): Howard, Neville, Heitinga, Senderos, Baines, Donovan (Anichebe 75), Fellaini, Osman▌, Pienaar▌, Cahill▌, Saha (Vaughan 90). **Subs not used:** Nash, Bilyaletdinov, Rodwell, Coleman, Duffy.

FEBRUARY

6th	● Liverpool	A	L 1–0	**Att:** 44,316. **Ref:** M Atkinson – (4-1-4-1): Howard, Neville, Distin, Heitinga▌, Baines, Fellaini (Arteta 40), Donovan, Osman (Yakubu 72), Cahill, Pienaar▌, Saha (Anichebe▌ 72). **Subs not used:** Nash, Bilyaletdinov, Senderos, Coleman.
10th	● Chelsea	H	W 2–1	**Att:** 36,411. **Ref:** A Wiley – (4-4-1-1): Howard, Neville, Heitinga, Distin, Baines, Arteta (Rodwell 74), Osman, Bilyaletdinov (Gosling 86), Cahill, Saha² (Senderos 90). **Subs not used:** Nash, Vaughan, Yakubu, Coleman.
16th	○ Sporting	H	W 2–1	**Att:** 28,131. **Ref:** D Ceferin – (4-4-1-1): Howard, Neville, Yobo, Distin▌, Baines, Donovan, Arteta (Rodwell 78), Osman, Pienaar¹, Cahill (Yakubu 62), Saha (Bilyaletdinov 83). **Subs not used:** Nash, Vaughan, Gosling, Coleman.
20th	● Man Utd	H	W 3–1	**Att:** 39,448. **Ref:** H Webb – (4-4-1-1): Howard, Neville, Heitinga, Distin, Baines, Donovan, Osman▌, Arteta▌, Bilyaletdinov¹ (Gosling¹ 70), Pienaar▌ (Rodwell▌ 88), Saha▌. **Subs not used:** Nash, Yobo, Vaughan, Yakubu, Coleman.
25th	○ Sporting	A	L 3–0	**Att:** 17,609. **Ref:** A Yefet – (4-4-2): Howard, Neville, Yobo, Senderos (Jagielka 52), Baines, Osman, Arteta, Pienaar▌, Bilyaletdinov (Rodwell 61), Saha, Donovan (Yakubu 73). **Subs not used:** Nash, Gosling, Anichebe, Coleman. Agg: 4–2.
28th	● Tottenham	A	L 2–1	**Att:** 35,912. **Ref:** S Bennett – (4-5-1): Howard, Neville▌, Heitinga, Distin, Baines, Anichebe (Donovan 63), Arteta▌, Pienaar▌, Osman (Jagielka 46), Rodwell (Vaughan 81), Yakubu¹. **Subs not used:** Nash, Yobo, Bilyaletdinov, Gosling.

MARCH

7th	● Hull	H	W 5–1	**Att:** 34,682. **Ref:** L Mason – (4-4-2): Howard, Neville, Jagielka, Distin, Baines, Osman (Rodwell 44), Heitinga, Arteta² (Pienaar 85), Yakubu, Anichebe (Donovan¹ 70). **Subs not used:** Nash, Hibbert, Yobo, Bilyaletdinov. Garcia OG.
13th	● Birmingham	A	D 2–2	**Att:** 24,579. **Ref:** L Probert – (4-4-1-1): Howard, Neville, Jagielka, Distin, Baines, Anichebe¹ (Gosling 79), Heitinga, Arteta, Pienaar, Cahill (Rodwell 76), Yakubu▌ (Donovan 67). **Subs not used:** Nash, Hibbert, Yobo, Bilyaletdinov.
20th	● Bolton	H	W 2–0	**Att:** 36,503. **Ref:** A Wiley – (4-4-1-1): Howard, Neville, Jagielka, Distin, Baines, Anichebe (Bilyaletdinov 15), Heitinga, Arteta¹, Pienaar¹, Cahill▌ (Saha 62), Yakubu (Osman 76). **Subs not used:** Nash, Hibbert, Yobo, Rodwell.
24th	● Man City	A	W 0–2	**Att:** 45,708. **Ref:** P Walton – (4-4-1-1): Howard, Neville, Jagielka, Distin, Baines, Osman, Heitinga, Arteta¹ (Yobo 90), Pienaar▌, Cahill¹, Saha (Rodwell 74). **Subs not used:** Nash, Hibbert, Bilyaletdinov, Gosling, Yakubu.
27th	● Wolverhampton	A	D 0–0	**Att:** 28,995. **Ref:** M Jones – (4-5-1): Howard, Neville, Jagielka, Distin, Baines, Osman (Gosling 83), Rodwell (Bilyaletdinov 88), Heitinga, Cahill, Pienaar▌, Saha (Yakubu 76). **Subs not used:** Nash, Hibbert, Yobo, Senderos.

APRIL

4th	● West Ham	H	D 2–2	**Att:** 37,451. **Ref:** H Webb – (4-5-1): Howard, Neville, Jagielka, Distin▌, Baines, Pienaar, Osman (Rodwell 83), Heitinga, Cahill▌, Bilyaletdinov¹ (Yakubu¹ 65), Saha. **Subs not used:** Turner, Hibbert, Senderos, Duffy, Wallace.
14th	● Aston Villa	A	D 2–2	**Att:** 38,729. **Ref:** M Atkinson – (4-5-1): Howard▌, Neville, Jagielka, Baines, Heitinga (Rodwell 50), Pienaar, Osman, Arteta (Yobo 89), Cahill▌², Yakubu (Saha 63). **Subs not used:** Turner, Hibbert, Senderos, Wallace.
17th	● Blackburn	A	W 2–3	**Att:** 27,022. **Ref:** A Marriner – (4-4-1-1): Howard, Hibbert (Yakubu¹ 78), Jagielka, Distin▌, Baines, Bilyaletdinov (Anichebe 69), Neville, Arteta▌▌, Pienaar, Cahill¹, Saha (Yobo 90). **Subs not used:** Turner, Senderos, Duffy, Wallace.
25th	● Fulham	H	W 2–1	**Att:** 35,578. **Ref:** L Mason – (4-4-1-1): Howard, Hibbert, Jagielka, Baines, Bilyaletdinov (Anichebe 46), Neville (Saha 60), Arteta¹, Pienaar, Cahill, Yakubu (Baxter 87). **Subs not used:** Turner, Yobo, Senderos, Wallace. Smalling OG.

MAY

| 1st | ● Stoke | A | D 0–0 | **Att:** 27,579. **Ref:** H Webb – (4-4-1-1): Howard, Yobo, Jagielka, Distin, Baines, Anichebe (Bilyaletdinov 90), Neville, Arteta, Osman (Rodwell 72), Cahill, Saha (Yakubu 72). **Subs not used:** Turner, Hibbert, Senderos, Baxter. |
| 9th | ● Portsmouth | H | W 1–0 | **Att:** 38,730. **Ref:** P Walton – (4-4-1-1): Howard, Hibbert, Jagielka, Distin, Baines, Anichebe (Bilyaletdinov¹ 66), Rodwell (Yakubu 55), Arteta (Heitinga 84), Pienaar, Osman, Saha. **Subs not used:** Turner, Yobo, Senderos, Baxter. |

● Barclays Premier League ● FA Cup ○ Carling Cup ○ UEFA Champions League ● Europa League ○ FA Community Shield   ▌ Yellow Card ▌ Red Card

EVERTON

BARCLAYS PREMIER LEAGUE GOALKEEPER STATS

Player	Minutes on pitch	Appearances	Match starts	Completed matches	Sub appearances	Subbed off	Saved with feet	Punched	Parried	Tipped over	Fumbled	Tipped round	Caught	Blocked	Clean sheets	Goals conceded	Save %	Saved	Resulting in goals	Opposition miss	Fouls committed	Free-kicks won	Yellow cards	Red cards
Tim Howard	3662	38	38	38	0	0	3	15	24	6	0	10	104	1	11	49	76.89	2	0	0	0	4	2	0

BARCLAYS PREMIER LEAGUE OUTFIELD PLAYER STATS

Player	Minutes on pitch	Appearances	Match starts	Completed matches	Substitute appearances	Subbed off	Goals scored	Assists	Shots on target	Shots off target	Crosses	Tackles made	Defensive clearances	Defensive blocks	Fouls committed	Free-kicks won	Caught offside	Yellow cards	Red cards
Keiran Agard	8	1	0	0	1	0	0	0	0	0	0	0	0	0	0	0	0	0	0
Victor Anichebe	512	11	6	0	5	6	1	2	9	3	7	7	0	1	12	10	3	1	0
Mikel Arteta	1106	13	11	8	2	3	6	2	17	4	26	21	2	1	16	28	0	3	0
Leighton Baines	3566	37	37	37	0	0	1	9	23	5	117	44	32	8	20	55	3	2	0
Jose Baxter	11	2	0	0	2	0	0	0	0	0	0	1	0	0	0	0	0	0	0
Diniyar Bilyaletdinov	1521	23	16	6	7	9	6	1	18	12	39	13	8	3	9	13	2	1	1
Tim Cahill	3050	33	33	27	0	6	8	5	38	26	19	25	32	6	74	71	18	8	0
Seamus Coleman	126	3	0	0	3	0	0	1	1	0	0	5	0	1	0	1	0	0	0
Sylvain Distin	2768	29	29	28	0	0	1	1	1	3	4	35	29	20	16	22	1	2	0
Landon Donovan	690	10	7	3	3	4	2	3	6	4	19	6	2	0	9	12	2	1	0
Marouane Fellaini	1882	23	20	17	3	3	2	3	22	11	11	28	15	2	57	30	9	6	0
Dan Gosling	384	11	3	1	8	2	2	0	7	1	8	4	1	0	3	8	1	0	0
Johnny Heitinga	2773	31	29	27	2	2	0	4	13	12	13	38	39	17	45	25	2	8	0
Tony Hibbert	1582	20	17	14	3	3	0	1	2	1	29	14	7	3	12	9	1	1	0
Phil Jagielka	1112	12	11	11	1	0	0	0	3	3	4	15	16	5	3	11	1	0	0
Joao Alves Jo	567	15	6	1	9	5	0	2	11	10	2	3	3	1	3	6	11	0	0
Joleon Lescott	95	1	1	1	0	0	0	0	0	0	0	0	0	0	0	0	0	0	0
Lucas Neill	994	12	10	10	2	0	0	2	0	0	5	18	11	4	12	7	0	1	0
Phil Neville	2090	23	22	20	1	2	0	1	1	4	32	15	15	7	24	11	1	1	0
Leon Osman	2064	26	25	10	1	15	2	1	21	19	20	22	10	5	27	26	2	3	0
Steven Pienaar	2833	30	30	24	0	5	4	4	27	13	58	46	2	2	40	91	3	9	1
Jack Rodwell	1744	26	17	12	9	5	2	2	22	20	5	19	11	6	16	8	0	4	0
Louis Saha	2448	33	26	8	7	18	13	1	44	40	11	13	18	1	30	46	30	2	0
Philippe Senderos	105	2	1	1	1	0	0	0	0	0	0	0	3	1	0	1	0	0	0
James Vaughan	92	8	0	0	8	0	1	0	2	0	0	2	1	0	4	1	1	0	0
Ayegbeni Yakubu	1196	25	9	3	16	6	5	4	17	12	7	5	0	1	24	21	3	1	0
Joseph Yobo	1267	17	14	12	3	2	1	0	2	2	0	11	13	8	10	7	0	2	0

SEASON TOTALS

Goals scored	60
Goals conceded	49
Clean sheets	11
Shots on target	307
Shots off target	205
Shots per goal	8.53
Pens awarded	8
Pens scored	5
Pens conceded	2
Offsides	95
Corners	230
Crosses	436
Players used	28
Fouls committed	466
Free-kicks won	524

LEAGUE POSITION AT THE END OF EACH MONTH

AUG	SEP	OCT	NOV	DEC	JAN	FEB	MAR	APR	MAY
16	9	13	16	11	9	10	8	8	8

SEASON INFORMATION
Highest position: 8
Lowest position: 20
Average goals scored per game: 1.58
Average goals conceded per game: 1.29

CARDS RECEIVED

58 2

SEQUENCES

Wins	3
(16/01/10–30/01/10)	
Losses	3
(21/11/09–29/11/09)	
Draws	4
(06/12/09–26/12/09)	
Undefeated	11
(07/03/10–09/05/10)	
Without win	7
(21/11/09–26/12/09)	
Undefeated home	12
(06/12/09–09/05/10)	
Undefeated away	6
(13/03/10–01/05/10)	
Without scoring	–
(–)	
Without conceding	3
(on two occasions)	
Scoring	9
(on two occasions)	
Conceding	12
(04/10/09–26/12/09)	

MATCH RECORDS

Goals scored per match

		W	D	L	Pts
Failed to score	6	0	2	4	2
Scored 1 goal	11	3	5	3	14
Scored 2 goals	16	9	5	2	32
Scored 3 goals	4	3	1	0	10
Scored 4+ goals	1	1	0	0	3

Goals conceded per match

		W	D	L	Pts
Clean sheet	11	9	2	0	29
Conceded 1 goal	13	6	5	2	23
Conceded 2 goals	9	1	5	3	8
Conceded 3 goals	4	0	1	3	1
Conceded 4+ goals	1	0	0	1	0

EARLIEST STRIKE
MIKEL ARTETA
(v Blackburn) 3:17

LATEST STRIKE
MIKEL ARTETA
(v Fulham) 93:43

Phil Jagielka

GOAL DETAILS

How the goals were struck

SCORED		CONCEDED
23	Right foot	21
18	Left foot	16
18	Header	11
1	Other	1

How the goals were struck

SCORED		CONCEDED
31	Open play	32
8	Cross	8
5	Corner	3
5	Penalty	0
2	Direct from free-kick	1
5	Free-kick	3
4	Own goal	2

Distance from goal

SCORED		CONCEDED
20	6YDS	13
33	18YDS	27
7	18+YDS	9

GOALS SCORED/CONCEDED
PER FIVE-MINUTE INTERVALS

MINS	5	10	15	20	25	30	35	40	45	50	55	60	65	70	75	80	85	90
FOR	2	1	2	4	4	1	4	2	4	2	5	1	4	0	3	3	7	11
AGN	0	1	2	6	2	6	3	2	1	4	2	5	1	3	1	4	1	5

FULHAM

CLUB SUMMARY

FORMED	1879
MANAGER	Roy Hodgson
GROUND	Craven Cottage
CAPACITY	25,350
NICKNAME	The Cottagers
WEBSITE	www.fulhamfc.co.uk

The New Football Pools PLAYER OF THE SEASON — Bobby Zamora

OVERALL

P	W	D	L	F	A	GD
63	26	15	22	80	70	10

BARCLAYS PREMIER LEAGUE

Pos	P	W	D	L	F	A	GD	Pts
12	38	12	10	16	39	46	-7	46

HOME

Pos	P	W	D	L	F	A	GD	Pts
8	19	11	3	5	27	15	12	36

AWAY

Pos	P	W	D	L	F	A	GD	Pts
15	19	1	7	11	12	31	-19	10

CUP PROGRESS DETAILS

Competition	Round reached	Knocked out by
Europa League	R-UP	Atlético Madrid
FA Cup	QF	Tottenham
Carling Cup	R3	Man City

BIGGEST WIN (ALL COMPS)
14/02/10 4–0 v Notts County

BIGGEST DEFEAT (ALL COMPS)
09/05/10 0–4 v Arsenal

THE PLAYER WITH THE MOST

GOALS SCORED	Bobby Zamora	**8**
SHOTS ON TARGET	Clinton Dempsey	**46**
SHOTS OFF TARGET	Clinton Dempsey	**46**
SHOTS WITHOUT SCORING	Chris Baird	**16**
ASSISTS	Bobby Zamora	**6**
OFFSIDES	Bobby Zamora	**33**
FOULS	Bobby Zamora	**57**
FOULS WITHOUT A CARD	David Elm	**9**
FREE-KICKS WON	Damien Duff	**58**
DEFENSIVE CLEARANCES	Brede Hangeland	**61**

actim INDEX — FOR THE 2009/10 BARCLAYS PREMIER LEAGUE SEASON

RANK	PLAYER	PTS
44	Mark Schwarzer	403
49	Damien Duff	394
72	Aaron Hughes	365

ATTENDANCE RECORD

HIGH	AVERAGE	LOW
25,700	23,909	20,831
v Arsenal (26/09/2009)		v Stoke (05/05/2010)

CLOCKWISE FROM ABOVE: Roy Hodgson consoles his players after their 2–1 defeat in the Europa League final; Simon Davies equalises for Fulham against Atlético Madrid in the Hamburg final; Bobby Zamora silences the critics with one of 19 goals during the season; Damien Duff scores in the win against Manchester United

FULHAM startled the whole continent by reaching the Europa League final following a fabulous 10-month run, while Roy Hodgson's men also continued to punch well above their weight at home.

As ever, Fulham started the season with their sights set on little more than Barclays Premier League survival – something they managed comfortably with 16 points separating them from the relegation zone. Crucially, it brought up a 10th successive campaign in the top flight, continuing a remarkable transformation of a club that finished near the bottom of what is now npower League 2 just 14 years ago.

The Europa League provided fans with their best memories of the season and probably of their lifetime supporting Fulham. Wins against continental giants Juventus, Shakhtar Donetsk and SV Hamburg were simply remarkable, and they were a credit to the Barclays Premier League when they ran Atlético Madrid close in the final.

However, for manager Roy Hodgson, staying in the Barclays Premier League was the primary objective. Hodgson, whose outstanding success saw him honoured with the League Managers' Association Manager of the Year award, gave a clear indication of what his priorities were when he initially fielded weakened teams in Europe. He ensured his strongest line-up – which was set in stone for most of the season – was fresh and ready for domestic duties.

It was only in the latter stages of the campaign, when the key objective of safety in the League had been obtained, that he reversed his policy. This invited an official complaint from relegation-battling West Ham, who took exception to Hodgson's decision to select a weakened side against Hull. The Premier League rejected the complaint and Fulham took revenge by beating the Hammers 3–2 with a similarly under-strength team five Barclays Premier League matches later.

Despite their glorious European run, there were highlights aplenty at home as Fulham registered magical victories over Manchester United and Liverpool. Beating and completely outplaying the defending Barclays Premier League champions will live long in the memory of fans, who giddily chanted 'we want four, we want four' after Damien Duff had rifled home the third goal.

Once again it was rock-solid home form that enabled Fulham to finish 12th, with 11 wins at Craven Cottage ultimately enough to keep them clear of the drop zone on their own. Their inability to challenge on the road continues under Hodgson, who oversaw just one away win all season, but seven draws point to a team that was still hard to beat on its travels.

Remarkably, the most successful season in the club's 131-year history was achieved playing a style of football that was easy on the eye. Praise for a swashbuckling passing game would be wide of the mark – they were happy to find Bobby Zamora with the long ball if necessary – but their pragmatic approach was laced with invention.

Zamora emerged as the star of the campaign as he ensured Andrew Johnson's season-ending injury was soon forgotten. The former Tottenham and West Ham forward's exploits as a goalscoring targetman swept him to the brink of England selection only for an Achilles injury to strike.

Flair was provided by Zoltan Gera, Duff and Simon Davies – all of whom have blossomed under Hodgson – while Brede Hangeland, Aaron Hughes and Dickson Etuhu provided the steel. Full-backs John Pantsil and Paul Konchesky were dangerous attacking weapons while, in goal, Mark Schwarzer was magnificent. Completing the first-choice line-up was the inspirational Danny Murphy, the former Liverpool and England player who lost his way during unsuccessful spells at Charlton and Tottenham, but who has been revitalised by Hodgson.

The challenge now facing Fulham and their chairman Mohamed Al Fayed is to keep the team together and, far more importantly, to prevent Hodgson from leaving for a bigger club. Hodgson has always insisted that it is the players who are the stars with management operating as facilitators, but his humility fails to mask the truth that he is the club's most valuable asset.

> Roy Hodgson led Fulham to the Europa League final in another season in which the stylish Cottagers punched well above their weight

FULHAM

RESULTS 2009/10

JULY
30th	● FK Vetra	A	W 0–3	**Att:** 12,000. **Ref:** F Stuchlik – (4-4-2): Schwarzer, Konchesky, Pantsil, Hangeland, Baird, A Johnson (Nevland 68), Gera, Murphy[1] (Riise 86), Hughes, Dempsey (Seol[1] 81), Zamora[1]. **Subs not used:** Stockdale, Kelly, Kamara, E Johnson.

AUGUST
6th	● FK Vetra	H	W 3–0	**Att:** 15,016. **Ref:** I Vad – (4-4-2): Schwarzer, Pantsil (Kelly 78), Hughes, Hangeland, Konchesky, Dempsey, Etuhu[1], Murphy, Gera (Riise 78), Zamora (E Johnson[2] 82), A Johnson. **Subs not used:** Stockdale, Baird, Seol, Nevland. Agg: 6–0.
15th	● Portsmouth	A	W 0–1	**Att:** 17,510. **Ref:** M Atkinson – (4-4-2): Schwarzer, Pantsil, Hughes, Hangeland, Konchesky, Gera (Seol 88), Murphy[1], Etuhu, Dempsey, A Johnson, Zamora[1] (Nevland 80). **Subs not used:** Zuberbuhler, Kelly, Baird, Kamara, Riise.
20th	● Amkar Perm	H	W 3–1	**Att:** 13,029. **Ref:** P Oliveira Alves Garcia – (4-4-2): Schwarzer, Pantsil, Hangeland, Hughes, Konchesky, Dempsey[1], Etuhu (Baird 77), Murphy, Gera (Duff 74), A Johnson[1] (Nevland 66), Zamora[1]. **Subs not used:** Stockdale, Kelly, Riise, E Johnson.
23rd	● Chelsea	H	L 0–2	**Att:** 25,404. **Ref:** A Marriner – (4-4-2): Schwarzer, Pantsil, Hughes, Hangeland, Konchesky, Gera (Kamara 62), Etuhu, Murphy (Baird 70), Duff, Dempsey, Zamora (Nevland 75). **Subs not used:** Zuberbuhler, Kelly, Seol, Riise.
27th	● Amkar Perm	A	L 1–0	**Att:** 20,000. **Ref:** M Strombergsson – (4-4-1-1): Schwarzer, Kelly, Hughes, Hangeland, Pantsil, Gera, Riise (Seol 75), Etuhu, Baird[1], Duff, Nevland (E Johnson, Smalling, Saunders, Anderson. Agg: 2–3.
30th	● Aston Villa	A	L 2–0	**Att:** 32,917. **Ref:** S Bennett – (4-5-1): Schwarzer, Pantsil, Hughes, Hangeland, Konchesky, Dempsey, Kamara, Greening[1], Etuhu[1], Duff, Nevland (E Johnson 75). **Subs not used:** Zuberbuhler, Kelly, Baird, Gera, Riise, Smalling.

SEPTEMBER
13th	● Everton	H	W 2–1	**Att:** 24,191. **Ref:** P Walton – (4-4-2): Stockdale, Pantsil, Hughes, Hangeland, Konchesky[1], Dempsey, Murphy[1], Etuhu, Duff[1] (Davies 86), Zamora, A Johnson (Kamara 89). **Subs not used:** Zuberbuhler, Baird, Nevland, Gera, Greening.
17th	● CSKA Sofia	A	D 1–1	**Att:** 28,000. **Ref:** D Ceferin – (4-4-2): Stockdale, Kelly, Pantsil, Baird, Smalling[1], Gera, Riise, Greening[1], Davies, Kamara[1], Nevland. **Subs not used:** Zuberbuhler, Watts, Saunders, Anderson, Uwezu, Marsh-Brown, Smith.
20th	● Wolverhampton	A	L 2–1	**Att:** 27,670. **Ref:** K Friend – (4-4-2): Schwarzer, Pantsil, Hughes, Hangeland, Konchesky (Greening 71), Duff, Etuhu (Kamara 77), Murphy[1], Dempsey (Davies 61), A Johnson, Zamora. **Subs not used:** Zuberbuhler, Baird, Gera, Smalling.
23rd	● Man City	A	L 2–1	**Att:** 24,507. **Ref:** S Attwell – (4-4-2): Stockdale, Stoor, Baird, Smalling, Kelly[1], Davies (Dikgacoi 71), Greening, Riise, Gera[1] (Anderson 120), Seol, E Johnson (Elm 91). **Subs not used:** Zuberbuhler, Watts, Saunders, Smith. AET – Score after 90 mins 1–1.
26th	● Arsenal	H	L 0–1	**Att:** 25,700. **Ref:** M Atkinson – (4-4-2): Schwarzer, Pantsil, Hughes, Hangeland, Konchesky, Duff (Gera 9), Etuhu (Greening 83), Murphy[1], Dempsey, Zamora[1], A Johnson. **Subs not used:** Zuberbuhler, Baird, Kamara, Riise, Smalling.

OCTOBER
1st	● Basle	H	W 1–0	**Att:** 16,100. **Ref:** M Weiner – (4-4-2): Schwarzer, Kelly, Baird[1], Smalling, Konchesky, Dempsey, Greening[1], Murphy[1], Riise, Zamora, A Johnson. **Subs not used:** Pantsil, Nevland, Gera, Kamara, Hughes, Saunders, Anderson.
4th	● West Ham	A	D 2–2	**Att:** 32,612. **Ref:** P Dowd – (4-4-2): Schwarzer, Pantsil, Hughes, Hangeland, Konchesky, Gera[1], Murphy[1], Dikgacoi[1], Dempsey (Riise 84), A Johnson[1] (Baird 46), Kamara (E Johnson 81). **Subs not used:** Zuberbuhler, Kelly, Greening, Nevland.
19th	● Hull	H	W 2–0	**Att:** 22,943. **Ref:** M Jones – (4-4-2): Schwarzer, Pantsil, Hughes, Hangeland, Konchesky[1], Duff (Gera 84), Murphy (Greening 60), Baird, Dempsey, Zamora[1], Kamara[1] (Nevland 87). **Subs not used:** Zuberbuhler, Kelly, Riise, Smalling.
22nd	● Roma	H	D 1–1	**Att:** 23,561. **Ref:** P Allaerts – (4-4-2): Schwarzer, Kelly[1], Hangeland[1], Hughes, Konchesky (Pantsil 46), Riise (Duff 75), Greening, Baird, Gera, Zamora (Nevland 61), Kamara. **Subs not used:** Stockdale, Dempsey, Smalling, Anderson.
25th	● Man City	A	D 2–2	**Att:** 44,906. **Ref:** K Friend – (4-4-2): Schwarzer, Pantsil, Hughes, Hangeland, Kelly, Duff[1], Greening, Baird, Dempsey[1], Kamara (Seol 90), Zamora. **Subs not used:** Zuberbuhler, Nevland, Gera, Riise, E Johnson, Smalling.
31st	● Liverpool	H	W 3–1	**Att:** 25,700. **Ref:** L Mason – (4-4-2): Schwarzer, Pantsil, Hughes, Hangeland, Konchesky, Dempsey[1], Baird[1], Greening (Etuhu 86), Duff (Nevland[1] 46), Zamora[1], Kamara (Gera 46). **Subs not used:** Zuberbuhler, Kelly, Riise, Smalling.

NOVEMBER
5th	● Roma	A	L 2–1	**Att:** 20,000. **Ref:** K Blom – (4-4-2): Schwarzer, Pantsil, Hughes, Hangeland, Konchesky, Riise (Zamora 70), Etuhu (Baird 77), Greening, Gera, Kamara[1] (Nevland 46), Dempsey. **Subs not used:** Stockdale, Smalling, Davies, Anderson.
8th	● Wigan	A	D 1–1	**Att:** 16,172. **Ref:** P Dowd – (4-4-2): Schwarzer, Pantsil, Hangeland, Hughes, Konchesky, Dempsey[1], Baird, Greening (Etuhu 79), Duff, Zamora, Kamara (Gera 85). **Subs not used:** Zuberbuhler, Kelly, Riise, Smalling, Dikgacoi.
21st	● Birmingham	A	L 1–0	**Att:** 23,659. **Ref:** C Foy – (4-4-2): Schwarzer, Kelly (Duff 74), Hughes, Hangeland, Konchesky, Davies, Baird (Etuhu 81), Greening, Gera, Dempsey, Zamora. **Subs not used:** Zuberbuhler, Pantsil, Riise, E Johnson, Smalling.
25th	● Blackburn	H	W 3–0	**Att:** 21,414. **Ref:** S Attwell – (4-4-2): Schwarzer, Pantsil, Hughes, Hangeland, Konchesky, Dempsey[2], Greening (Etuhu 81), Baird, Duff (Davies 85), Zamora (Gera 58), Nevland[1]. **Subs not used:** Zuberbuhler, Seol, Smalling, Dikgacoi.
28th	● Bolton	H	D 1–1	**Att:** 23,554. **Ref:** S Bennett – (4-4-2): Schwarzer, Pantsil (Davies 68), Hangeland, Hughes, Konchesky, Gera (Dikgacoi 80), Baird, Greening[1], Duff[1], Nevland, Dempsey. **Subs not used:** Stockdale, Seol, Riise, E Johnson, Smalling.

DECEMBER
3rd	● CSKA Sofia	H	W 1–0	**Att:** 23,604. **Ref:** P Balaj – (4-4-1-1): Schwarzer, Pantsil, Smalling, Hangeland (Hughes 46), Kelly, Riise, Baird[1], Murphy (Duff 78), Gera[1], Davies (Dempsey 70), Zamora. **Subs not used:** Stockdale, Saunders, Briggs, Uwezu.
6th	● Sunderland	H	W 1–0	**Att:** 23,168. **Ref:** M Dean – (4-4-2): Schwarzer, Pantsil, Hughes, Hangeland, Konchesky, Duff, Baird, Greening (Dikgacoi 86), Dempsey, Zamora[1], Nevland[1] (Gera 67). **Subs not used:** Zuberbuhler, Seol, Murphy, Riise, Smalling.
12th	● Burnley	A	D 1–1	**Att:** 18,397. **Ref:** M Jones – (4-4-2): Schwarzer, Pantsil, Hangeland, Hughes, Kelly, Greening[1], Baird, Dempsey, Duff, Nevland (Gera 77), Zamora[1]. **Subs not used:** Stockdale, Murphy, Riise, Smalling, Dikgacoi, Elm.
16th	● Basle	A	W 2–3	**Att:** 20,063. **Ref:** S Johannesson – (4-4-2): Schwarzer, Pantsil, Smalling, Hughes, Kelly, Riise, Etuhu, Murphy, Greening[1] (Dempsey 70), Gera[1], Zamora[2] (Duff 80). **Subs not used:** Stockdale, Hangeland, Saunders, Briggs, Uwezu.
19th	● Man Utd	H	W 3–0	**Att:** 25,700. **Ref:** H Webb – (4-4-2): Schwarzer, Pantsil, Hughes, Hangeland, Konchesky, Duff[1] (Greening 76), Murphy[1] (Dikgacoi 80), Baird, Gera, Dempsey, Zamora[1] (Nevland 90). **Subs not used:** Zuberbuhler, Riise, Etuhu, Smalling.
26th	● Tottenham	H	D 0–0	**Att:** 25,679. **Ref:** S Bennett – (4-4-2): Schwarzer, Pantsil[1], Hughes, Smalling, Konchesky, Duff, Murphy, Baird, Gera, Dempsey, Zamora. **Subs not used:** Stockdale, A Johnson, Nevland, Etuhu, Smalling, Greening, Kallio.
28th	● Chelsea	A	L 2–1	**Att:** 41,805. **Ref:** A Marriner – (4-4-1-1): Schwarzer, Pantsil (Etuhu 66), Hughes, Smalling, Konchesky, Duff (Riise 85), Murphy, Baird[1], Dempsey, Gera[1] (A Johnson 71), Zamora. **Subs not used:** Zuberbuhler, Nevland, Greening, Kallio.

JANUARY
2nd	● Swindon	H	W 1–0	**Att:** 19,623. **Ref:** A Taylor – (4-4-2): Schwarzer, Kelly, Hughes, Smalling, Konchesky, Riise, Greening, Dikgacoi, Dempsey, A Johnson (Gera 83), Zamora[1]. **Subs not used:** Stockdale, Baird, Nevland, Stoor, Kallio, Elm.

● Barclays Premier League ● FA Cup ● Carling Cup ● UEFA Champions League ● Europa League ● FA Community Shield   ▌ Yellow Card ▌ Red Card

RESULTS 2009/10

5th	● Stoke	A	L 3–2

Att: 25,104. **Ref:** M Clattenburg – (4-4-2): Schwarzer, Kelly, Hughes, Hangeland (Smalling 45), Konchesky, Gera, Murphy, Baird, Duff[1], A Johnson (Nevland 82), Zamora (Dempsey[1] 54). **Subs not used:** Zuberbuhler, Kallio, Greening, Dikgacoi.

17th	● Blackburn	A	L 2–0

Att: 21,287. **Ref:** K Friend – (4-4-2): Schwarzer, Kelly, Hughes, Hangeland, Konchesky (Kallio 46), Duff, Baird[1], Murphy, Gera[1], A Johnson, Dempsey (Nevland[1] 62). **Subs not used:** Zuberbuhler, Riise, Smalling, Greening, Dikgacoi.

23rd	● Accrington Stanley	A	W 1–3

Att: 3,712. **Ref:** S Attwell – (4-4-2): Schwarzer, Kelly, Hangeland, Hughes, Kallio (Elm 56), Gera[1] (Davies 84), Murphy, Baird[1], Duff[1] (Dikgacoi 68), Nevland[1], Riise. **Subs not used:** Zuberbuhler, Kamara, Smalling, Greening.

26th	● Tottenham	A	L 2–0

Att: 35,467. **Ref:** M Dean – (4-5-1): Schwarzer, Hughes, Hangeland, Smalling, Baird, Riise (Davies 64), Dikgacoi, Murphy, Gera (Kamara[1] 72), Duff, Zamora (Elm 79). **Subs not used:** Zuberbuhler, Nevland, Greening, Kallio.

30th	● Aston Villa	H	L 0–2

Att: 25,408. **Ref:** L Mason – (4-4-2): Schwarzer, Hughes, Smalling, Hangeland, Kelly (Riise 74), Duff, Murphy, Baird, Davies (Gera 24), Zamora, Nevland (Elm 65). **Subs not used:** Zuberbuhler, Stoor, Greening, Dikgacoi.

FEBRUARY

3rd	● Portsmouth	H	W 1–0

Att: 21,934. **Ref:** A Taylor – (4-4-2): Schwarzer, Kelly (Dikgacoi 55), Hughes, Hangeland, Shorey, Duff, Murphy, Baird, Greening[1], Okaka (Nevland 70), Zamora (Elm 77). **Subs not used:** Zuberbuhler, Riise, Stoor, Smalling.

6th	● Bolton	A	D 0–0

Att: 22,289. **Ref:** M Clattenburg – (4-4-2): Schwarzer, Baird, Hughes, Hangeland, Shorey, Duff, Dikgacoi (Etuhu 55), Murphy, Greening, Elm (Okaka 76), Nevland (Smalling 76). **Subs not used:** Zuberbuhler, Kelly, Riise, Stoor.

9th	● Burnley	H	W 3–0

Att: 23,005. **Ref:** C Foy – (4-4-2): Schwarzer, Shorey, Hangeland, Hughes, Baird, Duff (Riise 77), Etuhu[1], Murphy[1], Davies (Greening 62), Elm[1], Zamora[1] (Okaka 71). **Subs not used:** Zuberbuhler, Kelly, Nevland, Smalling.

14th	● Notts County	H	W 4–0

Att: 16,132. **Ref:** A Wiley – (4-4-2): Schwarzer, Baird, Hughes, Hangeland, Shorey, Duff[1] (Riise 75), Etuhu, Murphy (Greening 69), Davies[1], Zamora[1] (Okaka[1] 75), Elm. **Subs not used:** Zuberbuhler, Nevland, Stoor, Smalling.

18th	● Shakhtar Donetsk	H	W 2–1

Att: 21,832. **Ref:** S Gumienny – (4-4-2): Schwarzer, Baird, Hughes, Hangeland, Kelly, Davies, Etuhu, Murphy[1], Duff, Gera[1] (Elm 89), Zamora[1]. **Subs not used:** Zuberbuhler, Nevland, Riise, Smalling, Greening, Marsh-Brown.

21st	● Birmingham	H	W 2–1

Att: 21,758. **Ref:** P Dowd – (4-4-1-1): Schwarzer, Baird, Hughes, Hangeland, Shorey, Davies (Riise 83), Etuhu, Murphy (Smalling 90), Duff[1], Gera, Zamora[1]. **Subs not used:** Zuberbuhler, Kelly, Okaka, Greening, Elm.

25th	● Shakhtar Donetsk	A	D 1–1

Att: 47,509. **Ref:** S Oddvar Moen – (4-4-1-1): Schwarzer, Baird, Hangeland[1], Hughes, Kelly, Duff, Murphy[1], Etuhu, Davies (Riise 89), Gera[1], Zamora (Elm 72). **Subs not used:** Zuberbuhler, Nevland, Smalling, Greening, Marsh-Brown. Agg: 2–3.

28th	● Sunderland	A	D 0–0

Att: 40,192. **Ref:** M Atkinson – (4-4-2): Schwarzer, Baird[1], Hughes, Hangeland, Shorey, Duff, Etuhu, Murphy (Greening[1] 58), Davies, Gera, Zamora[1] (Elm 83). **Subs not used:** Zuberbuhler, Kelly, Okaka, Riise, Smalling.

MARCH

6th	● Tottenham	H	D 0–0

Att: 24,533. **Ref:** M Clattenburg – (4-4-2): Schwarzer, Baird, Hughes, Hangeland, Shorey, Duff, Greening, Etuhu[1], Davies (Elm 73), Gera, Zamora. **Subs not used:** Zuberbuhler, Kelly, Konchesky, Okaka, Riise, Smalling.

11th	● Juventus	A	L 3–1

Att: 11,406. **Ref:** F Meyer – (4-4-2): Schwarzer, Baird, Hangeland, Hughes, Konchesky, Duff, Davies (Dempsey 60), Etuhu[1], Greening[1], Gera, Zamora. **Subs not used:** Zuberbuhler, Kelly, Nevland, Smalling, Marsh-Brown.

14th	● Man Utd	A	L 3–0

Att: 75,207. **Ref:** M Jones – (4-4-1-1): Schwarzer, Kelly, Hangeland (Greening 62), Hughes, Shorey, Davies (Duff 46), Murphy[1], Baird, Dempsey (Nevland 72), Gera, Zamora. **Subs not used:** Zuberbuhler, Okaka, Stoor, Dikgacoi.

18th	● Juventus	H	W 4–1

Att: 23,458. **Ref:** B Kuipers – (4-4-1-1): Schwarzer, Kelly (Dempsey[1] 71), Hughes, Hangeland, Konchesky[1], Duff, Baird, Etuhu, Davies, Gera[2] (Riise 85), Zamora[1]. **Subs not used:** Zuberbuhler, Nevland, Smalling, Dikgacoi, Marsh-Brown. Agg: 5–4.

21st	● Man City	H	L 1–2

Att: 25,359. **Ref:** L Probert – (4-4-1-1): Schwarzer, Baird (Riise 80), Hughes, Smalling, Konchesky, Duff, Murphy[1], Etuhu, Davies, Gera (Okaka 55), Zamora (Dempsey 52). **Subs not used:** Zuberbuhler, Kelly, Shorey, Greening.

24th	● Tottenham	A	L 3–1

Att: 35,432. **Ref:** M Atkinson – (4-4-2): Schwarzer, Kelly[1] (Dempsey 69), Hangeland, Hughes, Duff, Etuhu, Murphy, Davies, Gera, Zamora[1] (Okaka 77). **Subs not used:** Zuberbuhler, Baird, Riise, Smalling, Greening.

27th	● Hull	A	L 2–0

Att: 24,361. **Ref:** C Foy – (4-4-1-1): Schwarzer, Shorey[1], Hangeland, Baird, Konchesky, Riise (Okaka 53), Smalling, Dikgacoi[1] (Greening 59), Davies[1], Gera[1], Dempsey. **Subs not used:** Zuberbuhler, Nevland, Hughes, Etuhu, Stoor.

APRIL

1st	● Wolfsburg	H	W 2–1

Att: 22,307. **Ref:** D Skomina – (4-4-1-1): Schwarzer, Davies, Hughes, Hangeland, Konchesky, Duff[1], Murphy (Baird 87), Etuhu, Dempsey, Gera, Zamora[1][1]. **Subs not used:** Zuberbuhler, Nevland, Riise, Smalling, Greening, Elm.

4th	● Wigan	H	W 2–1

Att: 22,730. **Ref:** M Clattenburg – (4-4-1-1): Schwarzer, Davies, Hughes, Hangeland[1], Konchesky, Duff, Murphy (Baird 88), Etuhu, Dempsey, Gera, Elm (Okaka[1] 46 (Nevland 88)). **Subs not used:** Zuberbuhler, Shorey, Smalling, Greening.

8th	● Wolfsburg	A	W 0–1

Att: 24,843. **Ref:** V Kassai – (4-2-3-1): Schwarzer, Baird[1], Hughes, Hangeland, Konchesky[1], Murphy, Etuhu, Duff, Gera (Nevland 82), Davies (Riise 86), Zamora[1]. **Subs not used:** Zuberbuhler, Kelly, Smalling, Greening, Dikgacoi. Agg: 1–3.

11th	● Liverpool	A	D 0–0

Att: 42,331. **Ref:** A Marriner – (4-4-2): Schwarzer, Baird, Hangeland, Hughes, Konchesky, Greening[1] (Riise 82), Murphy[1] (Dikgacoi 75), Etuhu, Duff[1], Nevland, Zamora (Okaka 68). **Subs not used:** Zuberbuhler, Kelly, Shorey, Smalling.

17th	● Wolverhampton	H	D 0–0

Att: 25,597. **Ref:** M Dean – (4-4-1-1): Schwarzer, Baird, Hughes, Smalling, Konchesky, Davies, Murphy, Etuhu, Duff, Gera, Zamora[1]. **Subs not used:** Zuberbuhler, Pantsil, Okaka, Nevland, Riise, Greening, Dikgacoi.

22nd	● Hamburg	A	D 0–0

Att: 49,000. **Ref:** C Bo Larsen – (4-4-2): Schwarzer, Baird[1], Hughes, Hangeland, Konchesky, Duff, Etuhu, Murphy, Davies, Zamora (Dempsey 52), Gera[1]. **Subs not used:** Zuberbuhler, Kelly, Nevland, Smalling, Greening, Dikgacoi.

25th	● Everton	A	L 2–1

Att: 35,578. **Ref:** L Mason – (4-4-2): Schwarzer, Pantsil[1], Smalling, Baird, Shorey, Dempsey, Dikgacoi, Greening, Riise, Okaka (Stoor 89), Nevland[1] (Elm 78). **Subs not used:** Zuberbuhler, Kelly, Teymourian, Briggs, Buchtmann.

29th	● Hamburg	H	W 2–1

Att: 25,700. **Ref:** C Cakir – (4-4-1-1): Schwarzer, Pantsil (Nevland 75), Hangeland[1], Hughes, Konchesky, Davies[1], Murphy, Etuhu, Duff, Gera[1], Zamora (Dempsey[1] 57). **Subs not used:** Zuberbuhler, Riise, Smalling, Greening, Dikgacoi. Agg: 2–1.

MAY

2nd	● West Ham	H	W 3–2

Att: 24,201. **Ref:** A Marriner – (4-4-2): Schwarzer, Pantsil, Baird, Smalling, Konchesky, Riise, Greening, Dikgacoi, Davies (Okaka[1] 70), Dempsey[1] (Elm 85), Nevland. **Subs not used:** Zuberbuhler, Kelly, Shorey, Gera, Etuhu. Cole OG.

5th	● Stoke	H	L 0–1

Att: 20,831. **Ref:** P Walton – (4-4-2): Schwarzer, Pantsil (Okaka 86), Hughes[1], Hangeland, Konchesky, Duff (Nevland 46), Murphy, Etuhu, Davies, Dempsey, Gera. **Subs not used:** Zuberbuhler, Kelly, Smalling, Dikgacoi.

9th	● Arsenal	A	L 4–0

Att: 60,039. **Ref:** M Jones – (4-4-2): Schwarzer, Pantsil (Kelly[1] 58), Baird, Smalling, Shorey, Riise (Elm 46), Greening, Dikgacoi, Dempsey (Stoor 67), Nevland, Okaka. **Subs not used:** Zuberbuhler, Gera, Murphy, Davies.

12th	● Atlético Madrid	N	L 2–1

Att: 49,000. **Ref:** N Rizzoli – (4-4-1-1): Schwarzer, Baird, Hughes, Hangeland[1], Konchesky, Duff (Nevland 84), Etuhu, Murphy (Greening 118), Davies[1], Gera, Zamora (Dempsey 55). **Subs not used:** Zuberbuhler, Pantsil, Riise, Dikgacoi. AET – Score after 90 mins 1–1.

● Barclays Premier League ● FA Cup ● Carling Cup ● UEFA Champions League ● Europa League ● FA Community Shield   ▮ Yellow Card ▮ Red Card

FULHAM

BARCLAYS PREMIER LEAGUE GOALKEEPER STATS

Player	Minutes on pitch	Appearances	Match starts	Completed matches	Sub appearances	Subbed off	Saved with feet	Punched	Parried	Tipped over	Fumbled	Tipped round	Caught	Blocked	Clean sheets	Goals conceded	Save %	Saved	Resulting in goals	Opposition miss	Fouls committed	Free-kicks won	Yellow cards	Red cards
Mark Schwarzer	3526	37	37	37	0	0	3	16	20	8	5	7	133	2	12	45	80.77	0	2	0	0	7	0	0
David Stockdale	96	1	1	1	0	0	0	0	2	0	0	0	1	0	0	1	75.00	0	0	0	0	0	0	0

BARCLAYS PREMIER LEAGUE OUTFIELD PLAYER STATS

Player	Minutes on pitch	Appearances	Match starts	Completed matches	Substitute appearances	Subbed off	Goals scored	Assists	Shots on target	Shots off target	Crosses	Tackles made	Defensive clearances	Defensive blocks	Fouls committed	Free-kicks won	Caught offside	Yellow cards	Red cards
Chris Baird	2814	32	29	27	3	2	0	3	6	10	18	41	28	9	28	21	1	4	0
Simon Davies	1055	17	12	7	5	5	0	2	5	1	17	15	5	2	5	10	0	1	0
Clinton Dempsey	2524	29	27	21	2	6	7	3	46	46	4	19	5	1	28	44	3	1	0
Kagisho Dikgacoi	633	12	7	4	5	2	0	0	2	3	2	10	2	2	9	5	0	1	1
Damien Duff	2663	32	30	21	2	9	6	5	35	18	79	29	8	3	16	58	7	2	0
David Elm	358	10	3	1	7	2	1	1	5	2	1	3	1	0	9	8	5	0	0
Dickson Etuhu	1416	20	14	12	6	2	0	0	3	3	1	21	3	3	34	7	0	3	0
Zoltan Gera	1981	27	19	13	8	6	2	3	24	13	15	31	9	1	36	31	3	2	0
Jonathan Greening	1588	23	15	10	8	5	1	1	3	3	17	30	9	3	31	15	0	5	0
Brede Hangeland	2967	32	32	30	0	2	1	0	2	4	0	46	61	16	26	25	1	2	0
Aaron Hughes	3239	34	34	34	0	0	0	0	1	0	5	38	46	18	7	23	0	2	0
Eddie Johnson	30	2	0	0	2	0	0	0	0	1	0	0	2	0	0	0	0	1	0
Andrew Johnson	627	8	7	4	1	3	0	1	7	5	1	2	0	1	8	10	11	0	0
Toni Kallio	48	1	0	0	1	0	0	0	0	0	0	0	0	0	0	0	0	0	0
Diomansy Kamara	478	9	5	1	4	4	1	1	2	4	2	3	0	0	6	11	4	1	0
Stephen Kelly	625	8	7	4	1	3	0	0	0	0	8	4	5	6	5	7	0	1	0
Paul Konchesky	2496	27	27	25	0	2	1	1	2	2	48	27	9	7	16	13	0	3	0
Danny Murphy	2247	25	25	18	0	7	5	0	13	9	23	50	9	6	32	16	0	5	0
Erik Nevland	1238	23	12	5	11	7	3	4	12	12	3	11	2	0	16	10	14	2	0
Stefano Okaka	478	11	3	0	8	3	2	0	8	6	0	5	1	0	18	9	5	1	0
John Pantsil	1997	22	22	18	0	4	0	1	3	2	25	18	16	4	21	22	0	5	0
Bjorn Helge Riise	448	12	5	2	7	3	0	1	2	9	3	0	1	5	13	1	0	0	0
Ki-Hyeon Seol	11	2	0	0	2	0	0	0	0	0	1	0	0	0	0	0	0	0	0
Nicky Shorey	860	9	9	9	0	0	0	0	1	1	19	11	7	5	1	4	0	1	0
Chris Smalling	938	12	9	9	3	0	0	0	2	1	0	13	10	4	8	8	1	0	0
Fredrik Stoor	33	2	0	0	2	0	0	0	0	0	0	0	0	0	0	0	0	0	0
Bobby Zamora	2321	27	27	16	0	11	8	6	28	23	16	8	26	0	57	57	33	3	0

SEASON TOTALS

Goals scored	39
Goals conceded	46
Clean sheets	12
Shots on target	211
Shots off target	171
Shots per goal	9.79
Pens awarded	4
Pens scored	4
Pens conceded	2
Offsides	89
Corners	183
Crosses	313
Players used	29
Fouls committed	422
Free-kicks won	434

LEAGUE POSITION AT THE END OF EACH MONTH

AUG	SEP	OCT	NOV	DEC	JAN	FEB	MAR	APR	MAY
15	17	11	10	9	11	9	12	12	12

SEASON INFORMATION
Highest position: 5
Lowest position: 18
Average goals scored per game: 1.03
Average goals conceded per game: 1.21

CARDS RECEIVED

46 | 1

SEQUENCES

Wins	2
(09/02/10–21/02/10)	
Losses	5
(28/12/09–30/01/10)	
Draws	2
(11/04/10–17/04/10)	
Undefeated	6
(25/11/09–26/12/09)	
Without win	6
(26/12/09–30/01/10)	
Undefeated home	7
(19/10/09–26/12/09)	
Undefeated away	3
(04/10/09–08/11/09)	
Without scoring	3
(17/01/10–30/01/10)	
Without conceding	3
(03/02/10–09/02/10)	
Scoring	5
(on two occasions)	
Conceding	6
(23/08/09–04/10/09)	

MATCH RECORDS

Goals scored per match

		W	D	L	Pts
Failed to score	16	0	5	11	5
Scored 1 goal	10	3	3	4	12
Scored 2 goals	7	4	2	1	14
Scored 3 goals	5	5	0	0	15
Scored 4+ goals	0	0	0	0	0

Goals conceded per match

		W	D	L	Pts
Clean sheet	12	7	5	0	26
Conceded 1 goal	10	4	3	3	15
Conceded 2 goals	13	1	2	10	5
Conceded 3 goals	2	0	0	2	0
Conceded 4+ goals	1	0	0	1	0

EARLIEST STRIKE

ZOLTAN GERA
(v Chelsea) 3:30

LATEST STRIKE

BOBBY ZAMORA
(v Birmingham) 90:03

Chris Smalling

GOAL DETAILS

How the goals were struck

SCORED		CONCEDED
21	Right foot	20
13	Left foot	13
3	Header	13
2	Other	0

How the goals were struck

SCORED		CONCEDED
28	Open play	27
2	Cross	4
2	Corner	2
4	Penalty	2
2	Direct from free-kick	1
0	Free-kick	5
1	Own goal	5

Distance from goal

SCORED		CONCEDED
13	6YDS	20
17	18YDS	22
9	18+YDS	4

GOALS SCORED/CONCEDED
PER FIVE-MINUTE INTERVALS

MINS	5	10	15	20	25	30	35	40	45	50	55	60	65	70	75	80	85	90
FOR	1	1	1	0	3	0	1	2	3	4	1	5	3	3	5	2	1	3
AGN	2	1	2	4	2	2	4	5	2	4	3	4	1	0	2	1	3	4

HULL CITY

CLUB SUMMARY

FORMED	1904
MANAGER	TBC
GROUND	KC Stadium
CAPACITY	25,404
NICKNAME	The Tigers
WEBSITE	www.hullcityafc.net

The New Football Pools PLAYER OF THE SEASON — George Boateng

OVERALL

P	W	D	L	F	A	GD
41	7	12	22	38	84	-46

BARCLAYS PREMIER LEAGUE

Pos	P	W	D	L	F	A	GD	Pts
19	38	6	12	20	34	75	-41	30

HOME

Pos	P	W	D	L	F	A	GD	Pts
18	19	6	6	7	22	29	-7	24

AWAY

Pos	P	W	D	L	F	A	GD	Pts
19	19	0	6	13	12	46	-34	6

CUP PROGRESS DETAILS

Competition	Round reached	Knocked out by
FA Cup	R3	Wigan
Carling Cup	R3	Everton

BIGGEST WIN (ALL COMPS)

25/08/09 3–1 v Southend

BIGGEST DEFEAT (ALL COMPS)

26/09/09 1–6 v Liverpool

THE PLAYER WITH THE MOST

GOALS SCORED Stephen Hunt	**6**
SHOTS ON TARGET Deiberson Geovanni	**27**
SHOTS OFF TARGET Jimmy Bullard	**17**
SHOTS WITHOUT SCORING Richard Garcia	**16**
ASSISTS Jozy Altidore	**7**
OFFSIDES Jozy Altidore	**16**
FOULS Craig Fagan	**56**
FOULS WITHOUT A CARD Jan Vennegoor of Hesselink	**39**
FREE-KICKS WON Stephen Hunt	**61**
DEFENSIVE CLEARANCES Anthony Gardner	**72**

actim INDEX FOR THE 2009/10 BARCLAYS PREMIER LEAGUE SEASON

RANK	PLAYER	PTS
58	Stephen Hunt	376
84	Andy Dawson	343
155	Boaz Myhill	260

ATTENDANCE RECORD

HIGH	AVERAGE	LOW
25,030	24,390	22,822
v Liverpool (09/05/2010)		v Wigan (03/10/2009)

CLOCKWISE FROM ABOVE: Andy Dawson helped his side to a memorable win over Everton in November by scoring the second goal; Nick Barmby and George Boateng show their emotions as Hull are relegated; Jimmy Bullard celebrates a goal against Manchester City by re-enacting the famous pitchside teamtalk once given by former manager Phil Brown, who is pictured above his successor at the KC Stadium, Iain Dowie

IT WILL be a much-changed Hull side that begins life in the npower Championship in the 2009/10 season following a Barclays Premier League campaign marked by struggles on and off the pitch.

The Tigers' two-year stay in the top flight effectively came to an end with a 1–0 defeat by Sunderland on 24th April and relegation was officially confirmed a week later with a 2–2 draw at Wigan.

Attention was drawn to the club's growing financial problems in October when chairman Paul Duffen resigned following a report from auditors that questioned the club's ability to continue as a going concern. Duffen was replaced by the returning Adam Pearson, who had led Hull from the brink of non-League football to the second tier before selling up in 2007.

In March, and with Hull stuck in the bottom three, Pearson dismissed manager Phil Brown, under whom the Tigers had achieved top-flight football for the first time in their history. Former Crystal Palace and Charlton boss Iain Dowie was brought in for the final nine games of the season, but he managed only one win and the club eventually finished in 19th place.

Hull had been tipped to be among the strugglers following their last-gasp escape in 2008/09 and they suffered a difficult start. A 5–1 home defeat by Tottenham came in only their second game and, although they

Hull's dreadful end to the previous season continued into 2009/10, with the Tigers eventually dropping out of the top flight

managed a 1–0 win over Bolton the week after, that was to be their only League victory in the opening two months of the season.

October began with a welcome win, 2–1 at home to Wigan, but that failed to inspire an upturn in form and their only other point that month came from a goalless draw with bottom side Portsmouth.

The pressure grew on Brown with the Tigers in the bottom three, but the return of a key figure finally led to them stringing together some results. Hull had spent a club-record £5million on Jimmy Bullard in January 2009, only for the midfielder to suffer a serious knee injury in his first game. But, having successfully completed his comeback, the former Fulham man was crowned as the Barclays Player of the Month for November as Hull posted wins over Stoke and Everton in an unbeaten spell of four games that also included draws with West Ham and high-flying Manchester City.

Bullard's luck did not last, though, and a 3–0 defeat by Aston Villa in December was made worse by another knee injury to the former Fulham and Wigan playmaker, ruling him out until March. The Tigers did not win again until February, when they followed up

a promising 1–1 draw with Chelsea by beating UEFA Champions League-chasing Manchester City 2–1.

Their bad luck with injuries continued as leading scorer Stephen Hunt suffered a foot problem that eventually ruled him out for the rest of the season while key defender Anthony Gardner missed two months with an ankle problem. The win over City was followed by five consecutive defeats, and the fourth of those – a last-gasp 2–1 loss to Arsenal – proved to be Brown's last as he was officially placed on 'gardening leave', with Dowie coming in.

The new manager faced a big task and, although Dowie secured a 2–0 win over Fulham in his second game in charge, a humiliating 4–1 home defeat by fellow strugglers Burnley proved to be a blow from which the club never recovered. They were even denied a first away League win of the season in their penultimate game at Wigan when the Latics scrambled a last-gasp equaliser, and they signed off with a 0–0 draw against Liverpool.

The priority for the KC Stadium club now is to reduce the high levels of debt and slash the wage bill as they prepare for life back in the second tier.

HULL CITY

RESULTS 2009/10

AUGUST

15th	● Chelsea	A	L 2–1	**Att:** 41,597. **Ref:** A Wiley – (4-5-1): Myhill, Mouyokolo, Turner, Gardner, Dawson, Mendy▪ (Geovanni 78), Olofinjana, Marney (Barmby▪ 44), Boateng, Hunt¹ (Ghilas 69), Folan. **Subs not used:** Duke, Halmosi, Zayatte, Cousin.
19th	● Tottenham	H	L 1–5	**Att:** 24,735. **Ref:** C Foy – (4-5-1): Myhill, Mouyokolo (Barmby 46), Turner▪, Gardner, Dawson, Mendy, Boateng (Ghilas 69), Olofinjana, Hunt▪, Folan▪, Cousin (Geovanni 22). **Subs not used:** Duke, Halmosi, Kilbane, Zayatte.
22nd	● Bolton	H	W 1–0	**Att:** 22,999. **Ref:** M Jones – (4-5-1): Myhill, Zayatte, Turner, Gardner, Dawson, Ghilas¹ (Fagan 86), Olofinjana▪, Geovanni▪ (Boateng 81), Kilbane, Hunt▪, Folan (Altidore 60). **Subs not used:** Warner, Barmby, Halmosi, Mouyokolo.
25th	● Southend	H	W 3–1	**Att:** 7,994. **Ref:** N Swarbrick – (4-4-2): Warner, Doyle▪, Mouyokolo, Cooper, Halmosi, Atkinson▪ (Ghilas 73), Cairney¹ (Kilbane 73), Featherstone, Barmby (Geovanni¹ 59), Fagan, Altidore¹. **Subs not used:** Duke, Mendy, Zayatte, Cousin.
29th	● Wolverhampton	A	D 1–1	**Att:** 27,906. **Ref:** S Attwell – (4-4-1-1): Myhill, Zayatte, Turner, Mouyokolo▪, Dawson▪, Ghilas (Fagan 73), Olofinjana, Kilbane, Hunt, Geovanni¹ (Barmby 82), Folan (Altidore 63). **Subs not used:** Warner, Halmosi, Boateng, Cooper.

SEPTEMBER

12th	● Sunderland	A	L 4–1	**Att:** 38,997. **Ref:** M Atkinson – (4-4-1-1): Myhill, Zayatte▪, McShane▪, Sonko, Dawson, Ghilas (Altidore 63), Kilbane (Mendy 76), Olofinjana▪, Hunt, Geovanni, Fagan (Vennegoor of Hesselink 58). **Subs not used:** Duke, Barmby, Halmosi, Boateng.
19th	● Birmingham	H	L 0–1	**Att:** 23,759. **Ref:** P Dowd – (4-4-2): Myhill, Dawson, Zayatte, Sonko, McShane, Hunt, Marney (Barmby 70), Olofinjana, Geovanni, Altidore (Ghilas 63), Vennegoor of Hesselink (Mendy 78). **Subs not used:** Warner, Halmosi, Kilbane, Boateng.
23rd	● Everton	H	L 0–4	**Att:** 13,558. **Ref:** S Bennett – (4-4-2): Duke, Mendy, Zayatte▪, Cooper, Halmosi, Barmby (Kilbane 65), Boateng (Marney 46), Featherstone (McShane 46), Cairney▪, Ghilas, Vennegoor of Hesselink. **Subs not used:** Warner, Fagan, Geovanni, Cousin.
26th	● Liverpool	A	L 6–1	**Att:** 44,392. **Ref:** P Walton – (4-4-2): Myhill, McShane▪, Sonko, Cooper, Dawson, Geovanni¹ (Altidore 83), Boateng, Kilbane▪ (Marney▪ 64), Hunt▪, Vennegoor of Hesselink (Cousin 63), Ghilas. **Subs not used:** Warner, Barmby, Zayatte, Olofinjana.

OCTOBER

3rd	● Wigan	H	W 2–1	**Att:** 22,822. **Ref:** M Clattenburg – (4-1-4-1): Myhill, McShane, Sonko, Kilbane, Dawson, Zayatte (Olofinjana 81), Barmby (Ghilas 64), Marney, Geovanni¹, Hunt, Vennegoor of Hesselink¹ (Mouyokolo 90). **Subs not used:** Duke, Altidore, Halmosi, Cairney.
19th	● Fulham	A	L 2–0	**Att:** 22,943. **Ref:** A Marriner – (4-1-4-1): Myhill, McShane, Sonko, Kilbane, Dawson▪, Zayatte, Ghilas (Bullard 58) Marney, Geovanni, Hunt (Altidore 69), Vennegoor of Hesselink (Mendy 80). **Subs not used:** Warner, Halmosi, Mouyokolo, Olofinjana.
24th	● Portsmouth	H	D 0–0	**Att:** 23,720. **Ref:** S Attwell – (4-4-2): Myhill▪, McShane, Gardner, Zayatte, Dawson, Mendy (Barmby 71), Marney▪ (Ghilas 89), Olofinjana, Hunt (Garcia 74), Geovanni, Vennegoor of Hesselink. **Subs not used:** Duke, Kilbane, Mouyokolo, Atkinson.
31st	● Burnley	A	L 2–0	**Att:** 20,219. **Ref:** M Jones – (4-4-1-1): Duke, McShane (Mendy▪ 59), Zayatte, Gardner, Dawson, Ghilas, Olofinjana, Marney, Hunt (Barmby 70), Geovanni▪▪, Vennegoor of Hesselink (Altidore▪ 58). **Subs not used:** Warner, Garcia, Kilbane, Mouyokolo.

NOVEMBER

8th	● Stoke	H	W 2–1	**Att:** 24,516. **Ref:** M Dean – (4-4-2): Duke, Mendy▪, Zayatte, Gardner, Dawson, Garcia (Barmby 52), Olofinjana¹, Bullard, Hunt, Fagan (Boateng 90), Altidore (Vennegoor of Hesselink¹ 83). **Subs not used:** Warner, McShane, Kilbane, Ghilas.
21st	● West Ham	H	D 3–3	**Att:** 24,909. **Ref:** M Clattenburg – (4-4-2): Duke, Mendy▪, Gardner, Zayatte¹, Dawson, Garcia (McShane 57), Marney, Bullard¹, Hunt (Geovanni 85), Fagan, Altidore (Vennegoor of Hesselink 73). **Subs not used:** Myhill, Barmby, Kilbane, Boateng. Cole OG.
25th	● Everton	H	W 3–2	**Att:** 24,685. **Ref:** M Atkinson – (4-4-1-1): Duke, McShane, Gardner, Zayatte▪, Dawson¹, Garcia (Barmby 78), Marney¹, Boateng, Hunt¹, Geovanni (Kilbane 87), Altidore (Vennegoor of Hesselink 75). **Subs not used:** Myhill, Mouyokolo, Ghilas, Cairney.
28th	● Man City	A	D 1–1	**Att:** 46,382. **Ref:** L Probert – (4-2-3-1): Duke, McShane▪, Gardner, Zayatte▪, Dawson▪, Bullard¹, Marney (Boateng 62), Garcia, Geovanni (Barmby 61), Hunt, Altidore (Vennegoor of Hesselink 73). **Subs not used:** Myhill, Kilbane, Mouyokolo, Ghilas.

DECEMBER

5th	● Aston Villa	A	L 3–0	**Att:** 39,748. **Ref:** S Attwell – (4-5-1): Duke▪, McShane, Zayatte, Gardner, Dawson, Garcia, Boateng, Bullard (Fagan▪ 19), Marney▪ (Vennegoor of Hesselink 77), Hunt, Altidore (Barmby 54). **Subs not used:** Myhill, Geovanni, Kilbane, Mouyokolo.
12th	● Blackburn	H	D 0–0	**Att:** 24,124. **Ref:** C Foy – (4-4-1-1): Myhill, McShane, Gardner, Zayatte, Dawson, Garcia (Altidore 66), Boateng, Marney▪ (Olofinjana 77), Hunt, Geovanni, Fagan (Vennegoor of Hesselink 77). **Subs not used:** Duke, Barmby, Mendy, Kilbane.
19th	● Arsenal	A	L 3–0	**Att:** 60,006. **Ref:** S Bennett – (4-1-4-1): Myhill, McShane, Zayatte▪, Gardner, Dawson, Boateng▪, Garcia (Cousin 61), Geovanni (Mendy 69), Barmby▪ (Olofinjana 46), Hunt, Fagan. **Subs not used:** Duke, Kilbane, Ghilas, Vennegoor of Hesselink.
27th	● Man Utd	H	L 1–3	**Att:** 24,627. **Ref:** A Wiley – (4-4-2): Myhill, Mendy, Gardner, Zayatte, Dawson, Garcia (Vennegoor of Hesselink 77), Boateng (Geovanni 83), Olofinjana, Hunt, Altidore (Ghilas 83), Fagan¹. **Subs not used:** Duke, Barmby, Kilbane, Cairney.
29th	● Bolton	A	D 2–2	**Att:** 20,696. **Ref:** P Dowd – (4-4-2): Myhill, Mendy▪, Zayatte, Gardner, Dawson▪, Garcia (Vennegoor of Hesselink 64), Boateng, Olofinjana (Geovanni 75), Hunt², Fagan, Altidore (Barmby 54). **Subs not used:** Duke, Kilbane, Mouyokolo, Ghilas.

JANUARY

2nd	● Wigan	A	L 4–1	**Att:** 5,335. **Ref:** A Marriner – (4-4-2): Myhill, Mendy, Mouyokolo, Zayatte, Kilbane, Garcia, Cairney, Halmosi (Boateng 71), Geovanni¹, Ghilas (Cullen▪ 67), Vennegoor of Hesselink (Altidore 79). **Subs not used:** Duke, Doyle, Dawson, Devitt.
16th	● Tottenham	A	D 0–0	**Att:** 35,729. **Ref:** M Atkinson – (4-3-2-1): Myhill, McShane, Zayatte, Gardner, Dawson, Garcia (Mouyokolo 83), Boateng, Hunt, Barmby▪ (Kilbane 65), Geovanni (Vennegoor of Hesselink 75), Fagan▪. **Subs not used:** Duke, Mendy, Ghilas, Cairney.
23rd	● Man Utd	A	L 4–0	**Att:** 73,933. **Ref:** S Bennett – (4-5-1): Myhill, McShane, Gardner, Zayatte, Dawson, Garcia (Ghilas 70), Barmby (Mendy 57), Boateng, Geovanni (Kilbane 74), Hunt, Fagan▪. **Subs not used:** Duke, Mouyokolo, Vennegoor of Hesselink, Cairney.
30th	● Wolverhampton	H	D 2–2	**Att:** 24,957. **Ref:** M Dean – (4-4-2): Myhill, McShane, Gardner, Mouyokolo, Dawson▪, Mendy (Garcia 80), Cairney, Boateng▪, Hunt¹, Altidore (Zaki 69), Vennegoor of Hesselink¹. **Subs not used:** Duke, Fagan, Barmby, Geovanni, Kilbane.

FEBRUARY

2nd	● Chelsea	H	D 1–1	**Att:** 24,957. **Ref:** M Clattenburg – (4-4-2): Myhill, McShane▪ (Zayatte 90), Gardner, Mouyokolo¹, Dawson, Fagan, Boateng, Cairney, Hunt, Altidore (Kilbane 85), Vennegoor of Hesselink (Zaki 66). **Subs not used:** Duke, Barmby, Geovanni, Mendy.
6th	● Man City	H	W 2–1	**Att:** 24,959. **Ref:** P Dowd – (4-4-2): Myhill, McShane, Gardner, Mouyokolo, Dawson▪, Fagan▪, Boateng¹ (Olofinjana 82), Cairney, Hunt, Altidore¹ (Zaki 66), Vennegoor of Hesselink (Kilbane 83). **Subs not used:** Duke, Barmby, Garcia, Zayatte.

● Barclays Premier League ● FA Cup ● Carling Cup ● UEFA Champions League ● Europa League ● FA Community Shield ▪ Yellow Card ▪ Red Card

BARCLAYS PREMIER LEAGUE

RESULTS 2009/10

| 10th | ● Blackburn | A | L 1–0 | **Att:** 23,518. **Ref:** L Probert – (4-4-2): Myhill, McShane▌ (Zaki 67), Mouyokolo, Gardner▌, Dawson (Zayatte 67), Fagan, Boateng▌, Cairney, Hunt, Altidore▌, Vennegoor of Hesselink (Olofinjana 44). **Subs not used:** Duke, Barmby, Garcia, Kilbane. |
| 20th | ● West Ham | A | L 3–0 | **Att:** 33,971. **Ref:** M Atkinson – (4-4-2): Myhill, McShane, Mouyokolo, Gardner, Dawson, Fagan▌, Boateng, Cairney (Altidore 64), Hunt (Barmby 65), Zaki (Olofinjana 65), Vennegoor of Hesselink. **Subs not used:** Duke, Garcia, Kilbane, Zayatte. |

MARCH

7th	● Everton	A	L 5–1	**Att:** 34,682. **Ref:** L Mason – (4-4-1-1): Myhill, McShane, Mouyokolo, Zayatte, Kilbane, Garcia▌, Bullard (Altidore 62), Boateng, Cairney[1], Barmby (Geovanni 60), Zaki (Vennegoor of Hesselink 69). **Subs not used:** Duke, Ghilas, Cooper, Olofinjana.
13th	● Arsenal	H	L 1–2	**Att:** 25,023. **Ref:** A Marriner – (4-4-2): Myhill, Mendy, Zayatte (Cooper 55), Mouyokolo, Dawson▌, Fagan, Boateng▌, Bullard[1], Marney, Vennegoor of Hesselink (Garcia 73), Altidore (Kilbane 82). **Subs not used:** Duke, Barmby, Zaki, Olofinjana.
20th	● Portsmouth	A	L 3–2	**Att:** 16,513. **Ref:** P Dowd – (4-4-2): Myhill▌, Mendy, McShane, Mouyokolo, Dawson (Garcia 70), Folan[2], Marney, Bullard, Kilbane, Fagan, Vennegoor of Hesselink (Barmby 66). **Subs not used:** Duke, Geovanni, Cooper, Olofinjana, Cairney.
27th	● Fulham	H	W 2–0	**Att:** 24,361. **Ref:** C Foy – (4-4-2): Myhill, McShane, Mouyokolo, Sonko, Kilbane▌, Garcia, Boateng, Bullard[1] (Olofinjana 85), Marney, Fagan[1], Altidore▌ (Vennegoor of Hesselink 78). **Subs not used:** Duke, Barmby, Geovanni, Mendy, Cairney.

APRIL

3rd	● Stoke	A	L 2–0	**Att:** 27,604. **Ref:** L Probert – (4-4-2): Myhill, Mendy▌, McShane, Mouyokolo, Kilbane, Garcia (Vennegoor of Hesselink 72), Boateng, Bullard, Marney (Geovanni 58), Fagan, Folan (Altidore 64). **Subs not used:** Duke, Dawson, Barmby, Olofinjana.
10th	● Burnley	H	L 1–4	**Att:** 24,369. **Ref:** M Atkinson – (4-4-2): Myhill, McShane (Geovanni 67), Sonko, Mouyokolo, Dawson (Barmby 51), Mendy▌, Boateng▌, Bullard, Kilbane▌, Fagan▌ (Vennegoor of Hesselink 74), Altidore▌. **Subs not used:** Duke, Folan, Marney, Cairney.
17th	● Birmingham	A	D 0–0	**Att:** 26,669. **Ref:** M Clattenburg – (4-5-1): Duke, McShane, Sonko, Mouyokolo, Dawson, Fagan, Bullard, Boateng, Cairney, Kilbane, Vennegoor of Hesselink (Altidore 75). **Subs not used:** Myhill, Barmby, Geovanni, Marney, Cooper, Olofinjana.
21st	● Aston Villa	H	L 0–2	**Att:** 23,842. **Ref:** M Dean – (4-4-1-1): Duke, McShane, Sonko, Mouyokolo, Dawson, Fagan▌, Cairney (Geovanni 70), Boateng, Kilbane (Olofinjana 84), Bullard, Vennegoor of Hesselink (Altidore 54). **Subs not used:** Myhill, Barmby, Cullen, Cooper.
24th	● Sunderland	H	L 0–1	**Att:** 25,012. **Ref:** L Probert – (4-4-2): Duke, Mendy, Gardner, Mouyokolo, Dawson, Barmby (Fagan 62), Boateng (Cullen 75), Bullard (Cairney 46), Geovanni▌, Folan, Altidore▌. **Subs not used:** Myhill, Kilbane, Sonko, Olofinjana.

MAY

| 3rd | ● Wigan | A | D 2–2 | **Att:** 20,242. **Ref:** P Dowd – (4-4-2): Duke, Mendy, Mouyokolo, Gardner, Dawson, Atkinson[1], Cairney, Boateng, Kilbane, Vennegoor of Hesselink (Folan 70), Cullen[1]. **Subs not used:** Myhill, Fagan, Barmby, Geovanni, Cooper, Olofinjana. |
| 9th | ● Liverpool | H | D 0–0 | **Att:** 25,030. **Ref:** A Marriner – (4-4-2): Duke, Mendy, Gardner, Mouyokolo, Dawson, Atkinson▌, Boateng, Cairney, Kilbane (Geovanni 76), Cullen, Vennegoor of Hesselink (Fagan 84). **Subs not used:** Myhill, McShane, Barmby, Cooper, Olofinjana. |

● Barclays Premier League ● FA Cup ● Carling Cup ● UEFA Champions League ● Europa League ● FA Community Shield ▌ Yellow Card ▎ Red Card

Stephen Hunt (right of picture) scores Hull's late equaliser at Bolton in December

HULL CITY

BARCLAYS PREMIER LEAGUE GOALKEEPER STATS

Player	Minutes on pitch	Appearances	Match starts	Completed matches	Sub appearances	Subbed off	SAVES BREAKDOWN								Clean sheets	Goals conceded	Save %	PENALTIES			Fouls committed	Free-kicks won	Yellow cards	Red cards
							Saved with feet	Punched	Parried	Tipped over	Fumbled	Tipped round	Caught	Blocked				Saved	Resulting in goals	Opposition miss				
Matt Duke	1073	11	11	11	0	0	1	4	11	1	1	2	36	0	2	17	76.39	0	4	0	1	1	1	0
Boaz Myhill	2603	27	27	27	0	0	1	24	41	6	3	13	96	2	5	58	75.93	1	3	0	1	5	2	0

BARCLAYS PREMIER LEAGUE OUTFIELD PLAYER STATS

Player	Minutes on pitch	Appearances	Match starts	Completed matches	Substitute appearances	Subbed off	Goals scored	Assists	Shots on target	Shots off target	Crosses	Tackles made	Defensive clearances	Defensive blocks	Fouls committed	Free-kicks won	Caught offside	Yellow cards	Red cards
Jozy Altidore	1554	28	16	2	12	13	1	7	13	12	8	11	2	2	25	56	16	4	1
Will Atkinson	193	2	2	2	0	0	1	0	2	0	1	2	0	0	4	3	0	1	0
Nick Barmby	836	20	6	0	14	6	0	0	7	6	8	24	1	3	10	7	1	4	0
George Boateng	2393	29	26	20	3	4	1	1	11	9	19	62	25	10	55	34	0	4	2
Jimmy Bullard	1134	14	13	9	1	4	5	2	17	17	35	8	2	0	7	23	1	0	0
Tom Cairney	952	11	10	8	1	2	1	0	3	5	20	27	2	6	8	13	1	1	0
Liam Cooper	138	2	1	1	1	0	0	0	0	0	0	1	9	4	0	1	0	0	0
Daniel Cousin	85	3	1	0	2	1	0	0	0	1	0	0	0	0	1	1	0	0	0
Mark Cullen	213	3	2	2	1	0	1	0	2	3	1	2	0	0	6	3	3	0	0
Andy Dawson	3284	35	35	32	0	3	1	0	6	2	46	81	31	20	30	23	0	7	0
Craig Fagan	1971	25	20	15	5	4	2	3	4	13	39	24	3	3	56	27	6	7	1
Caleb Folan	610	8	7	4	1	3	2	0	5	2	2	11	2	3	12	4	9	1	0
Richard Garcia	1165	18	14	4	4	10	0	1	10	6	13	19	9	3	15	20	2	1	0
Anthony Gardner	2318	24	24	24	0	0	0	0	2	5	0	39	72	19	17	19	1	1	0
Deiberson Geovanni	1656	26	16	7	10	8	3	0	27	16	36	45	0	2	27	51	5	4	1
Kamel Ghilas	632	13	6	2	7	4	1	1	7	4	8	20	1	0	6	8	12	0	0
Stephen Hunt	2457	27	27	21	0	6	6	5	14	8	108	76	9	8	41	61	3	4	0
Kevin Kilbane	1458	21	15	11	6	4	1	1	5	4	14	41	18	6	11	17	1	2	0
Dean Marney	1285	16	15	8	1	7	1	2	12	6	16	21	2	1	13	8	0	4	0
Paul McShane	2449	27	26	22	1	4	0	0	1	2	35	46	41	15	25	24	2	5	0
Bernard Mendy	1508	21	15	11	6	3	0	0	5	4	37	30	20	4	22	17	1	6	1
Steven Mouyokolo	1813	21	19	18	2	1	1	0	3	3	1	52	35	12	15	15	3	1	0
Seyi Olofinjana	1237	19	11	10	8	1	1	0	8	4	4	42	11	1	21	9	0	3	0
Ibrahima Sonko	872	9	9	9	0	0	0	0	0	0	3	11	18	8	5	5	0	0	0
Michael Turner	385	4	4	4	0	0	0	0	1	0	0	35	14	5	8	5	0	1	0
Jan Vennegoor of Hesselink	1586	31	17	3	14	14	3	4	9	14	4	10	9	2	39	21	14	0	0
Amr Zaki	245	6	2	0	4	2	0	0	2	2	2	2	0	0	7	7	2	0	0
Kamil Zayatte	1997	23	21	19	2	2	2	1	6	7	5	71	39	13	32	21	1	3	0

SEASON TOTALS

Goals scored	34
Goals conceded	75
Clean sheets	7
Shots on target	181
Shots off target	155
Shots per goal	9.88
Pens awarded	8
Pens scored	6
Pens conceded	8
Offsides	84
Corners	151
Crosses	465
Players used	30
Fouls committed	520
Free-kicks won	509

AUG	SEP	OCT	NOV	DEC	JAN	FEB	MAR	APR	MAY
14	19	18	15	19	19	18	18	18	19

LEAGUE POSITION AT THE END OF EACH MONTH

SEASON INFORMATION
Highest position: 11
Lowest position: 19
Average goals scored per game: 0.89
Average goals conceded per game: 1.97

CARDS RECEIVED

67   **6**

SEQUENCES

Wins	–
(–)	
Losses	5
(10/02/10–20/03/10)	
Draws	2
(on three occasions)	
Undefeated	4
(08/11/09–28/11/09)	
Without win	10
(28/11/09–02/02/10)	
Undefeated home	6
(03/10/09–12/12/09)	
Undefeated away	2
(on two occasions)	
Without scoring	3
(on three occasions)	
Without conceding	–
(–)	
Scoring	5
(15/08/09–12/09/09)	
Conceding	9
(23/01/10–20/03/10)	

MATCH RECORDS

Goals scored per match

		W	D	L	Pts
Failed to score	16	0	5	11	5
Scored 1 goal	12	1	3	8	6
Scored 2 goals	8	4	3	1	15
Scored 3 goals	2	1	1	0	4
Scored 4+ goals	0	0	0	0	0

Goals conceded per match

		W	D	L	Pts
Clean sheet	7	2	5	0	11
Conceded 1 goal	9	3	3	3	12
Conceded 2 goals	10	1	3	6	6
Conceded 3 goals	6	0	1	5	1
Conceded 4+ goals	6	0	0	6	0

GOALS SCORED/CONCEDED
PER FIVE-MINUTE INTERVALS

MINS	5	10	15	20	25	30	35	40	45	50	55	60	65	70	75	80	85	90
FOR	2	1	2	2	1	6	2	0	4	1	2	2	3	1	2	1	1	1
AGN	2	4	7	4	0	4	1	3	6	5	1	3	5	4	3	4	3	16

EARLIEST STRIKE
KEVIN KILBANE
(v Burnley) 2:09

LATEST STRIKE
JAN VENNEGOOR
(v Stoke) 90:23

George Boateng

GOAL DETAILS

How the goals were struck

SCORED		CONCEDED
12	Right foot	49
11	Left foot	16
10	Header	10
1	Other	0

How the goals were struck

SCORED		CONCEDED
13	Open play	43
7	Cross	8
2	Corner	4
6	Penalty	7
3	Direct from free-kick	5
3	Free-kick	2
0	Own goal	6

Distance from goal

SCORED		CONCEDED
9	6YDS	21
20	18YDS	42
5	18+YDS	12

LIVERPOOL

CLUB SUMMARY

FORMED	1892
MANAGER	TBC
GROUND	Anfield
CAPACITY	45,362
NICKNAME	The Reds
WEBSITE	www.liverpoolfc.tv

The New Football Pools PLAYER OF THE SEASON — Jose Reina

OVERALL
P	W	D	L	F	A	GD
56	26	11	19	84	54	30

BARCLAYS PREMIER LEAGUE
Pos	P	W	D	L	F	A	GD	Pts
7	38	18	9	11	61	35	26	63

HOME
Pos	P	W	D	L	F	A	GD	Pts
5	19	13	3	3	43	15	28	42

AWAY
Pos	P	W	D	L	F	A	GD	Pts
8	19	5	6	8	18	20	-2	21

CUP PROGRESS DETAILS
Competition	Round reached	Knocked out by
Champions League	Group E	–
Europa League	SF	Atlético Madrid
FA Cup	R3	Reading
Carling Cup	R4	Arsenal

BIGGEST WIN (ALL COMPS)
26/09/09 6–1 v Hull

BIGGEST DEFEAT (ALL COMPS)
1–3 on 2 occasions

THE PLAYER WITH THE MOST
GOALS SCORED Fernando Torres	18
SHOTS ON TARGET Steven Gerrard	54
SHOTS OFF TARGET Steven Gerrard	36
SHOTS WITHOUT SCORING Leiva Lucas	24
ASSISTS Steven Gerrard	7
OFFSIDES Fernando Torres	21
FOULS Javier Mascherano	67
FOULS WITHOUT A CARD Daniel Agger	11
FREE-KICKS WON Javier Mascherano	66
DEFENSIVE CLEARANCES Jamie Carragher	59

actim INDEX — FOR THE 2009/10 BARCLAYS PREMIER LEAGUE SEASON

RANK	PLAYER	PTS
21	Dirk Kuyt	494
24	Jose Reina	473
25	Steven Gerrard	471

ATTENDANCE RECORD
HIGH	AVERAGE	LOW
44,392	42,864	37,697
v Hull (26/09/2009)		v West Ham (19/04/2010)

THIS WAS supposed to be the season when Liverpool finally ended their 20-year wait for a championship title but it turned into their worst Barclays Premier League campaign for a decade and ended with the departure of manager Rafael Benitez.

High expectations of mounting a genuine challenge to defending champions Manchester United and eventual winners Chelsea faded by the end of October, by which time the Reds had already lost four times – twice as many defeats as in the whole of the previous season. From that point, Benitez found himself continually defending his team as Liverpool had to lower their sights from challenging for first to competing for fourth. That famously led to the Spaniard making his 'guarantee' of UEFA Champions League football in December – he later admitted it was to prevent confidence from falling further – which ultimately proved a hollow promise.

Liverpool eventually finished in seventh place, their worst result since 1999, and only just qualified for the Europa League.

The writing was on the wall within eight days of the season kicking off. An opening-day defeat at Tottenham, the team who eventually claimed the final Champions League place, was followed by a loss to Aston Villa at Anfield. Two defeats in three matches pointed to something more deep-rooted than just bad luck.

The sale of midfielder Xabi Alonso to Real Madrid for £30million was clearly a factor and his £20million replacement, Italian international Alberto Aquilani, struggled for fitness all season following his arrival from Roma.

Striker Fernando Torres initially looked jaded following his summer exertions for Spain at the Confederations Cup in South Africa but he appeared to put such fears behind him with five goals in two League matches, including a hat-trick in the 6–1 victory over Hull at Anfield. Unfortunately for Liverpool, that represented the peak of his impact as, in the coming months, he was hampered first by a hernia problem and then a knee injury which required two operations, one in January and the other in April. The second one ended his season.

Liverpool's luck had definitely changed for the worse and a 2–0 defeat at Chelsea in October was then followed by the most bizarre goal of the season when Sunderland

Liverpool endured their worst season in years as they struggled in the League and made an early exit in Europe

striker Darren Bent scored with the aid of a huge deflection off a beachball that had been thrown from the away end onto the pitch in the Black Cats' 1–0 victory at the Stadium of Light.

There were still some memorable moments for the fans to enjoy. Torres returned from injury to open the scoring in a 2–0 win at home to Manchester United in October, which looked to have reignited their title bid and left them six points behind leaders Chelsea, and the Reds won by the same margin in the Merseyside derby at Goodison Park at the end of November. However, defeats to Arsenal and then struggling Portsmouth meant they were down to seventh place at end of December. By that time they had also been eliminated from the Champions League at the group stage following two losses to Fiorentina and a 2–1 defeat to Lyon at Anfield.

January brought with it a five-week absence for Torres and, although Liverpool managed to get through that period relatively unscathed in the League, the after-effects were felt in the coming months. An FA Cup defeat to Coca-Cola Championship side Reading and a shock defeat at Wigan represented further lows, but it was not until the penultimate match of the season that fourth place was finally put out of reach thanks to a home defeat to eventual champions Chelsea.

The whole season was played out against a backdrop of difficulties behind the scenes. American co-owners Tom Hicks and George Gillett decided to put the club up for sale in April in a bid to find new owners 'committed to taking the club through the next level of growth and development'. British Airways boss Martin Broughton was brought in as chairman to oversee the sale before Benitez departed by mutual consent on 3rd June after six years in charge of the club.

CLOCKWISE FROM ABOVE: Liverpool stars look dejected following a goalless draw at Molineux in January; Rafael Benitez toils on the sidelines during a home defeat to Arsenal; Alberto Aquilani was hampered by injury during his first season at Anfield; Pepe Reina and David Ngog cheer a victory over rivals Manchester United at Anfield – a rare high point during a difficult campaign

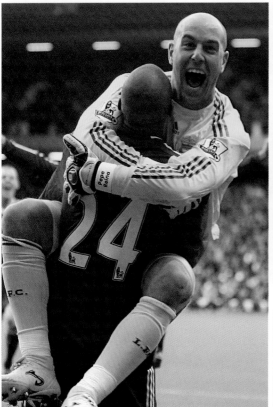

LIVERPOOL

RESULTS 2009/10

AUGUST

16th ● Tottenham A L 2–1 **Att:** 35,935. **Ref:** P Dowd – (4-4-1-1): Reina, Johnson, Carragher‖, Skrtel‖ (Ayala 75), Insua, Kuyt (Voronin 79), Mascherano‖, Lucas, Babel (Benayoun 67), Gerrard[1], Torres. **Subs not used:** Cavalieri, Spearing, Kelly, Dossena.

19th ● Stoke H W 4–0 **Att:** 44,318. **Ref:** P Walton – (4-2-3-1): Reina, Johnson[1], Carragher, Ayala, Insua, Mascherano, Lucas, Kuyt[1] (Riera 82), Gerrard (Voronin 81), Benayoun, Torres[1] (Ngog[1] 84). **Subs not used:** Cavalieri, Babel, Kelly, Dossena.

24th ● Aston Villa H L 1–3 **Att:** 43,667. **Ref:** M Atkinson – (4-2-3-1): Reina‖, Johnson, Carragher, Skrtel‖, Insua, Mascherano, Lucas (Voronin 66), Kuyt, Gerrard, Benayoun (Babel 75), Torres‖[1]. **Subs not used:** Cavalieri, Riera, Kelly, Dossena, Ayala.

29th ● Bolton A W 2–3 **Att:** 23,284. **Ref:** A Wiley – (4-2-3-1): Reina, Johnson[1], Kyrgiakos, Carragher, Insua, Mascherano (Voronin 74), Lucas, Kuyt (Dossena 89), Riera (Benayoun 63), Gerrard‖[1], Torres[1]. **Subs not used:** Gulacsi, Plessis, Kelly, Skrtel.

SEPTEMBER

12th ● Burnley H W 4–0 **Att:** 43,817. **Ref:** L Mason – (4-2-3-1): Reina, Johnson (Degen 64), Skrtel, Carragher, Insua, Gerrard, Lucas, Kuyt[1] (Voronin 69), Benayoun[3], Riera, Torres (Ngog 75). **Subs not used:** Cavalieri, Kyrgiakos, Spearing, Dossena.

16th ● Debrecen H W 1–0 **Att:** 41,591. **Ref:** P Proenca – (4-4-2): Reina, Johnson, Carragher, Skrtel, Insua, Benayoun (Mascherano 87), Lucas, Gerrard‖, Riera (Babel 80), Kuyt[1] (Aurelio 90), Torres. **Subs not used:** Cavalieri, Voronin, Kyrgiakos, Spearing.

19th ● West Ham A W 2–3 **Att:** 34,658. **Ref:** A Marriner – (4-2-3-1): Reina, Johnson, Carragher‖, Skrtel‖, Insua, Mascherano‖, Lucas, Kuyt[1] (Babel 60), Gerrard, Benayoun (Aurelio 85), Torres[2] (Riera 90). **Subs not used:** Cavalieri, Kyrgiakos, Degen, Dossena.

22nd ● Leeds A W 0–1 **Att:** 38,168. **Ref:** A Wiley – (4-4-1-1): Cavalieri, Degen (Johnson 71), Kyrgiakos‖, Carragher, Dossena, Aurelio, Mascherano, Spearing, Riera, Babel (Skrtel 90), Ngog[1] (Gerrard 78). **Subs not used:** Reina, Torres, Voronin, Plessis.

26th ● Hull H W 6–1 **Att:** 44,392. **Ref:** P Walton – (4-2-3-1): Reina, Johnson, Carragher, Skrtel‖, Insua, Lucas, Gerrard[1] (Mascherano 74), Benayoun (Voronin 77), Kuyt, Riera, Torres[3] (Babel[2] 67). **Subs not used:** Cavalieri, Aurelio, Kyrgiakos, Ngog.

29th ● Fiorentina A L 2–0 **Att:** 33,426. **Ref:** F Brych – (4-2-3-1): Reina, Johnson, Carragher, Skrtel, Insua (Babel 72), Gerrard, Lucas, Benayoun, Kuyt (Voronin 80), Aurelio, Torres. **Subs not used:** Cavalieri, Riera, Kyrgiakos, Spearing, Plessis.

OCTOBER

4th ● Chelsea A L 2–0 **Att:** 41,732. **Ref:** M Atkinson – (4-4-1-1): Reina, Johnson, Carragher, Skrtel‖, Insua (Aurelio 83), Kuyt, Mascherano, Lucas (Babel 76), Riera (Benayoun 67), Gerrard‖, Torres. **Subs not used:** Cavalieri, Agger, Kyrgiakos, Ngog.

17th ● Sunderland A L 1–0 **Att:** 47,327. **Ref:** M Jones – (4-4-1-1): Reina, Johnson, Agger, Skrtel (Voronin 72), Carragher, Babel (Ngog 81), Lucas, Aurelio, Spearing (Mascherano 72), Benayoun, Kuyt‖. **Subs not used:** Cavalieri, Riera, Insua, Kelly.

20th ● Lyon H L 1–2 **Att:** 41,562. **Ref:** A Undiano Mallenco – (4-2-3-1): Reina, Kelly (Skrtel 74), Carragher, Agger, Insua, Mascherano, Lucas, Kuyt, Gerrard (Aurelio 25), Benayoun[1] (Voronin 84), Ngog‖. **Subs not used:** Cavalieri, Babel, Spearing, Plessis.

25th ● Man Utd H W 2–0 **Att:** 44,188. **Ref:** A Marriner – (4-2-3-1): Reina, Johnson, Carragher‖, Agger, Insua, Lucas, Mascherano‖‖, Benayoun (Skrtel 90), Kuyt, Aurelio, Torres[1] (Ngog[1] 80). **Subs not used:** Cavalieri, Voronin, Babel, Spearing, Degen.

28th ● Arsenal A L 2–1 **Att:** 60,004. **Ref:** A Wiley – (4-4-2): Cavalieri, Degen (Eccleston 88), Skrtel, Kyrgiakos, Insua[1], Kuyt, Spearing, Plessis (Aquilani 76), Babel, Voronin, Ngog (Benayoun 74). **Subs not used:** Reina, Darby, Dossena, Ayala.

31st ● Fulham A L 3–1 **Att:** 25,700. **Ref:** L Mason – (4-4-1-1): Reina, Degen‖, Carragher‖, Kyrgiakos, Insua, Kuyt (Ayala 85), Mascherano, Lucas, Benayoun (Eccleston 78), Voronin, Torres[1] (Babel 63). **Subs not used:** Gulacsi, Spearing, Plessis, Dossena.

NOVEMBER

4th ● Lyon A D 1–1 **Att:** 39,180. **Ref:** F De Bleeckere – (4-2-3-1): Reina, Carragher, Agger‖, Kyrgiakos, Insua, Lucas, Mascherano, Kuyt, Voronin (Babel 68), Benayoun, Torres (Ngog 87). **Subs not used:** Cavalieri, Aquilani, Spearing, Darby, Ayala.

9th ● Birmingham H D 2–2 **Att:** 42,560. **Ref:** P Walton – (4-2-3-1): Reina, Johnson, Skrtel, Agger, Insua, Mascherano, Lucas (Aquilani 82), Kuyt, Benayoun (Babel 77), Riera (Gerrard[1] 45), Ngog‖[1]. **Subs not used:** Cavalieri, Kyrgiakos, Spearing, Darby.

21st ● Man City H D 2–2 **Att:** 44,164. **Ref:** P Dowd – (4-2-3-1): Reina, Carragher‖, Skrtel[1], Agger (Kyrgiakos 11), Insua, Mascherano, Lucas‖, Kuyt, Gerrard, Babel (Benayoun[1] 18 (Aurelio 85)), Ngog. **Subs not used:** Cavalieri, Aquilani, Riera, El Zhar.

24th ● Debrecen A W 0–1 **Att:** 41,500. **Ref:** B Kuipers – (4-4-1-1): Reina, Johnson, Carragher, Agger, Insua, Kuyt, Lucas, Mascherano, Aurelio (Dossena 89), Gerrard (Aquilani 90), Ngog[1] (Benayoun 77). **Subs not used:** Cavalieri, Kyrgiakos, Spearing, Skrtel.

29th ● Everton A W 0–2 **Att:** 39,652. **Ref:** A Wiley – (4-2-3-1): Reina, Johnson, Carragher, Agger, Insua, Mascherano, Lucas, Kuyt[1], Gerrard, Aurelio (Riera 78), Ngog (Benayoun 75). **Subs not used:** Cavalieri, Aquilani, Kyrgiakos, El Zhar, Skrtel. Yobo OG.

DECEMBER

5th ● Blackburn A D 0–0 **Att:** 29,660. **Ref:** M Atkinson – (4-2-3-1): Reina, Johnson, Carragher, Agger, Insua, Mascherano, Lucas, Benayoun (El Zhar 72), Gerrard, Riera (Ngog 52), Kuyt. **Subs not used:** Cavalieri, Aquilani, Kyrgiakos, Skrtel, Dossena.

9th ● Fiorentina H L 1–2 **Att:** 40,863. **Ref:** D Skomina – (4-2-3-1): Cavalieri, Darby, Skrtel, Agger, Insua, Aquilani (Pacheco 76), Mascherano (Aurelio 86), Benayoun[1], Gerrard, Dossena, Kuyt (Torres 65). **Subs not used:** Reina, Kyrgiakos, Carragher, Spearing.

13th ● Arsenal H L 1–2 **Att:** 43,853. **Ref:** H Webb – (4-2-3-1): Reina, Johnson (Degen 82), Carragher, Agger, Aurelio‖, Mascherano‖ (Aquilani 65), Lucas‖, Kuyt‖, Gerrard, Benayoun (Ngog 79), Torres. **Subs not used:** Cavalieri, Insua, Skrtel, Dossena.

16th ● Wigan H W 2–1 **Att:** 41,116. **Ref:** P Dowd – (4-4-2): Reina, Carragher, Skrtel, Agger, Insua, Benayoun (Aquilani 81), Mascherano‖, Gerrard, Aurelio (Lucas 60), Kuyt, Ngog[1] (Torres[1] 64). **Subs not used:** Cavalieri, Kyrgiakos, Darby, Dossena.

19th ● Portsmouth A L 2–0 **Att:** 20,534. **Ref:** L Mason – (4-4-1-1): Reina, Johnson‖, Carragher, Agger, Insua (Aurelio 68), Kuyt, Mascherano‖, Lucas‖ (Spearing 88), Dossena (Benayoun 53), Gerrard, Torres‖. **Subs not used:** Cavalieri, Babel, Ngog.

26th ● Wolverhampton H W 2–0 **Att:** 41,956. **Ref:** A Marriner – (4-2-3-1): Reina, Johnson, Carragher, Agger, Insua, Aquilani (Pacheco 84), Lucas, Benayoun[1] (Spearing 88), Gerrard[1], Aurelio (Kuyt 76), Torres. **Subs not used:** Cavalieri, Ngog, Darby, Skrtel.

29th ● Aston Villa A W 0–1 **Att:** 42,788. **Ref:** L Probert – (4-4-1-1): Reina, Johnson (Skrtel 89), Carragher, Agger, Insua, Kuyt, Lucas‖, Aquilani (Babel 77), Benayoun (Aurelio 90), Gerrard, Torres[1]. **Subs not used:** Cavalieri, Kyrgiakos, Ngog, Spearing.

JANUARY

2nd ● Reading A D 1–1 **Att:** 23,656. **Ref:** M Atkinson – (4-4-2): Reina, Darby, Skrtel, Carragher, Insua‖, Kuyt, Lucas, Gerrard[1], Aurelio (Benayoun 79), Torres, Ngog (Aquilani 68). **Subs not used:** Cavalieri, Kyrgiakos, Babel, Spearing, Degen.

● Barclays Premier League ● FA Cup ● Carling Cup ● UEFA Champions League ● Europa League ● FA Community Shield ‖ Yellow Card ▮ Red Card

RESULTS 2009/10

13th	● Reading	H	L 1–2	**Att:** 31,063. **Ref:** P Dowd – (4-2-3-1): Cavalieri, Degen▌ (Skrtel 91), Carragher, Agger, Insua, Lucas, Aquilani, Kuyt, Gerrard (Babel 46), Benayoun, Torres (Ngog 29). **Subs not used:** Gulacsi, Aurelio, Spearing, Pacheco. Bertrand OG. AET – Score after 90 mins 1–1.
16th	● Stoke	A	D 1–1	**Att:** 27,247. **Ref:** L Mason – (4-4-2): Reina▌, Carragher, Kyrgiakos[1], Skrtel, Insua, Degen (Maxi 78), Lucas▌, Mascherano, Aurelio, Kuyt, Ngog (Aquilani 87). **Subs not used:** Cavalieri, Riera, Spearing, Darby, Pacheco.
20th	● Tottenham	H	W 2–0	**Att:** 42,016. **Ref:** H Webb – (4-4-1-1): Reina, Carragher, Skrtel, Kyrgiakos, Insua, Degen (Darby 90), Mascherano▌, Lucas▌, Riera (Maxi 81), Aquilani (Ngog 79), Kuyt[2]. **Subs not used:** Cavalieri, Babel, Spearing, Pacheco.
26th	● Wolverhampton	A	D 0–0	**Att:** 28,763. **Ref:** P Walton – (4-4-1-1): Reina, Carragher, Skrtel▌, Kyrgiakos, Insua, Maxi, Lucas, Riera (Ngog 66), Gerrard, Kuyt. **Subs not used:** Cavalieri, Aquilani, Babel, Degen, Darby, Pacheco.
30th	● Bolton	H	W 2–0	**Att:** 43,413. **Ref:** S Bennett – (4-2-3-1): Reina, Carragher, Skrtel, Kyrgiakos, Insua, Aquilani (Lucas 65), Mascherano▌, Kuyt[1], Gerrard, Riera (Maxi 74), Ngog (Babel 84). **Subs not used:** Cavalieri, Agger, Darby, Pacheco. K Davies OG.

FEBRUARY

6th	● Everton	H	W 1–0	**Att:** 44,316. **Ref:** M Atkinson – (4-2-3-1): Reina, Carragher▌, Kyrgiakos▌, Agger, Insua, Mascherano, Lucas, Kuyt[1] (Skrtel 90), Gerrard▌, Maxi (Aurelio 90), Ngog (Babel 63). **Subs not used:** Cavalieri, Aquilani, Riera, Degen.
10th	● Arsenal	A	L 1–0	**Att:** 60,045. **Ref:** H Webb – (4-2-3-1): Reina, Carragher (Degen▌ 54), Skrtel, Agger, Insua, Lucas (Babel 78), Mascherano, Kuyt, Gerrard, Maxi▌, Ngog. **Subs not used:** Cavalieri, Riera, Aurelio, Spearing, Kelly.
18th	◖ Unirea Urziceni	H	W 1–0	**Att:** 40,450. **Ref:** E Braamhaar – (4-5-1): Reina, Carragher, Skrtel, Agger, Aurelio, Mascherano▌, Aquilani (Pacheco 75), Kuyt, Riera (Babel 63), Ngog[1] (Lucas 89). **Subs not used:** Cavalieri, Kyrgiakos, Insua, Degen.
21st	● Man City	A	D 0–0	**Att:** 47,203. **Ref:** P Walton – (4-2-3-1): Reina, Carragher, Skrtel, Agger, Insua, Mascherano▌, Lucas, Maxi (Benayoun 63), Gerrard▌, Babel▌ (Torres▌ 75), Kuyt (Aquilani 86). **Subs not used:** Cavalieri, Riera, Aurelio, Kelly.
25th	◖ Unirea Urziceni	A	W 1–3	**Att:** 25,000. **Ref:** S Johannesson – (4-5-1): Reina, Carragher (Kelly 61), Agger, Skrtel (Kyrgiakos 66), Insua, Babel▌[1], Gerrard[1], Lucas, Mascherano▌[1], Benayoun (Aurelio 77), Ngog. **Subs not used:** Cavalieri, Aquilani, Torres, Kuyt. Agg: 1–4.
28th	● Blackburn	H	W 2–1	**Att:** 42,795. **Ref:** A Wiley – (4-4-2): Reina, Mascherano, Carragher, Agger, Aurelio (Insua 38), Benayoun (Babel 81), Gerrard[1], Lucas▌, Maxi, Kuyt, Torres[1] (Ngog 89). **Subs not used:** Cavalieri, Aquilani, Kelly, Ayala.

MARCH

8th	● Wigan	A	L 1–0	**Att:** 17,427. **Ref:** A Marriner – (4-2-3-1): Reina, Mascherano, Carragher, Kyrgiakos▌, Insua▌, Lucas▌ (Johnson 55), Gerrard▌, Maxi, Kuyt (Babel 82), Benayoun (Aquilani 69), Torres▌. **Subs not used:** Cavalieri, Agger, Riera, Ngog.
11th	◖ Lille	A	L 1–0	**Att:** 18,000. **Ref:** A Larsen – (4-4-1-1): Reina, Johnson, Agger, Carragher, Insua▌, Kuyt (El Zhar 88), Mascherano, Lucas, Babel (Riera 73), Gerrard, Torres▌. **Subs not used:** Cavalieri, Aquilani, Kyrgiakos, Ngog, Kelly.
15th	◖ Portsmouth	H	W 4–1	**Att:** 40,316. **Ref:** S Attwell – (4-2-3-1): Reina, Johnson (Kelly 70), Carragher, Agger, Insua, Aquilani[1], Mascherano, Maxi, Gerrard (Benayoun 73), Babel[1], Torres[1] (Ngog 80). **Subs not used:** Cavalieri, Kyrgiakos, Kuyt, Lucas.
18th	◖ Lille	H	W 3–0	**Att:** 38,139. **Ref:** N Rizzoli – (4-2-3-1): Reina, Johnson, Carragher, Agger (Kyrgiakos 90), Insua▌, Kuyt, Mascherano, Lucas, Babel (Benayoun 80), Gerrard[1], Torres[2] (Ngog 90). **Subs not used:** Cavalieri, Degen, El Zhar, Kelly. Agg: 3–1.
21st	● Man Utd	A	L 2–1	**Att:** 75,216. **Ref:** H Webb – (4-2-3-1): Reina, Johnson, Carragher▌, Agger, Insua, Mascherano▌, Lucas (Benayoun 83), Kuyt (Aquilani 73), Gerrard, Maxi (Babel 76), Torres▌[1]. **Subs not used:** Cavalieri, Kyrgiakos, Ngog, Kelly.
28th	● Sunderland	H	W 3–0	**Att:** 43,121. **Ref:** P Dowd – (4-4-2): Reina, Johnson[1], Carragher, Agger, Insua, Maxi, Mascherano, Gerrard (El Zhar 81), Babel, Kuyt (Aquilani 71), Torres[2] (Ngog 78). **Subs not used:** Cavalieri, Benayoun, Kyrgiakos, Lucas.

APRIL

1st	◖ Benfica	A	L 2–1	**Att:** 62,629. **Ref:** J Eriksson – (4-2-3-1): Reina▌, Johnson, Agger[1], Carragher▌, Insua▌, Lucas, Mascherano, Kuyt, Gerrard (Benayoun 90), Babel▌, Torres (Ngog 82). **Subs not used:** Cavalieri, Kyrgiakos, Plessis, El Zhar, Pacheco.
4th	● Birmingham	A	D 1–1	**Att:** 27,909. **Ref:** M Atkinson – (4-4-2): Reina, Johnson, Carragher, Kyrgiakos, Insua, Benayoun (Babel 71), Gerrard[1], Lucas▌, Maxi, Torres (Ngog 65), Kuyt (Aquilani 81). **Subs not used:** Cavalieri, Agger, Mascherano, Degen.
8th	◖ Benfica	H	W 4–1	**Att:** 42,377. **Ref:** B Kuipers – (4-2-3-1): Reina, Johnson, Carragher, Kyrgiakos, Agger, Mascherano, Lucas[1], Kuyt[1], Gerrard (Aquilani 88), Benayoun (El Zhar 90), Torres[2] (Ngog 86). **Subs not used:** Cavalieri, Degen, Ayala, Pacheco. Agg: 5–3.
11th	● Fulham	H	D 0–0	**Att:** 42,331. **Ref:** A Marriner – (4-2-3-1): Reina, Johnson, Kyrgiakos, Carragher▌, Agger, Aquilani (Kuyt 65), Mascherano, Maxi, Lucas, Babel (Benayoun 71), Ngog (Pacheco 78). **Subs not used:** Cavalieri, Lucas, Degen, Ayala.
19th	● West Ham	H	W 3–0	**Att:** 37,697. **Ref:** P Walton – (4-4-2): Reina, Johnson, Carragher, Agger, Maxi, Gerrard (Mascherano 71), Lucas, Benayoun[1] (Degen 77), Kuyt, Ngog[1] (Babel 81). **Subs not used:** Cavalieri, Aquilani, El Zhar, Ayala. Green OG.
22nd	◖ Atlético Madrid	A	L 1–0	**Att:** 50,000. **Ref:** L Duhamel – (4-4-1-1): Reina, Johnson, Carragher, Kyrgiakos▌, Agger, Kuyt, Lucas, Maxi, Benayoun (El Zhar 83), Gerrard, Ngog (Babel 64). **Subs not used:** Cavalieri, Aquilani, Degen, Ayala, Pacheco.
25th	● Burnley	A	W 0–4	**Att:** 21,553. **Ref:** P Dowd – (4-4-1-1): Reina, Johnson, Carragher, Ayala, Agger (Lucas 78), Maxi[1], Aquilani, Mascherano, Babel[1], Gerrard▌[2] (Pacheco 82), Kuyt (Benayoun 48). **Subs not used:** Cavalieri, Kyrgiakos, Degen, El Zhar. Burnley are relegated.
29th	◖ Atlético Madrid	H	W 2–1	**Att:** 42,040. **Ref:** T Hauge – (4-2-3-1): Reina, Mascherano (Degen 110), Carragher▌, Agger, Johnson, Aquilani▌[1] (El Zhar 89), Lucas, Kuyt▌, Gerrard▌, Benayoun[1] (Pacheco 113), Babel. **Subs not used:** Cavalieri, Kyrgiakos, Ngog, Ayala. AET – Score after 90 mins 1–0. Agg: 2–2; Atletico Madrid win on away goals rule.

MAY

2nd	● Chelsea	H	L 0–2	**Att:** 44,375. **Ref:** A Wiley – (4-2-3-1): Reina, Mascherano▌, Kyrgiakos, Carragher (Ayala 57), Agger, Gerrard, Lucas, Maxi (Babel 42), Aquilani (Ngog 77), Benayoun, Kuyt. **Subs not used:** Cavalieri, Degen, El Zhar, Pacheco.
9th	● Hull	A	D 0–0	**Att:** 25,030. **Ref:** A Marriner – (4-2-3-1): Reina, Mascherano, Carragher, Kyrgiakos, Agger, Aquilani (Pacheco 73), Lucas, Gerrard, Babel (Robinson 87), Kuyt, El Zhar (Ngog 62). **Subs not used:** Cavalieri, Degen, Skrtel, Ayala.

● Barclays Premier League ● FA Cup ◖ Carling Cup ◖ UEFA Champions League ● Europa League ◖ FA Community Shield   ▌ Yellow Card ▐ Red Card

LIVERPOOL

BARCLAYS PREMIER LEAGUE GOALKEEPER STATS

Player	Minutes on pitch	Appearances	Match starts	Completed matches	Sub appearances	Subbed off	Saved with feet	Punched	Parried	Tipped over	Fumbled	Tipped round	Caught	Blocked	Clean sheets	Goals conceded	Save %	Saved	Resulting in goals	Opposition miss	Fouls committed	Free-kicks won	Yellow cards	Red cards
Jose Reina	3659	38	38	38	0	0	0	21	13	8	1	7	116	9	17	35	83.25	1	3	0	0	7	2	0

BARCLAYS PREMIER LEAGUE OUTFIELD PLAYER STATS

Player	Minutes on pitch	Appearances	Match starts	Completed matches	Substitute appearances	Subbed off	Goals scored	Assists	Shots on target	Shots off target	Crosses	Tackles made	Defensive clearances	Defensive blocks	Fouls committed	Free-kicks won	Caught offside	Yellow cards	Red cards
Daniel Agger	2108	23	23	21	0	2	0	0	4	15	7	38	27	6	11	29	0	0	0
Alberto Aquilani	872	18	9	2	9	7	1	6	10	9	11	27	2	1	10	23	0	0	0
Fabio Aurelio	722	14	8	4	6	4	0	3	4	2	35	0	4	0	8	4	1	1	0
Daniel Ayala	256	5	2	2	3	0	0	0	0	0	0	4	2	1	4	2	0	0	0
Ryan Babel	1051	25	9	3	16	6	4	1	14	12	17	2	2	1	18	8	5	1	0
Yossi Benayoun	1954	30	19	3	11	16	6	5	20	11	16	12	2	2	15	9	3	1	0
Jamie Carragher	3472	37	37	34	0	2	0	0	1	3	19	47	59	15	24	24	1	7	1
Stephen Darby	6	1	0	0	1	0	0	0	0	0	0	0	0	0	0	0	0	0	0
Philipp Degen	350	7	3	0	4	2	0	0	0	0	8	5	0	0	8	13	2	1	1
Andrea Dossena	61	2	1	0	1	1	0	0	1	0	1	1	0	0	2	0	0	0	0
Nathan Eccleston	16	1	0	0	1	0	0	0	0	0	0	0	0	0	1	0	0	0	0
Nabil El Zhar	95	3	1	0	2	1	0	0	2	0	3	0	0	0	0	3	0	0	0
Steven Gerrard	3016	33	32	26	1	6	9	7	54	36	134	34	10	4	28	32	0	6	0
Emiliano Insua	2913	31	30	28	1	2	0	5	5	9	67	30	18	6	28	19	0	1	0
Glen Johnson	2266	25	24	20	1	4	3	5	13	8	89	35	16	2	23	31	0	1	0
Martin Kelly	24	1	0	0	1	0	0	0	1	0	0	1	0	0	1	0	0	0	0
Dirk Kuyt	3190	37	35	22	2	13	9	4	37	23	64	23	19	2	43	33	11	3	0
Sotirios Kyrgiakos	1270	14	13	12	1	0	1	1	3	7	0	19	25	5	11	13	0	1	1
Leiva Lucas	3029	35	32	25	3	7	0	2	11	13	13	39	17	1	57	54	3	9	0
Javier Mascherano	2950	34	31	27	3	2	0	1	12	12	34	66	7	7	67	66	0	10	2
Maxi Rodriguez	1287	17	14	10	3	4	1	3	18	6	14	16	2	1	14	25	2	1	0
David Ngog	1108	24	10	3	14	7	5	3	18	13	12	7	5	0	14	21	10	1	0
Daniel Pacheco	58	4	0	0	4	0	0	0	3	0	2	1	0	0	0	1	1	0	0
Albert Riera	676	12	9	2	3	7	0	4	8	12	27	6	3	2	6	5	0	0	0
Jack Robinson	6	1	0	0	1	0	0	0	0	0	0	0	0	0	0	0	0	0	0
Martin Skrtel	1536	19	16	14	3	2	1	0	5	8	2	16	9	5	18	15	0	5	0
Jay Spearing	87	3	1	0	2	1	0	0	0	2	1	0	0	0	0	2	0	0	0
Fernando Torres	1800	22	20	10	2	10	18	3	40	28	22	10	8	1	34	47	21	5	0
Andriy Voronin	235	8	1	1	7	0	0	1	4	2	4	0	0	0	2	3	0	0	0

actim

BARCLAYS PREMIER LEAGUE

SEASON TOTALS

Goals scored	61
Goals conceded	35
Clean sheets	17
Shots on target	288
Shots off target	231
Shots per goal	8.51
Pens awarded	3
Pens scored	3
Pens conceded	4
Offsides	60
Corners	269
Crosses	602
Players used	30
Fouls committed	447
Free-kicks won	489

CARDS RECEIVED

56 5

SEQUENCES

Wins	4
(29/08/09–26/09/09)	
Losses	2
(04/10/09–17/10/09)	
Draws	2
(on two occasions)	
Undefeated	7
(26/12/09–06/02/10)	
Without win	3
(31/10/09–21/11/09)	
Undefeated home	10
(16/12/09–19/04/10)	
Undefeated away	3
(on two occasions)	
Without scoring	2
(on two occasions)	
Without conceding	4
(20/01/10–06/02/10)	
Scoring	7
(16/08/09–26/09/09)	
Conceding	4
(on two occasions)	

League position (graph)

AUG SEP OCT NOV DEC JAN FEB MAR APR MAY

LEAGUE POSITION AT THE END OF EACH MONTH: 7 3 5 5 7 5 6 6 7 7

SEASON INFORMATION

Highest position: 2
Lowest position: 15
Average goals scored per game: 1.61
Average goals conceded per game: 0.92

MATCH RECORDS

Goals scored per match

		W	D	L	Pts
Failed to score	11	0	5	6	5
Scored 1 goal	9	2	2	5	8
Scored 2 goals	9	7	2	0	23
Scored 3 goals	4	4	0	0	12
Scored 4+ goals	5	5	0	0	15

Goals conceded per match

		W	D	L	Pts
Clean sheet	17	12	5	0	41
Conceded 1 goal	9	4	2	3	14
Conceded 2 goals	10	2	2	6	8
Conceded 3 goals	2	0	0	2	0
Conceded 4+ goals	0	0	0	0	0

GOALS SCORED/CONCEDED PER FIVE-MINUTE INTERVALS

MINS	5	10	15	20	25	30	35	40	45	50	55	60	65	70	75	80	85	90
FOR	3	2	3	3	0	5	2	1	7	3	2	6	4	2	4	5	2	7
AGN	1	0	2	0	1	2	5	1	4	2	1	5	0	1	3	1	1	5

EARLIEST STRIKE

FERNANDO TORRES
(v Sunderland) 2:57

LATEST STRIKE

DAVID NGOG
(v Man Utd) 95:30

Dirk Kuyt

GOAL DETAILS

How the goals were struck

SCORED		CONCEDED
41	Right foot	15
12	Left foot	11
6	Header	8
2	Other	1

How the goals were struck

SCORED		CONCEDED
42	Open play	15
7	Cross	8
3	Corner	2
3	Penalty	3
0	Direct from free-kick	0
3	Free-kick	5
3	Own goal	2

Distance from goal

SCORED		CONCEDED
24	6YDS	18
31	18YDS	15
6	18+YDS	2

CLUB SUMMARY

FORMED	1880
MANAGER	Roberto Mancini
GROUND	City of Manchester Stadium
CAPACITY	48,000
NICKNAME	The Blues
WEBSITE	www.mcfc.co.uk

The New Football Pools PLAYER OF THE SEASON — *Carlos Tevez*

OVERALL
P	W	D	L	F	A	GD
48	25	14	9	95	57	38

BARCLAYS PREMIER LEAGUE
Pos	P	W	D	L	F	A	GD	Pts
5	38	18	13	7	73	45	28	67

HOME
Pos	P	W	D	L	F	A	GD	Pts
6	19	12	4	3	41	20	21	40

AWAY
Pos	P	W	D	L	F	A	GD	Pts
5	19	6	9	4	32	25	7	27

CUP PROGRESS DETAILS
Competition	Round reached	Knocked out by
FA Cup	R5	Stoke
Carling Cup	SF	Man Utd

BIGGEST WIN (ALL COMPS)
03/04/10 6–1 v Burnley

BIGGEST DEFEAT (ALL COMPS)
16/12/09 0–3 v Tottenham

THE PLAYER WITH THE MOST
GOALS SCORED	Carlos Tevez	**23**
SHOTS ON TARGET	Carlos Tevez	**66**
SHOTS OFF TARGET	Carlos Tevez	**43**
SHOTS WITHOUT SCORING	Robinho	**19**
ASSISTS	Craig Bellamy	**10**
OFFSIDES	Emmanuel Adebayor	**46**
FOULS	Gareth Barry	**57**
FOULS WITHOUT A CARD	Stephen Ireland	**6**
FREE-KICKS WON	Carlos Tevez	**62**
DEFENSIVE CLEARANCES	Kolo Toure	**50**

actim INDEX FOR THE 2009/10 BARCLAYS PREMIER LEAGUE SEASON

RANK	PLAYER	PTS
3	Carlos Tevez	673
18	Emmanuel Adebayor	505
20	Craig Bellamy	499

ATTENDANCE RECORD
HIGH	AVERAGE	Low
47,370	45,513	40,292
v Tottenham (05/05/2010)		v Blackburn (11/01/2010)

CLOCKWISE FROM ABOVE: Patrick Vieira scores in Manchester City's 6–1 thrashing of Burnley; Roberto Mancini congratulates Carlos Tevez after a goal against Manchester United in the Carling Cup semi-finals; Gareth Barry embraces Craig Bellamy after his strike in the win at Chelsea; Pablo Zabaleta shows his emotions after a defeat to Tottenham denies City a top-four finish

MANCHESTER City had to settle for Europa League qualification after they lost out in the battle to claim the fourth UEFA Champions League spot to Tottenham.

City utilised the wealth of their Middle Eastern backers to bring together a squad capable of upsetting the traditional 'big four', but they ultimately came up short as a defeat to rivals Spurs at Eastlands in the final week of the Barclays Premier League campaign ended their aspirations of reaching Europe's premier club competition for the first time in more than 40 years.

They did make an impression, with their victory at Chelsea's Stamford Bridge in February one of the stand-out performances by any team. They also had one of the top flight's best players in Argentinian Carlos Tevez, who finished the season with 23 goals in the League.

There were moments of magic, but at no stage did City put together a succession of performances and results that suggested they were worthy of a Champions League place.

To identify where it all went wrong is easy enough. Eight straight draws and a crushing defeat at Tottenham were a handicap that cost Mark Hughes his job in December and ultimately left too much ground to be made up.

There were some notable efforts during that winless streak but amid points gained at Villa Park and Anfield were those dropped against Burnley, Hull and Fulham on home soil, all from positions where any club with serious hopes of winning the title and, indeed, finishing in the top four would have expected to see out victories.

It was not the type of run anticipated by Sheikh Mansour and the Abu Dhabi United Group when they were ploughing £200million into player recruitment.

Still, Hughes' dismissal, or at least the manner of it, on 19th December was a surprise on a day when everyone seemed to know what was happening apart from the man himself. Hughes was left to take charge of one final game, at home to Sunderland, which he won before the dismissal was confirmed. New manager Roberto

Mancini landed in the middle of the turmoil to take charge of a team that had already reached the Carling Cup semi-finals. The Italian, who had led Internazionale to three Serie A titles, made an impressive start but he was quickly made aware that just achieving dominance in Manchester would not be easy, never mind over the rest of England.

The visit of United to Eastlands for the first leg of the Carling Cup semi-final was one of the highlights of the season. Trailing to Ryan Giggs' opener, Tevez scored twice against his old club. He scored in the return as well, but it was not enough as, for the second of what turned out to be three occasions, City fell to an injury-time goal against their neighbours.

Three meetings without a win against Stoke shortly afterwards cost City more points in the League and their place in the FA Cup, leaving just the top four to aim for, the position Mancini had specifically been brought in to attain.

It did not happen, even though he had Emmanuel Adebayor, Craig Bellamy, Patrick Vieira, Gareth Barry and Adam Johnson to call upon. Their collective attacking strength reached its peak with five first-half goals against Burnley, but it could not be sustained.

It is, however, worth remembering a few salient points. Firstly, Sheikh Mansour has never given the impression of being involved for the short term and, with the cash he can invest, City will only get better. Secondly, for all the recriminations that accompanied Hughes' exit after 18 months in charge, chairman Khaldoon al-Mubarak and chief executive Garry Cook moved with admirable speed to confirm that Mancini would remain at the helm even though he only has that Europa League place to show for his efforts so far. Finally, it is worth noting that 12 months previously City had finished in 10th spot. They were battling their way out of the third tier just 11 years ago.

Under Mancini the foundations have been laid. Now care and patience is required to ensure City's big ambitions are achieved.

City just missed out on a Champions League spot, but can look back on a season in which they established themselves at the top table

MANCHESTER CITY

RESULTS 2009/10

AUGUST

15th	● Blackburn	A	W 0–2	**Att:** 29,584. **Ref:** M Dean – (4-4-2): Given, Richards▮, Dunne, Toure, Bridge, Wright-Phillips, Ireland¹, Barry, Robinho (Tevez 69), Adebayor¹, Bellamy. **Subs not used:** Taylor, Onuoha, Zabaleta, Petrov, De Jong, Weiss.
22nd	● Wolverhampton	H	W 1–0	**Att:** 47,287. **Ref:** L Mason – (4-3-3): Given, Richards, Dunne, Toure, Bridge, Wright-Phillips, Ireland, Barry, Tevez (Bellamy 73), Adebayor¹, Robinho (De Jong 83). **Subs not used:** Taylor, Onuoha, Zabaleta, Petrov, Weiss.
27th	● Crystal Palace	A	W 0–2	**Att:** 14,725. **Ref:** D Deadman – (4-4-2): Given, Richards▮, Lescott, Toure, Bridge, Wright-Phillips¹, Ireland, Barry, Robinho (Bellamy 72), Adebayor, Tevez¹ (De Jong 86). **Subs not used:** Taylor, Onuoha, Zabaleta, Petrov, Weiss.
30th	● Portsmouth	A	W 0–1	**Att:** 17,826. **Ref:** H Webb – (4-3-3): Given, Richards (Zabaleta▮ 60), Toure, Lescott, Bridge, Wright-Phillips, Ireland (De Jong 76), Barry, Bellamy, Adebayor¹, Tevez. **Subs not used:** Taylor, Onuoha, Robinho, Petrov, Weiss.

SEPTEMBER

12th	● Arsenal	H	W 4–2	**Att:** 47,339. **Ref:** M Clattenburg – (4-4-2): Given, Richards, Toure, Lescott▮, Bridge, Wright-Phillips¹, Ireland (Petrov 73), Barry, De Jong▮, Adebayor▮¹, Bellamy¹. **Subs not used:** Taylor, Onuoha, Zabaleta, Sylvinho, Vidal, Weiss. Almunia OG.
20th	● Man Utd	A	L 4–3	**Att:** 75,066. **Ref:** M Atkinson – (4-5-1): Given, Richards, Lescott, Toure, Bridge, Wright-Phillips, Barry¹, De Jong (Petrov 83), Ireland, Bellamy¹², Tevez▮. **Subs not used:** Taylor, Zabaleta, Garrido, Weiss, Ball, Sylvinho.
23rd	● Fulham	H	W 2–1	**Att:** 24,507. **Ref:** S Attwell – (4-4-2): Given, Zabaleta, Toure¹, Lescott, Bridge, Wright-Phillips, De Jong (Weiss 91), Barry¹, Ireland (Petrov 75), Tevez, Bellamy. **Subs not used:** Taylor, Garrido, Sylvinho, Vidal, Ball. AET – Score after 90 mins 1–1.
28th	● West Ham	H	W 3–1	**Att:** 42,745. **Ref:** C Foy – (4-4-2): Given, Zabaleta, Toure, Lescott, Bridge▮, Wright-Phillips (Santa Cruz 80), De Jong, Barry (M Johnson 89), Petrov¹, Tevez², Bellamy. **Subs not used:** Taylor, Richards, Garrido, Sylvinho, Weiss.

OCTOBER

5th	● Aston Villa	A	D 1–1	**Att:** 37,924. **Ref:** M Dean – (4-3-3): Given, Zabaleta, Lescott, Toure, Bridge, De Jong▮ (Ireland 50), Barry, Wright-Phillips▮, Tevez (Santa Cruz 68), Bellamy¹, Adebayor. **Subs not used:** Taylor, Richards, Sylvinho, M Johnson, Petrov.
18th	● Wigan	A	D 1–1	**Att:** 20,005. **Ref:** A Wiley – (4-4-2): Given, Zabaleta▮, Richards, Lescott, Bridge, Wright-Phillips (Ireland 82), De Jong, Barry, Petrov¹, Tevez (Santa Cruz 82), Adebayor (Kompany 70). **Subs not used:** Taylor, M Johnson, Sylvinho, Weiss.
25th	● Fulham	H	D 2–2	**Att:** 44,906. **Ref:** K Friend – (4-3-3): Given, Richards, Toure (Kompany 90), Lescott¹, Bridge, De Jong (Ireland 72), Barry, Petrov¹ (Wright-Phillips 67), Bellamy, Adebayor, Tevez. **Subs not used:** Taylor, M Johnson, Sylvinho.
28th	● Scunthorpe	H	W 5–1	**Att:** 36,358. **Ref:** M Oliver – (4-4-2): Given, Zabaleta▮, Kompany, Lescott¹, Sylvinho, Wright-Phillips, De Jong▮, Barry (M Johnson¹ 72), Ireland¹ (Weiss 59), Tevez¹ (Mwaruwari 79), Santa Cruz¹. **Subs not used:** Taylor, Richards, Bridge, Bellamy.

NOVEMBER

1st	● Birmingham	A	D 0–0	**Att:** 21,462. **Ref:** M Dean – (4-4-2): Given, Zabaleta, Kompany, Lescott, Bridge▮, Wright-Phillips, De Jong (Ireland 60), Barry, Bellamy, Santa Cruz▮ (Petrov 66). **Subs not used:** Taylor, Richards, M Johnson, Sylvinho, Weiss.
7th	● Burnley	H	D 3–3	**Att:** 47,205. **Ref:** S Attwell – (4-4-2): Given, Zabaleta, Toure¹, Lescott, Bridge, Wright-Phillips¹, Ireland, Barry, Bellamy▮¹, Tevez (Petrov 73), Adebayor. **Subs not used:** Taylor, Richards, M Johnson, Santa Cruz, De Jong, Weiss.
21st	● Liverpool	A	D 2–2	**Att:** 44,164. **Ref:** P Dowd – (4-2-3-1): Given, Zabaleta, Toure (Onuoha 46), Lescott, Bridge, De Jong, Barry (Tevez 61), Wright-Phillips, Ireland¹, Bellamy, Adebayor¹. **Subs not used:** Taylor, M Johnson, Santa Cruz, Kompany, Weiss.
28th	● Hull	H	D 1–1	**Att:** 46,382. **Ref:** L Probert – (4-2-3-1): Given, Richards, Toure, Lescott, Bridge, De Jong▮, Ireland, Wright-Phillips¹, Tevez, Robinho (Bellamy 75), Adebayor (Santa Cruz 67). **Subs not used:** Taylor, Onuoha, M Johnson, Kompany, Weiss.

DECEMBER

2nd	● Arsenal	H	W 3–0	**Att:** 46,015. **Ref:** C Foy – (4-4-2): Given, Richards, Toure, Lescott, Bridge, Wright-Phillips¹ (Weiss¹ 77), Ireland, Barry, Bellamy▮, Tevez¹ (Kompany▮ 74), Adebayor. **Subs not used:** Taylor, Onuoha, M Johnson, Robinho, Santa Cruz.
5th	● Chelsea	H	W 2–1	**Att:** 47,348. **Ref:** H Webb – (4-2-3-1): Given, Richards (Onuoha 69), Toure, Lescott, Bridge (Kompany 76), De Jong, Barry¹, Wright-Phillips, Tevez¹, Robinho (Zabaleta 90), Adebayor¹. **Subs not used:** Taylor, M Johnson, Santa Cruz, Petrov.
12th	● Bolton	A	D 3–3	**Att:** 22,735. **Ref:** M Clattenburg – (4-4-2): Given, Richards¹, Toure, Lescott, Sylvinho▮, Wright-Phillips (Ireland 20), Kompany (Robinho 72), Barry, Bellamy▮▮, Adebayor (Santa Cruz 83), Tevez². **Subs not used:** Taylor, Onuoha, Zabaleta, Petrov.
16th	● Tottenham	A	L 3–0	**Att:** 35,891. **Ref:** A Wiley – (4-3-3): Given, Onuoha, Toure, Sylvinho▮, Ireland, De Jong▮ (Petrov 71), Barry, Tevez▮, Adebayor, Robinho (Santa Cruz 59). **Subs not used:** Taylor, Zabaleta, Mwaruwari, Kompany, Weiss.
19th	● Sunderland	H	W 4–3	**Att:** 44,735. **Ref:** A Marriner – (4-2-3-1): Given▮, Richards (Zabaleta▮ 22), Onuoha, Toure, Sylvinho, Ireland, Barry, Wright-Phillips (Kompany 52), Tevez¹, Bellamy¹ (Petrov 87), Santa Cruz². **Subs not used:** Taylor, Robinho, Adebayor, Weiss.
26th	● Stoke	H	W 2–0	**Att:** 47,325. **Ref:** L Mason – (4-2-3-1): Given, Zabaleta, Toure, Kompany, Sylvinho (Richards 66), De Jong, Barry, Robinho (Bellamy 70), Ireland, Petrov¹, Tevez¹ (Garrido 90). **Subs not used:** Taylor, Vidal, Weiss, Boyata.
28th	● Wolverhampton	A	W 0–3	**Att:** 28,957. **Ref:** M Jones – (4-5-1): Given, Zabaleta▮, Toure, Kompany, Richards, Petrov (Robinho 85), Ireland (Garrido¹ 55), De Jong, Barry, Bellamy, Tevez▮² (Sylvinho 90). **Subs not used:** Taylor, Vidal, Boyata, Weiss.

JANUARY

2nd	● Middlesbrough	A	W 0–1	**Att:** 12,474. **Ref:** S Attwell – (4-4-2): Given, Richards (Barry▮ 46), Garrido▮, Sylvinho, Kompany, Zabaleta, Petrov, Weiss (Bellamy 74), De Jong (Tevez 46), Mwaruwari¹, Boyata. **Subs not used:** Taylor, Vidal, Trippier, Tutte.
11th	● Blackburn	H	W 4–1	**Att:** 40,292. **Ref:** C Foy – (4-4-2): Given, Zabaleta▮, Richards¹, Kompany, Garrido, Petrov (Boyata 87), De Jong, Barry, Bellamy (Robinho 69), Tevez³, Mwaruwari (Santa Cruz 81). **Subs not used:** Taylor, Wright-Phillips, Sylvinho, Ibrahim.
16th	● Everton	A	L 2–0	**Att:** 37,378. **Ref:** A Marriner – (4-4-2): Given, Zabaleta, Richards, Kompany, Garrido, Petrov (Mwaruwari 46), De Jong, Barry, Bellamy, Tevez, Santa Cruz (Robinho 9 (Wright-Phillips 60)). **Subs not used:** Taylor, Onuoha, Sylvinho, Boyata.
19th	● Man Utd	H	W 2–1	**Att:** 46,067. **Ref:** M Dean – (4-3-3): Given, Zabaleta▮, Richards, Kompany (Boyata 69), Garrido, De Jong▮, Kompany, Barry, Wright-Phillips (Sylvinho 84), Tevez² (Mwaruwari 79), Bellamy. **Subs not used:** Taylor, Ireland, Robinho, Petrov.
24th	● Scunthorpe	A	W 2–4	**Att:** 8,861. **Ref:** K Friend – (4-3-3): Taylor, Onuoha¹, Boyata, Kompany, Sylvinho▮, Ibrahim, De Jong (Cunningham▮ 46), Ireland (Zabaleta 66), Mwaruwari, Robinho▮ (Bellamy 85), Petrov¹. **Subs not used:** Nielsen, Richards, Wright-Phillips, Barry.
27th	● Man Utd	A	L 3–1	**Att:** 74,576. **Ref:** H Webb – (4-3-3): Given, Richards, Kompany, Boyata, Garrido (Ireland 64), De Jong, Barry, Zabaleta, Wright-Phillips (Adebayor 72), Tevez▮¹, Bellamy. **Subs not used:** Taylor, Onuoha, Sylvinho, Petrov, Ibrahim. Agg: 4–3.

● Barclays Premier League ● FA Cup ● Carling Cup ● UEFA Champions League ● Europa League ● FA Community Shield　　▮ Yellow Card ▮ Red Card

RESULTS 2009/10

31st	● Portsmouth	H	W 2–0	**Att:** 44,015. **Ref:** M Atkinson – (4-3-1-2): Given, Zabaleta (Onuoha 37), Toure, Kompany[1] (Boyata 59), Garrido, De Jong[], Ireland, Barry, Petrov (Bellamy 73), Tevez, Adebayor[1]. **Subs not used:** Taylor, Wright-Phillips, Sylvinho, Ibrahim.

FEBRUARY

6th	● Hull	A	L 2–1	**Att:** 24,959. **Ref:** P Dowd – (4-4-2): Given, Zabaleta[], Toure[], Boyata[], Bridge (Petrov 85), Ireland (A Johnson 55), De Jong, Barry, Bellamy (Vieira[] 60), Tevez, Adebayor[1]. **Subs not used:** S Taylor, Onuoha, Wright-Phillips, Sylvinho.
9th	● Bolton	H	W 2–0	**Att:** 42,016. **Ref:** M Jones – (4-1-3-2): Given, Toure (Lescott 55), Kompany, Bridge (Wright-Phillips 68), De Jong, Vieira, Barry, A Johnson (Sylvinho 84), Tevez[1], Adebayor[1]. **Subs not used:** S Taylor, Onuoha, Ireland, Petrov.
13th	● Stoke	H	D 1–1	**Att:** 28,019. **Ref:** M Clattenburg – (4-4-1-1): Given, Zabaleta, Toure, Lescott, Bridge, Wright-Phillips[1], Barry, De Jong, Petrov (Santa Cruz 62), Ireland (Vieira 72), Adebayor. **Subs not used:** S Taylor, Onuoha, Garrido, Sylvinho, Boyata.
16th	● Stoke	A	D 1–1	**Att:** 26,778. **Ref:** A Wiley – (4-4-2): Given, Richards (Zabaleta 81), Toure, Lescott, Garrido (Wright-Phillips 60), A Johnson (Petrov 86), Vieira[], De Jong[], Barry[][], Santa Cruz, Adebayor. **Subs not used:** S Taylor, Bridge, Onuoha, Ireland.
21st	● Liverpool	H	D 0–0	**Att:** 47,203. **Ref:** P Walton – (4-5-1): Given, Zabaleta, Kompany, Lescott, Bridge, Wright-Phillips (Bellamy 68), Ireland (Ibrahim 75), De Jong, Barry[], A Johnson, Adebayor. **Subs not used:** Taylor, Richards, Santa Cruz, Sylvinho, Toure.
24th	● Stoke	A	L 3–1	**Att:** 21,813. **Ref:** S Bennett – (4-5-1): Given, Richards[], Onuoha, Lescott, Bridge (Santa Cruz 86), Zabaleta[], Ireland (Wright-Phillips 61), Kompany, Barry (Sylvinho 108), Bellamy[], Adebayor[]. **Subs not used:** Taylor, Garrido, De Jong, Boyata. AET – Score after 90 mins 1–1.
27th	● Chelsea	A	W 2–4	**Att:** 41,814. **Ref:** M Dean – (4-3-3): Given, Richards, Kompany, Lescott, Bridge (Santa Cruz 78), Zabaleta[], De Jong, Barry, Bellamy[2], Tevez[2] (Sylvinho 90), A Johnson (Wright-Phillips 60). **Subs not used:** S Taylor, Onuoha, Toure, Ibrahim.

MARCH

14th	● Sunderland	A	D 1–1	**Att:** 41,398. **Ref:** C Foy – (4-5-1): Given, Richards[] (Vieira 64), Kompany, Lescott, Bridge (Santa Cruz 32), Wright-Phillips[] (A Johnson[1] 72), Zabaleta, De Jong, Barry[], Bellamy, Tevez[]. **Subs not used:** S Taylor, Ireland, Sylvinho, Toure.
21st	● Fulham	A	W 1–2	**Att:** 25,359. **Ref:** L Probert – (4-4-2): Given, Zabaleta, Toure, Kompany, Garrido, A Johnson (Wright-Phillips 84), Vieira, Barry, Bellamy (Onuoha 90), Tevez[1], Santa Cruz[1] (De Jong 79). **Subs not used:** Taylor, Richards, Ireland, Sylvinho.
24th	● Everton	H	L 0–2	**Att:** 45,708. **Ref:** P Walton – (4-5-1): Given[], Richards (Vieira 75), Toure, Kompany, Zabaleta, A Johnson (Santa Cruz 57), Ireland (Wright-Phillips 41), De Jong[], Barry, Bellamy, Tevez[]. **Subs not used:** Taylor, Onuoha, Garrido, Sylvinho.
29th	● Wigan	H	W 3–0	**Att:** 43,534. **Ref:** S Attwell – (4-4-1-1): Given, Zabaleta, Toure, Kompany, Garrido[] (Onuoha 88), Wright-Phillips (Bellamy 46), Vieira, De Jong, A Johnson, Tevez[]3 (Sylvinho 88), Adebayor. **Subs not used:** S Taylor, Richards, Santa Cruz, Barry.

APRIL

3rd	● Burnley	A	W 1–6	**Att:** 21,330. **Ref:** A Wiley – (4-4-2): Given, Onuoha, Toure, Kompany[1], Sylvinho (De Jong 67), A Johnson, Vieira[1], Barry, Bellamy[1], Adebayor[2] (Santa Cruz 79), Tevez[1] (Nimely 83). **Subs not used:** Nielsen, Garrido, Wright-Phillips, Boyata.
11th	● Birmingham	H	W 5–1	**Att:** 45,209. **Ref:** P Dowd – (4-4-1-1): Given, Onuoha[1], Kompany, Toure, Garrido, A Johnson (Cunningham 90), De Jong, Barry, Bellamy (Wright-Phillips 80), Tevez[2] (Santa Cruz 87), Adebayor[2]. **Subs not used:** Nielsen, Kay, Boyata, Ibrahim.
17th	● Man Utd	H	L 0–1	**Att:** 47,019. **Ref:** M Atkinson – (4-4-2): Given, Onuoha, Kompany, Toure, Bridge, A Johnson[] (Vieira 65), De Jong (Ireland 78), Barry, Bellamy, Tevez, Adebayor (Wright-Phillips 74). **Subs not used:** Nielsen, Zabaleta, Santa Cruz, Boyata.
24th	● Arsenal	A	D 0–0	**Att:** 60,086. **Ref:** M Dean – (4-1-4-1): Given (Nielsen 73), Zabaleta[], Toure, Kompany, Bridge (Richards 27), De Jong, Vieira (Adebayor 52), Barry, A Johnson, Bellamy[], Tevez. **Subs not used:** Onuoha, Ireland, Wright-Phillips, Santa Cruz.

MAY

1st	● Aston Villa	H	W 3–1	**Att:** 47,102. **Ref:** M Clattenburg – (4-4-2): Fulop, Zabaleta, Toure, Kompany[], Bridge, A Johnson (Wright-Phillips 77), De Jong, Vieira, Bellamy[1], Adebayor[1], Tevez[1] (Richards 88). **Subs not used:** Nielsen, Onuoha, Santa Cruz, Garrido, Sylvinho.
5th	● Tottenham	H	L 0–1	**Att:** 47,370. **Ref:** S Bennett – (4-4-1-1): Fulop, Zabaleta, Toure, Kompany, Bridge, A Johnson (Wright-Phillips 71), De Jong, Barry (Vieira 57), Bellamy (Santa Cruz 84), Tevez, Adebayor. **Subs not used:** Nielsen, Richards, Onuoha, Sylvinho.
9th	● West Ham	A	D 1–1	**Att:** 34,989. **Ref:** H Webb – (4-4-2): Fulop, Zabaleta, Toure, Kompany, Sylvinho (Richards 73), Wright-Phillips[1], Vieira, De Jong, A Johnson (Cunningham 89), Santa Cruz (Tevez 73), Adebayor. **Subs not used:** Nielsen, Garrido, Boyata, Ibrahim.

● Barclays Premier League ● FA Cup ● Carling Cup ● UEFA Champions League ● Europa League ● FA Community Shield   ▌ Yellow Card ▌ Red Card

Emmanuel Adebayor celebrates his goal against former club Arsenal in Manchester City's 4–2 win in September

BARCLAYS PREMIER LEAGUE GOALKEEPER STATS

Player	Minutes on pitch	Appearances	Match starts	Completed matches	Sub appearances	Subbed off	SAVES BREAKDOWN								Clean sheets	Goals conceded	Save %	PENALTIES			Fouls committed	Free-kicks won	Yellow cards	Red cards
							Saved with feet	Punched	Parried	Tipped over	Fumbled	Tipped round	Caught	Blocked				Saved	Resulting in goals	Opposition miss				
Marton Fulop	289	3	3	3	0	0	1	2	3	1	0	0	7	0	0	3	33.33	0	0	0	0	1	0	0
Shay Given	3358	35	35	34	0	1	4	8	28	1	1	5	79	6	10	42	75.72	2	5	0	0	1	2	0
Gunnar Nielsen	26	1	0	0	1	0	0	1	0	0	0	0	0	1	0	0	0	0	0	0	0	0	0	0

BARCLAYS PREMIER LEAGUE OUTFIELD PLAYER STATS

Player	Minutes on pitch	Appearances	Match starts	Completed matches	Substitute appearances	Subbed off	Goals scored	Assists	Shots on target	Shots off target	Crosses	Tackles made	Defensive clearances	Defensive blocks	Fouls committed	Free-kicks won	Caught offside	Yellow cards	Red cards
Emmanuel Adebayor	2357	26	25	20	1	5	14	6	32	18	11	24	22	3	31	28	46	1	0
Gareth Barry	3211	34	34	31	0	3	2	8	14	11	31	104	27	4	57	53	4	4	0
Craig Bellamy	2555	32	26	19	6	6	10	10	36	18	55	30	1	1	24	25	22	5	1
Dedryk Boyata	138	3	1	1	2	0	0	0	0	0	0	6	5	0	3	1	0	1	0
Wayne Bridge	2007	23	23	17	0	6	0	0	10	1	22	52	10	10	12	16	0	2	0
Greg Cunningham	8	2	0	0	2	0	0	0	0	0	0	0	0	0	0	0	0	0	0
Nigel de Jong	2812	34	30	24	4	6	0	0	5	4	0	69	13	7	42	47	0	7	0
Richard Dunne	191	2	2	2	0	0	0	0	0	0	0	28	7	1	1	3	0	0	0
Javier Garrido	671	9	7	5	2	2	1	0	2	1	5	14	8	0	6	9	2	1	0
Abdisalam Ibrahim	20	1	0	0	1	0	0	0	0	0	1	0	0	0	0	2	0	0	0
Stephen Ireland	1562	22	16	10	6	6	2	2	8	8	3	44	7	5	6	15	2	0	0
Adam Johnson	1230	16	14	4	2	10	1	8	11	6	34	13	0	1	9	17	4	1	0
Michael Johnson	4	1	0	0	1	0	0	0	0	0	0	0	0	0	0	0	0	0	0
Vincent Kompany	2064	25	21	19	4	2	2	2	6	2		25	26	11	24	13	0	2	0
Joleon Lescott	1687	18	17	17	1	0	1	1	2	6	0	20	29	13	10	15	0	1	0
Benjani Mwaruwari	129	2	1	0	1	1	0	0	3	0	2	0	0	0	0	2	1	0	0
Alex Nimely	10	1	0	0	1	0	0	0	0	0	0	1	0	0	0	0	0	0	0
Nedum Onuoha	633	10	5	5	5	0	1	1	2	2	0	19	5	2	4	6	0	0	0
Martin Petrov	788	16	8	3	8	5	4	3	11	16	14	1	0	0	4	4	1	0	0
Micah Richards	1758	23	19	13	4	6	3	1	6	6	10	46	12	6	34	23	0	2	0
Robinho	566	10	6	0	4	7	0	3	9	10	2	27	0	0	3	13	7	0	0
Roque Santa Cruz	719	19	6	2	13	4	3	0	7	10	3	6	2	0	4	4	6	1	0
Sylvinho	532	10	6	3	4	3	0	2	0	0	2	15	0	5	4	2	0	2	0
Carlos Tevez	3041	35	32	21	3	11	23	7	66	43	16	38	0	2	36	62	17	6	0
Kolo Toure	2897	31	31	28	0	3	1	0	6	2	1	78	50	12	17	19	0	1	0
Patrick Vieira	879	13	8	7	5	1	1	2	7	0	1	14	7	0	21	20	0	2	0
Shaun Wright-Phillips	1886	30	19	12	11	7	4	8	15	17	30	39	4	4	18	42	6	2	0
Pablo Zabaleta	2267	27	23	21	4	1	0	1	1	9	2	42	17	3	34	30	1	9	1

actim

SEASON TOTALS

Goals scored	73
Goals conceded	45
Clean sheets	11
Shots on target	254
Shots off target	201
Shots per goal	6.23
Pens awarded	5
Pens scored	5
Pens conceded	7
Offsides	119
Corners	239
Crosses	262
Players used	31
Fouls committed	406
Free-kicks won	471

CARDS RECEIVED

52   2

SEQUENCES

Wins	4
(on two occasions)	
Losses	–
(–)	
Draws	7
(05/10/09–28/11/09)	
Undefeated	10
(28/09/09–12/12/09)	
Without win	7
(05/10/09–28/11/09)	
Undefeated home	13
(22/08/09–21/02/10)	
Undefeated away	7
(16/02/10–09/05/10)	
Without scoring	2
(17/04/10–24/04/10)	
Without conceding	3
(15/08/09–30/08/09)	
Scoring	9
(15/08/09–25/10/09)	
Conceding	7
(07/11/09–19/12/09)	

League position chart

AUG	SEP	OCT	NOV	DEC	JAN	FEB	MAR	APR	MAY
4	5	6	7	5	6	5	5	6	5

LEAGUE POSITION AT THE END OF EACH MONTH

SEASON INFORMATION

Highest position: 2
Lowest position: 9
Average goals scored per game: 1.92
Average goals conceded per game: 1.18

MATCH RECORDS

Goals scored per match

		W	D	L	Pts
Failed to score	8	0	3	5	3
Scored 1 goal	9	2	6	1	12
Scored 2 goals	8	6	2	0	20
Scored 3 goals	7	4	2	1	14
Scored 4+ goals	6	6	0	0	18

Goals conceded per match

		W	D	L	Pts
Clean sheet	11	8	3	0	27
Conceded 1 goal	15	7	6	2	27
Conceded 2 goals	7	2	2	3	8
Conceded 3 goals	4	1	2	1	5
Conceded 4+ goals	1	0	0	1	0

EARLIEST STRIKE

EMMANUEL ADEBAYOR
(v Blackburn) 2:29

LATEST STRIKE

STEPHEN IRELAND
(v Blackburn) 90:53

Nigel de Jong

GOAL DETAILS

How the goals were struck

SCORED		CONCEDED
44	Right foot	22
20	Left foot	11
9	Header	11
0	Other	1

How the goals were struck

SCORED		CONCEDED
50	Open play	28
7	Cross	4
7	Corner	2
5	Penalty	5
3	Direct from free-kick	1
1	Free-kick	4
0	Own goal	1

Distance from goal

SCORED		CONCEDED
27	6YDS	18
38	18YDS	19
8	18+YDS	8

GOALS SCORED/CONCEDED
PER FIVE-MINUTE INTERVALS

MINS	5	10	15	20	25	30	35	40	45	50	55	60	65	70	75	80	85	90
FOR	5	3	1	4	1	3	4	6	10	2	4	5	1	4	5	4	3	8
AGN	1	2	2	4	2	0	3	2	5	2	3	0	3	1	4	2	3	6

CLUB SUMMARY

FORMED	1878
MANAGER	Sir Alex Ferguson
GROUND	Old Trafford
CAPACITY	76,212
NICKNAME	The Red Devils
WEBSITE	www.manutd.com

The New **Football Pools** PLAYER OF THE SEASON — *Wayne Rooney*

OVERALL

P	W	D	L	F	A	GD
56	39	6	11	120	47	73

BARCLAYS PREMIER LEAGUE

Pos	P	W	D	L	F	A	GD	Pts
2	38	27	4	7	86	28	58	85

HOME

Pos	P	W	D	L	F	A	GD	Pts
2	19	16	1	2	52	12	40	49

AWAY

Pos	P	W	D	L	F	A	GD	Pts
1	19	11	3	5	34	16	18	36

CUP PROGRESS DETAILS

Competition	Round reached	Knocked out by
Champions League	QF	Bayern Munich
FA Cup	R3	Leeds
Carling Cup	WON	

BIGGEST WIN (ALL COMPS)

5-0 on 3 occasions

BIGGEST DEFEAT (ALL COMPS)

19/12/09 0-3 v Fulham

THE PLAYER WITH THE MOST

GOALS SCORED	Wayne Rooney	**26**
SHOTS ON TARGET	Wayne Rooney	**94**
SHOTS OFF TARGET	Wayne Rooney	**64**
SHOTS WITHOUT SCORING	Patrice Evra	**26**
ASSISTS	Ryan Giggs	**11**
OFFSIDES	Wayne Rooney	**26**
FOULS	Antonio Valencia	**42**
FOULS WITHOUT A CARD	John O'Shea	**12**
FREE-KICKS WON	Patrice Evra	**44**
DEFENSIVE CLEARANCES	Nemanja Vidic	**49**

actim INDEX FOR THE 2009/10 BARCLAYS PREMIER LEAGUE SEASON

RANK	PLAYER	PTS
7	Wayne Rooney	585
10	Patrice Evra	574
13	Antonio Valencia	544

ATTENDANCE RECORD

HIGH	AVERAGE	LOW
75,316	74,864	73,709
v Stoke (09/05/2010)		v Wolverhampton (15/12/2009)

CLOCKWISE FROM ABOVE: Nemanja Vidic reacts after defeat to Chelsea at Old Trafford; Nani shows his hurt after Manchester United are knocked out of the Champions League by Bayern Munich; Wayne Rooney scores one of his four goals in the 4-0 thrashing of Hull; Sir Alex Ferguson holds the Carling Cup trophy

MANCHESTER UNITED'S crown finally slipped following a hat-trick of Barclays Premier League titles as they lost out to Chelsea in the battle at the top of English football.

Wayne Rooney was the star of the season, but United just missed out on an unprecedented fourth title in a row

The eventual single-point margin made it look as though there was little to separate the two sides but, from the moment that the Blues' Joe Cole flicked the ball past Edwin Van der Sar at Old Trafford at the beginning of April, there was a sense of inevitability about the outcome.

There were a number of trigger points that led to United's downfall, the first coming in only the second game as they lost 1–0 at Burnley. It seems an astonishing result in retrospect. It was certainly a shock, although the Burnley of August were far removed from the team who sank towards relegation in the second half of the campaign. However, Michael Carrick's missed penalty against the Clarets was a microcosm of the season as a chance of history ultimately went begging.

No side has won four championships in a row. Considering the English League has been contended since 1888, that emphasises how gargantuan that achievement would be. And not many sides in the long history of the competition will have won a title having been forced to operate without two teams' worth of defenders, as United had to do on a couple of occasions, notably at Fulham just before Christmas. Losing seven times in a season is usually terminal these days too.

It is staggering to note, therefore, that had they beaten Blackburn in early April, rather than drawn 0–0 – a result that came in the aftermath of a shattering European exit to Bayern Munich – United would have been champions and a place in the record books would have been theirs.

It was always going to be a testing season goals-wise, with forwards Cristiano Ronaldo and Carlos Tevez having departed for Real Madrid and Manchester City respectively. However, Wayne Rooney relished the central striking role he was offered and ended the season considered firmly among the world's best players.

Rooney's performances were truly staggering at times. Better sides than Hull would have failed to stop him the day he netted all four against the Tigers. He also grabbed a hat-trick against Portsmouth and scored twice in a game on five occasions. When the major end-of-season awards were handed out, they were all marked for display on the England striker's mantelpiece.

United's problem was that, over the course of the season, Rooney lacked sufficient support. The fear of what would happen when he was not there to lead the attack was justified by those results against Chelsea and Blackburn, when the talismanic forward was missing with injuries sustained on European duty.

Ryan Giggs was majestic at the start of the season, rolling back the years with a string of performances that saw him crowned as the BBC Sports Personality of the Year in December. Fellow midfielder Paul Scholes was the veteran who shone in the latter part of this season.

Nani suddenly started to show the form that had persuaded Sir Alex Ferguson to sign him from Sporting Lisbon. Antonio Valencia gained more consistency in his debut United season, even if there is still plenty of room for improvement from the Ecuador winger.

Michael Owen missed much of the season with injury, although he did score in United's Carling Cup final win against Aston Villa.

Dimitar Berbatov once again displayed moments of sublime skill and, although they were countered by long periods of lethargy, he may still have a key role in 2010/11.

Against the backdrop of continuing anger from some sections of Old Trafford at the club's debts, now is a time for cool heads. Berbatov is one of the coolest of all, and if he can show his best side more often in the coming season then the title may not be absent for too long.

MANCHESTER UNITED

RESULTS 2009/10

AUGUST

9th	● Chelsea	N	D 2–2	**Att:** 85,896. **Ref:** C Foy – (4-4-2): Foster, O'Shea (F Da Silva 76), Ferdinand, J Evans, Evra, Park (Giggs 75), Fletcher (Scholes 75), Carrick, Nani▌ (Valencia 62), Rooney▌, Berbatov▌ (Owen▌ 75). **Subs not used:** Kuszczak, Gibson. Chelsea win 4–1 on penalties.
16th	● Birmingham	H	W 1–0	**Att:** 75,062. **Ref:** L Mason – (4-4-2): Foster, F Da Silva, O'Shea, J Evans (Brown 75), Evra, Valencia, Fletcher▌, Scholes, Nani (Giggs 46), Berbatov (Owen 74), Rooney¹. **Subs not used:** Kuszczak, Anderson, Gibson, De Laet.
19th	● Burnley	A	L 1–0	**Att:** 20,872. **Ref:** A Wiley – (4-4-2): Foster, O'Shea, J Evans, Brown (Neville 71), Evra, Park, Anderson (Valencia 59), Carrick, Giggs, Owen (Berbatov 63), Rooney▌. **Subs not used:** Kuszczak, Scholes, Gibson, De Laet.
22nd	● Wigan	A	W 0–5	**Att:** 18,164. **Ref:** H Webb – (4-4-2): Foster, Neville, Vidic, J Evans (O'Shea 72), Evra▌, Valencia, Fletcher, Scholes▌ (Gibson 72), Nani¹, Rooney² (Owen¹ 71), Berbatov¹. **Subs not used:** Kuszczak, Giggs, Welbeck, F Da Silva.
29th	● Arsenal	H	W 2–1	**Att:** 75,095. **Ref:** M Dean – (4-4-1-1): Foster, O'Shea, Brown▌, Vidic, Evra▌, Valencia (Park 63), Fletcher, Carrick, Nani, Giggs (Berbatov 85), Rooney▌. **Subs not used:** Kuszczak, Neville, Owen, Anderson, Scholes. Diaby OG.

SEPTEMBER

12th	● Tottenham	A	W 1–3	**Att:** 35,785. **Ref:** A Marriner – (4-4-2): Foster, O'Shea, Ferdinand, Vidic▌, Evra, Fletcher, Scholes▌, Anderson¹ (Nani 81), Giggs¹, Berbatov (Carrick 62), Rooney¹. **Subs not used:** Kuszczak, Owen, F Da Silva, J Evans, Valencia.
15th	● Besiktas	A	W 0–1	**Att:** 32,000. **Ref:** N Rizzoli – (4-5-1): Foster, Neville, J Evans, Vidic▌, Evra, Valencia (Park 83), Carrick (Berbatov 63), Scholes¹, Anderson, Nani, Rooney (Owen 64). **Subs not used:** Kuszczak, Brown, F Da Silva, Gibson.
20th	● Man City	H	W 4–3	**Att:** 75,066. **Ref:** M Atkinson – (4-4-2): Foster, O'Shea, Ferdinand, Vidic▌, Evra, Park (Valencia 62), Anderson▌ (Carrick 90), Fletcher², Giggs, Berbatov (Owen¹ 78), Rooney¹. **Subs not used:** Kuszczak, Neville, Nani, J Evans.
23rd	● Wolverhampton	H	W 1–0	**Att:** 51,160. **Ref:** P Walton – (4-4-2): Kuszczak, Neville, Brown, J Evans, F Da Silva▌, Welbeck¹ (King 81), Carrick, Gibson, Nani, Owen (Valencia 69), Macheda (De Laet 31). **Subs not used:** Amos, Ferdinand, Tosic, Eikrem.
26th	● Stoke	A	W 0–2	**Att:** 27,500. **Ref:** H Webb – (4-4-2): Foster, O'Shea▌, Ferdinand, Vidic▌, Evra, Valencia, Scholes▌ (Carrick 80), Fletcher, Nani (Giggs 55), Berbatov¹, Rooney (Owen 80). **Subs not used:** Kuszczak, Neville, Anderson, J Evans.
30th	● Wolfsburg	H	W 2–1	**Att:** 74,037. **Ref:** V Kassai – (4-4-2): Kuszczak, O'Shea, Ferdinand, Vidic▌, Evra, Valencia (Fletcher 82), Carrick▌, Anderson, Giggs¹, Owen (Berbatov 20), Rooney. **Subs not used:** Foster, Brown, Nani, Scholes, F Da Silva.

OCTOBER

3rd	● Sunderland	H	D 2–2	**Att:** 75,114. **Ref:** A Wiley – (4-4-2): Foster, O'Shea, Vidic, J Evans, Evra, Nani, Fletcher▌ (Carrick 71), Scholes▌ (Anderson 46), Welbeck (Valencia 71), Rooney, Berbatov¹. **Subs not used:** Kuszczak, Ferdinand, Brown, F Da Silva. Ferdinand OG.
17th	● Bolton	H	W 2–1	**Att:** 75,103. **Ref:** M Clattenburg – (4-4-2): Van der Sar, Neville, Ferdinand, J Evans (O'Shea 83), Valencia¹, Carrick, Anderson (Scholes 86), Giggs, Owen (Welbeck 83), Berbatov. **Subs not used:** Kuszczak, Brown, Nani, Macheda. Knight OG.
21st	● CSKA Moscow	A	W 0–1	**Att:** 37,500. **Ref:** C Bo Larsen – (4-1-4-1): Van der Sar, Neville, Ferdinand (Brown 57), Vidic, F Da Silva (Carrick 88), O'Shea, Valencia¹, Scholes (Owen 71), Anderson, Nani, Berbatov▌. **Subs not used:** Kuszczak, Welbeck, J Evans, Macheda.
25th	● Liverpool	A	L 2–0	**Att:** 44,188. **Ref:** A Marriner – (4-4-1-1): Van der Sar, Neville, O'Shea, Vidic▌, Evra▌, Valencia, Carrick, Scholes (Nani 74), Giggs, Berbatov (Owen 74), Rooney. **Subs not used:** Foster, Neville, Anderson, F Da Silva, J Evans.
27th	● Barnsley	A	W 0–2	**Att:** 20,019. **Ref:** C Foy – (4-4-2): Foster, Neville▌, Brown, J Evans, F Da Silva▌, Obertan, R Da Silva, Anderson, Welbeck¹ (Tosic▌ 53), Macheda, Owen¹ (De Laet 65). **Subs not used:** Amos, O'Shea, C Evans, King, James.
31st	● Blackburn	H	W 2–0	**Att:** 74,658. **Ref:** P Dowd – (4-4-2): Van der Sar, O'Shea, Brown, J Evans, Evra, Valencia, Carrick, Anderson, Nani (Obertan 63), Berbatov▌ (Owen 79), Rooney¹. **Subs not used:** Kuszczak, Scholes, F Da Silva, Fletcher, De Laet.

NOVEMBER

3rd	● CSKA Moscow	H	D 3–3	**Att:** 73,718. **Ref:** O Benquerenca – (4-4-2): Van der Sar, Neville, Brown, J Evans, F Da Silva (Evra 59), Valencia, Fletcher▌, Scholes¹, Nani (Rooney 58), Macheda (Obertan¹ 82), Owen¹. **Subs not used:** Kuszczak, Anderson, O'Shea, Gibson. Shchennikov OG.
8th	● Chelsea	A	L 1–0	**Att:** 41,836. **Ref:** M Atkinson – (4-3-3): Van der Sar, O'Shea, Brown, J Evans▌, Evra, Fletcher, Carrick, Anderson (Owen 84), Valencia▌, Rooney▌, Giggs (Obertan 84). **Subs not used:** Kuszczak, Park, F Da Silva, Gibson.
21st	● Everton	H	W 3–0	**Att:** 75,169. **Ref:** S Bennett – (4-4-2): Van der Sar, R Da Silva▌ (Scholes 63), Brown, Vidic, Evra, Valencia¹, Fletcher¹, Carrick¹▌ (Gibson 83), Giggs, Rooney, Owen (Obertan 74). **Subs not used:** Kuszczak, Anderson, Welbeck, De Laet.
25th	● Besiktas	H	L 0–1	**Att:** 74,242. **Ref:** S Lannoy – (4-4-2): Foster, Neville, Vidic, Brown, R Da Silva (Evra 73), Obertan, Gibson (Carrick 73), Anderson, Park (Owen 68), Macheda, Welbeck. **Subs not used:** Kuszczak, Nani, Scholes, Fletcher.
28th	● Portsmouth	A	W 1–4	**Att:** 20,482. **Ref:** M Dean – (4-4-1-1): Kuszczak, Neville▌, Brown, Vidic▌, Evra, Fletcher, Carrick (Anderson 76), Scholes▌, Giggs¹, Valencia, Rooney⁵. **Subs not used:** Foster, Owen, Berbatov, Park, Nani, De Laet.

DECEMBER

1st	● Tottenham	H	W 2–0	**Att:** 57,212. **Ref:** M Clattenburg – (4-4-2): Kuszczak, Neville, Brown, Vidic, De Laet▌, Park, Gibson¹² , Anderson (Tosic 82), Obertan (Carrick 62), Welbeck, Berbatov (Macheda 62). **Subs not used:** Amos, Owen, Giggs, Fletcher.
5th	● West Ham	A	W 0–4	**Att:** 34,980. **Ref:** P Walton – (4-2-3-1): Kuszczak, Fletcher, Neville (Carrick 34), Brown, Evra, Gibson¹ (Berbatov 67), Anderson, Valencia¹, Scholes¹▌, Giggs, Rooney¹ (Owen 72). **Subs not used:** Foster, Park, Nani, De Laet.
8th	● Wolfsburg	A	W 1–3	**Att:** 29,000. **Ref:** B Kuipers – (4-2-3-1): Kuszczak, Park, Fletcher, Carrick, Evra, Gibson, Scholes, Nani (Valencia 74), Welbeck (Obertan 74), Anderson, Owen⁵. **Subs not used:** Foster, Eikrem, James, Gill, Stewart.
12th	● Aston Villa	H	L 0–1	**Att:** 75,130. **Ref:** M Atkinson – (4-2-3-1): Kuszczak, Fletcher, Brown, Vidic, Evra, Carrick, Anderson (Gibson 68), Valencia, Giggs (Owen 46), Park (Berbatov 63), Rooney▌. **Subs not used:** Foster, Welbeck, Obertan, De Laet.
15th	● Wolverhampton	H	W 3–0	**Att:** 73,709. **Ref:** S Bennett – (4-4-2): Kuszczak, De Laet, Carrick, Vidic¹ (Fletcher 60), Evra, Valencia¹, Scholes, Gibson▌, Obertan (Welbeck 70), Berbatov, Rooney¹ (Owen 75). **Subs not used:** Foster, Anderson, Park, F Da Silva.
19th	● Fulham	A	L 3–0	**Att:** 25,700. **Ref:** H Webb – (4-4-2): Kuszczak, Fletcher, De Laet (F Da Silva 58), Carrick, Evra, Valencia, Scholes▌, Anderson, Gibson (Berbatov 58), Owen (Welbeck 72), Rooney. **Subs not used:** Foster, Park, Tosic, Obertan.
27th	● Hull	A	W 1–3	**Att:** 24,627. **Ref:** A Wiley – (4-4-2): Kuszczak, R Da Silva▌, Vidic, Brown, Evra▌, Valencia (Park 63), Carrick, Fletcher, Giggs (Obertan 78), Berbatov¹, Rooney¹. **Subs not used:** Foster, Owen, Welbeck, F Da Silva, De Laet. Dawson OG.
30th	● Wigan	H	W 5–0	**Att:** 74,560. **Ref:** L Mason – (4-4-2): Kuszczak, R Da Silva▌, Brown, Vidic (Anderson 68), Evra (F Da Silva 68), Valencia¹, Carrick¹, Fletcher, Park, Berbatov¹ (Welbeck 68), Rooney¹. **Subs not used:** Amos, Neville, Owen, Obertan.

● Barclays Premier League ● FA Cup ● Carling Cup ● UEFA Champions League ● Europa League ● FA Community Shield   ▌ Yellow Card ▌ Red Card

RESULTS 2009/10

JANUARY

3rd	● Leeds	H	L 0–1	**Att:** 74,526. **Ref:** C Foy – (4-4-2): Kuszczak, Neville, Brown∎, J Evans, F Da Silva, Welbeck (Valencia 57), Gibson∎, Anderson (Owen 69), Obertan (Giggs 57), Berbatov, Rooney. **Subs not used:** Amos, Tosic, Carrick, R Da Silva.
9th	● Birmingham	A	D 1–1	**Att:** 28,907. **Ref:** M Clattenburg – (4-5-1): Kuszczak, R Da Silva, Brown∎, J Evans, Evra, Valencia, Carrick, Scholes (Diouf 81), Fletcher∎∎, Park (Giggs 66), Rooney. **Subs not used:** Amos, Neville, Owen, Anderson, F Da Silva. Dann OG.
16th	◐ Burnley	H	W 3–0	**Att:** 75,120. **Ref:** L Probert – (4-4-2): Van der Sar, Neville, Brown, J Evans, Evra, Valencia, Carrick (Anderson 66), Scholes, Nani, Berbatov[1] (Owen 73), Rooney[1] Diouf[1] 74). **Subs not used:** Kuszczak, Park, F Da Silva, R Da Silva.
19th	◯ Man City	A	L 2–1	**Att:** 46,067. **Ref:** M Dean – (4-3-3): Van der Sar∎, R Da Silva (Diouf 90), Brown, J Evans, Evra, Anderson (Owen 72), Carrick, Fletcher, Valencia (Scholes 88), Rooney, Giggs[1]. **Subs not used:** Kuszczak, Neville, Park, F Da Silva.
23rd	● Hull	H	W 4–0	**Att:** 73,933. **Ref:** S Bennett – (4-4-2): Van der Sar, R Da Silva, Ferdinand, J Evans, Evra (F Da Silva 87), Nani, Scholes (Gibson 72), Fletcher, Park, Owen (Berbatov 72), Rooney∎[4]. **Subs not used:** Kuszczak, Brown, Carrick, Valencia.
27th	◯ Man City	H	W 3–1	**Att:** 74,576. **Ref:** H Webb – (4-3-3): Van der Sar, Brown (Brown 74), Ferdinand, J Evans, Evra, Fletcher, Scholes∎, Carrick[1], Nani∎ (Valencia 90), Rooney[1], Giggs. **Subs not used:** Kuszczak, Owen, Berbatov, Park, Vidic. Agg: 4–3.
31st	● Arsenal	A	W 1–3	**Att:** 60,091. **Ref:** C Foy – (4-3-3): Van der Sar, R Da Silva, J Evans, Brown, Evra, Scholes (Giggs 71), Carrick, Fletcher, Nani[1] (Berbatov 89), Rooney[1], Park[1] (Valencia 87). **Subs not used:** Kuszczak, Owen, Gibson, De Laet.

FEBRUARY

6th	● Portsmouth	H	W 5–0	**Att:** 74,684. **Ref:** L Mason – (4-4-2): Van der Sar, Neville, Brown, J Evans, Evra, Valencia, Carrick[1], Fletcher (Gibson 66), Nani, Berbatov[1] (Owen 66), Rooney[1] (Diouf∎ 66). **Subs not used:** Kuszczak, Park, F Da Silva, De Laet. Vanden Borre OG, Wilson OG.
10th	● Aston Villa	A	D 1–1	**Att:** 42,788. **Ref:** P Walton – (4-3-3): Van der Sar, R Da Silva, Brown, J Evans∎, Evra, Scholes (Valencia 46), Carrick, Fletcher, Nani∎, Rooney, Giggs (Berbatov 73). **Subs not used:** Foster, Neville, Owen, Park, Gibson. Collins OG.
16th	◐ AC Milan	A	W 2–3	**Att:** 80,000. **Ref:** O Benquerenca – (4-3-3): Van der Sar, R Da Silva (Brown 90), Ferdinand, J Evans, Evra, Nani (Valencia 64), Carrick∎∎, Scholes[1], Fletcher, Park, Rooney[2]. **Subs not used:** Kuszczak, Neville, Owen, Berbatov, Gibson.
20th	● Everton	A	L 3–1	**Att:** 39,448. **Ref:** H Webb – (4-3-3): Van der Sar, Neville, Brown, J Evans, Evra, Valencia (Owen 81), Fletcher∎, Carrick, Park (Obertan 66), Rooney, Berbatov[1] (Scholes 66). **Subs not used:** Foster, Vidic, R Da Silva, Gibson.
23rd	● West Ham	H	W 3–0	**Att:** 73,797. **Ref:** A Wiley – (4-4-2): Foster, Neville, Brown, Vidic, Evra, Valencia, Gibson, Scholes, Anderson (Park 19), Berbatov (Owen[1] 78), Rooney[2] (Diouf 78). **Subs not used:** Kuszczak, J Evans, R Da Silva, Fletcher.
28th	● Aston Villa	N	W 1–2	**Att:** 88,596. **Ref:** P Dowd – (4-4-2): Kuszczak, R Da Silva (Neville 66), Vidic∎, J Evans, Evra∎, Valencia, Fletcher, Carrick, Park (Gibson 85), Owen[1] (Rooney[1] 42), Berbatov. **Subs not used:** Foster, Brown, Scholes, Diouf.

MARCH

6th	● Wolverhampton	A	W 0–1	**Att:** 28,883. **Ref:** P Walton – (4-5-1): Van der Sar, Brown (Neville 46), Vidic∎, Ferdinand, Evra, Valencia, Gibson (Diouf 62), Scholes[1], Carrick, Nani (Park 73), Berbatov. **Subs not used:** Foster, R Da Silva, Fletcher, Obertan.
10th	◐ AC Milan	H	W 4–0	**Att:** 74,595. **Ref:** M Busacca – (4-3-3): Van der Sar, Neville (R Da Silva 66), Ferdinand, Vidic, Evra, Fletcher[1], Scholes∎ (Gibson 73), Park[1], Valencia, Nani, Rooney[2] (Berbatov 66). **Subs not used:** Kuszczak, J Evans, Obertan, Diouf. Agg: 7–2.
14th	● Fulham	H	W 3–0	**Att:** 75,207. **Ref:** M Jones – (4-4-2): Van der Sar, Neville (F Da Silva 87), Ferdinand, Vidic, Evra, Valencia∎ (Park 73), Carrick, Fletcher, Nani, Berbatov[1], Rooney[2]. **Subs not used:** Kuszczak, Obertan, C Evans, Diouf, Gill.
21st	● Liverpool	H	W 2–1	**Att:** 75,216. **Ref:** H Webb – (4-5-1): Van der Sar, Neville, Ferdinand, Vidic∎, Evra, Valencia∎, Fletcher, Carrick, Park[1] (Scholes 87), Nani (Giggs 79), Rooney[1]. **Subs not used:** Kuszczak, Berbatov, R Da Silva, J Evans, Obertan.
27th	● Bolton	A	W 0–4	**Att:** 25,370. **Ref:** M Atkinson – (4-2-3-1): Van der Sar, Neville, Vidic, J Evans, Evra, Fletcher (Gibson∎ 80), Scholes (Carrick 74), Valencia, Giggs (Macheda 84), Nani, Berbatov[2]. **Subs not used:** Kuszczak, Park, R Da Silva, De Laet. Samuel OG.
30th	◐ Bayern Munich	A	L 2–1	**Att:** 66,000. **Ref:** F De Bleeckere – (4-3-2-1): Van der Sar, Neville∎, Ferdinand, Vidic, Evra, Fletcher, Carrick (Valencia 70), Scholes∎, Nani (Giggs 82), Park (Berbatov 70), Rooney∎[1]. **Subs not used:** Kuszczak, R Da Silva, J Evans, Gibson.

APRIL

3rd	● Chelsea	H	L 1–2	**Att:** 75,217. **Ref:** M Dean – (4-5-1): Van der Sar, Neville∎, Ferdinand, Vidic, Evra, Valencia, Fletcher∎ (Gibson 86), Giggs, Scholes∎ (Nani 72), Park (Macheda[1] 71), Berbatov. **Subs not used:** Kuszczak, Carrick, R Da Silva, De Laet.
7th	◐ Bayern Munich	H	W 3–2	**Att:** 74,482. **Ref:** N Rizzoli – (4-3-3): Van der Sar, R Da Silva∎, Ferdinand, Vidic, Evra, Fletcher, Carrick (Berbatov 80), Gibson[1] (Giggs 80), Valencia, Rooney (O'Shea 55), Nani[2]. **Subs not used:** Kuszczak, Scholes, J Evans, Macheda. Agg: 4–4; Bayern Munich win on away goals.
11th	● Blackburn	A	D 0–0	**Att:** 29,912. **Ref:** P Walton – (4-4-2): Van der Sar, Neville∎, Ferdinand, Vidic, O'Shea (Evra 79), Valencia, Scholes, Giggs (Gibson∎ 57), Nani, Berbatov, Macheda (Park 65). **Subs not used:** Kuszczak, J Evans, Fletcher, Obertan.
17th	◯ Man City	A	W 0–1	**Att:** 47,019. **Ref:** M Atkinson – (4-3-3): Van der Sar, Neville, Vidic, J Evans, Evra∎, Fletcher, Scholes[1], Gibson (Nani 59), Valencia (Obertan 80), Berbatov (Park 74), Giggs. **Subs not used:** Kuszczak, Carrick, R Da Silva, O'Shea.
24th	● Tottenham	H	W 3–1	**Att:** 75,268. **Ref:** A Marriner – (4-3-3): Van der Sar, R Da Silva (Macheda 79), Vidic, J Evans, Evra (O'Shea 67), Fletcher, Scholes, Giggs[2], Valencia (Carrick 59), Berbatov, Nani∎[1]. **Subs not used:** Kuszczak, Hargreaves, Brown, Gibson.

MAY

| 2nd | ● Sunderland | A | W 0–1 | **Att:** 47,641. **Ref:** S Bennett – (4-4-2): Van der Sar, O'Shea, J Evans, Vidic∎, Evra, Nani[1] (Hargreaves 90), Scholes, Fletcher (Ferdinand 87), Giggs, Berbatov (Carrick 71), Rooney∎. **Subs not used:** Foster, Brown, Park, Macheda. |
| 9th | ● Stoke | H | W 4–0 | **Att:** 75,316. **Ref:** M Clattenburg – (4-4-2): Van der Sar, Neville, Ferdinand, Vidic∎, Evra, Nani, Fletcher[1], Scholes∎ (Gibson 62), Giggs[1], Berbatov (Macheda 62), Rooney (Park[1] 77). **Subs not used:** Foster, Carrick, O'Shea, J Evans. Higginbotham OG. |

● Barclays Premier League ● FA Cup ◐ Carling Cup ◐ UEFA Champions League ● Europa League ◐ FA Community Shield   ∎ Yellow Card ∎ Red Card

MANCHESTER UNITED

BARCLAYS PREMIER LEAGUE GOALKEEPER STATS

Player	Minutes on pitch	Appearances	Match starts	Completed matches	Sub appearances	Subbed off	SAVES BREAKDOWN								Clean sheets	Goals conceded	Save %	PENALTIES			Fouls committed	Free-kicks won	Yellow cards	Red cards
							Saved with feet	Punched	Parried	Tipped over	Fumbled	Tipped round	Caught	Blocked				Saved	Resulting in goals	Opposition miss				
Ben Foster	865	9	9	9	0	0	1	4	6	0	1	1	27	0	4	8	82.98	0	0	0	0	1	0	0
Tomasz Kuszczak	761	8	8	8	0	0	0	2	6	2	1	1	23	2	3	7	83.72	0	2	0	0	0	0	0
Edwin Van der Sar	2013	21	21	21	0	0	0	7	6	2	0	2	62	2	12	13	86.17	0	0	0	0	3	0	0

BARCLAYS PREMIER LEAGUE OUTFIELD PLAYER STATS

Player	Minutes on pitch	Appearances	Match starts	Completed matches	Substitute appearances	Subbed off	Goals scored	Assists	Shots on target	Shots off target	Crosses	Tackles made	Defensive clearances	Defensive blocks	Fouls committed	Free-kicks won	Caught offside	Yellow cards	Red cards
Oliveira Anderson	899	14	10	3	4	7	1	2	4	6	14	13	0	1	17	24	0	1	0
Dimitar Berbatov	2211	33	24	12	9	12	12	7	47	39	15	16	5	2	36	36	21	1	0
Wes Brown	1671	19	18	16	1	2	0	0	1	1	2	25	20	5	24	20	0	2	0
Michael Carrick	2268	30	22	19	8	3	3	1	18	13	5	28	11	2	14	24	0	1	0
Fabio Da Silva	168	5	1	1	4	0	0	0	0	0	1	8	0	2	0	3	1	0	0
Rafael Da Silva	722	8	8	6	0	2	1	1	2	0	25	15	3	3	14	12	0	2	0
Ritchie De Laet	152	2	2	1	0	1	0	0	0	0	3	5	1	0	2	1	0	0	0
Mame Diouf	109	5	0	0	5	0	1	0	2	6	3	0	1	0	3	0	2	1	0
Jonathan Evans	1685	18	18	16	0	2	0	0	3	4	1	43	19	9	20	15	0	2	0
Patrice Evra	3484	38	37	33	1	4	0	7	14	12	61	67	24	9	36	44	5	5	0
Rio Ferdinand	1158	13	12	12	1	0	0	0	1	2	1	11	15	2	2	9	0	0	0
Darren Fletcher	2716	30	29	23	1	5	4	7	20	13	40	66	7	5	35	32	0	5	1
Darron Gibson	631	15	6	2	9	4	2	3	16	13	4	17	6	1	8	3	0	2	0
Ryan Giggs	1919	25	20	13	5	7	5	11	18	12	79	19	11	0	12	19	5	0	0
Owen Hargreaves	5	1	0	0	1	0	0	0	0	0	0	0	0	0	0	0	0	0	0
Federico Macheda	142	5	1	0	4	1	1	1	3	0	1	0	0	0	3	1	0	0	0
Luis Nani	1678	23	19	12	4	7	4	9	30	26	90	37	5	1	23	37	3	1	1
Gary Neville	1430	17	15	13	2	2	0	1	1	3	41	32	10	5	16	18	1	3	0
John O'Shea	1204	15	12	11	3	1	1	1	1	0	6	23	4	1	12	1	0	0	0
Gabriel Obertan	192	7	1	0	6	1	0	0	3	2	4	2	0	1	5	2	0	0	0
Michael Owen	676	19	5	0	14	5	3	1	10	9	1	11	0	1	2	5	5	0	0
Ji-Sung Park	1022	17	10	3	7	7	3	1	10	9	14	16	0	0	8	25	4	0	0
Wayne Rooney	2868	32	32	23	0	9	26	6	94	64	47	22	3	1	24	31	26	6	0
Paul Scholes	2037	28	24	12	4	11	3	4	20	16	5	49	3	8	30	19	0	9	1
Antonio Valencia	2769	34	29	23	5	6	5	9	20	17	98	40	2	2	42	25	7	3	0
Nemanja Vidic	2231	24	24	21	0	2	1	0	6	3	2	59	49	22	28	23	0	8	0
Danny Welbeck	152	5	1	0	4	1	0	0	3	1	1	0	0	0	3	2	0	0	0

SEASON TOTALS

Goals scored	86
Goals conceded	28
Clean sheets	19
Shots on target	347
Shots off target	272
Shots per goal	7.20
Pens awarded	8
Pens scored	6
Pens conceded	2
Offsides	79
Corners	296
Crosses	571
Players used	30
Fouls committed	422
Free-kicks won	433

CARDS RECEIVED

52 **4**

SEQUENCES

Wins	5
(on two occasions)	
Losses	–
(–)	
Draws	–
(–)	
Undefeated	8
(27/12/09–10/02/10)	
Without win	2
(on two occasions)	
Undefeated home	8
(15/12/09–21/03/10)	
Undefeated away	5
(06/03/10–02/05/10)	
Without scoring	–
(–)	
Without conceding	3
(23/02/10–14/03/10)	
Scoring	15
(27/12/09–03/04/10)	
Conceding	3
(on two occasions)	

League position chart

AUG	SEP	OCT	NOV	DEC	JAN	FEB	MAR	APR	MAY
3	1	2	2	2	2	2	1	2	2

LEAGUE POSITION AT THE END OF EACH MONTH

SEASON INFORMATION

Highest position: 1
Lowest position: 13
Average goals scored per game: 2.26
Average goals conceded per game: 0.74

MATCH RECORDS

Goals scored per match

		W	D	L	Pts
Failed to score	6	0	1	5	1
Scored 1 goal	8	4	2	2	14
Scored 2 goals	6	5	1	0	16
Scored 3 goals	9	9	0	0	27
Scored 4+ goals	9	9	0	0	27

Goals conceded per match

		W	D	L	Pts
Clean sheet	19	18	1	0	55
Conceded 1 goal	13	8	2	3	26
Conceded 2 goals	3	0	1	2	1
Conceded 3 goals	3	1	0	2	3
Conceded 4+ goals	0	0	0	0	0

EARLIEST STRIKE

WAYNE ROONEY
(v Man City) 1:52

LATEST STRIKE

MICHAEL OWEN
(v Man City) 95:28

Nemanja Vidic

GOAL DETAILS

How the goals were struck

SCORED		CONCEDED
52	Right foot	16
16	Left foot	5
15	Header	7
3	Other	0

How the goals were struck

SCORED		CONCEDED
41	Open play	18
17	Cross	5
4	Corner	2
6	Penalty	2
3	Direct from free-kick	0
3	Free-kick	1
12	Own goal	0

Distance from goal

SCORED		CONCEDED
42	6YDS	10
37	18YDS	13
7	18+YDS	5

GOALS SCORED/CONCEDED PER FIVE-MINUTE INTERVALS

MINS	5	10	15	20	25	30	35	40	45	50	55	60	65	70	75	80	85	90
FOR	2	1	1	1	3	3	6	5	6	4	6	6	7	5	5	6	8	11
AGN	2	1	0	5	2	0	1	2	0	1	1	2	1	1	2	4	0	3

PORTSMOUTH

CLUB SUMMARY

FORMED	1898
MANAGER	TBC
GROUND	Fratton Park
CAPACITY	20,600
NICKNAME	Pompey
WEBSITE	www.pompeyfc.co.uk

The New Football Pools PLAYER OF THE SEASON — Jamie O'Hara

OVERALL
P	W	D	L	F	A	GD
49	15	8	26	60	77	-17

BARCLAYS PREMIER LEAGUE
Pos	P	W	D	L	F	A	GD	Pts
20	38	7	7	24	34	66	-32	19

HOME
Pos	P	W	D	L	F	A	GD	Pts
20	19	5	3	11	24	32	-8	18

AWAY
Pos	P	W	D	L	F	A	GD	Pts
17	19	2	4	13	10	34	-24	10

CUP PROGRESS DETAILS
Competition	Round reached	Knocked out by
FA Cup	R-UP	Chelsea
Carling Cup	QF	Aston Villa

BIGGEST WIN (ALL COMPS)
4–0 on 2 occasions

BIGGEST DEFEAT (ALL COMPS)
0–5 on 2 occasions

THE PLAYER WITH THE MOST
GOALS SCORED	Aruna Dindane	**8**
SHOTS ON TARGET	Jamie O'Hara	**44**
SHOTS OFF TARGET	Jamie O'Hara	**30**
SHOTS WITHOUT SCORING	Niko Kranjcar	**9**
ASSISTS	Jamie O'Hara	**5**
OFFSIDES	Frederic Piquionne	**36**
FOULS	Kevin-Prince Boateng	**46**
FOULS WITHOUT A CARD	Nwankwo Kanu	**12**
FREE-KICKS WON	Aruna Dindane	**55**
DEFENSIVE CLEARANCES	Marc Wilson	**46**

actim INDEX — FOR THE 2009/10 BARCLAYS PREMIER LEAGUE SEASON

RANK	PLAYER	PTS
184	Aruna Dindane	226
192	Marc Wilson	221
193	David James	220

ATTENDANCE RECORD
HIGH	AVERAGE	LOW
20,821	18,249	16,207
v Tottenham (17/10/2009)		v Blackburn (03/04/2010)

AVRAM GRANT joked that Portsmouth's season to forget would have made a good script for a movie, but it was one that did not end happily ever after – coming to a close instead with relegation from the Barclays Premier League and FA Cup final heartbreak.

Pompey had only just escaped relegation in 2008/09 under manager Paul Hart – aided by Brian Kidd as his assistant – and the warning signs were there again as continued off-the-field problems with their ownership showed no signs of abating. The wranglings had a direct impact on the team, with the lack of fresh investment meaning that Hart was unable to strengthen the squad. The club had been forced to offload several key players over the summer, with the likes of Glen Johnson, Peter Crouch, Niko Kranjcar, Sean Davis, Sol Campbell and Sylvain Distin all moving on.

The writing was on the wall from the start as Portsmouth opened the campaign with an unwanted record of losing their first seven Barclays Premier League matches, despite playing some entertaining football at times, and Hart, the former head of youth development at Fratton Park, was eventually dismissed.

Grant – who had been brought back to the club as director of football by then owner Ali Al Faraj – took over the reins, hoping that the financial problems would soon be cleared up. However, the expected – and much-needed – investment never materialised and Hong Kong-based businessman Balram Chainrai was the club's fourth owner of the season when they eventually went into administration. That resulted in an automatic nine-point deduction and the inevitable prospect of a return to the second tier.

Somehow, through all that, and not even knowing from one week to the next whether he would have a team to put out on matchday, Grant managed to keep things together on the pitch. 'You either smile or you can cry – and I will not cry. There was not even one moment that I thought of giving up,' said Grant.

In mid-December, Pompey put up a brave fight at Chelsea, losing only 2–1 after Frank Lampard had scored a penalty with 10 minutes left, while three days later Liverpool were resoundingly beaten 2–0 at Fratton Park thanks to goals from Nadir Belhadj and Frederic Piquionne. Heavy

A turbulent season on and off the pitch for Portsmouth fans ended in Wembley heartbreak rather than a fairytale success

home defeats to Arsenal and then Chelsea again and a 5–0 loss at Manchester United were perhaps understandable, but Grant's men continued to show plenty of fight, claiming three points from relegation rivals Hull in March as well as completing League doubles over relegation rivals Burnley and Wolves.

It was the FA Cup, though, that produced its own special magic once again as Pompey surprisingly made it to the semi-finals, where they claimed a shock win over former boss Harry Redknapp and his Tottenham team, who included several former Fratton Park players. That gave Grant and his charges the chance to end a season to forget with a day to remember at Wembley against double-chasing Chelsea.

It looked as though Pompey's name was set to be engraved on the Cup after all when Kevin-Prince Boateng stepped up to take a second-half penalty that would have put them in front, having already seen his side saved by the woodwork on no fewer than five occasions. However, it was not to be as Petr Cech's save was swiftly followed by Didier Drogba's decisive free-kick strike at the other end, and Pompey were denied the glorious finish to a season their fans will not be sorry to see the back of.

However, several players enhanced their reputations during a season of adversity, and none more so than Jamie O'Hara, who joined on loan from Tottenham and got the regular first-team football he craved. He soon established himself in midfield as a fans' favourite with his attitude and commitment – allied with a notable ability at set-pieces – and he was almost unanimously voted as the supporters' player of the season.

Pompey will begin life back in the second tier with a new manager following Grant's resignation less than a week after the end of the 2009/10 season.

CLOCKWISE FROM ABOVE: Kevin Prince-Boateng falls to the floor after failing to convert a crucial penalty in the FA Cup final at Wembley; Avram Grant addresses the travelling Pompey supporters after a final-day defeat to Everton at Goodison Park; administrator Andrew Andronikou speaks to the media in February; Tommy Smith receives treatment on a night that Pompey are beaten 5–0 at home by Chelsea

PORTSMOUTH

BARCLAYS PREMIER LEAGUE GOALKEEPER STATS

Player	Minutes on pitch	Appearances	Match starts	Completed matches	Sub appearances	Subbed off	Saved with feet	Punched	Parried	Tipped over	Fumbled	Tipped round	Caught	Blocked	Clean sheets	Goals conceded	Save %	Saved	Resulting in goals	Opposition miss	Fouls committed	Free-kicks won	Yellow cards	Red cards
								SAVES BREAKDOWN										**PENALTIES**						
Jamie Ashdown	484	6	5	5	1	0	1	4	4	0	0	4	30	3	2	8	85.19	0	0	0	0	1	0	0
Asmir Begovic	786	9	8	8	1	0	1	2	6	3	0	6	28	1	2	18	61.84	0	4	0	0	0	0	0
David James	2374	25	25	23	0	2	1	16	20	4	2	5	94	6	3	40	78.49	1	4	0	2	1	3	0

BARCLAYS PREMIER LEAGUE OUTFIELD PLAYER STATS

Player	Minutes on pitch	Appearances	Match starts	Completed matches	Substitute appearances	Subbed off	Goals scored	Assists	Shots on target	Shots off target	Crosses	Tackles made	Defensive clearances	Defensive blocks	Fouls committed	Free-kicks won	Caught offside	Yellow cards	Red cards
Angelos Basinas	837	12	7	5	5	2	0	0	3	3	6	10	5	2	6	7	0	3	0
Nadir Belhadj	1571	19	16	15	3	1	3	2	8	8	59	28	4	3	8	8	0	2	0
Tal Ben-Haim	2041	22	21	21	1	0	0	0	4	2	5	34	40	11	28	16	0	4	0
Kevin-Prince Boateng	1945	22	20	16	2	4	3	2	36	26	27	31	13	1	46	45	9	7	0
Michael Brown	2045	24	22	17	2	4	2	3	14	7	6	32	7	4	43	38	0	5	1
Aruna Dindane	1561	19	18	12	1	6	8	2	22	14	19	10	0	0	36	55	8	5	0
Papa Bouba Diop	755	12	9	3	3	6	0	0	1	6	1	18	14	1	20	18	1	1	0
Sylvain Distin	284	3	3	3	0	0	0	0	0	0	0	1	4	1	0	3	0	0	0
Steve Finnan	1918	21	20	16	1	4	0	1	1	0	31	26	18	5	13	12	0	2	0
Hermann Hreidarsson	1503	17	17	14	0	3	1	0	2	3	6	21	20	9	18	7	0	2	0
Richard Hughes	827	10	9	5	1	4	0	0	2	3	1	6	10	5	16	9	1	5	0
Younes Kaboul	1814	19	19	18	0	0	3	0	19	9	13	15	45	4	15	17	1	3	1
Nwankwo Kanu	924	23	6	3	17	3	2	3	5	8	2	10	5	1	12	17	6	0	0
Niko Kranjcar	378	4	4	4	0	0	0	0	5	4	4	0	0	1	5	7	0	0	0
Aaron Mokoena	1814	23	21	12	2	9	0	0	1	8	1	29	17	8	35	19	0	7	0
Hayden Mullins	1406	18	15	12	3	3	0	0	3	2	5	15	11	6	12	10	1	3	0
David Nugent	40	3	0	0	3	0	0	0	1	2	0	0	0	0	0	0	0	0	0
Jamie O'Hara	2389	26	25	21	1	4	2	5	44	30	96	22	16	2	29	30	3	8	0
Quincy Owusu-Abeyie	395	10	3	1	7	2	0	1	5	2	10	7	1	0	0	5	3	0	0
Frederic Piquionne	2419	34	26	14	8	12	5	4	28	25	20	13	20	2	27	25	36	2	0
Matt Ritchie	85	2	1	0	1	1	0	0	0	3	0	0	0	1	0	2	0	0	0
Ricardo Rocha	751	10	10	5	0	3	0	0	0	1	1	11	24	8	4	9	1	1	2
Tommy Smith	1060	16	12	3	4	9	1	1	14	8	23	7	2	1	7	7	1	0	0
Leonard Sowah	364	5	3	3	2	0	0	0	0	0	2	3	5	0	3	3	0	0	0
John Utaka	1134	18	10	8	8	2	1	3	13	18	10	3	1	0	11	18	11	1	0
Anthony Vanden Borre	1415	19	15	12	4	2	0	2	5	4	11	21	7	7	21	16	2	2	1
Joel Ward	157	3	1	1	2	0	0	0	1	0	1	4	1	1	1	3	0	0	0
Danny Webber	536	17	4	1	13	3	1	1	5	3	12	6	1	1	4	3	5	1	0
Marc Wilson	2557	28	28	25	0	3	0	0	3	5	1	34	46	25	33	19	0	2	0
Hassan Yebda	1349	18	15	8	3	7	2	0	12	8	19	20	2	0	31	13	3	2	0

BARCLAYS PREMIER LEAGUE

SEASON TOTALS

Goals scored	34
Goals conceded	66
Clean sheets	7
Shots on target	257
Shots off target	212
Shots per goal	13.79
Pens awarded	6
Pens scored	3
Pens conceded	9
Offsides	92
Corners	188
Crosses	392
Players used	33
Fouls committed	486
Free-kicks won	443

CARDS RECEIVED

71   5

SEQUENCES

Wins	–
(–)	
Losses	7
(15/08/09–26/09/09)	
Draws	2
(03/04/10–14/04/10)	
Undefeated	2
(on four occasions)	
Without win	8
(26/12/09–20/02/10)	
Undefeated home	2
(on two occasions)	
Undefeated away	2
(on two occasions)	
Without scoring	4
(24/03/10–14/04/10)	
Without conceding	2
(on two occasions)	
Scoring	6
(09/02/10–20/03/10)	
Conceding	14
(26/12/09–27/03/10)	

LEAGUE POSITION AT THE END OF EACH MONTH

AUG	SEP	OCT	NOV	DEC	JAN	FEB	MAR	APR	MAY
20	20	20	20	20	20	20	20	20	20

SEASON INFORMATION

Highest position: 11
Lowest position: 20
Average goals scored per game: 0.89
Average goals conceded per game: 1.74

MATCH RECORDS

Goals scored per match

		W	D	L	Pts
Failed to score	16	0	3	13	3
Scored 1 goal	14	1	3	10	6
Scored 2 goals	5	3	1	1	10
Scored 3 goals	2	2	0	0	6
Scored 4+ goals	1	1	0	0	3

Goals conceded per match

		W	D	L	Pts
Clean sheet	7	4	3	0	15
Conceded 1 goal	12	2	3	7	9
Conceded 2 goals	11	1	1	9	4
Conceded 3 goals	2	0	0	2	0
Conceded 4+ goals	6	0	0	6	0

GOALS SCORED/CONCEDED
PER FIVE-MINUTE INTERVALS

MINS	5	10	15	20	25	30	35	40	45	50	55	60	65	70	75	80	85	90
FOR	0	1	1	2	2	0	4	3	1	0	2	1	3	2	1	2	2	7
AGN	0	0	3	3	5	9	5	2	9	3	4	2	1	3	4	3	4	8

EARLIEST STRIKE

MICHAEL BROWN
(v Aston Villa) 9:01

LATEST STRIKE

ARUNA DINDANE
(v Sunderland) 94:32

Hassan Yebda

GOAL DETAILS

How the goals were struck

SCORED		CONCEDED
16	Right foot	33
11	Left foot	16
7	Header	14
0	Other	3

How the goals were struck

SCORED		CONCEDED
25	Open play	36
1	Cross	10
3	Corner	5
3	Penalty	8
1	Direct from free-kick	2
1	Free-kick	2
0	Own goal	3

Distance from goal

SCORED		CONCEDED
17	6YDS	26
14	18YDS	34
3	18+YDS	6

STOKE CITY

CLUB SUMMARY

FORMED	1863
MANAGER	Tony Pulis
GROUND	Britannia Stadium
CAPACITY	28,218
NICKNAME	The Potters
WEBSITE	www.stokecityfc.co.uk

The New **Football Pools** PLAYER OF THE SEASON — **Abdoulaye Faye**

OVERALL
P	W	D	L	F	A	GD
46	16	15	15	49	61	-12

BARCLAYS PREMIER LEAGUE
Pos	P	W	D	L	F	A	GD	Pts
11	38	11	14	13	34	48	-14	47

HOME
Pos	P	W	D	L	F	A	GD	Pts
13	19	7	6	6	24	21	3	27

AWAY
Pos	P	W	D	L	F	A	GD	Pts
9	19	4	8	7	10	27	-17	20

CUP PROGRESS DETAILS
Competition	Round reached	Knocked out by
FA Cup	QF	Chelsea
Carling Cup	R4	Portsmouth

BIGGEST WIN (ALL COMPS)
06/02/10 3–0 v Blackburn

BIGGEST DEFEAT (ALL COMPS)
25/04/10 0–7 v Chelsea

THE PLAYER WITH THE MOST
GOALS SCORED	Matthew Etherington	**5**
SHOTS ON TARGET	Ricardo Fuller	**30**
SHOTS OFF TARGET	Ricardo Fuller	**25**
SHOTS WITHOUT SCORING	Rory Delap	**17**
ASSISTS	Matthew Etherington	**9**
OFFSIDES	Ricardo Fuller	**29**
FOULS	Ricardo Fuller	**52**
FOULS WITHOUT A CARD	Mamady Sidibe	**25**
FREE-KICKS WON	Ricardo Fuller	**48**
DEFENSIVE CLEARANCES	Ryan Shawcross	**41**

actim INDEX ● FOR THE 2009/10 BARCLAYS PREMIER LEAGUE SEASON

RANK	PLAYER	PTS
46	Matthew Etherington	400
79	Ryan Shawcross	353
82	Thomas Sorensen	350

ATTENDANCE RECORD
HIGH	AVERAGE	LOW
27,604	27,162	25,104
v Hull (03/04/2010)		v Fulham (05/01/2010)

CLOCKWISE FROM ABOVE: Glenn Whelan celebrates in front of the Stoke fans after his winner at Tottenham; Ricardo Fuller scores in the FA Cup victory against Arsenal; Rory Delap takes one of his trademark throws; Stoke are left shell-shocked by a 7–0 thrashing at Chelsea

STOKE once again exceeded expectations under manager Tony Pulis to finish comfortably in mid-table.

Pulis has taken Stoke forward over the past couple of years to establish them as a Barclays Premier League club and after another season of progress he declared himself immensely proud of what his team had achieved.

Even though they lost 4–0 to Manchester United on the final day, the Potters finished in 11th place. In doing so they amassed 47 points, two more than the previous campaign when they had made their debut at Barclays Premier League level. So much for the so-called 'second-season syndrome' which has affected recently-promoted teams in the past.

The Potters can now prepare for a third successive campaign in the Barclays Premier League, having never looked to be in any serious danger of relegation at any point during 2009/10.

They started the season well and built a solid platform for the rest of the term. Seven points from their opening four games gave the team the confidence they needed, and they were always a step ahead of those clubs struggling around the drop zone.

Back-to-back victories against West Ham and Tottenham saw Pulis' side climb into the top half of the table in October.

However, while three straight defeats pushed them only four points above the relegation places at the turn of the year, the manager has engendered a collective mindset within the group that when the going gets tough, the team reacts positively.

The upturn began when non-League side York were beaten in the FA Cup in what proved to be the start of an 11-match unbeaten run. The streak included the Potters' victory over Arsenal in the fourth round at the end of the month, thanks to a Ricardo Fuller brace and a late Dean Whitehead strike.

Stoke then moved into the quarter-finals at the expense of big-spending Manchester City. A 1–1 draw at Eastlands, courtesy of a Fuller header, ensured the club were in the quarter-final draw for the first time in 38 years, and it got better still as a 3–1 victory

after extra-time in the replay secured a place in the last eight of the competition. The run was finally ended in March when a 2–0 defeat at Chelsea denied the club a first visit to the new Wembley Stadium.

Despite that Cup heartache, a vital victory in the Barclays Premier League soon arrived, against West Ham at Upton Park, with another wonderful winner from Fuller.

Hull were then beaten, and a point claimed at Wolves meant that Stoke could afford to relax.

Despite being well clear of the relegation zone, the Potters suffered their biggest defeat since returning to the top flight when they were thrashed 7–0 by Chelsea in April. While it was a poor display, the scale of the defeat was hardly down to complacency on Stoke's part. Carlo Ancelotti's side simply played with the kind of swagger that could have dismantled any team in the country. It may have been a setback, but even that humiliation could not detract from Stoke's achievements over the course of the campaign.

Away from the pitch, Pulis occasionally had to deal with the frustrations of those players who struggled for regular first-team action. However, any disagreements behind the scenes failed to alter the course of Stoke's successful campaign and Pulis believes that the majority of his squad still see their futures at the Britannia Stadium.

Looking ahead, the club are scheduled to move into a new £5million training complex at Clayton Wood before the start of the 2010/11 season, with the new facilities designed to suit the demands of the Barclays Premier League. It is all part of the gradual progression which the club hope will take them on to the next level.

Pulis said: 'We will be looking to improve step by step, but we must keep our feet firmly on the floor and not get ahead of ourselves too much. This club is simply a great place to be at the moment.

'It is a fantastic achievement to finish in mid-table. I worked much harder this season as a manager and I am sure it will be even harder next season.'

Tony Pulis' Stoke avoided the dreaded 'second-season syndrome' as they consolidated their position in the top flight

STOKE CITY

RESULTS 2009/10

AUGUST

15th ● Burnley H W 2-0 **Att:** 27,385. **Ref:** S Bennett – (4-4-2): Sorensen, Wilkinson, A Faye▮, Shawcross[1], Higginbotham, Lawrence, Delap, Whitehead, Etherington (Whelan 76), Beattie▮ (Kitson 67), Fuller (Cresswell 87). **Subs not used:** Simonsen, Griffin, Cort, Pugh. Jordan OG.

19th ● Liverpool A L 4-0 **Att:** 44,318. **Ref:** P Walton – (4-4-2): Sorensen, Wilkinson, Shawcross, A Faye, Higginbotham, Delap, Whelan, Whitehead▮ (Pugh 69), Etherington, Beattie (Fuller 62), Cresswell (Lawrence 62). **Subs not used:** Simonsen, Griffin, Cort, Kitson.

22nd ● Birmingham A D 0-0 **Att:** 21,694. **Ref:** C Foy – (4-4-2): Sorensen, Wilkinson, Shawcross, A Faye, Higginbotham, Lawrence, Whelan▮, Delap, Etherington (Whitehead▮ 76), Beattie (Kitson 11), Fuller▮. **Subs not used:** Simonsen, Griffin, Cort, Pugh, Cresswell.

26th ● Leyton Orient A W 0-1 **Att:** 2,742. **Ref:** M Russell – (4-4-2): Simonsen, Shotton (Griffin 48), Cort▮, Sonko (Davies 48), Dickinson, Soares (Moult▮ 62), Pugh, A Faye, Tonge, Cresswell, Kitson[1]. **Subs not used:** Parton, Lund, Wedderburn. AET – Score after 90 mins 0-0.

29th ● Sunderland H W 1-0 **Att:** 27,091. **Ref:** M Jones – (4-4-2): Sorensen, Wilkinson, Shawcross, A Faye, Higginbotham, Lawrence, Delap, Whelan, Etherington (Whitehead 78), Kitson[1] (Huth 90), Fuller (Tuncay 84). **Subs not used:** Simonsen, Griffin, Pugh, Cresswell.

SEPTEMBER

12th ● Chelsea H L 1-2 **Att:** 27,440. **Ref:** M Dean – (5-3-2): Sorensen (Simonsen 41), Wilkinson▮, Huth, A Faye[1], Shawcross▮, Collins, Delap▮, Whitehead, Whelan, Beattie (Fuller 12), Kitson (Tuncay 66). **Subs not used:** Higginbotham, Lawrence, Pugh, Etherington.

19th ● Bolton A D 1-1 **Att:** 20,265. **Ref:** M Clattenburg – (4-4-2): Sorensen, Shawcross, A Faye, Huth, Collins, Delap, Whitehead▮, Whelan, Etherington (Lawrence 63), Fuller▮ (Beattie 90), Kitson[1] (Pugh 78). **Subs not used:** Simonsen, Higginbotham, Cort, Tuncay.

22nd ● Blackpool H W 4-3 **Att:** 13,957. **Ref:** L Probert – (4-4-2): Simonsen, Wilkinson, Cort, Higginbotham[1], Griffin[1]▮, Lawrence, Arismendi (Tonge 46), Pugh, Soares (Etherington[1] 64), Tuncay, Beattie (Fuller[1] 64). **Subs not used:** Sorensen, Kitson, Shotton, Dickinson.

26th ● Man Utd H L 0-2 **Att:** 27,500. **Ref:** H Webb – (4-5-1): Sorensen, Huth▮, A Faye, Shawcross, Collins, Lawrence (Pugh 86), Whelan, Delap, Whitehead (Tuncay 72), Etherington, Kitson (Beattie 72). **Subs not used:** Simonsen, Higginbotham, Cort, Wilkinson.

OCTOBER

4th ● Everton A D 1-1 **Att:** 36,753. **Ref:** A Marriner – (4-4-1-1): Sorensen, Huth[1], A Faye, Shawcross▮, Collins, Delap, Diao▮ (Whelan 77), Whitehead, Etherington, Beattie, Fuller▮ (Kitson 90). **Subs not used:** Simonsen, Cort, Lawrence, Wilkinson, Tuncay.

17th ● West Ham H W 2-1 **Att:** 27,026. **Ref:** M Atkinson – (4-4-2): Sorensen, Huth, A Faye, Shawcross▮, Collins, Delap (Lawrence 68), Diao▮ (Whelan▮ 78), Whitehead, Etherington, Fuller, Beattie[2] (Kitson 83). **Subs not used:** Simonsen, Higginbotham, Tuncay, Wilkinson.

24th ● Tottenham A W 0-1 **Att:** 36,031. **Ref:** L Probert – (4-4-2): Simonsen, Wilkinson, A Faye, Shawcross, Collins, Delap (Whelan[1] 57), Whitehead, Diao▮, Etherington, Fuller▮ (Higginbotham 89), Beattie (Tuncay 70). **Subs not used:** Cort, Lawrence, Kitson, Pugh.

27th ● Portsmouth A L 4-0 **Att:** 11,251. **Ref:** P Walton – (4-4-2): Simonsen, Griffin▮, Higginbotham, Cort, Pugh, Lawrence (Soares 75), Arismendi, Whelan, Tonge▮, Tuncay (Moult 82), Kitson (Sidibe 55). **Subs not used:** Parton, Lund, Wedderburn, Connor.

31st ● Wolverhampton H D 2-2 **Att:** 27,500. **Ref:** C Foy – (4-4-2): Sorensen, Wilkinson, A Faye, Shawcross, Collins, Delap (Lawrence 80), Whelan, Whitehead, Etherington[1], Beattie (Sidibe 71), Fuller (Tuncay 75). **Subs not used:** Simonsen, Higginbotham, Cort, Pugh. Elokobi OG.

NOVEMBER

8th ● Hull A L 2-1 **Att:** 24,516. **Ref:** M Dean – (4-4-2): Sorensen, Huth▮, A Faye▮, Shawcross▮, Collins, Delap, Whelan▮, Whitehead, Etherington[1], Fuller (Tuncay 81 (Wilkinson 87)), Beattie (Kitson 61). **Subs not used:** Simonsen, Lawrence, Higginbotham, Cort.

22nd ● Portsmouth H W 1-0 **Att:** 27,069. **Ref:** K Friend – (4-4-2): Sorensen, Wilkinson, Shawcross, Huth, Collins, Delap, Diao (Lawrence 57), Whitehead▮, Etherington, Beattie (Sidibe 57), Fuller▮ (Tuncay 84). **Subs not used:** Simonsen, Higginbotham, Whelan, Pugh.

28th ● Blackburn A D 0-0 **Att:** 25,143. **Ref:** H Webb – (4-4-2): Sorensen, Wilkinson▮, Shawcross (A Faye 51), Huth, Collins, Lawrence, Whitehead▮, Diao, Etherington, Sidibe (Beattie 68), Fuller (Tuncay 83). **Subs not used:** Simonsen, Higginbotham, Whelan, Delap.

DECEMBER

5th ● Arsenal A L 2-0 **Att:** 60,048. **Ref:** M Clattenburg – (4-4-1-1): Sorensen, Wilkinson, Huth, A Faye, Collins, Lawrence (Fuller 75), Delap (Whelan 81), Diao, Etherington, Tuncay, Sidibe (Beattie 62). **Subs not used:** Simonsen, Higginbotham, Cort, Pugh.

12th ● Wigan H D 2-2 **Att:** 26,728. **Ref:** M Dean – (4-4-2): Sorensen, Wilkinson▮, Shawcross[1], A Faye▮, Huth▮, Delap, Diao▮ (Whelan 62), Whitehead, Etherington, Fuller (Beattie 83), Tuncay▮[1]. **Subs not used:** Simonsen, Higginbotham, Sidibe, Pugh, Collins.

19th ● Aston Villa A L 1-0 **Att:** 35,852. **Ref:** L Probert – (4-4-2): Sorensen, Wilkinson▮, Collins, A Faye, Higginbotham, Whitehead, Diao (Fuller 76), Whelan (Delap 84), Etherington, Sidibe (Beattie 84), Tuncay. **Subs not used:** Simonsen, Cort, Lawrence, Pugh.

26th ● Man City A L 2-0 **Att:** 47,325. **Ref:** L Mason – (4-5-1): Sorensen, Wilkinson (Huth 48), A Faye, Collins, Higginbotham, Tuncay (Fuller 59), Whitehead, Diao▮, Whelan▮, Etherington, Sidibe (Beattie 52). **Subs not used:** Simonsen, Lawrence, Pugh, Delap.

28th ● Birmingham H L 0-1 **Att:** 27,211. **Ref:** M Atkinson – (4-4-2): Sorensen, Huth, Shawcross▮, A Faye, Higginbotham, Lawrence (Sidibe 82), Delap▮, Whitehead, Etherington, Beattie (Fuller 70), Tuncay. **Subs not used:** Simonsen, Cort, Pugh, A Faye, Collins.

JANUARY

2nd ● York H W 3-1 **Att:** 15,586. **Ref:** M Jones – (4-4-2): Sorensen (Simonsen 46), Huth▮, Cort, Higginbotham, Collins, Lawrence, Delap▮, Whitehead, Etherington[1], Beattie (Tuncay 74), Fuller[1] (Sidibe 80). **Subs not used:** Whelan, Pugh, Tonge, Wilkinson. Parslow OG.

5th ● Fulham H W 3-2 **Att:** 25,104. **Ref:** M Clattenburg – (4-4-2): Simonsen, Huth, A Faye▮[1], Shawcross, Higginbotham, Lawrence (Diao 89), Delap (Whelan 66), Whitehead, Etherington, Tuncay[1] (Fuller 42), Sidibe[1]. **Subs not used:** St Louis-Hamilton, Collins, Wilkinson, Beattie.

16th ● Liverpool H D 1-1 **Att:** 27,247. **Ref:** L Mason – (4-4-2): Sorensen, Huth[1], A Faye (Wilkinson 26), Shawcross, Higginbotham, Delap (Lawrence 24), Whitehead, Diao▮, Etherington, Sidibe (Fuller 66), Tuncay. **Subs not used:** Simonsen, Whelan, Pugh, Collins.

24th ● Arsenal H W 3-1 **Att:** 19,735. **Ref:** M Atkinson – (4-4-2): Sorensen, Huth, Shawcross, Higginbotham, Collins, Delap (Diao 85), Whitehead[1], Whelan, Etherington (Pugh 90), Sidibe, Fuller[2] (Tuncay 85). **Subs not used:** Simonsen, Lawrence, Beattie, Wilkinson.

FEBRUARY

1st ● Sunderland A D 0-0 **Att:** 35,078. **Ref:** H Webb – (4-4-2): Sorensen, Huth, Shawcross, A Faye (Wilkinson▮ 17), Higginbotham, Diao (Delap 74), Whitehead▮, Whelan, Etherington, Tuncay (Fuller▮ 62), Sidibe. **Subs not used:** Simonsen, Lawrence, Beattie, Collins.

6th ● Blackburn H W 3-0 **Att:** 27,386. **Ref:** S Bennett – (4-4-2): Sorensen, Huth, Wilkinson, Shawcross▮, Higginbotham[1], Lawrence, Delap (Whelan 90), Whitehead, Etherington[1], Fuller▮ (Tuncay 79), Sidibe[1] (Beattie 81). **Subs not used:** Begovic, Pugh, Diao, Collins.

● Barclays Premier League ● FA Cup ● Carling Cup ● UEFA Champions League ● Europa League ● FA Community Shield ▮ Yellow Card ▮ Red Card

RESULTS 2009/10

9th	● Wigan	A	D 1-1	**Att:** 16,033. **Ref:** A Marriner – (4-4-1-1): Sorensen, Wilkinson, Huth▮, Shawcross▮, Higginbotham, Delap (Fuller 60), Whelan, Whitehead, Etherington▮, Tuncay¹ (Lawrence 88), Sidibe (Beattie 88). **Subs not used:** Begovic, Kitson, Pugh, Diao, Collins.
13th	● Man City	A	D 1-1	**Att:** 28,019. **Ref:** M Clattenburg – (4-4-2): Sorensen, Wilkinson▮ (Collins 55), Huth, Shawcross, Higginbotham, Etherington (Lawrence 14 (Delap 45)), Diao, Whelan, Tuncay, Sidibe, Fuller¹. **Subs not used:** Simonsen, Beattie, Kitson, Pugh.
16th	● Man City	H	D 1-1	**Att:** 26,778. **Ref:** A Wiley – (4-4-2): Sorensen, Huth, Shawcross, A Faye▮, Higginbotham (Collins 46), Delap, Whitehead, Whelan¹, Lawrence (Diao▮ 60), Sidibe, Fuller▮ (Beattie 80). **Subs not used:** Begovic, Kitson, Pugh, Tuncay.
20th	● Portsmouth	A	W 1-2	**Att:** 17,208. **Ref:** M Dean – (4-4-2): Sorensen, Wilkinson▮▮, Shawcross, Huth¹, Collins, Delap, Whitehead, Whelan, Tuncay (Diao¹ 76), Fuller (Kitson 90), Sidibe. **Subs not used:** Begovic, Lawrence, Beattie, Pugh, A Faye.
24th	● Man City	H	W 3-1	**Att:** 21,813. **Ref:** S Bennett – (4-4-2): Sorensen, Whitehead, Shawcross¹¹, Huth▮, Collins, Lawrence (Pugh¹ 72), Whelan, Diao (Tuncay¹ 54), Delap, Sidibe▮ (Kitson¹ 74), Fuller▮. **Subs not used:** Simonsen, Beattie, A Faye, Davies. AET – Score after 90 mins 1-1.
27th	● Arsenal	H	L 1-3	**Att:** 27,011. **Ref:** P Walton – (4-4-2): Sorensen, Huth, Shawcross▮, A Faye (Collins 60), Wilkinson, Delap, Whelan, Whitehead (Lawrence 77), Pugh¹, Sidibe, Fuller (Tuncay 80). **Subs not used:** Begovic, Beattie, Kitson, Diao.

MARCH

7th	● Chelsea	A	L 2-0	**Att:** 41,322. **Ref:** M Atkinson – (4-4-2): Sorensen, Wilkinson, A Faye, Huth, Collins, Whitehead, Whelan (Pugh 45), Delap, Tuncay (Lawrence 60), Sidibe (Kitson 61), Fuller. **Subs not used:** Simonsen, A Faye, Davies, Moult.
10th	● Burnley	A	D 1-1	**Att:** 20,323. **Ref:** H Webb – (4-4-2): Sorensen, Wilkinson, Collins, Lawrence (Pugh 63), Whitehead, Delap, Etherington, Tuncay¹ (Moult 85), Sidibe (Kitson 63). **Subs not used:** Begovic, A Faye, A Davies, Lund.
13th	● Aston Villa	H	D 0-0	**Att:** 27,598. **Ref:** K Friend – (4-4-2): Sorensen, Huth, A Faye, Higginbotham, Collins, Delap, Whelan, Whitehead, Etherington, Sidibe (Kitson 54), Tuncay (Fuller 53). **Subs not used:** Begovic, Lawrence, Pugh, Wilkinson, Moult.
20th	● Tottenham	H	L 1-2	**Att:** 27,575. **Ref:** M Dean – (4-4-2): Sorensen, Huth, A Faye, Higginbotham, Collins, Delap, Whelan (Tuncay 84), Whitehead▮, Etherington¹, Fuller▮, Kitson (Sidibe 84). **Subs not used:** Begovic, Lawrence, Pugh, Wilkinson, Moult.
27th	● West Ham	A	W 0-1	**Att:** 34,564. **Ref:** A Marriner – (4-4-2): Sorensen, Huth, A Faye (Wilkinson 25), Collins, Higginbotham, Lawrence, Delap▮, Whelan▮, Etherington (Fuller¹ 67), Sidibe, Kitson (Tuncay 48). **Subs not used:** Begovic, Pugh, A Faye, Moult.

APRIL

3rd	● Hull	H	W 2-0	**Att:** 27,604. **Ref:** L Probert – (4-4-2): Sorensen, Huth, A Faye▮, Higginbotham, Collins, Lawrence¹, Whelan (Whitehead 72), Delap, Etherington, Fuller¹ (Tuncay▮ 46), Kitson▮ (Sidibe 84). **Subs not used:** Begovic, Pugh, Shawcross, Wilkinson.
11th	● Wolverhampton	A	D 0-0	**Att:** 28,455. **Ref:** C Foy – (4-4-2): Sorensen, Huth, A Faye, Higginbotham, Collins, Delap, Whitehead, Whelan, Etherington, Sidibe (Lawrence 72), Kitson (Tuncay 69). **Subs not used:** Begovic, Pugh, Wilkinson, Lund, Moult.
17th	● Bolton	H	L 1-2	**Att:** 27,250. **Ref:** S Attwell – (4-4-2): Sorensen, Huth, A Faye, Higginbotham, Collins, Lawrence (Etherington 71), Whitehead, Whelan▮, Delap, Tuncay (Fuller 76), Kitson¹ (Beattie 82). **Subs not used:** Begovic, Pugh, Wilkinson, Moult.
25th	● Chelsea	A	L 7-0	**Att:** 41,013. **Ref:** S Bennett – (4-4-2): Sorensen (Begovic 35), Higginbotham, Huth▮, A Faye (Shawcross 9), Collins, Delap, Whitehead▮, Whelan▮, Etherington, Fuller, Kitson (Tuncay 59). **Subs not used:** Lawrence, Beattie, Pugh, Wilkinson.

MAY

1st	● Everton	H	D 0-0	**Att:** 27,579. **Ref:** H Webb – (4-4-2): Begovic, Wilkinson, Huth, Shawcross, Higginbotham, Delap (Pugh 88), Whelan, Whitehead, Etherington (Lawrence 87), Sidibe (Tuncay 88), Fuller. **Subs not used:** Simonsen, Diao, Collins, Moult.
5th	● Fulham	A	W 0-1	**Att:** 20,831. **Ref:** P Walton – (4-4-2): Begovic, Wilkinson, Huth▮, Shawcross▮, Higginbotham, Delap, Whelan, Whitehead, Etherington¹ (Diao 88), Fuller▮ (Lawrence 90), Sidibe (Tuncay 71). **Subs not used:** Simonsen, Pugh, Collins, Moult.
9th	● Man Utd	A	L 4-0	**Att:** 75,316. **Ref:** M Clattenburg – (4-4-2): Begovic, Wilkinson, Shawcross, Huth, Higginbotham (Collins 66), Delap, Whitehead (Diao 67), Whelan, Etherington, Sidibe (Pugh 66), Fuller. **Subs not used:** Simonsen, Lawrence, Tuncay, A Faye.

● Barclays Premier League ● FA Cup ● Carling Cup ● UEFA Champions League ● Europa League ● FA Community Shield   ▮ Yellow Card ▮ Red Card

Tuncay scores in the FA Cup fifth-round replay win against Manchester City in February

STOKE CITY

BARCLAYS PREMIER LEAGUE GOALKEEPER STATS

Player	Minutes on pitch	Appearances	Match starts	Completed matches	Sub appearances	Subbed off	SAVES BREAKDOWN								Clean sheets	Goals conceded	Save %	PENALTIES			Fouls committed	Free-kicks won	Yellow cards	Red cards
							Saved with feet	Punched	Parried	Tipped over	Fumbled	Tipped round	Caught	Blocked				Saved	Resulting in goals	Opposition miss				
Asmir Begovic	346	4	3	3	1	0	0	0	3	0	0	1	11	1	2	11	35.56	0	1	0	0	1	0	0
Steve Simonsen	261	3	2	2	1	0	0	0	2	1	0	3	13	0	1	4	82.61	0	0	0	0	0	0	0
Thomas Sorensen	3063	33	33	31	0	2	2	11	21	5	3	9	138	1	11	33	85.00	3	2	0	0	10	0	0

BARCLAYS PREMIER LEAGUE OUTFIELD PLAYER STATS

Player	Minutes on pitch	Appearances	Match starts	Completed matches	Substitute appearances	Subbed off	Goals scored	Assists	Shots on target	Shots off target	Crosses	Tackles made	Defensive clearances	Defensive blocks	Fouls committed	Free-kicks won	Caught offside	Yellow cards	Red cards
James Beattie	861	22	11	1	11	10	3	0	9	13	1	22	7	0	21	16	6	1	0
Danny Collins	2244	25	22	22	3	0	0	1	2	0	14	76	23	10	11	12	0	0	0
Richard Cresswell	70	2	1	0	1	1	0	0	0	1	0	0	4	0	3	1	0	0	0
Rory Delap	3073	36	34	25	2	9	0	1	8	9	23	104	26	6	31	11	1	3	0
Salif Diao	1012	16	11	5	5	6	1	0	1	4	2	53	3	1	32	6	0	7	0
Matthew Etherington	3071	34	33	26	1	7	5	9	13	14	75	67	4	2	14	38	5	1	0
Abdoulaye Faye	2541	31	30	23	1	5	2	0	8	16	5	102	31	13	23	13	1	5	2
Ricardo Fuller	2371	35	22	6	13	16	3	4	30	25	12	59	2	1	52	48	29	9	0
Danny Higginbotham	2141	24	23	21	1	2	1	2	6	7	10	59	11	12	10	15	4	0	0
Robert Huth	2952	32	30	30	2	0	3	1	10	14	5	88	28	25	26	20	0	6	0
Dave Kitson	998	18	10	0	8	10	3	2	9	9	5	30	4	2	31	18	5	1	0
Liam Lawrence	1484	25	14	7	11	7	1	2	13	2	44	45	2	0	14	21	1	0	0
Louis Moult	8	1	0	0	1	0	0	0	0	0	0	0	0	0	0	0	0	0	0
Danny Pugh	211	7	1	1	6	0	1	0	3	0	2	1	3	0	2	3	0	0	0
Tuncay	1398	30	13	4	17	9	4	2	15	8	6	23	0	1	20	27	18	2	0
Ryan Shawcross	2626	28	27	25	1	1	2	3	6	13	2	89	41	35	31	27	3	8	1
Mamady Sidibe	1614	24	19	6	5	13	2	1	6	6	3	12	9	1	25	28	8	0	0
Glenn Whelan	2544	33	25	22	8	3	2	2	17	18	24	83	11	13	32	18	0	9	0
Dean Whitehead	3107	36	33	28	3	4	0	0	11	4	9	86	14	8	47	32	1	8	1
Andy Wilkinson	2183	25	21	19	4	1	0	0	4	4	4	69	13	5	26	16	0	6	1

actim

BARCLAYS PREMIER LEAGUE

SEASON TOTALS

Goals scored	34
Goals conceded	48
Clean sheets	14
Shots on target	171
Shots off target	167
Shots per goal	9.94
Pens awarded	2
Pens scored	2
Pens conceded	6
Offsides	82
Corners	184
Crosses	246
Players used	23
Fouls committed	451
Free-kicks won	381

CARDS RECEIVED

66 **5**

SEQUENCES

Wins	2
(on two occasions)	
Losses	3
(19/12/09–28/12/09)	
Draws	2
(on three occasions)	
Undefeated	7
(05/01/10–20/02/10)	
Without win	6
(28/11/09–28/12/09)	
Undefeated home	4
(on two occasions)	
Undefeated away	6
(01/02/10–11/04/10)	
Without scoring	3
(19/12/09–28/12/09)	
Without conceding	3
(27/03/10–11/04/10)	
Scoring	6
(on two occasions)	
Conceding	7
(05/12/09–16/01/10)	

LEAGUE POSITION AT THE END OF EACH MONTH

AUG	SEP	OCT	NOV	DEC	JAN	FEB	MAR	APR	MAY
5	12	9	9	12	12	11	11	13	11

SEASON INFORMATION

Highest position: 3
Lowest position: 14
Average goals scored per game: 0.89
Average goals conceded per game: 1.26

MATCH RECORDS

Goals scored per match

		W	D	L	Pts
Failed to score	14	0	6	8	6
Scored 1 goal	16	5	6	5	21
Scored 2 goals	6	4	2	0	14
Scored 3 goals	2	2	0	0	6
Scored 4+ goals	0	0	0	0	0

Goals conceded per match

		W	D	L	Pts
Clean sheet	14	8	6	0	30
Conceded 1 goal	10	2	6	2	12
Conceded 2 goals	10	1	2	7	5
Conceded 3 goals	1	0	0	1	0
Conceded 4+ goals	3	0	0	3	0

EARLIEST STRIKE

RICARDO FULLER
(v Hull) 5:24

LATEST STRIKE

SALIF DIAO
(v Portsmouth) 90:46

Robert Huth

GOAL DETAILS

How the goals were struck

SCORED		CONCEDED
14	Right foot	24
10	Left foot	13
10	Header	11
0	Other	0

How the goals were struck

SCORED		CONCEDED
22	Open play	27
3	Cross	5
4	Corner	5
2	Penalty	3
0	Direct from free-kick	2
2	Free-kick	5
1	Own goal	1

Distance from goal

SCORED		CONCEDED
15	6YDS	27
17	18YDS	15
2	18+YDS	6

GOALS SCORED/CONCEDED
PER FIVE-MINUTE INTERVALS

MINS	5	10	15	20	25	30	35	40	45	50	55	60	65	70	75	80	85	90
FOR	0	3	3	2	1	1	3	2	3	2	1	0	1	3	4	0	1	4
AGN	1	0	2	0	1	2	5	1	4	3	3	1	5	1	1	4	5	9

CLUB SUMMARY

FORMED	1879
MANAGER	Steve Bruce
GROUND	Stadium of Light
CAPACITY	48,353
NICKNAME	The Black Cats
WEBSITE	www.safc.com

The New **Football Pools** PLAYER OF THE SEASON — *Darren Bent*

OVERALL

P	W	D	L	F	A	GD
43	14	12	17	58	59	-1

BARCLAYS PREMIER LEAGUE

Pos	P	W	D	L	F	A	GD	Pts
13	38	11	11	16	48	56	-8	44

HOME

Pos	P	W	D	L	F	A	GD	Pts
10	19	9	7	3	32	19	13	34

AWAY

Pos	P	W	D	L	F	A	GD	Pts
16	19	2	4	13	16	37	-21	10

CUP PROGRESS DETAILS

Competition	Round reached	Knocked out by
FA Cup	R4	Portsmouth
Carling Cup	R4	Aston Villa

BIGGEST WIN (ALL COMPS)
09/03/10 4–0 v Bolton

BIGGEST DEFEAT (ALL COMPS)
16/01/10 2–7 v Chelsea

THE PLAYER WITH THE MOST

GOALS SCORED	Darren Bent	**24**
SHOTS ON TARGET	Darren Bent	**61**
SHOTS OFF TARGET	Darren Bent	**36**
SHOTS WITHOUT SCORING	Steed Malbranque	**27**
ASSISTS	Andy Reid	**7**
OFFSIDES	Darren Bent	**56**
FOULS	Lorik Cana	**55**
FOULS WITHOUT A CARD	Matthew Kilgallon	**4**
FREE-KICKS WON	Kenwyne Jones	**55**
DEFENSIVE CLEARANCES	Michael Turner	**47**

actim INDEX FOR THE 2009/10 BARCLAYS PREMIER LEAGUE SEASON

RANK	PLAYER	PTS
8	Darren Bent	581
86	Kenwyne Jones	341
94	Michael Turner	331

ATTENDANCE RECORD

HIGH	AVERAGE	LOW
47,641	40,355	34,821
v Man Utd (02/05/2010)		v Aston Villa (15/12/2009)

CLOCKWISE FROM ABOVE: The impressive Craig Gordon saves at the feet of Fulham's Bobby Zamora; Fraizer Campbell and Alan Hutton celebrate Sunderland ending a long winless run with a thrashing of Bolton in March; Darren Bent scores the memorable 'beachball' goal to hand his side a win over Liverpool

IT IS a measure of manager Steve Bruce's ambition for Sunderland that he greeted the end of a season which saw the club finish comfortably in mid-table with disappointment.

The 49-year-old arrived at the Stadium of Light in the summer of 2009 charged with the task of transforming the club from one whose sole target was survival in the Barclays Premier League. This time around, top-flight status was mathematically guaranteed with two games to spare, but it had effectively been secured long before.

Bruce had his regrets, though. He said: 'I am disappointed after the season we have had because it could have been so very different. But, if I am being honest, from a team that was nearly relegated last year, I think there has been improvement.'

Sunderland started the 2009/10 season in optimistic mood having once again resorted to the power of owner Ellis Short's chequebook. An initial £10million secured the services of Tottenham striker Darren Bent, while there was also healthy investment in Lorik Cana, Lee Cattermole, Fraizer Campbell and, at the end of the summer transfer window, Michael Turner.

By the time the central defender had settled into his new surroundings, expectation was already soaring following a run of five successive League victories at the Stadium of Light, which came on the back of an opening-day win at Bolton. Chelsea's 3–1

An awful mid-season run ruined Steve Bruce's hopes of making the top half of the table, but there were signs of progress

success in the Black Cats' opening home fixture had become a distant memory and, despite away defeats at Stoke, Burnley and Birmingham, there was even talk on Wearside of a push for Europe.

Hope grew as Liverpool, followed by Arsenal, headed for the north-east and left empty-handed. The Reds did so courtesy of the famous 'beachball' goal, after Bruce's men had also come within seconds of victory over Manchester United at Old Trafford.

It was then that the wheels came off, however. The win against Arsenal on 21st November, which came courtesy of Bent's ninth goal for his new club, proved to be their last in a barren three months which saw 14 League games come and go with little reward. A 7–2 defeat, as Chelsea completed a double at Stamford Bridge on 16th January, was undoubtedly the low point for Bruce's side, and the alarm bells started ringing when Stoke, Wigan and Fulham in turn visited Wearside in quick succession and all left with a point to show for their efforts.

While Boudewijn Zenden, Alan Hutton and Benjani were brought in during the January transfer window, the Black Cats' fans had started to contemplate the possibility of

another relegation scrap as winter gave way to spring.

However, on 9th March, Bent made it 16 goals for the season as he claimed his first hat-trick in a red-and-white shirt against Bolton to lay the foundation for a 4–0 win.

It proved a significant turning point as the swagger with which Sunderland had played during the early part of the campaign gradually returned, and any fears were finally dispelled at Hull on 24th April when Bent's 24th League goal secured just their second away win and another season in the Barclays Premier League.

Bruce was left to reflect upon what might have been, and what he needs to do before the 2010/11 season gets under way to enhance his side's strengths and address its weaknesses. He has indicated that his new recruitment drive at the Stadium of Light will concentrate on quality rather than quantity as he attempts to bridge the gap between the relative safety of mid-table to the fringes of the top eight.

That will require greater resilience on the road in particular, and perhaps increased support for Bent on the goalscoring front with no teammate in double figures during 2009/10.

SUNDERLAND

RESULTS 2009/10

AUGUST

15th ● Bolton   A   W 0–1   **Att:** 22,247. **Ref:** A Marriner – (4-4-2): Fulop, Bardsley, Collins, Ferdinand, McCartney, Cana, Malbranque (Henderson 46), Cattermole, Richardson (Campbell 76), Bent[1], Jones. **Subs not used:** Gordon, Nosworthy, Edwards, Leadbitter, Healy.

18th ● Chelsea   H   L 1–3   **Att:** 41,179. **Ref:** S Bennett – (4-4-2): Fulop, Bardsley, Ferdinand, Collins, McCartney, Henderson, Cattermole (Leadbitter 62), Cana, Richardson (Reid 84), Jones (Campbell 62), Bent[1]. **Subs not used:** Gordon, Nosworthy, Edwards, Healy.

22nd ● Blackburn   H   W 2–1   **Att:** 37,106. **Ref:** A Wiley – (4-4-2): Fulop, Bardsley, Ferdinand, Collins, McCartney (Nosworthy 60), Malbranque (Henderson 79), Cana, Cattermole, Richardson, Bent (Campbell 90), Jones[2]. **Subs not used:** Gordon, Leadbitter, Reid, Healy.

24th ● Norwich   A   W 1–4   **Att:** 12,345. **Ref:** A Taylor – (4-4-2): Gordon, Edwards, Nosworthy, Da Silva, McCartney, Henderson, Tainio[1] (Healy 74), Leadbitter, Reid[2], Campbell (Malbranque 86), Jones (Murphy 46). **Subs not used:** Carson, Bardsley, Ferdinand, O'Donovan. Tudur Jones OG.

29th ● Stoke   A   L 1–0   **Att:** 27,091. **Ref:** M Jones – (4-4-2): Gordon, Bardsley, Ferdinand, Nosworthy, McCartney, Malbranque (Campbell 58), Cattermole (Henderson 80), Cana, Richardson (Reid 58), Jones, Bent. **Subs not used:** Carson, Collins, Leadbitter, Da Silva.

SEPTEMBER

12th ● Hull   H   W 4–1   **Att:** 38,997. **Ref:** M Atkinson – (4-4-2): Gordon, Bardsley (Mensah 77), Turner, Ferdinand, Richardson, Malbranque (Da Silva 80), Cana, Cattermole, Reid[1], Bent[2] (Jones 73), Campbell. **Subs not used:** Carson, Nosworthy, Murphy, Henderson. Zayatte OG.

19th ● Burnley   A   L 3–1   **Att:** 20,196. **Ref:** C Foy – (4-4-2): Gordon, Bardsley, Ferdinand, Turner, McCartney, Malbranque (Jones 62), Cana, Reid, Richardson, Campbell (Henderson 75), Bent[1]. **Subs not used:** Carson, Nosworthy, Mensah, Da Silva, Healy.

22nd ● Birmingham   H   W 2–0   **Att:** 20,576. **Ref:** M Dean – (4-4-2): Gordon, Mensah, Da Silva, Turner, Richardson, Malbranque (Healy 74), Cana (Nosworthy 86), Reid, Henderson[1], Campbell[1], Jones (Murphy 80). **Subs not used:** Carson, Ferdinand, Bardsley, Bent.

27th ● Wolverhampton   H   W 5–2   **Att:** 37,566. **Ref:** L Mason – (4-4-2): Gordon, Da Silva (Ferdinand 74), Turner, Mensah, Richardson, Malbranque, Cattermole (Henderson 46), Cana, Reid, Jones[2], Bent[1] (McCartney 90). **Subs not used:** Fulop, Nosworthy, Healy, Campbell. Mancienne OG.

OCTOBER

3rd ● Man Utd   A   D 2–2   **Att:** 75,114. **Ref:** A Wiley – (4-4-2): Gordon, Bardsley, Turner, Ferdinand, Richardson, Malbranque (McCartney 86), Cana, Cattermole, Reid (Henderson 74), Bent[1], Jones[1] (Campbell 84). **Subs not used:** Fulop, Nosworthy, Da Silva, Healy.

17th ● Liverpool   H   W 1–0   **Att:** 47,327. **Ref:** M Jones – (4-4-2): Gordon, Bardsley, Turner, Ferdinand, McCartney (Henderson 46), Malbranque, Cana, Cattermole (Zenden 58), Reid, Bent[1], Jones (Campbell 66). **Subs not used:** Fulop, Nosworthy, Da Silva, Healy.

24th ● Birmingham   A   L 2–1   **Att:** 21,723. **Ref:** M Atkinson – (4-4-2): Gordon, Bardsley, Ferdinand, Turner, Richardson, Malbranque (Campbell 68), Cana (Zenden 68), Henderson (McCartney 68), Reid, Bent, Jones. **Subs not used:** Fulop, Nosworthy, Da Silva, Healy. Damm OG.

27th ● Aston Villa   H   D 0–0   **Att:** 27,666. **Ref:** P Dowd – (4-4-2): Gordon, Da Silva, Turner, Nosworthy, McCartney (Ferdinand 78), Henderson, Cana, Richardson, Murphy (A Reid 73), Jones, Campbell (Malbranque 95). **Subs not used:** Fulop, Healy, Meyler, A Reid. AET – Score after 90 mins 0–0. Aston Villa win 3–1 on penalties.

31st ● West Ham   H   D 2–2   **Att:** 39,033. **Ref:** A Marriner – (4-4-2): Gordon, Da Silva, Nosworthy, Turner[1], Richardson[1], Malbranque (McCartney 81), Henderson, Cana[1], Reid[1], Jones[1], Bent[1]. **Subs not used:** Fulop, Ferdinand, Bardsley, Healy, Meyler, Murphy.

NOVEMBER

7th ● Tottenham   A   L 2–0   **Att:** 35,955. **Ref:** K Friend – (4-4-2): Gordon (Fulop 66), Bardsley (Ferdinand 77), Turner, Da Silva, McCartney, Malbranque (Healy 77), Henderson, Richardson, Reid, Bent, Campbell. **Subs not used:** Nosworthy, Murphy, Meyler, Reed.

21st ● Arsenal   H   W 1–0   **Att:** 44,918. **Ref:** A Wiley – (4-5-1): Fulop, Bardsley, Da Silva, Mensah (Ferdinand 82), McCartney, Malbranque (Campbell 66), Cana, Richardson, Henderson, Reid (Zenden 78), Bent[1]. **Subs not used:** Carson, Nosworthy, Murphy, Healy.

28th ● Wigan   A   L 1–0   **Att:** 20,447. **Ref:** M Atkinson – (4-5-1): Fulop, Bardsley, Da Silva (Zenden 84), Turner, McCartney (Healy 84), Malbranque (Campbell 46), Henderson, Cana, Richardson, Reid, Bent. **Subs not used:** Carson, Nosworthy, Ferdinand, Mensah.

DECEMBER

6th ● Fulham   A   L 1–0   **Att:** 23,168. **Ref:** M Dean – (4-4-2): Fulop, Bardsley, Ferdinand (Nosworthy 30), Turner, Richardson, Malbranque (Campbell 70), Henderson, Cana, Reid, Bent, Jones (Zenden 73). **Subs not used:** Carson, Murphy, Da Silva, Healy.

12th ● Portsmouth   H   D 1–1   **Att:** 37,578. **Ref:** S Bennett – (4-4-2): Fulop, Nosworthy, Turner, Da Silva, McCartney, Campbell, Henderson, Cana, Reid, Bent[1] (Malbranque 90), Jones (Murphy 85). **Subs not used:** Carson, Meyler, Healy, Anderson, R Noble.

15th ● Aston Villa   H   L 0–2   **Att:** 34,821. **Ref:** K Friend – (4-4-2): Fulop, Nosworthy, Turner (Mensah 82), Da Silva, McCartney, Henderson (Cattermole 71), Cana, Richardson, Reid, Bent, Jones (Bardsley 82). **Subs not used:** Carson, Malbranque, Campbell, Healy.

19th ● Man City   A   L 4–3   **Att:** 44,755. **Ref:** A Marriner – (4-5-1): Fulop, Nosworthy, Turner[1], Mensah[1] (Healy 76), McCartney, Campbell (Richardson 60), Henderson[1], Reid, Cattermole, Malbranque (Jones[1] 41), Bent. **Subs not used:** Carson, Bardsley, Murphy, Da Silva.

26th ● Everton   H   D 1–1   **Att:** 46,990. **Ref:** M Atkinson – (4-4-2): Fulop, McCartney, Mensah[1] (Nosworthy 71), Da Silva, Bardsley, Malbranque (Zenden 58), Cana, Henderson, Reid, Bent[1], Jones. **Subs not used:** Carson, Campbell, Murphy, Meyler, Healy.

28th ● Blackburn   A   D 2–2   **Att:** 25,656. **Ref:** M Dean – (4-4-2): Fulop, Bardsley, Nosworthy, Da Silva, McCartney, Henderson, Meyler, Cana, Murphy, Campbell, Bent[2]. **Subs not used:** Carson, Zenden, Healy, Reed, Anderson, R Noble, Liddle.

JANUARY

2nd ● Barrow   H   W 3–0   **Att:** 25,190. **Ref:** N Swarbrick – (4-4-2): Fulop, Bardsley, Cana, Da Silva, McCartney (Liddle 82), Malbranque[1], Meyler, Henderson, Murphy (Healy 77), Campbell[2], Bent (R Noble 72). **Subs not used:** Carson, O'Donovan, Reed, Anderson.

16th ● Chelsea   A   L 7–2   **Att:** 41,776. **Ref:** C Foy – (4-4-2): Fulop, Bardsley, Cana, Da Silva, McCartney, Malbranque (Zenden[1] 46), Henderson, Meyler, Murphy (Campbell 72), Bent[1], Jones. **Subs not used:** Carson, L Noble, Healy, R Noble, Liddle.

23rd ● Portsmouth   A   L 2–1   **Att:** 10,315. **Ref:** P Walton – (4-4-2): Gordon, Bardsley (Healy 85), Da Silva, Turner, Richardson, Henderson, Cana, Meyler (Reid 72), Zenden, Jones (Campbell 80), Bent[1]. **Subs not used:** Carson, Malbranque, Murphy, R Noble.

27th ● Everton   A   L 2–0   **Att:** 32,163. **Ref:** P Dowd – (4-4-1-1): Gordon, Mensah, Nosworthy (Da Silva 59), Kilgallon, McCartney, Henderson, Cattermole (Reid 46), Cana, Zenden, Richardson (Jones 25), Bent. **Subs not used:** Fulop, Malbranque, Campbell, Meyler.

FEBRUARY

1st ● Stoke   H   D 0–0   **Att:** 35,078. **Ref:** H Webb – (4-4-2): Gordon, Mensah[1], Turner, Kilgallon, McCartney, Malbranque (Campbell 69), Cattermole[1] (Henderson 89), Cana, Reid (Zenden 69), Bent, Jones. **Subs not used:** Fulop, Bardsley, Meyler, Da Silva.

● Barclays Premier League ● FA Cup ● Carling Cup ● UEFA Champions League ● Europa League ● FA Community Shield   ▮ Yellow Card ▮ Red Card

RESULTS 2009/10

6th	● Wigan	H	D 1–1	**Att:** 38,350. **Ref:** S Attwell – (4-4-2): Gordon, Hutton, Turner, Kilgallon, McCartney▌, Henderson (Zenden 69), Cattermole▌, Cana▌, Reid (Mwaruwari 87), Bent, Jones▌¹. **Subs not used:** Fulop, Bardsley, Malbranque, Campbell, P Da Silva.
9th	● Portsmouth	A	D 1–1	**Att:** 16,242. **Ref:** K Friend – (4-4-2): Gordon, Hutton, Turner, Kilgallon, McCartney, Malbranque (Zenden 45), Cana, Cattermole▌▌, Reid (Meyler▌ 85), Bent¹ (Bardsley 89), Jones. **Subs not used:** Carson, Da Silva, Mwaruwari, Liddle.
20th	● Arsenal	A	L 2–0	**Att:** 60,083. **Ref:** S Bennett – (4-4-2): Gordon, Hutton, Turner, Mensah▌, Turner▌, McCartney (Bardsley 85), Campbell, Cana▌, Ferdinand▌, Richardson▌ (Zenden 76), Bent, Jones (Mwaruwari 78). **Subs not used:** Carson, Malbranque, Da Silva, Kilgallon.
28th	● Fulham	H	D 0–0	**Att:** 40,192. **Ref:** M Atkinson – (4-4-2): Gordon, Hutton▌, Turner▌, Mensah (McCartney 83), Ferdinand, Campbell, Cana, Cattermole (Zenden 54), Richardson▌, Jones (Mwaruwari 80), Bent. **Subs not used:** Carson, Bardsley, Da Silva, Kilgallon.

MARCH

9th	● Bolton	H	W 4–0	**Att:** 36,087. **Ref:** S Bennett – (4-4-2): Gordon, Ferdinand, Turner, Mensah (Zenden 79), Hutton, Malbranque (Mwaruwari 85), Cana▌, Cattermole (Bardsley 70), Campbell▌, Jones, Bent▌³. **Subs not used:** Carson, McCartney, Da Silva, Kilgallon.
14th	● Man City	H	D 1–1	**Att:** 41,398. **Ref:** C Foy – (4-4-2): Gordon▌, Hutton, Turner, Mensah, Ferdinand, Campbell (Bardsley 83), Richardson, Meyler▌, Malbranque (Zenden 76), Jones¹ (Henderson 46), Bent. **Subs not used:** Carson, McCartney, Da Silva, Kilgallon.
20th	● Birmingham	H	W 3–1	**Att:** 37,962. **Ref:** P Walton – (4-4-2): Gordon, Hutton, Turner, Mensah (Bardsley 72), Ferdinand, Campbell¹, Meyler, Richardson, Cattermole (Cattermole 80), Bent², Mwaruwari (Henderson 72). **Subs not used:** Carson, Zenden, P Da Silva, Kilgallon.
24th	● Aston Villa	A	D 1–1	**Att:** 37,473. **Ref:** M Dean – (4-5-1): Gordon, Hutton, Turner, Mensah (P Da Silva 71), Ferdinand, Campbell¹, Henderson, Cattermole, Richardson, Malbranque (Cana 82), Bent. **Subs not used:** Carson, Bardsley, Zenden, Kilgallon, Mwaruwari.
28th	● Liverpool	A	L 3–0	**Att:** 43,121. **Ref:** P Dowd –(4-5-1): Gordon, Bardsley, Turner, Cana, Ferdinand, Campbell, Henderson (Zenden 78), Cattermole (Da Silva 46), Richardson, Malbranque (Jones 51), Bent▌. **Subs not used:** Carson, Kilgallon, Mwaruwari, Liddle.

APRIL

3rd	● Tottenham	H	W 3–1	**Att:** 43,184. **Ref:** L Mason – (4-4-2): Gordon, Ferdinand, Turner, Da Silva, Richardson, Henderson, Meyler, Cattermole▌, Malbranque▌ (Zenden¹ 78), Campbell (Bardsley 89), Bent² (Jones 78). **Subs not used:** Carson, Kilgallon, Mwaruwari, Liddle.
10th	● West Ham	A	L 1–0	**Att:** 34,685. **Ref:** M Jones – (4-4-2): Gordon▌, Ferdinand, Da Silva (Mwaruwari 88), Turner, Richardson, Henderson, Meyler (Jones 63), Cattermole▌, Malbranque (Zenden 72), Bent, Campbell▌. **Subs not used:** Carson, Bardsley, Hutton, Kilgallon.
17th	● Burnley	H	W 2–1	**Att:** 41,341. **Ref:** H Webb – (4-4-2): Gordon, Hutton, Turner, Mensah▌ (Ferdinand 46), Richardson, Campbell¹, Meyler▌ (Zenden 88), Henderson, Malbranque▌, Jones, Bent¹ (Mwaruwari 90). **Subs not used:** Carson, Bardsley, Da Silva, Kilgallon.
24th	● Hull	A	W 0–1	**Att:** 25,012. **Ref:** L Probert – (4-4-2): Gordon, Hutton▌, Turner (Ferdinand 46), Kilgallon, Richardson, Campbell▌, Henderson▌, Meyler▌, Malbranque (Bardsley 46), Bent¹, Jones (Cana 60). **Subs not used:** Carson, Zenden, Da Silva, Mwaruwari.

MAY

2nd	● Man Utd	H	L 0–1	**Att:** 47,641. **Ref:** S Bennett – (4-4-2): Gordon, Bardsley▌, Turner, Mensah (Kilgallon 17), Richardson▌, Henderson (Jones 74), Meyler (Cattermole 37), Cana, Malbranque▌, Campbell, Bent. **Subs not used:** Carson, Ferdinand, Zenden, Da Silva.
9th	● Wolverhampton	A	L 2–1	**Att:** 28,971. **Ref:** L Mason – (4-4-2): Gordon, Hutton, Turner▌, Kilgallon, Richardson, Campbell, Cana (Mwaruwari 73), Henderson (Zenden 46), Malbranque (Colback▌ 77), Bent, Jones¹. **Subs not used:** Carson, Bardsley, Ferdinand, Da Silva.

● Barclays Premier League ● FA Cup ● Carling Cup ● UEFA Champions League ● Europa League ● FA Community Shield ▌ Yellow Card ▌ Red Card

Boudewijn Zenden scores Sunderland's superb third goal in the victory over high-flying Tottenham in April

OFFICIAL FOOTBALL YEARBOOK OF THE ENGLISH & SCOTTISH LEAGUES 2010-2011

SUNDERLAND

BARCLAYS PREMIER LEAGUE GOALKEEPER STATS

Player	Minutes on pitch	Appearances	Match starts	Completed matches	Sub appearances	Subbed off	SAVES BREAKDOWN								Clean sheets	Goals conceded	Save %	PENALTIES			Fouls committed	Free-kicks won	Yellow cards	Red cards
							Saved with feet	Punched	Parried	Tipped over	Fumbled	Tipped round	Caught	Blocked				Saved	Resulting in goals	Opposition miss				
Marton Fulop	1177	13	12	12	1	0	2	6	7	2	1	2	41	0	2	25	68.18	0	2	0	0	3	0	0
Craig Gordon	2490	26	26	25	0	1	4	13	26	5	0	7	70	8	5	31	81.10	0	3	1	0	5	3	0

BARCLAYS PREMIER LEAGUE OUTFIELD PLAYER STATS

Player	Minutes on pitch	Appearances	Match starts	Completed matches	Substitute appearances	Subbed off	Goals scored	Assists	Shots on target	Shots off target	Crosses	Tackles made	Defensive clearances	Defensive blocks	Fouls committed	Free-kicks won	Caught offside	Yellow cards	Red cards
Phillip Bardsley	1834	26	18	16	8	2	0	0	6	7	31	47	27	9	36	15	0	8	0
Darren Bent	3609	38	38	31	0	7	24	4	61	36	18	26	24	1	41	30	56	5	0
Fraizer Campbell	2069	31	19	15	12	4	4	6	14	13	17	23	3	0	27	33	15	3	0
Lorik Cana	2773	31	29	26	2	2	0	1	5	17	8	79	36	6	55	41	0	10	1
Lee Cattermole	1582	22	19	9	3	9	0	3	6	4	5	56	9	2	37	10	0	8	1
Jack Colback	16	1	0	0	1	0	0	0	0	0	0	0	0	0	2	0	0	1	1
Danny Collins	287	3	3	3	0	0	0	0	0	0	0	4	6	4	3	5	0	0	0
Paulo Da Silva	1237	16	12	9	4	3	0	1	3	1	6	17	19	10	13	5	0	1	0
Anton Ferdinand	1909	24	19	18	5	1	0	1	0	0	6	53	31	16	9	10	1	2	0
David Healy	48	3	0	0	3	0	0	0	0	0	2	0	0	0	0	1	0	0	0
Jordan Henderson	2344	33	23	17	10	6	1	5	12	17	38	41	14	4	33	12	3	3	0
Alan Hutton	1017	11	11	10	0	0	0	1	4	2	17	22	5	0	11	10	1	1	1
Kenwyne Jones	2328	32	24	13	8	10	9	3	37	17	7	21	24	4	20	55	5	1	1
Matthew Kilgallon	669	7	6	6	1	0	0	0	0	1	2	8	9	1	4	1	0	0	0
Grant Leadbitter	30	1	0	0	1	0	0	0	0	0	0	0	0	0	1	1	0	0	0
Steed Malbranque	2144	31	30	4	1	26	0	6	18	9	45	57	5	5	41	43	1	3	0
George McCartney	1884	25	20	16	5	4	0	0	0	1	39	44	17	7	20	23	4	3	0
John Mensah	1118	16	14	5	2	9	1	0	2	4	2	29	12	5	17	17	0	4	0
David Meyler	773	10	9	5	1	3	0	0	2	2	6	13	7	2	19	12	1	4	1
Daryl Murphy	177	3	2	1	1	1	0	0	0	0	6	5	1	1	2	1	0	0	0
Benjani Mwaruwari	159	8	1	0	7	1	0	0	0	1	0	2	1	0	4	1	3	0	0
Nyron Nosworthy	761	10	7	6	3	1	0	0	1	0	5	31	14	2	14	10	0	3	0
Andy Reid	1750	21	18	13	3	5	2	2	7	12	130	22	4	2	21	29	1	2	0
Kieran Richardson	2568	29	28	22	1	5	1	1	12	15	51	55	10	3	49	29	2	8	1
Michael Turner	2724	29	29	25	0	2	2	1	6	4	1	54	47	17	35	27	0	8	2
Boudewijn Zenden	604	20	1	0	19	0	2	0	14	4	22	9	3	0	6	7	0	1	0

SEASON TOTALS

Goals scored	48
Goals conceded	56
Clean sheets	7
Shots on target	215
Shots off target	168
Shots per goal	7.98
Pens awarded	9
Pens scored	6
Pens conceded	6
Offsides	93
Corners	181
Crosses	464
Players used	28
Fouls committed	520
Free-kicks won	436

CARDS RECEIVED

82   9

SEQUENCES

Wins	2
(17/04/10–24/04/10)	
Losses	2
(on four occasions)	
Draws	3
(01/02/10–09/02/10)	
Undefeated	5
(28/02/10–24/03/10)	
Without win	14
(28/11/09–28/02/10)	
Undefeated home	9
(26/12/09–17/04/10)	
Undefeated away	–
(–)	
Without scoring	2
(on three occasions)	
Without conceding	2
(28/02/10–09/03/10)	
Scoring	7
(12/09/09–31/10/09)	
Conceding	9
(28/11/09–27/01/10)	

SEASON INFORMATION

Highest position: 5
Lowest position: 16
Average goals scored per game: 1.26
Average goals conceded per game: 1.47

LEAGUE POSITION AT THE END OF EACH MONTH

AUG	SEP	OCT	NOV	DEC	JAN	FEB	MAR	APR	MAY
9	8	8	8	10	13	14	13	10	13

MATCH RECORDS

Goals scored per match

		W	D	L	Pts
Failed to score	12	0	2	10	2
Scored 1 goal	14	4	6	4	18
Scored 2 goals	6	2	3	1	9
Scored 3 goals	3	2	0	1	6
Scored 4+ goals	3	3	0	0	9

Goals conceded per match

		W	D	L	Pts
Clean sheet	7	5	2	0	17
Conceded 1 goal	16	5	6	5	21
Conceded 2 goals	10	1	3	6	6
Conceded 3 goals	3	0	0	3	0
Conceded 4+ goals	2	0	0	2	0

EARLIEST STRIKE

DARREN BENT
(v Tottenham) 0:36

LATEST STRIKE

ANTON FERDINAND
(v Man Utd) 92:20

Kenwyne Jones

GOAL DETAILS

How the goals were struck

SCORED		CONCEDED
25	Right foot	33
12	Left foot	13
10	Header	8
1	Other	2

How the goals were struck

SCORED		CONCEDED
32	Open play	33
4	Cross	12
2	Corner	1
6	Penalty	5
1	Direct from free-kick	0
1	Free-kick	3
2	Own goal	2

Distance from goal

SCORED		CONCEDED
20	6YDS	20
23	18YDS	32
5	18+YDS	4

GOALS SCORED/CONCEDED
PER FIVE-MINUTE INTERVALS

MINS	5	10	15	20	25	30	35	40	45	50	55	60	65	70	75	80	85	90
FOR	5	5	3	3	4	1	1	3	0	2	2	2	4	2	4	1	1	5
AGN	2	4	3	3	3	4	3	2	2	2	6	2	3	4	1	3	2	7

TOTTENHAM HOTSPUR

CLUB SUMMARY

FORMED	1882
MANAGER	Harry Redknapp
GROUND	White Hart Lane
CAPACITY	36,236
NICKNAME	Spurs
WEBSITE	www.tottenhamhotspur.com

The New Football Pools PLAYER OF THE SEASON — Michael Dawson

OVERALL

P	W	D	L	F	A	GD
50	28	10	12	96	52	44

BARCLAYS PREMIER LEAGUE

Pos	P	W	D	L	F	A	GD	Pts
4	38	21	7	10	67	41	26	70

HOME

Pos	P	W	D	L	F	A	GD	Pts
4	19	14	2	3	40	12	28	44

AWAY

Pos	P	W	D	L	F	A	GD	Pts
6	19	7	5	7	27	29	-2	26

CUP PROGRESS DETAILS

Competition	Round reached	Knocked out by
FA Cup	SF	Portsmouth
Carling Cup	QF	Man Utd

BIGGEST WIN (ALL COMPS)
22/11/09 9–1 v Wigan

BIGGEST DEFEAT (ALL COMPS)
0–3 on 2 occasions

THE PLAYER WITH THE MOST

GOALS SCORED Jermain Defoe	**18**
SHOTS ON TARGET Jermain Defoe	**61**
SHOTS OFF TARGET Peter Crouch	**38**
SHOTS WITHOUT SCORING Younes Kaboul	**5**
ASSISTS Aaron Lennon	**9**
OFFSIDES Jermain Defoe	**52**
FOULS Wilson Palacios	**58**
FOULS WITHOUT A CARD Jonathan Woodgate	**2**
FREE-KICKS WON Aaron Lennon	**43**
DEFENSIVE CLEARANCES Michael Dawson	**35**

actim INDEX FOR THE 2009/10 BARCLAYS PREMIER LEAGUE SEASON

RANK	PLAYER	PTS
16	Jermain Defoe	523
40	Heurelho Gomes	415
48	Vedran Corluka	395

ATTENDANCE RECORD

HIGH	AVERAGE	LOW
36,041	35,794	35,318
v Arsenal (14/04/2010)		v Birmingham (29/08/2009)

TOTTENHAM will aim to rub shoulders with the European elite in the UEFA Champions League during the coming season after an extraordinary 2009/10 campaign for Harry Redknapp and his team.

The standard was set as early as the first month of the season when Spurs went four games unbeaten and proudly sat on top of the Barclays Premier League table. Their 5–1 win at Hull was a particular highlight with the Tigers' defence finding Jermain Defoe almost unplayable as he grabbed a hat-trick.

However, Spurs were brought down to earth in September when title holders Manchester United inflicted a 3–1 home defeat on Redknapp's side. Another loss, 3–0 at Chelsea, dampened the new-found optimism at White Hart Lane and a 3–0 defeat to archrivals Arsenal at the end of October was another setback. But five goals from England striker Defoe then put Spurs back on track as they walloped Wigan 9–1 at White Hart Lane.

It was Tottenham's inconsistency in the opening half of the season that most threatened their dream of earning a place in the top four. Redknapp was left scratching his head over how his side could lose to struggling Wolves one week and then beat fellow Champions League hopefuls Manchester City 3–0 the next.

Redknapp certainly had quality in abundance in attack with Defoe, Roman Pavlyuchenko, Robbie Keane and Peter Crouch all vying for a place in the first team. In January, the boss decided that he could do without one of them as he allowed Keane to go on loan to Celtic for the remainder of the season. Pavlyuchenko also looked certain to leave in the transfer window after outlining his unhappiness with life on the substitutes' bench, but the Russian remained and had a renaissance during the second half of the campaign.

Tottenham could also depend on some outstanding talents at the back, with Ledley King enjoying a marvellous season. His long-standing knee injury meant that he could hardly train and struggled to play more than once a week. However, Redknapp and his staff carefully managed the problem and actually did it so well that King eventually found himself alongside fellow Spurs defender Michael Dawson in Fabio Capello's 30-man provisional England squad for the World Cup.

Harry Redknapp's side ended a thrilling season by pipping Manchester City to qualification for the Champions League

A nine-game unbeaten run from 14th February until the end of March saw Tottenham's chances of breaking into the top four improve dramatically. They also progressed to the semi-finals of the FA Cup, but they would come unstuck against relegated Portsmouth in a 2–0 extra-time defeat at Wembley.

But it was over the next few games that Redknapp really got the best out of his side. Goalkeeper Heurelho Gomes, criticised in the past by Spurs fans, stepped up to the plate. The semi-final defeat was bad timing for Tottenham as they faced rivals Arsenal in midweek and title-chasing Chelsea the following Saturday. But to a man, they shook off the disappointment of missing out on a Cup final against Chelsea with a superb 2–1 win over the Gunners.

That game heralded the emergence of Gareth Bale. The Wales international, a left-back by trade, proved to be a sensation on the left side of midfield and he put his side 2–0 in front with a fabulous strike. Spurs had taken the lead thanks to a blockbuster of a goal from debutant Danny Rose and, although Arsenal fought back in the final stages, Gomes pulled off a string of stunning saves to give them an important win.

Spurs raised themselves again to beat Chelsea by the same scoreline, with Bale again on target, which put them in pole position for fourth spot. A 3–1 defeat at Manchester United was followed by a timely 1–0 success over Bolton at home to set up a vital clash against Manchester City in the battle for fourth place, with Redknapp knowing that victory would guarantee Champions League football for the 2010/11 season. Spurs went on the attack and outplayed Roberto Mancini's side throughout, and they were rewarded with Crouch's 82nd-minute winner and thus a place in Europe's top competition.

CLOCKWISE FROM ABOVE: Jermain Defoe is mobbed by his Spurs teammates after scoring five goals in a 9–1 win against Wigan in November; Gareth Bale became one of Tottenham's most influential players during the course of the campaign; Roman Pavlyuchenko enjoyed a new lease of life at Spurs, including a double against Wigan in February; Harry Redknapp attempts to rally his troops ahead of extra-time in the FA Cup semi-final against Portsmouth, but Spurs would lose out

TOTTENHAM HOTSPUR

RESULTS 2009/10

AUGUST

16th ● Liverpool H W 2–1 **Att:** 35,935. **Ref:** P Dowd – (4-4-2): Gomes▮, Corluka, King, Bassong▮, Assou-Ekotto▮, Lennon▮, Palacios, Huddlestone, Modric (O'Hara 83), Keane (Crouch 68), Defoe (Pavlyuchenko 90). **Subs not used:** Cudicini, Hutton, Bentley, Naughton.

19th ● Hull A W 1–5 **Att:** 24,735. **Ref:** C Foy – (4-4-2): Gomes (Cudicini 16), Hutton▮, Corluka, Bassong, Assou-Ekotto, Lennon, Palacios¹, Huddlestone, Modric (Bentley 85), Keane▮¹ (Crouch 81), Defoe³. **Subs not used:** Pavlyuchenko, Naughton, Chimbonda, O'Hara.

23rd ● West Ham A W 1–2 **Att:** 33,095. **Ref:** M Clattenburg – (4-4-2): Cudicini, Corluka, Bassong, King, Assou-Ekotto, Lennon¹, Huddlestone▮, Palacios, Modric (O'Hara 86), Keane (Crouch 81), Defoe¹ (Naughton 90). **Subs not used:** Button, Hutton, Bentley, Pavlyuchenko.

26th ● Doncaster A W 1–5 **Att:** 12,923. **Ref:** R Booth – (4-4-2): Cudicini (Button 82), Corluka, Bassong (Boateng 59), Huddlestone¹ (Rose 72), Naughton, Hutton, Giovani, Bentley¹, O'Hara¹, Pavlyuchenko¹, Crouch¹. **Subs not used:** Lennon, Palacios, Defoe.

29th ● Birmingham H W 2–1 **Att:** 35,318. **Ref:** P Walton – (4-4-2): Cudicini, Corluka, King (Hutton▮ 46), Bassong, Assou-Ekotto, Lennon¹, Palacios, Huddlestone▮, Modric (Crouch¹ 49), Keane, Defoe (Pavlyuchenko 80). **Subs not used:** Button, Bentley, Naughton, Giovani.

SEPTEMBER

12th ● Man Utd H L 1–3 **Att:** 35,785. **Ref:** A Marriner – (4-3-3): Cudicini, Corluka (Hutton 69), King▮, Bassong, Assou-Ekotto, Lennon, Huddlestone, Palacios▮ (Jenas▮ 46), Defoe¹, Crouch, Keane (Kranjcar 72). **Subs not used:** Gomes, Bentley, Pavlyuchenko, Naughton.

20th ● Chelsea A L 3–0 **Att:** 41,623. **Ref:** H Webb – (4-4-2): Cudicini, Corluka, King (Hutton 48), Bassong▮ (Kranjcar 82), Assou-Ekotto, Lennon, Jenas▮, Huddlestone, Palacios, Defoe (Crouch 67), Keane. **Subs not used:** Gomes, Bentley, Naughton, Giovani.

23rd ● Preston A W 1–5 **Att:** 16,533. **Ref:** P Dowd – (4-4-2): Gomes, Hutton▮, Huddlestone, Dawson (Corluka 80), Bale, Bentley, Jenas, Palacios, Giovani (Lennon 70), Crouch², Defoe¹ (Keane¹ 70). **Subs not used:** J Walker, Naughton, Rose, Dervite.

26th ● Burnley H W 5–0 **Att:** 35,462. **Ref:** M Dean – (4-4-2): Cudicini, Corluka, Huddlestone, Bassong (Dawson 88), Assou-Ekotto, Lennon (Bale 84), Jenas¹, Palacios▮, Kranjcar, Keane⁴, Defoe (Crouch 57). **Subs not used:** Gomes, Hutton, Bentley, Naughton.

OCTOBER

3rd ● Bolton A D 2–2 **Att:** 21,305. **Ref:** M Jones – (4-4-2): Cudicini, Corluka▮¹, Huddlestone, Bassong, Assou-Ekotto, Lennon, Jenas▮, Palacios, Kranjcar¹, Keane (Defoe 67), Crouch. **Subs not used:** Gomes, Hutton, Bale, Bentley, Naughton, Dawson.

17th ● Portsmouth A W 1–2 **Att:** 20,821. **Ref:** P Dowd – (4-4-2): Gomes, Corluka, King¹, Bassong, Assou-Ekotto, Lennon, Jenas▮, Huddlestone (Dawson 87), Kranjcar (Palacios¹ 66), Defoe▮¹, Keane (Crouch 56). **Subs not used:** Cudicini, Hutton, Bentley, Pavlyuchenko.

24th ● Stoke H L 0–1 **Att:** 36,031. **Ref:** L Probert – (4-4-2): Gomes, Corluka, Woodgate (Dawson 14), Bassong, Assou-Ekotto, Lennon, Huddlestone (Jenas 71), Palacios, Kranjcar, Keane (Pavlyuchenko 63), Crouch. **Subs not used:** Cudicini, Hutton, Bale, Naughton.

27th ● Everton H W 2–0 **Att:** 35,843. **Ref:** L Mason – (4-4-2): Gomes, Hutton, Bassong, Dawson, Assou-Ekotto, Bentley, Huddlestone¹, Palacios, Bale, Keane¹, Pavlyuchenko. **Subs not used:** Button, Jenas, Naughton, Corluka, Dervite, Parrett, Kane.

31st ● Arsenal A L 3–0 **Att:** 60,103. **Ref:** M Clattenburg – (4-5-1): Gomes, Corluka (Hutton 86), King, Bassong, Assou-Ekotto, Bentley, Huddlestone (Bale 55), Palacios, Jenas, Keane (Pavlyuchenko 65), Crouch▮. **Subs not used:** Button, Dawson, Kranjcar, Woodgate.

NOVEMBER

7th ● Sunderland H W 2–0 **Att:** 35,955. **Ref:** K Friend – (4-4-2): Gomes▮, Corluka, King (Dawson 59), Woodgate, Assou-Ekotto, Jenas, Huddlestone¹, Palacios, Keane¹ (Kranjcar 63), Crouch, Defoe. **Subs not used:** Alnwick, Hutton, Bale, Bentley, Pavlyuchenko.

22nd ● Wigan H W 9–1 **Att:** 35,650. **Ref:** P Walton – (4-4-2): Gomes, Corluka, Dawson, Woodgate, Assou-Ekotto (Bassong 81), Lennon¹ (Bentley 79), Huddlestone, Palacios (Jenas 84), Kranjcar¹, Defoe⁵, Crouch¹. **Subs not used:** Alnwick, Hutton, Pavlyuchenko, Keane. Kirkland OG.

28th ● Aston Villa A D 1–1 **Att:** 39,866. **Ref:** P Dowd – (4-4-2): Gomes, Corluka, Dawson¹, Bassong, Assou-Ekotto, Lennon, Huddlestone▮, Palacios (Jenas 66), Kranjcar (Keane 78), Defoe, Crouch. **Subs not used:** Alnwick, Hutton, Bale, Bentley, Rose.

DECEMBER

1st ● Man Utd A L 2–0 **Att:** 57,212. **Ref:** M Clattenburg – (4-4-2): Gomes, Hutton▮, Bassong, Dawson, Bale, Lennon, Jenas, Palacios (Huddlestone 46), Bentley, Defoe, Keane (Crouch 66). **Subs not used:** J Walker, Pavlyuchenko, Naughton, Corluka, Rose.

6th ● Everton A D 2–2 **Att:** 34,003. **Ref:** A Marriner – (4-4-2): Gomes, Corluka, Bassong, Dawson▮, Assou-Ekotto (Bale 46), Lennon, Huddlestone▮, Palacios (Hutton 90), Kranjcar (Jenas 88), Defoe¹, Crouch. **Subs not used:** Alnwick, Bentley, Pavlyuchenko, Keane.

12th ● Wolverhampton H L 0–1 **Att:** 36,012. **Ref:** S Attwell – (4-4-2): Gomes, Corluka, Bassong, Bassong, Assou-Ekotto, Lennon, Huddlestone, Palacios (Modric 58), Kranjcar (Giovani 78), Keane (Crouch 58), Defoe. **Subs not used:** Alnwick, Hutton, Bale, Rose.

16th ● Man City H W 3–0 **Att:** 35,891. **Ref:** A Wiley – (4-4-2): Gomes, Corluka, Dawson, Bassong, Assou-Ekotto (Bale 90), Lennon, Huddlestone, Palacios▮, Kranjcar▮² , Defoe¹ (Jenas 90), Crouch. **Subs not used:** Alnwick, Hutton, Pavlyuchenko, Keane, Modric.

19th ● Blackburn A W 0–2 **Att:** 26,490. **Ref:** P Walton – (4-4-2): Gomes, Corluka▮, Dawson, Bassong, Assou-Ekotto, Lennon (Hutton 90), Huddlestone, Palacios (Jenas 58), Kranjcar, Crouch², Defoe (Keane 67). **Subs not used:** Alnwick, Bale, Pavlyuchenko, Rose.

26th ● Fulham H D 0–0 **Att:** 25,679. **Ref:** S Bennett – (4-4-2): Gomes, Corluka, Dawson, Bassong (King 90), Assou-Ekotto, Lennon, Jenas, Palacios, Kranjcar (Modric 71), Keane (Defoe 71), Crouch. **Subs not used:** Alnwick, Bale, Huddlestone, Pavlyuchenko.

28th ● West Ham H W 2–0 **Att:** 35,994. **Ref:** C Foy – (4-4-2): Gomes, Corluka▮, Dawson, King, Assou-Ekotto (Bale 87), Lennon (Jenas 89), Palacios, Huddlestone, Modric¹ (Kranjcar 83), Crouch, Defoe▮. **Subs not used:** Alnwick, Hutton, Keane, Bassong.

JANUARY

2nd ● Peterborough H W 4–0 **Att:** 35,862. **Ref:** L Mason – (4-4-2): Gomes, Hutton, Dawson, Bassong, Bale (Naughton 79), Kranjcar² (Rose▮ 73), Huddlestone, Palacios, Modric, Keane▮, Defoe¹ (Pavlyuchenko 75). **Subs not used:** Alnwick, Crouch, Giovani, Corluka.

16th ● Hull H D 0–0 **Att:** 35,729. **Ref:** M Atkinson – (4-4-2): Gomes, Corluka, Dawson, Bassong▮, Bale, Modric, Huddlestone▮, Palacios▮ (Jenas▮ 55), Kranjcar, Defoe, Keane (Crouch 62). **Subs not used:** Alnwick, Bentley, Pavlyuchenko, Naughton, Rose.

20th ● Liverpool A L 2–0 **Att:** 42,016. **Ref:** H Webb – (4-4-2): Gomes, Corluka (Hutton 61), Dawson, King (Bassong 81), Bale▮, Modric, Jenas▮, Palacios▮, Kranjcar (Keane 65), Crouch, Defoe. **Subs not used:** Alnwick, Pavlyuchenko, Giovani, Rose.

23rd ● Leeds H D 2–2 **Att:** 35,750. **Ref:** A Wiley – (4-4-2): Gomes, Hutton▮, Bassong, Dawson, Bale, Kranjcar (Keane 71), Modric, Jenas, Rose (Palacios 56), Defoe, Crouch¹ (Pavlyuchenko¹ 71). **Subs not used:** Alnwick, Naughton, O'Hara, Dervite.

26th ● Fulham H W 2–0 **Att:** 35,467. **Ref:** M Dean – (4-4-2): Gomes, Corluka, Dawson▮, King, Bale, Bentley¹, Huddlestone, Palacios, Modric, Crouch¹, Defoe (Keane 81). **Subs not used:** Alnwick, Hutton, Jenas, Bassong, O'Hara, Rose.

● Barclays Premier League ● FA Cup ● Carling Cup ● UEFA Champions League ● Europa League ● FA Community Shield ▮ Yellow Card ▮ Red Card

RESULTS 2009/10

30th ● Birmingham   A   D 1–1   **Att:** 27,238. **Ref:** S Attwell – (4-4-2): Gomes, Corluka, Dawson, King, Bale, Bentley (Jenas 89), Huddlestone, Palacios▮, Modric, Crouch, Defoe▮[1] (Keane 78). **Subs not used:** Alnwick, Hutton, Bassong, Kranjcar, Rose.

FEBRUARY

3rd ● Leeds   A   W 1–3   **Att:** 37,704. **Ref:** A Marriner – (4-4-2): Gomes, Corluka, Dawson, Bassong, Bale, Bentley▮, Huddlestone, Jenas, Kranjcar, Crouch, Defoe[3]. **Subs not used:** Alnwick, Palacios, Modric, Rose, Dervite, Parrett, Fredericks.

6th ● Aston Villa   H   D 0–0   **Att:** 35,899. **Ref:** C Foy – (4-4-2): Gomes, Corluka, Dawson, King, Bale, Bentley, Huddlestone, Palacios, Modric, Defoe, Crouch. **Subs not used:** Alnwick, Kaboul, Jenas, Gudjohnsen, Bassong, Kranjcar, K Walker.

10th ● Wolverhampton   A   L 1–0   **Att:** 27,992. **Ref:** M Clattenburg – (4-4-2): Gomes, Kaboul, Dawson, Bassong, Bale, Bentley, Huddlestone, Jenas (Palacios▮ 46), Kranjcar (Modric 72), Defoe, Gudjohnsen (Crouch 63). **Subs not used:** Alnwick, Pavlyuchenko, Corluka, K Walker.

14th ● Bolton   A   D 1–1   **Att:** 13,596. **Ref:** P Dowd – (4-4-2): Gomes, Corluka, Dawson, King, Bale, Bentley, Huddlestone▮, Palacios▮, Modric (Kranjcar 63), Crouch, Defoe▮[1]. **Subs not used:** Alnwick, Pavlyuchenko, Gudjohnsen, Bassong, Rose, Dervite.

21st ● Wigan   A   W 0–3   **Att:** 16,165. **Ref:** A Wiley – (4-4-2): Gomes, Corluka, Dawson▮, King (Bassong 52), Bale, Bentley▮, Huddlestone▮, Palacios, Kranjcar (Modric 69), Crouch, Defoe▮[1] (Pavlyuchenko[2] 73). **Subs not used:** Alnwick, Kaboul, Gudjohnsen, Rose.

24th ● Bolton   H   W 4–0   **Att:** 31,436. **Ref:** P Walton – (4-4-2): Gomes, Assou-Ekotto, Dawson, Bassong, Bale, Bentley (Rose 70), Huddlestone, Palacios (Kranjcar 60), Modric, Pavlyuchenko[2], Defoe (Gudjohnsen 46). **Subs not used:** Alnwick, Dervite, Kane, M'Poku. Jaaskelainen OG, A O'Brien OG.

28th ● Everton   H   W 2–1   **Att:** 35,912. **Ref:** S Bennett – (4-4-2): Gomes, Corluka, Dawson, Bassong, Bale, Kranjcar, Huddlestone (Kaboul 52), Palacios, Modric▮[1], Pavlyuchenko[1] (Crouch 82), Defoe (Gudjohnsen 71). **Subs not used:** Alnwick, K Walker, Dervite, Assou-Ekotto.

MARCH

6th ● Fulham   A   D 0–0   **Att:** 24,533. **Ref:** M Clattenburg – (4-4-2): Gomes, Corluka, Dawson, Bassong, Assou-Ekotto, Modric, Palacios, Kranjcar, Bale, Crouch, Pavlyuchenko (Defoe 81). **Subs not used:** Alnwick, Gudjohnsen, Rose, Livermore, Dervite, Townsend.

13th ● Blackburn   H   W 3–1   **Att:** 35,474. **Ref:** H Webb – (4-4-2): Gomes, Corluka, Dawson, Bassong, Assou-Ekotto, Kranjcar, Modric (Gudjohnsen 89), Palacios, Bale, Pavlyuchenko[2], Defoe[1] (Crouch 82). **Subs not used:** Alnwick, Kaboul, Rose, K Walker, Livermore.

20th ● Stoke   A   W 1–2   **Att:** 27,575. **Ref:** M Dean – (4-4-2): Gomes, Corluka, Dawson, Bassong, Assou-Ekotto▮, Kranjcar▮[1] (Livermore 90), Kaboul, Modric, Bale, Crouch, Pavlyuchenko (Gudjohnsen[1] 36). **Subs not used:** Alnwick, Palacios, Dervite, Parrett, Townsend.

24th ● Fulham   H   W 3–1   **Att:** 35,432. **Ref:** M Atkinson – (4-4-2): Gomes, Corluka (Pavlyuchenko[1] 53), Bassong▮, Dawson, Assou-Ekotto (Huddlestone 46), Kranjcar (Bentley[1] 46), Palacios, Modric, Bale, Gudjohnsen[1], Crouch. **Subs not used:** Alnwick, Rose, Livermore, Townsend.

27th ● Portsmouth   H   W 2–0   **Att:** 35,870. **Ref:** K Friend – (4-4-2): Gomes, K Walker, Bassong, Dawson (Kaboul 62), Bale, Bentley, Huddlestone, Modric, Kranjcar[1] (Assou-Ekotto 66), Crouch[1], Gudjohnsen (Pavlyuchenko 79). **Subs not used:** Alnwick, Palacios, Rose, Livermore.

APRIL

3rd ● Sunderland   A   L 3–1   **Att:** 43,184. **Ref:** L Mason – (4-4-2): Gomes, K Walker, Kaboul, Bassong, Assou-Ekotto (Kranjcar 46), Bentley (Defoe 46), Palacios, Modric, Bale, Pavlyuchenko (Crouch[1] 71), Gudjohnsen. **Subs not used:** Alnwick, Rose, Livermore, Dervite.

11th ● Portsmouth   N   L 0–2   **Att:** 84,602. **Ref:** A Wiley – (4-4-2): Gomes, Corluka, Dawson, Bassong▮, Bale, Bentley (Kranjcar 79), Huddlestone▮ (Gudjohnsen 102), Palacios▮, Modric, Crouch, Defoe (Pavlyuchenko 59). **Subs not used:** Alnwick, Rose, Livermore, Assou-Ekotto. AET – Score after 90 mins 0–0.

14th ● Arsenal   H   W 2–1   **Att:** 36,041. **Ref:** M Clattenburg – (4-4-2): Gomes, Assou-Ekotto, Dawson▮, King, Bale[1], Kaboul▮, Huddlestone, Modric▮, Rose[1] (Bentley 46), Pavlyuchenko (Crouch 88), Defoe (Gudjohnsen 67). **Subs not used:** Alnwick, Bassong, K Walker, Livermore.

17th ● Chelsea   H   W 2–1   **Att:** 35,814. **Ref:** P Dowd – (4-4-2): Gomes, Kaboul, Dawson, Bassong, Assou-Ekotto, Bentley, Huddlestone▮, Modric, Bale[1], Pavlyuchenko▮ (Crouch 90), Defoe[1] (Gudjohnsen 78). **Subs not used:** Alnwick, Rose, K Walker, Livermore, Townsend.

24th ● Man Utd   A   L 3–1   **Att:** 75,268. **Ref:** A Marriner – (4-4-2): Gomes, Assou-Ekotto, Dawson, King[1], Bale, Bentley (Lennon 66), Huddlestone, Palacios, Modric, Defoe (Gudjohnsen 55), Pavlyuchenko (Crouch 75). **Subs not used:** Alnwick, Kaboul, Jenas, Bassong.

MAY

1st ● Bolton   H   W 1–0   **Att:** 35,852. **Ref:** C Foy – (4-4-2): Gomes, Kaboul, Dawson, King, Assou-Ekotto, Bentley (Lennon 73), Huddlestone[1], Modric, Bale, Pavlyuchenko (Gudjohnsen 87), Defoe (Crouch 72). **Subs not used:** Alnwick, Jenas, Palacios, Bassong.

5th ● Man City   A   W 0–1   **Att:** 47,370. **Ref:** S Bennett – (4-4-2): Gomes, Kaboul▮, Dawson, King, Assou-Ekotto▮, Lennon (Bentley 71), Huddlestone▮, Modric (Palacios 88), Bale, Crouch[1], Defoe (Pavlyuchenko 81). **Subs not used:** Alnwick, Jenas, Gudjohnsen, Bassong.

9th ● Burnley   A   L 4–2   **Att:** 21,161. **Ref:** M Dean – (4-4-2): Alnwick, Kaboul, Dawson, King, Assou-Ekotto, Lennon, Huddlestone (Palacios 64), Modric[1], Bale[1], Crouch (Gudjohnsen 85), Defoe (Pavlyuchenko 62). **Subs not used:** J Walker, Bentley, Jenas, Bassong.

● Barclays Premier League ● FA Cup ● Carling Cup ● UEFA Champions League ● Europa League ● FA Community Shield   ▮ Yellow Card ▮ Red Card

TOTTENHAM HOTSPUR

BARCLAYS PREMIER LEAGUE GOALKEEPER STATS

Player	Minutes on pitch	Appearances	Match starts	Completed matches	Sub appearances	Subbed off	SAVES BREAKDOWN								Clean sheets	Goals conceded	Save %	PENALTIES			Fouls committed	Free-kicks won	Yellow cards	Red cards
							Saved with feet	Punched	Parried	Tipped over	Fumbled	Tipped round	Caught	Blocked				Saved	Resulting in goals	Opposition miss				
Ben Alnwick	94	1	1	1	0	0	0	1	1	0	0	0	3	0	0	4	55.56	0	0	0	0	0	0	0
Carlo Cudicini	661	7	6	6	1	0	1	5	14	1	0	3	23	1	1	11	81.36	0	0	0	0	0	2	0
Heurelho Gomes	2924	31	31	30	0	1	1	28	28	3	5	5	90	5	12	26	86.02	3	6	0	2	6	2	0

BARCLAYS PREMIER LEAGUE OUTFIELD PLAYER STATS

Player	Minutes on pitch	Appearances	Match starts	Completed matches	Substitute appearances	Subbed off	Goals scored	Assists	Shots on target	Shots off target	Crosses	Tackles made	Defensive clearances	Defensive blocks	Fouls committed	Free-kicks won	Caught offside	Yellow cards	Red cards
Benoit Assou-Ekotto	2703	30	29	24	1	5	1	2	5	5	36	34	10	15	26	31	0	5	0
Gareth Bale	1861	23	18	18	5	0	3	6	23	16	61	28	8	1	24	29	3	2	0
Sebastien Bassong	2478	28	25	22	3	3	1	0	2	10	1	31	29	14	17	20	0	2	0
David Bentley	1050	15	11	7	4	4	2	2	19	10	27	13	3	0	12	23	4	1	0
Vedran Corluka	2736	29	29	26	0	3	1	2	3	2	21	43	25	7	23	12	0	3	0
Peter Crouch	2437	38	21	20	17	1	8	7	46	38	2	5	20	0	38	39	20	1	0
Michael Dawson	2514	29	25	24	4	1	2	0	7	5	3	43	35	23	18	25	0	4	0
Jermain Defoe	2696	34	31	12	3	18	18	5	61	35	14	11	0	0	31	42	52	3	1
Giovani Dos Santos	18	1	0	0	1	0	0	0	0	0	0	0	0	0	0	0	0	0	0
Eidur Gudjohnsen	436	11	3	1	8	2	1	0	5	2	1	8	4	0	1	5	0	0	0
Tom Huddlestone	3047	33	33	28	0	5	2	3	42	31	15	56	30	3	53	33	0	8	0
Alan Hutton	281	8	1	1	7	0	0	0	0	1	7	5	3	1	4	6	0	2	0
Jermaine Jenas	1035	19	9	8	10	1	1	2	7	7	5	9	5	4	11	19	2	6	0
Younes Kaboul	852	10	8	2	0	0	0	0	1	4	13	21	8	4	14	5	0	2	0
Robbie Keane	1223	20	15	3	5	12	6	2	14	5	4	11	2	0	6	14	13	1	0
Ledley King	1641	20	19	14	1	5	2	0	6	5	0	23	21	20	9	7	0	1	0
Niko Kranjcar	1765	24	19	9	5	10	6	6	29	19	41	14	6	2	30	28	2	3	0
Aaron Lennon	1922	22	20	15	2	5	3	9	20	5	31	11	2	1	6	43	6	1	0
Jake Livermore	5	1	0	0	1	0	0	0	0	0	0	0	0	0	0	0	0	0	0
Luka Modric	2043	25	21	14	4	7	3	3	19	26	20	30	1	2	17	39	0	2	0
Kyle Naughton	9	1	0	0	1	0	0	0	0	0	0	0	0	0	0	0	0	0	0
Jamie O'Hara	19	2	0	0	2	0	0	0	1	0	0	0	0	0	0	0	0	0	0
Wilson Palacios	2709	33	29	22	4	7	1	1	12	9	6	60	6	5	58	41	0	8	0
Roman Pavlyuchenko	800	16	8	1	8	7	5	3	25	14	3	8	0	0	17	11	8	1	0
Danny Rose	45	1	1	0	0	1	1	0	1	0	1	1	0	0	0	0	0	1	0
Kyle Walker	200	2	2	2	0	0	0	0	0	0	5	12	2	0	6	1	0	0	0
Jonathan Woodgate	207	3	3	2	0	1	0	0	0	1	0	5	3	0	2	0	0	0	0

SEASON TOTALS

Goals scored	67
Goals conceded	41
Clean sheets	13
Shots on target	348
Shots off target	250
Shots per goal	8.93
Pens awarded	3
Pens scored	2
Pens conceded	9
Offsides	112
Corners	243
Crosses	317
Players used	30
Fouls committed	419
Free-kicks won	486

LEAGUE POSITION AT THE END OF EACH MONTH

AUG	SEP	OCT	NOV	DEC	JAN	FEB	MAR	APR	MAY
2	4	4	3	4	4	4	4	4	4

SEASON INFORMATION
Highest position: 1
Lowest position: 7
Average goals scored per game: 1.76
Average goals conceded per game: 1.08

CARDS RECEIVED

58 1

SEQUENCES

Wins	5
(21/02/10–27/03/10)	
Losses	2
(on two occasions)	
Draws	2
(on two occasions)	
Undefeated	5
(on two occasions)	
Without win	3
(on two occasions)	
Undefeated home	11
(16/12/09–01/05/10)	
Undefeated away	4
(28/11/09–26/12/09)	
Without scoring	2
(on three occasions)	
Without conceding	5
(16/12/09–16/01/10)	
Scoring	5
(16/08/09–12/09/09)	
Conceding	6
(16/08/09–20/09/09)	

MATCH RECORDS

Goals scored per match

		W	D	L	Pts
Failed to score	9	0	3	6	3
Scored 1 goal	7	2	2	3	8
Scored 2 goals	16	13	2	1	41
Scored 3 goals	3	3	0	0	9
Scored 4+ goals	3	3	0	0	9

Goals conceded per match

		W	D	L	Pts
Clean sheet	13	10	3	0	33
Conceded 1 goal	16	11	2	3	35
Conceded 2 goals	3	0	2	1	2
Conceded 3 goals	5	0	0	5	0
Conceded 4+ goals	1	0	0	1	0

EARLIEST STRIKE
JERMAIN DEFOE
(v Man Utd) 0:48

LATEST STRIKE
AARON LENNON
(v Birmingham) 94:23

Michael Dawson

GOAL DETAILS

How the goals were struck

SCORED		CONCEDED
41	Right foot	17
14	Left foot	17
12	Header	6
0	Other	1

How the goals were struck

SCORED		CONCEDED
43	Open play	24
11	Cross	6
4	Corner	2
2	Penalty	6
2	Direct from free-kick	2
5	Free-kick	1
0	Own goal	0

Distance from goal

SCORED		CONCEDED
23	6YDS	21
36	18YDS	14
8	18+YDS	6

GOALS SCORED/CONCEDED
PER FIVE-MINUTE INTERVALS

MINS	5	10	15	20	25	30	35	40	45	50	55	60	65	70	75	80	85	90
FOR	2	3	5	1	0	5	3	2	7	3	5	4	1	4	4	5	5	8
AGN	3	2	0	0	2	2	1	0	4	1	2	6	2	1	2	3	2	8

WEST HAM UNITED

CLUB SUMMARY

FORMED	1895
MANAGER	Avram Grant
GROUND	Upton Park
CAPACITY	35,089
NICKNAME	The Hammers
WEBSITE	www.whufc.co.uk

The New Football Pools PLAYER OF THE SEASON — Scott Parker

OVERALL

P	W	D	L	F	A	GD
41	9	11	21	52	72	-20

BARCLAYS PREMIER LEAGUE

Pos	P	W	D	L	F	A	GD	Pts
17	38	8	11	19	47	66	-19	35

HOME

Pos	P	W	D	L	F	A	GD	Pts
14	19	7	5	7	30	29	1	26

AWAY

Pos	P	W	D	L	F	A	GD	Pts
18	19	1	6	12	17	37	-20	9

CUP PROGRESS DETAILS

Competition	Round reached	Knocked out by
FA Cup	R3	Arsenal
Carling Cup	R3	Bolton

BIGGEST WIN (ALL COMPS)
20/02/10 3-0 v Hull

BIGGEST DEFEAT (ALL COMPS)
05/12/09 0-4 v Man Utd

THE PLAYER WITH THE MOST

GOALS SCORED	Carlton Cole	**10**
SHOTS ON TARGET	Alessandro Diamanti	**46**
SHOTS OFF TARGET	Alessandro Diamanti	**38**
SHOTS WITHOUT SCORING	Mido	**15**
ASSISTS	Mark Noble, Alessandro Diamanti	**5**
OFFSIDES	Carlton Cole	**32**
FOULS	Carlton Cole	**64**
FOULS WITHOUT A CARD	Valon Behrami	**39**
FREE-KICKS WON	Scott Parker	**66**
DEFENSIVE CLEARANCES	Matthew Upson	**58**

actim INDEX — FOR THE 2009/10 BARCLAYS PREMIER LEAGUE SEASON

RANK	PLAYER	PTS
80	Robert Green	352
87	Matthew Upson	340
97	Scott Parker	323

ATTENDANCE RECORD

HIGH	AVERAGE	LOW
34,989	33,683	30,024
v Man City (09/05/2010)		v Aston Villa (04/11/2009)

CLOCKWISE FROM ABOVE: Ricardo Fuller compounded West Ham's relegation fears with Stoke's winner at Upton Park in March; Scott Parker's winner against Wigan in April effectively made sure that West Ham would remain in the top flight; Gianfranco Zola endured a turbulent season, and was sacked two days after the end of the campaign; Luis Jimenez puts his side five goals up against Burnley

STEERING West Ham to Barclays Premier League survival did not prove enough to save Gianfranco Zola from the sack after an eventful season at Upton Park.

Speculation had been rife that Zola would be replaced at the end of the season after the club finished 17th in the League and, less than 48 hours after the Hammers' final game of the season, the Italian's fate was sealed as co-owners David Gold and David Sullivan decided to terminate the former Chelsea striker's contract.

Zola's position at Upton Park certainly did not look in doubt when the club kicked off their 2009/10 campaign at newly-promoted Wolves. Goals from Matthew Upson and Mark Noble gave the Hammers a 2–0 win at Molineux to raise hopes that Zola could achieve a top-half finish in his first full season in charge.

However, signs that the recession had bitten hard on the club's Icelandic owners were beginning to tell as Zola was forced to allow defenders Lucas Neill and James Collins to leave the club in August, while the Italian was restricted to budget signings such as Fabio Daprela, Alessandro Diamanti and Guillermo Franco.

The Hammers then went nine games without a win to record their worst start to a season since they were relegated in 2002/03. A 2–1 win over Aston Villa in November halted the alarming run and dragged the team out of the bottom three to ease the pressure on Zola slightly.

The Hammers' performance for the first hour of their game against relegation rivals Burnley on 28th November was befitting of a side who should be challenging for Europe. But, having raced into a 5–0 lead, the team's defensive frailties were exposed as Burnley pulled three back and may well have earned a draw had they not run out of time.

Defeats against Manchester United, Bolton and Birmingham saw the Hammers slip to second from bottom in December.

To make matters worse for Zola, striker Dean Ashton announced his retirement at the age of 26 after being forced to admit defeat in his bid to recover from a long-term ankle injury.

A 2–0 win over Portsmouth added three more valuable points but, as the Hammers entered the new year, a six-match winless run meant that only goal difference kept them out of the relegation zone.

Gold and Sullivan then stepped in to rescue the club with a £50million takeover to provide Zola with funds to acquire the likes of Benni McCarthy, Ilan and Mido, before embarking upon a cost-cutting venture.

Gold and Sullivan had spent almost 17 years at Birmingham City, but never made any secret of their allegiance to the Hammers. Taking over was a dream come true, but they made no secret of the risks involved, having scrutinised the club's books.

The pair vowed to stand by Zola but they had to wait four weeks before they enjoyed their first win, which came against the pair's former club, Birmingham. The Hammers then rocketed up to 13th with a 3–0 win over Hull to seemingly ease fears of a relegation struggle.

Another six-match winless run again threw the spotlight on the manager and there were signs that his relationship with the owners was deteriorating when an irate Sullivan wrote an open letter to fans apologising for the performance during a 3–1 defeat to Wolves.

Zola fought on and defied his critics to secure the club's top-flight status with two games to spare. Scott Parker, often a rock in the centre of midfield, sealed Barclays Premier League football for the 2010/11 season with a 25-yard strike before racing down the touchline to hug Zola in a show of solidarity with his manager, who was then fired on 11th May.

Zola was replaced by Avram Grant, who arrived at Upton Park on a four-year contract following his success in leading Portsmouth to the FA Cup final. On his appointment, the former Chelsea boss said: 'I'm proud and honoured to be the manager of West Ham. It's an exciting challenge and I'm ready to do my best.'

Gianfranco Zola just about maintained West Ham's top-flight status, but it was not enough to keep the Italian in a job

WEST HAM UNITED

RESULTS 2009/10

AUGUST

15th ● Wolverhampton A W 0–2 **Att:** 28,674. **Ref:** C Foy – (4-4-2): Green, Faubert, Collins, Upson¹, Ilunga (Spector 65), Noble¹, Parker, Collison, Dyer (Stanislas 73), Cole (Nouble 90), Jimenez. **Subs not used:** Kurucz, Gabbidon, Payne, Hines.

23rd ● Tottenham H L 1–2 **Att:** 33,095. **Ref:** M Clattenburg – (4-3-3): Green, Faubert¹, Collins, Upson, Spector, Noble, Parker (Hines 85), Collison (Nouble 89), Jimenez▮ (Kovac 78), Cole¹, Stanislas. **Subs not used:** Kurucz, Gabbidon, Tomkins, Payne.

25th ● Millwall H W 3–1 **Att:** 24,492. **Ref:** P Taylor – (4-3-3): Green, Faubert, Gabbidon▮, Tomkins, Spector, Collison▮, Parker▮, Kovac (Nouble 62), Payne (Hines¹ 46), Cole▮ (Upson 109), Stanislas². **Subs not used:** Kurucz, Collins, Daprela, Lee, Hines. AET – Score after 90 mins 1–1.

29th ● Blackburn A D 0–0 **Att:** 23,421. **Ref:** P Dowd – (4-4-2): Green, Faubert, Collins▮, Upson, Spector, Jimenez (Dyer 66), Parker▮, Noble▮, Collison (Kovac 87), Cole, Stanislas. **Subs not used:** Kurucz, Gabbidon, Nouble, Tomkins, Hines.

SEPTEMBER

12th ● Wigan A L 1–0 **Att:** 17,142. **Ref:** A Wiley – (4-4-2): Green, Faubert, Upson, Tomkins, Gabbidon, Kovac (Behrami 63), Noble▮ (Nouble 86), Parker, Stanislas (Diamanti 63), Cole, Hines. **Subs not used:** Kurucz, Spector, Da Costa, Payne.

19th ● Liverpool H L 2–3 **Att:** 34,658. **Ref:** A Marriner – (4-3-3): Green, Faubert▮, Tomkins, Upson (Gabbidon 25), Ilunga, Behrami (Kovac 27), Parker▮, Noble, Diamanti¹ (Dyer 65), Cole▮¹, Hines. **Subs not used:** Kurucz, Spector, Nouble, Payne.

22nd ● Bolton A L 3–1 **Att:** 8,050. **Ref:** H Webb – (4-4-2): Green, Spector, Kovac, Tomkins, Ilunga¹, Dyer (Cole 75), Parker▮, Noble, Da Costa (N'Gala 63), Diamanti, Hines (Faubert 88). **Subs not used:** Kurucz, Nouble, Payne, Edgar. AET – Score after 90 mins 1–1.

28th ● Man City A L 3–1 **Att:** 42,745. **Ref:** C Foy – (4-5-1): Green, Faubert, Da Costa, Tomkins, Ilunga, Diamanti▮, Kovac (Stanislas 71), Parker, Noble, Jimenez (Hines 71), Cole¹. **Subs not used:** Kurucz, Spector, Nouble, Payne, N'Gala.

OCTOBER

4th ● Fulham H D 2–2 **Att:** 32,612. **Ref:** P Dowd – (4-3-3): Green, Faubert▮, Tomkins, Upson, Ilunga, Noble, Parker▮ (Behrami 72), Jimenez▮, Diamanti, Cole¹, Hines (Stanislas¹ 72). **Subs not used:** Kurucz, Spector, Da Costa, Payne, Nouble.

17th ● Stoke A L 2–1 **Att:** 27,026. **Ref:** M Atkinson – (4-4-1-1): Green, Faubert▮, Tomkins, Upson¹, Ilunga, Behrami, Kovac (Stanislas 83), Noble, Collison (Franco 89), Cole▮, Diamanti (Hines▮ 78). **Subs not used:** Kurucz, Jimenez, Spector, Da Costa.

25th ● Arsenal H D 2–2 **Att:** 34,442. **Ref:** C Foy – (4-4-2): Green, Spector, Tomkins, Upson, Ilunga, Behrami (Kovac 90), Parker▮▮, Noble (Diamanti¹ 56), Collison▮, Cole¹, Franco (Hines▮ 64). **Subs not used:** Kurucz, Faubert, Da Costa, Stanislas.

31st ● Sunderland A D 2–2 **Att:** 39,033. **Ref:** A Marriner – (4-4-2): Green, Spector, Tomkins, Upson, Ilunga▮, Behrami (Diamanti 67), Noble, Kovac▮, Collison, Franco¹ (Hines 72), Cole▮¹. **Subs not used:** Kurucz, Gabbidon, Jimenez, Faubert, Stanislas.

NOVEMBER

4th ● Aston Villa H W 2–1 **Att:** 30,024. **Ref:** S Bennett – (4-4-2): Green, Behrami, Upson, Faubert, Ilunga (Spector 8), Da Costa, Parker▮, Noble¹, Collison, Franco¹ (Jimenez 88), Cole (Hines¹ 32). **Subs not used:** Kurucz, Tomkins, Diamanti, Stanislas.

8th ● Everton H L 1–2 **Att:** 32,466. **Ref:** A Wiley – (4-1-3-2): Green, Faubert, Da Costa, Upson, Spector, Parker, Behrami, Jimenez (Diamanti 57), Collison (Stanislas 46), Franco, Hines. **Subs not used:** Kurucz, Tomkins, Daprela, Kovac, Noble. Hibbert OG.

21st ● Hull A D 3–3 **Att:** 24,909. **Ref:** M Clattenburg – (4-4-2): Green, Faubert, Da Costa¹, Upson, Gabbidon, Collison¹, Parker, Behrami (Hines▮ 60), Stanislas▮, Franco▮¹ (Jimenez¹ 70), Cole. **Subs not used:** Kurucz, Kovac, Spector, Ilunga, Nouble.

28th ● Burnley H W 5–3 **Att:** 34,003. **Ref:** C Foy – (4-4-2): Green, Spector, Da Costa, Gabbidon, Ilunga▮, Collison¹ (Faubert 77), Kovac▮, Parker, Stanislas¹, Cole¹ (Hines 46), Franco¹ (Jimenez¹ 59). **Subs not used:** Kurucz, Noble, Nouble, Tomkins.

DECEMBER

5th ● Man Utd H L 0–4 **Att:** 34,980. **Ref:** P Walton – (4-4-2): Green (Kurucz 73), Spector, Tomkins, Gabbidon, Ilunga, Collison, Kovac (Dyer 67), Parker, Stanislas, Franco, Hines (Diamanti 46). **Subs not used:** Faubert, Da Costa, Nouble, Payne.

12th ● Birmingham A L 1–0 **Att:** 28,203. **Ref:** L Mason – (4-4-2): Green, Faubert, Gabbidon, Tomkins, Ilunga (Nouble 83), Stanislas (Collison 69), Parker, Noble▮, Kovac▮ (Dyer 68), Diamanti▮, Franco. **Subs not used:** Kurucz, Spector, Da Costa, Payne.

15th ● Bolton A L 3–1 **Att:** 17,849. **Ref:** A Marriner – (4-4-2): Green, Faubert, Gabbidon, Tomkins, Ilunga, Dyer (Stanislas 21), Parker, Kovac, Collison (Da Costa 87), Franco▮, Diamanti¹. **Subs not used:** Kurucz, Spector, Nouble, Daprela, Payne.

20th ● Chelsea H D 1–1 **Att:** 33,388. **Ref:** M Dean – (4-4-2): Green, Faubert, Gabbidon (Tomkins 19), Upson▮, Ilunga, Noble▮, Kovac, Parker▮, Collison, Franco▮, Diamanti¹. **Subs not used:** Stech, Jimenez, Spector, Da Costa, Nouble, Stanislas.

26th ● Portsmouth H W 2–0 **Att:** 33,686. **Ref:** L Probert – (4-4-1-1): Green, Faubert, Tomkins, Upson, Ilunga, Collison, Kovac¹, Parker, Diamanti¹ (Behrami 72), Noble (Jimenez 16), Franco (Nouble 90). **Subs not used:** Stech, Spector, Da Costa, Stanislas.

28th ● Tottenham A L 2–0 **Att:** 35,994. **Ref:** C Foy – (4-5-1): Green, Faubert, Tomkins, Upson, Ilunga (Spector 19), Collison (Stanislas 79), Behrami, Kovac▮, Parker (Jimenez 12), Diamanti▮, Franco▮. **Subs not used:** Stech, Da Costa, Nouble, Payne.

JANUARY

3rd ● Arsenal H L 1–2 **Att:** 25,549. **Ref:** M Clattenburg – (4-5-1): Green, Faubert, Tomkins, Upson, Daprela▮, Behrami, Jimenez, Kovac, Diamanti¹, Stanislas (Edgar 87), Nouble (Sears 79). **Subs not used:** Stech, Da Costa, Payne, Lee, N'Gala.

17th ● Aston Villa A D 0–0 **Att:** 35,646. **Ref:** M Jones – (4-5-1): Green, Faubert, Tomkins, Upson, Spector, Noble, Kovac▮ (Stanislas▮ 62), Parker (Diamanti 57), Behrami, Collison▮, Nouble (Da Costa 90). **Subs not used:** Kurucz, Jimenez, Sears, Daprela.

26th ● Portsmouth A D 1–1 **Att:** 18,322. **Ref:** A Marriner – (4-5-1): Green, Faubert, Tomkins (Da Costa 80), Upson¹, Spector, Collison, Kovac, Noble▮, Behrami, Diamanti (Stanislas 87), Nouble (Cole 73). **Subs not used:** Stech, Jimenez, Sears, Daprela.

30th ● Blackburn H D 0–0 **Att:** 33,093. **Ref:** P Walton – (4-5-1): Green, Faubert, Tomkins, Upson, Spector, Collison, Noble, Kovac (Cole 57), Behrami (Parker 70), Diamanti, Nouble (Sears 78). **Subs not used:** Stech, Da Costa, Ilunga, Stanislas.

FEBRUARY

6th ● Burnley A L 2–1 **Att:** 21,001. **Ref:** H Webb – (4-1-2-1-2): Green, Faubert, Tomkins, Upson, Spector, Parker▮, Behrami, Collison (Stanislas 62), Noble (Ilan¹ 77), Cole, McCarthy (Mido 46). **Subs not used:** Stech, Kovac, Da Costa, Ilunga.

10th ● Birmingham H W 2–0 **Att:** 34,458. **Ref:** M Dean – (4-4-2): Green, Faubert, Tomkins, Upson▮, Ilunga (Spector 46), Diamanti¹, Parker (Noble 86), Kovac, Behrami, Mido (Ilan 66), Cole¹. **Subs not used:** Stech, Da Costa, Collison, Stanislas.

● Barclays Premier League ● FA Cup ● Carling Cup ● UEFA Champions League ● Europa League ● FA Community Shield ▮ Yellow Card ▮ Red Card

RESULTS 2009/10

| 20th | ● Hull | H | W 3–0 | **Att:** 33,971. **Ref:** M Atkinson – (4-4-2): Green, Faubert¹, Tomkins, Upson, Spector, Behrami¹, Parker‖, Kovac, Diamanti (Collison 85), Franco (Ilan 63), Cole¹ (Mido 79). **Subs not used:** Stech, Noble, Da Costa, Stanislas. |
| 23rd | ● Man Utd | A | L 3–0 | **Att:** 73,797. **Ref:** A Wiley – (4-4-2): Green, Faubert‖, Tomkins, Upson, Spector, Behrami (Collison 63), Noble, Kovac, Diamanti (Dyer 75), Franco (Mido 46), Cole. **Subs not used:** Stech, Ilan, Da Costa, Daprela. |

MARCH

6th	● Bolton	H	L 1–2	**Att:** 33,824. **Ref:** L Probert – (4-4-2): Green, Faubert (Dyer 47), Tomkins, Upson, Spector, Behrami, Parker, Kovac‖ (Stanislas 75), Diamanti‖, Cole, Franco (Mido 67). **Subs not used:** Stech, Ilan, Da Costa, Daprela.
13th	● Chelsea	A	L 4–1	**Att:** 41,755. **Ref:** M Clattenburg – (4-5-1): Green, Spector, Upson, Gabbidon, Daprela, Ilan (Diamanti 83), Parker¹, Kovac, Behrami, Dyer (Stanislas 68), Mido‖ (C Cole 67). **Subs not used:** Stech, McCarthy, Tomkins, Collison.
20th	● Arsenal	A	L 2–0	**Att:** 60,077. **Ref:** M Atkinson – (4-4-2): Green, Spector, Tomkins, Upson‖, Daprela‖, Diamanti‖, Kovac‖ (Noble 70), Behrami, Stanislas, Mido (McCarthy 75), Franco (C Cole 57). **Subs not used:** Stech, Ilan, Ilunga, Spence.
23rd	● Wolverhampton	H	L 1–3	**Att:** 33,988. **Ref:** A Marriner – (4-4-2): Green, Faubert, Tomkins (Spector 46), Upson, Daprela, Behrami, Parker, Kovac (Stanislas 46), Diamanti, Cole, McCarthy (Franco¹ 71). **Subs not used:** Stech, Ilan, Mido, Noble.
27th	● Stoke	H	L 0–1	**Att:** 34,564. **Ref:** A Marriner – (4-4-2): Green, Faubert, Da Costa, Upson, Spector, Dyer (Diamanti 46), Parker, Noble (Ilan 76), Behrami, Mido (McCarthy 84), Cole. **Subs not used:** Kurucz, Gabbidon, Kovac, Daprela.

APRIL

4th	● Everton	A	D 2–2	**Att:** 37,451. **Ref:** H Webb – (4-4-2): Green, Faubert, da Costa¹, Upson, Spector, Noble‖, Parker‖, Kovac, Stanislas (Gabbidon 90), Mido‖ (Ilan¹ 77), Cole. **Subs not used:** Kurucz, McCarthy, Daprela, Spence, Payne.
10th	● Sunderland	H	W 1–0	**Att:** 34,685. **Ref:** M Jones – (4-3-1-2): Green, Faubert, da Costa, Upson, Spector‖, Stanislas (Franco 74), Kovac, Behrami, Noble, Cole, Ilan¹ (Daprela 90). **Subs not used:** Kurucz, Gabbidon, McCarthy, Diamanti, Spence.
19th	● Liverpool	A	L 3–0	**Att:** 37,697. **Ref:** P Walton – (4-4-2): Green, Faubert‖, da Costa, Upson, Spector (Daprela 80), Behrami, Kovac‖, Noble, Stanislas (Franco 46), Cole (McCarthy 72), Ilan. **Subs not used:** Kurucz, Gabbidon, Mido, Diamanti.
24th	● Wigan	H	W 3–2	**Att:** 33,057. **Ref:** A Wiley – (4-4-2): Green, Faubert, da Costa, Upson, Spector¹, Behrami, Parker¹, Kovac¹, Noble (Daprela 90), Ilan¹ (Franco 71), Cole. **Subs not used:** Kurucz, Gabbidon, McCarthy, Diamanti, Stanislas.

MAY

| 2nd | ● Fulham | A | L 3–2 | **Att:** 24,201. **Ref:** A Marriner – (4-4-2): Green, Faubert (Diamanti 61), da Costa, Upson, Spector, Behrami (Stanislas 82), Kovac, Parker, Noble, Cole¹, Ilan (Franco¹ 61). **Subs not used:** Kurucz, Gabbidon, Boa Morte, Daprela. |
| 9th | ● Man City | H | D 1–1 | **Att:** 34,989. **Ref:** H Webb – (4-5-1): Green, Faubert, da Costa, Upson, Daprela‖, Ilan, Parker, Kovac, Boa Morte‖ (Stanislas 64), Diamanti (Spence 87), Cole (Franco 64). **Subs not used:** Kurucz, Gabbidon, McCarthy, Spector. |

● Barclays Premier League ● FA Cup ● Carling Cup ● UEFA Champions League ● Europa League ● FA Community Shield ‖ Yellow Card ▮ Red Card

Julien Faubert scores West Ham's third goal in the impressive win against Hull in February

WEST HAM UNITED

BARCLAYS PREMIER LEAGUE GOALKEEPER STATS

Player	Minutes on pitch	Appearances	Match starts	Completed matches	Sub appearances	Subbed off	SAVES BREAKDOWN								Clean sheets	Goals conceded	Save %	PENALTIES			Fouls committed	Free-kicks won	Yellow cards	Red cards
							Saved with feet	Punched	Parried	Tipped over	Fumbled	Tipped round	Caught	Blocked				Saved	Resulting in goals	Opposition miss				
Robert Green	3638	38	38	37	0	1	1	24	34	6	2	11	117	5	8	62	76.15	1	5	0	0	13	0	0
Peter Kurucz	21	1	0	0	1	0	0	0	0	0	0	0	0	0	0	4	0	0	0	0	0	0	0	0

BARCLAYS PREMIER LEAGUE OUTFIELD PLAYER STATS

Player	Minutes on pitch	Appearances	Match starts	Completed matches	Substitute appearances	Subbed off	Goals scored	Assists	Shots on target	Shots off target	Crosses	Tackles made	Defensive clearances	Defensive blocks	Fouls committed	Free-kicks won	Caught offside	Yellow cards	Red cards
Valon Behrami	2183	27	24	17	3	7	1	1	10	9	9	55	7	2	39	62	0	0	0
Luis Boa Morte	66	1	1	0	0	1	1	0	1	1	0	1	0	1	1	2	1	1	0
Carlton Cole	2439	30	26	20	4	6	10	4	42	34	10	21	21	3	64	35	32	3	0
James Collins	287	3	3	3	0	0	0	0	0	1	0	2	3	6	2	2	0	1	0
Jack Collison	1753	22	19	11	3	8	2	4	20	4	3	22	3	3	12	7	3	2	0
Fabio Daprela	407	7	4	4	3	0	0	0	0	0	0	3	5	2	10	8	0	2	0
Alessandro Diamanti	1933	27	18	11	9	7	7	5	46	38	28	14	0	0	43	41	3	5	0
Kieron Dyer	384	10	4	0	6	4	0	1	5	3	2	1	0	1	2	9	5	0	0
Julien Faubert	3017	33	32	30	1	2	1	3	4	5	42	57	12	7	27	27	0	6	0
Guillermo Franco	1458	23	16	6	7	10	5	3	15	12	3	3	5	1	29	29	14	5	0
Daniel Gabbidon	773	10	8	7	2	1	0	0	0	0	1	15	12	7	8	7	0	2	0
Zavon Hines	665	13	5	3	8	2	1	2	4	9	1	2	0	0	12	30	11	3	0
Araujo Ilan	617	11	6	2	5	4	4	0	8	5	1	7	0	1	6	9	4	0	0
Herita Ilunga	1285	16	16	11	0	5	0	0	3	0	5	18	5	6	14	18	1	2	0
Luis Jimenez	699	11	6	2	5	4	1	3	8	3	2	7	0	0	16	7	3	3	0
Radoslav Kovac	2397	31	27	16	4	10	2	2	6	10	1	26	14	6	34	29	1	8	1
Benedict McCarthy	167	5	2	0	3	2	0	0	1	3	0	2	0	0	3	2	1	0	0
Mido	516	9	5	0	4	5	0	0	7	8	5	7	8	1	13	0	5	2	0
Mark Noble	2252	27	25	18	2	6	2	5	19	9	33	40	3	6	36	17	2	6	1
Frank Nouble	284	8	3	0	5	3	0	0	2	1	2	3	0	0	5	1	1	0	0
Scott Parker	2741	31	30	24	1	5	2	3	21	14	4	54	9	17	32	66	3	9	1
Freddie Sears	16	1	0	0	1	0	0	0	0	0	0	0	0	0	0	0	0	0	0
Jonathan Spector	2394	27	22	21	5	1	0	1	2	3	12	36	16	7	20	26	0	2	0
Jordan Spence	6	1	0	0	1	0	0	0	0	0	0	0	0	0	0	0	0	0	0
Junior Stanislas	1351	26	11	6	15	5	3	3	21	11	20	16	3	0	12	8	3	2	0
James Tomkins	2130	23	22	20	1	2	0	0	3	7	3	50	31	24	10	14	0	0	0
Matthew Upson	3105	33	33	32	0	1	3	0	8	4	2	64	58	21	26	19	0	3	0
Manuel da Costa	1190	15	12	12	3	0	2	0	4	4	1	16	22	6	12	9	0	0	0

actim

BARCLAYS PREMIER LEAGUE

SEASON TOTALS

Goals scored	47
Goals conceded	66
Clean sheets	8
Shots on target	260
Shots off target	198
Shots per goal	9.74
Pens awarded	9
Pens scored	7
Pens conceded	6
Offsides	94
Corners	181
Crosses	190
Players used	30
Fouls committed	488
Free-kicks won	497

LEAGUE POSITION AT THE END OF EACH MONTH

AUG	SEP	OCT	NOV	DEC	JAN	FEB	MAR	APR	MAY
11	18	19	17	17	15	13	17	17	17

SEASON INFORMATION
Highest position: 4
Lowest position: 20
Average goals scored per game: 1.24
Average goals conceded per game: 1.74

CARDS RECEIVED

65   3

SEQUENCES

Wins	2
(10/02/10–20/02/10)	
Losses	6
(23/02/10–27/03/10)	
Draws	3
(17/01/10–30/01/10)	
Undefeated	3
(on two occasions)	
Without win	9
(23/08/09–31/10/09)	
Undefeated home	5
(20/12/09–20/02/10)	
Undefeated away	2
(on three occasions)	
Without scoring	2
(on three occasions)	
Without conceding	2
(10/02/10–20/02/10)	
Scoring	10
(19/09/09–28/11/09)	
Conceding	15
(12/09/09–20/12/09)	

MATCH RECORDS

Goals scored per match

		W	D	L	Pts
Failed to score	11	0	3	8	3
Scored 1 goal	13	1	3	9	6
Scored 2 goals	10	4	4	2	16
Scored 3 goals	3	2	1	0	7
Scored 4+ goals	1	1	0	0	3

Goals conceded per match

		W	D	L	Pts
Clean sheet	8	5	3	0	18
Conceded 1 goal	7	1	3	3	6
Conceded 2 goals	12	1	4	7	7
Conceded 3 goals	9	1	1	7	4
Conceded 4+ goals	2	0	0	2	0

EARLIEST STRIKE

VALON BEHRAMI
(v Hull) 2:08

LATEST STRIKE

ZAVON HINES
(v Aston Villa) 92:57

Kieron Dyer

GOAL DETAILS

How the goals were struck

SCORED		CONCEDED
21	Right foot	31
12	Left foot	18
13	Header	13
1	Other	4

How the goals were struck

SCORED		CONCEDED
25	Open play	38
3	Cross	9
4	Corner	5
7	Penalty	5
1	Direct from free-kick	4
7	Free-kick	2
0	Own goal	3

Distance from goal

SCORED		CONCEDED
15	6YDS	31
26	18YDS	26
6	18+YDS	9

GOALS SCORED/CONCEDED PER FIVE-MINUTE INTERVALS

MINS	5	10	15	20	25	30	35	40	45	50	55	60	65	70	75	80	85	90
FOR	2	0	1	3	3	3	1	6	1	3	2	3	4	1	2	1	8	
AGN	3	1	3	5	2	4	1	3	5	1	7	5	6	3	4	7	3	3

WIGAN ATHLETIC

CLUB SUMMARY

FORMED	1932
MANAGER	Roberto Martinez
GROUND	DW Stadium
CAPACITY	25,138
NICKNAME	The Latics
WEBSITE	www.wiganathletic.co.uk

The New Football Pools PLAYER OF THE SEASON — *Hugo Rodallega*

OVERALL

P	W	D	L	F	A	GD
42	10	10	22	44	88	-44

BARCLAYS PREMIER LEAGUE

Pos	P	W	D	L	F	A	GD	Pts
16	38	9	9	20	37	79	-42	36

HOME

Pos	P	W	D	L	F	A	GD	Pts
16	19	6	7	6	19	24	-5	25

AWAY

Pos	P	W	D	L	F	A	GD	Pts
14	19	3	2	14	18	55	-37	11

CUP PROGRESS DETAILS

Competition	Round reached	Knocked out by
FA Cup	R4	Notts County
Carling Cup	R2	Blackpool

BIGGEST WIN (ALL COMPS)
02/01/10 4–1 v Hull

BIGGEST DEFEAT (ALL COMPS)
22/11/09 1–9 v Tottenham

THE PLAYER WITH THE MOST

GOALS SCORED	Hugo Rodallega	**10**
SHOTS ON TARGET	Hugo Rodallega	**85**
SHOTS OFF TARGET	Hugo Rodallega	**48**
SHOTS WITHOUT SCORING	Marcelo Moreno	**18**
ASSISTS	Hugo Rodallega	**7**
OFFSIDES	Hugo Rodallega	**20**
FOULS	Hendry Thomas	**64**
FOULS WITHOUT A CARD	Marcelo Moreno	**11**
FREE-KICKS WON	Charles N'Zogbia	**61**
DEFENSIVE CLEARANCES	Titus Bramble	**65**

actim INDEX FOR THE 2009/10 BARCLAYS PREMIER LEAGUE SEASON

RANK	PLAYER	PTS
54	Titus Bramble	382
73	Charles N'Zogbia	365
103	Maynor Figueroa	316

ATTENDANCE RECORD

HIGH	AVERAGE	LOW
22,113	18,006	14,323
v Arsenal (18/04/2010)		v Portsmouth (14/04/2010)

CLOCKWISE FROM ABOVE: Wigan players stand shell-shocked during their 9–1 thrashing at Tottenham; the Latics celebrate victory against Arsenal following an incredible comeback; Titus Bramble opens the scoring against Chelsea; Roberto Martinez led Wigan to safety during his first season in the Barclays Premier League

WIGAN'S season was one of great inconsistency but, ultimately, progress.

Roberto Martinez suffered some heavy defeats in his first year as Latics boss but also claimed some notable scalps, and by the end of the campaign he was looking forward with optimism, despite the club only making sure of survival much later than they might have liked.

Martinez inherited a squad that needed to be reshaped in the summer of 2009 following the high-profile departures of Emile Heskey, Wilson Palacios and Antonio Valencia. The Spaniard, a Latics hero in his playing days, also brought with him a new footballing philosophy as he attempted to introduce a more slick passing style than had previously been employed at the club.

The results were mixed, with a hugely encouraging win over Aston Villa on the opening day of the Barclays Premier League season proving to be a false dawn. Wigan lost their next three games, including a 5–0 thrashing at the hands of Manchester United, and they were beaten 4–0 at Arsenal soon after.

Those results prolonged the club's record of having never beaten one of the 'big four' since their promotion to the top flight in 2005, and it seemed unlikely that they would end it as Chelsea paid a visit in late September. Yet, remarkably, Martinez's men overturned the odds and won 3–1, ending

Roberto Martinez's Wigan maintained their position in the Barclays Premier League despite a series of heavy defeats

the eventual champions' 100-percent start to the campaign.

While the victory over Chelsea was thoroughly deserved, Wigan then lost their way as they were beaten at struggling Hull in their next fixture and a 4–0 defeat at Portsmouth in October was described by Martinez as the team's worst performance of the season.

Others would have placed that label on the demoralising 9–1 loss they suffered at Tottenham in November. Wigan conceded seven second-half goals, five of them to Jermain Defoe. The fact that goalkeeper Chris Kirkland was still thought to be their man of the match underlined Spurs' dominance.

The Tottenham defeat marked the start of a three-month period during which Wigan won just three matches in the League. All the confidence generated by the Chelsea win had completely evaporated and Martinez's attempts to reverse the situation by playing attractive football were hampered by a poor pitch at the DW Stadium. That surface, battered by the harsh winter and the start of the rugby league season, was eventually relaid in March and that made an instant impact. Hugo Rodallega scored the only goal as the Latics beat Liverpool in the first game

on the new surface and their performance displayed all the characteristics that Martinez had been trying to instil.

It seemed as though safety was within reach, but it still took more than a month to secure it as the old inconsistencies remained. The Liverpool win was followed by a 4–0 defeat at neighbours Bolton and a run of just one win in six games.

In keeping with the rollercoaster nature of Wigan's season, it was not until an unexpected 3–2 victory over Arsenal in mid-April that planning could begin for a sixth campaign in the top flight. The manner of that win against the Gunners was also extraordinary, as Ben Watson, Titus Bramble and Charles N'Zogbia scored in the last 10 minutes to overturn a 2–0 deficit.

That proved to be their final win of the campaign and they signed off in inglorious fashion on the wrong end of an 8–0 drubbing by Chelsea at Stamford Bridge which left them in 16th place, just six points above the Barclays Premier League relegation zone.

However, the flashes of quality shown in isolation will give Martinez something to build on, as does the promise of youngsters such as James McCarthy and Victor Moses.

WIGAN ATHLETIC

RESULTS 2009/10

AUGUST

15th	● Aston Villa	A	W 0-2	Att: 35,578. **Ref:** M Clattenburg – (4-2-3-1): Kirkland, Melchiot, Bramble▌, Scharner, Figueroa▌, Brown, Thomas, N'Zogbia (Sinclair 68), Gomez, Koumas¹ (Cho 90), Rodallega¹ (Scotland 90). **Subs not used:** Pollitt, Edman, Boyce, King.
18th	● Wolverhampton	H	L 0-1	Att: 16,661. **Ref:** M Jones – (4-4-1-1): Kirkland, Melchiot, Scharner, Bramble, Figueroa, N'Zogbia, Thomas, Brown (Scotland 62), Koumas (Sinclair 62), Gomez, Rodallega. **Subs not used:** Pollitt, Edman, Watson, Boyce, King.
22nd	● Man Utd	H	L 0-5	Att: 18,164. **Ref:** H Webb – (4-4-1-1): Kirkland, Melchiot, Scharner▌, Bramble, Figueroa, N'Zogbia (Scotland 73), Thomas, Diame (McCarthy 74), Koumas (Sinclair 62), Gomez, Rodallega▌. **Subs not used:** Pollitt, Edman, Boyce, King.
26th	● Blackpool	A	L 4-1	Att: 8,089. **Ref:** M Oliver – (4-4-2): Pollitt, Boyce, Amaya▌, Scharner, Edman, McCarthy (Rodallega 65), Watson, Diame (Thomas 65), Sinclair, Scotland, King. **Subs not used:** Kingson, Cho, De Ridder, Bouaouzan, Figueroa.
30th	● Everton	A	L 2-1	Att: 35,122. **Ref:** L Probert – (4-5-1): Pollitt, Melchiot▌, Boyce▌, Bramble, Figueroa, N'Zogbia▌, Thomas▌ (Cho 73), Scharner¹, Diame▌ (Scotland 36), Gomez, Rodallega (Sinclair 82). **Subs not used:** Kingson, Edman, Koumas, King.

SEPTEMBER

12th	● West Ham	H	W 1-0	Att: 17,142. **Ref:** A Wiley – (4-1-4-1): Kirkland, Melchiot, Boyce, Bramble▌, Figueroa▌, Thomas, Koumas (Scharner 65), Gomez (Sinclair 90), Diame, N'Zogbia, Rodallega¹ (Scotland 72). **Subs not used:** Pollitt, Edman, Cho, King.
19th	● Arsenal	A	L 4-0	Att: 59,103. **Ref:** M Jones – (4-2-3-1): Kirkland, Melchiot, Boyce, Bramble, Figueroa, Thomas, Diame, N'Zogbia, Gomez▌ (Scotland 57), Koumas (Scharner▌ 57), Rodallega (Sinclair 87). **Subs not used:** Pollitt, Edman, Cho, King.
26th	● Chelsea	H	W 3-1	Att: 18,542. **Ref:** P Dowd – (4-1-3-2): Kirkland, Melchiot, Boyce, Bramble¹, Figueroa, Thomas▌, Rodallega¹, Diame, N'Zogbia, Scharner¹, Scotland (King 88). **Subs not used:** Pollitt, Amaya, Cho, Koumas, Gomez, De Ridder.

OCTOBER

3rd	● Hull	A	L 2-1	Att: 22,822. **Ref:** M Clattenburg – (4-5-1): Kirkland, Melchiot, Bramble, Boyce, Figueroa, N'Zogbia▌ (Sinclair¹ 84), Diame, Thomas (King 90), Rodallega, Scharner (Gomez▌ 66), Scotland. **Subs not used:** Pollitt, Cho, Koumas, Kapo.
18th	● Man City	H	D 1-1	Att: 20,005. **Ref:** A Wiley – (4-4-1-1): Kirkland, Melchiot, Boyce, Bramble, Figueroa▌, Rodallega, Thomas▌, Diame, N'Zogbia¹, Scharner (Gomez 72), Scotland. **Subs not used:** Pollitt, Cho, Koumas, Sinclair, Kapo, King.
24th	● Burnley	A	W 1-3	Att: 19,430. **Ref:** L Mason – (4-4-1-1): Kirkland, Melchiot, Boyce¹, Bramble, Figueroa (Gomez 28), N'Zogbia, Thomas, Diame, Rodallega² (Scharner (King 78), Scotland. **Subs not used:** Pollitt, Cho, Koumas, Sinclair, Kapo.
31st	● Portsmouth	A	L 4-0	Att: 18,212. **Ref:** A Wiley – (4-2-3-1): Kirkland, Melchiot, Boyce, Bramble, N'Zogbia, Diame, Thomas▌, Sinclair, Rodallega (Kapo 59), Scharner (Gomez 59), Scotland. **Subs not used:** Pollitt, Amaya, Cho, De Ridder, McCarthy.

NOVEMBER

8th	● Fulham	H	D 1-1	Att: 16,172. **Ref:** P Dowd – (4-5-1): Kirkland, Melchiot, Boyce¹, Bramble▌, Edman▌ (Sinclair 78), N'Zogbia, Thomas, Scharner, Diame, Rodallega, Scotland (Koumas 90). **Subs not used:** Pollitt, Amaya, Cho, Gomez, De Ridder.
22nd	● Tottenham	A	L 9-1	Att: 35,650. **Ref:** P Walton – (4-3-2-1): Kirkland, Melchiot, Bramble, Boyce, Edman, Thomas (Gomez 67), Diame, N'Zogbia, Scharner¹, Rodallega, Scotland. **Subs not used:** Pollitt, Koumas, Sinclair, Kapo, Figueroa.
28th	● Sunderland	H	W 1-0	Att: 20,447. **Ref:** M Atkinson – (4-5-1): Kirkland, Melchiot, Bramble, Boyce, Figueroa, N'Zogbia, Thomas, Scharner, Diame, Rodallega¹, Scotland (Gomez 54). **Subs not used:** Pollitt, Amaya, Cho, Koumas, Sinclair, McCarthy.

DECEMBER

5th	● Birmingham	H	L 2-3	Att: 18,797. **Ref:** L Probert – (4-5-1): Kirkland (Pollitt 24) Melchiot, Bramble, Boyce (Gomez¹ 76), Figueroa, N'Zogbia¹, Thomas▌, Scharner, Diame (Sinclair 69), Rodallega▌, Scotland. **Subs not used:** Amaya, Cho, Kapo, McCarthy.
12th	● Stoke	H	D 2-2	Att: 26,728. **Ref:** M Dean – (4-5-1): Kirkland, Melchiot, Boyce¹ (Sinclair 47), Bramble, Figueroa¹, Gomez, Koumas (Scotland 78), Diame, Scharner▌, N'Zogbia, Rodallega. **Subs not used:** Kingson, Amaya, Cho, De Ridder, McCarthy.
16th	● Liverpool	A	L 2-1	Att: 41,116. **Ref:** P Dowd – (4-1-4-1): Kirkland, Melchiot, Boyce, Bramble, Figueroa, Scharner, Gomez (Koumas 82), Diame (Scotland 58), Thomas▌, N'Zogbia, Rodallega. **Subs not used:** Kingson, Amaya, Cho, Sinclair, De Ridder.
26th	● Blackburn	H	D 1-1	Att: 20,243. **Ref:** M Clattenburg – (4-4-2): Kirkland, Melchiot, Bramble, Boyce, Figueroa, N'Zogbia, Scharner, Thomas▌, Gomez, Scotland, Rodallega¹. **Subs not used:** Kingson, Amaya, Cho, Sinclair, De Ridder, McCarthy, Bouaouzan.
30th	● Man Utd	A	L 5-0	Att: 74,560. **Ref:** L Mason – (4-5-1): Kirkland (Pollitt 46) Melchiot, Boyce, Bramble, Figueroa, Gomez, Thomas (Edman 71), Cho, Scharner, N'Zogbia▌ (Sinclair 67), Rodallega. **Subs not used:** Amaya, Scotland, Koumas, McCarthy.

JANUARY

2nd	● Hull	H	W 4-1	Att: 5,335. **Ref:** A Marriner – (4-5-1): Pollitt, Melchiot, Amaya, Bramble, Figueroa, Sinclair¹, Koumas (N'Zogbia² 46), McCarthy¹, Thomas, Rodallega (Watson 77), Scotland. **Subs not used:** Nicholls, Edman, Gomez, Boyce, Bouaouzan.
16th	● Wolverhampton	A	W 0-2	Att: 27,604. **Ref:** H Webb – (4-5-1): Kirkland, Melchiot, Caldwell, Bramble, Figueroa, N'Zogbia▌, Scharner (Gomez▌ 47), Diame, Thomas▌▌, McCarthy¹ (Sinclair 90), Rodallega. **Subs not used:** Stojkovic, Amaya, Watson, Scotland, Boyce.
23rd	● Notts County	A	D 2-2	Att: 9,073. **Ref:** M Clattenburg – (4-4-2): Stojkovic, Amaya (Gohouri 46), Bramble▌, Boyce, Figueroa▌, Sinclair (N'Zogbia 70), Gomez (Watson¹ 70), Diame, McCarthy, Scotland¹, Rodallega. **Subs not used:** Pollitt, Caldwell, Cywka, McManaman.
27th	● Blackburn	A	L 2-1	Att: 22,190. **Ref:** L Mason – (4-2-3-1): Stojkovic, Melchiot (Boyce 67), Caldwell¹, Bramble, Figueroa, Thomas (Scotland 85), Diame▌, N'Zogbia, Scharner, McCarthy (Sinclair 86), Rodallega. **Subs not used:** Pollitt, Gohouri, Amaya, Gomez.
30th	● Everton	A	L 0-1	Att: 16,869. **Ref:** L Probert – (4-3-3): Stojkovic, Boyce, Caldwell, Bramble, Figueroa, Diame (Scharner 58), Thomas (Gomez 88), McCarthy, N'Zogbia, Scotland (Sinclair 80), Rodallega. **Subs not used:** Pollitt, Amaya, Watson, Koumas.

FEBRUARY

2nd	● Notts County	H	L 0-2	Att: 5,519. **Ref:** K Friend – (4-5-1): Stojkovic, Boyce (Rodallega 86), Caldwell, Bramble, Figueroa, Sinclair, Scharner, Diame (McCarthy 61), Gomez▌, Koumas (N'Zogbia 61), Scotland. **Subs not used:** Pollitt, Amaya, Thomas, Watson.
6th	● Sunderland	A	D 1-1	Att: 38,350. **Ref:** S Attwell – (4-5-1): Kirkland, Boyce, Caldwell▌, Bramble, Figueroa▌, McCarthy▌, Scharner (Moreno 74), Thomas, Diame¹, N'Zogbia▌, Rodallega▌ (Moses 83). **Subs not used:** Stojkovic, Scotland, Gomez, Sinclair, Melchiot.
9th	● Stoke	H	D 1-1	Att: 16,033. **Ref:** A Marriner – (4-4-2): Kirkland, Boyce, Bramble, Caldwell▌, Figueroa, N'Zogbia, Scharner¹, Diame (Moreno 81), Rodallega▌, Scotland (Gomez 60), McCarthy (Thomas 54). **Subs not used:** Stojkovic, Moses, Sinclair, Melchiot.

● Barclays Premier League ● FA Cup ● Carling Cup ● UEFA Champions League ● Europa League ● FA Community Shield ▌ Yellow Card ▌ Red Card

RESULTS 2009/10

17th	● Bolton	H	D 0-0	**Att:** 18,089. **Ref:** H Webb – (4-3-3): Kirkland, Melchiot, Caldwell, Bramble (Scotland 51), Figueroa, Scharner, McCarthy, Diame, N'Zogbia, Moreno (Moses 80), Rodallega. **Subs not used:** Stojkovic, Thomas, Gomez, Sinclair, Boyce.
21st	● Tottenham	H	L 0-3	**Att:** 16,165. **Ref:** A Wiley – (4-3-3): Kirkland, Melchiot, Caldwell, Scharner, Figueroa‖, Thomas (Moses 56), Diame‖, McCarthy‖, N'Zogbia, Moreno (Sinclair 76), Rodallega. **Subs not used:** Stojkovic, Watson, Scotland, Gomez, Boyce.
27th	● Birmingham	A	L 1-0	**Att:** 25,921. **Ref:** A Taylor – (4-5-1): Kirkland, Melchiot, Caldwell‖, Bramble, Figueroa, Thomas, Scharner (Scotland 46), Diame, McCarthy (Gomez 84), N'Zogbia‖ (Moses 46), Rodallega‖. **Subs not used:** Stojkovic, Sinclair, Boyce, Moreno.

MARCH

8th	● Liverpool	H	W 1-0	**Att:** 17,427. **Ref:** A Marriner – (4-2-3-1): Kirkland, Boyce, Caldwell, Bramble‖, Figueroa, Diame (Thomas 82), McCarthy, N'Zogbia, Scharner, Rodallega¹ (Scotland 86), Moreno (Moses 67). **Subs not used:** Stojkovic, Amaya, Gomez, Sinclair.
13th	● Bolton	A	L 4-0	**Att:** 20,053. **Ref:** M Dean – (4-1-4-1): Kirkland, Boyce, Caldwell, Bramble, Figueroa, Scharner‖ (Scotland 54), N'Zogbia, Diame‖, Moses (Gomez 54), McCarthy, Rodallega (Thomas 78). **Subs not used:** Stojkovic, Amaya, Sinclair, Moreno.
16th	● Aston Villa	H	L 1-2	**Att:** 16,186. **Ref:** S Bennett – (4-3-3): Kirkland, Boyce (Scotland 90), Caldwell¹, Bramble‖, Figueroa, Thomas, McCarthy (Scharner 71), Diame, N'Zogbia (Moses 56), Moreno, Rodallega‖. **Subs not used:** Stojkovic, Amaya, Gomez, Sinclair.
20th	● Burnley	H	W 1-0	**Att:** 18,498. **Ref:** M Jones – (4-4-2): Kirkland, Melchiot, Caldwell, Bramble‖, Figueroa, McCarthy, Scharner (Scotland 33), Diame, Thomas (Moses 74), Moreno, Rodallega¹. **Subs not used:** Stojkovic, Gohouri, Amaya, Gomez, Sinclair.
29th	● Man City	A	L 3-0	**Att:** 43,534. **Ref:** S Attwell – (4-5-1): Stojkovic, Melchiot, Caldwell‖‖, Bramble‖, Figueroa, McCarthy, Diame, Thomas (N'Zogbia 52), Scharner‖, Rodallega (Scotland 81), Moreno (Gohouri 81). **Subs not used:** Moses, Pollitt, Gomez, Sinclair.

APRIL

4th	● Fulham	A	L 2-1	**Att:** 22,730. **Ref:** M Clattenburg – (4-5-1): Kirkland, Melchiot, Bramble, Scharner‖, Figueroa‖, McCarthy, Moreno (Sinclair 85), Diame, N'Zogbia (Watson 85), Rodallega, Scotland¹ (Moses 61). **Subs not used:** Stojkovic, Gohouri, Amaya, Gomez.
14th	● Portsmouth	H	D 0-0	**Att:** 14,323. **Ref:** M Dean – (4-3-3): Kirkland, Melchiot, Gohouri, Bramble‖, Figueroa, Diame, Scharner (Moreno 56), McCarthy, N'Zogbia, Scotland‖ (Moses 88), Rodallega. **Subs not used:** Stojkovic, Watson, Gomez, Sinclair, Boyce.
18th	● Arsenal	H	W 3-2	**Att:** 22,113. **Ref:** L Mason – (4-5-1): Kirkland, Melchiot, Gohouri, Bramble‖, Figueroa, Rodallega, Diame‖, Watson¹ (Scharner 90), McCarthy, N'Zogbia¹, Moreno (Moses 62). **Subs not used:** Stojkovic, Scotland, Gomez, Sinclair, Boyce.
24th	● West Ham	A	L 3-2	**Att:** 33,057. **Ref:** A Wiley – (4-3-3): Kirkland, Melchiot, Caldwell, Bramble‖, Figueroa, Watson, Diame (Scharner 90), McCarthy‖, N'Zogbia (Scotland 90), Moreno (Moses 38), Rodallega¹. **Subs not used:** Stojkovic, Gohouri, Sinclair, Boyce. Spector OG.

MAY

3rd	● Hull	H	D 2-2	**Att:** 20,242. **Ref:** P Dowd – (4-2-3-1): Stojkovic, Melchiot‖, Caldwell, Gohouri‖, Figueroa, Diame (Scharner 82), McCarthy (Sinclair 65), Gomez (Scotland 79), Watson, Moses¹, Rodallega. **Subs not used:** Pollitt, Thomas, Boyce, Mostoe. Hull are relegated.
9th	● Chelsea	A	L 8-0	**Att:** 41,383. **Ref:** M Atkinson – (4-1-4-1): Pollitt, Melchiot, Gohouri‖, Caldwell‖, Figueroa, Boyce, McCarthy, Watson (Thomas 61), Diame‖ (Scharner 72), N'Zogbia‖, Rodallega (Moses 82). **Subs not used:** Stojkovic, Scotland, Cywka, Mostoe.

● Barclays Premier League ● FA Cup ● Carling Cup ● UEFA Champions League ● Europa League ● FA Community Shield ‖ Yellow Card ∎ Red Card

Hugo Rodallega celebrates his winning goal against Liverpool in March

OFFICIAL FOOTBALL YEARBOOK OF THE ENGLISH & SCOTTISH LEAGUES 2010-2011 **153**

WIGAN ATHLETIC

BARCLAYS PREMIER LEAGUE GOALKEEPER STATS

Player	Minutes on pitch	Appearances	Match starts	Completed matches	Sub appearances	Subbed off	SAVES BREAKDOWN								Clean sheets	Goals conceded	Save %	PENALTIES			Fouls committed	Free-kicks won	Yellow cards	Red cards
							Saved with feet	Punched	Parried	Tipped over	Fumbled	Tipped round	Caught	Blocked				Saved	Resulting in goals	Opposition miss				
Chris Kirkland	2969	32	32	30	0	2	2	10	16	7	3	7	76	1	8	53	69.19	0	4	0	0	7	0	0
Mike Pollitt	309	4	2	2	2	0	0	2	3	1	0	1	16	2	0	18	58.14	0	3	0	0	0	0	0
Vladimir Stojkovic	389	4	4	4	0	0	0	2	5	1	0	0	8	0	0	8	66.67	0	0	0	0	1	0	0

BARCLAYS PREMIER LEAGUE OUTFIELD PLAYER STATS

Player	Minutes on pitch	Appearances	Match starts	Completed matches	Substitute appearances	Subbed off	Goals scored	Assists	Shots on target	Shots off target	Crosses	Tackles made	Defensive clearances	Defensive blocks	Fouls committed	Free-kicks won	Caught offside	Yellow cards	Red cards
Emmerson Boyce	2172	24	23	20	1	3	3	1	5	6	8	61	30	14	19	13	0	1	0
Titus Bramble	3337	35	35	34	0	1	2	0	5	8	1	114	65	32	27	23	0	10	0
Michael Brown	158	2	2	1	0	1	0	0	0	0	0	3	2	0	4	1	0	0	0
Gary Caldwell	1451	16	16	14	0	0	2	0	2	3	3	19	21	7	17	20	0	3	2
Won-Hee Cho	128	4	1	1	3	0	0	0	1	1	0	0	0	0	2	3	0	0	0
Mohamed Diame	3040	34	34	24	0	10	1	1	15	15	6	113	9	11	60	54	0	6	0
Erik Edman	197	3	2	1	1	1	0	0	1	1	0	6	1	0	3	3	0	1	0
Maynor Figueroa	3306	35	35	34	0	1	1	1	4	9	38	117	17	9	33	44	0	6	0
Steve Gohouri	398	5	4	4	1	0	1	0	1	0	1	12	1	0	5	2	0	2	0
Jordi Gomez	1371	23	11	7	12	4	1	1	19	21	12	37	6	2	21	41	2	3	0
Olivier Kapo	36	1	0	0	1	0	0	0	1	1	0	2	0	0	0	0	0	0	0
Marlon King	30	3	0	0	3	0	0	0	0	0	0	0	0	0	0	0	0	0	0
Jason Koumas	436	8	6	0	2	6	1	1	3	2	15	35	0	0	2	7	2	0	0
James McCarthy	1738	20	19	13	1	6	1	1	13	6	12	36	3	2	30	16	0	3	0
Mario Melchiot	3050	32	32	30	0	2	0	1	1	1	17	81	26	10	21	37	1	2	0
Marcelo Moreno	762	12	9	2	3	7	0	1	10	8	9	14	8	0	11	10	5	0	0
Victor Moses	506	14	2	1	12	1	1	3	6	5	14	10	0	0	3	12	2	0	0
Charles N'Zogbia	3225	36	35	27	1	8	5	6	45	25	67	61	3	1	53	61	8	7	0
Hugo Rodallega	3521	38	38	28	0	10	10	7	85	48	27	40	3	2	46	37	20	6	0
Paul Scharner	2688	38	30	20	8	10	4	4	20	37	12	70	24	5	43	38	4	6	0
Jason Scotland	1699	32	14	7	18	7	1	2	16	19	5	21	1	2	14	14	8	1	0
Scott Sinclair	429	18	1	1	17	0	1	0	3	5	6	18	0	0	3	3	0	0	0
Hendry Thomas	2478	31	27	17	4	9	0	0	6	12	4	69	23	10	64	34	1	8	1
Ben Watson	364	5	4	2	1	2	1	1	6	0	12	4	2	1	3	0	0	0	0

SEASON TOTALS

Goals scored	37
Goals conceded	79
Clean sheets	8
Shots on target	268
Shots off target	233
Shots per goal	13.54
Pens awarded	3
Pens scored	1
Pens conceded	7
Offsides	53
Corners	184
Crosses	269
Players used	27
Fouls committed	484
Free-kicks won	481

CARDS RECEIVED

65 **3**

SEQUENCES

Wins	–
(–)	
Losses	3
(18/08/09–30/08/09)	
Draws	3
(06/02/10–17/02/10)	
Undefeated	3
(06/02/10–17/02/10)	
Without win	7
(27/01/10–27/02/10)	
Undefeated home	5
(12/09/09–28/11/09)	
Undefeated away	–
(–)	
Without scoring	3
(17/02/10–27/02/10)	
Without conceding	–
(–)	
Scoring	7
(08/11/09–26/12/09)	
Conceding	8
(19/09/09–22/11/09)	

League position at the end of each month

AUG	SEP	OCT	NOV	DEC	JAN	FEB	MAR	APR	MAY
17	10	12	14	16	14	16	16	16	16

SEASON INFORMATION
Highest position: 5
Lowest position: 19
Average goals scored per game: 0.97
Average goals conceded per game: 2.08

MATCH RECORDS

Goals scored per match

		W	D	L	Pts
Failed to score	13	0	2	11	2
Scored 1 goal	16	4	5	7	17
Scored 2 goals	6	2	2	2	8
Scored 3 goals	3	3	0	0	9
Scored 4+ goals	0	0	0	0	0

Goals conceded per match

		W	D	L	Pts
Clean sheet	8	6	2	0	20
Conceded 1 goal	10	2	5	3	11
Conceded 2 goals	9	1	2	6	5
Conceded 3 goals	4	0	0	4	0
Conceded 4+ goals	7	0	0	7	0

EARLIEST STRIKE

HUGO RODALLEGA
(v Burnley) 10:40

LATEST STRIKE

HUGO RODALLEGA
(v Burnley) 92:46

Jordi Gomez

GOAL DETAILS

How the goals were struck

SCORED		CONCEDED
15	Right foot	49
10	Left foot	11
10	Header	18
2	Other	1

How the goals were struck

SCORED		CONCEDED
23	Open play	46
2	Cross	12
5	Corner	5
1	Penalty	7
2	Direct from free-kick	4
3	Free-kick	4
1	Own goal	1

Distance from goal

SCORED		CONCEDED
15	6YDS	29
16	18YDS	43
6	18+YDS	7

GOALS SCORED/CONCEDED PER FIVE-MINUTE INTERVALS

MINS	5	10	15	20	25	30	35	40	45	50	55	60	65	70	75	80	85	90
FOR	1	0	4	2	0	2	4	0	1	0	5	5	0	0	2	3	0	8
AGN	1	5	0	1	2	3	4	2	6	7	4	7	9	5	6	4	4	9

CLUB SUMMARY

FORMED	1877
MANAGER	Mick McCarthy
GROUND	Molineux
CAPACITY	28,525
NICKNAME	Wolves
WEBSITE	www.wolves.co.uk

The New Football Pools PLAYER OF THE SEASON — *Jody Craddock*

OVERALL
P	W	D	L	F	A	GD
43	10	13	20	36	62	-26

BARCLAYS PREMIER LEAGUE
Pos	P	W	D	L	F	A	GD	Pts
15	38	9	11	18	32	56	-24	38

HOME
Pos	P	W	D	L	F	A	GD	Pts
19	19	5	6	8	13	22	-9	21

AWAY
Pos	P	W	D	L	F	A	GD	Pts
11	19	4	5	10	19	34	-15	17

CUP PROGRESS DETAILS
Competition	Round reached	Knocked out by
FA Cup	R4	Crystal Palace
Carling Cup	R3	Man Utd

BIGGEST WIN (ALL COMPS)
23/03/10 3–1 v West Ham

BIGGEST DEFEAT (ALL COMPS)
21/11/09 0–4 v Chelsea

THE PLAYER WITH THE MOST
GOALS SCORED	Kevin Doyle	**9**
SHOTS ON TARGET	Kevin Doyle	**37**
SHOTS OFF TARGET	Kevin Doyle	**30**
SHOTS WITHOUT SCORING	Kevin Foley	**16**
ASSISTS	Matthew Jarvis	**5**
OFFSIDES	Kevin Doyle	**20**
FOULS	Karl Henry	**60**
FOULS WITHOUT A CARD	Chris Iwelumo	**11**
FREE-KICKS WON	Kevin Doyle	**73**
DEFENSIVE CLEARANCES	Christophe Berra	**41**

actim INDEX — FOR THE 2009/10 BARCLAYS PREMIER LEAGUE SEASON

RANK	PLAYER	PTS
38	Jody Craddock	418
95	Matthew Jarvis	329
135	Kevin Doyle	278

ATTENDANCE RECORD
HIGH	AVERAGE	LOW
29,023	28,366	26,668
v Portsmouth (03/10/2009)		v Birmingham (29/11/2009)

MICK McCARTHY'S faith in the side that had taken Wolves up to the Barclays Premier League proved to be justified as the Molineux men finished in 15th place in their first season back in the top flight.

McCarthy had led the club to the Coca-Cola Championship title and back into the elite for the first time in five years at the end of 2008/09. Predictably, the bookmakers and pundits tipped the Molineux outfit as one of the pre-season favourites to drop out of the top flight, but they were wrong.

Wolves' hold on their top-flight status did look to be under threat at more than one point during the course of the 2009/10 season, most notably in late November and then early February when they slipped into 19th position. But on both occasions they put together impressive sequences of results which ensured they kept their heads above water.

A low point was the 1–0 home defeat to Birmingham on 29th November, when they put in a particularly poor first-half performance. However, their response was to win three of the next four games, which lifted them briefly in to 12th spot.

The solitary loss during that run was against reigning champions Manchester United at Old Trafford, as McCarthy incurred the wrath of the Premier League. The club was given a suspended £25,000 fine for McCarthy's decision to make 10 changes for the 3–0 defeat against the Red Devils, clearly with one eye on the potential relegation clash with Burnley five days later.

Wolves faced a challenging period towards the back end of the season when they had to cope with successive away games at Burnley, Aston Villa and West Ham plus a home game with in-form Everton. Again the players dug deep in picking up eight points from a possible 12 to climb clear of the bottom three – and they remained outside of the relegation places right through until May.

McCarthy took several pivotal decisions that had a massive bearing on the final outcome. He had started the season with Wayne Hennessey in goal but in mid-November the former Sunderland and Republic of Ireland boss decided to switch allegiance to American veteran Marcus Hahnemann, and the former Reading player had a positive influence on Wolves'

back four as he turned in several point-saving performances. Hahnemann remained McCarthy's first choice for the rest of the season and it was no surprise when it was announced that he had been offered a new contract.

McCarthy made another significant change in late December, this time in terms of tactics rather than personnel, as he switched from a 4-4-2 to a 4-5-1 formation. He decided that his team needed to be more difficult to beat and opted to play with record signing Kevin Doyle as the lone striker. It was an inspired move, with Doyle – who had moved to Wolves from Reading ahead of the 2009/10 campaign – taking to the role immediately and causing constant problems for opponents.

Midfielder David Jones returned to fitness after a lengthy injury lay-off and the former Manchester United player provided the additional creative spark and support behind Doyle to offset the tireless work of captain Karl Henry. Jones has also been awarded a new deal.

Overall it was a successful season, but McCarthy knows that Wolves are a work in progress and that they will need to strengthen in the summer to ensure that they have a fighting chance of repeating their achievements in 2009/10.

While he may consider searching for another striker to complement Doyle in attack, McCarthy is certainly not craving goals for their own sake. Speaking at the end of the campaign he made it clear that the actual manner of Wolves' survival was irrelevant.

He said: 'I said early on in the season if we stayed up by virtue of there being three teams worse than us, am I bothered? If we had stayed up by one goal, that wouldn't have bothered me. The goals don't matter. All that mattered this season was finishing above the bottom three.'

> *Mick McCarthy's Barclays Premier League new boys surprised many pundits by surviving in relative comfort*

CLOCKWISE FROM ABOVE: Wolves boss Mick McCarthy celebrates after the 1–0 win against Tottenham in February; goalkeeper Marcus Hahnemann saves from Everton's Dan Gosling; defender Ronald Zubar (centre) is mobbed by teammates after scoring his side's second goal of the game in a 3–1 victory at West Ham; Sylvan Ebanks-Blake scores Wolves' first goal of the game from the penalty spot in the 1–1 draw with midlands rivals Aston Villa

WOLVERHAMPTON WANDERERS

AUGUST

15th ● West Ham H L 0–2 **Att:** 28,674. **Ref:** C Foy – (4-4-2): Hennessey, Foley (Vokes 75), Mancienne (Stearman 66), Craddock, Ward, Halford, Henry, Milijas (Edwards 80), Jarvis, Keogh, Ebanks-Blake. **Subs not used:** Hahnemann, Elokobi, Surman, Jones.

18th ● Wigan A W 0–1 **Att:** 16,661. **Ref:** M Jones – (4-5-1): Hennessey, Stearman, Craddock, Mancienne, Ward, Halford (Surman 65), Edwards, Henry, Milijas (Jones 56), Jarvis, Keogh (Vokes 81). **Subs not used:** Hahnemann, Elokobi, Zubar, Spray.

22nd ● Man City A L 1–0 **Att:** 47,287. **Ref:** L Mason – (4-1-4-1): Hennessey, Stearman, Craddock, Mancienne, Ward (Vokes 74), Henry, Halford (Elokobi 46), Edwards, Jarvis, Milijas (Doyle 46), Keogh. **Subs not used:** Hahnemann, Surman, Jones, Berra.

25th ● Swindon H D 0–0 **Att:** 11,416. **Ref:** K Hill – (4-4-2): Hahnemann, Zubar, Collins, Berra, Elokobi (Edwards 79), Mendez-Laing (Jarvis 62), Jones, Surman, Hill, Doyle (Keogh 62), Vokes. **Subs not used:** Ikeme, Stearman, Henry, Spray. AET – Score after 90 mins 0–0. Wolves win 6–5 on penalties.

29th ● Hull H D 1–1 **Att:** 27,906. **Ref:** S Attwell – (4-4-2): Hennessey, Stearman, Craddock, Mancienne, Elokobi, Halford, Henry, Milijas, Jarvis, Doyle, Keogh (Vokes 89). **Subs not used:** Hahnemann, Edwards, Surman, Jones, Berra, Zubar.

SEPTEMBER

12th ● Blackburn A L 3–1 **Att:** 24,845. **Ref:** S Bennett – (4-4-2): Hennessey, Stearman, Berra, Mancienne, Hill, Halford (Edwards 46), Henry, Milijas (Maierhofer 46), Jarvis, Doyle (Surman 78), Keogh. **Subs not used:** Hahnemann, Elokobi, Jones, Vokes.

20th ● Fulham H W 2–1 **Att:** 27,670. **Ref:** K Friend – (4-4-2): Hennessey, Halford, Mancienne, Berra, Elokobi, Edwards (Maierhofer 70), Henry, Castillo, Jarvis (Kightly 86), Doyle (Ebanks-Blake 77), Keogh. **Subs not used:** Hahnemann, Hill, Milijas, Zubar.

23rd ● Man Utd A L 1–0 **Att:** 51,160. **Ref:** P Walton – (4-4-2): Hahnemann, Foley, Berra, Craddock, Elokobi, Kightly (Keogh 77), Castillo (Milijas 46), Henry, Jones, Ebanks-Blake (Doyle 66), Maierhofer. **Subs not used:** Ikeme, Halford, Zubar, Hill.

27th ● Sunderland A L 5–2 **Att:** 37,566. **Ref:** L Mason – (4-4-2): Hennessey, Halford, Berra, Mancienne, Elokobi, Edwards, Henry, Castillo (Kightly 46), Jarvis, Doyle (Ebanks-Blake 76), Keogh (Maierhofer 77). **Subs not used:** Hahnemann, Craddock, Milijas, Foley. Mensah OG.

OCTOBER

3rd ● Portsmouth H L 0–1 **Att:** 29,023. **Ref:** H Webb – (4-4-2): Hennessey, Foley (Kightly 46), Mancienne, Berra, Elokobi (Maierhofer 80), Halford, Henry, Edwards, Jarvis, Doyle, Keogh (Ebanks-Blake 46). **Subs not used:** Hahnemann, Craddock, Milijas, Zubar.

17th ● Everton A D 1–1 **Att:** 39,319. **Ref:** S Attwell – (4-4-2): Hennessey, Zubar, Berra, Craddock, Elokobi, Kightly (Jarvis 58), Edwards, Henry, Halford (Castillo 66), Doyle, Ebanks-Blake (Maierhofer 79). **Subs not used:** Hahnemann, Stearman, Keogh, Milijas.

24th ● Aston Villa H D 1–1 **Att:** 28,734. **Ref:** P Walton – (4-4-2): Hennessey, Zubar, Craddock, Berra, Elokobi, Edwards (Milijas 75), Henry, Castillo, Kightly (Halford 86), Ebanks-Blake (Iwelumo 86), Doyle. **Subs not used:** Hahnemann, Stearman, Keogh, Jarvis.

31st ● Stoke A D 2–2 **Att:** 27,500. **Ref:** C Foy – (4-4-2): Hennessey, Zubar, Berra, Craddock, Elokobi (Stearman 59), Edwards, Castillo (Milijas 46), Henry, Kightly, Iwelumo (Maierhofer 73), Doyle. **Subs not used:** Hahnemann, Ebanks-Blake, Halford, Jarvis.

NOVEMBER

7th ● Arsenal H L 1–4 **Att:** 28,937. **Ref:** S Bennett – (4-4-2): Hennessey, Zubar, Craddock, Berra, Stearman, Edwards (Mancienne 80), Henry, Castillo (Kightly 65), Milijas (Jarvis 74), Doyle, Ebanks-Blake. **Subs not used:** Hahnemann, Keogh, Halford, Maierhofer.

21st ● Chelsea A L 4–0 **Att:** 41,786. **Ref:** L Mason – (3-5-2): Hennessey, Berra, Craddock, Stearman, Halford, Edwards, Henry, Castillo (Kightly 53), Surman, Ebanks-Blake (Keogh 62), Jarvis. **Subs not used:** Hahnemann, Elokobi, Milijas, Foley, Maierhofer.

29th ● Birmingham H L 0–1 **Att:** 26,668. **Ref:** M Clattenburg – (4-4-2): Hahnemann, Mancienne (Ward 46), Craddock, Berra, Stearman, Halford (Kightly 31 (Milijas 66)), Henry, Edwards, Jarvis, Ebanks-Blake, Doyle. **Subs not used:** Hennessey, Keogh, Maierhofer, Castillo.

DECEMBER

5th ● Bolton H W 2–1 **Att:** 27,362. **Ref:** C Foy – (4-4-2): Hahnemann, Stearman, Craddock, Berra, Ward, Milijas, Henry, Edwards (Mancienne 84), Jarvis, Doyle, Ebanks-Blake (Maierhofer 80). **Subs not used:** Hennessey, Keogh, Surman, Foley, Castillo.

12th ● Tottenham A W 0–1 **Att:** 36,012. **Ref:** S Attwell – (4-4-2): Hahnemann, Stearman (Iwelumo 79), Craddock, Berra, Ward, Milijas (Mancienne 70), Henry, Edwards (Foley 59), Jarvis, Ebanks-Blake, Doyle. **Subs not used:** Hennessey, Surman, Maierhofer, Castillo.

15th ● Man Utd A L 3–0 **Att:** 73,709. **Ref:** S Bennett – (4-4-1-1): Hahnemann, Zubar, Mancienne, Elokobi, Hill, Halford (Jones 76), Foley, Castillo, Friend (Jarvis 61), Surman, Maierhofer (Iwelumo 54). **Subs not used:** Hennessey, Henry, Ebanks-Blake, Berra.

20th ● Burnley H W 2–0 **Att:** 27,410. **Ref:** M Atkinson – (4-4-2): Hahnemann, Stearman, Craddock, Berra, Ward, Foley, Henry, Milijas (Mancienne 68), Jarvis (Iwelumo 87), Ebanks-Blake, Doyle (Elokobi 90). **Subs not used:** Hennessey, Surman, Maierhofer, Castillo.

26th ● Liverpool A L 2–0 **Att:** 41,956. **Ref:** A Marriner – (4-4-2): Hahnemann, Stearman, Craddock, Berra, Ward, Foley, Henry, Milijas (Mancienne 62), Jarvis, Ebanks-Blake (Iwelumo 66), Doyle (Elokobi 58). **Subs not used:** Hennessey, Surman, Maierhofer, Castillo.

28th ● Man City H L 0–3 **Att:** 28,957. **Ref:** M Jones – (4-4-2): Hahnemann, Zubar, Craddock, Berra (Stearman 46), Elokobi, Foley (Jarvis 79), Henry, Mancienne, Surman, Iwelumo, Doyle (Ebanks-Blake 73). **Subs not used:** Hennessey, Milijas, Maierhofer, Castillo.

JANUARY

3rd ● Tranmere A W 0–1 **Att:** 7,476. **Ref:** L Probert – (4-4-2): Hennessey, Foley, Stearman, Craddock, Ward, Milijas (Halford 89), Henry, Mancienne, Jarvis, Ebanks-Blake (Elokobi 89), Iwelumo (Vokes 76). **Subs not used:** Hahnemann, Surman, Jones, Zubar.

16th ● Wigan H L 0–2 **Att:** 27,604. **Ref:** H Webb – (4-4-2): Hahnemann, Stearman, Craddock, Mancienne, Ward, Foley, Henry, Milijas (Surman 82), Jarvis (Jones 46), Doyle, Ebanks-Blake (Iwelumo 68). **Subs not used:** Hennessey, Elokobi, Berra, Vokes.

23rd ● Crystal Palace H D 2–2 **Att:** 14,449. **Ref:** C Foy – (4-4-2): Hennessey, Zubar, Berra, Mancienne, Elokobi (Ward 72), Foley, Henry, Jones, Surman (Mujangi Bia 63), Ebanks-Blake (Doyle 63), Vokes. **Subs not used:** Hahnemann, Craddock, Iwelumo, Milijas.

26th ● Liverpool H D 0–0 **Att:** 28,763. **Ref:** P Walton – (4-4-1-1): Hahnemann, Zubar, Craddock, Berra, Ward, Foley, Henry, Mancienne, Jarvis (Guedioura 88), Milijas (Jones 73), Doyle. **Subs not used:** Hennessey, Stearman, Vokes, Iwelumo, Mujangi Bia.

30th ● Hull A D 2–2 **Att:** 24,957. **Ref:** M Dean – (4-5-1): Hahnemann, Zubar, Craddock, Berra, Ward (Stearman 90), Foley (Guedioura 90), Mancienne, Jones, Henry, Jarvis (Mujangi Bia 90), Doyle. **Subs not used:** Hennessey, Ebanks-Blake, Vokes, Milijas. Gardner OG.

FEBRUARY

2nd ● Crystal Palace A L 3–1 **Att:** 10,282. **Ref:** L Mason – (4-3-3): Hennessey, Stearman, Craddock, Berra, Zubar, Foley, Mancienne (Jones 76), Henry, Milijas, Mujangi Bia (Ebanks-Blake 59), Vokes (Iwelumo 58). **Subs not used:** Hahnemann, Surman, Halford, Castillo.

● Barclays Premier League ● FA Cup ● Carling Cup ● UEFA Champions League ● Europa League ● FA Community Shield ▮ Yellow Card ▮ Red Card

RESULTS 2009/10

7th	● Birmingham	A	L 2–1	Att: 24,165. Ref: L Probert – (4-5-1): Hahnemann, Zubar, Craddock, Berra▌, Ward, Foley (Ebanks-Blake 88), Henry▌, Mancienne▌, Jones▌ (Guedioura 67), Jarvis (Surman 88), Doyle¹. **Subs not used:** Hennessey, Elokobi, Vokes, Mujangi Bia.
10th	● Tottenham	H	W 1–0	Att: 27,992. Ref: M Clattenburg – (4-1-4-1): Hahnemann, Zubar, Craddock, Berra, Ward (Elokobi 60), Henry, Foley, Guedioura (Mancienne 72), Jones¹, Jarvis (Milijas 80), Doyle▌. **Subs not used:** Hennessey, Vokes, Ebanks-Blake, Mujangi Bia.
20th	● Chelsea	H	L 0–2	Att: 28,978. Ref: K Friend – (4-5-1): Hahnemann, Zubar, Craddock, Berra, Ward, Foley (Halford 76), Guedioura, Henry, Jones (Ebanks-Blake 76), Jarvis (Mujangi Bia 76), Doyle. **Subs not used:** Hennessey, Elokobi, Vokes, Milijas.
27th	● Bolton	A	L 1–0	Att: 21,261. Ref: A Marriner – (4-2-3-1): Hahnemann, Zubar, Craddock, Berra, Ward, Henry▌, Guedioura (Ebanks-Blake 68), Foley (Keogh▌ 73), Jones, Jarvis, Doyle. **Subs not used:** Hennessey, Elokobi, Vokes, Milijas, Mancienne.

MARCH

6th	● Man Utd	H	L 0–1	Att: 28,883. Ref: P Walton – (4-1-4-1): Hahnemann, Zubar, Craddock▌, Berra, Ward (Keogh 84), Henry, Foley, Guedioura (Ebanks-Blake 76), Jones, Jarvis, Doyle. **Subs not used:** Hennessey, Elokobi, Milijas, Mancienne.
13th	● Burnley	A	W 1–2	Att: 21,217. Ref: S Bennett – (4-5-1): Hahnemann, Zubar, Craddock, Berra▌, Ward, Foley, Guedioura▌ (Mancienne 59), Henry, Jones (Keogh▌ 70), Jarvis¹ (Ebanks-Blake 79), Doyle. **Subs not used:** Hennessey, Elokobi, Vokes, Milijas. Carlisle OG.
20th	● Aston Villa	A	D 2–2	Att: 37,562. Ref: M Clattenburg – (4-5-1): Hahnemann, Zubar▌, Craddock¹, Berra, Ward (Mancienne 64), Foley, Guedioura▌ (Elokobi 46), Henry, Jones, Jarvis (Iwelumo 89), Doyle. **Subs not used:** Hennessey, Ebanks-Blake, Keogh, Milijas. Milner OG.
23rd	● West Ham	A	W 1–3	Att: 33,988. Ref: P Dowd – (4-5-1): Hahnemann, Zubar▌▌ (Halford 80), Craddock, Berra, Elokobi, Foley, Mancienne▌ (Guedioura 86), Henry, Jones, Jarvis¹ (Ward 71), Doyle¹. **Subs not used:** Hennessey, Ebanks-Blake, Iwelumo, Milijas.
27th	● Everton	H	D 0–0	Att: 28,995. Ref: M Jones – (4-5-1): Hahnemann, Zubar, Craddock, Berra, Elokobi, Foley, Mancienne (Guedioura 70), Henry, Jones▌, Jarvis (Ward 90), Doyle (Iwelumo 90). **Subs not used:** Hennessey, Ebanks-Blake, Keogh, Milijas.

APRIL

3rd	● Arsenal	A	L 1–0	Att: 60,067. Ref: A Marriner – (4-5-1): Hahnemann, Zubar, Craddock, Berra, Elokobi, Foley, Henry▌, Mancienne▌, Jones (Edwards 69), Jarvis▌ (Ward 83), Doyle (Keogh 70). **Subs not used:** Hennessey, Iwelumo, Milijas, Guedioura.
11th	● Stoke	H	D 0–0	Att: 28,455. Ref: C Foy – (4-5-1): Hahnemann, Zubar, Craddock, Berra, Elokobi, Mancienne, Jones (Milijas 79), Edwards (Iwelumo 59), Foley, Jarvis, Doyle. **Subs not used:** Hennessey, Ebanks-Blake, Ward, Halford, Guedioura.
17th	● Fulham	A	D 0–0	Att: 25,597. Ref: M Dean – (4-4-1-1): Hahnemann, Zubar, Craddock, Berra, Elokobi, Mancienne, Jones (Milijas 72), Foley, Jarvis (Iwelumo 79), Edwards (Guedioura 70), Doyle. **Subs not used:** Hennessey, Ebanks-Blake, Ward, Halford.
24th	● Blackburn	H	D 1–1	Att: 28,967. Ref: M Clattenburg – (4-1-4-1): Hahnemann, Zubar, Craddock, Berra, Elokobi, Mancienne (Milijas 66), Foley (Ebanks-Blake¹ 79), Edwards (Iwelumo 37), Jones, Ward, Doyle. **Subs not used:** Hennessey, Stearman, Halford, Guedioura.

MAY

1st	● Portsmouth	A	L 3–1	Att: 19,213. Ref: M Jones – (4-5-1): Hahnemann, Zubar, Berra▌, Craddock, Elokobi, Foley (Guedioura 78), Henry, Mancienne (Ebanks-Blake 56), Jones, Mujangi Bia (Iwelumo 46), Doyle¹. **Subs not used:** Ikeme, Edwards, Stearman, Milijas.
9th	● Sunderland	H	W 2–1	Att: 28,971. Ref: L Mason – (4-4-2): Hahnemann, Zubar, Craddock, Berra, Elokobi, Guedioura¹, Henry, Jones (Edwards 61), Jarvis (Foley 85), Doyle¹ (Iwelumo 79), Ebanks-Blake. **Subs not used:** Ikeme, Stearman, Milijas, Mancienne.

● Barclays Premier League ● FA Cup ● Carling Cup ● UEFA Champions League ● Europa League ● FA Community Shield ▐ Yellow Card ▌ Red Card

Kevin Doyle scores in the end-of-season win against Sunderland

BARCLAYS PREMIER LEAGUE GOALKEEPER STATS

Player	Minutes on pitch	Appearances	Match starts	Completed matches	Sub appearances	Subbed off	Saved with feet	Punched	Parried	Tipped over	Fumbled	Tipped round	Caught	Blocked	Clean sheets	Goals conceded	Save %	Saved	Resulting in goals	Opposition miss	Fouls committed	Free-kicks won	Yellow cards	Red cards
Marcus Hahnemann	2394	25	25	25	0	0	2	16	16	6	1	6	117	6	7	30	84.92	1	2	0	0	5	3	0
Wayne Hennessey	1240	13	13	13	0	0	1	3	8	4	1	8	39	3	1	26	71.74	0	3	0	0	2	0	0

BARCLAYS PREMIER LEAGUE OUTFIELD PLAYER STATS

Player	Minutes on pitch	Appearances	Match starts	Completed matches	Substitute appearances	Subbed off	Goals scored	Assists	Shots on target	Shots off target	Crosses	Tackles made	Defensive clearances	Defensive blocks	Fouls committed	Free-kicks won	Caught offside	Yellow cards	Red cards
Christophe Berra	3011	32	32	31	0	1	0	4	3	8	1	44	41	13	45	31	1	6	0
Segundo Castillo	525	8	7	3	1	4	0	0	2	2	1	4	4	1	6	4	0	1	0
Jody Craddock	3156	33	33	33	0	0	5	2	13	7	0	75	39	23	35	26	0	1	0
Kevin Doyle	3051	34	33	24	1	9	9	1	37	30	22	31	15	2	44	73	20	4	0
Sylvan Ebanks-Blake	1260	23	12	6	11	6	2	0	18	12	4	9	0	2	16	7	10	2	0
David Edwards	1430	20	16	8	4	8	1	0	9	7	14	31	1	1	15	15	3	3	0
George Elokobi	1753	22	17	15	5	2	0	0	3	2	18	45	16	4	16	14	0	2	0
Kevin Foley	2080	25	23	14	2	9	0	1	7	9	21	8	8	3	23	16	5	1	0
George Friend	61	1	1	0	0	1	0	0	0	0	2	0	1	0	0	0	0	0	0
Adlene Guedioura	630	14	7	2	7	5	1	1	8	8	2	13	3	0	15	15	0	2	0
Greg Halford	939	15	12	6	3	6	0	0	6	7	11	28	8	3	16	5	2	2	0
Karl Henry	3226	34	34	33	0	0	0	0	7	7	8	68	13	4	60	45	0	6	1
Matthew Hill	188	2	2	2	0	0	0	0	0	0	1	5	0	0	3	2	0	0	0
Chris Iwelumo	480	15	2	1	13	1	0	0	1	3	0	2	1	0	11	3	3	0	0
Matthew Jarvis	2760	34	30	14	4	16	3	5	28	12	75	47	6	3	17	27	8	3	0
David Jones	1485	20	16	9	4	7	1	2	12	9	23	8	1	1	27	11	1	3	0
Andrew Keogh	788	13	8	4	5	4	1	1	11	11	6	17	9	1	14	6	11	4	0
Michael Kightly	455	9	3	0	6	3	0	2	1	8	9	0	1	6	7	0	3	0	
Stefan Maierhofer	209	8	1	0	7	1	1	0	1	3	0	5	1	0	5	2	0	1	1
Michael Mancienne	2118	30	22	16	8	6	0	0	4	4	1	55	13	11	26	11	0	6	0
Nenad Milijas	1024	19	12	2	7	10	2	3	17	11	31	30	0	2	20	11	0	1	0
Geoffrey Mujangi Bia	66	3	1	0	2	1	0	0	3	0	1	0	0	0	1	4	0	0	0
Richard Stearman	1192	16	12	10	4	1	0	0	6	3	6	47	5	7	15	20	1	5	0
Andrew Surman	348	7	3	3	4	0	0	0	2	1	6	2	0	0	4	2	0	0	0
Sam Vokes	60	5	0	0	5	0	0	0	1	3	0	5	0	0	2	1	0	0	0
Stephen Ward	1668	22	18	12	4	5	0	1	1	2	12	43	15	7	18	18	0	3	1
Ronald Zubar	2184	23	23	22	0	1	1	3	4	8	14	41	22	2	24	29	0	3	0

SEASON TOTALS

Goals scored	32
Goals conceded	56
Clean sheets	8
Shots on target	206
Shots off target	172
Shots per goal	11.81
Pens awarded	2
Pens scored	2
Pens conceded	6
Offsides	65
Corners	207
Crosses	286
Players used	29
Fouls committed	484
Free-kicks won	412

	AUG	SEP	OCT	NOV	DEC	JAN	FEB	MAR	APR	MAY

SEASON INFORMATION

Highest position: 11
Lowest position: 20
Average goals scored per game: 0.84
Average goals conceded per game: 1.47

13	16	16	19	15	17	17	14	15	15

LEAGUE POSITION AT THE END OF EACH MONTH

CARDS RECEIVED

65   **4**

SEQUENCES

Wins	2
(05/12/09–12/12/09)	
Losses	3
(on three occasions)	
Draws	3
(on two occasions)	
Undefeated	4
(13/03/10–27/03/10)	
Without win	8
(27/09/09–29/11/09)	
Undefeated home	4
(27/03/10–09/05/10)	
Undefeated away	3
(13/03/10–23/03/10)	
Without scoring	4
(on two occasions)	
Without conceding	2
(11/04/10–17/04/10)	
Scoring	4
(on two occasions)	
Conceding	13
(22/08/09–05/12/09)	

MATCH RECORDS

Goals scored per match

		W	D	L	Pts
Failed to score	17	0	4	13	4
Scored 1 goal	11	3	4	4	13
Scored 2 goals	9	5	3	1	18
Scored 3 goals	1	1	0	0	3
Scored 4+ goals	0	0	0	0	0

Goals conceded per match

		W	D	L	Pts
Clean sheet	8	4	4	0	16
Conceded 1 goal	15	5	4	6	19
Conceded 2 goals	8	0	3	5	3
Conceded 3 goals	4	0	0	4	0
Conceded 4+ goals	3	0	0	3	0

GOALS SCORED/CONCEDED
PER FIVE-MINUTE INTERVALS

MINS	5	10	15	20	25	30	35	40	45	50	55	60	65	70	75	80	85	90
FOR	2	2	1	1	1	3	1	1	1	7	1	1	3	1	0	2	2	2
AGN	3	2	2	6	2	3	1	3	4	1	1	3	2	9	4	3	2	5

EARLIEST STRIKE

JODY CRADDOCK
(v Bolton) 2:04

LATEST STRIKE

MICHAEL MANCIENNE
(v Sunderland) 90:49

Jody Craddock

GOAL DETAILS

How the goals were struck

SCORED		CONCEDED
15	Right foot	24
9	Left foot	17
6	Header	11
2	Other	4

How the goals were struck

SCORED		CONCEDED
15	Open play	34
1	Cross	6
3	Corner	6
2	Penalty	5
0	Direct from free-kick	1
7	Free-kick	1
4	Own goal	3

Distance from goal

SCORED		CONCEDED
14	6YDS	23
15	18YDS	23
3	18+YDS	10

COCA-COLA CHAMPIONSHIP

COCA-COLA CHAMPIONSHIP STATISTICS 2009/10

PLAYER OF THE SEASON
Kevin Nolan (Newcastle)

MANAGER OF THE SEASON
Chris Hughton (Newcastle)

THE PLAYER WITH THE MOST...

GOALS Nicky Maynard (Bristol City)		**20**
SHOTS ON TARGET Nicky Maynard (Bristol City)		**74**
SHOTS OFF TARGET Charlie Adam (Blackpool)		**69**
SHOTS WITHOUT SCORING Matt Oakley (Leicester)		**38**
SHOTS PER GOAL Marvin Elliott (Bristol City)		**52**
ASSISTS Graham Dorrans (West Brom)		**19**
OFFSIDES Martyn Waghorn (Leicester)		**66**
FOULS Jay Bothroyd (Cardiff)		**103**
FREE-KICKS WON Jay Bothroyd (Cardiff)		**115**
PENALTIES SCORED Peter Whittingham (Cardiff)		**7**
GOALS SCORED DIRECT FROM FREE-KICKS Clingan (Coventry), Sigurdsson (Reading), Dorrans (West Brom), Wallace (Preston)		**3**
SAVES MADE Keiren Westwood (Coventry)		**269**
DEFENSIVE CLEARANCES Gareth McAuley (Ipswich)		**109**
DEFENSIVE BLOCKS Sean St Ledger (Preston)		**42**

THE TEAM WITH THE MOST...

GOALS	Newcastle	90
SHOTS ON TARGET	Ipswich	373
SHOTS OFF TARGET	Blackpool	319
SHOTS PER GOAL	Ipswich	12.84
CORNERS	Reading	324
FOULS	Sheff Utd	627
WOODWORK STRIKES	Watford	19
OFFSIDES	Leicester	198
PENALTIES CONCEDED	Scunthorpe	12
PENALTIES AWARDED	Reading	12
PENALTIES SCORED	Reading	9
YELLOW CARDS	West Brom	90
RED CARDS	Scunthorpe, QPR	7

TOTALS 2009/10

GOALS

Total	1425
Home	830
Away	595

CARDS

Yellow	1673
Average per game	3.03
Reds	86
Average per game	0.16

ATTENDANCES

Total	9,918,196

FOLLOWING their shock relegation from the top flight, Newcastle were always likely to provide the main story of the 2009/10 Coca-Cola Championship season. All eyes were on the Magpies as they looked to secure an immediate return to the Barclays Premier League, but few people could have predicted the ease with which they adapted to life in the second tier.

Captain Kevin Nolan led by example with 17 goals in the League as Chris Hughton's side enjoyed a superb campaign, achieving promotion with six games to spare and remaining unbeaten at home as they finished on 102 points. Greater challenges undoubtedly lie ahead, but for now everyone connected with the Magpies can reflect on a job well done.

There was also joy for West Bromwich Albion, who secured the second automatic promotion spot. The Baggies were plagued by inconsistency throughout the first half of the season but they found their best form when it mattered the most, avoiding defeat in their final 12 games to secure a passage back to the Barclays Premier League. In Scotland international Graham Dorrans, they also had arguably the most exciting player in the division.

Although Newcastle and West Brom were successful in their bid to bounce back to the top flight at the first attempt, the same could not be said of Middlesbrough. Gareth Southgate was sacked in October with the club only one point off the top, but Boro were unable to sustain a promotion challenge under his successor, Gordon Strachan, with the departure of Adam Johnson to Manchester City in the January transfer window a significant blow.

Astute leadership

Nottingham Forest exceeded pre-season expectations under the astute leadership of Billy Davies, equalling a club record of 12 consecutive home wins in the League on their way to a third-place finish.

Next came Cardiff and Leicester – the latter in their first year back in the second tier – but it was the identity of the team who filled the final play-off place that provided arguably the biggest surprise. Many people had expected Blackpool to be embroiled in a relegation battle, but their fans were eventually left celebrating a first promotion to the top flight since 1970 as Ian Holloway worked miracles on a limited budget.

Swansea further enhanced their growing reputation as one of the best footballing

Newcastle swept to the title in style, but Sheffield Wednesday were among those to end the season in tears

sides in the division, but a lack of goals (40 in 46 games) eventually put paid to their hopes of a top-six finish, despite goalkeeper Dorus de Vries keeping a club-record 24 clean sheets at the other end of the pitch.

Sheffield United also fell short of the play-off places, but their disappointment paled in comparison to that of city rivals Sheffield Wednesday, who suffered relegation heartache on a dramatic final day. The Owls needed to beat Crystal Palace at Hillsborough to avoid the drop at the Eagles' expense, but a 2–2 draw meant Alan Irvine's men will be playing in npower League 1 in the coming season.

Palace will be relieved to have survived following a 10-point deduction in January for entering administration. Boss Neil Warnock left for QPR soon after that and he steered the west Londoners away from the relegation zone, while Paul Hart – who had spent a brief spell at Rangers earlier in the season – stepped in to take charge at Selhurst Park.

Peterborough finished bottom of the table following a difficult season in which four managers took charge at London Road, and Plymouth also went down despite the efforts of former Argyle player Paul Mariner, who replaced Paul Sturrock at the helm in December.

Gary Hooper's 19 Championship goals proved to be enough to help keep Scunthorpe up, and Reading went from relegation candidates to play-off hopefuls following the mid-season appointment of Brian McDermott. Keith Millen made a similarly positive impact as caretaker boss of Bristol City, although he will step aside to work under new boss Steve Coppell in the coming season.

Roy Keane's Ipswich overcame a shaky start to finish just below mid-table, alongside the likes of Doncaster, Derby, Preston and Barnsley, while 19th-place Coventry parted company with manager Chris Coleman having rounded off their campaign with a 4–0 defeat to Watford, who finished 16th.

actim▦

FINAL COCA-COLA CHAMPIONSHIP TABLE

Pos	Team	P	W	D	L	F	A	W	D	L	F	A	GD	Pts
1	Newcastle	46	18	5	0	56	13	12	7	4	34	22	55	102
2	West Brom	46	16	3	4	48	21	10	10	3	41	27	41	91
3	Nottm Forest	46	18	2	3	45	13	4	11	8	20	27	25	79
4	Cardiff	46	12	6	5	37	20	10	4	9	36	34	19	76
5	Leicester	46	13	6	4	40	18	8	7	8	21	27	16	76
6	Blackpool	46	13	6	4	46	22	6	7	10	28	36	16	70
7	Swansea	46	10	10	3	21	12	7	8	8	19	25	3	69
8	Sheff Utd	46	12	8	3	37	20	5	6	12	25	35	7	65
9	Reading	46	10	7	6	39	22	7	5	11	29	41	5	63
10	Bristol City	46	10	10	3	38	34	5	8	10	18	31	-9	63
11	Middlesbrough	46	9	8	6	25	21	7	6	10	33	29	8	62
12	Doncaster	46	9	7	7	32	29	6	8	9	27	29	1	60
13	QPR	46	8	9	6	36	28	6	6	11	22	37	-7	57
14	Derby	46	12	3	8	37	32	3	8	12	16	31	-10	56
15	Ipswich	46	8	11	4	24	23	4	9	10	26	38	-11	56
16	Watford	46	10	6	7	36	26	4	6	13	25	42	-7	54
17	Preston	46	9	10	4	35	26	4	5	14	23	47	-15	54
18	Barnsley	46	8	7	8	25	29	6	5	12	28	40	-16	54
19	Coventry	46	8	9	6	27	29	5	6	12	20	35	-17	54
20	Scunthorpe	46	10	7	6	40	32	4	3	16	22	52	-22	52
21	Crystal Palace*	46	8	5	10	24	27	6	12	5	26	26	-3	49
22	Sheff Wed	46	8	6	9	30	31	3	8	12	19	38	-20	47
23	Plymouth	46	5	6	12	20	30	6	2	15	23	38	-25	41
24	Peterborough	46	6	5	12	32	37	2	5	16	14	43	-34	34

*10 points deducted

Graham Dorrans (West Brom)

Gary O'Neil (Middlesbrough)

Martin Cranie (Coventry)

PLAY-OFF REVIEW

BLACKPOOL secured a fairytale promotion to the top flight with a 3–2 victory over Cardiff in the Coca-Cola Championship play-off final.

Ian Holloway's side – who defied all expectations by finishing in the top six – twice came from behind to secure victory in a thrilling clash at Wembley, with all five goals coming in the first half. Charlie Adam's superb free-kick cancelled out Michael Chopra's opener and, although Cardiff went in front again through Joe Ledley, goals from Gary Taylor-Fletcher and Brett Ormerod sent Blackpool into dreamland and clinched a place in the Barclays Premier League, estimated to be worth £90million.

The Seasiders booked their place in the final with a sensational 6–4 aggregate victory over Nottingham Forest. Chris Cohen gave the visitors the lead in the first leg at Bloomfield Road, but Keith Southern and Adam replied to give Blackpool a slender advantage. Forest led 2–1 in the return at the City Ground, with Robert Earnshaw scoring either side of DJ Campbell's strike. But Holloway's men then scored three times in seven second-half minutes, Campbell completing his hat-trick after Stephen Dobbie had restored Blackpool's aggregate lead. Dele Adebola grabbed an injury-time consolation for Forest, but the damage had already been done.

Cardiff overcame Leicester in the most dramatic of circumstances in the other semi-final. Peter Whittingham scored the only goal in the first leg at the Walkers Stadium, but the Foxes then claimed a 3–2 victory in south Wales to take the tie to extra-time and then a penalty shoot-out. It was to be the Bluebirds who held their nerve, with David Marshall saving from Yann Kermorgant and Martyn Waghorn, but Cardiff would ultimately fall short themselves in the final.

Newcastle's players celebrate their glorious Championship title triumph, with Chris Hughton having led his side to an immediate return to the top flight

COCA-COLA CHAMPIONSHIP

COCA-COLA CHAMPIONSHIP RESULTS

AWAY (columns) / HOME (rows)

HOME \ AWAY	BARNSLEY	BLACKPOOL	BRISTOL CITY	CARDIFF	COVENTRY	CRYSTAL PAL	DERBY	DONCASTER	IPSWICH	LEICESTER	MIDDLESBRO	NEWCASTLE	NOTTM FOREST	PETERBORO	PLYMOUTH	PRESTON	QPR	READING	SCUNTHORPE	SHEFF UTD	SHEFF WED	SWANSEA	WATFORD	WEST BROM
BARNSLEY	–	1-0	2-3	1-0	0-2	0-0	0-0	0-1	2-1	1-0	2-1	2-2	2-1	2-2	1-3	0-3	0-1	1-3	1-1	2-2	1-2	0-0	1-0	3-1
BLACKPOOL	1-2	–	1-1	1-1	3-0	2-2	0-0	2-0	1-0	1-2	2-0	2-1	3-1	2-0	2-0	1-1	2-2	2-0	4-1	3-0	1-2	5-1	3-2	2-3
BRISTOL CITY	5-3	2-0	–	0-6	1-1	1-0	2-1	2-5	0-0	1-1	2-1	2-2	1-1	1-1	3-1	4-2	1-0	1-1	1-1	2-3	1-1	1-0	2-2	2-1
CARDIFF	0-2	1-1	3-0	–	2-0	1-1	6-1	2-1	1-2	2-1	1-0	0-1	1-1	2-0	0-1	1-0	0-2	0-0	4-0	1-1	3-2	2-1	3-1	1-1
COVENTRY	3-1	1-1	0-1	1-2	–	1-1	1-0	1-0	2-1	1-1	2-2	0-2	1-0	3-2	1-1	1-1	1-0	1-3	2-1	3-2	1-1	0-1	0-4	0-0
CRYSTAL PAL	1-1	4-1	0-1	1-2	0-1	–	1-0	0-3	3-1	0-1	0-2	1-1	2-0	1-1	3-1	0-2	1-3	0-4	1-0	0-0	0-1	3-0	1-1	1-1
DERBY	2-3	0-2	1-0	2-0	2-1	1-1	–	0-2	1-3	1-0	2-2	3-0	1-0	2-1	2-1	5-3	2-4	2-1	1-4	0-1	3-0	0-1	2-0	2-2
DONCASTER	0-1	3-3	1-0	2-0	0-0	1-1	2-1	–	3-3	0-1	1-4	0-1	1-0	3-1	1-2	1-1	2-0	1-2	4-3	1-1	1-0	0-0	2-1	2-3
IPSWICH	1-0	3-1	0-0	2-0	3-2	1-3	1-0	1-1	–	0-0	1-1	0-4	1-1	0-0	3-0	2-1	1-0	0-3	0-0	1-1	1-1	1-1	1-1	1-1
LEICESTER	1-0	2-1	1-3	1-0	2-2	2-0	0-0	0-0	1-1	–	2-0	0-0	1-1	1-0	1-2	4-0	1-1	5-1	2-1	3-0	1-1	4-1	1-2	2-2
MIDDLESBRO	2-1	0-3	0-0	1-1	1-1	1-2	2-0	2-0	3-1	0-1	–	2-2	1-1	2-0	2-0	1-1	3-0	0-0	1-0	1-1	0-1	1-1	0-1	0-5
NEWCASTLE	6-1	4-1	0-0	5-1	4-1	2-0	0-0	2-1	2-2	1-0	2-0	–	2-0	3-1	3-1	5-0	2-1	2-0	1-0	3-0	2-1	3-0	2-4	0-1
NOTTM FOREST	1-0	0-1	1-1	0-0	2-0	2-0	3-2	4-1	3-0	5-1	1-0	1-0	–	1-0	3-0	3-0	5-0	2-1	2-0	1-0	2-1	1-0	2-4	0-1
PETERBORO	1-2	0-1	0-1	4-4	0-1	1-1	0-3	1-2	3-1	1-2	2-2	2-3	1-2	–	1-2	0-1	1-0	3-2	3-0	1-0	1-1	2-2	2-1	2-3
PLYMOUTH	0-0	0-2	3-2	1-3	0-1	0-1	1-0	2-1	1-1	1-1	0-2	0-2	0-1	1-2	–	1-1	1-1	4-1	2-1	0-1	1-3	1-1	0-1	0-1
PRESTON	1-4	0-0	2-2	3-0	3-2	1-1	0-0	1-1	2-0	0-1	2-2	0-1	3-2	2-0	2-0	–	2-2	1-2	2-1	2-2	2-2	1-1	1-1	0-0
QPR	5-2	1-1	2-1	0-1	2-2	1-1	1-1	2-1	1-2	1-2	1-5	0-1	1-1	1-1	2-0	4-0	–	4-1	0-1	1-1	1-1	1-1	1-1	3-1
READING	1-0	2-1	2-0	0-1	3-0	2-4	4-1	0-0	1-1	0-0	0-2	1-2	0-0	6-0	2-1	4-1	1-1	–	1-1	1-3	5-0	1-1	1-1	1-1
SCUNTHORPE	2-1	2-4	3-0	1-1	1-0	1-2	3-2	2-2	1-1	1-1	0-2	2-1	2-2	4-0	3-1	0-1	2-2	0-1	–	3-1	2-0	0-2	2-2	1-3
SHEFF UTD	0-0	3-0	2-0	3-4	1-0	2-0	1-1	1-1	3-3	1-1	1-0	0-1	0-0	1-0	4-3	1-1	3-0	0-1	0-1	–	3-2	2-0	2-0	2-2
SHEFF WED	2-2	2-0	0-1	3-1	2-2	0-0	0-1	2-0	0-1	1-3	2-1	2-1	2-1	1-2	2-0	0-2	4-0	1-1	0-0	0-1	–	0-2	2-1	0-4
SWANSEA	3-1	0-0	0-0	3-2	0-0	0-0	1-0	0-0	1-0	0-3	1-1	0-1	1-1	0-1	3-0	2-1	0-0	3-0	2-1	0-0	3-0	–	1-0	0-2
WATFORD	1-0	2-2	2-0	0-4	2-3	1-3	0-1	1-1	2-1	3-3	1-1	1-2	0-0	0-1	1-0	2-0	3-1	3-0	3-0	3-0	4-1	0-1	–	1-1
WEST BROM	1-1	3-2	4-1	0-2	1-0	0-1	3-1	3-1	2-0	3-0	2-0	1-1	1-3	2-0	3-1	3-2	2-2	3-1	2-0	3-1	1-0	0-1	5-0	–

Nicky Maynard (Bristol City)

LEADING SCORERS

PLAYER	TEAM	GLS
Nicky Maynard	Bristol City	20
Peter Whittingham	Cardiff	20
Gary Hooper	Scunthorpe	19
Andrew Carroll	Newcastle	17
Kevin Nolan	Newcastle	17
Charlie Adam	Blackpool	16
Gylfi Sigurdsson	Reading	16
Michael Chopra	Cardiff	16
Darren Ambrose	Crystal Palace	15
Robert Earnshaw	Nottm Forest	15

TEAM DISCIPLINE

TEAM	Y	R
Crystal Palace	87	5
West Brom	91	3
Nottm Forest	84	4
Sheff Utd	88	2
Barnsley	81	4
Scunthorpe	71	7
Derby	77	5
Bristol City	83	3
Coventry	75	4
Middlesbrough	72	4
Plymouth	76	2
QPR	60	7
Swansea	69	4
Ipswich	66	4
Reading	62	5
Newcastle	68	3
Preston	71	2
Cardiff	63	4
Leicester	60	3
Blackpool	58	3
Watford	58	3
Sheff Wed	60	0
Peterborough	48	2
Doncaster	43	3

Dorus De Vries (Swansea)

LEADING GOALKEEPERS

PLAYER	TEAM	CLEAN SHEET
Dorus De Vries	Swansea	24
Steve Harper	Newcastle	20
Lee Camp	Nottm Forest	19
Chris Weale	Leicester	16
Stephen Bywater	Derby	15
David Marshall	Cardiff	15
Neil Sullivan	Doncaster	13
Scott Carson	West Brom	13
Scott Loach	Watford	11
Mark Bunn	Sheff Utd	11

COCA-COLA CHAMPIONSHIP TABLES

HOME TABLE

	P	W	D	L	F	A	GD	PTS
Newcastle	23	18	5	0	56	13	43	59
Nottm Forest	23	18	2	3	45	13	32	56
West Brom	23	16	3	4	48	21	27	51
Blackpool	23	13	6	4	46	22	24	45
Leicester	23	13	6	4	40	18	22	45
Sheff Utd	23	12	8	3	37	20	17	44
Cardiff	23	12	6	5	37	20	17	42
Swansea	23	10	10	3	21	12	9	40
Bristol City	23	10	6	7	38	34	4	40
Derby	23	12	3	8	37	32	5	39
Reading	23	10	7	6	39	22	17	37
Preston	23	9	10	4	35	26	9	37
Scunthorpe	23	10	7	6	40	32	8	37
Watford	23	10	6	7	36	26	10	36
Middlesbrough	23	9	8	6	25	21	4	35
Ipswich	23	8	11	4	24	23	1	35
Doncaster	23	9	7	7	32	29	3	34
QPR	23	8	9	6	36	28	8	33
Coventry	23	8	9	6	27	29	-2	33
Barnsley	23	8	7	8	25	29	-4	31
Sheff Wed	23	8	6	9	30	31	-1	30
Crystal Palace	23	8	5	10	24	27	-3	29
Peterborough	23	6	5	12	32	37	-5	23
Plymouth	24	5	7	12	20	30	-10	22

AWAY TABLE

	P	W	D	L	F	A	GD	PTS
Newcastle	23	12	7	4	34	22	12	43
West Brom	23	10	10	3	41	27	14	40
Cardiff	23	10	4	9	36	34	2	34
Leicester	23	8	7	8	21	27	-6	31
Crystal Palace	23	6	12	5	26	26	0	30
Swansea	23	7	8	8	19	25	-6	29
Middlesbrough	23	7	6	10	33	29	4	27
Doncaster	23	6	8	9	27	29	-2	26
Reading	23	7	5	11	29	41	-12	26
Blackpool	23	6	7	10	28	36	-8	25
Barnsley	24	6	6	12	28	40	-12	24
QPR	23	6	6	11	22	37	-15	24
Nottm Forest	23	4	11	8	20	27	-7	23
Bristol City	23	5	8	10	18	31	-13	23
Sheff Utd	23	5	6	12	25	35	-10	21
Ipswich	23	4	9	10	26	38	-12	21
Coventry	23	5	6	12	20	35	-15	21
Plymouth	23	6	2	15	23	38	-15	20
Watford	23	4	6	13	25	42	-17	18
Derby	23	3	8	12	16	31	-15	17
Sheff Wed	23	3	8	12	19	38	-19	17
Preston	23	4	5	14	23	47	-24	17
Scunthorpe	23	4	3	16	22	52	-30	15
Peterborough	23	2	5	16	14	43	-29	11

FIRST-HALF TABLE

	P	W	D	L	F	A	GD	PTS
Newcastle	46	22	18	6	42	15	27	84
West Brom	46	19	21	6	43	19	24	78
Middlesbrough	46	21	15	10	29	16	13	78
Cardiff	46	18	18	10	41	26	15	72
Nottm Forest	46	17	19	10	29	15	14	70
Doncaster	46	17	19	10	28	21	7	70
QPR	46	18	15	13	31	26	5	69
Ipswich	46	14	22	10	26	22	4	64
Blackpool	46	15	19	12	26	25	1	64
Leicester	46	14	20	12	28	22	6	62
Reading	46	15	17	14	32	27	5	62
Swansea	46	10	31	5	17	14	3	61
Preston	46	14	17	15	31	32	-1	59
Watford	46	14	14	18	25	30	-5	56
Derby	46	12	20	14	18	24	-6	56
Bristol City	46	10	23	13	20	31	-11	53
Sheff Wed	46	11	19	16	26	34	-8	52
Coventry	46	11	19	16	21	30	-9	52
Sheff Utd	46	10	21	15	23	24	-1	51
Crystal Palace	46	10	21	15	22	24	-2	51
Scunthorpe	46	12	14	20	19	35	-16	50
Barnsley	47	8	23	16	23	34	-11	47
Plymouth	47	7	21	19	15	32	-17	42
Peterborough	46	5	12	29	12	49	-37	27

SECOND-HALF TABLE

	P	W	D	L	F	A	GD	PTS
Newcastle	46	25	15	6	48	20	28	90
West Brom	46	20	16	10	46	29	17	76
Nottm Forest	46	19	18	9	36	25	11	75
Sheff Utd	46	20	14	12	39	31	8	74
Blackpool	46	20	13	13	48	33	15	73
Leicester	46	18	18	10	33	23	10	72
Cardiff	46	19	14	13	32	28	4	71
Bristol City	46	16	17	13	36	34	2	65
Reading	46	17	13	16	36	36	0	64
Crystal Palace	46	16	15	15	28	29	-1	63
Barnsley	47	14	20	13	30	35	-5	62
Swansea	46	12	25	9	23	23	0	61
Derby	46	15	12	19	35	39	-4	57
Peterborough	46	11	22	13	34	31	3	55
Watford	46	14	13	19	36	38	-2	55
Middlesbrough	46	14	12	20	29	34	-5	54
Scunthorpe	46	14	12	20	43	49	-6	54
Doncaster	46	11	19	16	31	37	-6	52
Coventry	46	11	19	16	26	34	-8	52
Plymouth	47	14	9	24	28	36	-8	51
QPR	46	12	14	20	27	39	-12	50
Sheff Wed	46	11	17	18	23	35	-12	50
Ipswich	46	9	19	18	24	39	-15	46
Preston	46	9	18	19	27	41	-14	45

DISCIPLINARY RECORDS

Y=1PT/R=2PT

PLAYER	TEAM	FLS	Y	R
Ryan Shotton	Barnsley	41	10	2
Graham Dorrans	West Brom	32	11	1
Claude Davis	Crystal Palace	33	11	1
Charlie Adam	Blackpool	86	13	0
Ross Wallace	Preston	33	13	0
Cliff Byrne	Scunthorpe	56	6	3

PLAYER	TEAM	FLS	Y	R
Kevin Nolan	Newcastle	42	10	1
Jay Bothroyd	Cardiff	103	12	0
Clint Hill	Crystal Palace	62	12	0
Alan Smith	Newcastle	59	9	1
Rhys Williams	Middlesbrough	39	9	1
Chris Morgan	Sheff Utd	49	11	0

PENALTIES

TOTAL AWARDED	134
SCORED	101
SAVED	25
MISSED	8

EARLIEST STRIKE

BILLY CLARKE
(BLACKPOOL v Preston) 0:23

LATEST STRIKE

PABLO COUNAGO
(IPSWICH v Coventry) 96:12

Pablo Counago (Ipswich)

EARLIEST CARD

NICKY MAYNARD
(Nottm Forest v BRISTOL C) 0:26

SEQUENCES

Wins	Newcastle 7
24/10/2009–09/12/2009	
Losses	Plymouth 7
18/08/2009–27/09/2009	
Draws	Barnsley 4
30/03/2010–10/04/2010	
Undefeated	Nottm F 19
27/09/2009–26/01/2010	
Without win	Ipswich 14
09/08/2009–24/10/2009	
Undefeated home	Newcastle 23
15/08/2009–24/04/2010	
Undefeated away	Nottm F 13
08/08/2009–08/01/2010	
Without scoring	Sheff Wed 6
21/11/2009–19/12/2009	
Without conceding	Nottm F 5
08/12/2009–28/12/2009	
Scoring	Blackpool 15
31/10/2009–06/02/2010	
Conceding	QPR 22
20/10/2009–06/03/2010	

COCA-COLA CHAMPIONSHIP

KEVIN NOLAN had a season to remember in 2009/10, and he capped it off by finishing on top of the Coca-Cola Championship Actim Index.

The Newcastle midfielder was certainly the lynchpin of his side's title-winning campaign, scoring 17 goals in the League and producing a string of impressive displays. That consistent form meant that he led the way in the Index for much of the season, and his final tally of 834 points put him comfortably ahead of second-placed Graham Dorrans, who collected 769 points.

West Brom's Dorrans would easily have taken top spot in the 2008/09 season with

such a return, but he still had plenty to savour from a fine campaign. The former Livingston midfielder scored an impressive 13 Championship goals and made an impressive 19 assists as he helped the Baggies to make an immediate return to the Barclays Premier League.

Cardiff's Peter Whittingham capped a fine individual season by sealing third spot while Newcastle goalkeeper Steve Harper once again showed his class, making 234 saves on his way to completing a top four that barely changed all season.

Nicky Maynard made light of Bristol City's inconsistent season to finish in the top 10, a

position he achieved on the back of 20 goals in 3,723 minutes on the pitch – an average of a goal every two and a bit games.

Other players to excel in the top 20 were Scunthorpe striker Gary Hooper, who finished in 13th position with 19 goals from 46 shots on target, and Preston's Sean St Ledger, who finished 14th overall, making more winning tackles than any other player with 161 and more interceptions than all of his rivals with 73.

Cardiff's Michael Chopra produced the highest individual match score of the season, posting 88 points with a four-goal haul against Derby in September.

ACTIM PLAYER RANKINGS FOR THE 2009/2010 COCA-COLA CHAMPIONSHIP SEASON

	NAME	TEAM	INDEX SCORE		NAME	TEAM	INDEX SCORE		NAME	TEAM	INDEX SCORE
1	Kevin Nolan	Newcastle	834	34	Adam Federici	Reading	503	67	Anthony Gerrard	Cardiff	457
2	Graham Dorrans	West Brom	769	35	Julian Speroni	Crystal Palace	502	68	Neil Danns	Crystal Palace	453
3	Peter Whittingham	Cardiff	668	36	Gylfi Sigurdsson	Reading	501	69	Gareth McAuley	Ipswich	453
4	Steve Harper	Newcastle	659	37	Jack Hobbs	Leicester	500	70	Richie Wellens	Leicester	450
5	Darren Ambrose	Crystal Palace	641	38	Ian Evatt	Blackpool	500	71	Alan Tate	Swansea	448
6	Nicky Maynard	Bristol City	617	39	Jonas Gutierrez	Newcastle	500	72	Lloyd Doyley	Watford	446
7	Chris Burke	Cardiff	614	40	Michael Chopra	Cardiff	499	73	Brett Ormerod	Blackpool	446
8	Charlie Adam	Blackpool	602	41	Ross Wallace	Preston	498	74	Stephen Bywater	Derby	444
9	Wayne Routledge	Newcastle	598	42	Billy Sharp	Sheff Utd	497	75	Paul Gallagher	Leicester	443
10	Wes Morgan	Nottm Forest	594	43	James Coppinger	Doncaster	493	76	Martyn Waghorn	Leicester	442
11	Danny Guthrie	Newcastle	581	44	Paul Anderson	Nottm Forest	490	77	Hugo Colace	Barnsley	441
12	Ashley Williams	Swansea	575	45	Martin Cranie	Coventry	489	78	Gary O'Neil	Middlesbrough	441
13	Gary Hooper	Scunthorpe	573	46	Andy Lonergan	Preston	489	79	Angel Rangel	Swansea	438
14	Sean St Ledger	Preston	572	47	Bruno Berner	Leicester	484	80	Louis Carey	Bristol City	438
15	Lee Camp	Nottm Forest	570	48	Andrew Carroll	Newcastle	483	81	Richard Cresswell	Sheff Utd	437
16	David Marshall	Cardiff	566	49	Andy King	Leicester	483	82	Dean Gerken	Bristol City	437
17	Chris Gunter	Nottm Forest	566	50	Robbie Savage	Derby	483	83	Leon Best	Newcastle	436
18	Chris Cohen	Nottm Forest	565	51	Neil Sullivan	Doncaster	480	84	Tommy Spurr	Sheff Wed	435
19	Jay Bothroyd	Cardiff	562	52	Keiren Westwood	Coventry	480	85	James Chambers	Doncaster	434
20	Alex Baptiste	Blackpool	559	53	Tom Cleverley	Watford	477	86	Lee Grant	Sheff Wed	433
21	Billy Jones	Preston	554	54	Sanchez Jose Enrique	Newcastle	477	87	Robert Earnshaw	Nottm Forest	431
22	Danny Simpson	Newcastle	549	55	Gareth Roberts	Doncaster	475	88	David Wheater	Middlesbrough	424
23	Jonas Olsson	West Brom	545	56	Jonathan Walters	Ipswich	473	89	Darren Pratley	Swansea	424
24	Jimmy Kebe	Reading	543	57	Ryan Bertrand	Reading	470	90	Keith Southern	Blackpool	424
25	Chris Weale	Leicester	539	58	George Boyd	Nottm Forest	468	91	Youssouf Mulumbu	West Brom	423
26	Dorus De Vries	Swansea	533	59	Marcus Tudgay	Sheff Wed	467	92	Alan Lee	Crystal Palace	421
27	Chris Brunt	West Brom	532	60	Dexter Blackstock	Nottm Forest	467	93	Cole Skuse	Bristol City	420
28	Fabricio Coloccini	Newcastle	531	61	Jobi McAnuff	Reading	465	94	Joe Murphy	Scunthorpe	417
29	Paul Hayes	Scunthorpe	528	62	Bradley Orr	Bristol City	465	95	Darren Potter	Sheff Wed	416
30	Danny Graham	Watford	528	63	Adrian Mariappa	Watford	464	96	Clinton Morrison	Coventry	416
31	Stephen Crainey	Blackpool	527	64	Wayne Brown	Leicester	464	97	David Mirfin	Scunthorpe	416
32	Scott Carson	West Brom	524	65	Scott Loach	Watford	462	98	Marcus Williams	Scunthorpe	414
33	Craig Mackail-Smith	Peterborough	513	66	Chris Morgan	Sheff Utd	458	99	Clint Hill	Crystal Palace	414
								100	Stephen Wright	Coventry	413

LEADING PLAYERS IN THE ACTIM INDEX BY POSITION

TOP 5 GOALKEEPERS

Name	Index Score	Overall Index Rank	Team
Steve Harper	659	4	Newcastle
Lee Camp	570	15	Nottm Forest
David Marshall	566	16	Cardiff
Chris Weale	539	25	Leicester
Dorus De Vries	533	26	Swansea

TOP 5 MIDFIELDERS

Name	Index Score	Overall Index Rank	Team
Kevin Nolan	834	1	Newcastle
Graham Dorrans	769	2	West Brom
Peter Whittingham	668	3	Cardiff
Darren Ambrose	641	5	Crystal Palace
Chris Burke	614	7	Cardiff

TOP 5 DEFENDERS

Name	Index Score	Overall Index Rank	Team
Wes Morgan	594	10	Nottm Forest
Ashley Williams	575	12	Swansea
Sean St Ledger	572	14	Preston
Chris Gunter	566	17	Nottm Forest
Alex Baptiste	559	20	Blackpool

TOP 5 STRIKERS

Name	Index Score	Overall Index Rank	Team
Nicky Maynard	617	6	Bristol City
Gary Hooper	573	13	Scunthorpe
Jay Bothroyd	562	19	Cardiff
Paul Hayes	528	29	Scunthorpe
Danny Graham	528	30	Watford

Wes Morgan (Nottm Forest)

BEST INDIVIDUAL MATCH SCORES

Michael Chopra	Cardiff	88
29/09/2009: Cardiff 6–1 Derby		
Peter Whittingham	Cardiff	73
24/10/2009: Sheff Utd 3–4 Cardiff		
Kevin Nolan	Newcastle	67
26/09/2009: Ipswich 0–4 Newcastle		
Gary Hooper	Scunthorpe	66
17/04/2010: Scunthorpe 3–0 Bristol City		
Darius Henderson	Sheff Utd	65
28/11/2009: Bristol City 2–3 Sheff Utd		
Nicky Maynard	Bristol City	64
23/03/2010: Bristol City 5–3 Barnsley		
Paul Gallagher	Leicester	64
13/02/2010: Leicester 5–1 Scunthorpe		
Shola Ameobi	Newcastle	64
15/08/2009: Newcastle 3–0 Reading		

Daryl Murphy	Ipswich	62
09/03/2010: Ipswich 2–0 Cardiff		
Freddy Eastwood	Coventry	61
12/12/2009: Coventry 3–2 Peterborough		
Victor Moses	Crystal Palace	60
08/12/2009: Reading 2–4 Crystal Palace		
Billy Sharp	Doncaster	59
06/03/2010: Bristol City 2–5 Doncaster		
Robert Earnshaw	Nottm Forest	59
05/12/2009: Nottm Forest 5–1 Leicester		
George Boyd	Nottm Forest	58
24/10/2009: Peterborough 3–0 Scunthorpe		
Grzegorz Rasiak	Reading	58
27/02/2010: Reading 5–0 Sheff Wed		
Gylfi Sigurdsson	Reading	57
17/04/2010: Reading 6–0 Peterborough		

ACTIM INDEX TEAM OF THE SEASON

 **ASHLEY WILLIAMS**
(575) Swansea

 **DARREN AMBROSE**
(641) Crystal Palace

WES MORGAN
(594) Nottm Forest

KEVIN NOLAN
(834) Newcastle

GARY HOOPER
(573) Scunthorpe

STEVE HARPER
(659) Newcastle

GRAHAM DORRANS
(769) West Brom

NICKY MAYNARD
(617) Bristol City

SEAN ST LEDGER
(572) Preston

CHRIS GUNTER
(566) Nottm Forest

PETER WHITTINGHAM
(668) Cardiff

BY TEAM

	Score	Rank
BARNSLEY		
Hugo Colace	441	77
BLACKPOOL		
Charlie Adam	602	8
BRISTOL CITY		
Nicky Maynard	617	6
CARDIFF		
Peter Whittingham	668	3
COVENTRY		
Martin Cranie	489	45
CRYSTAL PALACE		
Darren Ambrose	641	5
DERBY		
Robbie Savage	483	50
DONCASTER		
Billy Sharp	497	42
IPSWICH		
Jonathan Walters	473	56
LEICESTER		
Chris Weale	539	25
MIDDLESBROUGH		
Gary O'Neil	441	78
NEWCASTLE		
Kevin Nolan	834	1
NOTTM FOREST		
Wes Morgan	594	10
PETERBOROUGH		
Craig Mackail-Smith	513	33
PLYMOUTH		
Jamie Mackie	334	164
PRESTON		
Sean St Ledger	572	14
QPR		
Jay Simpson	412	101
READING		
Jimmy Kebe	543	24
SCUNTHORPE		
Gary Hooper	573	13
SHEFF UTD		
Chris Morgan	458	66
SHEFF WED		
Marcus Tudgay	467	59
SWANSEA		
Ashley Williams	575	12
WATFORD		
Danny Graham	528	30
WEST BROM		
Graham Dorrans	769	2

BARNSLEY

CLUB SUMMARY

FORMED	1887
MANAGER	Mark Robins
GROUND	Oakwell
CAPACITY	23,000
NICKNAME	The Tykes
WEBSITE	www.barnsleyfc.co.uk

The New Football Pools PLAYER OF THE SEASON

Hugo Colace

OVERALL
P	W	D	L	F	A	GD
51	17	12	22	59	75	-16

COCA-COLA CHAMPIONSHIP
Pos	P	W	D	L	F	A	GD	Pts
18	46	14	12	20	53	69	-16	54

HOME
Pos	P	W	D	L	F	A	GD	Pts
20	23	8	7	8	25	29	-4	31

AWAY
Pos	P	W	D	L	F	A	GD	Pts
13	23	6	5	12	28	40	-12	23

CUP PROGRESS DETAILS
Competition	Round reached	Knocked out by
FA Cup	R3	Scunthorpe
Carling Cup	R4	Man Utd

BIGGEST WIN (ALL COMPS)
02/02/10 4-1 v Preston

BIGGEST DEFEAT (ALL COMPS)
06/03/10 1-6 v Newcastle

THE PLAYER WITH THE MOST
GOALS SCORED Daniel Bogdanovic	**11**
SHOTS ON TARGET Adam Hammill	**36**
SHOTS OFF TARGET Adam Hammill	**24**
SHOTS WITHOUT SCORING Filipe Teixeira	**30**
ASSISTS Hugo Colace, Emil Hallfredsson	**4**
OFFSIDES Daniel Bogdanovic	**42**
FOULS Jonathan Macken	**67**
FOULS WITHOUT A CARD Jamal Campbell-Ryce	**5**
FREE-KICKS WON Adam Hammill	**60**
DEFENSIVE CLEARANCES Stephen Foster	**65**

actim INDEX FOR THE 2009/10 COCA-COLA CHAMPIONSHIP SEASON

RANK	PLAYER	PTS
77	Hugo Colace	441
108	Adam Hammill	407
120	Luke Steele	394

ATTENDANCE RECORD
HIGH	AVERAGE	LOW
20,079	12,964	11,116
v Newcastle (12/12/2009)		v Reading (29/08/2009)

BARNSLEY manager Mark Robins and assistant John Breckin successfully completed their first task at Oakwell by keeping the Tykes in the Coca-Cola Championship.

The club had made a poor start to the season, failing to win any of their first six League matches, and were languishing in the bottom three when Robins replaced Simon Davey as manager in early September. Their multi-national squad responded to the change, and victory at Derby six days after Robins had been appointed kick-started a steady climb away from the lingering threat of relegation.

Three successive Championship wins soon followed, over West Brom, Ipswich and at local rivals Doncaster, and by February Barnsley had risen to ninth, just three points away from the top six.

Progress under Robins sparked a genuine belief among some fans that the Tykes could challenge for the play-offs, but the former Rotherham manager was mindful not to build false hopes. He had known there was little money available for new players when he first arrived and, although he supplemented his squad with canny loan signings such as Iceland international Emil Hallfredsson, Stoke pair Carl Dickinson and Ryan Shotton and later Filipe Teixeira from West Brom, he knew his small squad was vulnerable to injuries and loss of form during the run-in.

Robins briefly enjoyed the spotlight in October when Manchester United came to town. After an impressive home win over Barclays Premier League newcomers

Mark Robins raised his reputation by lifting Barnsley clear of the relegation battle

Burnley in the Carling Cup, the Tykes were rewarded with a fourth-round tie against Robins' former club, United. However, goals from United duo Danny Welbeck and Michael Owen ensured there was no upset.

There was to be no repeat of Barnsley's FA Cup heroics of recent years either following a 1–0 third-round defeat at Scunthorpe in January, which left the club to focus on their League campaign. Their fortunes peaked in February with wins at Cardiff and at home against Blackpool before a steady drop.

The Tykes beat Nottingham Forest 2–1 at Oakwell in mid-March, but that was their last win of the campaign as they slid back down the table to eventually finish in 18th place, seven points above the drop-zone.

A poor conclusion to the season clearly rankled Robins and an early-summer clear-out signalled his intentions for the future, with senior players Jonathan Macken, Darren Moore and Anderson De Silva among five released immediately following the end of the campaign.

Daniel Bogdanovic celebrates his first goal in a 2–1 win against Nottingham Forest

RESULTS 2009/10

AUGUST

8th	● Sheff Wed	A	D 2–2	Att: 30,644	Ref: A Taylor	**Scorers:** Butterfield, Macken. **Booked:** De Silva, Foster.
11th	● Lincoln	A	W 0–1	Att: 3,635	Ref: A Haines	**Scorers:** Bogdanovic. **Booked:** Foster.
15th	● Coventry	H	L 0–2	Att: 12,552	Ref: S Tanner	**Booked:** Kozluk, Butterfield. **Dismissed:** Kozluk.
18th	● Preston	H	L 0–3	Att: 11,850	Ref: D Whitestone	**Booked:** Butterfield, Odejayi, Potter, Bogdanovic.
22nd	● Leicester	A	L 1–0	Att: 21,799	Ref: A Penn	
25th	● Reading	A	W 1–2	Att: 5,576	Ref: G Horwood	**Scorers:** Bogdanovic[2]. **Booked:** El Haimour, Foster, Bogdanovic.
29th	● Reading	H	L 1–3	Att: 11,116	Ref: M Oliver	**Scorers:** A Gray.

SEPTEMBER

12th	● Watford	A	L 1–0	Att: 12,613	Ref: D Phillips	**Booked:** De Silva, Devaney.
15th	● Derby	A	W 2–3	Att: 27,609	Ref: N Miller	**Scorers:** De Silva, A Gray, Hammill. **Booked:** Colace.
19th	● Swansea	H	D 0–0	Att: 11,596	Ref: R Shoebridge	**Booked:** Hammill, Doyle.
22nd	● Burnley	H	W 3–2	Att: 6,270	Ref: M Clattenburg	**Scorers:** Colace, De Silva, Macken. **Booked:** Foster.
26th	● QPR	A	L 5–2	Att: 12,025	Ref: K Evans	**Scorers:** Foster, A Gray. **Booked:** Shotton, De Silva, Kozluk.
29th	● West Brom	H	W 3–1	Att: 12,191	Ref: S Mathieson	**Scorers:** Hammill, Hume, Martis OG. **Booked:** Dickinson.

OCTOBER

3rd	● Ipswich	H	W 2–1	Att: 12,224	Ref: P Gibbs	**Scorers:** Hume, Macken. **Booked:** Moore.
17th	● Doncaster	A	W 0–1	Att: 12,708	Ref: G Salisbury	**Scorers:** Hammill. **Booked:** Shotton, Doyle.
20th	● Nottm Forest	A	L 1–0	Att: 20,395	Ref: N Miller	**Booked:** Moore, Dickinson.
24th	● Bristol City	H	L 2–3	Att: 11,314	Ref: A Haines	**Scorers:** Bogdanovic, Hammill. **Booked:** Colace. **Dismissed:** Shotton.
27th	● Man Utd	H	L 0–2	Att: 20,019	Ref: C Foy	**Booked:** De Silva, Colace, Bogdanovic.
31st	● Peterborough	A	W 1–2	Att: 8,556	Ref: C Boyeson	**Scorers:** Bogdanovic, Macken. **Booked:** Bogdanovic, Shotton, Doyle, Foster.

NOVEMBER

| 9th | ● Sheff Utd | H | D 2–2 | Att: 12,998 | Ref: M Clattenburg | **Scorers:** Bogdanovic, De Silva. **Booked:** Shotton. |
| 21st | ● Cardiff | H | W 1–0 | Att: 11,903 | Ref: K Wright | **Scorers:** Dickinson. **Booked:** De Silva. |

DECEMBER

5th	● Blackpool	A	W 1–2	Att: 8,108	Ref: L Mason	**Scorers:** A Gray, Vaughan OG. **Booked:** Macken, Hammill.
9th	● Scunthorpe	H	D 1–1	Att: 11,657	Ref: E Ilderton	**Scorers:** Colace. **Booked:** Kozluk, Hume.
12th	● Newcastle	H	D 2–2	Att: 20,079	Ref: G Salisbury	**Scorers:** Hallfredsson, Hassell. **Booked:** Hassell, Moore.
19th	● Crystal Palace	A	D 1–1	Att: 14,279	Ref: K Hill	**Scorers:** Bogdanovic. **Booked:** Shotton, De Silva, Hume, Dickinson.
28th	● Middlesbrough	H	W 2–1	Att: 18,001	Ref: A Hall	**Scorers:** Colace, Foster. **Booked:** Hassell, Bogdanovic, Butterfield, Hallfredsson.

JANUARY

2nd	● Scunthorpe	A	L 1–0	Att: 5,457	Ref: D Foster	**Booked:** Butterfield.
9th	● Coventry	A	L 3–1	Att: 15,031	Ref: L Mason	**Scorers:** Macken. **Booked:** Hassell, Shotton, Dickinson.
16th	● Sheff Wed	H	L 1–2	Att: 17,844	Ref: A Penn	**Scorers:** Hallfredsson. **Booked:** Colace, Shotton.
26th	● Leicester	H	W 1–0	Att: 12,065	Ref: D Webb	**Scorers:** Colace.
30th	● Reading	A	L 1–0	Att: 15,580	Ref: J Linington	**Booked:** De Silva.

FEBRUARY

2nd	● Preston	A	W 1–4	Att: 12,453	Ref: N Miller	**Scorers:** De Silva, A Gray, Rodriguez, Hart OG. **Booked:** Hallfredsson, De Silva.
6th	● Watford	H	W 1–0	Att: 11,739	Ref: F Graham	**Scorers:** Hallfredsson. **Booked:** Colace. **Dismissed:** Shotton.
9th	● Middlesbrough	A	L 2–1	Att: 17,775	Ref: C Boyeson	**Scorers:** Colace.
13th	● Plymouth	H	L 1–3	Att: 11,661	Ref: K Evans	**Scorers:** Colace. **Booked:** Foster, Doyle.
16th	● Scunthorpe	A	L 2–1	Att: 5,648	Ref: C Webster	**Scorers:** Bogdanovic. **Booked:** Foster.
20th	● Cardiff	A	W 0–2	Att: 19,753	Ref: K Stroud	**Scorers:** Bogdanovic[2]. **Booked:** Potter, Teixeira.
27th	● Blackpool	H	W 1–0	Att: 12,347	Ref: J Singh	**Scorers:** Hume.

MARCH

6th	● Newcastle	A	L 6–1	Att: 44,464	Ref: G Hegley	**Scorers:** Bogdanovic. **Dismissed:** Steele.
13th	● Crystal Palace	H	D 0–0	Att: 11,416	Ref: T Kettle	**Booked:** Doyle.
16th	● Nottm Forest	H	W 2–1	Att: 13,174	Ref: K Friend	**Scorers:** Bogdanovic[2]. **Booked:** Hammill, Teixeira, Hume.
20th	● Ipswich	A	L 1–0	Att: 20,558	Ref: N Swarbrick	**Booked:** Shotton, Colace.
23rd	● Bristol City	A	L 5–3	Att: 13,009	Ref: G Scott	**Scorers:** Bogdanovic, Colace, A Gray. **Booked:** Hassell, Hallfredsson.
27th	● Doncaster	H	L 0–1	Att: 14,188	Ref: D Deadman	**Booked:** Colace, Shotton.
30th	● Plymouth	A	D 0–0	Att: 7,243	Ref: M Russell	**Booked:** Hallfredsson, Hammill, Shotton.

APRIL

3rd	● Sheff Utd	A	D 0–0	Att: 24,808	Ref: P Walton	**Booked:** Colace, Doyle, Moore, Devaney.
5th	● Peterborough	H	D 2–2	Att: 11,290	Ref: T Bates	**Scorers:** Hume[2]. **Booked:** Potter. Peterborough are relegated.
10th	● Derby	H	D 0–0	Att: 13,034	Ref: P Taylor	**Booked:** Foster.
17th	● Swansea	A	L 3–1	Att: 15,139	Ref: D Phillips	**Scorers:** Moore. **Booked:** A Gray, Devaney, Colace.
24th	● QPR	H	L 0–1	Att: 11,944	Ref: R Booth	**Booked:** Doyle, Potter.

MAY

| 2nd | ● West Brom | A | D 1–1 | Att: 25,297 | Ref: M Oliver | **Scorers:** Colace. |

● Coca-Cola Championship/Play-offs ● FA Cup ● Carling Cup

BARNSLEY

CHAMPIONSHIP GOALKEEPER STATS

Player	Minutes on pitch	Appearances	Match starts	Completed matches	Sub appearances	Subbed off	Saved with feet	Punched	Parried	Tipped over	Fumbled	Tipped round	Caught	Blocked	Clean sheets	Goals conceded	Save %	Saved	Resulting in goals	Opposition miss	Fouls committed	Free-kicks won	Yellow cards	Red cards
Bartosz Bialkowski	199	2	2	2	0	0	0	2	0	2	0	1	4	0	0	2	81.82	0	0	0	0	1	0	0
David Preece	537	6	5	5	1	0	0	1	6	0	0	0	9	0	2	14	53.33	0	1	0	0	0	0	0
Luke Steele	3697	39	39	38	0	0	2	16	30	6	3	9	144	2	9	54	79.47	1	6	1	2	8	0	1

CHAMPIONSHIP OUTFIELD PLAYER STATS

Player	Minutes on pitch	Appearances	Match starts	Completed matches	Substitute appearances	Subbed off	Goals scored	Assists	Shots on target	Shots off target	Crosses	Tackles made	Defensive clearances	Defensive blocks	Fouls committed	Free-kicks won	Caught offside	Yellow cards	Red cards
Jamil Adam	56	2	0	0	2	0	0	0	0	0	0	0	0	0	1	2	0	0	0
Daniel Bogdanovic	1777	29	20	4	9	16	11	2	27	10	14	28	0	4	33	20	42	3	0
Jacob Butterfield	1074	20	10	5	10	5	1	2	7	9	12	11	1	0	15	6	0	3	0
Jamal Campbell-Ryce	756	13	8	5	5	3	0	0	3	4	16	8	2	0	5	10	0	0	0
Hugo Colace	3880	41	41	38	0	3	7	4	24	16	10	98	28	1	47	18	2	8	0
Anderson De Silva	2172	31	25	12	6	13	3	3	18	14	25	20	17	2	56	27	1	7	0
Martin Devaney	624	11	6	2	5	4	0	2	4	3	10	10	1	0	7	8	7	3	0
Carl Dickinson	2594	28	27	26	1	1	1	1	5	6	34	67	17	6	16	15	0	4	0
Nathan Doyle	2966	34	32	24	2	8	0	1	0	15	11	63	25	5	39	29	0	7	0
Mounir El Haimour	188	2	2	2	0	0	0	0	1	0	3	4	3	2	3	4	0	0	0
Stephen Foster	3995	42	42	41	0	1	2	0	9	18	1	75	65	19	39	37	1	5	0
Julian Gray	226	5	1	1	4	0	0	0	0	3	0	2	2	0	1	4	1	0	0
Andy Gray	2016	30	19	16	11	3	6	3	11	8	6	16	5	0	22	39	23	1	0
Emil Hallfredsson	2035	27	22	13	5	9	3	4	20	21	39	35	11	1	29	24	2	4	0
Adam Hammill	2933	39	31	23	8	8	4	3	36	24	97	44	1	1	26	60	4	4	0
Bobby Hassell	2125	24	22	21	2	1	1	3	3	3	34	42	21	5	13	16	0	4	0
Iain Hume	1886	35	17	9	18	8	5	3	15	18	32	23	2	1	17	34	20	3	0
Robert Kozluk	1149	14	12	10	2	1	0	0	1	2	19	15	12	4	17	13	2	3	1
Jonathan Macken	2345	31	27	13	4	14	4	3	26	16	10	23	5	0	67	33	25	1	0
Darren Moore	3298	35	33	32	2	1	1	0	2	4	1	92	56	27	40	40	0	4	0
Reuben Noble-Lazarus	36	2	0	0	2	0	0	0	1	0	0	0	0	0	0	0	0	0	0
Kayode Odejayi	283	5	2	1	3	1	0	1	2	3	0	2	1	0	4	6	3	1	0
Luke Potter	1184	14	12	11	2	1	0	1	1	3	15	18	7	1	15	6	1	4	0
Jay Rodriguez	213	6	1	0	5	1	1	0	3	2	1	9	0	0	2	0	3	0	0
Ryan Shotton	2846	30	30	27	0	1	0	0	9	6	12	72	46	13	39	33	0	10	2
Onome Sodje	15	1	0	0	1	0	0	0	0	0	0	0	0	0	0	0	0	0	0
Alistair Taylor	13	1	0	0	1	0	0	0	0	0	0	0	0	0	0	1	0	0	0
Filipe Teixeira	1221	14	14	9	0	5	0	0	10	20	26	33	0	0	27	30	4	2	0
O'Neil Thompson	27	1	0	0	1	0	0	0	0	0	0	0	0	0	1	0	0	0	0
Kieran Trippier	210	3	3	1	0	2	0	0	0	0	1	13	3	4	3	5	0	0	0

actim

Coca-Cola CHAMPIONSHIP

SEASON TOTALS

Goals scored	53
Goals conceded	69
Clean sheets	11
Shots on target	245
Shots off target	230
Shots per goal	8.79
Pens awarded	5
Pens scored	3
Pens conceded	9
Offsides	146
Corners	245
Crosses	429
Players used	33
Fouls committed	592
Free-kicks won	532

SEASON INFORMATION
Highest position: 3
Lowest position: 24
Average goals scored per game: 1.15
Average goals conceded per game: 1.50

	AUG	SEP	OCT	NOV	DEC	JAN	FEB	MAR	APR	MAY

LEAGUE POSITION AT THE END OF EACH MONTH
24 · 21 · 17 · 15 · 15 · 15 · 11 · 14 · 18 · 18

CARDS RECEIVED

81   4

SEQUENCES

Wins	3
(29/09/09–17/10/09)	
Losses	5
(15/08/09–12/09/09)	
Draws	4
(30/03/10–10/04/10)	
Undefeated	8
(31/10/09–28/12/09)	
Without win	10
(20/03/10–02/05/10)	
Undefeated home	5
(09/11/09–28/12/09)	
Undefeated away	3
(31/10/09–19/12/09)	
Without scoring	3
(on two occasions)	
Without conceding	2
(on two occasions)	
Scoring	12
(24/10/09–26/01/10)	
Conceding	7
(on two occasions)	

MATCH RECORDS

Goals scored per match

		W	D	L	Pts
Failed to score	14	0	5	9	5
Scored 1 goal	16	5	3	8	18
Scored 2 goals	12	6	4	2	22
Scored 3 goals	3	2	0	1	6
Scored 4+ goals	1	1	0	0	3

Goals conceded per match

		W	D	L	Pts
Clean sheet	11	6	5	0	23
Conceded 1 goal	17	7	3	7	24
Conceded 2 goals	9	1	4	4	7
Conceded 3 goals	6	0	0	6	0
Conceded 4+ goals	3	0	0	3	0

EARLIEST STRIKE

HUGO COLACE
(v Bristol City) 2:58

LATEST STRIKE

JONATHAN MACKEN
(v Ipswich) 95:32

Jonathan Macken

GOALS SCORED/CONCEDED
PER FIVE-MINUTE INTERVALS

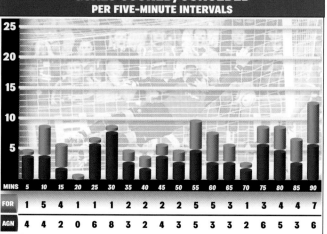

MINS	5	10	15	20	25	30	35	40	45	50	55	60	65	70	75	80	85	90
FOR	1	5	4	1	1	1	2	2	2	2	5	5	3	1	3	4	4	7
AGN	4	4	2	0	6	8	3	2	4	3	5	3	2	6	5	3	6

GOAL DETAILS

How the goals were struck

SCORED		CONCEDED
33	Right foot	34
9	Left foot	20
11	Header	14
0	Other	1

How the goals were struck

SCORED		CONCEDED
31	Open play	41
7	Cross	8
4	Corner	8
3	Penalty	7
1	Direct from free-kick	2
4	Free-kick	3
3	Own goal	0

Distance from goal

SCORED		CONCEDED
21	6YDS	24
24	18YDS	34
8	18+YDS	11

BLACKPOOL

CLUB SUMMARY

FORMED	1887
MANAGER	Ian Holloway
GROUND	Bloomfield Road
CAPACITY	12,555
NICKNAME	The Seasiders
WEBSITE	www.blackpoolfc.co.uk

The New Football Pools PLAYER OF THE SEASON — Charlie Adam

OVERALL
P	W	D	L	F	A	GD
53	24	13	16	93	72	21

COCA-COLA CHAMPIONSHIP
Pos	P	W	D	L	F	A	GD	Pts
6	46	19	13	14	74	58	16	70

HOME
Pos	P	W	D	L	F	A	GD	Pts
4	23	13	6	4	46	22	24	45

AWAY
Pos	P	W	D	L	F	A	GD	Pts
10	23	6	7	10	28	36	-8	25

CUP PROGRESS DETAILS
Competition	Round reached	Knocked out by
FA Cup	R3	Ipswich
Carling Cup	R3	Stoke

BIGGEST WIN (ALL COMPS)
23/03/10 5–1 v Swansea

BIGGEST DEFEAT (ALL COMPS)
1–4 on 2 occasions

THE PLAYER WITH THE MOST
GOALS SCORED	Charlie Adam	16
SHOTS ON TARGET	Charlie Adam	63
SHOTS OFF TARGET	Charlie Adam	69
SHOTS WITHOUT SCORING	Neal Eardley	20
ASSISTS	Charlie Adam	8
OFFSIDES	Brett Ormerod	27
FOULS	Charlie Adam	86
FOULS WITHOUT A CARD	Ben Burgess	30
FREE-KICKS WON	Charlie Adam	87
DEFENSIVE CLEARANCES	Ian Evatt	65

actim INDEX FOR THE 2009/10 COCA-COLA CHAMPIONSHIP SEASON

RANK	PLAYER	PTS
8	Charlie Adam	602
20	Alex Baptiste	559
31	Stephen Crainey	527

ATTENDANCE RECORD
HIGH	AVERAGE	LOW
12,296	8,611	6,855
v Bristol City (02/05/2010)		v Watford (23/01/2010)

Blackpool clinched an unlikely promotion thanks to a dramatic play-off final victory

BLACKPOOL'S fairytale victory over Cardiff in the Coca-Cola Championship play-off final secured the most lucrative promotion in the history of English football. The Lancashire outfit will return to the top flight for the first time since 1971 after clinching a place in the Barclays Premier League, estimated to be worth £90million.

Manager Ian Holloway's reward will be to rub shoulders with the likes of north-west neighbours Liverpool and Manchester United as his side become one of the smallest clubs to play in England's top tier since the Premier League's formation.

The Seasiders will be tipped to struggle, but there is a unity about Blackpool that has been evident since the former Leicester, QPR and Plymouth manager arrived in the summer of 2009 and breathed new life into the club.

When the charismatic boss was appointed, Blackpool were rated among the favourites for relegation from the Championship, having struggled during the previous campaign. Yet Holloway got the best out of well-travelled players like Brett Ormerod, utilised the loan market wisely and had one of the finest players in the Championship during 2009/10 in 19-goal midfielder Charlie Adam.

Charlie Adam scored a superb free-kick in the 3–2 play-off final win over Cardiff

The Seasiders began the campaign with four straight draws in the League, but gradually they built some winning momentum, beating Newcastle and Nottingham Forest in consecutive games. A run of six wins from their last eight games saw them hit form at just the right time and ultimately guaranteed them a place in the play-offs.

Having already despatched Forest over two legs in the semi-finals, the Seasiders' performance against Cardiff at Wembley summed up a season in which they were forced to show their resilience time and time again, as they twice came from behind to lead 3–2 at the break. That was an advantage they did not surrender and it ensured the Blackpool supporters – who made one half of Wembley a sea of brilliant orange – and Holloway can look forward to life in the top flight.

It is an achievement the manager feels will not truly sink in until Bloomfield Road's maiden Barclays Premier League campaign gets under way. 'I don't know about being a Premier League club yet but it feels real that we have done something special,' he said after the Wembley final.

'That probably won't be apparent until we play against all these other teams with a lot more than we have got. I'm delighted for these people and these lads have deserved it.'

Ian Holloway made an incredible impact in his first season at Blackpool

RESULTS 2009/10

AUGUST
8th	● QPR	A	D 1–1	**Att:** 14,013	**Ref:** A D'Urso	**Scorers:** Burgess. **Booked:** Adam.
11th	● Crewe	A	W 1–2	**Att:** 2,991	**Ref:** P Gibbs	**Scorers:** Nardiello, Nowland. **Booked:** Taylor-Fletcher.
15th	● Cardiff	H	D 1–1	**Att:** 7,698	**Ref:** G Hegley	**Scorers:** Evatt.
18th	● Derby	H	D 0–0	**Att:** 8,056	**Ref:** E Ilderton	
22nd	● Watford	A	D 2–2	**Att:** 12,745	**Ref:** D Deadman	**Scorers:** Baptiste, Taylor-Fletcher. **Booked:** Eardley, Evatt, Southern.
26th	● Wigan	H	W 4–1	**Att:** 8,089	**Ref:** M Oliver	**Scorers:** Adam, Burgess, Demontagnac, Taylor-Fletcher.
29th	● Coventry	H	W 3–0	**Att:** 8,239	**Ref:** N Miller	**Scorers:** Adam, Burgess, Taylor-Fletcher. **Booked:** Adam.

SEPTEMBER
12th	● Leicester	A	L 2–1	**Att:** 22,827	**Ref:** J Singh	**Scorers:** Adam. **Booked:** Crainey, Evatt, Bouazza.
16th	● Newcastle	H	W 2–1	**Att:** 9,647	**Ref:** J Moss	**Scorers:** Euell, Ormerod.
19th	● Nottm Forest	A	W 0–1	**Att:** 23,487	**Ref:** A Penn	**Scorers:** Adam.
22nd	● Stoke	A	L 4–3	**Att:** 13,957	**Ref:** L Probert	**Scorers:** Burgess, Clarke, Vaughan. **Booked:** Adam.
26th	● Peterborough	H	W 2–0	**Att:** 7,728	**Ref:** T Bates	**Scorers:** Bouazza, Euell.
29th	● Bristol City	A	L 2–0	**Att:** 13,673	**Ref:** R East	**Booked:** Adam.

OCTOBER
3rd	● Crystal Palace	A	L 4–1	**Att:** 15,749	**Ref:** A Taylor	**Scorers:** Baptiste. **Booked:** Baptiste.
17th	● Plymouth	H	W 2–0	**Att:** 7,765	**Ref:** D Webb	**Scorers:** Seip, Vaughan. **Booked:** Southern.
20th	● Sheff Utd	H	W 3–0	**Att:** 8,042	**Ref:** S Mathieson	**Scorers:** Adam, Euell, Seip. **Booked:** Eardley.
24th	● Swansea	A	D 0–0	**Att:** 14,724	**Ref:** A Hall	**Booked:** Bouazza, Adam, Euell.
31st	● Doncaster	A	D 3–3	**Att:** 10,312	**Ref:** M Oliver	**Scorers:** Burgess, Emmanuel-Thomas, Ormerod.

NOVEMBER
7th	● Scunthorpe	H	W 4–1	**Att:** 7,727	**Ref:** C Webster	**Scorers:** Adam, Baptiste, Burgess, Evatt.
21st	● Reading	A	L 2–1	**Att:** 15,945	**Ref:** G Scott	**Scorers:** Ormerod. **Booked:** Adam, Crainey, Seip.
30th	● Preston	H	D 1–1	**Att:** 9,861	**Ref:** K Friend	**Scorers:** Clarke. **Booked:** Baptiste, Clarke.

DECEMBER
5th	● Barnsley	H	L 1–2	**Att:** 8,108	**Ref:** L Mason	**Scorers:** Adam. **Booked:** Taylor-Fletcher.
8th	● Middlesbrough	A	W 0–3	**Att:** 18,089	**Ref:** R Shoebridge	**Scorers:** Adam, Taylor-Fletcher[2]. **Booked:** Crainey.
12th	● Ipswich	A	L 3–1	**Att:** 19,831	**Ref:** P Crossley	**Scorers:** Evatt. **Booked:** Bangura, Vaughan, Crainey, Evatt. **Dismissed:** Vaughan.
26th	● Derby	A	W 0–2	**Att:** 30,313	**Ref:** S Mathieson	**Scorers:** Ormerod, Buxton OG.

JANUARY
2nd	● Ipswich	H	L 1–2	**Att:** 7,332	**Ref:** E Ilderton	**Scorers:** Ormerod. **Booked:** Eardley. **Dismissed:** Evatt, Edwards.
9th	● Cardiff	A	D 1–1	**Att:** 19,147	**Ref:** G Ward	**Scorers:** Adam. **Booked:** Adam.
16th	● QPR	H	D 2–2	**Att:** 7,600	**Ref:** T Kettle	**Scorers:** Adam, Taylor-Fletcher. **Booked:** Adam.
19th	● Sheff Wed	H	L 1–2	**Att:** 8,007	**Ref:** A Hall	**Scorers:** Adam. **Booked:** Euell, Vaughan.
23rd	● Watford	H	W 3–2	**Att:** 6,855	**Ref:** C Boyeson	**Scorers:** Adam, Ormerod, Southern. **Booked:** Evatt.
30th	● Coventry	A	D 1–1	**Att:** 16,019	**Ref:** D Whitestone	**Scorers:** Bannan. **Booked:** Adam. **Dismissed:** Ormerod.

FEBRUARY
3rd	● West Brom	H	L 2–3	**Att:** 8,510	**Ref:** D Foster	**Scorers:** Dobbie, Southern. **Booked:** Butler.
6th	● Leicester	H	L 1–2	**Att:** 8,484	**Ref:** A Haines	**Scorers:** Dobbie. **Booked:** Adam.
9th	● Sheff Wed	A	L 2–0	**Att:** 19,058	**Ref:** G Eltrigham	
13th	● Preston	A	D 0–0	**Att:** 19,840	**Ref:** M Jones	**Booked:** Vaughan.
16th	● Middlesbrough	H	W 2–0	**Att:** 7,936	**Ref:** M Haywood	**Scorers:** Campbell, Ormerod. **Booked:** Adam, Southern. **Dismissed:** Edwards.
20th	● Reading	H	W 2–0	**Att:** 7,147	**Ref:** C Pawson	**Scorers:** Adam, Campbell. **Booked:** Southern.
27th	● Barnsley	A	L 1–0	**Att:** 12,347	**Ref:** J Singh	**Booked:** Ormerod, Vaughan, Baptiste.

MARCH
6th	● Ipswich	H	W 1–0	**Att:** 8,635	**Ref:** R Shoebridge	**Scorers:** Euell. **Booked:** Martin, Euell.
13th	● West Brom	A	L 3–2	**Att:** 21,592	**Ref:** J Moss	**Scorers:** Adam, Ormerod. **Booked:** Martin, Euell, Eardley, Baptiste.
16th	● Sheff Utd	A	L 3–0	**Att:** 22,555	**Ref:** O Langford	**Booked:** Southern.
20th	● Crystal Palace	H	D 2–2	**Att:** 9,702	**Ref:** P Gibbs	**Scorers:** Adam, Burgess. **Booked:** Baptiste, Evatt.
23rd	● Swansea	H	W 5–1	**Att:** 9,149	**Ref:** N Miller	**Scorers:** Burgess, Evatt, Ormerod[2], Taylor-Fletcher. **Booked:** Adam, Evatt.
27th	● Plymouth	A	W 0–2	**Att:** 10,614	**Ref:** J Linington	**Scorers:** Adam, Dobbie. **Booked:** Southern.

APRIL
2nd	● Scunthorpe	A	W 2–4	**Att:** 7,508	**Ref:** A Woolmer	**Scorers:** Campbell[2], Coleman, Wright OG. **Booked:** Evatt.
5th	● Doncaster	H	W 2–0	**Att:** 9,701	**Ref:** D Webb	**Scorers:** Campbell, Dobbie. **Booked:** Adam, Campbell.
10th	● Newcastle	A	L 4–1	**Att:** 47,010	**Ref:** M Russell	**Scorers:** Ormerod. **Booked:** Crainey.
17th	● Nottm Forest	H	W 3–1	**Att:** 11,164	**Ref:** A Taylor	**Scorers:** Adam, Campbell[2]. **Booked:** Adam.
24th	● Peterborough	A	W 0–1	**Att:** 7,812	**Ref:** C Webster	**Scorers:** Campbell.

MAY
2nd	● Bristol City	H	D 1–1	**Att:** 12,296	**Ref:** S Mathieson	**Scorers:** Ormerod.
8th	● Nottm Forest	H	W 2–1	**Att:** 11,805	**Ref:** P Dowd	**Scorers:** Adam, Southern. **Booked:** Evatt, Coleman, Vaughan.
11th	● Nottm Forest	A	W 3–4	**Att:** 28,358	**Ref:** M Clattenburg	**Scorers:** Campbell[3], Dobbie. **Booked:** Ormerod. Agg: 4–6.
22nd	● Cardiff	N	W 3–2	**Att:** 82,244	**Ref:** A Marriner	**Scorers:** Adam, Ormerod, Taylor-Fletcher.

● Coca-Cola Championship/Play-offs ● FA Cup ● Carling Cup

BLACKPOOL

CHAMPIONSHIP GOALKEEPER STATS

Player	Minutes on pitch	Appearances	Match starts	Completed matches	Sub appearances	Subbed off	Saved with feet	Punched	Parried	Tipped over	Fumbled	Tipped round	Caught	Blocked	Clean sheets	Goals conceded	Save %	Saved	Resulting in goals	Opposition miss	Fouls committed	Free-kicks won	Yellow cards	Red cards
Matthew Gilks	2491	26	26	26	0	0	1	11	22	4	0	8	106	3	10	32	82.89	1	3	0	0	3	0	0
Paul Rachubka	1916	20	20	20	0	0	1	10	9	2	1	4	75	2	6	26	79.84	0	2	0	0	7	0	0

CHAMPIONSHIP OUTFIELD PLAYER STATS

Player	Minutes on pitch	Appearances	Match starts	Completed matches	Substitute appearances	Subbed off	Goals scored	Assists	Shots on target	Shots off target	Crosses	Tackles made	Defensive clearances	Defensive blocks	Fouls committed	Free-kicks won	Caught offside	Yellow cards	Red cards
Charlie Adam	3848	43	41	30	2	11	16	8	63	69	128	88	15	8	86	87	1	13	0
Alhassan Bangura	192	9	2	0	7	2	0	0	0	2	0	4	1	1	9	5	0	1	0
Barry Bannan	809	20	8	0	12	8	1	2	3	7	36	14	1	2	5	5	3	0	0
Alex Baptiste	4002	42	42	41	0	1	3	1	16	14	39	129	60	29	21	23	1	5	0
Hameur Bouazza	1093	19	11	3	8	8	1	3	16	14	28	18	1	1	9	10	20	2	0
Ben Burgess	2032	35	20	10	15	10	6	1	28	20	3	31	12	0	30	19	25	0	0
Andy Butler	520	7	4	4	3	0	0	0	2	0	0	17	2	4	4	7	0	1	0
Dudley Campbell	1248	15	14	10	1	4	8	0	15	12	8	18	1	1	9	16	17	1	0
Billy Clarke	829	18	9	1	9	8	1	1	9	13	19	12	0	1	5	11	7	1	0
Danny Coid	45	1	1	0	0	1	0	0	0	0	0	2	0	1	1	0	0	0	0
Seamus Coleman	860	9	9	9	0	0	1	3	1	6	17	24	7	1	3	15	1	0	0
Stephen Crainey	3800	41	41	38	0	3	0	2	5	4	97	123	39	23	27	11	1	5	0
Ishmel Demontagnac	164	8	1	0	7	1	0	0	3	2	1	13	1	0	2	2	0	0	0
Stephen Dobbie	751	16	6	2	10	4	4	2	20	14	13	18	1	0	1	3	1	0	0
Neal Eardley	2009	24	22	18	2	4	0	3	5	15	72	38	16	8	10	17	0	3	0
Ashley Eastham	79	1	0	0	1	0	0	0	0	0	0	0	0	0	0	0	0	0	0
Rob Edwards	1775	21	19	17	2	1	0	1	1	4	2	77	16	12	13	18	2	0	1
Jay Emmanuel-Thomas	657	11	6	4	5	2	1	2	9	7	9	8	1	0	10	4	1	0	0
Jason Euell	2277	33	23	17	10	6	4	1	15	15	17	53	9	2	40	34	24	4	0
Ian Evatt	3332	36	35	32	1	3	4	1	17	12	7	131	65	28	45	27	2	7	0
Stephen Husband	62	3	1	0	2	1	0	0	0	0	0	4	1	0	0	0	0	0	0
Joe Martin	465	6	4	2	2	2	0	0	3	0	4	7	7	0	4	6	0	2	0
Daniel Nardiello	98	5	1	0	4	1	0	1	0	1	1	8	0	0	2	0	0	0	0
Brett Ormerod	2479	36	27	13	9	13	11	3	32	20	55	28	3	1	13	33	27	1	1
Marcel Seip	674	7	7	7	0	0	2	0	3	2	1	19	6	3	4	5	0	1	0
Keith Southern	4111	45	43	39	2	4	2	3	28	33	14	100	27	9	36	34	7	6	0
Gary Taylor-Fletcher	2234	32	26	9	6	17	6	5	24	15	22	56	5	3	36	23	15	1	0
David Vaughan	3473	41	37	27	4	9	1	6	15	18	45	96	13	12	36	47	6	4	1

SEASON TOTALS

Goals scored	74
Goals conceded	58
Clean sheets	16
Shots on target	333
Shots off target	319
Shots per goal	8.81
Pens awarded	3
Pens scored	3
Pens conceded	6
Offsides	161
Corners	262
Crosses	641
Players used	33
Fouls committed	458
Free-kicks won	474

LEAGUE POSITION AT THE END OF EACH MONTH

AUG	SEP	OCT	NOV	DEC	JAN	FEB	MAR	APR	MAY
10	7	6	6	8	7	8	7	6	6

SEASON INFORMATION
Highest position: 3
Lowest position: 15
Average goals scored per game: 1.61
Average goals conceded per game: 1.26

CARDS RECEIVED

58 3

SEQUENCES

Wins	4
(23/03/10–05/04/10)	
Losses	3
(03/02/10–09/02/10)	
Draws	4
(08/08/09–22/08/09)	
Undefeated	5
(on three occasions)	
Without win	5
(30/01/10–13/02/10)	
Undefeated home	9
(15/08/09–30/11/09)	
Undefeated away	3
(26/12/09–30/01/10)	
Without scoring	2
(09/02/10–13/02/10)	
Without conceding	3
(on two occasions)	
Scoring	15
(31/10/09–06/02/10)	
Conceding	8
(09/01/10–09/02/10)	

MATCH RECORDS

Goals scored per match

		W	D	L	Pts
Failed to score	7	0	3	4	3
Scored 1 goal	17	3	6	8	15
Scored 2 goals	13	8	3	2	27
Scored 3 goals	6	5	1	0	16
Scored 4+ goals	3	3	0	0	9

Goals conceded per match

		W	D	L	Pts
Clean sheet	16	13	3	0	42
Conceded 1 goal	11	4	6	1	18
Conceded 2 goals	12	2	3	7	9
Conceded 3 goals	5	0	1	4	1
Conceded 4+ goals	2	0	0	2	0

EARLIEST STRIKE

BILLY CLARKE
(v Preston) 0:23

LATEST STRIKE

CHARLIE ADAM
(v Sheff Wed) 95:40

Jason Euell

GOAL DETAILS

How the goals were struck

SCORED		CONCEDED
29	Right foot	28
32	Left foot	19
12	Header	11
1	Other	0

How the goals were struck

SCORED		CONCEDED
51	Open play	32
10	Cross	10
5	Corner	2
3	Penalty	5
0	Direct from free-kick	1
3	Free-kick	6
2	Own goal	2

Distance from goal

SCORED		CONCEDED
31	6YDS	23
35	18YDS	26
8	18+YDS	9

GOALS SCORED/CONCEDED PER FIVE-MINUTE INTERVALS

MINS	5	10	15	20	25	30	35	40	45	50	55	60	65	70	75	80	85	90
FOR	2	2	4	2	4	3	3	2	4	3	4	5	4	6	5	6	8	7
AGN	6	1	4	1	1	4	2	4	2	3	4	2	3	2	3	4	7	5

BRISTOL CITY

CLUB SUMMARY

FORMED	1897
MANAGER	Steve Coppell
GROUND	Ashton Gate
CAPACITY	21,479
NICKNAME	The Robins
WEBSITE	www.bcfc.co.uk

The New Football Pools PLAYER OF THE SEASON — Paul Hartley

OVERALL
P	W	D	L	F	A	GD
50	16	19	15	58	69	-11

COCA-COLA CHAMPIONSHIP
Pos	P	W	D	L	F	A	GD	Pts
10	46	15	18	13	56	65	-9	63

HOME
Pos	P	W	D	L	F	A	GD	Pts
9	23	10	10	3	38	34	4	40

AWAY
Pos	P	W	D	L	F	A	GD	Pts
14	23	5	8	10	18	31	-13	23

CUP PROGRESS DETAILS
Competition	Round reached	Knocked out by
FA Cup	R3	Cardiff
Carling Cup	R2	Carlisle

BIGGEST WIN (ALL COMPS)
23/03/10 5-3 v Barnsley

BIGGEST DEFEAT (ALL COMPS)
26/01/10 0-6 v Cardiff

THE PLAYER WITH THE MOST
GOALS SCORED	Nicky Maynard	**20**
SHOTS ON TARGET	Nicky Maynard	**74**
SHOTS OFF TARGET	Danny Haynes	**36**
SHOTS WITHOUT SCORING	Jamal Campbell-Ryce	**20**
ASSISTS	Paul Hartley	**6**
OFFSIDES	Nicky Maynard	**46**
FOULS	Marvin Elliott	**59**
FOULS WITHOUT A CARD	Chris Iwelumo	**9**
FREE-KICKS WON	Nicky Maynard	**69**
DEFENSIVE CLEARANCES	Louis Carey	**68**

actim INDEX FOR THE 2009/10 COCA-COLA CHAMPIONSHIP SEASON

RANK	PLAYER	PTS
6	Nicky Maynard	617
62	Bradley Orr	465
80	Louis Carey	438

ATTENDANCE RECORD
HIGH	AVERAGE	LOW
19,144	14,601	13,009
v Newcastle (20/03/2010)		v Barnsley (23/03/2010)

Gary Johnson can't bear to watch as Bristol City are thrashed 6–0 at home by Cardiff in January. Johnson went on to leave the club in March

A SEASON of disappointment at Ashton Gate looks set to be followed by a summer of change following the appointment of new manager Steve Coppell.

The long-serving Gary Johnson left the club on amicable terms in March after failing to put together a serious bid for the play-offs and, despite caretaker Keith Millen doing an admirable job, chairman Steve Lansdown opted to call on the experienced Coppell in a bid to take the club forward.

It had looked as though Johnson could do that himself at the beginning of 2009/10, with the Robins making a flying start. They had only lost three Coca-Cola Championship games by late November and had remained unbeaten at home for 11 months, only for Sheffield United to break that run with a late winner in a 3–2 victory.

That result triggered an alarming loss in form for City, with Johnson's side winning just four of their next 18 games, and it was after the last of those – a 3–2 defeat to Plymouth – that the manager moved on after five years in charge.

Millen took over the reins and presided over a six-game unbeaten run that briefly revived their play-off hopes. However, with so much ground to recover, they eventually came up short.

Former Crewe striker Nicky Maynard was once again one of the leading lights for the club, with the 23-year-old netting 21 goals in all competitions. There was a distinct correlation between the form of the forward and the success of the side. Maynard had reached 10 goals by the end of October but would add just a single

A tough season ended with Gary Johnson's departure and the arrival of Steve Coppell

strike to his tally before March.

Highlights of the campaign included an early-season 2–1 win over Middlesbrough, with Maynard scoring both goals, and a 3–1 victory at Leicester.

Former Celtic ace Paul Hartley added some grit to the midfield and, along with Maynard, was a key player, while goalkeeper Dean Gerken also had a positive impact after joining from Colchester.

The Robins lost only three times at home all season and will feel that, if they can improve their away form under Coppell, they will have a good chance of pushing for promotion. Ending the season with just one defeat in their last nine games will clearly also give the club a lift ahead of 2010/11.

While there is hope for the future in the npower Championship, City had little joy in either of the domestic knockout competitions during 2009/10. They were beaten by League One side Carlisle in the second round of the Carling Cup while Championship rivals Cardiff knocked them out of the FA Cup at the first hurdle.

RESULTS 2009/10

AUGUST

8th	● Preston	A	D 2–2	**Att:** 13,025	**Ref:** M Oliver	**Scorers:** Clarkson, Hartley. **Booked:** Clarkson, Elliott.
11th	● Brentford	A	W 0–1	**Att:** 3,024	**Ref:** P Crossley	**Scorers:** Maynard. **Booked:** Haynes, Skuse. **Dismissed:** Haynes.
15th	● Crystal Palace	H	W 1–0	**Att:** 14,603	**Ref:** R Shoebridge	**Scorers:** Maynard. **Booked:** Skuse.
18th	● QPR	H	W 1–0	**Att:** 14,571	**Ref:** P Gibbs	**Scorers:** Maynard. **Booked:** McAllister, Nyatanga, Hartley.
23rd	● Cardiff	A	L 3–0	**Att:** 20,853	**Ref:** K Friend	**Booked:** Johnson, Hartley, Gerken.
26th	● Carlisle	H	L 0–2	**Att:** 6,359	**Ref:** A Penn	
29th	● Middlesbrough	H	W 2–1	**Att:** 14,402	**Ref:** R Booth	**Scorers:** Maynard[2]. **Booked:** Haynes.

SEPTEMBER

12th	● Coventry	A	D 1–1	**Att:** 16,449	**Ref:** N Swarbrick	**Scorers:** Maynard. **Booked:** Saborio, Carey, Elliott.
15th	● Swansea	A	D 0–0	**Att:** 12,859	**Ref:** D Whitestone	**Booked:** Fontaine, Sno, McCombe, McAllister.
19th	● Scunthorpe	H	D 1–1	**Att:** 14,203	**Ref:** D McDermid	**Scorers:** Saborio. **Booked:** Hartley.
26th	● Derby	A	L 1–0	**Att:** 27,144	**Ref:** M Russell	**Booked:** Sno, McCombe, Maynard. **Dismissed:** McCombe.
29th	● Blackpool	H	W 2–0	**Att:** 13,673	**Ref:** R East	**Scorers:** Haynes, Maynard.

OCTOBER

3rd	● Newcastle	A	D 0–0	**Att:** 43,326	**Ref:** G Salisbury	**Booked:** Saborio, Carey.
17th	● Peterborough	H	D 1–1	**Att:** 13,833	**Ref:** K Hill	**Scorers:** Skuse. **Booked:** Haynes.
20th	● Plymouth	H	W 3–1	**Att:** 15,021	**Ref:** G Hegley	**Scorers:** Haynes, Maynard, McCombe.
24th	● Barnsley	A	W 2–3	**Att:** 11,314	**Ref:** A Haines	**Scorers:** Elliott, Maynard, Sno. **Booked:** Sno.
31st	● Sheff Wed	H	D 1–1	**Att:** 15,005	**Ref:** F Graham	**Scorers:** Maynard. **Booked:** McAllister.

NOVEMBER

7th	● Nottm Forest	A	D 1–1	**Att:** 21,467	**Ref:** A Taylor	**Scorers:** Haynes. **Booked:** Maynard, Sno, Elliott.
21st	● West Brom	A	L 4–1	**Att:** 23,444	**Ref:** M Oliver	**Scorers:** Hartley.
28th	● Sheff Utd	H	L 2–3	**Att:** 14,637	**Ref:** A Hall	**Scorers:** Carey, Saborio. **Booked:** Johnson, Carey, McAllister, Sproule.

DECEMBER

5th	● Ipswich	H	D 0–0	**Att:** 14,287	**Ref:** T Bates	**Booked:** Elliott, Sproule.
8th	● Leicester	A	W 1–3	**Att:** 19,349	**Ref:** S Cook	**Scorers:** Skuse, Sno, Sproule. **Booked:** Sproule, Sno.
12th	● Doncaster	A	L 1–0	**Att:** 9,572	**Ref:** J Singh	**Booked:** Orr.
19th	● Reading	H	D 1–1	**Att:** 14,366	**Ref:** M Haywood	**Scorers:** Hartley.
26th	● QPR	A	L 2–1	**Att:** 13,534	**Ref:** D Phillips	**Scorers:** Maynard. **Booked:** Haynes, Sno, Maynard.
28th	● Watford	H	D 2–2	**Att:** 16,035	**Ref:** J Linington	**Scorers:** Hartley, Haynes. **Booked:** Orr, Nyatanga. **Dismissed:** Nyatanga.

JANUARY

12th	● Cardiff	H	D 1–1	**Att:** 7,289	**Ref:** P Walton	**Scorers:** Williams. **Booked:** Orr, McAllister.
16th	● Preston	H	W 4–2	**Att:** 13,146	**Ref:** G Ward	**Scorers:** Carey, Fontaine, Haynes, Sno. **Booked:** Hartley, Saborio.
19th	● Cardiff	A	L 1–0	**Att:** 6,731	**Ref:** N Miller	**Booked:** Akinde, Hartley.
26th	● Cardiff	H	L 0–6	**Att:** 13,825	**Ref:** A D'Urso	**Booked:** Nyatanga.
30th	● Middlesbrough	A	D 0–0	**Att:** 17,865	**Ref:** C Webster	**Booked:** Nyatanga, Agyemang, Carey.

FEBRUARY

6th	● Coventry	H	D 1–1	**Att:** 13,852	**Ref:** G Horwood	**Scorers:** Clarkson. **Booked:** Hartley.
9th	● Watford	A	L 2–0	**Att:** 12,179	**Ref:** D McDermid	**Booked:** Skuse, Saborio, Nyatanga, Fontaine, Elliott.
13th	● Sheff Utd	A	L 2–0	**Att:** 22,613	**Ref:** D Deadman	**Booked:** Hartley, Nyatanga.
16th	● Leicester	H	D 1–1	**Att:** 13,746	**Ref:** S Hooper	**Scorers:** Clarkson. **Booked:** Haynes.
21st	● West Brom	H	W 2–1	**Att:** 14,374	**Ref:** N Swarbrick	**Scorers:** Iwelumo, Johnson. **Booked:** Johnson.
27th	● Ipswich	A	D 0–0	**Att:** 20,302	**Ref:** N Miller	**Booked:** Williams.

MARCH

6th	● Doncaster	H	L 2–5	**Att:** 13,401	**Ref:** D Phillips	**Scorers:** Orr[2]. **Booked:** Skuse.
9th	● Crystal Palace	A	W 0–1	**Att:** 12,844	**Ref:** M Russell	**Scorers:** Iwelumo. **Booked:** Campbell-Ryce, Akinde.
13th	● Reading	A	L 2–0	**Att:** 17,900	**Ref:** P Taylor	**Booked:** Johnson, Orr, Carey.
16th	● Plymouth	A	L 3–2	**Att:** 9,289	**Ref:** T Kettle	**Scorers:** Maynard[2]. **Booked:** Sproule, Campbell-Ryce, Carey. **Dismissed:** Campbell-Ryce.
20th	● Newcastle	H	D 2–2	**Att:** 19,144	**Ref:** A D'Urso	**Scorers:** Maynard, Nyatanga. **Booked:** McAllister.
23rd	● Barnsley	H	W 5–3	**Att:** 13,009	**Ref:** G Scott	**Scorers:** Hartley, Haynes[2], Maynard[2]. **Booked:** Haynes.
27th	● Peterborough	A	W 0–1	**Att:** 6,445	**Ref:** D Webb	**Scorers:** Clarkson. **Booked:** Hartley.

APRIL

3rd	● Nottm Forest	H	D 1–1	**Att:** 16,125	**Ref:** P Crossley	**Scorers:** Fontaine. **Booked:** Skuse, Campbell-Ryce.
5th	● Sheff Wed	A	W 0–1	**Att:** 19,688	**Ref:** G Salisbury	**Scorers:** Maynard. **Booked:** Orr, Haynes, Fontaine.
10th	● Swansea	H	W 1–0	**Att:** 14,719	**Ref:** M Dean	**Scorers:** Maynard.
17th	● Scunthorpe	A	L 3–0	**Att:** 5,430	**Ref:** M Russell	**Booked:** Nyatanga.
24th	● Derby	H	W 2–1	**Att:** 15,835	**Ref:** C Pawson	**Scorers:** Maynard[2]. **Booked:** Elliott.

MAY

2nd	● Blackpool	A	D 1–1	**Att:** 12,296	**Ref:** S Mathieson	**Scorers:** Maynard. **Booked:** Carey, Sproule, Hartley, Akinde.

● Coca-Cola Championship/Play-offs ● FA Cup ● Carling Cup

BRISTOL CITY

CHAMPIONSHIP GOALKEEPER STATS

Player	Minutes on pitch	Appearances	Match starts	Completed matches	Sub appearances	Subbed off	Saved with feet	Punched	Parried	Tipped over	Fumbled	Tipped round	Caught	Blocked	Clean sheets	Goals conceded	Save %	Saved	Resulting in goals	Opposition miss	Fouls committed	Free-kicks won	Yellow cards	Red cards
							SAVES BREAKDOWN											PENALTIES						
Adriano Basso	383	4	4	4	0	0	0	3	2	0	0	1	19	1	2	2	92.86	0	0	0	0	0	0	0
Dean Gerken	3775	39	39	39	0	0	4	16	34	4	4	10	119	3	8	60	76.00	0	3	0	1	6	1	0
Stephen Henderson	289	3	3	3	0	0	0	2	9	2	0	0	9	0	2	3	88.00	0	0	0	0	0	0	0

CHAMPIONSHIP OUTFIELD PLAYER STATS

Player	Minutes on pitch	Appearances	Match starts	Completed matches	Substitute appearances	Subbed off	Goals scored	Assists	Shots on target	Shots off target	Crosses	Tackles made	Defensive clearances	Defensive blocks	Fouls committed	Free-kicks won	Caught offside	Yellow cards	Red cards
Patrick Agyemang	518	7	5	4	2	1	0	0	2	3	3	2	1	0	8	8	2	1	0
John Akinde	235	7	0	0	7	0	0	0	2	0	2	3	0	0	8	8	3	2	0
Jamal Campbell-Ryce	1197	14	13	9	1	3	0	3	11	9	19	26	4	1	14	22	3	3	1
Louis Carey	3496	37	36	35	1	1	2	2	9	12	6	54	68	31	39	36	2	7	0
David Clarkson	1075	26	10	4	16	6	4	2	19	12	5	1	0	1	16	13	5	1	0
Marvin Elliott	3269	39	33	26	6	7	1	2	29	23	14	55	14	2	59	57	3	6	0
Liam Fontaine	3063	36	31	29	5	2	2	1	10	10	21	54	44	16	40	28	1	3	0
Paul Hartley	3347	40	36	22	4	14	5	2	22	19	72	40	14	6	40	33	5	8	0
Danny Haynes	2615	38	29	7	9	22	7	5	32	36	29	34	4	0	19	40	24	6	0
Chris Iwelumo	614	7	7	5	0	2	2	1	11	6	1	1	0	0	9	6	7	0	0
Lee Johnson	1812	28	18	12	10	6	1	0	13	6	18	29	5	2	16	14	1	4	0
Stefan Maierhofer	109	3	1	0	2	1	0	0	0	0	0	2	1	0	3	3	2	0	0
Nicky Maynard	3700	42	40	28	2	12	20	4	74	34	14	28	1	1	31	69	46	3	0
Jamie McAllister	2644	33	31	21	2	10	0	2	10	6	89	20	34	12	36	18	1	5	0
Jamie McCombe	1307	16	13	12	3	0	1	0	7	5	0	10	32	8	28	22	2	2	1
Lewin Nyatanga	3208	37	33	28	4	4	1	0	2	8	3	51	48	18	37	28	0	7	1
Bradley Orr	3625	39	38	37	1	1	2	2	8	9	70	66	42	13	42	19	4	4	0
Christian Ribeiro	434	5	5	4	0	1	0	0	0	0	2	9	5	0	1	5	0	0	0
Alvaro Saborio	937	19	11	2	8	9	2	2	9	8	4	5	1	0	30	13	12	4	0
Gary Sawyer	194	2	2	2	0	0	0	0	0	1	2	7	6	1	0	2	0	0	0
Cole Skuse	3599	43	39	30	4	4	2	2	17	11	21	57	20	6	32	35	4	4	0
Evander Sno	1455	24	16	4	8	12	3	0	14	11	6	21	12	0	25	25	6	6	0
Ivan Sproule	1134	30	8	5	22	3	1	1	10	7	21	12	1	0	11	15	7	5	0
Andrius Velicka	10	1	0	0	1	1	0	0	0	0	0	0	0	0	0	0	0	0	0
Gavin Williams	477	14	2	0	12	2	0	1	4	4	2	2	1	0	9	8	0	1	0
Brian Wilson	258	3	3	2	0	1	0	0	0	0	5	8	3	0	2	0	0	0	0

SEASON TOTALS

Goals scored	56
Goals conceded	65
Clean sheets	12
Shots on target	315
Shots off target	240
Shots per goal	9.91
Pens awarded	5
Pens scored	4
Pens conceded	3
Offsides	134
Corners	204
Crosses	429
Players used	29
Fouls committed	556
Free-kicks won	533

CARDS RECEIVED

83 3

SEQUENCES

Wins	2
(on four occasions)	
Losses	2
(on three occasions)	
Draws	3
(12/09/09–19/09/09)	
Undefeated	7
(29/09/09–07/11/09)	
Without win	6
(26/01/10–16/02/10)	
Undefeated home	8
(15/08/09–31/10/09)	
Undefeated away	3
(03/10/09–07/11/09)	
Without scoring	2
(on two occasions)	
Without conceding	2
(on three occasions)	
Scoring	7
(on two occasions)	
Conceding	7
(on two occasions)	

LEAGUE POSITION AT THE END OF EACH MONTH

AUG	SEP	OCT	NOV	DEC	JAN	FEB	MAR	APR	MAY
5	9	5	12	12	10	12	13	10	10

SEASON INFORMATION

Highest position: 1
Lowest position: 17
Average goals scored per game: 1.22
Average goals conceded per game: 1.41

MATCH RECORDS

Goals scored per match

		W	D	L	Pts
Failed to score	13	0	5	8	5
Scored 1 goal	18	6	10	2	28
Scored 2 goals	10	4	3	3	15
Scored 3 goals	3	3	0	0	9
Scored 4+ goals	2	2	0	0	6

Goals conceded per match

		W	D	L	Pts
Clean sheet	12	7	5	0	26
Conceded 1 goal	17	5	10	2	25
Conceded 2 goals	9	2	3	4	9
Conceded 3 goals	5	1	0	4	3
Conceded 4+ goals	3	0	0	3	0

EARLIEST STRIKE

DANNY HAYNES
(v Barnsley) 1:09

LATEST STRIKE

ALVARO SABORIO
(v Sheff Utd) 94:39

Danny Haynes

GOAL DETAILS

How the goals were struck

SCORED		CONCEDED
42	Right foot	39
6	Left foot	18
7	Header	8
1	Other	0

How the goals were struck

SCORED		CONCEDED
42	Open play	47
2	Cross	5
2	Corner	1
4	Penalty	3
2	Direct from free-kick	1
4	Free-kick	4
0	Own goal	4

Distance from goal

SCORED		CONCEDED
20	6YDS	18
27	18YDS	38
9	18+YDS	9

GOALS SCORED/CONCEDED PER FIVE-MINUTE INTERVALS

MINS	5	10	15	20	25	30	35	40	45	50	55	60	65	70	75	80	85	90
FOR	4	2	3	2	0	3	1	1	4	3	2	8	2	0	4	7	4	6
AGN	3	0	5	3	5	3	5	2	5	5	2	1	3	2	4	1	4	12

CARDIFF CITY

CLUB SUMMARY

FORMED	1899
MANAGER	Dave Jones
GROUND	Cardiff City Stadium
CAPACITY	26,828
NICKNAME	The Bluebirds
WEBSITE	www.cardiffcityfc.co.uk

The New
Football Pools
PLAYER OF THE SEASON

Peter Whittingham

OVERALL

P	W	D	L	F	A	GD
56	27	11	18	91	70	21

COCA-COLA CHAMPIONSHIP

Pos	P	W	D	L	F	A	GD	Pts
4	46	22	10	14	73	54	19	76

HOME

Pos	P	W	D	L	F	A	GD	Pts
7	23	12	6	5	37	20	17	42

AWAY

Pos	P	W	D	L	F	A	GD	Pts
3	23	10	4	9	36	34	2	34

CUP PROGRESS DETAILS

Competition	Round reached	Knocked out by
FA Cup	R5	Chelsea
Carling Cup	R3	Aston Villa

BIGGEST WIN (ALL COMPS)

26/01/10 6–0 v Bristol City

BIGGEST DEFEAT (ALL COMPS)

05/02/10 1–5 v Newcastle

THE PLAYER WITH THE MOST

GOALS SCORED	Peter Whittingham	**20**
SHOTS ON TARGET	Peter Whittingham	**55**
SHOTS OFF TARGET	Peter Whittingham	**43**
SHOTS WITHOUT SCORING	Darcy Blake	**10**
ASSISTS	Jay Bothroyd	**12**
OFFSIDES	Michael Chopra	**55**
FOULS	Jay Bothroyd	**103**
FOULS WITHOUT A CARD	Mark Kennedy	**10**
FREE-KICKS WON	Jay Bothroyd	**115**
DEFENSIVE CLEARANCES	Anthony Gerrard	**92**

actim INDEX FOR THE 2009/10 COCA-COLA CHAMPIONSHIP SEASON

RANK	PLAYER	PTS
3	Peter Whittingham	668
7	Chris Burke	614
16	David Marshall	566

ATTENDANCE RECORD

HIGH	AVERAGE	LOW
25,630	20,717	17,686
v Newcastle (13/09/2009)		v Peterborough (09/02/2010)

Cardiff claimed their best League finish in years, but lost a thrilling play-off final

A DRAMATIC campaign ended with Wembley agony for Cardiff as they lost out 3–2 to Blackpool in the Coca-Cola Championship play-off final.

The fixture – considered the most lucrative in world football – almost brought about a dream conclusion but it was not to be, leaving the club in the second tier but still looking forward thanks to investment from an Asian group. Departing chairman Peter Ridsdale, who makes way for the consortium headed by Dato Chan Tien Ghee, has urged the Bluebirds to be optimistic as he ends his five-year stay in the Welsh capital.

The funding promises a bright financial future for Cardiff and could not come at a better time following their lengthy High Court battles to stave off winding-up orders over unpaid taxes to HM Revenue & Customs. Ridsdale leaves having achieved his three-fold brief to seek new funding, to establish the club within the second tier and to assist in the construction of a new stadium.

The latter is where the 2009/10 season started as the club settled into their new state-of-the-art Cardiff City Stadium following an emotional switch from the iconic Ninian Park. Changes were also made on the pitch following their

Jay Bothroyd celebrates Cardiff's play-off semi-final win at Leicester

Dave Jones feels the pain at Wembley

heartbreaking failure to claim a play-off place on the final day of the 2008/09 season.

Dave Jones' side started the campaign in style, but as early as September it seemed clear that Newcastle and West Brom would be tough to beat to the automatic promotion positions, with Cardiff one of a number of teams perhaps already aiming only as high as the play-offs.

A 3–2 defeat at local rivals Swansea was hard to take but revenge was gained with a 2–1 home victory in April, while a 4–4 draw at Peterborough will be remembered for a long time, with the Bluebirds having been 4–0 ahead at half-time.

Ultimately, despite a fourth-place finish being their highest in the League for almost 40 years and the memories of a dramatic penalty shoot-out triumph over Leicester in the play-off semi-finals, City narrowly missed out on promotion in a thrilling Wembley match in which they led twice.

They will have learned a lot from the experience, however, and Jones must now target a top-two finish in 2010/11. He will hope out-of-contract midfielder Joe Ledley sticks around and Peter Whittingham can reproduce the form that made him the club's player of the season. Bolstered by a couple of new faces, the club stand a great chance of going one step further.

RESULTS 2009/10

AUGUST
8th	● Scunthorpe	H	W 4–0	**Att:** 22,264	**Ref:** J Moss	**Scorers:** Bothroyd, Chopra², Whittingham.
11th	● Dag & Red	H	W 3–1	**Att:** 5,545	**Ref:** A Penn	**Scorers:** Bothroyd, Rae, Whittingham.
15th	● Blackpool	A	D 1–1	**Att:** 7,698	**Ref:** G Hegley	**Scorers:** Chopra. **Booked:** Bothroyd, McPhail.
18th	● Plymouth	A	W 1–3	**Att:** 11,918	**Ref:** R Booth	**Scorers:** Chopra³. **Booked:** Capaldi, Matthews. **Dismissed:** Capaldi.
23rd	● Bristol City	H	W 3–0	**Att:** 20,853	**Ref:** K Friend	**Scorers:** Chopra, Rae, McCombe OG.
26th	● Bristol Rovers	H	W 3–1	**Att:** 9,767	**Ref:** R East	**Scorers:** Chopra, Magennis, Whittingham. **Booked:** Chopra.
29th	● Doncaster	A	L 2–0	**Att:** 9,742	**Ref:** E Ilderton	**Booked:** Chopra.

SEPTEMBER
13th	● Newcastle	H	L 0–1	**Att:** 25,630	**Ref:** A Hall	
16th	● Reading	A	W 0–1	**Att:** 16,687	**Ref:** P Taylor	**Scorers:** Burke. **Booked:** Ledley. **Dismissed:** McPhail.
19th	● QPR	H	L 0–2	**Att:** 20,121	**Ref:** L Probert	**Booked:** Quinn, Chopra.
23rd	● Aston Villa	A	L 1–0	**Att:** 22,527	**Ref:** A Taylor	**Booked:** Gyepes.
26th	● Sheff Wed	A	L 3–1	**Att:** 18,959	**Ref:** M Oliver	**Scorers:** Whittingham. **Booked:** Hudson, Bothroyd, Ledley, Rae. **Dismissed:** Ledley.
29th	● Derby	H	W 6–1	**Att:** 18,670	**Ref:** S Hooper	**Scorers:** Burke, Chopra⁴, Whittingham.

OCTOBER
3rd	● Watford	A	W 0–4	**Att:** 13,895	**Ref:** A Woolmer	**Scorers:** Bothroyd, Matthews, Whittingham². **Booked:** Rae, Bothroyd.
17th	● Crystal Palace	H	D 1–1	**Att:** 21,457	**Ref:** S Tanner	**Scorers:** Whittingham.
20th	● Coventry	H	W 2–0	**Att:** 19,038	**Ref:** M Russell	**Scorers:** Gerrard, Whittingham. **Booked:** Bothroyd.
24th	● Sheff Utd	A	W 3–4	**Att:** 25,021	**Ref:** T Kettle	**Scorers:** Bothroyd, Whittingham³. **Booked:** Ledley, Chopra.

NOVEMBER
1st	● Nottm Forest	H	D 1–1	**Att:** 20,413	**Ref:** G Salisbury	**Scorers:** Bothroyd. **Booked:** Whittingham, Chopra.
7th	● Swansea	A	L 3–2	**Att:** 18,209	**Ref:** L Probert	**Scorers:** Bothroyd, Hudson. **Booked:** Gerrard.
21st	● Barnsley	A	L 1–0	**Att:** 11,903	**Ref:** K Wright	**Booked:** Quinn, Hudson.
29th	● Ipswich	H	L 1–2	**Att:** 19,463	**Ref:** J Singh	**Scorers:** Whittingham.

DECEMBER
5th	● Preston	H	W 1–0	**Att:** 18,735	**Ref:** R East	**Scorers:** Burke. **Booked:** Bothroyd.
8th	● West Brom	A	W 0–2	**Att:** 20,742	**Ref:** P Taylor	**Scorers:** Burke, Whittingham. **Booked:** Whittingham, Chopra.
13th	● Middlesbrough	A	W 0–1	**Att:** 17,232	**Ref:** G Hegley	**Scorers:** Burke. **Booked:** Gerrard, Quinn.
26th	● Plymouth	H	L 0–1	**Att:** 24,010	**Ref:** P Gibbs	**Booked:** Bothroyd.
28th	● Peterborough	A	D 4–4	**Att:** 9,796	**Ref:** D Whitestone	**Scorers:** Bothroyd, Ledley², Whittingham. **Booked:** Quinn.

JANUARY
9th	● Blackpool	H	D 1–1	**Att:** 19,147	**Ref:** G Ward	**Scorers:** Hudson. **Booked:** Feeney, McCormack, McNaughton.
12th	● Bristol City	A	D 1–1	**Att:** 7,289	**Ref:** P Walton	**Scorers:** Chopra. **Booked:** McCormack.
16th	● Scunthorpe	A	D 1–1	**Att:** 5,032	**Ref:** S Mathieson	**Scorers:** Whittingham. **Booked:** Chopra, Bothroyd.
19th	● Bristol City	H	W 1–0	**Att:** 6,731	**Ref:** N Miller	**Scorers:** Orr OG. **Booked:** Gerrard.
23rd	● Leicester	H	W 4–2	**Att:** 10,961	**Ref:** P Crossley	**Scorers:** Bothroyd, Burke, McCormack, Whittingham. **Booked:** McCormack.
26th	● Bristol City	A	W 0–6	**Att:** 13,825	**Ref:** A D'Urso	**Scorers:** Chopra², McCormack², Whittingham, Fontaine OG.
30th	● Doncaster	H	W 2–1	**Att:** 19,730	**Ref:** G Scott	**Scorers:** Bothroyd, Chopra. **Booked:** Taiwo.

FEBRUARY
5th	● Newcastle	A	L 5–1	**Att:** 44,028	**Ref:** K Friend	**Scorers:** Wildig. **Booked:** Gyepes.
9th	● Peterborough	H	W 2–0	**Att:** 17,686	**Ref:** A Penn	**Scorers:** Burke, Gerrard.
13th	● Chelsea	A	L 4–1	**Att:** 40,827	**Ref:** A Marriner	**Scorers:** Chopra. **Booked:** Chopra, Gerrard.
16th	● West Brom	H	D 1–1	**Att:** 20,758	**Ref:** A Woolmer	**Scorers:** Whittingham.
20th	● Barnsley	H	L 0–2	**Att:** 19,753	**Ref:** K Stroud	**Booked:** Bothroyd.
27th	● Preston	A	L 3–0	**Att:** 11,777	**Ref:** A Hall	**Booked:** Gyepes, Quinn, Burke, McNaughton, Chopra.

MARCH
6th	● Middlesbrough	H	W 1–0	**Att:** 19,803	**Ref:** D Deadman	**Scorers:** Bothroyd. **Booked:** Burke, McCormack.
9th	● Ipswich	A	L 2–0	**Att:** 19,997	**Ref:** G Hegley	**Booked:** Chopra.
13th	● Leicester	A	L 1–0	**Att:** 22,767	**Ref:** K Evans	**Booked:** Gerrard.
16th	● Coventry	A	W 1–2	**Att:** 16,038	**Ref:** S Hooper	**Scorers:** Burke, Whittingham.
21st	● Watford	H	W 3–1	**Att:** 20,130	**Ref:** P Crossley	**Scorers:** Burke, McCormack, Whittingham. **Booked:** Bothroyd.
24th	● Sheff Utd	H	D 1–1	**Att:** 18,715	**Ref:** D McDermid	**Scorers:** Bothroyd. **Booked:** Blake, Bothroyd.
27th	● Crystal Palace	A	W 1–2	**Att:** 13,464	**Ref:** C Boyeson	**Scorers:** Burke, Gyepes. **Booked:** Feeney.
30th	● Leicester	H	W 2–1	**Att:** 20,438	**Ref:** F Graham	**Scorers:** McCormack, Whittingham. **Booked:** Quinn, Marshall. **Dismissed:** Gyepes.

APRIL
3rd	● Swansea	H	W 2–1	**Att:** 25,130	**Ref:** P Dowd	**Scorers:** Chopra². **Booked:** Bothroyd, Gerrard, Capaldi, Chopra.
5th	● Nottm Forest	A	D 0–0	**Att:** 22,185	**Ref:** C Foy	**Booked:** McCormack, Bothroyd, Chopra.
10th	● Reading	H	D 0–0	**Att:** 21,248	**Ref:** T Bates	
17th	● QPR	A	W 0–1	**Att:** 12,832	**Ref:** M Oliver	**Scorers:** Ledley.
24th	● Sheff Wed	H	W 3–2	**Att:** 23,304	**Ref:** P Taylor	**Scorers:** Bothroyd², Whittingham. **Booked:** Ledley.

MAY
2nd	● Derby	A	L 2–0	**Att:** 31,102	**Ref:** C Webster	**Booked:** Etuhu, McCormack, Quinn.
9th	● Leicester	A	W 0–1	**Att:** 29,165	**Ref:** A Wiley	**Scorers:** Whittingham. **Booked:** Bothroyd, Kennedy, Marshall.
12th	● Leicester	H	L 2–3	**Att:** 26,033	**Ref:** H Webb	**Scorers:** Chopra, Whittingham. **Booked:** Hudson, McPhail, Quinn, Whittingham. AET – Score after 90 mins 2–3. Agg: 3–3; Cardiff win 4–3 on penalties.
22nd	● Blackpool	N	L 3–2	**Att:** 82,244	**Ref:** A Marriner	**Scorers:** Chopra, Ledley.

● Coca-Cola Championship/Play-offs ● FA Cup ● Carling Cup

CHAMPIONSHIP GOALKEEPER STATS

Player	Minutes on pitch	Appearances	Match starts	Completed matches	Sub appearances	Subbed off	Saved with feet	Punched	Parried	Tipped over	Fumbled	Tipped round	Caught	Blocked	Clean sheets	Goals conceded	Save %	Saved	Resulting in goals	Opposition miss	Fouls committed	Free-kicks won	Yellow cards	Red cards
							SAVES BREAKDOWN											PENALTIES						
Peter Enckelman	335	4	3	3	1	0	0	1	0	1	0	2	8	0	0	9	57.14	0	1	0	0	1	0	0
David Marshall	4078	43	43	42	0	1	3	31	26	12	2	11	160	2	14	45	84.48	0	1	0	0	12	1	0

CHAMPIONSHIP OUTFIELD PLAYER STATS

Player	Minutes on pitch	Appearances	Match starts	Completed matches	Substitute appearances	Subbed off	Goals scored	Assists	Shots on target	Shots off target	Crosses	Tackles made	Defensive clearances	Defensive blocks	Fouls committed	Free-kicks won	Caught offside	Yellow cards	Red cards
Darcy Blake	1330	18	15	12	3	3	0	0	0	10	3	38	10	7	12	12	0	1	0
Jay Bothroyd	3565	40	40	29	0	11	11	12	46	33	29	55	42	2	103	115	45	12	0
Chris Burke	3632	44	38	28	6	10	9	7	34	21	90	71	5	5	6	64	2	2	0
Tony Capaldi	1039	15	10	7	5	5	0	0	0	0	7	36	3	4	9	12	0	2	1
Michael Chopra	3384	41	36	26	5	10	16	3	49	38	19	47	0	3	47	53	55	10	0
Miguel Comminges	3	1	0	0	1	0	0	0	0	0	0	0	0	0	0	0	0	0	0
Kelvin Etuhu	762	16	7	0	9	8	0	1	3	3	7	26	0	0	17	4	3	1	0
Warren Feeney	237	9	1	0	8	1	0	0	0	1	0	6	2	0	3	6	3	2	0
Anthony Gerrard	3658	39	39	37	0	2	2	3	5	15	4	107	92	21	26	34	1	4	0
Gabor Gyepes	1462	16	16	14	0	1	1	1	4	2	0	36	30	7	18	15	0	2	1
Mark Hudson	2545	27	26	26	1	0	2	0	5	8	2	79	74	13	20	21	1	2	0
Mark Kennedy	2412	30	25	20	5	5	0	1	2	5	29	50	26	5	10	14	3	0	0
Joe Ledley	2498	29	27	22	2	4	3	2	13	5	7	78	10	5	33	33	1	4	1
Josh Magennis	156	9	1	0	8	1	0	0	1	1	0	4	0	0	3	4	2	0	0
Adam Matthews	2398	32	24	18	8	6	1	1	3	4	33	51	16	5	5	19	0	1	0
Ross McCormack	2192	34	21	12	13	9	4	2	40	22	33	41	6	1	21	40	15	4	0
Kevin McNaughton	1713	21	20	15	1	5	0	0	0	1	12	86	12	5	6	21	0	2	0
Stephen McPhail	1780	21	21	12	0	8	0	6	0	5	8	76	5	2	33	28	0	1	1
Aaron Morris	9	1	0	0	1	0	0	0	0	0	0	0	0	0	0	0	0	0	0
Paul Quinn	1717	22	16	13	6	3	0	0	2	2	12	72	12	8	10	14	0	7	0
Gavin Rae	2912	37	28	22	9	6	1	3	10	11	5	47	10	4	34	17	0	2	0
Riccardo Scimeca	173	4	2	1	2	1	0	0	1	1	0	3	2	0	5	1	0	0	0
Solomon Taiwo	240	8	2	0	6	2	0	0	1	1	0	9	2	0	7	1	1	1	0
Peter Whittingham	3713	41	41	35	0	6	20	10	55	43	103	98	7	2	20	33	8	2	0
Aaron Wildig	517	11	4	2	7	2	1	0	1	2	0	10	2	0	4	2	0	0	0

SEASON TOTALS

Goals scored	73
Goals conceded	54
Clean sheets	14
Shots on target	276
Shots off target	234
Shots per goal	6.99
Pens awarded	9
Pens scored	8
Pens conceded	2
Offsides	141
Corners	218
Crosses	403
Players used	30
Fouls committed	452
Free-kicks won	576

CARDS RECEIVED

63 **4**

SEQUENCES

Wins	3
(on two occasions)	
Losses	3
(07/11/09–29/11/09)	
Draws	3
(28/12/09–16/01/10)	
Undefeated	10
(16/03/10–24/04/10)	
Without win	4
(on two occasions)	
Undefeated home	7
(06/03/10–24/04/10)	
Undefeated away	5
(08/12/09–26/01/10)	
Without scoring	2
(on four occasions)	
Without conceding	3
(on two occasions)	
Scoring	8
(on two occasions)	
Conceding	8
(09/03/10–03/04/10)	

League position at the end of each month

AUG	SEP	OCT	NOV	DEC	JAN	FEB	MAR	APR	MAY
3	5	4	8	4	4	6	4	4	4

LEAGUE POSITION AT THE END OF EACH MONTH

SEASON INFORMATION
Highest position: 1
Lowest position: 10
Average goals scored per game: 1.59
Average goals conceded per game: 1.17

MATCH RECORDS

Goals scored per match

		W	D	L	Pts
Failed to score	12	0	2	10	2
Scored 1 goal	15	5	7	3	22
Scored 2 goals	9	8	0	1	24
Scored 3 goals	4	4	0	0	12
Scored 4+ goals	6	5	1	0	16

Goals conceded per match

		W	D	L	Pts
Clean sheet	14	12	2	0	38
Conceded 1 goal	19	8	7	4	31
Conceded 2 goals	7	1	0	6	3
Conceded 3 goals	4	1	0	3	3
Conceded 4+ goals	2	0	1	1	1

GOALS SCORED/CONCEDED
PER FIVE-MINUTE INTERVALS

MINS	5	10	15	20	25	30	35	40	45	50	55	60	65	70	75	80	85	90
FOR	4	7	1	5	5	1	5	3	10	1	2	5	5	4	1	4	5	5
AGN	2	3	6	5	0	3	1	1	4	4	3	2	3	3	1	2	3	8

EARLIEST STRIKE
JAY BOTHROYD
(v Middlesbrough) 2:19

LATEST STRIKE
PETER WHITTINGHAM
(v Scunthorpe) 92:15

Stephen McPhail

GOAL DETAILS

How the goals were struck

SCORED		CONCEDED
29	Right foot	23
36	Left foot	21
8	Header	10
0	Other	0

How the goals were struck

SCORED		CONCEDED
46	Open play	35
5	Cross	6
3	Corner	3
8	Penalty	2
3	Direct from free-kick	3
6	Free-kick	3
2	Own goal	2

Distance from goal

SCORED		CONCEDED
28	6YDS	27
34	18YDS	21
11	18+YDS	6

COVENTRY CITY

CLUB SUMMARY

FORMED	1883
MANAGER	Aidy Boothroyd
GROUND	Ricoh Arena
CAPACITY	32,609
NICKNAME	The Sky Blues
WEBSITE	www.ccfc.co.uk

The New Football Pools PLAYER OF THE SEASON — Clinton Morrison

OVERALL
P	W	D	L	F	A	GD
49	13	16	20	49	68	-19

COCA-COLA CHAMPIONSHIP
Pos	P	W	D	L	F	A	GD	Pts
19	46	13	15	18	47	64	-17	54

HOME
Pos	P	W	D	L	F	A	GD	Pts
19	23	8	9	6	27	29	-2	33

AWAY
Pos	P	W	D	L	F	A	GD	Pts
17	23	5	6	12	20	35	-15	21

CUP PROGRESS DETAILS
Competition	Round reached	Knocked out by
FA Cup	R3	Portsmouth
Carling Cup	R1	Hartlepool

BIGGEST WIN (ALL COMPS)
09/01/10 3–1 v Barnsley

BIGGEST DEFEAT (ALL COMPS)
02/05/10 0–4 v Watford

THE PLAYER WITH THE MOST
GOALS SCORED	Clinton Morrison	**11**
SHOTS ON TARGET	Leon Best	**41**
SHOTS OFF TARGET	Clinton Morrison	**26**
SHOTS WITHOUT SCORING	Carl Baker	**22**
ASSISTS	Michael McIndoe	**6**
OFFSIDES	Leon Best	**56**
FOULS	Leon Best	**56**
FOULS WITHOUT A CARD	David Bell	**11**
FREE-KICKS WON	Aron Gunnarsson, Clinton Morrison	**61**
DEFENSIVE CLEARANCES	Richard Wood, Stephen Wright	**52**

actim INDEX FOR THE 2009/10 COCA-COLA CHAMPIONSHIP SEASON

RANK	PLAYER	PTS
45	Martin Cranie	489
52	Keiren Westwood	480
96	Clinton Morrison	416

ATTENDANCE RECORD
HIGH	AVERAGE	LOW
22,209	17,305	14,426
v Leicester (03/10/2009)		v Sheff Utd (15/09/2009)

COVENTRY'S disappointing end to the 2009/10 season led to manager Chris Coleman being replaced by Aidy Boothroyd over the summer.

Coleman was the Sky Blues' 15th manager in the last 10 years and the longest serving since Gordon Strachan's departure in 2001.

No one could have predicted the Welshman's exit in mid-March when the club were riding high in eighth place in the Coca-Cola Championship, just two points off the play-off places. But 11 winless games later, Coventry eventually finished 19th, just a single place higher than they had been when Coleman took over at the Ricoh Arena in February 2008.

The campaign started in promising fashion, despite the sale of defensive lynchpins Scott Dann and Danny Fox, as the Sky Blues claimed seven points from the opening nine available to sit in third place in the table. However, that soon changed, and just two wins from their next 17 matches saw the club fall to 20th place.

A 3–2 home triumph over bottom side Peterborough ended their unwanted sequence in mid-December – with Freddy Eastwood netting the club's first League hat-trick for seven years.

That kickstarted a run of form that took them back into the relative safety of mid-table, although the loss of their top scorer at the time, Leon Best, to Newcastle on the final day of the January transfer window left a question mark over their chances for the remainder of the season.

Their immediate response was positive as Coventry stormed to the fringes of the

A dreadful conclusion to the season led to the sacking of boss Chris Coleman

play-off places, and at that stage they appeared to be contenders for promotion. But their campaign fell away following a 2–1 home defeat to Cardiff, culminating in a final-day 4–0 reverse to Watford – their heaviest defeat of the season.

Ultimately, their small squad could not sustain a challenge in the upper reaches of the division and former Fulham boss Coleman paid the price within 48 hours of that thrashing by the Hornets.

Boothroyd left Colchester to take up the reins and, four years after he took Watford up to the Barclays Premier League, he is now charged with the task of repeating that feat at Coventry. While his priority should be to retain key players such as goalkeeper Keiren Westwood, Boothroyd must also add numbers to his squad if he is to be successful.

The new manager's appointment was met optimistically by Coventry fans, who can be safe in the knowledge that their club has overcome the financial difficulties that dogged them not so long ago.

Freddy Eastwood scores the first goal of his hat-trick against Peterborough

RESULTS 2009/10

AUGUST

9th	● Ipswich	H	W 2–1	Att: 16,279	Ref: R Booth	Scorers: Morrison[2].
12th	◐ Hartlepool	H	L 0–1	Att: 6,055	Ref: M Haywood	Booked: Wright.
15th	● Barnsley	A	W 0–2	Att: 12,552	Ref: S Tanner	Scorers: Best, Morrison. Booked: McIndoe.
18th	● Doncaster	A	D 0–0	Att: 9,484	Ref: C Boyeson	Booked: Gunnarsson.
22nd	● Swansea	H	L 0–1	Att: 16,307	Ref: P Crossley	Booked: Best, Van Aanholt, Clingan.
29th	● Blackpool	A	L 3–0	Att: 8,239	Ref: N Miller	

SEPTEMBER

12th	● Bristol City	H	D 1–1	Att: 16,449	Ref: N Swarbrick	Scorers: Best. Booked: Hall, Morrison, Eastwood.
15th	● Sheff Utd	H	W 3–2	Att: 14,426	Ref: A Taylor	Scorers: Best, Cranie, Morrison. Booked: Morrison.
19th	● Preston	A	L 3–2	Att: 11,230	Ref: D Deadman	Scorers: Clingan, Morrison. Booked: Morrison.
26th	● Middlesbrough	H	D 2–2	Att: 16,771	Ref: G Horwood	Scorers: Best, Morrison. Booked: Ward, Wright.
29th	● Watford	A	W 2–3	Att: 13,034	Ref: A Marriner	Scorers: Best[2], Clingan.

OCTOBER

3rd	● Leicester	H	D 1–1	Att: 22,209	Ref: M Oliver	Scorers: Clingan. Booked: Clingan, Best.
17th	● Sheff Wed	A	L 2–0	Att: 20,026	Ref: C Webster	Booked: Ward.
20th	● Cardiff	A	L 2–0	Att: 19,038	Ref: M Russell	Booked: Turner, Cork, Wright, Van Aanholt.
24th	● West Brom	H	D 0–0	Att: 20,871	Ref: K Stroud	Booked: Van Aanholt, Osbourne, Cork.
31st	● Reading	H	L 1–3	Att: 15,165	Ref: E Ilderton	Scorers: Eastwood. Booked: Hussey.

NOVEMBER

6th	● Derby	A	L 2–1	Att: 26,511	Ref: P Crossley	Scorers: Best. Booked: Barnett, Clarke, Van Aanholt, Hussey. Dismissed: Clarke.
21st	● Crystal Palace	H	D 1–1	Att: 18,400	Ref: J Singh	Scorers: Best. Booked: Best, Wright.
28th	● QPR	A	D 2–2	Att: 13,712	Ref: M Jones	Scorers: Best, Wood. Booked: Wood, Van Aanholt, Westwood, Cork, Wright. Dismissed: Wright.

DECEMBER

6th	● Scunthorpe	A	L 1–0	Att: 5,013	Ref: N Miller	
9th	● Newcastle	H	L 0–2	Att: 21,688	Ref: G Hegley	Booked: Cork.
12th	● Peterborough	H	W 3–2	Att: 15,190	Ref: R East	Scorers: Eastwood[3]. Booked: Barnett, Cranie.
19th	● Plymouth	A	W 0–1	Att: 8,347	Ref: K Stroud	Scorers: Eastwood. Booked: Gunnarsson.
26th	● Doncaster	H	W 1–0	Att: 19,221	Ref: R Shoebridge	Scorers: Morrison.
28th	● Nottm Forest	A	L 2–0	Att: 28,608	Ref: M Clattenburg	

JANUARY

2nd	● Portsmouth	A	D 1–1	Att: 11,214	Ref: P Dowd	Scorers: Bell. Booked: Wright, Wood.
9th	● Barnsley	H	W 3–1	Att: 15,031	Ref: L Mason	Scorers: Clingan, Eastwood, Morrison.
12th	● Portsmouth	H	L 1–2	Att: 7,097	Ref: M Jones	Scorers: Best. Booked: Bell, Cranie. AET – Score after 90 mins 1–1.
16th	● Ipswich	A	L 3–2	Att: 20,135	Ref: M Oliver	Scorers: Morrison, Wood. Booked: McPake, Morrison, McIndoe.
26th	● Swansea	A	D 0–0	Att: 13,868	Ref: D McDermid	Booked: Wright, Best.
30th	● Blackpool	H	D 1–1	Att: 16,019	Ref: D Whitestone	Scorers: Baptiste OG.

FEBRUARY

6th	● Bristol City	A	D 1–1	Att: 13,852	Ref: G Horwood	Scorers: Bell.
9th	● Nottm Forest	H	W 1–0	Att: 18,225	Ref: T Bates	Scorers: Eastwood. Booked: Wood, McPake, McIndoe, Baker.
13th	● QPR	H	W 1–0	Att: 15,247	Ref: D Foster	Scorers: Deegan. Booked: Wright, Cranie.
17th	● Newcastle	A	L 4–1	Att: 39,334	Ref: S Tanner	Scorers: Morrison. Booked: Deegan, Wright, Barnett, Gunnarsson. Dismissed: Barnett.
20th	● Crystal Palace	A	W 0–1	Att: 13,333	Ref: D Deadman	Scorers: Bell.
27th	● Scunthorpe	H	W 2–1	Att: 16,197	Ref: P Taylor	Scorers: Clingan, Stead. Booked: Barnett, McPake, Morrison. Dismissed: Barnett.

MARCH

6th	● Peterborough	A	W 0–1	Att: 10,469	Ref: R Booth	Scorers: Stead. Booked: Clingan.
13th	● Plymouth	H	D 1–1	Att: 18,127	Ref: A Haines	Scorers: McIndoe.
16th	● Cardiff	H	L 1–2	Att: 16,038	Ref: S Hooper	Scorers: Morrison. Booked: Wood, Eastwood, Westwood.
21st	● Leicester	A	D 2–2	Att: 23,093	Ref: L Mason	Scorers: Deegan, McPake.
24th	● West Brom	A	L 1–0	Att: 22,140	Ref: C Webster	Booked: McPake, Wood.
27th	● Sheff Wed	H	D 1–1	Att: 17,608	Ref: N Swarbrick	Scorers: Wood. Booked: Hall, Morrison, Cranie.

APRIL

3rd	● Derby	H	L 0–1	Att: 17,630	Ref: A D'Urso	Booked: Clingan, Wood.
5th	● Reading	A	L 3–0	Att: 17,435	Ref: A Woolmer	Booked: Gunnarsson, Morrison, Barnett, Deegan.
10th	● Sheff Utd	A	L 1–0	Att: 23,603	Ref: G Salisbury	
17th	● Preston	H	D 1–1	Att: 15,822	Ref: G Ward	Scorers: Eastwood. Booked: Clingan, Jeffers.
24th	● Middlesbrough	A	D 1–1	Att: 27,721	Ref: D McDermid	Scorers: Gunnarsson. Booked: Wright.

MAY

| 2nd | ● Watford | H | L 0–4 | Att: 19,103 | Ref: M Halsey | Booked: Eastwood. |

● Coca-Cola Championship/Play-offs ● FA Cup ◐ Carling Cup

COVENTRY CITY

CHAMPIONSHIP GOALKEEPER STATS

Player	Minutes on pitch	Appearances	Match starts	Completed matches	Sub appearances	Subbed off	Saved with feet	Punched	Parried	Tipped over	Fumbled	Tipped round	Caught	Blocked	Clean sheets	Goals conceded	Save %	Saved	Resulting in goals	Opposition miss	Fouls committed	Free-kicks won	Yellow cards	Red cards
Dimitrios Konstantopoulos	283	3	2	2	1	0	0	1	1	0	0	0	14	3	0	5	79.17	1	0	0	0	1	0	0
Keiren Westwood	4157	44	44	43	0	1	3	7	27	7	5	12	200	13	9	59	82.01	1	8	0	0	13	2	0

CHAMPIONSHIP OUTFIELD PLAYER STATS

Player	Minutes on pitch	Appearances	Match starts	Completed matches	Substitute appearances	Subbed off	Goals scored	Assists	Shots on target	Shots off target	Crosses	Tackles made	Defensive clearances	Defensive blocks	Fouls committed	Free-kicks won	Caught offside	Yellow cards	Red cards
Carl Baker	1446	22	14	11	8	3	0	3	10	12	52	28	1	2	15	20	1	1	0
Leon Barnett	1823	20	19	17	1	0	0	1	0	4	1	67	39	17	33	18	4	5	2
David Bell	1891	28	20	9	8	11	2	1	6	13	76	40	3	7	11	18	0	0	0
Leon Best	2333	27	25	16	2	9	9	4	41	21	18	32	17	3	56	38	56	4	0
Ashley Cain	42	2	0	0	2	0	0	0	0	1	2	0	0	0	0	0	0	0	0
Jordan Clarke	542	12	6	2	6	3	0	0	2	2	10	18	5	2	3	4	0	1	1
Sammy Clingan	2998	34	32	29	2	3	5	3	25	17	66	112	10	6	20	30	0	5	0
Jack Cork	1867	21	20	15	1	5	0	0	10	10	16	59	4	5	21	14	0	4	0
Martin Cranie	3663	40	38	34	2	4	1	3	4	0	35	111	47	30	42	22	1	3	0
Gary Deegan	1050	17	9	6	8	3	2	0	5	7	1	51	0	2	15	6	0	2	0
Freddy Eastwood	2151	36	21	10	15	11	8	2	26	15	28	41	4	0	37	8	11	3	0
Jermaine Grandison	192	3	1	1	2	0	0	0	2	1	3	4	5	2	2	0	0	0	0
Aron Gunnarsson	3165	40	34	24	6	10	1	0	20	20	41	100	13	14	50	61	2	4	0
Marcus Hall	584	8	7	3	1	0	0	1	0	1	1	11	8	4	6	9	4	2	0
Chris Hussey	235	8	1	0	7	1	0	0	0	0	9	6	2	1	3	7	0	2	0
Sean Jeffers	53	4	0	0	4	0	0	0	0	1	0	1	0	0	0	1	0	0	1
Gary Madine	91	9	0	0	9	0	0	0	2	2	0	3	0	0	3	2	0	0	0
Michael McIndoe	3469	40	38	27	2	11	1	6	18	13	146	40	10	5	34	51	17	3	0
Leon McKenzie	9	1	0	0	1	0	0	0	0	0	0	1	0	0	0	0	0	0	0
James McPake	1550	17	17	13	0	4	1	1	2	3	0	51	44	9	22	23	1	4	0
Clinton Morrison	3663	46	38	27	8	11	11	4	37	26	32	58	24	3	35	61	26	7	0
Isaac Osbourne	1124	15	12	9	3	3	0	2	1	3	13	23	8	1	24	6	1	1	0
Freddie Sears	391	10	3	2	7	1	0	0	3	1	10	10	1	0	3	5	4	0	0
Jonathan Stead	769	10	9	4	1	5	2	1	14	9	8	11	0	2	11	7	6	0	0
Ben Turner	1234	13	13	12	0	1	0	0	2	2	3	20	34	15	11	8	0	1	0
Patrick Van Aanholt	1784	20	19	15	1	4	0	1	9	5	30	56	6	3	9	11	0	5	0
Elliott Ward	467	8	4	4	4	0	0	2	2	2	1	28	5	4	7	3	0	2	0
Richard Wood	2145	24	22	22	2	0	3	0	8	3	5	90	52	13	30	17	2	5	0
Stephen Wright	3502	38	38	31	0	6	0	1	4	2	40	131	52	25	37	37	0	8	1

actim

Coca-Cola CHAMPIONSHIP

SEASON TOTALS	
Goals scored	47
Goals conceded	64
Clean sheets	10
Shots on target	253
Shots off target	196
Shots per goal	9.55
Pens awarded	3
Pens scored	1
Pens conceded	10
Offsides	132
Corners	240
Crosses	658
Players used	31
Fouls committed	544
Free-kicks won	499

SEASON INFORMATION
Highest position: 1
Lowest position: 20
Average goals scored per game: 1.02
Average goals conceded per game: 1.39

	AUG	SEP	OCT	NOV	DEC	JAN	FEB	MAR	APR	MAY
LEAGUE POSITION AT THE END OF EACH MONTH	12	10	16	17	17	14	10	12	16	19

CARDS RECEIVED

75   4

SEQUENCES

Wins	3
(on two occasions)	
Losses	3
(03/04/10–10/04/10)	
Draws	3
(26/01/10–06/02/10)	
Undefeated	5
(26/01/10–13/02/10)	
Without win	11
(13/03/10–02/05/10)	
Undefeated home	8
(12/12/09–13/03/10)	
Undefeated away	3
(20/02/10–21/03/10)	
Without scoring	3
(on three occasions)	
Without conceding	2
(on three occasions)	
Scoring	11
(30/01/10–21/03/10)	
Conceding	10
(22/08/09–20/10/09)	

MATCH RECORDS

Goals scored per match

		W	D	L	Pts
Failed to score	15	0	3	12	3
Scored 1 goal	19	6	9	4	27
Scored 2 goals	8	3	3	2	12
Scored 3 goals	4	4	0	0	12
Scored 4+ goals	0	0	0	0	0

Goals conceded per match

		W	D	L	Pts
Clean sheet	10	7	3	0	24
Conceded 1 goal	17	3	9	5	18
Conceded 2 goals	12	3	3	6	12
Conceded 3 goals	5	0	0	5	0
Conceded 4+ goals	2	0	0	2	0

GOALS SCORED/CONCEDED
PER FIVE-MINUTE INTERVALS

MINS	5	10	15	20	25	30	35	40	45	50	55	60	65	70	75	80	85	90
FOR	2	3	2	4	4	1	4	1	0	4	2	2	1	2	2	2	6	5
AGN	4	0	2	5	3	3	2	5	6	5	5	2	1	7	4	3	4	3

EARLIEST STRIKE
CLINTON MORRISON
(v Ipswich) 1:38

LATEST STRIKE
RICHARD WOOD
(v Ipswich) 95:02

Clinton Morrison

GOAL DETAILS

How the goals were struck

SCORED		CONCEDED
27	Right foot	36
7	Left foot	18
13	Header	10
0	Other	0

How the goals were struck

SCORED		CONCEDED
25	Open play	36
11	Cross	14
3	Corner	4
1	Penalty	8
4	Direct from free-kick	0
2	Free-kick	2
1	Own goal	0

Distance from goal

SCORED		CONCEDED
18	6YDS	23
21	18YDS	34
8	18+YDS	7

CRYSTAL PALACE

CLUB SUMMARY

FORMED	1905
MANAGER	TBC
GROUND	Selhurst Park
CAPACITY	26,400
NICKNAME	The Eagles
WEBSITE	www.cpfc.co.uk

The New Football Pools PLAYER OF THE SEASON

Julian Speroni

OVERALL
P	W	D	L	F	A	GD
53	17	19	17	62	65	-3

COCA-COLA CHAMPIONSHIP
Pos	P	W	D	L	F	A	GD	Pts
21	46	14	17	15	50	53	-3	49

HOME
Pos	P	W	D	L	F	A	GD	Pts
22	23	8	5	10	24	27	-3	29

AWAY
Pos	P	W	D	L	F	A	GD	Pts
5	23	6	12	5	26	26	0	30

CUP PROGRESS DETAILS
Competition	Round reached	Knocked out by
FA Cup	R5	Aston Villa
Carling Cup	R2	Man City

BIGGEST WIN (ALL COMPS)
03/10/09 4–1 v Blackpool

BIGGEST DEFEAT (ALL COMPS)
12/09/09 0–4 v Scunthorpe

THE PLAYER WITH THE MOST
GOALS SCORED	Darren Ambrose	**15**
SHOTS ON TARGET	Darren Ambrose	**69**
SHOTS OFF TARGET	Darren Ambrose	**45**
SHOTS WITHOUT SCORING	Johannes Ertl	**26**
ASSISTS	Darren Ambrose	**8**
OFFSIDES	Alan Lee	**23**
FOULS	Alan Lee	**76**
FOULS WITHOUT A CARD	Stern John	**12**
FREE-KICKS WON	Alan Lee	**89**
DEFENSIVE CLEARANCES	Clint Hill	**64**

actim INDEX FOR THE 2009/10 COCA-COLA CHAMPIONSHIP SEASON

RANK	PLAYER	PTS
5	Darren Ambrose	641
35	Julian Speroni	502
68	Neil Danns	453

ATTENDANCE RECORD
HIGH	AVERAGE	LOW
20,643	14,771	12,328
v Newcastle (22/08/2009)		v Swansea (09/02/2010)

Alan Lee celebrates his goal against Sheffield Wednesday in a thrilling final game

IN LATE January, Crystal Palace's squad boarded a plane bound for Newcastle looking for a victory that would have left them a point outside the play-off zone. By the time they landed later that evening, they found themselves embroiled in a relegation battle that went right to the wire.

The Eagles, more than £30million in debt, had been plunged into administration during the course of the trip to St James' Park and the subsequent 10-point penalty was to cost them a shot at promotion, their star player and their manager. Administrator Brendan Guilfoyle banned Neil Warnock from playing teenage striker Victor Moses at Newcastle for fear of him being injured before he was sold to Wigan for a cut-price £2million. Warnock eventually left to join QPR while Palace scrapped for their lives at the foot of the table.

Guilfoyle turned to Paul Hart, who had saved Portsmouth from relegation from the Barclays Premier League a year earlier, and Palace faced a do-or-die clash at Sheffield Wednesday on the final day of the campaign. The Eagles, needing only a point to stay up and send Wednesday down, secured a 2–2 draw courtesy of Darren Ambrose's 20th goal of the season. They had somehow survived, and the club then avoided extinction in the summer when the CPFC 2010 consortium agreed a deal in principle with Bank of Scotland over the purchase of Selhurst Park.

Palace's season had begun in bizarre circumstances when on-loan West Ham striker Freddie Sears had what appeared to

A season of financial instability ended in dramatic fashion with some last-day heroics

be a perfectly good 'goal' ruled out at Bristol City. The ball hit the back of the net and bounced out, but none of the officials saw it. Warnock was furious, especially as his side went on to lose the match, while Sears failed to register a goal in his 19 appearances for the club.

A month later, Warnock considered resigning after a 4–0 home defeat by Scunthorpe, only to be talked round by chairman Simon Jordan. Palace, inspired by the form of Moses, then went on to lose just three of their next 19 games until they took that fateful flight to Newcastle.

Warnock stayed for a further two months, guiding his side to the FA Cup fifth round courtesy of an amazing six-minute hat-trick from makeshift striker Danny Butterfield against Wolves. However, when QPR came calling, Warnock moved on and there are fears that some of the club's major players could follow even though Palace's immediate financial worries seem to have been eased.

RESULTS 2009/10

AUGUST

8th	● Plymouth	H	D 1–1	Att: 14,358	Ref: A Penn	Scorers: Lee.
11th	○ Torquay	H	W 2–1	Att: 3,140	Ref: D Phillips	Scorers: Ambrose[2]. Booked: Fonte.
15th	● Bristol City	A	L 1–0	Att: 14,603	Ref: R Shoebridge	Booked: Danns.
18th	● Ipswich	A	W 1–3	Att: 20,348	Ref: K Hill	Scorers: Ambrose[2], Danns. Booked: Hill.
22nd	● Newcastle	H	L 0–2	Att: 20,643	Ref: A D'Urso	Booked: Hill, McCarthy, Lee.
27th	○ Man City	H	L 0–2	Att: 14,725	Ref: D Deadman	
31st	● Peterborough	A	D 1–1	Att: 8,473	Ref: K Friend	Scorers: Lee. Booked: McCarthy. Dismissed: McCarthy.

SEPTEMBER

12th	● Scunthorpe	H	L 0–4	Att: 12,912	Ref: G Hegley	
19th	● Derby	H	W 1–0	Att: 12,760	Ref: M Oliver	Scorers: Ambrose. Booked: Speroni, McCarthy.
26th	● West Brom	A	W 0–1	Att: 21,007	Ref: R Booth	Scorers: N'Diaye. Booked: Derry, Carle.
29th	● Sheff Wed	H	D 0–0	Att: 12,476	Ref: T Kettle	Booked: Hill, Butterfield.

OCTOBER

3rd	● Blackpool	H	W 4–1	Att: 15,749	Ref: A Taylor	Scorers: Ambrose, Danns, Lee, N'Diaye. Booked: Ertl.
17th	● Cardiff	A	D 1–1	Att: 21,457	Ref: S Tanner	Scorers: Hudson OG. Booked: N'Diaye, Butterfield, Hill.
20th	● Leicester	A	L 2–0	Att: 22,220	Ref: R East	
24th	● Nottm Forest	H	D 1–1	Att: 15,692	Ref: G Horwood	Scorers: Ambrose. Booked: Hill, Moses.
31st	● Preston	A	D 1–1	Att: 12,558	Ref: D Foster	Scorers: Ambrose. Booked: Fonte, Davis.

NOVEMBER

3rd	● QPR	A	D 1–1	Att: 14,377	Ref: M Russell	Scorers: Ambrose. Booked: Davis.
7th	● Middlesbrough	H	W 1–0	Att: 15,321	Ref: J Linnington	Scorers: Ambrose. Booked: Butterfield.
21st	● Coventry	A	D 1–1	Att: 18,400	Ref: J Singh	Scorers: Ambrose. Booked: Fonte, Lee, Davis.
28th	● Watford	H	W 3–0	Att: 14,085	Ref: O Langford	Scorers: Ambrose, Lee, Moses. Booked: Davis, Danns.

DECEMBER

5th	● Doncaster	H	L 0–3	Att: 13,985	Ref: P Miller	
8th	● Reading	A	W 2–4	Att: 16,629	Ref: K Friend	Scorers: Ambrose, Clyne, Moses[2]. Booked: Butterfield, Clyne, Moses.
12th	● Sheff Utd	A	L 2–0	Att: 25,510	Ref: C Webster	Booked: Derry, Ertl, Danns, Hill.
19th	● Barnsley	H	D 1–1	Att: 14,279	Ref: K Hill	Scorers: Moses. Booked: Derry.
26th	● Ipswich	H	W 3–1	Att: 16,496	Ref: P Taylor	Scorers: Danns, Fonte, Moses. Booked: Hill, Danns, Davis, Sears.
28th	● Swansea	A	D 0–0	Att: 18,794	Ref: A Taylor	Booked: Hill.

JANUARY

2nd	● Sheff Wed	A	W 1–2	Att: 8,690	Ref: N Miller	Scorers: Andrew, Danns.
16th	● Plymouth	A	W 0–1	Att: 9,318	Ref: T Bates	Scorers: Moses. Booked: Davis, Moses, Derry, Danns, Hills.
23rd	● Wolverhampton	A	D 2–2	Att: 14,449	Ref: C Foy	Scorers: Ambrose, Lee.
27th	● Newcastle	A	L 2–0	Att: 37,886	Ref: R Booth	Booked: Butterfield.
30th	● Peterborough	H	W 2–0	Att: 14,699	Ref: G Salisbury	Scorers: Danns[2].

FEBRUARY

2nd	● Wolverhampton	H	W 3–1	Att: 10,282	Ref: L Mason	Scorers: Butterfield[3]. Booked: Derry, Lee.
6th	● Scunthorpe	A	W 1–2	Att: 7,543	Ref: P Tierney	Scorers: Ambrose, Danns. Booked: Lee, Derry, Butterfield, Lawrence, Davis.
9th	● Swansea	H	L 0–1	Att: 12,328	Ref: G Scott	
14th	● Aston Villa	H	D 2–2	Att: 20,486	Ref: K Friend	Scorers: Ambrose, Ertl. Booked: Carle, Davis, Butterfield, Lee.
17th	● Reading	H	L 1–3	Att: 13,259	Ref: D Whitestone	Scorers: Scannell. Booked: Scannell, Davis.
20th	● Coventry	H	L 0–1	Att: 13,333	Ref: D Deadman	
24th	● Aston Villa	A	L 3–1	Att: 31,874	Ref: M Atkinson	Scorers: Ambrose. Booked: Lawrence, Clyne.
27th	● Doncaster	A	D 1–1	Att: 9,779	Ref: N Swarbrick	Scorers: Djilali. Booked: Hill, Clyne, Lee.

MARCH

6th	● Sheff Utd	H	W 1–0	Att: 13,455	Ref: A Penn	Scorers: Lee. Booked: Derry, Davis, N'Diaye.
9th	● Bristol City	H	L 0–1	Att: 12,844	Ref: M Russell	Booked: Butterfield.
13th	● Barnsley	A	D 0–0	Att: 11,416	Ref: T Kettle	Booked: Lawrence, Ambrose, Derry.
16th	● Leicester	H	L 0–1	Att: 12,721	Ref: S Tanner	Booked: Davis, Danns. Dismissed: Davis.
20th	● Blackpool	A	D 2–2	Att: 9,702	Ref: P Gibbs	Scorers: Ambrose, Carle. Booked: Derry, Ertl, N'Diaye.
23rd	● Nottm Forest	A	L 2–0	Att: 20,025	Ref: A Hall	Booked: Lee. Dismissed: Lawrence.
27th	● Cardiff	H	L 1–2	Att: 13,464	Ref: C Boyeson	Scorers: Hill. Booked: Andrew, Hill.
30th	● Watford	A	W 1–3	Att: 15,134	Ref: P Taylor	Scorers: Danns, John, Scannell. Booked: Hills, Ertl, Lawrence. Dismissed: Hills.

APRIL

3rd	● Middlesbrough	A	D 1–1	Att: 18,428	Ref: G Salisbury	Scorers: N'Diaye. Booked: Davis, Lee, Speroni.
5th	● Preston	H	W 3–1	Att: 16,642	Ref: R East	Scorers: Ambrose, Andrew, Danns. Booked: Danns, Lawrence, Scannell, Andrew.
10th	● QPR	H	L 0–2	Att: 20,430	Ref: N Miller	Booked: McCarthy.
17th	● Derby	A	D 1–1	Att: 30,255	Ref: T Bates	Scorers: John. Booked: Hill, N'Diaye.
26th	● West Brom	H	D 1–1	Att: 17,798	Ref: D Whitestone	Scorers: Reid OG. Booked: Hill. Dismissed: Danns.

MAY

2nd	● Sheff Wed	A	D 2–2	Att: 37,121	Ref: M Dean	Scorers: Ambrose, Lee. Booked: Andrew, Ertl.

● Coca-Cola Championship/Play-offs ● FA Cup ○ Carling Cup

OFFICIAL FOOTBALL YEARBOOK OF THE ENGLISH & SCOTTISH LEAGUES 2010-2011 **189**

CRYSTAL PALACE

CHAMPIONSHIP GOALKEEPER STATS

Player	Minutes on pitch	Appearances	Match starts	Completed matches	Sub appearances	Subbed off	Saved with feet	Punched	Parried	Tipped over	Fumbled	Tipped round	Caught	Blocked	Clean sheets	Goals conceded	Save %	Saved	Resulting in goals	Opposition miss	Fouls committed	Free-kicks won	Yellow cards	Red cards
							SAVES BREAKDOWN											PENALTIES						
Darryl Flahavan	95	1	1	1	0	0	0	1	2	1	0	0	1	0	0	2	71.43	0	0	0	0	0	0	0
Julian Speroni	4356	45	45	45	0	0	0	16	24	5	1	18	179	5	10	51	82.89	2	2	0	0	7	2	0

CHAMPIONSHIP OUTFIELD PLAYER STATS

Player	Minutes on pitch	Appearances	Match starts	Completed matches	Substitute appearances	Subbed off	Goals scored	Assists	Shots on target	Shots off target	Crosses	Tackles made	Defensive clearances	Defensive blocks	Fouls committed	Free-kicks won	Caught offside	Yellow cards	Red cards
Darren Ambrose	4001	46	44	28	2	16	15	8	69	45	78	61	5	1	21	23	10	1	0
Calvin Andrew	1283	27	13	7	14	6	1	1	6	12	2	32	8	0	27	24	10	3	0
Danny Butterfield	3248	37	36	30	1	6	0	4	4	12	45	107	19	12	31	21	3	7	0
Nick Carle	1232	22	14	3	8	11	1	0	8	10	5	41	0	1	20	16	2	1	0
Nathaniel Clyne	1948	22	19	17	3	2	1	1	2	3	5	102	5	3	11	9	0	2	0
Neil Danns	3805	42	41	32	1	8	8	2	29	27	27	84	10	4	43	36	8	6	1
Claude Davis	1704	21	19	17	2	1	0	0	1	3	0	75	30	4	33	25	0	11	1
Shaun Derry	4364	46	46	44	0	2	0	3	7	11	7	144	32	4	59	34	0	8	0
Kieran Djilali	317	8	2	0	6	2	1	0	2	2	1	7	0	0	2	6	1	0	0
Johannes Ertl	2797	33	29	25	4	4	0	2	10	16	7	62	13	1	26	21	1	6	0
Jose Fonte	2122	22	22	22	0	0	1	0	4	5	3	36	27	7	41	19	0	2	0
Clint Hill	4163	43	43	43	0	0	1	0	8	10	23	119	64	13	62	39	1	12	0
Lee Hills	1000	19	10	5	9	4	0	3	1	2	15	43	3	1	12	2	1	2	1
Stern John	760	16	7	2	9	5	2	0	9	12	1	13	0	0	12	9	14	0	0
Matthew Lawrence	1547	18	14	11	4	2	0	0	0	1	5	65	16	1	15	8	0	4	1
Alan Lee	3017	42	33	11	9	22	6	5	28	16	6	47	22	1	76	89	23	6	0
Patrick McCarthy	1923	20	20	19	0	0	0	1	4	4	2	69	44	8	35	27	0	4	1
Victor Moses	1222	18	14	5	4	9	6	2	20	10	21	28	0	1	8	29	10	3	0
Alassane N'Diaye	1230	26	12	8	14	4	3	0	6	10	5	33	20	3	23	17	1	4	0
Sean Scannell	1356	26	11	3	15	8	2	3	7	10	8	24	1	1	11	16	2	2	0
Freddie Sears	1140	18	11	5	7	6	0	1	12	7	6	12	0	0	7	11	9	1	0
Ryan Smith	120	5	0	0	5	0	0	0	1	2	2	2	1	0	1	4	0	0	0
Wilfred Zaha	16	1	0	0	1	0	0	0	0	0	0	0	0	0	0	0	0	0	0

actim

Coca-Cola CHAMPIONSHIP

SEASON TOTALS

Goals scored	50
Goals conceded	53
Clean sheets	10
Shots on target	237
Shots off target	229
Shots per goal	9.32
Pens awarded	3
Pens scored	1
Pens conceded	4
Offsides	96
Corners	213
Crosses	275
Players used	25
Fouls committed	576
Free-kicks won	492

CARDS RECEIVED

87 **5**

SEQUENCES

Wins	2
(on two occasions)	
Losses	3
(09/02/10–20/02/10)	
Draws	3
(on two occasions)	
Undefeated	6
(24/10/09–28/11/09)	
Without win	6
(09/03/10–27/03/10)	
Undefeated home	6
(19/09/09–28/11/09)	
Undefeated away	4
(on four occasions)	
Without scoring	3
(09/03/10–16/03/10)	
Without conceding	3
(19/09/09–29/09/09)	
Scoring	6
(24/10/09–28/11/09)	
Conceding	6
(on two occasions)	

League position at the end of each month

AUG	SEP	OCT	NOV	DEC	JAN	FEB	MAR	APR	MAY
16	15	13	11	9	20	21	22	21	21

LEAGUE POSITION AT THE END OF EACH MONTH

SEASON INFORMATION
Highest position: 2
Lowest position: 20
Average goals scored per game: 1.09
Average goals conceded per game: 1.15

MATCH RECORDS

Goals scored per match

		W	D	L	Pts
Failed to score	16	0	3	13	3
Scored 1 goal	19	5	12	2	27
Scored 2 goals	4	2	2	0	8
Scored 3 goals	5	5	0	0	15
Scored 4+ goals	2	2	0	0	6

Goals conceded per match

		W	D	L	Pts
Clean sheet	10	7	3	0	24
Conceded 1 goal	23	6	12	5	30
Conceded 2 goals	10	1	2	7	5
Conceded 3 goals	2	0	0	2	0
Conceded 4+ goals	1	0	0	1	0

GOALS SCORED/CONCEDED
PER FIVE-MINUTE INTERVALS

MINS	5	10	15	20	25	30	35	40	45	50	55	60	65	70	75	80	85	90
FOR	3	2	1	2	2	2	3	4	3	3	5	2	8	4	0	0	1	5
AGN	4	2	3	5	4	0	2	1	3	4	3	3	2	3	1	2	6	5

EARLIEST STRIKE
VICTOR MOSES
(v Watford) 1:50

LATEST STRIKE
VICTOR MOSES
(v Ipswich) 93:41

Sean Scannell

GOAL DETAILS

How the goals were struck

SCORED		CONCEDED
28	Right foot	32
12	Left foot	13
10	Header	8
0	Other	0

How the goals were struck

SCORED		CONCEDED
37	Open play	37
5	Cross	5
3	Corner	3
1	Penalty	2
1	Direct from free-kick	1
1	Free-kick	4
2	Own goal	1

Distance from goal

SCORED		CONCEDED
21	6YDS	16
24	18YDS	28
5	18+YDS	9

DERBY COUNTY

CLUB SUMMARY

FORMED	1884
MANAGER	Nigel Clough
GROUND	Pride Park
CAPACITY	33,597
NICKNAME	The Rams
WEBSITE	www.dcfc.co.uk

The New Football Pools PLAYER OF THE SEASON — *Robbie Savage*

OVERALL

P	W	D	L	F	A	GD
51	16	13	22	58	69	-11

COCA-COLA CHAMPIONSHIP

Pos	P	W	D	L	F	A	GD	Pts
14	46	15	11	20	53	63	-10	56

HOME

Pos	P	W	D	L	F	A	GD	Pts
10	23	12	3	8	37	32	5	39

AWAY

Pos	P	W	D	L	F	A	GD	Pts
20	23	3	8	12	16	31	-15	17

CUP PROGRESS DETAILS

Competition	Round reached	Knocked out by
FA Cup	R5	Birmingham
Carling Cup	R1	Rotherham

BIGGEST WIN (ALL COMPS)
3–0 on 3 occasions

BIGGEST DEFEAT (ALL COMPS)
29/09/09 1-6 v Cardiff

THE PLAYER WITH THE MOST

GOALS SCORED	Rob Hulse	**12**
SHOTS ON TARGET	Rob Hulse	**46**
SHOTS OFF TARGET	Rob Hulse	**34**
SHOTS WITHOUT SCORING	Tomasz Cywka	**10**
ASSISTS	Kris Commons	**5**
OFFSIDES	Rob Hulse	**49**
FOULS	Rob Hulse	**74**
FOULS WITHOUT A CARD	Chris Porter	**13**
FREE-KICKS WON	Robbie Savage	**64**
DEFENSIVE CLEARANCES	Shaun Barker	**59**

actim INDEX — FOR THE 2009/10 COCA-COLA CHAMPIONSHIP SEASON

RANK	PLAYER	PTS
50	Robbie Savage	483
74	Stephen Bywater	444
105	Shaun Barker	409

ATTENDANCE RECORD

HIGH	AVERAGE	LOW
33,010	29,230	26,186
v Peterborough (08/08/2009)		v Plymouth (22/08/2009)

Despite some excellent home wins, it was a season of inconsistency for Nigel Clough's Rams

DERBY'S season was hampered by a string of injuries, which undoubtedly affected the course of their campaign. Manager Nigel Clough, in his first full season in charge of the club, rarely had more than 14 fit first-team professionals to call upon, so it is testament to his man-management skills that the Rams made the progress they did by improving upon the previous season's points tally and 18th-placed finish.

Clough also guided the club to only their third appearance in the FA Cup fifth round in the last 10 years, and only an injury-time goal from Birmingham's Liam Ridgewell denied them a place in the quarter-finals for the first time since 1999.

In the Carling Cup, it was always going to be a big ask for the Rams to repeat their heroics of the previous season, when they had reached the semi-finals before narrowly losing out to Manchester United 4–3 on aggregate. However, a first-round defeat at Coca-Cola League Two side Rotherham during the opening week of the campaign was a big surprise and that set the tone for the rest of the season in terms of their dreadful away form. County won just three times on their travels in the League and lost on 12 occasions.

While they struggled away from Pride Park, the Rams' home form continued to

Robbie Savage celebrates a win against rivals Nottingham Forest in January

keep them out of the relegation zone. A 2–0 victory against Cardiff on the final day ensured that no club outside of the top six won more home games than the Rams. Champions Newcastle, play-off contenders Nottingham Forest and Leicester and established Coca-Cola Championship clubs such as Reading and Preston were all beaten at Pride Park, while second-placed West Brom were held to a 2–2 draw in December.

The 2010/11 season is already looking as though it could hold more challenges, with Stephen Pearson set to miss the first month or so of the campaign following surgery on a serious knee injury he picked up in April. However, Clough has taken precautions to guard against a repeat of the injury problems suffered during the 2009/10 season by sending Steve Davies, Dean Leacock, Rob Hulse, Shaun Barker and David Martin for preemptive operations in the early summer.

The Rams boss has targeted a top-half finish in 2010/11, but whether that is achievable could depend on the club keeping hold of Hulse and Kris Commons. Both players have been the subject of intense interest from other managers in the last two transfer windows and may once again attract admiring glances during the close season.

Top scorer Rob Hulse grabs a goal in the home win over Coventry

AUGUST

8th	● Peterborough	H	W 2–1	Att: 33,010	Ref: P Taylor	Scorers: Addison, Teale. Booked: Buxton.
11th	● Rotherham	A	L 2–1	Att: 4,345	Ref: D Webb	Scorers: Teale. Booked: Connolly.
15th	● Scunthorpe	A	L 3–2	Att: 7,352	Ref: G Horwood	Scorers: Commons, Green.
18th	● Blackpool	A	D 0–0	Att: 8,056	Ref: E Ilderton	
22nd	● Plymouth	H	W 2–1	Att: 26,186	Ref: C Pawson	Scorers: Addison, Buxton. Booked: Addison.
29th	● Nottm Forest	A	L 3–2	Att: 28,143	Ref: M Atkinson	Scorers: Livermore, Morgan OG. Booked: Moxey, Buxton, Addison, Pearson.

SEPTEMBER

12th	● Sheff Utd	H	L 0–1	Att: 28,441	Ref: A D'Urso	Booked: Savage, Pearson.
15th	● Barnsley	H	L 2–3	Att: 27,609	Ref: N Miller	Scorers: Barker, Hulse. Booked: Croft.
19th	● Crystal Palace	A	L 1–0	Att: 12,760	Ref: M Oliver	Booked: Livermore, Croft.
26th	● Bristol City	H	W 1–0	Att: 27,144	Ref: M Russell	Scorers: Teale. Booked: Croft, Connolly.
29th	● Cardiff	A	L 6–1	Att: 18,670	Ref: S Hooper	Scorers: Hulse. Booked: Livermore.

OCTOBER

3rd	● Sheff Wed	H	W 3–0	Att: 30,116	Ref: C Foy	Scorers: Croft, Hulse, McEveley. Booked: Teale.
17th	● Leicester	A	D 0–0	Att: 28,875	Ref: M Dean	
20th	● Middlesbrough	A	L 2–0	Att: 17,459	Ref: J Moss	Booked: Hulse, Connolly.
24th	● QPR	H	L 2–4	Att: 30,135	Ref: M Haywood	Scorers: Dickov, Savage. Booked: Connolly.
31st	● Ipswich	A	L 1–0	Att: 20,299	Ref: A Taylor	Booked: Savage, Moxey.

NOVEMBER

6th	● Coventry	H	W 2–1	Att: 26,511	Ref: P Crossley	Scorers: Hulse2. Booked: Dickov.
20th	● Swansea	A	L 1–0	Att: 17,804	Ref: R East	Booked: Barker, Stoor, Connolly, Leacock.
28th	● Reading	H	W 2–1	Att: 30,174	Ref: A Haines	Scorers: Green, Hulse. Booked: Hulse, McEveley.

DECEMBER

5th	● West Brom	H	D 2–2	Att: 30,127	Ref: D Deadman	Scorers: Campbell, Dickov. Booked: Dickov, Leacock.
8th	● Preston	A	D 0–0	Att: 11,755	Ref: P Gibbs	Booked: Leacock, Dickov, Stoor.
12th	● Watford	A	W 0–1	Att: 14,063	Ref: K Stroud	Scorers: Porter. Booked: Connolly, Moxey, Pearson.
19th	● Doncaster	H	L 0–2	Att: 28,734	Ref: T Kettle	Booked: Bywater.
26th	● Blackpool	H	L 0–2	Att: 30,313	Ref: S Mathieson	Booked: Moxey. Dismissed: Moxey.
28th	● Newcastle	A	D 0–0	Att: 47,505	Ref: K Wright	Booked: McEveley, Hulse, Savage. Dismissed: McEveley.

JANUARY

2nd	● Millwall	A	D 1–1	Att: 10,531	Ref: J Linnington	Scorers: Commons. Booked: Hulse.
9th	● Scunthorpe	H	L 1–4	Att: 28,106	Ref: A Woolmer	Scorers: Williams OG.
12th	● Millwall	H	D 1–1	Att: 7,183	Ref: D Foster	Scorers: Davies. Booked: Pearson, Teale. AET – Score after 90 mins 0–0. Derby win 5–3 on penalties.
16th	● Peterborough	A	W 0–3	Att: 10,280	Ref: N Miller	Scorers: Campbell2, Davies. Booked: Hunt.
23rd	● Doncaster	H	W 1–0	Att: 11,316	Ref: C Webster	Scorers: McEveley.
26th	● Plymouth	A	L 1–0	Att: 7,996	Ref: A Hall	Booked: McEveley, Pearson, Hunt, Savage, Buxton, Davies.
30th	● Nottm Forest	H	W 1–0	Att: 32,674	Ref: N Swarbrick	Scorers: Hulse. Booked: Hulse, Pearson, Commons, Hunt, McEveley.

FEBRUARY

6th	● Sheff Utd	A	D 1–1	Att: 25,300	Ref: G Salisbury	Scorers: Savage.
9th	● Newcastle	H	W 3–0	Att: 28,607	Ref: A Taylor	Scorers: Barker, Commons, Hulse. Booked: Savage, Pearson, Buxton, Green.
13th	● Birmingham	H	L 1–2	Att: 21,043	Ref: M Atkinson	Scorers: McEveley. Booked: Savage.
16th	● Preston	H	W 5–3	Att: 26,993	Ref: C Pawson	Scorers: Barker, Commons, Hulse2, Jones OG. Booked: Savage.
20th	● Swansea	A	L 0–1	Att: 31,024	Ref: S Tanner	Booked: McEveley, Buxton. Dismissed: McEveley.
27th	● West Brom	A	L 3–1	Att: 23,335	Ref: P Crossley	Scorers: Porter. Booked: Barker, Moxey.

MARCH

6th	● Watford	H	W 2–0	Att: 29,492	Ref: G Horwood	Scorers: Porter, Tonge. Booked: Moxey, Hunt.
10th	● Reading	A	L 4–1	Att: 14,096	Ref: K Wright	Scorers: Sunu. Dismissed: Deeney.
13th	● Doncaster	A	L 2–1	Att: 11,858	Ref: S Hooper	Scorers: Hulse. Booked: Buxton.
16th	● Middlesbrough	H	D 2–2	Att: 27,143	Ref: D Phillips	Scorers: Porter, Tonge.
20th	● Sheff Wed	A	D 0–0	Att: 21,827	Ref: J Linington	Booked: Hulse, Anderson.
23rd	● QPR	A	D 1–1	Att: 12,569	Ref: M Russell	Scorers: Barker. Booked: Leacock.
27th	● Leicester	H	W 1–0	Att: 30,259	Ref: C Webster	Scorers: King OG. Booked: Pearson.

APRIL

3rd	● Coventry	A	W 0–1	Att: 17,630	Ref: A D'Urso	Scorers: Barker. Booked: Leacock.
5th	● Ipswich	H	L 1–3	Att: 28,137	Ref: J Moss	Scorers: Hulse. Booked: Hunt. Dismissed: Pearson.
10th	● Barnsley	A	D 0–0	Att: 13,034	Ref: P Taylor	Booked: Tonge.
17th	● Crystal Palace	H	D 1–1	Att: 30,255	Ref: T Bates	Scorers: Anderson. Booked: Davies.
24th	● Bristol City	A	L 2–1	Att: 15,835	Ref: C Pawson	Scorers: Pearson. Booked: Savage.

MAY

2nd	● Cardiff	H	W 2–0	Att: 31,102	Ref: C Webster	Scorers: D Martin, McEveley. Booked: Hunt, Pringle, Moxey, Savage.

● Coca-Cola Championship/Play-offs ● FA Cup ● Carling Cup

CHAMPIONSHIP GOALKEEPER STATS

Player	Minutes on pitch	Appearances	Match starts	Completed matches	Sub appearances	Subbed off	Saved with feet	Punched	Parried	Tipped over	Fumbled	Tipped round	Caught	Blocked	Clean sheets	Goals conceded	Save %	Saved	Resulting in goals	Opposition miss	Fouls committed	Free-kicks won	Yellow cards	Red cards
Stephen Bywater	3982	42	42	41	0	1	0	20	25	2	1	13	125	3	15	53	78.01	0	4	0	1	3	1	0
Saul Deeney	218	3	2	1	1	0	0	3	0	2	0	0	6	0	1	6	64.71	0	1	1	1	0	0	1
David Martin	195	2	2	2	0	0	0	0	1	0	1	0	8	0	0	4	69.23	0	1	0	0	0	0	0

CHAMPIONSHIP OUTFIELD PLAYER STATS

Player	Minutes on pitch	Appearances	Match starts	Completed matches	Substitute appearances	Subbed off	Goals scored	Assists	Shots on target	Shots off target	Crosses	Tackles made	Defensive clearances	Defensive blocks	Fouls committed	Free-kicks won	Caught offside	Yellow cards	Red cards
Miles Addison	1000	13	10	9	3	1	2	0	2	4	1	77	18	3	20	12	0	2	0
Russell Anderson	890	15	9	8	6	1	1	0	1	3	1	14	8	4	8	8	0	1	0
Callum Ball	8	1	0	0	1	0	0	0	0	0	0	0	0	0	0	0	0	0	0
Shaun Barker	3191	35	33	31	2	2	5	0	13	10	0	113	59	15	45	41	1	2	0
Jake Buxton	1811	19	19	17	0	2	1	2	6	5	1	138	21	9	27	14	0	6	0
Dudley Campbell	508	8	6	2	2	4	3	0	12	5	2	0	0	0	10	10	12	0	0
Kris Commons	1040	20	11	2	9	9	3	5	21	16	35	35	0	0	8	27	4	1	0
Ryan Connolley	3	1	0	0	1	0	0	0	0	0	0	0	0	0	0	0	0	0	0
Paul Connolly	1755	21	17	16	4	1	0	0	0	3	13	100	18	6	24	13	0	5	0
Lee Croft	1314	19	14	3	5	11	1	2	8	4	44	73	1	0	11	22	7	3	0
Tomasz Cywka	365	5	4	2	1	2	0	1	4	6	2	3	1	1	3	9	2	0	0
Steve Davies	683	18	7	0	11	7	1	1	9	11	3	15	0	0	11	9	5	2	0
Paul Dickov	949	16	10	1	6	9	2	3	5	12	7	22	0	0	25	23	22	3	0
Paul Green	2807	33	30	24	3	6	2	0	12	14	18	100	10	5	14	52	8	1	0
Lee Hendrie	415	9	4	0	5	4	0	3	4	3	8	2	1	1	2	10	0	0	0
Bryan Hughes	260	3	3	2	0	1	0	0	2	1	3	3	4	0	2	1	0	0	0
Rob Hulse	2996	37	30	20	7	10	12	2	46	34	6	70	13	0	74	56	49	5	0
Nicky Hunt	1854	21	20	15	1	5	0	0	1	2	39	71	19	4	16	16	0	6	0
Lee Johnson	331	4	4	2	0	2	0	0	2	0	6	4	0	1	2	1	0	0	0
Dean Leacock	1150	17	13	8	4	5	0	0	0	1	4	21	18	6	16	4	1	5	0
Jake Livermore	1051	16	11	5	5	6	1	0	7	3	9	62	4	1	14	13	1	2	0
Dave Martin	321	11	2	1	9	1	0	0	3	1	4	14	0	0	2	2	0	0	0
James McEveley	2644	33	28	23	5	3	2	3	5	8	51	101	23	15	30	19	2	5	2
Arnaud Mendy	4	1	0	0	1	0	0	0	0	0	0	0	0	0	0	0	0	0	0
Greg Mills	25	2	0	0	2	0	0	0	0	1	2	0	0	0	0	0	0	0	0
Dean Moxey	2648	30	27	25	3	1	0	0	3	5	41	121	19	9	23	30	0	7	1
Stephen Pearson	3304	37	34	29	3	4	1	1	7	13	26	101	15	3	25	28	1	7	1
Chris Porter	1148	21	11	5	10	6	4	0	13	11	1	15	0	0	13	24	20	1	0
Ben Pringle	146	5	1	1	4	0	0	1	1	0	1	13	1	0	2	2	1	1	0
Robbie Savage	4230	46	45	38	1	7	2	3	15	7	55	206	23	10	50	64	1	8	0
Fredrik Stoor	907	11	10	6	1	4	0	0	0	1	11	24	3	1	5	8	0	2	0
Gilles Sunu	556	9	6	0	3	7	1	0	2	2	4	11	0	0	1	15	5	0	0
Gary Teale	2184	28	21	19	7	2	2	4	14	18	74	73	1	0	14	22	8	1	0
Michael Tonge	1690	18	18	15	0	3	2	2	15	11	41	25	3	2	10	15	1	1	0
Luke Varney	13	1	0	0	1	0	0	0	0	1	0	0	0	0	0	0	0	0	0
James Vaughan	166	2	2	1	0	1	0	0	2	3	0	5	0	0	4	1	3	0	0
Javan Vidal	14	1	0	0	1	0	0	0	0	0	0	0	0	0	0	0	0	0	0

SEASON TOTALS

Goals scored	53
Goals conceded	63
Clean sheets	16
Shots on target	235
Shots off target	219
Shots per goal	8.57
Pens awarded	5
Pens scored	4
Pens conceded	7
Offsides	154
Corners	282
Crosses	513
Players used	40
Fouls committed	514
Free-kicks won	574

CARDS RECEIVED

77   5

SEQUENCES

Wins	2
(on two occasions)	
Losses	4
(29/08/09–19/09/09)	
Draws	3
(16/03/10–23/03/10)	
Undefeated	5
(16/03/10–03/04/10)	
Without win	5
(10/03/10–23/03/10)	
Undefeated home	3
(on three occasions)	
Undefeated away	4
(on two occasions)	
Without scoring	3
(19/12/09–28/12/09)	
Without conceding	2
(on three occasions)	
Scoring	5
(27/02/10–16/03/10)	
Conceding	7
(20/10/09–05/12/09)	

League position at the end of each month

AUG	SEP	OCT	NOV	DEC	JAN	FEB	MAR	APR	MAY
11	20	20	16	18	18	16	17	17	14

SEASON INFORMATION
Highest position: 2
Lowest position: 21
Average goals scored per game: 1.15
Average goals conceded per game: 1.37

MATCH RECORDS

Goals scored per match

		W	D	L	Pts
Failed to score	15	0	6	9	6
Scored 1 goal	15	5	3	7	18
Scored 2 goals	12	6	2	4	20
Scored 3 goals	3	3	0	0	9
Scored 4+ goals	1	1	0	0	3

Goals conceded per match

		W	D	L	Pts
Clean sheet	16	10	6	0	36
Conceded 1 goal	13	4	3	6	15
Conceded 2 goals	7	0	2	5	2
Conceded 3 goals	6	1	0	5	3
Conceded 4+ goals	4	0	0	4	0

EARLIEST STRIKE

MILES ADDISON
(v Peterborough) 4:00

LATEST STRIKE

SHAUN BARKER
(v Barnsley) 95:16

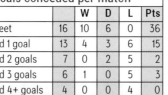

Shaun Barker

GOAL DETAILS

How the goals were struck

SCORED		CONCEDED
25	Right foot	42
12	Left foot	14
14	Header	7
2	Other	0

How the goals were struck

SCORED		CONCEDED
31	Open play	45
4	Cross	4
4	Corner	1
4	Penalty	6
1	Direct from free-kick	2
5	Free-kick	4
4	Own goal	1

Distance from goal

SCORED		CONCEDED
19	6YDS	15
26	18YDS	44
8	18+YDS	4

GOALS SCORED/CONCEDED
PER FIVE-MINUTE INTERVALS

MINS	5	10	15	20	25	30	35	40	45	50	55	60	65	70	75	80	85	90
FOR	1	2	1	5	1	1	1	3	2	6	1	4	6	3	4	4	2	6
AGN	4	3	3	2	2	1	1	4	4	1	1	5	3	5	1	5	8	10

DONCASTER ROVERS

CLUB SUMMARY

FORMED	1879
MANAGER	Sean O'Driscoll
GROUND	Keepmoat Stadium
CAPACITY	15,000
NICKNAME	Rovers
WEBSITE	www.doncasterroversfc.co.uk

The New Football Pools PLAYER OF THE SEASON — Billy Sharp

OVERALL
P	W	D	L	F	A	GD
50	17	15	18	62	64	-2

COCA-COLA CHAMPIONSHIP
Pos	P	W	D	L	F	A	GD	Pts
12	46	15	15	16	59	58	1	60

HOME
Pos	P	W	D	L	F	A	GD	Pts
17	23	9	7	7	32	29	3	34

AWAY
Pos	P	W	D	L	F	A	GD	Pts
8	23	6	8	9	27	29	-2	26

CUP PROGRESS DETAILS
Competition	Round reached	Knocked out by
FA Cup	R4	Derby
Carling Cup	R2	Tottenham

BIGGEST WIN (ALL COMPS)
06/03/10 5–2 v Bristol City

BIGGEST DEFEAT (ALL COMPS)
26/08/09 1–5 v Tottenham

THE PLAYER WITH THE MOST
GOALS SCORED Billy Sharp	**15**
SHOTS ON TARGET Billy Sharp	**52**
SHOTS OFF TARGET Billy Sharp	**29**
SHOTS WITHOUT SCORING Mark Wilson	**35**
ASSISTS John Oster, Billy Sharp	**6**
OFFSIDES Billy Sharp	**60**
FOULS James Chambers	**48**
FOULS WITHOUT A CARD Jay Emmanuel-Thomas	**14**
FREE-KICKS WON James Hayter	**50**
DEFENSIVE CLEARANCES James O'Connor	**51**

actim INDEX — FOR THE 2009/10 COCA-COLA CHAMPIONSHIP SEASON

RANK	PLAYER	PTS
42	Billy Sharp	497
43	James Coppinger	493
51	Neil Sullivan	480

ATTENDANCE RECORD
HIGH	AVERAGE	LOW
14,850	10,992	8,827
v Newcastle (23/03/2010)		v Reading (06/02/2010)

DONCASTER ended the season in 12th place as the club recorded its highest Football League finish in more than 50 years. Furthermore, they did so in style as Sean O'Driscoll's side continued to win admirers with their attractive passing game.

Rovers were one of the surprise packages of the 2008/09 Coca-Cola Championship season, but proved that was no fluke with an even better campaign. Their continued success is funded by one of the smallest budgets in the division, and it was no suprise that Barclays Premier League side Burnley considered O'Driscoll when looking for a new boss in January.

At Easter, briefly, there were hopes among some fans that Rovers were about to launch a play-off challenge and their eventual disappointment at not making the top six merely underlines the meteoric rise of a club that only won promotion from the Football Conference in 2003.

O'Driscoll had been concerned in August that the summer departures of midfielder Richie Wellens and central defender Matt Mills would seriously weaken his team, but he drafted in loanees Jason Shackell from Wolves and striker Billy Sharp from Sheffield United. Shackell proved a rock at the heart of the defence until a groin injury curtailed his season, while leading scorer Sharp went on to score 16 goals and win the players' player of the year award as well as becoming a fans' favourite.

Former Everton and Sunderland midfielder John Oster arrived on a free transfer and helped fill the gap left by Wellens, while O'Driscoll later boosted his

Rovers combined style with success as they enjoyed their best season in years

squad with Shelton Martis, in his second spell at the club, and Arsenal teenager Jay Emmanuel-Thomas. Each new addition made a telling contribution to Rovers' season, while the likes of James Coppinger, Brian Stock, Martin Woods, Mark Wilson and Dean Shiels also continued to blossom.

Chairman John Ryan, who has overseen the club's rise from the Conference during his 12-year tenure, labelled O'Driscoll's side 'the best in Doncaster's history, bar none' after their 2–0 home win over QPR in November, but he is also aware they should not rest on their laurels. Ryan believes Rovers have reached an important crossroads in their development and told fans that, in order to push on, the club needs bigger home crowds. Despite their lofty position, rarely did more than 10,000 fans turn out at the Keepmoat Stadium during the 2009/10 season and, if Rovers want to launch a serious play-off challenge in 2010/11, Ryan argues season-ticket sales must increase to fund a bigger budget for playing staff.

Billy Sharp heads home the winner against Sheffield Wednesday in December

RESULTS 2009/10

AUGUST
8th	● Watford	A	D 1–1	**Att:** 15,636	**Ref:** N Swarbrick	**Scorers:** Hayter.
11th	◐ Notts County	A	W 0–1	**Att:** 4,893	**Ref:** K Evans	**Scorers:** Coppinger.
15th	● Preston	H	D 1–1	**Att:** 10,070	**Ref:** M Russell	**Scorers:** Lockwood.
18th	● Coventry	H	D 0–0	**Att:** 9,484	**Ref:** C Boyeson	**Booked:** Coppinger.
22nd	● Middlesbrough	A	L 2–0	**Att:** 22,041	**Ref:** G Salisbury	**Booked:** Sullivan.
26th	◐ Tottenham	H	L 1–5	**Att:** 12,923	**Ref:** R Booth	**Scorers:** Woods.
29th	● Cardiff	H	W 2–0	**Att:** 9,742	**Ref:** E Ilderton	**Scorers:** Hayter, Lockwood.

SEPTEMBER
12th	● Reading	A	D 0–0	**Att:** 15,697	**Ref:** P Gibbs	**Booked:** Woods, Stock, Chambers.
15th	● West Brom	A	L 3–1	**Att:** 22,184	**Ref:** K Wright	**Scorers:** Fairhurst.
19th	● Ipswich	H	D 3–3	**Att:** 10,711	**Ref:** N Miller	**Scorers:** Fairhurst, Fortune, Woods.
26th	● Scunthorpe	A	D 2–2	**Att:** 7,945	**Ref:** K Stroud	**Scorers:** Sharp, Woods. **Booked:** Oster, Sharp, Woods. **Dismissed:** Oster, Fortune.
29th	● Swansea	H	D 0–0	**Att:** 8,833	**Ref:** A Haines	

OCTOBER
3rd	● Sheff Utd	A	D 1–1	**Att:** 26,211	**Ref:** L Probert	**Scorers:** Hayter. **Booked:** Roberts.
17th	● Barnsley	H	L 0–1	**Att:** 12,708	**Ref:** G Salisbury	
20th	● Peterborough	H	W 3–1	**Att:** 9,288	**Ref:** C Webster	**Scorers:** Shackell, Sharp, Shiels.
24th	● Newcastle	A	L 2–1	**Att:** 43,949	**Ref:** D Deadman	**Scorers:** Shiels. **Booked:** Shiels, O'Connor, Chambers, Sharp.
31st	● Blackpool	H	D 3–3	**Att:** 10,312	**Ref:** M Oliver	**Scorers:** Sharp[2], Woods. **Booked:** Woods, Chambers.

NOVEMBER
7th	● Plymouth	A	L 2–1	**Att:** 9,420	**Ref:** P Taylor	**Scorers:** Shiels. **Booked:** Woods. **Dismissed:** Woods.
21st	● QPR	H	W 2–0	**Att:** 10,821	**Ref:** T Bates	**Scorers:** Sharp, Shiels.
28th	● Nottm Forest	A	L 4–1	**Att:** 22,035	**Ref:** S Mathieson	**Scorers:** Sharp.

DECEMBER
5th	● Crystal Palace	A	W 0–3	**Att:** 13,985	**Ref:** P Miller	**Scorers:** Hayter, Sharp, Woods.
8th	● Sheff Wed	H	W 1–0	**Att:** 12,825	**Ref:** A Wiley	**Scorers:** Sharp. **Booked:** Shackell, O'Connor, Chambers.
12th	● Bristol City	H	W 1–0	**Att:** 9,572	**Ref:** J Singh	**Scorers:** Sharp. **Booked:** Gillett.
19th	● Derby	A	W 0–2	**Att:** 28,734	**Ref:** T Kettle	**Scorers:** Coppinger, Sharp. **Booked:** Roberts.
26th	● Coventry	A	L 1–0	**Att:** 19,221	**Ref:** R Shoebridge	

JANUARY
16th	● Watford	H	W 2–1	**Att:** 10,504	**Ref:** A Hall	**Scorers:** Roberts, Shiels. **Booked:** Wilson.
19th	● Brentford	A	W 0–1	**Att:** 2,883	**Ref:** G Hegley	**Scorers:** O'Connor.
23rd	● Derby	A	L 1–0	**Att:** 11,316	**Ref:** C Webster	
26th	● Middlesbrough	H	L 1–4	**Att:** 10,794	**Ref:** S Tanner	**Scorers:** Mutch. **Booked:** O'Connor.
30th	● Cardiff	A	L 2–1	**Att:** 19,730	**Ref:** G Scott	**Scorers:** Roberts. **Booked:** Shiels, Stock, Chambers.

FEBRUARY
6th	● Reading	H	L 1–2	**Att:** 8,827	**Ref:** K Stroud	**Scorers:** Sharp. **Booked:** Sharp.
9th	● Leicester	A	D 0–0	**Att:** 18,928	**Ref:** R Booth	**Booked:** Sharp.
13th	● Nottm Forest	H	W 1–0	**Att:** 12,768	**Ref:** A Penn	**Scorers:** Sharp. **Booked:** Chambers.
16th	● Sheff Wed	A	W 0–2	**Att:** 22,252	**Ref:** E Ilderton	**Scorers:** Ward, O'Connor OG.
20th	● QPR	A	L 2–1	**Att:** 11,178	**Ref:** D Whitestone	**Scorers:** Hayter.
23rd	● Leicester	H	L 0–1	**Att:** 11,027	**Ref:** A Woolmer	
27th	● Crystal Palace	H	D 1–1	**Att:** 9,779	**Ref:** N Swarbrick	**Scorers:** Coppinger. **Booked:** Ward.

MARCH
6th	● Bristol City	A	W 2–5	**Att:** 13,401	**Ref:** D Phillips	**Scorers:** Emmanuel-Thomas[2], Sharp[2], Orr OG.
9th	● Preston	A	D 1–1	**Att:** 11,942	**Ref:** P Crossley	**Scorers:** Hayter. **Booked:** Chambers, Wilson.
13th	● Derby	H	W 2–1	**Att:** 11,858	**Ref:** S Hooper	**Scorers:** Emmanuel-Thomas, Sharp. **Booked:** Sharp.
16th	● Peterborough	A	W 1–2	**Att:** 6,773	**Ref:** F Graham	**Scorers:** Oster, Roberts.
20th	● Sheff Utd	H	D 1–1	**Att:** 13,026	**Ref:** J Moss	**Scorers:** Hayter. **Booked:** Mutch.
23rd	● Newcastle	H	L 0–1	**Att:** 14,850	**Ref:** K Hill	
27th	● Barnsley	A	W 0–1	**Att:** 14,188	**Ref:** D Deadman	**Scorers:** Coppinger. **Booked:** Sharp, Oster.

APRIL
3rd	● Plymouth	H	L 1–2	**Att:** 10,179	**Ref:** K Wright	**Scorers:** Coppinger.
5th	● Blackpool	A	L 2–0	**Att:** 9,701	**Ref:** D Webb	**Booked:** Heffernan, Hayter.
10th	● West Brom	H	L 2–3	**Att:** 12,708	**Ref:** J Linington	**Scorers:** Emmanuel-Thomas, Hayter. **Booked:** Martis. West Brom are promoted.
17th	● Ipswich	A	D 1–1	**Att:** 19,943	**Ref:** A Penn	**Scorers:** Shiels.
24th	● Scunthorpe	H	W 4–3	**Att:** 12,124	**Ref:** A D'Urso	**Scorers:** Emmanuel-Thomas, Hayter, Martis, Mutch. **Booked:** Stock, Martis.

MAY
2nd	● Swansea	A	D 0–0	**Att:** 17,630	**Ref:** G Hegley	**Booked:** Mutch, Shiels.

● Coca-Cola Championship/Play-offs ● FA Cup ◐ Carling Cup

DONCASTER ROVERS

CHAMPIONSHIP GOALKEEPER STATS

Player	Minutes on pitch	Appearances	Match starts	Completed matches	Sub appearances	Subbed off	Saved with feet	Punched	Parried	Tipped over	Fumbled	Tipped round	Caught	Blocked	Clean sheets	Goals conceded	Save %	Saved	Resulting in goals	Opposition miss	Fouls committed	Free-kicks won	Yellow cards	Red cards
Benjamin Smith	110	2	1	1	1	0	0	2	0	0	0	0	3	0	1	4	55.56	0	0	0	0	0	0	0
Neil Sullivan	4308	45	45	44	0	1	2	16	15	8	2	11	143	3	13	54	78.57	0	3	1	2	8	1	0

CHAMPIONSHIP OUTFIELD PLAYER STATS

Player	Minutes on pitch	Appearances	Match starts	Completed matches	Substitute appearances	Subbed off	Goals scored	Assists	Shots on target	Shots off target	Crosses	Tackles made	Defensive clearances	Defensive blocks	Fouls committed	Free-kicks won	Caught offside	Yellow cards	Red cards
James Chambers	4089	43	43	40	0	3	0	2	5	3	27	132	38	8	48	40	2	7	0
James Coppinger	3475	39	38	21	1	17	4	3	44	19	68	52	13	1	27	47	11	1	0
Mustapha Dumbuya	36	3	0	0	3	0	0	0	0	0	1	7	0	0	1	0	0	0	0
Jay Emmanuel-Thomas	1105	14	12	6	2	6	3	5	22	12	14	9	3	0	14	7	11	0	0
Waide Fairhurst	216	6	2	1	4	1	2	0	2	0	0	1	0	0	2	4	2	0	0
Quinton Fortune	305	6	3	1	3	1	1	1	2	0	2	10	3	1	6	3	1	0	1
Simon Gillett	933	11	10	6	1	4	0	1	1	3	6	10	3	0	9	5	0	1	0
Lewis Guy	242	13	1	1	12	0	0	0	2	0	1	1	0	0	2	2	1	0	0
James Hayter	2883	38	29	24	9	5	9	3	21	27	10	47	5	5	31	50	12	1	0
Paul Heffernan	694	17	6	2	11	4	0	0	9	6	5	8	0	0	7	5	10	1	0
Sam Hird	2279	36	21	19	15	2	0	0	0	3	1	63	18	6	7	11	1	0	0
Adam Lockwood	1029	16	10	10	6	0	2	0	3	2	1	54	24	1	7	12	0	0	0
Shelton Martis	1193	14	13	10	1	3	0	0	1	1	2	34	16	5	11	4	0	2	0
Sean McDaid	11	1	0	0	1	0	0	1	0	0	0	0	0	0	0	0	0	0	0
Jordon Mutch	528	17	5	1	12	4	2	0	5	7	3	17	1	0	8	6	1	2	0
James O'Connor	3269	38	33	33	5	0	0	3		3	9	74	51	18	18	21	0	3	0
John Oster	3327	40	36	19	4	16	1	6	17	26	52	76	10	2	17	23	7	2	1
Gareth Roberts	3764	42	40	32	2	8	3	3	10	7	51	115	19	8	15	27	2	2	0
Jason Shackell	1836	21	20	18	1	2	1	0	1	4	4	66	41	8	15	24	1	1	0
Billy Sharp	3015	33	32	23	1	9	15	6	52	29	17	32	3	1	42	41	60	6	0
Dean Shiels	2281	38	25	7	13	18	6	2	28	26	25	46	0	0	19	33	9	3	0
John Spicer	861	20	9	2	11	7	0	0	2	5	3	36	4	1	7	8	0	1	0
Brian Stock	1358	15	15	10	0	5	0	1	14	17	21	30	5	1	23	24	0	3	0
Elliott Ward	576	6	6	6	0	0	1	0	2	1	0	12	15	4	5	5	2	1	0
Byron Webster	144	5	1	1	4	0	0	0	0	0	0	1	2	0	3	0	0	0	0
Mark Wilson	2689	35	29	18	6	11	0	1	21	14	12	61	8	2	29	23	0	2	0
Martin Woods	1914	24	21	15	3	5	4	5	25	21	44	33	6	5	32	27	1	4	1

actim ⊞

SEASON TOTALS

Goals scored	59
Goals conceded	58
Clean sheets	14
Shots on target	289
Shots off target	236
Shots per goal	8.90
Pens awarded	6
Pens scored	4
Pens conceded	4
Offsides	134
Corners	253
Crosses	379
Players used	29
Fouls committed	407
Free-kicks won	460

CARDS RECEIVED

43 **3**

SEQUENCES

Wins	4
(05/12/09–19/12/09)	
Losses	3
(on two occasions)	
Draws	4
(19/09/09–03/10/09)	
Undefeated	6
(27/02/10–20/03/10)	
Without win	7
(12/09/09–17/10/09)	
Undefeated home	6
(20/10/09–16/01/10)	
Undefeated away	4
(06/03/10–27/03/10)	
Without scoring	2
(18/08/09–22/08/09)	
Without conceding	4
(05/12/09–19/12/09)	
Scoring	10
(20/10/09–19/12/09)	
Conceding	9
(20/02/10–23/03/10)	

LEAGUE POSITION AT THE END OF EACH MONTH

	AUG	SEP	OCT	NOV	DEC	JAN	FEB	MAR	APR	MAY
	14	18	19	18	14	13	14	8	12	12

SEASON INFORMATION
Highest position: 7
Lowest position: 20
Average goals scored per game: 1.28
Average goals conceded per game: 1.26

MATCH RECORDS

Goals scored per match

		W	D	L	Pts
Failed to score	11	0	5	6	5
Scored 1 goal	20	4	7	9	19
Scored 2 goals	9	7	1	1	22
Scored 3 goals	4	2	2	0	8
Scored 4+ goals	2	2	0	0	6

Goals conceded per match

		W	D	L	Pts
Clean sheet	14	9	5	0	32
Conceded 1 goal	15	4	7	4	19
Conceded 2 goals	10	1	1	8	4
Conceded 3 goals	5	1	2	2	5
Conceded 4+ goals	2	0	0	2	0

EARLIEST STRIKE
JAY EMMANUEL-THOMAS
(v Bristol City) 1:34

LATEST STRIKE
JAMES COPPINGER
(v Derby) 93:08

Neil Sullivan

GOAL DETAILS

How the goals were struck

SCORED		CONCEDED
34	Right foot	27
15	Left foot	17
9	Header	13
1	Other	1

How the goals were struck

SCORED		CONCEDED
33	Open play	36
9	Cross	5
8	Corner	7
4	Penalty	3
0	Direct from free-kick	2
3	Free-kick	4
2	Own goal	1

Distance from goal

SCORED		CONCEDED
19	6YDS	23
32	18YDS	31
8	18+YDS	4

GOALS SCORED/CONCEDED
PER FIVE-MINUTE INTERVALS

MINS	5	10	15	20	25	30	35	40	45	50	55	60	65	70	75	80	85	90
FOR	3	1	6	3	3	2	3	3	4	3	2	2	6	2	1	3	8	4
AGN	0	2	2	4	2	5	2	1	3	0	2	2	3	6	7	7	3	7

IPSWICH TOWN

CLUB SUMMARY

FORMED	1878
MANAGER	Roy Keane
GROUND	Portman Road
CAPACITY	30,311
NICKNAME	The Tractor Boys
WEBSITE	www.itfc.co.uk

The New Football Pools PLAYER OF THE SEASON — Grant Leadbitter

OVERALL
P	W	D	L	F	A	GD
50	13	21	16	57	69	-12

COCA-COLA CHAMPIONSHIP
Pos	P	W	D	L	F	A	GD	Pts
15	46	12	20	14	50	61	-11	56

HOME
Pos	P	W	D	L	F	A	GD	Pts
16	23	8	11	4	24	23	1	35

AWAY
Pos	P	W	D	L	F	A	GD	Pts
16	23	4	9	10	26	38	-12	21

CUP PROGRESS DETAILS
Competition	Round reached	Knocked out by
FA Cup	R4	Southampton
Carling Cup	R2	Peterborough

BIGGEST WIN (ALL COMPS)
28/12/09 3–0 v QPR

BIGGEST DEFEAT (ALL COMPS)
26/09/09 0–4 v Newcastle

THE PLAYER WITH THE MOST
GOALS SCORED Jonathan Walters	**8**
SHOTS ON TARGET Grant Leadbitter	**49**
SHOTS OFF TARGET Jonathan Walters	**41**
SHOTS WITHOUT SCORING Damien Delaney	**20**
ASSISTS Grant Leadbitter	**8**
OFFSIDES Jonathan Walters	**31**
FOULS Jonathan Walters	**51**
FOULS WITHOUT A CARD Liam Trotter	**19**
FREE-KICKS WON Jonathan Walters	**48**
DEFENSIVE CLEARANCES Gareth McAuley	**109**

actim INDEX FOR THE 2009/10 COCA-COLA CHAMPIONSHIP SEASON

RANK	PLAYER	PTS
56	Jonathan Walters	473
69	Gareth McAuley	453
126	Damien Delaney	382

ATTENDANCE RECORD
HIGH	AVERAGE	LOW
27,059	20,841	19,283
v Newcastle (26/09/2009)		v Watford (20/10/2009)

Ipswich failed to mount a promotion push in a poor first year under Roy Keane

EXPECTATIONS were high at Portman Road as Roy Keane prepared for his first full season in charge of a side expected to be in the mix for promotion from the Coca-Cola Championship. With Town desperate to return to the top flight, the former Manchester United captain splashed the cash to bring in Tamas Priskin, Lee Martin, Colin Healy, Grant Leadbitter, Carlos Edwards and Damien Delaney while Liam Rosenior and Jack Colback arrived on loan.

However, defeat at Coventry on the opening weekend of the season was to prove a familiar feeling as Keane was forced to wait until the final day of October to savour his first win of the Championship campaign. Relegation remained a distinct possibility as late as January but a settled back four helped Town to pick up results and the arrival of two Murphys in March eventually led them to a mid-table finish. Daryl was signed on-loan from Keane's former club Sunderland and scored in his first three appearances while goalkeeper Brian looked an assured presence between the posts following his arrival from Bohemians.

Keane's side eventually finished in 15th place – some 14 points shy of the top six – and their troubles were not difficult to identify. The Tractor Boys drew a

Jonathan Stead enjoys one of his two goals in a 3–0 win against QPR

Roy Keane can't hide his frustration during a tough season at Ipswich

remarkable 20 games in the League and captain Jon Walters finished as top scorer with just eight goals to his name. Keane also gave more than 20 players a debut and will hope to find a consistent first XI if Ipswich are to challenge in 2010/11.

One major plus through the course of the season was the emergence of teenage striker Connor Wickham. The youngster was barely 16 when he scored twice in the Carling Cup game at Shrewsbury in August, and showed his confidence by scoring in the penalty shoot-out as Ipswich prevailed.

However, Wickham really found his feet after he signed a professional contract towards the end of the season. He scored three times in the final four games of the campaign, including a stunning finish at Newcastle, to suggest he has what it takes to lead the line full-time at Portman Road.

Keane plans to recruit heavily again over the summer and has no doubt what he needs. Last summer's purchases proved a mixed bag, with Priskin and Healy ending the season out on loan, but the former Republic of Ireland midfielder has revealed he wants players with leadership qualities to add to his young charges.

He said: 'I'll be bringing in characters. Forget stats, ages, the country they're from or what size boot they wear. It's all about characters.'

RESULTS 2009/10

AUGUST

9th	● Coventry	A	L 2–1	**Att:** 16,279	**Ref:** R Booth	**Scorers:** Walters.
11th	● Shrewsbury	A	D 3–3	**Att:** 4,184	**Ref:** M Russell	**Scorers:** Quinn, Wickham[2]. AET – Score after 90 mins 3–3. Ipswich win 4–2 on penalties.
15th	● Leicester	H	D 0–0	**Att:** 22,454	**Ref:** P Crossley	**Booked:** McAuley.
18th	● Crystal Palace	H	L 1–3	**Att:** 20,348	**Ref:** K Hill	**Scorers:** Bruce.
22nd	● West Brom	A	L 2–0	**Att:** 19,390	**Ref:** S Tanner	
25th	● Peterborough	A	L 2–1	**Att:** 5,451	**Ref:** R Shoebridge	**Scorers:** Priskin. **Booked:** Balkestein, Bruce.
29th	● Preston	H	D 1–1	**Att:** 19,454	**Ref:** P Taylor	**Scorers:** Walters. **Booked:** Walters, Smith.

SEPTEMBER

12th	● Middlesbrough	A	L 3–1	**Att:** 19,742	**Ref:** K Friend	**Scorers:** Walters. **Booked:** Leadbitter, Delaney, Colback, Bruce, Martin.
15th	● Nottm Forest	H	D 1–1	**Att:** 21,130	**Ref:** G Ward	**Scorers:** Leadbitter. **Booked:** Martin, Leadbitter, Colback. **Dismissed:** McAuley.
19th	● Doncaster	A	D 3–3	**Att:** 10,711	**Ref:** N Miller	**Scorers:** Colback, Martin, Priskin.
26th	● Newcastle	H	L 0–4	**Att:** 27,059	**Ref:** M Jones	**Booked:** Bruce, Walters.
29th	● Sheff Utd	A	D 3–3	**Att:** 28,366	**Ref:** E Ilderton	**Scorers:** Leadbitter, McAuley, Walters. **Booked:** Priskin.

OCTOBER

3rd	● Barnsley	A	L 2–1	**Att:** 12,224	**Ref:** P Gibbs	**Scorers:** Rosenior. **Booked:** Priskin, Leadbitter, Peters.
17th	● Swansea	H	D 1–1	**Att:** 19,667	**Ref:** K Wright	**Scorers:** Counago.
20th	● Watford	H	D 1–1	**Att:** 19,283	**Ref:** T Kettle	**Scorers:** McAuley. **Booked:** Counago, Leadbitter.
24th	● Plymouth	A	D 1–1	**Att:** 10,875	**Ref:** S Hooper	**Scorers:** Stead. **Booked:** McAuley.
31st	● Derby	H	W 1–0	**Att:** 20,299	**Ref:** A Taylor	**Scorers:** D Wright. **Booked:** Walters.

NOVEMBER

7th	● Reading	A	D 1–1	**Att:** 19,053	**Ref:** D Whitestone	**Scorers:** Stead.
21st	● Sheff Wed	H	D 0–0	**Att:** 19,636	**Ref:** A D'Urso	
29th	● Cardiff	A	W 1–2	**Att:** 19,463	**Ref:** J Singh	**Scorers:** Stead, Walters. **Booked:** John, Delaney, Garvan.

DECEMBER

5th	● Bristol City	A	D 0–0	**Att:** 14,287	**Ref:** T Bates	**Booked:** Walters.
8th	● Peterborough	H	D 0–0	**Att:** 19,975	**Ref:** A Hall	
12th	● Blackpool	H	W 3–1	**Att:** 19,831	**Ref:** P Crossley	**Scorers:** Colback, McAuley, Stead. **Booked:** Leadbitter, Walters.
26th	● Crystal Palace	A	L 3–1	**Att:** 16,496	**Ref:** P Taylor	**Scorers:** Peters. **Booked:** Colback. **Dismissed:** Stead.
28th	● QPR	H	W 3–0	**Att:** 25,349	**Ref:** S Tanner	**Scorers:** Stead[2], Walters.

JANUARY

2nd	● Blackpool	A	W 1–2	**Att:** 7,332	**Ref:** E Ilderton	**Scorers:** Colback, Garvan. **Booked:** Lee-Barrett, Wickham.
10th	● Leicester	A	D 1–1	**Att:** 20,758	**Ref:** M Haywood	**Scorers:** McGivern OG. **Booked:** Bruce.
16th	● Coventry	H	W 3–2	**Att:** 20,135	**Ref:** M Oliver	**Scorers:** Colback, Counago, John. **Booked:** Walters, Rosenior.
23rd	● Southampton	A	L 2–1	**Att:** 20,446	**Ref:** A Hall	**Scorers:** Counago. **Booked:** Counago, Leadbitter.
26th	● West Brom	H	D 1–1	**Att:** 19,574	**Ref:** S Attwell	**Scorers:** Leadbitter. **Booked:** Lee-Barrett, Leadbitter.
30th	● Preston	A	L 2–0	**Att:** 12,087	**Ref:** J Moss	**Booked:** McAuley, Leadbitter, Garvan, Rosenior, Norris.

FEBRUARY

6th	● Middlesbrough	H	D 1–1	**Att:** 21,243	**Ref:** K Hill	**Scorers:** D Murphy. **Booked:** Norris.
9th	● QPR	A	W 1–2	**Att:** 10,940	**Ref:** F Graham	**Scorers:** D Murphy, Norris. **Booked:** Norris, Walters.
16th	● Peterborough	A	L 3–1	**Att:** 9,428	**Ref:** J Linington	**Scorers:** D Murphy. **Booked:** Norris, Delaney.
20th	● Sheff Wed	A	W 0–1	**Att:** 21,641	**Ref:** M Russell	**Scorers:** Edwards.
23rd	● Scunthorpe	A	D 1–1	**Att:** 5,828	**Ref:** A Haines	**Scorers:** D Healy. **Booked:** D Wright, Wickham, Leadbitter.
27th	● Bristol City	H	D 0–0	**Att:** 20,302	**Ref:** N Miller	**Booked:** Wickham.

MARCH

6th	● Blackpool	A	L 1–0	**Att:** 8,635	**Ref:** R Shoebridge	**Booked:** Rosenior, Leadbitter.
9th	● Cardiff	H	W 2–0	**Att:** 19,997	**Ref:** G Hegley	**Scorers:** D Murphy[2]. **Booked:** Delaney, Norris.
13th	● Scunthorpe	H	W 1–0	**Att:** 19,378	**Ref:** P Miller	**Scorers:** Wickham. **Booked:** Colback. **Dismissed:** Delaney.
16th	● Watford	A	L 2–1	**Att:** 13,996	**Ref:** G Salisbury	**Scorers:** Colback.
20th	● Barnsley	H	W 1–0	**Att:** 20,558	**Ref:** N Swarbrick	**Scorers:** D Murphy. **Booked:** Colback, Counago, Norris.
23rd	● Plymouth	H	L 0–2	**Att:** 19,316	**Ref:** D Whitestone	
27th	● Swansea	A	D 0–0	**Att:** 14,902	**Ref:** C Pawson	

APRIL

3rd	● Reading	H	W 2–1	**Att:** 21,403	**Ref:** K Stroud	**Scorers:** McAuley, Walters. **Booked:** Norris, Walters, D Wright.
5th	● Derby	A	W 1–3	**Att:** 28,137	**Ref:** J Moss	**Scorers:** Edwards, McAuley, Wickham. **Booked:** Colback, McAuley, B Murphy.
10th	● Nottm Forest	A	L 3–0	**Att:** 23,459	**Ref:** D Foster	**Booked:** Leadbitter.
17th	● Doncaster	H	D 1–1	**Att:** 19,943	**Ref:** A Penn	**Scorers:** Wickham. **Booked:** Wickham.
24th	● Newcastle	A	D 2–2	**Att:** 52,181	**Ref:** C Boyeson	**Scorers:** Walters, Wickham. **Booked:** D Wright, Norris.

MAY

2nd	● Sheff Utd	H	L 0–3	**Att:** 23,003	**Ref:** A D'Urso	**Booked:** Eastman. **Dismissed:** Eastman.

● Coca-Cola Championship/Play-offs ● FA Cup ● Carling Cup

IPSWICH TOWN

CHAMPIONSHIP GOALKEEPER STATS

Player	Minutes on pitch	Appearances	Match starts	Completed matches	Sub appearances	Subbed off	Saves Breakdown: Saved with feet	Punched	Parried	Tipped over	Fumbled	Tipped round	Caught	Blocked	Clean sheets	Goals conceded	Save %	Penalties: Saved	Resulting in goals	Opposition miss	Fouls committed	Free-kicks won	Yellow cards	Red cards
Asmir Begovic	576	6	6	6	0	0	1	6	3	3	0	1	21	0	2	4	89.74	0	0	0	0	1	0	0
Arran Lee-Barrett	1226	13	12	12	1	0	0	4	3	2	2	4	54	0	3	16	80.72	0	0	0	1	3	1	0
Brian Murphy	1530	16	16	16	0	0	0	7	7	2	1	5	61	0	6	17	82.83	0	2	0	0	1	1	0
Richard Wright	1099	12	12	11	0	1	1	2	11	2	1	8	31	2	1	24	70.37	1	0	1	0	0	0	0

CHAMPIONSHIP OUTFIELD PLAYER STATS

Player	Minutes on pitch	Appearances	Match starts	Completed matches	Substitute appearances	Subbed off	Goals scored	Assists	Shots on target	Shots off target	Crosses	Tackles made	Defensive clearances	Defensive blocks	Fouls committed	Free-kicks won	Caught offside	Yellow cards	Red cards
Pim Balkestein	797	9	8	8	1	0	0	0	5	6	5	10	15	4	8	4	1	0	0
Troy Brown	31	1	0	0	1	0	0	0	1	0	0	1	0	0	0	0	0	0	0
Alex Bruce	1100	13	12	9	1	3	1	0	4	3	18	18	16	6	15	8	0	3	0
Billy Clark	44	3	0	0	3	0	0	0	0	0	0	0	0	0	0	0	0	0	0
Jack Colback	2895	37	29	25	8	4	4	4	15	13	56	74	12	8	41	46	3	6	0
Pablo Counago	1221	27	11	2	16	9	2	1	21	7	2	8	1	1	27	25	14	2	0
Damien Delaney	3337	36	36	32	0	3	0	1	9	11	26	89	64	24	36	26	1	4	1
Tom Eastman	59	1	1	0	0	0	0	0	0	0	0	0	0	0	3	1	0	1	1
Carlos Edwards	1850	28	21	8	7	13	2	2	8	16	67	18	6	4	11	25	0	0	0
Owen Garvan	1407	25	14	7	11	7	0	5	10	6	46	29	10	3	12	16	3	2	0
David Healy	482	12	5	0	7	5	1	1	13	8	4	14	0	2	9	7	10	0	0
Colin Healy	177	3	3	0	0	3	0	0	0	0	0	1	1	0	3	0	0	0	0
Stern John	383	7	5	1	2	4	1	1	3	3	0	3	1	0	5	12	8	1	0
Grant Leadbitter	3475	38	36	34	2	2	3	8	49	32	97	97	19	6	45	33	5	10	0
Lee Martin	877	16	9	4	7	5	1	1	6	13	19	6	3	0	15	13	4	2	0
Gareth McAuley	3818	41	40	38	1	1	5	0	22	18	3	119	109	30	44	30	2	4	1
Daryl Murphy	1389	18	18	4	0	14	6	1	31	12	10	27	2	0	16	9	17	0	0
David Norris	2037	24	24	15	0	9	1	0	19	11	10	75	6	7	43	31	1	8	0
Shane O'Connor	1030	12	11	9	1	2	0	0	0	0	29	20	4	4	6	9	0	0	0
Jaime Peters	2295	32	22	17	10	5	1	2	10	12	36	63	12	10	16	22	0	1	0
Tamas Priskin	856	17	9	2	8	7	1	0	10	6	8	8	1	0	15	18	12	1	0
Alan Quinn	911	19	8	1	11	7	0	0	9	5	13	2	9	4	5	9	1	0	0
Liam Rosenior	2523	29	26	24	3	2	1	2	6	3	84	84	25	15	18	15	1	3	0
Tommy Smith	1149	14	11	10	3	1	0	0	3	6	5	22	11	5	11	9	0	1	0
Jonathan Stead	1159	22	13	3	9	9	6	2	31	14	13	16	5	0	18	22	16	0	1
Liam Trotter	1057	12	11	9	1	2	0	0	6	5	4	10	7	0	19	6	1	0	0
Jonathan Walters	4058	43	43	37	0	6	8	2	47	41	83	56	14	2	51	48	31	8	0
Connor Wickham	1314	26	9	4	17	5	4	1	26	14	17	10	5	0	29	10	19	3	0
David Wright	2396	26	25	22	1	3	1	1	6	4	48	83	22	11	35	18	3	3	0

actim

Coca-Cola CHAMPIONSHIP

SEASON TOTALS

Goals scored	50
Goals conceded	61
Clean sheets	12
Shots on target	370
Shots off target	269
Shots per goal	12.78
Pens awarded	3
Pens scored	2
Pens conceded	4
Offsides	158
Corners	306
Crosses	701
Players used	33
Fouls committed	557
Free-kicks won	477

SEASON INFORMATION

Highest position: 11
Lowest position: 24
Average goals scored per game: 1.09
Average goals conceded per game: 1.33

LEAGUE POSITION AT THE END OF EACH MONTH

23 24 24 22 19 21 17 16 14 15

CARDS RECEIVED

66   4

SEQUENCES

Wins	2
(on two occasions)	
Losses	2
(18/08/09–22/08/09)	
Draws	3
(17/10/09–24/10/09)	
Undefeated	10
(17/10/09–12/12/09)	
Without win	14
(09/08/09–24/10/09)	
Undefeated home	14
(17/10/09–20/03/10)	
Undefeated away	4
(24/10/09–05/12/09)	
Without scoring	2
(on three occasions)	
Without conceding	2
(on two occasions)	
Scoring	7
(29/09/09–07/11/09)	
Conceding	12
(18/08/09–24/10/09)	

MATCH RECORDS

Goals scored per match

		W	D	L	Pts
Failed to score	13	0	6	7	6
Scored 1 goal	22	4	11	7	23
Scored 2 goals	5	4	1	0	13
Scored 3 goals	6	4	2	0	14
Scored 4+ goals	0	0	0	0	0

Goals conceded per match

		W	D	L	Pts
Clean sheet	12	6	6	0	24
Conceded 1 goal	17	5	11	1	26
Conceded 2 goals	8	1	1	6	4
Conceded 3 goals	8	0	2	6	2
Conceded 4+ goals	1	0	0	1	0

EARLIEST STRIKE

DARYL MURPHY
(v Middlesbrough) 0:23

LATEST STRIKE

PABLO COUNAGO
(v Coventry) 96:12

David Norris

GOAL DETAILS

How the goals were struck

SCORED		CONCEDED
23	Right foot	29
16	Left foot	15
11	Header	17
0	Other	0

How the goals were struck

SCORED		CONCEDED
32	Open play	35
7	Cross	11
7	Corner	7
2	Penalty	2
0	Direct from free-kick	3
1	Free-kick	3
1	Own goal	0

Distance from goal

SCORED		CONCEDED
15	6YDS	23
30	18YDS	25
5	18+YDS	13

GOALS SCORED/CONCEDED
PER FIVE-MINUTE INTERVALS

MINS	5	10	15	20	25	30	35	40	45	50	55	60	65	70	75	80	85	90
FOR	8	3	2	2	1	1	1	1	7	0	1	1	2	6	4	3	2	5
AGN	1	6	2	1	2	2	5	3	0	5	2	4	4	5	1	4	7	7

LEICESTER CITY

CLUB SUMMARY

FORMED	1884
MANAGER	Nigel Pearson
GROUND	The Walkers Stadium
CAPACITY	32,500
NICKNAME	The Foxes
WEBSITE	www.lcfc.co.uk

The New Football Pools PLAYER OF THE SEASON — Jack Hobbs

OVERALL
P	W	D	L	F	A	GD
52	24	13	15	71	55	16

COCA-COLA CHAMPIONSHIP
Pos	P	W	D	L	F	A	GD	Pts
5	46	21	13	12	61	45	16	76

HOME
Pos	P	W	D	L	F	A	GD	Pts
5	23	13	6	4	40	18	22	45

AWAY
Pos	P	W	D	L	F	A	GD	Pts
4	23	8	7	8	21	27	-6	31

CUP PROGRESS DETAILS
Competition	Round reached	Knocked out by
FA Cup	R4	Cardiff
Carling Cup	R2	Preston

BIGGEST WIN (ALL COMPS)
13/02/10 5–1 v Scunthorpe

BIGGEST DEFEAT (ALL COMPS)
05/12/09 1–5 v Nottm Forest

THE PLAYER WITH THE MOST
GOALS SCORED Martyn Waghorn	**12**
SHOTS ON TARGET Matt Fryatt	**43**
SHOTS OFF TARGET Martyn Waghorn	**33**
SHOTS WITHOUT SCORING Matt Oakley	**38**
ASSISTS Matt Fryatt, Richie Wellens	**5**
OFFSIDES Martyn Waghorn	**66**
FOULS Martyn Waghorn, Steve Howard	**55**
FOULS WITHOUT A CARD Yann Kermorgant	**16**
FREE-KICKS WON Richie Wellens	**91**
DEFENSIVE CLEARANCES Jack Hobbs	**88**

actim INDEX FOR THE 2009/10 COCA-COLA CHAMPIONSHIP SEASON

RANK	PLAYER	PTS
25	Chris Weale	539
37	Jack Hobbs	500
47	Bruno Berner	484

ATTENDANCE RECORD
HIGH	AVERAGE	LOW
31,759	23,943	18,928
v Nottm Forest (27/02/2010)		v Doncaster (09/02/2010)

Leicester's players feel the pain after their play-off defeat to Cardiff. The semi-final tie went to a penalty shoot-out, in which Leicester missed two kicks

PENALTY shoot-out heartbreak at Cardiff cost Leicester the chance of celebrating their 125th anniversary with a promotion showdown at Wembley.

The Foxes overturned a 1–0 first-leg deficit in the Coca-Cola Championship play-off semi-finals by winning 3–2 in the Welsh capital and forcing extra-time. However, with the penalty shoot-out delicately poised at 3–3, French striker Yann Kermorgant tried an audacious chip and his penalty was palmed away by Cardiff goalkeeper David Marshall. On-loan Sunderland striker Martyn Waghorn also had his spot-kick saved as Leicester lost 4–3 on penalties.

Leicester, who opted not to have a sponsor on their home shirts during the season, to commemorate their 125th birthday, began the campaign on the crest of a wave having gained promotion back to the second tier at the first time of asking by winning the League One title.

They started well and soon positioned themselves in the top half of the table, but a home defeat to Preston on 26th September – Leicester's first loss at the Walkers Stadium in a year – left some people wondering how they would react. The answer was emphatically, with a string of results that moved them into the play-off positions, where they would remain until the final month of the season.

Consistency and the ability to bounce back from disappointing results was the key to the Foxes' success. Manager Nigel Pearson refused to panic following heavy back-to-back defeats to Nottingham Forest

Leicester's dreams were shattered by an audacious penalty that went wrong

and Bristol City at the start of December, and his side responded by winning their next three fixtures. Likewise, after League defeats at Swansea and Barnsley either side of an FA Cup exit at Cardiff, the Foxes went on an eight-game run without defeat.

Leicester's character was tested again in March and April following an untimely four-match losing streak which saw them slip out of the top six. However, Pearson's players responded again by winning their final five games of the campaign and sealing a play-off spot with a match to spare. That run of results saw the Foxes go into the play-offs as the form team along with Cardiff, who they were to face in the semi-finals.

After such an unexpectedly successful campaign, Pearson acknowledges that expectations on his side will increase ahead of the 2010/11 season. Whether Leicester can seal a deal to keep Waghorn could hold the key to them repeating their achievements, or doing even better.

RESULTS 2009/10

AUGUST

8th	● Swansea	H	W 2–1	**Att:** 26,171	**Ref:** G Hegley	**Scorers:** N'Guessan, Waghorn. **Booked:** Brown, Wellens.
12th	● Macclesfield	A	W 0–2	**Att:** 2,197	**Ref:** A Hall	**Scorers:** Fryatt, N'Guessan. **Booked:** Powell.
15th	● Ipswich	A	D 0–0	**Att:** 22,454	**Ref:** P Crossley	**Booked:** Wellens, Howard, Waghorn, Weale.
18th	● Sheff Utd	A	D 1–1	**Att:** 26,069	**Ref:** N Miller	**Scorers:** Fryatt. **Booked:** Wellens, Fryatt, Oakley.
22nd	● Barnsley	H	W 1–0	**Att:** 21,799	**Ref:** A Penn	**Scorers:** Fryatt.
25th	● Preston	A	L 2–1	**Att:** 6,977	**Ref:** C Boyeson	**Scorers:** Adams.
31st	● Newcastle	A	L 1–0	**Att:** 38,813	**Ref:** N Swarbrick	**Booked:** Berner.

SEPTEMBER

12th	● Blackpool	H	W 2–1	**Att:** 22,827	**Ref:** J Singh	**Scorers:** Fryatt2. **Booked:** N'Guessan.
15th	● Peterborough	H	D 1–1	**Att:** 21,485	**Ref:** R Booth	**Scorers:** Fryatt. **Booked:** Oakley.
19th	● Watford	A	D 3–3	**Att:** 14,647	**Ref:** C Pawson	**Scorers:** Fryatt2, N'Guessan. **Booked:** Berner, King.
26th	● Preston	H	L 1–2	**Att:** 20,623	**Ref:** J Linnington	**Scorers:** Berner. **Booked:** Neilson, Howard, Waghorn.
29th	● Middlesbrough	A	W 0–1	**Att:** 18,577	**Ref:** M Haywood	**Scorers:** Dyer. **Booked:** Oakley.

OCTOBER

3rd	● Coventry	A	D 1–1	**Att:** 22,209	**Ref:** M Oliver	**Scorers:** Waghorn. **Booked:** Gallagher, Brown.
17th	● Derby	H	D 0–0	**Att:** 28,875	**Ref:** M Dean	**Booked:** Morrison, Howard.
20th	● Crystal Palace	H	W 2–0	**Att:** 22,220	**Ref:** R East	**Scorers:** Gallagher2.
26th	● Reading	A	W 0–1	**Att:** 16,192	**Ref:** K Hill	**Scorers:** Waghorn.
30th	● QPR	A	W 1–2	**Att:** 17,082	**Ref:** J Moss	**Scorers:** Fryatt2. **Booked:** Neilson, N'Guessan, Oakley.

NOVEMBER

7th	● West Brom	H	L 1–2	**Att:** 28,748	**Ref:** N Swarbrick	**Scorers:** Berner. **Booked:** Oakley, McGivern.
21st	● Plymouth	H	W 1–0	**Att:** 27,174	**Ref:** D McDermid	**Scorers:** King. **Booked:** Brown.
28th	● Scunthorpe	A	D 1–1	**Att:** 6,884	**Ref:** R Shoebridge	**Scorers:** Waghorn. **Booked:** Neilson.

DECEMBER

5th	● Nottm Forest	A	L 5–1	**Att:** 28,626	**Ref:** M Russell	**Scorers:** Waghorn. **Booked:** Howard.
8th	● Bristol City	H	L 1–3	**Att:** 19,349	**Ref:** S Cook	**Scorers:** Fryatt. **Booked:** Brown. **Dismissed:** Waghorn.
12th	● Sheff Wed	H	W 3–0	**Att:** 22,236	**Ref:** C Boyeson	**Scorers:** Howard, King2.
26th	● Sheff Utd	H	W 2–1	**Att:** 23,999	**Ref:** D Deadman	**Scorers:** Fryatt, Morrison.

JANUARY

2nd	● Swansea	H	W 2–1	**Att:** 12,307	**Ref:** P Taylor	**Scorers:** King, N'Guessan. **Booked:** Oakley, McGivern.
10th	● Ipswich	H	D 1–1	**Att:** 20,758	**Ref:** M Haywood	**Scorers:** Howard.
16th	● Swansea	A	L 1–0	**Att:** 15,037	**Ref:** F Graham	**Booked:** Morrison, Dyer, McGivern.
23rd	● Cardiff	A	L 4–2	**Att:** 10,961	**Ref:** P Crossley	**Scorers:** Morrison, N'Guessan. **Booked:** McGivern.
26th	● Barnsley	A	L 1–0	**Att:** 12,065	**Ref:** D Webb	**Booked:** Morrison.
30th	● Newcastle	H	D 0–0	**Att:** 29,067	**Ref:** A Marriner	**Booked:** Wellens, Berner, Oakley. **Dismissed:** Wellens.

FEBRUARY

6th	● Blackpool	A	W 1–2	**Att:** 8,484	**Ref:** A Haines	**Scorers:** Dyer, N'Guessan.
9th	● Doncaster	H	D 0–0	**Att:** 18,928	**Ref:** R Booth	**Booked:** Howard.
13th	● Scunthorpe	H	W 5–1	**Att:** 21,626	**Ref:** D Phillips	**Scorers:** Gallagher3, Morrison, Waghorn.
16th	● Bristol City	A	D 1–1	**Att:** 13,746	**Ref:** S Hooper	**Scorers:** Dyer. **Booked:** Berner, Wellens, Dyer.
20th	● Plymouth	A	D 1–1	**Att:** 11,581	**Ref:** R East	**Scorers:** Arnason OG. **Booked:** Brown, Gallagher.
23rd	● Doncaster	A	W 0–1	**Att:** 11,027	**Ref:** A Woolmer	**Scorers:** Waghorn. **Booked:** Berner.
27th	● Nottm Forest	H	W 3–0	**Att:** 31,759	**Ref:** L Probert	**Scorers:** Berner, Gallagher, King. **Booked:** Wellens, Hobbs, Waghorn, Gallagher, Oakley.

MARCH

6th	● Sheff Wed	A	L 2–0	**Att:** 21,647	**Ref:** P Gibbs	**Booked:** Berner.
13th	● Cardiff	H	W 1–0	**Att:** 22,767	**Ref:** K Evans	**Scorers:** Waghorn. **Booked:** Berner.
16th	● Crystal Palace	A	W 0–1	**Att:** 12,721	**Ref:** S Tanner	**Scorers:** Berner. **Booked:** Waghorn.
21st	● Coventry	H	D 2–2	**Att:** 23,093	**Ref:** L Mason	**Scorers:** King2. **Booked:** Gallagher.
24th	● Reading	H	L 1–2	**Att:** 20,108	**Ref:** D Foster	**Scorers:** Waghorn. **Booked:** Dyer, Waghorn, Solano.
27th	● Derby	A	L 1–0	**Att:** 30,259	**Ref:** C Webster	
30th	● Cardiff	A	L 2–1	**Att:** 20,438	**Ref:** F Graham	**Scorers:** Howard. **Booked:** Gallagher.

APRIL

2nd	● West Brom	A	L 3–0	**Att:** 23,334	**Ref:** D Deadman	**Booked:** Waghorn.
5th	● QPR	H	W 4–0	**Att:** 22,079	**Ref:** T Kettle	**Scorers:** Howard, King, Waghorn2.
10th	● Peterborough	A	W 1–2	**Att:** 9,651	**Ref:** G Scott	**Scorers:** Howard, King.
17th	● Watford	H	W 4–1	**Att:** 24,765	**Ref:** N Miller	**Scorers:** Gallagher, Spearing, Vaughan, Waghorn. **Booked:** Vaughan. **Dismissed:** Howard.
24th	● Preston	A	W 0–1	**Att:** 14,926	**Ref:** G Hegley	**Scorers:** King.

MAY

2nd	● Middlesbrough	H	W 2–0	**Att:** 30,223	**Ref:** A Taylor	**Scorers:** Kermorgant, Wellens.
9th	● Cardiff	H	L 0–1	**Att:** 29,165	**Ref:** A Wiley	**Booked:** Hobbs, Wellens.
12th	● Cardiff	A	W 2–3	**Att:** 26,033	**Ref:** H Webb	**Scorers:** Fryatt, King, Hudson OG. **Booked:** Dyer, Howard, King, Solano, Bruce, Wellens. AET – Score after 90 mins 2–3. Agg: 3–3; Cardiff win 4–3 on penalties.

● Coca-Cola Championship/Play-offs ● FA Cup ● Carling Cup

LEICESTER CITY

CHAMPIONSHIP GOALKEEPER STATS

Player	Minutes on pitch	Appearances	Match starts	Completed matches	Sub appearances	Subbed off	Saved with feet	Punched	Parried	Tipped over	Fumbled	Tipped round	Caught	Blocked	Clean sheets	Goals conceded	Save %	Saved	Resulting in goals	Opposition miss	Fouls committed	Free-kicks won	Yellow cards	Red cards
Conrad Logan	164	2	1	1	1	0	0	2	1	3	0	1	2	0	1	2	81.82	1	0	0	0	0	0	0
Chris Weale	4265	45	45	44	0	1	1	24	25	8	3	12	145	3	16	43	83.52	0	2	0	0	6	1	0

CHAMPIONSHIP OUTFIELD PLAYER STATS

Player	Minutes on pitch	Appearances	Match starts	Completed matches	Substitute appearances	Subbed off	Goals scored	Assists	Shots on target	Shots off target	Crosses	Tackles made	Defensive clearances	Defensive blocks	Fouls committed	Free-kicks won	Caught offside	Yellow cards	Red cards
Nicky Adams	421	18	1	0	17	1	0	0	3	3	15	13	0	1	1	5	1	0	0
Bruno Berner	3230	35	34	32	1	2	4	2	6	8	30	160	25	8	33	34	2	7	0
Wayne Brown	3621	39	38	37	1	1	0	0	1	3	9	138	84	23	30	38	0	5	0
Alex Bruce	139	3	2	1	1	1	0	0	0	0	0	6	0	0	1	0	0	0	0
Dudley Campbell	84	0	-3	0	3	-1	0	0	2	0	0	8	0	0	1	1	3	0	0
Paul Dickov	7	1	0	0	1	0	0	0	0	0	0	0	0	0	1	0	1	0	0
Lloyd Dyer	2352	33	25	12	8	13	3	1	24	16	33	83	0	2	8	31	5	3	0
Matt Fryatt	2067	29	26	7	3	19	11	5	43	20	14	43	1	2	22	22	59	1	0
Paul Gallagher	2867	41	31	11	10	20	7	4	33	28	104	69	7	1	24	36	10	5	0
Jack Hobbs	4187	44	44	43	0	1	0	0	5	13	6	181	88	25	28	23	1	1	0
Steve Howard	1886	36	17	10	19	6	5	3	25	28	3	43	6	0	55	47	26	5	1
Yann Kermorgant	824	20	9	2	11	7	1	0	9	7	4	43	11	0	16	9	1	0	0
Andy King	3618	43	37	35	6	2	9	1	19	22	9	146	24	4	19	31	0	1	0
Ryan McGivern	955	12	9	9	3	0	0	0	1	2	15	30	8	7	12	12	0	2	0
Michael Morrison	2830	31	30	28	1	2	6	5	6	5	20	149	40	9	24	23	4	3	0
Dany N'Guessan	1435	27	16	4	11	12	3	2	22	18	30	29	3	1	30	17	10	2	0
Robbie Neilson	1781	19	19	17	0	2	0	0	1	6	33	37	19	2	16	13	0	3	0
Luke O'Neill	48	1	0	0	1	0	0	0	0	0	0	0	0	0	0	0	0	0	0
Matt Oakley	3346	38	37	30	1	7	0	4	19	19	38	108	19	4	32	27	2	7	0
Chris Powell	190	2	2	2	0	0	0	0	0	0	0	1	2	0	0	1	0	0	0
Nolberto Solano	705	11	6	4	5	2	0	0	4	2	9	60	3	2	11	2	0	1	0
Jay Spearing	591	7	6	5	1	1	0	0	1	3	2	25	0	0	8	2	2	0	0
Aleksandar Tunchev	144	2	1	1	0	0	0	0	0	1	0	0	1	1	0	4	0	0	0
James Vaughan	355	8	2	0	6	2	1	1	6	3	3	3	1	0	7	6	5	1	0
Martyn Waghorn	2674	43	27	6	16	20	12	4	27	33	34	60	3	1	55	28	66	6	1
Richie Wellens	3734	41	41	34	0	6	1	5	17	17	31	145	6	1	45	91	0	6	1

SEASON TOTALS

Goals scored	61
Goals conceded	45
Clean sheets	17
Shots on target	276
Shots off target	257
Shots per goal	8.74
Pens awarded	8
Pens scored	6
Pens conceded	3
Offsides	198
Corners	262
Crosses	449
Players used	31
Fouls committed	479
Free-kicks won	509

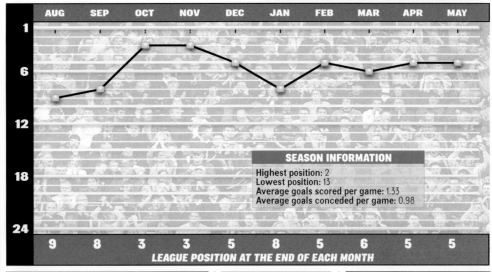

AUG	SEP	OCT	NOV	DEC	JAN	FEB	MAR	APR	MAY

SEASON INFORMATION
Highest position: 2
Lowest position: 13
Average goals scored per game: 1.33
Average goals conceded per game: 0.98

LEAGUE POSITION AT THE END OF EACH MONTH

9	8	3	3	5	8	5	6	5	5

CARDS RECEIVED

60   3

SEQUENCES

Wins	5
(05/04/10–02/05/10)	
Losses	4
(24/03/10–02/04/10)	
Draws	2
(on four occasions)	
Undefeated	8
(30/01/10–27/02/10)	
Without win	5
(21/03/10–02/04/10)	
Undefeated home	9
(12/12/09–21/03/10)	
Undefeated away	6
(19/09/09–28/11/09)	
Without scoring	3
(16/01/10–30/01/10)	
Without conceding	3
(17/10/09–26/10/09)	
Scoring	11
(20/10/09–10/01/10)	
Conceding	5
(on two occasions)	

MATCH RECORDS

Goals scored per match

		W	D	L	Pts
Failed to score	10	0	4	6	4
Scored 1 goal	21	8	7	6	31
Scored 2 goals	9	8	1	0	25
Scored 3 goals	3	2	1	0	7
Scored 4+ goals	3	3	0	0	9

Goals conceded per match

		W	D	L	Pts
Clean sheet	17	13	4	0	43
Conceded 1 goal	19	8	7	4	31
Conceded 2 goals	6	0	1	5	1
Conceded 3 goals	3	0	1	2	1
Conceded 4+ goals	1	0	0	1	0

GOALS SCORED/CONCEDED
PER FIVE-MINUTE INTERVALS

MINS	5	10	15	20	25	30	35	40	45	50	55	60	65	70	75	80	85	90
FOR	3	2	2	3	2	3	6	4	2	5	2	3	4	4	3	7		
AGN	1	2	1	4	0	1	5	5	3	2	4	2	2	2	0	5	1	5

EARLIEST STRIKE
MARTYN WAGHORN
(v Scunthorpe) 2:09

LATEST STRIKE
ANDY KING
(v Plymouth) 93:38

Wayne Brown

GOAL DETAILS

How the goals were struck

SCORED		CONCEDED
31	Right foot	29
19	Left foot	11
11	Header	4
0	Other	1

How the goals were struck

SCORED		CONCEDED
40	Open play	30
3	Cross	6
6	Corner	2
6	Penalty	2
2	Direct from free-kick	3
3	Free-kick	0
1	Own goal	2

Distance from goal

SCORED		CONCEDED
19	6YDS	17
34	18YDS	20
8	18+YDS	8

MIDDLESBROUGH

CLUB SUMMARY

FORMED	1876
MANAGER	Gordan Strachan
GROUND	Riverside Stadium
CAPACITY	35,049
NICKNAME	Boro
WEBSITE	www.mfc.co.uk

The New Football Pools PLAYER OF THE SEASON — Barry Robson

OVERALL
P	W	D	L	F	A	GD
48	16	14	18	59	53	6

COCA-COLA CHAMPIONSHIP
Pos	P	W	D	L	F	A	GD	Pts
11	46	16	14	16	58	50	8	62

HOME
Pos	P	W	D	L	F	A	GD	Pts
15	23	9	8	6	25	21	4	35

AWAY
Pos	P	W	D	L	F	A	GD	Pts
7	23	7	6	10	33	29	4	27

CUP PROGRESS DETAILS
Competition	Round reached	Knocked out by
FA Cup	R3	Man City
Carling Cup	R2	Nottm Forest

BIGGEST WIN (ALL COMPS)
05/12/09 5-1 v QPR

BIGGEST DEFEAT (ALL COMPS)
19/09/09 0-5 v West Brom

THE PLAYER WITH THE MOST
GOALS SCORED — Adam Johnson	11
SHOTS ON TARGET — Leroy Lita	42
SHOTS OFF TARGET — Leroy Lita, Adam Johnson	27
SHOTS WITHOUT SCORING — Julio Arca	26
ASSISTS — Gary O'Neil, Adam Johnson	6
OFFSIDES — Leroy Lita	54
FOULS — David Wheater	65
FOULS WITHOUT A CARD — Sean St. Ledger	16
FREE-KICKS WON — Leroy Lita	51
DEFENSIVE CLEARANCES — David Wheater	69

actim INDEX FOR THE 2009/10 COCA-COLA CHAMPIONSHIP SEASON

RANK	PLAYER	PTS
78	Gary O'Neil	441
88	David Wheater	424
102	Adam Johnson	411

ATTENDANCE RECORD
HIGH	AVERAGE	LOW
27,721	19,948	16,847
v Coventry (24/04/2010)		v Swansea (23/01/2010)

WHILE Gareth Southgate's response to relegation from the Barclays Premier League was characteristically defiant, it was not enough to save his job.

A man who had never shirked a challenge during his playing days began the Coca-Cola Championship campaign by simply rolling up his sleeves and fighting for a quick return to the Barclays Premier League following relegation in 2008/09.

Thirteen games into the campaign Middlesbrough sat fourth in the table, a point behind then-leaders West Brom and seemingly well placed for a promotion push. However, within hours of a 2–0 home victory over Derby on 20th October, which ended a run of three straight defeats at the Riverside, Southgate was clearing his desk as chairman Steve Gibson decided that, for once, the table did lie. As a replacement, Gibson opted for experience and a track record as he replaced the former England defender with Gordon Strachan.

The Scot took charge of his first game at home to Plymouth 11 days later and saw Adam Johnson miss a penalty as his side went down 1–0. Strachan had to wait five games to taste victory – a 5–1 win against QPR at Loftus Road – but successes proved to be few and far between. As the January transfer window approached, Strachan's focus was on how he could add experience to a youthful squad struggling to come to terms with life in the Championship.

The former Celtic manager did just that by raiding Parkhead for strikers Scott McDonald and Chris Killen, midfielders

A change of boss and a number of big-name departures made for a tough season at Boro

Barry Robson and Willo Flood and defender Stephen McManus, while Lee Miller arrived from Aberdeen and Kyle Naughton joined on a short-term deal from Tottenham. However, the pay-off was wing star Johnson's sale to Manchester City, as unpopular with the fans as the summer departures of international stars Stewart Downing, Robert Huth and Tuncay Sanli had been.

Robson and McManus made a major impact as the second half of the season unfolded but too many draws meant defeat at West Brom on 17th April ended Boro's hopes of making the play-offs.

There is little doubt that the upheaval sparked by Southgate's exit failed to substantially help Boro's cause and Strachan will hope to bed in his summer signings in time to make a better fist of it in 2010/11. However, with money tight on Teesside, he will need all his experience to get the club into the mix and keep it there.

Gordon Strachan arrived at Middlesbrough in October, but the new boss was soon bidding farewell to Adam Johnson, who was sold to Manchester City in January

RESULTS 2009/10

AUGUST

7th	●	Sheff Utd	H	D 0–0	Att: 23,541	Ref: L Mason	Booked: R Williams.
15th	●	Swansea	A	W 0–3	Att: 16,201	Ref: P Taylor	Scorers: Emnes, Johnson, Sanli. Booked: R Williams, O'Neil, McMahon, Huth.
18th	●	Scunthorpe	A	W 0–2	Att: 8,274	Ref: M Oliver	Scorers: Johnson[2]. Booked: Huth, Yeates.
22nd	●	Doncaster	H	W 2–0	Att: 22,041	Ref: G Salisbury	Scorers: Lita, Sanli. Booked: Arca, Lita.
25th	●	Nottm Forest	A	L 2–1	Att: 8,838	Ref: K Wright	Scorers: Johnson. AET – Score after 90 mins 1–1.
29th	●	Bristol City	A	L 2–1	Att: 14,402	Ref: R Booth	Scorers: Johnson. Booked: McMahon, Arca.

SEPTEMBER

12th	●	Ipswich	H	W 3–1	Att: 19,742	Ref: K Friend	Scorers: Aliadière[2], O'Neil. Booked: Johnson, Arca, O'Neil.
15th	●	Sheff Wed	A	W 1–3	Att: 21,722	Ref: T Bates	Scorers: Aliadière, Johnson, Purse OG. Booked: Aliadière, Hines.
19th	●	West Brom	H	L 0–5	Att: 22,725	Ref: T Kettle	Booked: R Williams, Arca.
26th	●	Coventry	A	D 2–2	Att: 16,771	Ref: G Horwood	Scorers: St. Ledger, R Williams. Booked: Bennett, Johnson, Lita.
29th	●	Leicester	H	L 0–1	Att: 18,577	Ref: M Haywood	

OCTOBER

3rd	●	Reading	A	W 0–2	Att: 17,638	Ref: N Swarbrick	Scorers: Lita, St. Ledger.
17th	●	Watford	H	L 0–1	Att: 18,957	Ref: S Mathieson	Booked: Arca.
20th	●	Derby	H	W 2–0	Att: 17,459	Ref: J Moss	Scorers: Johnson[2]. Booked: R Williams, Lita, Wheater.
24th	●	Preston	A	D 2–2	Att: 16,116	Ref: A Woolmer	Scorers: Johnson, O'Neil. Booked: Bennett, Digard, Johnson.
31st	●	Plymouth	H	L 0–1	Att: 21,141	Ref: M Russell	

NOVEMBER

7th	●	Crystal Palace	A	L 1–0	Att: 15,321	Ref: J Linnington	Booked: Osbourne.
21st	●	Nottm Forest	H	D 1–1	Att: 22,710	Ref: L Probert	Scorers: Lita. Booked: Osbourne, R Williams.
28th	●	Peterborough	A	D 2–2	Att: 10,772	Ref: D Phillips	Scorers: Kitson[2]. Booked: Kitson.

DECEMBER

5th	●	QPR	A	W 1–5	Att: 13,949	Ref: P Gibbs	Scorers: Kitson, Lita[2], O'Neil, Yeates. Booked: Lita, O'Neil.
8th	●	Blackpool	H	L 0–3	Att: 18,089	Ref: R Shoebridge	Booked: Pogatetz.
13th	●	Cardiff	H	L 0–1	Att: 17,232	Ref: G Hegley	
20th	●	Newcastle	A	L 2–0	Att: 49,644	Ref: K Friend	Booked: R Williams, Pogatetz.
26th	●	Scunthorpe	H	W 3–0	Att: 20,647	Ref: N Swarbrick	Scorers: Aliadière, Johnson, R Williams. Dismissed: Lita.
28th	●	Barnsley	A	L 2–1	Att: 18,001	Ref: A Hall	Scorers: Hoyte. Booked: R Williams, Wheater.

JANUARY

2nd	●	Man City	H	L 0–1	Att: 12,474	Ref: S Attwell	Booked: O'Neil.
16th	●	Sheff Utd	A	L 1–0	Att: 23,974	Ref: A D'Urso	Booked: O'Neil, Robson.
23rd	●	Swansea	H	D 1–1	Att: 16,847	Ref: A Penn	Scorers: Flood. Booked: Arca.
26th	●	Doncaster	A	W 1–4	Att: 10,794	Ref: S Tanner	Scorers: Franks, Johnson[2], Lita.
30th	●	Bristol City	H	D 0–0	Att: 17,865	Ref: C Webster	Booked: Robson. Dismissed: Robson.

FEBRUARY

6th	●	Ipswich	A	D 1–1	Att: 21,243	Ref: K Hill	Scorers: Wheater. Booked: O'Neil.
9th	●	Barnsley	H	W 2–1	Att: 17,775	Ref: C Boyeson	Scorers: Killen, O'Neil. Booked: O'Neil.
13th	●	Peterborough	H	W 1–0	Att: 18,412	Ref: J Moss	Scorers: Robson. Booked: Robson.
16th	●	Blackpool	A	L 2–0	Att: 7,936	Ref: M Haywood	Booked: Grounds, Robson.
20th	●	Nottm Forest	A	L 1–0	Att: 25,498	Ref: P Crossley	Booked: O'Neil.
27th	●	QPR	H	W 2–0	Att: 17,568	Ref: A Woolmer	Scorers: Robson[2]. Booked: Killen.

MARCH

6th	●	Cardiff	A	L 1–0	Att: 19,803	Ref: D Deadman	Booked: McManus, Robson, Lita.
13th	●	Newcastle	H	D 2–2	Att: 27,342	Ref: L Mason	Scorers: McDonald, Robson. Booked: McDonald.
16th	●	Derby	A	D 2–2	Att: 27,143	Ref: D Phillips	Scorers: Lita, Robson. Booked: Wheater, R Williams, Lita. Dismissed: R Williams.
20th	●	Reading	H	D 1–1	Att: 17,082	Ref: A Hall	Scorers: Killen. Booked: Arca, Robson, Killen.
23rd	●	Preston	H	W 2–0	Att: 16,974	Ref: S Tanner	Scorers: Franks, Killen. Booked: McManus.
27th	●	Watford	A	D 1–1	Att: 14,038	Ref: R East	Scorers: Lita. Booked: McManus, Killen, Wheater, O'Neil.

APRIL

3rd	●	Crystal Palace	H	D 1–1	Att: 18,428	Ref: G Salisbury	Scorers: McDonald.
5th	●	Plymouth	A	W 0–2	Att: 11,770	Ref: S Mathieson	Scorers: Franks, McManus. Booked: Lita, Hoyte, Robson, R Williams.
10th	●	Sheff Wed	H	W 1–0	Att: 19,932	Ref: J Moss	Scorers: McDonald. Booked: McManus.
17th	●	West Brom	A	L 2–0	Att: 22,548	Ref: G Hegley	Booked: O'Neil, McManus.
24th	●	Coventry	H	D 1–1	Att: 27,721	Ref: D McDermid	Scorers: McDonald.

MAY

2nd	●	Leicester	A	L 2–0	Att: 30,223	Ref: A Taylor	Dismissed: Jones.

● Coca-Cola Championship/Play-offs ● FA Cup ● Carling Cup

CHAMPIONSHIP GOALKEEPER STATS

Player	Minutes on pitch	Appearances	Match starts	Completed matches	Sub appearances	Subbed off	SAVES BREAKDOWN Saved with feet	Punched	Parried	Tipped over	Fumbled	Tipped round	Caught	Blocked	Clean sheets	Goals conceded	Save %	PENALTIES Saved	Resulting in goals	Opposition miss	Fouls committed	Free-kicks won	Yellow cards	Red cards
Danny Coyne	2212	23	22	22	1	0	1	10	8	1	0	9	73	1	8	26	79.84	0	2	0	0	4	0	0
Brad Jones	2204	24	24	23	0	0	2	15	18	3	3	5	72	3	5	24	83.10	1	0	0	1	3	0	1

CHAMPIONSHIP OUTFIELD PLAYER STATS

Player	Minutes on pitch	Appearances	Match starts	Completed matches	Substitute appearances	Subbed off	Goals scored	Assists	Shots on target	Shots off target	Crosses	Tackles made	Defensive clearances	Defensive blocks	Fouls committed	Free-kicks won	Caught offside	Yellow cards	Red cards
Jérémie Aliadière	1385	20	16	8	4	8	4	1	20	7	14	20	9	1	27	17	12	1	0
Julio Arca	2459	34	26	15	8	11	0	2	15	11	27	65	7	4	37	32	0	7	0
Joe Bennett	857	12	10	6	2	4	0	0	0	1	13	30	5	3	9	12	0	2	0
Marcus Bent	453	7	3	3	4	0	0	0	3	4	1	14	2	0	6	10	8	0	0
Didier Digard	421	9	4	2	5	2	0	0	2	5	1	17	3	1	10	3	0	1	0
Marvin Emnes	857	16	12	2	4	10	1	2	9	7	14	13	0	0	4	14	12	0	0
Willo Flood	987	11	11	9	0	2	1	0	5	3	15	45	3	4	10	17	2	0	0
Caleb Folan	64	1	0	0	1	0	0	0	0	0	0	0	0	0	2	2	0	0	0
Jonathan Franks	997	23	9	5	14	4	3	1	12	3	36	23	3	0	5	5	10	0	0
Jonathan Grounds	1616	20	16	14	4	4	0	1	0	0	5	60	25	9	16	12	0	1	0
Seb Hines	196	2	2	2	0	0	0	0	1	0	0	1	5	2	2	2	0	1	0
Justin Hoyte	2248	30	23	19	7	4	1	1	2	7	33	88	14	10	9	5	2	1	0
Robert Huth	381	4	4	4	0	0	0	0	0	1	0	25	8	3	2	5	0	2	0
Adam Johnson	2351	26	25	21	1	4	11	6	20	27	83	52	2	1	14	42	5	3	0
Chris Killen	1369	17	15	9	2	6	3	1	17	13	2	22	8	3	29	29	7	1	0
Dave Kitson	451	6	6	3	0	3	3	0	6	5	1	7	0	0	7	8	3	1	0
Leroy Lita	2481	40	23	10	17	12	8	3	42	27	12	49	2	2	29	51	54	7	1
Scott McDonald	1139	13	12	10	1	2	4	1	12	19	6	19	0	0	8	19	23	1	0
Tony McMahon	1935	21	20	18	1	2	0	1	3	3	57	55	18	8	27	17	0	2	0
Stephen McManus	1537	16	16	16	0	0	1	0	3	3	2	73	33	11	16	16	0	5	0
Lee Miller	492	10	6	1	4	5	0	0	5	8	1	20	1	0	6	11	6	0	0
Kyle Naughton	1256	15	12	10	3	2	0	0	1	4	25	53	8	1	1	6	0	0	0
Gary O'Neil	3361	36	35	32	1	3	4	6	30	25	76	70	17	5	59	44	3	9	0
James O'Shea	100	2	1	0	1	1	0	0	1	0	0	1	0	0	2	1	0	0	0
Isaiah Osbourne	859	9	9	9	0	0	0	0	2	4	2	20	3	0	10	6	0	2	0
Emanuel Pogatetz	1137	13	13	9	0	4	0	0	1	3	0	33	13	4	15	17	0	2	0
Chris Riggott	409	6	4	3	2	1	0	0	1	0	0	13	5	1	3	2	0	0	0
Barry Robson	1695	18	18	17	0	0	5	5	19	13	55	61	14	0	38	42	1	7	1
Tuncay Sanli	129	3	0	0	3	0	0	0	2	0	2	10	0	0	2	0	2	0	0
Sean St. Ledger	1357	15	14	14	1	0	2	0	5	2	1	43	12	14	16	20	3	0	0
Andrew Taylor	684	12	8	5	4	3	0	0	0	1	14	45	6	6	4	4	0	0	0
Joshua Walker	61	1	1	0	0	1	0	0	1	1	0	9	0	0	0	1	0	0	0
David Wheater	4036	42	42	42	0	0	1	0	4	21	0	183	69	33	65	32	2	4	0
Luke Williams	217	4	2	1	2	1	0	0	3	4	1	6	0	0	0	0	0	0	0
Rhys Williams	2937	32	31	27	1	3	2	1	17	9	13	98	19	7	39	29	1	9	1
Mark Yeates	1121	19	11	5	8	6	1	1	16	14	32	34	2	3	16	20	0	1	0

SEASON TOTALS

Goals scored	58
Goals conceded	50
Clean sheets	13
Shots on target	280
Shots off target	255
Shots per goal	9.22
Pens awarded	11
Pens scored	7
Pens conceded	3
Offsides	156
Corners	254
Crosses	549
Players used	38
Fouls committed	546
Free-kicks won	568

CARDS RECEIVED

72 **4**

SEQUENCES

Wins	3
(15/08/09–22/08/09)	
Losses	3
(08/12/09–20/12/09)	
Draws	3
(13/03/10–20/03/10)	
Undefeated	8
(13/03/10–10/04/10)	
Without win	5
(24/10/09–28/11/09)	
Undefeated home	12
(26/12/09–24/04/10)	
Undefeated away	4
(15/09/09–24/10/09)	
Without scoring	3
(08/12/09–20/12/09)	
Without conceding	4
(07/08/09–22/08/09)	
Scoring	8
(13/03/10–10/04/10)	
Conceding	9
(24/10/09–20/12/09)	

LEAGUE POSITION AT THE END OF EACH MONTH

AUG 4, SEP 4, OCT 7, NOV 10, DEC 11, JAN 9, FEB 9, MAR 9, APR 8, MAY 11

SEASON INFORMATION
Highest position: 1
Lowest position: 17
Average goals scored per game: 1.26
Average goals conceded per game: 1.09

MATCH RECORDS

Goals scored per match

		W	D	L	Pts
Failed to score	16	0	2	14	2
Scored 1 goal	11	2	7	2	13
Scored 2 goals	13	8	5	0	29
Scored 3 goals	4	4	0	0	12
Scored 4+ goals	2	2	0	0	6

Goals conceded per match

		W	D	L	Pts
Clean sheet	13	11	2	0	35
Conceded 1 goal	20	5	7	8	22
Conceded 2 goals	11	0	5	6	5
Conceded 3 goals	1	0	0	1	0
Conceded 4+ goals	1	0	0	1	0

GOALS SCORED/CONCEDED PER FIVE-MINUTE INTERVALS

MINS	5	10	15	20	25	30	35	40	45	50	55	60	65	70	75	80	85	90
FOR	1	1	4	3	4	4	3	4	5	4	5	4	1	3	3	1	3	5
AGN	3	0	0	3	2	3	1	0	4	2	3	4	7	1	3	2	5	7

EARLIEST STRIKE
LEROY LITA (v Nottm Forest) 4:33

LATEST STRIKE
JONATHAN FRANKS (v Plymouth) 93:06

Barry Robson

GOAL DETAILS

How the goals were struck

SCORED		CONCEDED
28	Right foot	29
16	Left foot	12
14	Header	8
0	Other	1

How the goals were struck

SCORED		CONCEDED
31	Open play	34
9	Cross	6
5	Corner	1
7	Penalty	2
2	Direct from free-kick	2
3	Free-kick	4
1	Own goal	1

Distance from goal

SCORED		CONCEDED
13	6YDS	15
38	18YDS	26
7	18+YDS	9

NEWCASTLE UNITED

CLUB SUMMARY

FORMED	1892
MANAGER	Chris Hughton
GROUND	St James' Park
CAPACITY	52,387
NICKNAME	The Magpies
WEBSITE	www.nufc.co.uk

The New Football Pools PLAYER OF THE SEASON — *Jose Enrique*

OVERALL
P	W	D	L	F	A	GD
51	32	13	6	99	44	55

COCA-COLA CHAMPIONSHIP
Pos	P	W	D	L	F	A	GD	Pts
1	46	30	12	4	90	35	55	102

HOME
Pos	P	W	D	L	F	A	GD	Pts
1	23	18	5	0	56	13	43	59

AWAY
Pos	P	W	D	L	F	A	GD	Pts
1	23	12	7	4	34	22	12	43

CUP PROGRESS DETAILS
Competition	Round reached	Knocked out by
FA Cup	R4	West Brom
Carling Cup	R3	Peterborough

BIGGEST WIN (ALL COMPS)
06/03/10 6–1 v Barnsley

BIGGEST DEFEAT (ALL COMPS)
09/02/10 0–3 v Derby

THE PLAYER WITH THE MOST
GOALS SCORED Andrew Carroll, Kevin Nolan	**17**
SHOTS ON TARGET Kevin Nolan	**53**
SHOTS OFF TARGET Andrew Carroll	**56**
SHOTS WITHOUT SCORING Alan Smith	**18**
ASSISTS Danny Guthrie	**13**
OFFSIDES Andrew Carroll	**34**
FOULS Andrew Carroll	**70**
FOULS WITHOUT A CARD Nile Ranger	**20**
FREE-KICKS WON Jonas Gutierrez	**95**
DEFENSIVE CLEARANCES Andrew Carroll	**39**

actim INDEX FOR THE 2009/10 COCA-COLA CHAMPIONSHIP SEASON

RANK	PLAYER	PTS
1	Kevin Nolan	834
4	Steve Harper	659
9	Wayne Routledge	598

ATTENDANCE RECORD
HIGH	AVERAGE	LOW
52,181	43,388	36,944
v Ipswich (24/04/2010)		v Reading (15/08/2009)

Chris Hughton defied the doubters to take Newcastle back to the top at the first attempt

AFTER the meltdown of relegation from the Barclays Premier League at the end of the 2008/09 season, Newcastle rose from the ashes to storm to the Coca-Cola Championship title.

After several big name departures over the summer, and the failure to recruit a permanent high-profile manager, Magpies supporters could have been forgiven for a pessimistic outlook ahead of the campaign. However, from the moment they launched their season with a hard-fought 1–1 draw at West Brom, there was a momentum about Newcastle's promotion push.

There were several memorable personal achievements along the way. Chris Hughton was installed as caretaker manager for a third time but proved to be so effective that he was handed the reins on a permanent basis before the end of October. On the pitch, striker Shola Ameobi plundered a hat-trick in the club's first home game, a 3–0 victory over Reading and, although injuries were to blight his campaign once again, Andy Carroll, Kevin Nolan and Peter Lovenkrands were there to pick up the goal-scoring baton.

There was only one real blip, when successive defeats at Nottingham Forest and Scunthorpe inside four days in October left some questioning the Magpies' ability

Kevin Nolan picks up the match ball after completing his hat-trick against Ipswich

Manager Chris Hughton poses with the Championship trophy

to sustain their push. However, the reverse at Glanford Park on 20th October proved something of a watershed and, remarkably, Newcastle were to lose only once more in the League – at Derby in February – in their remaining 33 games as they powered their way to promotion and then, ultimately, the Championship title.

There were times along the way when they had to grind out results, particularly on the road, but with January signing Wayne Routledge adding pace to Hughton's team, the Magpies became increasingly irresistible at St James' Park, where Barnsley were hit for six and Cardiff five amid a cascade of goals.

Promotion was clinched with six games to go and the title arrived at Plymouth on 19th April when sights were immediately set on top-flight survival.

Nolan, who was named the Championship's Player of the Year, said: 'It's going to be tough, it's going to be relentless again, but we are going to give it our best shot and hopefully make sure we stay a Premier League club for years.'

Newcastle will return to the big time knowing they have to strengthen on a limited budget and their aims, amongst the sensible at least, will be modest first time around as they attempt to avoid a repeat of the horrors of 2008/09.

RESULTS 2009/10

AUGUST

8th	● West Brom	A	D 1–1	Att: 23,502	Ref: M Dean	**Scorers:** Duff. **Booked:** Coloccini, Nolan.
15th	● Reading	H	W 3–0	Att: 36,944	Ref: A Taylor	**Scorers:** Ameobi[3]. **Booked:** Smith, Carroll, Barton.
19th	● Sheff Wed	H	W 1–0	Att: 43,904	Ref: P Dowd	**Scorers:** Ameobi. **Booked:** Smith, Coloccini, S Taylor.
22nd	● Crystal Palace	A	W 0–2	Att: 20,643	Ref: A D'Urso	**Scorers:** Nolan, R Taylor.
26th	● Huddersfield	H	W 4–3	Att: 23,815	Ref: T Bates	**Scorers:** Ameobi, Guthrie, Njitap, Nolan. **Booked:** Krul.
31st	● Leicester	H	W 1–0	Att: 38,813	Ref: N Swarbrick	**Scorers:** Guthrie. **Booked:** Guthrie.

SEPTEMBER

13th	● Cardiff	A	W 0–1	Att: 25,630	Ref: A Hall	**Scorers:** Coloccini. **Booked:** Jose Enrique, Guthrie, Smith. **Dismissed:** Smith.
16th	● Blackpool	A	L 2–1	Att: 9,647	Ref: J Moss	**Scorers:** Carroll. **Booked:** Carroll.
19th	● Plymouth	H	W 3–1	Att: 42,898	Ref: S Mathieson	**Scorers:** Carroll, Nolan, S Taylor. **Booked:** Carroll.
22nd	● Peterborough	A	L 2–0	Att: 10,298	Ref: K Stroud	**Booked:** Krul, Guthrie, S Taylor, R Taylor. **Dismissed:** Guthrie.
26th	● Ipswich	A	W 0–4	Att: 27,059	Ref: M Jones	**Scorers:** Nolan[3], R Taylor. **Booked:** Nolan.
30th	● QPR	H	D 1–1	Att: 38,923	Ref: R Shoebridge	**Scorers:** Harewood. **Booked:** Smith.

OCTOBER

3rd	● Bristol City	H	D 0–0	Att: 43,326	Ref: G Salisbury	**Booked:** Khizanishvili.
17th	● Nottm Forest	A	L 1–0	Att: 29,155	Ref: P Taylor	**Booked:** Smith, Khizanishvili, R Taylor.
20th	● Scunthorpe	A	L 2–1	Att: 8,921	Ref: A Penn	**Scorers:** Nolan. **Booked:** Smith.
24th	● Doncaster	H	W 2–1	Att: 43,949	Ref: D Deadman	**Scorers:** Carroll, Nolan. **Booked:** Harewood, Nolan, Butt. **Dismissed:** Khizanishvili.

NOVEMBER

2nd	● Sheff Utd	A	W 0–1	Att: 26,536	Ref: K Friend	**Scorers:** Morgan OG. **Booked:** Carroll, R Taylor.
7th	● Peterborough	H	W 3–1	Att: 43,067	Ref: A D'Urso	**Scorers:** Carroll, Gutierrez, Simpson.
23rd	● Preston	A	W 0–1	Att: 16,924	Ref: S Mathieson	**Scorers:** Nolan. **Booked:** Smith.
28th	● Swansea	H	W 3–0	Att: 42,616	Ref: M Haywood	**Scorers:** Harewood[2], Lovenkrands.

DECEMBER

5th	● Watford	H	W 2–0	Att: 43,050	Ref: J Moss	**Scorers:** Lovenkrands, Pancrate. **Booked:** Nolan. **Dismissed:** Nolan.
9th	● Coventry	A	W 0–2	Att: 21,688	Ref: G Hegley	**Scorers:** Ameobi, Ranger.
12th	● Barnsley	A	D 2–2	Att: 20,079	Ref: G Salisbury	**Scorers:** Harewood, Nolan. **Booked:** Carroll.
20th	● Middlesbrough	H	W 2–0	Att: 49,644	Ref: K Friend	**Scorers:** Ameobi, Harewood. **Booked:** Simpson.
26th	● Sheff Wed	A	D 2–2	Att: 30,030	Ref: S Attwell	**Scorers:** Ameobi, Nolan.
28th	● Derby	H	D 0–0	Att: 47,505	Ref: K Wright	**Booked:** Nolan.

JANUARY

2nd	● Plymouth	A	D 0–0	Att: 16,451	Ref: A Wiley	**Booked:** Ranger, R Taylor.
13th	● Plymouth	H	W 3–0	Att: 15,805	Ref: A D'Urso	**Scorers:** Lovenkrands[3].
18th	● West Brom	H	D 2–2	Att: 39,291	Ref: P Taylor	**Scorers:** Guthrie, Lovenkrands. **Booked:** Ameobi, Nolan.
23rd	● West Brom	A	L 4–2	Att: 16,102	Ref: J Linnington	**Scorers:** Carroll[2]. **Booked:** Kadar, Krul, Smith, Jose Enrique. **Dismissed:** R Taylor.
27th	● Crystal Palace	H	W 2–0	Att: 37,886	Ref: R Booth	**Scorers:** Ranger, Derry OG. **Booked:** Smith, Coloccini.
30th	● Leicester	A	D 0–0	Att: 29,067	Ref: A Marriner	**Booked:** Williamson.

FEBRUARY

5th	● Cardiff	H	W 5–1	Att: 44,028	Ref: K Friend	**Scorers:** Carroll[2], Lovenkrands[2], Gyepes OG. **Booked:** Best, Kadar.
9th	● Derby	A	L 3–0	Att: 28,607	Ref: A Taylor	**Booked:** Nolan.
13th	● Swansea	A	D 1–1	Att: 15,188	Ref: A Woolmer	**Scorers:** Carroll. **Booked:** Coloccini, Carroll.
17th	● Coventry	H	W 4–1	Att: 39,334	Ref: S Tanner	**Scorers:** Carroll, Lovenkrands, Routledge, R Taylor.
20th	● Preston	H	W 3–0	Att: 45,525	Ref: A Penn	**Scorers:** Lovenkrands, Nolan, R Taylor. **Booked:** Simpson.
27th	● Watford	A	W 1–2	Att: 17,120	Ref: T Bates	**Scorers:** Carroll, Coloccini. **Booked:** Best, Williamson, Nolan, Smith, Van Aanholt.

MARCH

6th	● Barnsley	H	W 6–1	Att: 44,464	Ref: G Hegley	**Scorers:** Guthrie[2], Gutierrez, Lovenkrands[2], Nolan.
13th	● Middlesbrough	A	D 2–2	Att: 27,342	Ref: L Mason	**Scorers:** Carroll, Lovenkrands. **Booked:** Hall, Simpson, Kadar, Carroll.
17th	● Scunthorpe	H	W 3–0	Att: 39,301	Ref: P Crossley	**Scorers:** Carroll[2], Lovenkrands. **Booked:** Carroll.
20th	● Bristol City	A	D 2–2	Att: 19,144	Ref: A D'Urso	**Scorers:** Carroll, Gutierrez. **Booked:** Coloccini, Guthrie.
23rd	● Doncaster	A	W 0–1	Att: 14,850	Ref: K Hill	**Scorers:** Carroll. **Booked:** R Taylor, Simpson, Nolan.
29th	● Nottm Forest	H	W 2–0	Att: 45,987	Ref: A Wiley	**Scorers:** Ameobi, Jose Enrique. **Booked:** Jose Enrique.

APRIL

3rd	● Peterborough	A	W 2–3	Att: 12,877	Ref: M Haywood	**Scorers:** Ameobi, Barton, Nolan. **Booked:** Best, Gutierrez.
5th	● Sheff Utd	H	W 2–1	Att: 48,270	Ref: A Hall	**Scorers:** Lovenkrands, Nolan. **Booked:** Routledge.
10th	● Blackpool	H	W 4–1	Att: 47,010	Ref: M Russell	**Scorers:** Carroll, Gutierrez, Nolan, Routledge. **Booked:** Guthrie.
13th	● Reading	A	W 1–2	Att: 23,163	Ref: F Graham	**Scorers:** Nolan[2]. **Booked:** Nolan, R Taylor, Ameobi.
19th	● Plymouth	A	W 0–2	Att: 13,111	Ref: C Pawson	**Scorers:** Carroll, Routledge. **Booked:** Carroll.
24th	● Ipswich	H	D 2–2	Att: 52,181	Ref: C Boyeson	**Scorers:** Ameobi, Carroll.

MAY

2nd	● QPR	A	W 0–1	Att: 16,819	Ref: D Deadman	**Scorers:** Lovenkrands. **Booked:** Williamson, R Taylor.

● Coca-Cola Championship/Play-offs ● FA Cup ● Carling Cup

NEWCASTLE UNITED

CHAMPIONSHIP GOALKEEPER STATS

Player	Minutes on pitch	Appearances	Match starts	Completed matches	Sub appearances	Subbed off	SAVES BREAKDOWN								Clean sheets	Goals conceded	Save %	PENALTIES			Fouls committed	Free-kicks won	Yellow cards	Red cards
							Saved with feet	Punched	Parried	Tipped over	Fumbled	Tipped round	Caught	Blocked				Saved	Resulting in goals	Opposition miss				
Steve Harper	4210	45	45	43	0	2	3	17	25	3	1	9	171	2	20	34	87.12	0	1	1	0	7	0	0
Tim Krul	192	3	1	1	2	0	0	3	4	1	0	2	13	0	1	1	95.83	0	0	0	0	0	0	0

CHAMPIONSHIP OUTFIELD PLAYER STATS

Player	Minutes on pitch	Appearances	Match starts	Completed matches	Substitute appearances	Subbed off	Goals scored	Assists	Shots on target	Shots off target	Crosses	Tackles made	Defensive clearances	Defensive blocks	Fouls committed	Free-kicks won	Caught offside	Yellow cards	Red cards
Shola Ameobi	1105	18	11	2	7	9	10	3	18	7	8	9	6	1	33	29	20	2	0
Joey Barton	800	15	8	2	7	6	1	2	10	1	14	12	2	4	16	6	0	1	0
Leon Best	658	13	6	2	7	4	0	2	7	7	2	11	0	0	13	4	8	3	0
Nicky Butt	1090	17	10	9	7	1	0	1	2	3	15	28	8	3	13	23	0	1	0
Andrew Carroll	3027	39	33	23	6	10	17	8	47	56	12	31	39	2	70	58	34	9	0
Fabricio Coloccini	3420	37	37	34	0	3	2	1	5	4	3	105	28	17	23	35	0	5	0
Ryan Donaldson	25	2	0	0	2	0	0	0	0	0	0	0	0	0	0	0	0	0	0
Damien Duff	96	1	1	1	0	0	1	0	2	1	2	0	0	0	1	3	0	0	0
Danny Guthrie	3212	38	36	19	2	17	4	13	29	17	96	108	4	0	22	39	2	4	0
Jonas Gutierrez	3082	37	34	22	3	12	4	8	26	17	71	50	2	0	22	95	3	1	0
Fitz Hall	602	7	7	4	0	3	0	1	1	0	1	43	5	5	4	1	0	1	0
Marlon Harewood	853	15	9	2	6	7	5	0	14	9	10	12	1	0	16	9	13	1	0
Sanchez Jose Enrique	3042	34	33	29	1	4	1	4	12	9	87	57	22	8	9	40	1	2	0
Tamas Kadar	699	13	6	5	7	1	0	0	2	1	0	15	6	2	6	3	0	2	0
Zurab Khizanishvili	582	7	6	5	1	0	0	0	0	0	1	15	5	3	4	10	0	2	1
Peter Lovenkrands	1650	29	19	5	10	14	13	2	24	21	18	30	1	0	20	21	19	0	0
Kazenga LuaLua	12	1	0	0	1	0	0	0	0	0	0	0	0	0	0	0	0	0	0
Geremi Njitap	311	7	3	2	4	1	0	1	2	4	10	4	1	0	1	3	4	0	0
Kevin Nolan	4066	44	44	38	0	5	17	5	53	28	16	132	21	10	42	31	20	10	1
Fabrice Pancrate	604	16	5	1	11	4	1	2	2	4	18	7	0	0	10	3	0	0	0
Nile Ranger	733	25	4	1	21	3	2	3	6	12	1	2	4	1	20	25	6	0	0
Wayne Routledge	1471	17	15	11	2	4	3	7	13	9	33	32	0	2	12	25	4	1	0
Danny Simpson	3583	39	39	34	0	5	1	2	2	3	33	101	23	15	22	23	1	4	0
Alan Smith	2907	32	31	27	1	3	0	1	13	5	7	90	29	7	59	42	0	9	1
Steven Taylor	2016	21	21	21	0	0	1	0	3	3	1	41	21	24	13	8	1	1	0
Ryan Taylor	2046	31	19	13	12	6	4	5	17	12	84	35	14	5	15	19	2	5	0
Ben Tozer	8	1	0	0	1	0	0	0	0	0	0	0	0	0	1	0	0	0	0
Patrick Van Aanholt	642	7	7	6	0	1	0	0	0	2	0	5	27	0	3	3	2	1	1
Haris Vuckic	24	2	0	0	2	0	0	0	0	0	0	0	0	0	1	0	0	0	0
Mike Williamson	1532	16	16	16	0	0	0	0	2	5	1	43	24	8	15	17	1	3	0
Xisco	53	2	0	0	2	0	0	0	0	0	0	0	0	0	1	0	0	0	0

actim

SEASON TOTALS

Goals scored	90
Goals conceded	35
Clean sheets	22
Shots on target	314
Shots off target	239
Shots per goal	6.14
Pens awarded	6
Pens scored	5
Pens conceded	2
Offsides	140
Corners	256
Crosses	549
Players used	33
Fouls committed	486
Free-kicks won	581

CARDS RECEIVED

68   3

SEQUENCES

Wins	7
(on two occasions)	
Losses	2
(17/10/09–20/10/09)	
Draws	3
(26/12/09–18/01/10)	
Undefeated	17
(13/02/10–02/05/10)	
Without win	4
(30/09/09–20/10/09)	
Undefeated home	23
(15/08/09–24/04/10)	
Undefeated away	9
(13/02/10–02/05/10)	
Without scoring	2
(03/10/09–17/10/09)	
Without conceding	5
(15/08/09–13/09/09)	
Scoring	11
(20/10/09–26/12/09)	
Conceding	4
(on two occasions)	

LEAGUE POSITION AT THE END OF EACH MONTH

AUG	SEP	OCT	NOV	DEC	JAN	FEB	MAR	APR	MAY
1	1	2	1	1	1	1	1	1	1

SEASON INFORMATION

Highest position: 1
Lowest position: 14
Average goals scored per game: 1.96
Average goals conceded per game: 0.76

MATCH RECORDS

Goals scored per match

		W	D	L	Pts
Failed to score	5	0	3	2	3
Scored 1 goal	12	7	3	2	24
Scored 2 goals	17	11	6	0	39
Scored 3 goals	7	7	0	0	21
Scored 4+ goals	5	5	0	0	15

Goals conceded per match

		W	D	L	Pts
Clean sheet	22	19	3	0	60
Conceded 1 goal	14	10	3	1	33
Conceded 2 goals	9	1	6	2	9
Conceded 3 goals	1	0	0	1	0
Conceded 4+ goals	0	0	0	0	0

GOALS SCORED/CONCEDED
PER FIVE-MINUTE INTERVALS

MINS	5	10	15	20	25	30	35	40	45	50	55	60	65	70	75	80	85	90
FOR	4	5	4	9	5	4	2	4	5	4	9	4	4	5	8	2	6	6
AGN	0	2	3	1	1	0	1	3	4	2	2	3	2	0	2	3	2	4

EARLIEST STRIKE

KEVIN NOLAN
(v Crystal Palace) 1:43

LATEST STRIKE

NILE RANGER
(v Crystal Palace) 93:59

Danny Guthrie

GOAL DETAILS

How the goals were struck

SCORED		CONCEDED
43	Right foot	20
22	Left foot	9
25	Header	5
0	Other	1

How the goals were struck

SCORED		CONCEDED
58	Open play	26
11	Cross	3
4	Corner	2
5	Penalty	1
4	Direct from free-kick	0
5	Free-kick	2
3	Own goal	1

Distance from goal

SCORED		CONCEDED
36	6YDS	15
41	18YDS	15
13	18+YDS	5

NOTTINGHAM FOREST

CLUB SUMMARY

FORMED	1865
MANAGER	Billy Davies
GROUND	City Ground
CAPACITY	30,602
NICKNAME	Forest
WEBSITE	www.nottinghamforest.co.uk

The New Football Pools PLAYER OF THE SEASON — Lee Camp

OVERALL

P	W	D	L	F	A	GD
53	24	14	15	74	49	25

COCA-COLA CHAMPIONSHIP

Pos	P	W	D	L	F	A	GD	Pts
3	46	22	13	11	65	40	25	79

HOME

Pos	P	W	D	L	F	A	GD	Pts
2	23	18	2	3	45	13	32	56

AWAY

Pos	P	W	D	L	F	A	GD	Pts
12	23	4	11	8	20	27	-7	23

CUP PROGRESS DETAILS

Competition	Round reached	Knocked out by
FA Cup	R3	Birmingham
Carling Cup	R3	Blackburn

BIGGEST WIN (ALL COMPS)
26/01/10 5-0 v QPR

BIGGEST DEFEAT (ALL COMPS)
27/02/10 0-3 v Leicester

THE PLAYER WITH THE MOST

GOALS SCORED Robert Earnshaw	**15**
SHOTS ON TARGET Robert Earnshaw	**45**
SHOTS OFF TARGET Dexter Blackstock	**30**
SHOTS WITHOUT SCORING Garath McCleary	**12**
ASSISTS Radoslaw Majewski	**9**
OFFSIDES Robert Earnshaw	**26**
FOULS Dexter Blackstock	**73**
FOULS WITHOUT A CARD George Boyd	**6**
FREE-KICKS WON Chris Gunter	**60**
DEFENSIVE CLEARANCES Wes Morgan	**77**

actim INDEX FOR THE 2009/10 COCA-COLA CHAMPIONSHIP SEASON

RANK	PLAYER	PTS
10	Wes Morgan	594
15	Lee Camp	570
17	Chris Gunter	566

ATTENDANCE RECORD

HIGH	AVERAGE	LOW
29,155	23,831	18,332
v Newcastle (17/10/2009)		v Scunthorpe (30/09/2009)

Forest players are left heartbroken by their play-off defeat to Blackpool

BILLY DAVIES transformed Nottingham Forest from relegation battlers to promotion contenders in his first full season as manager at the City Ground. Davies kept Forest in the Coca-Cola Championship during the 2008/09 campaign and at the midway point of the 2009/10 season they were mounting a serious challenge for automatic promotion.

An impressive 3–1 victory at West Brom on 8th January saw Forest usurp their midlands rivals in second place in the table but, rather than provide the springboard to push on and win automatic promotion, little did anyone know at the time that it would be a turning point in Forest's season for completely different reasons.

Forest's successful escape from relegation the previous season and the subsequent promotion challenge they had mounted was thanks, in large part, to a 10-month unbeaten run away from home. But that win at The Hawthorns was Forest's last on the road during the 2009/10 campaign as Davies' side lost eight of their remaining 10 away fixtures. Davies blamed the club's failure to add to the squad in January as the reason behind Forest's remarkable loss of form.

At least Forest's results at the City Ground were good. Between the end of November and the end of March, Davies' side won 12 successive home matches, equalling the club record set under the legendary Brian Clough in 1980. Blackpool's win at the City Ground on 19th September would be the last time Forest lost at home during the regular season and Davies' side

Forest lost out in the play-offs after a season in which away form cost them dear

went on to win 17 of their remaining 19 League fixtures at the City Ground from that point.

That played a large part in Forest finishing the season in third place and clinching a place in the play-offs where they would meet Blackpool – the only team to do the League double over Davies' side during the regular campaign.

Forest's poor away form continued as they lost the first leg 2–1 at Bloomfield Road, despite taking the lead through Chris Cohen's superb left-foot shot. Forest twice got back on level terms on aggregate in the second leg thanks to a Robert Earnshaw double but Blackpool hit back and DJ Campbell's hat-trick helped them win the second leg 4–3 to go through 6–4 on aggregate.

The future looks bright for Forest despite that disappointment and chairman Nigel Doughty has promised to 'invest sensibly and consistently'. Having now been out of the top flight for 10 years, Forest will be desperate for promotion to the Barclays Premier League in 2010/11.

AUGUST

8th	● Reading	A	D 0–0	Att: 19,640	Ref: P Crossley	Booked: Chambers, Majewski. Dismissed: Chambers.
12th	● Bradford	H	W 3–0	Att: 4,639	Ref: O Langford	Scorers: Anderson, Blackstock, McGugan. Booked: Garner.
15th	● West Brom	H	L 0–1	Att: 22,794	Ref: K Stroud	Booked: Garner, McKenna.
18th	● Watford	H	L 2–4	Att: 19,232	Ref: T Bates	Scorers: Adebola, Blackstock. Booked: Adebola.
22nd	● QPR	A	D 1–1	Att: 13,058	Ref: J Linington	Scorers: McGoldrick.
25th	● Middlesbrough	H	W 2–1	Att: 8,838	Ref: K Wright	Scorers: Chambers, Majewski. Booked: Gunter. AET – Score after 90 mins 1–1.
29th	● Derby	H	W 3–2	Att: 28,143	Ref: M Atkinson	Scorers: Blackstock, Majewski, Tyson. Booked: Garner, Earnshaw, McCleary.

SEPTEMBER

12th	● Sheff Wed	A	D 1–1	Att: 25,270	Ref: S Tanner	Scorers: Blackstock. Booked: Cohen, Garner.
15th	● Ipswich	A	D 1–1	Att: 21,130	Ref: G Ward	Scorers: Earnshaw. Booked: Garner, Gunter, Adebola, McGoldrick.
19th	● Blackpool	H	L 0–1	Att: 23,487	Ref: A Penn	
22nd	● Blackburn	H	L 0–1	Att: 11,553	Ref: M Oliver	
27th	● Plymouth	A	W 0–1	Att: 14,792	Ref: A Woolmer	Scorers: Gunter.
30th	● Scunthorpe	H	W 2–0	Att: 18,332	Ref: D Webb	Scorers: Blackstock, Chambers. Booked: Anderson, Camp.

OCTOBER

3rd	● Peterborough	A	W 1–2	Att: 12,711	Ref: J Moss	Scorers: Anderson, Majewski. Booked: McGoldrick, Tyson, Camp, Cohen.
17th	● Newcastle	H	W 1–0	Att: 29,155	Ref: P Taylor	Scorers: Blackstock. Booked: Garner.
20th	● Barnsley	H	W 1–0	Att: 20,395	Ref: N Miller	Scorers: Moussi. Booked: Tyson, Moussi. Dismissed: Moussi.
24th	● Crystal Palace	A	D 1–1	Att: 15,692	Ref: G Horwood	Scorers: McGoldrick. Booked: Gunter.

NOVEMBER

1st	● Cardiff	A	D 1–1	Att: 20,413	Ref: G Salisbury	Scorers: McGugan. Booked: Wilson.
7th	● Bristol City	H	D 1–1	Att: 21,467	Ref: A Taylor	Scorers: Morgan. Booked: Morgan, Cohen, Gunter, Moussi.
21st	● Middlesbrough	A	D 1–1	Att: 22,710	Ref: L Probert	Scorers: Earnshaw. Booked: McKenna, Cohen.
28th	● Doncaster	H	W 4–1	Att: 22,035	Ref: S Mathieson	Scorers: Earnshaw, McGugan, Morgan, Roberts OG.

DECEMBER

5th	● Leicester	H	W 5–1	Att: 28,626	Ref: M Russell	Scorers: Adebola, Anderson, Earnshaw[3]. Booked: Cohen.
8th	● Sheff Utd	A	D 0–0	Att: 26,490	Ref: A Haines	Booked: Cohen.
12th	● Swansea	A	W 0–1	Att: 16,690	Ref: S Hooper	Scorers: McGoldrick. Booked: Shorey, Morgan, Camp, McKenna.
19th	● Preston	H	W 3–0	Att: 21,582	Ref: F Graham	Scorers: Adebola, McGugan, McKenna.
26th	● Watford	A	D 0–0	Att: 17,086	Ref: A D'Urso	Booked: McGugan, McKenna.
28th	● Coventry	H	W 2–0	Att: 28,608	Ref: M Clattenburg	Scorers: Blackstock, Earnshaw. Booked: Tyson.

JANUARY

2nd	● Birmingham	H	D 0–0	Att: 20,975	Ref: S Bennett	Booked: Gunter.
8th	● West Brom	A	W 1–3	Att: 22,873	Ref: L Probert	Scorers: Blackstock, Cohen, Majewski. Booked: McKenna, Blackstock.
12th	● Birmingham	A	L 1–0	Att: 9,399	Ref: K Friend	Booked: McGoldrick.
16th	● Reading	H	W 2–1	Att: 27,635	Ref: D Deadman	Scorers: Anderson, Earnshaw. Booked: Anderson. Dismissed: Shorey.
26th	● QPR	H	W 5–0	Att: 23,293	Ref: E Ilderton	Scorers: Blackstock, Cohen, Earnshaw[2], Perch. Booked: McKenna.
30th	● Derby	A	L 1–0	Att: 32,674	Ref: N Swarbrick	Booked: Majewski, Morgan, Gunter.

FEBRUARY

6th	● Sheff Wed	H	W 2–1	Att: 27,900	Ref: T Kettle	Scorers: Blackstock[2]. Booked: Gunter, Anderson.
9th	● Coventry	A	L 1–0	Att: 18,225	Ref: T Bates	
13th	● Doncaster	A	L 1–0	Att: 12,768	Ref: A Penn	Booked: Majewski, Wilson. Dismissed: McCleary.
16th	● Sheff Utd	H	W 1–0	Att: 22,076	Ref: N Miller	Scorers: Earnshaw. Booked: Majewski, Perch.
20th	● Middlesbrough	H	W 1–0	Att: 25,498	Ref: P Crossley	Scorers: Cohen. Booked: Majewski, Perch, Blackstock.
27th	● Leicester	A	L 3–0	Att: 31,759	Ref: L Probert	Booked: Earnshaw, Majewski, Gunter, Perch, Morgan.

MARCH

6th	● Swansea	H	W 1–0	Att: 25,012	Ref: C Webster	Scorers: Chambers. Booked: Moussi.
13th	● Preston	A	L 3–2	Att: 14,426	Ref: M Haywood	Scorers: Blackstock, Earnshaw. Booked: Blackstock, Morgan, Wilson.
16th	● Barnsley	A	L 2–1	Att: 13,174	Ref: K Friend	Scorers: Blackstock. Booked: Moussi, Earnshaw, Majewski.
20th	● Peterborough	H	W 1–0	Att: 24,582	Ref: K Hill	Scorers: Earnshaw. Booked: Majewski, Wilson, Cohen.
23rd	● Crystal Palace	H	W 2–0	Att: 20,025	Ref: A Hall	Scorers: Morgan, Tyson. Booked: Wilson, Morgan.
29th	● Newcastle	A	L 2–0	Att: 45,987	Ref: A Wiley	Booked: Morgan, Wilson, McCleary.

APRIL

3rd	● Bristol City	A	D 1–1	Att: 16,125	Ref: P Crossley	Scorers: Moussi. Booked: Perch, Tyson, Chambers, Morgan.
5th	● Cardiff	H	D 0–0	Att: 22,185	Ref: C Foy	Booked: Blackstock, McGoldrick.
10th	● Ipswich	H	W 3–0	Att: 23,459	Ref: D Foster	Scorers: Chambers, Earnshaw, Moussi. Booked: Blackstock.
17th	● Blackpool	A	L 3–1	Att: 11,164	Ref: A Taylor	Scorers: Garner. Booked: Lynch.
24th	● Plymouth	H	W 3–0	Att: 22,602	Ref: N Swarbrick	Scorers: Anderson, Blackstock, Earnshaw.

MAY

2nd	● Scunthorpe	A	D 2–2	Att: 8,119	Ref: F Graham	Scorers: Boyd, Garner.
8th	● Blackpool	A	L 2–1	Att: 11,805	Ref: P Dowd	Scorers: Cohen. Booked: Blackstock, Perch, McKenna, Gunter, Earnshaw.
11th	● Blackpool	H	L 3–4	Att: 28,358	Ref: M Clattenburg	Scorers: Adebola, Earnshaw[2]. Booked: Perch. Agg: 4–6.

● Coca-Cola Championship/Play-offs ● FA Cup ● Carling Cup

NOTTINGHAM FOREST

CHAMPIONSHIP GOALKEEPER STATS

Player	Minutes on pitch	Appearances	Match starts	Completed matches	Sub appearances	Subbed off	Saved with feet	Punched	Parried	Tipped over	Fumbled	Tipped round	Caught	Blocked	Clean sheets	Goals conceded	Save %	Saved	Resulting in goals	Opposition miss	Fouls committed	Free-kicks won	Yellow cards	Red cards
							SAVES BREAKDOWN											**PENALTIES**						
Lee Camp	4357	45	45	45	0	0	4	15	27	12	2	18	135	5	19	38	85.04	1	4	0	0	12	3	0
Paul Smith	94	1	1	1	0	0	0	0	1	0	0	0	6	0	0	2	77.78	0	0	0	0	0	0	0

CHAMPIONSHIP OUTFIELD PLAYER STATS

Player	Minutes on pitch	Appearances	Match starts	Completed matches	Substitute appearances	Subbed off	Goals scored	Assists	Shots on target	Shots off target	Crosses	Tackles made	Defensive clearances	Defensive blocks	Fouls committed	Free-kicks won	Caught offside	Yellow cards	Red cards
Dele Adebola	1506	33	13	4	20	9	3	3	14	15	4	22	7	1	41	14	23	2	0
Paul Anderson	2758	37	33	10	4	23	4	7	23	14	58	70	3	4	18	31	6	3	0
Dexter Blackstock	2800	39	30	16	9	14	13	6	34	30	3	63	17	0	73	38	18	5	0
George Boyd	413	6	5	2	1	3	1	0	6	2	10	7	1	1	6	4	2	0	0
Luke Chambers	1808	23	17	15	6	1	3	1	7	3	13	68	17	10	18	9	1	2	1
Chris Cohen	4212	44	44	42	0	2	3	6	19	20	116	145	23	6	68	55	3	7	0
Robert Earnshaw	2034	32	20	7	12	13	15	1	45	21	7	25	1	0	9	21	26	3	0
Joe Garner	1091	18	14	3	4	11	2	0	13	12	11	38	2	2	25	24	2	5	0
Chris Gunter	4263	44	44	44	0	0	1	2	3	1	63	130	26	6	33	60	1	6	0
Joel Lynch	803	10	9	7	1	2	0	0	0	0	15	22	6	1	7	12	0	1	0
Radoslaw Majewski	2613	35	31	9	4	22	3	9	33	27	37	85	3	3	23	27	5	8	0
Garath McCleary	723	24	1	0	23	0	0	1	4	8	15	21	0	2	9	5	2	2	1
David McGoldrick	1800	33	18	7	15	11	3	2	13	15	9	38	1	4	25	15	15	3	0
Lewis McGugan	657	18	6	1	12	5	3	3	6	5	10	26	1	1	4	5	0	1	0
Paul McKenna	3294	35	35	33	0	2	1	1	10	13	23	106	28	1	42	35	2	6	0
Wes Morgan	4240	44	44	43	0	1	3	1	7	5	3	155	77	27	59	50	2	8	0
Guy Moussi	1998	27	21	15	6	5	3	1	11	6	10	56	9	6	25	21	0	4	1
James Perch	1333	17	14	12	3	2	1	3	2	6		47	19	9	16	20	0	4	0
Nicky Shorey	838	9	9	8	0	0	0	2	0	1	14	18	7	2	5	2	0	1	1
Nathan Tyson	1848	33	17	8	16	9	2	0	12	16	60	60	1	4	11	29	10	4	0
Kelvin Wilson	3361	35	35	34	0	1	0	0	0	6	0	90	50	17	44	39	0	6	0

Coca-Cola CHAMPIONSHIP

SEASON TOTALS

Goals scored	65
Goals conceded	40
Clean sheets	19
Shots on target	263
Shots off target	222
Shots per goal	7.46
Pens awarded	4
Pens scored	3
Pens conceded	5
Offsides	118
Corners	243
Crosses	487
Players used	26
Fouls committed	561
Free-kicks won	528

CARDS RECEIVED

84 4

SEQUENCES

Wins	5
(27/09/09–20/10/09)	
Losses	2
(on three occasions)	
Draws	4
(24/10/09–21/11/09)	
Undefeated	19
(27/09/09–26/01/10)	
Without win	4
(on two occasions)	
Undefeated home	19
(30/09/09–24/04/10)	
Undefeated away	13
(08/08/09–08/01/10)	
Without scoring	2
(on two occasions)	
Without conceding	5
(08/12/09–28/12/09)	
Scoring	11
(27/09/09–05/12/09)	
Conceding	7
(15/08/09–19/09/09)	

League position chart

AUG	SEP	OCT	NOV	DEC	JAN	FEB	MAR	APR	MAY
17	14	10	4	3	2	3	3	3	3

LEAGUE POSITION AT THE END OF EACH MONTH

SEASON INFORMATION

Highest position: 2
Lowest position: 23
Average goals scored per game: 1.41
Average goals conceded per game: 0.87

MATCH RECORDS

Goals scored per match

		W	D	L	Pts
Failed to score	11	0	4	7	4
Scored 1 goal	18	8	8	2	32
Scored 2 goals	9	6	1	2	19
Scored 3 goals	5	5	0	0	15
Scored 4+ goals	3	3	0	0	9

Goals conceded per match

		W	D	L	Pts
Clean sheet	19	15	4	0	49
Conceded 1 goal	19	6	8	5	26
Conceded 2 goals	4	1	1	2	4
Conceded 3 goals	3	0	0	3	0
Conceded 4+ goals	1	0	0	1	0

EARLIEST STRIKE

RADOSLAW MAJEWSKI
(v Derby) 0:50

LATEST STRIKE

PAUL ANDERSON
(v Plymouth) 92:38

Robert Earnshaw

GOAL DETAILS

How the goals were struck

SCORED		CONCEDED
33	Right foot	18
24	Left foot	13
6	Header	7
2	Other	2

How the goals were struck

SCORED		CONCEDED
48	Open play	24
4	Cross	4
4	Corner	3
3	Penalty	4
2	Direct from free-kick	2
3	Free-kick	1
1	Own goal	2

Distance from goal

SCORED		CONCEDED
26	6YDS	10
30	18YDS	23
9	18+YDS	7

GOALS SCORED/CONCEDED PER FIVE-MINUTE INTERVALS

MINS	5	10	15	20	25	30	35	40	45	50	55	60	65	70	75	80	85	90
FOR	3	0	3	6	3	2	4	0	8	4	3	7	1	0	3	10	3	5
AGN	3	0	1	2	2	1	4	2	0	2	3	0	5	1	2	4	3	5

PETERBOROUGH UNITED

CLUB SUMMARY

FORMED	1934
MANAGER	Gary Johnson
GROUND	London Road
CAPACITY	15,314
NICKNAME	The Posh
WEBSITE	www.theposh.com

The New Football Pools PLAYER OF THE SEASON — Joe Lewis

OVERALL
P	W	D	L	F	A	GD
51	11	10	30	56	90	-34

COCA-COLA CHAMPIONSHIP
Pos	P	W	D	L	F	A	GD	Pts
24	46	8	10	28	46	80	-34	34

HOME
Pos	P	W	D	L	F	A	GD	Pts
23	23	6	5	12	32	37	-5	23

AWAY
Pos	P	W	D	L	F	A	GD	Pts
24	23	2	5	16	14	43	-29	11

CUP PROGRESS DETAILS
Competition	Round reached	Knocked out by
FA Cup	R3	Tottenham
Carling Cup	R4	Blackburn

BIGGEST WIN (ALL COMPS)
11/08/09 4–0 v Wycombe

BIGGEST DEFEAT (ALL COMPS)
17/04/10 0–6 v Reading

THE PLAYER WITH THE MOST
GOALS SCORED Craig Mackail-Smith	**10**
SHOTS ON TARGET Craig Mackail-Smith	**44**
SHOTS OFF TARGET Lee Frecklington, Aaron Mclean	**32**
SHOTS WITHOUT SCORING Reuben Reid	**14**
ASSISTS George Boyd	**9**
OFFSIDES Craig Mackail-Smith	**45**
FOULS Lee Frecklington	**55**
FOULS WITHOUT A CARD Chris Whelpdale	**18**
FREE-KICKS WON Craig Mackail-Smith	**61**
DEFENSIVE CLEARANCES Craig Morgan	**79**

actim INDEX — FOR THE 2009/10 COCA-COLA CHAMPIONSHIP SEASON

Rank	Player	Pts
33	Craig Mackail-Smith	513
112	Joe Lewis	399
223	Craig Morgan	268

ATTENDANCE RECORD
High	Average	Low
12,877	8,913	6,445
v Newcastle (03/04/2010)		v Bristol City (27/03/2010)

WHEN Peterborough sealed a return to the second tier of English football in May 2009, fans were expecting an exciting season full of the attacking football that had carried them from Coca-Cola League 2 in back-to-back seasons under Darren Ferguson.

A year later, the Posh are back in npower League 1 following a disappointing campaign which saw them collect just eight League victories, using more than 40 players and four managers in the process.

Ferguson took eight games to gain the first of those wins, a 3–2 victory over Reading in late September, but his policy of giving the young players that had shone in League 1 the chance to prove themselves at a higher level ultimately proved unsuccessful.

Peterborough did enjoy a run in the Carling Cup, starting with a 4–0 victory at Wycombe and taking in a 2–1 win against Ipswich, but a 5–2 defeat at Barclays Premier League side Blackburn denied them a place in the quarter-finals.

The club surprisingly parted company with Ferguson in November and, while he took over at Championship rivals Preston in January, Kettering manager Mark Cooper was chosen to replace him at London Road. The 41-year-old – who had not managed in the Football League before – was then dismissed after just two months, during which time he won just a single game.

The Posh briefly rallied under the guidance of manager number three, Jim Gannon, who collected four wins as the club attempted to stave off relegation, but the departure of star forward George Boyd

A tumultuous season ended with the Posh making an immediate return to League One

to join promotion-chasing Nottingham Forest on loan in March ultimately proved crucial.

Relegation was finally confirmed following a 2–2 draw away to Barnsley on Easter Monday and Gary Johnson became the fourth manager of their season at the start of April after Gannon had declined to commit his future to the club beyond the end of the 2009/10 campaign.

Johnson's track record at Yeovil and Bristol City suggests he should make the Posh competitive back in League 1, and the 2–1 win at Plymouth on the final day of the campaign offered at least some encouragement to a group of supporters who had endured a season of turmoil.

Much will again be expected of strikers Aaron Mclean and Craig Mackail-Smith – if they stay at London Road. The self-styled 'Mac Attack' hit 44 goals between them last time the club were in League 1 and the club will hope they can provide the basis for a promotion challenge once again during 2010/11.

Goalkeeper Joe Lewis can't prevent Peterborough conceding yet another goal, on this occasion during the home defeat to Newcastle

RESULTS 2009/10

AUGUST

8th	● Derby	A	L 2–1	Att: 33,010	Ref: P Taylor	Scorers: Boyd. **Booked:** Keates, Batt, Boyd.
11th	● Wycombe	A	W 0–4	Att: 2,078	Ref: T Kettle	Scorers: Boyd, Frecklington, Mclean, Rowe.
15th	● Sheff Wed	H	D 1–1	Att: 10,747	Ref: A D'Urso	Scorers: Mackail-Smith.
18th	● West Brom	H	L 2–3	Att: 8,752	Ref: G Horwood	Scorers: Mackail-Smith, Mclean. **Booked:** Batt, Coutts.
22nd	● Preston	A	L 2–0	Att: 11,549	Ref: D Webb	**Booked:** Zakuani.
25th	● Ipswich	H	W 2–1	Att: 5,451	Ref: R Shoebridge	Scorers: Boyd, Frecklington. **Booked:** Rowe, Batt.
31st	● Crystal Palace	H	D 1–1	Att: 8,473	Ref: K Friend	Scorers: Batt. **Booked:** Boyd, Frecklington.

SEPTEMBER

12th	● QPR	A	D 1–1	Att: 11,814	Ref: O Langford	Scorers: Mclean. **Booked:** Zakuani, Batt.
15th	● Leicester	A	D 1–1	Att: 21,485	Ref: R Booth	Scorers: Boyd. **Booked:** Morgan, Frecklington, Mclean, Diagouraga.
19th	● Reading	H	W 3–2	Att: 8,521	Ref: C Sarginson	Scorers: Boyd, Mackail-Smith, Mclean.
22nd	● Newcastle	H	W 2–0	Att: 10,298	Ref: K Stroud	Scorers: Mackail-Smith, Williams. **Booked:** Diagouraga, Boyd.
26th	● Blackpool	A	L 2–0	Att: 7,728	Ref: T Bates	
29th	● Plymouth	H	L 1–2	Att: 7,114	Ref: A Hall	Scorers: Mackail-Smith. **Booked:** Mackail-Smith.

OCTOBER

3rd	● Nottm Forest	H	L 1–2	Att: 12,711	Ref: J Moss	Scorers: Mclean. **Booked:** Williams.
17th	● Bristol City	A	D 1–1	Att: 13,833	Ref: K Hill	Scorers: Boyd. **Booked:** Day, Morgan.
20th	● Doncaster	A	L 3–1	Att: 9,288	Ref: C Webster	Scorers: Mclean.
24th	● Scunthorpe	H	W 3–0	Att: 8,051	Ref: M Jones	Scorers: Boyd[2], Mackail-Smith. **Booked:** Mclean.
27th	● Blackburn	A	L 5–2	Att: 8,419	Ref: A Taylor	Scorers: Boyd, Whelpdale. **Dismissed:** Lewis.
31st	● Barnsley	H	L 1–2	Att: 8,556	Ref: C Boyeson	Scorers: Boyd.

NOVEMBER

7th	● Newcastle	A	L 3–1	Att: 43,067	Ref: A D'Urso	Scorers: Keates. **Booked:** Bennett.
21st	● Sheff Utd	A	L 1–0	Att: 25,144	Ref: G Hegley	
28th	● Middlesbrough	H	D 2–2	Att: 10,772	Ref: D Phillips	Scorers: Batt, Boyd. **Booked:** Mclean, Batt.

DECEMBER

5th	● Swansea	H	D 2–2	Att: 7,312	Ref: R Booth	Scorers: Mclean, Whelpdale. **Booked:** Griffiths.
8th	● Ipswich	A	D 0–0	Att: 19,975	Ref: A Hall	**Booked:** Boyd.
12th	● Coventry	A	L 3–2	Att: 15,190	Ref: R East	Scorers: Mackail-Smith[2]. **Booked:** Batt.
19th	● Watford	H	W 2–1	Att: 7,723	Ref: K Evans	Scorers: Frecklington, Geohaghon.
26th	● West Brom	A	L 2–0	Att: 24,924	Ref: M Jones	**Booked:** Frecklington, Zakuani, Morgan.
28th	● Cardiff	H	D 4–4	Att: 9,796	Ref: D Whitestone	Scorers: Boyd, Lee, Simpson[2]. **Booked:** Morgan, Batt.

JANUARY

2nd	● Tottenham	A	L 4–0	Att: 35,862	Ref: L Mason	**Booked:** Boyd, Lee.
16th	● Derby	H	L 0–3	Att: 10,280	Ref: N Miller	**Booked:** Coutts. **Dismissed:** Morgan, Bennett.
23rd	● Sheff Wed	A	L 2–1	Att: 24,882	Ref: D Foster	Scorers: Livermore. **Booked:** Livermore.
26th	● Preston	H	L 0–1	Att: 7,134	Ref: D Sheldrake	
30th	● Crystal Palace	A	L 2–0	Att: 14,699	Ref: G Salisbury	

FEBRUARY

6th	● QPR	H	W 1–0	Att: 8,933	Ref: D McDermid	Scorers: Mclean. **Booked:** Lee, Simpson, Bennett.
9th	● Cardiff	A	L 2–0	Att: 17,686	Ref: A Penn	
13th	● Middlesbrough	A	L 1–0	Att: 18,412	Ref: J Moss	**Booked:** Frecklington.
16th	● Ipswich	H	W 3–1	Att: 9,428	Ref: J Linington	Scorers: Dickinson, Frecklington, Morgan. **Booked:** Simpson.
27th	● Swansea	A	L 1–0	Att: 16,175	Ref: G Ward	

MARCH

6th	● Coventry	H	L 0–1	Att: 10,469	Ref: R Booth	
9th	● Sheff Utd	H	W 1–0	Att: 6,674	Ref: J Singh	Scorers: Mackail-Smith. **Booked:** Torres, Dickinson.
13th	● Watford	A	W 0–1	Att: 16,591	Ref: A Taylor	Scorers: Dickinson.
16th	● Doncaster	H	L 1–2	Att: 6,773	Ref: F Graham	Scorers: Lee.
20th	● Nottm Forest	A	L 1–0	Att: 24,582	Ref: K Hill	
23rd	● Scunthorpe	A	L 4–0	Att: 4,995	Ref: E Ilderton	**Booked:** Frecklington.
27th	● Bristol City	H	L 0–1	Att: 6,445	Ref: D Webb	**Booked:** Simpson.

APRIL

3rd	● Newcastle	H	L 2–3	Att: 12,877	Ref: M Haywood	Scorers: Dickinson, Green. **Booked:** Zakuani.
5th	● Barnsley	A	D 2–2	Att: 11,290	Ref: T Bates	Scorers: Bennett, Rowe. **Booked:** Geohaghon.
10th	● Leicester	H	L 1–2	Att: 9,651	Ref: G Scott	Scorers: Rowe. **Booked:** Rowe.
17th	● Reading	A	L 6–0	Att: 15,982	Ref: C Boyeson	
24th	● Blackpool	H	L 0–1	Att: 7,812	Ref: C Webster	**Booked:** Dickinson.

MAY

2nd	● Plymouth	A	W 1–2	Att: 8,557	Ref: S Tanner	Scorers: Mackail-Smith[2]. **Booked:** Koranteng, Andrew, Lee.

● Coca-Cola Championship/Play-offs ● FA Cup ● Carling Cup

CHAMPIONSHIP GOALKEEPER STATS

Player	Minutes on pitch	Appearances	Match starts	Completed matches	Sub appearances	Subbed off	SAVES BREAKDOWN								Clean sheets	Goals conceded	Save %	PENALTIES			Fouls committed	Free-kicks won	Yellow cards	Red cards
							Saved with feet	Punched	Parried	Tipped over	Fumbled	Tipped round	Caught	Blocked				Saved	Resulting in goals	Opposition miss				
Ben Amos	96	1	1	1	0	0	0	2	1	0	0	0	2	0	0	2	71.43	0	0	0	0	0	0	0
Joe Lewis	4028	43	43	41	0	2	8	13	29	11	3	9	185	5	5	69	79.03	0	4	0	0	6	0	0
James McKeown	293	4	2	2	2	0	0	0	10	1	0	0	13	0	0	9	72.73	0	0	0	0	0	0	0

CHAMPIONSHIP OUTFIELD PLAYER STATS

Player	Minutes on pitch	Appearances	Match starts	Completed matches	Substitute appearances	Subbed off	Goals scored	Assists	Shots on target	Shots off target	Crosses	Tackles made	Defensive clearances	Defensive blocks	Fouls committed	Free-kicks won	Caught offside	Yellow cards	Red cards
Danny Andrew	192	2	2	2	0	0	0	0	0	0	4	6	0	0	3	0	0	1	0
Shaun Batt	849	20	5	3	15	2	2	2	11	7	15	22	2	1	21	14	0	6	0
Ryan Bennett	1887	22	20	18	2	1	1	0	2	2	5	79	33	20	24	7	1	2	1
George Boyd	2974	32	32	28	0	4	9	9	31	21	89	91	10	2	23	28	9	3	0
Paul Coutts	1139	16	13	7	3	6	0	0	8	5	18	36	2	1	15	15	0	2	0
Jamie Day	262	5	2	1	3	1	0	0	2	4	5	17	1	0	2	4	0	1	0
Toumani Diagouraga	1483	19	18	11	1	7	0	0	4	5	1	66	6	5	16	5	0	1	0
Liam Dickinson	773	9	9	5	0	4	3	1	10	3	15	8	4	1	17	17	8	2	0
Lee Frecklington	2666	35	26	19	9	7	2	3	28	32	21	112	9	3	55	41	0	5	0
Exodus Geohaghon	1545	19	17	14	2	3	1	0	4	5	1	43	31	3	16	12	0	1	0
Kerrea Gilbert	715	10	7	5	3	2	0	0	0	1	10	23	8	0	4	9	0	0	0
Dominic Green	631	11	6	4	5	2	1	0	8	1	24	13	0	0	5	2	1	0	0
Scott Griffiths	1805	20	20	17	0	3	0	1	2	4	39	46	23	4	8	23	0	1	0
Dean Keates	285	6	2	1	4	1	1	0	1	0	1	12	3	2	4	3	0	1	0
Nathan Koranteng	281	4	3	1	1	2	0	0	2	4	4	4	0	0	7	4	1	1	0
Charlie Lee	2552	33	28	22	5	6	2	0	13	20	16	108	23	8	33	35	0	2	0
Mark Little	784	9	9	7	0	2	0	1	2	5	11	24	8	0	2	4	0	0	0
Jake Livermore	867	9	9	9	0	0	1	0	3	2	5	19	5	1	5	9	0	1	0
Craig Mackail-Smith	3652	43	39	31	4	8	10	2	44	22	21	63	0	3	34	61	45	1	0
Russell Martin	874	10	8	8	2	0	0	1	4	1	20	38	6	1	6	5	0	0	0
Romone McCrae	62	2	0	0	2	0	0	0	0	0	0	1	2	0	0	0	0	0	0
Izale McLeod	152	4	2	0	2	0	0	0	1	2	0	0	1	0	4	2	1	0	0
Aaron Mclean	2910	35	30	24	5	6	7	2	32	32	15	47	10	2	45	32	28	3	0
Danny Mills	145	3	1	0	2	1	0	0	0	0	1	2	1	1	4	1	1	0	0
Craig Morgan	3120	34	33	31	1	1	1	1	6	7	4	131	79	15	21	13	0	4	1
Krystian Pearce	50	2	0	0	2	0	0	0	0	0	0	5	0	0	2	0	0	0	0
Reuben Reid	718	13	5	1	8	4	0	0	8	6	11	10	3	0	13	12	3	0	0
Danny Rose	358	6	4	2	2	2	0	1	4	8	13	17	1	0	2	10	0	0	0
Tommy Rowe	2523	32	26	22	6	4	2	3	5	14	40	67	18	3	9	28	5	1	0
Josh Simpson	1198	21	8	7	13	1	2	0	11	3	12	28	2	0	15	20	2	3	0
Sergio Torres	548	9	7	2	2	5	0	0	5	4	10	6	2	1	5	14	0	1	0
Chris Whelpdale	2164	29	27	13	2	14	1	0	18	15	45	58	13	7	18	15	2	0	0
Tom Williams	1174	15	14	8	1	6	0	0	4	0	45	54	11	3	4	14	1	1	0
Ben Wright	89	4	0	0	4	0	0	0	1	1	0	1	0	1	2	0	1	0	0
Gabriel Zakuani	2539	29	28	23	1	5	0	0	3	11	0	72	63	18	30	22	0	4	0

actim

SEASON TOTALS

Goals scored	46
Goals conceded	80
Clean sheets	5
Shots on target	271
Shots off target	250
Shots per goal	11.33
Pens awarded	5
Pens scored	4
Pens conceded	4
Offsides	109
Corners	260
Crosses	521
Players used	38
Fouls committed	474
Free-kicks won	487

CARDS RECEIVED

48 **2**

SEQUENCES

Wins	2
(09/03/10–13/03/10)	
Losses	5
(16/03/10–03/04/10)	
Draws	3
(on two occasions)	
Undefeated	4
(31/08/09–19/09/09)	
Without win	9
(16/03/10–24/04/10)	
Undefeated home	4
(28/11/09–28/12/09)	
Undefeated away	2
(12/09/09–15/09/09)	
Without scoring	3
(20/03/10–27/03/10)	
Without conceding	2
(09/03/10–13/03/10)	
Scoring	7
(29/09/09–07/11/09)	
Conceding	13
(08/08/09–20/10/09)	

LEAGUE POSITION AT THE END OF EACH MONTH

AUG	SEP	OCT	NOV	DEC	JAN	FEB	MAR	APR	MAY
21	22	23	24	24	24	24	24	24	24

SEASON INFORMATION
Highest position: 15
Lowest position: 24
Average goals scored per game: 1.00
Average goals conceded per game: 1.74

MATCH RECORDS

Goals scored per match

		W	D	L	Pts
Failed to score	17	0	1	16	1
Scored 1 goal	17	3	5	9	14
Scored 2 goals	8	2	3	3	9
Scored 3 goals	3	3	0	0	9
Scored 4+ goals	1	0	1	0	1

Goals conceded per match

		W	D	L	Pts
Clean sheet	5	4	1	0	13
Conceded 1 goal	16	3	5	8	14
Conceded 2 goals	16	1	3	12	6
Conceded 3 goals	6	0	0	6	0
Conceded 4+ goals	3	0	1	2	1

EARLIEST STRIKE

RYAN BENNETT
(v Barnsley) 4:31

LATEST STRIKE

AARON MCLEAN
(v Swansea) 94:04

Jake Livermore

GOAL DETAILS

How the goals were struck

SCORED		CONCEDED
22	Right foot	39
10	Left foot	21
14	Header	20
0	Other	0

How the goals were struck

SCORED		CONCEDED
29	Open play	47
8	Cross	15
2	Corner	6
4	Penalty	4
1	Direct from free-kick	3
2	Free-kick	4
0	Own goal	1

Distance from goal

SCORED		CONCEDED
21	6YDS	35
17	18YDS	35
8	18+YDS	10

GOALS SCORED/CONCEDED PER FIVE-MINUTE INTERVALS

MINS	5	10	15	20	25	30	35	40	45	50	55	60	65	70	75	80	85	90
FOR	1	2	1	1	2	0	2	1	2	3	8	0	4	3	1	7	2	6
AGN	4	5	5	3	6	7	8	3	8	4	2	4	5	5	3	2	3	3

PLYMOUTH ARGYLE

CLUB SUMMARY

FORMED	1886
MANAGER	TBC
GROUND	Home Park
CAPACITY	21,118
NICKNAME	The Pilgrims
WEBSITE	www.pafc.co.uk

The New Football Pools PLAYER OF THE SEASON — *Carl Fletcher*

OVERALL

P	W	D	L	F	A	GD
49	11	9	29	44	73	-29

COCA-COLA CHAMPIONSHIP

Pos	P	W	D	L	F	A	GD	Pts
23	46	11	8	27	43	68	-25	41

HOME

Pos	P	W	D	L	F	A	GD	Pts
24	23	5	6	12	20	30	-10	21

AWAY

Pos	P	W	D	L	F	A	GD	Pts
18	23	6	2	15	23	38	-15	20

CUP PROGRESS DETAILS

Competition	Round reached	Knocked out by
FA Cup	R3	Newcastle
Carling Cup	R1	Gillingham

BIGGEST WIN (ALL COMPS)
28/12/09 4–1 v Reading

BIGGEST DEFEAT (ALL COMPS)
0–3 on 2 occasions

THE PLAYER WITH THE MOST

GOALS SCORED	Jamie Mackie	**8**
SHOTS ON TARGET	Jamie Mackie	**45**
SHOTS OFF TARGET	Jamie Mackie	**44**
SHOTS WITHOUT SCORING	Cillian Sheridan	**12**
ASSISTS	Chris Clark	**5**
OFFSIDES	Jamie Mackie	**50**
FOULS	Rory Fallon	**83**
FOULS WITHOUT A CARD	Bondz N'Gala	**8**
FREE-KICKS WON	Jamie Mackie	**55**
DEFENSIVE CLEARANCES	Kari Arnason	**51**

actim INDEX FOR THE 2009/10 COCA-COLA CHAMPIONSHIP SEASON

RANK	PLAYER	PTS
164	Jamie Mackie	334
170	Carl Fletcher	327
172	Karl Duguid	326

ATTENDANCE RECORD

HIGH	AVERAGE	LOW
14,792	10,316	7,243
v Nottm Forest (27/09/2009)		v Barnsley (30/03/2010)

A shortage of goals ultimately cost Plymouth their Championship status

PLYMOUTH endured a difficult season that ended with the club being relegated from the Coca-Cola Championship.

The Pilgrims made a poor start to the campaign as they failed to win in their first nine League games, a run in which they slumped to seven consecutive defeats.

Former Argyle and England striker Paul Mariner was appointed as head coach at Home Park in December, with Paul Sturrock moving upstairs into a business support role. But Mariner failed to turn the club's fortunes around and their six-year stay in the second tier was confirmed as over with two matches remaining when they were beaten 2–0 by champions Newcastle.

Mariner paid the price as chairman Sir Roy Gardner announced that the club would be looking for a more experienced manager, with Mariner set to stay on in a coaching capacity along with John Carver. Mariner said: 'I am disappointed we could not produce the results we wanted. I am a realist and understand why and how the board came to the conclusion that they have done.'

While Mariner is likely to stay at the club, Sturrock left Home Park – the second time he had departed the club following his move to Southampton in 2004 – in April having revealed that he was eager to return

Paul Mariner was sacked by Plymouth at the end of the campaign

to football management.

Plymouth's poor home form always seemed likely to leave them up against it in their battle to avoid the drop as they secured only five wins at Home Park all season. A lack of goals was also a major problem, with Argyle finding the back of the net a paltry 20 times at home and on just 43 occasions all season in the Championship.

Results in the knockout competitions were also disappointing. They fell at the point of entry in both the Carling Cup and FA Cup to Gillingham and Newcastle respectively.

Argyle finished the season with a run of five straight defeats, scoring just one goal in the process. With only 11 wins in the Championship all term, it meant that they finished second-bottom of the table and eight points adrift of Crystal Palace, who finished in 21st place, just above the relegation zone.

The experience of captain Carl Fletcher and fellow midfielder Damien Johnson will be vital for Argyle in 2010/11, when they will bid to secure an immediate return to the second tier. Keeping hold of Jamie Mackie, who scored eight League goals, will also be a priority, as the striker caught the eye of some rival Championship clubs during 2009/10.

Forward Bradley Wright-Phillips shows his frustration

AUGUST

8th	● Crystal Palace	A	D 1–1	Att: 14,358	Ref: A Penn	**Scorers:** Timar. **Booked:** Timar, Summerfield.
11th	◉ Gillingham	A	L 2–1	Att: 3,306	Ref: J Singh	**Scorers:** Summerfield. **Booked:** Mackie, Sawyer, Seip, Fallon.
15th	● QPR	H	D 1–1	Att: 11,588	Ref: R East	**Scorers:** Gorkss OG. **Booked:** Fletcher.
18th	● Cardiff	H	L 1–3	Att: 11,918	Ref: R Booth	**Scorers:** Gow. **Booked:** Sawyer.
22nd	● Derby	A	L 2–1	Att: 26,186	Ref: C Pawson	**Scorers:** Judge. **Booked:** Clark, Fletcher.
29th	● Sheff Wed	H	L 1–3	Att: 10,228	Ref: A Haines	**Scorers:** Gow. **Booked:** Arnason, Seip, Paterson.

SEPTEMBER

12th	● West Brom	A	L 3–1	Att: 22,190	Ref: G Salisbury	**Scorers:** Mackie.
15th	● Watford	A	L 0–1	Att: 8,703	Ref: G Scott	**Booked:** Timar, Arnason, McNamee.
19th	● Newcastle	A	L 3–1	Att: 42,898	Ref: S Mathieson	**Scorers:** Duguid. **Booked:** Gray, Mackie, Arnason.
27th	● Nottm Forest	H	L 0–1	Att: 14,792	Ref: A Woolmer	
29th	● Peterborough	A	W 1–2	Att: 7,114	Ref: A Hall	**Scorers:** Fallon, Mackie. **Booked:** Mackie, Fletcher.

OCTOBER

3rd	● Scunthorpe	H	W 2–1	Att: 9,780	Ref: A D'Urso	**Scorers:** Fallon, Judge. **Booked:** Fallon.
17th	● Blackpool	A	L 2–0	Att: 7,765	Ref: D Webb	**Booked:** Fletcher, Timar, Gray, Gow.
20th	● Bristol City	A	L 3–1	Att: 15,021	Ref: G Hegley	**Scorers:** Mackie.
24th	● Ipswich	H	D 1–1	Att: 10,875	Ref: S Hooper	**Scorers:** Fletcher. **Booked:** Lowry. **Dismissed:** Blake.
31st	● Middlesbrough	A	W 0–1	Att: 21,141	Ref: M Russell	**Scorers:** Mackie. **Booked:** Fletcher.

NOVEMBER

7th	● Doncaster	H	W 2–1	Att: 9,420	Ref: P Taylor	**Scorers:** Fallon, Judge. **Booked:** Gray, Mackie.
21st	● Leicester	A	L 1–0	Att: 27,174	Ref: D McDermid	**Booked:** Sawyer, Mackie.

DECEMBER

5th	● Sheff Utd	H	L 0–1	Att: 9,231	Ref: G Horwood	**Booked:** Lowry, Sawyer.
8th	● Swansea	A	L 1–0	Att: 14,004	Ref: S Tanner	**Booked:** Gray, Lowry, Judge, Fletcher. **Dismissed:** Lowry.
12th	● Preston	A	L 2–0	Att: 12,231	Ref: M Oliver	**Booked:** Blake.
19th	● Coventry	H	L 0–1	Att: 8,347	Ref: K Stroud	
26th	● Cardiff	A	W 0–1	Att: 24,010	Ref: P Gibbs	**Scorers:** Sawyer. **Booked:** R Johnson, Fallon, Larrieu, Fletcher.
28th	● Reading	H	W 4–1	Att: 12,091	Ref: S Hooper	**Scorers:** Arnason, Barnes, Judge[2]. **Booked:** R Johnson, Mackie.

JANUARY

2nd	● Newcastle	H	D 0–0	Att: 16,451	Ref: A Wiley	**Booked:** Arnason, Duguid, Fallon.
13th	● Newcastle	A	L 3–0	Att: 15,805	Ref: A D'Urso	
16th	● Crystal Palace	H	L 0–1	Att: 9,318	Ref: T Bates	**Booked:** Sawyer.
26th	● Derby	H	W 1–0	Att: 7,996	Ref: A Hall	**Scorers:** Mackie. **Booked:** Fallon, Sawyer.
30th	● Sheff Wed	A	L 2–1	Att: 22,590	Ref: K Wright	**Scorers:** Fallon. **Booked:** Duguid, R Johnson.

FEBRUARY

6th	● West Brom	H	L 0–1	Att: 12,053	Ref: S Tanner	**Booked:** Sawyer, D Johnson, Arnason.
9th	● Reading	A	L 2–1	Att: 15,484	Ref: O Langford	**Scorers:** Fletcher. **Booked:** Noone, Clark.
13th	● Barnsley	A	W 1–3	Att: 11,661	Ref: K Evans	**Scorers:** Fallon, Fletcher, Mackie. **Booked:** Fallon, Fletcher, Bolasie, R Johnson.
16th	● Swansea	H	D 1–1	Att: 9,185	Ref: K Hill	**Scorers:** D Johnson.
20th	● Leicester	H	D 1–1	Att: 11,581	Ref: R East	**Scorers:** Noone. **Booked:** Arnason.
27th	● Sheff Utd	A	L 4–3	Att: 24,886	Ref: C Sarginson	**Scorers:** Bolasie, Mackie, Mason. **Booked:** Stockdale, Mackie.

MARCH

6th	● Preston	H	D 1–1	Att: 9,582	Ref: A Woolmer	**Scorers:** D Johnson.
9th	● QPR	A	L 2–0	Att: 12,013	Ref: P Tierney	**Booked:** Duguid, Eckersley, Barker.
13th	● Coventry	A	D 1–1	Att: 18,127	Ref: A Haines	**Scorers:** Arnason. **Booked:** Duguid, Bolasie.
16th	● Bristol City	H	W 3–2	Att: 9,289	Ref: T Kettle	**Scorers:** Clark, Fletcher, Wright-Phillips. **Booked:** R Johnson, Stockdale.
20th	● Scunthorpe	A	L 2–1	Att: 5,153	Ref: A Taylor	**Scorers:** Mackie. **Booked:** R Johnson, Mackie.
23rd	● Ipswich	A	W 0–2	Att: 19,316	Ref: D Whitestone	**Scorers:** Mason, Wright-Phillips.
27th	● Blackpool	H	L 0–2	Att: 10,614	Ref: J Linington	**Booked:** Wright-Phillips, R Johnson.
30th	● Barnsley	H	D 0–0	Att: 7,243	Ref: M Russell	**Booked:** Bolasie.

APRIL

3rd	● Doncaster	A	W 1–2	Att: 10,179	Ref: K Wright	**Scorers:** Mason, Wright-Phillips. **Booked:** Wright-Phillips.
5th	● Middlesbrough	H	L 0–2	Att: 11,770	Ref: S Mathieson	**Booked:** Duguid.
10th	● Watford	A	L 1–0	Att: 14,246	Ref: W Atkins	**Booked:** Mackie.
19th	● Newcastle	H	L 0–2	Att: 13,111	Ref: C Pawson	
24th	● Nottm Forest	A	L 3–0	Att: 22,602	Ref: N Swarbrick	**Booked:** R Johnson, Eckersley, D Johnson.

MAY

2nd	● Peterborough	H	L 1–2	Att: 8,557	Ref: S Tanner	**Scorers:** Wright-Phillips. **Booked:** Judge.

● Coca-Cola Championship/Play-offs ● FA Cup ◉ Carling Cup

PLYMOUTH ARGYLE

CHAMPIONSHIP GOALKEEPER STATS

Player	Minutes on pitch	Appearances	Match starts	Completed matches	Sub appearances	Subbed off	Saved with feet	Punched	Parried	Tipped over	Fumbled	Tipped round	Caught	Blocked	Clean sheets	Goals conceded	Save %	Saved	Resulting in goals	Opposition miss	Fouls committed	Free-kicks won	Yellow cards	Red cards
							Saves breakdown											Penalties						
Romain Larrieu	2418	25	25	25	0	0	2	11	16	2	1	8	90	2	2	41	76.16	0	3	1	1	6	1	0
David Stockdale	2032	21	21	21	0	0	1	6	20	2	1	7	72	3	3	31	78.17	1	2	0	0	4	2	0

CHAMPIONSHIP OUTFIELD PLAYER STATS

Player	Minutes on pitch	Appearances	Match starts	Completed matches	Substitute appearances	Subbed off	Goals scored	Assists	Shots on target	Shots off target	Crosses	Tackles made	Defensive clearances	Defensive blocks	Fouls committed	Free-kicks won	Caught offside	Yellow cards	Red cards
Kari Arnason	3035	32	32	30	0	2	2	2	4	14	11	141	51	16	57	28	0	5	0
Chris Barker	1069	14	10	8	4	2	0	1	0	1	2	77	6	5	4	6	0	1	0
Ashley Barnes	256	7	3	0	4	3	1	0	5	3	0	7	1	0	7	5	1	0	0
Onismor Bhasera	600	7	7	4	0	3	0	1	0	0	10	22	4	0	3	8	0	0	0
Darcy Blake	430	7	5	1	2	3	0	0	1	2	6	48	5	3	5	3	0	1	1
Yannick Bolasie	935	16	8	5	8	3	1	2	8	10	21	17	0	1	15	22	3	3	0
James Chester	255	3	2	2	1	0	0	0	0	0	0	25	6	2	0	2	0	0	0
Chris Clark	2836	37	28	17	9	11	1	5	7	12	26	71	7	5	22	23	2	2	0
Kenny Cooper	167	7	0	0	7	0	0	0	1	1	0	6	0	0	2	5	0	0	0
Karl Duguid	3789	42	40	36	2	4	1	0	11	10	9	160	29	5	25	31	0	4	0
Richard Eckersley	528	7	7	4	0	3	0	0	0	0	3	32	2	1	9	5	0	2	0
Rory Fallon	2235	33	25	14	8	11	5	3	26	20	1	65	22	0	83	32	15	4	0
Carl Fletcher	3852	41	41	39	0	2	4	4	23	18	9	198	23	17	69	40	0	8	0
Yoann Folly	375	7	4	3	3	1	0	0	1	1	0	12	3	2	2	1	0	0	0
Alan Gow	812	14	8	2	6	6	2	2	7	8	5	44	1	2	4	14	6	1	0
David Gray	1084	12	12	10	0	2	0	0	0	2	10	46	7	4	15	6	0	4	0
Damien Johnson	1931	20	20	20	0	0	2	2	6	6	19	67	7	3	20	20	1	2	0
Reda Johnson	2078	25	23	19	2	4	0	0	4	8	0	67	34	6	33	28	0	8	0
Alan Judge	2521	37	28	10	9	18	5	2	21	24	62	96	4	2	18	47	2	2	0
Ryan Leonard	22	1	0	0	1	0	0	0	0	0	0	0	0	0	0	0	0	0	0
Shane Lowry	1253	13	13	12	0	0	0	0	2	1	2	43	28	12	16	9	0	3	1
Steven MacLean	183	3	3	0	0	3	0	0	1	0	1	12	0	0	1	3	3	0	0
Jamie Mackie	4057	42	42	40	0	2	8	2	45	44	13	96	6	1	67	55	50	8	0
Joe Mason	863	19	5	4	14	1	3	0	7	6	1	15	1	0	3	8	7	0	0
David McNamee	601	9	6	4	3	2	0	0	0	0	2	48	4	2	11	4	1	1	0
Bondz N'Gala	861	9	9	9	0	0	0	0	1	3	0	29	9	3	8	4	1	0	0
Craig Noone	549	17	3	1	14	0	0	0	4	2	13	17	0	0	9	13	3	1	0
James Paterson	973	12	11	7	1	4	0	0	1	4	20	75	4	2	10	5	1	1	0
Gary Sawyer	2700	29	28	24	1	4	0	1	3	6	33	143	23	5	22	12	0	6	0
Marcel Seip	483	5	5	5	0	0	0	0	0	1	0	53	9	2	9	5	0	1	0
Cillian Sheridan	602	13	5	3	8	2	0	1	6	6	6	28	4	0	4	5	7	0	0
Luke Summerfield	827	12	9	1	3	8	0	1	3	3	4	45	1	0	6	5	0	1	0
Krisztian Timar	605	7	6	6	1	0	1	0	1	4	0	27	15	5	13	5	0	3	0
Bradley Wright-Phillips	1064	15	12	4	3	8	4	0	13	12	5	14	4	0	14	7	7	2	0

SEASON TOTALS

Goals scored	43
Goals conceded	68
Clean sheets	5
Shots on target	222
Shots off target	238
Shots per goal	10.49
Pens awarded	7
Pens scored	5
Pens conceded	7
Offsides	112
Corners	239
Crosses	296
Players used	36
Fouls committed	591
Free-kicks won	482

SEASON INFORMATION

Highest position: 3
Lowest position: 24
Average goals scored per game: 0.93
Average goals conceded per game: 1.48

LEAGUE POSITION AT THE END OF EACH MONTH

AUG	SEP	OCT	NOV	DEC	JAN	FEB	MAR	APR	MAY
22	23	22	23	22	23	23	23	23	23

CARDS RECEIVED

77   2

SEQUENCES

Wins	2
(on three occasions)	
Losses	7
(18/08/09–27/09/09)	
Draws	2
(on two occasions)	
Undefeated	3
(on two occasions)	
Without win	9
(08/08/09–27/09/09)	
Undefeated home	4
(16/02/10–16/03/10)	
Undefeated away	2
(23/03/10–03/04/10)	
Without scoring	5
(21/11/09–19/12/09)	
Without conceding	0
(–)	
Scoring	6
(on two occasions)	
Conceding	14
(08/08/09–24/10/09)	

MATCH RECORDS

Goals scored per match

		W	D	L	Pts
Failed to score	17	0	1	16	1
Scored 1 goal	20	3	7	10	16
Scored 2 goals	5	5	0	0	15
Scored 3 goals	3	2	0	1	6
Scored 4+ goals	1	1	0	0	3

Goals conceded per match

		W	D	L	Pts
Clean sheet	5	4	1	0	13
Conceded 1 goal	22	6	7	9	25
Conceded 2 goals	12	1	0	11	3
Conceded 3 goals	6	0	0	6	0
Conceded 4+ goals	1	0	0	1	0

GOALS SCORED/CONCEDED
PER FIVE-MINUTE INTERVALS

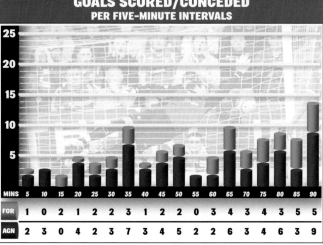

MINS	5	10	15	20	25	30	35	40	45	50	55	60	65	70	75	80	85	90
FOR	1	0	2	1	2	2	3	1	2	2	0	3	4	3	4	3	5	5
AGN	2	3	0	4	2	3	7	3	4	5	2	2	6	3	4	6	3	9

EARLIEST STRIKE

KRISZTIAN TIMAR
(v Crystal Palace) 4:28

LATEST STRIKE

CARL FLETCHER
(v Bristol City) 90:33

Karl Duguid

GOAL DETAILS

How the goals were struck

SCORED		CONCEDED
20	Right foot	35
12	Left foot	15
10	Header	17
1	Other	1

How the goals were struck

SCORED		CONCEDED
24	Open play	45
4	Cross	7
2	Corner	6
5	Penalty	5
1	Direct from free-kick	0
6	Free-kick	4
1	Own goal	1

Distance from goal

SCORED		CONCEDED
17	6YDS	28
22	18YDS	33
4	18+YDS	7

PRESTON NORTH END

CLUB SUMMARY

FORMED	1881
MANAGER	Darren Ferguson
GROUND	Deepdale
CAPACITY	22,226
NICKNAME	The Lilywhites
WEBSITE	www.pnefc.net

The New Football Pools PLAYER OF THE SEASON — Andy Lonergan

OVERALL
P	W	D	L	F	A	GD
51	16	15	20	73	82	-9

COCA-COLA CHAMPIONSHIP
Pos	P	W	D	L	F	A	GD	Pts
17	46	13	15	18	58	73	-15	54

HOME
Pos	P	W	D	L	F	A	GD	Pts
12	23	9	10	4	35	26	9	37

AWAY
Pos	P	W	D	L	F	A	GD	Pts
22	23	4	5	14	23	47	-24	17

CUP PROGRESS DETAILS
Competition	Round reached	Knocked out by
FA Cup	R4	Chelsea
Carling Cup	R3	Tottenham

BIGGEST WIN (ALL COMPS)
02/01/10 7–0 v Colchester

BIGGEST DEFEAT (ALL COMPS)
23/09/09 1–5 v Tottenham

THE PLAYER WITH THE MOST
GOALS SCORED Neil Mellor, Jon Parkin	10
SHOTS ON TARGET Neil Mellor	46
SHOTS OFF TARGET Ross Wallace	39
SHOTS WITHOUT SCORING Darren Carter	17
ASSISTS Ross Wallace	7
OFFSIDES Jon Parkin	36
FOULS Jon Parkin	73
FOULS WITHOUT A CARD Veliche Shumulikoski	12
FREE-KICKS WON Ross Wallace	50
DEFENSIVE CLEARANCES Neill Collins	56

actim INDEX — FOR THE 2009/10 COCA-COLA CHAMPIONSHIP SEASON

RANK	PLAYER	PTS
14	Sean St Ledger	572
21	Billy Jones	554
41	Ross Wallace	498

ATTENDANCE RECORD
HIGH	AVERAGE	LOW
19,840	12,992	10,270
v Blackpool (13/02/2010)		v Sheff Utd (09/02/2010)

Darren Ferguson replaced Alan Irvine as Preston manager in January

EYEBROWS were raised when Preston dismissed Alan Irvine midway through the campaign and replaced him with former Peterborough boss Darren Ferguson. Irvine had spent just over two years at Deepdale and his reign could certainly not be described as unsuccessful, having saved the Lancashire outfit from relegation in 2007/08 and then guided them into the Coca-Cola Championship play-offs the following year.

Chairman Derek Shaw's decision to usher the former Everton assistant boss out of the door was a surprise to many but Preston were struggling for form at the time and the North End hierarchy were clearly not convinced that Irvine was the man to engineer an upturn in fortunes.

So, in came Ferguson, who had guided his previous club to two successive promotions before his departure in November 2009. While acutely aware of the financial restrictions in place, Ferguson raised optimism at Deepdale by claiming that reaching the Barclays Premier League was not an unrealistic aim.

He quickly turned to his father for a helping hand as Manchester United manager Sir Alex allowed starlets Danny Welbeck and Matt James to join the Lilywhites on loan. Tom Williams and Paul Coutts also arrived from Peterborough, but Ferguson struggled to conjure any real consistency from his players.

Defensively they looked suspect, often frittering away winning positions during games to squander points. Instead of pushing towards the top six they found

Despite Alan Irvine's sacking, Preston could not overcome their defensive inadequacies

themselves languishing in the bottom half of the table towards the business end of the season.

His team's struggles served as a reality check for Ferguson, who could wield the axe in ruthless fashion ahead of 2010/11. James and Welbeck are set to return to Deepdale for season-long loan spells ahead of the new campaign, but the signs are that many players will depart, with Richard Chaplow, Darren Carter and Neil Mellor among the several players added to the transfer list shortly after the season's conclusion.

Speaking after a humiliating final-day 4–1 defeat at Reading, Ferguson said: 'I'm glad the 2009/10 season is over, to be honest, and now we can rebuild. I have already told a few players they are not in my plans. Much depends on if I can get them out of the club because from what I have seen there are some players who won't be wanted anywhere. Our squad needs big changes, but I am not the only manager who will be wanting to do that over the summer.'

RESULTS 2009/10

AUGUST

8th	● Bristol City	H	D 2–2	Att: 13,025	Ref: M Oliver	Scorers: Davidson, Parkin. Booked: Mawene, St Ledger.
11th	● Morecambe	H	W 5–1	Att: 5,407	Ref: C Pawson	Scorers: Brown, Elliott, Mellor, Nicholson, Trotman.
15th	● Doncaster	A	D 1–1	Att: 10,070	Ref: M Russell	Scorers: Brown. Booked: Chaplow.
18th	● Barnsley	A	W 0–3	Att: 11,850	Ref: D Whitestone	Scorers: Mellor, Parkin, Parry. Booked: Chilvers, Lonergan.
22nd	● Peterborough	H	W 2–0	Att: 11,549	Ref: D Webb	Scorers: Jones, Mellor. Booked: Nicholson, Carter, Davidson.
25th	● Leicester	H	W 2–1	Att: 6,977	Ref: C Boyeson	Scorers: Brown[2].
29th	● Ipswich	A	D 1–1	Att: 19,454	Ref: P Taylor	Scorers: Wallace. Booked: Wallace, Davidson. Dismissed: Davidson.

SEPTEMBER

12th	● Swansea	H	W 2–0	Att: 12,854	Ref: E Ilderton	Scorers: Elliott, Mellor. Booked: St Ledger, Elliott.
15th	● Scunthorpe	A	L 3–1	Att: 5,383	Ref: K Hill	Scorers: Parkin. Booked: Jones, Mawene, Sedgwick.
19th	● Coventry	H	W 3–2	Att: 11,230	Ref: D Deadman	Scorers: Brown[2], Mellor. Booked: Brown.
23rd	● Tottenham	H	L 1–5	Att: 16,533	Ref: P Dowd	Scorers: Brown. Booked: Nolan.
26th	● Leicester	A	W 1–2	Att: 20,623	Ref: J Linnington	Scorers: Chaplow, Mellor.
29th	● Reading	H	L 1–2	Att: 10,987	Ref: A Penn	Scorers: Parkin.

OCTOBER

3rd	● West Brom	H	D 0–0	Att: 12,489	Ref: T Bates	
17th	● QPR	A	L 4–0	Att: 12,810	Ref: R Booth	
20th	● Sheff Wed	A	W 1–2	Att: 20,882	Ref: R Shoebridge	Scorers: Mellor, Parkin. Booked: Carter, Collins.
24th	● Middlesbrough	H	D 2–2	Att: 16,116	Ref: A Woolmer	Scorers: Jones, Parry. Booked: Wallace.
31st	● Crystal Palace	H	D 1–1	Att: 12,558	Ref: D Foster	Scorers: Wallace. Booked: Chaplow.

NOVEMBER

7th	● Watford	A	L 2–0	Att: 13,524	Ref: K Wright	Booked: Hart, Parkin.
23rd	● Newcastle	H	L 0–1	Att: 16,924	Ref: S Mathieson	
30th	● Blackpool	A	D 1–1	Att: 9,861	Ref: K Friend	Scorers: Wallace. Booked: Jones, Wallace.

DECEMBER

5th	● Cardiff	A	L 1–0	Att: 18,735	Ref: R East	Booked: Sedgwick.
8th	● Derby	H	D 0–0	Att: 11,755	Ref: P Gibbs	Booked: Tonge, Wallace, Sedgwick.
12th	● Plymouth	H	W 2–0	Att: 12,231	Ref: M Oliver	Scorers: Chaplow, Wallace. Booked: Tonge.
19th	● Nottm Forest	A	L 3–0	Att: 21,582	Ref: F Graham	Booked: Wallace.
28th	● Sheff Utd	A	L 1–0	Att: 25,231	Ref: T Kettle	Booked: Parkin.

JANUARY

2nd	● Colchester	H	W 7–0	Att: 7,621	Ref: C Webster	Scorers: Brown, Carter, Parkin[3], Sedgwick, Williams OG.
16th	● Bristol City	A	L 4–2	Att: 13,146	Ref: G Ward	Scorers: Brown, Wallace. Booked: Wallace, Carter.
23rd	● Chelsea	H	L 0–2	Att: 23,119	Ref: M Dean	Booked: Hart.
26th	● Peterborough	A	W 0–1	Att: 7,134	Ref: D Sheldrake	Scorers: Mellor. Booked: Chaplow, Parkin.
30th	● Ipswich	H	W 2–0	Att: 12,087	Ref: J Moss	Scorers: Collins, Welbeck. Booked: Chaplow.

FEBRUARY

2nd	● Barnsley	H	L 1–4	Att: 12,453	Ref: N Miller	Scorers: Welbeck. Booked: Carter.
6th	● Swansea	A	L 2–0	Att: 14,659	Ref: P Gibbs	Booked: Wallace, Nolan, Parkin, Hart.
9th	● Sheff Utd	H	W 2–1	Att: 10,270	Ref: E Ilderton	Scorers: James, Parkin. Booked: Coutts.
13th	● Blackpool	H	D 0–0	Att: 19,840	Ref: M Jones	Booked: St Ledger.
16th	● Derby	A	L 5–3	Att: 26,993	Ref: C Pawson	Scorers: Brown, Parkin, Sedgwick. Booked: Parkin.
20th	● Newcastle	A	L 3–0	Att: 45,525	Ref: A Penn	
27th	● Cardiff	H	W 3–0	Att: 11,777	Ref: A Hall	Scorers: Brown, Parkin[2]. Booked: Coutts, Mawene. Dismissed: Coutts.

MARCH

6th	● Plymouth	A	D 1–1	Att: 9,582	Ref: A Woolmer	Scorers: St Ledger. Booked: Jones, Mawene.
9th	● Doncaster	H	D 1–1	Att: 11,942	Ref: P Crossley	Scorers: Mellor. Booked: Sedgwick.
13th	● Nottm Forest	H	W 3–2	Att: 14,426	Ref: M Haywood	Scorers: Davidson, James, Wallace. Booked: St Ledger, Wallace, Davidson, Chaplow.
16th	● Sheff Wed	H	D 2–2	Att: 12,311	Ref: C Boyeson	Scorers: Coutts, Mellor.
20th	● West Brom	A	L 3–2	Att: 21,343	Ref: J Singh	Scorers: Mellor, St Ledger. Booked: Sedgwick, Chaplow, Chilvers.
23rd	● Middlesbrough	A	L 2–0	Att: 16,974	Ref: S Tanner	Booked: Carter, Wallace, Mellor.
27th	● QPR	H	D 2–2	Att: 12,080	Ref: A Haines	Scorers: Davidson, Jones. Booked: Carter, Chaplow, St Ledger, Mellor.

APRIL

3rd	● Watford	H	D 1–1	Att: 12,534	Ref: R Shoebridge	Scorers: Davidson. Booked: Wallace.
5th	● Crystal Palace	A	L 3–1	Att: 16,642	Ref: R East	Scorers: Treacy. Booked: Parkin, Mellor.
10th	● Scunthorpe	H	W 3–2	Att: 12,441	Ref: T Kettle	Scorers: Jones, Parkin, Treacy.
17th	● Coventry	A	D 1–1	Att: 15,822	Ref: G Ward	Scorers: Davidson. Booked: Wallace.
24th	● Leicester	H	L 0–1	Att: 14,926	Ref: G Hegley	Booked: Wallace, Ward.

MAY

| 2nd | ● Reading | A | L 4–1 | Att: 19,239 | Ref: J Linnington | Scorers: Wallace. Booked: Wallace, Parkin. |

● Coca-Cola Championship/Play-offs ● FA Cup ● Carling Cup

PRESTON NORTH END

CHAMPIONSHIP GOALKEEPER STATS

Player	Minutes on pitch	Appearances	Match starts	Completed matches	Sub appearances	Subbed off	Saved with feet	Punched	Parried	Tipped over	Fumbled	Tipped round	Caught	Blocked	Clean sheets	Goals conceded	Save %	Saved	Resulting in goals	Opposition miss	Fouls committed	Free-kicks won	Yellow cards	Red cards
Wayne Henderson	145	2	1	1	1	0	0	2	3	0	0	0	7	0	0	5	70.59	0	0	0	0	0	0	0
Andy Lonergan	4285	45	45	44	0	1	7	26	41	6	3	15	165	6	10	68	79.64	2	4	0	0	8	1	0

CHAMPIONSHIP OUTFIELD PLAYER STATS

Player	Minutes on pitch	Appearances	Match starts	Completed matches	Substitute appearances	Subbed off	Goals scored	Assists	Shots on target	Shots off target	Crosses	Tackles made	Defensive clearances	Defensive blocks	Fouls committed	Free-kicks won	Caught offside	Yellow cards	Red cards
Adam Barton	45	1	1	0	0	1	0	0	0	0	0	0	1	0	1	0	0	0	0
Chris Brown	2450	43	24	14	19	10	6	2	23	23	14	34	22	2	40	40	23	1	0
Darren Carter	1316	23	11	7	12	4	0	0	5	12	9	27	3	5	25	18	0	6	0
Richard Chaplow	2615	31	29	22	2	7	2	3	19	20	31	62	11	4	48	18	4	7	0
Liam Chilvers	2058	23	20	19	3	1	0	1	2	2	2	51	49	16	14	17	1	2	0
Neill Collins	1872	21	19	19	2	0	1	0	5	5	1	52	56	27	25	11	0	1	0
Paul Coutts	1210	13	13	12	0	0	1	1	10	4	10	74	6	3	14	13	1	2	1
Callum Davidson	2358	27	25	19	2	5	5	0	2	4	47	62	19	10	24	18	1	3	1
Stephen Elliott	360	9	3	2	6	1	1	0	4	3	7	6	0	0	6	3	0	1	0
Michael Hart	941	11	10	9	1	1	0	0	1	1	23	19	14	1	14	7	1	2	0
Matthew James	1666	18	17	16	1	1	2	0	6	11	4	70	6	4	8	8	0	0	0
Billy Jones	4087	44	42	41	2	1	4	5	14	9	49	138	50	22	48	40	5	3	0
Youl Mawene	1552	19	18	14	1	4	0	1	2	6	4	64	53	9	16	16	0	4	0
Danny Mayor	429	7	4	2	3	2	0	0	2	2	22	13	0	2	3	5	0	0	0
Neil Mellor	2744	39	29	13	10	16	10	6	46	36	44	31	7	0	24	42	23	3	0
Barry Nicholson	162	4	3	1	1	2	0	0	0	1	0	10	0	0	2	1	0	1	0
Eddie Nolan	1482	19	15	13	4	2	0	2	6	4	36	35	25	11	7	15	0	1	0
Jon Parkin	2554	43	26	11	17	15	10	1	42	35	16	48	34	2	73	44	36	7	0
Paul Parry	1025	17	12	3	5	9	2	0	11	4	41	26	1	2	8	7	7	0	0
Jamie Proctor	16	1	0	0	1	0	0	0	1	0	0	0	0	0	0	0	0	0	0
Chris Sedgwick	2385	34	25	12	9	13	1	4	10	12	67	57	27	3	27	19	1	5	0
Veliche Shumulikoski	926	15	9	6	6	3	0	0	2	0	7	29	4	1	12	10	0	0	0
Sean St. Ledger	2885	30	30	29	0	1	2	1	7	6	4	118	55	28	29	42	0	5	0
Michael Tonge	663	7	7	6	0	1	0	0	4	5	6	8	1	2	15	5	0	2	0
Keith Treacy	845	17	8	2	9	6	2	2	12	6	25	20	4	4	9	9	2	0	0
Ross Wallace	3674	41	40	31	1	9	7	7	36	39	187	98	6	2	33	50	12	13	0
Elliott Ward	389	4	4	4	0	0	0	0	0	1	0	6	8	3	6	5	0	1	0
Danny Welbeck	742	8	8	6	0	2	2	0	3	4	2	11	2	1	12	11	6	0	0
Tom Williams	718	10	8	6	2	2	0	1	0	0	17	42	8	6	1	8	0	0	0

Coca-Cola
CHAMPIONSHIP

SEASON TOTALS

Goals scored	58
Goals conceded	73
Clean sheets	10
Shots on target	275
Shots off target	255
Shots per goal	9.14
Pens awarded	7
Pens scored	6
Pens conceded	6
Offsides	123
Corners	267
Crosses	675
Players used	31
Fouls committed	544
Free-kicks won	490

LEAGUE POSITION AT THE END OF EACH MONTH

AUG	SEP	OCT	NOV	DEC	JAN	FEB	MAR	APR	MAY
6	3	8	13	16	11	13	15	15	17

SEASON INFORMATION
Highest position: 2
Lowest position: 19
Average goals scored per game: 1.26
Average goals conceded per game: 1.59

CARDS RECEIVED

71   2

SEQUENCES

Wins	2
(on three occasions)	
Losses	3
(19/12/09–16/01/10)	
Draws	2
(on four occasions)	
Undefeated	6
(08/08/09–12/09/09)	
Without win	7
(24/10/09–08/12/09)	
Undefeated home	9
(09/02/10–10/04/10)	
Undefeated away	3
(15/08/09–29/08/09)	
Without scoring	2
(on four occasions)	
Without conceding	2
(on three occasions)	
Scoring	10
(08/08/09–29/09/09)	
Conceding	8
(17/10/09–05/12/09)	

MATCH RECORDS

Goals scored per match

		W	D	L	Pts
Failed to score	13	0	3	10	3
Scored 1 goal	14	1	8	5	11
Scored 2 goals	13	7	4	2	25
Scored 3 goals	6	5	0	1	15
Scored 4+ goals	0	0	0	0	0

Goals conceded per match

		W	D	L	Pts
Clean sheet	10	7	3	0	24
Conceded 1 goal	15	3	8	4	17
Conceded 2 goals	11	3	4	4	13
Conceded 3 goals	5	0	0	5	0
Conceded 4+ goals	5	0	0	5	0

EARLIEST STRIKE
KEITH TREACY
(v Crystal Palace) 7:18

LATEST STRIKE
CALLUM DAVIDSON
(v Bristol City) 95:36

Elliott Ward

GOAL DETAILS

How the goals were struck

SCORED		CONCEDED
29	Right foot	45
18	Left foot	22
11	Header	5
0	Other	1

How the goals were struck

SCORED		CONCEDED
33	Open play	48
10	Cross	8
4	Corner	1
6	Penalty	4
3	Direct from free-kick	6
2	Free-kick	4
0	Own goal	2

Distance from goal

SCORED		CONCEDED
19	6YDS	17
30	18YDS	41
9	18+YDS	15

GOALS SCORED/CONCEDED
PER FIVE-MINUTE INTERVALS

MINS	5	10	15	20	25	30	35	40	45	50	55	60	65	70	75	80	85	90
FOR	0	5	3	3	0	10	4	3	3	1	5	2	4	2	2	0	3	8
AGN	3	4	4	4	1	2	6	3	5	4	3	6	4	4	5	3	4	8

QUEENS PARK RANGERS

CLUB SUMMARY

FORMED	1882
MANAGER	Neil Warnock
GROUND	Loftus Road
CAPACITY	18,420
NICKNAME	The R's
WEBSITE	www.qprfc.co.uk

The New Football Pools PLAYER OF THE SEASON — Kaspars Gorkss

OVERALL

P	W	D	L	F	A	GD
51	16	16	19	68	71	-3

COCA-COLA CHAMPIONSHIP

Pos	P	W	D	L	F	A	GD	Pts
13	46	14	15	17	58	65	-7	57

HOME

Pos	P	W	D	L	F	A	GD	Pts
18	23	8	9	6	36	28	8	33

AWAY

Pos	P	W	D	L	F	A	GD	Pts
11	23	6	6	11	22	37	-15	24

CUP PROGRESS DETAILS

Competition	Round reached	Knocked out by
FA Cup	R3	Sheff Utd
Carling Cup	R3	Chelsea

BIGGEST WIN (ALL COMPS)
11/08/09 5-0 v Exeter

BIGGEST DEFEAT (ALL COMPS)
26/01/10 0-5 v Nottm Forest

THE PLAYER WITH THE MOST

GOALS SCORED	Jay Simpson	**12**
SHOTS ON TARGET	Adel Taarabt	**54**
SHOTS OFF TARGET	Adel Taarabt	**63**
SHOTS WITHOUT SCORING	Hogan Ephraim	**14**
ASSISTS	Wayne Routledge	**8**
OFFSIDES	Jay Simpson	**45**
FOULS	Kaspars Gorkss	**51**
FOULS WITHOUT A CARD	Rowan Vine	**23**
FREE-KICKS WON	Adel Taarabt	**79**
DEFENSIVE CLEARANCES	Kaspars Gorkss	**45**

actim INDEX — FOR THE 2009/10 COCA-COLA CHAMPIONSHIP SEASON

RANK	PLAYER	PTS
101	Jay Simpson	412
113	Kaspars Gorkss	398
168	Mikele Leigertwood	331

ATTENDANCE RECORD

HIGH	AVERAGE	LOW
17,082	13,349	10,940
v Leicester (30/10/2009)		v Ipswich (09/02/2010)

WHEN QPR won 2–1 at Sheffield Wednesday in November to move up to fourth place in the Coca-Cola Championship, it appeared as though chairman Flavio Briatore's promise of a return to the Barclays Premier League was finally coming to fruition. Jim Magilton's side were sweeping aside all before them, having just hit four goals past Preston, Reading and Derby in successive matches. But fast forward four months and Briatore was gone while Rangers had appointed their fifth manager of the season and were deep in relegation trouble.

Briatore may have saved the club from going bust in 2007, but his reign as chairman came to an end in February 2010. He was succeeded by Ishan Saksena, a 31-year-old financier who promised to bring some continuity to a club that had been through eight permanent bosses under the previous regime. One of Saksena's first moves was to negotiate the appointment of Neil Warnock as manager, having completed protracted compensation talks with Crystal Palace.

QPR's season had looked so different just a few months before as the club headed into December looking a comfortable bet for at least a play-off spot. However, a shock 5–1 home defeat to an out-of-form Middlesbrough side was the beginning of a slide, and two days later things got even worse in front of the TV cameras at Watford. Patrick Agyemang's refusal to celebrate the opening goal provided the first hint that all was not well in the Rangers camp, and after his side slipped to

Neil Warnock saved the day as Rangers survived another season of upheaval

a 3–1 defeat, Magilton let fly. His alleged confrontation with midfielder Akos Buzsaky led to the manager being suspended and he left the club later that month.

Youth coach Steve Gallen took over for a 2–2 draw at West Brom before the arrival of Paul Hart. However, the sense of chaos at Loftus Road was inflamed as the former Portsmouth and Nottingham Forest boss quit after just a month.

With promotion by now out of the question, Hart's assistant, Mick Harford, was given the reins until the end of the season. But results continued to suffer and, with relegation suddenly a real possibility, Saksena turned to Warnock.

The 61-year-old Yorkshireman was an instant hit as he used all his years of experience to guide Rangers clear of trouble. Having consolidated in the final few months of the campaign, Warnock has promised some changes to his squad over the summer and he will now begin moulding his own team for a shot at promotion in 2010/11.

Jim Magilton, Paul Hart and Neil Warnock were QPR's three full-time managers during a season in which the Loftus Road club failed to mount a promotion push

RESULTS 2009/10

AUGUST
8th	● Blackpool	H	D 1–1	Att: 14,013	Ref: A D'Urso	Scorers: Ramage. Booked: Helguson, Routledge, Buzsaky, Hall.
11th	◐ Exeter	A	W 0–5	Att: 4,614	Ref: S Bratt	Scorers: Ephraim, Pellicori, Routledge³. Booked: Ephraim.
15th	● Plymouth	A	D 1–1	Att: 11,588	Ref: R East	Scorers: Helguson.
18th	● Bristol City	A	L 1–0	Att: 14,571	Ref: P Gibbs	Booked: Faurlin, Buzsaky, Stewart.
22nd	● Nottm Forest	H	D 1–1	Att: 13,058	Ref: J Linington	Scorers: Leigertwood.
25th	◐ Accrington	H	W 2–1	Att: 5,203	Ref: C Pawson	Scorers: Ephraim, Routledge. Booked: Ramage.
29th	● Scunthorpe	A	W 0–1	Att: 5,866	Ref: G Salisbury	Scorers: Taarabt. Booked: Routledge.

SEPTEMBER
12th	● Peterborough	H	D 1–1	Att: 11,814	Ref: O Langford	Scorers: Routledge. Booked: Connolly, Borrowdale.
19th	● Cardiff	A	W 0–2	Att: 20,121	Ref: L Probert	Scorers: Simpson². Booked: Stewart, Pellicori.
23rd	◐ Chelsea	A	L 1–0	Att: 37,781	Ref: M Jones	
26th	● Barnsley	H	W 5–2	Att: 12,025	Ref: K Evans	Scorers: Buzsaky², Leigertwood, Simpson, Watson. Booked: Borrowdale.
30th	● Newcastle	A	D 1–1	Att: 38,923	Ref: R Shoebridge	Scorers: Watson. Booked: Stewart, Buzsaky, Leigertwood.

OCTOBER
3rd	● Swansea	A	L 2–0	Att: 14,444	Ref: K Hill	Booked: Rowlands, Gorkss, Watson. Dismissed: Rowlands, Watson.
17th	● Preston	H	W 4–0	Att: 12,810	Ref: R Booth	Scorers: Buzsaky, Routledge, Simpson, Taarabt.
20th	● Reading	H	W 4–1	Att: 11,900	Ref: A Hall	Scorers: Agyemang, Buzsaky, Simpson, Vine. Booked: Watson, Borrowdale, Faurlin. Dismissed: Watson.
24th	● Derby	A	W 2–4	Att: 30,135	Ref: M Haywood	Scorers: Buzsaky, Mahon, Simpson, Taarabt.
30th	● Leicester	H	L 1–2	Att: 17,082	Ref: J Moss	Scorers: Taarabt.

NOVEMBER
3rd	● Crystal Palace	H	D 1–1	Att: 14,377	Ref: M Russell	Scorers: Buzsaky. Booked: Routledge.
7th	● Sheff Wed	A	W 1–2	Att: 19,491	Ref: N Miller	Scorers: Gorkss, Simpson.
21st	● Doncaster	A	L 2–0	Att: 10,821	Ref: T Bates	Booked: Leigertwood.
28th	● Coventry	H	D 2–2	Att: 13,712	Ref: M Jones	Scorers: Buzsaky, Simpson.

DECEMBER
5th	● Middlesbrough	H	L 1–5	Att: 13,949	Ref: P Gibbs	Scorers: Agyemang. Booked: Hall.
7th	● Watford	A	L 3–1	Att: 15,058	Ref: A Penn	Scorers: Agyemang. Booked: Stewart, Borrowdale, Hall.
14th	● West Brom	A	D 2–2	Att: 21,565	Ref: A Taylor	Scorers: Gorkss, Olsson OG.
19th	● Sheff Utd	H	D 1–1	Att: 12,639	Ref: N Swarbrick	Scorers: Leigertwood. Booked: Stewart.
26th	● Bristol City	H	W 2–1	Att: 13,534	Ref: D Phillips	Scorers: Leigertwood, Simpson.
28th	● Ipswich	A	L 3–0	Att: 25,349	Ref: S Tanner	

JANUARY
3rd	● Sheff Utd	A	D 1–1	Att: 11,461	Ref: A Hall	Scorers: Simpson. Booked: Faurlin.
12th	● Sheff Utd	H	L 2–3	Att: 5,780	Ref: A Woolmer	Scorers: Buzsaky, Stewart. Booked: Gorkss.
16th	● Blackpool	A	D 2–2	Att: 7,600	Ref: T Kettle	Scorers: Connolly, Taarabt. Booked: Routledge.
26th	● Nottm Forest	A	L 5–0	Att: 23,293	Ref: E Ilderton	Booked: Buzsaky, Taarabt, Quashie.
30th	● Scunthorpe	H	L 0–1	Att: 13,105	Ref: G Hegley	

FEBRUARY
6th	● Peterborough	A	L 1–0	Att: 8,933	Ref: D McDermid	Booked: Ramage. Dismissed: Leigertwood, Ramage.
9th	● Ipswich	H	L 1–2	Att: 10,940	Ref: F Graham	Scorers: Simpson. Booked: Connolly.
13th	● Coventry	A	L 1–0	Att: 15,247	Ref: D Foster	Booked: Connolly, Faurlin, Gorkss.
20th	● Doncaster	H	W 2–1	Att: 11,178	Ref: D Whitestone	Scorers: German, Simpson.
27th	● Middlesbrough	A	L 2–0	Att: 17,568	Ref: A Woolmer	Booked: Gorkss.

MARCH
6th	● West Brom	H	W 3–1	Att: 14,578	Ref: S Attwell	Scorers: Buzsaky, Connolly, Simpson. Booked: Priskin, Faurlin.
9th	● Plymouth	H	W 2–0	Att: 12,013	Ref: P Tierney	Scorers: Stewart, Taarabt. Booked: Hill, Connolly.
13th	● Sheff Utd	A	D 1–1	Att: 23,456	Ref: T Bates	Scorers: Taarabt.
16th	● Reading	A	L 1–0	Att: 16,886	Ref: G Ward	Booked: Stewart, Faurlin, Leigertwood, Hill, Connolly. Dismissed: Stewart.
20th	● Swansea	H	D 1–1	Att: 15,502	Ref: C Boyeson	Scorers: German.
23rd	● Derby	H	D 1–1	Att: 12,569	Ref: M Russell	Scorers: Cook. Booked: Faurlin.
27th	● Preston	A	D 2–2	Att: 12,080	Ref: A Haines	Scorers: Priskin, Ramage. Booked: Hill, Taarabt.

APRIL
3rd	● Sheff Wed	H	D 1–1	Att: 13,405	Ref: C Webster	Scorers: Faurlin. Booked: Taarabt.
5th	● Leicester	A	L 4–0	Att: 22,079	Ref: T Kettle	Booked: Ephraim.
10th	● Crystal Palace	A	W 0–2	Att: 20,430	Ref: N Miller	Scorers: Buzsaky, Gorkss. Booked: Tosic.
17th	● Cardiff	H	L 0–1	Att: 12,832	Ref: M Oliver	Booked: Ramage, Taarabt.
20th	● Watford	H	W 1–0	Att: 13,171	Ref: P Miller	Scorers: Buzsaky. Booked: Buzsaky, Cook, Ephraim.
24th	● Barnsley	A	W 0–1	Att: 11,944	Ref: R Booth	Scorers: Leigertwood. Booked: Buzsaky.

MAY
2nd	● Newcastle	H	L 0–1	Att: 16,819	Ref: D Deadman	Dismissed: Ramage.

● Coca-Cola Championship/Play-offs ● FA Cup ◐ Carling Cup

QUEENS PARK RANGERS

CHAMPIONSHIP GOALKEEPER STATS

Player	Minutes on pitch	Appearances	Match starts	Completed matches	Sub appearances	Subbed off	SAVES BREAKDOWN								Clean sheets	Goals conceded	Save %	PENALTIES			Fouls committed	Free-kicks won	Yellow cards	Red cards
							Saved with feet	Punched	Parried	Tipped over	Fumbled	Tipped round	Caught	Blocked				Saved	Resulting in goals	Opposition miss				
Radek Cerny	2776	29	29	29	0	0	1	16	21	2	2	6	97	2	6	38	79.23	2	2	0	0	7	0	0
Carl Ikeme	1635	17	17	17	0	0	1	5	4	1	0	1	56	4	1	27	71.29	0	5	0	0	2	0	0

CHAMPIONSHIP OUTFIELD PLAYER STATS

Player	Minutes on pitch	Appearances	Match starts	Completed matches	Substitute appearances	Subbed off	Goals scored	Assists	Shots on target	Shots off target	Crosses	Tackles made	Defensive clearances	Defensive blocks	Fouls committed	Free-kicks won	Caught offside	Yellow cards	Red cards
Patrick Agyemang	736	17	5	3	12	2	3	0	6	6	4	8	3	1	12	9	8	0	0
Gareth Ainsworth	6	1	0	0	1	0	0	0	0	0	0	0	0	0	0	0	0	0	0
Angelo Balanta	100	4	1	0	3	1	0	0	0	3	1	10	0	0	1	0	0	0	0
Marcus Bent	148	3	2	1	1	1	0	0	2	3	1	0	0	0	0	2	0	0	0
Gary Borrowdale	1791	21	18	18	3	0	0	0	3	1	4	42	12	4	15	8	0	4	0
Lee Brown	6	1	0	0	1	0	0	0	0	0	0	0	0	0	0	0	0	0	0
Akos Buzsaky	2653	39	29	14	10	15	10	3	26	44	33	55	3	1	28	37	10	6	0
Matthew Connolly	1642	19	17	15	2	2	2	0	9	7	3	49	17	8	20	13	1	5	0
Lee Cook	806	16	8	4	8	4	1	0	7	5	23	13	4	0	6	16	5	1	0
Hogan Ephraim	1510	22	16	6	6	10	0	1	7	7	16	9	3	2	8	17	0	2	0
Alejandro Faurlin	3327	41	36	28	5	8	1	4	26	24	21	92	24	4	42	41	0	6	0
Antonio German	500	13	5	0	8	5	2	0	3	3	4	5	1	1	5	9	7	0	0
Kaspars Gorkss	3880	41	40	40	1	0	3	0	9	11	1	87	45	17	51	27	2	3	0
Fitz Hall	1064	14	12	9	2	3	0	0	2	1	2	36	14	5	15	11	0	3	0
Heidar Helguson	250	5	3	1	2	1	2	0	2	7	2	12	0	1	8	4	5	1	0
Matthew Hill	1466	16	15	14	1	1	0	0	2	0	3	45	7	5	22	12	0	3	0
Mikele Leigertwood	3716	40	39	37	1	4	1	5	14	25	11	85	35	9	45	23	0	3	1
Gavin Mahon	523	7	5	5	2	0	1	1	2	3	3	20	5	2	9	6	0	0	0
Joe Oastler	25	1	0	0	1	0	0	0	0	0	0	0	0	0	1	0	0	0	0
Josh Parker	153	4	1	1	3	0	0	0	0	0	0	3	0	0	5	2	0	0	0
Alessandro Pellicori	198	8	1	0	7	1	0	0	0	1	0	0	0	0	3	3	3	1	0
Tamas Priskin	1103	13	13	5	0	8	1	0	10	8	1	17	4	1	23	21	14	1	0
Nigel Quashie	294	4	4	2	0	2	0	0	1	0	0	2	2	0	6	5	0	1	0
Peter Ramage	2746	33	29	24	4	3	2	0	2	2	28	64	14	5	14	19	2	2	2
Steven Reid	110	2	1	1	1	0	0	0	1	0	0	3	0	0	2	1	0	0	0
Romone Rose	17	1	0	0	1	0	0	0	0	0	0	0	0	0	1	0	0	0	0
Wayne Routledge	2321	25	25	21	0	4	2	8	22	22	29	36	3	1	24	41	12	4	0
Martin Rowlands	435	6	5	3	1	2	1	0	2	3	0	15	2	1	10	3	0	1	1
Jay Simpson	3047	39	34	14	5	20	12	2	31	32	3	28	0	1	18	27	45	0	0
Damion Stewart	2645	30	30	26	0	3	1	1	3	5	0	55	44	17	41	15	2	6	1
Adel Taarabt	2913	41	32	11	9	21	7	6	54	63	25	40	1	0	10	79	14	4	0
Dusko Tosic	479	5	5	5	0	0	0	0	1	1	0	10	0	0	5	4	0	1	0
Rowan Vine	1267	31	8	2	23	6	2	2	19	14	4	13	0	0	23	14	18	0	0
Ben Watson	1438	16	14	14	0	2	2	2	10	10	17	19	11	4	10	13	1	2	2
Tom Williams	473	5	5	5	0	0	0	0	0	1	7	9	2	1	3	3	0	0	0

SEASON TOTALS

Goals scored	58
Goals conceded	65
Clean sheets	7
Shots on target	277
Shots off target	297
Shots per goal	9.90
Pens awarded	6
Pens scored	6
Pens conceded	9
Offsides	151
Corners	262
Crosses	248
Players used	37
Fouls committed	483
Free-kicks won	495

LEAGUE POSITION AT THE END OF EACH MONTH

AUG	SEP	OCT	NOV	DEC	JAN	FEB	MAR	APR	MAY
15	11	9	5	10	12	20	18	13	13

SEASON INFORMATION
Highest position: 4
Lowest position: 21
Average goals scored per game: 1.26
Average goals conceded per game: 1.41

CARDS RECEIVED

60   7

SEQUENCES

Wins	3
(17/10/09–24/10/09)	
Losses	5
(26/01/10–13/02/10)	
Draws	4
(20/03/10–03/04/10)	
Undefeated	6
(22/08/09–30/09/09)	
Without win	7
(on two occasions)	
Undefeated home	6
(on two occasions)	
Undefeated away	3
(29/08/09–30/09/09)	
Without scoring	3
(26/01/10–06/02/10)	
Without conceding	2
(20/04/10–24/04/10)	
Scoring	6
(on three occasions)	
Conceding	22
(20/10/09–06/03/10)	

MATCH RECORDS

Goals scored per match

		W	D	L	Pts
Failed to score	13	0	0	13	0
Scored 1 goal	18	3	11	4	20
Scored 2 goals	10	6	4	0	22
Scored 3 goals	1	1	0	0	3
Scored 4+ goals	4	4	0	0	12

Goals conceded per match

		W	D	L	Pts
Clean sheet	7	7	0	0	21
Conceded 1 goal	23	5	11	7	26
Conceded 2 goals	11	2	4	5	10
Conceded 3 goals	2	0	0	2	0
Conceded 4+ goals	3	0	0	3	0

GOALS SCORED/CONCEDED PER FIVE-MINUTE INTERVALS

MINS	5	10	15	20	25	30	35	40	45	50	55	60	65	70	75	80	85	90
FOR	2	3	4	3	3	1	6	7	2	3	2	4	2	5	3	4	4	2
AGN	2	6	1	3	1	0	2	7	4	3	7	4	3	4	7	3	5

EARLIEST STRIKE

MIKELE LEIGERTWOOD
(v Sheff Utd) 1:28

LATEST STRIKE

AKOS BUZSAKY
(v Derby) 90:01

Adel Taarabt

GOAL DETAILS

How the goals were struck

SCORED		CONCEDED
38	Right foot	37
14	Left foot	16
6	Header	11
0	Other	1

How the goals were struck

SCORED		CONCEDED
41	Open play	46
1	Cross	4
4	Corner	2
6	Penalty	7
3	Direct from free-kick	2
2	Free-kick	3
1	Own goal	1

Distance from goal

SCORED		CONCEDED
20	6YDS	28
24	18YDS	29
14	18+YDS	8

READING

CLUB SUMMARY

FORMED	1871
MANAGER	Brian McDermott
GROUND	Madejski Stadium
CAPACITY	24,200
NICKNAME	The Royals
WEBSITE	www.readingfc.co.uk

The New Football Pools PLAYER OF THE SEASON — Gylfi Sigurdsson

OVERALL
P	W	D	L	F	A	GD
54	21	14	19	85	76	9

COCA-COLA CHAMPIONSHIP
Pos	P	W	D	L	F	A	GD	Pts
9	46	17	12	17	68	63	5	63

HOME
Pos	P	W	D	L	F	A	GD	Pts
11	23	10	7	6	39	22	17	37

AWAY
Pos	P	W	D	L	F	A	GD	Pts
9	23	7	5	11	29	41	-12	26

CUP PROGRESS DETAILS
Competition	Round reached	Knocked out by
FA Cup	QF	Aston Villa
Carling Cup	R2	Barnsley

BIGGEST WIN (ALL COMPS)
17/04/10 6-0 v Peterborough

BIGGEST DEFEAT (ALL COMPS)
1–4 on 2 occasions

THE PLAYER WITH THE MOST
GOALS SCORED	Gylfi Sigurdsson	**16**
SHOTS ON TARGET	Gylfi Sigurdsson	**57**
SHOTS OFF TARGET	Gylfi Sigurdsson	**46**
SHOTS WITHOUT SCORING	Jem Karacan	**16**
ASSISTS	Jobi McAnuff	**10**
OFFSIDES	Simon Church	**35**
FOULS	Shane Long	**51**
FOULS WITHOUT A CARD	Shaun Cummings	**6**
FREE-KICKS WON	Ryan Bertrand	**65**
DEFENSIVE CLEARANCES	Matthew Mills	**28**

actim INDEX — FOR THE 2009/10 COCA-COLA CHAMPIONSHIP SEASON

RANK	PLAYER	PTS
24	Jimmy Kebe	543
34	Adam Federici	503
36	Gylfi Sigurdsson	501

ATTENDANCE RECORD
HIGH	AVERAGE	LOW
23,163	17,408	14,096
v Newcastle (13/04/2010)		v Derby (10/03/2010)

An FA Cup win at Liverpool inspired Reading to a superb end to the season

A TOP-HALF finish and a thrilling FA Cup perhaps mask some of the problems that Reading endured in adapting to life after Steve Coppell. The club legend resigned at the end of the 2008/09 campaign, but replacement Brendan Rodgers was sacked less than half way through the season, and it was left to rookie boss Brian McDermott to steer the Royals clear of relegation.

Rodgers arrived at the Madejski Stadium in the summer fresh from rescuing Watford from relegation trouble and, crucially, he was no stranger to the club, having spent several years coaching at the academy. He was handed the task of guiding the Royals back to the Barclays Premier League while also selling the family silver, as key men Kevin Doyle, Stephen Hunt, Marcus Hahnemann and Andre Bikey departed for top-flight outfits.

Rodgers instantly promoted from the youth set-up, handing debuts to Scott Davies, Hal Robson-Kanu, Ben Hamer, Nicholas Bignall and Michail Antonio, but he soon discovered that the Coca-Cola Championship is a tough league to blood young talent.

The poor home form which had stunted Coppell's last season in charge continued and by the time chairman Sir John Madejski lost patience and sacked Rodgers

Reading's players celebrate a famous FA Cup win at mighty Liverpool

in mid-December, the club were in severe danger of dropping into League One. Chief scout McDermott was the surprise choice to lead them away from danger and a tally of just two points from his first three games hardly indicated that the Royals had unearthed a managerial gem.

But the FA Cup was to prove the turning point in the club's season and a famous third-round replay win at Liverpool kicked McDermott's side into life. Burnley and West Brom were also swept aside as Reading reached the quarter-finals for the first time in 83 years while, in the League, their form was unrecognisable from their early-season woes.

McDermott was in charge for the final 20 games of the season on a permanent basis and collected a mammoth 40 points as the Royals climbed from 23rd place at the end of January to finish the campaign in ninth position.

Winger Jimmy Kebe was transformed from a fast but frustrating winger to a genuine goal threat, while in Gylfi Sigurdsson, McDermott possesses one of the gems of the Championship. If Reading can keep hold of the Icelandic midfielder then there is no reason why they should not be aiming for at least a play-off place during the 2010/11 season.

Icelandic midfielder Gylfi Sigurdsson was Reading's top scorer during the season

RESULTS 2009/10

AUGUST

8th	● Nottm Forest	H	D 0–0	Att: 19,640	Ref: P Crossley	Booked: Karacan.
11th	● Burton Albion	H	W 5–1	Att: 5,893	Ref: G Ward	Scorers: Bignall[2], Mooney[2], Sigurdsson.
15th	● Newcastle	A	L 3–0	Att: 36,944	Ref: A Taylor	
18th	● Swansea	A	D 0–0	Att: 12,775	Ref: S Hooper	Booked: Bertrand, Cisse, Rosenior, Pearce.
22nd	● Sheff Utd	H	L 1–3	Att: 16,025	Ref: M Russell	Scorers: Mills.
25th	● Barnsley	H	L 1–2	Att: 5,576	Ref: G Horwood	Scorers: Kozluk OG. Booked: Pearce.
29th	● Barnsley	A	W 1–3	Att: 11,116	Ref: M Oliver	Scorers: Hunt[2], Pearce. Booked: Rosenior.

SEPTEMBER

12th	● Doncaster	H	D 0–0	Att: 15,697	Ref: P Gibbs	
16th	● Cardiff	H	L 0–1	Att: 16,687	Ref: P Taylor	
19th	● Peterborough	A	L 3–2	Att: 8,521	Ref: C Sarginson	Scorers: Church, Sigurdsson. Booked: Howard, Pearce.
26th	● Watford	H	D 1–1	Att: 18,147	Ref: M Haywood	Scorers: Rasiak.
29th	● Preston	A	W 1–2	Att: 10,987	Ref: A Penn	Scorers: Church, Kebe. Booked: Mills, Kebe, Howard.

OCTOBER

3rd	● Middlesbrough	H	L 0–2	Att: 17,638	Ref: N Swarbrick	Booked: Karacan.
17th	● West Brom	A	L 3–1	Att: 20,935	Ref: A Taylor	Scorers: Mills. Booked: O'Dea.
20th	● QPR	A	L 4–1	Att: 11,900	Ref: A Hall	Scorers: Howard. Booked: Ingimarsson. Dismissed: Ingimarsson.
26th	● Leicester	H	L 0–1	Att: 16,192	Ref: K Hill	Booked: Matejovsky, Mills, Howard.
31st	● Coventry	A	W 1–3	Att: 15,165	Ref: E Ilderton	Scorers: McAnuff, Rasiak[2].

NOVEMBER

7th	● Ipswich	H	D 1–1	Att: 19,053	Ref: D Whitestone	Scorers: Church.
21st	● Blackpool	H	W 2–1	Att: 15,945	Ref: G Scott	Scorers: Rasiak, Sigurdsson. Booked: Matejovsky.
28th	● Derby	A	L 2–1	Att: 30,174	Ref: A Haines	Scorers: Sigurdsson. Booked: Kebe, Matejovsky, Pearce. Dismissed: Long.

DECEMBER

5th	● Sheff Wed	A	W 0–2	Att: 22,090	Ref: D Webb	Scorers: Cisse, Rasiak.
8th	● Crystal Palace	H	L 2–4	Att: 16,629	Ref: K Friend	Scorers: Pearce, Sigurdsson.
12th	● Scunthorpe	H	D 1–1	Att: 15,274	Ref: T Bates	Scorers: Rasiak. Booked: Rasiak, Cisse.
19th	● Bristol City	A	D 1–1	Att: 14,366	Ref: M Haywood	Scorers: Church. Booked: Church, Bertrand. Dismissed: Church.
26th	● Swansea	H	D 1–1	Att: 19,608	Ref: M Russell	Scorers: Sigurdsson. Booked: Gunnarsson.
28th	● Plymouth	A	L 4–1	Att: 12,091	Ref: S Hooper	Scorers: Sigurdsson. Booked: McAnuff.

JANUARY

2nd	● Liverpool	H	D 1–1	Att: 23,656	Ref: M Atkinson	Scorers: Church. Booked: Mills.
13th	● Liverpool	A	W 1–2	Att: 31,063	Ref: P Dowd	Scorers: Long, Sigurdsson. Booked: Karacan, Mills, Ingimarsson, Gunnarsson. AET – Score after 90 mins 1–1.
16th	● Nottm Forest	A	L 2–1	Att: 27,635	Ref: D Deadman	Scorers: Kebe. Booked: Mills.
23rd	● Burnley	H	W 1–0	Att: 12,910	Ref: A D'Urso	Scorers: Sigurdsson. Booked: Mills, Ingimarsson.
26th	● Sheff Utd	A	L 3–0	Att: 24,009	Ref: P Crossley	Booked: Griffin, Howard.
30th	● Barnsley	H	W 1–0	Att: 15,580	Ref: J Linington	Scorers: Long. Booked: Gunnarsson.

FEBRUARY

6th	● Doncaster	A	W 1–2	Att: 8,827	Ref: K Stroud	Scorers: Howard, Long. Booked: McAnuff, Bertrand. Dismissed: Mills.
9th	● Plymouth	H	W 2–1	Att: 15,484	Ref: O Langford	Scorers: Long[2].
13th	● West Brom	H	D 2–2	Att: 18,008	Ref: C Foy	Scorers: Church, Kebe. Booked: Howard. Dismissed: Long.
17th	● Crystal Palace	A	W 1–3	Att: 13,259	Ref: D Whitestone	Scorers: Church[2], Kebe. Booked: Griffin.
20th	● Blackpool	A	L 2–0	Att: 7,147	Ref: C Pawson	Booked: Bertrand.
24th	● West Brom	A	W 2–3	Att: 13,985	Ref: L Mason	Scorers: Howard, Kebe, Sigurdsson. Booked: Ingimarsson, Tabb, Kebe. AET – Score after 90 mins 2–2.
27th	● Sheff Wed	H	W 5–0	Att: 17,573	Ref: G Hegley	Scorers: Church, Kebe[2], Rasiak[2].

MARCH

7th	● Aston Villa	H	L 2–4	Att: 23,175	Ref: M Dean	Scorers: Long[2]. Booked: Sigurdsson, Tabb.
10th	● Derby	H	W 4–1	Att: 14,096	Ref: K Wright	Scorers: Bertrand, Church, Kebe, Long. Booked: Ingimarsson.
13th	● Bristol City	H	W 2–0	Att: 17,900	Ref: P Taylor	Scorers: Sigurdsson[2]. Booked: Gunnarsson, Mills.
16th	● QPR	H	W 1–0	Att: 16,886	Ref: G Ward	Scorers: Sigurdsson. Booked: Rasiak.
20th	● Middlesbrough	A	D 1–1	Att: 17,082	Ref: A Hall	Scorers: Wheater OG.
24th	● Leicester	A	W 1–2	Att: 20,108	Ref: D Foster	Scorers: Kebe, Sigurdsson. Booked: Howard, Griffin.
27th	● West Brom	H	D 1–1	Att: 20,515	Ref: A D'Urso	Scorers: Sigurdsson. Booked: Griffin, Bertrand, Mills, Sigurdsson.

APRIL

3rd	● Ipswich	A	L 2–1	Att: 21,403	Ref: K Stroud	Scorers: Sigurdsson. Booked: Gunnarsson, Sigurdsson, Bertrand. Dismissed: Mills.
5th	● Coventry	H	W 3–0	Att: 17,435	Ref: A Woolmer	Scorers: Church, Kebe, Rasiak. Booked: Mills, Robson-Kanu.
10th	● Cardiff	A	D 0–0	Att: 21,248	Ref: T Bates	Booked: Pearce.
13th	● Newcastle	H	L 1–2	Att: 23,163	Ref: F Graham	Scorers: Simpson OG. Booked: Pearce, Tabb.
17th	● Peterborough	H	W 6–0	Att: 15,982	Ref: C Boyeson	Scorers: Kebe, Long, McAnuff, Pearce, Sigurdsson[2]. Booked: Sigurdsson.
20th	● Scunthorpe	A	D 2–2	Att: 5,299	Ref: G Salisbury	Scorers: Pearce, Sigurdsson. Booked: Pearce, Khizanishvili, McAnuff, Sigurdsson.
24th	● Watford	A	L 3–0	Att: 15,949	Ref: K Friend	Booked: Griffin, Khizanishvili.

MAY

2nd	● Preston	H	W 4–1	Att: 19,239	Ref: J Linnington	Scorers: Church, Kebe, McAnuff, Sigurdsson. Booked: Pearce, Sigurdsson.

● Coca-Cola Championship/Play-offs ● FA Cup ● Carling Cup

READING

CHAMPIONSHIP GOALKEEPER STATS

Player	Minutes on pitch	Appearances	Match starts	Completed matches	Sub appearances	Subbed off	Saved with feet	Punched	Parried	Tipped over	Fumbled	Tipped round	Caught	Blocked	Clean sheets	Goals conceded	Save %	Saved	Resulting in goals	Opposition miss	Fouls committed	Free-kicks won	Yellow cards	Red cards
Adam Federici	4428	46	46	46	0	0	0	13	29	15	0	17	157	4	11	63	78.86	1	5	0	0	6	0	0

CHAMPIONSHIP OUTFIELD PLAYER STATS

Player	Minutes on pitch	Appearances	Match starts	Completed matches	Substitute appearances	Subbed off	Goals scored	Assists	Shots on target	Shots off target	Crosses	Tackles made	Defensive clearances	Defensive blocks	Fouls committed	Free-kicks won	Caught offside	Yellow cards	Red cards
Michail Antonio	20	1	0	0	1	0	0	0	0	0	1	0	0	0	1	1	0	0	0
Ryan Bertrand	4147	44	44	41	0	3	1	3	7	10	55	139	25	9	29	65	0	6	0
Nicholas Bignall	21	1	0	0	1	0	0	0	0	0	0	2	0	0	0	0	0	0	0
Simon Church	1946	36	22	4	14	17	10	1	24	27	7	27	2	1	17	26	35	1	1
Kalifa Cisse	1228	17	14	10	3	4	1	0	4	2	1	32	9	4	23	7	1	2	0
Shaun Cummings	769	8	8	8	0	0	0	0	2	0	19	15	9	1	6	7	0	0	0
Scott Davies	266	4	3	2	1	1	0	0	1	5	4	7	1	0	1	4	0	0	0
Andy Griffin	2002	21	21	19	0	2	0	1	1	3	17	83	14	2	16	20	0	5	0
Brynjar Gunnarsson	1712	26	18	11	8	7	0	1	3	5	7	36	9	0	22	20	0	4	0
James Harper	73	3	0	0	3	0	0	0	0	0	1	0	1	1	0	0	0	0	0
James Henry	129	3	1	0	2	1	0	0	0	0	6	7	1	0	3	1	2	0	0
Brian Howard	2744	34	30	19	4	11	2	5	25	25	51	49	4	0	34	49	4	5	0
Noel Hunt	545	10	5	1	5	4	2	0	6	2	7	13	1	1	3	4	9	0	0
Ivar Ingimarsson	2346	25	25	23	0	1	0	0	3	9	2	37	26	11	29	17	1	2	1
Jem Karacan	1820	27	19	10	8	9	0	2	3	13	12	54	11	3	19	25	0	2	0
Jimmy Kebe	3029	42	30	22	12	8	10	6	29	18	57	63	2	1	24	47	25	2	0
Zurab Khizanishvili	1159	15	12	11	3	1	0	0	1	1	0	53	23	1	12	19	0	2	0
Shane Long	2090	31	22	9	9	12	6	2	18	21	8	31	7	0	51	33	34	0	1
Marek Matejovsky	1196	15	13	10	2	3	0	0	7	7	14	11	4	2	19	21	0	3	0
Jobi McAnuff	3334	36	36	31	0	5	3	10	24	27	79	59	4	4	27	54	9	3	0
Matthew Mills	2042	23	22	19	1	1	2	1	6	5	2	74	28	17	28	15	0	6	2
Darren O'Dea	729	8	7	7	1	0	0	0	1	2	1	11	10	3	6	3	0	1	0
Alex Pearce	2377	25	24	24	1	0	4	0	10	4	1	66	21	6	41	25	0	7	0
Grzegorz Rasiak	1628	29	14	10	15	4	9	0	26	17	4	10	12	1	29	18	29	2	0
Hal Robson-Kanu	659	17	4	1	13	3	0	2	4	7	15	6	1	0	15	17	4	1	0
Liam Rosenior	481	5	5	5	0	0	0	0	0	0	5	26	4	2	3	2	0	2	0
Gylfi Sigurdsson	3031	38	32	23	6	9	16	8	57	46	59	66	17	1	31	38	6	5	0
Jay Tabb	2318	28	27	18	1	9	0	3	2	7	13	68	8	2	25	27	0	1	0
Gunnar Heidar Thorvaldsson	208	4	2	1	2	1	0	0	1	0	0	0	0	0	1	4	1	0	0

SEASON TOTALS

Goals scored	68
Goals conceded	63
Clean sheets	11
Shots on target	266
Shots off target	263
Shots per goal	7.78
Pens awarded	12
Pens scored	9
Pens conceded	6
Offsides	160
Corners	325
Crosses	447
Players used	30
Fouls committed	516
Free-kicks won	575

SEASON INFORMATION
Highest position: 9
Lowest position: 23
Average goals scored per game: 1.48
Average goals conceded per game: 1.37

LEAGUE POSITION AT THE END OF EACH MONTH

AUG	SEP	OCT	NOV	DEC	JAN	FEB	MAR	APR	MAY
18	19	21	21	20	22	18	11	11	9

CARDS RECEIVED

62   5

SEQUENCES

Wins	4
(on two occasions)	
Losses	4
(03/10/09–26/10/09)	
Draws	3
(12/12/09–26/12/09)	
Undefeated	7
(27/02/10–27/03/10)	
Without win	7
(08/12/09–26/01/10)	
Undefeated home	10
(12/12/09–05/04/10)	
Undefeated away	2
(on five occasions)	
Without scoring	3
(08/08/09–18/08/09)	
Without conceding	2
(on two occasions)	
Scoring	11
(31/10/09–16/01/10)	
Conceding	12
(16/09/09–28/11/09)	

MATCH RECORDS

Goals scored per match

		W	D	L	Pts
Failed to score	11	0	4	7	4
Scored 1 goal	17	2	7	8	13
Scored 2 goals	10	7	1	2	22
Scored 3 goals	4	4	0	0	12
Scored 4+ goals	4	4	0	0	12

Goals conceded per match

		W	D	L	Pts
Clean sheet	11	7	4	0	25
Conceded 1 goal	19	10	7	2	37
Conceded 2 goals	7	0	1	6	1
Conceded 3 goals	6	0	0	6	0
Conceded 4+ goals	3	0	0	3	0

GOALS SCORED/CONCEDED
PER FIVE-MINUTE INTERVALS

MINS	5	10	15	20	25	30	35	40	45	50	55	60	65	70	75	80	85	90
FOR	2	4	4	3	4	4	3	2	6	4	6	2	3	2	5	3	4	7
AGN	0	2	6	1	1	2	1	4	10	3	4	4	6	2	4	2	5	6

EARLIEST STRIKE
GRZEGORZ RASIAK
(v Coventry) 0:31

LATEST STRIKE
JIMMY KEBE
(v Nottm Forest) 93:24

Jobi McAnuff

GOAL DETAILS

How the goals were struck

SCORED		CONCEDED
36	Right foot	37
16	Left foot	10
13	Header	16
3	Other	0

How the goals were struck

SCORED		CONCEDED
41	Open play	37
6	Cross	9
3	Corner	9
9	Penalty	5
3	Direct from free-kick	1
4	Free-kick	2
2	Own goal	0

Distance from goal

SCORED		CONCEDED
29	6YDS	26
34	18YDS	27
5	18+YDS	10

CLUB SUMMARY

FORMED	1899
MANAGER	Nigel Adkins
GROUND	Glanford Park
CAPACITY	9,183
NICKNAME	The Iron
WEBSITE	www.scunthorpe-united.co.uk

The New Football Pools
PLAYER OF THE SEASON — Gary Hooper

OVERALL

P	W	D	L	F	A	GD
52	18	10	24	72	95	-23

COCA-COLA CHAMPIONSHIP

Pos	P	W	D	L	F	A	GD	Pts
20	46	14	10	22	62	84	-22	52

HOME

Pos	P	W	D	L	F	A	GD	Pts
13	23	10	7	6	40	32	8	37

AWAY

Pos	P	W	D	L	F	A	GD	Pts
23	23	4	3	16	22	52	-30	15

CUP PROGRESS DETAILS

Competition	Round reached	Knocked out by
FA Cup	R4	Man City
Carling Cup	R4	Man City

BIGGEST WIN (ALL COMPS)
4–0 on 2 occasions

BIGGEST DEFEAT (ALL COMPS)
1–5 on 2 occasions

THE PLAYER WITH THE MOST

GOALS SCORED	Gary Hooper	**19**
SHOTS ON TARGET	Paul Hayes	**47**
SHOTS OFF TARGET	Grant McCann, Paul Hayes	**38**
SHOTS WITHOUT SCORING	Josh Wright	**20**
ASSISTS	Paul Hayes	**9**
OFFSIDES	Gary Hooper	**47**
FOULS	Cliff Byrne	**56**
FOULS WITHOUT A CARD	Kenny Milne	**4**
FREE-KICKS WON	Grant McCann	**40**
DEFENSIVE CLEARANCES	Rob Jones	**88**

actim INDEX — FOR THE 2009/10 COCA-COLA CHAMPIONSHIP SEASON

RANK	PLAYER	PTS
13	Gary Hooper	573
29	Paul Hayes	528
94	Joe Murphy	417

ATTENDANCE RECORD

HIGH	AVERAGE	LOW
8,921	6,464	4,995
v Newcastle (20/10/2009)		v Peterborough (23/03/2010)

Scunthorpe boss Nigel Adkins was able to rely on Gary Hooper's goalscoring prowess

WHILE Scunthorpe's quality of football under Nigel Adkins has never been in question, doubts remained at the start of the 2009/10 season as to whether the Lincolnshire club could ever become a fixture in the second tier.

Having failed to survive in the Coca-Cola Championship when they were promoted three years ago, the Iron, with the smallest budget and lowest crowds in the division, were once again expected to make an instant return to the third tier this time around. But, thanks to manager Adkins' infectious positive attitude and an exceptional ability to motivate his players, they managed to stay up and secure back-to-back seasons in the division for the first time in 46 years.

It was not all down to Adkins of course, with star striker Gary Hooper scoring 20 goals in all competitions, while his forward partner, Paul Hayes, chipped in with 13 of his own. Ending the campaign with a flourish, Hooper grabbed six goals in the last four games of 2009/10 to put the seal on his and Scunthorpe's season, as the Iron ended five points clear of the relegation zone.

After getting into the play-offs in the 2008/09 season thanks to a last-gasp goal on the final day and then leaving it late to beat Millwall in the final, it was fitting that United secured their survival in equally dramatic fashion, with club stalwart Matt Sparrow's 90th-minute goal earning them a 2–2 draw with Reading.

The individual highlight of their season was undoubtedly the 2–1 home win over

Manager Nigel Adkins' motivational skills were a key factor as the Iron avoided relegation

champions Newcastle in October, while the early-season 4–0 win at Crystal Palace was also a memorable result, as was a 4–1 success at Derby in early January.

The form of goalkeeper Joe Murphy was another plus point for Adkins, with the highly rated Republic of Ireland international opting to extend his stay at Glanford Park by another year as a result of the club avoiding relegation.

Adkins' ability to spot a bargain in the transfer market was apparent again too, with the likes of midfield duo Josh Wright and Michael O'Connor, both of whom were signed in the summer of 2009, playing pivotal roles in their success.

Away from their impressive display in the League, Scunthorpe were knocked out of both Cup competitions by Barclays Premier League big boys Manchester City. They were soundly beaten 5–1 in the fourth round of the Carling Cup at Eastlands before restoring at least some credibility in a 4–2 home defeat in the FA Cup fourth round in January.

RESULTS 2009/10

AUGUST

8th	● Cardiff	A	L 4–0	Att: 22,264	Ref: J Moss	**Booked:** Togwell.
11th	● Chesterfield	H	W 2–1	Att: 2,501	Ref: D Whitestone	**Scorers:** Hayes, Sparrow.
15th	● Derby	H	W 3–2	Att: 7,352	Ref: G Horwood	**Scorers:** Hooper², Woolford.
18th	● Middlesbrough	H	L 0–2	Att: 8,274	Ref: M Oliver	**Booked:** O'Connor, Murphy, Hayes, Sparrow.
22nd	● Sheff Wed	A	L 4–0	Att: 20,215	Ref: A Hall	**Booked:** O'Connor.
25th	● Swansea	A	W 1–2	Att: 7,321	Ref: J Linnington	**Scorers:** Canavan, Hooper. **Booked:** Forte, Sparrow. AET – Score after 90 mins 1–1.
29th	● QPR	H	L 0–1	Att: 5,866	Ref: G Salisbury	**Booked:** Murphy.

SEPTEMBER

12th	● Crystal Palace	A	W 0–4	Att: 12,912	Ref: G Hegley	**Scorers:** Forte, Hayes, O'Connor, Togwell.
15th	● Preston	H	W 3–1	Att: 5,383	Ref: K Hill	**Scorers:** Hooper², McCann.
19th	● Bristol City	A	D 1–1	Att: 14,203	Ref: D McDermid	**Scorers:** McCann. **Booked:** Togwell.
22nd	● Port Vale	H	W 2–0	Att: 3,383	Ref: S Tanner	**Scorers:** Hayes, McCann. AET – Score after 90 mins 0–0.
26th	● Doncaster	H	D 2–2	Att: 7,945	Ref: K Stroud	**Scorers:** Byrne, McCann. **Booked:** Spence, O'Connor, Woolford.
30th	● Nottm Forest	A	L 2–0	Att: 18,332	Ref: D Webb	**Booked:** Spence, Murphy, McCann.

OCTOBER

3rd	● Plymouth	A	L 2–1	Att: 9,780	Ref: A D'Urso	**Scorers:** Hooper. **Booked:** J Wright, A Wright.
17th	● Sheff Utd	H	W 3–1	Att: 7,599	Ref: T Bates	**Scorers:** Hayes, McCann². **Booked:** O'Connor, Mirfin.
20th	● Newcastle	H	W 2–1	Att: 8,921	Ref: A Penn	**Scorers:** Woolford². **Booked:** Jones.
24th	● Peterborough	A	L 3–0	Att: 8,051	Ref: M Jones	**Booked:** Murphy, Woolford, Hayes.
28th	● Man City	A	L 5–1	Att: 36,358	Ref: M Oliver	**Scorers:** Forte.
31st	● Swansea	H	L 0–2	Att: 5,201	Ref: K Evans	**Booked:** Togwell, O'Connor.

NOVEMBER

7th	● Blackpool	A	L 4–1	Att: 7,727	Ref: C Webster	**Scorers:** Hayes. **Booked:** Hayes, A Wright. **Dismissed:** Murphy.
21st	● Watford	A	L 3–0	Att: 13,241	Ref: C Sarginson	**Booked:** Jones, J Wright.
28th	● Leicester	H	D 1–1	Att: 6,884	Ref: R Shoebridge	**Scorers:** Woolford. **Booked:** Mirfin.

DECEMBER

6th	● Coventry	H	W 1–0	Att: 5,013	Ref: N Miller	**Scorers:** Hooper. **Booked:** O'Connor.
9th	● Barnsley	A	D 1–1	Att: 11,657	Ref: E Ilderton	**Scorers:** Hayes. **Booked:** Byrne, Murphy.
12th	● Reading	A	D 1–1	Att: 15,274	Ref: T Bates	**Scorers:** Hooper. **Booked:** Byrne, A Wright, O'Connor.
26th	● Middlesbrough	A	L 3–0	Att: 20,647	Ref: N Swarbrick	**Booked:** Jones. **Dismissed:** Byrne.
28th	● West Brom	H	L 1–3	Att: 7,221	Ref: J Moss	**Scorers:** Jones. **Booked:** A Wright, Murphy. **Dismissed:** A Wright, McCann.

JANUARY

2nd	● Barnsley	H	W 1–0	Att: 5,457	Ref: D Foster	**Scorers:** Hayes.
9th	● Derby	A	W 1–4	Att: 28,106	Ref: A Woolmer	**Scorers:** Forte, Hooper, Thompson². **Booked:** A Wright.
16th	● Cardiff	H	D 1–1	Att: 5,032	Ref: S Mathieson	**Scorers:** O'Connor. **Booked:** O'Connor.
24th	● Man City	H	L 2–4	Att: 8,861	Ref: K Friend	**Scorers:** Hayes, Boyata OG.
27th	● Sheff Wed	H	W 2–0	Att: 7,038	Ref: M Clattenburg	**Scorers:** Hooper, McCann.
30th	● QPR	A	W 0–1	Att: 13,105	Ref: G Hegley	**Scorers:** Thompson. **Booked:** McCann.

FEBRUARY

6th	● Crystal Palace	H	L 1–2	Att: 7,543	Ref: P Tierney	**Scorers:** Mirfin. **Booked:** Hayes, Jones, Byrne. **Dismissed:** Williams.
9th	● West Brom	A	L 2–0	Att: 23,146	Ref: K Wright	**Booked:** Sparrow. **Dismissed:** Byrne.
13th	● Leicester	A	L 5–1	Att: 21,626	Ref: D Phillips	**Scorers:** Hayes.
16th	● Barnsley	H	W 2–1	Att: 5,648	Ref: C Webster	**Scorers:** Hayes, Hooper. **Booked:** McCann.
20th	● Watford	H	D 2–2	Att: 5,411	Ref: D Webb	**Scorers:** Hooper². **Booked:** Sparrow, Hooper, Williams, Byrne.
23rd	● Ipswich	H	D 1–1	Att: 5,828	Ref: A Haines	**Scorers:** Byrne. **Booked:** Togwell, Murphy.
27th	● Coventry	A	L 2–1	Att: 16,197	Ref: P Taylor	**Scorers:** McCann. **Booked:** Sparrow, Byrne.

MARCH

13th	● Ipswich	A	L 1–0	Att: 19,378	Ref: P Miller	**Booked:** Woolford, Williams. **Dismissed:** Byrne.
17th	● Newcastle	A	L 3–0	Att: 39,301	Ref: P Crossley	
20th	● Plymouth	H	W 2–1	Att: 5,153	Ref: A Taylor	**Scorers:** Thompson, Woolford. **Booked:** Woolford, Hayes, McCann.
23rd	● Peterborough	H	W 4–0	Att: 4,995	Ref: E Ilderton	**Scorers:** Hayes, Thompson², Togwell. **Booked:** Togwell.
28th	● Sheff Utd	A	W 0–1	Att: 23,005	Ref: R Booth	**Scorers:** Hayes. **Booked:** Forte.

APRIL

2nd	● Blackpool	H	L 2–4	Att: 7,508	Ref: A Woolmer	**Scorers:** Hooper, McCann. **Booked:** A Wright.
5th	● Swansea	A	L 3–0	Att: 14,830	Ref: D Whitestone	**Booked:** McNulty.
10th	● Preston	A	L 3–2	Att: 12,441	Ref: T Kettle	**Scorers:** Thompson².
17th	● Bristol City	H	W 3–0	Att: 5,430	Ref: M Russell	**Scorers:** Hooper³.
20th	● Reading	H	D 2–2	Att: 5,299	Ref: G Salisbury	**Scorers:** Hooper, Sparrow. **Booked:** Thompson, Hayes, A Wright, Byrne, Murphy.
24th	● Doncaster	A	L 4–3	Att: 12,124	Ref: A D'Urso	**Scorers:** Hayes, Hooper². **Booked:** Sparrow.

MAY

2nd	● Nottm Forest	H	D 2–2	Att: 8,119	Ref: F Graham	**Scorers:** Canavan, Thompson. **Booked:** McCann, Sparrow.

● Coca-Cola Championship/Play-offs ● FA Cup ● Carling Cup

SCUNTHORPE UNITED

CHAMPIONSHIP GOALKEEPER STATS

Player	Minutes on pitch	Appearances	Match starts	Completed matches	Sub appearances	Subbed off	Saved with feet	Punched	Parried	Tipped over	Fumbled	Tipped round	Caught	Blocked	Clean sheets	Goals conceded	Save %	Saved	Resulting in goals	Opposition miss	Fouls committed	Free-kicks won	Yellow cards	Red cards
Josh Lillis	688	8	6	6	2	0	0	4	6	1	2	0	29	3	0	12	78.18	0	1	0	1	2	0	0
Joe Murphy	3700	40	40	37	0	2	1	18	43	10	0	14	173	2	6	68	79.33	3	8	0	2	5	8	1
Sam Slocombe	31	1	0	0	1	0	0	0	0	0	1	0	4	0	0	4	50.00	0	0	0	0	0	0	0

CHAMPIONSHIP OUTFIELD PLAYER STATS

Player	Minutes on pitch	Appearances	Match starts	Completed matches	Substitute appearances	Subbed off	Goals scored	Assists	Shots on target	Shots off target	Crosses	Tackles made	Defensive clearances	Defensive blocks	Fouls committed	Free-kicks won	Caught offside	Yellow cards	Red cards
Cliff Byrne	3197	36	34	30	2	1	2	0	4	10	31	165	61	13	56	38	0	6	3
Niall Canavan	507	7	4	3	3	1	1	0	1	2	1	10	14	3	2	2	0	0	0
Jonathan Forte	794	28	6	3	22	3	2	2	8	9	5	43	0	2	16	12	11	1	0
George Friend	230	4	2	1	2	1	0	0	0	0	2	18	3	2	1	2	1	0	0
Paul Hayes	4094	45	45	34	0	11	9	9	47	38	66	96	19	2	49	33	41	6	0
Gary Hooper	2881	35	31	17	4	14	19	5	46	21	22	71	2	0	49	32	47	1	0
Rob Jones	2529	28	28	24	0	4	1	1	5	13	0	154	88	24	28	29	0	4	0
Ben May	6	1	0	0	1	0	0	0	0	0	0	0	0	0	1	0	0	0	0
Grant McCann	3326	42	36	24	6	11	8	3	34	38	85	151	38	4	35	40	3	5	1
Donal McDermott	515	9	4	1	5	3	0	1	3	6	5	8	0	0	4	9	1	0	0
Jim McNulty	243	3	2	2	1	0	0	0	0	0	3	6	1	0	2	3	0	1	0
Kenny Milne	377	4	4	3	0	1	0	0	0	1	0	7	6	2	4	1	0	0	0
David Mirfin	3313	37	37	33	0	4	1	0	4	7	6	150	71	34	28	39	1	2	0
Brendan Moloney	64	3	1	0	2	1	0	0	0	0	0	7	0	0	0	1	0	0	0
Ian Morris	263	3	2	2	1	0	0	0	0	1	3	29	0	0	3	1	0	0	0
Bondz N'Gala	64	2	0	0	2	0	0	0	0	0	0	9	1	0	2	1	0	0	0
Michael O'Connor	2112	32	23	10	9	13	2	2	20	21	45	107	18	6	43	28	1	8	0
Michael Raynes	1138	12	12	11	0	1	0	0	0	0	0	41	21	8	3	11	1	0	0
Matthew Sparrow	2016	30	22	13	8	9	1	1	10	7	24	53	3	4	51	11	2	6	0
Jordan Spence	845	9	9	8	0	1	0	1	2	1	12	31	12	2	7	12	0	2	0
Garry Thompson	2329	36	22	19	14	3	9	3	28	17	48	59	7	2	31	29	21	1	0
Sam Togwell	3061	41	33	19	8	14	2	1	16	13	17	154	18	14	42	31	2	5	0
Marcus Williams	3418	37	37	34	0	2	0	0	1	2	26	147	28	25	13	24	1	2	1
Martyn Woolford	2744	40	29	14	11	15	5	1	36	28	49	95	9	2	27	38	5	4	0
Andrew Wright	1384	19	13	12	6	0	0	1	1	3	9	45	19	4	18	22	0	7	1
Josh Wright	2481	35	24	18	11	6	0	0	9	11	27	73	22	7	15	24	1	2	0

SEASON TOTALS

Goals scored	62
Goals conceded	84
Clean sheets	6
Shots on target	275
Shots off target	249
Shots per goal	8.45
Pens awarded	5
Pens scored	4
Pens conceded	12
Offsides	139
Corners	220
Crosses	486
Players used	29
Fouls committed	533
Free-kicks won	480

CARDS RECEIVED

71   **7**

SEQUENCES

Wins	3
(20/03/10–28/03/10)	
Losses	4
(24/10/09–21/11/09)	
Draws	2
(on three occasions)	
Undefeated	4
(on three occasions)	
Without win	5
(on two occasions)	
Undefeated home	5
(16/02/10–23/03/10)	
Undefeated away	2
(on three occasions)	
Without scoring	3
(18/08/09–29/08/09)	
Without conceding	2
(on two occasions)	
Scoring	6
(28/12/09–06/02/10)	
Conceding	12
(15/09/09–28/11/09)	

League position at the end of each month

	AUG	SEP	OCT	NOV	DEC	JAN	FEB	MAR	APR	MAY
	20	17	18	20	21	16	19	19	20	20

LEAGUE POSITION AT THE END OF EACH MONTH

SEASON INFORMATION
Highest position: 8
Lowest position: 24
Average goals scored per game: 1.35
Average goals conceded per game: 1.83

MATCH RECORDS

Goals scored per match

		W	D	L	Pts
Failed to score	13	0	0	13	0
Scored 1 goal	15	3	6	6	15
Scored 2 goals	10	4	4	2	16
Scored 3 goals	5	4	0	1	12
Scored 4+ goals	3	3	0	0	9

Goals conceded per match

		W	D	L	Pts
Clean sheet	7	7	0	0	21
Conceded 1 goal	14	6	6	2	24
Conceded 2 goals	12	1	4	7	7
Conceded 3 goals	7	0	0	7	0
Conceded 4+ goals	6	0	0	6	0

GOALS SCORED/CONCEDED
PER FIVE-MINUTE INTERVALS

MINS	5	10	15	20	25	30	35	40	45	50	55	60	65	70	75	80	85	90
FOR	2	0	4	3	2	1	1	0	6	4	7	3	3	4	4	4	5	9
AGN	2	3	4	6	7	4	4	0	5	4	6	7	5	4	4	6	3	10

EARLIEST STRIKE
GARY HOOPER
(v Sheff Wed) 1:20

LATEST STRIKE
GARY HOOPER
(v Watford) 95:00

Garry Thompson

GOAL DETAILS

How the goals were struck

SCORED		CONCEDED
42	Right foot	42
16	Left foot	26
4	Header	16
0	Other	0

How the goals were struck

SCORED		CONCEDED
40	Open play	44
11	Cross	15
4	Corner	6
4	Penalty	9
1	Direct from free-kick	3
2	Free-kick	5
0	Own goal	2

Distance from goal

SCORED		CONCEDED
12	6YDS	22
43	18YDS	52
7	18+YDS	10

SHEFFIELD UNITED

CLUB SUMMARY

FORMED	1889
MANAGER	Kevin Blackwell
GROUND	Bramall Lane
CAPACITY	30,945
NICKNAME	The Blades
WEBSITE	www.sufc.co.uk

The New Football Pools PLAYER OF THE SEASON
Nick Montgomery

OVERALL

P	W	D	L	F	A	GD
50	18	15	17	67	62	5

COCA-COLA CHAMPIONSHIP

Pos	P	W	D	L	F	A	GD	Pts
8	46	17	14	15	62	55	7	65

HOME

Pos	P	W	D	L	F	A	GD	Pts
6	23	12	8	3	37	20	17	44

AWAY

Pos	P	W	D	L	F	A	GD	Pts
15	23	5	6	12	25	35	-10	21

CUP PROGRESS DETAILS

Competition	Round reached	Knocked out by
FA Cup	R4	Bolton
Carling Cup	R1	Port Vale

BIGGEST WIN (ALL COMPS)
3–0 on 3 occasions

BIGGEST DEFEAT (ALL COMPS)
0–3 on 2 occasions

THE PLAYER WITH THE MOST

GOALS SCORED Darius Henderson, Richard Cresswell	**12**	
SHOTS ON TARGET Darius Henderson	**38**	
SHOTS OFF TARGET Darius Henderson	**28**	
SHOTS WITHOUT SCORING Andy Taylor	**10**	
ASSISTS Mark Yeates	**7**	
OFFSIDES Darius Henderson	**38**	
FOULS Darius Henderson	**89**	
FOULS WITHOUT A CARD Glen Little	**7**	
FREE-KICKS WON Nick Montgomery	**67**	
DEFENSIVE CLEARANCES Chris Morgan	**49**	

actim INDEX FOR THE 2009/10 COCA-COLA CHAMPIONSHIP SEASON

RANK	PLAYER	PTS
66	Chris Morgan	458
81	Richard Cresswell	437
115	Stephen Quinn	397

ATTENDANCE RECORD

HIGH	AVERAGE	LOW
29,210	25,120	22,555
v Sheff Wed (18/09/2009)		v Blackpool (16/03/2010)

SHEFFIELD UNITED fans expected nothing less than a play-off finish when the 2009/10 season got under way so the Blades' failure to muster a serious challenge was undoubtedly a major disappointment.

Manager Kevin Blackwell had offered to quit following the club's Wembley play-off final defeat to Burnley at the end of the 2008/09 campaign, but he was persuaded to stay on by chairman Kevin McCabe and give it another go.

Blackwell knew it would be even harder to mount a promotion challenge this time around with a smaller budget, and the summer departures of several key players made it a taller order still.

What the former Leeds manager had not bargained for, though, was a succession of serious injuries and suspensions to senior players throughout a frustrating campaign. The problems caused him to regularly send out patched-up sides and at times he struggled to fill his substitutes' bench.

Three key members of Blackwell's starting line-up from the previous term – defender Kyle Naughton, midfielder Brian Howard and winger Greg Halford – were sold in the summer of 2009, while a fourth, Kyle Walker, moved to Tottenham but was then loaned back. Gary Naysmith and Derek Geary were sidelined with long-term knee injuries and another defender, Matt Kilgallon, was enticed away in January by top-flight club Sunderland. Added to all that, goalkeeper Paddy Kenny was unavailable for all but the last two games

Injury woes proved costly as Kevin Blackwell's side failed to meet expectations

of the season due to a drugs ban.

Despite their problems, it should be noted that the club had paid considerable sums in the close-season for Darius Henderson, Lee Williamson, Ched Evans and Andy Taylor, while Ryan France arrived on a free transfer from Hull.

Henri Camara and Glen Little were also drafted in on free transfers, while the Blades paid an undisclosed fee for Middlesbrough winger Mark Yeates in January. However, further injuries left them with no option other than to draft in more new recruits on loan, with half a dozen such players named in their starting line-up during the run-in.

There were still a number of moments to enjoy during the course of the campaign. The Blades took four points off city rivals Wednesday, including a thrilling 3–2 victory at Bramall Lane in which they were 3–0 up at half-time. Three wins and a draw from the last four games, culminating in a resounding win at Ipswich, at least provided some momentum for Blackwell's team to take into the close-season.

Jamie Ward enjoys scoring the opener in a derby win against Sheffield Wednesday

RESULTS 2009/10

AUGUST

7th	● Middlesbrough	A	D 0–0	Att: 23,541	Ref: L Mason	
11th	● Port Vale	H	L 1–2	Att: 7,627	Ref: K Hill	Scorers: Sharp.
15th	● Watford	H	W 2–0	Att: 24,638	Ref: M Oliver	Scorers: Evans, Ward. Booked: Treacy, Ward.
18th	● Leicester	H	D 1–1	Att: 26,069	Ref: N Miller	Scorers: Treacy. Booked: Taylor, Howard, Treacy.
22nd	● Reading	A	W 1–3	Att: 16,025	Ref: M Russell	Scorers: Cotterill, Quinn, Ward. Booked: Morgan, Cotterill.
29th	● West Brom	H	D 2–2	Att: 25,169	Ref: P Crossley	Scorers: Cotterill, Evans. Booked: Henderson.

SEPTEMBER

12th	● Derby	A	W 0–1	Att: 28,441	Ref: A D'Urso	Scorers: Kilgallon. Booked: Montgomery, Henderson, Morgan, Cotterill.
15th	● Coventry	A	L 3–2	Att: 14,426	Ref: A Taylor	Scorers: Harper, Ward.
18th	● Sheff Wed	H	W 3–2	Att: 29,210	Ref: A Wiley	Scorers: Henderson, Ward, Buxton OG. Booked: Davies, Montgomery, Henderson, Bunn, Cotterill, Morgan.
26th	● Swansea	A	L 2–1	Att: 14,324	Ref: D Deadman	Scorers: Quinn. Booked: Montgomery.
29th	● Ipswich	H	D 3–3	Att: 28,366	Ref: E Ilderton	Scorers: Henderson2, Morgan. Booked: Morgan, Taylor, Walker.

OCTOBER

3rd	● Doncaster	H	D 1–1	Att: 26,211	Ref: L Probert	Scorers: Cresswell.
17th	● Scunthorpe	A	L 3–1	Att: 7,599	Ref: T Bates	Scorers: Evans. Booked: Quinn.
20th	● Blackpool	A	L 3–0	Att: 8,042	Ref: S Mathieson	Booked: Cresswell.
24th	● Cardiff	H	L 3–4	Att: 25,021	Ref: T Kettle	Scorers: Harper, Henderson2. Booked: Evans, Walker.

NOVEMBER

2nd	● Newcastle	H	L 0–1	Att: 26,536	Ref: K Friend	Booked: Morgan.
9th	● Barnsley	A	D 2–2	Att: 12,998	Ref: M Clattenburg	Scorers: Henderson2. Booked: Henderson, Walker.
21st	● Peterborough	H	W 1–0	Att: 25,144	Ref: G Hegley	Scorers: Camara.
28th	● Bristol City	A	W 2–3	Att: 14,637	Ref: A Hall	Scorers: Henderson3. Booked: Ward, Walker, Henderson, Quinn, Stewart.

DECEMBER

5th	● Plymouth	A	W 0–1	Att: 9,231	Ref: G Horwood	Scorers: Harper. Booked: Montgomery, Williamson, Evans.
8th	● Nottm Forest	H	D 0–0	Att: 26,490	Ref: A Haines	Booked: Montgomery, Kilgallon.
12th	● Crystal Palace	H	W 2–0	Att: 25,510	Ref: C Webster	Scorers: Quinn, Williamson. Booked: Morgan.
19th	● QPR	A	D 1–1	Att: 12,639	Ref: N Swarbrick	Scorers: Cresswell. Booked: Morgan, Bunn.
26th	● Leicester	A	L 2–1	Att: 23,999	Ref: D Deadman	Scorers: Camara.
28th	● Preston	H	W 1–0	Att: 25,231	Ref: T Kettle	Scorers: Ward. Booked: Ward.

JANUARY

3rd	● QPR	H	D 1–1	Att: 11,461	Ref: A Hall	Scorers: Cresswell. Booked: Cresswell, Taylor, Geary.
12th	● QPR	A	W 2–3	Att: 5,780	Ref: A Woolmer	Scorers: Cresswell, Ward, Williamson. Booked: Evans, Seip, Quinn.
16th	● Middlesbrough	H	W 1–0	Att: 23,974	Ref: A D'Urso	Scorers: Cresswell. Booked: Cresswell, Quinn, Williamson.
23rd	● Bolton	A	L 2–0	Att: 14,572	Ref: A Marriner	Booked: Cresswell.
26th	● Reading	H	W 3–0	Att: 24,009	Ref: P Crossley	Scorers: Cresswell, Fortune, Morgan. Booked: Montgomery, Morgan, Harper, Quinn.
30th	● West Brom	A	L 3–1	Att: 22,193	Ref: M Russell	Scorers: Henderson. Booked: Quinn.

FEBRUARY

2nd	● Watford	A	L 3–0	Att: 13,076	Ref: K Hill	Booked: Harper, Quinn, Henderson, Montgomery, Nosworthy.
6th	● Derby	H	D 1–1	Att: 25,300	Ref: G Salisbury	Scorers: Williamson. Booked: Williamson, Kallio.
9th	● Preston	A	L 2–1	Att: 10,270	Ref: E Ilderton	Scorers: Yeates. Booked: Bartley.
13th	● Bristol City	H	W 2–0	Att: 22,613	Ref: D Deadman	Scorers: Camara, Henderson. Booked: Geary.
16th	● Nottm Forest	A	L 1–0	Att: 22,076	Ref: N Miller	Booked: Williamson, Yeates, Kallio, Cresswell. Dismissed: Henderson.
27th	● Plymouth	H	W 4–3	Att: 24,886	Ref: C Sarginson	Scorers: Camara, Cresswell, Ward2. Booked: Cresswell, Morgan.

MARCH

6th	● Crystal Palace	A	L 1–0	Att: 13,455	Ref: A Penn	Booked: Bartley, Williamson.
9th	● Peterborough	A	L 1–0	Att: 6,674	Ref: J Singh	Booked: Evans, Nosworthy, Yeates, Stewart.
13th	● QPR	H	D 1–1	Att: 23,456	Ref: T Bates	Scorers: Cresswell. Booked: Morgan.
16th	● Blackpool	H	W 3–0	Att: 22,555	Ref: O Langford	Scorers: Cresswell2, Montgomery. Booked: Seip.
20th	● Doncaster	A	D 1–1	Att: 13,026	Ref: J Moss	Scorers: Harper. Booked: Camara.
24th	● Cardiff	A	D 1–1	Att: 18,715	Ref: D McDermid	Scorers: Quinn. Booked: Connolly, Nosworthy, Quinn, Taylor, Williamson.
28th	● Scunthorpe	H	L 0–1	Att: 23,005	Ref: R Booth	

APRIL

3rd	● Barnsley	H	D 0–0	Att: 24,808	Ref: P Walton	Booked: Taylor, Morgan, Connolly. Dismissed: Connolly.
5th	● Newcastle	A	L 2–1	Att: 48,270	Ref: A Hall	Scorers: Cresswell. Booked: Seip.
10th	● Coventry	H	W 1–0	Att: 23,603	Ref: G Salisbury	Scorers: Cresswell.
18th	● Sheff Wed	A	D 1–1	Att: 35,485	Ref: C Foy	Scorers: Williamson. Booked: Taylor, Quinn.
24th	● Swansea	H	W 2–0	Att: 25,966	Ref: S Mathieson	Scorers: Cresswell, De Vries OG. Booked: Cresswell, Montgomery.

MAY

2nd	● Ipswich	A	W 0–3	Att: 23,003	Ref: A D'Urso	Scorers: Cresswell, Evans, Yeates.

● Coca-Cola Championship/Play-offs ● FA Cup ● Carling Cup

SHEFFIELD UNITED

CHAMPIONSHIP GOALKEEPER STATS

Player	Minutes on pitch	Appearances	Match starts	Completed matches	Sub appearances	Subbed off	Saved with feet	Punched	Parried	Tipped over	Fumbled	Tipped round	Caught	Blocked	Clean sheets	Goals conceded	Save %	Saved	Resulting in goals	Opposition miss	Fouls committed	Free-kicks won	Yellow cards	Red cards
Ian Bennett	365	5	4	3	1	1	0	1	5	0	1	0	15	0	0	8	72.41	1	1	0	0	3	0	0
Mark Bunn	3024	32	31	30	1	1	1	13	22	5	0	1	112	2	11	39	80.00	2	3	0	0	8	2	0
Carl Ikeme	194	2	2	2	0	0	0	1	1	0	0	0	6	2	1	2	25.64	0	0	0	0	0	0	0
Patrick Kenny	191	2	2	2	0	0	0	0	0	1	0	3	18	0	2	0	0	0	0	0	0	0	0	0
Steve Simonsen	674	7	7	7	0	0	0	2	5	0	1	2	34	1	2	6	88.00	0	1	0	0	2	0	0

CHAMPIONSHIP OUTFIELD PLAYER STATS

Player	Minutes on pitch	Appearances	Match starts	Completed matches	Substitute appearances	Subbed off	Goals scored	Assists	Shots on target	Shots off target	Crosses	Tackles made	Defensive clearances	Defensive blocks	Fouls committed	Free-kicks won	Caught offside	Yellow cards	Red cards
Kyle Bartley	1048	14	10	10	4	0	0	1	3	2	3	21	13	5	15	5	0	2	0
Henri Camara	1157	23	9	1	14	8	4	1	18	18	16	6	0	3	6	11	20	1	0
Paul Connolly	665	7	7	5	0	1	0	0	1	0	11	7	6	0	6	4	0	2	1
David Cotterill	580	14	3	0	11	3	2	1	1	1	34	19	0	1	8	7	0	3	0
Richard Cresswell	2663	31	28	21	3	7	12	1	21	15	29	21	10	3	51	30	23	5	0
Andrew Davies	746	8	7	7	1	0	0	0	3	6	3	3	11	4	11	15	0	1	0
Ched Evans	2033	33	21	8	12	13	4	4	34	27	12	20	3	1	36	28	20	3	0
Jonathan Fortune	357	5	3	3	2	0	1	0	0	0	3	3	3	1	3	3	0	0	0
Ryan France	387	9	3	2	6	1	0	0	3	2	4	6	2	1	6	1	0	0	0
Derek Geary	527	7	5	4	2	1	0	1	0	0	17	4	1	1	3	7	0	1	0
James Harper	2937	34	31	27	3	4	4	2	14	12	25	40	8	6	27	17	2	2	0
Darius Henderson	2622	32	28	22	4	5	12	1	38	28	18	17	18	0	89	40	38	6	1
Brian Howard	216	4	3	1	1	2	0	0	2	0	1	0	0	0	5	1	1	1	0
Toni Kallio	775	8	8	8	0	0	0	2	0	2	11	7	4	2	14	6	0	2	0
Matthew Kilgallon	1883	21	21	18	0	3	1	0	5	7	13	50	15	4	11	9	1	1	0
Glen Little	751	16	7	1	9	6	0	4	5	5	46	17	1	0	7	5	0	0	0
Matthew Lowton	94	2	1	1	1	0	0	0	0	2	1	2	4	0	1	3	1	0	0
Nick Montgomery	3702	39	39	37	0	2	1	2	5	11	17	102	21	3	80	67	1	8	0
Chris Morgan	3524	37	37	36	0	1	2	2	10	3	5	75	49	26	49	27	5	11	0
Gary Naysmith	164	2	2	1	0	1	0	1	0	0	1	1	2	0	2	0	0	0	0
Nyron Nosworthy	1827	19	19	18	0	1	0	1	0	1	8	42	46	5	20	14	2	3	0
Stephen Quinn	3612	44	38	28	6	10	4	3	34	19	61	43	10	6	29	59	14	8	0
Kyel Reid	118	7	0	0	7	0	0	0	0	0	2	6	3	0	0	1	3	0	0
Marcel Seip	461	6	5	3	1	2	0	0	1	1	0	1	9	2	7	3	0	2	0
Jordan Stewart	1514	23	15	11	8	4	0	0	5	4	29	20	13	7	21	29	1	2	0
Andy Taylor	1999	26	22	14	4	8	0	3	3	7	48	51	25	7	25	27	0	5	0
Keith Treacy	951	16	12	2	4	10	1	4	9	20	43	14	5	1	9	21	2	2	0
Kyle Walker	2433	26	26	24	0	2	0	1	2	4	29	52	12	11	16	34	1	4	0
Jamie Ward	2209	28	25	13	3	12	7	4	22	18	64	22	2	1	15	21	13	3	0
Lee Williamson	1220	20	14	5	6	9	3	1	5	6	11	18	3	2	35	16	0	6	0
Mark Yeates	1233	20	11	6	9	5	2	7	16	17	57	12	1	0	19	15	0	2	0

actim

SEASON TOTALS

Goals scored	62
Goals conceded	55
Clean sheets	16
Shots on target	260
Shots off target	240
Shots per goal	8.06
Pens awarded	4
Pens scored	4
Pens conceded	8
Offsides	146
Corners	259
Crosses	623
Players used	36
Fouls committed	627
Free-kicks won	541

LEAGUE POSITION AT THE END OF EACH MONTH

AUG	SEP	OCT	NOV	DEC	JAN	FEB	MAR	APR	MAY
7	6	15	14	7	6	7	10	9	8

SEASON INFORMATION
Highest position: 2
Lowest position: 20
Average goals scored per game: 1.35
Average goals conceded per game: 1.20

CARDS RECEIVED

88 2

SEQUENCES

Wins	3
(on two occasions)	
Losses	4
(17/10/09–02/11/09)	
Draws	2
(on two occasions)	
Undefeated	7
(09/11/09–19/12/09)	
Without win	8
(26/09/09–09/11/09)	
Undefeated home	11
(21/11/09–16/03/10)	
Undefeated away	4
(09/11/09–19/12/09)	
Without scoring	2
(on two occasions)	
Without conceding	3
(on two occasions)	
Scoring	11
(15/08/09–17/10/09)	
Conceding	10
(15/09/09–09/11/09)	

MATCH RECORDS

Goals scored per match

		W	D	L	Pts
Failed to score	10	0	3	7	3
Scored 1 goal	20	6	8	6	26
Scored 2 goals	7	4	2	1	14
Scored 3 goals	8	6	1	1	19
Scored 4+ goals	1	1	0	0	3

Goals conceded per match

		W	D	L	Pts
Clean sheet	16	13	3	0	42
Conceded 1 goal	14	1	8	5	11
Conceded 2 goals	8	2	2	4	8
Conceded 3 goals	7	1	1	5	4
Conceded 4+ goals	1	0	0	1	0

GOALS SCORED/CONCEDED PER FIVE-MINUTE INTERVALS

MINS	5	10	15	20	25	30	35	40	45	50	55	60	65	70	75	80	85	90
FOR	1	4	3	0	2	1	4	0	8	5	1	4	7	3	1	5	2	11
AGN	3	1	2	2	3	2	2	2	7	5	8	6	1	2	4	0	4	1

EARLIEST STRIKE

RICHARD CRESSWELL
(v Blackpool) 0:38

LATEST STRIKE

DARIUS HENDERSON
(v Bristol City) 95:39

Chris Morgan

GOAL DETAILS

How the goals were struck

SCORED		CONCEDED
31	Right foot	30
18	Left foot	16
12	Header	9
1	Other	0

How the goals were struck

SCORED		CONCEDED
36	Open play	28
11	Cross	9
3	Corner	7
4	Penalty	5
3	Direct from free-kick	2
3	Free-kick	3
2	Own goal	1

Distance from goal

SCORED		CONCEDED
27	6YDS	16
28	18YDS	29
7	18+YDS	10

SHEFFIELD WEDNESDAY

CLUB SUMMARY

FORMED	1867
MANAGER	Alan Irvine
GROUND	Hillsborough
CAPACITY	39,859
NICKNAME	The Owls
WEBSITE	www.swfc.co.uk

The New Football Pools PLAYER OF THE SEASON — Lee Grant

OVERALL

P	W	D	L	F	A	GD
49	12	14	23	53	73	-20

COCA-COLA CHAMPIONSHIP

Pos	P	W	D	L	F	A	GD	Pts
22	46	11	14	21	49	69	-20	47

HOME

Pos	P	W	D	L	F	A	GD	Pts
21	23	8	6	9	30	31	-1	30

AWAY

Pos	P	W	D	L	F	A	GD	Pts
21	23	3	8	12	19	38	-19	17

CUP PROGRESS DETAILS

Competition	Round reached	Knocked out by
FA Cup	R3	Crystal Palace
Carling Cup	R2	Port Vale

BIGGEST WIN (ALL COMPS)
22/08/09 4–0 v Scunthorpe

BIGGEST DEFEAT (ALL COMPS)
27/02/10 0–5 v Reading

THE PLAYER WITH THE MOST

GOALS SCORED Marcus Tudgay	**10**
SHOTS ON TARGET Luke Varney	**49**
SHOTS OFF TARGET Jermaine Johnson	**31**
SHOTS WITHOUT SCORING Mark Beevers	**8**
ASSISTS Marcus Tudgay	**8**
OFFSIDES Luke Varney, Leon Clarke	**36**
FOULS Marcus Tudgay	**71**
FOULS WITHOUT A CARD Sean McAllister	**6**
FREE-KICKS WON Marcus Tudgay	**53**
DEFENSIVE CLEARANCES Darren Purse	**60**

actim INDEX — FOR THE 2009/10 COCA-COLA CHAMPIONSHIP SEASON

RANK	PLAYER	PTS
59	Marcus Tudgay	467
84	Tommy Spurr	435
86	Lee Grant	433

ATTENDANCE RECORD

HIGH	AVERAGE	LOW
37,121	23,179	18,329
v Crystal Palace (02/05/2010)		v Swansea (19/12/2009)

Failure to beat Crystal Palace at home on the final day saw the Owls relegated once again

SHEFFIELD WEDNESDAY dropped out of the Coca-Cola Championship for the second time in five years having failed to secure the win that they needed to survive in their final-day relegation decider with Crystal Palace.

The Owls battled right to the end in a 2–2 draw against Palace after captain Darren Purse's late goal had hauled them level for a second time in the match. However, it was not meant to be for the South Yorkshire club.

Wednesday had finished in 12th place in 2008/09, leading to hopes from some of the club's fans that they could challenge for the play-offs this time around. But that optimism proved to be short-lived as they won just four games in the first half of the campaign.

By the turn of the year they were still in the bottom three and looking for a new manager. Brian Laws' three-year tenure at Hillsborough ended with his sacking in mid-December and, following Sean McAuley's brief spell as caretaker boss, the club announced that Alan Irvine was to take over.

Irvine's arrival had an immediate impact on their results, with the Scot claiming five wins from his first seven games in charge. That run lifted Wednesday out of the

A Sheffield Wednesday fan is left in tears after the Owls are relegated

Marcus Tudgay helps the Owls to a third consecutive win, against Peterborough

bottom three and up to 18th place in the table, but Irvine, who had been sacked by Preston shortly before being given the Owls job, was ultimately hamstrung by his new side's inability to convert their goalscoring chances.

A 5–0 defeat at fellow strugglers Reading in February first set the alarm bells ringing and, with a single win from their last 12 Championship matches, the writing was on the wall long before the decisive final-day showdown.

While relegation was the ultimate disaster for the Owls, it was also a difficult season from a parochial point of view, with Sheffield United beating them 3–2 at Bramall Lane in September. The Blades then played a part in Wednesday's drop by claiming a vital point at Hillsborough in the closing weeks of the season.

After a turbulent season on the pitch, there was upheaval in the boardroom in the close season as the club rejected an investment proposal from Chicago-based group Club 9 Sports. Owls chairman Lee Strafford then quit his position, leaving the Owls at something of a crossroads.

Former manager Howard Wilkinson, the club's technical advisor, was appointed interim chairman and will work closely with manager Irvine in building a new-look squad ahead of the 2010/11 season.

RESULTS 2009/10

AUGUST

8th	● Barnsley	H	D 2–2	Att: 30,644	Ref: A Taylor	Scorers: Gray, Johnson.
11th	● Rochdale	H	W 3–0	Att: 6,696	Ref: C Sarginson	Scorers: Esajas, Johnson[2].
15th	● Peterborough	A	D 1–1	Att: 10,747	Ref: A D'Urso	Scorers: O'Connor. Booked: O'Connor.
19th	● Newcastle	A	L 1–0	Att: 43,904	Ref: P Dowd	Booked: Buxton, Miller.
22nd	● Scunthorpe	H	W 4–0	Att: 20,215	Ref: A Hall	Scorers: Johnson, Potter, Tudgay, Wood.
25th	● Port Vale	A	L 2–0	Att: 6,667	Ref: G Salisbury	Dismissed: Jeffers.
29th	● Plymouth	A	W 1–3	Att: 10,228	Ref: A Haines	Scorers: Tudgay[2], Wood. Booked: Varney, Wood, Johnson.

SEPTEMBER

12th	● Nottm Forest	H	D 1–1	Att: 25,270	Ref: S Tanner	Scorers: Tudgay. Booked: Varney.
15th	● Middlesbrough	H	L 1–3	Att: 21,722	Ref: T Bates	Scorers: Varney.
18th	● Sheff Utd	A	L 3–2	Att: 29,210	Ref: A Wiley	Scorers: Esajas, Tudgay. Booked: O'Connor.
26th	● Cardiff	H	W 3–1	Att: 18,959	Ref: M Oliver	Scorers: Clarke, Esajas, Varney. Booked: Esajas.
29th	● Crystal Palace	A	D 0–0	Att: 12,476	Ref: T Kettle	Booked: O'Connor, Wood.

OCTOBER

3rd	● Derby	A	L 3–0	Att: 30,116	Ref: C Foy	Booked: Wood.
17th	● Coventry	H	W 2–0	Att: 20,026	Ref: C Webster	Scorers: Clarke, Purse. Booked: Clarke, Beevers.
20th	● Preston	H	L 1–2	Att: 20,882	Ref: R Shoebridge	Scorers: Gray. Booked: Purse.
23rd	● Watford	A	L 4–1	Att: 14,591	Ref: P Crossley	Scorers: Tudgay.
31st	● Bristol City	A	D 1–1	Att: 15,005	Ref: F Graham	Scorers: Varney. Booked: Varney, Simek.

NOVEMBER

7th	● QPR	H	L 1–2	Att: 19,491	Ref: N Miller	Scorers: Johnson.
21st	● Ipswich	A	D 0–0	Att: 19,636	Ref: A D'Urso	Booked: Simek, Hinds, Buxton.
28th	● West Brom	H	L 0–4	Att: 20,824	Ref: E Ilderton	Booked: Potter, Gray.

DECEMBER

5th	● Reading	H	L 0–2	Att: 22,090	Ref: D Webb	Booked: Hinds.
8th	● Doncaster	A	L 1–0	Att: 12,825	Ref: A Wiley	Booked: Purse, O'Connor, Clarke, Varney.
12th	● Leicester	A	L 3–0	Att: 22,236	Ref: C Boyeson	Booked: Tudgay, Beevers.
19th	● Swansea	H	L 0–2	Att: 18,329	Ref: O Langford	Booked: Spurr, Simek.
26th	● Newcastle	H	D 2–2	Att: 30,030	Ref: S Attwell	Scorers: O'Connor, Varney. Booked: Varney, Tudgay.

JANUARY

2nd	● Crystal Palace	H	L 1–2	Att: 8,690	Ref: N Miller	Scorers: Hill OG.
16th	● Barnsley	A	W 1–2	Att: 17,844	Ref: A Penn	Scorers: Johnson, Spurr. Booked: Potter, O'Connor.
19th	● Blackpool	A	W 1–2	Att: 8,007	Ref: A Hall	Scorers: Clarke, Soares. Booked: O'Connor, Purse, Soares, Buxton, Clarke.
23rd	● Peterborough	H	W 2–1	Att: 24,882	Ref: D Foster	Scorers: Tudgay[2]. Booked: Buxton.
27th	● Scunthorpe	A	L 2–0	Att: 7,038	Ref: M Clattenburg	
30th	● Plymouth	H	W 2–1	Att: 22,590	Ref: K Wright	Scorers: Varney[2]. Booked: Buxton.

FEBRUARY

6th	● Nottm Forest	A	L 2–1	Att: 27,900	Ref: T Kettle	Scorers: Varney. Booked: Gray, Varney.
9th	● Blackpool	H	W 2–0	Att: 19,058	Ref: G Eltrigham	Scorers: O'Connor, Potter.
16th	● Doncaster	H	L 0–2	Att: 22,252	Ref: E Ilderton	Booked: Gray.
20th	● Ipswich	H	L 0–1	Att: 21,641	Ref: M Russell	
27th	● Reading	A	L 5–0	Att: 17,573	Ref: G Hegley	

MARCH

6th	● Leicester	H	W 2–0	Att: 21,647	Ref: P Gibbs	Scorers: Clarke[2]. Booked: Potter, Tudgay, Varney.
9th	● West Brom	A	L 1–0	Att: 20,458	Ref: S Mathieson	Booked: Spurr.
13th	● Swansea	A	D 0–0	Att: 14,167	Ref: R Booth	Booked: O'Connor.
16th	● Preston	A	D 2–2	Att: 12,311	Ref: C Boyeson	Scorers: Miller, Tudgay.
20th	● Derby	H	D 0–0	Att: 21,827	Ref: J Linington	
24th	● Watford	H	W 2–1	Att: 18,449	Ref: D Deadman	Scorers: Nolan, Varney. Booked: Varney.
27th	● Coventry	A	D 1–1	Att: 17,608	Ref: N Swarbrick	Scorers: Varney. Booked: Purse, Spurr.

APRIL

3rd	● QPR	A	D 1–1	Att: 13,405	Ref: C Webster	Scorers: Soares.
5th	● Bristol City	H	L 0–1	Att: 19,688	Ref: G Salisbury	Booked: Soares.
10th	● Middlesbrough	A	L 1–0	Att: 19,932	Ref: J Moss	
18th	● Sheff Utd	H	D 1–1	Att: 35,485	Ref: C Foy	Scorers: Potter. Booked: O'Connor, Nolan.
24th	● Cardiff	A	L 3–2	Att: 23,304	Ref: P Taylor	Scorers: Johnson, Tudgay. Booked: Tudgay, Purse, Potter.

MAY

| 2nd | ● Crystal Palace | H | D 2–2 | Att: 37,121 | Ref: M Dean | Scorers: Clarke, Purse. Booked: Johnson. |

● Coca-Cola Championship/Play-offs ● FA Cup ● Carling Cup

CHAMPIONSHIP GOALKEEPER STATS

Player	Minutes on pitch	Appearances	Match starts	Completed matches	Sub appearances	Subbed off	Saved with feet	Punched	Parried	Tipped over	Fumbled	Tipped round	Caught	Blocked	Clean sheets	Goals conceded	Save %	Saved	Resulting in goals	Opposition miss	Fouls committed	Free-kicks won	Yellow cards	Red cards
Lee Grant	4434	46	46	46	0	0	2	10	39	20	1	14	134	2	8	69	76.21	0	3	0	1	10	0	0

CHAMPIONSHIP OUTFIELD PLAYER STATS

Player	Minutes on pitch	Appearances	Match starts	Completed matches	Substitute appearances	Subbed off	Goals scored	Assists	Shots on target	Shots off target	Crosses	Tackles made	Defensive clearances	Defensive blocks	Fouls committed	Free-kicks won	Caught offside	Yellow cards	Red cards
Mark Beevers	3122	35	32	31	3	1	0	1	3	5	1	111	42	11	38	29	0	2	0
Lewis Buxton	2630	28	28	26	0	2	0	0	1	2	30	121	17	9	30	15	0	5	0
Leon Clarke	2044	36	18	6	18	12	6	0	24	26	11	45	3	1	48	15	36	3	0
Etienne Esajas	766	20	5	0	15	5	2	3	14	11	25	15	0	0	14	6	0	1	0
Warren Feeney	16	1	0	0	1	0	0	0	0	0	0	0	0	0	0	0	0	0	0
Michael Gray	2281	30	27	15	3	12	2	4	12	12	72	80	6	2	12	26	3	3	0
Richard Hinds	770	11	7	7	4	0	0	0	1	0	0	11	11	2	5	9	0	2	0
Francis Jeffers	320	13	1	0	12	1	0	0	1	3	1	0	0	0	6	4	2	0	0
Jermaine Johnson	2263	34	29	9	5	20	5	1	37	31	44	55	1	0	33	45	14	2	0
Sean McAllister	593	12	5	2	7	3	0	0	3	2	2	34	1	1	6	10	0	0	0
Tommy Miller	1034	20	10	5	10	5	1	0	10	5	13	7	1	2	14	4	1	1	0
Eddie Nolan	1331	14	14	13	0	1	1	0	2	1	23	13	16	7	9	13	0	1	0
James O'Connor	3979	44	44	31	0	13	3	1	15	13	15	126	5	9	52	32	0	8	0
Darren Potter	4324	46	46	42	0	4	3	5	27	25	78	130	24	7	54	49	1	4	0
Darren Purse	3730	39	39	38	0	1	2	1	4	12	4	154	60	25	44	52	1	5	0
Frank Simek	956	12	9	8	3	1	0	0	0	2	7	9	5	6	11	5	0	3	0
Tom Soares	1716	25	17	9	8	8	2	1	11	9	14	75	8	3	16	19	2	2	0
Akpo Sodje	238	11	0	0	11	0	0	0	3	3	0	14	2	0	5	6	4	0	0
Tommy Spurr	4318	46	46	43	0	3	1	5	8	10	89	148	25	9	50	51	0	3	0
Marcus Tudgay	3883	43	41	37	2	4	10	8	40	29	9	85	35	6	71	53	24	4	0
Luke Varney	3004	39	32	19	7	13	9	4	49	19	26	29	10	3	61	39	36	8	0
Richard Wood	962	11	10	9	1	1	2	0	1	2	0	42	10	1	12	13	1	3	0

SEASON TOTALS

Goals scored	49
Goals conceded	69
Clean sheets	8
Shots on target	266
Shots off target	222
Shots per goal	9.96
Pens awarded	2
Pens scored	2
Pens conceded	3
Offsides	125
Corners	244
Crosses	464
Players used	23
Fouls committed	592
Free-kicks won	505

LEAGUE POSITION AT THE END OF EACH MONTH

AUG	SEP	OCT	NOV	DEC	JAN	FEB	MAR	APR	MAY
8	13	14	19	23	19	22	20	22	22

SEASON INFORMATION
Highest position: 7
Lowest position: 23
Average goals scored per game: 1.07
Average goals conceded per game: 1.50

CARDS RECEIVED

60   **0**

SEQUENCES

Wins	3
(16/01/10–23/01/10)	
Losses	5
(28/11/09–19/12/09)	
Draws	3
(13/03/10–20/03/10)	
Undefeated	6
(13/03/10–03/04/10)	
Without win	11
(20/10/09–26/12/09)	
Undefeated home	4
(26/12/09–09/02/10)	
Undefeated away	4
(13/03/10–03/04/10)	
Without scoring	6
(21/11/09–19/12/09)	
Without conceding	0
(–)	
Scoring	6
(22/08/09–26/09/09)	
Conceding	12
(28/11/09–06/02/10)	

MATCH RECORDS

Goals scored per match

		W	D	L	Pts
Failed to score	18	0	4	14	4
Scored 1 goal	11	0	6	5	6
Scored 2 goals	14	8	4	2	28
Scored 3 goals	2	2	0	0	6
Scored 4+ goals	1	1	0	0	3

Goals conceded per match

		W	D	L	Pts
Clean sheet	8	4	4	0	16
Conceded 1 goal	19	7	6	6	27
Conceded 2 goals	11	0	4	7	4
Conceded 3 goals	5	0	0	5	0
Conceded 4+ goals	3	0	0	3	0

GOALS SCORED/CONCEDED
PER FIVE-MINUTE INTERVALS

MINS	5	10	15	20	25	30	35	40	45	50	55	60	65	70	75	80	85	90
FOR	5	3	4	1	3	0	2	3	5	3	0	5	2	2	4	3	1	3
AGN	3	4	3	6	8	3	0	4	3	2	5	3	6	2	2	8	5	2

EARLIEST STRIKE
LUKE VARNEY
(v Middlesbrough) 1:50

LATEST STRIKE
MARCUS TUDGAY
(v Plymouth) 91:41

Jermaine Johnson

GOAL DETAILS

How the goals were struck

SCORED		CONCEDED
23	Right foot	32
12	Left foot	23
14	Header	13
0	Other	1

How the goals were struck

SCORED		CONCEDED
30	Open play	49
10	Cross	6
3	Corner	3
2	Penalty	3
3	Direct from free-kick	3
1	Free-kick	2
0	Own goal	3

Distance from goal

SCORED		CONCEDED
16	6YDS	23
25	18YDS	35
8	18+YDS	11

SWANSEA CITY

CLUB SUMMARY

FORMED	1912
MANAGER	Paulo Sousa
GROUND	Liberty Stadium
CAPACITY	20,532
NICKNAME	The Swans
WEBSITE	www.swanseacity.net

The New Football Pools PLAYER OF THE SEASON — Ashley Williams

OVERALL

P	W	D	L	F	A	GD
49	18	18	13	45	41	4

COCA-COLA CHAMPIONSHIP

Pos	P	W	D	L	F	A	GD	Pts
7	46	17	18	11	40	37	3	69

HOME

Pos	P	W	D	L	F	A	GD	Pts
8	23	10	10	3	21	12	9	40

AWAY

Pos	P	W	D	L	F	A	GD	Pts
6	23	7	8	8	19	25	-6	29

CUP PROGRESS DETAILS

Competition	Round reached	Knocked out by
FA Cup	R3	Leicester
Carling Cup	R2	Scunthorpe

BIGGEST WIN (ALL COMPS)
3–0 on 2 occasions

BIGGEST DEFEAT (ALL COMPS)
23/03/10 1–5 v Blackpool

THE PLAYER WITH THE MOST

GOALS SCORED Darren Pratley	**7**
SHOTS ON TARGET Darren Pratley	**30**
SHOTS OFF TARGET Nathan Dyer	**22**
SHOTS WITHOUT SCORING Stephen Dobbie	**21**
ASSISTS Mark Gower, Nathan Dyer	**4**
OFFSIDES Gorka Pintado	**26**
FOULS Darren Pratley	**58**
FOULS WITHOUT A CARD Thomas Butler	**13**
FREE-KICKS WON Darren Pratley	**77**
DEFENSIVE CLEARANCES Ashley Williams	**66**

actim INDEX FOR THE 2009/10 COCA-COLA CHAMPIONSHIP SEASON

RANK	PLAYER	PTS
12	Ashley Williams	575
26	Dorus De Vries	533
71	Alan Tate	448

ATTENDANCE RECORD

HIGH	AVERAGE	LOW
18,794	15,407	12,775
v Crystal Palace (28/12/2009)		v Reading (18/08/2009)

Paulo Sousa and his players are left dejected after missing out on the play-offs

PAULO SOUSA'S first season in charge of Swansea ended in disappointment after they missed out on a play-off place on the final day.

The Welsh side looked certain of a top-six finish in mid-March when they were 10 points better off than seventh-placed Blackpool. But Sousa's side took just 13 points from their last 13 games and a defeat at Sheffield United in their penultimate game saw the Swans drop out of the top six for the first time since December, with Blackpool replacing them.

Ian Holloway's side were held by Bristol City on a dramatic final day, but a lack of goals had been a problem for Swansea all season and they could only manage a goalless draw against Doncaster, having needed a victory to secure the final Coca-Cola Championship play-off position.

Former Portugal international Sousa arrived at the Liberty Stadium in the summer of 2009 following Roberto Martinez's departure for Wigan. The two-time Champions League winner persisted with Martinez's attractive brand of passing football, but the lack of a cutting edge proved to be costly as the Swans only scored 40 goals in their 46 games.

However, there were plenty of positives for Sousa to take from a campaign in which he had targeted a top-10 finish.

Swansea's stubborn defence conceded only 37 League goals and goalkeeper Dorus de Vries broke the club record for the number of clean sheets in a season, with the Dutchman keeping out the opposition in 24 games.

Paulo Sousa's Swansea were denied a play-off place on the final day of the season

Sousa guided the club to their highest finish since 1983 and that was achieved despite the fact that he had to cope without several key players due to injuries, particularly at the start of the season.

With a solid first season at the helm, the former QPR boss has enhanced his reputation as a manager, while Swansea's free-flowing football has ensured that they are regarded as among the most attractive teams to watch in the division.

The Swans will be looking to improve once more in 2010/11, but they will face a battle to keep hold of the likes of Welsh Player of the Year Ashley Williams, central midfielder Darren Pratley and playmaker Leon Britton, who was out of contract in the close season.

Sousa will almost certainly be in the market for a striker, as Pratley was the club's leading scorer during the 2009/10 season with just seven goals. The return of long-term absentee Ferrie Bodde, following a long and troublesome knee injury, will also seem like a new player for the Swans.

RESULTS 2009/10

AUGUST

8th	●	Leicester	A	L 2–1	Att: 26,171	Ref: G Hegley	Scorers: Williams. Booked: Gower.
11th	●	Brighton	H	W 3–0	Att: 6,400	Ref: G Scott	Scorers: Dobbie[2], Monk. Booked: Tate.
15th	●	Middlesbrough	H	L 0–3	Att: 16,201	Ref: P Taylor	Booked: Orlandi, Dobbie.
18th	●	Reading	H	D 0–0	Att: 12,775	Ref: S Hooper	Booked: Orlandi, Williams, Rangel.
22nd	●	Coventry	A	W 0–1	Att: 16,307	Ref: P Crossley	Scorers: Williams. Booked: Tate, Britton, Rangel.
25th	●	Scunthorpe	H	L 1–2	Att: 7,321	Ref: J Linnington	Scorers: Dobbie. Booked: Dyer, Pintado, Tate. Dismissed: Monk, Pintado, Rangel. AET – Score after 90 mins 1–1.
29th	●	Watford	H	D 1–1	Att: 14,172	Ref: A Taylor	Scorers: Tate. Booked: Painter, Williams, Orlandi.

SEPTEMBER

12th	●	Preston	A	L 2–0	Att: 12,854	Ref: E Ilderton	Booked: Williams, Painter, Richards.
15th	●	Bristol City	H	D 0–0	Att: 12,859	Ref: D Whitestone	Booked: Tate.
19th	●	Barnsley	A	D 0–0	Att: 11,596	Ref: R Shoebridge	
26th	●	Sheff Utd	H	W 2–1	Att: 14,324	Ref: D Deadman	Scorers: Butler, Trundle. Booked: Dyer, Lopez, De Vries. Dismissed: Lopez, Dyer.
29th	●	Doncaster	A	D 0–0	Att: 8,833	Ref: A Haines	Booked: Rangel.

OCTOBER

3rd	●	QPR	H	W 2–0	Att: 14,444	Ref: K Hill	Scorers: Gower, Trundle. Booked: Gower.
17th	●	Ipswich	A	D 1–1	Att: 19,667	Ref: K Wright	Scorers: Beattie. Booked: Rangel.
20th	●	West Brom	A	W 0–1	Att: 21,022	Ref: A D'Urso	Scorers: Beattie. Booked: Painter, Pratley.
24th	●	Blackpool	H	D 0–0	Att: 14,724	Ref: A Hall	
31st	●	Scunthorpe	A	W 0–2	Att: 5,201	Ref: K Evans	Scorers: Beattie, Van der Gun. Booked: Van der Gun.

NOVEMBER

7th	●	Cardiff	H	W 3–2	Att: 18,209	Ref: L Probert	Scorers: Dyer, Pratley[2]. Booked: Britton, Dyer.
20th	●	Derby	H	W 1–0	Att: 17,804	Ref: R East	Scorers: Bessone.
28th	●	Newcastle	A	L 3–0	Att: 42,616	Ref: M Haywood	Booked: Tate.

DECEMBER

5th	●	Peterborough	A	D 2–2	Att: 7,312	Ref: R Booth	Scorers: Trundle[2].
8th	●	Plymouth	H	W 1–0	Att: 14,004	Ref: S Tanner	Scorers: Trundle. Booked: Britton, Pintado.
12th	●	Nottm Forest	H	L 0–1	Att: 16,690	Ref: S Hooper	Booked: Tate.
19th	●	Sheff Wed	A	W 0–2	Att: 18,329	Ref: O Langford	Scorers: Pratley[2]. Booked: Williams.
26th	●	Reading	A	D 1–1	Att: 19,608	Ref: M Russell	Scorers: Pratley. Booked: Pratley, Dyer, Tate.
28th	●	Crystal Palace	H	D 0–0	Att: 18,794	Ref: A Taylor	Booked: Allen, Pintado, Britton. Dismissed: Serran.

JANUARY

2nd	●	Leicester	A	L 2–1	Att: 12,307	Ref: P Taylor	Scorers: Cotterill.
16th	●	Leicester	H	W 1–0	Att: 15,037	Ref: F Graham	Scorers: Pintado. Booked: De Vries.
23rd	●	Middlesbrough	A	D 1–1	Att: 16,847	Ref: A Penn	Scorers: Pintado.
26th	●	Coventry	H	D 0–0	Att: 13,868	Ref: D McDermid	

FEBRUARY

6th	●	Preston	H	W 2–0	Att: 14,659	Ref: P Gibbs	Scorers: Cotterill, Williams. Booked: Pratley, Dyer.
9th	●	Crystal Palace	A	W 0–1	Att: 12,328	Ref: G Scott	Scorers: Kuqi. Booked: Britton.
13th	●	Newcastle	H	D 1–1	Att: 15,188	Ref: A Woolmer	Scorers: Cotterill. Booked: Orlandi.
16th	●	Plymouth	A	D 1–1	Att: 9,185	Ref: K Hill	Scorers: Pratley. Booked: Gower, Orlandi, Monk, Kuqi.
20th	●	Derby	A	W 0–1	Att: 31,024	Ref: S Tanner	Scorers: Kuqi. Booked: Rangel, Dyer, Gower. Dismissed: Pintado.
27th	●	Peterborough	H	W 1–0	Att: 16,175	Ref: G Ward	Scorers: Cotterill.

MARCH

6th	●	Nottm Forest	A	L 1–0	Att: 25,012	Ref: C Webster	Booked: Kuqi.
9th	●	Watford	A	W 0–1	Att: 12,907	Ref: T Kettle	Scorers: Kuqi. Booked: Britton, Rangel.
13th	●	Sheff Wed	H	D 0–0	Att: 14,167	Ref: R Booth	
16th	●	West Brom	H	L 0–2	Att: 17,774	Ref: R East	Booked: Kuqi, Monk.
20th	●	QPR	A	D 1–1	Att: 15,502	Ref: C Boyeson	Scorers: Dyer. Booked: Richards.
23rd	●	Blackpool	A	L 5–1	Att: 9,149	Ref: N Miller	Scorers: Van der Gun. Booked: Bauza, Orlandi.
27th	●	Ipswich	H	D 0–0	Att: 14,902	Ref: C Pawson	Booked: Pratley.

APRIL

3rd	●	Cardiff	A	L 2–1	Att: 25,130	Ref: P Dowd	Scorers: Orlandi. Booked: Williams, Rangel, Pratley, Orlandi.
5th	●	Scunthorpe	H	W 3–0	Att: 14,830	Ref: D Whitestone	Scorers: Edgar, Kuqi, Williams.
10th	●	Bristol City	A	L 1–0	Att: 14,719	Ref: M Dean	Booked: Cotterill, Allen.
17th	●	Barnsley	H	W 3–1	Att: 15,139	Ref: D Phillips	Scorers: Kuqi, Pratley, Williams. Booked: Pratley, Monk, Britton.
24th	●	Sheff Utd	A	L 2–0	Att: 25,966	Ref: S Mathieson	Booked: Monk.

MAY

2nd	●	Doncaster	H	D 0–0	Att: 17,630	Ref: G Hegley	

● Coca-Cola Championship/Play-offs ● FA Cup ● Carling Cup

SWANSEA CITY

CHAMPIONSHIP GOALKEEPER STATS

Player	Minutes on pitch	Appearances	Match starts	Completed matches	Sub appearances	Subbed off	Saved with feet	Punched	Parried	Tipped over	Fumbled	Tipped round	Caught	Blocked	Clean sheets	Goals conceded	Save %	Saved	Resulting in goals	Opposition miss	Fouls committed	Free-kicks won	Yellow cards	Red cards
Dorus De Vries	4425	46	46	46	0	0	3	30	12	1	4	13	124	3	24	37	83.41	2	1	1	0	8	2	0

CHAMPIONSHIP OUTFIELD PLAYER STATS

Player	Minutes on pitch	Appearances	Match starts	Completed matches	Substitute appearances	Subbed off	Goals scored	Assists	Shots on target	Shots off target	Crosses	Tackles made	Defensive clearances	Defensive blocks	Fouls committed	Free-kicks won	Caught offside	Yellow cards	Red cards
Joe Allen	1087	21	13	2	8	11	0	2	7	11	1	35	4	3	9	25	0	2	0
Guillem Bauza	303	6	3	2	3	1	0	0	6	4	2	3	1	0	5	7	1	1	0
Craig Beattie	1091	23	12	3	11	9	3	2	24	13	5	16	9	0	10	20	9	0	0
Federico Bessone	1878	21	21	18	0	3	1	1	8	2	26	33	10	3	11	15	1	0	0
Ferrie Bodde	91	4	2	0	2	2	0	0	1	1	1	3	0	0	1	0	0	0	0
Chad Bond	67	1	1	0	0	1	0	0	1	0	0	0	0	0	0	0	0	0	0
Leon Britton	3239	36	35	27	1	8	0	0	2	2	7	59	5	4	29	47	0	7	0
Thomas Butler	1042	25	9	3	16	6	1	0	12	5	18	41	1	1	13	28	1	0	0
Matthew Collins	96	1	1	1	0	0	0	0	0	1	1	13	0	0	1	0	0	0	0
David Cotterill	1399	21	14	7	7	7	3	2	19	16	36	27	0	0	8	32	0	1	0
Stephen Dobbie	367	6	4	1	2	3	0	0	9	12	0	13	1	0	3	6	2	1	0
Nathan Dyer	3221	40	37	18	3	18	2	4	21	22	42	78	1	0	33	76	7	5	1
David Edgar	475	5	5	5	0	0	1	0	1	1	1	11	1	2	4	1	0	0	0
Mark Gower	2389	31	25	13	6	12	1	4	15	15	69	57	4	2	20	24	6	4	0
Besian Idrizaj	62	3	1	0	2	1	0	0	0	1	0	5	0	1	0	0	0	0	0
Shefki Kuqi	1394	20	14	7	6	7	5	1	23	16	1	21	14	0	13	13	9	3	0
Jordi Lopez	722	12	7	3	5	3	0	1	7	5	7	30	4	0	13	17	0	1	1
Shaun MacDonald	137	3	2	0	1	2	0	0	0	1	1	12	0	0	1	1	1	0	0
Garry Monk	2194	23	22	22	1	0	0	1	3	5	1	70	21	4	16	13	0	4	0
Kerry Morgan	147	3	1	1	2	0	0	0	1	3	0	1	0	0	0	4	0	0	0
Andrea Orlandi	1988	30	22	12	8	10	1	3	22	20	41	58	8	1	18	33	3	7	0
Marcos Painter	317	4	4	2	0	2	0	0	1	1	1	26	1	0	7	0	0	3	0
Gorka Pintado	1702	32	16	4	16	11	2	3	13	10	3	48	9	0	27	25	26	2	1
Darren Pratley	3130	36	33	28	3	5	7	2	30	19	32	82	6	1	58	77	7	6	0
Angel Rangel	3535	38	37	35	1	2	0	3	6	7	24	112	20	9	30	31	2	7	0
Ashley Richards	1080	15	10	10	5	0	0	0	0	0	3	36	6	1	7	8	1	2	0
Albert Serran	333	6	3	2	3	0	0	0	0	0	0	19	4	0	2	4	1	0	1
Alan Tate	3754	39	39	39	0	0	0	0	7	10	2	120	47	12	29	46	0	5	0
Casey Thomas	32	1	0	0	1	0	0	0	0	0	0	0	0	0	0	0	0	0	0
Lee Trundle	605	20	2	0	18	3	5	0	15	8	3	6	1	0	6	10	9	0	0
Cedric Van der Gun	1854	25	20	10	5	10	2	0	10	12	16	28	2	1	18	29	5	1	0
Ashley Williams	4347	46	45	45	1	0	5	1	7	16	0	146	66	21	32	26	2	5	0

SEASON TOTALS

Goals scored	40
Goals conceded	37
Clean sheets	24
Shots on target	270
Shots off target	240
Shots per goal	12.75
Pens awarded	3
Pens scored	2
Pens conceded	4
Offsides	93
Corners	280
Crosses	344
Players used	33
Fouls committed	424
Free-kicks won	626

CARDS RECEIVED

69   4

SEQUENCES

Wins	3
(31/10/09–20/11/09)	
Losses	2
(08/08/09–15/08/09)	
Draws	2
(on four occasions)	
Undefeated	12
(19/12/09–27/02/10)	
Without win	6
(13/03/10–03/04/10)	
Undefeated home	9
(18/08/09–08/12/09)	
Undefeated away	7
(05/12/09–20/02/10)	
Without scoring	3
(12/09/09–19/09/09)	
Without conceding	3
(on two occasions)	
Scoring	6
(06/02/10–27/02/10)	
Conceding	3
(on two occasions)	

LEAGUE POSITION AT THE END OF EACH MONTH

AUG	SEP	OCT	NOV	DEC	JAN	FEB	MAR	APR	MAY
19	16	11	7	6	5	4	5	7	7

SEASON INFORMATION

Highest position: 3
Lowest position: 24
Average goals scored per game: 0.87
Average goals conceded per game: 0.80

MATCH RECORDS

Goals scored per match

		W	D	L	Pts
Failed to score	18	0	10	8	10
Scored 1 goal	19	9	7	3	34
Scored 2 goals	6	5	1	0	16
Scored 3 goals	3	3	0	0	9
Scored 4+ goals	0	0	0	0	0

Goals conceded per match

		W	D	L	Pts
Clean sheet	24	14	10	0	52
Conceded 1 goal	12	2	7	3	13
Conceded 2 goals	7	1	1	5	4
Conceded 3 goals	2	0	0	2	0
Conceded 4+ goals	1	0	0	1	0

EARLIEST STRIKE

DARREN PRATLEY
(v Sheff Wed) 4:31

LATEST STRIKE

ALAN TATE
(v Watford) 92:19

Shefki Kuqi

GOAL DETAILS

How the goals were struck

SCORED		CONCEDED
19	Right foot	18
14	Left foot	9
7	Header	9
0	Other	1

How the goals were struck

SCORED		CONCEDED
23	Open play	25
5	Cross	1
5	Corner	5
2	Penalty	1
1	Direct from free-kick	1
4	Free-kick	3
0	Own goal	1

Distance from goal

SCORED		CONCEDED
15	6YDS	25
22	18YDS	10
3	18+YDS	2

GOALS SCORED/CONCEDED PER FIVE-MINUTE INTERVALS

MINS	5	10	15	20	25	30	35	40	45	50	55	60	65	70	75	80	85	90
FOR	1	2	1	4	1	3	3	2	0	4	3	2	1	3	2	1	5	2
AGN	0	1	2	0	1	2	5	0	3	1	2	1	1	3	2	2	3	8

WATFORD

CLUB SUMMARY

FORMED	1881
MANAGER	Malky Mackay
GROUND	Vicarage Road
CAPACITY	19,920
NICKNAME	The Hornets
WEBSITE	www.watfordfc.com

The New Football Pools PLAYER OF THE SEASON — *Tom Cleverley*

OVERALL
P	W	D	L	F	A	GD
49	15	12	22	64	75	-11

COCA-COLA CHAMPIONSHIP
Pos	P	W	D	L	F	A	GD	Pts
16	46	14	12	20	61	68	-7	54

HOME
Pos	P	W	D	L	F	A	GD	Pts
14	23	10	6	7	36	26	10	36

AWAY
Pos	P	W	D	L	F	A	GD	Pts
19	23	4	6	13	25	42	-17	18

CUP PROGRESS DETAILS
Competition	Round reached	Knocked out by
FA Cup	R3	Chelsea
Carling Cup	R2	Leeds

BIGGEST WIN (ALL COMPS)
02/05/10 4–0 v Coventry

BIGGEST DEFEAT (ALL COMPS)
0–5 on 2 occasions

THE PLAYER WITH THE MOST
GOALS SCORED Danny Graham	**14**
SHOTS ON TARGET Danny Graham	**42**
SHOTS OFF TARGET Heidar Helguson	**36**
SHOTS WITHOUT SCORING Ross Jenkins	**13**
ASSISTS Danny Graham	**6**
OFFSIDES Danny Graham	**63**
FOULS John Eustace	**67**
FOULS WITHOUT A CARD Mike Williamson	**10**
FREE-KICKS WON Henri Lansbury	**69**
DEFENSIVE CLEARANCES Adrian Mariappa	**64**

actim INDEX — FOR THE 2009/10 COCA-COLA CHAMPIONSHIP SEASON

RANK	PLAYER	PTS
30	Danny Graham	528
53	Tom Cleverley	477
63	Adrian Mariappa	464

ATTENDANCE RECORD
HIGH	AVERAGE	LOW
17,120	14,345	12,179
v Newcastle (27/02/2010)		v Bristol City (09/02/2010)

FINANCIAL worries and a mid-season goal drought made for a tough campaign at Vicarage Road, with rookie boss Malky Mackay emerging as a hero by saving the Hornets from relegation.

The cash problems had been on the cards for some time, a lingering hangover from their relegation in 2007 after a one-year stay in the Barclays Premier League. The parachute payments came to an end in the summer so key players like Tommy Smith, Tamas Priskin, Jobi McAnuff and Mike Williamson had to be sold to balance the books.

The financial situation then came to a head over Christmas when, at the club's AGM, chairman Jimmy Russo resigned and called in a loan of nearly £5million, pushing the club to the brink of administration. Thankfully that has so far been avoided.

While the Hornets looked to trim the wage bill in summer 2009, they were also looking for a new manager after Brendan Rodgers defected to Reading. Eventually the club turned to Mackay, who had had a successful stint as caretaker manager at Vicarage Road during 2008/09. The canny Scot had to rely largely on loan signings to replace the outgoing players and unearthed a couple of gems in Henri Lansbury of Arsenal and Manchester United's Tom Cleverley – the latter hitting 11 goals from midfield.

Mackay was able to make one permanent signing, bringing in Carlisle striker Danny Graham, who initially settled in well and scored seven goals by November. Former Vicarage Road hero

Malky Mackay excelled in tough circumstances to preserve Watford's Championship status

Heidar Helguson returned on loan from QPR to partner former Middlesbrough forward Graham and suddenly the Hornets were dark horses for a promotion push.

A 3–1 televised win over QPR in December, including a first career goal in 279 matches for defender and crowd favourite Lloyd Doyley, lifted them into the play-off places. But the goals dried up – Graham found the net just once more in 21 games – and Watford slumped down the Championship table. Just four wins in 24 matches left them in the relegation mire until a 3–0 victory over Reading secured their survival with just a week to spare.

Despite recent injury problems, Helguson looks set to make a permanent switch back to Hertfordshire while Mackay will be active in the loan market once again. Youngsters Ross Jenkins, Lee Hodson and Dale Bennett have impressed and will be a year older and wiser for their experiences in a rollercoaster first season at Vicarage Road.

Don Cowie is congratulated after scoring in a 3–0 win against Sheffield United

AUGUST

8th	● Doncaster	H	D 1–1	Att: 15,636	Ref: N Swarbrick	Scorers: Graham.
11th	● Barnet	A	W 0–2	Att: 3,139	Ref: S Cook	Scorers: Severin, Williamson. Booked: Hodson. AET – Score after 90 mins 0–0.
15th	● Sheff Utd	A	L 2–0	Att: 24,638	Ref: M Oliver	Booked: Mariappa, Sordell.
18th	● Nottm Forest	A	W 2–4	Att: 19,232	Ref: T Bates	Scorers: Cleverley, Graham, Smith, Williamson. Booked: Cleverley.
22nd	● Blackpool	H	D 2–2	Att: 12,745	Ref: D Deadman	Scorers: Cleverley, Smith.
25th	● Leeds	A	L 2–1	Att: 14,681	Ref: A Hall	Scorers: Sordell. Booked: Eustace, Doyley, Mariappa. AET – Score after 90 mins 1–1.
29th	● Swansea	A	D 1–1	Att: 14,172	Ref: A Taylor	Scorers: Graham. Booked: Loach.

SEPTEMBER

12th	● Barnsley	H	W 1–0	Att: 12,613	Ref: D Phillips	Scorers: Graham. Booked: Bennett.
15th	● Plymouth	A	W 0–1	Att: 8,703	Ref: G Scott	Scorers: Cleverley.
19th	● Leicester	H	D 3–3	Att: 14,647	Ref: C Pawson	Scorers: Graham, Helguson[2].
26th	● Reading	A	D 1–1	Att: 18,147	Ref: M Haywood	Scorers: Graham. Booked: Graham, Ellington. Dismissed: Ellington.
29th	● Coventry	H	L 2–3	Att: 13,034	Ref: A Marriner	Scorers: Cleverley, Hoskins.

OCTOBER

3rd	● Cardiff	H	L 0–4	Att: 13,895	Ref: A Woolmer	Booked: Mariappa.
17th	● Middlesbrough	A	W 0–1	Att: 18,957	Ref: S Mathieson	Scorers: Cleverley. Booked: Doyley.
20th	● Ipswich	A	D 1–1	Att: 19,283	Ref: T Kettle	Scorers: Ellington. Booked: Harley, Jenkins.
23rd	● Sheff Wed	H	W 4–1	Att: 14,591	Ref: P Crossley	Scorers: Harley, Lansbury[2], Mariappa.
31st	● West Brom	A	L 5–0	Att: 21,421	Ref: N Miller	Booked: Hodson.

NOVEMBER

7th	● Preston	H	W 2–0	Att: 13,524	Ref: K Wright	Scorers: Cleverley, Helguson. Booked: Lansbury, Helguson.
21st	● Scunthorpe	H	W 3–0	Att: 13,241	Ref: C Sarginson	Scorers: Graham, Helguson[2]. Booked: Lansbury.
28th	● Crystal Palace	A	L 3–0	Att: 14,085	Ref: O Langford	Booked: Harley.

DECEMBER

5th	● Newcastle	A	L 2–0	Att: 43,050	Ref: J Moss	Booked: Cathcart, Lansbury.
7th	● QPR	H	W 3–1	Att: 15,058	Ref: A Penn	Scorers: Cleverley, Cowie, Doyley.
12th	● Derby	H	L 0–1	Att: 14,063	Ref: K Stroud	Booked: Harley, Eustace, Cleverley, Mariappa, Helguson.
19th	● Peterborough	A	L 2–1	Att: 7,723	Ref: K Evans	Scorers: Eustace. Booked: Graham, Cleverley.
26th	● Nottm Forest	H	D 0–0	Att: 17,086	Ref: A D'Urso	Booked: Helguson.
28th	● Bristol City	A	D 2–2	Att: 16,035	Ref: J Linington	Scorers: Cleverley, Eustace. Booked: Lansbury, Eustace.

JANUARY

3rd	● Chelsea	A	L 5–0	Att: 40,912	Ref: K Friend	Booked: Lansbury, Eustace, Cleverley.
16th	● Doncaster	A	L 2–1	Att: 10,504	Ref: A Hall	Scorers: Helguson. Booked: Cleverley, Lansbury.
23rd	● Blackpool	A	L 3–2	Att: 6,855	Ref: C Boyeson	Scorers: Cleverley, Lansbury.

FEBRUARY

2nd	● Sheff Utd	H	W 3–0	Att: 13,076	Ref: K Hill	Scorers: Cleverley, Cowie, Helguson.
6th	● Barnsley	A	L 1–0	Att: 11,739	Ref: F Graham	Booked: Mariappa.
9th	● Bristol City	H	W 2–0	Att: 12,179	Ref: D McDermid	Scorers: Helguson, Taylor.
20th	● Scunthorpe	A	D 2–2	Att: 5,411	Ref: D Webb	Scorers: Eustace, Graham. Booked: Eustace, Loach, DeMerit. Dismissed: Cleverley.
27th	● Newcastle	H	L 1–2	Att: 17,120	Ref: T Bates	Scorers: Hoskins. Booked: Helguson, Harley.

MARCH

6th	● Derby	A	L 2–0	Att: 29,492	Ref: G Horwood	Booked: Eustace.
9th	● Swansea	H	L 0–1	Att: 12,907	Ref: T Kettle	Booked: Helguson, Lansbury.
13th	● Peterborough	H	L 0–1	Att: 16,591	Ref: A Taylor	Booked: Lansbury, Helguson.
16th	● Ipswich	H	W 2–1	Att: 13,996	Ref: G Salisbury	Scorers: Hoskins, Lansbury. Booked: Eustace.
21st	● Cardiff	A	L 3–1	Att: 20,130	Ref: P Crossley	Scorers: Helguson. Booked: McGinn.
24th	● Sheff Wed	A	L 2–1	Att: 18,449	Ref: D Deadman	Scorers: Cleverley.
27th	● Middlesbrough	H	D 1–1	Att: 14,038	Ref: R East	Scorers: Eustace. Booked: Lansbury, Cowie.
30th	● Crystal Palace	H	L 1–3	Att: 15,134	Ref: P Taylor	Scorers: Graham. Booked: Eustace, Helguson.

APRIL

3rd	● Preston	A	D 1–1	Att: 12,534	Ref: R Shoebridge	Scorers: Buckley. Booked: Buckley, Lansbury.
5th	● West Brom	H	D 1–1	Att: 14,555	Ref: S Tanner	Scorers: Graham. Booked: Harley, Eustace, Graham. Dismissed: Harley.
10th	● Plymouth	H	W 1–0	Att: 14,246	Ref: W Atkins	Scorers: Helguson. Booked: Henderson.
17th	● Leicester	A	L 4–1	Att: 24,765	Ref: N Miller	Scorers: Taylor.
20th	● QPR	A	L 1–0	Att: 13,171	Ref: P Miller	Booked: Mariappa, Eustace.
24th	● Reading	H	W 3–0	Att: 15,949	Ref: K Friend	Scorers: Graham[2], Helguson. Booked: Eustace, Graham, Taylor.

MAY

2nd	● Coventry	A	W 0–4	Att: 19,103	Ref: M Halsey	Scorers: Graham[2], Lansbury, Sordell.

● Coca-Cola Championship/Play-offs ● FA Cup ● Carling Cup

WATFORD

CHAMPIONSHIP GOALKEEPER STATS

Player	Minutes on pitch	Appearances	Match starts	Completed matches	Sub appearances	Subbed off	Saved with feet	Punched	Parried	Tipped over	Fumbled	Tipped round	Caught	Blocked	Clean sheets	Goals conceded	Save %	Saved	Resulting in goals	Opposition miss	Fouls committed	Free-kicks won	Yellow cards	Red cards
Scott Loach	4449	46	46	46	0	0	2	19	36	13	1	12	136	0	11	68	76.22	0	6	0	0	11	2	0

CHAMPIONSHIP OUTFIELD PLAYER STATS

Player	Minutes on pitch	Appearances	Match starts	Completed matches	Substitute appearances	Subbed off	Goals scored	Assists	Shots on target	Shots off target	Crosses	Tackles made	Defensive clearances	Defensive blocks	Fouls committed	Free-kicks won	Caught offside	Yellow cards	Red cards
Dale Bennett	770	10	8	7	2	1	0	0	0	0	0	16	11	3	5	5	0	1	0
Michael Bryan	141	7	1	0	6	1	0	2	2	0	3	0	0	0	2	0	0	0	0
William Buckley	336	6	4	1	2	3	1	1	1	2	13	6	0	1	1	11	1	1	0
Craig Cathcart	1107	12	12	11	0	1	0	0	2	3	3	43	26	9	17	9	0	1	0
Tom Cleverley	3016	33	33	22	0	10	11	5	41	31	79	65	4	4	30	58	1	4	1
Don Cowie	3542	41	40	24	1	16	2	4	11	24	108	75	9	3	22	31	13	1	0
Jay DeMerit	2522	27	25	24	2	1	0	0	0	2	3	52	37	9	16	37	1	1	0
Lloyd Doyley	4091	44	43	40	1	3	1	0	3	5	27	106	42	20	25	34	1	1	0
Nathan Ellington	493	17	2	0	15	2	1	0	10	15	11	14	5	0	11	9	3	1	1
John Eustace	3873	42	39	36	3	3	4	4	20	18	32	88	35	5	67	43	2	9	0
Danny Graham	3582	46	37	23	9	14	14	6	42	25	37	33	6	1	29	29	63	4	0
Jon Harley	2070	38	20	11	18	8	1	2	13	7	52	33	17	5	38	35	8	5	1
Heidar Helguson	2469	29	26	16	3	10	11	4	32	36	23	34	20	1	44	50	41	7	0
Liam Henderson	197	13	0	0	13	0	0	0	3	1	2	5	1	0	8	8	1	1	0
Lee Hodson	2705	31	29	23	2	6	0	2	1	1	47	81	13	11	15	20	0	1	0
Will Hoskins	566	18	5	0	13	5	3	0	5	7	3	4	0	0	5	10	9	0	0
Ross Jenkins	1831	24	21	12	3	9	0	1	7	6	5	16	5	2	15	17	1	1	0
Henri Lansbury	3130	37	34	21	3	13	5	4	32	27	49	94	22	6	43	69	5	9	0
Adrian Mariappa	4423	46	46	44	0	2	1	1	11	10	40	127	64	18	32	60	1	5	0
Gavin Massey	6	1	0	0	1	0	0	0	0	0	0	1	0	0	0	0	0	0	0
Jobi McAnuff	216	3	3	0	0	3	0	0	0	1	6	3	0	0	4	1	0	0	0
Stephen McGinn	279	9	2	1	7	1	0	0	0	1	1	3	0	0	3	2	0	1	0
Eddie Oshodi	17	1	0	0	1	0	0	0	0	0	0	0	0	0	0	0	0	0	0
Scott Severin	389	9	4	2	5	2	0	0	1	4	2	7	1	0	3	10	1	0	0
Tommy Smith	384	4	4	4	0	0	2	5	6	3	10	3	0	1	3	10	3	0	0
Marvin Sordell	186	6	1	0	5	1	1	0	2	2	1	2	0	0	6	3	4	1	0
Martin Taylor	1660	19	17	15	2	2	2	1	7	7	3	43	20	5	19	8	3	1	0
Mike Williamson	384	4	4	4	0	0	1	0	1	0	2	0	8	12	4	10	6	0	0

SEASON TOTALS

Goals scored	61
Goals conceded	68
Clean sheets	11
Shots on target	253
Shots off target	241
Shots per goal	8.10
Pens awarded	3
Pens scored	2
Pens conceded	6
Offsides	161
Corners	272
Crosses	558
Players used	29
Fouls committed	471
Free-kicks won	588

SEASON INFORMATION

Highest position: 6
Lowest position: 23
Average goals scored per game: 1.33
Average goals conceded per game: 1.48

LEAGUE POSITION AT THE END OF EACH MONTH

AUG	SEP	OCT	NOV	DEC	JAN	FEB	MAR	APR	MAY
13	12	12	9	13	17	15	21	19	16

CARDS RECEIVED

58 3

SEQUENCES

Wins	2
(on three occasions)	
Losses	4
(27/02/10–13/03/10)	
Draws	2
(on four occasions)	
Undefeated	7
(18/08/09–26/09/09)	
Without win	6
(on two occasions)	
Undefeated home	4
(on two occasions)	
Undefeated away	6
(18/08/09–20/10/09)	
Without scoring	3
(06/03/10–13/03/10)	
Without conceding	2
(on two occasions)	
Scoring	9
(16/03/10–17/04/10)	
Conceding	12
(20/02/10–05/04/10)	

MATCH RECORDS

Goals scored per match

		W	D	L	Pts
Failed to score	12	0	1	11	1
Scored 1 goal	18	4	7	7	19
Scored 2 goals	8	3	3	2	12
Scored 3 goals	5	4	1	0	13
Scored 4+ goals	3	3	0	0	9

Goals conceded per match

		W	D	L	Pts
Clean sheet	11	10	1	0	31
Conceded 1 goal	15	3	7	5	16
Conceded 2 goals	11	1	3	7	6
Conceded 3 goals	6	0	1	5	1
Conceded 4+ goals	3	0	0	3	0

GOALS SCORED/CONCEDED
PER FIVE-MINUTE INTERVALS

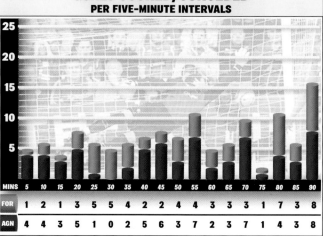

MINS	5	10	15	20	25	30	35	40	45	50	55	60	65	70	75	80	85	90
FOR	1	2	1	3	5	5	4	2	2	4	3	3	3	1	7	3	8
AGN	4	4	3	5	1	0	2	5	6	3	7	2	3	7	1	4	3	8

EARLIEST STRIKE

TOM CLEVERLEY
(v Plymouth) 3:46

LATEST STRIKE

TOM CLEVERLEY
(v QPR) 93:59

Lloyd Doyley

GOAL DETAILS

How the goals were struck

SCORED		CONCEDED
37	Right foot	29
11	Left foot	20
12	Header	18
1	Other	1

How the goals were struck

SCORED		CONCEDED
36	Open play	37
15	Cross	13
2	Corner	5
2	Penalty	6
3	Direct from free-kick	2
3	Free-kick	5
0	Own goal	0

Distance from goal

SCORED		CONCEDED
27	6YDS	26
26	18YDS	32
8	18+YDS	10

WEST BROMWICH ALBION

CLUB SUMMARY

FORMED	1878
MANAGER	Roberto Di Matteo
GROUND	The Hawthorns
CAPACITY	27,877
NICKNAME	The Baggies
WEBSITE	www.wbafc.co.uk

The New Football Pools PLAYER OF THE SEASON — Graham Dorrans

OVERALL
P	W	D	L	F	A	GD
53	30	14	9	105	60	45

COCA-COLA CHAMPIONSHIP
Pos	P	W	D	L	F	A	GD	Pts
2	46	26	13	7	89	48	41	91

HOME
Pos	P	W	D	L	F	A	GD	Pts
3	23	16	3	4	48	21	27	51

AWAY
Pos	P	W	D	L	F	A	GD	Pts
2	23	10	10	3	41	27	14	40

CUP PROGRESS DETAILS
Competition	Round reached	Knocked out by
FA Cup	R5	Reading
Carling Cup	R3	Arsenal

BIGGEST WIN (ALL COMPS)
5–0 on 2 occasions

BIGGEST DEFEAT (ALL COMPS)
1–3 on 3 occasions

THE PLAYER WITH THE MOST
GOALS SCORED — Graham Dorrans, Chris Brunt	13
SHOTS ON TARGET — Chris Brunt	56
SHOTS OFF TARGET — Chris Brunt	55
SHOTS WITHOUT SCORING — Abdoulaye Meite	6
ASSISTS — Graham Dorrans	19
OFFSIDES — Roman Bednar	53
FOULS — Chris Brunt	57
FOULS WITHOUT A CARD — Filipe Teixeira	7
FREE-KICKS WON — Jerome Thomas	60
DEFENSIVE CLEARANCES — Jonas Olsson	75

actim INDEX — FOR THE 2009/10 COCA-COLA CHAMPIONSHIP SEASON

RANK	PLAYER	PTS
2	Graham Dorrans	769
23	Jonas Olsson	545
27	Chris Brunt	532

ATTENDANCE RECORD
HIGH	AVERAGE	LOW
25,297	22,199	19,390
v Barnsley (02/05/2010)		v Ipswich (22/08/2009)

New boss Roberto Di Matteo helped the Baggies to yet another promotion

WEST BROM fans must have experienced more than the odd feeling of déjà vu over the past 12 months but they will certainly look back on the 2009/10 season as mission accomplished.

Back in the summer of 2009 they were despondent after yet again tasting relegation from the Barclays Premier League and preparing for another campaign in the Coca-Cola Championship. But those same supporters are now celebrating a fourth promotion to the top flight in the space of nine seasons – in the process recording their highest points tally in a single season to finish runners-up behind Newcastle.

It all started in the summer of 2009 with the departure of manager Tony Mowbray for Celtic and the arrival of the relatively inexperienced MK Dons boss Roberto Di Matteo. The decision was perhaps a gamble for chairman Jeremy Peace but it paid off in a big way with the Italian going on to prove himself as one of the hottest young properties in the English game.

Despite the loss of playmaker Jonathan Greening to Fulham, Albion won six and drew two of their opening eight games in the League – laying down a marker for themselves and the rest of the division. However, the club's early form dipped after

Gianni Zuiverloon scores in the 5–0 thrashing of Watford in October

West Brom's players savour promotion back to the Barclays Premier League

their unbeaten record fell and sporadic results led to a mixed return over the closing months of 2009.

The Baggies remained in second place behind fellow pre-season promotion favourites Newcastle until Nottingham Forest launched an assault on the top two, culminating in a 3–1 victory at The Hawthorns in early January. The manner of the defeat was a turning point in Albion's season and – with a new 4-5-1 formation and fresh approach – the club went on to lose just two of their remaining 22 League fixtures, getting better and better as the season progressed.

Scotland midfielder Graham Dorrans proved key to their success, contributing 13 goals – including five in Cup competitions – and a number of stunning displays to scoop a series of deserved accolades in his first full season in English football. Despite interest from some established Barclays Premier League teams, West Brom are determined to keep Dorrans at the club, along with the core of their promotion-winning side.

Di Matteo now faces the task of adding suitable signings, particularly with top-flight experience, to help West Brom follow in the footsteps of neighbours Wolves and Birmingham by going up to the top flight *and* staying there.

RESULTS 2009/10

AUGUST

8th	● Newcastle	H	D 1–1	Att: 23,502	Ref: M Dean	Scorers: Martis.
11th	● Bury	A	W 0–2	Att: 3,077	Ref: R Shoebridge	Scorers: Dorrans, Jones OG. Booked: R Reid.
15th	● Nottm Forest	A	W 0–1	Att: 22,794	Ref: K Stroud	Scorers: Cohen OG. Booked: Zuiverloon, Martis, Carson, Cech.
18th	● Peterborough	A	W 2–3	Att: 8,752	Ref: G Horwood	Scorers: Brunt, Moore2. Booked: Dorrans, Martis. Dismissed: Dorrans.
22nd	● Ipswich	H	W 2–0	Att: 19,390	Ref: S Tanner	Scorers: Koren, Mulumbu.
26th	● Rotherham	H	W 4–3	Att: 10,659	Ref: G Hegley	Scorers: Beattie2, Cox, Dorrans. AET – Score after 90 mins 2–2.
29th	● Sheff Utd	A	D 2–2	Att: 25,169	Ref: P Crossley	Scorers: Bednar2. Booked: Mulumbu, Koren, Thomas, Mattock, Bednar.

SEPTEMBER

12th	● Plymouth	H	W 3–1	Att: 22,190	Ref: G Salisbury	Scorers: Cech2, Martis. Booked: Dorrans.
15th	● Doncaster	H	W 3–1	Att: 22,184	Ref: K Wright	Scorers: Olsson2, Wood. Booked: Mattock, Olsson.
19th	● Middlesbrough	A	W 0–5	Att: 22,725	Ref: T Kettle	Scorers: Bednar, Brunt2, Mulumbu, Thomas. Booked: Thomas, Olsson, Mattock, Dorrans, Martis.
22nd	● Arsenal	A	L 2–0	Att: 56,592	Ref: L Mason	Booked: Cox. Dismissed: Thomas.
26th	● Crystal Palace	H	L 0–1	Att: 21,007	Ref: R Booth	Booked: Bednar, Mulumbu, Cox.
29th	● Barnsley	A	L 3–1	Att: 12,191	Ref: S Mathieson	Scorers: Brunt. Booked: Mattock.

OCTOBER

3rd	● Preston	A	D 0–0	Att: 12,489	Ref: T Bates	
17th	● Reading	H	W 3–1	Att: 20,935	Ref: A Taylor	Scorers: Mulumbu, Thomas2. Booked: Zuiverloon.
20th	● Swansea	H	L 0–1	Att: 21,022	Ref: A D'Urso	Booked: Jara.
24th	● Coventry	A	D 0–0	Att: 20,871	Ref: K Stroud	Booked: Thomas, Moore, Jara.
31st	● Watford	H	W 5–0	Att: 21,421	Ref: N Miller	Scorers: Cox, Dorrans, Moore, Olsson, Zuiverloon. Booked: Moore.

NOVEMBER

7th	● Leicester	A	W 1–2	Att: 28,748	Ref: N Swarbrick	Scorers: Dorrans, Jara.
21st	● Bristol City	H	W 4–1	Att: 23,444	Ref: M Oliver	Scorers: Brunt, Cox, Thomas, Carey OG. Booked: Cox.
28th	● Sheff Wed	A	W 0–4	Att: 20,824	Ref: E Ilderton	Scorers: Brunt, Cox2, Thomas. Booked: Brunt.

DECEMBER

5th	● Derby	A	D 2–2	Att: 30,127	Ref: D Deadman	Scorers: Cox, Dorrans. Booked: Dorrans.
8th	● Cardiff	H	L 0–2	Att: 20,742	Ref: P Taylor	Booked: Jara, Olsson. Dismissed: Carson.
14th	● QPR	H	D 2–2	Att: 21,565	Ref: A Taylor	Scorers: Cox, Thomas. Booked: Brunt, Cox.
26th	● Peterborough	H	W 2–0	Att: 24,924	Ref: M Jones	Scorers: Moore, Bennett OG. Booked: Mattock, Cox.
28th	● Scunthorpe	A	W 1–3	Att: 7,221	Ref: J Moss	Scorers: Dorrans2, Zuiverloon. Booked: Thomas, Jara.

JANUARY

2nd	● Huddersfield	A	W 0–2	Att: 13,472	Ref: K Wright	Scorers: Dorrans, Wood. Booked: Brunt.
8th	● Nottm Forest	H	L 1–3	Att: 22,873	Ref: L Probert	Scorers: Bednar. Booked: Mattock, Tamas.
18th	● Newcastle	A	D 2–2	Att: 39,291	Ref: P Taylor	Scorers: Bednar, Olsson. Booked: Tamas, Bednar, Olsson, Jara, Dorrans.
23rd	● Newcastle	H	W 4–2	Att: 16,102	Ref: J Linnington	Scorers: Dorrans2, Olsson, Thomas.
26th	● Ipswich	A	D 1–1	Att: 19,574	Ref: S Attwell	Scorers: Brunt. Booked: Mulumbu, Dorrans, Olsson.
30th	● Sheff Utd	H	W 3–1	Att: 22,193	Ref: M Russell	Scorers: Bednar, Dorrans, Thomas. Booked: Jara, Brunt, Cech.

FEBRUARY

3rd	● Blackpool	A	W 2–3	Att: 8,510	Ref: D Foster	Scorers: Bednar2, Dorrans.
6th	● Plymouth	A	W 0–1	Att: 12,053	Ref: S Tanner	Scorers: Cox. Booked: Meite, Mattock, Bednar. Dismissed: Thomas.
9th	● Scunthorpe	H	W 2–0	Att: 23,146	Ref: K Wright	Scorers: Bednar, Zuiverloon. Booked: Brunt.
13th	● Reading	A	D 2–2	Att: 18,008	Ref: C Foy	Scorers: Koren, Mattock. Booked: Mulumbu, Tamas. Dismissed: Mulumbu.
16th	● Cardiff	A	D 1–1	Att: 20,758	Ref: A Woolmer	Scorers: Zuiverloon. Booked: Tamas, Dorrans, Koren, Mattock.
21st	● Bristol City	A	L 2–1	Att: 14,374	Ref: N Swarbrick	Scorers: Dorrans. Booked: Brunt.
24th	● Reading	H	L 2–3	Att: 13,985	Ref: L Mason	Scorers: Koren2. Booked: Carson, Cech. AET – Score after 90 mins 2–2.
27th	● Derby	H	W 3–1	Att: 23,335	Ref: P Crossley	Scorers: Brunt2, Cox. Booked: Brunt, Tamas.

MARCH

6th	● QPR	A	L 3–1	Att: 14,578	Ref: S Attwell	Scorers: Brunt. Booked: Cech, Brunt.
9th	● Sheff Wed	H	W 1–0	Att: 20,458	Ref: S Mathieson	Scorers: Koren.
13th	● Blackpool	H	W 3–2	Att: 21,592	Ref: J Moss	Scorers: Dorrans, Koren, Miller. Booked: Koren, S Reid.
16th	● Swansea	A	W 0–2	Att: 17,774	Ref: R East	Scorers: Dorrans, Miller. Booked: Dorrans, Miller.
20th	● Preston	H	W 3–2	Att: 21,343	Ref: J Singh	Scorers: Brunt, Dorrans, Watson. Booked: Meite.
24th	● Coventry	H	W 1–0	Att: 22,140	Ref: C Webster	Scorers: S Reid. Booked: Barnes.
27th	● Reading	A	D 1–1	Att: 20,515	Ref: A D'Urso	Scorers: Tamas. Booked: S Reid, Watson.

APRIL

2nd	● Leicester	H	W 3–0	Att: 23,334	Ref: D Deadman	Scorers: Koren2, Morrison. Booked: Carson, Tamas.
5th	● Watford	A	D 1–1	Att: 14,555	Ref: S Tanner	Scorers: Brunt. Booked: Dorrans, Bednar, Olsson, Tamas, Brunt.
10th	● Doncaster	A	W 2–3	Att: 12,708	Ref: J Linington	Scorers: Bednar, Brunt, Dorrans. Booked: S Reid. West Brom are promoted.
17th	● Middlesbrough	H	W 2–0	Att: 22,548	Ref: G Hegley	Scorers: Bednar, Cox.
26th	● Crystal Palace	A	D 1–1	Att: 17,798	Ref: D Whitestone	Scorers: Tamas. Booked: Cox, S Reid, Bednar, Olsson, Dorrans.

MAY

2nd	● Barnsley	H	D 1–1	Att: 25,297	Ref: M Oliver	Scorers: Dorrans. Booked: Dorrans.

● Coca-Cola Championship/Play-offs ● FA Cup ● Carling Cup

WEST BROMWICH ALBION

CHAMPIONSHIP GOALKEEPER STATS

Player	Minutes on pitch	Appearances	Match starts	Completed matches	Sub appearances	Subbed off	Saved with feet	Punched	Parried	Tipped over	Fumbled	Tipped round	Caught	Blocked	Clean sheets	Goals conceded	Save %	Saved	Resulting in goals	Opposition miss	Fouls committed	Free-kicks won	Yellow cards	Red cards
Scott Carson	4090	43	43	41	0	1	1	14	21	3	0	10	119	1	13	43	79.72	0	5	1	1	2	2	1
Dean Kiely	344	5	3	3	2	0	0	0	6	0	0	0	7	0	1	5	72.22	1	0	0	0	0	0	0

CHAMPIONSHIP OUTFIELD PLAYER STATS

Player	Minutes on pitch	Appearances	Match starts	Completed matches	Substitute appearances	Subbed off	Goals scored	Assists	Shots on target	Shots off target	Crosses	Tackles made	Defensive clearances	Defensive blocks	Fouls committed	Free-kicks won	Caught offside	Yellow cards	Red cards
Giles Barnes	300	9	1	0	8	1	0	0	1	1	3	1	2	0	5	8	0	1	0
Leon Barnett	44	2	0	0	2	0	0	0	0	0	0	4	0	0	1	0	0	0	0
Craig Beattie	76	3	0	0	3	0	0	0	0	1	2	4	0	0	2	3	1	0	0
Roman Bednar	1972	27	21	13	6	8	11	4	28	23	19	6	6	1	38	27	53	7	0
Chris Brunt	3526	40	39	26	1	13	13	6	56	55	92	56	12	3	57	16	13	8	0
Marek Cech	2625	33	29	21	4	8	2	1	7	8	43	47	13	4	28	18	4	3	0
Simon Cox	1664	28	17	6	11	11	9	2	29	20	13	17	0	1	21	10	16	6	0
Shaun Cummings	289	3	3	3	0	0	0	1	0	1	8	1	1	0	5	3	0	0	0
Graham Dorrans	4076	45	42	38	3	3	13	19	45	35	81	82	3	4	32	37	5	11	1
Jonathan Greening	192	2	2	2	0	0	0	0	1	1	10	18	2	0	3	2	0	0	0
Gonzalo Jara	1971	22	20	19	2	1	1	1	5	5	19	42	9	3	17	18	0	6	0
Robert Koren	2397	34	26	10	8	16	5	3	33	22	28	32	4	0	10	24	2	3	0
Shelton Martis	982	13	10	10	3	0	2	0	3	4	1	20	20	10	16	11	0	3	0
Joe Mattock	2384	29	26	20	3	6	0	1	2	1	54	61	14	10	26	23	0	8	0
Abdoulaye Meite	1669	20	16	16	4	0	0	0	3	3	1	30	20	6	22	5	0	2	0
Ishmael Miller	563	15	4	0	11	4	2	0	17	7	5	8	2	0	6	7	8	1	0
Luke Moore	1844	26	23	7	3	16	4	0	32	21	3	15	1	0	26	24	32	2	0
James Morrison	517	11	5	1	6	4	1	1	4	6	4	6	0	0	3	4	1	0	0
Youssouf Mulumbu	3313	40	35	29	5	6	3	1	6	8	9	63	13	3	53	31	0	3	0
Frank Nouble	230	3	3	1	0	2	0	2	2	0	7	2	0	1	1	2	0	0	0
Jonas Olsson	4060	43	43	40	0	3	4	2	8	13	4	81	75	20	43	33	3	8	0
Steven Reid	883	10	10	8	0	2	1	0	4	3	4	27	4	2	15	10	0	4	0
Reuben Reid	86	4	0	0	4	0	0	0	1	1	0	0	0	0	1	0	0	0	0
Andwele Slory	193	6	1	0	5	1	0	1	1	3	1	4	0	0	1	3	0	0	0
Gabriel Tamas	2226	23	23	23	0	0	2	0	10	7	6	45	29	9	21	26	0	6	0
Filipe Teixeira	331	9	1	1	8	0	0	0	3	1	13	7	0	0	7	6	0	0	0
Jerome Thomas	2042	27	22	11	5	10	7	2	32	18	49	13	1	1	25	60	6	4	1
George Thorne	6	1	0	0	1	0	0	0	0	0	0	0	0	0	0	0	0	0	0
Borja Valero	9	1	0	0	1	0	0	0	0	0	0	0	0	0	1	0	0	0	0
Ben Watson	585	7	6	5	1	1	1	1	6	1	1	23	13	1	11	2	0	1	0
Chris Wood	770	18	6	2	12	4	4	0	8	9	1	4	1	0	6	8	13	0	0
Gianni Zuiverloon	2489	30	26	21	4	5	4	2	7	12	62	51	21	4	36	25	1	2	0

actim

Coca-Cola CHAMPIONSHIP

SEASON TOTALS

Goals scored	89
Goals conceded	48
Clean sheets	14
Shots on target	354
Shots off target	290
Shots per goal	7.24
Pens awarded	9
Pens scored	6
Pens conceded	7
Offsides	158
Corners	298
Crosses	543
Players used	34
Fouls committed	539
Free-kicks won	450

CARDS RECEIVED

91 **3**

SEQUENCES

Wins	5
(09/03/10–24/03/10)	
Losses	2
(26/09/09–29/09/09)	
Draws	2
(on two occasions)	
Undefeated	12
(09/03/10–02/05/10)	
Without win	3
(on three occasions)	
Undefeated home	10
(30/01/10–02/05/10)	
Undefeated away	11
(03/10/09–16/02/10)	
Without scoring	2
(20/10/09–24/10/09)	
Without conceding	2
(on two occasions)	
Scoring	8
(08/08/09–19/09/09)	
Conceding	6
(28/12/09–03/02/10)	

League position chart

AUG	SEP	OCT	NOV	DEC	JAN	FEB	MAR	APR	MAY
2	2	1	2	2	3	2	2	2	2

LEAGUE POSITION AT THE END OF EACH MONTH

SEASON INFORMATION
Highest position: 1
Lowest position: 24
Average goals scored per game: 1.93
Average goals conceded per game: 1.04

MATCH RECORDS

Goals scored per match

		W	D	L	Pts
Failed to score	5	0	2	3	2
Scored 1 goal	15	4	7	4	19
Scored 2 goals	10	6	4	0	22
Scored 3 goals	12	12	0	0	36
Scored 4+ goals	4	4	0	0	12

Goals conceded per match

		W	D	L	Pts
Clean sheet	15	13	2	0	41
Conceded 1 goal	17	8	7	2	31
Conceded 2 goals	11	5	4	2	19
Conceded 3 goals	3	0	0	3	0
Conceded 4+ goals	0	0	0	0	0

GOALS SCORED/CONCEDED
PER FIVE-MINUTE INTERVALS

MINS	5	10	15	20	25	30	35	40	45	50	55	60	65	70	75	80	85	90
FOR	3	3	4	5	4	4	5	9	6	5	4	1	5	6	1	4	7	13
AGN	0	5	4	4	2	0	1	0	3	5	5	5	2	2	1	2	4	3

EARLIEST STRIKE
LUKE MOORE
(v Peterborough) 2:18

LATEST STRIKE
CHRIS BRUNT
(v Watford) 94:59

Roman Bednar

GOAL DETAILS

How the goals were struck

SCORED		CONCEDED
50	Right foot	22
27	Left foot	16
12	Header	10
0	Other	0

How the goals were struck

SCORED		CONCEDED
54	Open play	28
8	Cross	2
8	Corner	4
6	Penalty	5
4	Direct from free-kick	3
6	Free-kick	3
3	Own goal	3

Distance from goal

SCORED		CONCEDED
29	6YDS	23
40	18YDS	19
20	18+YDS	6

COCA-COLA LEAGUE 1

COCA-COLA LEAGUE 1 STATISTICS 2009/10

PLAYER OF THE SEASON
Jermaine Beckford (Leeds)

MANAGER OF THE SEASON
Paul Lambert (Norwich)

THE PLAYER WITH THE MOST...

GOALS Rickie Lambert (Southampton)	**31**
SHOTS ON TARGET Jermaine Beckford (Leeds)	**77**
SHOTS OFF TARGET Richard Lambert (Southampton)	**78**
SHOTS WITHOUT SCORING Simon Lappin (Norwich)	**51**
SHOTS PER GOAL Therry Racon (Charlton)	**38**
ASSISTS Jon-Paul McGovern (Swindon)	**16**
OFFSIDES Kevin Lisbie (Colchester)	**115**
FOULS Kevin Lisbie (Colchester)	**91**
FREE-KICKS WON Kevin Lisbie (Colchester)	**164**
PENALTIES SCORED Kevin Lisbie (Colchester)	**9**
GOALS SCORED DIRECT FROM FREE-KICKS Henry (Millwall), Lambert (Southampton)	**4**
SAVES MADE Owain Fon Williams (Stockport)	**255**
DEFENSIVE CLEARANCES Sean Gregan (Oldham)	**122**
DEFENSIVE BLOCKS Adam Barrett (Southend)	**32**

THE TEAM WITH THE MOST...

GOALS	Norwich	89
SHOTS ON TARGET	Leeds	309
SHOTS OFF TARGET	Leeds	323
SHOTS PER GOAL	Stockport	12.77
CORNERS	Huddersfield	326
FOULS	Milton Keynes Dons	629
WOODWORK STRIKES	Huddersfield	20
OFFSIDES	Brighton	175
PENALTIES CONCEDED	Bristol Rovers	11
PENALTIES AWARDED	Swindon	9
PENALTIES SCORED	Swindon	8
YELLOW CARDS	Milton Keynes Dons	132
RED CARDS	Brighton	10

TOTALS 2009/10

GOALS

Total	1459
Home	848
Away	611

CARDS

Yellow	1759
Average per game	3.19
Reds	102
Average per game	0.18

ATTENDANCES

Total	5,047,281

NORWICH started and ended their Coca-Cola League 1 season with home defeats, but spent the 44 games in between collecting 95 points as they claimed the title in style.

Their opening-day loss was no ordinary defeat as the Canaries were thrashed 7–1 at home by Colchester. The result prompted the sacking of manager Bryan Gunn just six days later. Paul Lambert, the man who had masterminded Colchester's win at Carrow Road, was chosen as Gunn's successor and 29 wins later he had won the first title of his managerial career.

The goals of Grant Holt, who scored 24 in the League and 30 in total, were pivotal to the Canaries' success, with the captain ably supported by Chris Martin with 23 and Wes Hoolahan's 14 strikes.

Meanwhile, Leeds ended their three-year stay in the division by securing automatic promotion, but they were very nearly forced to settle for the play-offs again. Simon Grayson's men topped the table from the start of the season until February but a run of just three wins from 16 games early in 2010 nearly cost them their automatic promotion hopes. Fittingly, a goal from Jermaine Beckford – a man who has dominated the headlines during their time in the third tier – took them up as they beat Bristol Rovers at Elland Road on the final day.

Leeds' promotion meant Millwall, Charlton, Swindon and Huddersfield were forced to settle for the play-off places, having all gone into the final round of fixtures with a chance of going up automatically.

Swindon's story was the most eye-catching, with Danny Wilson taking a side that had finished 15th a year previously into the top six. The 19 League goals of Charlie Austin, a former bricklayer, allied with 26 from Billy Paynter helped their cause, while the other three play-off sides also boasted predatory forwards.

Millwall's Steve Morison enjoyed a stunning first season in the Football League as he ended the campaign with 20 goals, while Jordan Rhodes netted 19 for Huddersfield. For Charlton, Deon Burton claimed 13, with Nicky Bailey adding 12 from midfield, while the performances of 18-year-old midfielder Jonjo Shelvey earned him a move to Liverpool.

The final-day drama did not only come at the top of the table, with things at the bottom just as tense. Stockport's financial plight meant they were down long before

Norwich recovered from an awful start to claim the title, while Leeds ended their three-year spell in the third tier

the last games kicked off, with Southend and Wycombe also joining them in the final reckoning. That left Exeter, Gillingham and Tranmere all on tenterhooks, with Hartlepool also forced to endure a nervy finale as they were deducted three points for fielding an ineligible player.

In the end it was Gillingham who were relegated to npower League Two, with Exeter and Tranmere snatching wins, and Hartlepool a draw, to send the Kent club down on goal difference.

Gallant late run

Alan Pardew's Southampton made a gallant late run for the play-offs and would have made them had it not been for a pre-season 10-point deduction, but the goals of Rickie Lambert, 37 of them in total, should give the Saints a solid base on which to build in the coming season.

Nine managers left their clubs in total, with Brighton, Gillingham, Leyton Orient, Milton Keynes Dons, Oldham, Tranmere and Wycombe all joining Colchester and Norwich in making changes at the helm.

Paul Ince's departure from the Dons came after they had stalled badly and finished in mid-table, while Oldham parted company with Dave Penney with just a game to go following a season of struggle at Boundary Park.

Carlisle, whose veteran defender Ian Harte scored an incredible 18 goals, ended the campaign in mid-table, along with Bristol Rovers, Colchester, Walsall and Yeovil, who all showed varying degrees of potential at one stage or another over the course of the year.

Closer to the bottom, Brighton sacked Russell Slade and replaced him with former Leeds and Tottenham assistant manager Gus Poyet, with their late-season performances suggesting that the Uruguayan could be a shrewd appointment. Meanwhile, Slade returned to football at Leyton Orient following the departure of Geraint Williams and managed to keep the London club in the division.

actim

FINAL COCA-COLA LEAGUE 1 TABLE

Pos	Team	P	HOME					AWAY					GD	Pts
			W	D	L	F	A	W	D	L	F	A		
1	Norwich	46	17	3	3	48	22	12	5	6	41	25	42	95
2	Leeds	46	14	6	3	41	19	11	5	7	36	25	33	86
3	Millwall	46	17	5	1	48	15	7	8	8	28	29	32	85
4	Charlton	46	14	6	3	41	22	9	9	5	30	26	23	84
5	Swindon	46	13	8	2	42	25	9	8	6	31	32	16	82
6	Huddersfield	46	14	8	1	52	22	9	3	11	30	34	26	80
7	Southampton*	46	15	5	3	48	21	8	9	6	37	26	38	73
8	Colchester	46	15	5	3	37	21	5	7	11	27	31	12	72
9	Brentford	46	9	12	2	34	21	5	8	10	21	31	3	62
10	Walsall	46	10	8	5	36	26	6	6	11	24	37	-3	62
11	Bristol Rovers	46	13	3	7	32	30	6	2	15	27	40	-11	62
12	Milton Keynes Dons	46	10	5	8	31	28	7	4	12	29	40	-8	60
13	Brighton	46	7	4	12	26	30	8	10	5	30	30	-4	59
14	Carlisle	46	10	4	9	34	28	5	9	9	29	38	-3	58
15	Yeovil	46	9	7	7	36	26	4	7	12	19	33	-4	53
16	Oldham	46	7	7	9	23	28	6	6	11	16	29	-18	52
17	Leyton Orient	46	10	6	7	35	25	3	6	14	18	38	-10	51
18	Exeter	46	9	10	4	30	20	2	8	13	18	40	-12	51
19	Tranmere	46	11	3	9	30	32	3	6	14	15	40	-27	51
20	Hartlepool**	46	10	6	7	33	26	4	5	14	26	41	-8	50
21	Gillingham	46	12	8	3	35	15	0	6	17	13	49	-16	50
22	Wycombe	46	6	7	10	26	31	4	8	11	30	45	-20	45
23	Southend	46	7	10	6	29	27	3	3	17	22	45	-21	43
24	Stockport	46	2	6	15	21	51	3	4	16	14	44	-60	25

*10 points deducted **3 points deducted

Charlie Austin
(Swindon)

Jordan Rhodes
(Huddersfield)

Rickie Lambert
(Southampton)

MILLWALL'S rock-solid defence formed the basis of their promotion through the play-offs 12 months after they had fallen at the final hurdle.

Kenny Jackett's men had been beaten 3–2 by Scunthorpe in a thriller at the end of the 2008/09 season, but they dusted themselves down sufficiently well to complete the job this time around.

Paul Robinson's first-half goal was enough to earn a 1–0 win over Swindon at Wembley, with the Lions having also gone through their two semi-finals against Huddersfield without conceding. The first game between the two at the Galpharm Stadium ended goalless before Steve Morison and Robinson scored in a 2–0 second-leg win.

Swindon made it to Wembley following a see-saw battle with Charlton. Charlie Austin and Daniel Ward gave the Robins a two-goal lead in the first leg of the semi-final, only for Deon Burton to score and set up a tense return fixture at The Valley.

Simon Ferry's own goal levelled matters early on, then David Mooney put Charlton ahead in the tie for the first time. Gordon Greer was sent off, leaving Swindon staring down the barrel of elimination, before Ward sneaked in to score and take the tie to a penalty shoot-out. Charlton, who had seen Miguel Angel Llera sent off, were the first to lose their nerve in the penalty shoot-out, with Nicky Bailey's miss putting Swindon through.

The Robins were unable to repeat their heroics in the final, though, as Lions skipper Robinson's 39th-minute goal proved decisive. Austin wasted a glorious chance to level for Swindon in the second half, firing wide when clean through, but nothing could spoil the day for jubilant Millwall.

Norwich's players savour the moment of being handed the Coca-Cola League 1 trophy following a superb title-winning season

COCA-COLA LEAGUE 1

COCA-COLA LEAGUE 1 RESULTS

AWAY

HOME	BRENTFORD	BRIGHTON	BRISTOL R	CARLISLE	CHARLTON	COLCHESTER	EXETER	GILLINGHAM	HARTLEPOOL	HUDDERSFIELD	LEEDS	LEYTON ORIENT	MILLWALL	MK DONS	NORWICH	OLDHAM	SOUTHAMPTON	SOUTHEND	STOCKPORT	SWINDON	TRANMERE	WALSALL	WYCOMBE	YEOVIL
BRENTFORD	–	0-0	1-3	3-1	1-1	1-0	0-0	4-0	0-0	3-0	0-0	1-0	2-2	3-3	2-1	1-1	1-1	2-1	2-0	2-3	2-1	1-1	1-1	1-1
BRIGHTON	3-0	–	2-1	1-2	0-2	1-2	2-0	2-0	3-3	0-0	0-3	0-0	0-1	0-1	1-2	0-2	2-2	2-3	2-4	0-1	3-0	0-1	1-0	1-0
BRISTOL R	0-0	1-1	–	3-2	2-1	3-2	1-0	2-1	2-0	1-0	0-4	1-2	2-0	1-0	0-3	1-0	1-5	4-3	1-0	3-0	0-0	0-1	2-3	1-2
CARLISLE	1-3	0-2	3-1	–	3-1	2-1	0-1	2-0	3-2	1-2	1-3	2-2	1-3	5-0	0-1	1-2	1-1	2-1	0-0	0-1	3-0	1-1	1-0	1-0
CHARLTON	2-0	1-2	4-2	1-0	–	1-0	2-1	2-2	2-1	2-1	1-0	0-1	4-4	5-1	0-1	0-0	1-1	1-0	2-0	2-2	1-1	2-0	3-2	2-0
COLCHESTER	3-3	0-0	1-0	2-1	3-0	–	2-2	2-1	2-0	1-0	1-2	1-0	1-2	2-0	0-5	1-0	2-1	2-0	2-0	3-0	1-1	2-1	1-1	2-1
EXETER	3-0	0-1	1-0	2-3	1-1	2-0	–	1-1	3-1	2-1	2-0	0-0	1-1	1-2	1-1	1-1	1-0	0-1	1-1	2-1	2-1	1-1	1-1	
GILLINGHAM	0-1	1-1	1-0	0-0	1-1	0-0	3-0	–	0-1	2-0	3-2	1-1	2-0	2-2	1-1	1-0	2-1	3-0	3-1	5-0	0-1	0-0	3-2	2-1
HARTLEPOOL	0-0	2-0	1-2	4-1	0-2	3-1	1-1	1-1	–	0-2	2-2	1-0	3-0	0-5	0-2	2-1	1-3	3-0	3-0	0-1	1-0	3-0	1-1	1-1
HUDDERSFIELD	0-0	7-1	0-0	1-1	1-1	2-1	4-0	2-1	2-2	–	2-2	4-0	1-0	1-0	1-3	2-0	3-1	2-1	0-0	2-2	3-3	4-3	6-0	2-1
LEEDS	1-1	1-1	2-1	1-1	0-0	2-1	2-1	4-1	3-1	2-2	–	1-0	0-2	4-1	2-1	2-0	1-0	2-0	0-3	3-0	1-2	1-1		4-0
LEYTON ORIENT	2-1	1-1	5-0	2-2	1-2	0-1	1-1	3-1	1-3	0-2	1-1	–	1-0	1-2	2-1	1-2	2-2	1-2	2-0	0-0	2-1	2-0	2-0	2-0
MILLWALL	1-1	1-1	2-0	0-0	4-0	2-1	1-0	4-0	1-0	3-1	2-1	2-1	–	3-2	2-1	2-0	1-0	5-0	3-2	5-0	2-1	0-2	0-0	
MK DONS	0-1	0-0	2-1	3-4	0-1	2-1	1-1	2-0	0-0	2-3	0-1	1-3		–	2-1	0-0	0-3	3-1	4-1	2-1	1-0	1-0	2-3	2-2
NORWICH	1-0	4-1	5-1	0-2	2-2	1-7	3-1	2-0	2-1	3-0	1-0	4-0	2-0	1-1	–	2-0	0-2	2-1	2-1	1-0	2-0	0-0	5-2	3-0
OLDHAM	2-3	0-2	2-1	2-0	0-2	2-2	2-0	1-0	0-3	0-1	2-0	0-1	2-0	0-1	2-1	–	1-3	2-2	0-0	2-2	0-0	1-0	2-2	0-0
SOUTHAMPTON	1-1	1-3	2-3	3-2	1-0	0-0	3-1	4-1	3-2	5-0	1-0	2-1	1-1	3-1	2-2		–	3-1	2-0	0-1	3-0	5-1	1-0	2-0
SOUTHEND	2-2	0-1	2-1	2-2	1-2	1-2	0-0	1-1	3-2	2-2	0-0	3-0	0-0	2-1	0-3	0-1	1-3	–	2-1	2-2	1-1	3-0	1-1	0-0
STOCKPORT	0-1	1-1	0-2	1-2	1-2	2-2	1-3	0-0	0-2	0-6	2-4	2-1	0-4	1-3	1-3	0-1	1-1	0-2	–	0-1	0-3	1-1	4-3	1-3
SWINDON	3-2	2-1	0-4	2-0	1-1	1-1	3-2	2-1	3-0	3-2	1-1	0-0	1-1	4-2	1-0	2-1	4-1			–	3-0	1-1	1-1	3-1
TRANMERE	1-0	2-1	2-0	0-0	0-4	1-1	3-1	4-2	0-0	0-2	1-4	2-1	2-0	0-1	3-1	0-1	2-1	2-0	0-1	1-4	–	2-3	0-3	2-1
WALSALL	2-1	1-2	0-0	2-2	1-1	1-0	3-0	0-0	3-1	2-1	1-2	2-2	2-2	2-1	1-2	3-0	1-3	2-2	2-0	1-1	2-1	–	2-1	0-1
WYCOMBE	1-0	2-5	2-1	0-0	1-2	1-1	2-2	3-0	2-0	1-2	0-1	0-1	1-0	0-1	0-1	2-2	0-0	1-1	2-1	2-2	0-1	2-3	–	1-4
YEOVIL	2-0	2-2	0-3	3-1	1-1	0-1	2-1	0-0	4-0	0-0	1-2	3-3	1-1	1-0	3-3	3-0	0-1	1-0	2-2	0-1	2-0	1-3	4-0	–

Rickie Lambert (Southampton)

LEADING SCORERS

PLAYER	TEAM	GLS
Rickie Lambert	Southampton	31
Billy Paynter	Swindon	26
Jermaine Beckford	Leeds	25
Grant Holt	Norwich	24
Lee Barnard	Southampton	24
Steve Morison	Millwall	20
Charlie Austin	Swindon	19
Jordan Rhodes	Huddersfield	19
Chris Martin	Norwich	17
Ian Harte	Carlisle	16

TEAM DISCIPLINE

TEAM	Y	R
Milton Keynes Dons	132	8
Brighton	78	10
Tranmere	83	8
Colchester	89	6
Stockport	77	7
Southend	70	7
Charlton	81	3
Yeovil	81	3
Oldham	84	2
Gillingham	80	3
Walsall	66	7
Leeds	79	2
Exeter	59	8
Hartlepool	72	3
Millwall	75	2
Southampton	78	1
Huddersfield	67	3
Carlisle	65	3
Leyton Orient	65	3
Bristol Rovers	66	2
Norwich	57	4
Brentford	53	3
Swindon	52	2
Wycombe	49	2

Fraser Forster (Norwich)

LEADING GOALKEEPERS

PLAYER	TEAM	CLEAN SHEET
Fraser Forster	Norwich	20
David Forde	Millwall	18
Alex Smithies	Huddersfield	17
Ben Williams	Colchester	15
Scott Flinders	Hartlepool	14
Mikkel Andersen	Bristol Rovers	12
Alex McCarthy	Yeovil	12
Willy Gueret	MK Dons	11
Kelvin Davis	Southampton	11
Dean Brill	Oldham	11

COCA-COLA LEAGUE 1 TABLES

HOME TABLE

	P	W	D	L	F	A	GD	PTS
Millwall	23	17	5	1	48	15	33	56
Norwich	23	17	3	3	48	22	26	54
Huddersfield	23	14	8	1	52	22	30	50
Southampton	23	15	5	3	48	21	27	50
Colchester	23	15	5	3	37	21	16	50
Leeds	23	14	6	3	41	19	22	48
Charlton	23	14	6	3	41	22	19	48
Swindon	23	13	8	2	42	25	17	47
Gillingham	23	12	8	3	35	15	20	44
Bristol Rovers	23	13	3	7	32	30	2	42
Brentford	23	9	12	2	34	21	13	39
Walsall	23	10	8	5	36	26	10	38
Exeter	23	9	10	4	30	20	10	37
Leyton Orient	23	10	6	7	35	25	10	36
Hartlepool	23	10	6	7	33	26	7	36
Tranmere	23	11	3	9	30	32	-2	36
Milton Keynes Dons	23	10	5	8	31	28	3	35
Yeovil	23	9	7	7	36	26	10	34
Carlisle	23	10	4	9	34	28	6	34
Southend	23	7	10	6	29	27	2	31
Oldham	23	7	7	9	23	28	-5	28
Brighton	23	7	4	12	26	30	-4	25
Wycombe	23	6	7	10	26	31	-5	25
Stockport	23	2	6	15	21	51	-30	12

AWAY TABLE

	P	W	D	L	F	A	GD	PTS
Norwich	23	12	5	6	41	25	16	41
Leeds	23	11	5	7	36	25	11	38
Charlton	23	9	9	5	30	26	4	36
Swindon	23	9	8	6	31	32	-1	35
Brighton	23	8	10	5	30	30	0	34
Southampton	23	8	9	6	37	26	11	33
Huddersfield	23	9	3	11	30	34	-4	30
Millwall	23	7	8	8	28	29	-1	29
Milton Keynes Dons	23	7	4	12	29	40	-11	25
Carlisle	23	5	9	9	29	38	-9	24
Walsall	23	6	6	11	24	37	-13	24
Oldham	23	6	6	11	16	29	-13	24
Brentford	23	5	8	10	21	31	-10	23
Colchester	23	5	7	11	27	31	-4	22
Bristol Rovers	23	6	2	15	27	40	-13	20
Wycombe	23	4	8	11	30	45	-15	20
Yeovil	23	4	7	12	19	33	-14	19
Hartlepool	23	4	5	14	26	41	-15	17
Leyton Orient	23	3	6	14	18	38	-20	15
Tranmere	23	3	6	14	15	40	-25	15
Exeter	23	2	8	13	18	40	-22	14
Stockport	23	3	4	16	14	44	-30	13
Southend	23	3	3	17	22	45	-23	12
Gillingham	23	0	6	17	13	49	-36	6

FIRST-HALF TABLE

	P	W	D	L	F	A	GD	PTS
Huddersfield	46	20	19	7	33	18	15	79
Southampton	46	19	21	6	39	18	21	78
Charlton	46	20	15	11	35	22	13	75
Leeds	46	17	22	7	31	16	15	73
Swindon	46	20	13	13	33	27	6	73
Colchester	46	16	19	11	35	24	11	67
Norwich	46	17	15	14	32	29	3	66
Brighton	46	15	20	11	30	29	1	65
Millwall	46	16	16	14	33	24	9	64
Yeovil	46	17	11	18	29	31	-2	62
Milton Keynes Dons	46	14	19	13	28	25	3	61
Bristol Rovers	46	12	24	10	35	27	8	60
Walsall	46	14	17	15	29	32	-3	59
Gillingham	46	12	21	13	26	28	-2	57
Brentford	46	11	24	11	22	25	-3	57
Hartlepool	46	14	13	19	36	35	1	55
Carlisle	46	10	24	12	29	29	0	54
Leyton Orient	46	9	26	11	19	24	-5	53
Exeter	46	11	18	17	16	26	-10	51
Tranmere	46	9	22	15	21	33	-12	49
Oldham	46	7	25	14	12	25	-13	46
Wycombe	46	8	20	18	19	32	-13	44
Southend	46	7	23	16	18	31	-13	44
Stockport	46	4	19	23	14	44	-30	31

SECOND-HALF TABLE

	P	W	D	L	F	A	GD	PTS
Norwich	46	29	11	6	57	18	39	98
Millwall	46	25	13	8	43	20	23	88
Leeds	46	24	9	13	46	28	18	81
Swindon	46	21	16	9	40	30	10	79
Charlton	46	14	26	6	36	26	10	68
Southampton	46	16	19	11	46	29	17	67
Huddersfield	46	17	16	13	49	38	11	67
Brentford	46	16	17	13	33	27	6	65
Walsall	46	17	14	15	31	31	0	65
Colchester	46	15	18	13	29	28	1	63
Leyton Orient	46	18	8	20	34	39	-5	62
Exeter	46	14	18	14	32	34	-2	60
Wycombe	46	14	18	14	37	44	-7	60
Brighton	46	13	18	15	26	31	-5	57
Yeovil	46	13	16	17	26	28	-2	55
Hartlepool	46	13	16	17	23	32	-9	55
Oldham	46	13	15	18	27	32	-5	54
Southend	46	13	14	19	33	41	-8	53
Carlisle	46	11	19	16	34	37	-3	52
Milton Keynes Dons	46	12	15	19	32	43	-11	51
Bristol Rovers	46	11	15	20	24	43	-19	48
Tranmere	46	11	14	21	24	39	-15	47
Gillingham	46	8	15	23	22	36	-14	39
Stockport	46	7	14	25	21	51	-30	35

DISCIPLINARY RECORDS

Y=1PT/R=2PT

PLAYER	TEAM	FLS	Y	R
Alan McCormack	Southend	54	15	1
JP Kalala	Yeovil	64	15	1
Glenn Murray	Brighton	75	10	2
Josh Gowling	Gillingham	28	10	2
Troy Deeney	Walsall	55	9	2
Marlon Broomes	Tranmere	39	11	1

PLAYER	TEAM	FLS	Y	R
Richard Duffy	Exeter	33	11	1
Anthony Grant	Southend	55	13	0
Peter Leven	MK Dons	37	10	1
Kemal Izzet	Colchester	51	10	1
Sean Thornton	Leyton Orient	39	12	0
J F Christophe	Southend	63	7	2

PENALTIES

TOTAL AWARDED	155
SCORED	120
SAVED	29
MISSED	6

EARLIEST STRIKE

CHRIS MARTIN
(MK Dons v NORWICH) 0:17

LATEST STRIKE

THERRY RACON
(Bristol R v CHARLTON) 96:26

EARLIEST CARD

DOMINIC BLIZZARD
(BRISTOL R v Charlton) 0:26

Dominic Blizzard (Bristol R)

SEQUENCES

Wins	Norwich 8
19/12/2009–30/01/2010	
Losses	Stockport 12
17/10/2009–19/01/2010	
Draws	Southend 4
08/08/2009–21/08/2009	
Undefeated	Norwich 16
24/10/2009–30/01/2010	
Without win	Stockport 17
17/10/2009–13/02/2010	
Undefeated home	Brentford 17
24/10/2009–08/05/2010	
Undefeated away	Brighton 8
28/12/2009–20/03/2010	
Without scoring	Stockport 6
02/03/2010–27/03/2010	
Without conceding	Leeds 5
27/10/2009–01/12/2009	
Scoring	Norwich 25
14/09/2009–13/02/2010	
Conceding	Southend 19
14/11/2009–06/03/2010	

BRENTFORD

BRENTFORD will look back on a successful season of consolidation under their increasingly impressive manager, Andy Scott.

The Bees were promoted as Coca-Cola League Two champions in 2008/09 and at times they made the step up look simple. A 3–1 opening-day win at Carlisle started a five-game unbeaten run and proved that they could hold their own in their new surroundings.

Scott's astute use of the loan market once again unearthed a few gems, notably Arsenal's Polish goalkeeper Wojciech Szczesny, who will no doubt have caught the eye of Gunners boss Arsène Wenger following a string of impressive performances. Leon Legge, a signing from non-League Tonbridge, was another bargain.

Striker Charlie MacDonald missed the first month of the campaign through injury but still managed to weigh in with 17 goals to top the scoring charts at Griffin Park again, while captain Kevin O'Connor racked up his 400th appearance for the club.

CLUB SUMMARY

FORMED	1889
MANAGER	Andy Scott
GROUND	Griffin Park
CAPACITY	12,763
NICKNAME	The Bees
WEBSITE	www.brentfordfc.co.uk

The New **Football Pools** PLAYER OF THE SEASON

Charlie MacDonald

OVERALL

P	W	D	L	F	A	GD
52	16	21	15	63	59	4

COCA-COLA FOOTBALL LEAGUE 1

Pos	P	W	D	L	F	A	GD	Pts
9	46	14	20	12	55	52	3	62

HOME

Pos	P	W	D	L	F	A	GD	Pts
11	23	9	12	2	34	21	13	39

AWAY

Pos	P	W	D	L	F	A	GD	Pts
13	23	5	8	10	21	31	-10	23

CUP PROGRESS DETAILS

Competition	Round reached	Knocked out by
FA Cup	R3	Doncaster
Carling Cup	R1	Bristol City
JP Trophy	R1	Norwich

BIGGEST WIN (ALL COMPS)

06/02/10 4–0 v Gillingham

BIGGEST DEFEAT (ALL COMPS)

0–3 on 2 occasions

ATTENDANCE RECORD

High	Average	Low
9,031	6,018	4,200
v Leeds (12/12/2009)		v Colchester (01/12/2009)

RESULTS 2009/10

AUGUST

8th	● Carlisle	A	W 1–3	Att: 6,367	Scorers: Weston2, Wood.
11th	● Bristol City	H	L 0–1	Att: 3,024	
15th	● Brighton	H	D 0–0	Att: 6,950	
18th	● Norwich	H	W 2–1	Att: 7,395	Scorers: Dickson, Hunt.
22nd	● Southampton	A	D 1–1	Att: 19,169	Scorers: Taylor. Booked: Foster, Hunt.
29th	● Oldham	H	D 1–1	Att: 5,125	Scorers: O'Connor.

SEPTEMBER

1st	● Norwich	A	L 1–0	Att: 12,540	Booked: Bean.
5th	● Charlton	A	L 2–0	Att: 16,399	Booked: O'Connor, Taylor.
12th	● Huddersfield	A	D 0–0	Att: 12,020	Booked: O'Connor.
19th	● Bristol Rovers	H	L 1–3	Att: 6,528	Scorers: MacDonald.
26th	● Yeovil	A	L 2–0	Att: 4,249	Booked: Bean, Foster .
29th	● Southend	H	W 2–1	Att: 5,578	Scorers: O'Connor2. Booked: Phillips, Bean.

OCTOBER

3rd	● Swindon	H	L 2–3	Att: 6,471	Scorers: Cort, MacDonald. Booked: Bean.
9th	● Hartlepool	A	D 0–0	Att: 3,105	
17th	● Leyton Orient	A	L 2–1	Att: 4,781	Scorers: Cort. Booked: Bean, Phillips.
24th	● Stockport	H	W 2–0	Att: 5,045	Scorers: MacDonald, Weston. Booked: Hunt.
31st	● Exeter	A	L 3–0	Att: 5,355	Booked: Phillips, Dickson.

NOVEMBER

7th	● Gateshead	A	D 2–2	Att: 1,150	Scorers: Cort, O'Connor. Booked: Dickson, Bean.
14th	● Millwall	H	D 2–2	Att: 6,408	Scorers: Bostock2.
17th	● Gateshead	H	W 5–2	Att: 1,960	Scorers: MacDonald2, Strevens, Weston2.
21st	● Walsall	H	D 1–1	Att: 4,492	Scorers: Strevens.
24th	● Wycombe	A	L 1–0	Att: 5,181	Booked: Bean, Osborne, Szczesny. Dismissed: Wilson.
28th	● Walsall	H	W 1–0	Att: 2,611	Scorers: Legge.

DECEMBER

1st	● Colchester	H	W 1–0	Att: 4,200	Scorers: MacDonald.
5th	● Tranmere	A	L 1–0	Att: 4,839	Booked: Legge.
12th	● Leeds	H	D 0–0	Att: 9,031	
19th	● Milton Keynes Dons	A	W 0–1	Att: 9,520	Scorers: MacDonald. Booked: Strevens.
26th	● Gillingham	A	W 0–1	Att: 7,019	Scorers: Strevens. Booked: MacDonald, Balkestein, Wood, Weston. Dismissed: MacDonald.
28th	● Charlton	H	D 1–1	Att: 8,387	Scorers: Cort. Booked: Foster , Bostock, Price.

JANUARY

16th	● Carlisle	H	W 3–1	Att: 5,089	Scorers: Dickson, Weston2. Booked: Legge, Szczesny.
19th	● Doncaster	H	L 0–1	Att: 2,883	
23rd	● Norwich	A	L 1–0	Att: 24,979	Booked: Bean, O'Connor.
26th	● Southampton	H	D 1–1	Att: 6,501	Scorers: Legge. Booked: Dickson.

FEBRUARY

6th	● Gillingham	H	W 4–0	Att: 6,036	Scorers: MacDonald2, Weston2. Booked: Weston.
13th	● Wycombe	H	D 1–1	Att: 5,740	Scorers: Weston.
20th	● Walsall	A	L 2–1	Att: 3,616	Scorers: MacDonald. Booked: Smith.

MARCH

6th	● Leeds	A	D 1–1	Att: 25,445	Scorers: Strevens.
13th	● Milton Keynes Dons	H	D 3–3	Att: 5,209	Scorers: Cort, Strevens, Wood. Booked: Phillips, Dickson, Strevens.
16th	● Brighton	A	L 3–0	Att: 5,539	Booked: O'Connor, Bennett. Dismissed: Bennett.
20th	● Stockport	A	W 0–1	Att: 3,707	Scorers: MacDonald. Booked: Foster , Strevens.
23rd	● Colchester	A	D 3–3	Att: 3,915	Scorers: Hunt, Legge, MacDonald.
27th	● Leyton Orient	H	W 1–0	Att: 6,369	Scorers: Grabban. Booked: Saunders.
30th	● Oldham	A	W 2–3	Att: 2,833	Scorers: Balkestein, MacDonald2. Booked: O'Connor, Legge.

APRIL

2nd	● Millwall	A	D 1–1	Att: 14,025	Scorers: Cort. Booked: Osborne, Weston, Bean.
5th	● Exeter	H	D 0–0	Att: 6,017	
10th	● Huddersfield	H	W 3–0	Att: 5,209	Scorers: Grabban, MacDonald2. Booked: Szczesny.
13th	● Southend	H	D 2–2	Att: 6,838	Scorers: Cort, MacDonald. Booked: Legge, Diagouraga.
17th	● Bristol Rovers	A	D 0–0	Att: 6,048	
20th	● Tranmere	H	W 2–1	Att: 4,341	Scorers: O'Connor, Strevens. Booked: Osborne.
24th	● Yeovil	H	D 1–1	Att: 5,395	Scorers: Saunders.

MAY

1st	● Swindon	A	L 3–2	Att: 10,465	Scorers: Hunt, Strevens. Booked: Legge.
8th	● Hartlepool	H	D 0–0	Att: 6,893	Booked: Hunt.

● Coca-Cola League 1/Play-Offs ● FA Cup ● Carling Cup ● Johnstone's Paint Trophy

LEAGUE 1 GOALKEEPER STATS

Player	Appearances	Match starts	Completed matches	Sub appearances	Subbed off	Clean sheets	Yellow cards	Red cards
Nikki Bull	6	5	5	1	0	1	0	0
Simon Moore	1	0	0	1	0	0	0	0
Lewis Price	13	13	13	0	0	4	1	0
Wojciech Szczesny	28	28	26	0	2	9	3	0

LEAGUE 1 OUTFIELD PLAYER STATS

Player	Appearances	Match starts	Completed matches	Substitute appearances	Subbed off	Goals scored	Yellow cards	Red cards
Lionel Ainsworth	9	1	0	8	1	0	0	0
John Akinde	2	2	0	0	2	0	0	0
Pim Balkestein	14	14	13	0	1	1	1	0
Marcus Bean	31	25	21	6	4	0	7	0
Alan Bennett	13	11	9	2	1	0	1	1
Ryan Blake	1	0	0	1	0	0	0	0
John Bostock	9	9	3	0	6	2	1	0
Carl Cort	28	16	15	12	1	6	0	0
Toumani Diagouraga	20	20	18	0	2	0	1	0
Ryan Dickson	27	26	22	1	4	2	3	0
Danny Foster	36	32	30	4	2	0	4	0
Lewis Grabban	7	7	2	0	5	2	0	0
David Hunt	24	18	12	6	6	3	3	0
Steven Kabba	10	3	1	7	2	0	0	0
Leon Legge	29	28	25	1	3	2	5	0
Charlie MacDonald	40	39	32	1	6	15	1	1
Rhys Murphy	5	1	0	4	2	0	0	0
Kevin O'Connor	43	43	42	0	1	4	5	0
Karleigh Osborne	19	13	12	6	1	0	3	0
Mark Phillips	22	19	15	3	4	0	4	0
Sam Saunders	26	15	6	11	9	1	1	0
Tommy Smith	8	8	8	0	0	0	0	0
Ben Strevens	25	20	13	5	7	6	3	0
Cleveland Taylor	12	8	4	4	4	1	1	0
Myles Weston	40	32	23	8	9	8	3	0
James Wilson	13	13	12	0	0	0	0	1
Sam Wood	43	37	24	6	13	2	1	0

SEASON INFORMATION

Highest position: 3
Lowest position: 19
Average goals scored per game: 1.20
Average goals conceded per game: 1.13

LEAGUE POSITION AT THE END OF EACH MONTH

AUG	SEP	OCT	NOV	DEC	JAN	FEB	MAR	APR	MAY
6	10	16	18	11	10	14	11	10	9

LONGEST SEQUENCES

Wins	2		Undefeated home	17
(on two occasions)			(24/10/09–08/05/10)	
Losses	2		Undefeated away	6
(19/09/09–26/09/09)			(20/03/10–17/04/10)	
Draws	2		Without scoring	2
(on five occasions)			(on two occasions)	
Undefeated	11		Without conceding	3
(20/03/10–24/04/10)			(12/12/09–26/12/09)	
Without win	6		Scoring	6
(22/08/09–26/09/09)			(26/01/10–13/03/10)	

CARDS RECEIVED

53   3

EARLIEST STRIKE

CARL CORT
(v Leyton Orient) 3:52

LATEST STRIKE

KEVIN O'CONNOR
(v Southend) 94:17

GOALS SCORED/CONCEDED
PER FIVE-MINUTE INTERVALS

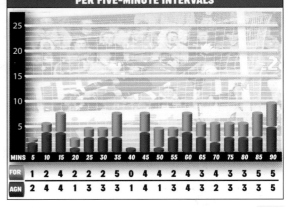

MINS	5	10	15	20	25	30	35	40	45	50	55	60	65	70	75	80	85	90
FOR	1	2	4	2	2	2	5	0	4	4	2	4	3	4	3	3	5	5
AGN	2	4	4	1	3	3	3	1	4	1	3	4	3	2	3	3	3	5

BRIGHTON & HOVE ALBION

GUS POYET proved the saviour as Brighton somehow steered themselves clear of relegation trouble. The former Chelsea and Tottenham midfielder was chosen to replace Russell Slade, whose heroics in pulling off the great escape the previous season could not save him when he was sacked in November with Albion just a point above the drop zone.

Poyet began his first managerial role with a stunning 3–1 win at Southampton. Slow progress followed and the Uruguayan had to wait four months to register his first League victory at the Withdean Stadium, a 2–0 success over Exeter in late February, which came hard on the heels of a fine win at promotion-chasing Charlton.

Just two defeats from their final 16 games secured a comfortable mid-table finish, but their hopes for the coming season could rest on being able to attract loan signings with the class of 2009/10 successes Marcos Painter, Kazenga LuaLua and Ashley Barnes.

CLUB SUMMARY

FORMED	1901
MANAGER	Gus Poyet
GROUND	Withdean Stadium
CAPACITY	8,850
NICKNAME	The Seagulls
WEBSITE	www.seagulls.co.uk

The New **Football Pools** PLAYER OF THE SEASON

Andrew Crofts

OVERALL
P	W	D	L	F	A	GD
53	18	15	20	68	73	-5

COCA-COLA FOOTBALL LEAGUE 1
Pos	P	W	D	L	F	A	GD	Pts
13	46	15	14	17	56	60	-4	59

HOME
Pos	P	W	D	L	F	A	GD	Pts
22	23	7	4	12	26	30	-4	25

AWAY
Pos	P	W	D	L	F	A	GD	Pts
5	23	8	10	5	30	30	0	34

CUP PROGRESS DETAILS
Competition	Round reached	Knocked out by
FA Cup	R4	Aston Villa
Carling Cup	R1	Swansea
JP Trophy	R2	Leyton Orient

BIGGEST WIN (ALL COMPS)
28/12/09 5–2 v Wycombe

BIGGEST DEFEAT (ALL COMPS)
18/08/09 1–7 v Huddersfield

ATTENDANCE RECORD
HIGH	AVERAGE	Low
7,784	6,467	4,711
v Southampton (01/04/2010)		v Huddersfield (09/02/2010)

RESULTS 2009/10

AUGUST
8th	Walsall	H	L 0–1	Att: 6,504	Booked: Navarro.
11th	Swansea	A	L 3–0	Att: 6,400	Booked: J Wright, Virgo.
15th	Brentford	A	D 0–0	Att: 6,950	Booked: Murray.
18th	Huddersfield	A	L 7–1	Att: 11,269	Scorers: Dickinson. Booked: G Smith, Forster. Dismissed: Kuipers.
22nd	Stockport	H	L 2–4	Att: 5,270	Scorers: Dickinson, Forster. Booked: Elphick, Dickinson. Dismissed: Elphick, Hawkins.
28th	Millwall	A	D 1–1	Att: 10,138	Scorers: Forster. Booked: Whing, Virgo, Hart.

SEPTEMBER
5th	Wycombe	H	W 1–0	Att: 5,895	Scorers: Forster. Booked: Dickinson, Bennett, Kuipers.
12th	Carlisle	A	W 0–2	Att: 5,368	Scorers: Forster². Booked: El-Abd, Dicker, Dickinson, A Davies.
19th	Southend	H	L 2–3	Att: 6,287	Scorers: Forster².
26th	Bristol Rovers	A	D 1–1	Att: 8,098	Scorers: Tunnicliffe. Booked: Tunnicliffe, Virgo. Dismissed: Virgo.

OCTOBER
3rd	Milton Keynes Dons	H	L 0–1	Att: 6,419	Booked: Dickinson. Dismissed: El-Abd.
6th	Leyton Orient	A	L 1–0	Att: 1,457	
10th	Yeovil	A	D 2–2	Att: 4,412	Scorers: Crofts, Dickinson. Booked: Forster, J Wright, Murray.
13th	Gillingham	H	W 2–0	Att: 5,960	Scorers: Bennett, Elphick. Booked: Elphick.
17th	Tranmere	A	L 2–1	Att: 5,250	Scorers: Murray. Booked: Murray, Bennett, Hart. Dismissed: Murray.
24th	Oldham	H	L 0–2	Att: 6,205	
31st	Hartlepool	H	D 3–3	Att: 5,694	Scorers: Dickinson, Forster².

NOVEMBER
7th	Wycombe	A	D 4–4	Att: 2,749	Scorers: Bennett, Forster, Murray². Booked: Virgo, Murray. Dismissed: Hoyte.
15th	Southampton	A	W 1–3	Att: 21,932	Scorers: Crofts, Murray². Booked: Dicker, Murray.
18th	Wycombe	H	W 2–0	Att: 3,383	Scorers: Bennett, Crofts. Booked: Dicker.
21st	Leeds	H	L 0–3	Att: 7,615	
24th	Norwich	A	L 4–1	Att: 24,617	Scorers: Tunnicliffe. Booked: Crofts, Cox, Murray, El-Abd.
28th	Rushden & D'monds	H	W 3–2	Att: 3,638	Scorers: Dickinson², Forster. Booked: El-Abd.

DECEMBER
1st	Charlton	H	L 0–2	Att: 6,769	Booked: El-Abd, Elphick, Dicker.
5th	Exeter	A	W 0–1	Att: 5,456	Scorers: Crofts. Booked: Crofts, Navarro, Hoyte.
11th	Colchester	A	L 1–2	Att: 5,898	Scorers: Dicker. Booked: McNulty.
19th	Swindon	A	L 2–1	Att: 7,068	Scorers: Forster. Booked: McNulty, Elphick.
26th	Leyton Orient	H	D 0–0	Att: 6,690	Booked: Crofts, Elphick, Dickinson. Dismissed: Crofts.
28th	Wycombe	H	W 2–5	Att: 6,126	Scorers: Forster, Murray⁴. Booked: Murray.

JANUARY
2nd	Torquay	A	W 0–1	Att: 4,028	Scorers: Crofts. Booked: Virgo.
16th	Walsall	A	W 1–2	Att: 3,450	Scorers: Forster, Murray. Booked: Elphick, Calderon.
23rd	Aston Villa	A	L 3–2	Att: 39,755	Scorers: Elphick, Forster. Booked: Navarro, Dickinson.
26th	Stockport	A	D 1–1	Att: 3,636	Scorers: Crofts. Booked: Painter, Navarro.
30th	Millwall	H	L 0–1	Att: 6,610	Booked: Elphick, Calderon.

FEBRUARY
6th	Leyton Orient	A	D 1–1	Att: 6,027	Scorers: Murray. Booked: Murray, Dicker, Kuipers, Calderon.
9th	Huddersfield	H	D 0–0	Att: 4,711	
13th	Norwich	H	L 1–2	Att: 7,258	Scorers: Bennett. Booked: Carole, Calderon.
20th	Leeds	A	D 1–1	Att: 24,120	Scorers: Murray. Booked: Navarro, Elphick, Brezovan, Dicker. Dismissed: Virgo.
23rd	Charlton	A	W 1–2	Att: 17,508	Scorers: Bennett, Calderon.
27th	Exeter	H	W 2–0	Att: 6,952	Scorers: Dicker, Elphick.

MARCH
8th	Colchester	A	D 0–0	Att: 3,914	Booked: Calderon, Murray, Dicker.
13th	Swindon	H	L 0–1	Att: 6,946	
16th	Brentford	H	W 3–0	Att: 5,539	Scorers: Forster, Murray, Virgo. Booked: El-Abd, Murray.
20th	Oldham	A	W 0–2	Att: 4,059	Scorers: Bennett, Worthington OG. Booked: Elphick, Navarro.
27th	Tranmere	H	W 3–0	Att: 6,812	Scorers: Barnes, Crofts, Murray.

APRIL
1st	Southampton	H	D 2–2	Att: 7,784	Scorers: Barnes, Bennett. Booked: Murray, Bennett.
5th	Hartlepool	A	L 2–0	Att: 3,466	Booked: Calderon.
10th	Carlisle	H	L 1–2	Att: 6,673	Scorers: Elphick. Booked: Barnes.
13th	Gillingham	A	D 1–1	Att: 7,977	Scorers: El-Abd.
17th	Southend	A	W 0–1	Att: 8,503	Scorers: Barnes. Booked: Crofts.
24th	Bristol Rovers	H	W 2–1	Att: 6,922	Scorers: Barnes, Bennett. Booked: El-Abd, Hoyte, Bennett. Dismissed: Murray.

MAY
1st	Milton Keynes Dons	A	D 0–0	Att: 12,023	Booked: Crofts, Hoyte. Dismissed: Arismendi.
8th	Yeovil	H	W 1–0	Att: 7,323	Scorers: Bennett.

● Coca-Cola League 1/Play-Offs ● FA Cup ● Carling Cup ● Johnstone's Paint Trophy

actim

LEAGUE 1 GOALKEEPER STATS

Player	Appearances	Match starts	Completed matches	Sub appearances	Subbed off	Clean sheets	Yellow cards	Red cards
Peter Brezovan	20	20	20	0	0	9	1	0
Michel Kuipers	20	20	19	0	0	5	2	1
Graeme Smith	6	5	5	1	0	0	1	0
Mitchell Walker	1	1	1	0	0	1	0	0

LEAGUE 1 OUTFIELD PLAYER STATS

Player	Appearances	Match starts	Completed matches	Substitute appearances	Subbed off	Goals scored	Yellow cards	Red cards
Diego Arismendi	6	3	0	3	2	0	0	1
Ashley Barnes	8	4	4	4	0	4	1	0
Elliott Bennett	43	43	39	0	4	7	4	0
Inigo Calderon	19	19	17	0	2	1	6	0
Sebastien Carole	9	7	0	2	7	0	1	0
Jake Caskey	1	0	0	1	0	0	0	0
Dean Cox	21	9	2	12	7	0	1	0
Andrew Crofts	44	44	42	0	1	5	5	1
Craig Davies	5	0	0	5	0	0	0	0
Arron Davies	7	7	1	0	6	0	1	0
Gary Dicker	42	33	27	9	6	2	6	0
Liam Dickinson	27	17	9	10	8	4	5	0
Lewis Dunk	1	1	1	0	0	0	0	0
Adam El-Abd	35	33	27	2	5	1	5	0
Tommy Elphick	44	43	41	1	1	3	9	0
Nicky Forster	27	23	9	4	14	13	2	0
Gary Hart	17	1	0	16	1	0	2	0
Colin Hawkins	1	0	0	1	0	0	0	0
Lee Hendrie	8	6	1	2	5	0	0	0
Chris Holroyd	13	5	1	8	4	0	0	0
Gavin Hoyte	18	16	14	2	2	0	3	0
Kazenga LuaLua	11	9	2	2	7	0	0	0
Kevin McLeod	5	2	1	3	1	0	0	0
Jim McNulty	8	5	4	3	1	0	2	0
Glenn Murray	32	25	15	7	8	12	10	2
Alan Navarro	36	31	16	5	15	0	5	0
Marcos Painter	19	18	16	1	2	0	1	0
Jamie Smith	2	1	0	1	1	0	0	0
Matt Thornhill	7	3	1	4	2	0	0	0
James Tunnicliffe	17	17	16	0	1	2	1	0
Adam Virgo	25	20	18	5	0	1	2	2
Andrew Whing	9	9	6	0	3	0	1	0
Mark Wright	4	2	1	2	1	0	0	0
Jake Wright	6	4	3	2	1	0	1	0

SEASON INFORMATION

Highest position: 12
Lowest position: 23
Average goals scored per game: 1.22
Average goals conceded per game: 1.30

AUG SEP OCT NOV DEC JAN FEB MAR APR MAY

LEAGUE POSITION AT THE END OF EACH MONTH

23 20 20 20 20 20 16 13 13 13

LONGEST SEQUENCES

Wins	3	Undefeated home		3
(16/03/10–27/03/10)		(16/03/10–01/04/10)		
Losses	3	Undefeated away		8
(21/11/09–01/12/09)		(28/12/09–20/03/10)		
Draws	2	Without scoring		2
(06/02/10–09/02/10)		(on two occasions)		
Undefeated	5	Without conceding		3
(13/04/10–08/05/10)		(16/03/10–27/03/10)		
Without win	6	Scoring		7
(26/01/10–20/02/10)		(18/08/09–26/09/09)		

CARDS RECEIVED

78 10

EARLIEST STRIKE

NICKY FORSTER
(v Carlisle) 3:07

LATEST STRIKE

ELLIOTT BENNETT
(v Bristol Rovers) 95:02

GOALS SCORED/CONCEDED
PER FIVE-MINUTE INTERVALS

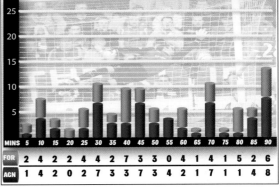

MINS	5	10	15	20	25	30	35	40	45	50	55	60	65	70	75	80	85	90
FOR	2	4	2	2	4	4	2	7	3	3	0	4	1	4	1	5	2	6
AGN	1	4	2	0	2	7	3	3	7	3	4	2	1	7	1	1	4	8

BRISTOL ROVERS

INCONSISTENCY proved to be Bristol Rovers' major downfall as they failed to mount a promotion push despite having made a promising start to the season.

Following a defeat on the opening day of the campaign against Leyton Orient, Paul Trollope's side won six of their next seven Coca-Cola League 1 games to raise hopes of a push for promotion, despite star striker Rickie Lambert's move to Southampton.

However, while they continued to pick up points at home, the Pirates endured a miserable run of seven consecutive away defeats which proved to be costly as they missed out on the play-offs and finished well off the pace down in 11th place.

Trollope's side won just six times on the road in the League all season and, having conceded five goals at Norwich, Leyton Orient and Southampton, they will have to improve on their travels in 2010/11 if they are to have any hope of securing promotion.

CLUB SUMMARY

FORMED	1883
MANAGER	Paul Trollope
GROUND	Memorial Stadium
CAPACITY	9,400
NICKNAME	The Pirates
WEBSITE	www.bristolrovers.co.uk

The New **Football Pools** PLAYER OF THE SEASON — *Mikkel Andersen*

OVERALL
P	W	D	L	F	A	GD
50	20	6	24	64	77	-13

COCA-COLA FOOTBALL LEAGUE 1
Pos	P	W	D	L	F	A	GD	Pts
11	46	19	5	22	59	70	-11	62

HOME
Pos	P	W	D	L	F	A	GD	Pts
10	23	13	3	7	32	30	2	42

AWAY
Pos	P	W	D	L	F	A	GD	Pts
15	23	6	2	15	27	40	-13	20

CUP PROGRESS DETAILS
Competition	Round reached	Knocked out by
FA Cup	R1	Southampton
Carling Cup	R2	Cardiff
JP Trophy	R1	Hereford

BIGGEST WIN (ALL COMPS)
06/03/10 4-0 v Swindon

BIGGEST DEFEAT (ALL COMPS)
02/02/10 0-5 v Leyton Orient

ATTENDANCE RECORD
HIGH	AVERAGE	LOW
11,448	7,043	5,322
v Leeds (27/10/2009)		v Stockport (02/03/2010)

RESULTS 2009/10

AUGUST
8th	● Leyton Orient	H	L 1-2	Att: 7,745	Scorers: Lambert. Booked: Kuffour.
11th	● Aldershot	H	W 2-1	Att: 3,644	Scorers: Duffy². Booked: Pipe, Lines.
15th	● Stockport	A	W 0-2	Att: 4,084	Scorers: Coles, Kuffour. Booked: Campbell.
18th	● Hartlepool	A	W 1-2	Att: 3,137	Scorers: Kuffour, Lescott. Booked: Hughes.
22nd	● Huddersfield	H	W 1-0	Att: 6,952	Scorers: Hughes. Booked: Hughes, Coles.
26th	● Cardiff	A	L 3-1	Att: 9,767	Scorers: Elliott.
29th	● Wycombe	A	L 2-1	Att: 5,214	Scorers: Lines. Booked: Coles, Hunt.

SEPTEMBER
1st	● Hereford	A	D 0-0	Att: 970	Booked: Regan. Hereford win 4-2 on penalties.
5th	● Millwall	H	W 2-0	Att: 6,038	Scorers: Hughes, Lines. Booked: Regan.
12th	● Oldham	H	W 1-0	Att: 6,674	Scorers: Kuffour. Booked: Anthony.
19th	● Brentford	A	W 1-3	Att: 6,528	Scorers: Dickson², Lescott. Booked: Andersen.
26th	● Brighton	H	D 1-1	Att: 8,098	Scorers: Kuffour.
29th	● Southampton	A	W 2-3	Att: 19,724	Scorers: Dickson, Kuffour, Williams. Booked: Hughes, Coles, Regan.

OCTOBER
3rd	● Norwich	A	L 5-1	Att: 24,117	Scorers: Hughes.
17th	● Southend	A	L 2-1	Att: 6,853	Scorers: Grant OG. Booked: Kuffour, Anthony, Lescott.
24th	● Yeovil	H	L 1-2	Att: 7,812	Scorers: Dickson. Booked: Anthony, Campbell.
27th	● Leeds	H	L 0-4	Att: 11,448	Booked: Elliott.
31st	● Milton Keynes Dons	A	L 2-1	Att: 9,711	Scorers: Duffy. Booked: Elliott.

NOVEMBER
6th	● Southampton	H	L 2-3	Att: 6,446	Scorers: Duffy, Hughes. Booked: Williams.
14th	● Carlisle	H	W 3-2	Att: 5,862	Scorers: Hughes, Kuffour, Lines. Booked: Regan, Williams.
21st	● Gillingham	H	W 2-1	Att: 6,210	Scorers: Hughes, Lines. Booked: Hughes, Campbell.
24th	● Charlton	A	L 4-2	Att: 15,885	Scorers: Hughes, Lines. Booked: Baldwin, Campbell, Coles, Lines, Duffy.

DECEMBER
1st	● Exeter	H	W 1-0	Att: 7,313	Scorers: Duffy.
5th	● Colchester	A	L 1-0	Att: 4,942	Booked: Hughes, Coles.
12th	● Swindon	H	W 3-0	Att: 7,613	Scorers: Hughes, Kuffour, Williams. Booked: Reece.
19th	● Tranmere	A	L 2-0	Att: 4,755	Booked: Lescott, Hughes.
28th	● Millwall	A	L 2-0	Att: 10,014	Booked: Baldwin.

JANUARY
19th	● Huddersfield	A	D 0-0	Att: 12,624	
23rd	● Hartlepool	H	W 2-0	Att: 5,794	Scorers: Duffy, Lines. Booked: Anthony.
30th	● Wycombe	H	L 2-3	Att: 6,688	Scorers: Lines². Booked: Lines, Coles.

FEBRUARY
2nd	● Leyton Orient	A	L 5-0	Att: 2,931	
6th	● Walsall	A	D 0-0	Att: 3,886	
9th	● Walsall	H	L 0-1	Att: 5,919	Booked: Anthony.
15th	● Charlton	H	W 2-1	Att: 7,624	Scorers: Elliott, Heffernan. Booked: Blizzard, Campbell.
20th	● Gillingham	A	L 1-0	Att: 5,302	Booked: Anthony, Hughes.
27th	● Colchester	H	W 3-2	Att: 6,023	Scorers: Blizzard, Kuffour, Lines. Booked: Elliott.

MARCH
2nd	● Stockport	H	W 1-0	Att: 5,322	Scorers: Hughes.
6th	● Swindon	A	W 0-4	Att: 10,341	Scorers: Heffernan, Hughes, Kuffour, Lines. Booked: Anthony, Lines.
13th	● Tranmere	H	D 0-0	Att: 6,477	
17th	● Exeter	A	L 1-0	Att: 5,269	Booked: Anthony, Blizzard.
20th	● Yeovil	A	W 0-3	Att: 5,968	Scorers: Heffernan, Kuffour². Booked: Coles, Elliott.
27th	● Southend	H	W 4-3	Att: 6,476	Scorers: Hughes², Kuffour, Grant OG. Booked: Anthony, Lines.

APRIL
2nd	● Carlisle	A	L 3-1	Att: 5,407	Scorers: Heffernan. Booked: Campbell. Dismissed: Hughes.
5th	● Milton Keynes Dons	H	W 1-0	Att: 6,406	Scorers: Kuffour. Booked: Regan, Williams.
10th	● Oldham	A	L 2-1	Att: 3,769	Scorers: Kuffour. Booked: Lines, Elliott, Coles.
13th	● Southampton	H	L 1-5	Att: 8,607	Scorers: Hughes. Booked: Blizzard.
17th	● Brentford	H	D 0-0	Att: 6,048	
24th	● Brighton	A	L 2-1	Att: 6,922	Scorers: Williams. Booked: Hughes, Coles, Jones. Dismissed: Coles.

MAY
1st	● Norwich	H	L 0-3	Att: 8,836	Booked: Anthony, Lines.
8th	● Leeds	A	L 2-1	Att: 38,234	Scorers: Duffy. Booked: Jones, Duffy. Leeds are promoted.

● Coca-Cola League 1/Play-Offs ● FA Cup ● Carling Cup ● Johnstone's Paint Trophy

actim

LEAGUE 1 GOALKEEPER STATS

Player	Appearances	Match starts	Completed matches	Sub appearances	Subbed off	Clean sheets	Yellow cards	Red cards
Mikkel Andersen	39	39	39	0	0	12	1	0
Rhys Evans	3	3	3	0	0	1	0	0
Fraser Forster	4	4	4	0	0	2	0	0

LEAGUE 1 OUTFIELD PLAYER STATS

Player	Appearances	Match starts	Completed matches	Substitute appearances	Subbed off	Goals scored	Yellow cards	Red cards
Byron Anthony	37	37	35	0	2	0	10	0
Pat Baldwin	6	6	6	0	0	0	2	0
Dominic Blizzard	34	22	7	12	15	1	3	0
Wayne Brown	4	3	1	1	2	0	0	0
Stuart Campbell	46	46	45	0	1	0	6	0
Danny Coles	36	36	35	0	0	1	9	1
Chris Dickson	14	10	1	4	9	4	0	0
Darryl Duffy	30	15	4	15	11	4	2	0
Steve Elliott	21	21	20	0	1	1	5	0
Paul Heffernan	11	11	8	0	3	4	0	0
Jeff Hughes	44	44	37	0	6	12	8	1
Ben Hunt	2	0	0	2	0	0	1	0
Daniel Jones	17	17	17	0	0	0	2	0
Jo Kuffour	42	42	33	0	9	14	2	0
Richard Lambert	1	1	1	0	0	1	0	0
Aaron Lescott	24	23	16	1	7	2	2	0
Chris Lines	42	41	36	1	5	10	6	0
David Pipe	7	5	4	2	1	0	0	0
Charles Reece	14	5	2	9	3	0	1	0
Carl Regan	35	32	32	3	0	0	4	0
Elliot Richard	5	0	0	5	0	0	0	0
Ben Swallow	23	6	3	17	3	0	0	0
Andrew Williams	43	18	8	25	10	3	2	0
Mark Wright	24	19	5	5	14	0	0	0

SEASON INFORMATION
Highest position: 3
Lowest position: 17
Average goals scored per game: 1.28
Average goals conceded per game: 1.52

LEAGUE POSITION AT THE END OF EACH MONTH

LONGEST SEQUENCES

Wins	3	Undefeated home	6
(on three occasions)		(15/02/10–05/04/10)	
Losses	5	Undefeated away	2
(03/10/09–31/10/09)		(on two occasions)	
Draws	–	Without scoring	3
(–)		(on two occasions)	
Undefeated	5	Without conceding	3
(05/09/09–29/09/09)		(02/03/10–13/03/10)	
Without win	6	Scoring	13
(10/04/10–08/05/10)		(08/08/09–24/10/09)	

CARDS RECEIVED

66 **2**

EARLIEST STRIKE
JO KUFFOUR
(v Stockport) 2:03

LATEST STRIKE
ANDREW WILLIAMS
(v Southampton) 95:13

GOALS SCORED/CONCEDED
PER FIVE-MINUTE INTERVALS

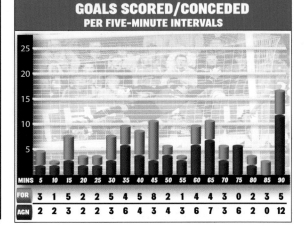

MINS	5	10	15	20	25	30	35	40	45	50	55	60	65	70	75	80	85	90
FOR	3	1	5	2	2	5	4	5	8	2	1	4	4	3	0	2	3	5
AGN	2	2	3	2	2	3	6	4	3	4	3	6	7	3	6	2	0	12

CARLISLE UNITED

CARLISLE were expected to be involved in a relegation struggle after releasing eight players during the close season. However, their third-tier status never looked in doubt during the campaign, and the Cumbrians also rewarded their fans with a day out at Wembley in the Johnstone's Paint Trophy final.

Unfortunately, Greg Abbott's side were swept away by Southampton in a lop-sided final and had little to play for during the run-in but there were enough high points to give supporters optimism for the 2010/11 campaign.

Carlisle registered League wins over Charlton, Colchester, MK Dons and Norwich, who they also beat in the FA Cup to earn a fourth-round clash at Everton where they impressed despite a 3–1 defeat.

Adam Clayton, on loan from Manchester City, was a key performer while Richard Keogh was a rock at the back and Matty Robson, a shrewd free signing from Hartlepool, won the fans' player of the year award.

CLUB SUMMARY

FORMED	1903
MANAGER	Greg Abbott
GROUND	Brunton Park
CAPACITY	16,651
NICKNAME	The Cumbrians
WEBSITE	www.carlisleunited.co.uk

Ian Harte
PLAYER OF THE SEASON

OVERALL
P	W	D	L	F	A	GD
60	23	15	22	91	88	3

COCA-COLA FOOTBALL LEAGUE 1
Pos	P	W	D	L	F	A	GD	Pts
14	46	15	13	18	63	66	-3	58

HOME
Pos	P	W	D	L	F	A	GD	Pts
19	23	10	4	9	34	28	6	34

AWAY
Pos	P	W	D	L	F	A	GD	Pts
10	23	5	9	9	29	38	-9	24

CUP PROGRESS DETAILS
Competition	Round reached	Knocked out by
FA Cup	R3	Everton
Carling Cup	R3	Portsmouth
JP Trophy	R-UP	Southampton

BIGGEST WIN (ALL COMPS)
13/02/10 5–0 v Milton Keynes Dons

BIGGEST DEFEAT (ALL COMPS)
1–4 on 2 occasions

ATTENDANCE RECORD
High	Average	Low
8,728	5,210	3,731
v Leeds (13/04/2010)		v Yeovil (16/03/2010)

RESULTS 2009/10

AUGUST
8th	● Brentford	H	L 1–3	Att: 6,367	Scorers: Harte. Booked: Taiwo.
11th	● Oldham	H	W 1–0	Att: 2,509	Scorers: Dobie. Booked: Kavanagh.
15th	● Millwall	A	D 0–0	Att: 9,055	Booked: Pidgeley, Harte.
18th	● Stockport	A	W 1–2	Att: 4,009	Scorers: Anyinsah, Hurst. Booked: Robson, Dobie.
22nd	● Exeter	H	L 0–1	Att: 5,156	Booked: Pidgeley, Murphy.
26th	● Bristol City	A	W 0–2	Att: 6,359	Scorers: Dobie, Madine.
29th	● Leyton Orient	A	D 2–2	Att: 3,546	Scorers: Robson, Thirlwell. Booked: Thirlwell, Robson.

SEPTEMBER
1st	● Morecambe	A	D 2–2	Att: 2,016	Scorers: Kavanagh[2]. Booked: Murphy, Kavanagh. Carlisle win 4–2 on penalties.
5th	● Tranmere	H	W 3–0	Att: 5,269	Scorers: Anyinsah, Harte, Livesey. Booked: Raven.
12th	● Brighton	A	L 0–2	Att: 5,368	Booked: Anyinsah.
19th	● Oldham	A	L 2–0	Att: 4,268	Booked: Kavanagh, Livesey.
22nd	● Portsmouth	H	L 1–3	Att: 7,042	Scorers: Harte.
26th	● Southampton	H	D 1–1	Att: 7,000	Scorers: Dobie. Booked: Raven.
29th	● Leeds	A	D 1–1	Att: 19,673	Scorers: Dobie. Booked: Kavanagh.

OCTOBER
3rd	● Walsall	A	D 2–2	Att: 3,572	Scorers: Keogh, Robson. Booked: Keogh.
6th	● Macclesfield	H	W 4–2	Att: 1,753	Scorers: Bridge-Wilkinson, Dobie[2], Robson. Booked: Horwood.
10th	● Norwich	H	L 0–1	Att: 6,825	Booked: Kavanagh, Keogh.
17th	● Yeovil	A	L 3–1	Att: 4,333	Scorers: Harte. Booked: Livesey, Bridge-Wilkinson, Offiong.
24th	● Southend	H	W 2–1	Att: 4,551	Scorers: Anyinsah, Pericard.
31st	● Charlton	H	W 3–1	Att: 6,077	Scorers: Harte, Kavanagh[2]. Booked: Dobie.

NOVEMBER
7th	● Morecambe	H	D 2–2	Att: 4,181	Scorers: Harte, Pericard.
10th	● Chesterfield	A	W 1–3	Att: 2,878	Scorers: Clayton, Murphy, Robson. Booked: Keogh, Anyinsah.
14th	● Bristol Rovers	A	L 3–2	Att: 5,862	Scorers: Harte, Keogh. Booked: Taiwo.
17th	● Morecambe	A	W 0–1	Att: 3,307	Scorers: Anyinsah. Booked: Clayton.
21st	● Swindon	H	L 0–1	Att: 4,339	
24th	● Milton Keynes Dons	A	W 3–4	Att: 9,459	Scorers: Anyinsah, Hurst, Pericard[2]. Booked: Clayton, Taiwo, Kavanagh. Dismissed: Taiwo.
28th	● Norwich	H	W 3–1	Att: 3,946	Scorers: Hurst, Keogh, Pericard. Booked: Kavanagh.

DECEMBER
1st	● Hartlepool	H	W 3–2	Att: 4,109	Scorers: Harte, Robson, Taiwo. Booked: Taiwo.
5th	● Gillingham	A	D 0–0	Att: 7,214	Booked: Clayton.
12th	● Wycombe	H	W 1–0	Att: 4,528	Scorers: Pericard.
15th	● Bradford	H	W 3–0	Att: 3,176	Scorers: Dobie, Keogh, Robson.
28th	● Tranmere	A	D 0–0	Att: 6,313	Booked: Kavanagh, Horwood, Pericard, Clayton.

JANUARY
2nd	● Everton	A	L 3–1	Att: 31,196	Scorers: Hurst. Booked: Collin.
16th	● Brentford	A	L 3–1	Att: 5,089	Scorers: Harte. Booked: Keogh, Kavanagh, Offiong.
19th	● Leeds	A	W 1–2	Att: 13,011	Scorers: Anyinsah, Kavanagh. Booked: Hurst.
23rd	● Stockport	H	D 0–0	Att: 4,966	Booked: Keogh, Horwood, Anyinsah. Dismissed: Dobie.
26th	● Exeter	A	W 2–3	Att: 4,106	Scorers: Anyinsah[2], Offiong. Booked: Keogh.
30th	● Leyton Orient	H	D 2–2	Att: 4,687	Scorers: Anyinsah, Harte. Booked: Harte.

FEBRUARY
2nd	● Colchester	A	L 2–1	Att: 3,903	Scorers: Harte. Booked: Harte.
6th	● Huddersfield	A	D 1–1	Att: 14,132	Booked: Marshall.
9th	● Leeds	H	L 2–3	Att: 9,430	Scorers: Clayton, Hurst. Booked: Keogh, Clayton. Agg: 4–4; Carlisle win 6–5 on penalties.
13th	● Milton Keynes Dons	H	W 5–0	Att: 4,930	Scorers: Anyinsah, Dobie, Duffy, Harte, Robson. Booked: Dobie.
16th	● Huddersfield	H	L 1–2	Att: 5,236	Scorers: Anyinsah. Booked: Murphy.
20th	● Swindon	A	L 2–0	Att: 7,704	
23rd	● Hartlepool	A	L 4–1	Att: 2,975	Scorers: Dobie. Booked: Hurst, Livesey.
27th	● Gillingham	H	W 2–0	Att: 4,646	Scorers: Harte[2].

MARCH
6th	● Wycombe	A	D 0–0	Att: 4,876	
9th	● Millwall	H	L 1–3	Att: 3,853	Scorers: Livesey. Booked: Clayton, Harte, Offiong.
13th	● Colchester	H	W 2–1	Att: 4,469	Scorers: Marshall, Price. Booked: Taiwo, Price. Dismissed: Taiwo.
16th	● Yeovil	H	W 1–0	Att: 3,731	Scorers: Clayton.
20th	● Southend	A	D 2–2	Att: 6,384	Scorers: Dobie, Marshall.
28th	● Southampton	N	L 1–4	Att: 73,476	Scorers: Madine. Booked: Murphy, Keogh.

APRIL
2nd	● Bristol Rovers	H	W 3–1	Att: 5,407	Scorers: Harte[2], Price. Booked: Thirlwell, Robson, Harte.
5th	● Charlton	A	L 1–0	Att: 17,229	Booked: Thirlwell, Dobie.
10th	● Brighton	A	W 1–2	Att: 6,673	Scorers: Harte, Madine. Booked: Thirlwell, Taiwo, Horwood, Keogh.
13th	● Leeds	H	L 1–3	Att: 8,728	Scorers: Keogh. Booked: Clayton, Marshall.
17th	● Oldham	H	L 1–2	Att: 4,484	Scorers: Madine.
24th	● Southampton	A	L 3–2	Att: 18,908	Scorers: Harte, Madine. Booked: Horwood.

MAY
1st	● Walsall	H	D 1–1	Att: 5,114	Scorers: Price. Booked: Price, Keogh.
8th	● Norwich	A	W 0–2	Att: 25,181	Scorers: Madine, Price. Booked: Thirlwell.

● Coca-Cola League 1/Play-Offs ● FA Cup ● Carling Cup ● Johnstone's Paint Trophy

actim

LEAGUE 1 GOALKEEPER STATS

Player	Appearances	Match starts	Completed matches	Sub appearances	Subbed off	Clean sheets	Yellow cards	Red cards
Adam Collin	29	29	28	0	1	8	0	0
Mark Gillespie	1	0	0	1	0	0	0	0
Lenny Pidgeley	17	17	17	0	0	2	2	0

LEAGUE 1 OUTFIELD PLAYER STATS

Player	Appearances	Match starts	Completed matches	Substitute appearances	Subbed off	Goals scored	Yellow cards	Red cards
Tom Aldred	5	4	3	1	1	0	0	0
Joe Anyinsah	28	20	14	8	6	9	2	0
Ryan Bowman	6	0	0	6	0	0	0	0
Marc Bridge-Wilkinson	19	6	2	13	4	0	1	0
Adam Clayton	28	28	25	0	3	1	5	0
Scott Dobie	39	24	11	15	12	5	4	1
Darryl Duffy	8	7	6	1	1	1	0	0
Ian Harte	45	45	43	0	2	16	5	0
Evan Horwood	32	31	27	1	4	0	4	0
Kevan Hurst	33	30	13	3	17	2	1	0
Tony Kane	4	1	1	3	0	0	0	0
Graham Kavanagh	29	28	16	1	12	2	6	0
Richard Keogh	41	41	40	0	1	3	7	0
Danny Livesey	38	38	33	0	5	2	3	0
Gary Madine	20	6	6	14	0	4	0	0
Ben Marshall	20	11	7	9	4	3	1	0
Peter Murphy	16	12	8	4	4	0	2	0
Richard Offiong	15	2	0	13	2	1	3	0
Vincent Pericard	10	10	7	0	3	4	1	0
Jason Price	9	8	2	1	6	4	2	0
David Raven	16	14	14	2	0	0	2	0
Matthew Robson	39	39	37	0	2	4	3	0
Gavin Rothery	1	0	0	1	0	0	0	0
Tom Taiwo	35	30	19	5	9	1	6	2
Cleveland Taylor	1	1	1	0	0	0	0	0
Paul Thirlwell	28	24	17	4	7	1	5	0

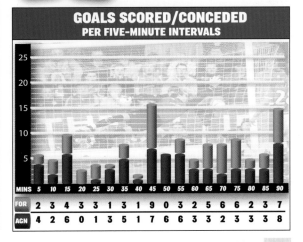

SEASON INFORMATION
Highest position: 4
Lowest position: 23
Average goals scored per game: 1.37
Average goals conceded per game: 1.43

LEAGUE POSITION AT THE END OF EACH MONTH

16 18 15 17 15 12 13 12 14 14

LONGEST SEQUENCES

Wins (on three occasions)	2	Undefeated home (01/12/09–13/02/10)	5
Losses (on two occasions)	3	Undefeated away (on two occasions)	3
Draws (26/09/09–03/10/09)	3	Without scoring (12/09/09–19/09/09)	2
Undefeated (24/11/09–28/12/09)	5	Without conceding (05/12/09–28/12/09)	3
Without win (12/09/09–17/10/09)	7	Scoring (26/01/10–16/02/10)	6

CARDS RECEIVED
65 3

EARLIEST STRIKE
GARY MADINE
(v Norwich) 0:54

LATEST STRIKE
GARY MADINE
(v Southampton) 93:58

GOALS SCORED/CONCEDED
PER FIVE-MINUTE INTERVALS

MINS	5	10	15	20	25	30	35	40	45	50	55	60	65	70	75	80	85	90
FOR	2	3	4	3	3	1	3	1	9	0	0	3	2	5	6	6	2	3	7
AGN	4	2	6	0	1	3	5	1	7	6	6	3	3	2	3	3	3	8

CHARLTON ATHLETIC

CHARLTON failed to secure an immediate return to the npower Championship following defeat in the play-off semi-finals to Swindon.

The Addicks had fallen from the Barclays Premier League to Coca-Cola League 1 following two relegations in three seasons, but were considered among the promotion favourites at the start of 2009/10.

While Norwich roared off into the distance, the Addicks stayed on the coat-tails of second-placed Leeds but, like the rest of the chasing pack, were unable to take advantage of the mid-season jitters at Elland Road.

A 4–0 reverse at neighbours Millwall in March hit their hopes hard and even an early May victory over Leeds could not lift them into the top two. Their semi-final defeat by Swindon encapsulated their season – leading 3–2 on aggregate at The Valley and with the visitors down to 10 men, the finish line was in sight. However, undermined by nerves, they conceded an equaliser and lost out in a penalty shoot-out.

CLUB SUMMARY

FORMED	1905
MANAGER	Phil Parkinson
GROUND	The Valley
CAPACITY	27,111
NICKNAME	The Addicks
WEBSITE	www.cafc.co.uk

The New **Football Pools** PLAYER OF THE SEASON — *Christian Dailly*

OVERALL
P	W	D	L	F	A	GD
52	25	15	12	79	56	23

COCA-COLA FOOTBALL LEAGUE 1
Pos	P	W	D	L	F	A	GD	Pts
4	46	23	15	8	71	48	23	84

HOME
Pos	P	W	D	L	F	A	GD	Pts
7	23	14	6	3	41	22	19	48

AWAY
Pos	P	W	D	L	F	A	GD	Pts
3	23	9	9	5	30	26	4	36

CUP PROGRESS DETAILS
Competition	Round reached	Knocked out by
FA Cup	R1	Northwich
Carling Cup	R1	Hereford
JP Trophy	QF	Southampton

BIGGEST WIN (ALL COMPS)
14/11/09 5–1 v Milton Keynes Dons

BIGGEST DEFEAT (ALL COMPS)
13/03/10 0–4 v Millwall

ATTENDANCE RECORD
HIGH	AVERAGE	LOW
23,198	17,407	14,636
v Leeds (01/05/2010)		v Hartlepool (19/01/2010)

RESULTS 2009/10

AUGUST
8th	● Wycombe	H	W 3–2	Att: 16,552	Scorers: Bailey, Dailly, Llera. Booked: Bailey, Llera.
11th	● Hereford	A	L 1–0	Att: 2,017	Booked: McLeod, Stavrinou. AET – Score after 90 mins 0–0.
15th	● Hartlepool	H	W 0–2	Att: 4,408	Scorers: Bailey, Burton. Booked: Youga, Semedo.
18th	● Leyton Orient	A	W 1–2	Att: 7,376	Scorers: Burton, Shelvey. Booked: Shelvey, Sam, Racon.
22nd	● Walsall	H	W 2–0	Att: 15,306	Scorers: Llera, Wagstaff. Booked: Llera.
29th	● Tranmere	A	W 0–4	Att: 5,417	Scorers: Bailey, Sam2, Semedo. Booked: Llera.

SEPTEMBER
5th	● Brentford	H	W 2–0	Att: 16,399	Scorers: Burton, Sam.
12th	● Southampton	H	D 1–1	Att: 19,441	Scorers: Burton. Booked: Racon, Richardson, Youga.
19th	● Norwich	A	D 2–2	Att: 24,018	Scorers: Burton, Shelvey. Booked: Elliot, Semedo, Llera, McLeod, Wagstaff.
26th	● Exeter	H	W 2–1	Att: 16,867	Scorers: Bailey, McLeod. Booked: McLeod.
29th	● Colchester	A	L 3–0	Att: 7,098	Booked: Burton, Shelvey.

OCTOBER
3rd	● Leeds	A	D 0–0	Att: 31,838	Booked: S Sodje.
6th	● Barnet	H	W 4–1	Att: 4,522	Scorers: Bailey, McLeod, Tuna, Wagstaff.
10th	● Oldham	H	D 0–0	Att: 16,441	
17th	● Huddersfield	H	W 2–1	Att: 16,991	Scorers: McLeod, S Sodje. Booked: Spring, McLeod.
24th	● Gillingham	A	D 1–1	Att: 10,304	Scorers: Nutter OG. Booked: Burton, S Sodje, Dailly.
31st	● Carlisle	A	L 3–1	Att: 6,077	Scorers: Burton. Booked: Dailly.

NOVEMBER
8th	● Northwich	A	L 1–0	Att: 2,153	Booked: Semedo.
11th	● Southampton	A	L 2–1	Att: 13,906	Scorers: McKenzie. Booked: Dailly.
14th	● Milton Keynes Dons	H	W 5–1	Att: 17,188	Scorers: Bailey, Burton, Mooney, Sam, S Sodje. Booked: Sam, McKenzie.
21st	● Yeovil	A	L 2–1	Att: 5,632	Scorers: A Sodje. Booked: Semedo, Youga. Dismissed: S Sodje.
24th	● Bristol Rovers	H	W 4–2	Att: 15,885	Scorers: Bailey, Burton, Mooney, A Sodje. Booked: Omozusi, Dailly, Sam.

DECEMBER
1st	● Brighton	A	W 0–2	Att: 6,769	Scorers: Burton, Wagstaff. Booked: S Sodje, Semedo, Elliot, Mooney.
5th	● Southend	H	W 1–0	Att: 17,445	Scorers: Burton. Booked: Racon, Bailey.
12th	● Stockport	A	W 1–2	Att: 4,277	Scorers: S Sodje, Wagstaff. Booked: Basey, Sam.
19th	● Millwall	H	D 4–4	Att: 19,105	Scorers: Bailey, Burton2, Morison OG. Booked: Sam, Mooney, A Sodje.
26th	● Swindon	H	D 2–2	Att: 17,977	Scorers: Llera, Shelvey. Booked: Burton, Basey. Dismissed: S Sodje, Burton.
28th	● Brentford	A	D 1–1	Att: 8,387	Scorers: Bailey. Booked: Semedo.

JANUARY
16th	● Wycombe	A	W 1–2	Att: 6,123	Scorers: Bailey, Shelvey. Booked: Basey.
19th	● Hartlepool	H	W 2–1	Att: 14,636	Scorers: Mooney, Wagstaff. Booked: Dickson.
25th	● Leyton Orient	H	L 0–1	Att: 15,955	Booked: Llera, Elliot, Basey.
30th	● Tranmere	H	D 1–1	Att: 16,168	Scorers: Bailey. Booked: Burton.

FEBRUARY
2nd	● Walsall	A	D 1–1	Att: 3,417	Scorers: Burton. Booked: Reid.
6th	● Swindon	A	D 1–1	Att: 9,552	Scorers: Bailey. Booked: Burton.
15th	● Bristol Rovers	A	L 2–1	Att: 7,624	Scorers: Racon. Booked: Bailey, Semedo, Racon, Burton.
20th	● Yeovil	H	W 2–0	Att: 15,991	Scorers: Mooney, Reid. Booked: Dailly.
23rd	● Brighton	H	L 1–2	Att: 17,508	Scorers: A Sodje.
26th	● Southend	A	W 1–2	Att: 9,724	Scorers: Reid, A Sodje. Booked: Bailey, Reid.

MARCH
6th	● Stockport	H	W 2–0	Att: 16,609	Scorers: A Sodje, Huntington OG. Booked: Llera.
13th	● Millwall	A	L 4–0	Att: 17,632	Booked: Llera.
20th	● Gillingham	H	D 2–2	Att: 20,024	Scorers: Mooney, Richardson.
27th	● Huddersfield	A	D 1–1	Att: 14,459	Scorers: Reid. Booked: Dailly, Semedo.

APRIL
3rd	● Milton Keynes Dons	A	W 0–1	Att: 10,869	Scorers: Forster. Booked: Racon, Randolph, Borrowdale, Shelvey.
5th	● Carlisle	H	W 1–0	Att: 17,229	Scorers: S Sodje. Booked: Semedo.
10th	● Southampton	A	L 1–0	Att: 23,061	
13th	● Colchester	H	W 1–0	Att: 17,427	Scorers: Forster. Booked: Semedo, S Sodje.
17th	● Norwich	H	L 0–1	Att: 20,023	
24th	● Exeter	A	D 1–1	Att: 6,835	Scorers: Reid. Booked: Sam, Reid, Semedo.

MAY
1st	● Leeds	H	W 1–0	Att: 23,198	Scorers: Naylor OG. Booked: S Sodje, Semedo, A Sodje.
8th	● Oldham	A	W 0–2	Att: 5,686	Scorers: Bailey, Llera. Booked: Sam.
14th	● Swindon	A	L 2–1	Att: 13,560	Scorers: Burton.
17th	● Swindon	H	W 2–1	Att: 21,521	Scorers: Mooney, Ferry OG. Booked: Semedo, Burton. Dismissed: Llera. AET – Score after 90 mins 2–1. Agg: 3–3; Swindon win 5–4 on penalties.

● Coca-Cola League 1/Play-offs ● FA Cup ● Carling Cup ● Johnstone's Paint Trophy

LEAGUE 1 GOALKEEPER STATS

Player	Appearances	Match starts	Completed matches	Sub appearances	Subbed off	Clean sheets	Yellow cards	Red cards
Rob Elliot	33	33	31	0	2	10	3	0
Carl Ikeme	4	4	4	0	0	0	0	0
Darren Randolph	11	9	9	2	0	5	1	0

LEAGUE 1 OUTFIELD PLAYER STATS

Player	Appearances	Match starts	Completed matches	Substitute appearances	Subbed off	Goals scored	Yellow cards	Red cards
Nicky Bailey	44	43	42	1	1	12	4	0
Grant Basey	19	14	12	5	2	0	4	0
Gary Borrowdale	10	10	9	0	1	0	1	0
Deon Burton	39	35	23	4	11	13	6	1
Christian Dailly	44	44	44	0	0	1	5	0
Chris Dickson	5	1	0	4	1	0	1	0
Nicky Forster	8	8	2	0	6	2	0	0
Andy Gray	2	0	0	2	0	0	0	0
Johnnie Jackson	4	4	2	0	2	0	0	0
Miguel Angel Llera	25	23	20	2	2	4	7	0
Leon McKenzie	12	0	0	12	0	0	1	0
Izale McLeod	11	3	0	8	3	2	3	0
David Mooney	28	20	8	8	12	5	2	0
Elliot Omozusi	9	7	4	2	3	0	1	0
Therry Racon	36	36	25	0	11	1	5	0
Kyel Reid	17	11	7	6	4	4	3	0
Frazer Richardson	38	37	33	1	4	1	1	0
Lloyd Sam	43	40	20	3	20	4	7	0
Jose Vitor Semedo	38	35	27	3	8	1	11	0
Jonjo Shelvey	24	19	8	5	11	4	3	0
Akpo Sodje	25	10	4	15	6	5	2	0
Sam Sodje	27	24	21	3	1	4	5	2
Chris Solly	8	1	0	7	1	0	0	0
Matthew Spring	12	7	5	5	2	0	1	0
Tamer Tuna	1	0	0	1	0	0	0	0
Scott Wagstaff	31	10	5	21	5	4	1	0
Kelly Youga	18	18	17	0	1	0	3	0

AUG SEP OCT NOV DEC JAN FEB MAR APR MAY

LEAGUE POSITION AT THE END OF EACH MONTH

| 1 | 2 | 2 | 2 | 2 | 3 | 3 | 5 | 5 | 4 |

SEASON INFORMATION

Highest position: 1
Lowest position: 5
Average goals scored per game: 1.54
Average goals conceded per game: 1.04

LONGEST SEQUENCES

Wins	6	Undefeated home	13	
(08/08/09–05/09/09)		(08/08/09–19/01/10)		
Losses	–	Undefeated away	7	
(–)		(21/11/09–06/02/10)		
Draws	3	Without scoring	3	
(on two occasions)		(29/09/09–10/10/09)		
Undefeated	11	Without conceding	3	
(14/11/09–19/01/10)		(22/08/09–05/09/09)		
Without win	5	Scoring	14	
(25/01/10–15/02/10)		(17/10/09–19/01/10)		

CARDS RECEIVED

81 3

EARLIEST STRIKE

DAVID MOONEY
(v Bristol Rovers) 3:16

LATEST STRIKE

THERRY RACON
(v Bristol Rovers) 96:26

GOALS SCORED/CONCEDED
PER FIVE-MINUTE INTERVALS

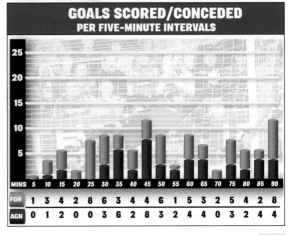

MINS	5	10	15	20	25	30	35	40	45	50	55	60	65	70	75	80	85	90
FOR	1	3	4	2	8	6	3	4	4	6	1	5	3	2	5	4	2	8
AGN	0	1	2	0	0	3	6	2	8	3	2	4	4	0	3	2	4	4

COLCHESTER UNITED

COLCHESTER'S season began in spectacular fashion before a poor second half of the campaign cost them a shot at promotion.

The fall-out of the sensational 7–1 opening-day win at Norwich was that the Canaries sacked their own manager and promptly tempted U's boss Paul Lambert across East Anglia. Unfortunately for Colchester, while the Carrow Road club celebrated romping to the title, the U's fell away.

Aidy Boothroyd came in to replace Lambert at the start of September and, for a while, the transition was seamless. The U's were unbeaten in Boothroyd's first nine matches and moved up to third place.

However, cracks started to appear when they were thrashed 7–0 by Preston and 5–0 by Lambert's Norwich at the start of 2010, and a run of just two wins from their final 15 matches saw them slip out of the play-off picture.

Boothroyd departed for Coventry in May, with his former assistant John Ward taking over.

CLUB SUMMARY

FORMED	1937
MANAGER	John Ward
GROUND	Community Stadium
CAPACITY	10,064
NICKNAME	The U's
WEBSITE	www.cu-fc.com

The New Football Pools PLAYER OF THE SEASON — **Anthony Wordsworth**

OVERALL
P	W	D	L	F	A	GD
51	22	13	16	71	62	9

COCA-COLA FOOTBALL LEAGUE 1
Pos	P	W	D	L	F	A	GD	Pts
8	46	20	12	14	64	52	12	72

HOME
Pos	P	W	D	L	F	A	GD	Pts
5	23	15	5	3	37	21	16	50

AWAY
Pos	P	W	D	L	F	A	GD	Pts
14	23	5	7	11	27	31	-4	22

CUP PROGRESS DETAILS
Competition	Round reached	Knocked out by
FA Cup	R3	Preston
Carling Cup	R1	Leyton Orient
JP Trophy	R1	Gillingham

BIGGEST WIN (ALL COMPS)
08/08/09 7–1 v Norwich

BIGGEST DEFEAT (ALL COMPS)
02/01/10 0–7 v Preston

ATTENDANCE RECORD
High	Average	Low
10,064	5,530	3,601
v Norwich (16/01/2010)		v Milton Keynes Dons (26/01/2010)

RESULTS 2009/10

AUGUST
8th	● Norwich	A	W 1–7	Att: 25,217	Scorers: Fox, Lisbie2, Perkins, Platt2, Vernon. Booked: Tierney, Fox.
11th	● Leyton Orient	H	L 1–2	Att: 3,308	Scorers: Hackney. Dismissed: Platt.
15th	● Yeovil	H	W 2–1	Att: 4,263	Scorers: Fox, Vincent. Booked: Hackney, Vincent.
18th	● Gillingham	H	W 2–1	Att: 4,849	Scorers: Lisbie, Vernon.
22nd	● Milton Keynes Dons	A	L 2–1	Att: 8,633	Scorers: Vernon.
29th	● Leeds	H	L 1–2	Att: 8,810	Scorers: Lisbie. Booked: Maybury, Izzet, Vincent, Tierney, Perkins.

SEPTEMBER
1st	● Gillingham	A	D 1–1	Att: 1,725	Scorers: Platt. Booked: Izzet, Wordsworth. Gillingham win 4–3 on penalties.
5th	● Southampton	A	D 0–0	Att: 17,070	Booked: Lisbie, Vincent. Dismissed: Izzet.
12th	● Swindon	A	D 1–1	Att: 6,621	Scorers: Vincent. Booked: Wordsworth.
19th	● Hartlepool	H	W 2–0	Att: 4,259	Scorers: Lisbie2. Booked: Tierney.
26th	● Tranmere	A	D 1–1	Att: 5,314	Scorers: O'Toole. Booked: Lisbie, Wordsworth, O'Toole, Tierney.
29th	● Charlton	H	W 3–0	Att: 7,098	Scorers: Odejayi2, Llera OG.

OCTOBER
3rd	● Huddersfield	H	W 1–0	Att: 5,154	Scorers: Odejayi. Booked: Batth.
10th	● Leyton Orient	A	W 0–1	Att: 5,410	Scorers: Odejayi. Booked: Platt, O'Toole.
17th	● Wycombe	A	D 1–1	Att: 5,394	Scorers: Odejayi. Booked: Batth, Tierney, O'Toole, Wordsworth, White.
24th	● Walsall	H	W 2–1	Att: 4,880	Scorers: Lisbie2.
31st	● Millwall	A	L 2–1	Att: 10,036	Scorers: Wordsworth. Booked: O'Toole, Wordsworth.

NOVEMBER
7th	● Bromley	A	W 0–4	Att: 4,242	Scorers: Gillespie, Hackney, Odejayi, Platt. Booked: O'Toole, Okuonghae.
14th	● Exeter	H	D 2–2	Att: 5,208	Scorers: Platt2. Booked: Platt, Payne. Dismissed: Elito.
21st	● Oldham	A	D 2–2	Att: 3,607	Scorers: Fox, Odejayi. Booked: Tierney, White. Dismissed: Tierney.
24th	● Stockport	H	W 2–0	Att: 3,818	Scorers: Lisbie, Platt. Booked: Izzet.
28th	● Hereford	A	W 0–1	Att: 2,225	Scorers: Lisbie. Booked: Izzet, O'Toole.

DECEMBER
1st	● Brentford	A	L 1–0	Att: 4,200	Booked: Wordsworth, O'Toole.
5th	● Bristol Rovers	H	W 1–0	Att: 4,942	Scorers: Lisbie. Booked: O'Toole.
11th	● Brighton	A	W 1–2	Att: 5,898	Scorers: Ifil, Wordsworth. Booked: Wordsworth, Platt, Hackney, Okuonghae.
26th	● Southend	A	W 1–2	Att: 10,329	Scorers: Ifil, Wordsworth. Booked: O'Toole, Reid.
28th	● Southampton	H	W 2–1	Att: 8,514	Scorers: Gillespie, Wordsworth. Booked: O'Toole.

JANUARY
2nd	● Preston	A	L 7–0	Att: 7,621	Booked: Thomas.
16th	● Norwich	H	L 0–5	Att: 10,064	Booked: Okuonghae, Platt, Tierney, Lisbie, Batth, Izzet. Dismissed: Henderson.
23rd	● Gillingham	A	D 0–0	Att: 4,948	Booked: Izzet, Gillespie.
26th	● Milton Keynes Dons	H	W 2–0	Att: 3,601	Scorers: Lisbie, Prutton. Booked: Prutton.
30th	● Leeds	A	L 2–0	Att: 23,425	Booked: Izzet.

FEBRUARY
2nd	● Carlisle	H	W 2–1	Att: 3,903	Scorers: Odejayi, Platt. Booked: Platt.
8th	● Southend	H	W 2–0	Att: 6,466	Scorers: Wordsworth2. Booked: Izzet.
13th	● Stockport	A	D 2–2	Att: 3,642	Scorers: Prutton, Wordsworth. Booked: Okuonghae.
16th	● Yeovil	A	W 0–1	Att: 3,469	Scorers: Odejayi. Booked: Prutton.
20th	● Oldham	H	W 1–0	Att: 5,321	Scorers: Batth. Booked: Prutton.
27th	● Bristol Rovers	A	L 3–2	Att: 6,023	Scorers: O'Toole, Odejayi. Booked: Wordsworth, Batth, Ifil, Tierney.

MARCH
8th	● Brighton	H	D 0–0	Att: 3,914	Booked: Prutton, Izzet, White.
13th	● Carlisle	A	L 2–1	Att: 4,469	Scorers: Platt. Booked: Henderson.
20th	● Walsall	A	L 1–0	Att: 3,510	Booked: Prutton.
23rd	● Brentford	H	D 3–3	Att: 3,915	Scorers: Prutton, Wordsworth, Hunt OG. Booked: Lisbie.
27th	● Wycombe	H	D 1–1	Att: 5,593	Scorers: Henderson. Booked: Gillespie, Izzet, Williams, Prutton.

APRIL
2nd	● Exeter	A	L 2–0	Att: 6,297	Booked: Izzet, Gillespie.
5th	● Millwall	H	L 1–2	Att: 7,393	Scorers: Lisbie. Booked: Lisbie, Wordsworth, White.
10th	● Swindon	A	W 3–0	Att: 5,111	Scorers: Vincent, Wordsworth2. Booked: Wordsworth, Izzet.
13th	● Charlton	A	L 1–0	Att: 17,427	Booked: Lisbie, Vincent, White. Dismissed: Lisbie.
17th	● Hartlepool	A	L 3–1	Att: 3,126	Scorers: Henderson. Booked: Okuonghae, Hackney.
24th	● Tranmere	H	D 1–1	Att: 4,353	Scorers: Wordsworth. Booked: Prutton, Lisbie, Gillespie, Izzet. Dismissed: Prutton.

MAY
1st	● Huddersfield	A	L 2–1	Att: 17,950	Scorers: Hackney. Booked: Reid, Tierney.
8th	● Leyton Orient	H	W 1–0	Att: 5,751	Scorers: Lisbie. Booked: Lisbie.

● Coca-Cola League 1/Play-Offs ● FA Cup ● Carling Cup ● Johnstone's Paint Trophy

actim

Coca-Cola LEAGUE 1

LEAGUE 1 GOALKEEPER STATS

Player	Appearances	Match starts	Completed matches	Sub appearances	Subbed off	Clean sheets	Yellow cards	Red cards
Ben Williams	46	46	46	0	0	15	1	0

LEAGUE 1 OUTFIELD PLAYER STATS

Player	Appearances	Match starts	Completed matches	Substitute appearances	Subbed off	Goals scored	Yellow cards	Red cards
Pat Baldwin	7	6	5	1	1	0	0	0
Danny Batth	17	16	12	1	4	1	4	0
Lee Beevers	4	4	3	0	1	0	0	0
Thomas Bender	1	0	0	1	0	0	0	0
Medy Elito	3	0	0	3	0	0	0	1
David Fox	18	15	9	3	6	3	1	0
Steven Gillespie	30	8	0	22	8	1	4	0
Jamie Guy	1	0	0	1	1	0	0	0
Simon Hackney	17	9	3	8	6	1	3	0
Dean Hammond	2	2	2	0	0	0	0	0
Matt Heath	18	13	13	5	0	0	0	0
Ian Henderson	13	6	0	7	5	2	1	0
Philip Ifil	27	15	7	12	8	2	1	0
Kemal Izzet	37	31	27	6	3	0	10	1
Kevin Lisbie	41	35	20	6	14	13	8	1
Matthew Lockwood	1	1	0	0	1	0	0	0
Alan Maybury	2	1	1	1	0	0	1	0
John-Joe O'Toole	31	30	27	1	3	2	8	0
Kayode Odejayi	28	19	7	9	12	9	0	0
Magnus Okuonghae	44	44	43	0	1	0	4	0
Josh Payne	3	2	0	1	2	0	1	0
David Perkins	5	0	0	5	0	1	1	0
Clive Platt	41	36	19	5	17	7	5	0
David Prutton	19	18	16	1	1	3	7	1
Franck Queudrue	3	3	2	0	1	0	0	0
Paul Reid	12	10	10	2	0	0	2	0
Christian Ribeiro	2	2	1	0	1	0	0	0
Joel Thomas	4	0	0	4	0	0	0	0
Marc Tierney	41	41	40	0	0	0	9	1
Scott Vernon	7	4	2	3	2	3	0	0
Ashley Vincent	19	15	4	4	11	3	4	0
John White	39	38	34	1	4	0	5	0
Anthony Wordsworth	41	36	31	5	5	11	9	0

League position graph (AUG–MAY)

LEAGUE POSITION AT THE END OF EACH MONTH: 5 4 4 3 4 4 4 6 8 8

SEASON INFORMATION
- Highest position: 1
- Lowest position: 9
- Average goals scored per game: 1.39
- Average goals conceded per game: 1.13

LONGEST SEQUENCES

Wins (05/12/09–28/12/09)	4	Undefeated home (19/09/09–28/12/09)	8
Losses (on four occasions)	2	Undefeated away (05/09/09–17/10/09)	5
Draws (on three occasions)	2	Without scoring (16/01/10–23/01/10)	2
Undefeated (05/09/09–24/10/09)	9	Without conceding (29/09/09–10/10/09)	3
Without win (27/02/10–05/04/10)	8	Scoring (12/09/09–24/11/09)	12

CARDS RECEIVED

89 6

EARLIEST STRIKE
ANTHONY WORDSWORTH
(v Southend) 2:58

LATEST STRIKE
KAYODE ODEJAYI
(v Carlisle) 91:52

GOALS SCORED/CONCEDED
PER FIVE-MINUTE INTERVALS

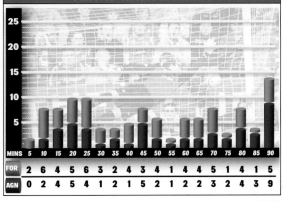

MINS	5	10	15	20	25	30	35	40	45	50	55	60	65	70	75	80	85	90
FOR	2	6	4	5	6	3	2	4	3	4	1	4	4	5	1	4	1	5
AGN	0	2	4	5	4	1	2	1	5	2	1	2	2	3	2	4	3	9

EXETER CITY

LIFE in Coca-Cola League 1 was never going to be easy for Exeter after Paul Tisdale had led the club to two successive promotions, but they survived in dramatic style on the last afternoon of the season.

Relegation appeared to be almost certain when the Grecians were being held 1–1 by high-flying Huddersfield at half-time in their final game, but Ryan Harley netted a late winning goal to secure the club's status for another season.

The final stages of the campaign were emotional for the Grecians after star striker Adam Stansfield was diagnosed with bowel cancer in April. Stansfield later underwent a successful operation to remove part of his colon and the fans will be hoping to see him back in action in the coming season.

Exeter picked up some big results along the road to survival, including a 2–0 win over Leeds, and they will be looking to consolidate in 2010/11 to avoid such a tense finale.

CLUB SUMMARY

FORMED	1904
MANAGER	Paul Tisdale
GROUND	St James Park
CAPACITY	8,830
NICKNAME	The Grecians
WEBSITE	www.exetercityfc.co.uk

The New Football Pools PLAYER OF THE SEASON — Ryan Harley

OVERALL
P	W	D	L	F	A	GD
50	12	19	19	56	70	-14

COCA-COLA FOOTBALL LEAGUE 1
Pos	P	W	D	L	F	A	GD	Pts
18	46	11	18	17	48	60	-12	51

HOME
Pos	P	W	D	L	F	A	GD	Pts
13	23	9	10	4	30	20	10	37

AWAY
Pos	P	W	D	L	F	A	GD	Pts
21	23	2	8	13	18	40	-22	14

CUP PROGRESS DETAILS
Competition	Round reached	Knocked out by
FA Cup	R2	Milton Keynes Dons
Carling Cup	R1	QPR
JP Trophy	R2	Swindon

BIGGEST WIN (ALL COMPS)
07/11/09 4–0 v Nuneaton

BIGGEST DEFEAT (ALL COMPS)
11/08/09 0–5 v QPR

ATTENDANCE RECORD
HIGH	AVERAGE	LOW
8,549	5,832	4,106
v Leeds (16/01/2010)		v Carlisle (26/01/2010)

RESULTS 2009/10

AUGUST
8th	● Leeds	A	L 2–1	Att: 27,681	Scorers: Russell. Booked: Edwards, Golbourne, Harley. Dismissed: Corr.
11th	● QPR	H	L 0–5	Att: 4,614	Dismissed: Golbourne.
15th	● Norwich	H	D 1–1	Att: 6,357	Scorers: Logan. Booked: Harley.
18th	● Yeovil	H	D 1–1	Att: 6,650	Scorers: Stam OG.
22nd	● Carlisle	A	W 0–1	Att: 5,156	Scorers: Stewart. Booked: Logan.
29th	● Milton Keynes Dons	H	L 1–2	Att: 5,333	Scorers: Corr. Booked: Corr, M Taylor.

SEPTEMBER
5th	● Gillingham	A	L 3–0	Att: 5,107	Booked: Duffy.
12th	● Leyton Orient	A	D 1–1	Att: 4,703	Scorers: Noone. Booked: Russell, Duffy.
19th	● Tranmere	H	W 2–1	Att: 4,901	Scorers: Stansfield[2]. Booked: Seaborne.
26th	● Charlton	A	L 2–1	Att: 16,867	Scorers: Cozic. Booked: Archibald-Henville.
29th	● Swindon	H	D 1–1	Att: 5,337	Scorers: Logan. Booked: Archibald-Henville.

OCTOBER
3rd	● Hartlepool	H	W 3–1	Att: 4,706	Scorers: Dunne, Fleetwood, Harley. Booked: Fleetwood.
6th	● Swindon	H	D 1–1	Att: 2,006	Scorers: Fleetwood. Booked: Cozic. Swindon win 4–3 on penalties.
10th	● Huddersfield	A	L 4–0	Att: 13,438	
17th	● Walsall	A	L 3–0	Att: 4,063	Booked: Duffy. Dismissed: Duffy.
24th	● Wycombe	H	D 1–1	Att: 5,227	Scorers: Corr. Booked: Logan, Edwards, Corr.
31st	● Brentford	H	W 3–0	Att: 5,355	Scorers: Cozic, Noone, Tully. Booked: Stewart. Dismissed: Stewart.

NOVEMBER
7th	● Nuneaton	A	W 0–4	Att: 2,452	Scorers: Corr, M Taylor[2], Hadland OG.
14th	● Colchester	A	D 2–2	Att: 5,208	Scorers: Fleetwood, Harley.
21st	● Stockport	A	W 1–3	Att: 4,101	Scorers: Harley, Logan, Stansfield. Booked: Cozic.
24th	● Millwall	H	D 1–1	Att: 5,732	Scorers: Stansfield. Booked: Tully, Fleetwood, Corr. Dismissed: Tully.
28th	● Milton Keynes Dons	A	L 4–3	Att: 4,867	Scorers: Corr[2], Stansfield. Booked: Russell, Dunne.

DECEMBER
1st	● Bristol Rovers	A	L 1–0	Att: 7,313	
5th	● Brighton	H	L 0–1	Att: 5,456	
12th	● Oldham	A	L 2–0	Att: 6,230	Booked: Duffy.
19th	● Southend	H	W 1–0	Att: 4,839	Scorers: Stansfield. Booked: Duffy. Dismissed: Corr.
26th	● Southampton	A	L 3–1	Att: 30,890	Scorers: M Taylor. Booked: Stewart, Seaborne. Dismissed: Archibald-Henville.
28th	● Gillingham	H	D 1–1	Att: 5,761	Scorers: Duffy. Booked: Cozic.

JANUARY
9th	● Norwich	A	L 3–1	Att: 24,955	Scorers: Stewart. Booked: Duffy, Stewart.
16th	● Leeds	H	W 2–0	Att: 8,549	Scorers: Harley[2]. Booked: Stewart.
23rd	● Yeovil	A	L 2–1	Att: 6,282	Scorers: Stansfield. Booked: Duffy.
26th	● Carlisle	H	L 2–3	Att: 4,106	Scorers: Harley, Stansfield.
30th	● Milton Keynes Dons	A	D 1–1	Att: 8,740	Scorers: Corr. Booked: M Taylor, Logan, Stansfield.

FEBRUARY
6th	● Southampton	H	D 1–1	Att: 7,654	Scorers: M Taylor.
13th	● Millwall	A	L 1–0	Att: 9,104	Booked: M Taylor, Duffy, Cozic. Dismissed: Corr.
20th	● Stockport	H	L 0–1	Att: 4,990	Booked: Logan.
27th	● Brighton	A	L 2–0	Att: 6,952	Booked: Edwards, Duffy, Harley, Dunne.

MARCH
6th	● Oldham	H	D 1–1	Att: 4,997	Scorers: Harley. Booked: Golbourne, Dunne.
13th	● Southend	A	D 0–0	Att: 6,761	
17th	● Bristol Rovers	H	W 1–0	Att: 5,269	Scorers: Dunne. Booked: Duffy.
20th	● Wycombe	A	D 2–2	Att: 5,054	Scorers: Logan, Sercombe. Booked: Logan.
27th	● Walsall	H	W 2–1	Att: 5,887	Scorers: Harley, M Taylor. Booked: M Taylor, Edwards, Tully.

APRIL
2nd	● Colchester	H	W 2–0	Att: 6,297	Scorers: Fleetwood, Harley. Booked: Dunne.
5th	● Brentford	A	D 0–0	Att: 6,017	
10th	● Leyton Orient	H	D 0–0	Att: 5,522	Booked: Golbourne, Tully.
12th	● Swindon	A	D 1–1	Att: 8,753	Scorers: Dunne. Booked: Golbourne, R Taylor, Burnell.
17th	● Tranmere	A	L 3–1	Att: 5,466	Scorers: Fleetwood. Booked: Dunne. Dismissed: Dunne.
24th	● Charlton	H	D 1–1	Att: 6,835	Scorers: Friend. Booked: Duffy.

MAY
1st	● Hartlepool	A	D 1–1	Att: 3,983	Scorers: M Taylor. Booked: Tully.
8th	● Huddersfield	H	W 2–1	Att: 8,383	Scorers: Harley, M Taylor.

● Coca-Cola League 1/Play-Offs ● FA Cup ● Carling Cup ● Johnstone's Paint Trophy

actim

Coca-Cola LEAGUE 1

LEAGUE 1 GOALKEEPER STATS

Player	Appearances	Match starts	Completed matches	Sub appearances	Subbed off	Clean sheets	Yellow cards	Red cards
Oscar Jansson	7	7	7	0	0	0	0	0
Paul Jones	26	26	26	0	0	8	0	0
Andy Marriott	13	13	13	0	0	1	0	0

LEAGUE 1 OUTFIELD PLAYER STATS

Player	Appearances	Match starts	Completed matches	Substitute appearances	Subbed off	Goals scored	Yellow cards	Red cards
Troy Archibald-Henville	15	13	9	2	3	0	2	1
Joe Burnell	8	4	0	4	4	0	1	0
Barry Corr	34	17	4	17	10	3	3	3
Bertrand Cozic	29	21	10	8	11	2	3	1
Richard Duffy	42	41	37	1	3	1	11	1
James Dunne	23	18	11	5	6	3	4	1
Rob Edwards	21	17	11	4	6	0	4	0
Stuart Fleetwood	27	16	1	11	15	4	2	0
George Friend	13	13	12	0	1	1	0	0
Scott Golbourne	34	30	29	4	1	0	4	0
Marcus Haber	5	3	0	2	3	0	0	0
Ryan Harley	44	43	41	1	2	10	3	0
Richard Logan	34	4	2	30	2	4	5	0
Craig McAllister	4	0	0	4	0	0	0	0
Craig Noone	7	7	3	0	4	2	0	0
James Norwood	3	2	0	1	2	0	0	0
Alex Russell	29	27	20	2	7	1	1	0
Neil Saunders	6	2	1	4	1	0	0	0
Daniel Seaborne	19	17	17	2	0	0	2	0
Liam Sercombe	28	25	23	3	2	1	0	0
Adam Stansfield	27	19	6	8	13	7	1	0
Marcus Stewart	41	36	16	5	19	2	4	1
Matthew Taylor	46	46	45	0	1	5	4	0
Ryan Taylor	7	3	0	4	3	0	1	0
Steve Tully	38	36	29	2	6	1	4	1
Ben Watson	1	0	0	1	0	0	0	0

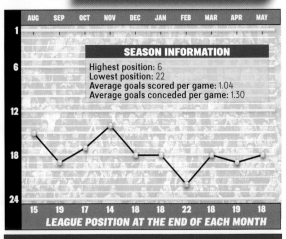

| AUG | SEP | OCT | NOV | DEC | JAN | FEB | MAR | APR | MAY |

SEASON INFORMATION
Highest position: 6
Lowest position: 22
Average goals scored per game: 1.04
Average goals conceded per game: 1.30

LEAGUE POSITION AT THE END OF EACH MONTH

| 15 | 19 | 17 | 14 | 18 | 18 | 22 | 18 | 19 | 18 |

LONGEST SEQUENCES

Wins	2		Undefeated home	7	
(27/03/10–02/04/10)			(06/03/10–08/05/10)		
Losses	3		Undefeated away	4	
(on two occasions)			(13/03/10–12/04/10)		
Draws	3		Without scoring	3	
(05/04/10–12/04/10)			(on two occasions)		
Undefeated	9		Without conceding	3	
(06/03/10–12/04/10)			(02/04/10–10/04/10)		
Without win	9		Scoring	9	
(23/01/10–13/03/10)			(19/12/09–06/02/10)		

CARDS RECEIVED

59 **8**

EARLIEST STRIKE
RYAN HARLEY
(v Leeds) 3:46

LATEST STRIKE
RICHARD LOGAN
(v Stockport) 93:35

GOALS SCORED/CONCEDED
PER FIVE-MINUTE INTERVALS

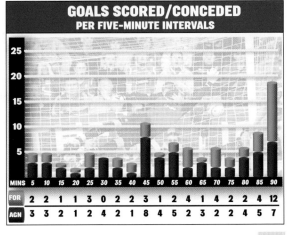

MINS	5	10	15	20	25	30	35	40	45	50	55	60	65	70	75	80	85	90
FOR	2	2	1	1	3	0	2	2	3	1	2	4	1	4	2	2	4	12
AGN	3	3	2	1	2	4	2	1	8	4	5	2	3	2	2	4	5	7

GILLINGHAM

GILLINGHAM suffered the heartbreak of relegation on the final day of the season despite heading into their last game at Wycombe two points above the drop zone.

The Gills needed just a point to ensure they would not make an immediate return to npower League Two, but their poor away form cost them yet again as they suffered a 3–0 defeat to go down on goal difference. Manager Mark Stimson was sacked two days later on the back of a campaign in which they failed to win a single game away from the Priestfield Stadium.

The Gills began the season in some style with a 5–0 victory at home to Swindon when star striker Simeon Jackson netted a hat-trick.

They had looked destined to retain their League 1 status when they won their final two home games, but it was not to be as last-day heartache loomed.

Andy Hessenthaler, who had managed the club from 2000–04, returned to Priestfield in the summer as Stimson's replacement.

CLUB SUMMARY

FORMED	1893
MANAGER	Andy Hessenthaler
GROUND	Priestfield Stadium
CAPACITY	11,582
NICKNAME	The Gills
WEBSITE	www.gillinghamfootballclub.com

The New **Football Pools** PLAYER OF THE SEASON — *Simeon Jackson*

OVERALL
P	W	D	L	F	A	GD
53	15	15	23	56	71	-15

COCA-COLA FOOTBALL LEAGUE 1
Pos	P	W	D	L	F	A	GD	Pts
21	46	12	14	20	48	64	-16	50

HOME
Pos	P	W	D	L	F	A	GD	Pts
9	23	12	8	3	35	15	20	44

AWAY
Pos	P	W	D	L	F	A	GD	Pts
24	23	0	6	17	13	49	-36	6

CUP PROGRESS DETAILS
Competition	Round reached	Knocked out by
FA Cup	R3	Accrington
Carling Cup	R2	Blackburn
JP Trophy	R2	Norwich

BIGGEST WIN (ALL COMPS)
08/08/09 5–0 v Swindon

BIGGEST DEFEAT (ALL COMPS)
0–4 on 2 occasions

ATTENDANCE RECORD
HIGH	AVERAGE	Low
10,304	6,335	3,840
v Charlton (24/10/2009)		v Tranmere (09/02/2010)

RESULTS 2009/10

AUGUST
8th	● Swindon	H	W 5–0	Att: 6,852	Scorers: Bentley, Jackson³, Miller.
11th	● Plymouth	H	W 2–1	Att: 3,306	Scorers: Barcham, Jackson. Booked: Richards.
15th	● Tranmere	A	L 4–2	Att: 5,590	Scorers: Barcham, Weston. Booked: Barcham.
18th	● Colchester	A	L 2–1	Att: 4,849	Scorers: Weston.
22nd	● Hartlepool	H	L 0–1	Att: 4,969	Booked: Miller, Nutter.
25th	● Blackburn	H	L 1–3	Att: 7,293	Scorers: Jackson. Booked: Gowling, Fuller.
29th	● Walsall	A	D 0–0	Att: 3,331	Booked: Oli, Gowling.

SEPTEMBER
1st	● Colchester	H	D 1–1	Att: 1,725	Scorers: Jackson. Booked: Rooney. Gillingham win 4–3 on penalties.
5th	● Exeter	H	W 3–0	Att: 5,107	Scorers: Jackson², Rooney.
12th	● Millwall	H	W 2–0	Att: 8,097	Scorers: Barcham, Weston.
19th	● Leeds	A	L 4–1	Att: 21,026	Scorers: Barcham.
26th	● Norwich	H	D 1–1	Att: 7,550	Scorers: Jackson. Booked: Fuller, Bentley, Gowling.

OCTOBER
3rd	● Southampton	A	L 4–1	Att: 19,457	Scorers: Rooney. Booked: Weston, Gowling.
6th	● Norwich	H	L 0–1	Att: 2,814	Booked: Miller, Nutter, Weston.
10th	● Wycombe	H	W 3–2	Att: 5,316	Scorers: Gowling, Jackson, Weston. Booked: Bentley, Payne, Oli, Jackson.
13th	● Brighton	A	L 2–0	Att: 5,960	Booked: Miller, Fuller, Lewis.
17th	● Milton Keynes Dons	A	L 2–0	Att: 11,764	
24th	● Charlton	H	D 1–1	Att: 10,304	Scorers: Jackson. Booked: Nutter, Weston, Gowling.
30th	● Southend	A	L 1–0	Att: 7,830	Booked: Fry, Nutter, Gowling, Oli, Fuller.

NOVEMBER
7th	● Southend	H	W 3–0	Att: 4,605	Scorers: Bentley, Brandy, Weston. Booked: Fry, Fuller.
14th	● Oldham	H	W 1–0	Att: 4,787	Scorers: Weston.
21st	● Bristol Rovers	A	L 2–1	Att: 6,210	Scorers: Barcham. Booked: Fry, Gowling, McCammon.
24th	● Yeovil	A	W 1–0	Att: 4,450	Scorers: Jackson. Booked: Gowling, Brandy.
28th	● Burton Albion	H	W 1–0	Att: 4,996	Scorers: Weston. Booked: Weston.

DECEMBER
1st	● Leyton Orient	A	L 3–1	Att: 3,183	Scorers: Weston.
5th	● Carlisle	H	D 0–0	Att: 7,214	Booked: Fuller, Jackson, Gowling.
12th	● Huddersfield	A	L 2–1	Att: 13,844	Scorers: Jackson. Booked: Fry, Maher.
19th	● Stockport	H	W 3–1	Att: 4,769	Scorers: Brandy, Nutter, Oli. Booked: Jackson, Fry.
26th	● Brentford	H	L 0–1	Att: 7,019	Booked: Gowling, Weston, Fuller. Dismissed: Gowling.
28th	● Exeter	A	D 1–1	Att: 5,761	Scorers: Lewis. Booked: McCammon.

JANUARY
16th	● Swindon	A	L 3–1	Att: 6,773	Scorers: Palmer. Booked: Bentley.
19th	● Accrington Stanley	A	L 1–0	Att: 1,322	Booked: Bentley.
23rd	● Colchester	H	D 0–0	Att: 4,948	Booked: Barcham, Wynter.
26th	● Hartlepool	A	D 1–1	Att: 2,465	Scorers: Jackson. Booked: Howe, Jackson.
30th	● Walsall	H	D 0–0	Att: 4,796	Booked: Wynter.

FEBRUARY
6th	● Brentford	A	L 4–0	Att: 6,036	Booked: Maher, Payne, Rooney.
9th	● Tranmere	H	L 0–1	Att: 3,840	Booked: Weston, Bentley, Dennehy.
13th	● Yeovil	A	D 0–0	Att: 3,853	Booked: Miller.
20th	● Bristol Rovers	H	W 1–0	Att: 5,302	Scorers: Jackson. Booked: Nutter, Fuller.
23rd	● Leyton Orient	H	D 1–1	Att: 4,753	Scorers: Dickson. Booked: Dickson.
27th	● Carlisle	A	L 2–1	Att: 4,646	

MARCH
6th	● Huddersfield	H	W 2–0	Att: 5,388	Scorers: Jackson². Booked: Lewis, Weston.
13th	● Stockport	A	D 0–0	Att: 3,894	Booked: Miller.
20th	● Charlton	A	D 2–2	Att: 20,024	Scorers: Barcham, Oli. Booked: Oli, Weston.
27th	● Milton Keynes Dons	H	D 2–2	Att: 5,465	Scorers: Barcham, Miller. Booked: Nutter, Oli, Howe. Dismissed: Oli.

APRIL
3rd	● Oldham	A	L 1–0	Att: 3,486	Booked: Howe, Nutter.
5th	● Southend	H	W 3–0	Att: 7,657	Scorers: Barcham, Howe, Oli. Booked: Weston, Barcham, Jackman.
10th	● Millwall	A	L 4–0	Att: 13,174	Booked: Miller.
13th	● Brighton	H	D 1–1	Att: 7,977	Scorers: Miller. Booked: Miller. Dismissed: Gowling.
17th	● Leeds	H	W 3–2	Att: 9,649	Scorers: Bentley, Miller, Naylor OG. Booked: Payne.
24th	● Norwich	A	L 2–0	Att: 25,227	Booked: Weston, Dennehy.

MAY
1st	● Southampton	H	W 2–1	Att: 9,504	Scorers: Gowling, Howe. Booked: Howe.
8th	● Wycombe	A	L 3–0	Att: 7,110	Booked: Gowling, Howe, Payne, Miller.

● Coca-Cola League 1/Play-Offs ● FA Cup ● Carling Cup ● Johnstone's Paint Trophy

actim

LEAGUE 1 GOALKEEPER STATS

Player	Appearances	Match starts	Completed matches	Sub appearances	Subbed off	Clean sheets	Yellow cards	Red cards
Alan Julian	30	30	29	0	1	8	0	0
Simon Royce	17	16	16	1	0	6	0	0

LEAGUE 1 OUTFIELD PLAYER STATS

Player	Appearances	Match starts	Completed matches	Substitute appearances	Subbed off	Goals scored	Yellow cards	Red cards
Andy Barcham	42	38	33	4	5	7	3	0
Mark Bentley	36	34	24	2	10	2	4	0
Febian Brandy	7	5	2	2	3	1	1	0
Darren Dennehy	19	19	17	0	2	0	2	0
Chris Dickson	9	4	2	5	2	1	1	0
Jacob Erskine	4	0	0	4	0	0	0	0
Matt Fry	11	11	10	0	1	0	4	0
Barry Fuller	36	35	32	1	3	0	6	0
Josh Gowling	30	29	27	1	0	2	10	2
Rene Howe	18	18	9	0	9	2	5	0
Danny Jackman	22	21	17	1	4	0	1	0
Simeon Jackson	42	34	29	8	5	14	4	0
Stuart Lewis	20	16	11	4	5	1	2	0
Kevin Maher	26	21	13	5	8	0	2	0
Mark McCammon	14	3	1	11	2	0	2	0
Adam Miller	26	22	17	4	5	4	7	0
John Nutter	35	32	30	3	2	1	6	0
Dennis Oli	36	23	10	13	12	3	5	1
Chris Palmer	20	16	14	4	2	1	0	0
Jack Payne	19	14	10	5	4	0	4	0
Tristan Plummer	2	2	0	0	2	0	0	0
Garry Richards	16	16	14	0	2	0	2	0
Luke Rooney	13	2	0	11	2	2	1	0
Scott Vernon	1	1	0	0	1	0	0	0
James Walker	5	2	0	3	2	0	0	0
Curtis Weston	39	36	26	3	10	6	8	0
Tom Wynter	8	4	3	4	1	0	2	0
Rashid Yussuff	8	2	2	6	0	0	0	0

AUG SEP OCT NOV DEC JAN FEB MAR APR MAY

SEASON INFORMATION
Highest position: 2
Lowest position: 22
Average goals scored per game: 1.04
Average goals conceded per game: 1.39

LEAGUE POSITION AT THE END OF EACH MONTH
18 13 19 15 17 19 18 17 20 21

LONGEST SEQUENCES

Wins	2	Undefeated home	9
(05/09/09–12/09/09)		(05/09/09–19/12/09)	
Losses	3	Undefeated away	2
(15/08/09–22/08/09)		(13/03/10–20/03/10)	
Draws	3	Without scoring	4
(on two occasions)		(30/01/10–13/02/10)	
Undefeated	4	Without conceding	3
(06/03/10–27/03/10)		(29/08/09–12/09/09)	
Without win	9	Scoring	6
(26/12/09–13/02/10)		(05/09/09–10/10/09)	

CARDS RECEIVED
80   3

EARLIEST STRIKE
SIMEON JACKSON
(v Huddersfield) 2:42

LATEST STRIKE
SIMEON JACKSON
(v Bristol Rovers) 91:52

GOALS SCORED/CONCEDED
PER FIVE-MINUTE INTERVALS

MINS	5	10	15	20	25	30	35	40	45	50	55	60	65	70	75	80	85	90
FOR	2	6	2	4	0	3	4	3	2	5	3	0	2	2	2	2	3	3
AGN	3	1	2	2	1	4	5	3	7	3	2	3	6	4	6	5	2	5

HARTLEPOOL UNITED

HARTLEPOOL'S survival went down to the wire for the second successive season, with the club only avoiding relegation on goal difference following a controversial points deduction.

Director of sport Chris Turner had promised changes after a nailbiting end to the 2008/09 campaign and he kept his word, bringing 14 new faces to Victoria Park at different points during the season. The most inspired signing was striker Roy O'Donovan, on loan from Sunderland, but even his nine goals in 15 games could not prevent another nervy finish.

Pools' cause was not helped by the deduction of three points after they had selected suspended defender Gary Liddle in a 2–0 win against Brighton.

Season highlights included an O'Donovan hat-trick against Southend in March and Antony Sweeney's last-gasp header to rescue a point at home to Leeds, but it was the point from a 0–0 draw at Brentford on the final day of the campaign that ultimately proved vital.

CLUB SUMMARY

FORMED	1908
MANAGER	Chris Turner
GROUND	Victoria Park
CAPACITY	7,691
NICKNAME	The Pools
WEBSITE	www.hartlepoolunited.co.uk

The New Football Pools
PLAYER OF THE SEASON

Andy Monkhouse

OVERALL

P	W	D	L	F	A	GD
50	15	11	24	61	72	-11

COCA-COLA FOOTBALL LEAGUE 1

Pos	P	W	D	L	F	A	GD	Pts
20	46	14	11	21	59	67	-8	50

HOME

Pos	P	W	D	L	F	A	GD	Pts
15	23	10	6	7	33	26	7	36

AWAY

Pos	P	W	D	L	F	A	GD	Pts
18	23	4	5	14	26	41	-15	17

CUP PROGRESS DETAILS

Competition	Round reached	Knocked out by
FA Cup	R1	Kettering
Carling Cup	R2	Burnley
JP Trophy	R2	Grimsby

BIGGEST WIN (ALL COMPS)
23/02/10 4–1 v Carlisle

BIGGEST DEFEAT (ALL COMPS)
16/01/10 0–5 v Milton Keynes Dons

ATTENDANCE RECORD

High	Average	Low
5,115	3,444	2,465
v Leeds (06/02/2010)		v Gillingham (26/01/2010)

RESULTS 2009/10

AUGUST

8th	● Milton Keynes Dons	A	D 0–0	Att: 8,965	Booked: Liddle.
12th	● Coventry	A	W 0–1	Att: 6,055	Scorers: Boyd. Booked: Monkhouse.
15th	● Charlton	H	L 0–2	Att: 4,408	Booked: Sweeney, Fredriksen.
18th	● Bristol Rovers	H	L 1–2	Att: 3,137	Scorers: Behan. Booked: Collins, Haslam, Fredriksen.
22nd	● Gillingham	A	W 0–1	Att: 4,969	Scorers: Brown. Booked: Hartley, McSweeney.
25th	● Burnley	H	L 1–2	Att: 3,501	Scorers: Boyd. Booked: Sweeney, Collins. AET – Score after 90 mins 1–1.
29th	● Norwich	H	L 0–2	Att: 4,470	Booked: Monkhouse.

SEPTEMBER

4th	● Oldham	A	W 0–3	Att: 4,014	Scorers: Behan, Brown, McSweeney. Booked: Jones.
12th	● Wycombe	H	D 1–1	Att: 3,326	Scorers: Boyd. Booked: Collins.
19th	● Colchester	A	L 2–0	Att: 4,259	Booked: Monkhouse.
26th	● Walsall	H	W 3–0	Att: 3,334	Scorers: Larkin, Monkhouse[2]. Booked: Flinders.
29th	● Stockport	A	D 2–2	Att: 3,780	Scorers: Behan, Boyd. Booked: Behan.

OCTOBER

3rd	● Exeter	A	L 3–1	Att: 4,706	Scorers: Behan. Booked: Austin, Fredriksen.
6th	● Grimsby	H	L 0–2	Att: 1,675	
9th	● Brentford	H	D 0–0	Att: 3,105	
17th	● Swindon	A	W 0–2	Att: 7,096	Scorers: Brown, Monkhouse. Booked: Jones, Liddle, Monkhouse.
24th	● Tranmere	H	W 1–0	Att: 3,428	Scorers: Hartley. Booked: Behan.
31st	● Brighton	A	D 3–3	Att: 5,694	Scorers: Boyd, Jones, Monkhouse. Booked: Hartley, Behan.

NOVEMBER

7th	● Kettering	H	L 0–1	Att: 2,645	
14th	● Leyton Orient	H	W 1–0	Att: 3,119	Scorers: Boyd. Booked: Liddle, Collins.
21st	● Huddersfield	A	L 2–1	Att: 12,518	Scorers: Liddle. Booked: Boyd, Liddle, Austin.
24th	● Southampton	H	L 1–3	Att: 3,818	Scorers: Monkhouse. Booked: Jones. Dismissed: Jones.

DECEMBER

1st	● Carlisle	A	L 3–2	Att: 4,109	Scorers: Bjornsson, Monkhouse.
5th	● Millwall	H	W 3–0	Att: 3,153	Scorers: Bjornsson, Boyd, Hartley.
12th	● Southend	A	L 3–2	Att: 7,737	Scorers: Boyd, Grant OG. Booked: Clark. Dismissed: Clark.
19th	● Yeovil	H	D 1–1	Att: 2,778	Scorers: Monkhouse. Booked: Monkhouse.
26th	● Leeds	A	L 3–1	Att: 30,191	Scorers: Bjornsson. Booked: McSweeney, Collins, Bjornsson.

JANUARY

2nd	● Oldham	H	W 2–1	Att: 2,634	Scorers: Jones, Monkhouse. Booked: Hartley. Dismissed: Hartley.
16th	● Milton Keynes Dons	H	L 0–5	Att: 3,211	Booked: Liddle, Monkhouse, Austin.
19th	● Charlton	A	L 2–1	Att: 14,636	Scorers: Behan. Booked: Behan, Collins, Monkhouse, Gamble.
23rd	● Bristol Rovers	A	L 2–0	Att: 5,794	Booked: Humphreys, Liddle, Monkhouse.
26th	● Gillingham	H	D 1–1	Att: 2,465	Scorers: Austin. Booked: Collins.
30th	● Norwich	A	L 2–1	Att: 25,506	Scorers: Austin. Booked: Monkhouse, Boyd, Liddle.

FEBRUARY

6th	● Leeds	H	D 2–2	Att: 5,115	Scorers: Boyd, Sweeney. Booked: Austin.
20th	● Huddersfield	H	L 0–2	Att: 4,452	Booked: Liddle, Monkhouse, Gamble.
23rd	● Carlisle	H	W 4–1	Att: 2,975	Scorers: Gamble, Jones[2], Sweeney. Booked: O'Donovan.
27th	● Millwall	A	L 1–0	Att: 10,818	Booked: Liddle.

MARCH

6th	● Southend	H	W 3–0	Att: 3,299	Scorers: O'Donovan[3]. Booked: McSweeney, Sweeney.
13th	● Yeovil	A	L 4–0	Att: 4,169	Booked: Collins, Monkhouse, McSweeney.
19th	● Tranmere	A	D 0–0	Att: 5,409	
23rd	● Southampton	A	L 3–2	Att: 18,072	Scorers: Austin, Monkhouse.
27th	● Swindon	H	L 0–1	Att: 3,536	

APRIL

3rd	● Leyton Orient	A	W 1–3	Att: 3,604	Scorers: Liddle[2], O'Donovan. Booked: Liddle.
5th	● Brighton	H	W 2–0	Att: 3,466	Scorers: Monkhouse, O'Donovan. Booked: Haslam, Bjornsson.
10th	● Wycombe	A	L 2–0	Att: 4,342	
13th	● Stockport	H	W 3–0	Att: 2,869	Scorers: Gamble, Monkhouse, O'Donovan. Booked: McSweeney, Brown.
17th	● Colchester	H	W 3–1	Att: 3,126	Scorers: Brown, O'Donovan[2]. Booked: McSweeney.
24th	● Walsall	A	L 3–1	Att: 3,457	Scorers: O'Donovan. Booked: Collins.

MAY

1st	● Exeter	H	D 1–1	Att: 3,983	Scorers: Behan. Booked: McSweeney, Austin.
8th	● Brentford	A	D 0–0	Att: 6,893	Booked: O'Donovan, McSweeney, Monkhouse, Behan.

● Coca-Cola League 1/Play-Offs ● FA Cup ● Carling Cup ● Johnstone's Paint Trophy

LEAGUE 1 GOALKEEPER STATS

Player	Appearances	Match starts	Completed matches	Sub appearances	Subbed off	Clean sheets	Yellow cards	Red cards
Scott Flinders	46	46	46	0	0	14	1	0

LEAGUE 1 OUTFIELD PLAYER STATS

Player	Appearances	Match starts	Completed matches	Substitute appearances	Subbed off	Goals scored	Yellow cards	Red cards
Neil Austin	39	36	35	3	1	3	5	0
Denis Behan	29	21	6	8	15	6	5	0
Armann Bjornsson	18	10	5	8	5	3	2	0
Adam Boyd	40	25	9	15	16	7	2	0
James Brown	32	19	5	13	14	4	1	0
Julian Cherel	1	1	1	0	0	0	0	0
Ben Clark	11	6	5	5	0	0	1	1
Sam Collins	44	44	43	0	1	0	8	0
David Foley	2	0	0	2	0	0	0	0
Jon-Andre Fredriksen	12	4	0	8	4	0	3	0
Joe Gamble	22	22	15	0	7	2	2	0
Billy Greulich	4	0	0	4	0	0	0	0
Peter Hartley	38	38	34	0	3	2	3	1
Steven Haslam	15	15	15	0	0	0	2	0
Ritchie Humphreys	38	33	20	5	13	0	1	0
Ritchie Jones	33	22	13	11	8	4	3	1
Colin Larkin	22	10	5	12	5	1	0	0
Gary Liddle	40	40	39	0	1	3	10	0
Michael Mackay	1	0	0	1	0	0	0	0
Leon McSweeney	31	24	10	7	14	1	8	0
Andy Monkhouse	43	43	38	0	5	11	11	0
Roy O'Donovan	15	15	11	0	4	9	2	0
Alan Power	2	0	0	2	0	0	0	0
Jonny Rowell	6	0	0	6	0	0	0	0
Antony Sweeney	42	32	28	10	4	2	2	0

AUG SEP OCT NOV DEC JAN FEB MAR APR MAY

SEASON INFORMATION

Highest position: 7
Lowest position: 21
Average goals scored per game: 1.28
Average goals conceded per game: 1.46

LEAGUE POSITION AT THE END OF EACH MONTH

21 12 11 12 16 16 17 20 16 20

LONGEST SEQUENCES

Wins	2		Undefeated home	5	
(on three occasions)			(12/09/09–14/11/09)		
Losses	3		Undefeated away	3	
(on two occasions)			(08/08/09–04/09/09)		
Draws	2		Without scoring	2	
(01/05/10–08/05/10)			(on two occasions)		
Undefeated	5		Without conceding	3	
(09/10/09–14/11/09)			(09/10/09–24/10/09)		
Without win	7		Scoring	12	
(16/01/10–20/02/10)			(17/10/09–02/01/10)		

CARDS RECEIVED

72   3

EARLIEST STRIKE

JAMES BROWN
(v Swindon) 1:38

LATEST STRIKE

ANTONY SWEENEY
(v Leeds) 92:52

GOALS SCORED/CONCEDED
PER FIVE-MINUTE INTERVALS

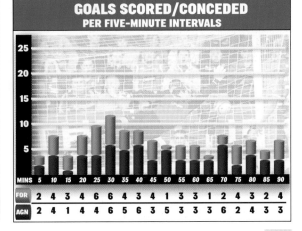

MINS	5	10	15	20	25	30	35	40	45	50	55	60	65	70	75	80	85	90
FOR	2	4	3	4	6	6	4	3	4	1	3	3	1	2	4	3	2	4
AGN	2	4	1	4	4	6	5	6	3	5	3	3	3	6	2	4	3	3

HUDDERSFIELD TOWN

HUDDERSFIELD'S season ultimately ended in disappointment after losing out to Millwall in the semi-finals of the play-offs – but the Terriers will start the 2010/11 season among the promotion favourites.

In lifelong Town supporter Dean Hoyle – who sold his Card Factory retail business for a reported £350million in April – Terriers fans have a chairman who has provided manager Lee Clark with serious financial backing.

Clark, in his first full season, assembled a progressive, young squad whose enterprising passing game won many admirers on their way to a top-six finish, and they were the division's top scorers on home soil, where they were only beaten once in the League.

Although Town's young manager could not hide his bitter disappointment at seeing his side freeze against Millwall in the play-offs, he will use the experience to ready the club for another crack at reaching the npower Championship in the coming season.

CLUB SUMMARY

FORMED	1908
MANAGER	Lee Clark
GROUND	Galpharm Stadium
CAPACITY	24,500
NICKNAME	The Terriers
WEBSITE	www.htafc.com

 Peter Clarke

PLAYER OF THE SEASON

OVERALL
P	W	D	L	F	A	GD
55	27	13	15	100	70	30

COCA-COLA FOOTBALL LEAGUE 1
Pos	P	W	D	L	F	A	GD	Pts
6	46	23	11	12	82	56	26	80

HOME
Pos	P	W	D	L	F	A	GD	Pts
3	23	14	8	1	52	22	30	50

AWAY
Pos	P	W	D	L	F	A	GD	Pts
7	23	9	3	11	30	34	-4	30

CUP PROGRESS DETAILS
Competition	Round reached	Knocked out by
FA Cup	R3	West Brom
Carling Cup	R2	Newcastle
JP Trophy	R2	Chesterfield

BIGGEST WIN (ALL COMPS)
18/08/09 7–1 v Brighton

BIGGEST DEFEAT (ALL COMPS)
02/03/10 0–5 v Southampton

ATTENDANCE RECORD
HIGH	AVERAGE	Low
21,764	14,507	11,269
v Leeds (27/02/2010)		v Brighton (18/08/2009)

RESULTS 2009/10

AUGUST
8th	● Southend	A	D 2–2	Att: 8,059	Scorers: Pilkington, Rhodes. Booked: Kay, Rhodes. Dismissed: Collins.
11th	● Stockport	H	W 3–1	Att: 5,120	Scorers: Rhodes², Robinson.
15th	● Southampton	H	W 3–1	Att: 12,449	Scorers: Kay, Rhodes².
18th	● Brighton	H	W 7–1	Att: 11,269	Scorers: P Clarke, Drinkwater, Kay, Novak, Roberts, Robinson². Booked: Butler.
22nd	● Bristol Rovers	A	L 1–0	Att: 6,952	Booked: Smithies.
26th	● Newcastle	A	L 4–3	Att: 23,815	Scorers: Rhodes, Robinson². Booked: Pilkington, Butler, Skarz, Berrett.
29th	● Yeovil	H	W 2–1	Att: 12,646	Scorers: Collins, Robinson. Booked: Simpson.

SEPTEMBER
1st	● Rotherham	A	W 1–2	Att: 2,246	Scorers: P Clarke, Simpson. Booked: Collins.
5th	● Milton Keynes Dons	A	W 2–3	Att: 9,772	Scorers: Kay, Rhodes, Robinson. Booked: Pilkington, Rhodes, Kay.
12th	● Brentford	H	D 0–0	Att: 12,020	Booked: P Clarke.
19th	● Millwall	A	L 3–1	Att: 8,502	Scorers: Rhodes.
26th	● Stockport	H	D 0–0	Att: 14,921	Booked: Pilkington.
29th	● Walsall	A	L 2–1	Att: 3,419	Scorers: Robinson. Booked: Goodwin, Skarz.

OCTOBER
3rd	● Colchester	A	L 1–0	Att: 5,154	Booked: Goodwin, P Clarke, Pilkington. Dismissed: P Clarke.
6th	● Chesterfield	A	D 3–3	Att: 3,003	Scorers: N Clarke, Pilkington². Booked: Berrett. Chesterfield win 4–2 on penalties.
10th	● Exeter	H	W 4–0	Att: 13,438	Scorers: Novak, Rhodes³. Booked: Peltier.
17th	● Charlton	A	L 2–1	Att: 16,991	Scorers: Pilkington. Booked: Roberts, Peltier.
24th	● Leyton Orient	H	W 4–0	Att: 13,396	Scorers: N Clarke, Collins, Rhodes, Roberts.

NOVEMBER
1st	● Oldham	A	W 0–1	Att: 8,569	Scorers: Williams. Booked: Rhodes, Smithies.
6th	● Dag & Red	H	W 6–1	Att: 5,858	Scorers: Novak², Rhodes, Roberts², Williams.
14th	● Wycombe	H	W 6–0	Att: 14,869	Scorers: P Clarke², Pilkington, Roberts, Robinson, Duberry OG. Booked: Novak, Williams.
21st	● Hartlepool	H	W 2–1	Att: 12,518	Scorers: Kay, Hartley OG. Booked: Kay.
24th	● Swindon	A	L 2–1	Att: 6,630	Scorers: Novak.
28th	● Port Vale	A	W 0–1	Att: 5,311	Scorers: N Clarke. Booked: Kay, Berrett.

DECEMBER
1st	● Tranmere	H	D 3–3	Att: 13,509	Scorers: Collins, Kay, Novak.
5th	● Leeds	A	D 2–2	Att: 36,723	Scorers: Novak, Rhodes. Booked: Collins, Pilkington.
12th	● Gillingham	H	W 2–1	Att: 13,844	Scorers: Novak, Rhodes. Booked: Kay, Collins.
19th	● Norwich	A	L 3–0	Att: 25,004	Booked: Pilkington, Roberts, Collins.
28th	● Milton Keynes Dons	H	W 1–0	Att: 16,086	Scorers: Pilkington. Booked: Peltier.

JANUARY
2nd	● West Brom	H	L 0–2	Att: 13,472	
16th	● Southend	H	W 2–1	Att: 14,200	Scorers: Rhodes².
19th	● Bristol Rovers	H	D 0–0	Att: 12,624	Booked: Kay.
30th	● Yeovil	A	W 0–1	Att: 4,110	Scorers: Eccleston. Booked: Trotman, Roberts.

FEBRUARY
6th	● Carlisle	H	D 1–1	Att: 14,132	Scorers: Pilkington. Booked: Kay, Eccleston, P Clarke.
9th	● Brighton	H	D 0–0	Att: 4,711	
13th	● Swindon	H	D 2–2	Att: 14,610	Scorers: P Clarke, Kay.
16th	● Carlisle	A	W 1–2	Att: 5,236	Scorers: Novak, Rhodes. Booked: Drinkwater, Heffernan, Pilkington.
20th	● Hartlepool	A	W 0–2	Att: 4,452	Scorers: Roberts, Trotman. Booked: Heffernan, T Clarke.
23rd	● Tranmere	A	W 0–2	Att: 5,793	Scorers: Novak².
27th	● Leeds	H	D 2–2	Att: 21,764	Scorers: Pilkington, Roberts. Booked: Kay.

MARCH
2nd	● Southampton	A	L 5–0	Att: 19,821	Booked: T Clarke, Trotman, Kay.
6th	● Gillingham	A	L 2–0	Att: 5,388	Booked: Smithies, Rhodes, Williams, P Clarke, Drinkwater. Dismissed: Eccleston.
13th	● Norwich	H	L 1–3	Att: 17,959	Scorers: Trotman. Booked: Roberts.
20th	● Leyton Orient	A	W 0–2	Att: 4,119	Scorers: Rhodes, Robinson. Booked: Heffernan, Pilkington.
27th	● Charlton	H	D 1–1	Att: 14,459	Scorers: Rhodes. Booked: Peltier.

APRIL
3rd	● Wycombe	A	W 1–2	Att: 5,288	Scorers: Rhodes, Robinson. Booked: Trotman, Kay.
6th	● Oldham	H	W 2–0	Att: 14,561	Scorers: Robinson². Booked: Smithies.
10th	● Brentford	A	L 3–0	Att: 5,209	Booked: Drinkwater.
13th	● Walsall	H	W 4–3	Att: 14,396	Scorers: Kay, Novak, Rhodes, Robinson. Booked: Kay, Novak.
16th	● Millwall	H	W 1–0	Att: 16,050	Scorers: P Clarke. Booked: P Clarke, Roberts.
24th	● Stockport	A	W 0–6	Att: 6,887	Scorers: Drinkwater, Novak, Pilkington, Rhodes, Roberts, Robinson.

MAY
1st	● Colchester	H	W 2–1	Att: 17,950	Scorers: Novak, Robinson. Booked: P Clarke, Peltier.
8th	● Exeter	A	L 2–1	Att: 8,383	Scorers: Roberts. Booked: Rhodes.
15th	● Millwall	H	D 0–0	Att: 14,654	
18th	● Millwall	A	L 2–0	Att: 15,463	Booked: Pilkington, Kay, Peltier. Agg: 2–0.

● Coca-Cola League 1/Play-offs ● FA Cup ● Carling Cup ● Johnstone's Paint Trophy

actim

LEAGUE 1 GOALKEEPER STATS

Player	Appearances	Match starts	Completed matches	Sub appearances	Subbed off	Clean sheets	Yellow cards	Red cards
Alex Smithies	46	46	46	0	0	16	4	0

LEAGUE 1 OUTFIELD PLAYER STATS

Player	Appearances	Match starts	Completed matches	Substitute appearances	Subbed off	Goals scored	Yellow cards	Red cards
Lionel Ainsworth	11	2	0	9	2	0	0	0
James Berrett	9	2	1	7	1	0	0	0
Andy Butler	11	10	10	1	0	0	1	0
Tom Clarke	21	15	13	6	2	0	2	0
Peter Clarke	46	46	45	0	0	5	6	1
Nathan Clarke	17	15	15	2	0	1	0	0
Michael Collins	28	23	17	5	5	3	3	1
Daniel Drinkwater	33	27	23	6	4	2	3	0
Nathan Eccleston	11	4	1	7	2	1	1	1
Jim Goodwin	5	3	1	2	2	0	2	0
Dean Heffernan	15	15	12	0	3	0	3	0
Antony Kay	40	38	31	2	7	6	10	0
Lee Novak	37	24	11	13	13	12	2	0
Krystian Pearce	1	0	0	1	0	0	0	0
Lee Peltier	42	42	38	0	4	0	5	0
Anthony Pilkington	43	42	35	1	7	7	8	0
Jordan Rhodes	45	43	22	2	21	19	5	0
Gary Roberts	43	40	25	3	15	7	5	0
Theo Robinson	36	17	11	19	6	13	0	0
Robbie Simpson	13	4	1	9	3	0	1	0
Joe Skarz	15	14	14	1	0	0	1	0
Neal Trotman	21	21	20	0	1	2	3	0
Robbie Williams	17	13	11	4	2	2	2	0

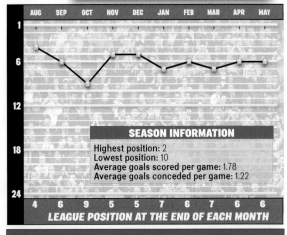

LEAGUE POSITION AT THE END OF EACH MONTH

SEASON INFORMATION

Highest position: 2
Lowest position: 10
Average goals scored per game: 1.78
Average goals conceded per game: 1.22

LONGEST SEQUENCES

Wins	4	Undefeated home	17
(on two occasions)		(15/08/09–27/02/10)	
Losses	3	Undefeated away	5
(02/03/10–13/03/10)		(30/01/10–23/02/10)	
Draws	3	Without scoring	2
(06/02/10–13/02/10)		(02/03/10–06/03/10)	
Undefeated	11	Without conceding	3
(28/12/09–27/02/10)		(24/10/09–14/11/09)	
Without win	5	Scoring	10
(12/09/09–03/10/09)		(10/10/09–12/12/09)	

CARDS RECEIVED

67 3

EARLIEST STRIKE

ANTHONY PILKINGTON
(v Stockport) 1:32

LATEST STRIKE

LEE NOVAK
(v Colchester) 94:10

GOALS SCORED/CONCEDED
PER FIVE-MINUTE INTERVALS

MINS	5	10	15	20	25	30	35	40	45	50	55	60	65	70	75	80	85	90
FOR	3	4	1	3	5	4	2	5	6	8	4	6	4	6	3	7	8	
AGN	2	5	3	2	3	1	2	0	0	4	1	6	2	5	4	4	9	3

LEEDS UNITED

LEEDS clinched promotion on the final day of the season to end their three-year stay in Coca-Cola League 1, but not before making life nervous for their fans.

The tense win over Bristol Rovers at Elland Road neatly reflected their season. Trailing 1–0 and down to 10 men after an hour, with results elsewhere going against them, Leeds finally pulled themselves together to stumble over the finishing line.

Simon Grayson's side had held an 11-point advantage over eventual champions Norwich heading into their FA Cup clash at Manchester United in January, but after pulling off a stunning upset against the Red Devils and then pushing Tottenham to a replay in the next round, their form in the League deserted them.

Norwich cruised past them in the table and it required a last-day winner from talismanic striker Jermaine Beckford to edge out Millwall, Swindon, Charlton and Huddersfield in the race for the second automatic promotion spot.

CLUB SUMMARY

FORMED	1919
MANAGER	Simon Grayson
GROUND	Elland Road
CAPACITY	40,296
NICKNAME	The Whites
WEBSITE	www.leedsunited.com

The New **Football Pools** PLAYER OF THE SEASON — *Patrick Kisnorbo*

OVERALL
P	W	D	L	F	A	GD
60	34	13	13	103	59	44

COCA-COLA FOOTBALL LEAGUE 1
Pos	P	W	D	L	F	A	GD	Pts
2	46	25	11	10	77	44	33	86

HOME
Pos	P	W	D	L	F	A	GD	Pts
6	23	14	6	3	41	19	22	48

AWAY
Pos	P	W	D	L	F	A	GD	Pts
2	23	11	5	7	36	25	11	38

CUP PROGRESS DETAILS
Competition	Round reached	Knocked out by
FA Cup	R4	Tottenham
Carling Cup	R3	Liverpool
JP Trophy	F (N)	Carlisle

BIGGEST WIN (ALL COMPS)
08/12/09 5–1 v Kettering

BIGGEST DEFEAT (ALL COMPS)
0–3 on 2 occasions

ATTENDANCE RECORD
High	Average	Low
38,234	24,818	17,635
v Bristol Rovers (08/05/2010)		v Oldham (23/02/2010)

RESULTS 2009/10

AUGUST
8th	● Exeter	H	W 2–1	Att: 27,681	Scorers: Beckford². Booked: Showunmi.
10th	● Darlington	A	W 0–1	Att: 4,487	Scorers: Showunmi.
15th	● Wycombe	A	W 0–1	Att: 8,400	Scorers: Becchio. Booked: Beckford, Howson.
18th	● Walsall	A	W 1–2	Att: 8,483	Scorers: Beckford, Johnson. Booked: Snodgrass.
22nd	● Tranmere	H	W 3–0	Att: 21,692	Scorers: Becchio, Beckford, Johnson. Booked: Doyle.
25th	● Watford	H	W 2–1	Att: 14,681	Scorers: Snodgrass². Booked: Kisnorbo, Snodgrass. AET – Score after 90 mins 1–1.
29th	● Colchester	A	W 1–2	Att: 8,810	Scorers: Beckford, Johnson. Booked: Johnson, Beckford.

SEPTEMBER
5th	● Stockport	H	W 2–0	Att: 22,870	Scorers: Grella, Michalik. Booked: Doyle.
11th	● Southend	A	D 0–0	Att: 10,123	Booked: Crowe, Hughes.
19th	● Gillingham	H	W 4–1	Att: 21,026	Scorers: Beckford, Howson, Johnson². Booked: Bromby.
22nd	● Liverpool	A	L 0–1	Att: 38,168	Booked: Crowe.
26th	● Milton Keynes Dons	A	W 0–1	Att: 16,713	Scorers: Snodgrass. Booked: Snodgrass.
29th	● Carlisle	H	D 1–1	Att: 19,673	Scorers: Beckford.

OCTOBER
3rd	● Charlton	H	D 0–0	Att: 31,838	Booked: Bromby.
6th	● Darlington	H	W 2–1	Att: 8,429	Scorers: Kandol, Robinson.
19th	● Norwich	H	W 2–1	Att: 19,912	Scorers: Beckford, Johnson. Booked: Naylor, Doyle, Johnson, Crowe.
24th	● Millwall	A	L 2–1	Att: 14,165	Scorers: Kisnorbo.
27th	● Bristol Rovers	A	W 0–4	Att: 11,448	Scorers: Beckford², Kandol, Vokes. Booked: Johnson, Doyle.
31st	● Yeovil	H	W 4–0	Att: 24,482	Scorers: Beckford, Gradel, Johnson, Kandol.

NOVEMBER
7th	● Oldham	A	W 0–2	Att: 5,552	Scorers: Grella, Howson. Booked: Howson, Kilkenny, Doyle.
10th	● Grimsby	H	W 3–1	Att: 10,430	Scorers: Beckford, Kilkenny, Lancashire OG.
21st	● Brighton	H	W 0–3	Att: 7,615	Scorers: Beckford, Kilkenny, Snodgrass. Booked: Michalik.
24th	● Leyton Orient	H	W 1–0	Att: 19,744	Scorers: Gradel. Booked: Bromby.
29th	● Kettering	A	D 1–1	Att: 4,837	Scorers: Beckford.

DECEMBER
1st	● Oldham	A	W 0–2	Att: 7,793	Scorers: Becchio, Kilkenny.
5th	● Huddersfield	H	D 2–2	Att: 36,723	Scorers: Gradel, Snodgrass. Booked: Capaldi, Crowe.
8th	● Kettering	H	W 5–1	Att: 10,670	Scorers: Becchio, Beckford, Grella², Kandol. Booked: Snodgrass. AET – Score after 90 mins 1–1.
12th	● Brentford	A	D 0–0	Att: 9,031	Booked: Capaldi.
15th	● Accrington Stanley	H	W 2–0	Att: 12,696	Scorers: Ephraim, Kilkenny.
19th	● Southampton	H	W 1–0	Att: 25,948	Scorers: Snodgrass. Booked: Kisnorbo.
26th	● Hartlepool	H	W 3–1	Att: 30,191	Scorers: Becchio, Beckford². Booked: Kilkenny, Becchio, Johnson.
28th	● Stockport	A	W 2–4	Att: 7,768	Scorers: Beckford², Bromby, Snodgrass. Booked: Snodgrass, Becchio, Bromby, Ankergren, Naylor, Kisnorbo.

JANUARY
3rd	● Man Utd	A	W 0–1	Att: 74,526	Scorers: Beckford. Booked: Naylor, Johnson.
9th	● Wycombe	H	D 1–1	Att: 24,383	Scorers: Howson. Booked: Doyle, Gradel.
16th	● Exeter	A	L 2–0	Att: 8,549	Booked: Beckford, Johnson, Doyle, Kilkenny.
19th	● Carlisle	H	L 1–2	Att: 13,011	Scorers: Crowe. Booked: Johnson.
23rd	● Tottenham	A	D 2–2	Att: 35,750	Scorers: Beckford². Booked: Bromby, Doyle, Crowe, Kisnorbo, Kilkenny, Johnson.
26th	● Swindon	A	L 3–0	Att: 14,508	Booked: Bromby, Snodgrass, Ankergren, Gradel.
30th	● Colchester	H	W 2–0	Att: 23,425	Scorers: Beckford². Booked: Michalik.

FEBRUARY
3rd	● Tottenham	H	L 1–3	Att: 37,704	Scorers: Becchio. Booked: Johnson, Beckford.
6th	● Hartlepool	A	D 2–2	Att: 5,115	Scorers: Becchio².
9th	● Carlisle	A	W 2–3	Att: 9,430	Scorers: Crowe, Grella, Snodgrass. Booked: Crowe, Howson, Gradel. Agg: 4–4; Carlisle win 6–5 on penalties.
13th	● Leyton Orient	A	D 1–1	Att: 8,013	Scorers: Daniels OG.
16th	● Walsall	H	L 1–2	Att: 18,941	Scorers: McSheffrey. Booked: Beckford.
20th	● Brighton	A	D 1–1	Att: 24,120	Scorers: Snodgrass. Booked: Hughes, Kisnorbo.
23rd	● Oldham	H	W 2–0	Att: 17,635	Scorers: Becchio². Booked: Lowry.
27th	● Huddersfield	A	D 2–2	Att: 21,764	Scorers: Becchio, Howson. Booked: Lowry, Naylor, Becchio.

MARCH
6th	● Brentford	H	D 1–1	Att: 25,445	Scorers: Beckford. Booked: Snodgrass.
9th	● Tranmere	A	W 1–4	Att: 8,346	Scorers: Becchio, Beckford², Snodgrass. Booked: Becchio.
13th	● Southampton	A	L 1–0	Att: 30,794	Booked: Howson, Kisnorbo, Gradel.
22nd	● Millwall	H	L 0–2	Att: 21,348	
27th	● Norwich	A	L 1–0	Att: 25,445	Booked: Naylor, Snodgrass, Lowry. Dismissed: Kandol.

APRIL
3rd	● Swindon	H	L 0–3	Att: 27,881	Booked: Howson.
5th	● Yeovil	A	W 1–2	Att: 6,308	Scorers: Naylor². Booked: Collins, Beckford, Kilkenny, Bromby.
10th	● Southend	H	W 2–0	Att: 21,650	Scorers: Becchio, Gradel. Booked: Johnson, Doyle.
13th	● Carlisle	A	W 1–3	Att: 8,728	Scorers: Becchio², Gradel. Booked: Naylor.
17th	● Gillingham	A	L 3–2	Att: 9,649	Scorers: Becchio, Beckford. Booked: Collins, Naylor, Gradel.
24th	● Milton Keynes Dons	H	W 4–1	Att: 25,964	Scorers: Becchio, Beckford², Gradel. Booked: Johnson, Hughes, Collins.

MAY
1st	● Charlton	A	L 1–0	Att: 23,198	Booked: Johnson, Naylor, Lowry.
8th	● Bristol Rovers	H	W 2–1	Att: 38,234	Scorers: Beckford, Howson. Booked: Doyle, Becchio. Dismissed: Gradel.

● Coca-Cola League 1/Play-Offs ● FA Cup ● Carling Cup ● Johnstone's Paint Trophy

actim

LEAGUE 1 GOALKEEPER STATS

Player	Appearances	Match starts	Completed matches	Sub appearances	Subbed off	Clean sheets	Yellow cards	Red cards
Casper Ankergren	29	27	27	2	0	10	2	0
Shane Higgs	19	19	17	0	2	5	0	0

LEAGUE 1 OUTFIELD PLAYER STATS

Player	Appearances	Match starts	Completed matches	Substitute appearances	Subbed off	Goals scored	Yellow cards	Red cards
Luciano Becchio	37	32	10	5	22	15	5	0
Jermaine Beckford	42	38	27	4	11	25	5	0
Leigh Bromby	32	31	29	1	2	1	6	0
Tony Capaldi	3	3	3	0	0	0	2	0
Neill Collins	9	9	9	0	0	0	3	0
Jason Crowe	17	16	12	1	4	0	3	0
Paul Dickov	4	1	1	3	0	0	0	0
Michael Doyle	42	42	30	0	12	0	8	0
Hogan Ephraim	3	1	0	2	1	0	0	0
Max Gradel	32	11	6	21	4	6	4	1
Mike Grella	17	3	1	14	2	1	0	0
Jonathan Howson	45	39	33	6	6	4	3	0
Andy Hughes	39	38	28	1	10	0	3	0
Bradley Johnson	36	26	21	10	5	7	8	0
Tresor Kandol	10	0	0	10	0	2	0	1
Neil Kilkenny	35	24	17	11	7	2	3	0
Patrick Kisnorbo	29	29	28	0	1	1	4	0
Shane Lowry	11	11	9	0	2	0	4	0
Rui Marques	5	5	4	0	1	0	0	0
Gary McSheffrey	10	9	4	1	5	1	0	0
Lubomir Michalik	13	7	7	6	0	1	2	0
Richard Naylor	29	29	26	0	3	2	7	0
Ben Parker	4	2	0	2	2	0	0	0
David Prutton	6	1	1	5	0	0	0	0
Andy Robinson	6	0	0	6	0	0	0	0
Enoch Showunmi	7	0	0	7	0	0	1	0
Robert Snodgrass	44	40	22	4	18	7	6	0
Sam Vokes	8	8	1	0	7	1	0	0
Sanchez Watt	6	1	0	5	1	0	0	0
Aidan White	8	4	1	4	3	0	0	0

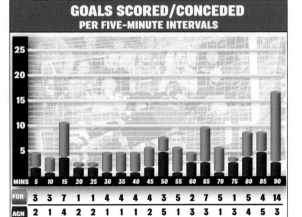

SEASON INFORMATION
Highest position: 1
Lowest position: 4
Average goals scored per game: 1.67
Average goals conceded per game: 0.96

LEAGUE POSITION AT THE END OF EACH MONTH

AUG 2 · SEP 1 · OCT 1 · NOV 1 · DEC 1 · JAN 2 · FEB 2 · MAR 2 · APR 2 · MAY 2

LONGEST SEQUENCES

Wins	6	Undefeated home	14
(08/08/09–05/09/09)		(08/08/09–30/01/10)	
Losses	4	Undefeated away	5
(13/03/10–03/04/10)		(on two occasions)	
Draws	2	Without scoring	4
(on four occasions)		(13/03/10–03/04/10)	
Undefeated	12	Without conceding	5
(08/08/09–19/10/09)		(27/10/09–01/12/09)	
Without win	4	Scoring	9
(on two occasions)		(30/01/10–09/03/10)	

CARDS RECEIVED

79 **2**

EARLIEST STRIKE
ROBERT SNODGRASS
(v Huddersfield) 1:25

LATEST STRIKE
ROBERT SNODGRASS
(v Brighton) 94:26

GOALS SCORED/CONCEDED
PER FIVE-MINUTE INTERVALS

MINS	5	10	15	20	25	30	35	40	45	50	55	60	65	70	75	80	85	90
FOR	3	3	7	1	1	4	4	4	3	5	2	7	5	1	5	4	14	
AGN	2	1	4	2	2	1	1	1	2	5	1	3	3	1	3	4	5	3

LEYTON ORIENT

MANAGER Russell Slade pulled off his second rescue act in as many seasons to save Orient from the drop. Slade, who had kept Brighton up the previous term, was drafted in by chairman Barry Hearn to replace Geraint Williams with six games remaining and proved his survival skills once again.

Williams had saved the O's in the 2008/09 season but, despite a nine-game unbeaten run at the turn of the year, they remained in trouble and Hearn acted after a 3–1 home defeat by Hartlepool which left them a point above the relegation zone.

The 'Slade effect' produced the three wins they needed to stay up, including a 2–1 success against champions Norwich, and saw him offered the manager's job permanently.

During the course of the campaign, veteran striker Scott McGleish showed no signs of slowing down at 36 as he topped the scoring charts with 12 goals, while defender Tamika Mkandawire remains a class act at this level.

CLUB SUMMARY

FORMED	1881
MANAGER	Russell Slade
GROUND	Brisbane Road
CAPACITY	9,271
NICKNAME	The O's
WEBSITE	www.leytonorient.com

The New **Football Pools** PLAYER OF THE SEASON — *Tamika Mkandawire*

OVERALL
P	W	D	L	F	A	GD
52	15	14	23	58	68	-10

COCA-COLA FOOTBALL LEAGUE 1
Pos	P	W	D	L	F	A	GD	Pts
17	46	13	12	21	53	63	-10	51

HOME
Pos	P	W	D	L	F	A	GD	Pts
14	23	10	6	7	35	25	10	36

AWAY
Pos	P	W	D	L	F	A	GD	Pts
19	23	3	6	14	18	38	-20	15

CUP PROGRESS DETAILS
Competition	Round reached	Knocked out by
FA Cup	R1	Tranmere
Carling Cup	R2	Stoke
JP Trophy	QF	Hereford

BIGGEST WIN (ALL COMPS)
02/02/10 5–0 v Bristol Rovers

BIGGEST DEFEAT (ALL COMPS)
0–4 on 2 occasions

ATTENDANCE RECORD
HIGH	AVERAGE	LOW
8,013	4,937	2,669
v Leeds (13/02/2010)		v Yeovil (19/01/2010)

RESULTS 2009/10

AUGUST
8th	● Bristol Rovers	A	W 1–2	Att: 7,745	**Scorers:** Melligan, Smith. **Booked:** Thornton, Chorley, Jones.
11th	● Colchester	A	W 1–2	Att: 3,308	**Scorers:** Melligan, Patulea. **Booked:** Mkandawire, Morris, Smith.
15th	● Oldham	H	L 1–2	Att: 4,061	**Scorers:** Jarvis. **Booked:** Demetriou, Purches, Thornton.
18th	● Charlton	H	L 1–2	Att: 7,376	**Scorers:** Mkandawire. **Booked:** Demetriou, Thornton.
22nd	● Yeovil	A	D 3–3	Att: 3,827	**Scorers:** Jarvis, McGleish, Townsend. **Booked:** Mkandawire, Smith.
26th	● Stoke	H	L 0–1	Att: 2,742	**Booked:** Chorley. AET – Score after 90 mins 0–0.
29th	● Carlisle	H	D 2–2	Att: 3,546	**Scorers:** McGleish². **Booked:** Ashworth.

SEPTEMBER
4th	● Southend	A	L 3–0	Att: 8,836	**Booked:** Ashworth.
12th	● Exeter	H	D 1–1	Att: 4,703	**Scorers:** Stewart OG. **Booked:** Demetriou.
19th	● Stockport	A	L 2–1	Att: 4,091	**Scorers:** Mkandawire. **Booked:** Demetriou.
26th	● Millwall	H	W 1–0	Att: 5,255	**Scorers:** Townsend. **Booked:** Cave-Brown.
29th	● Norwich	A	L 4–0	Att: 23,981	**Booked:** Smith, Scowcroft. **Dismissed:** Melligan.

OCTOBER
3rd	● Wycombe	A	W 0–1	Att: 4,798	**Scorers:** McGleish. **Booked:** Cave-Brown.
6th	● Brighton	H	W 1–0	Att: 1,457	**Scorers:** Patulea. **Booked:** Demetriou.
10th	● Colchester	H	L 0–1	Att: 5,410	**Booked:** McGleish, Townsend.
17th	● Brentford	H	W 2–1	Att: 4,781	**Scorers:** McGleish, Foster OG. **Booked:** Daniels, Purches.
24th	● Huddersfield	A	L 4–0	Att: 13,396	**Booked:** Daniels, Scowcroft.
31st	● Southampton	H	D 2–2	Att: 7,544	**Scorers:** Mkandawire, Trotman OG.

NOVEMBER
7th	● Tranmere	A	D 1–1	Att: 3,180	**Scorers:** Ashworth. **Booked:** Chorley, Smith.
10th	● Hereford	H	D 1–1	Att: 1,282	**Scorers:** Demetriou. Hereford win 3–2 on penalties.
14th	● Hartlepool	A	L 1–0	Att: 3,119	
17th	● Tranmere	H	L 0–1	Att: 1,518	
21st	● Tranmere	H	W 2–1	Att: 4,620	**Scorers:** McGleish². **Booked:** Daniels.
24th	● Leeds	A	L 1–0	Att: 19,744	

DECEMBER
1st	● Gillingham	H	W 3–1	Att: 3,183	**Scorers:** Jarvis, Smith, Thornton.
5th	● Swindon	A	L 3–2	Att: 6,815	**Scorers:** Thornton². **Booked:** Chorley, Scowcroft, Thornton. **Dismissed:** Mkandawire.
12th	● Milton Keynes Dons	H	L 1–2	Att: 3,959	**Scorers:** McGleish.
19th	● Walsall	A	D 2–2	Att: 3,616	**Scorers:** Jarvis, Mkandawire. **Booked:** Jones.
26th	● Brighton	A	D 0–0	Att: 6,690	**Booked:** Thornton, Chambers.
28th	● Southend	H	L 1–2	Att: 5,680	**Scorers:** Chambers. **Booked:** Chorley, Pires.

JANUARY
19th	● Yeovil	H	W 2–0	Att: 2,669	**Scorers:** McGleish, Mkandawire. **Booked:** Thornton.
25th	● Charlton	A	W 0–1	Att: 15,955	**Scorers:** McGleish. **Booked:** Chambers.
30th	● Carlisle	A	D 2–2	Att: 4,687	**Scorers:** Jarvis, Livesey OG.

FEBRUARY
2nd	● Bristol Rovers	H	W 5–0	Att: 2,931	**Scorers:** Demetriou, Jarvis, Purches, Tehoue, Andersen OG.
6th	● Brighton	H	D 1–1	Att: 6,027	**Scorers:** McGleish. **Booked:** Chorley, Demetriou, McGleish, Thornton.
13th	● Leeds	H	D 1–1	Att: 8,013	**Scorers:** Mkandawire. **Booked:** Tehoue.
20th	● Tranmere	A	L 2–1	Att: 5,357	**Scorers:** Tehoue. **Booked:** Pires.
23rd	● Gillingham	A	D 1–1	Att: 4,753	**Scorers:** Mkandawire. **Booked:** Chorley.
27th	● Swindon	H	D 0–0	Att: 4,574	

MARCH
6th	● Milton Keynes Dons	A	L 1–0	Att: 14,323	**Booked:** Smith, Tehoue.
9th	● Oldham	A	L 2–0	Att: 3,126	**Booked:** Chambers, Daniels.
13th	● Walsall	H	W 2–0	Att: 3,685	**Scorers:** Thornton². **Booked:** Thornton.
20th	● Huddersfield	H	L 0–2	Att: 4,119	**Booked:** Cave-Brown, Chorley.
27th	● Brentford	A	L 1–0	Att: 6,369	**Booked:** Tehoue, Lichaj, Thornton, Scowcroft.

APRIL
3rd	● Hartlepool	H	L 1–3	Att: 3,604	**Scorers:** Patulea. **Booked:** Thornton.
5th	● Southampton	A	L 2–1	Att: 21,559	**Scorers:** Spicer. **Booked:** Chambers.
10th	● Exeter	A	D 0–0	Att: 5,522	
13th	● Norwich	H	W 2–1	Att: 7,520	**Scorers:** Thornton². **Booked:** McGleish, Smith, Lichaj.
17th	● Stockport	H	W 2–0	Att: 4,373	**Scorers:** Jarvis, Lichaj. **Booked:** Smith.
24th	● Millwall	A	L 2–1	Att: 13,011	**Scorers:** Chorley. **Booked:** Smith, Chambers, Thornton.

MAY
1st	● Wycombe	H	W 2–0	Att: 5,918	**Scorers:** Jarvis, McGleish. **Booked:** Thornton, Baker.
8th	● Colchester	A	L 1–0	Att: 5,751	**Booked:** Chambers. **Dismissed:** Ashworth.

● Coca-Cola League 1/Play-Offs ● FA Cup ● Carling Cup ● Johnstone's Paint Trophy

LEAGUE 1 GOALKEEPER STATS

Player	Appearances	Match starts	Completed matches	Sub appearances	Subbed off	Clean sheets	Yellow cards	Red cards
Jamie Jones	36	36	35	0	1	10	2	0
Glenn Morris	11	10	10	1	0	1	0	0

LEAGUE 1 OUTFIELD PLAYER STATS

Player	Appearances	Match starts	Completed matches	Substitute appearances	Subbed off	Goals scored	Yellow cards	Red cards
Nicky Adams	6	6	5	0	1	0	0	0
Luke Ashworth	10	7	6	3	0	0	2	1
Harry Baker	4	0	0	4	0	0	1	0
Matthew Briggs	1	1	1	0	0	0	0	0
Andrew Cave-Brown	16	12	11	4	1	0	3	0
Adam Chambers	29	26	20	3	6	1	6	0
Ben Chorley	42	42	41	0	1	1	6	0
Charlie Daniels	41	40	38	1	2	0	4	0
Jason Demetriou	39	29	25	10	4	1	5	0
Aaron Doran	6	6	2	0	4	0	0	0
Ryan Jarvis	42	34	12	8	22	8	5	0
Eric Lichaj	9	9	9	0	0	1	2	0
Scott McGleish	42	36	19	6	17	12	3	0
John Melligan	16	14	8	2	5	1	0	1
Tamika Mkandawire	43	43	41	0	1	7	1	0
Kristian O'Leary	3	1	0	2	1	0	0	0
Adrian Patulea	21	4	1	17	3	1	0	0
Loick Pires	8	0	0	8	0	0	2	0
Stephen Purches	31	30	27	1	3	1	2	0
James Scowcroft	26	13	6	13	7	0	4	0
Jimmy Smith	40	34	30	6	4	2	6	0
John Spicer	9	9	4	0	5	1	0	0
Luke Summerfield	14	14	13	0	1	0	0	0
Jonathan Tehoue	16	5	0	11	6	2	3	0
Sean Thornton	30	28	20	2	8	7	12	0
Andros Townsend	22	17	13	5	4	2	1	0

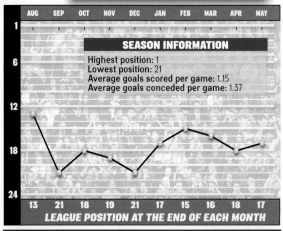

SEASON INFORMATION
Highest position: 1
Lowest position: 21
Average goals scored per game: 1.15
Average goals conceded per game: 1.37

LEAGUE POSITION AT THE END OF EACH MONTH

13	21	18	19	21	17	15	16	18	17

LONGEST SEQUENCES

Wins	2	Undefeated home	6	
(on two occasions)		(19/01/10–13/03/10)		
Losses	4	Undefeated away	4	
(20/03/10–05/04/10)		(19/12/09–30/01/10)		
Draws	2	Without scoring	3	
(on four occasions)		(27/02/10–09/03/10)		
Undefeated	6	Without conceding	2	
(19/01/10–13/02/10)		(19/01/10–25/01/10)		
Without win	7	Scoring	9	
(on two occasions)		(28/12/09–23/02/10)		

CARDS RECEIVED

65   **3**

EARLIEST STRIKE
RYAN JARVIS
(v Walsall) 1:10

LATEST STRIKE
CHARLIE DANIELS
(v Leeds) 94:23

GOALS SCORED/CONCEDED
PER FIVE-MINUTE INTERVALS

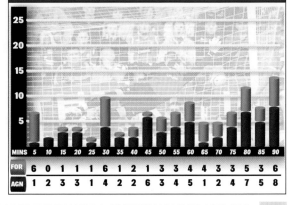

MINS	5	10	15	20	25	30	35	40	45	50	55	60	65	70	75	80	85	90
FOR	6	0	1	1	1	6	1	2	1	3	4	4	3	3	5	3	6	
AGN	1	2	3	3	1	4	2	2	6	3	4	5	1	2	4	7	5	8

MILLWALL

PAUL ROBINSON was the hero as Millwall made it back to the npower Championship. Injury had seen the Lions' captain restricted to a substitute appearance in the 2008/09 play-off final, as his side were beaten 3–2 by Scunthorpe. However, manager Kenny Jackett rallied his team for a second attempt and Robinson scored the goal that beat Swindon in the Wembley showpiece in late May.

A promotion bid looked to be out of the question following a poor start to the campaign, in which Millwall won only two of their opening 10 games in the League. But after a slow start, Steve Morison – Jackett's £130,000 summer signing from Stevenage – began to score regularly, and he finished the season with an impressive 23 goals.

The Lions were briefly in the second automatic promotion spot on the final day of the regular season, but they were edged out by Leeds and had to settle for third. However, this time they made no mistake at Wembley.

CLUB SUMMARY

FORMED	1885
MANAGER	Kenny Jackett
GROUND	The New Den
CAPACITY	20,146
NICKNAME	The Lions
WEBSITE	www.millwallfc.co.uk

The New Football Pools PLAYER OF THE SEASON

Steve Morison

OVERALL
P	W	D	L	F	A	GD
57	29	17	11	95	53	42

COCA-COLA FOOTBALL LEAGUE 1
Pos	P	W	D	L	F	A	GD	Pts
3	46	24	13	9	76	44	32	85

HOME
Pos	P	W	D	L	F	A	GD	Pts
1	23	17	5	1	48	15	33	56

AWAY
Pos	P	W	D	L	F	A	GD	Pts
8	23	7	8	8	28	29	-1	29

CUP PROGRESS DETAILS
Competition	Round reached	Knocked out by
FA Cup	R3	Derby
Carling Cup	R2	West Ham
JP Trophy	R1	Barnet

BIGGEST WIN (ALL COMPS)
5–0 on 2 occasions

BIGGEST DEFEAT (ALL COMPS)
05/12/09 0–3 v Hartlepool

ATTENDANCE RECORD
HIGH	AVERAGE	Low
17,632	10,835	6,617
v Charlton (13/03/2010)		v Yeovil (29/09/2009)

RESULTS 2009/10

AUGUST
8th	● Southampton	A	D 1–1	Att: 20,103	Scorers: Abdou.
11th	● Bournemouth	H	W 4–0	Att: 3,552	Scorers: Alexander, Harris³.
15th	● Carlisle	H	D 0–0	Att: 9,055	Booked: Fuseini.
18th	● Oldham	H	W 2–0	Att: 7,369	Scorers: Harris, Martin. Booked: Craig, Fuseini, Friend, Harris.
21st	● Southend	A	D 0–0	Att: 8,435	Booked: Martin, Friend, Laird, Alexander, Smith.
25th	● West Ham	A	L 3–1	Att: 24,492	Scorers: Harris. Booked: Frampton, Laird, Barron. AET – Score after 90 mins 1–1.
28th	● Brighton	H	D 1–1	Att: 10,138	Scorers: Price. Booked: Dunne.

SEPTEMBER
1st	● Barnet	A	L 2–0	Att: 1,623	Booked: Dunne.
5th	● Bristol Rovers	A	L 2–0	Att: 6,038	Booked: Frampton, Smith, Fuseini.
12th	● Gillingham	A	L 2–0	Att: 8,097	Booked: Abdou, Smith, Martin.
19th	● Huddersfield	H	W 3–1	Att: 8,502	Scorers: Hackett, Harris, Morison. Booked: Dunne, Forde.
26th	● Leyton Orient	A	L 1–0	Att: 5,255	
29th	● Yeovil	H	D 0–0	Att: 6,617	Booked: Forde, Alexander, Fuseini.

OCTOBER
3rd	● Tranmere	H	W 5–0	Att: 8,046	Scorers: Frampton, Henry³, Morison. Booked: Martin.
10th	● Swindon	A	D 1–1	Att: 7,222	Scorers: Schofield. Booked: Forde, Schofield, Harris. Dismissed: Frampton.
17th	● Stockport	A	W 0–4	Att: 4,394	Scorers: Harris³, Robinson.
24th	● Leeds	H	W 2–1	Att: 14,165	Scorers: Alexander, Harris. Booked: Robinson, Alexander.
31st	● Colchester	H	W 2–1	Att: 10,036	Scorers: Dunne, Henry. Booked: Laird, Robinson.

NOVEMBER
9th	● AFC Wimbledon	H	W 4–1	Att: 9,453	Scorers: Harris, Price², Schofield. Booked: Abdou.
14th	● Brentford	A	D 2–2	Att: 6,408	Scorers: Henry, Robinson.
21st	● Wycombe	H	L 0–2	Att: 9,728	
24th	● Exeter	A	D 1–1	Att: 5,732	Scorers: Martin. Booked: Smith, Martin, Frampton, Morison.
28th	● Staines Town	A	D 1–1	Att: 2,753	Scorers: Robinson. Booked: Morison, Price, Robinson, Grimes.

DECEMBER
1st	● Milton Keynes Dons	H	W 3–2	Att: 7,883	Scorers: Frampton, Hackett, Morison.
5th	● Hartlepool	A	L 3–0	Att: 3,153	Booked: Morison.
9th	● Staines Town	H	W 4–0	Att: 3,452	Scorers: Dunne, Morison, Schofield, Smith. Booked: Robinson, Dunne, Abdou.
12th	● Walsall	H	W 2–1	Att: 8,174	Scorers: Morison².
19th	● Charlton	A	D 4–4	Att: 19,105	Scorers: Martin, Morison², Schofield. Booked: Martin, Smith, Laird. Dismissed: Abdou.
26th	● Norwich	A	L 2–0	Att: 25,242	Booked: Dunne.
28th	● Bristol Rovers	H	W 2–0	Att: 10,014	Scorers: Morison, Baldwin OG. Booked: Abdou, Morison, Grabban.

JANUARY
2nd	● Derby	H	D 1–1	Att: 10,531	Scorers: Grabban. Booked: Smith, Morison.
12th	● Derby	A	D 1–1	Att: 7,183	Scorers: Morison. AET – Score after 90 mins 0–0. Derby win 5–3 on penalties.
16th	● Southampton	H	D 1–1	Att: 11,524	Scorers: Trotter. Booked: Robinson.
23rd	● Oldham	A	W 0–1	Att: 3,656	Scorers: Harris. Booked: Martin, Craig, Schofield, Smith, Morison, Ward.
26th	● Southend	H	W 2–0	Att: 7,612	Scorers: Batt, Schofield. Booked: Batt, Abdou, Trotter.
30th	● Brighton	A	W 0–1	Att: 6,610	Scorers: Morison. Booked: Abdou, Craig.

FEBRUARY
6th	● Norwich	H	W 2–1	Att: 14,374	Scorers: Craig, Harris.
13th	● Exeter	H	W 1–0	Att: 9,104	Scorers: Harris. Booked: Morison.
20th	● Wycombe	A	L 1–0	Att: 5,774	Booked: Trotter, Robinson, Schofield, Harris, Ward.
23rd	● Milton Keynes Dons	A	W 1–3	Att: 10,610	Scorers: Harris², Schofield. Booked: Robinson, Morison.
27th	● Hartlepool	H	W 1–0	Att: 10,818	Scorers: Harris.

MARCH
6th	● Walsall	A	D 2–2	Att: 3,835	Scorers: Dunne, Morison.
9th	● Carlisle	A	W 1–3	Att: 3,853	Scorers: Morison², Schofield. Booked: Dunne, Morison, Forde.
13th	● Charlton	H	W 4–0	Att: 17,632	Scorers: Morison², Ward, Dailly OG.
22nd	● Leeds	A	W 0–2	Att: 21,348	Scorers: Batt, Morison.
27th	● Stockport	H	W 5–0	Att: 11,116	Scorers: Morison, Obika, Schofield, Swailes OG, Huntington OG.

APRIL
2nd	● Brentford	H	D 1–1	Att: 14,025	Scorers: Robinson. Booked: Trotter.
5th	● Colchester	A	W 1–2	Att: 7,393	Scorers: Morison, Batth OG. Booked: Ward, Schofield, Robinson, Craig.
10th	● Gillingham	H	W 4–0	Att: 13,174	Scorers: Batt, Craig, Harris, Schofield.
13th	● Yeovil	A	D 1–1	Att: 4,713	Scorers: Obika.
16th	● Huddersfield	A	L 1–0	Att: 16,050	Booked: Smith.
24th	● Leyton Orient	H	W 2–1	Att: 13,011	Scorers: Morison, Robinson.

MAY
1st	● Tranmere	A	L 2–0	Att: 8,694	Booked: Robinson, Trotter, Alexander.
8th	● Swindon	H	W 3–2	Att: 17,083	Scorers: Morison², Greer OG. Booked: Morison, Batt.
15th	● Huddersfield	A	D 0–0	Att: 14,654	Booked: Robinson, Harris, Alexander.
18th	● Huddersfield	H	W 2–0	Att: 15,463	Scorers: Morison, Robinson. Booked: Craig. Agg: 2–0.
29th	● Swindon	N	W 1–0	Att: 73,108	Scorers: Robinson.

● Coca-Cola League 1/Play-offs ■ FA Cup ● Carling Cup ● Johnstone's Paint Trophy

actim

LEAGUE 1 GOALKEEPER STATS

Player	Appearances	Match starts	Completed matches	Sub appearances	Subbed off	Clean sheets	Yellow cards	Red cards
David Forde	46	46	46	0	0	16	4	0

LEAGUE 1 OUTFIELD PLAYER STATS

Player	Appearances	Match starts	Completed matches	Substitute appearances	Subbed off	Goals scored	Yellow cards	Red cards
Nadjim Abdou	43	43	39	0	3	1	4	1
Gary Alexander	15	8	5	7	3	1	4	0
Scott Barron	23	12	10	11	2	0	0	0
Shaun Batt	16	10	2	6	8	3	2	0
Adam Bolder	11	5	1	6	4	0	0	0
Tony Craig	30	29	27	1	2	2	4	0
Alan Dunne	32	29	29	3	0	2	4	0
Andy Frampton	21	20	16	1	3	2	2	1
George Friend	6	4	4	2	0	0	2	0
Ali Fuseini	15	10	7	5	3	0	4	0
Lewis Grabban	11	5	0	6	6	0	1	0
Ashley Grimes	4	2	1	2	1	0	0	0
Chris Hackett	40	34	18	6	16	2	0	0
Neil Harris	32	21	11	11	10	13	3	0
James Henry	9	6	3	3	3	5	0	0
Kiernan Hughes-Mason	1	0	0	1	0	0	0	0
Marc Laird	20	17	10	3	7	0	3	0
John Marquis	1	0	0	1	0	0	0	0
Dave Martin	20	16	4	4	12	3	6	0
Steve Morison	43	42	27	1	15	20	8	0
Jonathan Obika	12	0	0	12	0	2	0	0
Jason Price	15	5	0	10	5	1	0	0
Paul Robinson	34	34	34	0	0	4	7	0
Danny Schofield	36	28	25	8	3	7	4	0
Jack Smith	31	30	27	1	3	0	7	0
Liam Trotter	20	20	18	0	2	4	4	0
Darren Ward	31	30	29	1	1	1	3	0

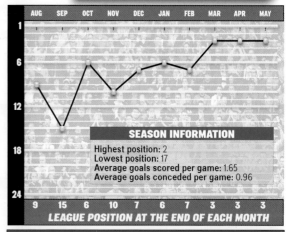

SEASON INFORMATION

Highest position: 2
Lowest position: 17
Average goals scored per game: 1.65
Average goals conceded per game: 0.96

LEAGUE POSITION AT THE END OF EACH MONTH

LONGEST SEQUENCES

Wins	5	Undefeated home	14
(23/01/10–13/02/10)		(01/12/09–08/05/10)	
Losses	2	Undefeated away	6
(05/09/09–12/09/09)		(23/02/10–13/04/10)	
Draws	2	Without scoring	2
(on two occasions)		(on two occasions)	
Undefeated	11	Without conceding	3
(23/02/10–13/04/10)		(on three occasions)	
Without win	4	Scoring	11
(21/08/09–12/09/09)		(23/02/10–13/04/10)	

CARDS RECEIVED

76   2

EARLIEST STRIKE

NEIL HARRIS
(v Leeds) 2:38

LATEST STRIKE

LIAM TROTTER
(v Southampton) 94:59

GOALS SCORED/CONCEDED
PER FIVE-MINUTE INTERVALS

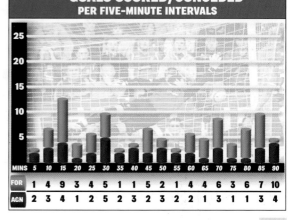

MINS	5	10	15	20	25	30	35	40	45	50	55	60	65	70	75	80	85	90
FOR	1	4	9	3	4	5	1	1	5	2	1	4	4	6	3	6	7	10
AGN	2	3	4	1	2	5	2	3	2	3	2	2	1	3	1	1	3	4

MILTON KEYNES DONS

KARL ROBINSON became the youngest manager in the Football League in May when the 29-year-old took over at stadium:mk following the end of Paul Ince's short-lived second spell in charge.

Ince won the Coca-Cola League Two title and Johnstone's Paint Trophy in his first stint, before departing for Blackburn, and was expected to mount another promotion push in 2009/10. However, a crippling injury list and a poor disciplinary record undermined his side's chances and they fell away badly in the spring after a bright enough start – the Dons failing to win any of their last 11 League games as they finished in 12th place.

Chairman Pete Winkelman's budget cuts for the 2010/11 season paved the way for the departure of Ince, who resigned in April, with Robinson handed the reins. The new manager will be assisted by former Liverpool and Germany midfielder Dietmar Hamann, who joined as a first-team coach in May.

CLUB SUMMARY

FORMED	1889
MANAGER	Karl Robinson
GROUND	stadium:mk
CAPACITY	22,000
NICKNAME	The Dons
WEBSITE	www.mkdons.com

The New Football Pools PLAYER OF THE SEASON

Luke Chadwick

OVERALL
P	W	D	L	F	A	GD
56	23	9	24	80	84	-4

COCA-COLA FOOTBALL LEAGUE 1
Pos	P	W	D	L	F	A	GD	Pts
12	46	17	9	20	60	68	-8	60

HOME
Pos	P	W	D	L	F	A	GD	Pts
17	23	10	5	8	31	28	3	35

AWAY
Pos	P	W	D	L	F	A	GD	Pts
9	23	7	4	12	29	40	-11	25

CUP PROGRESS DETAILS
Competition	Round reached	Knocked out by
FA Cup	R3	Burnley
Carling Cup	R1	Swindon
JP Trophy	F (S)	Southampton

BIGGEST WIN (ALL COMPS)
16/01/10 5–0 v Hartlepool

BIGGEST DEFEAT (ALL COMPS)
13/02/10 0–5 v Carlisle

ATTENDANCE RECORD
High	Average	Low
16,713	10,290	8,528
v Leeds (26/09/2009)		v Oldham (13/04/2010)

RESULTS 2009/10

AUGUST
8th	● Hartlepool	H	D 0–0	Att: 8,965	**Booked:** McCracken, Howell.
11th	● Swindon	H	L 1–4	Att: 4,812	**Scorers:** Easter.
15th	● Swindon	A	D 0–0	Att: 6,692	**Booked:** Howell, Darren Powell, Gueret.
18th	● Tranmere	A	W 0–1	Att: 5,744	**Scorers:** Ibehre. **Booked:** Gleeson, McCracken, Howell, Ibehre.
22nd	● Colchester	H	W 2–1	Att: 8,633	**Scorers:** Carrington, Easter. **Booked:** Johnson, Gueret, Howell, Gleeson, Ibehre.
29th	● Exeter	A	W 1–2	Att: 5,333	**Scorers:** Easter². **Booked:** Easter.

SEPTEMBER
1st	● Dag & Red	H	W 3–1	Att: 4,413	**Scorers:** Easter², Lewington.
5th	● Huddersfield	H	L 2–3	Att: 9,772	**Scorers:** Easter, Johnson. **Booked:** Howell, Easter, L Gobern.
14th	● Norwich	H	W 2–1	Att: 10,354	**Scorers:** Leven, Puncheon. **Booked:** Chadwick.
19th	● Wycombe	A	W 0–1	Att: 6,127	**Scorers:** Doumbe.
26th	● Leeds	H	L 0–1	Att: 16,713	**Booked:** Lewington, Gleeson, Johnson, Doumbe, Darren Powell. **Dismissed:** Puncheon.
29th	● Oldham	A	L 2–1	Att: 3,630	**Scorers:** Brill OG. **Booked:** Doumbe, Leven, Howell, Lewington, Johnson.

OCTOBER
3rd	● Brighton	A	W 0–1	Att: 6,419	**Scorers:** Easter. **Booked:** Partridge, Leven, Doumbe, Gleeson, Davis.
6th	● Southend	H	W 2–0	Att: 4,792	**Scorers:** Carrington, Doran. **Booked:** Wilbraham.
10th	● Walsall	H	W 1–0	Att: 8,919	**Scorers:** Easter.
17th	● Gillingham	H	W 2–0	Att: 11,764	**Scorers:** Easter, Wilbraham. **Booked:** Leven, Easter.
24th	● Southampton	A	L 3–1	Att: 21,387	**Scorers:** Puncheon.
31st	● Bristol Rovers	H	W 2–1	Att: 9,711	**Scorers:** Leven, Puncheon.

NOVEMBER
7th	● Macclesfield	H	W 1–0	Att: 4,868	**Scorers:** L Gobern.
10th	● Northampton	H	W 3–1	Att: 8,886	**Scorers:** S Baldock², Wilbraham. **Booked:** L Gobern, Darren Powell, McCracken.
14th	● Charlton	A	L 5–1	Att: 17,188	**Scorers:** Wilbraham. **Booked:** Davis, Leven, Darren Powell, Puncheon, Woodards.
20th	● Southend	A	L 2–1	Att: 6,957	**Scorers:** S Baldock. **Booked:** Howell, Chadwick, S Baldock, McCracken, Puncheon.
24th	● Carlisle	H	L 3–4	Att: 9,459	**Scorers:** S Baldock, Chadwick². **Booked:** Swailes.
28th	● Exeter	H	W 4–3	Att: 4,867	**Scorers:** S Baldock², Devaney, Easter. **Booked:** Devaney, Easter.

DECEMBER
1st	● Millwall	A	L 3–2	Att: 7,883	**Scorers:** Easter². **Booked:** Quashie, Puncheon, Wilbraham, Easter.
5th	● Yeovil	H	D 2–2	Att: 8,965	**Scorers:** S Baldock, Leven. **Booked:** McCracken, Puncheon, Leven.
12th	● Leyton Orient	A	W 1–2	Att: 3,959	**Scorers:** Morgan, Quashie. **Booked:** D Powell, Howell, Woodards, Gueret.
15th	● Hereford	A	W 1–4	Att: 1,367	**Scorers:** S Baldock, Easter, Puncheon, Wilbraham. **Booked:** Gleeson, L Gobern.
19th	● Brentford	H	L 0–1	Att: 9,520	**Booked:** Howell, Wilbraham, Leven.
26th	● Stockport	H	W 4–1	Att: 9,661	**Scorers:** Easter, Puncheon², Quashie. **Booked:** Easter, Puncheon.
28th	● Huddersfield	A	L 1–0	Att: 16,086	**Booked:** Chadwick, Stirling, Easter.

JANUARY
2nd	● Burnley	H	L 1–2	Att: 11,816	**Scorers:** Morgan. **Booked:** Doumbe, Easter.
16th	● Hartlepool	A	W 0–5	Att: 3,211	**Scorers:** S Baldock, Easter, Leven, Puncheon, Liddle OG. **Booked:** Puncheon, Easter.
20th	● Southampton	H	L 0–1	Att: 7,918	**Booked:** Randall, Gleeson.
23rd	● Tranmere	H	W 1–0	Att: 9,438	**Scorers:** Puncheon. **Booked:** Gleeson.
26th	● Colchester	A	L 2–0	Att: 3,601	**Booked:** Randall, Gleeson, Lewington, Woodards. **Dismissed:** Stirling.
30th	● Exeter	H	D 1–1	Att: 8,740	**Scorers:** S Baldock. **Booked:** Townsend, Darren Powell, Lewington, McCracken, Gleeson, Wilbraham.

FEBRUARY
6th	● Stockport	A	W 1–3	Att: 3,720	**Scorers:** Easter, Townsend, Wilbraham. **Booked:** Woodards, Easter, Townsend, L Gobern.
9th	● Southampton	A	L 3–1	Att: 29,901	**Booked:** Wilbraham. Agg: 4–1.
13th	● Carlisle	A	L 5–0	Att: 4,930	**Booked:** Gleeson, Chadwick, Townsend, Davis.
20th	● Southend	H	W 3–1	Att: 9,801	**Scorers:** Carrington², Townsend.
23rd	● Millwall	H	L 1–3	Att: 10,610	**Scorers:** Wilbraham.
27th	● Yeovil	A	L 1–0	Att: 3,844	**Booked:** Gleeson, Leven, Townsend, McCracken.

MARCH
6th	● Leyton Orient	H	W 1–0	Att: 14,323	**Scorers:** Carrington. **Booked:** Wilbraham, Lewington, Randall, Stirling.
9th	● Swindon	H	W 2–1	Att: 8,764	**Scorers:** Tunnicliffe, Wilbraham. **Booked:** Stirling, Carrington.
13th	● Brentford	A	D 3–3	Att: 5,209	**Scorers:** Easter, Wilbraham². **Booked:** Randall, Woodards, Easter.
20th	● Southampton	H	L 0–1	Att: 10,750	**Booked:** Leven, Lewington, McCracken, Wilbraham.
27th	● Gillingham	A	D 2–2	Att: 5,465	**Scorers:** Easter, McCracken. **Booked:** McCracken, Lewington, Easter, Leven, Gleeson.

APRIL
3rd	● Charlton	H	L 0–1	Att: 10,869	**Booked:** Chicksen, Chadwick.
5th	● Bristol Rovers	A	L 1–0	Att: 6,406	**Booked:** Woodards, Easter, Doumbe, Searle, McCracken, Randall. **Dismissed:** Doumbe.
10th	● Norwich	A	D 1–1	Att: 24,888	**Scorers:** Wilbraham. **Booked:** Randall, Leven, Wilbraham, Chadwick, O'Hanlon, Darren Powell, Davis, Carrington. **Dismissed:** Wilbraham.
13th	● Oldham	H	D 0–0	Att: 8,528	
17th	● Wycombe	H	L 2–3	Att: 10,561	**Scorers:** Wilbraham². **Booked:** Chadwick.
24th	● Leeds	A	L 4–1	Att: 25,964	**Scorers:** Lewington. **Booked:** Lewington, Randall. **Dismissed:** Doumbe, McCracken, Leven.

MAY
1st	● Brighton	H	D 0–0	Att: 12,023	**Booked:** Davis, Darren Powell, Lewington. **Dismissed:** Rae.
8th	● Walsall	A	L 2–1	Att: 4,772	**Scorers:** Daniel Powell. **Booked:** Darren Powell.

● Coca-Cola League 1/Play-Offs ● FA Cup ● Carling Cup ● Johnstone's Paint Trophy

actim

LEAGUE 1 GOALKEEPER STATS

Player	Appearances	Match starts	Completed matches	Sub appearances	Subbed off	Clean sheets	Yellow cards	Red cards
Willy Gueret	43	43	43	0	0	11	3	0
Stuart Searle	3	3	3	0	0	1	1	0

LEAGUE 1 OUTFIELD PLAYER STATS

Player	Appearances	Match starts	Completed matches	Substitute appearances	Subbed off	Goals scored	Yellow cards	Red cards
Sam Baldock	20	11	5	9	6	5	1	0
George Baldock	1	0	0	1	0	0	0	0
Michael Bridges	1	0	0	1	0	0	0	0
Mark Carrington	20	15	10	5	5	4	2	0
Luke Chadwick	40	39	17	1	22	2	7	0
Adam Chicksen	6	4	3	2	1	0	1	0
Charlie Collins	2	2	0	0	2	0	0	0
Sol Davis	10	5	3	5	2	0	5	0
Martin Devaney	5	4	1	1	3	0	0	0
Aaron Doran	4	2	1	2	1	0	0	0
Mathias Doumbe	33	29	24	4	3	1	4	2
Jermaine Easter	36	32	17	4	15	14	11	0
Tom Flanagan	1	0	0	1	0	0	0	0
Stephen Gleeson	29	26	24	3	2	0	10	0
Oscar Gobern	2	0	0	2	0	0	0	0
Lewis Gobern	19	7	0	12	7	0	2	0
Luke Howell	29	17	12	12	5	0	9	0
Jabo Ibehre	10	3	1	7	2	1	2	0
Jemal Johnson	17	12	6	5	6	1	3	0
Peter Leven	31	26	21	5	4	4	10	1
Dean Lewington	42	42	40	0	2	1	9	0
David McCracken	41	41	35	0	5	1	9	0
Dean Morgan	9	1	0	8	1	1	0	0
Sean O'Hanlon	6	3	1	3	2	0	1	0
Richie Partridge	5	1	0	4	1	0	1	0
Daniel Powell	2	2	0	0	1	0	0	0
Darren Powell	24	19	16	5	3	0	8	0
Jason Puncheon	24	23	20	1	2	7	6	1
Nigel Quashie	7	6	2	1	4	2	1	0
Alex Rae	3	2	0	1	1	0	0	0
Mark Randall	16	12	8	4	4	0	6	0
Jude Stirling	9	1	0	8	2	0	3	1
Danny Swailes	2	2	2	0	0	0	1	0
Andros Townsend	9	8	1	1	0	2	4	0
James Tunnicliffe	9	9	7	0	1	0	0	0
Aaron Wilbraham	35	31	29	4	1	10	6	1
Dan Woodards	29	23	12	6	11	0	6	0

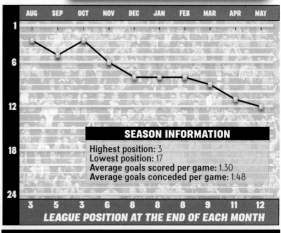

SEASON INFORMATION

Highest position: 3
Lowest position: 17
Average goals scored per game: 1.30
Average goals conceded per game: 1.48

LEAGUE POSITION AT THE END OF EACH MONTH

LONGEST SEQUENCES

Wins	3	Undefeated home	4
(on two occasions)		(26/12/09–20/02/10)	
Losses	4	Undefeated away	4
(14/11/09–01/12/09)		(15/08/09–19/09/09)	
Draws	2	Without scoring	2
(on two occasions)		(on two occasions)	
Undefeated	5	Without conceding	3
(08/08/09–29/08/09)		(on two occasions)	
Without win	11	Scoring	12
(13/03/10–08/05/10)		(29/09/09–12/12/09)	

CARDS RECEIVED

132 **8**

EARLIEST STRIKE

JERMAINE EASTER
(v Exeter) 0:33

LATEST STRIKE

AARON WILBRAHAM
(v Brentford) 92:11

GOALS SCORED/CONCEDED
PER FIVE-MINUTE INTERVALS

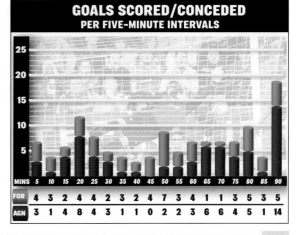

MINS	5	10	15	20	25	30	35	40	45	50	55	60	65	70	75	80	85	90
FOR	4	3	2	4	4	2	3	2	4	7	3	4	1	1	3	5	3	5
AGN	3	1	4	8	4	3	1	1	0	2	2	3	6	6	4	5	1	14

NORWICH CITY

FEW PEOPLE would have predicted that Norwich would end the campaign as Coca-Cola League 1 champions when Colchester pulled off a stunning 7–1 win at Carrow Road on the opening day of the season, but ultimately the Canaries went up in style.

Norwich sacked manager Bryan Gunn just six days after that opening defeat, but showed their clout in the third tier by enticing the architect of their humiliation, U's boss Paul Lambert, to take over at Carrow Road.

Lambert made sweeping changes to the side, with Australian goalkeeper Michael Theoklitos among those to leave the club having made just one appearance. However, it was one of Gunn's signings who had the biggest impact, with Grant Holt scoring 30 goals to fire the Canaries to the title.

With 18,500 season tickets sold by March, there is plenty of expectation from Norwich fans that their team can enjoy more success in the npower Championship in 2010/11.

CLUB SUMMARY

FORMED	1902
MANAGER	Paul Lambert
GROUND	Carrow Road
CAPACITY	26,034
NICKNAME	The Canaries
WEBSITE	www.canaries.co.uk

The New **Football Pools**
PLAYER OF THE SEASON

Wes Hoolahan

OVERALL

P	W	D	L	F	A	GD
54	33	10	11	106	56	50

COCA-COLA FOOTBALL LEAGUE 1

Pos	P	W	D	L	F	A	GD	Pts
1	46	29	8	9	89	47	42	95

HOME

Pos	P	W	D	L	F	A	GD	Pts
2	23	17	3	3	48	22	26	54

AWAY

Pos	P	W	D	L	F	A	GD	Pts
1	23	12	5	6	41	25	16	41

CUP PROGRESS DETAILS

Competition	Round reached	Knocked out by
FA Cup	R2	Carlisle
Carling Cup	R2	Sunderland
JP Trophy	SF	Southampton

BIGGEST WIN (ALL COMPS)
07/11/09 7–0 v Paulton

BIGGEST DEFEAT (ALL COMPS)
08/08/09 1–7 v Colchester

ATTENDANCE RECORD

HIGH	AVERAGE	Low
25,506	24,756	23,041
v Hartlepool (30/01/2010)		v Walsall (05/09/2009)

RESULTS 2009/10

AUGUST
8th	● Colchester	H	L 1–7	Att: 25,217	Scorers: McDonald. Booked: Doherty.
11th	● Yeovil	A	W 0–4	Att: 3,860	Scorers: Holt³, Hoolahan.
15th	● Exeter	A	D 1–1	Att: 6,357	Scorers: Berthel Askou. Booked: Holt.
18th	● Brentford	A	L 2–1	Att: 7,395	Scorers: Tudur Jones. Booked: Holt, C Martin.
22nd	● Wycombe	H	W 5–2	Att: 23,428	Scorers: Berthel Askou, Holt², Otsemobor, Smith.
24th	● Sunderland	H	L 1–4	Att: 12,345	Scorers: Hoolahan. Dismissed: Spillane.
29th	● Hartlepool	A	W 0–2	Att: 4,470	Scorers: Hughes, Nelson.

SEPTEMBER
1st	● Brentford	H	W 1–0	Att: 12,540	Scorers: C Martin.
5th	● Walsall	A	D 0–0	Att: 23,041	
14th	● Milton Keynes Dons	A	L 2–1	Att: 10,354	Scorers: C Martin.
19th	● Charlton	H	D 2–2	Att: 24,018	Scorers: Holt, Hoolahan. Booked: Berthel Askou.
26th	● Gillingham	A	D 1–1	Att: 7,550	Scorers: Russell. Booked: Lappin, Drury, Holt. Dismissed: Forster.
29th	● Leyton Orient	H	W 4–0	Att: 23,981	Scorers: Cureton, Holt, C Martin, Spillane.

OCTOBER
3rd	● Bristol Rovers	H	W 5–1	Att: 24,117	Scorers: Cureton, Holt², Hoolahan, C Martin. Booked: Berthel Askou, Lappin, Drury.
6th	● Gillingham	A	W 0–1	Att: 2,814	Scorers: McDonald. Booked: Francomb.
10th	● Carlisle	A	W 0–1	Att: 6,825	Scorers: Hoolahan. Booked: Lappin, McDonald.
19th	● Leeds	A	L 2–1	Att: 19,912	Scorers: Holt. Booked: Hughes, Russell, Holt.
24th	● Swindon	H	W 1–0	Att: 24,959	Scorers: C Martin.
31st	● Stockport	A	W 1–3	Att: 5,218	Scorers: Holt², Hoolahan. Booked: Lappin, Drury, Hoolahan.

NOVEMBER
7th	● Paulton	A	W 0–7	Att: 2,070	Scorers: Holt², Hoolahan, C Martin⁴. Booked: Lappin, Holt.
10th	● Swindon	A	D 0–0	Att: 4,978	Booked: Berthel Askou. Norwich win 5–3 on penalties.
14th	● Tranmere	H	W 2–0	Att: 25,025	Scorers: Doherty, Hoolahan.
21st	● Southampton	A	D 2–2	Att: 21,362	Scorers: Hoolahan, Hughes. Booked: Russell, C Martin.
24th	● Brighton	H	W 4–1	Att: 24,617	Scorers: Holt, Hoolahan, C Martin, Elphick OG. Booked: Doherty, Russell.
28th	● Carlisle	H	L 3–1	Att: 3,946	Scorers: Holt.

DECEMBER
1st	● Southend	A	W 0–3	Att: 8,732	Scorers: Holt², Smith. Booked: Holt.
5th	● Oldham	H	W 2–0	Att: 24,404	Scorers: Holt, Hoolahan.
12th	● Yeovil	A	D 3–3	Att: 4,964	Scorers: Doherty, C Martin, Russell. Booked: Drury, Forster, Doherty.
15th	● Southampton	A	D 2–2	Att: 15,453	Scorers: Doherty, Nelson, C Martin, R Martin. Booked: Doherty. Holt. Southampton win 6–5 on penalties.
19th	● Huddersfield	H	W 3–0	Att: 25,004	Scorers: Doherty, Hoolahan, C Martin. Booked: Doherty.
26th	● Millwall	H	W 2–0	Att: 25,242	Scorers: Holt, Hoolahan.

JANUARY
2nd	● Wycombe	A	W 0–1	Att: 7,171	Scorers: Smith. Booked: Lappin.
9th	● Exeter	H	W 3–1	Att: 24,955	Scorers: Holt², C Martin. Booked: Russell.
16th	● Colchester	A	W 0–5	Att: 10,064	Scorers: Doherty, Holt, Johnson, C Martin². Booked: Hoolahan, C Martin, Holt, Doherty.
23rd	● Brentford	H	W 1–0	Att: 24,979	Scorers: C Martin. Booked: Russell, Drury, Johnson. Dismissed: Holt.
26th	● Walsall	A	W 1–2	Att: 5,022	Scorers: C Martin, McDonald.
30th	● Hartlepool	H	W 2–1	Att: 25,506	Scorers: McDonald, Rose.

FEBRUARY
6th	● Millwall	A	L 2–1	Att: 14,374	Scorers: C Martin.
13th	● Brighton	A	W 1–2	Att: 7,258	Scorers: Doherty, Holt. Booked: Lappin, Forster.
20th	● Southampton	H	L 0–2	Att: 25,103	Booked: C Martin. Dismissed: Russell.
23rd	● Southend	H	W 2–1	Att: 24,824	Scorers: Johnson². Booked: R Martin.
27th	● Oldham	A	W 0–1	Att: 5,344	Scorers: Holt.

MARCH
6th	● Yeovil	H	W 3–0	Att: 24,868	Scorers: Holt, Hoolahan, C Martin.
13th	● Huddersfield	A	W 1–3	Att: 17,959	Scorers: Elliott², Holt. Booked: Russell.
20th	● Swindon	A	D 1–1	Att: 11,972	Scorers: Holt.
27th	● Leeds	H	W 1–0	Att: 25,445	Scorers: C Martin. Booked: Smith, Holt, Drury.

APRIL
2nd	● Tranmere	A	L 3–1	Att: 6,263	Scorers: Holt. Booked: R Martin. Dismissed: Forster.
5th	● Stockport	H	W 2–1	Att: 25,353	Scorers: Holt, McNamee.
10th	● Milton Keynes Dons	H	D 1–1	Att: 24,888	Scorers: C Martin, Holt.
13th	● Leyton Orient	A	L 2–1	Att: 7,520	Scorers: Smith. Booked: Johnson, C Martin, Drury, Russell.
17th	● Charlton	A	W 0–1	Att: 20,023	Scorers: Nelson. Booked: Drury, Hughes, Forster, Spillane.
24th	● Gillingham	H	W 2–0	Att: 25,227	Scorers: Nelson, Russell. Booked: Nelson.

MAY
1st	● Bristol Rovers	A	W 0–3	Att: 8,836	Scorers: Hughes, Johnson, C Martin.
8th	● Carlisle	H	L 0–2	Att: 25,181	

● Coca-Cola League 1/Play-Offs ● FA Cup ● Carling Cup ● Johnstone's Paint Trophy

actim

LEAGUE 1 GOALKEEPER STATS

Player	Appearances	Match starts	Completed matches	Sub appearances	Subbed off	Clean sheets	Yellow cards	Red cards
Ben Alnwick	3	3	3	0	0	0	0	0
Fraser Forster	38	38	35	0	1	18	3	2
Declan Rudd	7	4	4	3	0	1	0	0
Michael Theoklitos	1	1	1	0	0	0	0	0

LEAGUE 1 OUTFIELD PLAYER STATS

Player	Appearances	Match starts	Completed matches	Substitute appearances	Subbed off	Goals scored	Yellow cards	Red cards
Tom Adeyemi	11	2	0	9	2	0	0	0
Jens Berthel Askou	22	21	21	1	0	2	2	0
Jamie Cureton	6	3	0	3	3	2	0	0
Luke Daley	7	3	1	4	2	0	0	0
Gary Doherty	38	38	38	0	0	5	5	0
Adam Drury	35	35	31	0	4	0	8	0
Stephen Elliott	10	4	0	6	4	2	0	0
George Francomb	2	2	0	0	2	0	0	0
Matthew Gill	8	5	2	3	3	0	0	0
Grant Holt	39	39	32	0	6	24	8	1
Wes Hoolahan	37	36	21	1	15	11	2	0
Stephen Hughes	29	12	5	17	7	3	2	0
Oli Johnson	17	4	0	13	4	4	2	0
Simon Lappin	44	42	32	2	10	0	6	0
Russell Martin	26	26	25	0	1	0	2	0
Chris Martin	42	36	25	6	11	17	6	0
Cody McDonald	17	4	2	13	2	3	1	0
Anthony McNamee	17	7	4	10	3	1	0	0
Paul McVeigh	9	4	1	5	3	0	0	0
Michael Nelson	31	28	24	3	4	3	1	0
Jon Otsemobor	13	12	11	1	1	1	0	0
Michael Rose	12	11	11	1	0	0	0	0
Darel Russell	35	34	29	1	4	3	7	1
Korey Smith	37	36	21	1	15	4	1	0
Michael Spillane	13	10	8	3	2	1	1	0
Owain Tudur Jones	3	2	2	1	0	1	0	0
Simon Whaley	3	3	2	0	1	0	0	0
Zak Whitbread	4	1	1	3	0	0	0	0

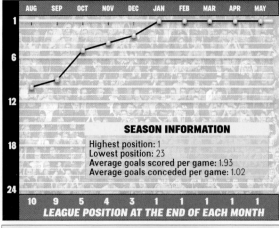

SEASON INFORMATION
Highest position: 1
Lowest position: 23
Average goals scored per game: 1.93
Average goals conceded per game: 1.02

LEAGUE POSITION AT THE END OF EACH MONTH

10 9 5 4 3 1 1 1 1 1

LONGEST SEQUENCES

Wins	8	Undefeated home	14
(19/12/09–30/01/10)		(22/08/09–30/01/10)	
Losses	–	Undefeated away	7
(–)		(31/10/09–26/01/10)	
Draws	2	Without scoring	–
(19/09/09–26/09/09)		(–)	
Undefeated	16	Without conceding	3
(24/10/09–30/01/10)		(on two occasions)	
Without win	4	Scoring	25
(05/09/09–26/09/09)		(14/09/09–13/02/10)	

CARDS RECEIVED

57 **4**

EARLIEST STRIKE

CHRIS MARTIN
(v Milton Keynes Dons) 0:17

LATEST STRIKE

DAREL RUSSELL
(v Gillingham) 96:07

GOALS SCORED/CONCEDED
PER FIVE-MINUTE INTERVALS

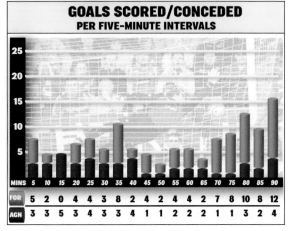

MINS	5	10	15	20	25	30	35	40	45	50	55	60	65	70	75	80	85	90
FOR	5	2	0	4	4	3	8	2	4	2	4	4	2	7	8	10	8	12
AGN	3	3	5	3	4	3	3	4	1	1	2	2	2	1	1	3	2	4

OLDHAM just about avoided a relegation fight but manager Dave Penney left by mutual consent with one game of the season remaining.

A run of three wins and three draws from seven games in April was enough to lift the Latics clear of the drop zone but their 16th-place finish saw Penney depart. While the club accepted that the manager had been hampered by a string of injuries, chief executive Alan Hardy stated that worries over falling attendances played a part in Penney's departure.

Three straight wins at the end of September had left the Latics outside of the play-off places on goal difference alone, but they ultimately paid the price for a lack of cutting edge, with 13-goal striker Pawel Abbott the only player to score more than three during 2009/10.

There were only two victories to celebrate between October and the end of January – a run that left the Latics struggling near the foot of the table before their end-of-season resurgence preserved their third-tier status.

CLUB SUMMARY

FORMED	1895
MANAGER	TBC
GROUND	Boundary Park
CAPACITY	13,595
NICKNAME	The Latics
WEBSITE	www.oldhamathletic.co.uk

Pawel Abbott
PLAYER OF THE SEASON

OVERALL

P	W	D	L	F	A	GD
49	13	13	23	40	62	-22

COCA-COLA FOOTBALL LEAGUE 1

Pos	P	W	D	L	F	A	GD	Pts
16	46	13	13	20	39	57	-18	52

HOME

Pos	P	W	D	L	F	A	GD	Pts
21	23	7	7	9	23	28	-5	28

AWAY

Pos	P	W	D	L	F	A	GD	Pts
12	23	6	6	11	16	29	-13	24

CUP PROGRESS DETAILS

Competition	Round reached	Knocked out by
FA Cup	R1	Leeds
Carling Cup	R1	Carlisle
JP Trophy	R1	Accrington

BIGGEST WIN (ALL COMPS)
2–0 on 4 occasions

BIGGEST DEFEAT (ALL COMPS)
0–3 on 3 occasions

ATTENDANCE RECORD

High	Average	Low
8,569	4,630	2,833
v Huddersfield (01/11/2009)		v Brentford (30/03/2010)

RESULTS 2009/10

AUGUST
8th	● Stockport	H	D 0–0	Att: 6,918	Booked: Whitaker.
11th	● Carlisle	A	L 1–0	Att: 2,509	Booked: Hazell.
15th	● Leyton Orient	A	W 1–2	Att: 4,061	Scorers: Abbott². Booked: Holdsworth, Gilbert, Parker, Worthington, Marrow.
18th	● Millwall	A	L 2–0	Att: 7,369	Booked: Taylor, Worthington, Furman.
22nd	● Swindon	H	D 2–2	Att: 4,229	Scorers: Lee, Marrow. Booked: Worthington.
29th	● Brentford	A	D 1–1	Att: 5,125	Scorers: Blackman.

SEPTEMBER
1st	● Accrington	H	L 1–2	Att: 1,619	Scorers: Whitaker. Booked: Hazell, Gregan.
4th	● Hartlepool	H	L 0–3	Att: 4,014	
12th	● Bristol Rovers	A	L 1–0	Att: 6,674	Booked: Marrow, Sheehan.
19th	● Carlisle	H	W 2–0	Att: 4,268	Scorers: Abbott, Parker.
26th	● Southend	A	W 0–1	Att: 6,979	Scorers: Abbott. Booked: Taylor, Furman.
29th	● Milton Keynes Dons	H	W 2–1	Att: 3,630	Scorers: Parker, Sheehan. Booked: Marrow.

OCTOBER
3rd	● Yeovil	H	D 0–0	Att: 4,208	Booked: Worthington.
10th	● Charlton	A	D 0–0	Att: 16,441	Booked: Lomax, Brill.
17th	● Southampton	H	L 1–3	Att: 5,341	Scorers: Abbott. Booked: Lomax.
24th	● Brighton	A	W 0–2	Att: 6,205	Scorers: Abbott, Hazell. Booked: Gregan, Furman, Abbott.

NOVEMBER
1st	● Huddersfield	H	L 0–1	Att: 8,569	Booked: Hazell, Holdsworth, Abbott.
7th	● Leeds	H	L 0–2	Att: 5,552	Booked: Furman, Smalley.
14th	● Gillingham	A	L 1–0	Att: 4,787	Booked: Taylor, Marrow, Holdsworth, Furman, Hazell, Parker.
21st	● Colchester	H	D 2–2	Att: 3,607	Scorers: Brooke, Taylor. Booked: Colbeck.
24th	● Walsall	A	L 3–0	Att: 3,191	Booked: Smalley, Parker. Dismissed: Hills.

DECEMBER
1st	● Leeds	H	L 0–2	Att: 7,793	Booked: Marrow, Black.
5th	● Norwich	A	L 2–0	Att: 24,404	Booked: Furman, Gregan.
12th	● Exeter	H	W 2–0	Att: 6,230	Scorers: Heffernan, Smalley. Booked: Colbeck, Smalley, Gregan, Marrow, Stephens.
19th	● Wycombe	A	D 2–2	Att: 4,160	Scorers: Hazell, Whitaker. Booked: Stephens, Furman, Smalley, Lee, Hazell.

JANUARY
2nd	● Hartlepool	A	L 2–1	Att: 2,634	Scorers: Abbott. Booked: Goodwin, Gregan.
20th	● Tranmere	H	D 0–0	Att: 3,688	Booked: Marrow.
23rd	● Millwall	H	L 0–1	Att: 3,656	Booked: Gregan.

FEBRUARY
6th	● Tranmere	A	W 0–1	Att: 5,518	Scorers: Abbott. Booked: Stephens, Smalley.
9th	● Swindon	A	L 4–2	Att: 6,183	Scorers: Colbeck, Price. Booked: Hazell.
13th	● Walsall	H	W 1–0	Att: 3,968	Scorers: Abbott. Booked: Smalley.
20th	● Colchester	A	L 1–0	Att: 5,321	
23rd	● Leeds	A	L 2–0	Att: 17,635	Booked: Furman, Taylor, Smalley, Gregan.
27th	● Norwich	H	L 0–1	Att: 5,344	Booked: Stephens.

MARCH
6th	● Exeter	A	D 1–1	Att: 4,997	Scorers: Gregan. Booked: Stephens, Hazell, Furman, Taylor.
9th	● Leyton Orient	H	W 2–0	Att: 3,126	Scorers: Smalley, Stephens. Booked: Gregan.
13th	● Wycombe	H	D 2–2	Att: 3,846	Scorers: Abbott, Hazell. Booked: Hazell.
16th	● Stockport	A	W 0–1	Att: 4,283	Scorers: Abbott. Booked: Eaves.
20th	● Brighton	H	L 0–2	Att: 4,059	Booked: Worthington, Furman, Eaves.
30th	● Brentford	H	L 2–3	Att: 2,833	Scorers: Abbott².

APRIL
3rd	● Gillingham	H	W 1–0	Att: 3,486	Scorers: Guy. Booked: Gregan, Millar.
6th	● Huddersfield	A	L 2–0	Att: 14,561	Booked: Lee. Dismissed: Lee.
10th	● Bristol Rovers	H	W 2–1	Att: 3,769	Scorers: Guy, Smalley.
13th	● Milton Keynes Dons	A	D 0–0	Att: 8,528	Booked: Stephens.
17th	● Carlisle	A	W 1–2	Att: 4,484	Scorers: Guy, Stephens. Booked: Furman.
20th	● Southampton	A	D 0–0	Att: 18,366	Booked: Abbott, Marrow.
24th	● Southend	H	D 2–2	Att: 4,225	Scorers: Black, Whitaker. Booked: Stephens, Smalley, Furman.

MAY
1st	● Yeovil	A	L 3–0	Att: 4,513	Booked: Gregan, Taylor.
8th	● Charlton	H	L 0–2	Att: 5,686	Booked: Gregan.

● Coca-Cola League 1/Play-Offs ● FA Cup ● Carling Cup ● Johnstone's Paint Trophy

LEAGUE 1 GOALKEEPER STATS

Player	Appearances	Match starts	Completed matches	Sub appearances	Subbed off	Clean sheets	Yellow cards	Red cards
Dean Brill	28	28	28	0	0	11	1	0
Darryl Flahavan	18	18	18	0	0	4	0	0

LEAGUE 1 OUTFIELD PLAYER STATS

Player	Appearances	Match starts	Completed matches	Substitute appearances	Subbed off	Goals scored	Yellow cards	Red cards
Pawel Abbott	39	38	22	1	16	13	3	0
Lewis Alessandra	1	0	0	1	0	0	0	0
Hasney Aljofree	1	1	1	0	0	0	0	0
Paul Black	13	12	11	1	1	1	1	0
Nick Blackman	12	6	3	6	3	1	0	0
Ryan Brooke	15	2	1	13	1	1	0	0
Darren Byfield	3	0	0	3	0	0	0	0
Joe Colbeck	27	18	7	9	11	1	2	0
Tom Eaves	15	0	0	15	0	0	2	0
Dean Furman	38	32	23	6	9	0	11	0
Peter Gilbert	5	5	5	0	0	0	1	0
Jim Goodwin	8	8	7	0	1	0	1	0
Sean Gregan	46	46	46	0	0	1	10	0
Lewis Guy	12	12	7	0	5	3	0	0
Reuben Hazell	41	41	40	0	1	3	6	0
Paul Heffernan	4	4	1	0	3	1	0	0
Lee Hills	3	3	1	0	1	0	0	1
Andy Holdsworth	12	11	8	1	3	0	3	0
Joe Jacobson	15	14	13	1	1	0	0	0
Kieran Lee	24	16	14	8	1	1	2	1
Kelvin Lomax	15	11	9	4	2	0	2	0
Alex Marrow	32	26	21	6	5	1	8	0
Kirk Millar	6	2	0	4	2	0	1	0
Daniel Nardiello	2	2	0	0	2	0	0	0
Keigan Parker	27	17	5	10	12	2	3	0
Jason Price	7	7	5	0	2	1	0	0
Chris Rowney	1	0	0	1	0	0	0	0
Alan Sheehan	8	8	8	0	0	1	1	0
Deane Smalley	29	23	13	6	10	3	7	0
Dale Stephens	26	24	22	2	2	2	7	0
Chris Taylor	32	27	17	5	10	1	6	0
Krisztian Timar	2	2	1	0	1	0	0	0
Danny Whitaker	41	31	24	10	7	2	1	0
Jonathan Worthington	16	11	5	5	6	0	5	0

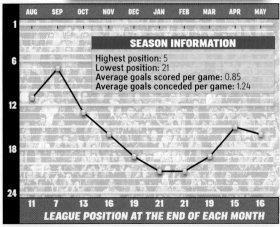

SEASON INFORMATION

Highest position: 5
Lowest position: 21
Average goals scored per game: 0.85
Average goals conceded per game: 1.24

LEAGUE POSITION AT THE END OF EACH MONTH

11 7 13 16 19 21 21 19 15 16

LONGEST SEQUENCES

Wins	3	Undefeated home	3
(19/09/09–29/09/09)		(on two occasions)	
Losses	3	Undefeated away	3
(on two occasions)		(on two occasions)	
Draws	2	Without scoring	3
(on three occasions)		(on two occasions)	
Undefeated	5	Without conceding	2
(on two occasions)		(on two occasions)	
Without win	6	Scoring	4
(01/11/09–05/12/09)		(06/03/10–16/03/10)	

CARDS RECEIVED

84 2

EARLIEST STRIKE

DANNY WHITAKER
(v Southend) 1:11

LATEST STRIKE

KIERAN LEE
(v Swindon) 93:33

GOALS SCORED/CONCEDED
PER FIVE-MINUTE INTERVALS

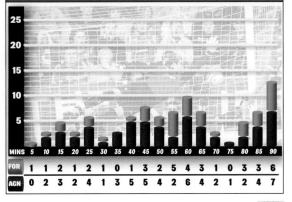

MINS	5	10	15	20	25	30	35	40	45	50	55	60	65	70	75	80	85	90
FOR	1	1	2	1	2	1	0	1	3	2	5	4	3	1	0	3	3	6
AGN	0	2	3	2	4	1	3	5	5	4	2	6	4	2	1	2	4	7

SOUTHAMPTON

DESPITE a 10-point penalty for going into administration, Southampton made a decent fist of gatecrashing the play-offs with some sparkling late-season form. Eventually they fell just short, but would have finished in fifth place had they not been penalised.

Markus Liebherr had taken over the club following relegation in 2008/09, and appointed Alan Pardew as manager ahead of the new season. However, despite several purchases, the Saints had to wait eight games to record their first League win.

The signing of Rickie Lambert proved to be £1 million well spent as the striker scored 36 goals while Jason Puncheon, José Fonte and Lee Barnard were also astute buys, offering hope that the club could make a genuine challenge for promotion in 2010/11.

While the season was frustrating in some ways, the 4–1 Johnstone's Paint Trophy final win over Carlisle at least saw the Saints claim their first piece of silverware at Wembley since 1976.

CLUB SUMMARY

FORMED	1885
MANAGER	Alan Pardew
GROUND	St Mary's Stadium
CAPACITY	32,551
NICKNAME	The Saints
WEBSITE	www.saintsfc.co.uk

The New Football Pools PLAYER OF THE SEASON — Rickie Lambert

OVERALL

P	W	D	L	F	A	GD
59	32	16	11	112	65	47

COCA-COLA FOOTBALL LEAGUE 1

Pos	P	W	D	L	F	A	GD	Pts
7	46	23	14	9	85	47	38	73

HOME

Pos	P	W	D	L	F	A	GD	Pts
4	23	15	5	3	48	21	27	50

AWAY

Pos	P	W	D	L	F	A	GD	Pts
6	23	8	9	6	37	26	11	33

CUP PROGRESS DETAILS

Competition	Round reached	Knocked out by
FA Cup	R5	Portsmouth
Carling Cup	R2	Birmingham
JP Trophy	WON	

BIGGEST WIN (ALL COMPS)
02/03/10 5–0 v Huddersfield

BIGGEST DEFEAT (ALL COMPS)
13/02/10 1–4 v Portsmouth

ATTENDANCE RECORD

High	Average	Low
30,890	20,982	16,402
v Exeter (26/12/2009)		v Wycombe (01/12/2009)

RESULTS 2009/10

AUGUST

8th	● Millwall	H	D 1–1	Att: 20,103	Scorers: Paterson.	
11th	● Northampton	H	W 2–0	Att: 10,921	Scorers: Lallana, Lambert.	
15th	● Huddersfield	A	L 3–1	Att: 12,449	Scorers: Lambert. Booked: Wotton, Thomas, Lallana.	
18th	● Swindon	A	L 1–0	Att: 11,007	Booked: Paterson, Schneiderlin, Wotton.	
22nd	● Brentford	A	D 1–1	Att: 19,169	Scorers: Harding. Booked: Paterson, Harding.	
25th	● Birmingham	H	L 1–2	Att: 11,753	Scorers: Lallana. Booked: Perry.	
29th	● Stockport	A	D 1–1	Att: 4,680	Scorers: Lambert. Booked: Trotman.	

SEPTEMBER

5th	● Colchester	H	D 0–0	Att: 17,070	Booked: Mellis, James, Mills.
12th	● Charlton	A	D 1–1	Att: 19,441	Scorers: Lallana. Booked: Hammond, Thomas.
19th	● Yeovil	H	W 2–0	Att: 19,907	Scorers: Lambert². Booked: Hammond, Trotman, James, Papa Waigo.
26th	● Carlisle	A	D 1–1	Att: 7,000	Scorers: Jaidi.
29th	● Bristol Rovers	H	L 2–3	Att: 19,724	Scorers: Lallana, Lambert. Booked: Hammond.

OCTOBER

3rd	● Gillingham	H	W 4–1	Att: 19,457	Scorers: Lallana², Lambert, Papa Waigo. Booked: Trotman.
6th	● Torquay	H	D 2–2	Att: 9,319	Scorers: Papa Waigo². Booked: James, Davis. Southampton win 5–3 on penalties.
9th	● Southend	A	W 1–3	Att: 8,281	Scorers: Lallana², Trotman. Booked: Harding, Schneiderlin.
17th	● Oldham	A	W 1–3	Att: 5,341	Scorers: Connolly, Hammond, Lambert. Booked: Connolly.
24th	● Milton Keynes Dons	H	W 3–1	Att: 21,387	Scorers: Connolly, Hammond, Lambert. Booked: Jaidi.
31st	● Leyton Orient	A	D 2–2	Att: 7,544	Scorers: Lambert². Booked: Papa Waigo, Trotman.

NOVEMBER

6th	● Bristol Rovers	A	W 2–3	Att: 6,446	Scorers: Antonio, Connolly². Booked: Harding, O Gobern, Jaidi, Davis.
11th	● Charlton	H	W 2–1	Att: 13,906	Scorers: Lambert, Thomas.
15th	● Brighton	H	L 1–3	Att: 21,932	Scorers: Lambert.
21st	● Norwich	H	D 2–2	Att: 21,362	Scorers: Connolly, Lallana. Booked: James, Lallana, Jaidi.
24th	● Hartlepool	A	W 1–3	Att: 3,818	Scorers: Lallana², Lambert. Booked: Schneiderlin, Trotman, Wotton.
28th	● Northampton	A	W 2–3	Att: 4,858	Scorers: Hammond, Lallana, Papa Waigo.

DECEMBER

1st	● Wycombe	H	W 1–0	Att: 16,402	Scorers: Lambert. Booked: Antonio.
5th	● Walsall	H	W 1–3	Att: 5,681	Scorers: Connolly, Hammond, Lambert. Booked: Harding, Jaidi.
12th	● Tranmere	H	W 3–0	Att: 19,800	Scorers: Harding, Lambert². Booked: Lambert, Schneiderlin.
15th	● Norwich	H	D 2–2	Att: 15,453	Scorers: Papa Waigo². Southampton win 6–5 on penalties.
19th	● Leeds	A	L 1–0	Att: 25,948	Booked: Lallana, Lambert.
26th	● Exeter	H	W 3–1	Att: 30,890	Scorers: James, Papa Waigo, Trotman. Booked: Perry.
28th	● Colchester	A	L 2–1	Att: 8,514	Scorers: Lambert. Booked: Antonio, Trotman, Thomas.

JANUARY

2nd	● Luton	H	W 1–0	Att: 18,786	Scorers: Lambert. Booked: Schneiderlin.
16th	● Millwall	A	D 1–1	Att: 11,524	Scorers: Lambert. Booked: Seaborne, Fonte.
20th	● Milton Keynes Dons	A	W 0–1	Att: 7,918	Scorers: Antonio. Booked: Davis, James, Thomas, Holmes. Dismissed: Schneiderlin.
23rd	● Ipswich	H	W 2–1	Att: 20,446	Scorers: Antonio, Thomas.
26th	● Brentford	A	D 1–1	Att: 6,501	Scorers: James. Booked: Wotton.
30th	● Stockport	H	W 2–0	Att: 18,308	Scorers: Lambert, Papa Waigo. Booked: Mills.

FEBRUARY

6th	● Exeter	A	D 1–1	Att: 7,654	Scorers: Lallana. Booked: Seaborne, Schneiderlin, Fonte.
9th	● Milton Keynes Dons	H	W 3–1	Att: 29,901	Scorers: Lallana, Lambert, Woodards OG. Booked: Thomas. Agg: 4–1.
13th	● Portsmouth	H	L 1–4	Att: 31,385	Scorers: Lambert. Booked: Hammond.
20th	● Norwich	A	W 0–2	Att: 25,103	Scorers: Barnard². Booked: Jaidi, Hammond, Davis, Harding.
23rd	● Wycombe	A	D 0–0	Att: 6,232	Booked: Harding.
27th	● Walsall	H	W 5–1	Att: 20,461	Scorers: Barnard², Lallana, Lambert, Puncheon.

MARCH

2nd	● Huddersfield	H	W 5–0	Att: 19,821	Scorers: Barnard, Hammond, Lambert, Papa Waigo, Puncheon.
6th	● Tranmere	A	L 2–1	Att: 6,187	Scorers: Barnard. Booked: Schneiderlin, Puncheon, Fonte.
13th	● Leeds	H	W 1–0	Att: 30,794	Scorers: Harding. Booked: Puncheon, Hammond.
16th	● Swindon	H	L 0–1	Att: 20,752	Booked: Puncheon, Harding.
20th	● Milton Keynes Dons	A	W 0–3	Att: 10,570	Scorers: Lambert³. Booked: Schneiderlin, Barnard, Fonte.
23rd	● Hartlepool	H	W 3–2	Att: 18,072	Scorers: Barnard, Lambert, Papa Waigo.
28th	● Carlisle	N	W 1–4	Att: 73,476	Scorers: Antonio, Lallana, Lambert, Papa Waigo.

APRIL

1st	● Brighton	A	D 2–2	Att: 7,784	Scorers: Barnard, Hammond. Booked: Hammond, Barnard.
5th	● Leyton Orient	H	W 2–1	Att: 21,559	Scorers: Lallana².
10th	● Charlton	H	W 1–0	Att: 23,061	Scorers: Antonio. Booked: Hammond.
13th	● Bristol Rovers	A	W 1–5	Att: 8,607	Scorers: Lallana, Lambert², Puncheon, Schneiderlin. Booked: Schneiderlin.
17th	● Yeovil	A	W 0–1	Att: 7,484	Scorers: Barnard. Booked: Barnard, Fonte, Papa Waigo. Dismissed: Schneiderlin.
20th	● Oldham	H	D 0–0	Att: 18,366	Booked: Harding.
24th	● Carlisle	H	W 3–2	Att: 18,908	Scorers: Antonio², Lambert. Booked: Davis.

MAY

1st	● Gillingham	A	L 2–1	Att: 9,504	Scorers: Connolly. Booked: Fonte, Mills, Martin.
8th	● Southend	H	W 3–1	Att: 25,289	Scorers: Lallana, Lambert². Booked: Lallana.

● Coca-Cola League 1/Play-Offs ● FA Cup ● Carling Cup ● Johnstone's Paint Trophy

LEAGUE 1 GOALKEEPER STATS

Player	Appearances	Match starts	Completed matches	Sub appearances	Subbed off	Clean sheets	Yellow cards	Red cards
Bartosz Bialkowski	7	6	6	1	0	2	0	0
Kelvin Davis	40	40	39	0	1	11	2	0

LEAGUE 1 OUTFIELD PLAYER STATS

Player	Appearances	Match starts	Completed matches	Substitute appearances	Subbed off	Goals scored	Yellow cards	Red cards
Michail Antonio	28	14	3	14	11	3	2	0
Lee Barnard	20	14	2	6	12	9	3	0
David Connolly	20	9	3	11	6	5	1	0
Jose Fonte	21	21	20	0	1	0	6	0
Simon Gillett	2	0	0	2	0	0	0	0
Oscar Gobern	4	0	0	4	0	0	0	0
Dean Hammond	40	40	37	0	3	5	7	0
Dan Harding	42	42	40	0	2	3	7	0
Lee Holmes	5	2	2	3	0	0	0	0
Radhi Jaidi	27	26	22	1	4	1	4	0
Lloyd James	30	28	21	2	7	2	3	0
Adam Lallana	44	44	34	0	10	15	4	0
Rickie Lambert	45	44	32	1	12	30	2	0
Oliver Lancashire	2	1	0	1	1	0	0	0
Aaron Martin	2	2	2	0	0	0	1	0
Callum McNish	1	0	0	1	0	0	0	0
Jacob Mellis	12	7	3	5	4	0	1	0
Joseph Mills	16	8	5	8	3	0	3	0
Graeme Murty	6	5	5	1	0	0	0	0
Jon Otsemobor	19	19	16	0	3	0	0	0
Alex Oxlade-Chamberlain	2	0	0	2	0	0	0	0
Ndiaye Papa Waigo	35	11	2	24	9	5	3	0
Matthew Paterson	7	4	0	3	4	1	2	0
Chris Perry	12	11	8	1	3	0	1	0
Jason Puncheon	19	19	16	0	3	3	3	0
Grzegorz Rasiak	3	1	1	2	0	0	0	0
Marek Saganowski	6	3	1	3	2	0	0	0
Morgan Schneiderlin	37	35	19	2	15	1	8	1
Daniel Seaborne	16	11	11	5	0	0	2	0
Wayne Thomas	15	10	7	5	3	0	3	0
Jake Thomson	4	0	0	4	0	0	0	0
Neal Trotman	18	17	15	1	2	0	6	0
Paul Wotton	26	12	6	14	6	0	4	0

AUG SEP OCT NOV DEC JAN FEB MAR APR MAY

SEASON INFORMATION
Highest position: 7
Lowest position: 24
Average goals scored per game: 1.85
Average goals conceded per game: 1.02

LEAGUE POSITION AT THE END OF EACH MONTH

24 24 22 21 13 11 11 10 7 7

LONGEST SEQUENCES

Wins (on three occasions)	4	Undefeated home (21/11/09–13/03/10)	8
Losses (15/08/09–18/08/09)	2	Undefeated away (29/08/09–05/12/09)	8
Draws (22/08/09–12/09/09)	4	Without scoring (–)	–
Undefeated (20/03/10–24/04/10)	9	Without conceding (on two occasions)	2
Without win (08/08/09–12/09/09)	7	Scoring (12/09/09–12/12/09)	15

CARDS RECEIVED
78 1

EARLIEST STRIKE
LLOYD JAMES
(v Brentford) 3:55

LATEST STRIKE
RADHI JAIDI
(v Carlisle) 95:01

GOALS SCORED/CONCEDED
PER FIVE-MINUTE INTERVALS

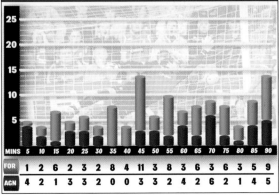

MINS	5	10	15	20	25	30	35	40	45	50	55	60	65	70	75	80	85	90
FOR	1	2	6	2	3	2	8	4	11	3	8	3	6	3	6	3	5	9
AGN	4	2	1	3	3	2	0	0	3	3	2	4	2	6	2	1	4	5

SOUTHEND UNITED

IT WAS certainly a season to forget for Southend, who returned to the bottom tier of English football for the first time in five years as well as dealing with major financial worries.

The Essex club were faced with winding-up orders from HM Revenue and Customs and, despite eventually settling their debt in April, the Shrimpers continued to struggle on the pitch and were relegated with two games remaining.

Steve Tilson's side had made an encouraging start to the campaign, losing just one of their first eight games in the League. However, they went on to win just 10 games overall and paid the price.

Tilson knows what it takes to build a promotion-winning side having previously lifted the Shrimpers from the basement division to the Coca-Cola Championship and, although he faces a big rebuilding job, the club will expect to be in the hunt for promotion straight back up to npower League 1 during 2010/11.

CLUB SUMMARY

FORMED	1906
MANAGER	Steve Tilson
GROUND	Roots Hall
CAPACITY	12,306
NICKNAME	The Shrimpers
WEBSITE	www.southendunited.co.uk

The New **Football Pools** PLAYER OF THE SEASON — **Simon Francis**

OVERALL
P	W	D	L	F	A	GD
50	11	13	26	54	81	-27

COCA-COLA FOOTBALL LEAGUE 1
Pos	P	W	D	L	F	A	GD	Pts
23	46	10	13	23	51	72	-21	43

HOME
Pos	P	W	D	L	F	A	GD	Pts
20	23	7	10	6	29	27	2	31

AWAY
Pos	P	W	D	L	F	A	GD	Pts
23	23	3	3	17	22	45	-23	12

CUP PROGRESS DETAILS
Competition	Round reached	Knocked out by
FA Cup	R1	Gillingham
Carling Cup	R2	Hull
JP Trophy	R2	Milton Keynes Dons

BIGGEST WIN (ALL COMPS)
3–0 on 2 occasions

BIGGEST DEFEAT (ALL COMPS)
0–3 on 4 occasions

ATTENDANCE RECORD
HIGH	AVERAGE	Low
10,329	7,718	6,382
v Colchester (26/12/2009)		v Tranmere (13/02/2010)

RESULTS 2009/10

AUGUST
8th	● Huddersfield	H	D 2–2	Att: 8,059	Scorers: Barnard, Moussa. Booked: Heath.
11th	● Cheltenham	A	W 1–2	Att: 1,918	Scorers: Barnard². Booked: Francis, Grant.
15th	● Walsall	A	D 2–2	Att: 3,658	Scorers: Barnard, Freedman.
18th	● Wycombe	A	D 1–1	Att: 4,607	Scorers: Christophe. Booked: McCormack.
21st	● Millwall	H	D 0–0	Att: 8,435	Booked: Grant, McCormack.
25th	● Hull	A	L 3–1	Att: 7,994	Scorers: Moussa. Booked: Christophe, Sawyer.
29th	● Swindon	A	L 2–1	Att: 6,417	Scorers: Scannell. Booked: Christophe, Mvoto, Grant, Francis. Dismissed: Christophe.

SEPTEMBER
4th	● Leyton Orient	H	W 3–0	Att: 8,836	Scorers: Barnard³. Booked: McCormack.
11th	● Leeds	H	D 0–0	Att: 10,123	Booked: McCormack.
19th	● Brighton	A	W 2–3	Att: 6,287	Scorers: Barnard, Laurent, O'Donovan.
26th	● Oldham	H	L 0–1	Att: 6,979	Booked: Christophe, Barnard.
29th	● Brentford	A	L 2–1	Att: 5,578	Scorers: Francis. Booked: Barnard, Grant, Moussa, Francis.

OCTOBER
3rd	● Stockport	A	W 0–2	Att: 4,102	Scorers: Barnard². Booked: Grant.
6th	● Milton Keynes Dons	A	L 2–0	Att: 4,792	Booked: Christophe, Francis, Sawyer.
9th	● Southampton	H	L 1–3	Att: 8,281	Scorers: Friend.
17th	● Bristol Rovers	H	W 2–1	Att: 6,853	Scorers: Barnard². Booked: Barrett, Grant, Barnard.
24th	● Carlisle	A	L 2–1	Att: 4,551	Scorers: Laurent. Booked: Grant, McCormack, Barnard.
30th	● Gillingham	H	W 1–0	Att: 7,830	Scorers: Barnard. Booked: Grant, Barnard, Walker, McCormack.

NOVEMBER
7th	● Gillingham	A	L 3–0	Att: 4,605	
14th	● Yeovil	A	L 1–0	Att: 3,906	Booked: McCormack, Grant. Dismissed: Morrison.
20th	● Milton Keynes Dons	H	W 2–1	Att: 6,957	Scorers: Barnard, Wilbraham OG. Booked: Christophe, Grant, Barnard, Barrett.
24th	● Tranmere	A	L 2–0	Att: 4,317	Booked: McCormack, Laurent, Barrett.

DECEMBER
1st	● Norwich	H	L 0–3	Att: 8,732	Booked: Scannell, Christophe.
5th	● Charlton	A	L 1–0	Att: 17,445	Booked: Moussa, Malone, Francis.
12th	● Hartlepool	H	W 3–2	Att: 7,737	Scorers: Barnard², Laurent. Booked: Grant.
19th	● Exeter	A	L 1–0	Att: 4,839	Booked: Barrett. Dismissed: Ibehre.
26th	● Colchester	H	L 1–2	Att: 10,329	Scorers: Barnard. Booked: Moussa, McCormack.
28th	● Leyton Orient	A	W 1–2	Att: 5,680	Scorers: Barrett, McCormack. Booked: Scannell.

JANUARY
16th	● Huddersfield	A	L 2–1	Att: 14,200	Scorers: Spencer.
23rd	● Wycombe	H	D 1–1	Att: 6,675	Scorers: McCormack. Booked: McCormack.
26th	● Millwall	A	L 2–0	Att: 7,612	Booked: Grant, McCormack, Malone.
30th	● Swindon	H	D 2–2	Att: 6,669	Scorers: Baldwin, Spencer.

FEBRUARY
8th	● Colchester	A	L 2–0	Att: 6,466	Booked: Laurent.
13th	● Tranmere	H	D 1–1	Att: 6,382	Scorers: Vernon. Booked: Christophe.
20th	● Milton Keynes Dons	A	L 3–1	Att: 9,801	Scorers: Paterson. Booked: McCormack, Christophe.
23rd	● Norwich	A	L 2–1	Att: 24,824	Scorers: Vernon.
26th	● Charlton	H	L 1–2	Att: 9,724	Scorers: Paterson. Booked: Watt. Dismissed: Christophe.

MARCH
6th	● Hartlepool	A	L 3–0	Att: 3,299	Booked: McCormack. Dismissed: McCormack.
13th	● Exeter	H	D 0–0	Att: 6,761	Booked: Scannell.
20th	● Carlisle	H	D 2–2	Att: 6,384	Scorers: Barrett, Moussa. Booked: Barrett, Baldwin. Dismissed: Barrett.
23rd	● Walsall	H	W 3–0	Att: 6,432	Scorers: Moussa², Spencer.
27th	● Bristol Rovers	A	L 4–3	Att: 6,476	Scorers: Spencer, Vernon². Booked: McCormack, Grant. Dismissed: Moussa.

APRIL
3rd	● Yeovil	H	D 0–0	Att: 6,854	Booked: Grant.
5th	● Gillingham	A	L 3–0	Att: 7,657	Booked: Laurent, Baldwin.
10th	● Leeds	A	L 2–0	Att: 21,650	Booked: Christophe, Laurent.
13th	● Brentford	H	D 2–2	Att: 6,838	Scorers: Laurent². Booked: McCormack.
17th	● Brighton	A	L 0–1	Att: 8,503	Booked: Moussa.
24th	● Oldham	A	D 2–2	Att: 4,225	Scorers: Laurent, Mvoto. Booked: Crawford.

MAY
1st	● Stockport	H	W 2–1	Att: 7,145	Scorers: Crawford, McCormack. Booked: Mvoto.
8th	● Southampton	A	L 3–1	Att: 25,289	Scorers: Moussa.

● Coca-Cola League 1/Play-Offs ● FA Cup ● Carling Cup ● Johnstone's Paint Trophy

actim

LEAGUE 1 GOALKEEPER STATS

Player	Appearances	Match starts	Completed matches	Sub appearances	Subbed off	Clean sheets	Yellow cards	Red cards
Ian Joyce	2	2	2	0	0	0	0	0
Steve Mildenhall	44	44	44	0	0	8	0	0

LEAGUE 1 OUTFIELD PLAYER STATS

Player	Appearances	Match starts	Completed matches	Substitute appearances	Subbed off	Goals scored	Yellow cards	Red cards
Pat Baldwin	18	18	18	0	0	1	2	0
Lee Barnard	25	25	21	0	4	15	6	0
Adam Barrett	41	41	39	0	1	2	5	1
Kevin Betsy	2	0	0	2	0	0	0	0
Jean Francois Christophe	36	31	21	5	8	1	7	2
Harry Crawford	7	2	2	5	0	1	1	0
Simon Francis	45	45	45	0	0	1	3	0
Dougie Freedman	20	9	1	11	8	1	0	0
George Friend	6	5	5	1	0	1	0	0
Anthony Grant	38	38	28	0	10	0	13	0
Matt Heath	4	4	4	0	0	0	1	0
Johnny Herd	20	17	16	3	1	0	0	0
Jabo Ibehre	4	4	2	0	1	0	0	1
Francis Laurent	35	28	16	7	12	6	4	0
Scott Malone	17	15	13	2	2	0	2	0
Alan McCormack	41	40	36	1	3	3	15	1
Marcus Milner	1	0	0	1	0	0	0	0
Sean Morrison	8	8	7	0	0	0	0	1
Franck Moussa	43	41	34	2	6	5	4	1
Jean Yves Mvoto	17	15	11	2	4	1	2	0
Roy O'Donovan	4	3	0	1	3	1	0	0
Stuart O'Keefe	7	3	2	4	1	0	0	0
Matthew Paterson	16	9	1	7	8	2	0	0
Alex Revell	3	1	0	2	1	0	0	0
Osei Sankofa	12	10	9	2	1	0	0	0
Lee Sawyer	6	0	0	6	0	0	0	0
Damian Scannell	25	15	9	10	6	1	3	0
Scott Spencer	12	5	1	7	4	4	0	0
Scott Vernon	17	17	13	0	4	4	0	0
James Walker	13	2	1	11	1	0	1	0
Sanchez Watt	4	4	1	0	3	0	1	0
John White	5	5	5	0	0	0	0	0

AUG	SEP	OCT	NOV	DEC	JAN	FEB	MAR	APR	MAY

SEASON INFORMATION

Highest position: 8
Lowest position: 23
Average goals scored per game: 1.11
Average goals conceded per game: 1.57

19	14	10	11	12	15	20	22	23	23

LEAGUE POSITION AT THE END OF EACH MONTH

LONGEST SEQUENCES

Wins	–	Undefeated home	5
(–)		(13/03/10–13/04/10)	
Losses	4	Undefeated away	2
(20/02/10–06/03/10)		(15/08/09–18/08/09)	
Draws	4	Without scoring	3
(08/08/09–21/08/09)		(on two occasions)	
Undefeated	4	Without conceding	2
(08/08/09–21/08/09)		(04/09/09–11/09/09)	
Without win	12	Scoring	6
(16/01/10–20/03/10)		(29/09/09–30/10/09)	

CARDS RECEIVED

70   **7**

EARLIEST STRIKE

SCOTT VERNON
(v Bristol Rovers) 4:33

LATEST STRIKE

LEE BARNARD
(v Stockport) 94:21

GOALS SCORED/CONCEDED
PER FIVE-MINUTE INTERVALS

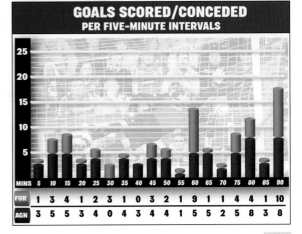

MINS	5	10	15	20	25	30	35	40	45	50	55	60	65	70	75	80	85	90
FOR	1	3	4	1	2	3	1	0	3	2	1	9	1	1	4	4	1	10
AGN	3	5	5	3	4	0	4	3	4	4	1	5	5	2	5	8	3	8

STOCKPORT COUNTY

STOCKPORT were relegated to npower League Two following a difficult season on and off the pitch for the Hatters.

The Edgeley Park club began the campaign in administration and their failure to find a new buyer appeared to have a negative impact on the team.

County won just five games in the course of the whole League season and lost 31 overall, scoring a meagre 35 goals in the process. Their last League victory came courtesy of a 4–3 success at home to Wycombe in February, with 12 of their last 14 games ending in defeat.

Gary Ablett faced a tough task in his first season in charge and revealed his frustration after his side lost 6–0 at home to Huddersfield in April – their heaviest home defeat since 1961. He said: 'It's difficult to motivate players who possibly don't want to be motivated and can't wait for the season to finish.'

After a humiliating season, a major rebuilding job now looks to be on the cards for County.

CLUB SUMMARY

FORMED	1883
MANAGER	Gary Ablett
GROUND	Edgeley Park
CAPACITY	10,852
NICKNAME	The Hatters
WEBSITE	www.stockportcounty.com

The New Football Pools
PLAYER OF THE SEASON

Greg Tansey

OVERALL
P	W	D	L	F	A	GD
51	7	10	34	46	106	-60

COCA-COLA FOOTBALL LEAGUE 1
Pos	P	W	D	L	F	A	GD	Pts
24	46	5	10	31	35	95	-60	25

HOME
Pos	P	W	D	L	F	A	GD	Pts
24	23	2	6	15	21	51	-30	12

AWAY
Pos	P	W	D	L	F	A	GD	Pts
22	23	3	4	16	14	44	-30	13

CUP PROGRESS DETAILS
Competition	Round reached	Knocked out by
FA Cup	R2	Torquay
Carling Cup	R1	Huddersfield
JP Trophy	R2	Port Vale

BIGGEST WIN (ALL COMPS)
07/11/09 5–0 v Tooting & Mitcham

BIGGEST DEFEAT (ALL COMPS)
24/04/10 0–6 v Huddersfield

ATTENDANCE RECORD
HIGH	AVERAGE	Low
7,768	4,420	3,281
v Leeds (28/12/2009)		v Swindon (19/01/2010)

RESULTS 2009/10

AUGUST
8th	Oldham	A	D 0–0	Att: 6,918	Booked: Havern, Fon Williams.
11th	Huddersfield	A	L 3–1	Att: 5,120	Scorers: Griffin.
15th	Bristol Rovers	H	L 0–2	Att: 4,084	Booked: Turnbull.
18th	Carlisle	H	L 1–2	Att: 4,009	Scorers: Keogh OG. Booked: Raynes, Havern.
22nd	Brighton	A	W 2–4	Att: 5,270	Scorers: Baker[3], O Johnson. Booked: Bridcutt, Rose. Dismissed: Bridcutt.
29th	Southampton	A	D 1–1	Att: 4,680	Scorers: Baker. Booked: Baker.

SEPTEMBER
1st	Crewe	A	W 1–4	Att: 2,331	Scorers: Baker[3], Bignall. Booked: Halls.
5th	Leeds	A	L 2–0	Att: 22,870	Booked: Rose, Mullins, Fon Williams.
12th	Yeovil	A	D 2–2	Att: 3,519	Scorers: Baker[2]. Booked: Vincent.
19th	Leyton Orient	H	W 2–1	Att: 4,091	Scorers: Bignall, Tansey. Booked: Raynes.
26th	Huddersfield	H	D 0–0	Att: 14,921	Booked: Huntington, Bridcutt.
29th	Hartlepool	H	D 2–2	Att: 3,780	Scorers: Bignall, Raynes. Booked: Tansey.

OCTOBER
3rd	Southend	H	L 0–2	Att: 4,102	Booked: Tansey, Poole, Raynes, Mullins, Rose, Bridcutt. Dismissed: Huntington.
6th	Port Vale	A	L 3–1	Att: 3,154	Scorers: Bridcutt. Booked: Turnbull, Havern.
12th	Tranmere	A	W 0–1	Att: 5,645	Scorers: Baker.
17th	Millwall	H	L 0–4	Att: 4,394	Booked: Tansey.
24th	Brentford	A	L 2–0	Att: 5,045	Booked: Mullins.
31st	Norwich	H	L 1–3	Att: 5,218	Scorers: Thompson. Booked: Mullins, Bridcutt.

NOVEMBER
7th	Tooting & Mitcham	H	W 5–0	Att: 3,076	Scorers: Baker, Poole, Thompson, Turnbull[2].
14th	Walsall	A	L 2–0	Att: 4,143	Booked: Griffin.
21st	Exeter	H	L 1–3	Att: 4,101	Scorers: Rose.
24th	Colchester	A	L 2–0	Att: 3,818	Booked: Griffin.

DECEMBER
5th	Wycombe	A	L 2–1	Att: 4,343	Scorers: Baker. Booked: Mullins.
12th	Charlton	H	L 1–2	Att: 4,277	Scorers: Elliot OG. Booked: Poole, Turnbull, O Johnson. Dismissed: Baker.
15th	Torquay	N	L 0–4	Att: 1,690	Booked: Tansey.
19th	Gillingham	A	L 3–1	Att: 4,769	Scorers: Rose. Booked: Rose, McNeil.
26th	Milton Keynes Dons	A	L 4–1	Att: 9,661	Scorers: Thompson. Booked: Raynes, Griffin, Mullins.
28th	Leeds	H	L 2–4	Att: 7,768	Scorers: Baker, Mullins. Booked: Thompson, Poole. Dismissed: Poole.

JANUARY
19th	Swindon	H	L 0–1	Att: 3,281	Booked: Pilkington, Swailes, Rose.
23rd	Carlisle	A	D 0–0	Att: 4,966	Booked: Ibehre, Raynes. Dismissed: Ibehre.
26th	Brighton	H	D 1–1	Att: 3,636	Booked: Pilkington. Booked: J Johnson.
30th	Southampton	A	L 2–0	Att: 18,308	

FEBRUARY
6th	Milton Keynes Dons	H	L 1–3	Att: 3,720	Scorers: Donnelly. Booked: Sadler, Mullins, Pilkington.
13th	Colchester	H	D 2–2	Att: 3,642	Scorers: Ibehre[2]. Booked: Mullins, Ibehre, Swailes, Huntington.
20th	Exeter	A	W 0–1	Att: 4,990	Scorers: J Johnson. Booked: Fon Williams.
23rd	Swindon	A	L 4–1	Att: 7,063	Scorers: Tansey.
27th	Wycombe	H	W 4–3	Att: 3,740	Scorers: Donnelly[2], J Johnson, Partridge.

MARCH
2nd	Bristol Rovers	A	L 1–0	Att: 5,322	Booked: Poole, Perkins, Turnbull. Dismissed: Poole.
6th	Charlton	A	L 2–0	Att: 16,609	
13th	Gillingham	H	D 0–0	Att: 3,894	Booked: Perkins.
16th	Oldham	H	L 0–1	Att: 4,283	Booked: Turnbull, Mullins. Dismissed: Swailes.
20th	Brentford	H	L 0–1	Att: 3,707	Booked: Tansey, Donnelly, Sadler, Partridge.
27th	Millwall	A	L 5–0	Att: 11,116	Booked: Swailes, J Johnson.

APRIL
3rd	Walsall	H	D 1–1	Att: 3,580	Scorers: Ibehre.
5th	Norwich	A	L 2–1	Att: 25,353	Scorers: Ibehre. Booked: J Johnson.
10th	Yeovil	H	L 1–3	Att: 3,587	Scorers: Donnelly. Stockport are relegated.
13th	Hartlepool	A	L 3–0	Att: 2,869	Booked: Donnelly, Perkins, Halls.
17th	Leyton Orient	A	L 2–0	Att: 4,373	Booked: Ibehre, Barnes, Huntington.
24th	Huddersfield	H	L 0–6	Att: 6,887	Booked: Perkins, Halls.

MAY
1st	Southend	A	L 2–1	Att: 7,145	Scorers: Ibehre. Booked: Turnbull.
8th	Tranmere	H	L 0–3	Att: 7,208	Booked: Ibehre, Halls.

● Coca-Cola League 1/Play-Offs ● FA Cup ● Carling Cup ● Johnstone's Paint Trophy

actim

Coca-Cola LEAGUE 1

LEAGUE 1 GOALKEEPER STATS

Player	Appearances	Match starts	Completed matches	Sub appearances	Subbed off	Clean sheets	Yellow cards	Red cards
Owain Fon Williams	44	44	44	0	0	6	3	0
Lloyd Rigby	2	2	2	0	0	0	0	0

LEAGUE 1 OUTFIELD PLAYER STATS

Player	Appearances	Match starts	Completed matches	Substitute appearances	Subbed off	Goals scored	Yellow cards	Red cards
Carl Baker	20	19	16	1	2	9	1	1
Sam Barnes	2	2	2	0	0	0	1	0
Nicholas Bignall	11	11	3	0	8	2	0	0
Liam Bridcutt	15	15	13	0	1	0	4	1
George Donnelly	19	16	10	3	6	4	2	0
Declan Edwards	1	0	0	1	0	0	0	0
Tom Fisher	1	0	0	1	0	0	0	0
Adam Griffin	18	9	6	9	3	0	3	0
Andy Halls	11	8	8	3	0	0	3	0
Gianluca Havern	7	7	7	0	0	0	2	0
Paul Huntington	26	26	24	0	1	0	3	1
Jabo Ibehre	20	20	19	0	0	5	4	1
Oli Johnson	16	4	1	12	3	1	1	0
Jemal Johnson	16	14	6	2	8	2	3	0
Matty McNeil	5	4	4	1	0	0	1	0
Johnny Mullins	36	36	34	0	2	1	9	0
Richie Partridge	22	20	9	2	11	1	1	0
David Perkins	22	22	21	0	1	0	4	0
Danny Pilkington	29	10	5	19	5	1	2	0
David Poole	36	29	13	7	14	0	4	2
Michael Raynes	25	24	23	1	1	1	5	0
Christian Ribeiro	7	7	6	0	1	0	0	0
Michael Rose	24	24	24	0	0	2	5	0
Daniel Rowe	4	0	0	4	0	0	0	0
Mathew Sadler	20	20	20	0	0	0	2	0
Danny Swailes	20	20	19	0	0	0	3	1
Greg Tansey	32	25	21	7	4	2	4	0
Peter Thompson	22	14	9	8	5	2	1	0
Paul Turnbull	30	24	21	6	3	0	5	0
James Vincent	34	30	18	4	12	0	1	0

AUG SEP OCT NOV DEC JAN FEB MAR APR MAY

SEASON INFORMATION

Highest position: 11
Lowest position: 24
Average goals scored per game: 0.76
Average goals conceded per game: 2.07

LEAGUE POSITION AT THE END OF EACH MONTH

14 16 21 23 24 24 24 24 24 24

LONGEST SEQUENCES

Wins	–	Undefeated home	3
(–)		(on two occasions)	
Losses	12	Undefeated away	3
(17/10/09–19/01/10)		(12/09/09–12/10/09)	
Draws	2	Without scoring	6
(on two occasions)		(02/03/10–27/03/10)	
Undefeated	4	Without conceding	–
(12/09/09–29/09/09)		(–)	
Without win	17	Scoring	5
(17/10/09–13/02/10)		(on two occasions)	

CARDS RECEIVED

77 7

EARLIEST STRIKE

PAUL HUNTINGTON
(v Charlton) 6:48

LATEST STRIKE

CARL BAKER
(v Southampton) 94:19

GOALS SCORED/CONCEDED
PER FIVE-MINUTE INTERVALS

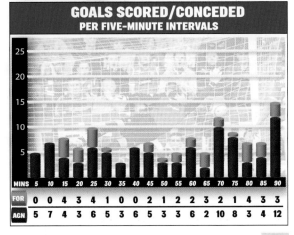

MINS	5	10	15	20	25	30	35	40	45	50	55	60	65	70	75	80	85	90
FOR	0	0	4	3	4	1	0	0	2	1	2	2	3	2	1	4	3	3
AGN	5	7	4	3	6	5	3	6	5	3	3	6	2	10	8	3	4	12

SWINDON TOWN

SWINDON will look back on their campaign as one of huge progress, although it ended in disappointment following their play-off final defeat to Millwall at Wembley.

Twelve months ago, Town had just staved off the threat of relegation from Coca-Cola League 1 and 32-goal leading scorer Simon Cox was on his way to West Brom. But this time around, Danny Wilson worked wonders in his first full season in charge of the club to transform them into promotion contenders, eventually finishing in fifth place.

Experienced players such as Jonathan Douglas and David Lucas were brought in, while Wilson also got the best out of Jon-Paul McGovern and Billy Paynter. Talented young forward Charlie Austin also enjoyed a superb campaign, scoring 20 goals on his step up from non-League football.

Wilson will now look to keep his squad together and strengthen in the transfer market to go one better in 2010/11.

CLUB SUMMARY

FORMED	1881
MANAGER	Danny Wilson
GROUND	County Ground
CAPACITY	14,800
NICKNAME	The Robins
WEBSITE	www.swindontownfc.co.uk

The New Football Pools PLAYER OF THE SEASON — *Charlie Austin*

OVERALL
P	W	D	L	F	A	GD
56	26	19	11	83	64	19

COCA-COLA FOOTBALL LEAGUE 1
Pos	P	W	D	L	F	A	GD	Pts
5	46	22	16	8	73	57	16	82

HOME
Pos	P	W	D	L	F	A	GD	Pts
8	23	13	8	2	42	25	17	47

AWAY
Pos	P	W	D	L	F	A	GD	Pts
4	23	9	8	6	31	32	-1	35

CUP PROGRESS DETAILS
Competition	Round reached	Knocked out by
FA Cup	R3	Fulham
Carling Cup	R2	Wolverhampton
JP Trophy	QF	Norwich

BIGGEST WIN (ALL COMPS)
4–1 on 3 occasions

BIGGEST DEFEAT (ALL COMPS)
08/08/09 0–5 v Gillingham

ATTENDANCE RECORD
HIGH	AVERAGE	Low
14,508	8,360	6,183
v Leeds (26/01/2010)		v Oldham (09/02/2010)

RESULTS 2009/10

AUGUST
8th	● Gillingham	A	L 5–0	Att: 6,852	Booked: Timlin, Morrison.
11th	● Milton Keynes Dons	A	W 1–4	Att: 4,812	Scorers: McGovern, Paynter2, McCracken OG.
15th	● Milton Keynes Dons	H	D 0–0	Att: 6,692	Booked: Douglas.
18th	● Southampton	H	W 1–0	Att: 11,007	Scorers: Morrison. Booked: Jean-Francois.
22nd	● Oldham	A	D 2–2	Att: 4,229	Scorers: McGovern, Paynter.
25th	● Wolverhampton	A	D 0–0	Att: 11,416	Booked: Paynter, Amankwaah.
					AET – Score after 90 mins 0–0. Wolverhampton win 6–5 on penalties.
29th	● Southend	H	W 2–1	Att: 6,417	Scorers: Cuthbert, Obadeyi. Booked: Jean-Francois.

SEPTEMBER
5th	● Yeovil	A	W 0–1	Att: 4,807	Scorers: Forbes OG. Booked: Macklin.
12th	● Colchester	H	D 1–1	Att: 6,621	Scorers: Obadeyi. Booked: Hutchinson.
19th	● Walsall	A	D 1–1	Att: 4,148	Scorers: Paynter. Booked: Jean-Francois, Morrison, Obadeyi.
26th	● Wycombe	H	D 1–1	Att: 6,929	Scorers: Amankwaah. Booked: Douglas, Jean-Francois.
29th	● Exeter	A	D 1–1	Att: 5,337	Scorers: Amankwaah. Booked: Cuthbert.

OCTOBER
3rd	● Brentford	A	W 2–3	Att: 6,471	Scorers: Hutchinson, Revell2. Booked: Greer, Macklin, Timlin.
6th	● Exeter	A	D 1–1	Att: 2,006	Scorers: McNamee. Swindon win 4–3 on penalties.
10th	● Millwall	H	D 1–1	Att: 7,222	Scorers: Cuthbert. Booked: McNamee, Amankwaah, Timlin. Dismissed: Douglas.
17th	● Hartlepool	H	L 0–2	Att: 7,096	
24th	● Norwich	A	L 1–0	Att: 24,959	Booked: Timlin.
31st	● Tranmere	A	W 1–4	Att: 5,811	Scorers: Ferry, McNamee, Paynter2. Booked: Jean-Francois.

NOVEMBER
7th	● Woking	H	W 1–0	Att: 4,805	Scorers: Paynter.
10th	● Norwich	H	D 0–0	Att: 4,978	Booked: Greer. Norwich win 5–3 on penalties.
21st	● Carlisle	A	W 0–1	Att: 4,339	Scorers: Austin.
24th	● Huddersfield	H	W 2–1	Att: 6,630	Scorers: Austin, Paynter.
28th	● Wrexham	A	W 0–1	Att: 3,011	Scorers: Greer. Booked: Hutchinson, Sheehan, Greer.

DECEMBER
5th	● Leyton Orient	H	W 3–2	Att: 6,815	Scorers: Austin2, Paynter. Booked: Austin.
12th	● Bristol Rovers	A	L 3–0	Att: 7,613	Booked: Cuthbert.
19th	● Brighton	H	W 2–1	Att: 7,068	Scorers: Austin, Paynter. Booked: Douglas, Paynter, Sheehan.
26th	● Charlton	A	D 2–2	Att: 17,977	Scorers: Austin, Paynter. Booked: Hutchinson.
28th	● Yeovil	H	W 3–1	Att: 8,509	Scorers: Austin, Paynter, Ward.

JANUARY
2nd	● Fulham	A	L 1–0	Att: 19,623	Booked: Lucas.
16th	● Gillingham	H	W 3–1	Att: 6,773	Scorers: Austin, Cuthbert, Paynter. Booked: Ward, Ferry, Jean-Francois.
19th	● Stockport	A	W 0–1	Att: 3,281	Scorers: Paynter.
26th	● Leeds	H	W 3–0	Att: 14,508	Scorers: Austin, Paynter2. Booked: McGovern, Amankwaah.
30th	● Southend	A	D 2–2	Att: 6,669	Scorers: Austin, Paynter. Booked: Greer.

FEBRUARY
6th	● Charlton	H	D 1–1	Att: 9,552	Scorers: Amankwaah.
9th	● Oldham	H	W 4–2	Att: 6,183	Scorers: Austin, Paynter2, Ward.
13th	● Huddersfield	A	D 2–2	Att: 14,610	Scorers: Austin, Ward. Booked: Amankwaah.
20th	● Carlisle	H	W 2–0	Att: 7,704	Scorers: Austin, Paynter.
23rd	● Stockport	H	W 4–1	Att: 7,063	Scorers: Ferry, Paynter2, Ward. Booked: Morrison.
27th	● Leyton Orient	A	D 0–0	Att: 4,574	Booked: Sheehan.

MARCH
6th	● Bristol Rovers	H	L 0–4	Att: 10,341	Booked: Ferry, Greer, Sheehan, Douglas.
9th	● Milton Keynes Dons	A	L 2–1	Att: 8,764	Scorers: Ward.
13th	● Brighton	A	W 0–1	Att: 6,946	Scorers: Austin.
16th	● Southampton	A	W 0–1	Att: 20,752	Scorers: Austin. Booked: Ferry, Douglas. Dismissed: Ferry.
20th	● Norwich	H	D 1–1	Att: 11,972	Scorers: Greer. Booked: Easton.
27th	● Hartlepool	A	W 0–1	Att: 3,536	Scorers: Austin.

APRIL
3rd	● Leeds	A	W 0–3	Att: 27,881	Scorers: Austin, Paynter2.
5th	● Tranmere	H	W 3–0	Att: 9,495	Scorers: Austin, Paynter, Gordon OG.
10th	● Colchester	A	L 3–0	Att: 5,111	Booked: Douglas.
12th	● Exeter	H	D 1–1	Att: 8,753	Scorers: Taylor OG. Booked: Ward.
17th	● Walsall	H	D 1–1	Att: 8,467	Scorers: Austin. Booked: Austin.
24th	● Wycombe	A	D 2–2	Att: 7,459	Scorers: Paynter, Sheehan. Booked: Sheehan, Paynter, Cuthbert, Marshall.

MAY
1st	● Brentford	H	W 3–2	Att: 10,465	Scorers: Paynter2, Ward.
8th	● Millwall	A	L 3–2	Att: 17,083	Scorers: Paynter, Ward. Booked: Jean-Francois, Paynter.
14th	● Charlton	H	W 2–1	Att: 13,560	Scorers: Austin, Ward. Booked: McGovern.
17th	● Charlton	A	L 2–1	Att: 21,521	Scorers: Ward. Booked: Douglas, Austin. Dismissed: Greer.
					AET – Score after 90 mins 2–1. Agg: 3–3; Swindon win 5–4 on penalties.
29th	● Millwall	N	L 1–0	Att: 73,108	Booked: Jean-Francois.

● Coca-Cola League 1/Play-offs ● FA Cup ● Carling Cup ● Johnstone's Paint Trophy

LEAGUE 1 GOALKEEPER STATS

Player	Appearances	Match starts	Completed matches	Sub appearances	Subbed off	Clean sheets	Yellow cards	Red cards
David Lucas	41	41	40	0	1	11	0	0
Phil Smith	6	5	5	1	0	1	0	0

LEAGUE 1 OUTFIELD PLAYER STATS

Player	Appearances	Match starts	Completed matches	Substitute appearances	Subbed off	Goals scored	Yellow cards	Red cards
Kevin Amankwaah	36	33	30	3	3	3	3	0
Charlie Austin	33	29	10	4	19	19	2	0
Scott Cuthbert	39	39	36	0	3	3	3	0
Stephen Darby	12	12	8	0	4	0	0	0
Jonathan Douglas	43	43	42	0	0	0	6	1
Craig Easton	12	2	1	10	1	0	1	0
Simon Ferry	40	40	25	0	14	2	3	1
Gordon Greer	44	43	41	1	1	1	3	0
Ben Hutchinson	10	6	0	4	6	1	2	0
Lescinel Jean-Francois	33	27	22	6	5	0	7	0
Callum Kennedy	8	4	3	4	1	0	0	0
Lloyd Macklin	9	1	0	8	1	0	2	0
Mark Marshall	7	1	0	6	1	0	1	0
Jon-Paul McGovern	45	45	42	0	3	1	1	0
Anthony McNamee	17	14	5	3	9	1	1	0
Sean Morrison	9	8	7	1	1	1	3	0
Frank Nouble	8	3	0	5	3	0	0	0
Alan O'Brien	9	3	0	6	3	0	0	0
Temitope Obadeyi	12	9	5	3	4	2	1	0
Billy Paynter	42	37	29	5	8	26	3	0
Lee Peacock	4	0	0	4	0	0	0	0
Vincent Pericard	14	2	0	12	2	0	0	0
Alex Revell	10	7	1	3	6	4	0	0
Matt Ritchie	4	0	0	4	0	0	0	0
Alan Sheehan	22	22	21	0	1	1	4	0
Michael Timlin	21	6	3	15	3	0	4	0
Daniel Ward	28	24	15	4	9	7	2	0

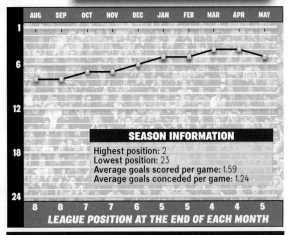

SEASON INFORMATION
Highest position: 2
Lowest position: 23
Average goals scored per game: 1.59
Average goals conceded per game: 1.24

LEAGUE POSITION AT THE END OF EACH MONTH

8 8 7 7 6 5 5 4 4 5

LONGEST SEQUENCES

Wins	4		Undefeated home	10	
(on two occasions)			(24/11/09–23/02/10)		
Losses	2		Undefeated away	5	
(on two occasions)			(on two occasions)		
Draws	4		Without scoring	2	
(12/09/09–29/09/09)			(on three occasions)		
Undefeated	13		Without conceding	3	
(19/12/09–27/02/10)			(27/03/10–05/04/10)		
Without win	4		Scoring	12	
(on two occasions)			(19/12/09–23/02/10)		

CARDS RECEIVED

52 2

EARLIEST STRIKE
BILLY PAYNTER
(v Southend) 0:45

LATEST STRIKE
DANIEL WARD
(v Milton Keynes Dons) 92:52

GOALS SCORED/CONCEDED
PER FIVE-MINUTE INTERVALS

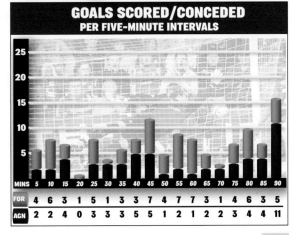

MINS	5	10	15	20	25	30	35	40	45	50	55	60	65	70	75	80	85	90
FOR	4	6	3	1	5	1	3	3	7	4	7	7	3	1	4	6	3	5
AGN	2	2	4	0	3	3	3	5	5	1	2	1	2	2	3	4	4	11

TRANMERE ROVERS

LES PARRY emerged at the centre of one of the most heart-warming stories of the 2009/10 season as he steered Tranmere to safety on the final day of the campaign.

The long-serving physiotherapist had been a shock choice to take over the reins at Prenton Park following John Barnes' dismissal in October. At the time, Rovers were heading for relegation to the basement division at a pace but, despite his lack of tactical experience, Parry was able to turn things around.

His organisational and motivational skills came to the fore when it mattered most and, with players like Ian Thomas-Moore making key contributions, Tranmere ended the season with two successive wins to ensure their survival.

Parry said after the finale: 'If I'm not in the manager's job next season then hopefully I can stay at Tranmere and go back to the physio role.' However, it seems unlikely that Parry will be removed from his unlikely position after his success so far in the Prenton Park hot-seat.

CLUB SUMMARY

FORMED	1884
MANAGER	Les Parry
GROUND	Prenton Park
CAPACITY	16,567
NICKNAME	Rovers
WEBSITE	www.tranmererovers.co.uk

The New **Football Pools** PLAYER OF THE SEASON — **Ian Thomas-Moore**

OVERALL
P	W	D	L	F	A	GD
54	17	11	26	54	78	-24

COCA-COLA FOOTBALL LEAGUE 1
Pos	P	W	D	L	F	A	GD	Pts
19	46	14	9	23	45	72	-27	51

HOME
Pos	P	W	D	L	F	A	GD	Pts
16	23	11	3	9	30	32	-2	36

AWAY
Pos	P	W	D	L	F	A	GD	Pts
20	23	3	6	14	15	40	-25	15

CUP PROGRESS DETAILS
Competition	Round reached	Knocked out by
FA Cup	R3	Wolves
Carling Cup	R2	Bolton
JP Trophy	R2	Bury

BIGGEST WIN (ALL COMPS)
11/08/09 4-0 v Grimsby

BIGGEST DEFEAT (ALL COMPS)
03/10/09 0-5 v Millwall

ATTENDANCE RECORD
High	Average	Low
8,694	5,671	4,317
v Millwall (01/05/2010)		v Southend (24/11/2009)

RESULTS 2009/10

AUGUST
8th	Yeovil	A	L 2-0	Att: 4,349	**Booked:** Logan, Welsh.
11th	Grimsby	H	W 4-0	Att: 3,527	**Scorers:** Curran, Edds, McLaren, Thomas-Moore.
15th	Gillingham	H	W 4-2	Att: 5,590	**Scorers:** Gornell, Thomas-Moore2, Welsh.
18th	Milton Keynes Dons	H	L 0-1	Att: 5,744	**Booked:** Welsh.
22nd	Leeds	A	L 3-0	Att: 21,692	**Booked:** McLaren, Goodison.
25th	Bolton	H	L 0-1	Att: 5,381	**Booked:** Cresswell.
29th	Charlton	H	L 0-4	Att: 5,417	**Booked:** Logan, McLaren, Gornell.

SEPTEMBER
5th	Carlisle	A	L 3-0	Att: 5,269	**Booked:** Logan. **Dismissed:** Logan.
12th	Walsall	H	L 2-3	Att: 4,858	**Scorers:** Mahon, Shuker.
19th	Exeter	A	L 2-1	Att: 4,901	**Scorers:** Ricketts. **Booked:** Ricketts, Broomes.
26th	Colchester	H	D 1-1	Att: 5,314	**Scorers:** Welsh. **Booked:** Logan, Cresswell, Broomes, McLaren.
29th	Wycombe	A	W 0-1	Att: 3,899	**Scorers:** Thomas-Moore.

OCTOBER
3rd	Millwall	A	L 5-0	Att: 8,046	**Booked:** Goodison, Broomes, Logan, Cresswell. **Dismissed:** Broomes.
6th	Bury	A	L 2-1	Att: 1,903	**Scorers:** Curran.
12th	Stockport	H	L 0-1	Att: 5,645	**Dismissed:** Daniels.
17th	Brighton	H	W 2-1	Att: 5,250	**Scorers:** Edds, Welsh. **Booked:** Bakayogo, Broomes, D Martin.
24th	Hartlepool	A	L 1-0	Att: 3,428	**Booked:** Welsh. **Dismissed:** Barnett.
31st	Swindon	H	L 1-4	Att: 5,811	**Scorers:** Shuker. **Booked:** Welsh, Thomas-Moore.

NOVEMBER
7th	Leyton Orient	H	D 1-1	Att: 3,180	**Scorers:** Shuker. **Booked:** Logan.
14th	Norwich	A	L 2-0	Att: 25,025	**Booked:** Welsh, Goodison.
17th	Leyton Orient	A	W 0-1	Att: 1,518	**Scorers:** Taylor. **Booked:** Logan, Thomas-Moore, Taylor, Barnett.
21st	Leyton Orient	A	L 2-1	Att: 4,620	**Scorers:** Barnett. **Booked:** Curran, Taylor.
24th	Southend	H	W 2-0	Att: 4,317	**Scorers:** Goodison, Gornell. **Booked:** Broomes.
28th	Aldershot	H	D 0-0	Att: 3,742	**Booked:** Gornell.

DECEMBER
1st	Huddersfield	A	D 3-3	Att: 13,509	**Scorers:** Curran, Taylor, Thomas-Moore. **Booked:** Curran.
5th	Brentford	H	W 1-0	Att: 4,839	**Scorers:** Curran. **Booked:** Logan, Thomas-Moore, Gornell.
8th	Aldershot	A	W 1-2	Att: 4,060	**Scorers:** Gornell, Thomas-Moore. **Booked:** Bakayogo, Gornell, Daniels.
12th	Southampton	A	L 3-0	Att: 19,800	**Booked:** Goodison, Broomes, Curran.
19th	Bristol Rovers	H	W 2-0	Att: 4,755	**Scorers:** Curran, Edds.
28th	Carlisle	H	D 0-0	Att: 6,313	**Booked:** McLaren.

JANUARY
3rd	Wolverhampton	H	L 0-1	Att: 7,476	
20th	Oldham	A	D 0-0	Att: 3,688	**Booked:** Logan.
23rd	Milton Keynes Dons	A	L 1-0	Att: 9,438	**Booked:** Welsh, Goodison, Logan.
26th	Yeovil	H	W 2-1	Att: 4,584	**Scorers:** Taylor, Thomas-Moore. **Booked:** Shuker, McLaren, Daniels.
30th	Charlton	A	D 1-1	Att: 16,168	**Scorers:** Sodje OG. **Booked:** Taylor, Bakayogo, Daniels. **Dismissed:** Bakayogo.

FEBRUARY
6th	Oldham	H	L 0-1	Att: 5,518	**Booked:** Goodison.
9th	Gillingham	A	W 0-1	Att: 3,840	**Scorers:** Thomas-Moore. **Booked:** Curran, Sordell, Gornell, Daniels, McLaren.
13th	Southend	A	D 1-1	Att: 6,382	**Scorers:** Goodison. **Booked:** McLaren, Logan, Curran, Welsh.
20th	Leyton Orient	H	W 2-1	Att: 5,357	**Scorers:** Sordell, Thomas-Moore. **Booked:** McLaren, Gornell.
23rd	Huddersfield	H	L 0-2	Att: 5,793	**Booked:** Daniels.

MARCH
6th	Southampton	H	W 2-1	Att: 6,187	**Scorers:** Broomes, Thomas-Moore.
9th	Leeds	H	L 1-4	Att: 8,346	**Scorers:** Welsh.
13th	Bristol Rovers	A	D 0-0	Att: 6,477	**Booked:** McLaren, Bakayogo, Welsh, Thomas-Moore. **Dismissed:** Bakayogo.
19th	Hartlepool	H	D 0-0	Att: 5,409	**Booked:** Taylor.
27th	Brighton	A	L 3-0	Att: 6,812	**Booked:** Gordon, Broomes. **Dismissed:** Robinson.

APRIL
2nd	Norwich	H	W 3-1	Att: 6,263	**Scorers:** Curran, Thomas-Moore2. **Booked:** McLaren, Daniels, Broomes.
5th	Swindon	A	L 3-0	Att: 9,495	**Dismissed:** Gornell.
10th	Walsall	A	L 2-1	Att: 3,841	**Scorers:** Smith OG. **Booked:** Gordon.
13th	Wycombe	H	L 0-3	Att: 4,956	**Booked:** Broomes.
17th	Exeter	H	W 3-1	Att: 5,466	**Scorers:** Curran, Edds, Labadie. **Booked:** Goodison, Labadie.
20th	Brentford	A	L 2-1	Att: 4,341	**Scorers:** Labadie. **Booked:** Welsh, Thomas-Moore.
24th	Colchester	A	D 1-1	Att: 4,353	**Scorers:** Thomas-Moore. **Booked:** Curran, Labadie.

MAY
1st	Millwall	H	W 2-0	Att: 8,694	**Scorers:** Robinson, Thomas-Moore. **Booked:** Broomes, Thomas-Moore, Robinson.
8th	Stockport	A	W 0-3	Att: 7,208	**Scorers:** Goodison, Labadie, Thomas-Moore. **Booked:** Broomes.

● Coca-Cola League 1/Play-Offs ● FA Cup ● Carling Cup ● Johnstone's Paint Trophy

LEAGUE 1 GOALKEEPER STATS

Player	Appearances	Match starts	Completed matches	Sub appearances	Subbed off	Clean sheets	Yellow cards	Red cards
Joe Collister	3	1	1	2	0	0	0	0
Luke Daniels	37	37	35	0	1	9	5	1
Peter Gulacsi	5	5	5	0	0	2	0	0
David Martin	3	3	3	0	0	0	1	0

LEAGUE 1 OUTFIELD PLAYER STATS

Player	Appearances	Match starts	Completed matches	Substitute appearances	Subbed off	Goals scored	Yellow cards	Red cards
Kithson Bain	10	0	0	10	0	0	0	0
Zoumana Bakayogo	29	29	27	0	0	0	3	2
Charlie Barnett	7	1	0	6	0	1	0	1
Marlon Broomes	31	31	29	0	1	1	11	1
Sebastien Carole	4	4	0	4	0	0	0	0
Aaron Cresswell	14	13	12	1	1	0	2	0
Craig Curran	43	38	25	5	13	5	6	0
Gareth Edds	35	24	17	11	7	3	0	0
Ryan Fraughan	6	1	0	5	1	0	0	0
Ian Goodison	44	44	41	0	3	3	7	0
Ben Gordon	4	4	4	0	0	0	2	0
Terry Gornell	27	18	8	9	9	2	4	1
Gavin Gunning	6	6	5	0	1	0	0	0
Joss Labadie	9	5	4	4	1	3	2	0
Shaleum Logan	33	32	31	1	0	0	9	1
Alan Mahon	16	8	2	8	6	1	0	0
Chris McCready	8	8	7	0	1	0	0	0
Paul McLaren	38	36	29	2	7	0	10	0
Luke O'Neill	4	4	3	0	1	0	0	0
Michael Ricketts	12	7	2	5	5	1	1	0
Andy Robinson	5	3	0	2	2	1	1	1
Bas Savage	13	10	8	3	2	0	1	0
Chris Shuker	26	16	9	10	7	2	1	0
Marvin Sordell	8	6	0	2	6	1	1	0
Ash Taylor	33	27	25	6	2	2	3	0
Ian Thomas-Moore	43	41	35	2	6	13	5	0
John Welsh	45	44	36	1	8	4	9	0

AUG	SEP	OCT	NOV	DEC	JAN	FEB	MAR	APR	MAY

SEASON INFORMATION

Highest position: 11
Lowest position: 24
Average goals scored per game: 0.98
Average goals conceded per game: 1.57

22	22	23	24	22	22	19	21	21	19

LEAGUE POSITION AT THE END OF EACH MONTH

LONGEST SEQUENCES

Wins	2	Undefeated home	5
(01/05/10–08/05/10)		(24/11/09–26/01/10)	
Losses	6	Undefeated away	4
(18/08/09–19/09/09)		(30/01/10–13/03/10)	
Draws	2	Without scoring	4
(on two occasions)		(18/08/09–05/09/09)	
Undefeated	3	Without conceding	3
(on four occasions)		(19/12/09–20/01/10)	
Without win	7	Scoring	4
(18/08/09–26/09/09)		(on two occasions)	

CARDS RECEIVED

83   **8**

EARLIEST STRIKE

MARLON BROOMES
(v Southampton) 2:25

LATEST STRIKE

IAN THOMAS-MOORE
(v Gillingham) 93:11

GOALS SCORED/CONCEDED
PER FIVE-MINUTE INTERVALS

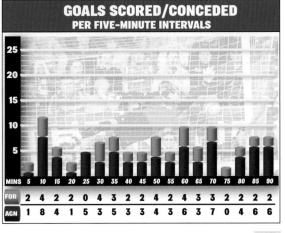

MINS	5	10	15	20	25	30	35	40	45	50	55	60	65	70	75	80	85	90
FOR	2	4	2	2	0	4	3	2	2	4	2	4	3	3	2	2	2	2
AGN	1	8	4	1	5	3	5	3	3	4	3	6	3	7	0	4	6	6

WALSALL will look back on 2009/10 with mixed emotions. The Saddlers momentarily flirted with the play-offs and were just a point off the top six after beating Yeovil at the start of December but, while they fell back into more familiar mid-table surroundings, their performances point to a bright future.

Their inconsistency was summed up in February by their losing to struggling Oldham only to then claim a superb victory at high-flying Leeds, which ended the Yorkshire club's unbeaten home record. However, their 10th-place finish – their highest since their relegation from the second tier in 2003/04 – does point towards progress on a tight budget.

The team looks stronger under manager Chris Hutchings and they are now firmly established in the third tier, with Troy Deeney and Darren Byfield forming a solid partnership up front. Deeney's 14-goal haul in all competitions saw him voted as the club's player of the year, while Steve Jones also reached double figures.

CLUB SUMMARY

FORMED	1888
MANAGER	Chris Hutchings
GROUND	Banks's Stadium
CAPACITY	11,300
NICKNAME	The Saddlers
WEBSITE	www.saddlers.co.uk

The New
Football Pools
PLAYER OF THE SEASON

Troy Deeney

OVERALL
P	W	D	L	F	A	GD
50	17	15	18	62	66	-4

COCA-COLA FOOTBALL LEAGUE 1
Pos	P	W	D	L	F	A	GD	Pts
10	46	16	14	16	60	63	-3	62

HOME
Pos	P	W	D	L	F	A	GD	Pts
12	23	10	8	5	36	26	10	38

AWAY
Pos	P	W	D	L	F	A	GD	Pts
11	23	6	6	11	24	37	-13	24

CUP PROGRESS DETAILS
Competition	Round reached	Knocked out by
FA Cup	R2	Brentford
Carling Cup	R1	Accrington
JP Trophy	R1	Bury

BIGGEST WIN (ALL COMPS)
3–0 on 2 occasions

BIGGEST DEFEAT (ALL COMPS)
27/02/10 1–5 v Southampton

ATTENDANCE RECORD
HIGH	AVERAGE	LOW
8,483	4,029	2,929
v Leeds (18/08/2009)		v Yeovil (23/02/2010)

RESULTS 2009/10

AUGUST
8th	● Brighton	A	W 0–1	Att: 6,504	Scorers: Whing OG. Booked: Mattis, Richards, Parkin.
11th	● Accrington	A	L 2–1	Att: 1,041	Scorers: Nicholls. Booked: Weston. Dismissed: Weston.
15th	● Southend	H	D 2–2	Att: 3,658	Scorers: Jones, Parkin. Booked: Mattis. Dismissed: Mattis.
18th	● Leeds	H	L 1–2	Att: 8,483	Scorers: Parkin.
22nd	● Charlton	A	L 2–0	Att: 15,306	
29th	● Gillingham	H	D 0–0	Att: 3,331	

SEPTEMBER
1st	● Bury	H	D 0–0	Att: 2,314	Bury win 5–4 on penalties.
5th	● Norwich	A	D 0–0	Att: 23,041	
12th	● Tranmere	A	W 2–3	Att: 4,858	Scorers: Byfield, Deeney[2]. Booked: Vincent, Westlake, Nicholls.
19th	● Swindon	H	D 1–1	Att: 4,148	Scorers: Deeney. Booked: Mattis, Westlake.
26th	● Hartlepool	A	L 3–0	Att: 3,334	Booked: Deeney, Westlake.
29th	● Huddersfield	H	W 2–1	Att: 3,419	Scorers: Byfield, Mattis. Booked: Deeney.

OCTOBER
3rd	● Carlisle	H	D 2–2	Att: 3,572	Scorers: Byfield, Jones. Booked: McDonald.
10th	● Milton Keynes Dons	A	L 1–0	Att: 8,919	Booked: McDonald, Hughes.
17th	● Exeter	H	W 3–0	Att: 4,063	Scorers: Deeney, Jones[2]. Booked: Weston.
24th	● Colchester	A	L 2–1	Att: 4,880	Scorers: Deeney, Sansara.
31st	● Wycombe	A	W 2–3	Att: 5,046	Scorers: Hughes, Jones, Nicholls. Booked: Deeney, Jones, Sansara, Nicholls.

NOVEMBER
7th	● Stourbridge	A	W 0–1	Att: 2,014	Scorers: Jones. Booked: Weston, Hughes.
14th	● Stockport	H	W 2–0	Att: 4,143	Scorers: Byfield, Richards. Booked: Byfield.
21st	● Brentford	A	D 1–1	Att: 4,492	Scorers: Jones.
24th	● Oldham	H	W 3–0	Att: 3,191	Scorers: Deeney[2], Jones. Booked: O'Keefe, Hughes, Sansara.
28th	● Brentford	A	L 1–0	Att: 2,611	Booked: Mattis, Sansara, Smith.

DECEMBER
1st	● Yeovil	A	W 1–3	Att: 3,508	Scorers: Byfield, Jones, Parkin.
5th	● Southampton	H	L 1–3	Att: 5,681	Scorers: Byfield. Booked: Bradley, Deeney, Weston, Hughes.
12th	● Millwall	A	L 2–1	Att: 8,174	Scorers: Smith. Booked: Hughes.
19th	● Leyton Orient	H	D 2–2	Att: 3,616	Scorers: Deeney[2]. Booked: Bradley.

JANUARY
16th	● Brighton	H	L 1–2	Att: 3,450	Scorers: Richards.
26th	● Norwich	H	L 1–2	Att: 5,022	Scorers: Deeney. Booked: Parkin.
30th	● Gillingham	A	D 0–0	Att: 4,796	Booked: Vincent.

FEBRUARY
2nd	● Charlton	H	D 1–1	Att: 3,417	Scorers: Deeney. Booked: Mattis, McDonald, Deeney, Vincent. Dismissed: Deeney.
6th	● Bristol Rovers	H	D 0–0	Att: 3,886	
9th	● Bristol Rovers	A	W 0–1	Att: 5,919	Scorers: Taundry. Booked: Vincent, Mattis.
13th	● Oldham	A	L 1–0	Att: 3,968	Booked: Deeney, Westlake, McDonald, Byfield.
16th	● Leeds	A	W 1–2	Att: 18,941	Scorers: Mattis, McDonald. Booked: McDonald, Westlake.
20th	● Brentford	H	W 2–1	Att: 3,616	Scorers: Deeney, Nicholls. Booked: McDonald, Deeney, Smith.
23rd	● Yeovil	H	L 0–1	Att: 2,929	Booked: Nicholls, McDonald.
27th	● Southampton	A	L 5–1	Att: 20,461	Scorers: Richards. Booked: Westlake, Deeney.

MARCH
6th	● Millwall	H	D 2–2	Att: 3,835	Scorers: Nicholls, Taundry. Booked: Richards, Nicholls. Dismissed: Richards.
13th	● Leyton Orient	A	L 2–0	Att: 3,685	
20th	● Colchester	H	W 1–0	Att: 3,510	Scorers: Byfield. Booked: Taundry. Dismissed: Hughes.
23rd	● Southend	A	L 3–0	Att: 6,432	Booked: Nicholls, Mattis. Dismissed: McDonald.
27th	● Exeter	A	L 2–1	Att: 5,887	Scorers: Gray. Booked: Smith, Vincent.

APRIL
3rd	● Stockport	A	D 1–1	Att: 3,580	Scorers: Gray. Dismissed: Deeney.
5th	● Wycombe	H	W 2–1	Att: 3,618	Scorers: Gray, Smith. Booked: Byfield.
10th	● Tranmere	H	W 2–1	Att: 3,841	Scorers: Byfield, Smith.
13th	● Huddersfield	A	L 4–3	Att: 14,396	Scorers: Deeney[2], Nicholls. Booked: Byfield. Dismissed: Hughes.
17th	● Swindon	A	D 1–1	Att: 8,467	Scorers: Jones. Booked: Nicholls.
24th	● Hartlepool	H	W 3–1	Att: 3,457	Scorers: Deeney, Gray, Taundry. Booked: Smith.

MAY
1st	● Carlisle	A	D 1–1	Att: 5,114	Scorers: Byfield. Booked: Smith, Gray.
8th	● Milton Keynes Dons	H	W 2–1	Att: 4,772	Scorers: Richards, Smith.

● Coca-Cola League 1/Play-Offs ● FA Cup ● Carling Cup ● Johnstone's Paint Trophy

actim

LEAGUE 1 GOALKEEPER STATS

Player	Appearances	Match starts	Completed matches	Sub appearances	Subbed off	Clean sheets	Yellow cards	Red cards
Rene Gilmartin	22	22	21	0	1	2	0	0
Clayton Ince	25	24	24	1	0	7	0	0

LEAGUE 1 OUTFIELD PLAYER STATS

Player	Appearances	Match starts	Completed matches	Substitute appearances	Subbed off	Goals scored	Yellow cards	Red cards
Sam Adkins	1	0	0	1	0	0	0	0
Mark Bradley	28	19	16	9	3	0	2	0
Darren Byfield	37	31	17	6	14	10	4	0
Troy Deeney	42	42	32	0	8	14	9	2
Julian Gray	18	17	15	1	2	4	1	0
Mark Hughes	26	24	22	2	0	1	4	2
Steve Jones	30	25	8	5	17	9	1	0
Dwayne Mattis	34	34	29	0	4	2	6	1
Clayton McDonald	26	24	19	2	4	1	7	1
Alex Nicholls	37	20	11	17	9	4	6	0
Josh O'Keefe	13	8	4	5	4	0	1	0
Sam Parkin	24	7	7	17	0	3	2	0
Matthew Richards	40	39	33	1	5	4	2	1
Stephen Roberts	1	1	0	0	1	0	0	0
Netan Sansara	17	17	15	0	2	0	3	0
Emmanuele Smith	33	30	30	3	0	4	4	0
Richard Taundry	30	24	21	6	3	3	1	0
Peter Till	28	18	6	10	12	0	0	0
Jamie Vincent	38	37	37	1	0	0	5	0
Darryl Westlake	22	20	18	2	2	0	6	0
Rhys Weston	27	23	21	4	2	0	2	0

AUG SEP OCT NOV DEC JAN FEB MAR APR MAY

SEASON INFORMATION
Highest position: 1
Lowest position: 19
Average goals scored per game: 1.30
Average goals conceded per game: 1.37

LEAGUE POSITION AT THE END OF EACH MONTH

17	11	12	9	10	13	10	14	12	10

LONGEST SEQUENCES

Wins	2	Undefeated home	7
(on four occasions)		(29/08/09–24/11/09)	
Losses	2	Undefeated away	3
(on five occasions)		(31/10/09–01/12/09)	
Draws	3	Without scoring	3
(30/01/10–06/02/10)		(22/08/09–05/09/09)	
Undefeated	5	Without conceding	2
(31/10/09–01/12/09)		(on two occasions)	
Without win	8	Scoring	12
(05/12/09–06/02/10)		(17/10/09–26/01/10)	

CARDS RECEIVED
66 **7**

EARLIEST STRIKE
DARREN BYFIELD
(v Carlisle) 1:35

LATEST STRIKE
DARREN BYFIELD
(v Colchester) 93:16

GOALS SCORED/CONCEDED
PER FIVE-MINUTE INTERVALS

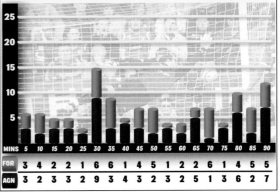

MINS	5	10	15	20	25	30	35	40	45	50	55	60	65	70	75	80	85	90
FOR	3	4	2	2	1	6	6	1	4	5	1	2	2	6	1	4	5	5
AGN	3	2	3	3	2	9	3	4	3	2	3	2	5	1	3	6	2	7

WYCOMBE WANDERERS

A SEASON of struggle at Adams Park ended in relegation back to npower League Two after just a single year.

Peter Taylor had guided the Chairboys to promotion during the 2008/09 campaign but survival this time around was always going to be a tough ask.

The signings of experienced defenders Michael Duberry and Chris Westwood looked to be a good move but the duo failed to click as Taylor's side made a poor start. However, the manager's exit at the start of October was still a surprise as the club turned to Aldershot boss Gary Waddock instead.

The new manager took time to settle in, with a televised 6–0 defeat in November at Huddersfield a particular low point.

A late rally that included wins over Hartlepool, Tranmere and MK Dons gave the club hope of beating the drop but it was left to former favourite Scott McGleish to send them down with a winner for Leyton Orient in May.

CLUB SUMMARY

FORMED	1887
MANAGER	Gary Waddock
GROUND	Adams Park
CAPACITY	10,284
NICKNAME	The Chairboys
WEBSITE	www.wycombewanderers.co.uk

The New
Football Pools
PLAYER OF THE SEASON

Jon-Paul Pittman

OVERALL
P	W	D	L	F	A	GD
50	10	17	23	62	88	-26

COCA-COLA FOOTBALL LEAGUE 1
Pos	P	W	D	L	F	A	GD	Pts
22	46	10	15	21	56	76	-20	45

HOME
Pos	P	W	D	L	F	A	GD	Pts
23	23	6	7	10	26	31	-5	25

AWAY
Pos	P	W	D	L	F	A	GD	Pts
16	23	4	8	11	30	45	-15	20

CUP PROGRESS DETAILS
Competition	Round reached	Knocked out by
FA Cup	R1	Brighton
Carling Cup	R1	Peterborough
JP Trophy	R1	Northampton

BIGGEST WIN (ALL COMPS)
3–0 on 2 occasions

BIGGEST DEFEAT (ALL COMPS)
14/11/09 0–6 v Huddersfield

ATTENDANCE RECORD
High	Average	Low
8,400	5,544	3,899
v Leeds (15/08/2009)		v Tranmere (29/09/2009)

RESULTS 2009/10

AUGUST
8th	● Charlton	A	L 3–2	Att: 16,552	Scorers: Zebroski².
11th	● Peterborough	H	L 0–4	Att: 2,078	
15th	● Leeds	H	L 0–1	Att: 8,400	
18th	● Southend	H	D 1–1	Att: 4,607	Scorers: Harrold.
22nd	● Norwich	A	L 5–2	Att: 23,428	Scorers: Harrold, Pittman. Booked: Johnson.
29th	● Bristol Rovers	A	W 2–1	Att: 5,214	Scorers: Phillips, Pittman.

SEPTEMBER
1st	● Northampton	H	D 2–2	Att: 1,035	Scorers: Pittman². Booked: Johnson, Phillips. Northampton win 3–0 on penalties.
5th	● Brighton	A	L 1–0	Att: 5,895	
12th	● Hartlepool	A	D 1–1	Att: 3,326	Scorers: Beavon. Booked: Pack.
19th	● Milton Keynes Dons	H	L 0–1	Att: 6,127	
26th	● Swindon	A	D 1–1	Att: 6,929	Scorers: Chambers. Booked: Zebroski, Hunt.
29th	● Tranmere	H	L 0–1	Att: 3,899	

OCTOBER
3rd	● Leyton Orient	H	L 0–1	Att: 4,798	
10th	● Gillingham	A	L 3–2	Att: 5,316	Scorers: Woodman, Bentley OG. Booked: Westlake, Hunt.
17th	● Colchester	H	D 1–1	Att: 5,394	Scorers: Pittman. Booked: Harrold, Pittman, Woodman.
24th	● Exeter	A	D 1–1	Att: 5,227	Scorers: Harrold. Booked: Shearer, Davies.
31st	● Walsall	H	L 2–3	Att: 5,046	Scorers: Davies². Booked: Zebroski, Woodman.

NOVEMBER
7th	● Brighton	H	D 4–4	Att: 2,749	Scorers: Davies, Harrold², Pittman. Booked: Johnson, Shearer. Dismissed: Woodman.
14th	● Huddersfield	A	L 6–0	Att: 14,869	Booked: Davies.
18th	● Brighton	A	L 2–0	Att: 3,383	Booked: Phillips.
21st	● Millwall	A	W 0–2	Att: 9,728	Scorers: Betsy, Westwood. Booked: S Davies.
24th	● Brentford	H	W 1–0	Att: 5,181	Scorers: Harrold. Booked: Harrold.

DECEMBER
1st	● Southampton	A	L 1–0	Att: 16,402	Booked: Betsy, Oliver.
5th	● Stockport	H	W 2–1	Att: 4,343	Scorers: Davies, Westwood. Booked: Mousinho, Shearer.
12th	● Carlisle	A	L 1–0	Att: 4,528	Booked: Davies.
19th	● Oldham	H	D 2–2	Att: 4,160	Scorers: Akinde, Harrold. Booked: Doherty. Dismissed: Akinde.
26th	● Yeovil	A	L 4–0	Att: 5,055	Booked: Oliver.
28th	● Brighton	H	L 2–5	Att: 6,126	Scorers: Mousinho, Pittman. Booked: Beavon.

JANUARY
2nd	● Norwich	H	L 0–1	Att: 7,171	Booked: Hinshelwood, Doherty.
9th	● Leeds	A	D 1–1	Att: 24,383	Scorers: Pittman. Booked: Hunt.
16th	● Charlton	H	L 1–2	Att: 6,123	Scorers: Pittman.
23rd	● Southend	A	D 1–1	Att: 6,675	Scorers: Payne. Booked: Woodman, Payne, Mousinho.
30th	● Bristol Rovers	H	W 2–3	Att: 6,688	Scorers: Beavon, Harrold, Revell. Booked: Harrold, Revell.

FEBRUARY
6th	● Yeovil	H	L 1–4	Att: 4,793	Scorers: Harrold. Booked: Oliver.
13th	● Brentford	A	D 1–1	Att: 5,740	Scorers: Betsy. Booked: Oliver.
20th	● Millwall	H	W 1–0	Att: 5,774	Scorers: Kelly. Dismissed: Ainsworth.
23rd	● Southampton	H	D 0–0	Att: 6,232	Booked: Bennett.
27th	● Stockport	A	L 4–3	Att: 3,740	Scorers: Phillips², Fon Williams OG. Booked: McLeod.

MARCH
6th	● Carlisle	H	D 0–0	Att: 4,876	Booked: Kelly, Hinshelwood.
13th	● Oldham	A	D 2–2	Att: 3,846	Scorers: Betsy, Harrold.
20th	● Exeter	H	D 2–2	Att: 5,054	Scorers: Ainsworth, Beavon.
27th	● Colchester	A	D 1–1	Att: 5,593	Scorers: Ainsworth. Booked: Hinshelwood, Keates.

APRIL
3rd	● Huddersfield	H	L 1–2	Att: 5,288	Scorers: Keates. Booked: McLeod.
5th	● Walsall	A	L 2–1	Att: 3,618	Scorers: Hinshelwood.
10th	● Hartlepool	H	W 2–0	Att: 4,342	Scorers: Phillips, Pittman. Booked: Mousinho.
13th	● Tranmere	A	W 0–3	Att: 4,956	Scorers: Bloomfield, Revell². Booked: Bloomfield, Mousinho, Ainsworth.
17th	● Milton Keynes Dons	A	W 2–3	Att: 10,561	Scorers: Betsy, Revell².
24th	● Swindon	H	D 2–2	Att: 7,459	Scorers: Bloomfield, Revell. Booked: Woodman, Revell, Betsy.

MAY
1st	● Leyton Orient	A	L 2–0	Att: 5,918	
8th	● Gillingham	H	W 3–0	Att: 7,110	Scorers: Bennett, Betsy, Phillips. Booked: Mousinho.

● Coca-Cola League 1/Play-Offs ● FA Cup ● Carling Cup ● Johnstone's Paint Trophy

actim

Coca-Cola LEAGUE 1

LEAGUE 1 GOALKEEPER STATS

Player	Appearances	Match starts	Completed matches	Sub appearances	Subbed off	Clean sheets	Yellow cards	Red cards
Tom Heaton	16	16	16	0	0	6	0	0
Scott Shearer	29	29	29	0	0	2	2	0
Jamie Young	1	1	1	0	0	0	0	0

LEAGUE 1 OUTFIELD PLAYER STATS

Player	Appearances	Match starts	Completed matches	Substitute appearances	Subbed off	Goals scored	Yellow cards	Red cards
Gareth Ainsworth	14	12	9	2	2	2	1	1
John Akinde	6	4	2	2	1	1	0	1
Stuart Beavon	25	14	5	11	9	3	1	0
Alan Bennett	6	6	6	0	0	1	1	0
Kevin Betsy	39	35	31	4	4	5	2	0
Matt Bloomfield	14	8	7	6	1	2	1	0
Ashley Chambers	3	0	0	3	0	1	0	0
Scott Davies	15	14	13	1	1	3	4	0
Tommy Doherty	12	11	10	1	1	0	2	0
Michael Duberry	18	18	18	0	0	0	0	0
Stuart Green	13	10	3	3	7	0	0	0
Kadeem Harris	2	0	0	2	0	0	0	0
Matt Harrold	36	29	14	7	15	8	3	0
Adam Hinshelwood	13	13	10	0	3	1	3	0
Lewis Hunt	27	26	21	1	5	0	3	0
Leon Johnson	5	5	5	0	0	0	1	0
Dean Keates	13	13	12	0	1	1	1	0
Julian Kelly	9	9	8	0	1	1	1	0
Kevin McLeod	11	8	6	3	2	0	2	0
Thomas Moncur	4	4	3	0	1	0	0	0
Lewis Montrose	14	11	6	3	5	0	0	0
John Mousinho	39	37	30	2	7	1	5	0
Luke Oliver	23	19	19	4	0	0	4	0
Marlon Pack	8	7	6	1	1	0	1	0
Josh Payne	3	3	2	0	1	1	1	0
Matt Phillips	36	18	13	18	5	5	0	0
Jon-Paul Pittman	41	21	10	20	11	7	1	0
Alex Revell	15	11	7	4	4	6	2	0
Adam Smith	3	3	1	0	2	0	0	0
Ian Westlake	9	7	0	2	7	0	1	0
Chris Westwood	28	28	25	0	3	2	0	0
Craig Woodman	44	44	43	0	1	1	4	0
Chris Zebroski	15	12	10	3	2	2	2	0

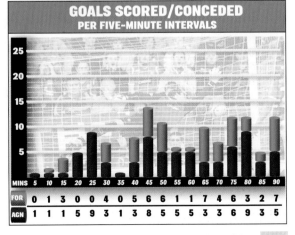

	AUG	SEP	OCT	NOV	DEC	JAN	FEB	MAR	APR	MAY

SEASON INFORMATION
Highest position: 17
Lowest position: 24
Average goals scored per game: 1.22
Average goals conceded per game: 1.65

LEAGUE POSITION AT THE END OF EACH MONTH
20 23 24 22 23 23 23 23 22 22

LONGEST SEQUENCES

Wins	3	Undefeated home	4
(10/04/10–17/04/10)		(20/02/10–20/03/10)	
Losses	3	Undefeated away	4
(on two occasions)		(09/01/10–13/02/10)	
Draws	4	Without scoring	2
(06/03/10–27/03/10)		(29/09/09–03/10/09)	
Undefeated	4	Without conceding	2
(on two occasions)		(on three occasions)	
Without win	11	Scoring	9
(05/09/09–14/11/09)		(13/03/10–24/04/10)	

CARDS RECEIVED
49   **2**

EARLIEST STRIKE
JOHN AKINDE
(v Oldham) 8:42

LATEST STRIKE
KEVIN BETSY
(v Milton Keynes Dons) 94:31

GOALS SCORED/CONCEDED
PER FIVE-MINUTE INTERVALS

MINS	5	10	15	20	25	30	35	40	45	50	55	60	65	70	75	80	85	90
FOR	0	1	3	0	0	4	0	5	6	6	1	1	7	4	6	3	2	7
AGN	1	1	1	5	9	3	1	3	8	5	5	5	3	6	9	9	3	5

YEOVIL TOWN

TERRY SKIVERTON continued to make steady progress in his first full season in charge at Huish Park.

Survival was only secured on the penultimate weekend with an emphatic 3–0 win over Oldham but the Glovers looked safe well before then and were never in the bottom four as they finished in 15th spot, an improvement of two places on the 2008/09 season.

Yeovil stayed up despite the news of the talismanic Darren Way's retirement in February, as the midfielder failed to fully recover from the injuries he sustained in a car accident in December 2008.

Player/manager Skiverton did not feature on the pitch during the course of the season and confirmed after the final game of the campaign that he will now concentrate solely on the manager's job.

The supporters will be hoping to see some new faces arrive at Huish Park as their side look to push further up the table in 2010/11.

CLUB SUMMARY

FORMED	1895
MANAGER	Terry Skiverton
GROUND	Huish Park
CAPACITY	9,665
NICKNAME	The Glovers
WEBSITE	www.ytfc.net

The New Football Pools PLAYER OF THE SEASON

Steven Caulker

OVERALL
P	W	D	L	F	A	GD
49	13	14	22	56	66	-10

COCA-COLA FOOTBALL LEAGUE 1
Pos	P	W	D	L	F	A	GD	Pts
15	46	13	14	19	55	59	-4	53

HOME
Pos	P	W	D	L	F	A	GD	Pts
18	23	9	7	7	36	26	10	34

AWAY
Pos	P	W	D	L	F	A	GD	Pts
17	23	4	7	12	19	33	-14	19

CUP PROGRESS DETAILS
Competition	Round reached	Knocked out by
FA Cup	R1	Oxford
Carling Cup	R1	Norwich
JP Trophy	R1	Bournemouth

BIGGEST WIN (ALL COMPS)
4–0 on 2 occasions

BIGGEST DEFEAT (ALL COMPS)
0–4 on 2 occasions

ATTENDANCE RECORD
High	Average	Low
7,484	4,664	3,469
v Southampton (17/04/2010)		v Colchester (16/02/2010)

RESULTS 2009/10

AUGUST
8th	● Tranmere	H	W 2–0	Att: 4,349	Scorers: Bowditch, Tomlin.
11th	● Norwich	H	L 0–4	Att: 3,860	Booked: Schofield, Jones.
15th	● Colchester	A	L 2–1	Att: 4,263	Scorers: Mason. Booked: O'Callaghan.
18th	● Exeter	A	D 1–1	Att: 6,650	Scorers: Mason. Booked: Stam.
22nd	● Leyton Orient	H	D 3–3	Att: 3,827	Scorers: Obika, Schofield, Tomlin. Booked: Murtagh.
29th	● Huddersfield	A	L 2–1	Att: 12,646	Scorers: Murtagh. Booked: Tomlin, Smith.

SEPTEMBER
1st	● Bournemouth	A	L 2–1	Att: 2,655	Scorers: Obika. Booked: S Williams, Murtagh, Smith, O'Callaghan.
5th	● Swindon	H	L 0–1	Att: 4,807	Booked: Smith, Lindegaard, Mason, Jones.
12th	● Stockport	H	D 2–2	Att: 3,519	Scorers: Tomlin, S Williams. Booked: Obika. Dismissed: McCarthy.
19th	● Southampton	A	L 2–0	Att: 19,907	Booked: Jones.
26th	● Brentford	H	W 2–0	Att: 4,249	Scorers: Alcock, Welsh. Booked: Welsh, Kalala.
29th	● Millwall	A	D 0–0	Att: 6,617	Booked: S Williams, C Davies, Jones, Forbes.

OCTOBER
3rd	● Oldham	A	D 0–0	Att: 4,208	Booked: Kalala, C Davies, Tomlin, Smith.
10th	● Brighton	H	D 2–2	Att: 4,412	Scorers: Murray[2]. Booked: S Williams, Kalala, Obika.
17th	● Carlisle	H	W 3–1	Att: 4,333	Scorers: Mason[2], Murtagh.
24th	● Bristol Rovers	A	W 1–2	Att: 7,812	Scorers: Forbes, Obika. Booked: Kalala.
31st	● Leeds	A	L 4–0	Att: 24,482	Booked: Welsh, Kalala.

NOVEMBER
7th	● Oxford	A	L 1–0	Att: 6,144	Booked: Forbes, Mason, Murtagh.
14th	● Southend	H	W 1–0	Att: 3,906	Scorers: Bowditch. Booked: Kalala, O'Callaghan.
21st	● Charlton	H	D 1–1	Att: 5,632	Scorers: Obika. Booked: Stam, Hutchins.
24th	● Gillingham	A	L 1–0	Att: 4,450	Booked: S Williams, Stam, Bowditch, Kalala. Dismissed: Kalala.

DECEMBER
1st	● Walsall	H	L 1–3	Att: 3,508	Scorers: Obika. Booked: Hutchins.
5th	● Milton Keynes Dons	A	D 2–2	Att: 8,965	Scorers: Bowditch, MacDonald. Booked: Forbes, Kalala.
12th	● Norwich	H	D 3–3	Att: 4,964	Scorers: Bowditch, MacDonald, Obika. Booked: Tomlin, Obika, Mason, Forbes.
19th	● Hartlepool	A	D 1–1	Att: 2,778	Scorers: S Williams. Booked: Tomlin, Alcock.
26th	● Wycombe	H	W 4–0	Att: 5,055	Scorers: Kalala, Murtagh, Obika, S Williams. Booked: Kalala, Murray.
28th	● Swindon	A	L 3–1	Att: 8,509	Scorers: Tomlin. Booked: S Williams, Mason, Forbes.

JANUARY
19th	● Leyton Orient	A	L 2–0	Att: 2,669	Booked: Kalala, Jones, Smith.
23rd	● Exeter	H	W 2–1	Att: 6,282	Scorers: Mason, Stam.
26th	● Tranmere	A	L 2–1	Att: 4,584	Scorers: Mason. Booked: Stam.
30th	● Huddersfield	H	L 0–1	Att: 4,110	Booked: S Williams, Kalala.

FEBRUARY
6th	● Wycombe	A	W 1–4	Att: 4,793	Scorers: Bowditch[2], Tudur Jones, Welsh. Booked: Tomlin, Smith.
13th	● Gillingham	H	D 0–0	Att: 3,853	Booked: Alcock.
16th	● Colchester	H	L 0–1	Att: 3,469	
20th	● Charlton	A	L 2–0	Att: 15,991	Booked: Smith.
23rd	● Walsall	A	W 0–1	Att: 2,929	Scorers: S Williams. Booked: Forbes, Smith.
27th	● Milton Keynes Dons	H	W 1–0	Att: 3,844	Scorers: MacDonald. Booked: S Williams, Tomlin.

MARCH
6th	● Norwich	A	L 3–0	Att: 24,868	Booked: Kalala.
13th	● Hartlepool	H	W 4–0	Att: 4,169	Scorers: Bowditch, Tomlin, G Williams, Collins OG. Booked: Kalala, Tomlin. Dismissed: G Williams.
16th	● Carlisle	A	L 1–0	Att: 3,731	Booked: Forbes.
20th	● Bristol Rovers	H	L 0–3	Att: 5,968	Booked: Kalala, Caulker.

APRIL
3rd	● Southend	A	D 0–0	Att: 6,854	Booked: Smith, Alcock.
5th	● Leeds	H	L 1–2	Att: 6,308	Scorers: Bowditch. Booked: Tomlin.
10th	● Stockport	A	W 1–3	Att: 3,587	Scorers: Bowditch, G Williams[2]. Booked: Forbes, Tomlin.
13th	● Millwall	H	D 1–1	Att: 4,713	Scorers: Bowditch. Booked: Smith.
17th	● Southampton	H	L 0–1	Att: 7,484	Booked: Caulker, G Williams.
24th	● Brentford	A	D 1–1	Att: 5,395	Scorers: Tomlin. Booked: Alcock, Ayling.

MAY
1st	● Oldham	H	W 3–0	Att: 4,513	Scorers: Tomlin, G Williams[2]. Booked: Kalala.
8th	● Brighton	A	L 1–0	Att: 7,323	Booked: Ayling.

● Coca-Cola League 1/Play-Offs ● FA Cup ● Carling Cup ● Johnstone's Paint Trophy

actim

Coca-Cola LEAGUE 1

LEAGUE 1 GOALKEEPER STATS

Player	Appearances	Match starts	Completed matches	Sub appearances	Subbed off	Clean sheets	Yellow cards	Red cards
Richard Martin	3	2	2	1	0	0	0	0
Alex McCarthy	44	44	43	0	0	12	0	1

LEAGUE 1 OUTFIELD PLAYER STATS

Player	Appearances	Match starts	Completed matches	Substitute appearances	Subbed off	Goals scored	Yellow cards	Red cards
Craig Alcock	42	39	37	3	2	1	4	0
Luke Ayling	4	1	0	3	1	0	2	0
Dean Bowditch	30	26	15	4	11	10	1	0
Steven Caulker	44	44	44	0	0	0	2	0
Scott Davies	4	4	2	0	2	0	0	0
Craig Davies	4	2	1	2	1	0	2	0
Arron Davies	10	4	1	6	3	0	0	0
Aidan Downes	5	2	0	3	2	0	0	0
Terrell Forbes	38	35	35	3	0	1	7	0
Danny Hutchins	7	4	2	3	2	0	2	0
Nathan Jones	18	18	17	0	1	0	4	0
JP Kalala	34	32	27	2	4	1	15	1
Andy Lindegaard	5	2	1	3	1	0	1	0
Shaun MacDonald	31	31	31	0	0	3	0	0
Ryan Mason	28	26	13	2	13	6	3	0
Andre McCollin	2	0	0	2	0	0	0	0
Scott Murray	20	10	4	10	6	2	1	0
Kieran Murtagh	27	13	8	14	5	3	1	0
George O'Callaghan	12	7	7	5	0	0	2	0
Jonathan Obika	22	13	7	9	6	6	3	0
Danny Schofield	4	4	3	0	1	1	0	0
Nathan Smith	34	27	26	7	1	0	9	0
Stefan Stam	18	18	13	0	5	1	4	0
Gavin Tomlin	35	29	14	6	15	7	9	0
Owain Tudur Jones	6	6	5	0	1	1	0	0
Andrew Welsh	42	28	9	14	19	2	2	0
Gavin Williams	8	7	4	1	2	5	1	1
Sam Williams	34	28	23	6	5	4	6	0

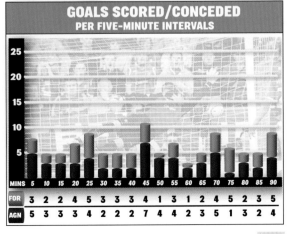

SEASON INFORMATION
Highest position: 4
Lowest position: 23
Average goals scored per game: 1.20
Average goals conceded per game: 1.28

LEAGUE POSITION AT THE END OF EACH MONTH
12 17 14 13 14 14 12 15 17 15

LONGEST SEQUENCES

Wins	2	Undefeated home	6	
(on two occasions)		(12/09/09–21/11/09)		
Losses	2	Undefeated away	3	
(on six occasions)		(on two occasions)		
Draws	3	Without scoring	3	
(on two occasions)		(on two occasions)		
Undefeated	6	Without conceding	3	
(26/09/09–24/10/09)		(26/09/09–03/10/09)		
Without win	7	Scoring	6	
(15/08/09–19/09/09)		(01/12/09–28/12/09)		

CARDS RECEIVED
81 **3**

EARLIEST STRIKE
DEAN BOWDITCH
(v Milton Keynes Dons) 0:27

LATEST STRIKE
RYAN MASON
(v Tranmere) 91:03

GOALS SCORED/CONCEDED
PER FIVE-MINUTE INTERVALS

MINS	5	10	15	20	25	30	35	40	45	50	55	60	65	70	75	80	85	90
FOR	3	2	2	4	5	3	3	3	4	1	3	1	2	4	5	2	3	5
AGN	5	3	3	3	4	2	2	2	7	4	4	2	3	5	1	3	2	4

COCA-COLA LEAGUE 2

COCA-COLA LEAGUE 2 STATISTICS 2009/10

PLAYER OF THE SEASON
Craig Dawson (Rochdale)

MANAGER OF THE SEASON
Keith Hill (Rochdale)

THE PLAYER WITH THE MOST...

GOALS Lee Hughes (Notts County)	**30**
SHOTS ON TARGET Brett Pitman (Bournemouth)	**119**
SHOTS OFF TARGET Brett Pitman (Bournemouth)	**101**
SHOTS WITHOUT SCORING John Brayford (Crewe)	**35**
SHOTS PER GOAL John McGrath (Burton Albion)	**45**
ASSISTS Ben Davies (Notts County)	**14**
OFFSIDES Ryan Lowe (Bury)	**75**
FOULS Adebayo Akinfenwa (Northampton)	**80**
FREE-KICKS WON Ben Davies (Notts County)	**99**
PENALTIES SCORED Adam Le Fondre (Rotherham)	**10**
GOALS SCORED DIRECT FROM FREE-KICKS Davies (Notts County), Westwood (Crewe)	**3**
SAVES MADE Adam Bartlett (Hereford)	**261**
DEFENSIVE CLEARANCES Ian Sharps (Rotherham)	**94**
DEFENSIVE BLOCKS Paul Morgan (Macclesfield)	**33**

THE TEAM WITH THE MOST...

GOALS	Notts County	96
SHOTS ON TARGET	Notts County	355
SHOTS OFF TARGET	Dag & Red	308
SHOTS PER GOAL	Darlington	12.33
CORNERS	Dag & Red	359
FOULS	Northampton	580
WOODWORK STRIKES	Morecambe	23
OFFSIDES	Hereford	183
PENALTIES CONCEDED	Accrington	12
PENALTIES AWARDED	Chesterfield	12
PENALTIES SCORED	Rotherham	10
YELLOW CARDS	Notts County	84
RED CARDS	Grimsby	8

TOTALS 2009/10

GOALS

Total	1446
Home	816
Away	630

CARDS

Yellow	1510
Average per game	2.74
Reds	94
Average per game	0.17

ATTENDANCES

Total	2,122,879

NOTTS COUNTY dominated the 2009/10 Coca-Cola League 2 season both on and off the pitch.

A high-profile multi-million pound takeover in the summer propelled the Magpies into the national news and that exposure was only heightened by the surprise appointment of former England manager Sven-Goran Eriksson as director of football. Ex-Arsenal and Tottenham defender Sol Campbell soon followed on a five-year deal and, with other money-spinning signings, County were expected to take the division by storm.

It was not that easy, though. An inconsistent start saw manager Ian McParland depart in October, while his replacement Hans Backe stepped down after just seven weeks at the helm. Sol Campbell had already left Meadow Lane by then, having played just one game and Eriksson did likewise as the financial backing failed to materialise. All in all, things were not exactly going to plan by the early part of 2010.

The appointment of former Burnley boss Steve Cotterill proved to be crucial as he galvanised the side and took them on a 20-game unbeaten streak that helped them to overhaul runaway leaders Rochdale and take the title.

In normal circumstances, Dale may have been slightly disappointed that they let such a significant lead slip but, considering that their eventual third-place finish gave them a first promotion since 1969, it is unlikely that too many people at Spotland will be complaining.

The season marked a dramatic turnaround for Bournemouth, who had only maintained their Football League status on the final day of the 2008/09 campaign. Eddie Howe proved to be one of the finest young managers in the League as he made light of a season-long transfer embargo and a lengthy injury list to lead his side to an impressive second-place finish.

Morecambe produced a fine end-of-season run of just three defeats in their final 12 games to ensure a fourth-place finish, the highest in the club's history.

Rotherham were among the favourites to go up automatically following a summer of heavy spending but they suffered a blow in the early part of the season when manager Mark Robins joined Barnsley. Returning hero Ronnie Moore took the reins and, thanks to the goals of Adam Le Fondre, the Millers finished fifth, while

Notts County may have claimed the title, but nothing else about their rollercoaster season was predictable

Aldershot and Dagenham held off the challenging pack to also make the play-offs, spelling disappointment for the likes of Bury, Northampton, Chesterfield and Port Vale, who were unable sneak into the top seven.

Brief hope

At the other end of the table, it was a season of despair for Grimsby and Darlington, who slipped out of the Football League. The Mariners had looked dead and buried for much of the campaign but a late-season surge gave them brief hope of survival. However, a final-day defeat at Burton and a win for Barnet meant that it was the Bees who stayed up.

The writing was on the wall for Darlington from early in the campaign following a summer of turmoil at the club. New manager Colin Todd began his reign with just two players on the books and, despite quickly building a squad, he left his post in September without a win to his name. Former Republic of Ireland boss Steve Staunton was appointed as his replacement but he was unable to stem the tide, lasting only until April. Finally, Simon Davey came in to inherit a team that ended with just eight wins.

Macclesfield finished in mid-table but their campaign was overshadowed by the tragic death of their manager Keith Alexander in March, while former Blackburn and England striker Chris Sutton had a mixed season on his first step into management at Lincoln, who finished just above the relegation zone.

Shrewsbury suffered a hangover from their play-off final defeat of 2008/09 as they were unable to mount a promotion challenge. Their failure to do so ultimately cost Paul Simpson his job, while Bradford and Crewe will also be disappointed not to have made a stronger push for the promotion places.

Torquay and Burton performed admirably following their ascent from the Conference as they finished in mid-table, along with Accrington and Hereford.

FINAL COCA-COLA LEAGUE 2 TABLE

Pos	Team	P	HOME					AWAY					GD	Pts
			W	D	L	F	A	W	D	L	F	A		
1	Notts County	46	16	6	1	58	14	11	6	6	38	17	65	93
2	Bournemouth	46	16	3	4	33	16	9	5	9	28	28	17	83
3	Rochdale	46	14	3	6	45	20	11	4	8	37	28	34	82
4	Morecambe	46	14	6	3	44	24	6	7	10	29	40	9	73
5	Rotherham	46	10	9	4	29	18	11	1	11	26	34	3	73
6	Aldershot	46	12	7	4	43	24	8	5	10	26	32	13	72
7	Dag & Red	46	15	2	6	46	27	5	10	8	23	31	11	72
8	Chesterfield	46	14	3	6	38	27	7	4	12	23	35	-1	70
9	Bury	46	11	6	6	29	23	8	6	9	25	36	-5	69
10	Port Vale	46	8	8	7	32	25	9	9	5	29	25	11	68
11	Northampton	46	9	9	5	29	21	9	4	10	33	32	9	67
12	Shrewsbury	46	10	6	7	30	20	7	6	10	25	34	1	63
13	Burton	46	9	5	9	38	34	8	6	9	33	37	0	62
14	Bradford	46	8	8	7	28	27	8	6	9	31	35	-3	62
15	Accrington	46	11	1	11	38	39	7	6	10	24	35	-12	61
16	Hereford	46	12	4	7	32	25	5	4	14	22	40	-11	59
17	Torquay	46	9	6	8	34	24	5	9	9	30	31	9	57
18	Crewe	46	7	4	12	35	36	8	6	9	33	37	-5	55
19	Macclesfield	46	7	8	8	27	28	5	10	8	22	30	-9	54
20	Lincoln	46	9	7	7	25	26	4	4	15	17	39	-23	50
21	Barnet	46	8	10	5	30	18	4	2	17	17	45	-16	48
22	Cheltenham	46	5	8	10	34	38	5	10	8	20	33	-17	48
23	Grimsby	46	4	9	10	25	36	5	8	10	20	35	-26	44
24	Darlington	46	3	3	17	14	40	5	3	15	19	47	-54	30

Adam Le Fondre
(Rotherham)

Shaun Harrad
(Burton)

Calvin Zola
(Crewe)

PLAY-OFF REVIEW

DAGENHAM AND REDBRIDGE secured a place in English football's third tier for the first time in their history by beating favourites Rotherham in the final of the Coca-Cola League 2 play-offs.

John Still's men capped a remarkable season by edging an enthralling Wembley clash against the Millers 3–2.

Paul Benson and Danny Green twice put the Daggers ahead, but Rotherham striker Ryan Taylor pulled his side level on both occasions with his first goals in more than a year. Jon Nurse proved to be the Daggers' hero when he struck the decisive goal with 20 minutes remaining.

There was little doubt that Dagenham would be in the showpiece following the first leg of their semi-final against Morecambe, as they beat Sammy McIlroy's side 6–0 at Victoria Road. Josh Scott was the man of the moment, scoring four goals, with Benson grabbing two.

The Shrimps battled back in the second leg, with goals from Mark Duffy and David Artell either side of another Benson strike earning them a 2–1 win, but the damage had already been done and Dagenham advanced comfortably, heading to Wembley on the back of a 7–2 aggregate victory.

Rotherham booked their first Wembley appearance in 14 years thanks to a 3–0 aggregate win over Aldershot.

Striker Adam Le Fondre capitalised on a late defensive error to earn his side a 1–0 win in the first leg at the Recreation Ground, and he scored his second of the tie in the return leg at the Don Valley Stadium before Kevin Ellison's header finished the job.

That set up the final at Wembley, where Dagenham upset the odds to clinch a famous victory.

Notts County players celebrate capturing the Coca-Cola League 2 trophy having overcome a turbulent campaign with an impressive unbeaten run towards the end of the season

COCA-COLA LEAGUE 2

COCA-COLA LEAGUE 2 RESULTS

HOME / AWAY	ACCRINGTON	ALDERSHOT	BARNET	BOURNEMOUTH	BRADFORD	BURTON	BURY	CHELTENHAM	CHESTERFIELD	CREWE	DAG & RED	DARLINGTON	GRIMSBY	HEREFORD	LINCOLN	MACCLESFIELD	MORECAMBE	NORTHAMPTON	NOTTS COUNTY	PORT VALE	ROCHDALE	ROTHERHAM	SHREWSBURY	TORQUAY
ACCRINGTON	–	2-1	1-0	0-1	2-0	0-2	2-4	4-0	2-0	5-3	0-1	2-1	2-3	1-2	1-0	1-1	3-2	0-3	0-3	1-2	2-4	2-1	1-3	4-2
ALDERSHOT	3-1	–	4-0	2-1	1-0	0-2	2-3	4-1	1-0	1-1	2-3	3-1	1-1	2-2	3-1	0-0	4-1	2-1	1-1	1-1	1-1	3-0	2-0	0-2
BARNET	1-2	3-0	–	1-1	2-2	1-1	0-0	1-1	3-1	1-2	2-0	3-0	3-0	0-0	1-2	1-2	2-0	0-0	1-0	0-0	1-0	0-1	2-2	1-1
BOURNEMOUTH	2-0	1-0	3-0	–	1-0	1-0	1-2	0-0	1-2	1-0	0-0	2-0	3-1	2-1	3-1	1-1	1-0	0-2	2-1	4-0	0-4	1-0	1-0	2-1
BRADFORD	1-1	2-1	2-1	1-1	–	1-1	0-1	1-1	3-0	2-3	3-3	1-0	0-0	1-0	0-2	1-2	2-0	2-0	0-0	0-0	0-3	2-4	1-3	2-0
BURTON	0-2	6-1	2-0	0-2	1-1	–	0-0	5-6	2-2	1-2	0-1	1-2	3-0	3-2	1-0	1-1	5-2	3-2	1-4	1-0	1-0	0-1	1-1	0-2
BURY	0-2	1-2	2-0	0-3	2-1	3-0	–	0-1	2-1	3-0	0-0	1-1	0-1	1-0	2-0	2-1	0-0	2-2	3-3	1-1	1-0	2-1	1-0	0-3
CHELTENHAM	1-1	1-2	5-1	0-1	4-5	0-1	5-2	–	0-1	0-4	1-1	3-3	2-1	0-1	1-0	1-2	2-0	2-2	1-1	1-1	1-4	1-1	1-2	1-1
CHESTERFIELD	1-0	0-1	1-0	2-1	1-1	5-2	1-0	1-0	–	2-3	2-2	5-2	3-2	1-2	2-1	4-1	1-1	1-0	2-1	0-5	2-0	0-1	0-1	1-0
CREWE	5-1	1-2	2-2	1-2	0-1	2-1	2-3	1-2	0-1	–	1-2	3-0	4-2	1-0	0-0	2-1	1-2	3-2	0-1	1-2	2-2	2-3	0-3	1-1
DAG & RED	3-1	2-5	4-1	1-0	2-1	2-1	3-1	0-2	2-1	2-0	–	2-0	2-0	2-1	3-0	3-1	1-1	0-1	0-3	1-1	1-2	0-1	5-0	5-3
DARLINGTON	0-0	1-2	1-2	0-2	0-1	1-0	0-1	1-1	2-3	0-1	0-2	–	0-2	0-1	1-1	0-1	0-4	1-2	0-5	1-3	0-2	2-0	2-1	1-3
GRIMSBY	2-2	1-2	2-0	3-2	0-3	1-2	1-1	1-0	2-2	0-4	1-1	1-1	–	1-0	2-2	1-1	1-1	1-2	0-1	1-2	1-2	1-2	3-0	0-3
HEREFORD	2-0	2-0	2-1	2-1	2-0	3-4	1-3	1-1	1-0	1-1	1-1	2-1	0-1	–	2-0	0-2	0-1	0-2	0-2	2-2	2-1	3-0	1-0	1-0
LINCOLN	2-1	1-0	1-1	0-1	2-1	0-2	1-0	1-1	2-1	1-1	1-1	3-0	0-0	3-1	–	0-0	1-3	1-1	0-3	1-2	1-3	1-2	0-2	0-0
MACCLESFIELD	0-0	1-1	1-1	3-2	2-2	1-1	2-0	1-0	2-0	4-1	2-2	0-2	0-0	3-1	0-1	–	2-2	0-2	0-4	2-0	0-1	1-3	0-1	2-1
MORECAMBE	1-2	1-0	2-1	5-0	0-0	3-2	3-0	1-0	0-1	4-3	1-0	2-0	1-1	2-2	3-1	2-2	–	2-4	2-1	1-0	3-3	2-0	1-1	2-0
NORTHAMPTON	4-0	0-3	1-3	2-0	2-2	1-1	1-1	2-1	0-0	2-2	1-0	2-0	0-0	1-3	1-0	0-0	2-0	–	0-1	1-1	1-2	3-1	2-0	0-0
NOTTS COUNTY	1-2	0-0	2-0	2-2	5-0	1-1	5-0	5-0	1-0	2-0	3-0	4-0	1-1	5-0	3-1	1-0	4-1	5-2	–	3-1	1-0	1-0	1-1	2-2
PORT VALE	2-2	1-1	0-2	0-0	2-1	3-1	0-1	1-1	1-2	0-1	3-1	1-0	4-0	2-0	4-0	0-0	0-2	1-3	2-1	–	1-1	1-2	1-1	2-2
ROCHDALE	1-2	1-0	2-1	0-0	0-1	1-2	3-0	0-1	2-3	2-0	3-1	0-1	4-1	1-1	3-0	4-1	1-0	2-0	1-3	0-0	–	4-0	4-0	2-1
ROTHERHAM	1-0	0-0	3-0	1-3	1-2	2-2	1-0	0-0	3-1	0-0	2-0	1-2	2-1	1-1	2-0	3-1	0-0	1-0	0-0	1-2	2-1	–	1-1	1-1
SHREWSBURY	0-1	3-1	2-0	1-0	1-2	3-1	1-1	0-0	1-1	2-0	2-1	0-2	0-0	3-1	1-0	2-2	2-3	3-0	0-1	0-1	0-1	2-0	–	1-1
TORQUAY	2-1	1-1	0-1	1-2	1-2	2-3	1-1	3-0	2-0	1-1	0-0	5-0	0-2	1-0	2-3	1-0	2-2	1-0	0-0	1-2	5-0	0-2	2-1	–

Lee Hughes (Notts County)

Kasper Schmeichel (Notts County)

LEADING SCORERS

PLAYER	TEAM)	GLS
Lee Hughes	Notts County	30
Brett Pitman	Bournemouth	26
Adam Le Fondre	Rotherham	25
Chris O'Grady	Rochdale	22
Shaun Harrad	Burton	21
Chris Dagnall	Rochdale	20
Marc Richards	Port Vale	20
Phil Jevons	Morecambe	18
Ryan Lowe	Bury	18
Adebayo Akinfenwa	Northampton	17

TEAM DISCIPLINE

TEAM	Y	R
Grimsby	81	8
Lincoln	82	6
Northampton	69	7
Notts County	84	2
Port Vale	69	5
Bournemouth	74	3
Torquay	73	3
Barnet	69	4
Accrington	68	4
Aldershot	70	3
Bradford	60	5
Shrewsbury	63	4
Chesterfield	69	2
Burton	61	4
Darlington	70	1
Dag & Red	63	3
Hereford	52	6
Morecambe	58	3
Bury	49	5
Macclesfield	58	2
Rotherham	50	4
Cheltenham	51	3
Crewe	32	4
Rochdale	35	3

LEADING GOALKEEPERS

PLAYER	TEAM	CLEAN SHEET
Kasper Schmeichel	Notts County	23
Shwan Jalal	Bournemouth	18
Andy Warrington	Rotherham	18
Barry Roche	Morecambe	15
Jake Cole	Barnet	13
Wayne Brown	Bury	13
Tony Roberts	Dag & Red	13
Chris Dunn	Northampton	12
Jon Brain	Macclesfield	11
David Button	Shrewsbury	11

COCA-COLA LEAGUE 2 TABLES

HOME TABLE

	P	W	D	L	F	A	GD	PTS
Notts County	23	16	6	1	58	14	44	54
Bournemouth	23	16	3	4	33	16	17	51
Morecambe	23	14	6	3	44	24	20	48
Dag & Red	23	15	2	6	46	27	19	47
Rochdale	23	14	3	6	45	20	25	45
Chesterfield	23	14	3	6	38	27	11	45
Aldershot	23	12	7	4	43	24	19	43
Rotherham	24	10	10	4	29	18	11	40
Hereford	23	12	4	7	32	25	7	40
Bury	23	11	6	6	29	23	6	39
Shrewsbury	23	10	6	7	30	20	10	36
Northampton	23	9	9	5	29	21	8	36
Barnet	23	8	10	5	30	18	12	34
Accrington	23	11	1	11	38	39	-1	34
Lincoln	23	9	7	7	25	26	-1	34
Torquay	23	9	6	8	34	24	10	33
Port Vale	23	8	8	7	32	25	7	32
Burton	23	9	5	9	38	34	4	32
Bradford	23	8	8	7	28	27	1	32
Macclesfield	23	7	8	8	27	28	-1	29
Crewe	23	7	4	12	35	36	-1	25
Cheltenham	23	5	8	10	34	38	-4	23
Grimsby	23	4	9	10	25	36	-11	21
Darlington	23	3	3	17	14	40	-26	12

FIRST-HALF TABLE

	P	W	D	L	F	A	GD	PTS
Notts County	46	25	15	6	48	17	31	90
Macclesfield	46	17	21	8	31	21	10	72
Rochdale	46	17	20	9	30	21	9	71
Dag & Red	47	17	17	13	30	24	6	68
Shrewsbury	46	18	14	14	30	30	0	68
Port Vale	46	17	16	13	31	26	5	67
Rotherham	47	14	24	9	24	17	7	66
Bradford	46	15	18	13	27	29	-2	63
Burton	46	16	14	16	37	31	6	62
Morecambe	46	15	17	14	31	28	3	62
Aldershot	46	14	20	12	24	25	-1	62
Bury	46	12	24	10	23	20	3	60
Chesterfield	46	14	17	15	24	22	2	59
Bournemouth	46	12	23	11	20	21	-1	59
Torquay	46	13	19	14	27	20	7	58
Barnet	46	12	22	12	28	28	0	58
Northampton	46	12	19	15	23	26	-3	55
Hereford	46	13	15	18	24	28	-4	54
Accrington	46	11	19	16	18	24	-6	52
Grimsby	46	10	21	15	20	32	-12	51
Crewe	46	10	18	18	32	36	-4	48
Cheltenham	46	10	18	18	35	51	-16	48
Darlington	46	11	11	24	16	43	-27	44
Lincoln	46	7	20	19	16	29	-13	41

AWAY TABLE

	P	W	D	L	F	A	GD	PTS
Notts County	23	11	6	6	38	17	21	39
Rochdale	23	11	4	8	37	28	9	37
Port Vale	23	9	9	5	29	25	4	36
Rotherham	23	11	1	11	26	34	-8	34
Bournemouth	23	9	5	9	28	28	0	32
Northampton	23	9	4	10	33	32	1	31
Burton	23	8	6	9	33	37	-4	30
Crewe	23	8	6	9	33	37	-4	30
Bradford	23	8	6	9	31	35	-4	30
Bury	23	8	6	9	25	36	-11	30
Aldershot	23	8	5	10	26	32	-6	29
Shrewsbury	23	7	6	10	25	34	-9	27
Accrington	23	7	6	10	24	35	-11	27
Dag & Red	24	5	11	8	23	31	-8	26
Macclesfield	23	5	10	8	22	30	-8	25
Morecambe	23	6	7	10	29	40	-11	25
Chesterfield	23	7	4	12	23	35	-12	25
Cheltenham	23	5	10	8	20	33	-13	25
Torquay	23	5	9	9	30	31	-1	24
Grimsby	23	5	8	10	20	35	-15	23
Hereford	23	5	4	14	22	40	-18	19
Darlington	23	5	3	15	19	47	-28	18
Lincoln	23	4	4	15	17	39	-22	16
Barnet	23	4	2	17	17	45	-28	14

SECOND-HALF TABLE

	P	W	D	L	F	A	GD	PTS
Notts County	46	24	16	6	48	14	34	88
Rochdale	46	23	13	10	52	27	25	82
Bournemouth	46	21	17	8	41	23	18	80
Northampton	46	21	14	11	39	27	12	77
Aldershot	46	17	18	11	45	31	14	69
Shrewsbury	46	18	13	15	25	24	1	67
Dag & Red	47	16	17	14	39	34	5	65
Morecambe	46	15	18	13	42	36	6	63
Rotherham	47	17	12	18	31	35	-4	63
Burton	46	15	17	14	34	40	-6	62
Torquay	46	15	16	15	37	35	2	61
Chesterfield	46	15	16	15	37	40	-3	61
Port Vale	46	13	21	12	30	24	6	60
Crewe	46	15	15	16	36	37	-1	60
Cheltenham	46	15	15	16	35	36	-1	60
Accrington	46	15	14	17	44	50	-6	59
Bury	46	15	13	18	31	39	-8	58
Bradford	46	13	16	17	32	33	-1	55
Hereford	46	12	19	15	30	37	-7	55
Lincoln	46	12	14	20	26	36	-10	50
Grimsby	46	9	18	19	25	39	-14	45
Barnet	46	10	15	21	19	35	-16	45
Darlington	46	9	17	20	17	44	-27	44
Macclesfield	46	8	16	22	18	37	-19	40

PENALTIES

TOTAL AWARDED	169
SCORED	120
SAVED	38
MISSED	11

EARLIEST STRIKE

LUKE RODGERS
(Lincoln v NOTTS CO) 0:14

LATEST STRIKE

DANNY HONE
(Darlington v LINCOLN) 96:33

Danny Hone (Lincoln)

EARLIEST CARD

SHANE CANSDELL-SHERRIFF
(Torquay v SHREWSBURY) 0:25

SEQUENCES

Wins	Morecambe 7	31/10/2009-12/12/2009
Losses	Torquay 6	22/08/2009-26/09/2009
Draws	Torquay 5	29/09/2009-24/10/2009
Undefeated	Notts Co 16	17/02/2010-20/04/2010
Without win	Grimsby 25	26/09/2009-27/02/2010
Undefeated home	Bury 14	26/09/2009-09/03/2010
Undefeated away	Rochdale 8	17/10/2009-23/01/2010
Without scoring	Rochdale 4	03/04/2010-13/04/2010
Without conceding	Notts Co 6	20/03/2010-10/04/2010
Scoring	Notts Co 17	24/11/2009-20/03/2010
Conceding	Lincoln 23	12/12/2009-17/04/2010

DISCIPLINARY RECORDS   Y=1PT/R=2PT

PLAYER	TEAM	FLS	Y	R
Mark Hughes	Barnet	73	13	1
Shane Cansdell-Sherriff	Shrewsbury	59	12	1
Peter Gain	Dag & Red	64	14	0
Guy Branston	Torquay	66	7	3
Ryan Valentine	Hereford	26	11	1
Lee Hughes	Notts County	69	11	1
Nick Fenton	Rotherham	36	8	2
Tommy Fraser	Port Vale	40	10	1
Dean Holden	Shrewsbury	38	10	1
Lee Bullock	Bradford	57	10	1
John Thompson	Notts County	34	12	0
Robert Page	Chesterfield	54	11	0

OFF-THE-FIELD problems made life difficult for Accrington in 2009/10, although on the pitch it was still an encouraging season.

Stanley were on course for a play-off place before a run of eight defeats in nine games through March and April ended their hopes of finishing in the top seven. However, arguably the biggest story of their campaign was their fight for financial survival. The club were on the brink of going out of business in November before being rescued at the 11th hour by lifelong fan Ilyas Khan. The former merchant banker stepped in and announced that the club's tax bill had been paid to avoid a winding-up order in the High Court.

Boss John Coleman will be looking to push on in 2010/11 but their chances of mounting a promotion bid may depend on whether they can hold on to sought-after strike duo Michael Symes and Bobby Grant. Both were prolific this season, scoring a healthy 27 goals between them in the League.

CLUB SUMMARY

FORMED	1891
MANAGER	John Coleman
GROUND	Fraser Eagle Stadium
CAPACITY	5,057
NICKNAME	The Stans
WEBSITE	www.accringtonstanley.co.uk

The New **Football Pools**
PLAYER OF THE SEASON

Michael Symes

OVERALL

P	W	D	L	F	A	GD
57	25	8	24	79	88	-9

COCA-COLA FOOTBALL LEAGUE 2

Pos	P	W	D	L	F	A	GD	Pts
15	46	18	7	21	62	74	-12	61

HOME

Pos	P	W	D	L	F	A	GD	Pts
14	23	11	1	11	38	39	-1	34

AWAY

Pos	P	W	D	L	F	A	GD	Pts
13	23	7	6	10	24	35	-11	27

CUP PROGRESS DETAILS

Competition	Round reached	Knocked out by
FA Cup	R4	Fulham
Carling Cup	R2	QPR
JP Trophy	SF	Leeds

BIGGEST WIN (ALL COMPS)
10/10/09 4-0 v Cheltenham

BIGGEST DEFEAT (ALL COMPS)
24/04/10 1-5 v Crewe

ATTENDANCE RECORD

HIGH	AVERAGE	Low
3,396	1,980	1,210
v Bradford (20/02/2010)		v Macclesfield (09/03/2010)

RESULTS 2009/10

AUGUST

8th	● Rotherham	A	L 1-0	Att: 3,254	Booked: Martin.
11th	● Walsall	H	W 2-1	Att: 1,041	Scorers: Grant, P Mullin.
15th	● Lincoln	H	W 1-0	Att: 1,498	Scorers: Kempson.
18th	● Northampton	H	L 0-3	Att: 1,561	Booked: Joyce.
22nd	● Aldershot	A	L 3-1	Att: 2,276	Scorers: Edwards. Booked: P Mullin, Procter.
25th	○ QPR	A	L 2-1	Att: 5,203	Scorers: Symes. Booked: Ryan.
29th	● Shrewsbury	H	L 1-3	Att: 1,447	Scorers: Symes.

SEPTEMBER

1st	● Oldham	A	W 1-2	Att: 1,619	Scorers: Edwards, Gregan OG. Booked: Kempson, Grant.
5th	● Bury	A	W 0-2	Att: 3,082	Scorers: Grant².
11th	● Darlington	H	W 2-1	Att: 3,228	Scorers: Kee, Procter.
19th	● Hereford	A	L 2-0	Att: 2,013	Booked: Kempson, Lees.
25th	● Crewe	H	W 5-3	Att: 2,764	Scorers: Grant², Procter, Symes².
29th	● Port Vale	A	D 2-2	Att: 4,326	Scorers: Edwards, Procter. Booked: Winnard.

OCTOBER

3rd	● Chesterfield	A	L 1-0	Att: 3,104	Booked: Kee, Symes, Dunbavin.
10th	● Cheltenham	H	W 4-0	Att: 1,843	Scorers: Edwards, Grant², Turner. Booked: Joyce.
17th	● Bournemouth	H	L 0-1	Att: 1,858	Booked: Symes, Winnard.
20th	● Shrewsbury	H	W 2-0	Att: 819	Scorers: G King, Winnard. Booked: Ryan, Lees.
24th	● Rochdale	A	W 1-2	Att: 3,206	Scorers: Grant, Symes. Booked: Edwards, Kempson, Symes.
30th	● Grimsby	H	D 2-2	Att: 4,325	Scorers: Edwards, G King. Booked: Lees, G King, Joyce.

NOVEMBER

7th	● Salisbury	H	W 2-1	Att: 1,379	Scorers: Ryan, Symes. Booked: Kempson, Grant, McConville.
10th	● Bury	H	W 3-2	Att: 1,637	Scorers: Grant, Symes². Booked: Grant, Joyce.
14th	● Dag & Red	H	L 0-1	Att: 1,538	
21st	● Bradford	A	D 1-1	Att: 11,176	Scorers: Symes. Booked: Procter, McConville, Grant.
28th	● Barnet	H	D 2-2	Att: 1,501	Scorers: Grant, Symes. Booked: Grant, Symes, Kempson. Dismissed: Miles.

DECEMBER

1st	● Burton	A	W 0-2	Att: 2,027	Scorers: Kee, Symes. Booked: Winnard, Edwards, Kee.
5th	● Torquay	H	W 4-2	Att: 1,351	Scorers: Edwards, Grant, Joyce, Procter.
8th	● Barnet	A	W 0-1	Att: 1,288	Scorers: Grant. Booked: Bouzanis, Procter, Murphy.
12th	● Notts County	A	W 1-2	Att: 5,855	Scorers: Ryan, Symes.
15th	● Leeds	A	L 2-0	Att: 12,696	
26th	● Morecambe	A	W 1-2	Att: 3,478	Scorers: Edwards². Booked: Grant, Edwards, Ryan.
28th	● Bury	H	L 2-4	Att: 3,138	Scorers: McConville, Symes. Booked: Ryan, Joyce, Kee.

JANUARY

19th	● Gillingham	H	W 1-0	Att: 1,322	Scorers: Miles.
23rd	● Fulham	A	L 1-3	Att: 3,712	Scorers: Symes. Booked: Kempson. Dismissed: Kempson.
26th	● Aldershot	H	W 2-1	Att: 1,279	Scorers: Kee, Procter. Booked: Edwards, Grant.
30th	● Shrewsbury	A	W 0-1	Att: 5,319	Scorers: Grant. Booked: Procter, Bouzanis. Dismissed: Procter.

FEBRUARY

6th	● Morecambe	H	W 3-2	Att: 2,372	Scorers: Grant², Ryan. Booked: McConville, Edwards, Symes, Kee.
9th	● Northampton	A	L 4-0	Att: 3,206	Booked: Lees.
13th	● Macclesfield	A	D 0-0	Att: 1,729	
16th	● Lincoln	A	L 2-1	Att: 2,779	Scorers: Grant. Booked: Miles.
20th	● Bradford	H	W 2-0	Att: 3,396	Scorers: Miles². Booked: Ryan.
27th	● Torquay	A	L 2-1	Att: 2,503	Scorers: Symes. Booked: Edwards.

MARCH

6th	● Notts County	H	L 0-3	Att: 2,123	Booked: Edwards, Procter, Symes.
9th	● Macclesfield	H	D 1-1	Att: 1,210	Scorers: Kee. Booked: Lees.
13th	● Barnet	A	W 1-2	Att: 1,559	Scorers: Edwards, Kee. Booked: Joyce, Winnard, Procter. Dismissed: Dunbavin.
16th	● Rotherham	H	W 2-1	Att: 1,440	Scorers: Ryan, Symes. Booked: Procter, Ryan.
20th	● Rochdale	H	L 2-4	Att: 3,025	Scorers: Miles, Symes. Booked: Joyce. Dismissed: Symes.
23rd	● Burton	H	L 0-2	Att: 1,270	Booked: Winnard, Joyce.
27th	● Bournemouth	A	L 2-0	Att: 5,413	Booked: Edwards, Lees.

APRIL

3rd	● Dag & Red	A	L 3-1	Att: 2,031	Scorers: Grant. Booked: J Mullin, Turner.
5th	● Grimsby	H	L 2-3	Att: 1,839	Scorers: Kee, Symes.
10th	● Darlington	A	D 0-0	Att: 1,545	
13th	● Port Vale	H	L 1-2	Att: 2,205	Scorers: Procter, Lees, Edwards.
17th	● Hereford	H	L 1-2	Att: 1,420	Scorers: Symes.
24th	● Crewe	A	L 5-1	Att: 3,810	Scorers: Brayford OG. Dismissed: Dunbavin.
27th	● Barnet	H	W 1-0	Att: 1,268	Scorers: Kee. Booked: Murphy, Winnard, Grant, Procter.

MAY

1st	● Chesterfield	H	W 2-0	Att: 2,475	Scorers: Kee². Booked: McConville, Kee.
8th	● Cheltenham	A	D 1-1	Att: 3,856	Scorers: Turner.

● Coca-Cola League 2/Play-Offs ● FA Cup ● Carling Cup ● Johnstone's Paint Trophy

LEAGUE 2 GOALKEEPER STATS

Player	Appearances	Match starts	Completed matches	Sub appearances	Subbed off	Clean sheets	Yellow cards	Red cards
Dean Bouzanis	14	12	12	2	0	2	1	0
Ian Dunbavin	27	27	25	0	0	7	1	2
Alan Martin	7	7	7	0	0	1	1	0

LEAGUE 2 OUTFIELD PLAYER STATS

Player	Appearances	Match starts	Completed matches	Substitute appearances	Subbed off	Goals scored	Yellow cards	Red cards
Adam Black	1	0	0	1	0	0	0	0
Phil Edwards	46	46	44	0	2	8	9	0
Jonathan Flynn	8	6	6	2	0	0	0	0
Robert Grant	42	41	36	1	5	14	4	0
Luke Joyce	41	36	28	5	8	1	7	0
Billy Kee	36	15	6	21	9	9	5	0
Darran Kempson	40	40	37	0	3	1	2	0
Chris King	1	1	0	0	1	0	0	0
Gary King	8	3	0	5	3	1	1	0
Tom Lees	39	39	35	0	4	0	6	0
Jamie McCarten	1	1	1	0	0	0	0	0
Sean McConville	28	14	6	14	8	1	3	0
John Miles	36	32	19	4	13	3	1	0
Paul Mullin	4	4	3	0	1	0	1	0
John Mullin	3	1	0	2	1	0	1	0
Peter Murphy	10	5	2	5	3	0	1	0
Andrew Procter	44	44	40	0	3	5	8	1
Leam Richardson	2	2	2	0	0	0	0	0
James Ryan	39	36	28	3	8	3	4	0
Michael Symes	41	39	37	2	1	13	5	1
Chris Turner	24	11	5	13	6	2	1	0
Dean Winnard	44	44	43	0	1	0	6	0

SEASON INFORMATION

Highest position: 2
Lowest position: 23
Average goals scored per game: 1.35
Average goals conceded per game: 1.61

LEAGUE POSITION AT THE END OF EACH MONTH

AUG	SEP	OCT	NOV	DEC	JAN	FEB	MAR	APR	MAY
23	13	14	17	11	10	12	14	13	15

LONGEST SEQUENCES

Wins	4	Undefeated home	3	
(01/12/09–26/12/09)		(on two occasions)		
Losses	5	Undefeated away	7	
(20/03/10–05/04/10)		(24/10/09–30/01/10)		
Draws	–	Without scoring	2	
(–)		(on two occasions)		
Undefeated	5	Without conceding	2	
(21/11/09–26/12/09)		(27/04/10–01/05/10)		
Without win	9	Scoring	9	
(20/03/10–24/04/10)		(21/11/09–06/02/10)		

CARDS RECEIVED

68 4

EARLIEST STRIKE

ROBERT GRANT
(v Crewe) 2:54

LATEST STRIKE

DARRAN KEMPSON
(v Torquay) 94:22

GOALS SCORED/CONCEDED
PER FIVE-MINUTE INTERVALS

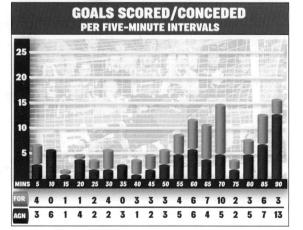

MINS	5	10	15	20	25	30	35	40	45	50	55	60	65	70	75	80	85	90
FOR	4	0	1	1	2	4	0	3	3	3	4	6	7	10	2	3	6	3
AGN	3	6	1	4	2	2	3	1	2	3	5	6	4	5	2	5	7	13

AFC BOURNEMOUTH

MANAGER Eddie Howe guided Bournemouth to promotion in his first full season in charge.

Howe masterminded the Cherries' return to the third tier, despite having to cope with a transfer embargo and a lengthy injury list for much of the season.

The south-coast outfit won a club-record eight of their first nine Coca-Cola League 2 games and never looked back from that point. Their only real disappointment came in the Cups, in which they were beaten by Millwall and Notts County.

Howe rejected the opportunity to take over at Championship side Peterborough in November and his decision to stick with the Cherries was vindicated when they secured automatic promotion with two games remaining by beating Burton.

They had only eight senior players fit at one point during the season and, with the embargo lifted, they will now look to strengthen in order to be competitive in npower League 1.

CLUB SUMMARY

FORMED	1899
MANAGER	Eddie Howe
GROUND	Dean Court
CAPACITY	10,770
NICKNAME	The Cherries
WEBSITE	www.afcb.co.uk

The New Football Pools PLAYER OF THE SEASON — Shwan Jalal

OVERALL
P	W	D	L	F	A	GD
51	27	8	16	68	54	14

COCA-COLA FOOTBALL LEAGUE 2
Pos	P	W	D	L	F	A	GD	Pts
2	46	25	8	13	61	44	17	83

HOME
Pos	P	W	D	L	F	A	GD	Pts
2	23	16	3	4	33	16	17	51

AWAY
Pos	P	W	D	L	F	A	GD	Pts
5	23	9	5	9	28	28	0	32

CUP PROGRESS DETAILS
Competition	Round reached	Knocked out by
FA Cup	R2	Notts County
Carling Cup	R1	Millwall
JP Trophy	R2	Northampton

BIGGEST WIN (ALL COMPS)
01/05/10 4-0 v Port Vale

BIGGEST DEFEAT (ALL COMPS)
12/12/09 0-5 v Morecambe

ATTENDANCE RECORD
High	Average	Low
9,055	5,720	4,019
v Port Vale (01/05/2010)		v Barnet (23/02/2010)

RESULTS 2009/10

AUGUST
8th	● Bury	A	W 0-3	Att: 2,998	Scorers: Molesley, Pitman, Robinson.
11th	● Millwall	A	L 4-0	Att: 3,552	
15th	● Rotherham	H	W 1-0	Att: 5,091	Scorers: Garry. Booked: Molesley, Bradbury, Cummings.
18th	● Aldershot	H	W 1-0	Att: 5,556	Scorers: Pearce. Booked: Bradbury.
22nd	● Northampton	A	L 2-0	Att: 4,102	Booked: Robinson, Fletcher, Cummings, Molesley.
29th	● Crewe	H	W 1-0	Att: 4,563	Scorers: Feeney. Booked: Molesley, Pitman, Bartley.

SEPTEMBER
1st	● Yeovil	H	W 2-1	Att: 2,655	Scorers: Connell, Pitman. Booked: Robinson.
5th	● Torquay	A	W 1-2	Att: 3,881	Scorers: Fletcher, Pitman. Booked: Pitman.
12th	● Lincoln	H	W 3-1	Att: 5,385	Scorers: Igoe[2], Pitman.
19th	● Darlington	A	W 0-2	Att: 1,999	Scorers: Pitman[2].
26th	● Burton	H	W 1-0	Att: 6,327	Scorers: Pitman. Booked: Robinson.
29th	● Hereford	A	L 2-1	Att: 2,104	Scorers: Fletcher. Booked: Bradbury.

OCTOBER
3rd	● Port Vale	A	D 0-0	Att: 4,905	Booked: Hollands, Pitman, Bradbury.
6th	● Northampton	A	L 2-1	Att: 1,718	Scorers: Hollands. Booked: Tindall, Stockley.
10th	● Chesterfield	H	L 1-2	Att: 5,896	Scorers: Hollands. Booked: Garry, Pitman.
17th	● Accrington	A	W 0-1	Att: 1,858	Scorers: Hollands. Booked: Feeney, Pearce.
24th	● Grimsby	H	W 3-1	Att: 5,270	Scorers: Connell, Pitman, Linwood OG.
31st	● Rochdale	H	L 0-4	Att: 6,378	Booked: Garry, Cummings.

NOVEMBER
7th	● Chesterfield	A	W 1-3	Att: 3,277	Scorers: Connell[2], Igoe.
14th	● Bradford	A	D 1-1	Att: 11,732	Scorers: Pitman. Booked: Pearce.
21st	● Macclesfield	A	W 1-2	Att: 1,413	Scorers: Pitman[2]. Booked: Garry, Bradbury.
24th	● Dag & Red	H	D 0-0	Att: 6,881	Booked: Hollands.
28th	● Notts County	H	L 1-2	Att: 6,082	Scorers: Pitman. Booked: Bartley, Connell.

DECEMBER
1st	● Barnet	A	D 1-1	Att: 2,030	Scorers: Pitman. Booked: Robinson, Bradbury.
5th	● Shrewsbury	H	W 1-0	Att: 4,652	Scorers: Dunfield OG.
12th	● Morecambe	A	L 5-0	Att: 2,034	Booked: Pearce, Garry. Dismissed: Bartley.
26th	● Cheltenham	A	W 0-1	Att: 4,114	Scorers: Feeney. Booked: Partington, Hollands, Jalal, Cummings, Goulding.
28th	● Torquay	H	W 2-1	Att: 7,626	Scorers: Feeney, Pitman. Booked: Goulding, Bradbury, Connell, Partington, Cummings.

JANUARY
2nd	● Northampton	H	L 0-2	Att: 5,715	Booked: Hollands, Fletcher.
16th	● Bury	H	L 1-2	Att: 4,516	Scorers: Pitman.
23rd	● Aldershot	A	L 2-1	Att: 4,387	Scorers: Pitman. Booked: Garry, Pearce, Pitman. Dismissed: Cummings.
30th	● Crewe	A	W 1-2	Att: 3,741	Scorers: Fletcher, Robinson.

FEBRUARY
2nd	● Rotherham	A	W 1-3	Att: 3,180	Scorers: Hollands[2], Pitman. Booked: Fletcher.
6th	● Cheltenham	H	D 0-0	Att: 5,259	
9th	● Notts County	H	W 2-1	Att: 5,472	Scorers: Hollands[2]. Booked: Bradbury, Robinson.
13th	● Dag & Red	A	L 1-0	Att: 2,215	Booked: Bartley.
20th	● Macclesfield	H	D 1-1	Att: 4,549	Scorers: Connell. Booked: Hollands, Feeney, Wiggins.
23rd	● Barnet	H	W 3-0	Att: 4,019	Scorers: Fletcher, Pitman[2]. Booked: Pearce.
27th	● Shrewsbury	A	L 1-0	Att: 6,061	Booked: Bartley, Cummings.

MARCH
6th	● Morecambe	H	W 1-0	Att: 5,103	Scorers: Robinson.
15th	● Notts County	A	D 2-2	Att: 6,120	Scorers: Goulding, Pitman. Booked: Wiggins.
20th	● Grimsby	A	L 3-2	Att: 4,428	Scorers: Bradbury, Feeney. Booked: Hollands, Bradbury, Jalal. Dismissed: Goulding.
27th	● Accrington	H	W 2-0	Att: 5,413	Scorers: Feeney, Pitman. Booked: Hollands.

APRIL
3rd	● Bradford	H	W 1-0	Att: 6,239	Scorers: Pitman.
5th	● Rochdale	A	D 0-0	Att: 5,027	Booked: Bartley.
10th	● Lincoln	A	L 2-1	Att: 3,040	Scorers: Pitman. Booked: Jalal, Robinson.
13th	● Hereford	H	W 2-1	Att: 6,128	Scorers: Pitman[2]. Booked: Bartley, Pitman.
17th	● Darlington	A	W 2-0	Att: 6,464	Scorers: Pitman, Robinson. Booked: Pearce, Bartley.
24th	● Burton	A	W 0-2	Att: 3,977	Scorers: Connell, Pitman. Booked: Pearce, Bradbury.

MAY
1st	● Port Vale	H	W 4-0	Att: 9,055	Scorers: Connell[2], McQuoid, Pitman. Booked: Bartley.
8th	● Chesterfield	A	L 2-1	Att: 7,702	Scorers: Talbot OG. Booked: Bartley, Bradbury, Hollands.

● Coca-Cola League 2/Play-Offs ● FA Cup ● Carling Cup ● Johnstone's Paint Trophy

LEAGUE 2 GOALKEEPER STATS

Player	Appearances	Match starts	Completed matches	Sub appearances	Subbed off	Clean sheets	Yellow cards	Red cards
Shwan Jalal	44	44	43	0	1	18	3	0
Marek Stech	1	1	1	0	0	0	0	0
Dan Thomas	2	1	1	1	0	1	0	0

LEAGUE 2 OUTFIELD PLAYER STATS

Player	Appearances	Match starts	Completed matches	Substitute appearances	Subbed off	Goals scored	Yellow cards	Red cards
Marvin Bartley	34	24	16	10	7	0	8	1
Lee Bradbury	44	43	40	1	3	1	11	0
Alan Connell	38	19	3	19	16	5	1	0
Shaun Cooper	6	6	5	0	1	0	0	0
Warren Cummings	34	27	24	7	2	0	6	1
Anthony Edgar	3	2	1	1	1	0	0	0
Liam Feeney	44	44	23	0	21	5	2	0
Steve Fletcher	45	31	14	14	17	4	3	0
Ryan Garry	34	33	26	1	7	1	5	0
Jeff Goulding	17	3	0	14	3	1	2	1
Scott Guyett	9	6	5	3	1	0	0	0
Danny Hollands	39	37	36	2	1	6	8	0
Sammy Igoe	21	15	5	6	10	2	0	0
Josh McQuoid	29	9	1	20	8	1	0	0
Mark Molesley	10	10	6	0	4	1	3	0
Joe Partington	11	4	3	7	1	0	2	0
Jason Pearce	39	39	39	0	0	1	7	0
Brett Pitman	46	46	42	0	4	26	6	0
Anton Robinson	44	43	42	1	1	4	5	0
Jayden Stockley	2	0	0	2	0	0	0	0
George Webb	1	0	0	1	0	0	0	0
Rhys Wiggins	19	19	18	0	1	0	2	0

SEASON INFORMATION

Highest position: 1
Lowest position: 5
Average goals scored per game: 1.33
Average goals conceded per game: 0.96

LEAGUE POSITION AT THE END OF EACH MONTH

AUG	SEP	OCT	NOV	DEC	JAN	FEB	MAR	APR	MAY
3	1	1	1	2	2	2	3	3	2

LONGEST SEQUENCES

Wins	5	Undefeated home	10
(29/08/09–26/09/09)		(06/02/10–01/05/10)	
Losses	3	Undefeated away	5
(02/01/10–23/01/10)		(03/10/09–01/12/09)	
Draws	2	Without scoring	–
(24/11/09–01/12/09)		(–)	
Undefeated	5	Without conceding	3
(on two occasions)		(on three occasions)	
Without win	3	Scoring	6
(on two occasions)		(29/08/09–29/09/09)	

CARDS RECEIVED

74   3

EARLIEST STRIKE

DANNY HOLLANDS
(v Notts County) 1:29

LATEST STRIKE

BRETT PITMAN
(v Torquay) 94:12

GOALS SCORED/CONCEDED
PER FIVE-MINUTE INTERVALS

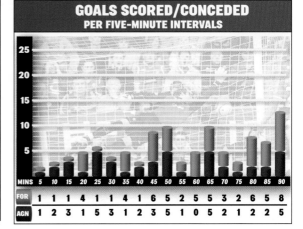

MINS	5	10	15	20	25	30	35	40	45	50	55	60	65	70	75	80	85	90
FOR	1	1	1	4	1	1	4	1	6	5	2	5	5	3	2	6	5	8
AGN	1	2	3	1	5	3	1	2	3	5	1	0	5	2	1	2	2	5

ALDERSHOT TOWN

KEVIN DILLON excelled throughout a successful first season at the helm as Aldershot reached the play-off semi-finals. Dillon replaced Gary Waddock in November 2009 and led the Shots to an impressive sixth-place finish in only the club's second season back in the Football League.

Dillon's men suffered a 3–0 aggregate defeat to Rotherham in the play-off semi-finals but, despite missing out on a trip to Wembley and the potential for a place in npower League 1, the Hampshire club have made huge progress on the field.

The Shots maintained their solid home form, losing just four games in the League at the Recreation Ground, while they also showed decent form on their travels by claiming 29 points to maintain their play-off push.

Aldershot will be expected to be in and around the top seven again in the coming season and, with Dillon in charge, optimism is high for a bright future.

CLUB SUMMARY

FORMED	1926
MANAGER	Kevin Dillon
GROUND	Recreation Ground
CAPACITY	7,100
NICKNAME	The Shots
WEBSITE	www.theshots.co.uk

The New **Football Pools** PLAYER OF THE SEASON — **Marvin Morgan**

OVERALL

P	W	D	L	F	A	GD
53	21	14	18	75	65	10

COCA-COLA FOOTBALL LEAGUE 2

Pos	P	W	D	L	F	A	GD	Pts
6	46	20	12	14	69	56	13	72

HOME

Pos	P	W	D	L	F	A	GD	Pts
7	23	12	7	4	43	24	19	43

AWAY

Pos	P	W	D	L	F	A	GD	Pts
11	23	8	5	10	26	32	-6	29

CUP PROGRESS DETAILS

Competition	Round reached	Knocked out by
FA Cup	R2	Tranmere
Carling Cup	R1	Bristol Rovers
JP Trophy	R2	Hereford

BIGGEST WIN (ALL COMPS)
26/12/09 4–0 v Barnet

BIGGEST DEFEAT (ALL COMPS)
12/12/09 1–6 v Burton Albion

ATTENDANCE RECORD

HIGH	AVERAGE	LOW
4,506	3,086	2,053
v Lincoln City (01/05/2010)		v Dag & Red (23/02/2010)

RESULTS 2009/10

AUGUST
8th	● Darlington	H	W 3–1	Att: 2,866	Scorers: M Morgan, Sandell, Soares.
11th	● Bristol Rovers	A	L 2–1	Att: 3,644	Scorers: M Morgan. Booked: Hinshelwood, Halls, M Morgan.
15th	● Rochdale	A	L 1–0	Att: 2,465	Booked: Halls.
18th	● Bournemouth	A	L 1–0	Att: 5,556	Booked: Harding, M Morgan.
22nd	● Accrington	H	W 3–1	Att: 2,276	Scorers: Donnelly2, M Morgan. Booked: Harding, Winfield.
29th	● Grimsby	H	W 1–2	Att: 3,757	Scorers: Donnelly2. Booked: Blackburn.

SEPTEMBER
5th	● Hereford	H	D 2–2	Att: 3,094	Scorers: Hylton, M Morgan. Booked: Donnelly.
12th	● Port Vale	H	D 1–1	Att: 3,406	Scorers: Soares. Booked: Charles, Winfield.
19th	● Crewe	A	W 1–2	Att: 3,661	Scorers: Donnelly, Hudson. Booked: Charles.
26th	● Cheltenham	H	W 4–1	Att: 2,964	Scorers: Charles, Donnelly, M Morgan, Winfield. Booked: Parrett, M Morgan.
29th	● Torquay	A	D 1–1	Att: 2,271	Scorers: M Morgan. Booked: Chalmers.

OCTOBER
3rd	● Lincoln	A	L 1–0	Att: 4,131	Booked: Parrett.
6th	● Hereford	A	D 2–2	Att: 897	Scorers: Hudson, Soares. Booked: Soares, Straker. Hereford win 4–3 on penalties.
10th	● Morecambe	A	W 4–1	Att: 2,974	Scorers: Hudson, M Morgan, Soares, Stanley OG. Booked: M Morgan.
17th	● Bury	A	L 2–3	Att: 3,196	Scorers: Soares, Winfield. Booked: Hinshelwood, Chalmers.
24th	● Shrewsbury	A	L 3–1	Att: 5,417	Scorers: Soares. Booked: Sandell, Jaimez-Ruiz, Chalmers. Dismissed: Winfield.
31st	● Rotherham	A	D 0–0	Att: 3,002	Booked: Grant.

NOVEMBER
7th	● Bury	H	W 2–0	Att: 2,519	Scorers: Donnelly, Soares. Booked: Hudson.
14th	● Macclesfield	H	D 0–0	Att: 2,646	
21st	● Notts County	A	D 0–0	Att: 6,500	Booked: Sandell, Straker.
24th	● Northampton	H	W 2–1	Att: 2,761	Scorers: Donnelly, M Morgan. Booked: Herd, Sandell.
28th	● Tranmere	A	D 0–0	Att: 3,742	Booked: Sandell.

DECEMBER
1st	● Dag & Red	A	W 2–5	Att: 1,876	Scorers: Charles, Jackson, M Morgan, Sandell, Soares.
5th	● Chesterfield	H	W 1–0	Att: 2,977	Scorers: Charles. Booked: Chalmers.
8th	● Tranmere	H	L 1–2	Att: 4,060	Scorers: Bozanic.
12th	● Burton	A	L 6–1	Att: 2,547	Scorers: Grant. Booked: Blackburn. Dismissed: Charles.
26th	● Barnet	H	W 4–0	Att: 3,231	Scorers: Donnelly, Grant2, Sandell.

JANUARY
19th	● Rochdale	H	D 1–1	Att: 2,453	Scorers: Soares.
23rd	● Bournemouth	H	W 2–1	Att: 4,387	Scorers: Sandell, Straker. Booked: Bozanic, Blackburn, Harding, Herd, Sandell.
26th	● Accrington	A	L 2–1	Att: 1,279	Scorers: Sandell. Booked: Bozanic, Soares.
30th	● Grimsby	A	D 1–1	Att: 3,195	Scorers: Hylton. Booked: Soares, Blackburn, Donnelly.

FEBRUARY
6th	● Barnet	A	L 3–0	Att: 2,145	Booked: M Morgan.
12th	● Northampton	A	W 0–3	Att: 4,718	Scorers: Hudson, M Morgan2. Booked: Donnelly, Straker, Herd, Charles.
16th	● Hereford	A	L 2–0	Att: 1,576	Booked: Sandell.
20th	● Notts County	H	D 1–1	Att: 4,016	Scorers: Bozanic. Booked: Charles, Straker.
23rd	● Dag & Red	H	L 2–3	Att: 2,053	Scorers: Donnelly, Hudson.
27th	● Chesterfield	A	W 0–1	Att: 3,827	Scorers: Hylton. Booked: Hylton.

MARCH
2nd	● Bradford	H	W 1–0	Att: 2,311	Scorers: Charles. Booked: Henderson.
6th	● Burton	H	L 0–2	Att: 2,784	Booked: Herd, Blackburn, Straker, Hylton.
13th	● Bradford	A	L 2–1	Att: 11,272	Scorers: Straker. Booked: Straker.
20th	● Shrewsbury	H	W 2–0	Att: 2,681	Scorers: Bozanic, M Morgan. Booked: Charles, Jaimez-Ruiz.
23rd	● Darlington	A	W 1–2	Att: 1,296	Scorers: Brown, M Morgan. Booked: M Morgan, Spencer.
27th	● Bury	H	W 1–2	Att: 2,795	Scorers: Donnelly2. Booked: Blackburn, Herd. Dismissed: Jaimez-Ruiz.

APRIL
3rd	● Macclesfield	A	D 1–1	Att: 1,428	Scorers: Donnelly.
5th	● Rotherham	H	W 3–0	Att: 3,573	Scorers: Howell, D Morgan, M Morgan. Booked: Charles, Winfield, Donnelly.
10th	● Port Vale	A	D 1–1	Att: 5,399	Scorers: D Morgan. Booked: Herd.
13th	● Torquay	H	L 0–2	Att: 3,652	
17th	● Crewe	H	D 1–1	Att: 2,966	Scorers: Harding. Booked: Winfield, Bozanic.
24th	● Cheltenham	A	W 1–2	Att: 3,386	Scorers: Donnelly, D Morgan. Booked: Young, M Morgan, Sandell.

MAY
1st	● Lincoln	H	W 3–1	Att: 4,506	Scorers: D Morgan, M Morgan2. Booked: Donnelly, Brown.
8th	● Morecambe	A	L 1–0	Att: 5,268	Booked: Soares.
15th	● Rotherham	H	L 0–1	Att: 5,470	Booked: Donnelly, Charles.
19th	● Rotherham	A	L 2–0	Att: 7,082	Booked: D Morgan. Agg: 3–0.

● Coca-Cola League 2/Play-offs ● FA Cup ● Carling Cup ● Johnstone's Paint Trophy

actim⊞

Coca-Cola LEAGUE 2

LEAGUE 2 GOALKEEPER STATS

Player	Appearances	Match starts	Completed matches	Sub appearances	Subbed off	Clean sheets	Yellow cards	Red cards
Stephen Henderson	8	8	8	0	0	3	1	0
Mikhael Jaimez-Ruiz	30	30	28	0	1	6	2	1
Clark Masters	1	0	0	1	0	0	0	0
Jamie Young	9	8	8	1	0	1	1	0

LEAGUE 2 OUTFIELD PLAYER STATS

Player	Appearances	Match starts	Completed matches	Substitute appearances	Subbed off	Goals scored	Yellow cards	Red cards
Chris Blackburn	42	36	36	6	0	0	6	0
Oliver Bozanic	25	19	11	6	8	2	3	0
Aaron Brown	12	12	11	0	1	1	1	0
Lewis Chalmers	23	19	11	4	8	0	4	0
Anthony Charles	33	32	28	1	3	4	6	1
Reece Connolly	3	0	0	3	0	0	0	0
Scott Donnelly	43	42	28	1	14	13	5	0
Antonio German	3	2	1	1	1	0	0	0
John Grant	17	5	1	12	4	3	1	0
John Halls	16	10	10	6	0	0	1	0
Ben Harding	33	28	22	5	6	1	3	0
Ben Herd	34	33	32	1	1	0	6	0
Adam Hinshelwood	15	13	9	2	4	0	1	0
Bobby Hopkinson	1	0	0	1	0	0	0	0
Dean Howell	3	0	0	3	0	1	0	0
Kirk Hudson	34	24	13	10	11	4	0	0
Danny Hylton	21	5	2	16	3	3	2	0
Marlon Jackson	22	18	4	4	14	1	0	0
Dean Morgan	9	8	6	1	2	4	0	0
Marvin Morgan	40	36	25	4	11	15	6	0
Dean Parrett	4	4	1	0	3	0	2	0
Omer Riza	1	0	0	1	0	0	0	0
Andy Sandell	29	29	24	0	5	5	6	0
Louie Soares	36	28	22	8	6	7	3	0
Damian Spencer	12	3	1	9	2	0	1	0
Anthony Straker	37	35	29	2	6	2	5	0
Dave Winfield	25	19	17	6	1	2	4	1

AUG	SEP	OCT	NOV	DEC	JAN	FEB	MAR	APR	MAY

LEAGUE POSITION AT THE END OF EACH MONTH

7	7	10	8	6	8	10	7	5	6

SEASON INFORMATION

Highest position: 3
Lowest position: 16
Average goals scored per game: 1.50
Average goals conceded per game: 1.22

LONGEST SEQUENCES

Wins	3	Undefeated home	8
(on two occasions)		(14/11/09–20/02/10)	
Losses	2	Undefeated away	5
(on three occasions)		(23/03/10–24/04/10)	
Draws	3	Without scoring	3
(31/10/09–21/11/09)		(31/10/09–21/11/09)	
Undefeated	7	Without conceding	3
(22/08/09–29/09/09)		(31/10/09–21/11/09)	
Without win	5	Scoring	9
(17/10/09–21/11/09)		(24/11/09–30/01/10)	

CARDS RECEIVED

70   **3**

EARLIEST STRIKE

MARVIN MORGAN
(v Darlington) 2:49

LATEST STRIKE

SCOTT DONNELLY
(v Cheltenham) 91:35

GOALS SCORED/CONCEDED
PER FIVE-MINUTE INTERVALS

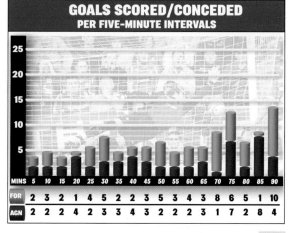

MINS	5	10	15	20	25	30	35	40	45	50	55	60	65	70	75	80	85	90
FOR	2	3	2	1	4	5	2	2	5	3	4	3	8	6	5	1	10	
AGN	2	2	2	4	2	3	3	4	3	2	2	2	3	1	7	2	8	4

BARNET

BARNET secured their npower Football League status following a dramatic relegation battle that went right down to the wire.

It was a rollercoaster season for the Bees, who spent time at both ends of the table.

Ian Hendon's side made a bright start to the campaign, with four wins from their first six League games and a 2–0 victory against Coca-Cola League 1 high-flyers Millwall in the Johnstone's Paint Trophy. They were even top of the table at one point following a win at Northampton. However, a poor run of form, including a 13-game winless streak, saw their season unravel and after five straight defeats they were suddenly involved in a fight to stay up.

Hendon was sacked in April with two games of the season remaining and former boss Paul Fairclough returned as caretaker manager. Despite losing to relegation rivals Grimsby in the penultimate fixture, Fairclough guided the club to safety, with Mark Stimson taking over on a permanent basis in June.

CLUB SUMMARY

FORMED	1888
MANAGER	Mark Stimson
GROUND	Underhill
CAPACITY	5,568
NICKNAME	The Bees
WEBSITE	www.barnetfc.com

The New Football Pools PLAYER OF THE SEASON

Jake Cole

OVERALL
P	W	D	L	F	A	GD
52	14	13	25	55	73	-18

COCA-COLA FOOTBALL LEAGUE 2
Pos	P	W	D	L	F	A	GD	Pts
21	46	12	12	22	47	63	-16	48

HOME
Pos	P	W	D	L	F	A	GD	Pts
13	23	8	10	5	30	18	12	34

AWAY
Pos	P	W	D	L	F	A	GD	Pts
24	23	4	2	17	17	45	-28	14

CUP PROGRESS DETAILS
Competition	Round reached	Knocked out by
FA Cup	R2	Accrington
Carling Cup	R1	Watford
JP Trophy	R2	Charlton

BIGGEST WIN (ALL COMPS)
3–0 on 3 occasions

BIGGEST DEFEAT (ALL COMPS)
24/11/09 1–5 v Cheltenham

ATTENDANCE RECORD
High	Average	Low
4,638	2,059	1,298
v Rochdale (08/05/2010)		v Morecambe (18/08/2009)

RESULTS 2009/10

AUGUST
8th	● Lincoln	A	L 1–0	Att: 3,753	Booked: Hughes.
11th	● Watford	H	L 0–2	Att: 3,139	Booked: Furlong, O'Neill. AET – Score after 90 mins 0–0.
15th	● Shrewsbury	H	D 2–2	Att: 1,835	Scorers: J Hyde². Booked: Leach, Furlong.
18th	● Morecambe	H	W 2–0	Att: 1,298	Scorers: Furlong, Jarrett. Booked: Furlong, J Hyde, Tabiri.
22nd	● Torquay	A	W 0–1	Att: 2,856	Scorers: Adomah. Booked: O'Neill, Furlong.
29th	● Notts County	H	W 1–0	Att: 2,858	Scorers: J Hyde. Booked: Hughes, M Hyde.

SEPTEMBER
1st	● Millwall	H	W 2–0	Att: 1,623	Scorers: J Hyde, Yakubu. Booked: Devera, Kamdjo.
4th	● Northampton	A	W 1–3	Att: 4,206	Scorers: Deen, Furlong, O'Flynn. Booked: O'Neill.
12th	● Macclesfield	A	D 1–1	Att: 1,125	Scorers: Morgan OG. Booked: O'Neill, Hughes, Furlong.
19th	● Bradford	H	D 2–2	Att: 2,282	Scorers: Hughes, O'Flynn. Booked: Kamdjo.
26th	● Rotherham	A	L 3–0	Att: 3,823	Booked: Leach, Jarrett.
29th	● Dag & Red	H	W 2–0	Att: 2,093	Scorers: Furlong, O'Flynn. Booked: Hughes, M Hyde, Yakubu.

OCTOBER
3rd	● Grimsby	H	W 3–0	Att: 2,497	Scorers: Adomah, Bolasie, O'Flynn.
6th	● Charlton	A	L 4–1	Att: 4,522	Scorers: O'Flynn.
10th	● Rochdale	A	L 2–1	Att: 2,648	Scorers: J Hyde. Booked: Cole, Hughes.
17th	● Burton	A	L 2–0	Att: 2,935	Booked: Jarrett.
24th	● Darlington	H	W 3–0	Att: 2,313	Scorers: Bolasie, Deverdics, Yakubu. Booked: Furlong, M Hyde.
31st	● Chesterfield	A	L 1–0	Att: 3,585	Booked: Hughes.

NOVEMBER
7th	● Darlington	H	W 3–1	Att: 1,654	Scorers: M Hyde, O'Flynn². Booked: Yakubu.
14th	● Hereford	H	D 0–0	Att: 1,965	
21st	● Port Vale	H	D 0–0	Att: 1,939	Booked: Bolasie.
24th	● Cheltenham	A	L 5–1	Att: 2,331	Scorers: O'Flynn. Booked: Leach, Gillet, Hughes.
28th	● Accrington	A	D 2–2	Att: 1,501	Scorers: O'Flynn, Yakubu. Booked: M Hyde, O'Flynn.

DECEMBER
1st	● Bournemouth	H	D 1–1	Att: 2,030	Scorers: O'Flynn. Booked: Cole.
5th	● Bury	A	L 2–0	Att: 2,511	Booked: Hughes. Dismissed: Hughes.
8th	● Accrington	H	L 0–1	Att: 1,288	
12th	● Crewe	H	L 1–2	Att: 1,841	Scorers: Sinclair. Booked: Butcher.
26th	● Aldershot	A	L 4–0	Att: 3,231	Booked: Hughes, Yakubu, Devera.
28th	● Northampton	H	D 0–0	Att: 2,237	Booked: Sinclair. Dismissed: Sinclair.

JANUARY
16th	● Lincoln	H	L 1–2	Att: 1,810	Scorers: Yakubu. Booked: Deen, Sawyer, M Hyde.
23rd	● Morecambe	A	L 2–1	Att: 1,558	Scorers: Lockwood.
26th	● Torquay	H	D 1–1	Att: 1,331	Scorers: Sawyer. Booked: Breen, Jarrett.
30th	● Notts County	A	L 2–0	Att: 6,444	Booked: Sawyer, Hughes.

FEBRUARY
6th	● Aldershot	H	W 3–0	Att: 2,145	Scorers: M Hyde, O'Flynn².
9th	● Shrewsbury	A	L 2–0	Att: 4,328	Booked: Hughes.
13th	● Cheltenham	H	D 1–1	Att: 1,667	Scorers: Adomah. Booked: Devera.
20th	● Port Vale	A	W 0–2	Att: 4,571	Scorers: O'Flynn². Booked: Adomah, Livermore.
23rd	● Bournemouth	A	L 3–0	Att: 4,019	Booked: Devera, Jarrett.
27th	● Bury	H	D 0–0	Att: 1,949	Booked: Lockwood.

MARCH
6th	● Crewe	A	D 2–2	Att: 3,551	Scorers: Lockwood, O'Flynn. Booked: Breen.
13th	● Accrington	H	L 1–2	Att: 1,559	Scorers: O'Flynn. Booked: Hughes. Dismissed: Kamdjo.
20th	● Darlington	A	W 1–2	Att: 1,463	Scorers: Adomah, Livermore. Booked: J Hyde.
27th	● Burton	H	D 1–1	Att: 1,842	Scorers: Hughes. Booked: Gillet, Upson.

APRIL
3rd	● Hereford	A	L 2–1	Att: 2,146	Scorers: Rose OG.
5th	● Chesterfield	H	W 3–1	Att: 1,916	Scorers: Furlong², J Hyde. Booked: Hughes, M Hyde.
10th	● Macclesfield	H	L 1–2	Att: 1,433	Scorers: Upson. Booked: Livermore, Upson.
13th	● Dag & Red	A	L 4–1	Att: 2,004	Scorers: J Hyde. Booked: Gillet. Dismissed: Leach.
17th	● Bradford	A	L 2–1	Att: 11,138	Scorers: Adomah. Booked: Livermore.
24th	● Rotherham	H	L 0–1	Att: 1,884	Booked: M Hyde, Lockwood.
27th	● Accrington	A	L 1–0	Att: 1,268	Booked: Livermore, Furlong.

MAY
1st	● Grimsby	A	L 2–0	Att: 7,033	Booked: M Hyde, Adomah.
8th	● Rochdale	H	W 1–0	Att: 4,638	Scorers: Jarrett. Booked: Jarrett.

● Coca-Cola League 2/Play-Offs ● FA Cup ● Carling Cup ● Johnstone's Paint Trophy

LEAGUE 2 GOALKEEPER STATS

Player	Appearances	Match starts	Completed matches	Sub appearances	Subbed off	Clean sheets	Yellow cards	Red cards
Jake Cole	46	46	46	0	0	13	2	0

LEAGUE 2 OUTFIELD PLAYER STATS

Player	Appearances	Match starts	Completed matches	Substitute appearances	Subbed off	Goals scored	Yellow cards	Red cards
Albert Adomah	45	37	24	8	13	5	2	0
Yannick Bolasie	22	14	8	8	6	2	1	0
Gary Breen	25	25	25	0	0	0	2	0
Calum Butcher	3	3	3	0	0	0	1	0
Elliott Charles	3	0	0	3	0	0	0	0
Ahmed Deen	16	12	11	4	1	1	1	0
Joe Devera	33	31	29	2	2	0	3	0
Nicky Deverdics	16	4	2	12	2	1	0	0
Paul Furlong	38	31	23	7	8	5	6	0
Kenny Gillet	37	31	25	6	6	0	3	0
Danny Hart	1	0	0	1	0	0	0	0
Mark Hughes	41	40	33	1	6	2	13	1
Jake Hyde	34	17	6	17	11	6	2	0
Micah Hyde	41	41	33	0	8	1	7	0
Chris James	2	0	0	2	0	0	0	0
Albert Jarrett	45	33	21	12	12	2	5	0
Clovis Kamdjo	15	14	12	1	1	0	1	1
Daniel Leach	13	12	11	1	0	0	3	1
David Livermore	14	11	8	3	3	1	4	0
Kofi Lockhart-Adams	1	0	0	1	0	0	0	0
Matthew Lockwood	19	19	18	0	1	2	2	0
Craig McAllister	5	4	0	1	4	0	0	0
Luke Medley	1	0	0	1	0	0	0	0
John O'Flynn	36	31	15	5	16	12	0	0
Ryan O'Neill	15	11	8	4	3	0	3	0
Lee Sawyer	7	4	1	3	3	1	2	0
Dean Sinclair	3	2	0	1	1	1	1	0
Joe Tabiri	5	2	0	3	2	0	1	0
Edward Upson	9	5	2	4	3	1	2	0
Mauro Vilhete	2	1	0	1	1	0	0	0
Ben Wright	3	0	0	3	0	0	0	0
Ismail Yakubu	25	25	23	0	2	2	2	0

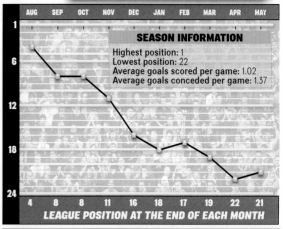

SEASON INFORMATION
Highest position: 1
Lowest position: 22
Average goals scored per game: 1.02
Average goals conceded per game: 1.37

LEAGUE POSITION AT THE END OF EACH MONTH

LONGEST SEQUENCES

Wins	4	Undefeated home	10
(18/08/09–04/09/09)		(15/08/09–01/12/09)	
Losses	6	Undefeated away	3
(10/04/10–01/05/10)		(22/08/09–12/09/09)	
Draws	2	Without scoring	3
(on three occasions)		(on two occasions)	
Undefeated	7	Without conceding	3
(15/08/09–19/09/09)		(18/08/09–29/08/09)	
Without win	13	Scoring	9
(31/10/09–30/01/10)		(06/03/10–17/04/10)	

CARDS RECEIVED 69 4

EARLIEST STRIKE
PAUL FURLONG
(v Morecambe) 2:01

LATEST STRIKE
JAKE HYDE
(v Notts County) 93:14

GOALS SCORED/CONCEDED
PER FIVE-MINUTE INTERVALS

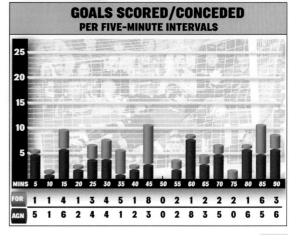

MINS	5	10	15	20	25	30	35	40	45	50	55	60	65	70	75	80	85	90
FOR	1	1	4	1	3	4	5	1	8	0	2	1	2	2	2	1	6	3
AGN	5	1	6	2	4	4	1	2	3	0	2	8	3	5	0	6	5	6

BRADFORD CITY

THERE are signs that Peter Taylor could be the man to lead Bradford out of the bottom tier in the coming season following an encouraging end to 2009/10. The former England coach took over from fans' favourite Stuart McCall in February and the Bantams finished the campaign on a six-game unbeaten run.

Club legend McCall had been persuaded to stay on ahead of 2009/10, and City's squad was boosted in the close season by the likes of Michael Flynn, Simon Ramsden and Gareth Evans, while striker James Hanson proved to be one of the division's bargain buys following his arrival from Guiseley.

However, a 5–0 defeat at Notts County on the opening day of the season did not bode well and by the turn of the year the club had slumped to 16th place in the table.

On the back of that run, McCall soon made way for Taylor, who managed to guide the Bantams to eight wins from their last 17 matches to restore some stability.

CLUB SUMMARY

FORMED	1903
MANAGER	Peter Taylor
GROUND	Valley Parade
CAPACITY	25,136
NICKNAME	The Bantams
WEBSITE	www.bradfordcityfc.co.uk

The New **Football Pools** PLAYER OF THE SEASON — **Simon Ramsden**

OVERALL
P	W	D	L	F	A	GD
52	17	16	19	66	75	-9

COCA-COLA FOOTBALL LEAGUE 2
Pos	P	W	D	L	F	A	GD	Pts
14	46	16	14	16	59	62	-3	62

HOME
Pos	P	W	D	L	F	A	GD	Pts
19	23	8	8	7	28	27	1	32

AWAY
Pos	P	W	D	L	F	A	GD	Pts
9	23	8	6	9	31	35	-4	30

CUP PROGRESS DETAILS
Competition	Round reached	Knocked out by
FA Cup	R1	Notts County
Carling Cup	R1	Nottm Forest
JP Trophy	SF	Carlise

BIGGEST WIN (ALL COMPS)
3–0 on 2 occasions

BIGGEST DEFEAT (ALL COMPS)
08/08/09 0–5 v Notts County

ATTENDANCE RECORD
HIGH	AVERAGE	Low
12,403	11,423	10,831
v Northampton (01/05/2010)		v Cheltenham (02/01/2010)

RESULTS 2009/10

AUGUST
8th	● Notts County	A	L 5–0	Att: 9,396	Booked: Bullock.
12th	● Nottm Forest	A	L 3–0	Att: 4,639	Booked: Williams, Bullock. Dismissed: Bateson.
15th	● Port Vale	H	D 0–0	Att: 11,333	Booked: Brandon.
18th	● Lincoln	H	L 0–2	Att: 11,242	Booked: Ramsden, Brandon, Colbeck.
22nd	● Cheltenham	A	W 4–5	Att: 3,073	Scorers: Evans, Hanson, J O'Brien, Ramsden, Williams.
29th	● Torquay	H	W 2–0	Att: 11,123	Scorers: Brandon, Hanson.

SEPTEMBER
1st	● Rochdale	A	W 1–2	Att: 1,800	Scorers: Flynn, Neilson. Booked: Williams.
5th	● Shrewsbury	A	W 1–2	Att: 5,525	Scorers: Evans, Flynn. Booked: Bullock, Eastwood.
12th	● Burton	H	D 1–1	Att: 11,439	Scorers: Evans. Booked: Ramsden, Williams.
19th	● Barnet	A	D 2–2	Att: 2,282	Scorers: Hanson, Rehman. Booked: J O'Brien.
26th	● Chesterfield	H	W 3–0	Att: 11,664	Scorers: Brandon, Flynn, Neilson. Booked: Rehman.
29th	● Morecambe	A	D 0–0	Att: 3,116	Booked: Bullock. Dismissed: Evans.

OCTOBER
3rd	● Northampton	A	D 2–2	Att: 4,391	Scorers: M Boulding, Ramsden. Booked: Rehman, M Boulding, Eastwood, J O'Brien.
6th	● Notts County	H	D 2–2	Att: 3,701	Scorers: M Boulding, Brandon. Booked: Brandon. Bradford win 3–2 on penalties.
10th	● Crewe	H	L 2–3	Att: 11,757	Scorers: M Boulding, Hanson.
17th	● Dag & Red	A	L 2–1	Att: 2,446	Scorers: Flynn.
24th	● Hereford	H	W 1–0	Att: 11,107	Scorers: Evans. Booked: Bullock. Dismissed: Bullock.
31st	● Macclesfield	A	D 2–2	Att: 2,526	Scorers: Hanson, Williams. Booked: Flynn.

NOVEMBER
6th	● Notts County	A	L 2–1	Att: 4,213	Scorers: M Boulding. Booked: L O'Brien, J O'Brien, Bullock.
10th	● Port Vale	H	D 2–2	Att: 5,096	Scorers: Flynn, Hanson. Booked: Williams. Bradford win 5–4 on penalties.
14th	● Bournemouth	H	D 1–1	Att: 11,732	Scorers: Evans.
21st	● Accrington	H	D 1–1	Att: 11,176	Scorers: Edwards OG. Booked: Rehman, Bullock, L O'Brien, Flynn.
24th	● Grimsby	A	W 0–3	Att: 3,646	Scorers: Hanson, Whaley, Williams.

DECEMBER
1st	● Rochdale	H	L 0–3	Att: 11,472	
5th	● Darlington	A	W 0–1	Att: 2,744	Scorers: Williams. Booked: Neilson.
12th	● Rotherham	H	L 2–4	Att: 11,578	Scorers: Bullock, Flynn. Booked: Bullock, Flynn, Ramsden, Clarke.
15th	● Carlisle	A	L 3–0	Att: 3,176	Booked: Ramsden, Clarke. Dismissed: Ramsden.
28th	● Shrewsbury	H	L 1–3	Att: 11,522	Scorers: Hanson. Booked: Clarke. Dismissed: Clarke.

JANUARY
2nd	● Cheltenham	H	D 1–1	Att: 10,831	Scorers: J O'Brien. Booked: Williams, Ramsden. Dismissed: Williams.
19th	● Bury	A	L 2–1	Att: 2,930	Scorers: M Boulding. Booked: Bateson.
23rd	● Lincoln	A	L 2–1	Att: 3,803	Scorers: M Boulding. Booked: Williams, Bullock.
30th	● Torquay	A	W 1–2	Att: 2,592	Scorers: Evans2. Booked: Ramsden, Williams, Clarke.

FEBRUARY
6th	● Bury	H	L 0–1	Att: 11,965	Booked: Evans, Flynn.
13th	● Grimsby	H	D 0–0	Att: 11,321	
20th	● Accrington	A	L 2–0	Att: 3,396	
23rd	● Rochdale	A	W 1–3	Att: 3,055	Scorers: Clarke, Evans, Threlfall. Booked: Bullock.
27th	● Darlington	H	W 1–0	Att: 11,532	Scorers: Hanson. Booked: Flynn, McCammon, Clarke.

MARCH
2nd	● Aldershot	A	L 1–0	Att: 2,311	Booked: Hanson, Daley, Clarke.
6th	● Rotherham	A	W 1–2	Att: 4,185	Scorers: Flynn, Hanson.
9th	● Port Vale	A	L 2–1	Att: 3,728	Scorers: Threlfall.
13th	● Aldershot	H	W 2–1	Att: 11,272	Scorers: Daley, Hanson. Booked: Hanson, Daley.
20th	● Hereford	A	L 2–0	Att: 1,926	Booked: Bullock, Oliver.
23rd	● Notts County	H	D 0–0	Att: 11,630	Booked: Bolder, Daley, Oliver.
27th	● Dag & Red	H	D 3–3	Att: 11,064	Scorers: Hanson2, Kendall. Booked: L O'Brien, Kendall.

APRIL
3rd	● Bournemouth	A	L 1–0	Att: 6,239	Booked: Bullock, Grant.
5th	● Macclesfield	H	L 1–2	Att: 11,395	Scorers: Oliver. Booked: Threlfall.
10th	● Burton Albion	A	D 1–1	Att: 2,648	Scorers: Oliver. Booked: Threlfall.
13th	● Morecambe	H	W 2–0	Att: 11,027	Scorers: Bolder, Rehman. Booked: J O'Brien.
17th	● Barnet	H	W 2–1	Att: 11,138	Scorers: Flynn, L O'Brien.
24th	● Chesterfield	A	D 1–1	Att: 4,109	Scorers: Evans. Dismissed: Daley.

MAY
1st	● Northampton	H	W 2–0	Att: 12,403	Scorers: Evans2.
8th	● Crewe	A	W 0–1	Att: 5,172	Scorers: Kendall. Booked: Williams.

● Coca-Cola League 2/Play-Offs ● FA Cup ● Carling Cup ● Johnstone's Paint Trophy

LEAGUE 2 GOALKEEPER STATS

Player	Appearances	Match starts	Completed matches	Sub appearances	Subbed off	Clean sheets	Yellow cards	Red cards
Simon Eastwood	22	22	22	0	0	7	2	0
Matthew Glennon	17	17	17	0	0	3	0	0
Jon McLaughlin	7	7	7	0	0	3	0	0

LEAGUE 2 OUTFIELD PLAYER STATS

Player	Appearances	Match starts	Completed matches	Substitute appearances	Subbed off	Goals scored	Yellow cards	Red cards
Jonathan Bateson	21	14	13	7	1	0	1	0
Adam Bolder	14	14	12	0	2	1	1	0
Michael Boulding	21	9	6	12	3	4	1	0
Rory Boulding	2	0	0	2	0	0	0	0
Chris Brandon	20	14	2	6	12	2	2	0
Lee Bullock	41	41	35	0	5	1	10	1
Matthew Clarke	21	20	18	1	1	1	5	1
Joe Colbeck	5	3	1	2	2	0	1	0
Omar Daley	14	6	1	8	4	1	3	1
Luke Dean	1	0	0	1	0	0	0	0
Gareth Evans	43	38	27	5	10	11	1	1
Michael Flynn	42	41	39	1	2	6	5	0
Gavin Grant	11	7	2	4	5	0	1	0
James Hanson	34	33	32	1	1	12	2	0
Ryan Harrison	1	0	0	1	0	0	0	0
Louis Horne	1	0	0	1	0	0	0	0
Ryan Kendall	6	2	0	4	2	2	1	0
Mark McCammon	4	2	0	2	2	0	1	0
Scott Neilson	23	18	9	5	9	1	1	0
James O'Brien	23	15	5	8	10	2	3	0
Luke O'Brien	43	39	34	4	5	1	2	0
Steve O'Leary	7	4	1	3	3	0	0	0
Luke Oliver	7	7	7	0	0	2	2	0
Leon Osborne	12	5	4	7	1	0	0	0
Simon Ramsden	31	30	28	1	2	2	5	0
Zesh Rehman	38	36	31	2	5	2	3	0
Luke Sharry	1	0	0	1	0	0	0	0
Peter Thorne	7	4	2	3	2	0	0	0
Robbie Threlfall	17	17	15	0	2	2	2	0
Simon Whaley	6	5	2	1	3	1	0	0
Steve Williams	39	36	33	3	2	4	5	1

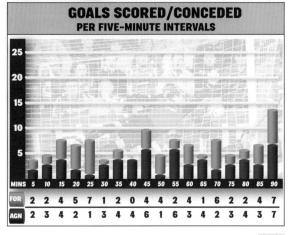

SEASON INFORMATION
Highest position: 5
Lowest position: 24
Average goals scored per game: 1.28
Average goals conceded per game: 1.35

LEAGUE POSITION AT THE END OF EACH MONTH

LONGEST SEQUENCES

Wins	3	Undefeated home	5
(22/08/09–05/09/09)		(13/02/10–27/03/10)	
Losses	2	Undefeated away	5
(on four occasions)		(22/08/09–03/10/09)	
Draws	3	Without scoring	3
(31/10/09–21/11/09)		(on two occasions)	
Undefeated	8	Without conceding	2
(22/08/09–03/10/09)		(26/09/09–29/09/09)	
Without win	6	Scoring	8
(20/03/10–10/04/10)		(03/10/09–24/11/09)	

CARDS RECEIVED
60   **5**

EARLIEST STRIKE
JAMES O'BRIEN
(v Cheltenham) 1:38

LATEST STRIKE
JAMES HANSON
(v Rotherham) 94:12

GOALS SCORED/CONCEDED
PER FIVE-MINUTE INTERVALS

MINS	5	10	15	20	25	30	35	40	45	50	55	60	65	70	75	80	85	90
FOR	2	2	4	5	7	1	2	0	4	2	4	2	4	1	6	2	2	4	7
AGN	2	3	4	2	1	3	4	4	6	1	6	3	4	2	3	4	3	7

BURTON ALBION

BURTON ALBION'S first Football League campaign was a successful one – and the same can be said of Paul Peschisolido's first season in management.

The Canadian took over at the helm of the 2008/09 Conference champions in the close season, but he found life tough to start with as the club won just two of their opening 12 games. However, Burton and Peschisolido soon found their feet and an immediate return to non-League football was never a worry.

Indeed Albion appeared to be capable of making the play-offs until March. Ultimately, a poor home record in 2010 was mostly to blame for their failure to do so, with their struggles on their own ground illustrated best by an amazing 6–5 defeat to Cheltenham in which they conceded four times in the last six minutes.

They were one of just four teams to concede more than 70 League goals in 2009/10 and Peschisolido has vowed to improve that, along with their home record, in the coming season.

CLUB SUMMARY

FORMED	1950
MANAGER	Paul Peschisolido
GROUND	Pirelli Stadium
CAPACITY	7,028
NICKNAME	The Brewers
WEBSITE	www.burtonalbionfc.co.uk

The New Football Pools PLAYER OF THE SEASON — Shaun Harrad

OVERALL

P	W	D	L	F	A	GD
50	18	11	21	76	84	-8

COCA-COLA FOOTBALL LEAGUE 2

Pos	P	W	D	L	F	A	GD	Pts
13	46	17	11	18	71	71	0	62

HOME

Pos	P	W	D	L	F	A	GD	Pts
18	23	9	5	9	38	34	4	32

AWAY

Pos	P	W	D	L	F	A	GD	Pts
7	23	8	6	9	33	37	-4	30

CUP PROGRESS DETAILS

Competition	Round reached	Knocked out by
FA Cup	R2	Gillingham
Carling Cup	R1	Reading
JP Trophy	R1	Chesterfield

BIGGEST WIN (ALL COMPS)
12/12/09 6–1 v Aldershot

BIGGEST DEFEAT (ALL COMPS)
1–5 on 2 occasions

ATTENDANCE RECORD

HIGH	AVERAGE	Low
5,801	3,213	2,027
v Notts County (28/12/2009)		v Accrington (01/12/2009)

RESULTS 2009/10

AUGUST
8th	● Shrewsbury	A	L 3–1	Att: 6,438	Scorers: Pearson. Booked: Branston.
11th	● Reading	A	L 5–1	Att: 5,893	Scorers: Phillips. Booked: Simpson.
15th	● Morecambe	H	W 5–2	Att: 2,742	Scorers: Harrad, McGrath, Pearson², Penn.
18th	● Torquay	H	L 0–2	Att: 2,670	
22nd	● Lincoln	A	W 0–2	Att: 3,590	Scorers: Austin, Penn. Booked: Boertien.
29th	● Northampton	H	W 3–2	Att: 3,321	Scorers: Harrad, Simpson². Booked: Boertien.

SEPTEMBER
1st	● Chesterfield	H	L 1–5	Att: 1,493	Scorers: McGrath. Booked: Branston.
5th	● Notts County	A	D 1–1	Att: 8,891	Scorers: Walker. Booked: Branston, Simpson.
12th	● Bradford	A	D 1–1	Att: 11,439	Scorers: Boertien.
19th	● Dag & Red	H	L 0–1	Att: 2,689	Booked: Maghoma. Dismissed: Branston.
26th	● Bournemouth	A	L 1–0	Att: 6,327	Booked: Harrad, Shroot, Boertien.
29th	● Macclesfield	H	D 1–1	Att: 2,332	Scorers: Pearson. Booked: Pearson.

OCTOBER
4th	● Rochdale	H	W 1–0	Att: 3,119	Scorers: Walker. Booked: Simpson.
10th	● Grimsby	A	W 1–2	Att: 4,002	Scorers: Corbett, Phillips.
17th	● Barnet	H	W 2–0	Att: 2,935	Scorers: Austin, Maghoma.
24th	● Chesterfield	A	L 5–2	Att: 4,218	Scorers: Harrad, Webster. Booked: Webster.
31st	● Bury	H	D 0–0	Att: 3,373	

NOVEMBER
8th	● Oxford City	H	W 3–2	Att: 2,207	Scorers: Austin, Harrad, Maghoma. Booked: Simpson.
14th	● Darlington	A	L 1–0	Att: 2,404	
21st	● Hereford	H	W 3–2	Att: 2,796	Scorers: Harrad², Webster.
24th	● Crewe	A	L 2–1	Att: 3,446	Scorers: Walker. Booked: Webster, Walker.
28th	● Gillingham	A	L 1–0	Att: 4,996	Booked: Penn, Branston, Webster.

DECEMBER
1st	● Accrington	H	L 0–2	Att: 2,027	Booked: Branston, Kabba.
5th	● Rotherham	A	D 2–2	Att: 3,177	Scorers: Pearson, Webster.
12th	● Aldershot	H	W 6–1	Att: 2,547	Scorers: Harrad, Kabba², Pearson³. Booked: Gilroy, McGrath.
28th	● Notts County	H	L 1–4	Att: 5,801	Scorers: Kabba. Booked: Krysiak, Harrad.

JANUARY
16th	● Shrewsbury	H	D 1–1	Att: 3,139	Scorers: Pearson. Booked: Branston. Dismissed: Branston.
19th	● Port Vale	A	L 3–1	Att: 4,458	Scorers: Harrad. Booked: Penn, Boertien. Dismissed: Krysiak.
23rd	● Torquay	A	W 2–3	Att: 2,629	Scorers: Harrad, Penn, Taylor. Booked: Penn.
27th	● Lincoln	H	W 1–0	Att: 2,109	Scorers: Taylor. Booked: Penn, Pearson.
30th	● Northampton	A	D 1–1	Att: 4,552	Scorers: Harrad. Booked: Harrad, Parkes.

FEBRUARY
6th	● Port Vale	H	W 1–0	Att: 4,644	Scorers: Maghoma. Booked: Harrad, Webster, Penn, Krysiak.
9th	● Cheltenham	A	W 0–1	Att: 2,593	Scorers: Harrad. Booked: Phillips, Parkes, Kabba.
12th	● Crewe	H	L 1–2	Att: 2,985	Scorers: Harrad.
16th	● Morecambe	A	L 3–2	Att: 1,537	Scorers: Harrad, Maghoma. Booked: Corbett, Harrad.
20th	● Hereford	A	W 3–4	Att: 2,253	Scorers: Harrad, James, Taylor, Webster. Booked: Webster, Taylor. Dismissed: Webster.
27th	● Rotherham	A	L 0–1	Att: 3,568	Booked: Kabba.

MARCH
6th	● Aldershot	A	W 0–2	Att: 2,784	Scorers: Kabba, Parkes. Booked: Taylor, Kabba.
13th	● Cheltenham	H	L 5–6	Att: 2,500	Scorers: Harrad², Kabba², Townsend OG. Booked: Taylor.
20th	● Chesterfield	H	D 2–2	Att: 3,696	Scorers: Pearson, Penn. Booked: Boertien, Kabba, Harrad.
23rd	● Accrington	A	W 0–2	Att: 1,270	Scorers: Harrad, Pearson. Booked: Boertien.
27th	● Barnet	A	D 1–1	Att: 1,842	Scorers: Pearson. Booked: Parkes.

APRIL
3rd	● Darlington	H	L 1–2	Att: 2,779	Scorers: Pearson.
5th	● Bury	A	L 3–0	Att: 2,710	Booked: McGrath, James, Taylor.
10th	● Bradford	H	D 1–1	Att: 2,648	Scorers: Harrad. Booked: McGrath.
13th	● Macclesfield	A	D 1–1	Att: 1,588	Scorers: Tipton OG.
17th	● Dag & Red	A	L 2–1	Att: 1,891	Scorers: Harrad. Booked: Parkes, Penn.
24th	● Bournemouth	H	L 0–2	Att: 3,977	Booked: McGrath, Pearson. Bournemouth are promoted.

MAY
1st	● Rochdale	A	W 1–2	Att: 3,749	Scorers: Harrad, Taylor. Booked: Penn, Parkes.
8th	● Grimsby	H	W 3–0	Att: 5,510	Scorers: Harrad², Pearson. Booked: Boco, James, Taylor.

● Coca-Cola League 2/Play-Offs ● FA Cup ● Carling Cup ● Johnstone's Paint Trophy

actim

LEAGUE 2 GOALKEEPER STATS

Player	Appearances	Match starts	Completed matches	Sub appearances	Subbed off	Clean sheets	Yellow cards	Red cards
Artur Krysiak	38	38	37	0	0	9	2	1
Kevin Poole	6	5	5	1	0	1	0	0
Shane Redmond	3	3	3	0	0	0	0	0

LEAGUE 2 OUTFIELD PLAYER STATS

Player	Appearances	Match starts	Completed matches	Substitute appearances	Subbed off	Goals scored	Yellow cards	Red cards
Ryan Austin	18	18	18	0	0	2	0	0
Romuald Boco	8	3	1	5	2	0	1	0
Paul Boertien	34	33	30	1	3	1	6	0
Guy Branston	19	18	16	1	0	0	4	2
Aaron Brown	1	1	1	0	0	0	0	0
Kieron Cadogan	2	2	0	0	2	0	0	0
Andrew Corbett	34	32	26	2	6	1	1	0
Marc Edworthy	1	1	1	0	0	0	0	0
Keith Gilroy	8	4	2	4	2	0	1	0
Marc Goodfellow	3	0	0	3	0	0	0	0
Shaun Harrad	42	35	23	7	12	21	6	0
Richard Jackson	5	4	3	1	1	0	0	0
Tony James	42	42	42	0	0	1	2	0
Steven Kabba	23	18	11	5	7	6	5	0
Shaun Kelly	4	2	2	2	0	0	0	0
Jacques Maghoma	35	24	17	11	7	3	1	0
Serge Makofo	2	0	0	2	0	0	0	0
John McGrath	45	44	42	1	2	1	4	0
Tom Parkes	22	21	20	1	1	1	5	0
Greg Pearson	42	24	11	18	13	14	3	0
Russell Penn	40	34	28	6	6	4	6	0
Jimmy Phillips	24	19	4	5	15	1	1	0
Robin Shroot	7	4	1	3	3	0	0	0
Michael Simpson	24	20	17	4	3	2	2	0
Darren Stride	9	5	4	4	1	0	0	0
Cleveland Taylor	24	23	13	1	10	4	5	0
O'Neil Thompson	2	1	1	0	0	0	0	0
Richard Walker	17	10	4	7	6	3	1	0
Aaron Webster	24	18	17	6	0	4	4	1

SEASON INFORMATION

Highest position: 6
Lowest position: 21
Average goals scored per game: 1.54
Average goals conceded per game: 1.54

LEAGUE POSITION AT THE END OF EACH MONTH

AUG	SEP	OCT	NOV	DEC	JAN	FEB	MAR	APR	MAY
8	14	11	12	14	14	13	12	14	13

LONGEST SEQUENCES

Wins	3	Undefeated home	5
(04/10/09–17/10/09)		(29/09/09–21/11/09)	
Losses	2	Undefeated away	4
(on five occasions)		(20/02/10–27/03/10)	
Draws	2	Without scoring	2
(on two occasions)		(on two occasions)	
Undefeated	5	Without conceding	2
(23/01/10–09/02/10)		(06/02/10–09/02/10)	
Without win	7	Scoring	13
(27/03/10–24/04/10)		(05/12/09–20/02/10)	

CARDS RECEIVED

61 **4**

EARLIEST STRIKE

CLEVELAND TAYLOR
(v Lincoln City) 0:54

LATEST STRIKE

TONY JAMES
(v Hereford) 95:44

GOALS SCORED/CONCEDED
PER FIVE-MINUTE INTERVALS

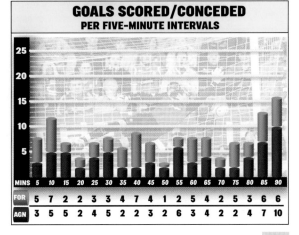

MINS	5	10	15	20	25	30	35	40	45	50	55	60	65	70	75	80	85	90
FOR	5	7	2	2	3	3	4	7	4	1	2	5	4	5	3	6	6	
AGN	3	5	5	2	4	5	2	2	3	2	6	3	4	2	2	4	7	10

BURY

A DISAPPOINTING loss of form in the second half of the season cost Alan Knill's men a shot at promotion.

Bury were second in the table at Christmas and looked to be a solid bet for automatic promotion, but results fell away to such an extent that they finished down in ninth place.

A 5–0 away defeat to eventual champions Notts County in early April was the low point of the campaign, coming at the end of an eight-game winless run. That slump ultimately put paid to their ambitions of a play-off place, and in the end they missed out on the top seven by three points.

Their form away from the League was of little consolation, as they lost at the first hurdle in both the FA Cup and the League Cup, while they were eliminated at the quarter-final stage of the Johnstone's Paint Trophy by Accrington.

The majority of Bury's players were out of contract at the end of 2009/10 and Knill says he is planning a major overhaul.

CLUB SUMMARY

FORMED	1885
MANAGER	Alan Knill
GROUND	Gigg Lane
CAPACITY	11,669
NICKNAME	The Shakers
WEBSITE	www.buryfc.co.uk

The New Football Pools PLAYER OF THE SEASON — Ryan Lowe

OVERALL
P	W	D	L	F	A	GD
51	20	13	18	58	67	-9

COCA-COLA FOOTBALL LEAGUE 2
Pos	P	W	D	L	F	A	GD	Pts
9	46	19	12	15	54	59	-5	69

HOME
Pos	P	W	D	L	F	A	GD	Pts
10	23	11	6	6	29	23	6	39

AWAY
Pos	P	W	D	L	F	A	GD	Pts
10	23	8	6	9	25	36	-11	30

CUP PROGRESS DETAILS
Competition	Round reached	Knocked out by
FA Cup	R1	Aldershot
Carling Cup	R1	West Brom
JP Trophy	QF	Accrington

BIGGEST WIN (ALL COMPS)
3–0 on 2 occasions

BIGGEST DEFEAT (ALL COMPS)
03/04/10 0–5 v Notts County

ATTENDANCE RECORD
High	Average	Low
6,528	3,029	2,123
v Rochdale (01/02/2010)		v Darlington (09/03/2010)

RESULTS 2009/10

AUGUST
8th	● Bournemouth	H	L 0–3	**Att:** 2,998
11th	● West Brom	H	L 0–2	**Att:** 3,077 **Booked:** Dawson.
15th	● Darlington	A	W 0–1	**Att:** 2,310 **Scorers:** Robertson. **Booked:** Brown.
18th	● Hereford	A	W 1–3	**Att:** 2,321 **Scorers:** Jones, Lowe². **Booked:** Dawson.
22nd	● Grimsby	H	L 0–1	**Att:** 2,799
29th	● Rochdale	A	L 3–0	**Att:** 4,534 **Booked:** Scott, Robertson, Futcher, Sodje.

SEPTEMBER
1st	● Walsall	A	D 0–0	**Att:** 2,314 **Booked:** Sodje. Bury win 5–4 on penalties.
5th	● Accrington	H	L 0–2	**Att:** 3,082
12th	● Cheltenham	H	L 0–1	**Att:** 2,130 **Booked:** Worrall.
19th	● Port Vale	A	W 0–1	**Att:** 5,461 **Scorers:** Lowe. **Booked:** Cresswell, Brown. **Dismissed:** Cresswell.
26th	● Lincoln	H	W 2–0	**Att:** 2,554 **Scorers:** Lowe, Worrall.
29th	● Crewe	A	W 2–3	**Att:** 3,534 **Scorers:** Dawson, Elliott, Lowe. **Booked:** Newey, Baker.

OCTOBER
3rd	● Torquay	A	D 1–1	**Att:** 2,524 **Scorers:** Jones. **Booked:** Cresswell, Dawson, Sodje.
6th	● Tranmere	H	W 2–1	**Att:** 1,903 **Scorers:** Jones, Worrall.
10th	● Northampton	H	D 2–2	**Att:** 2,863 **Scorers:** Lowe, Worrall. **Booked:** Elliott, Worrall.
17th	● Aldershot	A	W 2–3	**Att:** 3,196 **Scorers:** Barry-Murphy, Dawson, Sodje. **Booked:** Brown, Dawson.
24th	● Rotherham	H	W 2–1	**Att:** 3,496 **Scorers:** Baker, Lowe. **Booked:** Newey, Cresswell, Sodje.
31st	● Burton	A	D 0–0	**Att:** 3,373

NOVEMBER
7th	● Aldershot	A	L 2–0	**Att:** 2,519 **Booked:** Scott, Sodje.
10th	● Accrington	A	L 3–2	**Att:** 1,637 **Scorers:** Jones, Racchi. **Booked:** Futcher.
14th	● Notts County	A	D 3–3	**Att:** 3,602 **Scorers:** Dawson, Morrell, Nardiello.
21st	● Shrewsbury	A	D 1–1	**Att:** 5,070 **Scorers:** Nardiello.
24th	● Chesterfield	H	W 2–1	**Att:** 2,504 **Scorers:** Morrell². **Booked:** Sodje, Futcher.

DECEMBER
1st	● Morecambe	A	L 3–0	**Att:** 1,875 **Booked:** Buchanan, Nardiello.
5th	● Barnet	H	W 2–0	**Att:** 2,511 **Scorers:** Nardiello, Worrall. **Booked:** Baker.
12th	● Dag & Red	A	L 3–1	**Att:** 1,915 **Scorers:** Nardiello. **Booked:** Nardiello.
28th	● Accrington	H	W 2–4	**Att:** 3,138 **Scorers:** Jones, Lowe, Morrell². **Booked:** Sodje.

JANUARY
2nd	● Grimsby	A	D 1–1	**Att:** 3,463 **Scorers:** Lowe. **Booked:** Brown, Newey.
16th	● Bournemouth	A	W 1–2	**Att:** 4,516 **Scorers:** Dawson, Worrall.
19th	● Bradford	H	W 2–1	**Att:** 2,930 **Scorers:** Jones, Lowe. **Booked:** Sodje, Futcher.
23rd	● Hereford	H	W 1–0	**Att:** 2,797 **Scorers:** Jones.

FEBRUARY
1st	● Rochdale	H	W 1–0	**Att:** 6,528 **Scorers:** Lowe. **Booked:** Sodje.
6th	● Bradford	A	W 0–1	**Att:** 11,965 **Scorers:** Morrell.
9th	● Macclesfield	H	W 2–1	**Att:** 2,169 **Scorers:** Bishop, Lowe. **Booked:** Dawson.
13th	● Chesterfield	A	L 1–0	**Att:** 4,122 **Booked:** Lowe.
19th	● Shrewsbury	H	W 1–0	**Att:** 3,720 **Scorers:** Lowe. **Booked:** Sodje, Hewson.
23rd	● Morecambe	H	D 0–0	**Att:** 2,222
27th	● Barnet	A	D 0–0	**Att:** 1,949

MARCH
6th	● Dag & Red	H	D 0–0	**Att:** 2,886
9th	● Darlington	H	D 1–1	**Att:** 2,123 **Scorers:** Lowe.
13th	● Macclesfield	A	L 2–0	**Att:** 2,740 **Booked:** Futcher, Lowe, Baker, Sodje. **Dismissed:** Lowe.
20th	● Rotherham	A	L 1–0	**Att:** 3,521 **Booked:** Sodje.
27th	● Aldershot	H	L 1–2	**Att:** 2,795 **Scorers:** Bishop. **Booked:** Dawson, Futcher.

APRIL
3rd	● Notts County	A	L 5–0	**Att:** 7,005
5th	● Burton	H	W 3–0	**Att:** 2,710 **Scorers:** Morrell², James OG. **Booked:** Jones. **Dismissed:** Jones.
10th	● Cheltenham	A	L 5–2	**Att:** 3,071 **Scorers:** Lowe². **Dismissed:** Brown.
13th	● Crewe	H	W 3–0	**Att:** 2,178 **Scorers:** Bishop, Lowe, Morrell.
17th	● Port Vale	H	D 1–1	**Att:** 4,570 **Scorers:** Sodje. **Booked:** Dawson.
24th	● Lincoln	A	L 1–0	**Att:** 3,403 **Booked:** Bishop.

MAY
1st	● Torquay	H	L 0–3	**Att:** 3,492 **Booked:** Buchanan, Sodje.
8th	● Northampton	A	D 1–1	**Att:** 5,234 **Scorers:** Lowe. **Dismissed:** Poole.

● Coca-Cola League 2/Play-Offs ● FA Cup ● Carling Cup ● Johnstone's Paint Trophy

LEAGUE 2 GOALKEEPER STATS

Player	Appearances	Match starts	Completed matches	Sub appearances	Subbed off	Clean sheets	Yellow cards	Red cards
Cameron Belford	7	5	5	2	0	1	0	0
Wayne Brown	41	41	39	0	1	13	4	1

LEAGUE 2 OUTFIELD PLAYER STATS

Player	Appearances	Match starts	Completed matches	Substitute appearances	Subbed off	Goals scored	Yellow cards	Red cards
Richie Baker	14	7	2	7	5	1	3	0
Brian Barry-Murphy	46	46	46	0	0	1	0	0
Andy Bishop	25	12	4	13	8	3	1	0
David Buchanan	38	37	36	1	1	0	2	0
Danny Carlton	7	1	1	6	0	0	0	0
Ryan Cresswell	28	24	22	4	1	0	3	1
Stephen Dawson	45	45	41	0	4	4	6	0
Tom Elliott	16	7	6	9	1	1	1	0
Ben Futcher	32	29	29	3	0	0	5	0
Sam Hewson	7	1	0	6	1	0	1	0
Simon Johnson	4	1	0	3	1	0	0	0
Mike Jones	41	36	22	5	13	5	1	1
Ryan Lowe	39	34	18	5	15	18	2	1
Andrew Morrell	32	25	11	7	14	9	0	0
Daniel Nardiello	6	6	3	0	3	4	2	0
Tom Newey	32	29	27	3	2	0	3	0
Keigan Parker	2	2	0	0	2	0	0	0
James Poole	9	4	1	5	2	0	0	1
Danny Racchi	22	10	2	12	8	0	0	0
Jordan Robertson	4	4	1	0	3	1	1	0
Domaine Rouse	4	1	0	3	1	0	0	0
Paul Scott	30	26	23	4	3	0	1	0
Efetobore Sodje	39	39	36	0	3	2	11	0
David Worrall	40	34	22	6	12	4	2	0

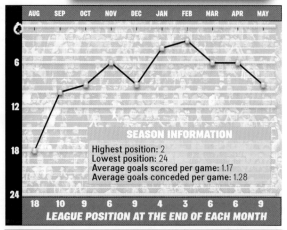

SEASON INFORMATION
Highest position: 2
Lowest position: 24
Average goals scored per game: 1.17
Average goals conceded per game: 1.28

LEAGUE POSITION AT THE END OF EACH MONTH

LONGEST SEQUENCES

Wins	6	Undefeated home	14	
(16/01/10–09/02/10)		(26/09/09–09/03/10)		
Losses	4	Undefeated away	6	
(on two occasions)		(19/09/09–21/11/09)		
Draws	4	Without scoring	4	
(23/02/10–09/03/10)		(22/08/09–12/09/09)		
Undefeated	11	Without conceding	4	
(19/09/09–24/11/09)		(19/02/10–06/03/10)		
Without win	8	Scoring	10	
(23/02/10–03/04/10)		(05/12/09–09/02/10)		

CARDS RECEIVED

49 5

EARLIEST STRIKE
MIKE JONES
(v Hereford) 1:54

LATEST STRIKE
DAVID WORRALL
(v Lincoln City) 93:15

GOALS SCORED/CONCEDED
PER FIVE-MINUTE INTERVALS

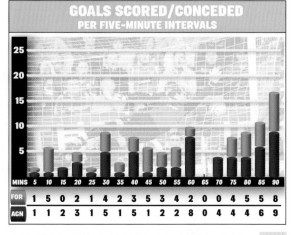

MINS	5	10	15	20	25	30	35	40	45	50	55	60	65	70	75	80	85	90
FOR	1	5	0	2	1	4	2	3	5	3	4	2	0	0	4	5	5	8
AGN	1	1	2	3	1	5	1	5	1	2	2	8	0	4	4	4	6	9

CHELTENHAM TOWN

CHELTENHAM
TOWN FC

CHELTENHAM avoided relegation on the final day of the season but their escape act in May provided little reason for cheer.

There is no doubt that Football League survival is to be celebrated as it at least assures the Robins' financial health. However, having been relegated from Coca-Cola League 1 just 12 months earlier, Cheltenham were expected to spend the season looking up the table rather than over their shoulders.

Martin Allen began the season in charge but his reign came to an end by mutual consent in December, with the club languishing in the lower reaches of the League 2 table. Mark Yates took over and brought with him a fresh approach, which eventually paid dividends.

Veteran striker Julian Alsop returned to break the club's all-time goalscoring record while the Robins also went through a re-branding process off the pitch. However, the real work for Yates begins this summer when he will no doubt look to make the squad his own.

CLUB SUMMARY

FORMED	1892
MANAGER	Mark Yates
GROUND	Abbey Business Stadium
CAPACITY	7,066
NICKNAME	The Robins
WEBSITE	www.ctfc.co.uk

The New **Football Pools** PLAYER OF THE SEASON

Michael Pook

OVERALL
P	W	D	L	F	A	GD
49	10	18	21	57	79	-22

COCA-COLA FOOTBALL LEAGUE 2
Pos	P	W	D	L	F	A	GD	Pts
22	46	10	18	18	54	71	-17	48

HOME
Pos	P	W	D	L	F	A	GD	Pts
22	23	5	8	10	34	38	-4	23

AWAY
Pos	P	W	D	L	F	A	GD	Pts
18	23	5	10	8	20	33	-13	25

CUP PROGRESS DETAILS
Competition	Round reached	Knocked out by
FA Cup	R1	Torquay
Carling Cup	R1	Southend
JP Trophy	R1	Torquay

BIGGEST WIN (ALL COMPS)
24/11/09 5–1 v Barnet

BIGGEST DEFEAT (ALL COMPS)
01/05/10 0–5 v Notts County

ATTENDANCE RECORD
HIGH	AVERAGE	Low
4,134	3,186	2,331
v Notts County (03/10/2009)		v Barnet (24/11/2009)

RESULTS 2009/10

AUGUST
8th	● Grimsby	H	W 2–1	Att: 3,654	Scorers: Hayles, Ridley. Booked: Hayles.
11th	● Southend	H	L 1–2	Att: 1,918	Scorers: Hammond.
15th	● Hereford	A	D 1–1	Att: 3,280	Scorers: Alsop. Booked: Diallo.
18th	● Rochdale	A	W 0–1	Att: 2,311	Scorers: Alsop. Booked: Diallo.
22nd	● Bradford	H	L 4–5	Att: 3,073	Scorers: Hammond, Richards2, Townsend.
29th	● Darlington	D	D 1–1	Att: 1,840	Scorers: Richards. Booked: Haynes.

SEPTEMBER
1st	● Torquay	H	L 1–3	Att: 1,397	Scorers: Low. Booked: Hayles, Artus.
5th	● Dag & Red	H	D 1–1	Att: 2,969	Scorers: Townsend. Booked: Alsop.
12th	● Bury	A	W 0–1	Att: 2,130	Scorers: Hayles.
19th	● Rotherham	H	D 1–1	Att: 3,088	Scorers: Alsop. Booked: Low.
26th	● Aldershot	A	L 4–1	Att: 2,964	Scorers: Richards. Booked: Townsend.
29th	● Shrewsbury	H	L 1–2	Att: 2,928	Scorers: Hayles. Booked: Pook.

OCTOBER
3rd	● Notts County	H	D 1–1	Att: 4,134	Scorers: Hammond.
10th	● Accrington	A	L 4–0	Att: 1,843	Booked: Low.
16th	● Macclesfield	H	L 1–2	Att: 2,930	Scorers: Hammond.
24th	● Port Vale	A	D 1–1	Att: 4,979	Scorers: Pook. Booked: Eyjolfsson, Low.
31st	● Crewe	H	L 0–4	Att: 3,124	Booked: Eyjolfsson, Hayles.

NOVEMBER
7th	● Torquay	A	L 3–1	Att: 2,370	Scorers: Lewis. Booked: Low. Dismissed: Ridley.
14th	● Lincoln	A	D 1–1	Att: 3,008	Scorers: Richards. Booked: Alsop. Dismissed: Richardson.
21st	● Morecambe	A	L 1–0	Att: 1,567	Booked: Labadie.
24th	● Barnet	H	W 5–1	Att: 2,331	Scorers: Gallinagh, Marshall2, Richards, Yakubu OG. Booked: Hayles.

DECEMBER
1st	● Torquay	A	L 3–0	Att: 2,122	Booked: Labadie, Pipe.
5th	● Northampton	H	D 2–2	Att: 2,824	Scorers: Hayles2. Booked: Pipe, Alsop.
12th	● Chesterfield	A	L 1–0	Att: 3,145	Booked: Labadie.
26th	● Bournemouth	H	L 0–1	Att: 4,114	Booked: Hayles, Pipe.
28th	● Dag & Red	A	W 0–2	Att: 2,028	Scorers: Low, Richards. Booked: Eastham, Low, Hutton.

JANUARY
2nd	● Bradford	A	D 1–1	Att: 10,831	Scorers: Richards. Booked: Labadie.
16th	● Grimsby	A	D 0–0	Att: 3,334	Booked: Eastham, Townsend, Low, S P Brown. Dismissed: Eastham.
23rd	● Rochdale	H	L 1–4	Att: 3,460	Scorers: Townsend. Booked: Townsend.

FEBRUARY
6th	● Bournemouth	A	D 0–0	Att: 5,259	Booked: Pook, Hammond.
9th	● Burton	H	L 0–1	Att: 2,593	Booked: Pook, Andrew, Labadie, Hayles. Dismissed: Andrew.
13th	● Barnet	A	D 1–1	Att: 1,667	Scorers: Thornhill. Booked: Thornhill, Lewis, Townsend, Haynes.
20th	● Morecambe	H	W 2–0	Att: 2,806	Scorers: Alsop, Thornhill. Booked: Pook.
23rd	● Torquay	H	D 1–1	Att: 2,607	Scorers: Hayles. Booked: Alsop.
27th	● Northampton	A	L 2–1	Att: 4,428	Scorers: Watkins. Booked: Low, Eastham, Watkins.

MARCH
2nd	● Hereford	H	L 0–1	Att: 3,273	Booked: Pook.
6th	● Chesterfield	H	L 0–1	Att: 3,006	
13th	● Burton	A	W 5–6	Att: 2,500	Scorers: Elito, Pook3, Richards2. Booked: Pook.
20th	● Port Vale	H	D 1–1	Att: 3,503	Scorers: Elito.
27th	● Macclesfield	A	L 1–0	Att: 1,572	

APRIL
3rd	● Lincoln	H	W 1–0	Att: 3,708	Scorers: Alsop.
5th	● Crewe	A	W 1–2	Att: 3,488	Scorers: Richards2. Booked: Hayles.
10th	● Bury	H	W 5–2	Att: 3,071	Scorers: Hayles, Low2, Richards, Thornhill.
13th	● Shrewsbury	A	D 0–0	Att: 4,967	Booked: Alsop.
17th	● Rotherham	A	D 0–0	Att: 3,478	
20th	● Darlington	H	D 3–3	Att: 2,836	Scorers: Elito, Pook, Richards.
24th	● Aldershot	H	L 1–2	Att: 3,386	Scorers: Richards. Booked: Richards.

MAY
1st	● Notts County	A	L 5–0	Att: 11,331	
8th	● Accrington	H	D 1–1	Att: 3,856	Scorers: Low.

● Coca-Cola League 2/Play-Offs ● FA Cup ● Carling Cup ● Johnstone's Paint Trophy

actim

LEAGUE 2 GOALKEEPER STATS

Player	Appearances	Match starts	Completed matches	Sub appearances	Subbed off	Clean sheets	Yellow cards	Red cards
Scott P Brown	46	46	46	0	0	9	1	0

LEAGUE 2 OUTFIELD PLAYER STATS

Player	Appearances	Match starts	Completed matches	Substitute appearances	Subbed off	Goals scored	Yellow cards	Red cards
Louis Almond	4	2	0	2	2	0	0	0
Julian Alsop	41	21	11	20	10	4	5	0
Danny Andrew	10	9	8	1	0	0	1	1
Frankie Artus	7	7	3	0	4	0	0	0
David Bird	37	35	30	2	5	0	0	0
Oliver Bozanic	4	4	1	0	3	0	0	0
Scott Brown	1	0	0	1	0	0	0	0
Sam Cox	1	1	1	0	0	0	0	0
Tom Denton	2	1	0	1	1	0	0	0
Drissa Diallo	18	17	17	1	0	0	1	0
Shane Duff	11	11	9	0	2	0	0	0
Ashley Eastham	20	18	17	2	0	0	3	1
Medy Elito	12	12	11	0	1	3	0	0
Holmar Orn Eyjolfsson	4	4	1	0	3	0	2	0
Andy Gallinagh	39	35	30	4	5	1	0	0
Elvis Hammond	24	14	8	10	6	4	1	0
Barry Hayles	39	23	10	16	13	7	6	0
Kyle Haynes	13	6	3	7	3	0	0	0
David Hutton	25	14	7	11	7	0	1	0
Joss Labadie	11	11	10	0	1	0	5	0
Jake Lee	1	0	0	1	0	0	0	0
Aaron Lescott	8	7	7	1	0	0	0	0
Theo Lewis	15	9	5	6	4	0	1	0
Joshua Low	39	35	33	4	2	4	6	0
Ben Marshall	6	6	4	0	2	2	0	0
David Pipe	8	7	6	1	1	0	3	0
Michael Pook	35	31	27	4	4	5	6	0
Justin Richards	44	39	26	5	13	15	1	0
Lee Ridley	27	26	20	1	6	1	0	0
Romone Rose	1	1	0	0	1	0	0	0
Matt Thornhill	17	16	12	1	4	3	1	0
Michael Townsend	34	34	30	0	4	3	4	0
Marley Watkins	13	4	0	9	4	1	1	0

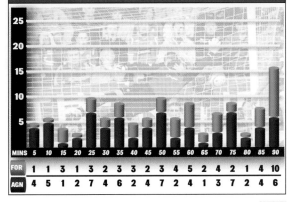

SEASON INFORMATION
Highest position: 3
Lowest position: 22
Average goals scored per game: 1.17
Average goals conceded per game: 1.54

LEAGUE POSITION AT THE END OF EACH MONTH

AUG 9 · SEP 12 · OCT 21 · NOV 20 · DEC 21 · JAN 22 · FEB 22 · MAR 22 · APR 21 · MAY 22

LONGEST SEQUENCES

Wins	3	Undefeated home	4	
(03/04/10–10/04/10)		(20/03/10–20/04/10)		
Losses	3	Undefeated away	5	
(27/02/10–06/03/10)		(28/12/09–13/02/10)		
Draws	3	Without scoring	2	
(13/04/10–20/04/10)		(on four occasions)		
Undefeated	6	Without conceding	2	
(03/04/10–20/04/10)		(13/04/10–17/04/10)		
Without win	10	Scoring	11	
(19/09/09–21/11/09)		(08/08/09–03/10/09)		

CARDS RECEIVED

51   3

EARLIEST STRIKE
ELVIS HAMMOND
(v Bradford) 3:10

LATEST STRIKE
MICHAEL POOK
(v Burton Albion) 94:00

GOALS SCORED/CONCEDED
PER FIVE-MINUTE INTERVALS

MINS	5	10	15	20	25	30	35	40	45	50	55	60	65	70	75	80	85	90
FOR	1	1	3	1	3	2	3	2	3	2	3	4	2	5	2	4	2	1	4	10
AGN	4	5	1	2	7	4	6	2	4	7	2	4	1	3	7	2	4	6

CHESTERFIELD

CHESTERFIELD said goodbye to Saltergate at the end of 2009/10 but they were unable to provide the perfect send off by winning promotion.

The Spireites had looked to be heading for at least a play-off place back in March, but an untimely run of just one win from 11 matches leading up to the final game of the season at home to Bournemouth meant that their hopes faded. However, the Football League's oldest ground did get a fitting finale. Chesterfield's longest-serving player, Derek Niven, scored the final goal in Saltergate's 139-year history deep into injury-time to secure a 2–1 victory against the Cherries.

It meant that the Spireites finished in eighth place, just missing out on the play-offs. They will now begin a new era at the 10,500 all-seater b2net Stadium still in npower League 2.

John Sheridan, in his first full season as manager, acknowledged his side should have finished higher and he will hope for a sustained promotion challenge in the coming season.

CLUB SUMMARY

FORMED	1866
MANAGER	John Sheridan
GROUND	b2net Stadium
CAPACITY	8,504
NICKNAME	The Spireites
WEBSITE	www.chesterfield-fc.co.uk

The New Football Pools PLAYER OF THE SEASON — Tommy Lee

OVERALL
P	W	D	L	F	A	GD
51	22	8	21	72	74	-2

COCA-COLA FOOTBALL LEAGUE 2
Pos	P	W	D	L	F	A	GD	Pts
8	46	21	7	18	61	62	-1	70

HOME
Pos	P	W	D	L	F	A	GD	Pts
6	23	14	3	6	38	27	11	45

AWAY
Pos	P	W	D	L	F	A	GD	Pts
17	23	7	4	12	23	35	-12	25

CUP PROGRESS DETAILS
Competition	Round reached	Knocked out by
FA Cup	R1	Bournemouth
Carling Cup	R1	Scunthorpe
JP Trophy	QF	Carlisle

BIGGEST WIN (ALL COMPS)
01/09/09 5–1 v Burton

BIGGEST DEFEAT (ALL COMPS)
13/03/10 0–5 v Port Vale

ATTENDANCE RECORD
High	Average	Low
7,702	3,967	3,104
v Bournemouth (08/05/2010)		v Accrington Stanley (03/10/2009)

RESULTS 2009/10

AUGUST
8th	● Torquay	A	L 2–0	Att: 3,966		
11th	● Scunthorpe	A	L 2–1	Att: 2,501	Scorers: Currie.
15th	● Northampton	H	W 1–0	Att: 3,700	Scorers: McDermott.
19th	● Notts County	H	W 2–1	Att: 6,196	Scorers: Lowry². Booked: Allott, Talbot, Lester.
22nd	● Shrewsbury	A	D 1–1	Att: 5,086	Scorers: Lowry.
29th	● Morecambe	H	D 1–1	Att: 3,210	Scorers: Lester. Booked: Breckin.

SEPTEMBER
1st	● Burton	A	W 1–5	Att: 1,493	Scorers: Lowry, Small², Talbot². Booked: Allott.
5th	● Rotherham	A	L 3–1	Att: 4,458	Scorers: Lowry. Booked: Robertson, Page.
12th	● Dag & Red	A	L 2–1	Att: 1,819	Scorers: McDermott. Booked: Austin.
19th	● Macclesfield	H	W 4–1	Att: 3,138	Scorers: Lester, Lowry, McDermott, Small.
26th	● Bradford	A	L 3–0	Att: 11,664	Booked: Page, Lester.
30th	● Grimsby	H	W 3–2	Att: 3,329	Scorers: Lester, McDermott, Niven. Booked: Page, Robertson.

OCTOBER
3rd	● Accrington	H	W 1–0	Att: 3,104	Scorers: Small. Booked: Page, McDermott, Small.
6th	● Huddersfield	H	D 3–3	Att: 3,003	Scorers: Bowery, Talbot². Chesterfield win 4–2 on penalties.
10th	● Bournemouth	A	W 1–2	Att: 5,896	Scorers: Talbot². Booked: Lee, Bowery.
17th	● Hereford	A	L 1–0	Att: 2,574	Booked: Page, Picken.
24th	● Burton	H	W 5–2	Att: 4,218	Scorers: Allott, Hall, Lester, McDermott, Talbot. Booked: Robertson, Allott.
31st	● Barnet	H	W 1–0	Att: 3,585	Scorers: Boden. Booked: Robertson.

NOVEMBER
7th	● Bournemouth	H	L 1–3	Att: 3,277	Scorers: Lester. Booked: Little. Dismissed: Little.
10th	● Carlisle	H	L 1–3	Att: 2,878	Scorers: Currie. Booked: Allott.
14th	● Rochdale	A	W 2–3	Att: 3,011	Scorers: Lester², Perkins. Booked: Picken.
21st	● Darlington	H	W 5–2	Att: 3,460	Scorers: Allott, Boden², Djilali, Page. Booked: Little.
24th	● Bury	A	L 2–1	Att: 2,504	Scorers: Small.

DECEMBER
2nd	● Crewe	H	L 2–3	Att: 3,267	Scorers: Lester, Talbot. Booked: Page, Breckin.
5th	● Aldershot	A	L 1–0	Att: 2,977	Booked: Page.
12th	● Cheltenham	H	W 1–0	Att: 3,145	Scorers: Lester.
26th	● Lincoln	A	L 2–1	Att: 4,604	Scorers: Boden. Booked: Niven.

JANUARY
2nd	● Shrewsbury	H	L 0–1	Att: 3,601	Booked: Somma.
16th	● Torquay	H	W 1–0	Att: 3,215	Scorers: Conlon. Booked: Niven, Boden.
23rd	● Northampton	A	D 0–0	Att: 4,513	Booked: Conlon.
26th	● Rotherham	H	L 0–1	Att: 4,951	Booked: Gray.
30th	● Morecambe	A	W 0–1	Att: 1,967	Scorers: Gritton. Booked: Artus, Gray. Dismissed: Artus.

FEBRUARY
6th	● Lincoln	H	W 2–1	Att: 3,573	Scorers: Conlon, Green. Booked: Boshell.
9th	● Port Vale	A	W 1–2	Att: 4,090	Scorers: Downes, Green. Booked: Goodall, Gray.
13th	● Bury	H	W 1–0	Att: 4,122	Scorers: Boden. Booked: Page.
20th	● Darlington	A	W 2–3	Att: 2,209	Scorers: Talbot, Whaley, Byrne OG. Booked: Rundle.
24th	● Crewe	A	W 0–1	Att: 3,278	Scorers: Talbot. Booked: Gray.
27th	● Aldershot	H	L 0–1	Att: 3,827	

MARCH
6th	● Cheltenham	A	W 0–1	Att: 3,006	Scorers: Conlon.
9th	● Notts County	A	L 1–0	Att: 7,341	Booked: Gray, Conlon.
13th	● Port Vale	H	L 0–5	Att: 4,138	Booked: Whing, Niven. Dismissed: Goodall.
20th	● Burton	A	D 2–2	Att: 3,696	Scorers: Boden, Demontagnac. Booked: Boden, Whing.
27th	● Hereford	H	L 1–2	Att: 3,593	Scorers: Conlon. Booked: Goodall, Picken.

APRIL
3rd	● Rochdale	H	W 2–0	Att: 4,471	Scorers: Conlon². Booked: Whing, Rundle.
5th	● Barnet	A	L 3–1	Att: 1,916	Scorers: Small. Booked: Demontagnac, Breckin, Picken.
10th	● Dag & Red	H	D 2–2	Att: 3,588	Scorers: Conlon, Demontagnac. Booked: Whing, Breckin.
13th	● Grimsby	A	D 2–2	Att: 5,648	Scorers: Lester². Booked: Lester, Page, Whing, Boshell, Allott.
17th	● Macclesfield	A	L 2–0	Att: 2,143	Booked: Demontagnac, Small, Boshell, Page.
24th	● Bradford	H	D 1–1	Att: 4,109	Scorers: Demontagnac. Booked: Demontagnac.

MAY
1st	● Accrington	A	L 2–0	Att: 2,475	Booked: Demontagnac.
8th	● Bournemouth	H	W 2–1	Att: 7,702	Scorers: Lester, Niven. Booked: Breckin, Allott, Page.

● Coca-Cola League 2/Play-Offs ● FA Cup ● Carling Cup ● Johnstone's Paint Trophy

actim

LEAGUE 2 GOALKEEPER STATS

Player	Appearances	Match starts	Completed matches	Sub appearances	Subbed off	Clean sheets	Yellow cards	Red cards
Mark Crossley	4	4	4	0	0	1	0	0
Tommy Lee	42	42	42	0	0	10	1	0

LEAGUE 2 OUTFIELD PLAYER STATS

Player	Appearances	Match starts	Completed matches	Substitute appearances	Subbed off	Goals scored	Yellow cards	Red cards
Mark Allott	45	45	42	0	3	2	4	0
Frankie Artus	3	2	1	1	0	0	1	1
Kevin Austin	19	14	12	5	2	0	1	0
Scott Boden	35	5	3	30	2	6	2	0
Danny Boshell	9	3	2	6	1	0	3	0
Jordan Bowery	10	2	2	8	0	0	1	0
Ian Breckin	42	41	40	1	1	0	5	0
Barry Conlon	19	15	5	4	10	7	2	0
Darren Currie	4	2	0	2	2	0	0	0
Ishmel Demontagnac	10	10	9	0	1	3	4	0
Kieran Djilali	8	8	7	0	1	1	1	0
Aaron Downes	7	7	6	0	1	1	0	0
Alan Goodall	17	17	14	0	2	0	2	1
Dan Gray	19	16	14	3	2	0	5	0
Dominic Green	10	10	7	0	3	2	0	0
Martin Gritton	9	2	0	7	2	1	0	0
Daniel Hall	7	5	2	2	3	1	0	0
Paul Harsley	3	0	0	3	0	0	0	0
Jack Lester	29	27	14	2	13	11	3	0
Terrell Lewis	1	0	0	1	0	0	0	0
Mark Little	12	12	12	0	0	0	1	0
Jamie Lowry	13	13	10	0	3	5	0	0
Gary Madine	4	2	0	2	2	0	0	0
Donal McDermott	15	13	9	2	4	5	1	0
Ian Morris	7	7	5	0	2	0	0	0
Derek Niven	39	28	13	11	15	2	3	0
Robert Page	39	38	37	1	1	1	11	0
David Perkins	13	11	9	2	2	1	0	0
Phil Picken	21	20	17	1	3	0	4	0
Gregor Robertson	10	8	8	2	0	0	4	0
Adam Rundle	16	12	7	4	5	0	2	0
Wade Small	27	24	10	3	14	4	2	0
Davide Somma	3	1	0	2	1	0	1	0
Drew Talbot	30	26	16	4	10	6	1	0
Simon Whaley	6	5	5	1	0	0	0	0
Andrew Whing	11	9	8	2	1	0	5	0

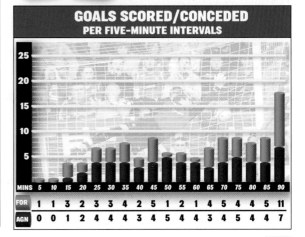

LEAGUE POSITION AT THE END OF EACH MONTH

AUG	SEP	OCT	NOV	DEC	JAN	FEB	MAR	APR	MAY
10	11	6	5	7	7	4	5	9	8

SEASON INFORMATION

Highest position: 2
Lowest position: 23
Average goals scored per game: 1.33
Average goals conceded per game: 1.35

LONGEST SEQUENCES

Wins	6	Undefeated home	9
(30/01/10–24/02/10)		(15/08/09–21/11/09)	
Losses	3	Undefeated away	6
(24/11/09–05/12/09)		(23/01/10–06/03/10)	
Draws	2	Without scoring	2
(on two occasions)		(on two occasions)	
Undefeated	6	Without conceding	2
(30/01/10–24/02/10)		(16/01/10–23/01/10)	
Without win	6	Scoring	7
(05/04/10–01/05/10)		(15/08/09–19/09/09)	

CARDS RECEIVED

69 **2**

EARLIEST STRIKE

WADE SMALL
(v Macclesfield) 3:12

LATEST STRIKE

DEREK NIVEN
(v Bournemouth) 95:16

GOALS SCORED/CONCEDED
PER FIVE-MINUTE INTERVALS

MINS	5	10	15	20	25	30	35	40	45	50	55	60	65	70	75	80	85	90
FOR	1	1	3	2	3		4	2	5	1	2	1	4	5	4	4	5	11
AGN	0	0	1	2	4	4	4	3	4	5	4	4	3	4	5	4	4	7

CREWE ALEXANDRA

VETERAN manager Dario Gradi took charge of Crewe for the third time as Alex finished their first season back in England's fourth tier in 18th place. The popular boss was appointed as caretaker manager when Gudjon Thordarson was sacked at the start of October following a run of five League defeats in which Alex had conceded 15 goals.

A leaky defence continued to be Crewe's downfall throughout the season – a fact perhaps best illustrated by their defeat at Morecambe in April, where Alex led 3–1 with three minutes to go but somehow lost 4–3.

Their inability to keep clean sheets also cost them dear in the knockout competitions, most notably as they surrendered a lead to lose 3–2 at non-League York in the FA Cup first round.

Alex conceded in excess of 70 goals in the League over the course of the campaign and they will need to strengthen at the back as a priority if they are to mount a promotion challenge in 2010/11.

CLUB SUMMARY

FORMED	1877
MANAGER	Dario Gradi
GROUND	Gresty Road
CAPACITY	10,046
NICKNAME	The Railwaymen
WEBSITE	www.crewealex.net

John Brayford
PLAYER OF THE SEASON

OVERALL
P	W	D	L	F	A	GD
49	15	10	24	72	82	-10

COCA-COLA FOOTBALL LEAGUE 2
Pos	P	W	D	L	F	A	GD	Pts
18	46	15	10	21	68	73	-5	55

HOME
Pos	P	W	D	L	F	A	GD	Pts
21	23	7	4	12	35	36	-1	25

AWAY
Pos	P	W	D	L	F	A	GD	Pts
8	23	8	6	9	33	37	-4	30

CUP PROGRESS DETAILS
Competition	Round reached	Knocked out by
FA Cup	R1	York
Carling Cup	R1	Blackpool
JP Trophy	R1	Stockport

BIGGEST WIN (ALL COMPS)
24/04/10 5–1 v Accrington

BIGGEST DEFEAT (ALL COMPS)
1–4 on 2 occasions

ATTENDANCE RECORD
High	Average	Low
6,943	4,075	3,272
v Port Vale (17/10/2009)		v Grimsby (09/03/2010)

RESULTS 2009/10

AUGUST
8th	● Dag & Red	H	L 1–2	Att: 3,936	Scorers: Moore.
11th	● Blackpool	H	L 1–2	Att: 2,991	Scorers: Zola. Booked: Ada.
15th	● Grimsby	A	W 0–4	Att: 5,007	Scorers: Jones, Moore, Zola[2]. Booked: Jones.
18th	● Darlington	A	W 0–1	Att: 1,821	Scorers: Zola.
22nd	● Hereford	H	W 1–0	Att: 3,731	Scorers: Jones.
29th	● Bournemouth	A	L 1–0	Att: 4,563	Booked: Jones, Verma.

SEPTEMBER
1st	● Stockport	H	L 1–4	Att: 2,331	Scorers: Zola. Booked: Walton.
5th	● Macclesfield	H	W 2–1	Att: 4,151	Scorers: Grant, Zola. Booked: Ada.
12th	● Shrewsbury	A	L 2–0	Att: 6,204	Booked: Miller.
19th	● Aldershot	H	L 1–2	Att: 3,661	Scorers: Miller. Booked: Worley, Walton, Zola.
25th	● Accrington	A	L 5–3	Att: 2,764	Scorers: Grant[2], Murphy.
29th	● Bury	H	L 2–3	Att: 3,534	Scorers: Worley, Zola. Booked: Murphy. Dismissed: Jones, Ada.

OCTOBER
3rd	● Rotherham	H	L 2–3	Att: 4,253	Scorers: Schumacher, Zola.
10th	● Bradford	A	W 2–3	Att: 11,757	Scorers: Schumacher, Zola[2]. Booked: Mitchel-King, Westwood, Bailey.
17th	● Port Vale	H	L 1–2	Att: 6,943	Scorers: Miller. Booked: Miller, Westwood.
24th	● Notts County	A	L 2–0	Att: 6,545	
31st	● Cheltenham	A	W 0–4	Att: 3,124	Scorers: Schumacher, Shelley, Zola[2].

NOVEMBER
7th	● York	A	L 3–2	Att: 3,070	Scorers: Grant, Zola.
14th	● Morecambe	H	L 1–2	Att: 4,113	Scorers: Schumacher.
21st	● Northampton	A	D 2–2	Att: 3,876	Scorers: Donaldson, Johnson OG.
24th	● Burton	H	W 2–1	Att: 3,446	Scorers: Donaldson, Grant.

DECEMBER
2nd	● Chesterfield	A	W 2–3	Att: 3,267	Scorers: Donaldson, Murphy, Westwood. Booked: Mitchel-King.
5th	● Lincoln	H	D 0–0	Att: 3,632	
12th	● Barnet	A	W 1–2	Att: 1,841	Scorers: Donaldson, Grant. Booked: Tootle, Westwood.
26th	● Rochdale	H	D 2–2	Att: 5,563	Scorers: Tootle, Westwood.
28th	● Macclesfield	A	L 4–1	Att: 3,449	Scorers: Zola. Booked: Westwood.

JANUARY
16th	● Dag & Red	A	L 2–0	Att: 1,951	
19th	● Hereford	A	D 1–1	Att: 1,367	Scorers: Donaldson. Booked: Miller.
23rd	● Darlington	H	W 3–0	Att: 3,717	Scorers: Grant, Zola[2]. Booked: Miller.
30th	● Bournemouth	H	L 1–2	Att: 3,741	Scorers: Murphy. Booked: Schumacher, Donaldson.

FEBRUARY
2nd	● Torquay	H	D 1–1	Att: 3,421	Scorers: Miller.
6th	● Rochdale	A	L 2–0	Att: 3,164	
12th	● Burton	A	W 1–2	Att: 2,985	Scorers: Donaldson, Miller. Booked: Worley.
20th	● Northampton	H	W 3–2	Att: 4,036	Scorers: Walton, Westwood[2]. Booked: Miller, Walton.
24th	● Chesterfield	H	L 0–1	Att: 3,278	
27th	● Lincoln City	A	D 1–1	Att: 3,110	Scorers: Miller.

MARCH
6th	● Barnet	H	D 2–2	Att: 3,551	Scorers: Donaldson[2].
9th	● Grimsby	H	W 4–2	Att: 3,272	Scorers: Donaldson, Grant, Moore, Westwood. Dismissed: Martin.
13th	● Torquay	A	D 1–1	Att: 2,507	Scorers: Donaldson.
20th	● Notts County	H	L 0–1	Att: 5,003	Dismissed: Westwood.
27th	● Port Vale	A	W 0–1	Att: 7,232	Scorers: Miller. Booked: Schumacher.

APRIL
2nd	● Morecambe	A	L 4–3	Att: 2,347	Scorers: Donaldson, Grant, Miller. Booked: Miller.
5th	● Cheltenham	H	L 1–2	Att: 3,488	Scorers: Martin.
10th	● Shrewsbury	A	L 0–3	Att: 4,283	Booked: Schumacher, Walton.
13th	● Bury	A	L 3–0	Att: 2,178	
17th	● Aldershot	A	D 1–1	Att: 2,966	Scorers: Donaldson. Booked: Zola.
24th	● Accrington	H	W 5–1	Att: 3,810	Scorers: Donaldson, Grant, Westwood, Zola[2]. Booked: Donaldson, Walton.

MAY
1st	● Rotherham	A	D 0–0	Att: 4,142	
8th	● Bradford	H	L 0–1	Att: 5,172	

● Coca-Cola League 2/Play-Offs ● FA Cup ● Carling Cup ● Johnstone's Paint Trophy

actim

LEAGUE 2 GOALKEEPER STATS

Player	Appearances	Match starts	Completed matches	Sub appearances	Subbed off	Clean sheets	Yellow cards	Red cards
Adam Bogdan	1	1	1	0	0	0	0	0
David Button	10	10	10	0	0	2	0	0
Steve Collis	1	1	1	0	0	0	0	0
Adam Legzdins	6	6	6	0	0	3	0	0
Steve Phillips	28	28	28	0	0	3	0	0

LEAGUE 2 OUTFIELD PLAYER STATS

Player	Appearances	Match starts	Completed matches	Substitute appearances	Subbed off	Goals scored	Yellow cards	Red cards
Patrick Ada	18	16	14	2	1	0	1	1
James Bailey	21	20	16	1	4	0	1	0
John Brayford	45	45	44	0	1	0	0	0
Harry Davis	1	0	0	1	0	0	0	0
Clayton Donaldson	37	28	21	9	7	13	2	0
Anthony Elding	10	4	2	6	2	0	0	0
Danny Gardner	2	0	0	2	0	0	0	0
Joel Grant	43	41	22	2	19	9	0	0
Billy Jones	11	10	9	1	0	2	2	1
Ajay Leitch-Smith	1	0	0	1	0	0	0	0
Carl Martin	6	1	0	5	1	1	0	1
Shaun Miller	33	22	11	11	11	7	6	0
Mat Mitchel-King	32	31	29	1	2	0	2	0
Byron Moore	32	13	9	19	4	3	0	0
Luke Murphy	32	24	15	8	9	3	1	0
Daniel O'Donnell	27	27	24	0	3	0	0	0
Steven Schumacher	32	27	18	5	9	4	3	0
Danny Shelley	19	7	3	12	4	1	0	0
Chris Stokes	2	2	1	0	1	0	0	0
Matt Tootle	28	26	22	2	4	1	1	0
Aman Verma	7	5	3	2	2	0	1	0
Simon Walton	31	26	20	5	6	1	4	0
Ashley Westwood	36	34	29	2	4	6	4	1
Harry Worley	23	21	20	2	1	1	2	0
Calvin Zola	34	30	22	4	8	15	2	0

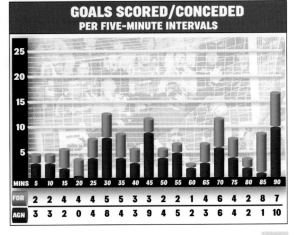

SEASON INFORMATION

Highest position: 2
Lowest position: 22
Average goals scored per game: 1.48
Average goals conceded per game: 1.59

LEAGUE POSITION AT THE END OF EACH MONTH

LONGEST SEQUENCES

Wins	3	Undefeated home	4
(15/08/09–22/08/09)		(24/11/09–23/01/10)	
Losses	5	Undefeated away	4
(12/09/09–03/10/09)		(on two occasions)	
Draws	2	Without scoring	2
(27/02/10–06/03/10)		(10/04/10–13/04/10)	
Undefeated	6	Without conceding	3
(21/11/09–26/12/09)		(15/08/09–22/08/09)	
Without win	5	Scoring	6
(on two occasions)		(19/09/09–17/10/09)	

CARDS RECEIVED

32   4

EARLIEST STRIKE

CLAYTON DONALDSON
(v Aldershot) 0:54

LATEST STRIKE

BYRON MOORE
(v Grimsby) 93:16

GOALS SCORED/CONCEDED
PER FIVE-MINUTE INTERVALS

MINS	5	10	15	20	25	30	35	40	45	50	55	60	65	70	75	80	85	90
FOR	2	2	4	4	5	5	3	2	2	1	4	6	4	2	8	7		
AGN	3	3	2	0	4	8	4	3	9	4	5	2	3	6	4	2	1	10

DAGENHAM & REDBRIDGE

THE DAGGERS completed a fairytale promotion with victory over Rotherham in the Coca-Cola League 2 play-off final at Wembley.

Manager John Still faced a tough task to lift his players at the start of the season and keep up his record of improving the club's League position every year since 2004, with the Daggers having missed out on the play-offs by a single point in 2008/09 and then lost key players Ben Strevens and Sam Saunders in the close season.

However, Still was again able to work wonders at Victoria Road.

Paul Benson's 22 goals proved decisive, but strike partner Josh Scott stole the show in the play-off semi-final when he scored four times in a memorable 6–0 defeat of Morecambe before Benson was again on target in the second leg to seal a 7–2 aggregate win.

Benson, Danny Green and Jon Nurse then struck at Wembley to help Still's side beat the Millers and seal a place in npower League 1.

CLUB SUMMARY

FORMED	1992
MANAGER	John Still
GROUND	Victoria Road
CAPACITY	6,078
NICKNAME	The Daggers
WEBSITE	www.daggers.co.uk

The New Football Pools PLAYER OF THE SEASON — Danny Green

OVERALL

P	W	D	L	F	A	GD
52	22	12	18	82	74	8

COCA-COLA FOOTBALL LEAGUE 2

Pos	P	W	D	L	F	A	GD	Pts
7	46	20	12	14	69	58	11	72

HOME

Pos	P	W	D	L	F	A	GD	Pts
4	23	15	2	6	46	27	19	47

AWAY

Pos	P	W	D	L	F	A	GD	Pts
14	23	5	10	8	23	31	-8	25

CUP PROGRESS DETAILS

Competition	Round reached	Knocked out by
FA Cup	R1	Huddersfield
Carling Cup	R1	Cardiff
JP Trophy	R1	Milton Keynes Dons

BIGGEST WIN (ALL COMPS)
16/05/10 6–0 v Morecambe

BIGGEST DEFEAT (ALL COMPS)
06/11/09 1–6 v Huddersfield

ATTENDANCE RECORD

High	Average	Low
3,721	2,089	1,683
v Macclesfield (20/03/2010)		v Shrewsbury (18/08/2009)

RESULTS 2009/10

AUGUST
8th	Crewe	A	W 1–2	Att: 3,936	Scorers: Benson, Nurse. Booked: Doe, Gain.
11th	Cardiff	A	L 3–1	Att: 5,545	Scorers: Scott.
15th	Torquay	H	W 5–3	Att: 1,824	Scorers: Gain, Green[2], Scott, Thomas.
18th	Shrewsbury	H	W 5–0	Att: 1,683	Scorers: Benson[4], Griffiths. Booked: Scott, Arber.
22nd	Notts County	A	L 3–0	Att: 6,562	
29th	Lincoln	H	W 3–0	Att: 1,810	Scorers: Green, Nurse[2].

SEPTEMBER
1st	Milton Keynes Dons	A	L 3–1	Att: 4,413	Scorers: Scott. Booked: Scott.
5th	Cheltenham	A	D 1–1	Att: 2,969	Scorers: Benson. Booked: Gain.
12th	Chesterfield	H	W 2–1	Att: 1,819	Scorers: Antwi, Benson. Booked: Benson, Doe.
19th	Burton	A	W 0–1	Att: 2,689	Scorers: Benson. Booked: Thurgood.
26th	Morecambe	H	D 1–1	Att: 1,770	Scorers: Scott. Booked: Arber, Roberts.
29th	Barnet	A	L 2–0	Att: 2,093	Booked: Doe.

OCTOBER
3rd	Hereford	A	D 1–1	Att: 2,253	Scorers: Thomas.
10th	Darlington	H	W 2–0	Att: 1,981	Scorers: Green, Scott. Booked: Griffiths.
17th	Bradford	H	W 2–1	Att: 2,446	Scorers: Benson, Ogogo.
24th	Macclesfield	A	D 2–2	Att: 1,574	Scorers: Arber, Thomas. Booked: Thurgood, Gain, Arber. Dismissed: Ogogo.
31st	Port Vale	H	D 1–1	Att: 2,003	Scorers: Scott. Booked: Gain.

NOVEMBER
6th	Huddersfield	A	L 6–1	Att: 5,858	Scorers: Benson.
14th	Accrington	A	W 0–1	Att: 1,538	Scorers: Arber. Booked: Benson, Doe.
21st	Rochdale	H	L 1–2	Att: 2,235	Scorers: Gain. Dismissed: Thomas.
24th	Bournemouth	A	D 0–0	Att: 6,881	Booked: Doe.

DECEMBER
1st	Aldershot	H	L 2–5	Att: 1,876	Scorers: Arber, Ofori-Twumasi.
5th	Grimsby	A	D 1–1	Att: 3,090	Scorers: Nurse. Booked: Green.
12th	Bury	H	W 3–1	Att: 1,915	Scorers: Benson[2], Ofori-Twumasi. Booked: Nurse, Green.
26th	Northampton	A	L 1–0	Att: 4,108	Booked: Day, Gain, Ofori-Twumasi.
28th	Cheltenham	H	L 0–2	Att: 2,028	

JANUARY
16th	Crewe	H	W 2–0	Att: 1,951	Scorers: Green, Scott.
23rd	Shrewsbury	A	L 2–1	Att: 4,812	Scorers: Benson. Booked: Ogogo, Gain, Vincelot. Dismissed: Doe.
26th	Notts County	H	L 0–3	Att: 1,916	Booked: Green.

FEBRUARY
6th	Northampton	H	L 0–1	Att: 2,206	Booked: Gain.
9th	Rotherham	A	L 2–0	Att: 2,604	Booked: Arber, Benson.
13th	Bournemouth	H	W 1–0	Att: 2,215	Scorers: Arber. Booked: Ogogo, Pack.
20th	Rochdale	A	L 3–1	Att: 3,153	Scorers: Scott. Booked: Gain, Green, Ogogo.
23rd	Aldershot	A	W 2–3	Att: 2,053	Scorers: Benson[2], Scott. Booked: McCrory, Thomas.
27th	Grimsby	H	W 2–0	Att: 2,190	Scorers: Green, Scott. Booked: Pack.

MARCH
2nd	Torquay	A	D 0–0	Att: 2,140	Booked: McCrory, Gain.
6th	Bury	A	D 0–0	Att: 2,886	Booked: Arber, Gain.
13th	Rotherham	H	L 0–1	Att: 1,862	
16th	Lincoln	A	D 1–1	Att: 2,457	Scorers: Nurse.
20th	Macclesfield	H	W 3–1	Att: 3,721	Scorers: Green[2], Ogogo. Booked: Gain.
27th	Bradford	A	D 3–3	Att: 11,064	Scorers: Nurse, Williams OG, Oliver OG. Booked: Ogogo.

APRIL
3rd	Accrington	H	W 3–1	Att: 2,031	Scorers: Benson, Gain, Green. Booked: Ogogo.
5th	Port Vale	A	L 3–1	Att: 4,572	Scorers: Pack. Booked: Benson, Gain, Vincelot.
10th	Chesterfield	A	D 2–2	Att: 3,588	Scorers: Green[2]. Booked: Green, McCrory, Roberts.
13th	Barnet	H	W 4–1	Att: 2,004	Scorers: Benson, Green[2], Scott. Booked: Nurse, Green, Gain, Benson.
17th	Burton	H	W 2–1	Att: 1,891	Scorers: Montgomery, Vincelot. Booked: Vincelot, Arber.
24th	Morecambe	A	L 1–0	Att: 2,100	Booked: Gain.

MAY
1st	Hereford	H	W 2–1	Att: 2,663	Scorers: Benson, Montgomery. Booked: Doe.
8th	Darlington	A	W 0–2	Att: 2,720	Scorers: Nurse, Scott. Booked: Arber, Green.
16th	Morecambe	H	W 6–0	Att: 4,566	Scorers: Benson[2], Scott[4]. Booked: Vincelot.
20th	Morecambe	A	L 2–1	Att: 4,972	Scorers: Benson. Booked: Ogogo, Gain. Agg: 2–7.
30th	Rotherham	N	W 3–2	Att: 32,054	Scorers: Benson, Green, Nurse. Booked: Green, Vincelot.

● Coca-Cola League 2/Play-offs ● FA Cup ● Carling Cup ● Johnstone's Paint Trophy

actim

LEAGUE 2 GOALKEEPER STATS

Player	Appearances	Match starts	Completed matches	Sub appearances	Subbed off	Clean sheets	Yellow cards	Red cards
Tony Roberts	46	46	46	0	0	12	2	0

LEAGUE 2 OUTFIELD PLAYER STATS

Player	Appearances	Match starts	Completed matches	Substitute appearances	Subbed off	Goals scored	Yellow cards	Red cards
Will Antwi	19	19	18	0	1	1	0	0
Mark Arber	41	41	40	0	1	4	7	0
Paul Benson	45	45	44	0	1	17	5	0
Billy Bingham	2	0	0	2	0	0	0	0
Joao Carlos	1	0	0	1	0	0	0	0
Darren Currie	16	5	3	11	2	0	0	0
Jamie Day	8	8	8	0	0	0	1	0
Harlee Dean	1	0	0	1	0	0	0	0
Scott Doe	42	40	33	2	6	0	6	1
Yoann Folly	7	5	4	2	1	0	0	0
Peter Gain	43	43	42	0	1	3	14	0
Danny Green	46	45	23	1	22	13	7	0
Scott Griffiths	13	13	12	0	1	1	1	0
Matthew Lockwood	4	4	4	0	0	0	0	0
Damien McCrory	20	20	20	0	0	0	3	0
Adam Miller	8	8	7	0	1	0	0	0
Graeme Montgomery	17	4	1	13	3	2	0	0
Jon Nurse	38	30	15	8	15	7	2	0
Seth Ofori-Twumasi	8	8	8	0	0	2	1	0
Abu Ogogo	30	27	26	3	0	2	5	1
Marlon Pack	17	17	12	0	5	1	2	0
Josh Scott	40	36	15	4	21	10	1	0
Daniel Spiller	10	7	5	3	2	0	0	0
Solomon Taiwo	4	4	4	0	0	0	0	0
Tommy Tejan-Sie	3	1	1	2	0	0	0	0
Wesley Thomas	23	3	0	20	3	3	1	1
Stuart Thurgood	17	17	16	0	1	0	2	0
Anwar Uddin	6	3	3	3	0	0	0	0
Romain Vincelot	9	7	7	0	1	0	3	0
Phil Walsh	9	0	0	9	0	0	0	0

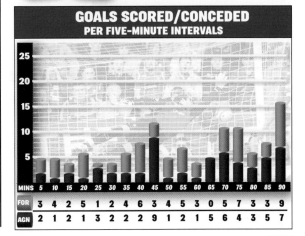

SEASON INFORMATION
Highest position: 1
Lowest position: 13
Average goals scored per game: 1.50
Average goals conceded per game: 1.26

LEAGUE POSITION AT THE END OF EACH MONTH

1	3	3	4	5	9	9	9	11	7

LONGEST SEQUENCES

Wins	3	Undefeated home	8
(08/08/09–18/08/09)		(15/08/09–31/10/09)	
Losses	4	Undefeated away	5
(23/01/10–09/02/10)		(on two occasions)	
Draws	2	Without scoring	3
(on two occasions)		(on two occasions)	
Undefeated	6	Without conceding	3
(03/10/09–14/11/09)		(27/02/10–06/03/10)	
Without win	4	Scoring	8
(on three occasions)		(16/03/10–17/04/10)	

CARDS RECEIVED
63 **3**

EARLIEST STRIKE
PETER GAIN
(v Rochdale) 2:46

LATEST STRIKE
GRAEME MONTGOMERY
(v Burton Albion) 94:28

GOALS SCORED/CONCEDED
PER FIVE-MINUTE INTERVALS

MINS	5	10	15	20	25	30	35	40	45	50	55	60	65	70	75	80	85	90
FOR	3	4	2	5	1	2	4	6	3	4	5	3	0	5	7	3	3	9
AGN	2	1	2	1	3	2	2	2	9	1	2	1	5	6	4	3	5	7

DARLINGTON'S 19-year stay in the Football League came to an end as they were relegated to the Conference.

It was a season of struggle for the Quakers, who had their fate confirmed on 13th April with six games still remaining, despite a 1–0 win at promotion-bound Rochdale.

Managers Colin Todd and Steve Staunton were both sacked during the course of a campaign in which the club won just eight of their 46 League matches. Former Barnsley boss Simon Davey was appointed in April and will now lead their bid to bounce straight back.

Darlington failed to win any of their first 12 League games, with Todd departing in September. Former Ireland coach Staunton arrived soon afterwards and drafted in plenty of his own players, but results failed to improve, leading the club to turn to Davey.

At the end of the campaign, the club announced that they had released 17 players as part of their rebuilding process.

CLUB SUMMARY

FORMED	1883
MANAGER	Simon Davey
GROUND	Darlington Arena
CAPACITY	25,000
NICKNAME	The Quakers
WEBSITE	www.darlington-fc.net

The New Football Pools PLAYER OF THE SEASON

Ian Miller

OVERALL
P	W	D	L	F	A	GD
50	9	6	35	36	93	-57

COCA-COLA FOOTBALL LEAGUE 2
Pos	P	W	D	L	F	A	GD	Pts
24	46	8	6	32	33	87	-54	30

HOME
Pos	P	W	D	L	F	A	GD	Pts
24	23	3	3	17	14	40	-26	12

AWAY
Pos	P	W	D	L	F	A	GD	Pts
22	23	5	3	15	19	47	-28	18

CUP PROGRESS DETAILS
Competition	Round reached	Knocked out by
FA Cup	R1	Barnet
Carling Cup	R1	Leeds
JP Trophy	R2	Leeds

BIGGEST WIN (ALL COMPS)
2–0 on 3 occasions

BIGGEST DEFEAT (ALL COMPS)
0–5 on 2 occasions

ATTENDANCE RECORD
HIGH	AVERAGE	Low
2,744	1,943	1,296
v Bradford (05/12/2009)		v Aldershot (23/03/2010)

RESULTS 2009/10

AUGUST
8th	Aldershot	A	L 3–1	Att: 2,866	Scorers: Dowson. Booked: Chandler.
10th	Leeds	H	L 0–1	Att: 4,487	Booked: Chandler.
15th	Bury	A	L 0–1	Att: 2,310	
18th	Crewe	H	L 0–1	Att: 1,821	
22nd	Port Vale	A	L 1–0	Att: 4,561	Booked: Chandler.
29th	Cheltenham	H	D 1–1	Att: 1,840	Scorers: Gall. Booked: Gall, Windass.

SEPTEMBER
1st	Lincoln	H	W 1–0	Att: 828	Scorers: Thorpe. Booked: Arnison, Thorpe.
5th	Lincoln	A	L 3–0	Att: 3,005	
11th	Accrington	A	L 2–1	Att: 3,228	Scorers: Gall.
19th	Bournemouth	H	L 0–2	Att: 1,999	Booked: Kane.
26th	Grimsby	A	D 1–1	Att: 4,014	Scorers: Main. Dismissed: Chandler.
29th	Rochdale	H	L 0–1	Att: 1,748	

OCTOBER
3rd	Macclesfield	H	L 0–1	Att: 1,763	Booked: Devitt.
6th	Leeds	A	L 2–1	Att: 8,429	Scorers: Convery. Dismissed: Liversedge.
10th	Dag & Red	A	L 2–0	Att: 1,981	Booked: Arnison.
17th	Shrewsbury	H	W 2–1	Att: 1,958	Scorers: Devitt, Thomas. Booked: Chandler, Devitt.
24th	Barnet	A	L 3–0	Att: 2,313	Booked: Collins, Davis.
31st	Hereford	A	L 2–1	Att: 2,238	Scorers: Collins.

NOVEMBER
7th	Barnet	A	L 3–1	Att: 1,654	Scorers: Diop. Booked: G Smith.
14th	Burton	H	W 1–0	Att: 2,404	Scorers: Main. Booked: Davis, Thomas, Chandler.
21st	Chesterfield	A	L 5–2	Att: 3,460	Scorers: Collins, Hogg. Booked: Giddings, Thomas, Davis.
24th	Morecambe	H	L 0–4	Att: 1,698	Booked: Barnes, Giddings, Collins.

DECEMBER
1st	Notts County	A	L 4–0	Att: 4,606	Booked: Thorpe, Hall.
5th	Bradford	H	L 0–1	Att: 2,744	Booked: Hall, Harsley, Hogg, Thorpe.
12th	Torquay	A	L 5–0	Att: 2,434	Booked: Collins, Harsley, G Smith.

JANUARY
19th	Rotherham	A	W 1–2	Att: 3,234	Scorers: Purcell, G Smith. Booked: Giddings, G Smith, White.
23rd	Crewe	A	L 3–0	Att: 3,717	Booked: Arnison.
26th	Northampton	H	L 1–2	Att: 1,694	Scorers: Purcell.

FEBRUARY
6th	Rotherham	H	W 2–0	Att: 2,231	Scorers: Purcell, Waite. Booked: White, Main, Madden.
9th	Lincoln	H	D 1–1	Att: 1,697	Scorers: Dempsey. Booked: Purcell, Waite.
13th	Morecambe	A	L 2–0	Att: 1,741	Booked: Miller, Byrne, Mulligan.
20th	Chesterfield	H	L 2–3	Att: 2,209	Scorers: Purcell[2]. Booked: Byrne, Mulligan, Groves, Madden.
27th	Bradford	A	L 1–0	Att: 11,532	Booked: Diop, Gray.

MARCH
2nd	Port Vale	H	L 1–3	Att: 1,582	Scorers: Purcell. Booked: White.
6th	Torquay	H	L 1–3	Att: 1,819	Scorers: Main. Booked: White.
9th	Bury	A	D 1–1	Att: 2,123	Scorers: Purcell. Booked: G Smith, Purcell, Dempsey, Diop.
13th	Northampton	A	L 2–0	Att: 4,755	
20th	Barnet	H	L 1–2	Att: 1,463	Scorers: Breen OG. Booked: Miller.
23rd	Aldershot	H	L 1–2	Att: 1,296	Scorers: Arnison. Booked: Waite, Gray, White.
27th	Shrewsbury	A	W 0–2	Att: 5,081	Scorers: Diop, Purcell. Booked: Arnison.

APRIL
3rd	Burton	A	W 1–2	Att: 2,779	Scorers: Gray, White. Booked: G Smith, Dempsey, Main.
5th	Hereford	H	L 0–1	Att: 2,131	
10th	Accrington	H	D 0–0	Att: 1,545	Booked: Giddings.
13th	Rochdale	A	W 0–1	Att: 5,371	Scorers: Mulligan. Booked: Miller, Redmond. Darlington are relegated.
17th	Bournemouth	A	L 2–0	Att: 6,464	Booked: G Smith, Mulligan, Dempsey, Miller.
20th	Cheltenham	H	D 3–3	Att: 2,836	Scorers: Diop, Purcell, Eastham OG.
24th	Grimsby	H	L 0–2	Att: 1,911	Booked: Diop.
27th	Notts County	H	L 0–5	Att: 2,112	

MAY
1st	Macclesfield	A	W 0–2	Att: 1,716	Scorers: Miller, M Smith.
8th	Dag & Red	H	L 0–2	Att: 2,720	Booked: White.

● Coca-Cola League 2/Play-Offs ● FA Cup ● Carling Cup ● Johnstone's Paint Trophy

LEAGUE 2 GOALKEEPER STATS

Player	Appearances	Match starts	Completed matches	Sub appearances	Subbed off	Clean sheets	Yellow cards	Red cards
Russell Hoult	6	6	6	0	0	0	0	0
Ashlee Jones	1	1	1	0	0	0	0	0
David Knight	7	7	7	0	0	0	0	0
Nick Liversedge	13	13	13	0	0	2	0	0
Shane Redmond	19	19	19	0	0	4	1	0

LEAGUE 2 OUTFIELD PLAYER STATS

Player	Appearances	Match starts	Completed matches	Substitute appearances	Subbed off	Goals scored	Yellow cards	Red cards
Paul Arnison	18	17	13	1	4	1	3	0
Rikki Bains	4	3	2	1	1	0	0	0
Corey Barnes	6	4	3	2	1	0	1	0
Moses Barnett	4	4	4	0	0	0	0	0
James Bennett	4	3	1	1	0	0	0	0
Mark Bower	13	12	9	1	3	0	0	0
Dan Burn	4	2	1	2	1	0	0	0
Richie Byrne	4	2	1	2	1	0	2	0
Jamie Chandler	14	12	11	2	0	0	4	1
Ross Chisholm	3	2	1	1	1	0	0	0
James Collins	7	5	5	2	0	2	3	0
Mark Convery	21	9	5	12	4	0	0	0
Jordan Cook	5	4	2	1	2	1	0	0
David Davis	5	5	3	0	2	0	3	0
Patrick Deane	10	0	0	10	0	0	0	0
Gary Dempsey	24	24	17	0	7	1	3	0
Jamie Devitt	6	5	4	1	1	1	2	0
Mor Diop	23	18	8	5	10	2	3	0
David Dowson	10	6	0	4	6	1	0	0
Stephen Foster	16	15	14	1	1	0	0	0
Kevin Gall	10	9	8	1	1	2	1	0
Stuart Giddings	22	22	20	0	2	0	4	0
Josh Gray	27	10	4	17	6	1	2	0
Danny Groves	16	8	4	8	4	0	1	0
Daniel Hall	3	3	3	0	0	0	2	0
Paul Harsley	3	3	3	0	0	0	1	0
Jonathan Hogg	5	5	5	0	0	1	1	0
Anthony Kane	4	4	3	0	1	0	1	0
Chris Lumsdon	2	2	1	0	0	0	0	0
Simon Madden	15	13	13	2	0	0	2	0
Curtis Main	26	12	4	14	8	3	2	0
Jordan Marshall	3	0	0	3	0	0	0	0
John McReady	4	3	3	1	0	0	0	0
Ian Miller	38	38	37	0	1	0	4	0
Andrew Milne	15	14	12	1	2	0	0	0
Chris Moore	11	8	4	3	4	0	0	0
Nathan Mulligan	16	10	1	6	9	1	3	0
Matt Plummer	8	5	5	3	0	0	0	0
Nathan Porritt	5	4	2	1	2	0	0	0
Tadgh Purcell	22	22	20	0	2	9	2	0
Jeff Smith	24	22	14	2	8	0	0	0
Gary Smith	34	32	23	2	9	1	5	0
Michael Smith	7	3	2	4	1	0	0	0
Simon Thomas	7	7	4	0	3	1	2	0
Lee Thorpe	8	7	3	1	4	0	2	0
Gareth Waite	14	14	13	0	1	1	2	0
Noel Whelan	3	2	0	1	3	0	0	0
Alan White	24	23	21	1	2	1	6	0
Dean Windass	6	3	1	3	2	0	1	0

AUG	SEP	OCT	NOV	DEC	JAN	FEB	MAR	APR	MAY

SEASON INFORMATION

Highest position: 21
Lowest position: 24
Average goals scored per game: 0.72
Average goals conceded per game: 1.89

LEAGUE POSITION AT THE END OF EACH MONTH

24	24	24	24	24	24	24	24	24	24

LONGEST SEQUENCES

Wins	2	Undefeated home	2
(27/03/10–03/04/10)		(on two occasions)	
Losses	5	Undefeated away	3
(on two occasions)		(27/03/10–13/04/10)	
Draws	–	Without scoring	4
(–)		(24/11/09–12/12/09)	
Undefeated	2	Without conceding	2
(on three occasions)		(10/04/10–13/04/10)	
Without win	12	Scoring	4
(08/08/09–10/10/09)		(20/03/10–03/04/10)	

CARDS RECEIVED

70 1

EARLIEST STRIKE

TADGH PURCELL
(v Cheltenham) 1:50

LATEST STRIKE

MOR DIOP
(v Shrewsbury) 86:55

GOALS SCORED/CONCEDED
PER FIVE-MINUTE INTERVALS

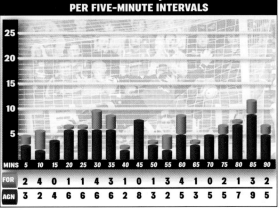

MINS	5	10	15	20	25	30	35	40	45	50	55	60	65	70	75	80	85	90
FOR	2	4	0	1	1	4	3	1	0	1	3	4	1	0	2	1	3	2
AGN	3	2	4	6	6	6	6	2	8	3	2	5	3	5	5	7	9	5

GRIMSBY TOWN

GRIMSBY'S 99-year stay in the Football League is over following the heartbreak of relegation to the Conference.

A 3–0 defeat at Burton on the final day of the season condemned them to the drop but, in truth, the Mariners had done well to take it that far. A club-record run of 25 League matches without a win between September and March had left them well adrift of safety but four victories in the last six matches prior to the trip to the Pirelli Stadium gave them a fighting chance of survival.

Manager Mike Newell was sacked at the start of September following six defeats in the opening seven games of the season. First-team coach Neil Woods took over later that month but was ultimately unable to complete a rescue act.

Despite such a disappointing end to Woods' first season in senior management, the Grimsby board opted to retain faith in the former Mariners striker, giving him the chance to help restore their League status.

CLUB SUMMARY

FORMED	1878
MANAGER	Neil Woods
GROUND	Blundell Park
CAPACITY	9,953
NICKNAME	The Mariners
WEBSITE	www.gtfc.co.uk

Peter Bore — PLAYER OF THE SEASON

OVERALL

P	W	D	L	F	A	GD
50	10	17	23	48	80	-32

COCA-COLA FOOTBALL LEAGUE 2

Pos	P	W	D	L	F	A	GD	Pts
23	46	9	17	20	45	71	-26	44

HOME

Pos	P	W	D	L	F	A	GD	Pts
23	23	4	9	10	25	36	-11	21

AWAY

Pos	P	W	D	L	F	A	GD	Pts
20	23	5	8	10	20	35	-15	23

CUP PROGRESS DETAILS

Competition	Round reached	Knocked out by
FA Cup	R1	Bath City
Carling Cup	R1	Tranmere
JP Trophy	QF	Leeds

BIGGEST WIN (ALL COMPS)
06/03/10 3–0 v Shrewsbury

BIGGEST DEFEAT (ALL COMPS)
0–4 on 3 occasions

ATTENDANCE RECORD

HIGH	AVERAGE	LOW
7,033	4,428	3,090
v Barnet (01/05/2010)		v Dag & Red (05/12/2009)

RESULTS 2009/10

AUGUST
8th	● Cheltenham	A	L 2–1	Att: 3,654	Scorers: Conlon. Booked: Conlon, Bennett.
11th	● Tranmere	A	L 4–0	Att: 3,527	Booked: Akpa Akpro.
15th	● Crewe	H	L 0–4	Att: 5,007	
18th	● Rotherham	H	L 1–2	Att: 4,156	Scorers: Sweeney. Booked: Sweeney, Hegarty.
22nd	● Bury	A	W 0–1	Att: 2,799	Scorers: Conlon. Booked: Sweeney.
29th	● Aldershot	H	L 1–2	Att: 3,757	Scorers: Conlon. Booked: Proudlock, Stockdale, Bennett. Dismissed: Conlon, Proudlock.

SEPTEMBER
5th	● Port Vale	A	L 4–0	Att: 5,056	Booked: Stockdale, Boshell. Dismissed: Boshell.
12th	● Hereford	H	W 1–0	Att: 3,173	Scorers: North. Booked: Widdowson.
19th	● Torquay	A	W 0–2	Att: 2,575	Scorers: Sweeney, Nicholson OG. Booked: Linwood.
26th	● Darlington	H	D 1–1	Att: 4,014	Scorers: Atkinson.
30th	● Chesterfield	A	L 3–2	Att: 3,329	Scorers: Proudlock, Sweeney. Booked: Sweeney, Proudlock, Colgan.

OCTOBER
3rd	● Barnet	A	L 3–0	Att: 2,497	Booked: Widdowson, Bennett, Wood, North. Dismissed: Conlon.
6th	● Hartlepool	A	W 0–2	Att: 1,675	Scorers: Proudlock, Sweeney. Booked: Boshell, Sweeney. Dismissed: Boshell.
10th	● Burton	H	L 1–2	Att: 4,002	Scorers: Jones. Booked: Wood, Widdowson, North.
17th	● Rochdale	H	L 0–2	Att: 3,754	Booked: Wood, Bore.
24th	● Bournemouth	A	L 3–1	Att: 5,270	Scorers: Linwood. Booked: Bore, Magennis.
30th	● Accrington	H	D 2–2	Att: 4,325	Scorers: Conlon, Forbes. Booked: Sweeney, Boshell, Akpa Akpro. Dismissed: Lancashire.

NOVEMBER
7th	● Bath City	H	L 0–2	Att: 2,103	Booked: Linwood, Shahin.
10th	● Leeds	A	L 3–1	Att: 10,430	Scorers: Sweeney.
14th	● Northampton	A	D 0–0	Att: 4,028	Booked: Leary, McCrory. Dismissed: Atkinson.
21st	● Lincoln	A	D 0–0	Att: 4,981	Booked: Bore, Leary, Sweeney.
24th	● Bradford	H	L 0–3	Att: 3,646	
28th	● Macclesfield	A	D 0–0	Att: 1,409	Booked: McCrory.

DECEMBER
5th	● Dag & Red	H	D 1–1	Att: 3,090	Scorers: Coulson. Booked: Lancashire, Sweeney.
12th	● Shrewsbury	A	D 0–0	Att: 4,850	Booked: Linwood, Featherstone, Akpa Akpro, Leary, McCrory.
18th	● Morecambe	H	D 1–1	Att: 3,119	Scorers: Sweeney.
28th	● Port Vale	H	L 1–2	Att: 4,401	Scorers: Conlon. Booked: Bore, Proudlock, Sweeney.

JANUARY
2nd	● Bury	H	D 1–1	Att: 3,463	Scorers: Akpa Akpro. Booked: Linwood.
16th	● Cheltenham	H	D 0–0	Att: 3,334	Booked: Linwood, Proudlock, Jarman, North.
23rd	● Rotherham	A	L 2–1	Att: 3,751	Scorers: Fletcher. Booked: Sweeney.
30th	● Aldershot	A	D 1–1	Att: 3,195	Scorers: Grant OG.

FEBRUARY
6th	● Notts County	H	L 0–1	Att: 4,452	Booked: T Wright.
13th	● Bradford	A	D 0–0	Att: 11,321	Booked: Atkinson, Leary.
17th	● Notts County	A	L 5,163	Att: 5,163	Scorers: Devitt. Booked: Proudlock, T Wright, Sweeney.
20th	● Lincoln	H	D 2–2	Att: 6,395	Scorers: Peacock². Booked: Devitt.
23rd	● Macclesfield	H	D 1–1	Att: 4,813	Scorers: Devitt. Booked: Devitt. Dismissed: Jarman.
27th	● Dag & Red	A	L 2–0	Att: 2,190	

MARCH
6th	● Shrewsbury	H	W 3–0	Att: 3,651	Scorers: Akpa Akpro, Sinclair². Booked: Lancashire, Akpa Akpro.
9th	● Crewe	A	L 4–2	Att: 3,272	Scorers: Akpa Akpro, Sinclair. Booked: Sweeney, Linwood, Sinclair.
13th	● Morecambe	A	D 1–1	Att: 1,882	Scorers: Coulson.
20th	● Bournemouth	H	W 3–2	Att: 4,428	Scorers: Chambers, Coulson, Devitt. Booked: Peacock.
27th	● Rochdale	A	L 4–1	Att: 4,724	Scorers: Chambers. Booked: Atkinson.

APRIL
2nd	● Northampton	H	L 1–2	Att: 6,482	Scorers: Coulson. Booked: Akpa Akpro. Dismissed: Lancashire.
5th	● Accrington	A	W 2–3	Att: 1,839	Scorers: Coulson, Devitt, Hudson.
10th	● Hereford	A	W 0–1	Att: 2,143	Scorers: Devitt. Booked: Hudson, Colgan, T Wright.
13th	● Chesterfield	H	D 2–2	Att: 5,648	Scorers: Akpa Akpro, T Wright. Booked: Hudson, Devitt.
17th	● Torquay	H	L 0–3	Att: 5,702	Booked: T Wright.
24th	● Darlington	A	W 0–2	Att: 1,911	Scorers: Akpa Akpro, Lancashire. Booked: Atkinson, Leary, Widdowson.

MAY
1st	● Barnet	H	W 2–0	Att: 7,033	Scorers: Atkinson, Hudson. Booked: Peacock, Leary, Devitt, Hudson.
8th	● Burton	A	L 3–0	Att: 5,510	Booked: Sinclair.

● Coca-Cola League 2/Play-Offs ● FA Cup ● Carling Cup ● Johnstone's Paint Trophy

LEAGUE 2 GOALKEEPER STATS

Player	Appearances	Match starts	Completed matches	Sub appearances	Subbed off	Clean sheets	Yellow cards	Red cards
Nick Colgan	35	35	35	0	0	10	2	0
Tommy Forecast	4	4	4	0	0	1	0	0
Josh Lillis	4	4	4	0	0	2	0	0
Mark Oxley	3	3	3	0	0	0	0	0

LEAGUE 2 OUTFIELD PLAYER STATS

Player	Appearances	Match starts	Completed matches	Substitute appearances	Subbed off	Goals scored	Yellow cards	Red cards
Jean-Louis Akpa Akpro	36	26	13	10	13	5	4	0
Robert Atkinson	37	37	34	0	2	2	3	1
Ryan Bennett	13	13	13	0	0	0	3	0
Peter Bore	40	37	35	3	2	0	4	0
Danny Boshell	6	5	4	1	0	0	2	1
Ashley Chambers	4	2	0	2	2	2	0	0
Jamie Clarke	13	9	6	4	3	0	0	0
Barry Conlon	16	7	4	9	1	5	1	2
Michael Coulson	29	28	17	1	11	5	0	0
Paris Cowan Hall	3	0	0	3	0	0	0	0
Jamie Devitt	15	15	9	0	6	5	4	0
Nicky Featherstone	8	7	4	1	3	0	1	0
Wes Fletcher	6	1	0	5	1	1	0	0
Adrian Forbes	13	8	1	5	7	1	0	0
Josh Fuller	5	2	1	3	1	0	0	0
Nick Hegarty	9	5	1	4	4	0	1	0
Matthew Heywood	1	1	1	0	0	0	0	0
Mark Hudson	16	11	11	5	0	2	3	0
Nathan Jarman	7	2	0	5	1	0	1	1
Chris Jones	7	6	3	1	3	1	0	0
Oliver Lancashire	25	24	20	1	2	1	2	2
Michael Leary	28	19	15	9	4	0	6	0
Paul Linwood	28	23	22	5	1	1	5	0
Josh Magennis	2	1	0	1	1	0	1	0
Damien McCrory	10	10	10	0	0	0	3	0
Arnaud Mendy	1	1	1	0	0	0	0	0
Danny North	17	9	6	8	3	1	3	0
Lee Peacock	17	14	10	3	4	2	2	0
Adam Proudlock	27	14	2	13	11	1	5	1
Jammal Shahin	5	4	1	1	3	0	0	0
Dean Sinclair	16	16	10	0	6	3	2	0
Jude Stirling	4	2	1	2	1	0	0	0
Robbie Stockdale	8	8	8	0	0	0	2	0
Peter Sweeney	40	36	31	4	5	4	10	0
Joe Widdowson	38	36	35	2	1	0	4	0
Bradley Wood	8	7	7	1	0	0	3	0
Ben Wright	2	1	0	1	1	0	0	0
Tommy Wright	14	13	2	1	11	1	4	0

| AUG | SEP | OCT | NOV | DEC | JAN | FEB | MAR | APR | MAY |

SEASON INFORMATION

Highest position: 11
Lowest position: 24
Average goals scored per game: 0.98
Average goals conceded per game: 1.54

LEAGUE POSITION AT THE END OF EACH MONTH

22 21 23 23 23 23 23 23 23 23

LONGEST SEQUENCES

Wins	2	Undefeated home	4
(on three occasions)		(20/02/10–20/03/10)	
Losses	5	Undefeated away	4
(30/09/09–24/10/09)		(14/11/09–12/12/09)	
Draws	4	Without scoring	4
(on two occasions)		(14/11/09–28/11/09)	
Undefeated	4	Without conceding	2
(on two occasions)		(on three occasions)	
Without win	25	Scoring	9
(26/09/09–27/02/10)		(06/03/10–13/04/10)	

CARDS RECEIVED

81   8

EARLIEST STRIKE

CHRIS JONES
(v Burton Albion) 3:50

LATEST STRIKE

BARRY CONLON
(v Accrington Stanley) 94:44

GOALS SCORED/CONCEDED
PER FIVE-MINUTE INTERVALS

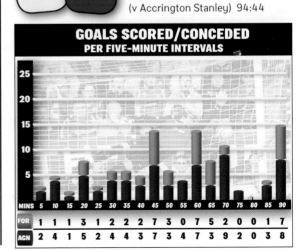

MINS	5	10	15	20	25	30	35	40	45	50	55	60	65	70	75	80	85	90
FOR	1	1	3	1	2	2	2	7	3	0	7	5	2	0	0	1	7	
AGN	2	4	1	5	2	4	4	3	7	3	4	7	3	9	2	0	3	8

HEREFORD UNITED

HEREFORD successfully avoided a relegation battle, although they may look back on their campaign with some disappointment.

The Bulls had hoped to challenge for an immediate return to the third tier following their relegation in the previous season, but in the end they finished 16th on the back of seven wins from their last 10 games.

Boss John Trewick left Edgar Street in March, with chairman Graham Turner stepping back into the dugout for a second spell as manager until the end of the 2009/10 season.

Having assured their safety with that fine end-of-season run, which included a 2–1 win over promoted Rochdale, Turner now faces the challenge of finding a successor to take over the helm, while his own 15-year involvement with the Bulls could be set to come to an end this summer as his shares in the club are up for sale.

Before Christmas, the Bulls reached the regional semi-finals of the Johnstone's Paint Trophy, but suffered a 4–0 defeat to MK Dons.

CLUB SUMMARY

FORMED	1924
MANAGER	Graham Turner
GROUND	Edgar Street
CAPACITY	8,843
NICKNAME	The Bulls
WEBSITE	www.herefordunited.net

The New Football Pools PLAYER OF THE SEASON — Adam Bartlett

OVERALL
P	W	D	L	F	A	GD
54	19	11	24	62	77	-15

COCA-COLA FOOTBALL LEAGUE 2
Pos	P	W	D	L	F	A	GD	Pts
16	46	17	8	21	54	65	-11	59

HOME
Pos	P	W	D	L	F	A	GD	Pts
8	23	12	4	7	32	25	7	40

AWAY
Pos	P	W	D	L	F	A	GD	Pts
21	23	5	4	14	22	40	-18	19

CUP PROGRESS DETAILS
Competition	Round reached	Knocked out by
FA Cup	R2	Colchester
Carling Cup	R2	Portsmouth
JP Trophy	SF	Milton Keynes Dons

BIGGEST WIN (ALL COMPS)
08/05/10 3–0 v Rotherham

BIGGEST DEFEAT (ALL COMPS)
27/02/10 0–5 v Notts County

ATTENDANCE RECORD
High	Average	Low
3,280	2,139	1,208
v Cheltenham (15/08/2009)		v Morecambe (16/03/2010)

RESULTS 2009/10

AUGUST
8th	● Morecambe	A	D 2–2	Att: 2,119	Scorers: Pugh2.
11th	● Charlton	H	W 1–0	Att: 2,017	Scorers: Godsmark. AET – Score after 90 mins 0–0.
15th	● Cheltenham	H	D 1–1	Att: 3,280	Scorers: Godsmark.
18th	● Bury	H	L 1–3	Att: 2,321	Scorers: Constantine. Booked: D Valentine, Southam, Dennehy. Dismissed: D Valentine.
22nd	● Crewe	A	L 1–0	Att: 3,731	Booked: Plummer, C Jones.
25th	● Portsmouth	A	L 4–1	Att: 6,645	Scorers: Plummer.
29th	● Port Vale	H	D 2–2	Att: 2,434	Scorers: Plummer, Pugh.

SEPTEMBER
1st	● Bristol Rovers	H	D 0–0	Att: 970	Booked: J Tolley. Hereford win 4–2 on penalties.
5th	● Aldershot	A	D 2–2	Att: 3,094	Scorers: Plummer2. Booked: J Tolley, Southam.
12th	● Grimsby	A	L 1–0	Att: 3,173	Booked: D Jones, Rose, Gwynne.
19th	● Accrington	H	W 2–0	Att: 2,013	Scorers: King, R Valentine.
26th	● Rochdale	A	L 4–1	Att: 2,620	Scorers: Pugh. Booked: D Jones, Green, Gwynne. Dismissed: Green.
29th	● Bournemouth	H	W 2–1	Att: 2,104	Scorers: Pugh2. Booked: Dennehy.

OCTOBER
3rd	● Dag & Red	H	D 1–1	Att: 2,253	Scorers: Walker.
6th	● Aldershot	H	D 2–2	Att: 897	Scorers: Manset, Walker. Hereford win 4–3 on penalties.
10th	● Rotherham	A	D 1–1	Att: 3,452	Scorers: McCallum.
17th	● Chesterfield	H	W 1–0	Att: 2,574	Scorers: R Valentine. Booked: King, R Valentine, Gwynne.
24th	● Bradford	A	L 1–0	Att: 11,107	Booked: R Valentine, Gwynne, Sonko.
31st	● Darlington	H	W 2–1	Att: 2,238	Scorers: D Jones, Lowe.

NOVEMBER
7th	● Sutton Utd	H	W 2–0	Att: 1,713	Scorers: Manset, R Valentine. Dismissed: Manset.
10th	● Leyton Orient	A	D 1–1	Att: 1,282	Scorers: Constantine. Booked: Marshall. Hereford win 3–2 on penalties.
14th	● Barnet	A	D 0–0	Att: 1,965	
21st	● Burton	A	L 3–2	Att: 2,796	Scorers: Constantine2.
24th	● Shrewsbury	H	W 2–1	Att: 2,913	Scorers: McCallum, R Valentine. Booked: D Jones, R Valentine.
28th	● Colchester	H	L 0–1	Att: 2,225	

DECEMBER
1st	● Northampton	A	W 1–3	Att: 3,524	Scorers: D Jones, King, Manset. Booked: Godsmark.
5th	● Notts County	H	L 0–2	Att: 2,727	
12th	● Macclesfield	A	L 3–1	Att: 1,406	Scorers: Constantine.
15th	● Milton Keynes Dons	H	L 1–4	Att: 1,367	Scorers: Constantine.
26th	● Torquay	A	L 1–0	Att: 3,792	Booked: Mutch, R Valentine.

JANUARY
19th	● Crewe	H	D 1–1	Att: 1,367	Scorers: Constantine. Booked: Lunt, D Jones.
23rd	● Bury	A	L 1–0	Att: 2,797	
30th	● Port Vale	A	L 2–0	Att: 4,686	Booked: R Valentine, Gwynne. Dismissed: R Valentine.

FEBRUARY
2nd	● Lincoln	H	W 2–0	Att: 1,429	Scorers: McCallum2. Booked: Lunt, Gwynne.
6th	● Torquay	H	W 1–0	Att: 2,123	Scorers: McCallum. Booked: D Jones.
13th	● Shrewsbury	A	L 3–1	Att: 6,098	Scorers: Constantine. Booked: Lunt.
16th	● Aldershot	H	W 2–0	Att: 1,576	Scorers: McCallum, Blackburn OG. Booked: Downing, R Valentine.
20th	● Burton	H	L 3–4	Att: 2,253	Scorers: Lunt, McQuilken, Pugh. Booked: R Valentine.
23rd	● Northampton	A	L 0–2	Att: 1,266	Booked: R Valentine.
27th	● Notts County	A	L 5–0	Att: 6,036	Booked: Preston. Dismissed: Adamson, Downing.

MARCH
2nd	● Cheltenham	A	W 0–1	Att: 3,273	Scorers: Green. Booked: McQuilken, McCallum, Pugh. Dismissed: McQuilken.
6th	● Macclesfield	H	L 0–2	Att: 1,919	
12th	● Lincoln	A	L 3–1	Att: 6,012	Scorers: Pugh. Booked: R Valentine.
16th	● Morecambe	H	L 0–1	Att: 1,208	
20th	● Bradford	H	W 2–0	Att: 1,926	Scorers: Jervis, Manset.
27th	● Chesterfield	A	W 1–2	Att: 3,593	Scorers: Jervis, Pugh. Booked: Jervis.

APRIL
3rd	● Barnet	H	W 2–1	Att: 2,146	Scorers: McQuilken, Breen OG.
5th	● Darlington	A	W 0–1	Att: 2,131	Scorers: Pugh. Booked: Jervis.
10th	● Grimsby	H	L 0–1	Att: 2,143	Booked: Manset, R Valentine.
13th	● Bournemouth	A	L 2–1	Att: 6,128	Scorers: Pugh. Booked: McCallum.
17th	● Accrington	A	W 1–2	Att: 1,420	Scorers: McCallum2. Booked: D Jones, Manset.
24th	● Rochdale	H	W 2–1	Att: 1,975	Scorers: King, R Valentine. Booked: Green.

MAY
1st	● Dag & Red	A	L 2–1	Att: 2,663	Scorers: Pugh. Booked: R Valentine.
8th	● Rotherham	H	W 3–0	Att: 3,005	Scorers: D Jones, Manset, Pugh. Booked: Manset.

● Coca-Cola League 2/Play-Offs ● FA Cup ● Carling Cup ● Johnstone's Paint Trophy

actim

LEAGUE 2 GOALKEEPER STATS

Player	Appearances	Match starts	Completed matches	Sub appearances	Subbed off	Clean sheets	Yellow cards	Red cards
Chris Adamson	1	1	0	0	0	0	0	1
Adam Bartlett	46	45	45	1	0	10	0	0

LEAGUE 2 OUTFIELD PLAYER STATS

Player	Appearances	Match starts	Completed matches	Substitute appearances	Subbed off	Goals scored	Yellow cards	Red cards
Astrit Ajdarevic	1	0	0	1	0	0	0	0
Daniel Blanchett	13	13	12	0	1	0	0	0
Leon Constantine	35	25	15	10	10	6	0	0
Darren Dennehy	7	6	5	1	1	0	2	0
Matt Done	20	7	2	13	5	0	0	0
Paul Downing	6	6	5	0	0	0	1	1
Lateef Elford-Alliyu	1	1	0	0	1	0	0	0
Jonny Godsmark	8	7	2	1	5	1	1	0
Ryan Green	31	31	28	0	2	1	2	1
Sam Gwynne	26	21	17	5	4	0	6	0
Marlon Jackson	5	2	0	3	2	2	0	0
Jake Jervis	7	5	2	2	3	2	2	0
Darren Jones	40	39	39	1	0	3	6	0
Lee Jones	1	1	1	0	0	0	1	0
Craig Jones	1	1	1	0	0	0	1	0
Craig King	26	22	13	4	9	3	1	0
Keith Lowe	19	17	15	2	2	1	0	0
Kenny Lunt	42	42	42	0	0	1	3	0
Mathieu Manset	29	16	7	13	9	3	3	0
Mark Marshall	8	8	7	0	1	0	0	0
Gavin McCallum	27	20	13	7	7	8	2	0
James McQuilken	22	20	18	2	1	2	1	1
Lee Morris	12	5	2	7	3	0	0	0
Jordon Mutch	3	3	3	0	0	1	0	0
Tristan Plummer	5	4	3	1	1	3	1	0
Daniel Preston	4	4	4	0	0	0	1	0
Marc Pugh	40	39	36	1	3	13	1	0
Richard Rose	25	22	20	3	2	0	1	0
Edrissa Sonko	10	5	4	5	1	0	1	0
Glen Southam	6	5	2	1	3	0	2	0
Christopher Tolley	1	0	0	1	0	0	0	0
Jamie Tolley	9	6	4	3	2	0	1	0
Ryan Valentine	38	38	35	0	2	4	11	1
David Valentine	2	2	0	0	1	0	1	1
James Walker	6	6	4	0	2	1	0	0
Nathaniel Wedderburn	3	3	2	0	1	0	0	0
Tyler Weir	3	3	2	0	0	0	0	0
Lewis Young	6	5	1	1	4	0	0	0

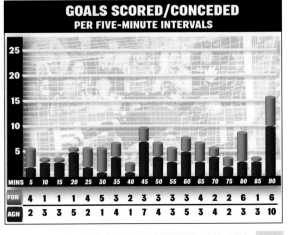

LEAGUE POSITION AT THE END OF EACH MONTH

AUG	SEP	OCT	NOV	DEC	JAN	FEB	MAR	APR	MAY
20	18	17	16	20	21	18	17	16	16

SEASON INFORMATION
Highest position: 6
Lowest position: 23
Average goals scored per game: 1.17
Average goals conceded per game: 1.41

LONGEST SEQUENCES

Wins	4	Undefeated home	7
(20/03/10–05/04/10)		(29/08/09–24/11/09)	
Losses	3	Undefeated away	2
(on three occasions)		(27/03/10–05/04/10)	
Draws	2	Without scoring	2
(on three occasions)		(on two occasions)	
Undefeated	4	Without conceding	2
(on two occasions)		(02/02/10–06/02/10)	
Without win	7	Scoring	6
(08/08/09–12/09/09)		(19/09/09–17/10/09)	

CARDS RECEIVED

52   **6**

EARLIEST STRIKE
TRISTAN PLUMMER
(v Aldershot) 3:15

LATEST STRIKE
MARC PUGH
(v Bournemouth) 93:25

GOALS SCORED/CONCEDED
PER FIVE-MINUTE INTERVALS

MINS	5	10	15	20	25	30	35	40	45	50	55	60	65	70	75	80	85	90
FOR	4	1	1	1	4	5	3	2	3	3	3	4	2	2	6	1	6
AGN	2	3	3	5	2	1	4	1	7	4	3	5	3	4	2	3	3	10

LINCOLN CITY

CHRIS SUTTON made a solid start to his managerial career at Lincoln. The appointment of the former Blackburn and Norwich striker as Peter Jackson's successor in September raised some eyebrows due to his lack of experience, but Sutton achieved his remit of keeping the club in the Football League.

Working within a tight budget, good loan signings proved to be the key to Sutton's success. Defenders Adam Watts and Nathan Baker and midfielder Chris Herd were particularly astute signings, although it was Davide Somma's goals – nine in all – that really kept Lincoln clear of the relegation zone.

Sutton also guided the club to the FA Cup third round for the first time in a decade, where they were beaten by Barclays Premier League side Bolton.

The manager has promised new faces in time for the coming season but there will also be changes in the boardroom, with Steff Wright due to step down as chairman.

CLUB SUMMARY

FORMED	1884
MANAGER	Chris Sutton
GROUND	Sincil Bank
CAPACITY	10,147
NICKNAME	The Imps
WEBSITE	www.redimps.com

The New **Football Pools** PLAYER OF THE SEASON — Robert Burch

OVERALL
P	W	D	L	F	A	GD
51	15	11	25	48	73	-25

COCA-COLA FOOTBALL LEAGUE 2
Pos	P	W	D	L	F	A	GD	Pts
20	46	13	11	22	42	65	-23	50

HOME
Pos	P	W	D	L	F	A	GD	Pts
15	23	9	7	7	25	26	-1	34

AWAY
Pos	P	W	D	L	F	A	GD	Pts
23	23	4	4	15	17	39	-22	16

CUP PROGRESS DETAILS
Competition	Round reached	Knocked out by
FA Cup	R3	Bolton
Carling Cup	R1	Barnsley
JP Trophy	R1	Darlington

BIGGEST WIN (ALL COMPS)
05/09/09 3–0 v Darlington

BIGGEST DEFEAT (ALL COMPS)
0–4 on 2 occasions

ATTENDANCE RECORD
High	Average	Low
6,012	3,670	2,457
v Hereford (12/03/2010)		v Dag & Red (16/03/2010)

RESULTS 2009/10

AUGUST
8th	● Barnet	H	W 1-0	Att: 3,753	Scorers: Kovacs. Booked: Oakes, Swaibu, Kovacs, Butcher.
11th	● Barnsley	H	L 0-1	Att: 3,635	
15th	● Accrington	A	L 1-0	Att: 1,498	Booked: Hughton, Howe, Heath, Kerr, Kovacs, Hutchinson.
18th	● Bradford	A	W 0-2	Att: 11,242	Scorers: Fagan, Howe. Booked: Kerr, Fagan, Brown, S Clarke.
22nd	● Burton	H	L 0-2	Att: 3,590	Booked: S Clarke.
29th	● Dag & Red	A	L 3-0	Att: 1,810	Booked: Kovacs, Kerr.

SEPTEMBER
1st	● Darlington	A	L 1-0	Att: 828	Booked: S Clarke, Hone.
5th	● Darlington	H	W 3-0	Att: 3,005	Scorers: Fagan, Howe[2]. Booked: Hutchinson.
12th	● Bournemouth	A	L 3-1	Att: 5,385	Scorers: Fagan.
19th	● Shrewsbury	H	L 0-2	Att: 3,234	Booked: Swaibu, Kerr.
26th	● Bury	A	L 2-0	Att: 2,554	Booked: Kovacs, Hughton.
29th	● Notts County	H	L 0-3	Att: 5,527	Booked: Swaibu, Howe.

OCTOBER
3rd	● Aldershot	H	W 1-0	Att: 4,131	Scorers: Torres. Booked: Kovacs.
10th	● Macclesfield	A	W 0-1	Att: 2,006	Scorers: Howe. Booked: Oakes.
17th	● Northampton	A	L 1-0	Att: 4,341	Booked: Pulis, Torres, S Clarke, Hone, Kovacs, Howe.
24th	● Torquay	H	D 0-0	Att: 3,604	Booked: Baker.
31st	● Morecambe	A	L 3-1	Att: 1,701	Scorers: Howe. Booked: J Clarke. Dismissed: Lichaj.

NOVEMBER
7th	● AFC Telford	A	W 1-3	Att: 2,809	Scorers: Brown, J Clarke, Torres. Booked: Howe.
14th	● Cheltenham	H	D 1-1	Att: 3,008	Scorers: J Clarke. Booked: Pulis. Dismissed: Brown, Pearce.
21st	● Grimsby	H	D 0-0	Att: 4,981	
24th	● Rotherham	A	L 2-0	Att: 2,901	
28th	● Northwich	A	W 1-3	Att: 3,544	Scorers: J Clarke[2], Fagan. Booked: Herd, Smith.

DECEMBER
1st	● Port Vale	H	L 1-2	Att: 2,569	Scorers: Martin OG.
5th	● Crewe	A	D 0-0	Att: 3,632	Booked: Herd.
12th	● Rochdale	H	L 1-3	Att: 3,293	Scorers: Herd. Booked: Lichaj, Hughton, Herd.
26th	● Chesterfield	H	W 2-1	Att: 4,604	Scorers: Facey, Hughton. Booked: Baker, Heath, Watts, Burch.

JANUARY
2nd	● Bolton	A	L 4-0	Att: 11,193	Booked: Kerr.
16th	● Barnet	A	W 1-2	Att: 1,810	Scorers: Hughton, John-Lewis. Booked: Herd.
23rd	● Bradford	H	W 2-1	Att: 3,803	Scorers: Gilmour, Herd.
27th	● Burton	A	L 1-0	Att: 2,109	Booked: Watts, Kerr, Green, Hughton.

FEBRUARY
2nd	● Hereford	A	L 2-0	Att: 1,429	Booked: Swaibu.
6th	● Chesterfield	A	L 2-1	Att: 3,573	Scorers: Swaibu. Booked: Herd, Hughton, Kerr.
9th	● Darlington	A	D 1-1	Att: 1,697	Scorers: Hone. Booked: Kerr, Herd, Hone.
13th	● Rotherham	H	L 1-2	Att: 4,152	Scorers: Lennon. Dismissed: Swaibu.
16th	● Accrington	H	W 2-1	Att: 2,779	Scorers: Lennon, Kempson OG.
20th	● Grimsby	A	D 2-2	Att: 6,595	Scorers: Somma, Herd. Booked: Herd, Hughton, Kerr, Broughton.
23rd	● Port Vale	A	L 4-0	Att: 3,231	Booked: Gilmour, Herd, Pearce.
27th	● Crewe	H	D 1-1	Att: 3,110	Scorers: Somma. Booked: Hughton.

MARCH
6th	● Rochdale	A	D 1-1	Att: 3,453	Scorers: Herd. Booked: Broughton, Somma, Lennon, Burch.
12th	● Hereford	H	W 3-1	Att: 6,012	Scorers: Saunders[2], Somma.
16th	● Dag & Red	H	D 1-1	Att: 2,457	Scorers: Somma.
20th	● Torquay	A	W 2-3	Att: 2,547	Scorers: Hughton, Somma[2]. Booked: Hughton.
27th	● Northampton	H	D 1-1	Att: 3,964	Scorers: Saunders. Booked: Herd, Saunders.

APRIL
3rd	● Cheltenham	A	L 1-0	Att: 3,708	Booked: Kerr.
5th	● Morecambe	H	L 1-3	Att: 3,109	Scorers: Hughton. Booked: Hughton.
10th	● Bournemouth	H	W 2-1	Att: 3,040	Scorers: Somma[2]. Booked: Hughton.
13th	● Notts County	A	L 3-1	Att: 7,501	Scorers: Lennon. Booked: Saunders, Lennon, Somma, Kerr. Dismissed: Swaibu.
17th	● Shrewsbury	A	L 1-0	Att: 4,932	
24th	● Bury	H	W 1-0	Att: 3,403	Scorers: Somma. Booked: Kerr.

MAY
1st	● Aldershot	A	L 3-1	Att: 4,506	Scorers: Somma. Booked: Saunders, Hughton, Keltie.
8th	● Macclesfield	H	D 0-0	Att: 3,291	Booked: Keltie. Dismissed: Somma.

● Coca-Cola League 2/Play-Offs ● FA Cup ● Carling Cup ● Johnstone's Paint Trophy

actim

COCA-COLA LEAGUE 2

LEAGUE 2 GOALKEEPER STATS

Player	Appearances	Match starts	Completed matches	Sub appearances	Subbed off	Clean sheets	Yellow cards	Red cards
Robert Burch	46	46	46	0	0	10	2	0

LEAGUE 2 OUTFIELD PLAYER STATS

Player	Appearances	Match starts	Completed matches	Substitute appearances	Subbed off	Goals scored	Yellow cards	Red cards
Nathan Adams	2	0	0	2	0	0	0	0
Joe Anderson	23	23	22	0	1	0	0	0
Nathan Baker	18	17	12	1	5	0	2	0
Lee Bennett	1	0	0	1	0	0	0	0
Drewe Broughton	7	7	4	0	3	0	2	0
Aaron Brown	17	14	13	3	0	0	1	1
Richard Butcher	15	10	9	5	1	0	1	0
Jamie Clarke	20	14	5	6	9	1	1	0
Shane Clarke	29	21	17	8	4	0	3	0
Luca Coleman-Carr	1	0	0	1	0	0	0	0
Paul Connor	15	8	4	7	4	0	0	0
Delroy Facey	10	9	4	1	5	1	0	0
Chris Fagan	13	10	3	3	7	3	1	0
Brian Gilmour	16	14	6	2	8	2	1	0
Michael Gordon	5	4	3	1	1	0	0	0
Paul Green	15	13	13	2	0	0	1	0
Joe Heath	4	3	2	1	1	0	2	0
Chris Herd	20	20	14	0	6	4	8	0
Danny Hone	17	16	12	1	4	1	2	0
Rene Howe	17	14	13	3	1	5	3	0
Cian Hughton	41	41	38	0	3	4	11	0
Andrew Hutchinson	10	0	0	10	0	0	2	0
Lenell John-Lewis	24	7	3	17	4	1	0	0
Clark Keltie	11	9	7	2	2	0	2	0
Scott Kerr	39	36	29	3	7	0	11	0
Janos Kovacs	14	14	14	0	0	1	6	0
Steven Lennon	19	15	13	4	2	3	2	0
Eric Lichaj	6	6	5	0	0	0	1	1
Stefan Oakes	16	11	1	5	10	0	2	0
Ian Pearce	10	5	3	5	1	0	1	1
Anthony Pulis	7	7	4	0	3	0	2	0
Matthew Saunders	18	17	15	1	2	3	3	0
Khano Smith	5	4	1	1	3	0	0	0
Davide Somma	14	14	13	0	0	9	2	0
David Stephens	3	3	3	0	0	0	0	0
Moses Swaibu	34	29	26	5	1	1	4	2
Sergio Torres	8	7	4	1	3	1	1	0
Michael Uwezu	2	0	0	2	0	0	0	0
Adam Watts	18	18	15	0	3	0	2	0

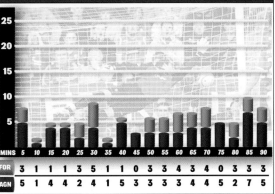

| AUG | SEP | OCT | NOV | DEC | JAN | FEB | MAR | APR | MAY |

SEASON INFORMATION
Highest position: 4
Lowest position: 22
Average goals scored per game: 0.91
Average goals conceded per game: 1.41

| 17 | 22 | 19 | 21 | 22 | 19 | 19 | 18 | 20 | 20 |

LEAGUE POSITION AT THE END OF EACH MONTH

LONGEST SEQUENCES

Wins	3	Undefeated home	5
(26/12/09–23/01/10)		(16/02/10–27/03/10)	
Losses	4	Undefeated away	2
(12/09/09–29/09/09)		(on three occasions)	
Draws	2	Without scoring	3
(on two occasions)		(19/09/09–29/09/09)	
Undefeated	6	Without conceding	2
(27/02/10–27/03/10)		(03/10/09–10/10/09)	
Without win	9	Scoring	6
(17/10/09–12/12/09)		(27/02/10–27/03/10)	

CARDS RECEIVED

82 **6**

EARLIEST STRIKE
IAN PEARCE
(v Port Vale) 0:20

LATEST STRIKE
DANNY HONE
(v Darlington) 96:13

GOALS SCORED/CONCEDED
PER FIVE-MINUTE INTERVALS

MINS	5	10	15	20	25	30	35	40	45	50	55	60	65	70	75	80	85	90
FOR	3	1	1	1	3	5	1	1	0	3	3	4	3	4	0	3	3	3
AGN	5	1	4	4	2	4	1	5	3	3	3	3	4	4	5	2	7	5

OFFICIAL FOOTBALL YEARBOOK OF THE ENGLISH & SCOTTISH LEAGUES 2010-2011   **349**

FOOTBALL was put into perspective for everyone at Macclesfield following the shock death of manager Keith Alexander. The former Lincoln boss, a hugely popular figure in the game, was only 53 when he passed away on 3rd March.

Events on the pitch understandably took a back seat in light of that tragedy, but it was a fitting tribute to Alexander that the Silkmen won their battle against relegation with ease. Gary Simpson, formerly Alexander's trusted right-hand man, was appointed as the club's new manager and guided them to safety with room to spare.

His challenge in 2010/11 will be to take the club forward with a relatively small playing budget as they aim to push towards the top half of the table.

Colin Daniel, Carl Tremarco, Ross Draper and Emile Sinclair have all agreed new contracts to give Simpson a solid foundation on which to build at Moss Rose.

CLUB SUMMARY

FORMED	1874
MANAGER	Gary Simpson
GROUND	Moss Rose
CAPACITY	6,335
NICKNAME	The Silkmen
WEBSITE	www.mtfc.co.uk

The New
Football Pools
PLAYER OF THE SEASON

Lee Bell

OVERALL
P	W	D	L	F	A	GD
49	12	18	19	51	65	-14

COCA-COLA FOOTBALL LEAGUE 2
Pos	P	W	D	L	F	A	GD	Pts
19	46	12	18	16	49	58	-9	54

HOME
Pos	P	W	D	L	F	A	GD	Pts
20	23	7	8	8	27	28	-1	29

AWAY
Pos	P	W	D	L	F	A	GD	Pts
15	23	5	10	8	22	30	-8	25

CUP PROGRESS DETAILS
Competition	Round reached	Knocked out by
FA Cup	R1	Milton Keynes Dons
Carling Cup	R1	Leicester
JP Trophy	R2	Carlisle

BIGGEST WIN (ALL COMPS)
28/12/09 4–1 v Crewe

BIGGEST DEFEAT (ALL COMPS)
15/08/09 0–4 v Notts County

ATTENDANCE RECORD
HIGH	AVERAGE	Low
3,449	1,929	1,035
v Crewe (28/12/2009)		v Northampton (20/01/2010)

RESULTS 2009/10

AUGUST
8th	● Northampton	A	D 0–0	Att: 4,064	**Booked:** Rooney.
12th	● Leicester	H	L 0–2	Att: 2,197	**Booked:** Brisley, Draper.
15th	● Notts County	H	L 0–4	Att: 2,785	
18th	● Port Vale	H	W 2–0	Att: 3,433	**Scorers:** Bencherif, Tipton. **Booked:** Bencherif, Daniel, Tremarco.
22nd	● Morecambe	A	D 2–2	Att: 1,757	**Scorers:** Draper, Tipton. **Booked:** Wright.
29th	● Rotherham	H	L 1–3	Att: 1,972	**Scorers:** Tipton. **Booked:** Brisley, Tremarco.

SEPTEMBER
5th	● Crewe	A	L 2–1	Att: 4,151	**Scorers:** Sappleton. **Booked:** Bencherif, Draper.
12th	● Barnet	H	D 1–1	Att: 1,125	**Scorers:** Sappleton. **Booked:** Tremarco, Sappleton.
19th	● Chesterfield	A	L 4–1	Att: 3,138	**Scorers:** Bencherif. **Booked:** Brown.
26th	● Torquay	H	W 2–1	Att: 1,745	**Scorers:** Bencherif². **Booked:** Daniel.
29th	● Burton	A	D 1–1	Att: 2,332	**Scorers:** Sinclair. **Booked:** Bencherif.

OCTOBER
3rd	● Darlington	A	W 0–1	Att: 1,763	**Scorers:** Smith OG. **Booked:** Bell.
6th	● Carlisle	A	L 4–2	Att: 1,753	**Scorers:** Brisley, Rooney.
10th	● Lincoln	H	L 0–1	Att: 2,006	**Booked:** Bell, Brisley, Bencherif.
16th	● Cheltenham	A	W 1–2	Att: 2,930	**Scorers:** Rooney, Sappleton.
24th	● Dag & Red	H	D 2–2	Att: 1,574	**Scorers:** Sappleton, Tipton. **Booked:** Sappleton, Tipton, Tremarco, Sinclair. **Dismissed:** Tipton.
31st	● Bradford	H	D 2–2	Att: 2,526	**Scorers:** Bencherif, Daniel. **Booked:** Tremarco.

NOVEMBER
7th	● Milton Keynes Dons	A	L 1–0	Att: 4,868	
14th	● Aldershot	A	D 0–0	Att: 2,646	
21st	● Bournemouth	H	L 1–2	Att: 1,413	**Scorers:** Brisley. **Booked:** Tremarco.
28th	● Grimsby	H	D 0–0	Att: 1,409	

DECEMBER
5th	● Rochdale	A	L 3–0	Att: 3,003	**Booked:** Tremarco. **Dismissed:** Brisley.
12th	● Hereford	H	W 3–1	Att: 1,406	**Scorers:** Sinclair², Wright. **Booked:** Bolland.
26th	● Shrewsbury	A	D 2–2	Att: 5,942	**Scorers:** Brown, Daniel. **Booked:** Draper, Morgan, Hessey.
28th	● Crewe	H	W 4–1	Att: 3,449	**Scorers:** Bolland, Daniel, Sappleton, Wright. **Booked:** Draper, Sappleton.

JANUARY
20th	● Northampton	H	L 0–2	Att: 1,035	**Booked:** Bell.
23rd	● Port Vale	A	D 0–0	Att: 5,167	**Booked:** Brown.
26th	● Morecambe	H	D 2–2	Att: 1,046	**Scorers:** Lindfield, Sappleton. **Booked:** Tremarco, Brown.

FEBRUARY
6th	● Shrewsbury	H	L 0–1	Att: 2,058	**Booked:** Daniel.
9th	● Bury	A	L 2–1	Att: 2,169	**Scorers:** Butcher. **Booked:** Bell, Daniel.
13th	● Accrington	H	D 0–0	Att: 1,729	
20th	● Bournemouth	A	D 1–1	Att: 4,549	**Scorers:** Brown. **Booked:** Sappleton, Draper, Brain, Bell.
23rd	● Grimsby	A	D 1–1	Att: 4,813	**Scorers:** Butcher. **Booked:** Sappleton, Tipton, Hessey.
27th	● Rochdale	H	L 0–1	Att: 2,462	**Booked:** Draper.

MARCH
2nd	● Notts County	A	L 1–0	Att: 4,672	**Booked:** Draper.
6th	● Hereford	A	W 0–2	Att: 1,919	**Scorers:** Sappleton, Sinclair. **Booked:** Bell.
9th	● Accrington	A	D 1–1	Att: 1,210	**Scorers:** Tipton. **Booked:** Brisley, Morgan.
13th	● Bury	H	W 2–0	Att: 2,740	**Scorers:** Lindfield, Wright. **Booked:** Draper.
20th	● Dag & Red	A	L 3–1	Att: 3,721	**Scorers:** Bell. **Booked:** Brisley.
23rd	● Rotherham	A	L 3–1	Att: 2,873	**Scorers:** Wright.
27th	● Cheltenham	H	W 1–0	Att: 1,572	**Scorers:** Wright.

APRIL
3rd	● Aldershot	H	D 1–1	Att: 1,428	**Scorers:** Brown. **Booked:** Mukendi.
5th	● Bradford	A	W 1–2	Att: 11,395	**Scorers:** Sinclair, Wright.
10th	● Barnet	A	W 1–2	Att: 1,433	**Scorers:** Bell, Sinclair. **Booked:** Sinclair.
13th	● Burton	H	D 1–1	Att: 1,588	**Scorers:** Brown.
17th	● Chesterfield	H	W 2–0	Att: 2,143	**Scorers:** Mukendi, Sinclair. **Booked:** Brain.
24th	● Torquay	A	L 1–0	Att: 2,570	

MAY
1st	● Darlington	H	L 0–2	Att: 1,716	
8th	● Lincoln	A	D 0–0	Att: 3,291	**Booked:** Rooney, Tremarco, Hessey.

● Coca-Cola League 2/Play-Offs ● FA Cup ● Carling Cup ● Johnstone's Paint Trophy

actim

Coca-Cola LEAGUE 2

LEAGUE 2 GOALKEEPER STATS

Player	Appearances	Match starts	Completed matches	Sub appearances	Subbed off	Clean sheets	Yellow cards	Red cards
Jon Brain	41	41	41	0	0	11	2	0
Jose Veiga	5	5	5	0	0	1	0	0

LEAGUE 2 OUTFIELD PLAYER STATS

Player	Appearances	Match starts	Completed matches	Substitute appearances	Subbed off	Goals scored	Yellow cards	Red cards
Lee Bell	42	37	29	5	8	2	6	0
Hamza Bencherif	19	19	17	0	2	5	4	0
Paul Bolland	27	17	13	10	4	1	1	0
Shaun Brisley	33	29	24	4	4	1	4	1
Nathaniel Brown	38	37	35	1	2	4	3	0
Richard Butcher	8	8	7	0	1	2	0	0
Colin Daniel	38	34	23	4	11	3	4	0
Ross Draper	29	28	24	1	4	1	7	0
Sean Hessey	27	27	25	0	2	0	3	0
Craig Lindfield	18	12	4	6	8	2	0	0
Matthew Lowe	10	7	6	3	1	0	0	0
Greg Mills	1	0	0	1	0	1	0	0
Paul Morgan	36	35	33	1	2	0	2	0
Vinny Mukendi	9	8	6	1	2	1	1	0
Izak Reid	37	34	34	3	0	0	0	0
John Rooney	25	14	7	11	7	1	2	0
Reneil Sappleton	24	18	6	6	12	7	5	0
Emile Sinclair	42	33	13	9	20	7	2	0
Michael Thomas	4	0	0	4	0	0	0	0
Mathew Tipton	31	11	1	20	9	5	2	1
Carl Tremarco	29	27	25	2	2	0	9	0
Kyle Wilson	4	0	0	4	0	0	0	0
Ben Wright	39	25	16	14	9	6	1	0

SEASON INFORMATION
Highest position: 8
Lowest position: 23
Average goals scored per game: 1.07
Average goals conceded per game: 1.26

LEAGUE POSITION AT THE END OF EACH MONTH

AUG	SEP	OCT	NOV	DEC	JAN	FEB	MAR	APR	MAY
19	20	18	19	17	17	21	20	19	19

LONGEST SEQUENCES

Wins	2	Undefeated home	5
(05/04/10–10/04/10)		(13/03/10–17/04/10)	
Losses	2	Undefeated away	4
(on five occasions)		(29/09/09–14/11/09)	
Draws	3	Without scoring	2
(on two occasions)		(on four occasions)	
Undefeated	6	Without conceding	–
(27/03/10–17/04/10)		(–)	
Without win	10	Scoring	11
(20/01/10–02/03/10)		(06/03/10–17/04/10)	

CARDS RECEIVED

58 2

EARLIEST STRIKE
NATHANIEL BROWN
(v Burton Albion) 2:20

LATEST STRIKE
RENEIL SAPPLETON
(v Crewe) 91:25

GOALS SCORED/CONCEDED
PER FIVE-MINUTE INTERVALS

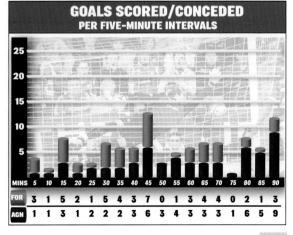

MINS	5	10	15	20	25	30	35	40	45	50	55	60	65	70	75	80	85	90
FOR	3	1	5	2	1	5	4	3	7	0	1	3	4	4	0	2	1	3
AGN	1	1	3	1	2	2	2	3	6	3	4	3	3	3	1	6	5	9

MORECAMBE

MORECAMBE can look back on the 2009/10 season with immense pride after finishing fourth in Coca-Cola League 2 – their highest-ever placing.

The Shrimps only entered the Football League in 2007 and have now become a respected force under the guidance of manager Sammy McIlroy.

The former Macclesfield boss took his side into the play-offs, only to see them suffer a 6–0 defeat in the first leg of the semi-final against Dagenham & Redbridge. However, the spirit and desire that McIlroy has instilled into his players was evident in the second leg. The Shrimps won 2–1 to end their 89-year stay at Christie Park on a high ahead of the move to a new era at their new home – the Globe Arena.

McIlroy said: 'We let ourselves down in the first leg at Dagenham but we got some pride back at Christie Park and we're looking forward to maintaining the progress and playing at the Globe Arena next season.'

CLUB SUMMARY

FORMED	1920
MANAGER	Sammy McIlroy
GROUND	Globe Arena
CAPACITY	6,400
NICKNAME	The Shrimps
WEBSITE	www.morecambefc.com

The New Football Pools PLAYER OF THE SEASON — Barry Roche

OVERALL

P	W	D	L	F	A	GD
52	21	15	16	80	81	-1

COCA-COLA FOOTBALL LEAGUE 2

Pos	P	W	D	L	F	A	GD	Pts
4	46	20	13	13	73	64	9	73

HOME

Pos	P	W	D	L	F	A	GD	Pts
3	23	14	6	3	44	24	20	48

AWAY

Pos	P	W	D	L	F	A	GD	Pts
16	23	6	7	10	29	40	-11	25

CUP PROGRESS DETAILS

Competition	Round reached	Knocked out by
FA Cup	R1	Carlisle
Carling Cup	R1	Preston
JP Trophy	R1	Carlisle

BIGGEST WIN (ALL COMPS)
12/12/09 5–0 v Bournemouth

BIGGEST DEFEAT (ALL COMPS)
16/05/10 0–6 v Dag & Red

ATTENDANCE RECORD

High	Average	Low
5,268	2,262	1,537
v Aldershot (08/05/2010)		v Burton (16/02/2010)

RESULTS 2009/10

AUGUST
8th	● Hereford	H	D 2–2	Att: 2,119	Scorers: Drummond, Stanley. Booked: Adams, Stanley.
11th	● Preston	A	L 5–1	Att: 5,407	Scorers: Twiss. Booked: Moss.
15th	● Burton Albion	A	L 5–2	Att: 2,742	Scorers: Craney, Jevons. Dismissed: Duffy.
18th	● Barnet	A	L 2–0	Att: 1,298	Booked: Wilson, Moss.
22nd	● Macclesfield	H	D 2–2	Att: 1,757	Scorers: Artell, Twiss. Booked: Roche.
29th	● Chesterfield	A	D 1–1	Att: 3,210	Scorers: Jevons. Booked: Panther.

SEPTEMBER
1st	● Carlisle	H	D 2–2	Att: 2,016	Scorers: Curtis, Hunter. Carlisle win 4–2 on penalties.
4th	● Rochdale	H	D 3–3	Att: 2,367	Scorers: Craney, Jevons2.
12th	● Rotherham	A	D 0–0	Att: 3,172	Booked: Bentley.
19th	● Notts County	H	W 2–1	Att: 3,335	Scorers: Bentley, Mullin. Booked: Bentley, Hunter.
26th	● Dag & Red	A	D 1–1	Att: 1,770	Scorers: Jevons. Booked: Hunter, Craney.
29th	● Bradford	H	D 0–0	Att: 3,116	Booked: Curtis, Wilson.

OCTOBER
3rd	● Shrewsbury	H	D 1–1	Att: 2,105	Scorers: Drummond. Booked: Stanley, Parrish. Dismissed: Adams.
10th	● Aldershot	A	L 4–1	Att: 2,974	Scorers: Mullin.
17th	● Torquay	A	D 2–2	Att: 2,614	Scorers: Duffy, Mullin. Booked: Adams, Jevons, Craney, Duffy.
24th	● Northampton	H	L 2–4	Att: 2,041	Scorers: Drummond, Jevons.
31st	● Lincoln City	H	W 3–1	Att: 1,701	Scorers: Drummond, Jevons, Mullin. Booked: Wilson, Adams, Curtis.

NOVEMBER
7th	● Carlisle	A	D 2–2	Att: 4,181	Scorers: Duffy, Jevons. Booked: Wainwright, Wilson, Hunter. Dismissed: Drummond.
14th	● Crewe	A	W 1–2	Att: 4,113	Scorers: Bentley, Jevons. Booked: Hunter.
17th	● Carlisle	H	L 0–1	Att: 3,307	Booked: Twiss, Mullin, Stanley.
21st	● Cheltenham	H	W 1–0	Att: 1,567	Scorers: Wilson.
24th	● Darlington	A	W 0–4	Att: 1,698	Scorers: Curtis, Drummond, Jevons, Wilson. Booked: Haining.

DECEMBER
1st	● Bury	H	W 3–0	Att: 1,875	Scorers: Jevons2, Futcher OG.
5th	● Port Vale	A	W 0–2	Att: 4,679	Scorers: Jevons, Mullin.
12th	● Bournemouth	H	W 5–0	Att: 2,034	Scorers: Drummond, Duffy, Jevons, Stanley, Wilson. Booked: Duffy.
18th	● Grimsby	H	D 1–1	Att: 3,119	Scorers: Mullin.
26th	● Accrington Stanley	H	L 1–2	Att: 3,478	Scorers: Hunter. Booked: Artell.
28th	● Rochdale	A	L 4–1	Att: 4,309	Scorers: Curtis. Booked: Hunter, Wilson.

JANUARY
23rd	● Barnet	H	W 2–1	Att: 1,558	Scorers: Drummond, Duffy. Booked: Duffy.
26th	● Macclesfield	A	D 2–2	Att: 1,046	Scorers: Drummond, Haining. Booked: Wilson.
30th	● Chesterfield	H	L 0–1	Att: 1,967	Booked: Wilson.

FEBRUARY
6th	● Accrington Stanley	A	L 3–2	Att: 2,372	Scorers: Artell2. Booked: Wilson, Twiss.
13th	● Darlington	H	W 2–0	Att: 1,741	Scorers: Jevons, Mullin. Booked: Wainwright, Wilson.
16th	● Burton Albion	H	W 3–2	Att: 1,537	Scorers: Drummond, Jevons, Mullin. Booked: Stanley.
20th	● Cheltenham	A	L 2–0	Att: 2,806	Booked: Artell.
23rd	● Bury	A	D 0–0	Att: 2,222	Booked: Panther, Wilson, Mullin.
27th	● Port Vale	H	W 1–0	Att: 2,064	Scorers: Jevons.

MARCH
6th	● Bournemouth	A	L 1–0	Att: 5,103	Booked: Parrish.
13th	● Grimsby	H	D 1–1	Att: 1,882	Scorers: Mullin.
16th	● Hereford	A	W 0–1	Att: 1,208	Scorers: Bentley.
20th	● Northampton	A	L 2–0	Att: 4,210	Booked: Parrish, Curtis.
27th	● Torquay	H	W 2–0	Att: 1,734	Scorers: Mullin, Stanley. Booked: Roche.

APRIL
2nd	● Crewe	H	W 4–3	Att: 2,347	Scorers: Artell, Curtis, Jevons, Mullin. Booked: Hackney, Duffy, Wilson. Dismissed: Parrish.
5th	● Lincoln City	A	W 1–3	Att: 3,109	Scorers: Curtis, Mullin, Stanley. Booked: Jevons, Moss, Artell.
10th	● Rotherham	H	W 2–0	Att: 2,337	Scorers: Hackney, Jevons.
13th	● Bradford	A	L 2–0	Att: 11,027	
17th	● Notts County	A	L 4–1	Att: 8,500	Scorers: Artell. Booked: Stanley, Drummond, Artell.
24th	● Dag & Red	H	W 1–0	Att: 2,100	Scorers: Moss. Booked: Moss.

MAY
1st	● Shrewsbury	A	W 2–3	Att: 5,340	Scorers: Artell2, Duffy. Booked: Artell, Haining.
8th	● Aldershot	H	W 1–0	Att: 5,268	Scorers: Hunter. Booked: Haining, Bentley.
16th	● Dag & Red	A	L 6–0	Att: 4,566	
20th	● Dag & Red	H	W 2–1	Att: 4,972	Scorers: Artell, Duffy. Booked: Wilson. Agg: 2–7.

● Coca-Cola League 2/Play-offs ● FA Cup ● Carling Cup ● Johnstone's Paint Trophy

LEAGUE 2 GOALKEEPER STATS

Player	Appearances	Match starts	Completed matches	Sub appearances	Subbed off	Clean sheets	Yellow cards	Red cards
Scott Davies	1	1	1	0	0	0	0	0
Barry Roche	42	42	42	0	0	15	2	0
Benjamin Smith	3	3	3	0	0	0	0	0

LEAGUE 2 OUTFIELD PLAYER STATS

Player	Appearances	Match starts	Completed matches	Substitute appearances	Subbed off	Goals scored	Yellow cards	Red cards
Danny Adams	17	15	13	2	1	0	3	1
David Artell	37	33	30	4	3	7	5	0
Jim Bentley	28	27	25	1	2	3	3	0
Ian Craney	16	16	10	0	6	2	2	0
Wayne Curtis	35	9	7	26	2	4	3	0
Stewart Drummond	43	41	39	2	2	9	1	0
Mark Duffy	35	24	13	11	10	4	4	1
Simon Hackney	8	8	2	0	6	1	1	0
Will Haining	32	28	24	4	4	1	3	0
Garry Hunter	31	26	18	5	8	2	4	0
Phil Jevons	40	40	20	0	20	18	2	0
Fraser McLachlan	1	1	0	0	1	0	0	0
Henry McStay	2	0	0	2	0	0	0	0
Darren Moss	16	13	12	3	1	1	3	0
Paul Mullin	38	36	24	2	12	12	1	0
Diarmuid O'Carroll	1	1	1	0	0	0	0	0
Emmanuel Panther	18	13	10	5	3	0	2	0
Andy Parrish	35	34	31	1	2	0	3	1
Craig Stanley	40	31	28	9	3	4	4	0
Aaron Taylor	3	0	0	3	0	0	0	0
Michael Twiss	26	18	13	8	5	1	1	0
Neil Wainwright	17	5	2	12	3	0	1	0
Laurence Wilson	41	41	35	0	6	3	10	0

AUG	SEP	OCT	NOV	DEC	JAN	FEB	MAR	APR	MAY

LEAGUE POSITION AT THE END OF EACH MONTH

21	19	20	13	10	11	11	10	8	4

SEASON INFORMATION
Highest position: 4
Lowest position: 23
Average goals scored per game: 1.59
Average goals conceded per game: 1.39

LONGEST SEQUENCES

Wins	7		Undefeated home		9
(31/10/09–12/12/09)			(13/02/10–08/05/10)		
Losses	2		Undefeated away		5
(on four occasions)			(17/10/09–18/12/09)		
Draws	4		Without scoring		2
(22/08/09–12/09/09)			(20/02/10–23/02/10)		
Undefeated	8		Without conceding		5
(on two occasions)			(21/11/09–12/12/09)		
Without win	7		Scoring		16
(08/08/09–12/09/09)			(03/10/09–26/01/10)		

CARDS RECEIVED
58   **3**

EARLIEST STRIKE
PHIL JEVONS
(v Port Vale) 0:25

LATEST STRIKE
DAVID ARTELL
(v Crewe) 94:22

GOALS SCORED/CONCEDED
PER FIVE-MINUTE INTERVALS

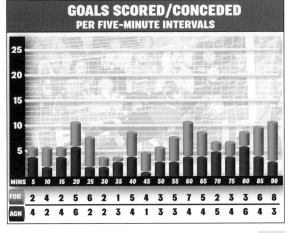

MINS	5	10	15	20	25	30	35	40	45	50	55	60	65	70	75	80	85	90
FOR	2	4	2	5	6	2	1	5	4	3	5	7	5	2	3	3	6	8
AGN	4	2	4	6	2	2	3	4	1	3	3	4	4	5	4	6	4	3

NORTHAMPTON TOWN

NORTHAMPTON'S hopes of making an immediate return to the third tier were dashed as they finished in mid-table.

Prior to the start of the campaign, chairman David Cardoza had gone public with his belief that the Cobblers could win promotion from Coca-Cola League 2 at the first attempt, but it was to prove a disappointing 2009/10 season at Sixfields.

Several key players had departed over the summer, and manager Stuart Gray was faced with the job of rebuilding. However, he was sacked in September following a poor start.

Assistant Ian Sampson took charge and, having taken time to settle in to his new role, he led his side on a remarkable run which saw them lose just twice in 21 games.

At that stage they looked capable of mounting a serious play-off challenge, but top scorer Adebayo Akinfenwa suffered an ankle injury over Easter and the Cobblers finished five points down on the top seven.

CLUB SUMMARY

FORMED	1897
MANAGER	Ian Sampson
GROUND	Sixfields Stadium
CAPACITY	7,653
NICKNAME	The Cobblers
WEBSITE	www.ntfc.co.uk

The New **Football Pools** PLAYER OF THE SEASON

Adebayo Akinfenwa

OVERALL
P	W	D	L	F	A	GD
52	20	14	18	71	65	6

COCA-COLA FOOTBALL LEAGUE 2
Pos	P	W	D	L	F	A	GD	Pts
11	46	18	13	15	62	53	9	67

HOME
Pos	P	W	D	L	F	A	GD	Pts
12	23	9	9	5	29	21	8	36

AWAY
Pos	P	W	D	L	F	A	GD	Pts
6	23	9	4	10	33	32	1	31

CUP PROGRESS DETAILS
Competition	Round reached	Knocked out by
FA Cup	R2	Southampton
Carling Cup	R1	Southampton
JP Trophy	QF	Milton Keynes Dons

BIGGEST WIN (ALL COMPS)
09/02/10 4-0 v Accrington

BIGGEST DEFEAT (ALL COMPS)
12/09/09 2-5 v Notts County

ATTENDANCE RECORD
HIGH	AVERAGE	LOW
5,647	4,375	3,206
v Notts County (10/04/2010)		v Accrington (09/02/2010)

RESULTS 2009/10

AUGUST
8th	● Macclesfield	H	D 0-0	Att: 4,064	Booked: Akinfenwa, Dyer, Rodgers.
11th	● Southampton	A	L 2-0	Att: 10,921	
15th	● Chesterfield	A	L 1-0	Att: 3,700	Booked: Osman, Curtis, Guinan.
18th	● Accrington	A	W 0-3	Att: 1,561	Scorers: Akinfenwa, Guinan, Mckay.
22nd	● Bournemouth	H	W 2-0	Att: 4,102	Scorers: Akinfenwa, Marshall. Booked: Gilligan, Marshall, Rodgers.
29th	● Burton	A	L 3-2	Att: 3,321	Scorers: Gilligan, Guinan. Booked: Osman, Marshall, Gilligan.

SEPTEMBER
1st	● Wycombe	A	D 2-2	Att: 1,035	Scorers: Gilligan, Guinan. Northampton win 3-0 on penalties.
4th	● Barnet	H	L 1-3	Att: 4,206	Scorers: Marshall. Booked: Gilligan.
12th	● Notts County	A	L 5-2	Att: 7,154	Scorers: Dyer, Holt. Booked: Curtis. Dismissed: McCready.
19th	● Rochdale	H	L 1-2	Att: 4,048	Scorers: Gilligan.
26th	● Shrewsbury	A	L 3-0	Att: 5,548	
29th	● Rotherham	H	W 3-1	Att: 4,017	Scorers: Gilligan, Herbert, Sharps OG. Booked: Johnson, Holt, Guttridge.

OCTOBER
3rd	● Bradford	H	D 2-2	Att: 4,391	Scorers: Dyer, Johnson. Booked: Gilligan.
6th	● Bournemouth	H	W 2-1	Att: 1,718	Scorers: Gilligan, Guinan. Booked: Gilligan.
10th	● Bury	A	D 2-2	Att: 2,863	Scorers: Akinfenwa, Herbert. Booked: Hinton, Curtis, Guinan, McCready.
17th	● Lincoln	H	W 1-0	Att: 4,341	Scorers: Guinan.
24th	● Morecambe	A	W 2-4	Att: 2,041	Scorers: Akinfenwa, Guinan, Holt, Johnson.
31st	● Torquay	A	L 1-0	Att: 2,732	Booked: Johnson, Gilligan.

NOVEMBER
7th	● Fleetwood Town	H	W 2-1	Att: 3,077	Scorers: Guttridge[2]. Booked: Beckwith, Akinfenwa.
10th	● Milton Keynes Dons	A	L 3-1	Att: 8,886	Scorers: Dunn. Booked: Dunn, Rodgers.
14th	● Grimsby	H	D 0-0	Att: 4,028	Booked: Curtis. Dismissed: Gilbert.
21st	● Crewe	H	D 2-2	Att: 3,876	Scorers: Akinfenwa[2].
24th	● Aldershot	A	L 2-1	Att: 2,761	Scorers: Guttridge. Booked: Rodgers, Guttridge, Mulligan, Guinan.
28th	● Southampton	H	L 2-3	Att: 4,858	Scorers: Gilligan, Hammond OG.

DECEMBER
1st	● Hereford	H	L 1-3	Att: 3,524	Scorers: Gilligan. Booked: Swailes, Johnson.
5th	● Cheltenham	A	D 2-2	Att: 2,824	Scorers: Akinfenwa[2]. Booked: Hinton.
12th	● Port Vale	H	D 1-1	Att: 4,132	Scorers: Akinfenwa. Booked: Swailes, Johnson, Dunn.
26th	● Dag & Red	H	W 1-0	Att: 4,108	Scorers: Mckay. Booked: Gilligan, Holt. Dismissed: Holt.
28th	● Barnet	A	D 0-0	Att: 2,237	Booked: Benjamin, Rodgers.

JANUARY
2nd	● Bournemouth	A	W 0-2	Att: 5,715	Scorers: Gilligan, Guttridge. Booked: Guttridge, Osman.
20th	● Macclesfield	A	W 0-2	Att: 1,035	Scorers: Akinfenwa, Guttridge. Booked: Hinton.
23rd	● Chesterfield	H	D 0-0	Att: 4,513	Booked: Gilligan.
26th	● Darlington	A	W 1-2	Att: 1,694	Scorers: Gilligan, Mckay.
30th	● Burton	H	D 1-1	Att: 4,552	Scorers: Holt. Booked: Thornton.

FEBRUARY
6th	● Dag & Red	A	W 0-1	Att: 2,206	Scorers: Johnson. Booked: Beckwith.
9th	● Accrington	H	W 4-0	Att: 3,206	Scorers: Akinfenwa, Guttridge, Mckay[2].
12th	● Aldershot	H	L 0-3	Att: 4,718	Booked: Akinfenwa, Gilligan. Dismissed: Thornton.
20th	● Crewe	A	L 3-2	Att: 4,036	Scorers: Akinfenwa, Gilligan. Booked: Hinton, Gilbert, Beckwith, Gilligan, Guttridge.
23rd	● Hereford	A	W 0-2	Att: 1,266	Scorers: Akinfenwa, Mckay. Booked: Curtis.
27th	● Cheltenham	H	W 2-1	Att: 4,428	Scorers: Akinfenwa, Harris.

MARCH
6th	● Port Vale	A	W 1-3	Att: 4,861	Scorers: Akinfenwa, Mckay, Osman. Booked: Osman.
13th	● Darlington	H	W 2-0	Att: 4,755	Scorers: Johnson, Osman.
20th	● Morecambe	H	W 2-0	Att: 4,210	Scorers: Davis, Gilligan. Booked: Osman.
27th	● Lincoln	A	D 1-1	Att: 3,964	Scorers: Johnson. Booked: Johnson, Osman.

APRIL
2nd	● Grimsby	A	W 1-2	Att: 6,482	Scorers: Akinfenwa, Davis. Booked: Gilligan, Gilbert, Beckwith.
5th	● Torquay	H	D 0-0	Att: 5,515	Booked: Beckwith, Herbert.
10th	● Notts County	H	L 0-1	Att: 5,647	Booked: Guinan, Thornton.
13th	● Rotherham	A	L 1-0	Att: 3,325	Booked: Rodgers. Dismissed: Hinton, Guttridge.
17th	● Rochdale	A	L 1-0	Att: 5,025	Booked: Beckwith, Gilbert.
24th	● Shrewsbury	H	W 2-0	Att: 5,019	Scorers: Mckay, Thornton. Booked: Gilbert.

MAY
1st	● Bradford	A	L 2-0	Att: 12,403	Booked: Johnson. Dismissed: Beckwith.
8th	● Bury	H	D 1-1	Att: 5,234	Scorers: Akinfenwa.

● Coca-Cola League 2/Play-Offs ● FA Cup ● Carling Cup ● Johnstone's Paint Trophy

LEAGUE 2 GOALKEEPER STATS

Player	Appearances	Match starts	Completed matches	Sub appearances	Subbed off	Clean sheets	Yellow cards	Red cards
Simon Brown	2	2	2	0	0	0	0	0
Chris Dunn	29	29	29	0	0	12	1	0
Billy Lumley	2	2	2	0	0	1	0	0
Jason Steele	13	13	13	0	0	4	0	0

LEAGUE 2 OUTFIELD PLAYER STATS

Player	Appearances	Match starts	Completed matches	Substitute appearances	Subbed off	Goals scored	Yellow cards	Red cards
Adebayo Akinfenwa	40	36	17	4	19	17	2	0
Dean Beckwith	38	37	35	1	1	0	5	1
Joe Benjamin	3	2	1	1	1	0	1	0
Luke Boden	4	4	1	0	3	0	0	0
John Curtis	19	18	11	1	7	0	5	0
Liam Davis	17	13	3	4	10	2	0	0
Alex Dyer	20	4	2	16	2	2	1	0
Peter Gilbert	30	30	25	0	4	0	4	1
Ryan Gilligan	42	41	35	1	6	8	10	0
Steve Guinan	28	19	10	9	9	4	4	0
Luke Guttridge	31	24	21	7	2	4	4	1
Seb Harris	9	0	0	9	0	1	0	0
Courtney Herbert	23	8	1	15	7	2	1	0
Craig Hinton	40	38	33	2	4	0	4	0
Andrew Holt	31	31	28	0	2	3	2	1
John Johnson	36	36	35	0	1	5	6	0
Patrick Kanyuka	3	3	3	0	0	0	0	0
Ben Marshall	15	11	8	4	3	2	2	0
Chris McCready	14	13	11	1	1	0	1	1
Billy Mckay	40	29	9	11	20	8	0	0
Gary Mulligan	9	2	1	7	1	0	1	0
Stephen O'Flynn	5	0	0	5	0	0	0	0
Abdul Osman	30	26	23	4	3	2	6	0
Paul Rodgers	31	24	14	7	10	0	5	0
Romone Rose	1	0	0	1	0	0	0	0
Danny Swailes	3	3	2	0	1	0	2	0
Kevin Thornton	11	4	1	7	2	1	2	1
Robbie Threlfall	4	1	1	3	0	0	0	0
Joshua Walker	3	3	2	0	1	0	0	0

SEASON INFORMATION

Highest position: 4
Lowest position: 22
Average goals scored per game: 1.35
Average goals conceded per game: 1.15

LEAGUE POSITION AT THE END OF EACH MONTH

AUG	SEP	OCT	NOV	DEC	JAN	FEB	MAR	APR	MAY
12	17	16	18	18	13	8	8	10	11

LONGEST SEQUENCES

Wins	5	Undefeated home	5
(23/02/10–20/03/10)		(on two occasions)	
Losses	5	Undefeated away	6
(29/08/09–26/09/09)		(05/12/09–06/02/10)	
Draws	2	Without scoring	4
(on three occasions)		(05/04/10–17/04/10)	
Undefeated	11	Without conceding	5
(05/12/09–09/02/10)		(26/12/09–23/01/10)	
Without win	7	Scoring	8
(31/10/09–12/12/09)		(20/02/10–02/04/10)	

CARDS RECEIVED

69 7

EARLIEST STRIKE

RYAN GILLIGAN
(v Hereford) 0:37

LATEST STRIKE

ADEBAYO AKINFENWA
(v Bury) 93:23

GOALS SCORED/CONCEDED
PER FIVE-MINUTE INTERVALS

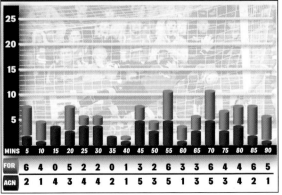

MINS	5	10	15	20	25	30	35	40	45	50	55	60	65	70	75	80	85	90
FOR	6	4	0	5	2	2	0	1	3	2	6	3	3	6	4	4	6	5
AGN	2	1	4	3	4	4	2	1	5	3	5	1	3	5	3	4	2	1

A ROLLERCOASTER season ended with Notts County being crowned as champions.

The campaign had begun with the takeover of the club by consortium Munto Finance and the arrival of former England manager Sven-Goran Eriksson as director of football. There were also the high-profile signings of Kasper Schmeichel and Sol Campbell. However, Campbell left having played just one game and manager Ian McParland was sacked shortly afterwards.

Eriksson appointed Hans Backe as McParland's successor but the club suffered a major blow when Munto Finance withdrew their investment and Backe resigned. Despite the financial concerns, County avoided administration and new owner Ray Trew stepped in to save the club and appointed Steve Cotterill as manager.

On the pitch, the Magpies made light of their problems and clinched the title with two games remaining. However, Cotterill left the club in May after just three months in charge, with former Meadow Lane favourite Craig Short taking over.

CLUB SUMMARY

FORMED	1862
MANAGER	Craig Short
GROUND	Meadow Lane
CAPACITY	20,300
NICKNAME	The Magpies
WEBSITE	www.nottscountyfc.co.uk

The New **Football Pools** PLAYER OF THE SEASON

Lee Hughes

OVERALL
P	W	D	L	F	A	GD
54	31	14	9	108	43	65

COCA-COLA FOOTBALL LEAGUE 2
Pos	P	W	D	L	F	A	GD	Pts
1	46	27	12	7	96	31	65	93

HOME
Pos	P	W	D	L	F	A	GD	Pts
1	23	16	6	1	58	14	44	54

AWAY
Pos	P	W	D	L	F	A	GD	Pts
1	23	11	6	6	38	17	21	39

CUP PROGRESS DETAILS
Competition	Round reached	Knocked out by
FA Cup	R5	Fulham
Carling Cup	R1	Doncaster
JP Trophy	R2	Bradford

BIGGEST WIN (ALL COMPS)
5–0 on 5 occasions

BIGGEST DEFEAT (ALL COMPS)
14/02/10 0–4 v Fulham

ATTENDANCE RECORD
High	Average	Low
11,331	7,353	4,606
v Cheltenham (01/05/2010)		v Darlington (01/12/2009)

RESULTS 2009/10

AUGUST
8th	● Bradford	H	W 5-0	Att: 9,396	Scorers: Davies, Hughes³, Moloney. Booked: Rodgers.
11th	● Doncaster	H	L 0-1	Att: 4,893	Booked: Edwards.
15th	● Macclesfield	A	W 0-4	Att: 2,785	Scorers: Hunt, Ravenhill, Westcarr, Wright OG.
19th	● Chesterfield	A	L 2-1	Att: 6,196	Scorers: Edwards. Booked: Ravenhill.
22nd	● Dag & Red	H	W 3-0	Att: 6,562	Scorers: Hawley, Hughes, Jackson.
29th	● Barnet	A	L 1-0	Att: 2,858	Booked: Hughes, Moloney.

SEPTEMBER
5th	● Burton	H	D 1-1	Att: 8,891	Scorers: Hawley. Booked: Davies, Edwards.
12th	● Northampton	H	W 5-2	Att: 7,154	Scorers: Hughes³, Ritchie². Booked: Thompson, Hawley, Facey.
19th	● Morecambe	A	L 2-1	Att: 3,335	Scorers: Davies.
26th	● Port Vale	H	W 3-1	Att: 7,561	Scorers: Hughes², Collins OG.
29th	● Lincoln	A	W 0-3	Att: 5,527	Scorers: Rodgers³. Booked: Hughes, Ritchie, Thompson, Jones.

OCTOBER
3rd	● Cheltenham	A	D 1-1	Att: 4,134	Scorers: Rodgers.
6th	● Bradford	A	D 2-2	Att: 3,701	Scorers: Facey, Westcarr. Booked: Lee, Edwards, Schmeichel, Westcarr. Dismissed: Lee. Bradford win 3-2 on penalties.
11th	● Torquay	H	D 2-2	Att: 8,812	Scorers: Davies, Westcarr. Booked: Hughes.
17th	● Rotherham	A	D 0-0	Att: 5,738	Booked: Thompson.
24th	● Crewe	H	W 2-0	Att: 6,545	Scorers: Rodgers, Westcarr. Booked: Lee, Rodgers, Thompson, Akinbiyi.
31st	● Shrewsbury	H	D 1-1	Att: 7,562	Scorers: Lee. Booked: Bishop.

NOVEMBER
6th	● Bradford	H	W 2-1	Att: 4,213	Scorers: Hawley, Jackson. Booked: Edwards, Davies, Bishop.
14th	● Bury	A	D 3-3	Att: 3,602	Scorers: Hughes², Ritchie. Booked: Edwards.
21st	● Aldershot	H	D 0-0	Att: 6,500	Booked: Hughes.
24th	● Rochdale	A	L 2-1	Att: 2,779	Scorers: Flynn OG. Booked: Jackson, Lee, Hunt.
28th	● Bournemouth	H	W 1-2	Att: 6,082	Scorers: Hughes, Westcarr. Booked: Lee, Hughes.

DECEMBER
1st	● Darlington	H	W 4-0	Att: 4,606	Scorers: Davies, Hughes², Rodgers. Booked: Thompson.
5th	● Hereford	A	W 0-2	Att: 2,727	Scorers: Edwards, Westcarr. Booked: Schmeichel.
12th	● Accrington	H	L 1-2	Att: 5,855	Scorers: Hughes. Booked: Moloney.
28th	● Burton	H	W 1-4	Att: 5,801	Scorers: Hughes³, Ravenhill. Booked: Ravenhill, Hughes.

JANUARY
19th	● Forest Green	H	W 2-1	Att: 4,389	Scorers: Hughes, Hunt.
23rd	● Wigan	A	D 2-2	Att: 9,073	Scorers: Davies, Hughes. Booked: Jackson, Westcarr, Hughes.
26th	● Dag & Red	A	W 0-3	Att: 1,916	Scorers: Davies, Hughes, Ogogo OG. Booked: Edwards, Hamshaw.
30th	● Barnet	H	W 2-0	Att: 6,444	Scorers: Davies, Hawley. Booked: Bishop, Hunt.

FEBRUARY
2nd	● Wigan	A	W 0-2	Att: 5,519	Scorers: Hunt, Caldwell OG. Booked: Ravenhill.
6th	● Grimsby	A	W 0-1	Att: 4,452	Scorers: Hughes. Booked: Ravenhill, Jackson, Hunt, Edwards.
9th	● Bournemouth	A	L 2-1	Att: 5,472	Scorers: Bishop. Booked: Bishop, Hunt.
14th	● Fulham	A	L 4-0	Att: 16,132	
17th	● Grimsby	H	D 1-1	Att: 5,163	Scorers: Hughes. Booked: Edwards, Hughes. Dismissed: Hughes.
20th	● Aldershot	A	D 1-1	Att: 4,016	Scorers: Davies. Booked: Ravenhill, Lee, Rodgers.
27th	● Hereford	H	W 5-0	Att: 6,036	Scorers: Rodgers², Westcarr³. Booked: Thompson, Rodgers, Hamshaw.

MARCH
2nd	● Macclesfield	H	W 1-0	Att: 4,672	Scorers: Clapham.
6th	● Accrington	A	W 0-3	Att: 2,123	Scorers: Davies, Hughes, Rodgers. Booked: Thompson, Lee, Bishop.
9th	● Chesterfield	H	W 1-0	Att: 7,341	Scorers: Davies. Booked: Ravenhill, Davies, Bishop, Thompson, Hughes.
15th	● Bournemouth	H	D 2-2	Att: 6,120	Scorers: Hughes². Booked: Hughes.
20th	● Crewe	A	W 0-1	Att: 5,003	Scorers: Edwards. Booked: Ravenhill, Hunt, Thompson, Lee, Rodgers. Dismissed: Rodgers.
23rd	● Bradford	A	D 0-0	Att: 11,630	
27th	● Rotherham	H	W 1-0	Att: 9,015	Scorers: Rodgers. Booked: Thompson, Hughes, Rodgers.

APRIL
3rd	● Bury	H	W 5-0	Att: 7,005	Scorers: Davies, Edwards, Facey, Hughes, Westcarr.
5th	● Shrewsbury	A	W 0-1	Att: 6,287	Scorers: Davies. Booked: Rodgers, Lee, Hughes.
10th	● Northampton	A	W 0-1	Att: 5,647	Scorers: Davies. Booked: Edwards, Westcarr, Ravenhill, Davies.
13th	● Lincoln	H	W 3-1	Att: 7,501	Scorers: Facey, Hughes, Lee. Booked: Hughes, Lee.
17th	● Morecambe	H	W 4-1	Att: 8,500	Scorers: Davies, Hughes², Ravenhill. Booked: Thompson.
20th	● Rochdale	H	W 1-0	Att: 10,536	Scorers: Hughes. Booked: Lee.
24th	● Port Vale	A	L 2-1	Att: 7,459	Scorers: Lee. Booked: Lee.
27th	● Darlington	A	W 0-5	Att: 2,112	Scorers: Edwards, Jackson, Rodgers², Westcarr. Booked: Hunt.

MAY
1st	● Cheltenham	H	W 5-0	Att: 11,331	Scorers: Davies, Hughes², Lee, Rodgers. Booked: Bishop, Thompson, Ravenhill.
8th	● Torquay	A	D 0-0	Att: 5,124	Booked: Edwards, Bishop, Rodgers.

● Coca-Cola League 2/Play-Offs ● FA Cup ● Carling Cup ● Johnstone's Paint Trophy

LEAGUE 2 GOALKEEPER STATS

Player	Appearances	Match starts	Completed matches	Sub appearances	Subbed off	Clean sheets	Yellow cards	Red cards
Russell Hoult	4	3	3	1	0	2	0	0
Kasper Schmeichel	43	43	42	0	1	23	1	0

LEAGUE 2 OUTFIELD PLAYER STATS

Player	Appearances	Match starts	Completed matches	Substitute appearances	Subbed off	Goals scored	Yellow cards	Red cards
Ade Akinbiyi	10	1	1	9	0	0	1	0
Neal Bishop	43	39	35	4	4	1	7	0
Sol Campbell	1	1	1	0	0	0	0	0
Sean Canham	1	0	0	1	0	0	0	0
Jamie Clapham	30	17	15	13	2	1	0	0
Ben Davies	45	45	34	0	11	14	3	0
Mike Edwards	40	37	37	3	0	5	7	0
Delroy Facey	18	7	4	11	3	2	1	0
Nathan Fox	1	0	0	1	0	0	0	0
Matthew Hamshaw	20	2	1	18	1	0	2	0
Karl Hawley	31	14	5	17	9	3	1	0
Lee Hughes	39	39	20	0	18	30	11	1
Stephen Hunt	32	32	30	0	2	1	6	0
Johnnie Jackson	24	20	16	4	4	2	2	0
Daniel Jones	7	7	6	0	1	0	1	0
Graeme Lee	32	31	30	1	1	4	9	0
Brendan Moloney	18	18	17	0	1	1	2	0
Richard Ravenhill	40	40	32	0	8	3	8	0
Matt Ritchie	16	12	5	4	7	3	1	0
Luke Rodgers	42	27	7	15	19	13	8	1
John Thompson	40	38	36	2	2	0	12	0
Craig Westcarr	42	33	14	9	19	9	1	0

LEAGUE POSITION AT THE END OF EACH MONTH

AUG	SEP	OCT	NOV	DEC	JAN	FEB	MAR	APR	MAY
5	6	4	7	4	5	7	2	1	1

SEASON INFORMATION

Highest position: 1
Lowest position: 18
Average goals scored per game: 2.09
Average goals conceded per game: 0.67

LONGEST SEQUENCES

Wins	7	Undefeated home	12
(27/03/10–20/04/10)		(30/01/10–01/05/10)	
Losses	–	Undefeated away	6
(–)		(20/02/10–10/04/10)	
Draws	3	Without scoring	–
(on two occasions)		(–)	
Undefeated	16	Without conceding	6
(17/02/10–20/04/10)		(20/03/10–10/04/10)	
Without win	4	Scoring	17
(31/10/09–24/11/09)		(24/11/09–20/03/10)	

CARDS RECEIVED

84   2

EARLIEST STRIKE

LUKE RODGERS
(v Lincoln City) 0:14

LATEST STRIKE

BEN DAVIES
(v Aldershot) 90:53

GOALS SCORED/CONCEDED
PER FIVE-MINUTE INTERVALS

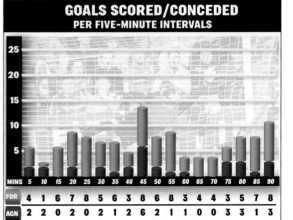

MINS	5	10	15	20	25	30	35	40	45	50	55	60	65	70	75	80	85	90
FOR	4	1	6	7	8	5	6	3	8	6	8	3	4	4	3	5	7	8
AGN	2	2	0	2	0	2	1	2	6	2	1	1	0	0	3	3	1	3

PORT VALE

PORT VALE missed out on a play-off place on the final day, but even that could not take the gloss off a season of progress.

Under Lee Sinnott and then Dean Glover, the Valiants had ended 2008/09 in 18th place, having flirted with the relegation places. However, they have been transformed under the shrewd stewardship of Micky Adams and for much of this campaign they were genuine promotion contenders.

It was not always an easy ride, though, and a poor run of form in September memorably led to Adams putting his entire squad up for sale, seemingly as a motivational tactic.

With more time to mould his team in the close season, the former Fulham and Leicester boss is now aiming to turn them into a force to be reckoned with in 2010/11. Star striker Marc Richards will be key to their hopes of mounting a sustained challenge having scored an impressive 22 goals in all competitions during the 2009/10 season.

CLUB SUMMARY

FORMED	1876
MANAGER	Micky Adams
GROUND	Vale Park
CAPACITY	18,982
NICKNAME	The Valiants
WEBSITE	www.port-vale.co.uk

The New **Football Pools** PLAYER OF THE SEASON

Marc Richards

OVERALL

P	W	D	L	F	A	GD
54	21	19	14	72	58	14

COCA-COLA FOOTBALL LEAGUE 2

Pos	P	W	D	L	F	A	GD	Pts
10	46	17	17	12	61	50	11	68

HOME

Pos	P	W	D	L	F	A	GD	Pts
17	23	8	8	7	32	25	7	32

AWAY

Pos	P	W	D	L	F	A	GD	Pts
3	23	9	9	5	29	25	4	36

CUP PROGRESS DETAILS

Competition	Round reached	Knocked out by
FA Cup	R2	Huddersfield
Carling Cup	R3	Scunthorpe
JP Trophy	QF	Bradford

BIGGEST WIN (ALL COMPS)
13/03/10 5–0 v Chesterfield

BIGGEST DEFEAT (ALL COMPS)
01/05/10 0–4 v Bournemouth

ATTENDANCE RECORD

High	Average	Low
8,467	5,080	3,231

v Shrewsbury (08/05/2010)   v Lincoln City (23/02/2010)

RESULTS 2009/10

AUGUST
8th	● Rochdale	H	D 1–1	Att: 6,158	Scorers: Richards.
11th	● Sheff Utd	A	W 1–2	Att: 7,627	Scorers: Richards². Booked: Stockley, Fraser.
15th	● Bradford	A	D 0–0	Att: 11,333	Booked: Griffith.
18th	● Macclesfield	A	L 2–0	Att: 3,433	Booked: Collins, Fraser.
22nd	● Darlington	H	W 1–0	Att: 4,561	Booked: Griffith.
25th	● Sheff Wed	H	W 2–0	Att: 6,667	Scorers: R Taylor, K Taylor. Booked: Griffith.
29th	● Hereford	A	D 2–2	Att: 2,434	Scorers: Dodds, R Taylor. Booked: R Taylor.

SEPTEMBER
5th	● Grimsby	H	W 4–0	Att: 5,056	Scorers: Collins, Dodds, Owen, Richards. Booked: Loft.
12th	● Aldershot	A	D 1–1	Att: 3,406	Scorers: R Taylor. Booked: Loft.
19th	● Bury	H	L 0–1	Att: 5,461	Booked: Owen.
22nd	● Scunthorpe	A	L 2–0	Att: 3,383	Booked: Fraser, Stockley, Griffith, Haldane, Owen. AET – Score after 90 mins 0–0.
26th	● Notts County	A	L 3–1	Att: 7,561	Scorers: Richards. Booked: McCrory, Fraser, R Taylor.
29th	● Accrington	H	D 2–2	Att: 4,326	Scorers: Dodds, Fraser.

OCTOBER
3rd	● Bournemouth	H	D 0–0	Att: 4,905	Booked: Richards, Owen, Dodds.
6th	● Stockport	H	W 3–1	Att: 3,154	Scorers: Dodds, Haldane, Richards. Booked: Haldane.
10th	● Shrewsbury	A	W 0–1	Att: 7,096	Scorers: McCombe. Booked: Dodds, Griffith, Stockley, Martin.
17th	● Crewe	A	W 1–2	Att: 6,943	Scorers: Richards, K Taylor. Booked: McCombe, Jarrett.
24th	● Cheltenham	H	D 1–1	Att: 4,979	Scorers: Richards. Booked: Griffith, Stockley.
31st	● Dag & Red	A	D 1–1	Att: 2,003	Scorers: Dodds. Booked: Jarrett, Stockley.

NOVEMBER
7th	● Stevenage	H	D 1–1	Att: 3,999	Scorers: Yates. Booked: Griffith, Collins.
10th	● Bradford	A	D 2–2	Att: 5,096	Scorers: McCombe, R Taylor. Booked: Dodds. Bradford win 5–4 on penalties.
14th	● Rotherham	H	L 1–2	Att: 4,788	Scorers: Prosser. Booked: Richards, Prosser. Dismissed: Prosser.
17th	● Stevenage	A	W 0–1	Att: 2,914	Scorers: Dodds. Booked: K Taylor.
21st	● Barnet	A	D 0–0	Att: 1,939	Booked: Jarrett. Dismissed: Fraser.
24th	● Torquay	H	D 2–2	Att: 3,996	Scorers: Loft, R Taylor.
28th	● Huddersfield	H	L 0–1	Att: 5,311	

DECEMBER
1st	● Lincoln	A	W 1–2	Att: 2,569	Scorers: Dodds, Richards. Booked: Griffith, Loft.
5th	● Morecambe	H	L 0–2	Att: 4,679	Booked: Rigg.
12th	● Northampton	A	D 1–1	Att: 4,132	Scorers: Richards. Booked: Fraser, K Taylor. Dismissed: McCombe.
28th	● Grimsby	A	W 1–2	Att: 4,401	Scorers: Rigg, R Taylor. Booked: Fraser, R Taylor, Griffith. Dismissed: R Taylor.

JANUARY
19th	● Burton	H	W 3–1	Att: 4,458	Scorers: Richards², Rigg. Booked: Fraser, Griffith, Dodds.
23rd	● Macclesfield	H	D 0–0	Att: 5,167	
26th	● Rochdale	A	D 0–0	Att: 3,081	Booked: Fraser.
30th	● Hereford	H	W 2–0	Att: 4,686	Scorers: Davies, Richards. Booked: Haldane, K Taylor, Howland, Richards. Dismissed: Haldane.

FEBRUARY
6th	● Burton	A	L 1–0	Att: 4,644	Booked: Dodds.
9th	● Chesterfield	H	L 1–2	Att: 4,090	Scorers: Davies. Booked: McCombe.
13th	● Torquay	A	W 1–2	Att: 2,563	Scorers: Haldane, Richards. Booked: Griffith.
20th	● Barnet	H	L 0–2	Att: 4,571	Booked: Rigg, Richards, Fraser, Owen.
23rd	● Lincoln	H	W 4–0	Att: 3,231	Scorers: Davies, McCombe, R Taylor, Pearce OG. Booked: Fraser.
27th	● Morecambe	A	L 1–0	Att: 2,064	Booked: Dodds.

MARCH
2nd	● Darlington	A	W 1–3	Att: 1,582	Scorers: Dodds, Haldane, Loft.
6th	● Northampton	H	L 1–3	Att: 4,861	Scorers: Loft. Booked: Fraser.
9th	● Bradford	H	W 2–1	Att: 3,728	Scorers: Richards, R Taylor. Booked: Collins.
13th	● Chesterfield	A	W 0–5	Att: 4,138	Scorers: Davies, Richards³, R Taylor. Booked: Davies.
20th	● Cheltenham	A	D 1–1	Att: 3,503	Scorers: McCombe. Booked: Haldane, Davies.
27th	● Crewe	H	L 0–1	Att: 7,232	Booked: Owen, R Taylor, Griffith.

APRIL
3rd	● Rotherham	A	W 1–2	Att: 3,721	Scorers: Davies, Richards.
5th	● Dag & Red	H	W 3–1	Att: 4,572	Scorers: Davies, Haldane, R Taylor. Booked: Griffith.
10th	● Aldershot	H	D 1–1	Att: 5,399	Scorers: Rigg. Booked: Collins, Richards.
13th	● Accrington Stanley	A	W 1–2	Att: 2,205	Scorers: Davies, K Taylor. Booked: Griffith.
17th	● Bury	A	D 1–1	Att: 4,570	Scorers: Richards.
24th	● Notts County	H	W 2–1	Att: 7,459	Scorers: Richards, K Taylor. Booked: Fraser.

MAY
1st	● Bournemouth	A	L 4–0	Att: 9,055	Booked: Griffith, K Taylor, Yates, R Taylor.
8th	● Shrewsbury	H	D 1–1	Att: 8,467	Scorers: Richards. Booked: McCombe.

● Coca-Cola League 2/Play-Offs ● FA Cup ● Carling Cup ● Johnstone's Paint Trophy

Coca-Cola LEAGUE 2

LEAGUE 2 GOALKEEPER STATS

Player	Appearances	Match starts	Completed matches	Sub appearances	Subbed off	Clean sheets	Yellow cards	Red cards
Joe Anyon	7	7	7	0	0	2	0	0
Chris Martin	39	39	39	0	0	9	1	0

LEAGUE 2 OUTFIELD PLAYER STATS

Player	Appearances	Match starts	Completed matches	Substitute appearances	Subbed off	Goals scored	Yellow cards	Red cards
Lee Collins	45	45	45	0	0	1	3	0
Craig Davies	24	22	11	2	11	7	2	0
Louis Dodds	44	33	14	11	19	6	5	0
Tommy Fraser	38	33	24	5	8	1	10	1
Danny Glover	3	0	0	3	0	0	0	0
Anthony Griffith	40	38	25	2	13	0	11	0
Jamie Guy	3	0	0	3	0	0	0	0
Lewis Haldane	37	29	10	8	18	3	2	1
Geoff Horsfield	9	1	0	8	1	0	0	0
David Howland	5	0	0	5	0	0	1	0
Jason Jarrett	9	7	5	2	2	0	3	0
Claus Bech Jorgensen	4	0	0	4	0	0	0	0
James Lawrie	3	0	0	3	0	0	0	0
Doug Loft	32	21	10	11	11	3	3	0
John McCombe	40	37	32	3	4	3	3	1
Damien McCrory	5	2	2	3	0	0	1	0
Sam Morsy	1	0	0	1	0	0	0	0
Gareth Owen	40	40	37	0	3	1	4	0
Luke Prosser	2	2	1	0	0	1	1	0
Marc Richards	46	45	41	1	4	20	5	0
Simon Richman	5	0	0	5	0	0	0	0
Sean Rigg	26	9	5	17	4	3	2	0
Sam Stockley	9	8	4	1	4	0	3	0
Robert Taylor	38	25	12	13	12	8	5	1
Kris Taylor	41	38	34	3	4	3	3	0
Adam Yates	32	25	22	7	3	0	1	0

| AUG | SEP | OCT | NOV | DEC | JAN | FEB | MAR | APR | MAY |

SEASON INFORMATION
Highest position: 7
Lowest position: 22
Average goals scored per game: 1.33
Average goals conceded per game: 1.09

| 16 | 16 | 13 | 14 | 13 | 12 | 14 | 13 | 7 | 10 |

LEAGUE POSITION AT THE END OF EACH MONTH

LONGEST SEQUENCES

Wins	2	Undefeated home	4
(on four occasions)		(05/04/10–08/05/10)	
Losses	2	Undefeated away	8
(on two occasions)		(10/10/09–26/01/10)	
Draws	2	Without scoring	2
(on five occasions)		(on two occasions)	
Undefeated	6	Without conceding	3
(on three occasions)		(23/01/10–30/01/10)	
Without win	5	Scoring	6
(on two occasions)		(03/04/10–24/04/10)	

CARDS RECEIVED
69   5

EARLIEST STRIKE
ROBERT TAYLOR
(v Lincoln City) 2:33

LATEST STRIKE
MARC RICHARDS
(v Hereford) 91:26

GOALS SCORED/CONCEDED
PER FIVE-MINUTE INTERVALS

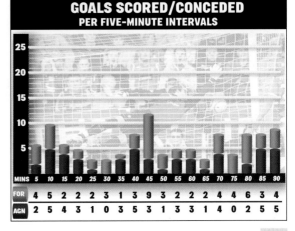

MINS	5	10	15	20	25	30	35	40	45	50	55	60	65	70	75	80	85	90
FOR	4	5	2	2	2	3	1	3	9	3	2	2	2	4	4	6	3	4
AGN	2	5	4	3	1	0	3	5	3	1	3	3	1	4	0	2	5	5

ROCHDALE

ROCHDALE finally clinched their first promotion since 1969 after two years of play-off heartache.

Dale had been in the bottom tier of English football since 1974 but, under manager Keith Hill, they can now look forward to life in the third tier following an outstanding Coca-Cola League 2 campaign in which they won many admirers.

Hill used the loan market astutely, utilising the services of Will Atkinson, Jason Taylor and Frank Fielding to his advantage as Rochdale romped to promotion.

They were the first side to seal their ascent but, instead of going on to clinch the title, they let their momentum slip, losing their last four games and winning just two of their last 10 fixtures to finish in third place behind Notts County and Bournemouth.

Hill and his assistant, Dave Flitcroft, signed new two-year deals towards the end of the campaign and will be hopeful of making the most of the opportunity to progress.

CLUB SUMMARY

FORMED	1907
MANAGER	Keith Hill
GROUND	Spotland
CAPACITY	10,249
NICKNAME	The Dale
WEBSITE	www.rochdalefc.co.uk

The New Football Pools
PLAYER OF THE SEASON
Craig Dawson

OVERALL
P	W	D	L	F	A	GD
50	25	8	17	86	58	28

COCA-COLA FOOTBALL LEAGUE 2
Pos	P	W	D	L	F	A	GD	Pts
3	46	25	7	14	82	48	34	82

HOME
Pos	P	W	D	L	F	A	GD	Pts
5	23	14	3	6	45	20	25	45

AWAY
Pos	P	W	D	L	F	A	GD	Pts
2	23	11	4	8	37	28	9	37

CUP PROGRESS DETAILS
Competition	Round reached	Knocked out by
FA Cup	R1	Luton
Carling Cup	R1	Sheff Wed
JP Trophy	R1	Bradford

BIGGEST WIN (ALL COMPS)
4–0 on 3 occasions

BIGGEST DEFEAT (ALL COMPS)
10/04/10 0–5 v Torquay

ATTENDANCE RECORD
High	Average	Low
5,371	3,443	2,311
v Darlington (13/04/2010)		v Cheltenham (18/08/2009)

RESULTS 2009/10

AUGUST
8th	● Port Vale	A	D 1–1	Att: 6,158	Scorers: Thompson.
11th	● Sheff Wed	A	L 3–0	Att: 6,696	Booked: T Kennedy.
15th	● Aldershot	H	W 1–0	Att: 2,465	Scorers: T Kennedy. **Dismissed:** Stanton.
18th	● Cheltenham	H	L 0–1	Att: 2,311	
23rd	● Rotherham	A	L 2–1	Att: 3,602	Scorers: Dagnall. Booked: Stanton.
29th	● Bury	H	W 3–0	Att: 4,534	Scorers: Dagnall, T Kennedy, Thompson. Booked: Dagnall, Flynn, T Kennedy.

SEPTEMBER
1st	● Bradford	H	L 1–2	Att: 1,800	Scorers: Dawson. Booked: Rundle.
4th	● Morecambe	A	D 3–3	Att: 2,367	Scorers: Dagnall, Stephens, Thompson.
12th	● Torquay	H	W 2–1	Att: 2,407	Scorers: Dagnall[2].
19th	● Northampton	A	W 1–2	Att: 4,048	Scorers: Buckley, O'Grady.
26th	● Hereford	H	W 4–1	Att: 2,620	Scorers: Buckley, Dagnall, Dawson, Whaley. Booked: J Kennedy.
29th	● Darlington	A	W 0–2	Att: 1,748	Scorers: Buckley, O'Grady.

OCTOBER
4th	● Burton	A	L 1–0	Att: 3,119	Booked: T Kennedy.
10th	● Barnet	H	W 2–1	Att: 2,648	Scorers: Dagnall, T Kennedy. Booked: Jones.
17th	● Grimsby	A	W 0–2	Att: 3,754	Scorers: O'Grady, Rundle.
24th	● Accrington	H	L 1–2	Att: 3,206	Scorers: Dagnall.
31st	● Bournemouth	A	W 0–4	Att: 6,378	Scorers: Dagnall, O'Grady[2], Whaley. Booked: T Kennedy, Whaley. **Dismissed:** Stanton.

NOVEMBER
7th	● Luton	A	D 3–3	Att: 3,167	Scorers: Dawson, Thompson[2].
11th	● Luton	H	L 0–2	Att: 1,982	
14th	● Chesterfield	H	L 2–3	Att: 3,011	Scorers: Dawson, O'Grady. Booked: Wiseman.
21st	● Dag & Red	A	W 1–2	Att: 2,235	Scorers: Dawson, Higginbotham. Booked: T Kennedy.
24th	● Notts County	H	W 2–1	Att: 2,779	Scorers: Dagnall, O'Grady.

DECEMBER
1st	● Bradford	A	W 0–3	Att: 11,472	Scorers: Dagnall[2], O'Grady. Booked: T Kennedy.
5th	● Macclesfield	H	W 3–0	Att: 3,003	Scorers: Atkinson, Taylor, Wiseman. Booked: Stanton, J Kennedy.
12th	● Lincoln	A	W 1–3	Att: 3,293	Scorers: Dawson, O'Grady, Thompson.
19th	● Shrewsbury	H	W 4–0	Att: 2,596	Scorers: Dawson, O'Grady[2].
26th	● Crewe	H	D 2–2	Att: 5,563	Scorers: Dawson, Higginbotham. Booked: T Kennedy.
28th	● Morecambe	H	W 4–1	Att: 4,309	Scorers: Atkinson[2], Dagnall, O'Grady.

JANUARY
19th	● Aldershot	A	D 1–1	Att: 2,453	Scorers: Dagnall.
23rd	● Cheltenham	A	W 1–4	Att: 3,460	Scorers: Dawson, O'Grady[3].
26th	● Port Vale	H	D 0–0	Att: 3,081	

FEBRUARY
1st	● Bury	A	L 1–0	Att: 6,528	Booked: T Kennedy, Wiseman.
6th	● Crewe	A	W 2–0	Att: 3,164	Scorers: O'Grady, Tootle OG.
20th	● Dag & Red	H	W 3–1	Att: 3,153	Scorers: Jones, O'Grady, Obadeyi.
23rd	● Bradford	H	L 1–3	Att: 3,055	Scorers: Dagnall. Booked: Obadeyi, Stanton.
27th	● Macclesfield	A	W 0–1	Att: 2,462	Scorers: O'Grady. Booked: Atkinson.

MARCH
2nd	● Rotherham	H	W 4–0	Att: 3,502	Scorers: Dagnall, Dawson, O'Grady, Green OG. Booked: Dawson, T Kennedy, Atkinson.
6th	● Lincoln	H	D 1–1	Att: 3,453	Scorers: Dagnall. Booked: Dagnall.
13th	● Shrewsbury	A	W 0–1	Att: 6,081	Scorers: Thompson. Booked: O'Grady.
20th	● Accrington	A	W 2–4	Att: 3,025	Scorers: Higginbotham, Jones[2], O'Grady. Booked: Dagnall. **Dismissed:** Taylor.
27th	● Grimsby	H	W 4–1	Att: 4,724	Scorers: Dagnall[3], Thompson. Booked: O'Grady.

APRIL
3rd	● Chesterfield	A	L 2–0	Att: 4,471	Booked: McArdle.
5th	● Bournemouth	H	D 0–0	Att: 5,027	Booked: Higginbotham, Dagnall.
10th	● Torquay	A	L 5–0	Att: 3,093	Booked: Fielding.
13th	● Darlington	H	L 0–1	Att: 5,371	
17th	● Northampton	H	W 1–0	Att: 5,025	Scorers: O'Grady. Booked: Stanton.
20th	● Notts County	A	L 1–0	Att: 10,536	
24th	● Hereford	A	L 2–1	Att: 1,975	Scorers: Jones. Booked: Jones, McArdle.

MAY
1st	● Burton	H	L 1–2	Att: 3,749	Scorers: O'Grady.
8th	● Barnet	A	L 1–0	Att: 4,638	Booked: Holness.

● Coca-Cola League 2/Play-Offs ● FA Cup ● Carling Cup ● Johnstone's Paint Trophy

actim

Coca-Cola LEAGUE 2

LEAGUE 2 GOALKEEPER STATS

Player	Appearances	Match starts	Completed matches	Sub appearances	Subbed off	Clean sheets	Yellow cards	Red cards
Kenny Arthur	15	15	15	0	0	4	0	0
Frank Fielding	18	18	18	0	0	6	1	0
Tom Heaton	12	12	12	0	0	4	0	0
Josh Lillis	1	1	1	0	0	1	0	0

LEAGUE 2 OUTFIELD PLAYER STATS

Player	Appearances	Match starts	Completed matches	Substitute appearances	Subbed off	Goals scored	Yellow cards	Red cards
Will Atkinson	15	15	8	0	7	3	2	0
William Buckley	15	12	7	3	5	3	0	0
Chris Dagnall	45	45	34	0	11	20	4	0
Craig Dawson	42	40	38	2	2	9	1	0
Matthew Flynn	10	7	5	3	2	0	1	0
Danny Glover	2	0	0	2	0	0	0	0
Reece Gray	2	0	0	2	0	0	0	0
Andrew Haworth	7	3	0	4	3	0	0	0
Kallum Higginbotham	29	6	3	23	3	3	1	0
Marcus Holness	11	7	7	4	0	0	1	0
Gary Jones	34	32	28	2	4	4	2	0
Thomas Kennedy	44	44	42	0	2	3	8	0
Jason Kennedy	42	40	36	2	4	0	2	0
Adam Le Fondre	1	0	0	1	0	0	0	0
Marcus Magna	2	0	0	2	0	0	0	0
Rory McArdle	20	17	15	3	2	0	2	0
Chris O'Grady	43	43	35	0	8	22	2	0
Temitope Obadeyi	11	5	0	6	5	1	1	0
Adam Rundle	12	6	1	6	5	1	0	0
Jon Shaw	1	0	0	1	0	0	0	0
Scott Spencer	4	0	0	4	0	0	0	0
Nathan Stanton	38	37	32	1	3	0	4	2
Dale Stephens	6	3	2	3	1	1	0	0
Jason Taylor	23	23	17	0	5	1	0	1
Joe Thompson	36	27	15	9	12	6	0	0
Ciaran Toner	13	7	4	6	3	0	0	0
Simon Whaley	9	8	5	1	3	2	1	0
Scott Wiseman	36	33	30	3	3	1	2	0

AUG SEP OCT NOV DEC JAN FEB MAR APR MAY

SEASON INFORMATION

Highest position: 1
Lowest position: 20
Average goals scored per game: 1.78
Average goals conceded per game: 1.04

League position at the end of each month: 13 2 2 2 1 1 1 1 2 3

LEAGUE POSITION AT THE END OF EACH MONTH

LONGEST SEQUENCES

Wins	6	Undefeated home	7
(21/11/09–19/12/09)		(24/11/09–20/02/10)	
Losses	4	Undefeated away	8
(20/04/10–08/05/10)		(17/10/09–23/01/10)	
Draws	–	Without scoring	4
(–)		(03/04/10–13/04/10)	
Undefeated	11	Without conceding	2
(21/11/09–26/01/10)		(on two occasions)	
Without win	4	Scoring	15
(on two occasions)		(10/10/09–23/01/10)	

CARDS RECEIVED

35   **3**

EARLIEST STRIKE

CRAIG DAWSON
(v Shrewsbury) 7:32

LATEST STRIKE

KALLUM HIGGINBOTHAM
(v Accrington Stanley) 94:19

GOALS SCORED/CONCEDED
PER FIVE-MINUTE INTERVALS

MINS	5	10	15	20	25	30	35	40	45	50	55	60	65	70	75	80	85	90
FOR	0	4	3	5	4	2	1	2	9	4	3	6	5	7	9	4	6	8
AGN	2	2	0	0	3	4	5	1	4	0	1	0	8	3	2	4	3	6

ROTHERHAM UNITED

ROTHERHAM are facing a fourth consecutive season in npower League 2 after their 2009/10 campaign ended in disappointment with a play-off final defeat at Wembley.

Despite a summer of investment, with strikers Tom Pope and Adam Le Fondre brought in, the Millers were unable to complete the job started by manager Mark Robins, who departed for Barnsley in September. While replacement Ronnie Moore was welcomed as a returning hero, he could not maintain a top-three place as the Millers had to settle for the play-offs.

There were plenty of positives, though. Le Fondre proved a good acquisition, scoring 30 goals, and Nicky Law also had a fine season.

The 2009/10 season was far from a smooth ride with the club playing in Sheffield – ahead of the completion of their new 12,000-seater stadium – and training in Doncaster, but chairman Tony Stewart will be determined to guide the club into the third tier by the time they move into their new home in 2011.

CLUB SUMMARY

FORMED	1870
MANAGER	Ronnie Moore
GROUND	Don Valley Stadium
CAPACITY	25,000
NICKNAME	The Millers
WEBSITE	www.themillers.co.uk

The New Football Pools PLAYER OF THE SEASON

Adam Le Fondre

OVERALL
P	W	D	L	F	A	GD
55	25	11	19	71	69	2

COCA-COLA FOOTBALL LEAGUE 2
Pos	P	W	D	L	F	A	GD	Pts
5	46	21	10	15	55	52	3	73

HOME
Pos	P	W	D	L	F	A	GD	Pts
9	23	10	9	4	29	18	11	39

AWAY
Pos	P	W	D	L	F	A	GD	Pts
4	23	11	1	11	26	34	-8	34

CUP PROGRESS DETAILS
Competition	Round reached	Knocked out by
FA Cup	R2	Luton
Carling Cup	R2	West Brom
JP Trophy	R1	Huddersfield

BIGGEST WIN (ALL COMPS)
26/09/09 3–0 v Barnet

BIGGEST DEFEAT (ALL COMPS)
02/03/10 0–4 v Rochdale

ATTENDANCE RECORD
HIGH	AVERAGE	Low
5,738	3,513	2,604
v Notts County (17/10/2009)		v Dag & Red (09/02/2010)

RESULTS 2009/10

AUGUST
8th	● Accrington	H	W 1–0	Att: 3,254	Scorers: Warne.
11th	● Derby	H	W 2–1	Att: 4,345	Scorers: Ellison, Warne.
15th	● Bournemouth	A	L 1–0	Att: 5,091	Booked: Warne.
18th	● Grimsby	A	W 1–2	Att: 4,156	Scorers: Cummins, Le Fondre. Booked: Cummins.
23rd	● Rochdale	H	W 2–1	Att: 3,602	Scorers: Le Fondre, Warne.
26th	● West Brom	A	L 4–3	Att: 10,659	Scorers: Cummins, Pope². Booked: Joseph. AET – Score after 90 mins 2–2.
29th	● Macclesfield	A	W 1–3	Att: 1,972	Scorers: Harrison, Le Fondre, Pope.

SEPTEMBER
1st	● Huddersfield	H	L 1–2	Att: 2,246	Scorers: Le Fondre.
5th	● Chesterfield	H	W 3–1	Att: 4,458	Scorers: Ellison, Harrison, Le Fondre. Booked: Joseph.
12th	● Morecambe	H	D 0–0	Att: 3,172	Booked: Ellison.
19th	● Cheltenham	A	D 1–1	Att: 3,088	Scorers: Le Fondre. Booked: Law.
26th	● Barnet	H	W 3–0	Att: 3,823	Scorers: Ellison, Law, Le Fondre.
29th	● Northampton	A	L 3–1	Att: 4,017	Scorers: Le Fondre. Booked: R Taylor.

OCTOBER
3rd	● Crewe	A	W 2–3	Att: 4,253	Scorers: Broughton, Ellison, Le Fondre. Booked: Fenton, Sharps.
10th	● Hereford	H	D 1–1	Att: 3,452	Scorers: Le Fondre. Booked: Sharps.
17th	● Notts County	H	D 0–0	Att: 5,738	Booked: Fenton, Warne. Dismissed: Fenton.
24th	● Bury	A	L 2–1	Att: 3,496	Scorers: Ellison.
31st	● Aldershot	H	D 0–0	Att: 3,002	

NOVEMBER
8th	● Wealdstone	A	W 2–3	Att: 1,638	Scorers: Broughton, Ellison, Le Fondre. Booked: Tonge, Nicholas, Brogan.
14th	● Port Vale	A	W 1–2	Att: 4,788	Scorers: Brogan, Law. Booked: Sharps, Fenton, Nicholas.
21st	● Torquay	A	W 0–2	Att: 2,551	Scorers: Ellison, Le Fondre. Booked: Lynch.
24th	● Lincoln	H	W 2–0	Att: 2,901	Scorers: Le Fondre².
28th	● Luton	H	D 2–2	Att: 3,210	Scorers: Brogan, Le Fondre.

DECEMBER
1st	● Shrewsbury	A	L 2–0	Att: 4,522	Booked: Fenton, Roberts.
5th	● Burton	H	D 2–2	Att: 3,177	Scorers: Le Fondre². Dismissed: Fenton.
8th	● Luton	A	L 3–0	Att: 2,518	Booked: Harrison.
12th	● Bradford	A	W 2–4	Att: 11,578	Scorers: Broughton, Ellison², Roberts. Booked: Broughton.

JANUARY
19th	● Darlington	H	L 1–2	Att: 3,234	Scorers: Cummins. Booked: Roberts, Mills.
23rd	● Grimsby	H	W 2–1	Att: 3,751	Scorers: Le Fondre².
26th	● Chesterfield	A	W 0–1	Att: 4,951	Scorers: Pope. Booked: Roberts, Pope.

FEBRUARY
2nd	● Bournemouth	H	L 1–3	Att: 3,180	Scorers: Pope. Booked: Cummins, Roberts.
6th	● Darlington	A	L 2–0	Att: 2,231	Booked: Broughton.
9th	● Dag & Red	H	W 2–0	Att: 2,604	Scorers: Le Fondre². Booked: Fenton.
13th	● Lincoln	A	W 1–2	Att: 4,152	Scorers: Le Fondre, Roberts. Booked: Harrison.
19th	● Torquay	H	D 1–1	Att: 3,339	Scorers: Harrison. Booked: Gunning, Roberts. Dismissed: Roberts.
22nd	● Shrewsbury	H	D 1–1	Att: 2,869	Scorers: Le Fondre. Booked: Gunning.
27th	● Burton	A	W 0–1	Att: 3,568	Scorers: Le Fondre. Booked: J Walker, Sharps.

MARCH
2nd	● Rochdale	A	L 4–0	Att: 3,502	
6th	● Bradford	H	L 1–2	Att: 4,185	Scorers: Le Fondre. Booked: Fenton, Pope.
13th	● Dag & Red	A	W 0–1	Att: 1,862	Scorers: Le Fondre. Booked: Lynch, Fenton, Tonge.
16th	● Accrington	A	L 2–1	Att: 1,440	Scorers: J Walker. Booked: Sharps.
20th	● Bury	H	W 1–0	Att: 3,521	Scorers: J Walker. Booked: Sharps.
23rd	● Macclesfield	H	W 3–1	Att: 2,873	Scorers: Broughton, Harrison, Le Fondre.
27th	● Notts County	A	L 1–0	Att: 9,015	Booked: Harrison.

APRIL
3rd	● Port Vale	H	L 1–2	Att: 3,721	Scorers: J Walker.
5th	● Aldershot	A	L 3–0	Att: 3,573	Booked: Harrison, Sharps.
10th	● Morecambe	A	L 2–0	Att: 2,337	Booked: Broughton.
13th	● Northampton	H	W 1–0	Att: 3,325	Scorers: Le Fondre. Booked: Mills, Marshall. Dismissed: Harrison.
17th	● Cheltenham	H	D 0–0	Att: 3,478	Booked: Gunning, Mills.
24th	● Barnet	A	W 0–1	Att: 1,884	Scorers: Ellison. Booked: Gunning, Fenton.

MAY
1st	● Crewe	H	D 0–0	Att: 4,142	Booked: Ellison.
8th	● Hereford	A	L 3–0	Att: 3,005	
15th	● Aldershot	A	W 0–1	Att: 5,470	Scorers: Le Fondre.
19th	● Aldershot	H	W 2–0	Att: 7,082	Scorers: Ellison, Le Fondre. Booked: Gunning, Ellison. Agg: 3–0.
30th	● Dag & Red	N	L 3–2	Att: 32,054	Scorers: R Taylor². Booked: Sharps, Le Fondre, R Taylor.

● Coca-Cola League 2/Play-offs ● FA Cup ● Carling Cup ● Johnstone's Paint Trophy

actim

LEAGUE 2 GOALKEEPER STATS

Player	Appearances	Match starts	Completed matches	Sub appearances	Subbed off	Clean sheets	Yellow cards	Red cards
Andy Warrington	46	46	46	0	0	16	0	0

LEAGUE 2 OUTFIELD PLAYER STATS

Player	Appearances	Match starts	Completed matches	Substitute appearances	Subbed off	Goals scored	Yellow cards	Red cards
Abdulai Bell-Baggie	11	2	0	9	2	0	0	0
Stephen Brogan	5	1	1	4	0	1	0	0
Drewe Broughton	16	6	1	10	5	3	3	0
Michael Cummins	15	6	4	9	2	2	2	0
Kevin Ellison	39	36	24	3	12	8	2	0
Nick Fenton	35	34	30	1	2	0	8	2
Jamie Green	19	14	13	5	1	0	0	0
Gavin Gunning	21	21	17	0	4	0	4	0
Danny Harrison	37	32	29	5	2	4	3	1
Marc Joseph	15	11	10	4	1	0	1	0
Nicky Law	42	41	34	1	7	2	1	0
Adam Le Fondre	44	43	37	1	6	25	0	0
Andy Liddell	2	0	0	2	0	0	0	0
Mark Lynch	23	21	19	2	2	0	2	0
Marcus Marshall	22	13	7	9	6	0	1	0
Craig McAllister	8	7	2	1	5	0	0	0
Pablo Mills	37	34	30	3	4	0	3	0
Andrew Nicholas	7	7	5	0	2	0	1	0
Tom Pope	35	26	9	9	17	3	2	0
Gary Roberts	13	11	8	2	2	2	5	1
Adam Rundle	4	4	0	0	4	0	0	0
Ian Sharps	44	44	40	0	4	0	7	0
Jason Taylor	2	2	0	0	2	0	0	0
Ryan Taylor	19	3	0	16	3	0	1	0
Dale Tonge	21	18	16	3	2	0	1	0
Joshua Walker	15	15	11	0	4	3	1	0
Paul Warne	14	8	4	6	4	2	2	0

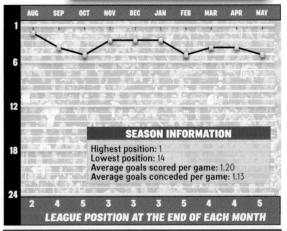

SEASON INFORMATION

Highest position: 1
Lowest position: 14
Average goals scored per game: 1.20
Average goals conceded per game: 1.13

LEAGUE POSITION AT THE END OF EACH MONTH

2	4	5	3	3	3	5	4	4	5

LONGEST SEQUENCES

Wins	4	Undefeated home	10
(18/08/09–05/09/09)		(08/08/09–05/12/09)	
Losses	4	Undefeated away	3
(27/03/10–10/04/10)		(18/08/09–19/09/09)	
Draws	2	Without scoring	2
(on three occasions)		(05/04/10–10/04/10)	
Undefeated	7	Without conceding	4
(18/08/09–26/09/09)		(13/04/10–01/05/10)	
Without win	4	Scoring	6
(on two occasions)		(05/12/09–02/02/10)	

CARDS RECEIVED

50   4

EARLIEST STRIKE

KEVIN ELLISON
(v Barnet) 4:15

LATEST STRIKE

ADAM LE FONDRE
(v Torquay) 93:56

GOALS SCORED/CONCEDED
PER FIVE-MINUTE INTERVALS

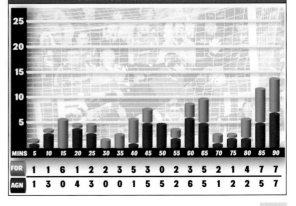

MINS	5	10	15	20	25	30	35	40	45	50	55	60	65	70	75	80	85	90
FOR	1	1	6	1	2	2	3	5	3	0	2	3	5	2	1	4	7	7
AGN	1	3	0	4	3	0	0	1	5	5	2	6	5	1	2	2	5	7

SHREWSBURY TOWN

THE LOSS of several key players hit Shrewsbury hard as they suffered a disappointing campaign. The pre-season departures of star striker Grant Holt and influential goalscoring midfielder Ben Davies – who between them had netted 32 goals en route to the Coca-Cola League 2 play-off final in 2008/2009 – proved just too much of a hurdle to overcome.

Town failed to find the goals necessary to secure a top-seven finish and the problems caused by the squad's lack of depth ultimately cost manager Paul Simpson his job just before the end of the campaign.

An early Johnstone's Paint Trophy exit to Accrington was followed by the club being on the wrong end of an FA Cup first-round upset at the hands of non-League Staines Town.

Chairman Roland Wycherley now has the task of finding a new Shrewsbury boss who can bolster the ranks accordingly and bring in the necessary experience to fire the club back up the League.

CLUB SUMMARY

FORMED	1886
MANAGER	TBC
GROUND	Prostar Stadium
CAPACITY	10,000
NICKNAME	The Shrews
WEBSITE	www.shrewsburytown.com

The New **Football Pools** PLAYER OF THE SEASON

Kelvin Langmead

OVERALL
P	W	D	L	F	A	GD	
49	17	13	19	58	60	-2	

COCA-COLA FOOTBALL LEAGUE 2
Pos	P	W	D	L	F	A	GD	Pts
12	46	17	12	17	55	54	1	63

HOME
Pos	P	W	D	L	F	A	GD	Pts
11	23	10	6	7	30	20	10	36

AWAY
Pos	P	W	D	L	F	A	GD	Pts
12	23	7	6	10	25	34	-9	27

CUP PROGRESS DETAILS
Competition	Round reached	Knocked out by
FA Cup	R1	Staines Town
Carling Cup	R1	Ipswich
JP Trophy	R2	Accrington

BIGGEST WIN (ALL COMPS)
3–0 on 2 occasions

BIGGEST DEFEAT (ALL COMPS)
18/08/09 0–5 v Dag & Red

ATTENDANCE RECORD
HIGH	AVERAGE	Low
7,096	5,482	4,328
v Port Vale (10/10/2009)		v Barnet (09/02/2010)

RESULTS 2009/10

AUGUST
8th	● Burton	H	W 3–1	Att: 6,438	Scorers: Hibbert, Labadie, Robinson.
11th	● Ipswich	H	D 3–3	Att: 4,184	Scorers: Cansdell-Sherriff, Hibbert, Robinson. Booked: Coughlan. AET – Score after 90 mins 3–3. Ipswich win 4–2 on penalties.
15th	● Barnet	A	D 2–2	Att: 1,835	Scorers: Elder, Hibbert. Booked: Murray, Holden.
18th	● Dag & Red	A	L 5–0	Att: 1,683	Booked: Cansdell-Sherriff.
22nd	● Chesterfield	H	D 1–1	Att: 5,086	Scorers: Leslie. Booked: Murray.
29th	● Accrington	A	W 1–3	Att: 1,447	Scorers: Hibbert, Langmead, Leslie. Booked: Elder, Holden.

SEPTEMBER
5th	● Bradford	H	L 1–2	Att: 5,525	Scorers: Hibbert. Booked: Langmead.
12th	● Crewe	H	W 2–0	Att: 6,204	Scorers: Hibbert, Labadie. Booked: Holden.
19th	● Lincoln	A	W 0–2	Att: 3,234	Scorers: Hibbert, Robinson. Booked: Labadie, McIntyre.
26th	● Northampton	H	W 3–0	Att: 5,548	Scorers: Labadie, Langmead, Robinson. Booked: Cansdell-Sherriff.
29th	● Cheltenham	H	W 1–0	Att: 2,928	Scorers: Hibbert, Labadie. Booked: Murray, McIntyre.

OCTOBER
3rd	● Morecambe	A	D 1–1	Att: 2,105	Scorers: Labadie. Booked: Langmead, Labadie. Dismissed: Labadie.
10th	● Port Vale	H	L 0–1	Att: 7,096	Booked: Coughlan, Holden. Dismissed: Coughlan.
17th	● Darlington	A	L 2–1	Att: 1,958	Scorers: Neal. Booked: Cansdell-Sherriff, Neal, Labadie.
20th	● Accrington	A	L 2–0	Att: 819	
24th	● Aldershot	H	W 3–1	Att: 5,417	Scorers: Elder, Fairhurst, Neal. Booked: Neal.
31st	● Notts County	A	D 1–1	Att: 7,562	Scorers: Devitt. Booked: Holden, Labadie.

NOVEMBER
7th	● Staines Town	H	L 0–1	Att: 3,539	Booked: Hibbert.
14th	● Torquay	H	D 1–1	Att: 5,072	Scorers: Hibbert. Booked: Murray.
21st	● Bury	H	D 1–1	Att: 5,070	Scorers: Coughlan.
24th	● Hereford	A	L 2–1	Att: 2,913	Scorers: Fairhurst. Booked: McIntyre, Cansdell-Sherriff.

DECEMBER
1st	● Rotherham	H	W 2–0	Att: 4,522	Scorers: Devitt, Fairhurst. Booked: Holden, Langmead, Devitt.
5th	● Bournemouth	A	L 1–0	Att: 4,652	Booked: Cansdell-Sherriff, Holden, Langmead.
12th	● Grimsby	H	D 0–0	Att: 4,850	Booked: Holden, Dunfield.
19th	● Rochdale	A	L 4–0	Att: 2,596	Booked: Holden.
26th	● Macclesfield	H	D 2–2	Att: 5,942	Scorers: Fairhurst, Hibbert. Booked: Cansdell-Sherriff.
28th	● Bradford	A	W 1–3	Att: 11,522	Scorers: Dunfield, Hibbert, McIntyre. Booked: Cansdell-Sherriff, Leslie.

JANUARY
2nd	● Chesterfield	A	W 0–1	Att: 3,601	Scorers: Hibbert. Booked: Button, J Taylor. Dismissed: Holden.
16th	● Burton	A	D 1–1	Att: 3,139	Scorers: Hibbert. Booked: Murray, Cansdell-Sherriff.
23rd	● Dag & Red	H	W 2–1	Att: 4,812	Scorers: Hibbert, Leslie. Booked: Skarz.
30th	● Accrington	H	L 0–1	Att: 5,319	

FEBRUARY
6th	● Macclesfield	A	W 0–1	Att: 2,058	Scorers: Leslie. Booked: McIntyre, Hibbert.
9th	● Barnet	H	W 2–0	Att: 4,328	Scorers: Disley, Leslie. Booked: Coughlan.
13th	● Hereford	H	W 3–1	Att: 6,098	Scorers: Cansdell-Sherriff, Coughlan, Langmead.
19th	● Bury	A	L 1–0	Att: 3,720	Booked: Dunfield, Skarz.
22nd	● Rotherham	A	D 1–1	Att: 2,869	Scorers: Leslie. Booked: Cansdell-Sherriff.
27th	● Bournemouth	H	W 1–0	Att: 6,061	Scorers: Dunfield. Booked: Holden.

MARCH
6th	● Grimsby	A	L 3–0	Att: 3,651	
13th	● Rochdale	H	L 0–1	Att: 6,081	Dismissed: Cansdell-Sherriff.
20th	● Aldershot	A	L 2–0	Att: 2,681	Booked: Bright.
27th	● Darlington	H	L 0–2	Att: 5,081	Booked: Dunfield, Leslie.

APRIL
3rd	● Torquay	A	L 2–1	Att: 3,094	Scorers: Bevan OG. Booked: Cansdell-Sherriff, Skarz.
5th	● Notts County	H	L 0–1	Att: 6,287	Booked: Dunfield, McIntyre, Bright.
10th	● Crewe	A	W 0–3	Att: 4,283	Scorers: Bradshaw², Hibbert. Booked: Skarz.
13th	● Cheltenham	H	D 0–0	Att: 4,967	Booked: Cansdell-Sherriff.
17th	● Lincoln	H	W 1–0	Att: 4,932	Scorers: Bright.
24th	● Northampton	A	L 2–0	Att: 5,019	Booked: Bright.

MAY
1st	● Morecambe	H	L 2–3	Att: 5,340	Scorers: Bradshaw, Van den Broek. Booked: Skarz.
8th	● Port Vale	A	D 1–1	Att: 8,467	Scorers: Bright. Booked: Cansdell-Sherriff.

● Coca-Cola League 2/Play-Offs ● FA Cup ● Carling Cup ● Johnstone's Paint Trophy

LEAGUE 2 GOALKEEPER STATS

Player	Appearances	Match starts	Completed matches	Sub appearances	Subbed off	Clean sheets	Yellow cards	Red cards
Andres Arestidou	2	2	2	0	0	0	0	0
David Button	26	26	26	0	0	9	1	0
Chris Neal	7	7	7	0	0	0	0	0
Steve Phillips	11	11	11	0	0	3	0	0

LEAGUE 2 OUTFIELD PLAYER STATS

Player	Appearances	Match starts	Completed matches	Substitute appearances	Subbed off	Goals scored	Yellow cards	Red cards
Tom Bradshaw	6	1	1	5	0	3	0	0
Kris Bright	26	4	2	22	2	2	3	0
Shane Cansdell-Sherriff	41	41	39	0	1	1	12	1
Graham Coughlan	36	36	32	0	3	2	2	1
Jamie Cureton	12	10	3	2	7	0	0	0
Jamie Devitt	9	8	3	1	5	2	1	0
Craig Disley	18	16	10	2	6	1	0	0
Terry Dunfield	30	28	24	2	4	2	4	0
Nathan Elder	19	9	1	10	8	2	1	0
Waide Fairhurst	10	10	0	0	10	4	0	0
Andre Gray	4	0	0	4	0	0	0	0
Dave Hibbert	38	37	19	1	18	14	1	0
Dean Holden	37	37	34	0	2	0	10	1
Harry Hooman	2	1	1	0	0	0	0	0
Joss Labadie	13	11	9	2	1	5	4	1
Kelvin Langmead	44	44	44	0	0	3	4	0
Steven Leslie	34	21	16	13	5	6	2	0
Kevin McIntyre	45	43	43	2	0	1	5	0
Paul Murray	27	25	16	2	9	0	5	0
Lewis Neal	29	21	12	8	9	2	2	0
Omer Riza	8	1	0	7	2	0	0	0
Jake Robinson	34	15	6	19	9	3	0	0
Jake Simpson	18	14	3	4	11	0	0	0
Joe Skarz	20	20	19	0	1	0	5	0
Danny Taylor	3	2	2	1	0	0	0	0
Jon Taylor	2	0	0	2	0	0	1	0
Benjamin Van den Broek	11	5	2	6	3	1	0	0

AUG SEP OCT NOV DEC JAN FEB MAR APR MAY

SEASON INFORMATION

Highest position: 1
Lowest position: 22
Average goals scored per game: 1.20
Average goals conceded per game: 1.17

LEAGUE POSITION AT THE END OF EACH MONTH

11 5 7 9 8 6 6 11 12 12

LONGEST SEQUENCES

Wins	4	Undefeated home	7	
(12/09/09–29/09/09)		(24/10/09–23/01/10)		
Losses	6	Undefeated away	4	
(06/03/10–05/04/10)		(on two occasions)		
Draws	3	Without scoring	4	
(31/10/09–21/11/09)		(06/03/10–27/03/10)		
Undefeated	5	Without conceding	3	
(on two occasions)		(on two occasions)		
Without win	6	Scoring	8	
(06/03/10–05/04/10)		(22/08/09–03/10/09)		

CARDS RECEIVED

63　4

EARLIEST STRIKE

NATHAN ELDER
(v Barnet) 1:33

LATEST STRIKE

DAVE HIBBERT
(v Macclesfield) 95:37

GOALS SCORED/CONCEDED
PER FIVE-MINUTE INTERVALS

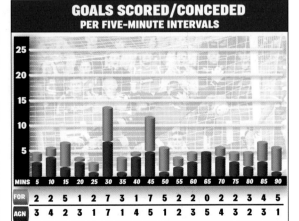

MINS	5	10	15	20	25	30	35	40	45	50	55	60	65	70	75	80	85	90
FOR	2	2	5	1	2	7	3	1	7	5	2	2	0	2	2	3	4	5
AGN	3	4	2	3	1	7	1	4	5	1	2	3	5	4	3	2	3	1

TORQUAY UNITED

TORQUAY proved once again that the gap between the Conference and Coca-Cola League 2 can be successfully bridged as they ensured survival in their first season back in the Football League.

It took them until April to complete the job but Paul Buckle's side – promoted via the Conference play-offs in 2008/09 – ultimately did enough to stay up.

The Gulls managed just two wins from their opening 10 games in the League and at that stage they appeared to be set for a difficult campaign. However, a run of just two defeats from their last 16 games, including a 5–0 success over then-leaders Rochdale, proved that they could match anybody in the division on their day.

If Torquay can recapture that form on a consistent basis in the coming season they could challenge in the top half of the table, although Buckle is likely to try and add some new faces to his squad first.

CLUB SUMMARY

FORMED	1899
MANAGER	Paul Buckle
GROUND	Plainmoor
CAPACITY	6,104
NICKNAME	The Gulls
WEBSITE	www.torquayunited.com

The New **Football Pools** PLAYER OF THE SEASON — *Lee Mansell*

OVERALL
P	W	D	L	F	A	GD
52	17	16	19	77	62	15

COCA-COLA FOOTBALL LEAGUE 2
Pos	P	W	D	L	F	A	GD	Pts
17	46	14	15	17	64	55	9	57

HOME
Pos	P	W	D	L	F	A	GD	Pts
16	23	9	6	8	34	24	10	33

AWAY
Pos	P	W	D	L	F	A	GD	Pts
19	23	5	9	9	30	31	-1	24

CUP PROGRESS DETAILS
Competition	Round reached	Knocked out by
FA Cup	R3	Brighton
Carling Cup	R1	Crystal Palace
JP Trophy	R2	Southampton

BIGGEST WIN (ALL COMPS)
5–0 on 2 occasions

BIGGEST DEFEAT (ALL COMPS)
15/08/09 3–5 v Dag & Red

ATTENDANCE RECORD
High	Average	Low
5,124	2,856	2,122
v Notts County (08/05/2010)		v Cheltenham (01/12/2009)

RESULTS 2009/10

AUGUST
8th	● Chesterfield	H	W 2-0	Att: 3,966	Scorers: Mansell, Rendell.
11th	● Crystal Palace	A	L 2-1	Att: 3,140	Scorers: Sills. Booked: Robertson, Todd.
15th	● Dag & Red	A	L 5-3	Att: 1,824	Scorers: Benyon, Carayol, Wroe. Booked: Todd, Hargreaves.
18th	● Burton	A	W 0-2	Att: 2,670	Scorers: Benyon, Rendell. Booked: Hargreaves, Charnock.
22nd	● Barnet	A	L 0-1	Att: 2,856	Booked: Todd, Carayol.
29th	● Bradford	A	L 2-0	Att: 11,123	Booked: Robertson.

SEPTEMBER
1st	● Cheltenham	A	W 1-3	Att: 1,397	Scorers: Benyon, Stevens[2]. Booked: Charnock, Wroe.
5th	● Bournemouth	H	L 1-2	Att: 3,881	Scorers: Todd. Booked: Wroe, Nicholson.
12th	● Rochdale	A	L 2-1	Att: 2,407	Scorers: Hargreaves. Booked: Robertson.
19th	● Grimsby	H	L 0-2	Att: 2,575	Booked: Poke.
26th	● Macclesfield	A	L 2-1	Att: 1,745	Scorers: Benyon. Booked: Carlisle.
29th	● Aldershot	H	D 1-1	Att: 2,271	Scorers: Sills. Booked: Sills. Dismissed: Sills.

OCTOBER
3rd	● Bury	H	D 1-1	Att: 2,524	Scorers: Benyon. Booked: Ellis, Robertson.
6th	● Southampton	A	D 2-2	Att: 9,319	Scorers: Sills, Wroe. Southampton win 5–3 on penalties.
11th	● Notts County	A	D 2-2	Att: 8,812	Scorers: Ellis, Sills. Booked: Sills.
17th	● Morecambe	H	D 2-2	Att: 2,614	Scorers: Carlisle, Wroe. Booked: Rendell.
24th	● Lincoln	A	D 0-0	Att: 3,604	Booked: Hargreaves.
31st	● Northampton	H	W 1-0	Att: 2,732	Scorers: Hargreaves. Booked: Charnock, Thomson.

NOVEMBER
7th	● Cheltenham	H	W 3-1	Att: 2,370	Scorers: Wroe[3]. Booked: Wroe.
14th	● Shrewsbury	A	D 1-1	Att: 5,072	Scorers: Hargreaves. Booked: Mansell, Poke. Dismissed: Charnock.
21st	● Rotherham	H	L 0-2	Att: 2,551	Booked: Wroe, Thompson.
24th	● Port Vale	A	D 2-2	Att: 3,996	Scorers: Rendell, Wroe. Booked: Mansell, Smith, Wroe.

DECEMBER
1st	● Cheltenham	H	W 3-0	Att: 2,122	Scorers: Rendell, Thomson, Zebroski. Booked: Ellis.
5th	● Accrington	A	L 4-2	Att: 1,351	Scorers: Wroe, Zebroski.
12th	● Darlington	H	W 5-0	Att: 2,434	Scorers: Benyon, Carlisle, Rendell, Zebroski[2].
15th	● Stockport	N	W 0-4	Att: 1,690	Scorers: Benyon[3], Rendell.
26th	● Hereford	H	W 1-0	Att: 3,792	Scorers: Wroe. Booked: Smith, Mansell, Poke.
28th	● Bournemouth	A	L 2-1	Att: 7,626	Scorers: Rendell. Booked: Wroe, Thomson, Carlisle, Mansell, Smith, Robertson, Poke.

JANUARY
2nd	● Brighton	H	L 0-1	Att: 4,028	Booked: Mansell, Hargreaves, Smith.
16th	● Chesterfield	A	L 1-0	Att: 3,215	Booked: Hargreaves.
23rd	● Burton	H	L 2-3	Att: 2,629	Scorers: Rendell, Robertson. Booked: Hargreaves, Robertson, Smith.
26th	● Barnet	A	D 1-1	Att: 1,331	Scorers: Furlong OG.
30th	● Bradford	H	L 1-2	Att: 2,592	Scorers: Robertson. Booked: Zebroski, Benyon.

FEBRUARY
2nd	● Crewe	A	D 1-1	Att: 3,421	Scorers: Zebroski.
6th	● Hereford	A	L 1-0	Att: 2,123	Booked: Thompson, Cox, Benyon, Wroe, Stevens.
13th	● Port Vale	H	L 1-2	Att: 2,563	Scorers: Benyon. Booked: O'Kane.
19th	● Rotherham	A	D 1-1	Att: 3,339	Scorers: Benyon.
23rd	● Cheltenham	A	D 1-1	Att: 2,607	Scorers: Carayol. Booked: Ellis.
27th	● Accrington	H	W 2-1	Att: 2,503	Scorers: Mansell, Kempson OG. Booked: Rowe-Turner, Mansell.

MARCH
2nd	● Dag & Red	H	D 0-0	Att: 2,140	Booked: Barnes, Zebroski.
6th	● Darlington	A	W 1-3	Att: 1,819	Scorers: Carayol, Ellis, O'Kane. Booked: Barnes, Mansell.
13th	● Crewe	H	D 1-1	Att: 2,507	Scorers: Rendell. Booked: Zebroski, Carlisle, Mansell.
20th	● Lincoln	A	L 2-3	Att: 2,547	Scorers: Wroe, Zebroski. Booked: Benyon, Smith.
27th	● Morecambe	A	L 2-0	Att: 1,734	Booked: Ellis, Branston.

APRIL
3rd	● Shrewsbury	H	W 2-1	Att: 3,094	Scorers: Ellis, Rendell. Booked: Branston, Carayol.
5th	● Northampton	A	D 0-0	Att: 5,515	Booked: Rendell.
10th	● Rochdale	H	W 5-0	Att: 3,093	Scorers: Benyon[2], Carayol, Rendell, Wroe.
13th	● Aldershot	A	W 0-2	Att: 3,652	Scorers: Benyon, Rendell.
17th	● Grimsby	A	W 0-3	Att: 5,702	Scorers: Benyon, Carayol, Wroe. Booked: Ellis, Branston. Dismissed: Branston.
24th	● Macclesfield	H	W 1-0	Att: 2,570	Scorers: Wroe.

MAY
1st	● Bury	A	W 0-3	Att: 3,492	Scorers: Carayol, Rendell, Stevens. Booked: Mansell.
8th	● Notts County	H	D 0-0	Att: 5,124	Booked: Mansell, Ellis, Charnock.

● Coca-Cola League 2/Play-Offs ● FA Cup ● Carling Cup ● Johnstone's Paint Trophy

actim

LEAGUE 2 GOALKEEPER STATS

Player	Appearances	Match starts	Completed matches	Sub appearances	Subbed off	Clean sheets	Yellow cards	Red cards
Scott Bevan	18	17	16	1	1	4	0	0
Steve Collis	1	1	1	0	0	1	0	0
Michael Poke	29	28	27	1	1	9	4	0

LEAGUE 2 OUTFIELD PLAYER STATS

Player	Appearances	Match starts	Completed matches	Substitute appearances	Subbed off	Goals scored	Yellow cards	Red cards
Ashley Barnes	6	6	3	0	3	0	2	0
Elliot Benyon	45	31	11	14	20	11	3	0
Guy Branston	16	16	15	0	0	0	3	1
Michael Brough	1	0	0	1	0	0	0	0
Mohammed Camara	2	2	1	0	1	0	0	0
Mustapha Carayol	20	11	4	9	7	6	2	0
Wayne Carlisle	24	20	17	4	3	2	3	0
Kieran Charnock	24	22	19	2	2	0	3	1
Sam Cox	3	1	1	2	0	0	1	0
Mark Ellis	27	25	24	2	1	3	6	0
Chris Hargreaves	23	21	19	2	2	3	5	0
Lee Hodges	5	2	1	3	1	0	0	0
Lloyd Macklin	4	3	0	1	3	0	0	0
Lee Mansell	39	35	33	4	2	2	9	0
Danny Mills	2	0	0	2	0	0	0	0
Kevin Nicholson	27	23	22	4	1	0	1	0
Eunan O'Kane	16	5	0	11	5	1	1	0
Scott Rendell	35	28	17	7	11	12	2	0
Chris Robertson	45	45	44	0	1	2	5	0
Lathanial Rowe-Turner	6	5	5	1	0	0	1	0
Tim Sills	18	12	8	6	3	2	2	1
Adam Smith	16	16	14	0	2	0	5	0
Danny Stevens	27	16	5	11	10	1	2	0
Tyrone Thompson	24	17	11	7	6	0	2	0
Jake Thomson	15	13	6	2	7	1	2	0
Chris Todd	9	9	7	0	2	1	2	0
Marvin Williams	4	1	1	3	0	0	0	0
Nicky Wroe	45	45	42	0	3	9	5	0
Chris Zebroski	30	30	28	0	2	6	3	0

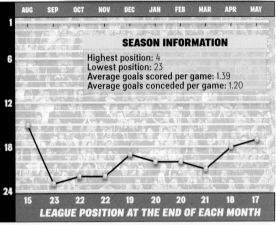

SEASON INFORMATION

Highest position: 4
Lowest position: 23
Average goals scored per game: 1.39
Average goals conceded per game: 1.20

LEAGUE POSITION AT THE END OF EACH MONTH

| 15 | 23 | 22 | 22 | 19 | 20 | 20 | 21 | 18 | 17 |

LONGEST SEQUENCES

Wins	5	Undefeated home		4
(10/04/10–01/05/10)		(on two occasions)		
Losses	6	Undefeated away		4
(22/08/09–26/09/09)		(on two occasions)		
Draws	5	Without scoring		2
(29/09/09–24/10/09)		(22/08/09–29/08/09)		
Undefeated	8	Without conceding		2
(03/04/10–08/05/10)		(on two occasions)		
Without win	11	Scoring		6
(22/08/09–24/10/09)		(24/11/09–28/12/09)		

CARDS RECEIVED

73   3

EARLIEST STRIKE

CHRIS ZEBROSKI
(v Crewe) 6:55

LATEST STRIKE

SCOTT RENDELL
(v Bury) 90:51

GOALS SCORED/CONCEDED
PER FIVE-MINUTE INTERVALS

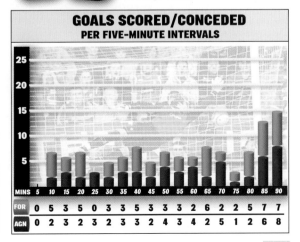

MINS	5	10	15	20	25	30	35	40	45	50	55	60	65	70	75	80	85	90
FOR	0	5	3	5	0	3	3	5	3	3	3	2	6	2	2	5	7	7
AGN	0	2	3	2	3	2	3	3	2	4	3	4	2	5	1	2	6	8

COMMITMENT TO FOOTBALL FANS AND THEIR COMMUNITIES

DURING this season, The New Football Pools began funding a number of community-related schemes linked to Clydesdale Bank Premier League and Irn-Bru Scottish Football League clubs. More than £1.2million has been donated by The New Football Pools across all four Leagues in community initiatives that will have a positive impact on the lives and welfare of the fans of the 42 football club communities involved over the next two to three years.

FIT FANS

Some £300,000 of funding from The New Football Pools will be injected into the newly formed Scottish Premier League Trust next season.

The SPL Trust has been set up to drive investment into community programmes across the 12 SPL clubs with a focus on health, citizenship and achievement.

The New Football Pools has contributed more than £1.1 billion to the arts, sporting and good causes since 1923, with almost £530 million given to British football alone. Whilst in the past we have invested in infrastructure and bricks and mortar, including £5 million given to the Scottish Football Association to re-build Hampden Park and a major contribution going towards Murrayfield, we are currently heavily focused on community programmes and the many social aspects in and around football.

FIT FOR FOOTBALL, FIT FOR LIFE

In an unprecedented partnership between The New Football Pools and the Scottish Football League, a donation of more than £900,000 from The New Football Pools was made to fund Fit for Football, Fit for Life. The multi-channelled scheme, which has been involved in heart screening for young people, alcohol awareness schemes, U17 and U19 training as well as the donation of a defibrillators to every League club across Scotland, will benefit the local communities of the 30 Football League clubs over the next two to three years.

Dundee star Leigh Griffiths holds one of the defibrillators that were given to every Scottish Football League club (above). In the past the Pools provided funds for renovations at Hampden Park (below)

Mr Menzies from Dundee was one of our Top Prize winners in March 2010

THE NEW FOOTBALL POOLS PLAYER OF THE SEASON

The New Football Pools Panel of football experts and pundits has once again produced its definitive 2009/10 'Player of the Season' for The Official Football Yearbook, having analysed player performances across all Scottish Premier League and Football League clubs.

With outstanding individual displays across the Leagues during this season, selecting the players to receive this accolade proved difficult. However, combining criteria such as clean sheets, goals scored, games played, assists and man-of-the-match performances, we selected those players who made the biggest impact during the campaign.

We'd like to congratulate each winner of this accolade. Read on to see whether your favourite player matches our verdict.

Miller (Hibernian)

Lilley (Queen of Sth)

FREEZE WISE MEN

An action-packed 10 months of highs and lows for fans all over the UK was only temporarily disrupted by the weather this winter, but nowhere more so than in Scotland as The New Football Pools' Pools Panel dealt with their busiest Saturday for more than 25 years.

Former Scotland, Albion Rovers, Blackpool and Newcastle United midfielder Tony Green (pictured), who sits weekly alongside England World Cup winners Gordon Banks and Roger Hunt, was called into action to deliberate for more than two hours on one Saturday in January, as the Panel had to decide the outcome of 40 postponed games. Not since the early 1980s have so many games been postponed over a single weekend.

January's arctic weather draws parallels with the time when the Pools Panel was founded. Forty-seven years ago, the winter of 1962/63 saw sub-zero temperatures play havoc with British football and the Pools results and on 26th January, 1963, the Panel of former players and referees provided expert opinion on 52 of the 55 postponed games that week.

Tony, who became Scotland's most expensive player when he moved from Blackpool to Newcastle for £150,000 in 1971, has sat on the panel for 34 years, after his career was cut short at the age of 26 with a serious knee injury. The Glaswegian originally decided to join the Panel on the understanding that it would be for just 12 months. Only Panel chairman Roger Hunt has more years on Green – one more in fact, having served for 35 years.

The Pools Panel decisions are taken very seriously – after all, they could be making the difference between someone becoming very rich or not. In fact, only the week before the 'big freeze' in January, one lucky Pools player won just over £118,000, with three of his winning selections being decided by the Pools Panel after freezing weather caused matches that week to be postponed.

Pools Panel members Roger Hunt and Gordon Banks were kept busy when a huge number of games were postponed in January

CLYDESDALE BANK PREMIER LEAGUE

CLYDESDALE BANK PREMIER LEAGUE STATISTICS 2009/10

PLAYER OF THE SEASON
David Weir (Rangers)

MANAGER OF THE SEASON
Walter Smith (Rangers)

THE PLAYER WITH THE MOST...

GOALS	Kris Boyd (Rangers)	**23**
SHOTS ON TARGET	Derek Riordan (Hibernian)	**58**
SHOTS OFF TARGET	Derek Riordan (Hibernian)	**42**
SHOTS WITHOUT SCORING	John Rankin (Hibernian)	**34**
SHOTS PER GOAL	James McArthur (Hamilton)	**44**
ASSISTS	McGeady (Celtic), Davis (Rangers)	**14**
OFFSIDES	Anthony Stokes (Hibernian)	**56**
FOULS	Kevin Kyle (Kilmarnock)	**82**
FREE-KICKS WON	Jim O'Brien (Motherwell)	**94**
PENALTIES SCORED	Simon Mensing (Hamilton)	**5**
GOALS SCORED DIRECT FROM FREE-KICKS	Derek Riordan (Hibernian)	**4**
SAVES MADE	Jamie Langfield (Aberdeen)	**196**
DEFENSIVE CLEARANCES	David Weir (Rangers)	**71**
DEFENSIVE BLOCKS	Darren Dods (Dundee Utd)	**19**

THE TEAM WITH THE MOST...

GOALS	Rangers	82
SHOTS ON TARGET	Celtic	326
SHOTS OFF TARGET	Celtic	240
SHOTS PER GOAL	Falkirk	11.71
CORNERS	Celtic	304
FOULS	Hibernian	548
WOODWORK STRIKES	Celtic	20
OFFSIDES	Hibernian	128
PENALTIES CONCEDED	Hibernian	10
PENALTIES AWARDED	Celtic	9
PENALTIES SCORED	Dundee Utd	6
YELLOW CARDS	Hearts	79
RED CARDS	Aberdeen	10

TOTALS 2009/10

GOALS

Total	585
Home	321
Away	264

CARDS

Yellow	749
Average per game	3.29
Reds	50
Average per game	0.22

ATTENDANCES

Total	3,180,623

IT WAS another season to remember in the Clydesdale Bank Premier League, with Rangers emerging victorious following a fascinating title race.

The Old Firm occupied the top two places, but behind them there was plenty of entertainment, with the jostling for position, the race for European qualification and the battle for survival all making for a thrilling finale.

The men from Ibrox ultimately won the championship with some room to spare, as Walter Smith guided them to a second successive title success. Having already claimed the Co-operative Insurance Cup in March, the Gers could celebrate a domestic double, achieved despite Smith and assistant Ally McCoist having to work under tough financial restrictions all season.

The good news for Rangers fans is that, following some uncertainty over his future, Smith has signed a new one-year contract and will be back again in 2010/11 to try and make it a title hat-trick.

Rangers were forced to produce their best in the closing weeks of the season, as a resurgent Celtic side rallied to finish the campaign strongly under interim boss Neil Lennon. The Northern Irishman had been handed the job in March following the departure of Tony Mowbray, and brought at least some joy to the Bhoys' fans following a difficult few months.

Managerial changes

Mowbray's exit from Celtic Park was one of 12 managerial changes over the course of the season. Indeed, of those in charge of SPL clubs at the end of 2008/09, only Smith, St Johnstone's Derek McInnes and Hamilton's Billy Reid remained at their respective clubs come the end of the 2009/10 campaign.

Jimmy Calderwood had parted company with Aberdeen prior to the start of the campaign, paving the way for Motherwell's Mark McGhee to return to Pittodrie, where he had enjoyed a successful spell as a player in the 1980s. However, a difficult first year back in the Granite City followed for the new Dons boss, and Aberdeen eventually ended the term down in ninth place.

Over at Hibernian, John Hughes was brought in to replace Mixu Paatelainen. Hughes had impressed at Falkirk and he enjoyed a good start to his tenure at Easter Road thanks to an impressive 12-game unbeaten run in the League, which sparked

Rangers stormed to title glory while Dundee United enjoyed their best campaign in years

talk of the club splitting the Old Firm. A series of disappointing results ultimately prevented them from doing that, but a fourth-place finish on the final day secured them Europa League football for the 2010/11 season.

Dundee United said a fond farewell to Craig Levein when he left to take the Scotland job midway through the season, although his assistant, Peter Houston, ensured that the transition was a relatively smooth one when he stepped into the role and led the Terrors to third place in the SPL and success in the Active Nation Scottish Cup.

Former national-team boss Craig Brown helped to lift the fortunes of Motherwell, having replaced Jim Gannon over the festive period, and the club were ultimately unfortunate to lose out to Hibs in the race for fourth spot.

Hearts ensured a top-six finish in a campaign that saw the return of Jim Jefferies for a second spell as manager when he was named as Csaba László's successor.

At Rugby Park, Calderwood stepped in to take on the challenge of keeping Kilmarnock in the top flight, and he achieved it following a tense goalless draw against Falkirk on the final day of the season, which simultaneously relegated the Bairns and their new manager, Steven Pressley.

St Mirren survived a relegation scrap and also reached the final of the Co-operative Insurance Cup, only to lose to nine-man Rangers in heartbreaking fashion at Hampden Park. Manager Gus MacPherson's seven-year association with the Paisley club ended within a few days of the campaign coming to a close, and his will be big shoes to fill.

There was also satisfaction for St Johnstone – who enjoyed a tremendous return to the top flight by finishing in eighth place – and Hamilton, who went one better by finishing in seventh, as Reid took the club to its highest finish in the League for 75 years.

actim

FINAL CLYDESDALE BANK PREMIER LEAGUE TABLE

Pos	Team	P	HOME					AWAY					GD	Pts
			W	D	L	F	A	W	D	L	F	A		
1	Rangers	38	15	4	0	52	13	11	5	3	30	15	54	87
2	Celtic	38	14	4	1	42	14	11	2	6	33	25	36	81
3	Dundee Utd	38	8	4	7	22	21	9	8	2	33	26	8	63
4	Hibernian	38	9	4	6	29	21	6	5	8	29	34	3	54
5	Motherwell	38	8	5	5	29	25	5	9	6	23	29	−2	53
6	Hearts	38	9	4	6	19	20	4	5	10	16	26	−11	48
7	Hamilton	38	6	7	6	19	17	7	3	9	20	29	−7	49
8	St Johnstone	38	6	6	7	31	28	6	5	8	26	33	−4	47
9	Aberdeen	38	6	4	10	20	31	4	7	7	16	21	−16	41
10	St Mirren	38	5	9	5	18	18	2	4	13	18	31	−13	34
11	Kilmarnock	38	5	6	8	23	27	3	3	13	6	24	−22	33
12	Falkirk	38	3	6	10	17	29	3	7	9	14	28	−26	31

Prince Buaben
(Dundee Utd)

Brian McLean
(Falkirk)

It's celebration time for Rangers as Walter Smith's team lift the Clydesdale Bank Premier League trophy

CLYDESDALE BANK PREMIER LEAGUE RESULTS

	Aberdeen	Celtic	Dundee Utd	Falkirk	Hamilton	Hearts	Hibernian	Kilmarnock	Motherwell	Rangers	St Johnstone	St Mirren
Aberdeen	–	1–3, 4–4	0–2, 2–2	0–1, 1–0	1–2, 1–3	1–1, 0–1	0–2	1–0, 1–2	0–0, 0–3	1–0	2–1, 1–3	1–0, 2–1
Celtic	3–0	–	1–1, 1–0	1–1	2–0	2–1, 2–0	1–2, 3–2	3–0, 3–1	0–0, 2–1, 4–0	1–1, 2–1	5–2, 3–0	3–1
Dundee Utd	0–1	2–1, 0–2	–	2–1, 3–0	1–1, 0–2	2–0, 1–0	1–0, 0–2	0–0	0–1, 3–0	0–3, 0–0, 1–2	3–3	3–2
Falkirk	0–0, 3–1	3–3, 0–2	1–4	–	2–0, 0–1	0–1	1–3, 1–3	0–0, 0–1	0–0	1–3	1–2, 0–0	1–3, 2–1, 1–1
Hamilton	0–3, 1–1	1–2, 0–1	0–1	0–0, 2–2	–	2–1	2–0, 4–1	0–0, 3–0	2–2, 0–0	0–1	0–2, 1–0	1–0, 0–0
Hearts	0–3	2–1, 1–2	0–0, 0–0	0–0, 3–2	2–1, 2–0	–	0–0, 2–1	1–0, 1–0	1–0, 0–2	1–2, 1–4	1–2	1–0
Hibernian	2–0, 2–2	0–1, 0–1	1–1, 2–4	2–0	5–1	1–1, 1–2	–	1–0, 1–0	2–0	1–4, 0–1	3–0, 1–1	2–1, 2–1
Kilmarnock	1–1, 2–0	1–0	0–2, 4–4	1–2, 0–0	3–0, 1–2	1–2	1–1	–	0–3	0–0, 0–2	2–1, 3–2, 1–2	1–2, 1–1
Motherwell	1–1	2–3	2–2, 2–3	1–0, 0–1	1–0	1–0, 3–1	1–3, 1–0, 6–6	3–1, 1–0	–	0–0, 1–1	1–3	2–0
Rangers	0–0, 3–1	2–1, 1–0	7–1	4–1, 3–0	4–1, 1–0	1–1, 2–0	1–1, 3–0	3–0	6–1, 3–3	–	3–0	2–1, 3–1
St Johnstone	1–0, 1–1	1–4	2–3, 0–1	3–1, 1–1	1–1, 2–3	2–2, 1–0	5–1	0–1	2–2, 1–2	1–2, 4–1	–	1–0, 2–2
St Mirren	1–0, 0–1	0–2, 4–0	0–0, 1–2	1–1	0–2, 0–0	2–1, 1–1	1–1	1–0, 1–0	3–3, 0–0	0–2	1–1, 1–1	–

STADIUM STATISTICS

GROUND	TEAM	M	GLS	G/M	GROUND	TEAM	M	GLS	G/M	GROUND	TEAM	M	GLS	G/M
Ibrox	Rangers	19	65	3.42	Rugby Park	Kilmarnock	19	50	2.63	Tannadice Park	Dundee Utd	19	43	2.26
McDiarmid Park	St Johnstone	19	59	3.11	Easter Road	Hibernian	19	50	2.63	Tynecastle	Hearts	19	39	2.05
Fir Park	Motherwell	18	54	3.00	Pittodrie	Aberdeen	20	51	2.55	St Mirren Park	St Mirren	19	36	1.89
Celtic Park	Celtic	19	56	2.95	Falkirk Stadium	Falkirk	19	46	2.42	New Douglas Park	Hamilton	19	36	1.89

Kris Boyd (Rangers)

TEAM DISCIPLINE

TEAM	Y	R
Hearts	79	9
Aberdeen	74	10
Dundee Utd	64	9
Hibernian	66	4
St Mirren	59	5
St Johnstone	71	1
Rangers	58	5
Kilmarnock	63	1
Falkirk	66	0
Celtic	52	4
Hamilton	60	1
Motherwell	36	1

John Ruddy (Motherwell)

LEADING SCORERS

PLAYER	TEAM	GLS
Kris Boyd	Rangers	23
Anthony Stokes	Hibernian	21
Kenny Miller	Rangers	18
Derek Riordan	Hibernian	13
Jon Daly	Dundee Utd	13
Robbie Keane	Celtic	12
John Sutton	Motherwell	12
Lukas Jutkiewicz	Motherwell	12
Georgios Samaras	Celtic	10
Marc-Antoine Fortuné	Celtic	10

LATE GOALS
IN THE LAST 10 MINUTES OF MATCHES

TEAM	F	A
Aberdeen	5	4
Celtic	9	10
Dundee Utd	11	6
Falkirk	4	8
Hamilton	6	5
Hearts	2	9
Hibernian	9	7
Kilmarnock	2	6
Motherwell	8	7
Rangers	12	4
St Johnstone	8	9
St Mirren	9	10

LEADING GOALKEEPERS

PLAYER	TEAM	CLEAN SHEET
John Ruddy	Motherwell	15
Allan McGregor	Rangers	14
Jamie Langfield	Aberdeen	11
Artur Boruc	Celtic	11
Robert Olejnik	Falkirk	10
Tomas Cerny	Hamilton	9
Dusan Pernis	Dundee Utd	7
Paul Gallacher	St Mirren	7
Nicky Weaver	Dundee Utd	6
Marian Kello	Hearts	6

CLYDESDALE BANK PREMIER LEAGUE TABLES

HOME TABLE

	P	W	D	L	F	A	GD	PTS
Rangers	19	15	4	0	52	13	39	49
Celtic	19	14	4	1	42	14	28	46
Hibernian	19	9	4	6	29	21	8	31
Hearts	19	9	4	6	19	20	-1	31
Motherwell	18	8	5	5	29	25	4	29
Dundee Utd	19	8	4	7	22	21	1	28
Hamilton	19	6	7	6	19	17	2	25
St Johnstone	19	6	6	7	31	28	3	24
St Mirren	19	5	9	5	18	18	0	24
Aberdeen	20	6	4	10	20	31	-11	22
Kilmarnock	19	5	6	8	23	27	-4	21
Falkirk	19	3	6	10	17	29	-12	15

AWAY TABLE

	P	W	D	L	F	A	GD	PTS
Rangers	19	11	5	3	30	15	15	38
Celtic	19	11	2	6	33	25	8	35
Dundee Utd	19	9	8	2	33	26	7	35
Motherwell	20	5	9	6	23	29	-6	24
Hamilton	19	7	3	9	20	29	-9	24
Hibernian	19	6	5	8	29	34	-5	23
St Johnstone	19	6	5	8	26	33	-7	23
Aberdeen	18	4	7	7	16	21	-5	19
Hearts	19	4	5	10	16	26	-10	17
Falkirk	19	3	7	9	14	28	-14	16
Kilmarnock	19	3	3	13	6	24	-18	12
St Mirren	19	2	4	13	18	31	-13	10

FIRST-HALF TABLE

	P	W	D	L	F	A	GD	PTS
Rangers	38	20	13	5	37	15	22	73
Celtic	38	15	18	5	32	18	14	63
Hamilton	38	10	19	9	18	17	1	49
Dundee Utd	38	11	16	11	25	25	0	49
Hearts	38	10	19	9	17	17	0	49
St Johnstone	38	12	13	13	27	28	-1	49
Motherwell	38	10	18	10	20	20	0	48
Aberdeen	38	12	12	14	20	23	-3	48
Hibernian	38	10	17	11	28	28	0	47
Kilmarnock	38	5	23	10	10	20	-10	38
Falkirk	38	6	19	13	16	26	-10	37
St Mirren	38	4	19	15	11	24	-13	31

SECOND-HALF TABLE

	P	W	D	L	F	A	GD	PTS
Rangers	38	21	13	4	45	13	32	76
Celtic	38	20	10	8	43	21	22	70
Dundee Utd	38	17	14	7	30	22	8	65
Hibernian	38	18	8	12	30	27	3	62
Motherwell	38	13	14	11	32	34	-2	53
St Johnstone	38	14	9	15	30	33	-3	51
St Mirren	38	11	14	13	25	25	0	47
Hearts	38	10	13	15	18	29	-11	43
Kilmarnock	38	9	12	17	19	31	-12	39
Hamilton	38	6	17	15	21	29	-8	35
Aberdeen	38	6	17	15	16	29	-13	35
Falkirk	38	3	19	16	15	31	-16	28

REFEREE STATISTICS

	GAMES	Y	R	AVE
Chris Boyle	4	8	0	2.00
William Collum	23	50	6	2.43
Stevie O'Reilly	13	33	1	2.62
Douglas McDonald	23	68	5	3.17
Crawford Allan	9	28	1	3.22
Brian Winter	13	38	4	3.23
Mike Tumilty	16	49	3	3.25
Calum Murray	13	42	3	3.46
Craig Thomson	21	70	4	3.52
Iain Brines	18	62	3	3.61
Charlie Richmond	14	48	3	3.64
Euan Norris	12	45	1	3.83
Steve Conroy	17	68	4	4.24
David Somers	5	18	4	4.40
Alan Muir	14	61	3	4.57
Stephen Finnie	9	41	1	4.67
Steven Nicholls	3	15	2	5.67
Steven McLean	1	5	2	7.00

DISCIPLINARY RECORDS

Y=1PT/R=2PT

PLAYER	TEAM	FLS	Y	R
Lee McCulloch	Rangers	53	11	1
Eggert Jonsson	Hearts	46	8	2
Morgaro Gomis	Dundee Utd	55	10	1
Colin Nish	Hibernian	67	6	2
Prince Buaben	Dundee Utd	36	6	2
Graham Gartland	St Johnstone	28	8	1
Jamie Hamill	Kilmarnock	45	10	0
Lee Mair	St Mirren	32	5	2
Aiden McGeady	Celtic	23	7	1
Ian Black	Hearts	37	9	0
Scott Arfield	Falkirk	61	9	0
Daniel Swanson	Dundee Utd	29	4	2
Michael Stewart	Hearts	24	4	2
Scott Brown	Celtic	40	6	1
Liam Miller	Hibernian	59	6	1
Richard Foster	Aberdeen	18	6	1
Michael Duberry	St Johnstone	32	8	0
Mark McLaughlin	Hamilton	58	8	0
Sasa Papac	Rangers	41	8	0
Murray Davidson	St Johnstone	41	8	0
Chris Innes	St Mirren	30	5	1
Michael Higdon	St Mirren	54	5	1

PENALTIES

TOTAL AWARDED	61
SCORED	46
SAVED	15
MISSED	0

EARLIEST STRIKE
ANTHONY STOKES
(HIBERNIAN v Rangers) 0:13

LATEST STRIKE
PAUL SHEERIN
(ST JOHNSTONE v St Mirren)
93:47

Paul Sheerin (St Johnstone)

EARLIEST CARD
CHARLIE MULGREW
(Rangers v ABERDEEN) 0:50

SEQUENCES

Wins	Celtic 8
27/03/2010-09/05/2010	
Losses	Hibernian 6
31/03/2010-01/05/2010	
Draws	Falkirk 3
14/09/2009-26/09/2009	
Undefeated	Rangers 17
05/12/2009-27/03/2010	
Without win	St Mirren 11
16/01/2010-13/03/2010	
Undefeated home	Rangers 19
15/08/2009-09/05/2010	
Undefeated away	Rangers 9
05/12/2009-27/03/2010	
Without scoring	Kilmarnock 5
26/12/2009-26/01/2010	
Without conceding	Aberdeen 5
22/08/2009-26/09/2009	
Scoring	Rangers 20
05/12/2009-07/04/2010	
Conceding	St Mirren 14
29/08/2009-19/12/2009	

ABERDEEN

CLUB SUMMARY

FORMED	1903
MANAGER	Mark McGhee
GROUND	Pittodrie
CAPACITY	21,421
NICKNAME	The Dons
WEBSITE	www.afc.co.uk

The New Football Pools PLAYER OF THE SEASON — Richard Foster

OVERALL

P	W	D	L	F	A	GD
44	11	12	21	42	65	-23

CLYDESDALE BANK PREMIER LEAGUE

Pos	P	W	D	L	F	A	GD	Pts
9	38	10	11	17	36	52	-16	41

HOME

Pos	P	W	D	L	F	A	GD	Pts
10	20	6	4	10	20	31	-11	22

AWAY

Pos	P	W	D	L	F	A	GD	Pts
8	18	4	7	7	16	21	-5	19

CUP PROGRESS DETAILS

Competition	Round reached	Knocked out by
Europa League	Q3	Olomouc
Scottish Cup	R5	Raith
Co-op Insurance Cup	R3	Dundee

BIGGEST WIN (ALL COMPS)
3-0 on 2 occasions

BIGGEST DEFEAT (ALL COMPS)
30/07/09 1-5 v Olomouc

THE PLAYER WITH THE MOST

GOALS SCORED Steven MacLean		**5**
SHOTS ON TARGET Charlie Mulgrew		**30**
SHOTS OFF TARGET Charlie Mulgrew		**25**
SHOTS WITHOUT SCORING Richard Foster		**19**
ASSISTS Paton, Mackie, Mulgrew, MacLean		**3**
OFFSIDES Darren Mackie, Steven MacLean		**15**
FOULS Lee Miller		**42**
FOULS WITHOUT A CARD Sone Aluko		**15**
FREE-KICKS WON Lee Miller		**57**
DEFENSIVE CLEARANCES Jerel Ifil		**45**

ATTENDANCE RECORD

HIGH	AVERAGE	LOW
16,803	10,461	6,097
v Celtic (15/08/2009)		v Kilmarnock (05/05/2010)

Steven MacLean grabs a late equaliser in the 4-4 draw with Celtic in February

ABERDEEN failed to finish in the top six of the Clydesdale Bank Premier League for the first time in six years as Mark McGhee endured what he described as a 'torrid' first season in charge.

McGhee had arrived at the club amid a wave of optimism having led Motherwell into Europe twice, but he struggled to instil his attacking ethos into his new team, who then appeared to suffer badly from a loss of confidence in the latter part of the campaign.

Previous manager Jimmy Calderwood had paid the price for his failure to lead the Dons to a major Cup final but McGhee fared no better, with his side falling to Irn-Bru First Division sides Dundee and Raith Rovers in the knockout competitions. Indeed, McGhee's reign began with Cup disappointment as Aberdeen fell to an 8-1 aggregate defeat by Czech side Sigma Olomouc in the Europa League qualifying rounds.

Aberdeen's SPL campaign also started badly as they conceded three first-half goals to Celtic. However, they ensured respectability by scoring the only goal of the second period against the Hoops and then embarked on a seven-match unbeaten run in the League, which included a draw against Rangers at Ibrox.

Consistency gradually deserted them, although they were in the top half of the table following a 1-0 victory over Rangers at Pittodrie in November, which came courtesy of Lee Miller's strike.

The Dons failed to register a point in December and a defeat to Motherwell at

The high expectations, brought about by Mark McGhee's arrival, failed to materialise

the end of January heralded a run of 11 games without a single victory. They were also dumped out of the Active Nation Scottish Cup following a fifth-round replay defeat to Raith.

Victory over St Mirren kept alive the club's slim hopes of making the top six in the SPL, but those dreams were soon ended with a 2-0 defeat to Calderwood's Kilmarnock.

Aberdeen closed the season with two wins from their last seven games to leave McGhee and his backroom team facing a testing rebuilding job. The former Wolves manager, who won the European Cup Winners' Cup as a player with Aberdeen in 1983, entered the summer with just 12 first-team players under contract, but he has spoken of his determination to bring about an improvement in their fortunes.

McGhee will be aided by promising young players such as midfielder Fraser Fyvie who, at 16 years and 10 months, became the youngest ever SPL scorer when he netted in the 3-0 win over Hearts at Tynecastle in January.

RESULTS 2009/10

JULY

| 30th | ● Olomouc | H | L 1–5 | Att: 13,973 | Ref: J Laperriere | Scorers: Mulgrew. Booked: Foster. |

AUGUST

6th	● Olomouc	A	L 3–0	Att: 7,405	Ref: M Weiner	Booked: Langfield, Foster. Agg: 8–1.
15th	● Celtic	H	L 1–3	Att: 16,803	Ref: C Thomson	Scorers: Aluko. Booked: Ifil.
22nd	● Hamilton	A	W 0–3	Att: 3,347	Ref: B Winter	Scorers: Considine, Maguire, Mulgrew. Booked: Mackie, Ifil, Considine.
29th	● Motherwell	H	D 0–0	Att: 11,320	Ref: C Boyle	Booked: Crawford.

SEPTEMBER

14th	● Falkirk	A	D 0–0	Att: 4,724	Ref: A Muir	Booked: Fyvie, Pawlett, Miller.
19th	● St Mirren	H	W 1–0	Att: 10,103	Ref: C Thomson	Scorers: Mulgrew.
22nd	● Dundee	A	L 3–2	Att: 6,131	Ref: S Conroy	Scorers: Paton[2]. Booked: Pawlett. AET – Score after 90 mins 2–2.
26th	● Rangers	A	D 0–0	Att: 47,968	Ref: I Brines	Booked: Mulgrew, Duff.

OCTOBER

3rd	● Kilmarnock	A	D 1–1	Att: 4,997	Ref: W Collum	Scorers: McDonald. Booked: Maguire.
17th	● Hearts	H	D 1–1	Att: 11,629	Ref: D McDonald	Scorers: Miller. Booked: Considine.
24th	● Dundee Utd	H	L 0–2	Att: 11,766	Ref: S Conroy	Booked: Kerr, Miller, Fyvie.
31st	● Hibernian	A	L 2–0	Att: 13,885	Ref: S Nicholls	Booked: Ifil, Ross, Maguire. Dismissed: Ross, Maguire.

NOVEMBER

7th	● St Johnstone	H	W 2–1	Att: 10,894	Ref: E Norris	Scorers: Aluko, Miller. Booked: Considine, Pawlett, Langfield, Foster.
21st	● Motherwell	A	D 1–1	Att: 4,668	Ref: C Allan	Scorers: McDonald. Booked: McDonald. Dismissed: McDonald.
28th	● Rangers	H	W 1–0	Att: 16,153	Ref: C Thomson	Scorers: Miller. Booked: Kerr, Mulgrew, Pawlett. Dismissed: Kerr.

DECEMBER

5th	● Celtic	A	L 3–0	Att: 56,010	Ref: M Tumilty	Booked: Mulgrew, Young, Foster. Dismissed: Ifil.
12th	● Hamilton	H	L 1–2	Att: 9,499	Ref: A Muir	Scorers: McDonald. Booked: Miller, Grassi, Wright.
19th	● Hibernian	H	L 0–2	Att: 9,096	Ref: D McDonald	Booked: Young, Mackie. Dismissed: Miller.

JANUARY

2nd	● Dundee Utd	A	W 0–1	Att: 10,032	Ref: C Murray	Scorers: Mulgrew. Booked: Mackie, Pawlett. Dismissed: Grassi.
9th	● Hearts	H	W 2–0	Att: 8,226	Ref: S Conroy	Scorers: Mackie, Miller.
12th	● St Mirren	A	L 1–0	Att: 3,867	Ref: W Collum	
23rd	● Kilmarnock	H	W 1–0	Att: 12,150	Ref: I Brines	Scorers: Young.
27th	● Hearts	A	W 0–3	Att: 14,219	Ref: M Tumilty	Scorers: Fyvie, Mackie, Young. Booked: Foster, Mulgrew.
30th	● Motherwell	H	L 0–3	Att: 9,555	Ref: S Conroy	Booked: Mulgrew, Maguire.

FEBRUARY

2nd	● Falkirk	H	L 0–1	Att: 7,741	Ref: S Finnie	Booked: Fyvie.
6th	● Raith	A	D 1–1	Att: 7,045	Ref: W Collum	Scorers: McDonald. Booked: Ifil, Aluko.
10th	● Hibernian	A	D 2–2	Att: 10,469	Ref: C Thomson	Scorers: MacLean, Paton. Booked: McDonald.
13th	● Celtic	H	D 4–4	Att: 14,898	Ref: I Brines	Scorers: MacLean[2], Mackie, Paton. Booked: Mackie, Paterson.
16th	● Raith	H	L 0–1	Att: 8,153	Ref: D Somers	Booked: Paterson.
20th	● Falkirk	A	L 3–1	Att: 4,643	Ref: C Richmond	Scorers: Mulgrew. Booked: Foster, Fyvie, Grassi.
27th	● Hearts	H	L 0–1	Att: 8,316	Ref: W Collum	Booked: Kerr, McDonald, Diamond.

MARCH

6th	● Hamilton	A	D 1–1	Att: 2,030	Ref: S Finnie	Scorers: Diamond. Booked: Young, Paton, Diamond.
16th	● St Johnstone	A	L 1–0	Att: 3,826	Ref: C Richmond	Booked: MacLean.
20th	● Dundee Utd	H	D 2–2	Att: 9,316	Ref: I Brines	Scorers: Diamond, Paton. Booked: Foster, Diamond, Young.
27th	● St Mirren	H	W 2–1	Att: 8,764	Ref: B Winter	Scorers: Aluko, Diamond. Booked: MacLean. Dismissed: MacLean.

APRIL

4th	● Kilmarnock	A	L 2–0	Att: 4,825	Ref: M Tumilty	Booked: Paton, Mulgrew, Mackie, Fyvie.
7th	● Rangers	A	L 3–1	Att: 47,061	Ref: W Collum	Scorers: Mackie. Booked: Grassi.
11th	● St Johnstone	H	L 1–3	Att: 7,568	Ref: C Murray	Scorers: Mackie. Booked: Grassi.
17th	● Falkirk	H	W 1–0	Att: 10,461	Ref: B Winter	Scorers: MacLean. Booked: Mackie, Duff.
24th	● St Johnstone	A	D 1–1	Att: 3,295	Ref: D McDonald	Scorers: MacLean. Booked: Marshall, MacLean.

MAY

1st	● Hamilton	H	L 1–3	Att: 7,099	Ref: S McLean	Scorers: Young. Booked: Grassi, Foster, Duff, Diamond, MacLean. Dismissed: Foster, Diamond.
5th	● Kilmarnock	H	L 1–2	Att: 6,097	Ref: C Allan	Scorers: Kerr. Booked: Kerr.
8th	● St Mirren	A	W 0–1	Att: 4,022	Ref: S O'Reilly	Scorers: Mair OG.

● Clydesdale Bank Premier League ● Scottish Cup ● Co-op Insurance Cup ● UEFA Champions League ● Europa League

ABERDEEN

CLYDESDALE BANK PREMIER LEAGUE GOALKEEPER STATS

Player	Minutes on pitch	Appearances	Match starts	Completed matches	Sub appearances	Subbed off	Saved with feet	Punched	Parried	Tipped over	Fumbled	Tipped round	Caught	Blocked	Clean sheets	Goals conceded	Save %	Saved	Resulting in goals	Opposition miss	Fouls committed	Free-kicks won	Yellow cards	Red cards
Jamie Langfield	3295	35	35	35	0	0	2	14	36	8	3	7	126	3	11	46	80.99	0	2	0	0	4	1	0
Stuart Nelson	283	3	3	3	0	0	1	0	3	0	0	1	18	0	0	6	79.31	0	0	0	0	0	0	0

Saves Breakdown spans: Saved with feet, Punched, Parried, Tipped over, Fumbled, Tipped round, Caught, Blocked. Penalties spans: Saved, Resulting in goals, Opposition miss.

CLYDESDALE BANK PREMIER LEAGUE OUTFIELD PLAYER STATS

Player	Minutes on pitch	Appearances	Match starts	Completed matches	Substitute appearances	Subbed off	Goals scored	Assists	Shots on target	Shots off target	Crosses	Corners taken	Defensive clearances	Defensive blocks	Fouls committed	Free-kicks won	Caught offside	Yellow cards	Red cards
Sone Aluko	1463	22	15	5	7	10	3	0	11	15	19	11	4	1	15	24	7	0	0
Andrew Considine	1423	16	15	15	1	0	1	0	2	4	1	0	14	7	20	14	0	3	0
Jonathan Crawford	113	2	2	0	0	2	0	0	0	0	0	0	0	0	3	0	0	1	0
Zander Diamond	1416	16	15	13	1	1	3	0	5	5	2	0	23	10	21	24	0	4	1
Stuart Duff	1076	17	11	9	6	2	0	0	2	3	18	0	9	0	21	11	1	3	0
Richard Foster	3444	37	37	35	0	1	0	1	9	10	45	2	17	5	18	30	1	6	1
Fraser Fyvie	1684	26	17	8	9	9	1	1	5	6	18	43	11	1	18	22	3	5	0
Dominico Gibson	56	1	1	0	0	1	0	0	1	0	0	0	0	0	1	0	0	0	0
Davide Grassi	1633	23	16	12	7	3	0	1	2	5	20	0	12	3	25	17	2	5	1
Jack Grimmer	27	2	0	0	2	0	0	0	0	0	0	0	0	0	0	0	0	0	0
Jerel Ifil	2256	27	25	22	2	2	0	0	6	1	5	0	45	6	32	18	0	3	1
Mark Kerr	3427	37	37	35	0	1	1	1	12	14	10	1	21	1	36	34	3	4	1
Nicky Low	10	1	0	0	1	0	0	0	0	0	0	0	0	0	0	0	0	0	0
Steven MacLean	1371	16	15	12	1	2	5	3	13	2	9	0	0	1	28	27	15	4	1
Darren Mackie	2069	32	21	13	11	8	4	3	18	16	14	1	1	0	39	33	15	6	0
Christopher Maguire	672	17	5	1	12	3	1	0	6	7	12	4	1	0	20	16	6	3	1
Paul Marshall	506	9	6	1	3	5	1	3	3	3	9	16	0	1	8	7	0	1	0
Gary McDonald	2143	24	24	21	0	2	3	0	13	8	5	1	12	4	26	16	5	3	1
Mitchel Megginson	8	2	0	0	2	0	0	0	0	0	0	0	0	0	1	0	0	0	0
Lee Miller	1683	18	18	17	0	0	3	0	14	15	1	0	6	1	42	57	13	3	1
Charlie Mulgrew	3437	37	37	35	0	2	4	3	30	25	108	92	34	11	30	31	0	6	0
Jim Paterson	467	7	7	3	0	4	0	2	0	1	7	3	2	2	3	3	1	1	0
Michael Paton	2082	35	22	6	13	16	3	3	9	8	23	7	5	0	18	16	5	2	0
Peter Pawlett	906	14	11	2	3	9	0	0	4	10	0	9	4	2	15	17	1	4	0
Clark Robertson	92	3	1	0	2	1	0	0	1	0	2	0	1	0	1	1	0	0	0
Maurice Ross	520	6	6	4	0	1	0	1	0	0	1	0	2	0	2	2	0	1	1
Tommy Wright	56	3	0	0	3	0	0	0	0	0	0	0	0	0	2	0	0	1	0
Derek Young	1436	20	16	11	4	5	3	1	6	6	11	0	8	1	27	13	0	4	0

actim

Clydesdale Bank PREMIER LEAGUE

SEASON TOTALS

Goals scored	36
Goals conceded	52
Clean sheets	11
Shots on target	172
Shots off target	164
Shots per goal	9.33
Pens awarded	3
Pens scored	3
Pens conceded	2
Offsides	78
Corners	206
Crosses	340
Players used	30
Fouls committed	472
Free-kicks won	437

CARDS RECEIVED

74 **10**

SEQUENCES

Wins	2
(23/01/10–27/01/10)	
Losses	3
(on two occasions)	
Draws	3
(26/09/09–17/10/09)	
Undefeated	7
(22/08/09–17/10/09)	
Without win	9
(30/01/10–20/03/10)	
Undefeated home	3
(29/08/09–17/10/09)	
Undefeated away	4
(22/08/09–03/10/09)	
Without scoring	2
(on three occasions)	
Without conceding	5
(22/08/09–26/09/09)	
Scoring	3
(on two occasions)	
Conceding	13
(30/01/10–11/04/10)	

LEAGUE POSITION AT THE END OF EACH MONTH

AUG	SEP	OCT	NOV	DEC	JAN	FEB	MAR	APR	MAY
6	5	7	6	8	7	7	8	9	9

SEASON INFORMATION
Highest position: 4
Lowest position: 9
Average goals scored per game: 0.95
Average goals conceded per game: 1.37

MATCH RECORDS

Goals scored per match

		W	D	L	Pts
Failed to score	13	0	3	10	3
Scored 1 goal	18	6	5	7	23
Scored 2 goals	4	2	2	0	8
Scored 3 goals	2	2	0	0	6
Scored 4+ goals	1	0	1	0	1

Goals conceded per match

		W	D	L	Pts
Clean sheet	11	8	3	0	27
Conceded 1 goal	11	2	5	4	11
Conceded 2 goals	8	0	2	6	2
Conceded 3 goals	7	0	0	7	0
Conceded 4+ goals	1	0	1	0	1

EARLIEST STRIKE
CHARLIE MULGREW
(v Falkirk) 4:41

LATEST STRIKE
STEVEN MACLEAN
(v Celtic) 87:58

Darren Mackie

GOAL DETAILS

How the goals were struck

SCORED		CONCEDED
19	Right foot	28
14	Left foot	10
3	Header	13
0	Other	1

How the goals were struck

SCORED		CONCEDED
21	Open play	30
2	Cross	8
2	Corner	6
3	Penalty	2
4	Direct from free-kick	0
3	Free-kick	4
1	Own goal	2

Distance from goal

SCORED		CONCEDED
13	6YDS	25
18	18YDS	19
5	18+YDS	8

GOALS SCORED/CONCEDED
PER FIVE-MINUTE INTERVALS

MINS	5	10	15	20	25	30	35	40	45	50	55	60	65	70	75	80	85	90
FOR	1	1	4	3	2	3	2	2	2	2	0	1	2	2	3	1	3	2
AGN	2	1	2	0	5	3	3	4	3	3	3	1	6	2	4	6	0	4

OFFICIAL FOOTBALL YEARBOOK OF THE ENGLISH & SCOTTISH LEAGUES 2010-2011 **377**

CELTIC

CLUB SUMMARY

FORMED	1888
MANAGER	TBC
GROUND	Celtic Park
CAPACITY	60,355
NICKNAME	The Bhoys
WEBSITE	www.celticfc.net

The New Football Pools PLAYER OF THE SEASON — Robbie Keane

OVERALL

P	W	D	L	F	A	GD
54	31	9	14	97	57	40

CLYDESDALE BANK PREMIER LEAGUE

Pos	P	W	D	L	F	A	GD	Pts
2	38	25	6	7	75	39	36	81

HOME

Pos	P	W	D	L	F	A	GD	Pts
2	19	14	4	1	42	14	28	46

AWAY

Pos	P	W	D	L	F	A	GD	Pts
2	19	11	2	6	33	25	8	35

CUP PROGRESS DETAILS

Competition	Round reached	Knocked out by
Champions League	QR4	Arsenal
Europa League	Group C	–
Scottish Cup	SF	Ross County
Co-op Insurance Cup	QF	Hearts

BIGGEST WIN (ALL COMPS)

4-0 on 2 occasions

BIGGEST DEFEAT (ALL COMPS)

24/03/10 0-4 v St Mirren

THE PLAYER WITH THE MOST

GOALS SCORED Robbie Keane	12
SHOTS ON TARGET Aiden McGeady	45
SHOTS OFF TARGET Aiden McGeady	39
SHOTS WITHOUT SCORING Landry N'Guemo	18
ASSISTS Aiden McGeady	14
OFFSIDES Scott McDonald	27
FOULS Scott Brown	40
FOULS WITHOUT A CARD Marc Crosas	11
FREE-KICKS WON Aiden McGeady	65
DEFENSIVE CLEARANCES Josh Thompson	30

ATTENDANCE RECORD

HIGH	AVERAGE	LOW
58,500	45,582	24,000
v St Johnstone (22/08/2009)		v Motherwell (01/05/2010)

CELTIC endured a difficult season as Old Firm rivals Rangers retained the Clydesdale Bank Premier League title as well as picking up the Co-operative Insurance Cup. A shock Active Nation Scottish Cup semi-final defeat to Irn-Bru First Division side Ross County meant that there were no trophies to parade at Celtic Park for the first time in seven years.

Things had looked set to unfold differently when Tony Mowbray took over from Gordon Strachan as the club's manager in the summer of 2009. There was plenty of optimism around the east end of Glasgow at the time as the former Hoops defender promised the supporters a fresh, expansive brand of football.

However, Celtic ultimately failed to overhaul their great rivals in the race for the SPL title and a disappointing European campaign ended at the group stages of the Europa League after they had already lost to Arsenal in the UEFA Champions League qualifiers.

Mowbray made plenty of changes to his squad, including the addition of Marc-Antoine Fortuné, Landry N'Guémo and Danny Fox. There was a feeling that, given time, the side would settle down and gel together. However, that did not happen as the manager would have liked and the former Hibernian and West Brom boss felt compelled to shuffle his side again in the January transfer window.

The Hoops battled through the winter and did not always pick up the points that their performances perhaps deserved as they gradually slipped behind Rangers in

Celtic's end-of-season form proved little comfort after a trophyless campaign

the title race. There was little between the two teams in all four of the Old Firm encounters during 2009/10, but the bottom line was that the Gers emerged from those games with two wins and a draw.

Mowbray departed in March following a 4-0 defeat at St Mirren that confirmed the end of Celtic's title challenge. Reserves coach and former Hoops captain Neil Lennon took over on an interim basis and asked his former Celtic Park teammate, Johan Mjallby, to assist him.

Lennon was at the helm for that surprise defeat to Ross County in the Scottish Cup, but he lifted his side to a record eight straight SPL victories as they finished the season on a winning note. Their end-of-season form will give the club's supporters plenty of hope that Celtic can regroup and challenge again during the 2010/11 campaign as they begin the task of trying to win back the League title from their great rivals.

In a tough season for Celtic, even loan signing Robbie Keane's goals could not alleviate the gloom. Manager Tony Mowbray paid the price by losing his job in March

RESULTS 2009/10

JULY
| 29th | ● Dinamo Moscow | H | L 0–1 | Att: 54,184 | Ref: N Rizzoli | Booked: Hinkel, Killen. |

AUGUST
5th	● Dinamo Moscow	A	W 0–2	Att: 12,000	Ref: J Eriksson	Scorers: McDonald, Samaras. Booked: N'Guemo. Agg: 1–2.
15th	● Aberdeen	A	W 1–3	Att: 16,803	Ref: C Thomson	Scorers: McDonald, McGeady[2].
18th	● Arsenal	H	L 0–2	Att: 58,000	Ref: M Busacca	Booked: Fox, N'Guemo, Loovens.
22nd	● St Johnstone	H	W 5–2	Att: 58,500	Ref: W Collum	Scorers: Fortuné[2], Maloney[2], McDonald.
26th	● Arsenal	A	L 3–1	Att: 59,962	Ref: M Gonzalez	Scorers: Donati. Booked: Caldwell, McGeady, Brown. Agg: 5–1.
30th	● Hibernian	A	W 0–1	Att: 14,221	Ref: D McDonald	Scorers: Samaras. Booked: McGeady, N'Guemo, Boruc. Dismissed: McGeady.

SEPTEMBER
12th	● Dundee Utd	H	D 1–1	Att: 58,500	Ref: S Conroy	Scorers: McDonald. Booked: McDonald.
17th	● Hapoel Tel-Aviv	A	L 2–1	Att: 15,500	Ref: P Allaerts	Scorers: Samaras. Booked: McGeady, McDonald.
20th	● Hearts	H	W 2–1	Att: 58,024	Ref: D McDonald	Scorers: Killen, Loovens. Booked: Brown, Fox.
23rd	● Falkirk	A	W 0–4	Att: 5,669	Ref: M Tumilty	Scorers: Killen, McCourt, McDonald[2]. Booked: Wilson.
26th	● St Mirren	A	W 0–2	Att: 6,164	Ref: C Richmond	Scorers: Maloney, McCourt. Booked: Brown, Killen.

OCTOBER
1st	● Rapid Vienna	H	D 1–1	Att: 42,013	Ref: B Paixao	Scorers: McDonald. Booked: N'Guemo.
4th	● Rangers	A	L 2–1	Att: 50,276	Ref: C Thomson	Scorers: McGeady. Booked: Maloney, Wilson, Brown, Loovens.
17th	● Motherwell	H	D 0–0	Att: 58,000	Ref: C Boyle	Booked: McManus.
22nd	● Hamburg	H	L 0–1	Att: 38,821	Ref: G Rocchi	Booked: McManus, Naylor.
25th	● Hamilton	A	W 1–2	Att: 4,689	Ref: I Brines	Scorers: Maloney, McDonald. Booked: McGeady, Robson.
28th	● Hearts	H	L 0–1	Att: 18,675	Ref: C Thomson	Booked: Fox. Dismissed: McManus.
31st	● Kilmarnock	H	W 3–0	Att: 46,000	Ref: W Collum	Scorers: McGeady, McGinn, Samaras. Booked: McGeady.

NOVEMBER
5th	● Hamburg	A	D 0–0	Att: 45,037	Ref: C Carballo	Booked: Caldwell, Samaras, Robson.
8th	● Falkirk	A	D 3–3	Att: 6,795	Ref: B Winter	Scorers: Caldwell, McDonald[2]. Booked: Samaras, Fox.
22nd	● Dundee Utd	A	L 2–1	Att: 11,098	Ref: D McDonald	Scorers: Robson. Booked: Loovens.
28th	● St Mirren	H	W 3–1	Att: 41,000	Ref: S Conroy	Scorers: McDonald[2], Samaras. Booked: Caldwell.

DECEMBER
2nd	● Hapoel Tel-Aviv	H	W 2–0	Att: 32,000	Ref: T Asumaa	Scorers: Robson, Samaras.
5th	● Aberdeen	H	W 3–0	Att: 56,010	Ref: M Tumilty	Scorers: McDonald, Samaras[2].
12th	● Motherwell	A	W 2–3	Att: 7,807	Ref: C Richmond	Scorers: Fortuné, McGeady, Samaras. Booked: Robson, McGeady.
17th	● Rapid Vienna	A	D 3–3	Att: 48,000	Ref: R Malek	Scorers: Fortuné[2], McGowan.
20th	● Hearts	A	L 2–1	Att: 16,223	Ref: W Collum	Scorers: Samaras. Booked: Robson. Dismissed: Caldwell.
26th	● Hamilton	H	W 2–0	Att: 36,827	Ref: S O'Reilly	Scorers: Loovens, McGinn.

JANUARY
3rd	● Rangers	H	D 1–1	Att: 58,300	Ref: S Conroy	Scorers: McDonald.
16th	● Falkirk	H	D 1–1	Att: 50,000	Ref: A Muir	Scorers: Samaras.
19th	● Morton	A	W 0–1	Att: 10,191	Ref: C Thomson	Scorers: McGinn.
24th	● St Johnstone	A	W 1–4	Att: 7,743	Ref: W Collum	Scorers: Fortuné[2], McCourt, Samaras. Booked: Samaras.
27th	● Hibernian	H	L 1–2	Att: 41,000	Ref: I Brines	Scorers: Fortuné. Booked: Samaras, Boruc.
30th	● Hamilton	A	W 0–1	Att: 4,922	Ref: C Murray	Scorers: Rasmussen. Booked: Rasmussen.

FEBRUARY
2nd	● Kilmarnock	A	L 1–0	Att: 9,308	Ref: M Tumilty	Booked: McGeady, N'Guemo.
7th	● Dunfermline	A	W 2–4	Att: 8,933	Ref: C Richmond	Scorers: Kamara, Keane, Rasmussen, Woods OG. Booked: Caddis.
10th	● Hearts	H	W 2–0	Att: 44,500	Ref: B Winter	Scorers: Fortuné, Loovens. Booked: McGeady.
13th	● Aberdeen	A	D 4–4	Att: 14,898	Ref: I Brines	Scorers: Fortuné, Kamara, Keane, McGeady. Booked: O'Dea, McGeady. Dismissed: O'Dea.
20th	● Dundee Utd	H	W 1–0	Att: 49,000	Ref: C Thomson	Scorers: Keane. Booked: Hinkel, Braafheid, Keane.
28th	● Rangers	A	L 1–0	Att: 50,320	Ref: D McDonald	Booked: Fortuné, N'Guemo. Dismissed: Brown.

MARCH
7th	● Falkirk	A	W 0–2	Att: 6,792	Ref: B Winter	Scorers: Keane[2].
13th	● Kilmarnock	A	W 0–3	Att: 7,351	Ref: I Brines	Scorers: Keane[3].
20th	● St Johnstone	H	W 3–0	Att: 30,000	Ref: C Murray	Scorers: Keane, Samaras, Thompson.
24th	● St Mirren	A	L 4–0	Att: 5,018	Ref: C Richmond	Booked: Thompson.
27th	● Kilmarnock	H	W 3–1	Att: 41,000	Ref: D McDonald	Scorers: Brown, Keane[2]. Booked: N'Guemo.

APRIL
4th	● Hibernian	A	W 0–1	Att: 10,523	Ref: C Richmond	Scorers: Keane. Booked: O'Dea, N'Guemo, Fortuné.
10th	● Ross County	H	L 0–2	Att: 24,535	Ref: W Collum	Booked: O'Dea.
13th	● Motherwell	H	W 2–1	Att: 27,750	Ref: I Brines	Scorers: Thompson[2]. Booked: Naylor.
17th	● Hibernian	H	W 3–2	Att: 29,650	Ref: S Finnie	Scorers: Fortuné, Keane, Rasmussen.
25th	● Dundee Utd	A	W 0–2	Att: 8,638	Ref: I Brines	Scorers: Kamara, Keane. Booked: N'Guemo, Brown.

MAY
1st	● Motherwell	H	W 4–0	Att: 24,000	Ref: A Muir	Scorers: Forrest, Keane, McGeady, O'Dea.
4th	● Rangers	H	W 2–1	Att: 58,000	Ref: C Murray	Scorers: Fortuné, Naylor. Booked: Kamara, Brown, Hinkel, O'Dea.
9th	● Hearts	A	W 1–2	Att: 14,389	Ref: C Thomson	Scorers: Keane, Zhi. Booked: Brown, Hinkel, Zhi.

● Clydesdale Bank Premier League ● Scottish Cup ● Co-op Insurance Cup ● UEFA Champions League ● Europa League

CELTIC

CLYDESDALE BANK PREMIER LEAGUE GOALKEEPER STATS

Player	Minutes on pitch	Appearances	Match starts	Completed matches	Sub appearances	Subbed off	SAVES BREAKDOWN Saved with feet	Punched	Parried	Tipped over	Fumbled	Tipped round	Caught	Blocked	Clean sheets	Goals conceded	Save %	PENALTIES Saved	Resulting in goals	Opposition miss	Fouls committed	Free-kicks won	Yellow cards	Red cards
Artur Boruc	2595	28	28	27	0	1	1	20	14	3	0	2	49	2	11	25	78.45	0	4	0	0	6	2	0
Lukasz Zaluska	975	11	10	10	1	0	0	5	8	1	1	2	22	2	3	14	74.07	0	1	0	0	0	0	0

CLYDESDALE BANK PREMIER LEAGUE OUTFIELD PLAYER STATS

Player	Minutes on pitch	Appearances	Match starts	Completed matches	Substitute appearances	Subbed off	Goals scored	Assists	Shots on target	Shots off target	Crosses	Corners taken	Defensive clearances	Defensive blocks	Fouls committed	Free-kicks won	Caught offside	Yellow cards	Red cards
Edson Braafheid	808	10	9	6	1	3	0	1	2	3	24	20	6	1	8	10	0	1	0
Scott Brown	1815	21	19	17	2	1	1	5	5	6	6	2	10	1	40	41	2	6	1
Paul Caddis	482	10	3	3	7	0	1	1	1	1	12	15	1	1	4	9	0	0	0
Gary Caldwell	1252	14	14	13	0	0	1	0	6	3	2	0	20	5	18	16	0	1	1
Marc Crosas	1208	17	14	9	3	5	0	2	3	5	8	16	4	0	11	8	0	0	0
Massimo Donati	150	2	2	1	0	1	0	0	0	1	2	0	0	0	3	3	0	0	0
Willo Flood	25	1	0	0	1	0	0	0	0	0	0	0	0	0	1	0	0	0	0
James Forrest	16	2	0	0	2	0	1	0	1	0	0	0	0	0	0	0	0	0	0
Marc-Antoine Fortuné	2049	30	22	11	8	11	10	3	36	30	27	0	3	0	34	51	20	2	0
Daniel Fox	1388	15	15	14	0	1	0	3	7	4	39	53	7	1	11	10	3	2	0
Andreas Hinkel	2724	31	30	26	1	4	0	6	4	6	36	0	15	3	25	27	0	3	0
Jos Hooiveld	150	2	2	1	0	1	0	0	0	1	0	0	0	0	0	0	0	0	0
Diomansy Kamara	751	9	8	6	1	2	2	3	5	7	10	21	1	0	12	11	3	1	0
Robbie Keane	1406	16	15	12	1	3	12	3	32	15	11	0	0	0	5	14	24	1	0
Ki Sung Yueng	575	10	5	4	5	1	0	1	7	2	12	40	2	0	5	11	0	0	0
Chris Killen	217	5	2	1	3	1	1	0	5	2	0	0	1	0	6	5	1	0	0
Glenn Loovens	1623	20	20	14	0	6	3	0	6	5	1	0	20	5	16	11	1	2	0
Shaun Maloney	718	9	8	5	1	3	4	2	14	5	8	24	2	0	5	10	3	1	0
Patrick McCourt	340	9	3	0	6	3	2	0	10	2	6	6	0	0	6	2	0	0	0
Scott McDonald	1339	18	16	8	2	8	10	2	28	17	3	1	0	0	11	16	27	1	0
Aiden McGeady	3139	35	35	25	0	9	7	14	45	39	85	10	2	0	23	65	3	7	1
Niall McGinn	713	17	6	2	11	4	2	0	11	12	11	9	1	0	2	13	2	0	0
Paul McGowan	221	5	2	1	3	1	0	3	3	2	2	0	0	0	0	0	0	0	0
Stephen McManus	604	8	6	5	2	1	0	0	0	0	1	0	6	0	12	5	0	1	0
Koki Mizuno	15	1	0	0	1	0	0	0	0	0	0	0	0	0	0	0	0	0	0
Landry N'Guemo	2701	30	30	26	0	4	0	2	10	8	3	0	13	5	35	42	0	6	0
Lee Naylor	1000	12	11	8	1	3	1	2	7	3	31	41	3	1	7	11	0	1	0
Darren O'Dea	1621	19	16	14	3	1	1	0	3	6	2	0	19	6	16	11	0	3	1
Morten Rasmussen	317	10	2	0	8	2	2	1	6	2	0	0	0	0	6	6	1	1	0
Barry Robson	763	10	9	6	1	3	1	2	5	7	22	41	0	2	18	29	0	3	0
Thomas Rogne	185	4	3	1	1	2	0	0	1	0	0	0	4	1	1	1	0	0	0
Georgios Samaras	1994	32	20	12	12	8	10	2	40	33	17	2	13	0	31	44	12	3	0
Josh Thompson	1606	18	16	16	2	0	3	1	5	4	0	0	30	6	14	9	0	1	0
Mark Wilson	771	10	8	7	2	1	0	0	0	2	15	0	3	1	6	11	2	1	0
Zheng Zhi	849	16	9	4	7	5	1	1	10	6	2	3	1	3	13	11	0	1	0

actim

Clydesdale Bank PREMIER LEAGUE

SEASON TOTALS

Goals scored	75
Goals conceded	39
Clean sheets	14
Shots on target	318
Shots off target	240
Shots per goal	7.44
Pens awarded	9
Pens scored	5
Pens conceded	5
Offsides	105
Corners	304
Crosses	398
Players used	37
Fouls committed	405
Free-kicks won	531

LEAGUE POSITION AT THE END OF EACH MONTH

AUG	SEP	OCT	NOV	DEC	JAN	FEB	MAR	APR	MAY
2	1	1	1	2	2	2	2	2	2

SEASON INFORMATION

Highest position: 1
Lowest position: 3
Average goals scored per game: 1.97
Average goals conceded per game: 1.03

CARDS RECEIVED

52 | 4

SEQUENCES

Wins	8
(27/03/10–09/05/10)	
Losses	–
(–)	
Draws	2
(03/01/10–16/01/10)	
Undefeated	8
(27/03/10–09/05/10)	
Without win	2
(on three occasions)	
Undefeated home	10
(22/08/09–16/01/10)	
Undefeated away	3
(on two occasions)	
Without scoring	–
(–)	
Without conceding	2
(on two occasions)	
Scoring	14
(25/10/09–30/01/10)	
Conceding	4
(03/01/10–27/01/10)	

MATCH RECORDS

Goals scored per match

		W	D	L	Pts
Failed to score	4	0	1	3	1
Scored 1 goal	11	4	3	4	15
Scored 2 goals	10	10	0	0	30
Scored 3 goals	9	8	1	0	25
Scored 4+ goals	4	3	1	0	10

Goals conceded per match

		W	D	L	Pts
Clean sheet	14	13	1	0	40
Conceded 1 goal	14	9	3	2	30
Conceded 2 goals	7	3	0	4	9
Conceded 3 goals	1	0	1	0	1
Conceded 4+ goals	2	0	1	1	1

GOALS SCORED/CONCEDED PER FIVE-MINUTE INTERVALS

MINS	5	10	15	20	25	30	35	40	45	50	55	60	65	70	75	80	85	90
FOR	3	1	4	3	4	5	2	5	5	4	5	1	6	3	4	11	1	8
AGN	1	4	1	2	0	2	1	4	3	1	2	1	3	0	2	2	5	5

EARLIEST STRIKE

DIOMANSY KAMARA
(v Aberdeen) 2:19

LATEST STRIKE

ROBBIE KEANE
(v Dundee Utd) 93:42

Scott Brown

GOAL DETAILS

How the goals were struck

SCORED		CONCEDED
42	Right foot	26
16	Left foot	7
17	Header	6
0	Other	0

How the goals were struck

SCORED		CONCEDED
54	Open play	22
5	Cross	6
7	Corner	2
5	Penalty	5
1	Direct from free-kick	0
3	Free-kick	4
0	Own goal	0

Distance from goal

SCORED		CONCEDED
34	6YDS	16
36	18YDS	17
5	18+YDS	6

DUNDEE UNITED

CLUB SUMMARY

FORMED	1909
MANAGER	Peter Houston
GROUND	Tannadice Park
CAPACITY	14,223
NICKNAME	The Terrors
WEBSITE	www.dundeeunitedfc.co.uk

The New **Football Pools**
PLAYER OF THE SEASON

Andy Webster

OVERALL

P	W	D	L	F	A	GD
47	24	13	10	72	52	20

CLYDESDALE BANK PREMIER LEAGUE

Pos	P	W	D	L	F	A	GD	Pts
3	38	17	12	9	55	47	8	63

HOME

Pos	P	W	D	L	F	A	GD	Pts
6	19	8	4	7	22	21	1	28

AWAY

Pos	P	W	D	L	F	A	GD	Pts
3	19	9	8	2	33	26	7	35

CUP PROGRESS DETAILS

Competition	Round reached	Knocked out by
Scottish Cup	WON	
Co-op Insurance Cup	QF	St Johnstone

BIGGEST WIN (ALL COMPS)
24/01/10 4–1 v Falkirk

BIGGEST DEFEAT (ALL COMPS)
30/12/09 1–7 v Rangers

THE PLAYER WITH THE MOST

GOALS SCORED	Jon Daly	**13**
SHOTS ON TARGET	Jon Daly	**29**
SHOTS OFF TARGET	David Goodwillie	**26**
SHOTS WITHOUT SCORING	Paul Dixon	**12**
ASSISTS	Craig Conway	**8**
OFFSIDES	David Goodwillie	**23**
FOULS	Morgaro Gomis	**53**
FOULS WITHOUT A CARD	Damian Casalinuovo	**19**
FREE-KICKS WON	Craig Conway	**82**
DEFENSIVE CLEARANCES	Darren Dods	**65**

ATTENDANCE RECORD

HIGH	AVERAGE	LOW
11,100	7,864	5,598
v Rangers (14/04/2010)		v Hamilton (10/02/2010)

Despite losing Craig Levein, the Terrors ended the season as Scottish Cup winners

DUNDEE UNITED coped admirably with the loss of manager Craig Levein as they went on to end the season by lifting the Active Nation Scottish Cup.

Levein had long been linked with jobs away from Tannadice and was widely tipped as a future boss of one of the Old Firm clubs. However, when the call came that finally lured him away from Tayside, it was not from Rangers or Celtic but from the Scottish Football Association. The opportunity to manage his country proved too great a challenge to turn down and Levein departed in December.

The Terrors initially struggled following Levein's departure. His former assistant, Peter Houston, took over temporarily, but a difficult start to his tenure, including a 7–1 defeat to Rangers at Ibrox, meant that he initially ruled himself out of the running for the job on a permanent basis.

Chairman Stephen Thompson launched a search for Levein's successor, and Bohemians manager Pat Fenlon looked set to be appointed. However, the move broke down in January when United and the Irish club were unable to agree a compensation package.

Gradually, results began to improve under Houston, prompting him into a change of heart over wanting the job, and

United boss Peter Houston lifts the Scottish Cup at Hampden Park

he was soon given the green light to take charge of team affairs until the end of the season.

The 51-year-old went on to add some significant entries to his managerial CV as United completed one of their most successful campaigns in recent memory.

They secured a comfortable third-place finish behind the Old Firm in the Clydesdale Bank Premier League, guaranteeing Europa League football for 2010/11.

However, arguably an even greater achievement came in the Scottish Cup, as they beat Partick, St Johnstone, holders Rangers and then Raith to book their place in the final.

United headed for Hampden as huge favourites against Ross County, despite having claimed the trophy just once in their history, 16 years earlier. A David Goodwillie strike and a double from Craig Conway sealed their first piece of silverware since that 1994 victory.

The celebrations continued on Tayside when Houston revealed that he had taken the manager's job on a three-year deal.

Houston said: 'The chairman and I have now spoken and he has asked me to become the permanent manager of Dundee United, and I'm absolutely thrilled and honoured to take on the role at this fabulous club.'

Jon Daly was prolific in front of goal throughout the Terrors' season

RESULTS 2009/10

AUGUST

17th	● Hearts	H	W 2–0	Att: 8,253	Ref: S Conroy	Scorers: Cadamarteri[2]. Booked: Webster, Kovacevic, Swanson, Dixon.
22nd	● St Mirren	A	D 0–0	Att: 4,775	Ref: D McDonald	
25th	● Alloa	A	W 0–2	Att: 1,000	Ref: E Norris	Scorers: Goodwillie, Shala.
29th	● Falkirk	H	W 2–1	Att: 6,979	Ref: C Thomson	Scorers: Cadamarteri, Goodwillie. Booked: Dixon, Gomis.

SEPTEMBER

12th	● Celtic	A	D 1–1	Att: 58,500	Ref: S Conroy	Scorers: Goodwillie. Booked: Swanson, Gomis, S Robertson, Dixon. Dismissed: S Robertson.
19th	● Motherwell	H	L 0–1	Att: 7,196	Ref: D Somers	Booked: Buaben, Goodwillie, Kovacevic.
22nd	● Ross County	A	W 0–2	Att: 1,986	Ref: C Thomson	Scorers: Russell, Wilkie. Booked: Myrie-Williams.
26th	● St Johnstone	A	W 2–3	Att: 7,225	Ref: D McDonald	Scorers: Cadamarteri, Casalinuovo, Webster. Booked: Goodwillie. Dismissed: Swanson.

OCTOBER

3rd	● Hibernian	A	D 1–1	Att: 13,056	Ref: M Tumilty	Scorers: Webster. Dismissed: Buaben.
17th	● Hamilton	H	D 1–1	Att: 5,944	Ref: I Brines	Scorers: Kenneth. Booked: Fotheringham, Gomis.
24th	● Aberdeen	A	W 0–2	Att: 11,766	Ref: S Conroy	Scorers: Casalinuovo, Gomis. Booked: Gomis, Myrie-Williams, Dods.
27th	● St Johnstone	A	L 2–1	Att: 5,146	Ref: S Conroy	Scorers: Buaben.

NOVEMBER

7th	● Kilmarnock	A	W 0–2	Att: 4,753	Ref: S O'Reilly	Scorers: Casalinuovo[2]. Booked: Gomis.
22nd	● Celtic	H	W 2–1	Att: 11,098	Ref: D McDonald	Scorers: Daly, Dods. Booked: Dods.
28th	● Motherwell	A	D 2–2	Att: 4,593	Ref: A Muir	Scorers: Daly, Webster. Booked: Myrie-Williams, Buaben, Daly. Dismissed: Buaben, Swanson.

DECEMBER

5th	● St Mirren	H	W 3–2	Att: 6,259	Ref: B Winter	Scorers: Casalinuovo, Conway, Myrie-Williams. Booked: Goodwillie, Myrie-Williams. Dismissed: Gomis.
12th	● Hearts	A	D 0–0	Att: 14,873	Ref: E Norris	
15th	● Rangers	H	L 0–3	Att: 10,037	Ref: M Tumilty	Booked: Cadamarteri.
26th	● Kilmarnock	H	D 0–0	Att: 6,692	Ref: C Thomson	Booked: Kenneth.
30th	● Rangers	A	L 7–1	Att: 48,721	Ref: W Collum	Scorers: Casalinuovo. Booked: Swanson.

JANUARY

2nd	● Aberdeen	H	L 0–1	Att: 10,032	Ref: C Murray	Booked: Kenneth, Conway, Webster.
9th	● Partick	A	W 0–2	Att: 4,002	Ref: D McDonald	Scorers: Casalinuovo, Goodwillie. Booked: Kenneth, Dixon.
13th	● Hamilton	A	W 0–1	Att: 2,033	Ref: I Brines	Scorers: Goodwillie. Booked: Buaben, Daly.
16th	● Hibernian	H	W 1–0	Att: 7,812	Ref: S Conroy	Scorers: Swanson.
24th	● Falkirk	A	W 1–4	Att: 4,378	Ref: E Norris	Scorers: Daly[3], Goodwillie. Booked: Kovacevic.
27th	● St Johnstone	H	D 3–3	Att: 6,600	Ref: S O'Reilly	Scorers: Daly, Myrie-Williams, Swanson. Booked: Kenneth, Dods, Buaben, Dixon.
30th	● Kilmarnock	A	D 4–4	Att: 4,587	Ref: D McDonald	Scorers: Buaben, Conway[2], Daly.

FEBRUARY

6th	● St Johnstone	A	W 0–1	Att: 5,636	Ref: C Thomson	Scorers: Goodwillie.
10th	● Hamilton	H	L 0–2	Att: 5,598	Ref: A Muir	Booked: Conway, Dods.
13th	● St Mirren	A	W 1–2	Att: 3,944	Ref: E Norris	Scorers: Goodwillie, Swanson. Booked: Mihadjuks, D Robertson, Dods, Kenneth.
20th	● Celtic	A	L 1–0	Att: 49,000	Ref: C Thomson	Booked: Kenneth, Dillon, Buaben.
27th	● Falkirk	H	W 3–0	Att: 6,352	Ref: C Murray	Scorers: Gomis[2], Goodwillie. Booked: Gomis.

MARCH

7th	● Hearts	H	W 1–0	Att: 6,683	Ref: M Tumilty	Scorers: Gomis.
14th	● Rangers	A	D 3–3	Att: 24,096	Ref: D McDonald	Scorers: Kovacevic, Shala, Whittaker OG. Booked: Pernis, Dillon, Dods.
20th	● Aberdeen	A	D 2–2	Att: 9,316	Ref: I Brines	Scorers: Daly[2]. Booked: Webster.
24th	● Rangers	H	W 1–0	Att: 11,898	Ref: D McDonald	Scorers: D Robertson. Booked: Kenneth, D Robertson, Goodwillie.
27th	● Motherwell	H	W 3–0	Att: 7,609	Ref: W Collum	Scorers: Buaben, Goodwillie, Swanson. Dismissed: Dixon.
31st	● Hibernian	A	W 2–4	Att: 9,185	Ref: S O'Reilly	Scorers: Daly, Goodwillie, Sandaza, Swanson. Booked: Gomis.

APRIL

5th	● St Johnstone	A	W 0–1	Att: 5,769	Ref: S Conroy	Scorers: Daly. Booked: Gomis.
11th	● Raith	N	W 2–0	Att: 17,671	Ref: C Thomson	Scorers: Goodwillie, Webster.
14th	● Rangers	H	D 0–0	Att: 11,100	Ref: B Winter	Dismissed: Kovacevic.
18th	● Motherwell	A	W 2–3	Att: 3,544	Ref: C Murray	Scorers: Conway, Daly[2]. Booked: Gomis.
25th	● Celtic	H	L 0–2	Att: 8,638	Ref: I Brines	Booked: Goodwillie, Myrie-Williams, Gomis, Kenneth, Buaben, Pernis. Dismissed: Myrie-Williams.

MAY

1st	● Rangers	H	L 1–2	Att: 10,003	Ref: S O'Reilly	Scorers: Casalinuovo. Booked: Watson, D Robertson.
5th	● Hearts	A	D 0–0	Att: 12,325	Ref: S Finnie	Booked: S Robertson, Swanson.
9th	● Hibernian	H	L 0–2	Att: 6,527	Ref: C Richmond	Booked: Cameron.
15th	● Ross County	N	W 3–0	Att: 47,122	Ref: D McDonald	Scorers: Conway[2], Goodwillie. Booked: Goodwillie, Gomis.

● Clydesdale Bank Premier League ● Scottish Cup ● Co-op Insurance Cup ● UEFA Champions League ● Europa League

DUNDEE UNITED

CLYDESDALE BANK PREMIER LEAGUE GOALKEEPER STATS

Player	Minutes on pitch	Appearances	Match starts	Completed matches	Sub appearances	Subbed off	Saved with feet	Punched	Parried	Tipped over	Fumbled	Tipped round	Caught	Blocked	Clean sheets	Goals conceded	Save %	Saved	Resulting in goals	Opposition miss	Fouls committed	Free-kicks won	Yellow cards	Red cards
Steve Banks	93	1	1	1	0	0	0	2	0	0	1	0	0	1	0	0		0	0	0	0	1	0	0
Dusan Pernis	1799	19	19	19	0	0	1	16	9	4	1	9	57	3	7	24	80.49	1	2	0	1	1	1	0
Nicky Weaver	1704	18	18	18	0	0	1	11	9	5	0	4	38	1	6	24	74.19	0	3	0	0	4	0	0

CLYDESDALE BANK PREMIER LEAGUE OUTFIELD PLAYER STATS

Player	Minutes on pitch	Appearances	Match starts	Completed matches	Substitute appearances	Subbed off	Goals scored	Assists	Shots on target	Shots off target	Crosses	Corners taken	Defensive clearances	Defensive blocks	Fouls committed	Free-kicks won	Caught offside	Yellow cards	Red cards
Prince Buaben	3038	34	33	28	1	3	2	1	17	11	13	3	19	5	35	48	1	6	2
Danny Cadamarteri	1233	21	15	5	6	10	4	0	10	9	24	1	2	0	31	9	12	1	0
Greg Cameron	38	1	0	0	1	0	0	0	0	0	1	0	0	0	1	0	0	1	0
Damian Casalinuovo	1513	25	16	6	9	10	7	0	16	22	8	0	5	1	19	10	10	0	0
Craig Conway	2467	33	29	15	4	14	4	8	16	18	110	113	7	0	20	82	6	2	0
Jon Daly	1597	23	16	10	7	6	13	0	29	21	4	0	5	0	17	15	12	2	0
Sean Dillon	2462	33	24	23	9	1	0	1	2	2	38	1	22	4	27	12	0	1	0
Paul Dixon	2143	25	25	20	0	4	0	3	4	8	66	29	15	8	25	22	0	4	0
Darren Dods	2312	27	23	22	4	1	1	0	5	6	2	0	65	19	41	20	0	5	0
Ryan Dow	119	2	0	0	2	0	0	1	0	1	2	7	0	0	2	1	0	0	0
Mark Fotheringham	227	3	2	2	1	0	0	1	0	4	4	6	1	0	2	5	0	1	0
Morgaro Gomis	2839	31	31	27	0	3	4	3	9	10	20	0	11	2	53	29	0	10	1
David Goodwillie	2112	33	23	4	10	19	8	2	24	26	14	0	1	2	38	44	23	4	0
Craig Hill	96	1	1	1	0	0	0	0	0	0	0	0	0	0	1	0	0	0	0
Dale Hilson	24	2	0	0	2	0	0	1	0	0	0	0	0	0	0	1	0	0	0
Garry Kenneth	2471	28	26	26	2	0	1	1	9	11	15	0	58	9	29	13	1	6	0
Mihael Kovacevic	2182	26	25	19	1	5	0	0	1	4	11	0	13	11	35	5	0	3	1
Pavels Mihadjuks	149	3	3	0	0	3	0	0	0	0	0	0	4	1	4	1	0	1	0
Jennison Myrie-Williams	1288	24	11	6	13	4	2	1	11	9	21	13	1	0	21	28	2	4	1
David Robertson	771	14	8	4	6	4	0	0	1	3	10	3	2	1	16	14	2	2	0
Scott Robertson	850	13	8	5	5	2	0	0	1	3	10	0	11	1	10	12	0	2	1
Francisco Sandaza	174	7	1	0	6	1	1	0	2	3	1	0	2	0	5	2	0	0	0
Andis Shala	330	12	2	1	10	1	0	1	2	2	3	0	2	0	6	4	0	0	0
Kevin Smith	136	3	2	0	1	2	0	0	0	0	1	0	1	0	1	3	0	0	0
Ross Smith	49	1	0	0	1	0	0	0	0	0	0	0	0	0	1	0	0	0	0
Daniel Swanson	2012	31	22	7	9	13	5	5	14	16	31	45	4	1	29	39	1	4	2
Keith Watson	685	8	7	7	1	0	0	0	0	0	6	0	3	0	4	5	0	1	0
Andy Webster	2280	26	26	22	0	4	3	1	8	7	3	0	52	9	40	36	0	3	0
Lee Wilkie	74	1	1	0	0	1	0	0	1	1	0	0	2	1	3	1	0	0	0

SEASON TOTALS

Goals scored	55
Goals conceded	47
Clean sheets	14
Shots on target	184
Shots off target	202
Shots per goal	6.89
Pens awarded	8
Pens scored	6
Pens conceded	6
Offsides	77
Corners	225
Crosses	417
Players used	32
Fouls committed	522
Free-kicks won	479

CARDS RECEIVED

64 **9**

SEQUENCES

Wins	3
(on three occasions)	
Losses	2
(on two occasions)	
Draws	2
(on two occasions)	
Undefeated	9
(26/09/09–12/12/09)	
Without win	5
(12/12/09–02/01/10)	
Undefeated home	4
(27/02/10–14/04/10)	
Undefeated away	8
(22/08/09–12/12/09)	
Without scoring	3
(12/12/09–26/12/09)	
Without conceding	2
(on five occasions)	
Scoring	8
(26/09/09–05/12/09)	
Conceding	6
(on two occasions)	

LEAGUE POSITION AT THE END OF EACH MONTH

AUG	SEP	OCT	NOV	DEC	JAN	FEB	MAR	APR	MAY
3	4	5	4	4	4	3	3	3	3

SEASON INFORMATION
Highest position: 2
Lowest position: 6
Average goals scored per game: 1.45
Average goals conceded per game: 1.24

MATCH RECORDS

Goals scored per match

		W	D	L	Pts
Failed to score	12	0	5	7	5
Scored 1 goal	9	4	3	2	15
Scored 2 goals	8	6	2	0	20
Scored 3 goals	6	5	1	0	16
Scored 4+ goals	3	2	1	0	7

Goals conceded per match

		W	D	L	Pts
Clean sheet	14	9	5	0	32
Conceded 1 goal	10	4	3	3	15
Conceded 2 goals	10	4	2	4	14
Conceded 3 goals	2	0	1	1	1
Conceded 4+ goals	2	0	1	1	1

GOALS SCORED/CONCEDED
PER FIVE-MINUTE INTERVALS

MINS	5	10	15	20	25	30	35	40	45	50	55	60	65	70	75	80	85	90
FOR	2	2	1	3	2	5	3	3	4	4	1	4	0	2	3	5	5	6
AGN	2	1	2	5	3	6	1	1	4	0	1	1	3	3	6	2	3	3

EARLIEST STRIKE
DANNY CADAMARTERI
(v Hearts) 3:29

LATEST STRIKE
DAVID GOODWILLIE
(v St Mirren) 93:11

Garry Kenneth

GOAL DETAILS

How the goals were struck

SCORED		CONCEDED
38	Right foot	20
9	Left foot	12
8	Header	14
0	Other	1

How the goals were struck

SCORED		CONCEDED
34	Open play	23
7	Cross	7
4	Corner	6
6	Penalty	5
1	Direct from free-kick	1
3	Free-kick	3
0	Own goal	2

Distance from goal

SCORED		CONCEDED
23	6YDS	20
26	18YDS	23
6	18+YDS	4

FALKIRK

CLUB SUMMARY

FORMED	1876
MANAGER	Steven Pressley
GROUND	Falkirk Stadium
CAPACITY	9,120
NICKNAME	The Bairns
WEBSITE	www.falkirkfc.co.uk

The New Football Pools PLAYER OF THE SEASON — Darren Barr

OVERALL

P	W	D	L	F	A	GD
42	7	13	22	32	64	-32

CLYDESDALE BANK PREMIER LEAGUE

Pos	P	W	D	L	F	A	GD	Pts
12	38	6	13	19	31	57	-26	31

HOME

Pos	P	W	D	L	F	A	GD	Pts
12	19	3	6	10	17	29	-12	15

AWAY

Pos	P	W	D	L	F	A	GD	Pts
10	19	3	7	9	14	28	-14	16

CUP PROGRESS DETAILS

Competition	Round reached	Knocked out by
Europa League	Q2	FC Vaduz
Scottish Cup	R4	Kilmarnock
Co-op Insurance Cup	R3	Celtic

BIGGEST WIN (ALL COMPS)
20/02/10 3–1 v Aberdeen

BIGGEST DEFEAT (ALL COMPS)
23/09/09 0–4 v Celtic

THE PLAYER WITH THE MOST

GOALS SCORED Pedro Moutinho		**6**
SHOTS ON TARGET Ryan Flynn		**24**
SHOTS OFF TARGET Scott Arfield		**26**
SHOTS WITHOUT SCORING Vitor Lima		**33**
ASSISTS Ryan Flynn		**6**
OFFSIDES Enoch Showunmi		**23**
FOULS Scott Arfield		**61**
FOULS WITHOUT A CARD Ryan Flynn		**13**
FREE-KICKS WON Ryan Flynn		**69**
DEFENSIVE CLEARANCES Brian McLean		**51**

ATTENDANCE RECORD

HIGH	AVERAGE	LOW
7,049	5,635	4,321
v Kilmarnock (10/02/2010)		v Motherwell (27/01/2010)

Carl Finnigan celebrates a goal, while boss Steven Pressley encourages his team

FALKIRK lost their Clydesdale Bank Premier League status having failed to emulate last season's final-day escape.

The Bairns were bottom of the table for much of the campaign, but they were always within touching distance of the rest of the SPL and manager Steven Pressley remained supremely confident that they would escape the drop. However, a goalless draw at Kilmarnock on the final weekend ended their five-year stay in the top flight.

They began the season under boss Eddie May, who suffered a Europa League exit at the hands of Vaduz of Liechtenstein, 2–1 on aggregate, in his first two competitive games in charge. He also faced a major rebuilding job following the departure of more than 10 players during the close season.

Falkirk placed their emphasis on youth, but they failed to win any of their first 11 SPL matches, despite keeping four clean sheets.

May was given funds to supplement his squad and he brought in experienced players such as former club favourite Pedro Moutinho, Leeds striker Enoch Showunmi and Ipswich midfielder Colin Healy.

The Bairns' first SPL win of the season, a 2–0 triumph over Hamilton, followed a 3–3 draw against Celtic and they went on to draw at Celtic Park during an improved run of results.

Falkirk, who exited both the Cups at the first hurdle, moved off the bottom of the SPL table in February for the first time in almost five months as Healy's goal gave them victory against Aberdeen at Pittodrie

The Bairns' failure to turn good displays into points proved crucial as they were relegated

for the first time since 1958. However, they slipped back down the standings eight days later following a 1–0 home defeat by Kilmarnock, which heralded the end of May's tenure.

Pressley took charge and, after insisting that the club would not go down, guided his team to a 3–1 triumph over Aberdeen in his first home match.

Falkirk then went six games without a victory before recording consecutive wins over Motherwell and St Mirren to draw level on points with the latter. However, they lost 1–0 to both Aberdeen and Hamilton after the split and then let 10-man St Mirren off the hook at the Falkirk Stadium as Stephen O'Donnell's late equaliser all but secured Saints' safety.

Another home draw, this time against St Johnstone, meant that Falkirk needed to win at Rugby Park on the final day in order to stay up, rekindling memories of their 1–0 triumph at Inverness a year earlier. But Ryan Flynn volleyed their best chance over from 10 yards as some desperate late pressure came to nothing.

RESULTS 2009/10

JULY

16th	● FC Vaduz	H	W 1–0	Att: 5,763	Ref: D Ledentu	Scorers: Flynn. Booked: Arfield, Finnigan, McNamara, Robertson.
23rd	● FC Vaduz	A	L 2–0	Att: 1,842	Ref: D Kovacic	Booked: Barr, Scobbie, Finnigan, Flynn. AET – Score after 90 mins 1–0. Agg: 2–1.

AUGUST

15th	● Rangers	A	L 4–1	Att: 50,239	Ref: M Tumilty	Scorers: Finnigan. Booked: McNamara.
22nd	● Hibernian	H	L 1–3	Att: 6,059	Ref: S Conroy	Scorers: Flynn. Booked: Scobbie, Arfield, Finnigan.
29th	● Dundee Utd	A	L 2–1	Att: 6,979	Ref: C Thomson	Scorers: Finnbogason. Booked: Mitchell.

SEPTEMBER

14th	● Aberdeen	H	D 0–0	Att: 4,724	Ref: A Muir	Booked: Olejnik, Arfield.
19th	● Hamilton	A	D 0–0	Att: 2,640	Ref: W Collum	Booked: O'Brien, Lynch.
23rd	● Celtic	H	L 0–4	Att: 5,669	Ref: M Tumilty	
26th	● Kilmarnock	H	D 0–0	Att: 5,394	Ref: S Finnie	Booked: McLean, Marceta, Scobbie, Finnigan.

OCTOBER

3rd	● Motherwell	A	L 1–0	Att: 4,337	Ref: E Norris	Booked: Lynch, McNamara.
17th	● St Mirren	H	L 1–3	Att: 5,084	Ref: C Allan	Scorers: McLean. Booked: McNamara.
24th	● Hearts	A	D 0–0	Att: 14,127	Ref: C Boyle	Booked: Barr, Stewart, Arfield.
31st	● St Johnstone	A	L 3–1	Att: 4,423	Ref: D McDonald	Scorers: Finnigan. Booked: Lima.

NOVEMBER

8th	● Celtic	H	D 3–3	Att: 6,795	Ref: B Winter	Scorers: Arfield, Moutinho, Stewart. Booked: Arfield, Moutinho.
21st	● Hamilton	H	W 2–0	Att: 5,268	Ref: M Tumilty	Scorers: Bullen, Mitchell. Booked: Lima, Finnigan.
28th	● Hibernian	A	L 2–0	Att: 13,305	Ref: D Somers	Booked: MacDonald, Bullen.

DECEMBER

5th	● Rangers	H	L 1–3	Att: 6,903	Ref: W Collum	Scorers: Moutinho. Booked: McLean, Mitchell.
12th	● St Mirren	A	D 1–1	Att: 4,033	Ref: C Thomson	Scorers: Finnigan.
19th	● Kilmarnock	A	W 1–2	Att: 4,472	Ref: C Allan	Scorers: Finnigan, Flynn. Booked: Finnigan.
26th	● Hearts	H	L 0–1	Att: 6,082	Ref: C Murray	

JANUARY

16th	● Celtic	A	D 1–1	Att: 50,000	Ref: A Muir	Scorers: Finnigan. Booked: Finnigan, Barr, Bullen.
18th	● Kilmarnock	A	L 1–0	Att: 3,378	Ref: M Tumilty	
24th	● Dundee Utd	H	L 1–4	Att: 4,378	Ref: E Norris	Scorers: Moutinho. Booked: Lima, Healy.
27th	● Motherwell	H	D 0–0	Att: 4,321	Ref: C Richmond	Booked: Barr, Twaddle, Compton, Murdoch.
30th	● Rangers	A	L 3–0	Att: 45,907	Ref: C Allan	Booked: McLean, Healy.

FEBRUARY

2nd	● Aberdeen	A	W 0–1	Att: 7,741	Ref: S Finnie	Scorers: Healy. Booked: McLean, Twaddle, Barr, Olejnik.
10th	● Kilmarnock	H	L 0–1	Att: 7,049	Ref: W Collum	
13th	● Hearts	A	L 3–2	Att: 14,078	Ref: D McDonald	Scorers: Moutinho, Kucharski OG. Booked: Arfield.
20th	● Aberdeen	H	W 3–1	Att: 4,643	Ref: C Richmond	Scorers: Barr, Moutinho, Showunmi.
27th	● Dundee Utd	A	L 3–0	Att: 6,352	Ref: C Murray	Booked: Arfield, Healy.

MARCH

7th	● Celtic	H	L 0–2	Att: 6,792	Ref: B Winter	Booked: McLean, Twaddle.
13th	● St Johnstone	H	L 1–2	Att: 5,895	Ref: S O'Reilly	Scorers: Twaddle. Booked: Scobbie, Twaddle.
20th	● Hamilton	A	D 2–2	Att: 2,461	Ref: D McDonald	Scorers: Arfield, Flynn. Booked: Moutinho, Twaddle, McLean.
23rd	● St Johnstone	A	D 1–1	Att: 3,107	Ref: E Norris	Scorers: Flynn. Booked: Lynch, Scobbie.
27th	● Hibernian	H	L 1–3	Att: 5,460	Ref: M Tumilty	Scorers: Stewart. Booked: Showunmi, Arfield.

APRIL

3rd	● Motherwell	A	W 0–1	Att: 4,268	Ref: C Thomson	Scorers: Flynn.
10th	● St Mirren	H	W 2–1	Att: 5,671	Ref: D McDonald	Scorers: Moutinho, Higdon OG. Booked: Moutinho.
17th	● Aberdeen	A	L 1–0	Att: 10,461	Ref: B Winter	Booked: Twaddle, Compton.
24th	● Hamilton	H	L 0–1	Att: 5,118	Ref: C Murray	Booked: Arfield, Duffie.

MAY

1st	● St Mirren	H	D 1–1	Att: 5,919	Ref: W Collum	Scorers: Arfield. Booked: Duffie, Arfield.
5th	● St Johnstone	H	D 0–0	Att: 5,502	Ref: C Thomson	
8th	● Kilmarnock	A	D 0–0	Att: 10,662	Ref: D McDonald	Booked: Twaddle.

● Clydesdale Bank Premier League ● Scottish Cup ● Co-op Insurance Cup ● UEFA Champions League ● Europa League

FALKIRK

CLYDESDALE BANK PREMIER LEAGUE GOALKEEPER STATS

Player	Minutes on pitch	Appearances	Match starts	Completed matches	Sub appearances	Subbed off	Saved with feet	Punched	Parried	Tipped over	Fumbled	Tipped round	Caught	Blocked	Clean sheets	Goals conceded	Save %	Saved	Resulting in goals	Opposition miss	Fouls committed	Free-kicks won	Yellow cards	Red cards
Robert Olejnik	3594	38	38	38	0	0	3	26	24	5	2	11	118	2	10	57	76.83	1	5	0	0	6	2	0

CLYDESDALE BANK PREMIER LEAGUE OUTFIELD PLAYER STATS

Player	Minutes on pitch	Appearances	Match starts	Completed matches	Substitute appearances	Subbed off	Goals scored	Assists	Shots on target	Shots off target	Crosses	Corners taken	Defensive clearances	Defensive blocks	Fouls committed	Free-kicks won	Caught offside	Yellow cards	Red cards
Brian Allison	373	4	4	4	0	0	0	0	0	0	3	0	1	0	4	1	0	0	0
Scott Arfield	3202	36	35	32	1	3	3	2	21	26	18	14	7	1	61	35	3	9	0
Darren Barr	3594	38	38	38	0	0	1	0	8	10	20	1	36	16	33	30	0	4	0
Lee Bullen	231	9	0	0	9	0	1	0	2	1	0	0	2	1	3	3	3	2	0
Jack Compton	461	13	3	1	10	2	0	1	6	2	22	13	0	0	5	8	1	2	0
Kieran Duffie	483	6	5	4	1	1	0	0	1	0	6	0	3	0	6	3	0	1	0
Kjartan Finnbogason	591	7	7	4	0	3	1	0	8	6	4	0	1	0	11	11	7	0	0
Carl Finnigan	1768	27	20	10	7	10	5	2	14	15	14	0	7	0	59	52	17	5	0
Ryan Flynn	3109	36	36	19	0	17	5	6	24	15	29	15	5	1	13	69	5	0	0
Colin Healy	1564	19	17	12	2	5	1	0	7	4	18	27	4	1	31	18	2	3	0
Vitor Lima	1975	26	22	18	4	4	0	0	14	19	7	6	4	3	19	32	0	3	0
Sean Lynch	270	8	3	1	5	2	0	0	0	0	1	0	0	0	1	0	1	3	0
Alex MacDonald	585	11	4	1	7	3	0	1	6	11	8	10	1	0	9	6	3	1	0
Danijel Marceta	786	15	8	2	7	6	0	0	9	8	18	4	0	0	10	12	0	1	0
Brian McLean	3308	36	36	34	0	2	1	0	8	6	1	1	51	11	32	36	0	6	0
Jackie McNamara	1105	13	13	10	0	3	0	0	0	0	12	0	13	3	11	9	0	3	0
Chris Mitchell	510	8	5	5	3	0	1	0	2	4	20	14	4	2	6	5	0	2	0
Pedro Moutinho	1771	25	20	5	5	15	6	4	21	18	39	58	2	0	21	31	14	3	0
Stewart Murdoch	97	3	0	0	3	0	0	0	0	0	4	0	1	0	2	2	0	1	0
Burton O'Brien	2207	27	23	19	4	4	0	2	3	9	25	16	13	5	15	22	0	1	0
Pedro Pele	560	9	7	5	2	2	0	1	2	1	1	0	3	2	11	3	0	0	0
Dayne Robertson	5	1	0	0	1	0	0	0	0	0	0	0	0	0	0	0	0	0	0
Thomas Scobbie	1719	20	19	14	1	5	0	1	3	19	1	25	7	18	23	1	4	0
Enoch Showunmi	1584	21	15	13	6	2	1	3	10	15	11	0	12	0	41	24	23	1	0
Mark Stewart	939	19	7	5	12	2	2	0	6	11	6	3	0	0	13	9	4	1	0
Marc Twaddle	2820	33	30	29	3	1	1	0	1	2	22	5	21	7	27	19	0	7	0
Toufik Zerara	269	3	3	2	0	1	0	0	1	1	5	13	0	0	6	2	0	0	0

actim

Clydesdale Bank PREMIER LEAGUE

SEASON TOTALS

Goals scored	31
Goals conceded	57
Clean sheets	10
Shots on target	175
Shots off target	187
Shots per goal	11.68
Pens awarded	2
Pens scored	2
Pens conceded	6
Offsides	84
Corners	201
Crosses	333
Players used	28
Fouls committed	468
Free-kicks won	471

CARDS RECEIVED

66 **0**

SEQUENCES

Wins	2
(03/04/10–10/04/10)	
Losses	3
(on two occasions)	
Draws	3
(on two occasions)	
Undefeated	3
(on two occasions)	
Without win	11
(15/08/09–08/11/09)	
Undefeated home	2
(on three occasions)	
Undefeated away	3
(on two occasions)	
Without scoring	4
(14/09/09–03/10/09)	
Without conceding	3
(14/09/09–26/09/09)	
Scoring	6
(13/03/10–10/04/10)	
Conceding	9
(10/02/10–27/03/10)	

LEAGUE POSITION AT THE END OF EACH MONTH

AUG	SEP	OCT	NOV	DEC	JAN	FEB	MAR	APR	MAY
11	11	12	12	12	12	12	12	12	12

SEASON INFORMATION
Highest position: 10
Lowest position: 12
Average goals scored per game: 0.82
Average goals conceded per game: 1.50

MATCH RECORDS

Goals scored per match

		W	D	L	Pts
Failed to score	16	0	7	9	7
Scored 1 goal	15	2	4	9	10
Scored 2 goals	5	3	1	1	10
Scored 3 goals	2	1	1	0	4
Scored 4+ goals	0	0	0	0	0

Goals conceded per match

		W	D	L	Pts
Clean sheet	10	3	7	0	16
Conceded 1 goal	12	3	4	5	13
Conceded 2 goals	5	0	1	4	1
Conceded 3 goals	9	0	1	8	1
Conceded 4+ goals	2	0	0	2	0

EARLIEST STRIKE
CARL FINNIGAN
(v Kilmarnock) 2:48

LATEST STRIKE
PEDRO MOUTINHO
(v Dundee Utd) 90:11

Scott Arfield

GOAL DETAILS

How the goals were struck

SCORED		CONCEDED
24	Right foot	31
4	Left foot	15
3	Header	11
0	Other	0

How the goals were struck

SCORED		CONCEDED
18	Open play	33
2	Cross	7
3	Corner	4
2	Penalty	5
2	Direct from free-kick	4
2	Free-kick	2
2	Own goal	2

Distance from goal

SCORED		CONCEDED
11	6YDS	26
16	18YDS	23
4	18+YDS	8

GOALS SCORED/CONCEDED
PER FIVE-MINUTE INTERVALS

MINS	5	10	15	20	25	30	35	40	45	50	55	60	65	70	75	80	85	90
FOR	1	0	1	3	2	3	1	0	5	1	1	2	3	2	1	1	2	2
AGN	3	1	2	5	1	2	4	3	5	2	2	6	3	3	4	3	2	6

HAMILTON ACADEMICAL

CLUB SUMMARY

FORMED	1874
MANAGER	Billy Reid
GROUND	New Douglas Park
CAPACITY	6,078
NICKNAME	The Accies
WEBSITE	www.acciesfc.co.uk

The New Football Pools PLAYER OF THE SEASON — James McArthur

OVERALL

P	W	D	L	F	A	GD
41	13	11	17	43	53	-10

CLYDESDALE BANK PREMIER LEAGUE

Pos	P	W	D	L	F	A	GD	Pts
7	38	13	10	15	39	46	-7	49

HOME

Pos	P	W	D	L	F	A	GD	Pts
7	19	6	7	6	19	17	2	25

AWAY

Pos	P	W	D	L	F	A	GD	Pts
5	19	7	3	9	20	29	-9	24

CUP PROGRESS DETAILS

Competition	Round reached	Knocked out by
Scottish Cup	R4	Rangers
Co-op Insurance Cup	R2	Ross County

BIGGEST WIN (ALL COMPS)
10/04/10 4–1 v Hibernian

BIGGEST DEFEAT (ALL COMPS)
23/01/10 1–5 v Hibernian

THE PLAYER WITH THE MOST

GOALS SCORED	Simon Mensing	8
SHOTS ON TARGET	James McArthur	24
SHOTS OFF TARGET	Marco Paixao	36
SHOTS WITHOUT SCORING	Alex Neil	7
ASSISTS	Dougie Imrie	5
OFFSIDES	Mickael Antoine-Curier	42
FOULS	James McArthur, Mark McLaughlin	58
FOULS WITHOUT A CARD	Joël Thomas	13
FREE-KICKS WON	James McArthur	58
DEFENSIVE CLEARANCES	Martin Canning	44

ATTENDANCE RECORD

HIGH	AVERAGE	LOW
5,343	3,005	2,003
v Rangers (16/01/2010)		v Hearts (06/12/2009)

HAMILTON enjoyed one of their best seasons in three-quarters of a century as they finished seventh in the Clydesdale Bank Premier League. It is 75 years since the Accies occupied such a lofty position among the elite and Billy Reid's side actually ended the campaign with more points than sixth-placed Hearts, but finished below them following the League's split.

Reid, who led the club into Scotland's top flight for the first time in 19 years in 2008, had lost two of his star players to Barclays Premier League clubs in the summer, with James McCarthy sold to Wigan and Brian Easton departing for Burnley. There were also several new faces brought in as the number of summer signings at New Douglas Park reached double figures.

On the pitch, the club made a slow start to the campaign with four straight defeats, including a shock Co-operative Insurance Cup exit at Ross County.

The Accies went into December having won only two of their first 14 games in all competitions. However, a 2–1 victory over Hearts just before Christmas proved to be crucial as the club's form picked up. Accies proved increasingly hard to beat and they held Rangers to a 3–3 draw in the Active Nation Scottish Cup fourth round – one of three games in 10 days against Walter Smith's men. They lost the other two – including the replay in the Cup – and they also went down 5–1 at Hibernian.

In the January transfer window they made a signing that helped to transform

Manager Billy Reid led the impressive Accies to their best season in 75 years

their season. Striker Dougie Imrie arrived from Inverness on transfer deadline day and, although he suffered defeat on his debut, Hamilton subsequently embarked on a run that saw them lose just two of their final 16 games.

Imrie only scored twice for the club but the diminutive forward caused defences all sorts of problems with his tireless running and unselfish play for the remainder of the campaign. The squad was also boosted in the winter transfer window by the loan return of former players Easton and Joël Thomas from Colchester.

The Accies went into the split all but safe after beating Hibernian 4–1, before mathematically confirming a third successive SPL campaign with a 3–0 victory over Kilmarnock.

Wins at Falkirk, Aberdeen and St Johnstone followed, with the only blip coming in a goalless home draw against St Mirren. That match saw James McArthur bid an emotional farewell to New Douglas Park, as Reid braced himself to lose more key men ahead of 2010/11.

Simon Mensing, pictured scoring against Hearts, and goalkeeper Tomas Cerny were two of Hamilton's key players during the 2009/10 season

RESULTS 2009/10

AUGUST

15th	● Kilmarnock	A	L 3–0	**Att:** 5,307	**Ref:** C Boyle	**Booked:** Mensing.
22nd	○ Aberdeen	H	L 0–3	**Att:** 3,347	**Ref:** B Winter	**Booked:** F Paixao, Wilkie.
25th	○ Ross County	A	L 2–1	**Att:** 764	**Ref:** C Boyle	**Scorers:** Mensing.
29th	● Rangers	A	L 4–1	**Att:** 47,633	**Ref:** S O'Reilly	**Scorers:** McLaughlin. **Booked:** Knight.

SEPTEMBER

13th	● Hibernian	H	W 2–0	**Att:** 4,023	**Ref:** D Somers	**Scorers:** Antoine-Curier, Mensing. **Booked:** McLaughlin, Wesolowski.
19th	● Falkirk	H	D 0–0	**Att:** 2,640	**Ref:** W Collum	**Booked:** Wesolowski.
26th	● Hearts	A	L 2–1	**Att:** 13,025	**Ref:** A Muir	**Scorers:** M Paixao. **Booked:** Canning, McLaughlin, McArthur, Mason.

OCTOBER

3rd	● St Johnstone	H	L 0–2	**Att:** 2,199	**Ref:** C Richmond	**Booked:** Wesolowski.
17th	● Dundee Utd	A	D 1–1	**Att:** 5,944	**Ref:** I Brines	**Scorers:** Antoine-Curier. **Booked:** McLaughlin, Wesolowski.
25th	● Celtic	H	L 1–2	**Att:** 4,689	**Ref:** I Brines	**Scorers:** Antoine-Curier.
31st	● St Mirren	A	W 0–2	**Att:** 4,022	**Ref:** S Finnie	**Scorers:** Canning, M Paixao. **Booked:** Wesolowski, Antoine-Curier, Evans.

NOVEMBER

7th	● Motherwell	H	D 2–2	**Att:** 3,583	**Ref:** C Thomson	**Scorers:** Mensing, M Paixao. **Booked:** Beuzelin, Hastings, McClenahan. **Dismissed:** Beuzelin.
21st	● Falkirk	A	L 2–0	**Att:** 5,268	**Ref:** M Tumilty	
28th	● St Johnstone	A	D 1–1	**Att:** 3,426	**Ref:** W Collum	**Scorers:** Antoine-Curier.

DECEMBER

6th	● Hearts	H	W 2–1	**Att:** 2,003	**Ref:** D Somers	**Scorers:** McArthur, Mensing.
12th	● Aberdeen	A	W 1–2	**Att:** 9,499	**Ref:** A Muir	**Scorers:** Antoine-Curier, Wesolowski. **Booked:** Neil, Mensing, McClenahan.
26th	● Celtic	A	L 2–0	**Att:** 36,827	**Ref:** S O'Reilly	**Booked:** McLaughlin.

JANUARY

10th	● Rangers	H	D 3–3	**Att:** 3,940	**Ref:** C Richmond	**Scorers:** Antoine-Curier, Mensing, M Paixao. **Booked:** Antoine-Curier, Hastings, Canning. **Dismissed:** Hastings.
13th	● Dundee Utd	H	L 0–1	**Att:** 2,033	**Ref:** I Brines	
16th	● Rangers	H	L 0–1	**Att:** 5,343	**Ref:** M Tumilty	**Booked:** McLaughlin.
19th	● Rangers	A	L 2–0	**Att:** 21,856	**Ref:** C Richmond	**Booked:** Mensing, Elebert. AET – Score after 90 mins 0–0.
23rd	● Hibernian	A	L 5–1	**Att:** 11,481	**Ref:** B Winter	**Scorers:** F Paixao. **Booked:** Neil, McLaughlin.
26th	● Kilmarnock	H	D 0–0	**Att:** 2,018	**Ref:** S Finnie	**Booked:** McArthur.
30th	● Celtic	H	L 0–1	**Att:** 4,922	**Ref:** C Murray	

FEBRUARY

6th	● Motherwell	A	L 1–0	**Att:** 4,777	**Ref:** M Tumilty	**Booked:** Imrie.
10th	● Dundee Utd	A	W 0–2	**Att:** 5,598	**Ref:** A Muir	**Scorers:** M Paixao, F Paixao. **Booked:** Imrie, F Paixao, Mensing.
13th	● Motherwell	H	D 0–0	**Att:** 3,133	**Ref:** C Richmond	**Booked:** M Paixao.
21st	● Hearts	A	L 2–0	**Att:** 13,496	**Ref:** S Conroy	**Booked:** Elebert.
27th	● St Mirren	A	D 0–0	**Att:** 3,628	**Ref:** C Allan	**Booked:** Easton, McLaughlin, Elebert, Neil.

MARCH

6th	● Aberdeen	H	D 1–1	**Att:** 2,030	**Ref:** S Finnie	**Scorers:** F Paixao. **Booked:** McLaughlin, Mensing, Elebert, Canning.
13th	● St Mirren	H	W 1–0	**Att:** 2,179	**Ref:** E Norris	**Scorers:** F Paixao. **Booked:** Mensing, Antoine-Curier, Neil, McArthur, F Paixao.
20th	● Falkirk	H	D 2–2	**Att:** 2,461	**Ref:** D McDonald	**Scorers:** Antoine-Curier, Mensing. **Booked:** Mensing, Wesolowski.
24th	● Kilmarnock	A	W 1–2	**Att:** 4,068	**Ref:** C Thomson	**Scorers:** Antoine-Curier, Mensing. **Booked:** McArthur, Canning.
27th	● St Johnstone	H	W 1–0	**Att:** 2,245	**Ref:** C Allan	**Scorers:** Wesolowski. **Booked:** McArthur.

APRIL

3rd	● Rangers	A	L 1–0	**Att:** 48,068	**Ref:** S O'Reilly	**Booked:** Neil.
10th	● Hibernian	H	W 4–1	**Att:** 2,520	**Ref:** S Conroy	**Scorers:** Mensing[2], Thomas[2].
17th	● Kilmarnock	H	W 3–0	**Att:** 2,628	**Ref:** D McDonald	**Scorers:** Imrie, F Paixao, Thomas. **Booked:** Antoine-Curier, McArthur.
24th	● Falkirk	A	W 0–1	**Att:** 5,118	**Ref:** C Murray	**Scorers:** M Paixao. **Booked:** M Paixao, Imrie.

MAY

1st	● Aberdeen	A	W 1–3	**Att:** 7,099	**Ref:** S McLean	**Scorers:** Mensing, F Paixao, Wesolowski.
5th	● St Mirren	H	D 0–0	**Att:** 3,102	**Ref:** I Brines	**Booked:** Neil, Imrie.
8th	● St Johnstone	A	W 2–3	**Att:** 3,188	**Ref:** W Collum	**Scorers:** Imrie, McLaughlin, Wesolowski. **Booked:** Murdoch.

● Clydesdale Bank Premier League ● Scottish Cup ● Co-op Insurance Cup ● UEFA Champions League ● Europa League

HAMILTON ACADEMICAL

CLYDESDALE BANK PREMIER LEAGUE GOALKEEPER STATS

Player	Minutes on pitch	Appearances	Match starts	Completed matches	Sub appearances	Subbed off	Saved with feet	Punched	Parried	Tipped over	Fumbled	Tipped round	Caught	Blocked	Clean sheets	Goals conceded	Save %	Saved	Resulting in goals	Opposition miss	Fouls committed	Free-kicks won	Yellow cards	Red cards
Tomas Cerny	3142	34	34	32	0	2	5	9	20	5	1	4	122	2	9	42	79.90	4	1	0	0	10	0	0
Sean Murdoch	444	6	4	4	2	0	1	6	1	1	0	2	12	0	2	4	85.19	1	0	0	2	0	1	0

CLYDESDALE BANK PREMIER LEAGUE OUTFIELD PLAYER STATS

Player	Minutes on pitch	Appearances	Match starts	Completed matches	Substitute appearances	Subbed off	Goals scored	Assists	Shots on target	Shots off target	Crosses	Corners taken	Defensive clearances	Defensive blocks	Fouls committed	Free-kicks won	Caught offside	Yellow cards	Red cards
Marvin Andrews	148	2	2	1	0	1	0	0	0	1	0	0	1	0	1	0	0	0	0
Mickael Antoine-Curier	2179	26	25	14	1	11	7	2	22	15	3	0	10	1	29	27	42	3	0
Guillaume Beuzelin	222	7	3	0	4	2	0	0	0	2	0	3	1	0	4	2	0	1	1
Martin Canning	3469	37	37	36	0	1	1	0	3	5	11	0	44	11	39	20	0	3	0
Ali Crawford	94	7	0	0	7	0	0	0	1	1	4	3	0	1	0	4	0	0	0
Brian Easton	1066	12	12	9	0	3	0	2	4	3	27	35	7	0	8	12	0	1	0
David Elebert	1575	25	15	12	10	3	0	1	1	2	1	0	7	5	17	9	1	3	0
Stuart Elliott	155	5	2	0	3	2	0	1	2	0	0	0	0	0	2	1	0	0	0
Grant Evans	519	9	5	2	4	3	0	1	1	2	6	0	1	3	13	2	0	1	0
Grant Gillespie	2	1	0	0	1	0	0	0	0	0	0	0	0	0	0	0	0	0	0
Richard Hastings	1436	17	17	10	0	7	0	1	4	1	29	40	8	0	18	20	0	1	0
Dougie Imrie	1469	16	16	12	0	4	2	5	13	12	33	22	4	0	28	53	10	4	0
Izzy Iriekpen	184	2	2	2	0	0	0	0	0	0	0	0	4	0	3	2	0	0	0
Jordan Kirkpatrick	194	5	1	0	4	1	0	0	2	1	0	0	0	0	1	0	1	0	0
John Kissock	99	2	2	0	0	2	0	0	0	0	0	0	0	0	1	1	0	0	0
Leon Knight	174	6	0	0	6	0	0	1	3	1	0	0	0	0	2	2	2	1	0
David Louhoungou	253	6	0	0	6	0	0	1	2	0	1	0	0	0	2	3	0	0	0
Derek Lyle	307	5	2	1	2	2	0	0	2	1	3	3	0	0	2	4	0	0	0
Gary Mason	338	5	5	1	0	4	0	0	0	1	0	0	2	1	7	4	0	1	0
James McArthur	3310	35	35	35	0	0	1	2	24	20	20	4	18	5	58	58	8	6	0
Trent McClenahan	2112	27	23	18	4	5	0	1	1	0	6	0	6	4	16	27	0	2	0
Mark McLaughlin	2877	32	32	25	0	7	2	0	5	9	2	0	41	11	58	56	1	8	0
Brian McQueen	16	1	0	0	1	0	0	0	0	0	0	0	0	0	0	0	0	0	0
Simon Mensing	3405	37	37	33	0	4	8	4	19	18	11	1	30	3	53	25	4	6	0
Stuart Mills	48	2	0	0	2	0	0	0	0	0	0	0	0	0	1	0	0	0	0
Alex Neil	2011	22	22	19	0	3	0	0	2	5	8	3	9	2	35	18	0	6	0
Richard Offiong	92	1	1	1	0	0	0	0	1	2	0	0	1	0	0	2	1	0	0
Flavio Paixao	1847	25	18	14	7	4	6	2	17	14	42	24	5	0	27	34	5	3	0
Marco Paixao	2160	33	23	13	10	10	5	3	23	36	37	55	3	1	24	28	6	2	0
Luis Rubiales	276	3	3	3	0	0	0	1	2	1	4	9	1	1	5	4	0	0	0
John Sullivan	69	2	1	0	1	1	0	0	0	0	0	0	0	0	2	0	0	0	0
Stuart Taylor	32	1	0	0	1	0	0	0	0	0	0	0	0	0	0	0	0	0	0
Joël Thomas	331	11	2	1	9	1	3	0	5	4	0	0	0	0	13	4	5	0	0
Kevin Welsh	45	1	1	0	0	1	0	0	0	0	0	0	0	0	0	0	0	0	0
James Wesolowski	2441	29	27	17	2	10	4	4	10	8	11	2	10	2	28	47	0	6	0
Kyle Wilkie	467	12	3	2	9	1	0	0	2	3	4	4	2	0	8	9	0	1	0
David van Zanten	372	6	4	2	2	2	0	0	1	0	0	0	0	0	3	1	0	0	0

actim

Clydesdale Bank PREMIER LEAGUE

SEASON TOTALS

Goals scored	39
Goals conceded	46
Clean sheets	12
Shots on target	168
Shots off target	174
Shots per goal	8.77
Pens awarded	5
Pens scored	5
Pens conceded	6
Offsides	86
Corners	209
Crosses	269
Players used	39
Fouls committed	509
Free-kicks won	490

CARDS RECEIVED

60 **1**

SEQUENCES

Wins	4
(10/04/10–01/05/10)	
Losses	4
(26/12/09–23/01/10)	
Draws	2
(27/02/10–06/03/10)	
Undefeated	6
(on two occasions)	
Without win	7
(26/12/09–06/02/10)	
Undefeated home	8
(13/02/10–05/05/10)	
Undefeated away	3
(24/04/10–08/05/10)	
Without scoring	3
(on three occasions)	
Without conceding	2
(on three occasions)	
Scoring	5
(06/03/10–27/03/10)	
Conceding	9
(07/11/09–23/01/10)	

LEAGUE POSITION AT THE END OF EACH MONTH

AUG	SEP	OCT	NOV	DEC	JAN	FEB	MAR	APR	MAY
12	10	11	10	9	10	11	9	8	7

SEASON INFORMATION
Highest position: 6
Lowest position: 12
Average goals scored per game: 1.03
Average goals conceded per game: 1.21

MATCH RECORDS

Goals scored per match

		W	D	L	Pts
Failed to score	16	0	5	11	5
Scored 1 goal	10	3	3	4	12
Scored 2 goals	8	6	2	0	20
Scored 3 goals	3	3	0	0	9
Scored 4+ goals	1	1	0	0	3

Goals conceded per match

		W	D	L	Pts
Clean sheet	12	7	5	0	26
Conceded 1 goal	13	5	3	5	18
Conceded 2 goals	9	1	2	6	5
Conceded 3 goals	2	0	0	2	0
Conceded 4+ goals	2	0	0	2	0

GOALS SCORED/CONCEDED
PER FIVE-MINUTE INTERVALS

MINS	5	10	15	20	25	30	35	40	45	50	55	60	65	70	75	80	85	90
FOR	3	2	2	2	4	1	1	0	3	2	0	3	4	2	1	3	3	3
AGN	0	0	3	2	2	6	2	1	1	2	2	3	4	5	2	6	2	3

EARLIEST STRIKE
FLAVIO PAIXAO
(v Aberdeen) 0:40

LATEST STRIKE
FLAVIO PAIXAO
(v St Mirren) 91:20

Mickael Antoine-Curier

GOAL DETAILS

How the goals were struck

SCORED		CONCEDED
23	Right foot	28
4	Left foot	11
12	Header	7
0	Other	0

How the goals were struck

SCORED		CONCEDED
17	Open play	28
8	Cross	8
8	Corner	3
5	Penalty	1
1	Direct from free-kick	3
0	Free-kick	3
0	Own goal	0

Distance from goal

SCORED		CONCEDED
19	6YDS	15
17	18YDS	25
3	18+YDS	6

HEART OF MIDLOTHIAN

CLUB SUMMARY

FORMED	1874
MANAGER	Jim Jefferies
GROUND	Tynecastle
CAPACITY	17,402
NICKNAME	The Jambos
WEBSITE	www.heartsfc.co.uk

The New Football Pools PLAYER OF THE SEASON — Lee Wallace

OVERALL

P	W	D	L	F	A	GD
44	16	9	19	40	54	-14

CLYDESDALE BANK PREMIER LEAGUE

Pos	P	W	D	L	F	A	GD	Pts
6	38	13	9	16	35	46	-11	48

HOME

Pos	P	W	D	L	F	A	GD	Pts
4	19	9	4	6	19	20	-1	31

AWAY

Pos	P	W	D	L	F	A	GD	Pts
9	19	4	5	10	16	26	-10	17

CUP PROGRESS DETAILS

Competition	Round reached	Knocked out by
Europa League	QR4	Dinamo Zagreb
Scottish Cup	R4	Aberdeen
Co-op Insurance Cup	SF	St Mirren

BIGGEST WIN (ALL COMPS)

2–0 on 2 occasions

BIGGEST DEFEAT (ALL COMPS)

20/08/09 0–4 v Dinamo Zagreb

THE PLAYER WITH THE MOST

GOALS SCORED	Suso Santana	6
SHOTS ON TARGET	Suso Santana	25
SHOTS OFF TARGET	David Obua	21
SHOTS WITHOUT SCORING	Laryea Kingston	19
ASSISTS	Craig Thomson	4
OFFSIDES	David Obua	30
FOULS	David Obua	53
FOULS WITHOUT A CARD	David Witteveen	6
FREE-KICKS WON	Suso Santana	43
DEFENSIVE CLEARANCES	Marius Zaliukas	33

ATTENDANCE RECORD

High	Average	Low
17,126	14,497	12,325
v Hibernian (20/03/2010)		v Dundee Utd (05/05/2010)

Club favourite Jim Jefferies returned to Hearts and quickly made his presence felt

HEARTS' season was memorable in the most part for two dramatic hours in January that saw Csaba László depart as manager and Jim Jefferies return.

The Jambos acted swiftly to replace László with Tynecastle legend Jefferies, whose first spell in charge had ended almost a decade earlier. Jefferies subsequently guided them to a top-six place in the Clydesdale Bank Premier League prior to the split and he came close to snatching a Europa League place.

László had earned praise a year ago for transforming a side that had finished eighth the previous campaign into one that ended 2008/09 in third place behind the Old Firm.

However, the Hungarian's hopes of emulating, or even bettering, that feat were hit by the summer departure of key players Christos Karipidis, Bruno Aguiar and Robbie Neilson, with the Jambos having already lost captain Christophe Berra.

Hearts' Europa League adventure proved to be brief as they lost 4–0 to Dinamo Zagreb, although they did win the second leg 2–0. They also got off to a slow start in the League, winning only two of their first 12 SPL games. However, they did manage an impressive 1–0 Co-operative Insurance Cup victory at Celtic during that period to

Jim Jefferies returned to Tynecastle in January, replacing Csaba László

Michael Stewart scores a penalty in the Co-operative Insurance Cup win at Celtic

earn a semi-final place.

Their season hit a low when they lost 2–1 at Hamilton in December, but there was still plenty of reason for cheer as the club saw several young players establish themselves in the first team during the course of the campaign. The likes of Craig Thomson, Gary Glen and Scott Robinson all made encouraging progress as Hearts continue to look to the future.

A seven-match unbeaten run in the SPL lifted them up the table, although that was tempered by a defeat at Aberdeen in the Active Nation Scottish Cup fourth round. The Dons also ended Hearts' positive sequence in the League, and that match proved to be László's last in charge.

Jefferies soon arrived in the dugout, but his hopes of making an instant impact were hit by three successive defeats, including to St Mirren in the Co-operative Insurance Cup semi-final.

An injury crisis that had dogged the club all season also reached its nadir before the new manager steadied the ship with a hat-trick of victories.

Although European football ultimately proved beyond them, Hearts did end the season with two memorable Edinburgh derby triumphs over archrivals Hibernian. Now Jefferies will be focused on ensuring the club progress in 2010/11.

RESULTS 2009/10

AUGUST

17th	● Dundee Utd	A	L 2–0	**Att:** 8,253	**Ref:** S Conroy	**Booked:** Obua, M Stewart, Santana, Black. **Dismissed:** M Stewart.
20th	● Dinamo Zagreb	A	L 4–0	**Att:** 22,000	**Ref:** N Ivanov	**Booked:** Nade, Zaliukas.
23rd	● Rangers	H	L 1–2	**Att:** 16,284	**Ref:** C Thomson	**Scorers:** Witteveen. **Booked:** Santana, Nade, Palazuelos, Obua.
27th	● Dinamo Zagreb	H	W 2–0	**Att:** 11,769	**Ref:** K Kircher	**Scorers:** M Stewart, Zaliukas. **Booked:** M Stewart, Black. Agg: 2–4.
30th	● St Johnstone	A	D 2–2	**Att:** 5,825	**Ref:** M Tumilty	**Scorers:** Goncalves, Obua. **Booked:** L Wallace, Goncalves, C Thomson, Nade, Obua.

SEPTEMBER

15th	● Kilmarnock	H	W 1–0	**Att:** 13,576	**Ref:** W Collum	**Scorers:** Driver.
20th	● Celtic	A	L 2–1	**Att:** 58,024	**Ref:** D McDonald	**Scorers:** Santana. **Booked:** Palazuelos, Black.
23rd	● Dunfermline	H	W 2–1	**Att:** 6,126	**Ref:** B Winter	**Scorers:** Glen, M Stewart. **Booked:** Santana.
26th	● Hamilton	H	W 2–1	**Att:** 13,025	**Ref:** A Muir	**Scorers:** Santana, M Stewart. **Booked:** Black.

OCTOBER

3rd	● St Mirren	A	L 2–1	**Att:** 4,652	**Ref:** B Winter	**Scorers:** Goncalves. **Booked:** Bouzid.
17th	● Aberdeen	A	D 1–1	**Att:** 11,629	**Ref:** D McDonald	**Scorers:** Driver.
24th	● Falkirk	H	D 0–0	**Att:** 14,127	**Ref:** C Boyle	**Booked:** Obua.
28th	● Celtic	A	W 0–1	**Att:** 18,675	**Ref:** C Thomson	**Scorers:** M Stewart. **Booked:** Bouzid, Jonsson, Goncalves.
31st	● Motherwell	A	L 1–0	**Att:** 4,830	**Ref:** D Somers	**Booked:** Palazuelos, Novikovas. **Dismissed:** Jonsson.

NOVEMBER

7th	● Hibernian	H	D 0–0	**Att:** 16,762	**Ref:** S Conroy	**Booked:** Driver.
21st	● St Johnstone	H	L 1–2	**Att:** 13,416	**Ref:** S O'Reilly	**Scorers:** Nade. **Booked:** Black, Nade. **Dismissed:** Goncalves.
28th	● Kilmarnock	A	W 1–2	**Att:** 4,707	**Ref:** S Nicholls	**Scorers:** Jonsson, Nade. **Booked:** Palazuelos.

DECEMBER

6th	● Hamilton	A	L 2–1	**Att:** 2,003	**Ref:** D Somers	**Scorers:** Jonsson. **Booked:** Santana, C Thomson, Bouzid. **Dismissed:** M Stewart, Bouzid.
12th	● Dundee Utd	H	D 0–0	**Att:** 14,873	**Ref:** E Norris	**Booked:** Goncalves, M Stewart, Kingston.
20th	● Celtic	H	W 2–1	**Att:** 16,223	**Ref:** W Collum	**Scorers:** Bouzid, M Stewart. **Booked:** L Wallace, Bouzid, Jonsson, Goncalves, Templeton.
26th	● Falkirk	A	W 0–1	**Att:** 6,082	**Ref:** C Murray	**Scorers:** M Stewart. **Booked:** Kello.
30th	● Motherwell	H	W 1–0	**Att:** 14,411	**Ref:** C Allan	**Scorers:** M Stewart. **Booked:** L Wallace, Kucharski.

JANUARY

3rd	● Hibernian	A	D 1–1	**Att:** 16,949	**Ref:** C Richmond	**Scorers:** Smith. **Booked:** Santana, Templeton, M Stewart. **Dismissed:** Palazuelos.
9th	● Aberdeen	A	L 2–0	**Att:** 8,226	**Ref:** S Conroy	
16th	● St Mirren	H	W 1–0	**Att:** 12,821	**Ref:** S O'Reilly	**Scorers:** M Stewart. **Booked:** Jonsson, Obua.
23rd	● Rangers	A	D 1–1	**Att:** 47,031	**Ref:** C Murray	**Scorers:** Robinson. **Booked:** Bouzid, Nade. **Dismissed:** Nade.
27th	● Aberdeen	H	L 0–3	**Att:** 14,219	**Ref:** M Tumilty	**Booked:** Black.
30th	● St Johnstone	A	L 1–0	**Att:** 4,752	**Ref:** E Norris	**Booked:** M Stewart.

FEBRUARY

2nd	● St Mirren	N	L 0–1	**Att:** 9,170	**Ref:** C Richmond	**Booked:** Black, L Wallace, Nade.
10th	● Celtic	A	L 2–0	**Att:** 44,500	**Ref:** B Winter	**Booked:** Mulrooney, Zaliukas, Jonsson, Black.
13th	● Falkirk	H	W 3–2	**Att:** 14,078	**Ref:** D McDonald	**Scorers:** Black, Santana, L Wallace. **Booked:** Black.
21st	● Hamilton	H	W 2–0	**Att:** 13,496	**Ref:** S Conroy	**Scorers:** Obua, Templeton. **Booked:** Zaliukas, Jonsson.
27th	● Aberdeen	A	W 0–1	**Att:** 8,316	**Ref:** W Collum	**Scorers:** Jonsson. **Booked:** Jonsson, Mulrooney, Balogh. **Dismissed:** Kingston.

MARCH

7th	● Dundee Utd	A	L 1–0	**Att:** 6,683	**Ref:** M Tumilty	
13th	● Motherwell	A	L 3–1	**Att:** 4,448	**Ref:** S Finnie	**Scorers:** Templeton. **Booked:** Santana, Jonsson, L Wallace, Kucharski.
20th	● Hibernian	H	W 2–1	**Att:** 17,126	**Ref:** W Collum	**Scorers:** Driver, Glen. **Booked:** Glen.
27th	● Rangers	H	L 1–4	**Att:** 16,832	**Ref:** C Murray	**Scorers:** Santana. **Booked:** Santana, C Thomson.

APRIL

3rd	● St Mirren	A	D 1–1	**Att:** 4,204	**Ref:** I Brines	**Scorers:** Zaliukas. **Booked:** J Thomson.
10th	● Kilmarnock	H	W 1–0	**Att:** 14,015	**Ref:** E Norris	**Scorers:** Santana. **Booked:** Jonsson, Santana.
18th	● Rangers	A	L 2–0	**Att:** 47,590	**Ref:** I Brines	**Booked:** Obua, C Thomson, Kingston, Black, Robinson. **Dismissed:** Jonsson.
24th	● Motherwell	H	L 0–2	**Att:** 13,447	**Ref:** B Winter	**Booked:** Black.

MAY

1st	● Hibernian	A	W 1–2	**Att:** 11,277	**Ref:** D McDonald	**Scorers:** Obua, Santana. **Booked:** Zaliukas, Elliot.
5th	● Dundee Utd	H	D 0–0	**Att:** 12,325	**Ref:** S Finnie	**Booked:** Bouzid, Jonsson.
9th	● Celtic	H	L 1–2	**Att:** 14,389	**Ref:** C Thomson	**Scorers:** Zaliukas. **Booked:** Stevenson, Obua, J Thomson.

● Clydesdale Bank Premier League ● Scottish Cup ● Co-op Insurance Cup ● UEFA Champions League ● Europa League

HEART OF MIDLOTHIAN

CLYDESDALE BANK PREMIER LEAGUE GOALKEEPER STATS

Player	Minutes on pitch	Appearances	Match starts	Completed matches	Sub appearances	Subbed off	Saved with feet	Punched	Parried	Tipped over	Fumbled	Tipped round	Caught	Blocked	Clean sheets	Goals conceded	Save %	Saved	Resulting in goals	Opposition miss	Fouls committed	Free-kicks won	Yellow cards	Red cards
Janos Balogh	1470	16	16	15	0	1	0	9	15	1	0	3	53	0	3	19	81.00	1	1	0	0	3	1	0
Marian Kello	1324	14	14	14	0	0	0	9	8	5	2	2	70	0	6	13	87.85	1	1	0	0	4	1	0
Jamie MacDonald	801	9	8	8	1	0	1	3	6	3	0	4	19	2	2	14	73.08	0	2	0	0	3	0	0

CLYDESDALE BANK PREMIER LEAGUE OUTFIELD PLAYER STATS

Player	Minutes on pitch	Appearances	Match starts	Completed matches	Substitute appearances	Subbed off	Goals scored	Assists	Shots on target	Shots off target	Crosses	Corners taken	Defensive clearances	Defensive blocks	Fouls committed	Free-kicks won	Caught offside	Yellow cards	Red cards
Ian Black	1694	26	17	9	9	8	1	0	13	15	12	8	8	3	37	32	1	9	0
Ismael Bouzid	2435	26	26	24	0	1	1	0	4	3	6	0	29	9	41	19	0	5	1
Marius Cinikas	136	2	1	1	1	0	0	0	0	0	3	0	0	0	2	1	0	0	0
Andrew Driver	1004	12	11	6	1	5	3	0	7	2	19	22	1	0	10	6	0	1	0
Calum Elliot	631	13	6	2	7	4	0	1	3	3	0	1	4	0	5	16	5	1	0
Gary Glen	959	18	10	2	8	8	1	0	7	17	1	0	1	0	4	4	8	1	0
Jose Goncalves	1785	19	19	18	0	0	2	0	4	5	7	0	12	10	21	31	0	3	1
Eggert Jonsson	2527	28	27	25	1	0	3	2	12	5	8	0	13	4	46	38	1	8	2
Laryea Kingston	938	14	10	5	4	4	0	0	5	14	13	13	0	0	16	12	0	2	1
Dawid Kucharski	770	14	10	7	4	3	0	0	0	0	2	0	8	4	13	9	0	2	0
Jamie Mole	343	7	5	0	2	5	0	0	0	2	3	0	0	0	3	5	5	0	0
Paul Mulrooney	258	6	3	0	3	3	0	0	1	0	2	0	0	0	3	2	0	2	0
Christian Nade	1489	23	15	5	8	9	2	3	6	15	7	0	3	0	40	28	21	4	1
Arvydas Novikovas	591	13	5	0	8	5	0	1	7	3	11	14	6	1	8	8	4	1	0
David Obua	2811	32	30	25	2	5	3	1	12	21	21	1	20	1	53	24	30	7	0
Ruben Palazuelos	2396	27	26	24	1	1	0	1	5	7	15	0	15	1	26	21	1	4	1
Scott Robinson	689	13	7	1	6	6	1	0	1	5	2	7	0	2	4	8	2	1	0
Suso Santana	1926	27	21	9	6	12	6	3	25	20	25	27	8	1	14	43	14	7	0
Gordon Smith	227	8	2	0	6	2	1	0	2	3	0	0	0	0	1	1	1	0	0
Ryan Stevenson	876	11	9	6	2	3	0	0	7	7	4	5	4	1	13	8	1	1	0
Michael Stewart	2118	25	24	19	1	3	5	0	2	15	13	4	7	0	24	30	2	4	2
Jonathan Stewart	5	1	0	0	1	0	0	0	0	0	0	0	0	0	1	1	0	0	0
David Templeton	874	16	7	5	9	2	2	2	11	7	11	31	1	0	13	12	1	2	0
Jason Thomson	1396	16	15	14	1	0	0		3		25	0	14	4	21	15	1	2	0
Craig Thomson	1460	20	15	12	5	3	0	4	7	9	52	74	6	3	25	20	1	4	0
Rocky Visconte	86	2	1	0	1	1	0	0	0	0	3	0	0	0	1	0	0	0	0
Ryan Wallace	45	2	0	0	2	0	0	0	0	1	0	0	0	0	0	1	0	1	0
Lee Wallace	2911	32	32	30	0	2	1	1	2	6	26	1	8	4	30	24	1	4	0
David Witteveen	473	10	5	5	5	5	0	0	3	7	1	0	0	1	6	8	6	0	0
Marius Zaliukas	1839	22	21	17	1	4	2	0	5	4	3	0	33	11	20	27	0	3	0

actim

Clydesdale Bank PREMIER LEAGUE

SEASON TOTALS

Goals scored	35
Goals conceded	46
Clean sheets	11
Shots on target	152
Shots off target	198
Shots per goal	10.00
Pens awarded	4
Pens scored	4
Pens conceded	6
Offsides	107
Corners	208
Crosses	295
Players used	33
Fouls committed	502
Free-kicks won	459

CARDS RECEIVED

80 **9**

SEQUENCES

Wins	3
(on two occasions)	
Losses	3
(27/01/10–10/02/10)	
Draws	2
(17/10/09–24/10/09)	
Undefeated	7
(12/12/09–23/01/10)	
Without win	6
(03/10/09–21/11/09)	
Undefeated home	4
(on two occasions)	
Undefeated away	3
(26/12/09–23/01/10)	
Without scoring	3
(on two occasions)	
Without conceding	2
(on two occasions)	
Scoring	7
(23/08/09–17/10/09)	
Conceding	5
(on two occasions)	

LEAGUE POSITION AT THE END OF EACH MONTH

AUG	SEP	OCT	NOV	DEC	JAN	FEB	MAR	APR	MAY
10	7	8	7	5	6	6	6	6	6

SEASON INFORMATION

Highest position: 5
Lowest position: 11
Average goals scored per game: 0.92
Average goals conceded per game: 1.21

MATCH RECORDS

Goals scored per match

		W	D	L	Pts
Failed to score	12	0	4	8	4
Scored 1 goal	18	6	4	8	22
Scored 2 goals	7	6	1	0	19
Scored 3 goals	1	1	0	0	3
Scored 4+ goals	0	0	0	0	0

Goals conceded per match

		W	D	L	Pts
Clean sheet	11	7	4	0	25
Conceded 1 goal	12	5	4	3	19
Conceded 2 goals	12	1	1	10	4
Conceded 3 goals	2	0	0	2	0
Conceded 4+ goals	1	0	0	1	0

EARLIEST STRIKE

SUSO SANTANA
(v Celtic) 4:32

LATEST STRIKE

DAVID OBUA
(v Hibernian) 88:49

Ruben Palazuelos

GOAL DETAILS

How the goals were struck

SCORED		CONCEDED
17	Right foot	24
11	Left foot	9
7	Header	13
0	Other	0

How the goals were struck

SCORED		CONCEDED
21	Open play	25
4	Cross	3
3	Corner	5
4	Penalty	4
0	Direct from free-kick	3
3	Free-kick	5
0	Own goal	1

Distance from goal

SCORED		CONCEDED
13	6YDS	16
17	18YDS	26
5	18+YDS	4

GOALS SCORED/CONCEDED
PER FIVE-MINUTE INTERVALS

MINS	5	10	15	20	25	30	35	40	45	50	55	60	65	70	75	80	85	90
FOR	2	0	0	1	2	1	6	2	3	1	0	3	4	3	2	3	0	2
AGN	4	0	2	0	4	0	1	1	5	4	5	2	4	1	1	3	3	6

HIBERNIAN

CLUB SUMMARY

FORMED	1875
MANAGER	John Hughes
GROUND	Easter Road
CAPACITY	20,250
NICKNAME	The Hibees
WEBSITE	www.hibernianfc.co.uk

The New Football Pools PLAYER OF THE SEASON — Liam Miller

OVERALL

P	W	D	L	F	A	GD
44	18	10	16	73	63	10

CLYDESDALE BANK PREMIER LEAGUE

Pos	P	W	D	L	F	A	GD	Pts
4	38	15	9	14	58	55	3	54

HOME

Pos	P	W	D	L	F	A	GD	Pts
3	19	9	4	6	29	21	8	31

AWAY

Pos	P	W	D	L	F	A	GD	Pts
6	19	6	5	8	29	34	-5	23

CUP PROGRESS DETAILS

Competition	Round reached	Knocked out by
Scottish Cup	QF	Ross County
Co-op Insurance Cup	R3	St Johnstone

BIGGEST WIN (ALL COMPS)
5–1 on 2 occasions

BIGGEST DEFEAT (ALL COMPS)
17/02/10 1–5 v St Johnstone

THE PLAYER WITH THE MOST

GOALS SCORED	Anthony Stokes	**21**
SHOTS ON TARGET	Derek Riordan	**58**
SHOTS OFF TARGET	Derek Riordan	**42**
SHOTS WITHOUT SCORING	John Rankin	**34**
ASSISTS	Derek Riordan	**7**
OFFSIDES	Anthony Stokes	**56**
FOULS	Colin Nish	**67**
FOULS WITHOUT A CARD	Alan Gow	**6**
FREE-KICKS WON	Colin Nish	**47**
DEFENSIVE CLEARANCES	Souleymane Bamba	**60**

ATTENDANCE RECORD

High	Average	Low
16,949	12,164	9,185
v Hearts (03/01/2010)		v Dundee Utd (31/03/2010)

Impressive Irish striker Anthony Stokes celebrates a goal against St Johnstone

Hibs' season of ups and downs ended in a European spot and high hopes for 2010/11

HIBERNIAN had a rollercoaster season, which ended with them snatching the Clydesdale Bank Premier League's last guaranteed Europa League spot on the final day. But it was their penultimate match that perhaps best summed up their campaign, an epic 6–6 draw at Motherwell, which had left their European ambitions hanging in the balance. Hibs stormed into a 6–2 lead but ended up holding on for a draw in what was the highest-scoring match in SPL history.

John Hughes was the first managerial appointment of the summer of 2009, the 45-year-old leaving Falkirk to take charge. Hibs' new manager then pulled off arguably the two biggest coups of the summer, signing Anthony Stokes from Sunderland and, later, Liam Miller.

The Easter Road side made a bright start to the campaign, winning their first three games before back-to-back defeats to Celtic and Hamilton. They responded with a 12-match unbeaten run in the SPL, with the only black mark being a Co-operative Insurance Cup exit at the hands of St Johnstone.

Their good start in the League led to talk of Hibs splitting the Old Firm, and that looked even more likely when Stokes put them 1–0 up against Rangers after just 12.4 seconds in December – another SPL record. However, the champions hit back to win 4–1.

Hibs rallied to keep their challenge on track, winning 2–1 at Celtic to stay in touch at the top of the table. That result came just a few days after Hughes had publicly challenged his players to finish no lower than third in the table, a feat which soon looked unlikely.

Two weeks after earning victory at Celtic Park, Hibs embarked on a run that saw them beat only the SPL's bottom two sides, Kilmarnock and Falkirk, during a poor 17-match spell in all competitions.

The second half of the season brought an end to their Active Nation Scottish Cup ambitions, despite being handed a series of favourable draws. Each round saw Hibs land a home tie against one of the lowest-ranked teams left in the competition. They began with a fourth-round clash against Junior side Irvine Meadow, eventually beating them with ease. Next came the Scottish Football League's bottom club, Montrose. And when they avoided an SPL team yet again in the quarter-finals, they appeared Hampden-bound. However, they did not reckon with Ross County.

Hibs' struggles continued until a victory at Dundee United on the final day ended their season on a high, and guaranteed them European qualification.

RESULTS 2009/10

AUGUST
15th	● St Mirren	H	W 2–1	**Att:** 12,313	**Ref:** A Muir	**Scorers:** Benjelloun, Wotherspoon. **Booked:** Nish, Hanlon, Galbraith.
22nd	● Falkirk	A	W 1–3	**Att:** 6,059	**Ref:** S Conroy	**Scorers:** Bamba, Riordan². **Booked:** van Zanten, Hogg, Bamba, Rankin, McBride, Cregg.
26th	● Brechin	H	W 3–0	**Att:** 7,047	**Ref:** S McLean	**Scorers:** Hanlon, Riordan, Nimmo OG.
30th	● Celtic	H	L 0–1	**Att:** 14,221	**Ref:** D McDonald	**Booked:** Cregg, McBride, Bamba.

SEPTEMBER
13th	● Hamilton	A	L 2–0	**Att:** 4,023	**Ref:** D Somers	**Booked:** Riordan, Nish. **Dismissed:** Nish.
19th	● St Johnstone	H	W 3–0	**Att:** 10,817	**Ref:** E Norris	**Scorers:** Riordan, Stokes².
22nd	● St Johnstone	H	L 1–3	**Att:** 7,078	**Ref:** C Richmond	**Scorers:** Stokes. **Booked:** McBride, Stokes.
26th	● Motherwell	A	W 1–3	**Att:** 5,221	**Ref:** S Conroy	**Scorers:** Nish, Riordan, Zemmama. **Booked:** Miller, Wotherspoon.

OCTOBER
3rd	● Dundee Utd	H	D 1–1	**Att:** 13,056	**Ref:** M Tumilty	**Scorers:** Zemmama. **Booked:** Benjelloun.
17th	● Kilmarnock	H	W 1–0	**Att:** 10,922	**Ref:** C Thomson	**Scorers:** Benjelloun. **Booked:** Miller.
24th	● Rangers	A	D 1–1	**Att:** 46,892	**Ref:** C Richmond	**Scorers:** Stokes. **Booked:** Stokes, Nish, Stevenson.
31st	● Aberdeen	H	W 2–0	**Att:** 13,885	**Ref:** S Nicholls	**Scorers:** Miller, Nish. **Booked:** Zemmama, Riordan, Nish.

NOVEMBER
7th	● Hearts	A	D 0–0	**Att:** 16,762	**Ref:** S Conroy	**Booked:** Stokes, Murray.
21st	● St Mirren	A	D 1–1	**Att:** 4,681	**Ref:** W Collum	**Scorers:** Riordan. **Booked:** Hogg.
28th	● Falkirk	H	W 2–0	**Att:** 13,305	**Ref:** D Somers	**Scorers:** Riordan, McLean OG. **Booked:** Murray.

DECEMBER
5th	● Motherwell	H	W 2–0	**Att:** 11,240	**Ref:** I Brines	**Scorers:** Stokes². **Booked:** Riordan.
12th	● Kilmarnock	A	D 1–1	**Att:** 5,132	**Ref:** S Conroy	**Scorers:** Stokes. **Booked:** Wotherspoon.
19th	● Aberdeen	A	W 0–2	**Att:** 9,096	**Ref:** D McDonald	**Scorers:** Stokes². **Booked:** Bamba, Murray.
27th	● Rangers	H	L 1–4	**Att:** 16,894	**Ref:** I Brines	**Scorers:** Stokes. **Booked:** Bamba.

JANUARY
3rd	● Hearts	H	D 1–1	**Att:** 16,949	**Ref:** C Richmond	**Scorers:** Stokes. **Booked:** Murray, McBride. **Dismissed:** McCormack.
9th	● Irvine Meadow	H	W 3–0	**Att:** 10,197	**Ref:** E Norris	**Scorers:** Hanlon, Riordan, Zemmama. **Booked:** Hogg.
16th	● Dundee Utd	A	L 1–0	**Att:** 7,812	**Ref:** S Conroy	**Booked:** Rankin, Benjelloun.
23rd	● Hamilton	H	W 5–1	**Att:** 11,481	**Ref:** B Winter	**Scorers:** Nish, Riordan², Stokes². **Booked:** Rankin.
27th	● Celtic	A	W 1–2	**Att:** 41,000	**Ref:** I Brines	**Scorers:** Galbraith, Stokes. **Booked:** Rankin, McBride, Galbraith.
30th	● St Mirren	H	W 2–1	**Att:** 11,476	**Ref:** W Collum	**Scorers:** Miller, Ross OG.

FEBRUARY
6th	● Montrose	H	W 5–1	**Att:** 9,068	**Ref:** A Muir	**Scorers:** Benjelloun, Gow, Nish², Riordan.
10th	● Aberdeen	H	D 2–2	**Att:** 10,469	**Ref:** C Thomson	**Scorers:** Benjelloun, Stokes. **Booked:** McBride, Bamba, Zemmama, Miller.
14th	● Rangers	A	L 3–0	**Att:** 48,161	**Ref:** S Conroy	**Booked:** Hogg.
17th	● St Johnstone	A	L 5–1	**Att:** 4,100	**Ref:** B Winter	**Scorers:** Stokes. **Dismissed:** Nish.
20th	● Motherwell	A	L 1–0	**Att:** 5,055	**Ref:** E Norris	**Dismissed:** Miller.
27th	● St Johnstone	H	D 1–1	**Att:** 12,174	**Ref:** A Muir	**Scorers:** Stokes. **Booked:** Bamba, Nish, Hogg, Miller.

MARCH
6th	● Kilmarnock	H	W 1–0	**Att:** 10,359	**Ref:** S O'Reilly	**Scorers:** Riordan.
13th	● Ross County	H	D 2–2	**Att:** 9,857	**Ref:** B Winter	**Scorers:** Nish, Riordan. **Booked:** Riordan.
20th	● Hearts	A	L 2–1	**Att:** 17,126	**Ref:** W Collum	**Scorers:** Riordan. **Booked:** Stevenson.
23rd	● Ross County	A	L 2–1	**Att:** 5,607	**Ref:** B Winter	**Scorers:** Stokes. **Booked:** Nish.
27th	● Falkirk	A	W 1–3	**Att:** 5,460	**Ref:** M Tumilty	**Scorers:** Bamba, Riordan, Twaddle OG. **Booked:** Murray, Thicot.
31st	● Dundee Utd	H	L 2–4	**Att:** 9,185	**Ref:** S O'Reilly	**Scorers:** Cregg, Stokes. **Booked:** Miller, Cregg.

APRIL
4th	● Celtic	H	L 0–1	**Att:** 10,523	**Ref:** C Richmond	**Booked:** Miller, Thicot, Nish, Bamba, McCormack.
10th	● Hamilton	A	L 4–1	**Att:** 2,520	**Ref:** S Conroy	**Scorers:** Nish.
17th	● Celtic	A	L 3–2	**Att:** 29,650	**Ref:** S Finnie	**Scorers:** Riordan, Stokes. **Booked:** McBride, Murray, McCormack.
25th	● Rangers	H	L 0–1	**Att:** 10,573	**Ref:** W Collum	**Booked:** Stokes.

MAY
1st	● Hearts	H	L 1–2	**Att:** 11,277	**Ref:** D McDonald	**Scorers:** Stokes. **Booked:** Hogg, Murray.
5th	● Motherwell	A	D 6–6	**Att:** 6,241	**Ref:** W Collum	**Scorers:** Nish³, Riordan, Stokes².
9th	● Dundee Utd	A	W 0–2	**Att:** 6,527	**Ref:** C Richmond	**Scorers:** Nish².

● Clydesdale Bank Premier League ● Scottish Cup ◉ Co-op Insurance Cup ◉ UEFA Champions League ● Europa League

HIBERNIAN

CLYDESDALE BANK PREMIER LEAGUE GOALKEEPER STATS

Player	Minutes on pitch	Appearances	Match starts	Completed matches	Sub appearances	Subbed off	Saved with feet	Punched	Parried	Tipped over	Fumbled	Tipped round	Caught	Blocked	Clean sheets	Goals conceded	Save %	Saved	Resulting in goals	Opposition miss	Fouls committed	Free-kicks won	Yellow cards	Red cards
Yves Ma-Kalambay	611	7	6	6	1	0	1	7	3	4	0	3	10	0	2	7	80.00	0	0	0	0	0	0	0
Graeme Smith	1125	12	12	12	0	0	1	12	6	3	2	5	44	0	1	24	74.74	2	2	0	1	7	0	0
Graham Stack	1842	20	20	19	0	1	1	12	11	2	1	6	61	0	5	24	79.49	0	6	0	1	3	0	0

CLYDESDALE BANK PREMIER LEAGUE OUTFIELD PLAYER STATS

Player	Minutes on pitch	Appearances	Match starts	Completed matches	Substitute appearances	Subbed off	Goals scored	Assists	Shots on target	Shots off target	Crosses	Corners taken	Defensive clearances	Defensive blocks	Fouls committed	Free-kicks won	Caught offside	Yellow cards	Red cards
Souleymane Bamba	2760	30	30	29	0	1	2	2	5	7	2	0	60	8	53	41	2	7	0
Abdessalam Benjelloun	1109	28	8	3	20	5	3	0	8	10	5	0	1	0	22	38	2	2	0
Kurtis Byrne	121	4	0	0	4	0	0	1	1	1	1	1	0	0	1	0	1	0	0
Patrick Cregg	771	15	10	3	5	7	1	0	2	2	5	0	1	2	15	12	0	3	0
Daniel Galbraith	258	14	0	0	14	0	1	1	3	1	5	3	1	0	3	4	0	2	0
Alan Gow	259	7	3	1	4	2	0	0	1	2	2	0	0	0	6	4	0	0	0
Paul Hanlon	1572	18	16	15	2	1	0	0	3	6	5	1	18	5	15	11	0	1	0
Chris Hogg	3057	33	33	32	0	1	0	0	2	4	11	1	50	12	34	30	0	5	0
Kevin McBride	1930	26	21	16	5	5	0	0	1	1	8	0	13	4	30	17	0	6	0
Kevin McCann	71	1	1	0	0	1	0	0	0	0	8	0	3	1	0	0	0	0	0
Darren McCormack	644	9	7	5	2	1	0	1	0	1	8	0	2	1	6	7	2	2	1
Liam Miller	2879	33	32	28	1	3	2	5	9	5	14	0	14	5	59	41	1	6	1
Ian Murray	3201	34	34	34	0	0	0	1	5	4	18	0	22	9	54	30	4	7	0
Colin Nish	2217	32	23	12	9	9	9	4	22	18	3	0	26	0	67	47	31	6	2
John Rankin	2841	33	30	26	3	4	0	5	12	22	29	39	30	2	57	30	1	4	0
Derek Riordan	3133	37	35	22	2	13	13	7	58	42	54	93	1	0	23	30	23	3	0
Lewis Stevenson	691	10	7	5	3	2	0	0	0	0	3	0	5	1	10	5	0	2	0
Anthony Stokes	3145	37	36	21	1	15	21	2	53	34	23	2	2	0	34	34	56	3	0
Steven Thicot	836	10	8	7	2	1	0	1	0	2	9	0	9	3	7	4	0	2	0
David Wotherspoon	2841	33	30	25	3	5	1	4	12	6	41	2	20	4	31	23	3	2	0
Merouane Zemmama	1200	21	15	5	6	10	2	1	11	10	28	26	1	0	15	24	2	2	0
David van Zanten	92	1	1	1	0	0	0	0	0	0	1	0	2	0	4	1	0	1	0

actim

SEASON TOTALS

Goals scored	58
Goals conceded	55
Clean sheets	9
Shots on target	208
Shots off target	178
Shots per goal	6.66
Pens awarded	8
Pens scored	5
Pens conceded	10
Offsides	128
Corners	168
Crosses	283
Players used	25
Fouls committed	548
Free-kicks won	443

CARDS RECEIVED

66 **4**

SEQUENCES

Wins	3
(23/01/10–30/01/10)	
Losses	6
(31/03/10–01/05/10)	
Draws	2
(07/11/09–21/11/09)	
Undefeated	12
(19/09/09–19/12/09)	
Without win	7
(31/03/10–05/05/10)	
Undefeated home	6
(on two occasions)	
Undefeated away	6
(26/09/09–19/12/09)	
Without scoring	2
(30/08/09–13/09/09)	
Without conceding	2
(on two occasions)	
Scoring	7
(21/11/09–03/01/10)	
Conceding	11
(27/12/09–27/02/10)	

LEAGUE POSITION AT THE END OF EACH MONTH

AUG	SEP	OCT	NOV	DEC	JAN	FEB	MAR	APR	MAY
4	3	2	3	3	3	4	4	5	4

SEASON INFORMATION

Highest position: 2
Lowest position: 6
Average goals scored per game: 1.53
Average goals conceded per game: 1.45

MATCH RECORDS

Goals scored per match

		W	D	L	Pts
Failed to score	8	0	1	7	1
Scored 1 goal	13	2	6	5	12
Scored 2 goals	11	8	1	2	25
Scored 3 goals	4	4	0	0	12
Scored 4+ goals	2	1	1	0	4

Goals conceded per match

		W	D	L	Pts
Clean sheet	9	8	1	0	25
Conceded 1 goal	18	7	6	5	27
Conceded 2 goals	4	0	1	3	1
Conceded 3 goals	2	0	0	2	0
Conceded 4+ goals	5	0	1	4	1

GOALS SCORED/CONCEDED
PER FIVE-MINUTE INTERVALS

MINS	5	10	15	20	25	30	35	40	45	50	55	60	65	70	75	80	85	90
FOR	3	2	2	2	3	5	4	4	3	2	7	4	2	1	2	3	2	7
AGN	3	4	1	5	4	2	2	4	3	1	2	2	2	4	5	4	2	5

EARLIEST STRIKE

ANTHONY STOKES
(v Rangers) 0:13

LATEST STRIKE

LIAM MILLER
(v Aberdeen) 92:13

Liam Miller

GOAL DETAILS

How the goals were struck

SCORED		CONCEDED
37	Right foot	29
13	Left foot	17
8	Header	9
0	Other	0

How the goals were struck

SCORED		CONCEDED
35	Open play	39
5	Cross	2
3	Corner	4
5	Penalty	8
6	Direct from free-kick	1
1	Free-kick	0
3	Own goal	1

Distance from goal

SCORED		CONCEDED
21	6YDS	20
25	18YDS	30
12	18+YDS	5

KILMARNOCK

CLUB SUMMARY

FORMED	1869
MANAGER	TBC
GROUND	Rugby Park
CAPACITY	18,128
NICKNAME	Killie
WEBSITE	www.kilmarnockfc.co.uk

The New Football Pools PLAYER OF THE SEASON — *Craig Bryson*

OVERALL

P	W	D	L	F	A	GD
43	11	9	23	37	57	-20

CLYDESDALE BANK PREMIER LEAGUE

Pos	P	W	D	L	F	A	GD	Pts
11	38	8	9	21	29	51	-22	33

HOME

Pos	P	W	D	L	F	A	GD	Pts
11	19	5	6	8	23	27	-4	21

AWAY

Pos	P	W	D	L	F	A	GD	Pts
11	19	3	3	13	6	24	-18	12

CUP PROGRESS DETAILS

Competition	Round reached	Knocked out by
Scottish Cup	QF	Celtic
Co-op Insurance Cup	R3	St Mirren

BIGGEST WIN (ALL COMPS)
3–0 on 2 occasions

BIGGEST DEFEAT (ALL COMPS)
0–3 on 5 occasions

THE PLAYER WITH THE MOST

GOALS SCORED	Kevin Kyle	**8**
SHOTS ON TARGET	Kevin Kyle	**35**
SHOTS OFF TARGET	Kevin Kyle	**34**
SHOTS WITHOUT SCORING	Mehdi Taouil	**20**
ASSISTS	Garry Hay	**4**
OFFSIDES	Kevin Kyle	**43**
FOULS	Kevin Kyle	**82**
FOULS WITHOUT A CARD	David Fernandez	**20**
FREE-KICKS WON	Kevin Kyle, Craig Bryson	**54**
DEFENSIVE CLEARANCES	Frazer Wright	**36**

ATTENDANCE RECORD

HIGH	AVERAGE	LOW
10,662	5,919	4,068
v Falkirk (08/05/2010)		v Hamilton (24/03/2010)

KILMARNOCK avoided relegation from the Clydesdale Bank Premier League on the final day of the season with a goalless draw against bottom side Falkirk at Rugby Park. Defeat would have sent them down to the Irn-Bru First Division, but they ground out the priceless point they needed to survive.

It had been a difficult season for the oldest club in the SPL. Kilmarnock started the campaign with Jim Jefferies in charge, and a 3–0 win over Hamilton on the opening day led to plenty of optimism. However, things did not go so smoothly for them after that.

The club's Co-operative Insurance Cup campaign ended in the third round with a 2–1 defeat to St Mirren before a 3–0 loss at home to Celtic ended their hopes of silverware in the Active Nation Scottish Cup for another year. Meanwhile, in the SPL, points proved hard to come by as they struggled to string together a run of positive results.

Dogged defending and a never-say-die attitude kept Killie away from the foot of the table, although they were never able to pull away from trouble completely.

Jefferies used all of his experience to make sure that his charges kept their heads above water. However, after almost eight years at the helm, Scotland's longest-serving boss parted company with the Ayrshire club in January and a few days later took over at his former club Hearts.

Former Aberdeen boss Jimmy Calderwood was appointed as his replacement, starting his reign with a 3–0

Killie maintained their SPL status thanks to a home draw on the last day of the campaign

home loss to Motherwell. However, Killie then went on a tremendous unbeaten run of seven games – including a first win over Celtic in nine years – until they lost to Motherwell again, this time at Fir Park.

The final few weeks of the season were difficult for even an experienced manager such as Calderwood, with consecutive defeats against Hearts, Hamilton, St Mirren and St Johnstone leaving his side very much in trouble.

They went into the final-day clash with Falkirk knowing that another loss would send them down, and they were forced to withstand heavy late pressure from the Bairns. Falkirk threw men forward in a bid to snatch the victory they required but Ryan Flynn missed the best chance of the game when he volleyed over from 10 yards in the 88th minute.

The draw was enough to see Killie survive, but not sufficient to tempt Calderwood to stay with the club as he resigned in late May.

Kilmarnock enjoy a win against Celtic, while Kevin Kyle was a key man once again

Clydesdale Bank PREMIER LEAGUE

RESULTS 2009/10

AUGUST
15th	● Hamilton	H	W 3–0	Att: 5,307	Ref: C Boyle	Scorers: Hamill, Kyle 2.
22nd	● Motherwell	A	L 3–1	Att: 5,093	Ref: C Allan	Scorers: Hamill. Booked: Old, Sammon, Wright.
25th	● Morton	H	W 3–1	Att: 3,645	Ref: M Tumilty	Scorers: Kyle, Sammon 2. Booked: Skelton, Kyle.
29th	● St Mirren	H	L 1–2	Att: 5,645	Ref: E Norris	Scorers: Sammon. Booked: Clancy, Taouil.

SEPTEMBER
15th	● Hearts	A	L 1–0	Att: 13,576	Ref: W Collum	Booked: Clancy.
19th	● Rangers	H	D 0–0	Att: 10,310	Ref: S Conroy	Booked: Pascali, Hamill, Kyle, Sammon, Taouil. Dismissed: Pascali.
22nd	● St Mirren	H	L 1–2	Att: 3,561	Ref: D McDonald	Scorers: Kyle. Booked: Pascali.
26th	● Falkirk	A	D 0–0	Att: 5,394	Ref: S Finnie	Booked: Invincibile, Sammon, Skelton.

OCTOBER
3rd	● Aberdeen	H	D 1–1	Att: 4,997	Ref: W Collum	Scorers: Invincibile. Booked: Wright.
17th	● Hibernian	A	L 1–0	Att: 10,922	Ref: C Thomson	Booked: Hamill.
24th	● St Johnstone	H	W 2–1	Att: 4,643	Ref: A Muir	Scorers: Kyle 2. Booked: Kyle.
31st	● Celtic	A	L 3–0	Att: 46,000	Ref: W Collum	Booked: Taouil, Wright.

NOVEMBER
7th	● Dundee Utd	H	L 0–2	Att: 4,753	Ref: S O'Reilly	
21st	● Rangers	A	L 3–0	Att: 45,358	Ref: A Muir	Booked: Kyle, Taouil.
28th	● Hearts	H	L 1–2	Att: 4,707	Ref: S Nicholls	Scorers: Bryson. Booked: Wright.

DECEMBER
5th	● St Johnstone	A	W 0–1	Att: 3,518	Ref: C Murray	Scorers: Kyle. Booked: Hamill.
12th	● Hibernian	H	D 1–1	Att: 5,132	Ref: S Conroy	Scorers: Burchill.
19th	● Falkirk	H	L 1–2	Att: 4,472	Ref: C Allan	Scorers: Invincibile.
26th	● Dundee Utd	A	D 0–0	Att: 6,692	Ref: C Thomson	Booked: Skelton, Invincibile.

JANUARY
2nd	● St Mirren	A	L 1–0	Att: 4,917	Ref: A Muir	Booked: Pascali, Bryson, Wright.
16th	● Motherwell	H	L 0–3	Att: 5,354	Ref: C Thomson	Booked: Hamill, Kyle.
18th	● Falkirk	H	W 1–0	Att: 3,378	Ref: M Tumilty	Scorers: Pascali. Booked: Pascali.
23rd	● Aberdeen	A	L 1–0	Att: 12,150	Ref: I Brines	
26th	● Hamilton	A	D 0–0	Att: 2,018	Ref: S Finnie	Booked: Hamill.
30th	● Dundee Utd	H	D 4–4	Att: 4,587	Ref: D McDonald	Scorers: Bryson, Ford, Kyle, Pascali. Booked: Pascali.

FEBRUARY
2nd	● Celtic	H	W 1–0	Att: 9,308	Ref: M Tumilty	Scorers: Maguire.
6th	● Inverness CT	H	W 3–0	Att: 4,473	Ref: C Murray	Scorers: Kelly 2, Sammon. Booked: Pascali, Invincibile.
10th	● Falkirk	A	W 0–1	Att: 7,049	Ref: W Collum	Scorers: Bryson. Booked: Clancy, Maguire.
13th	● St Johnstone	H	W 3–2	Att: 4,605	Ref: S Finnie	Scorers: Hay, Kyle, Maguire. Booked: Bryson.
20th	● St Mirren	H	D 1–1	Att: 5,501	Ref: A Muir	Scorers: Maguire. Booked: Kelly, Kyle.
27th	● Motherwell	A	L 1–0	Att: 4,178	Ref: I Brines	Booked: Fowler.

MARCH
6th	● Hibernian	A	L 1–0	Att: 10,359	Ref: S O'Reilly	Booked: Fowler.
9th	● Rangers	H	L 0–2	Att: 8,906	Ref: A Muir	Booked: Wright, Maguire, Fowler.
13th	● Celtic	H	L 0–3	Att: 7,351	Ref: I Brines	Booked: Clancy.
24th	● Hamilton	H	L 1–2	Att: 4,068	Ref: C Thomson	Scorers: Maguire. Booked: Hamill, Bryson, Kyle.
27th	● Celtic	A	L 3–1	Att: 41,000	Ref: D McDonald	Scorers: Bryson. Booked: Kelly, Invincibile, Hamill.

APRIL
4th	● Aberdeen	H	W 2–0	Att: 4,825	Ref: M Tumilty	Scorers: Russell, Grassi OG. Booked: Russell, Hay.
10th	● Hearts	A	L 1–0	Att: 14,015	Ref: E Norris	Booked: Russell, Burchill.
17th	● Hamilton	A	L 3–0	Att: 2,628	Ref: D McDonald	Booked: Kelly, Hamill, Clancy.
24th	● St Mirren	A	L 1–0	Att: 5,639	Ref: C Thomson	Booked: Bryson, Kyle.

MAY
1st	● St Johnstone	H	L 1–2	Att: 4,679	Ref: I Brines	Scorers: Wright. Booked: Wright, Hamill, Hay.
5th	● Aberdeen	A	W 1–2	Att: 6,097	Ref: C Allan	Scorers: Kelly, Kyle.
8th	● Falkirk	H	D 0–0	Att: 10,662	Ref: D McDonald	Booked: Hamill, Clancy, Fowler.

● Clydesdale Bank Premier League ● Scottish Cup ● Co-op Insurance Cup ● UEFA Champions League ● Europa League

KILMARNOCK

CLYDESDALE BANK PREMIER LEAGUE GOALKEEPER STATS

Player	Minutes on pitch	Appearances	Match starts	Completed matches	Sub appearances	Subbed off	SAVES BREAKDOWN								Clean sheets	Goals conceded	Save %	PENALTIES			Fouls committed	Free-kicks won	Yellow cards	Red cards
							Saved with feet	Punched	Parried	Tipped over	Fumbled	Tipped round	Caught	Blocked				Saved	Resulting in goals	Opposition miss				
Cameron Bell	1893	21	21	20	0	1	0	10	10	5	0	7	75	0	5	32	76.98	0	2	0	0	3	0	0
Mark Brown	1316	14	14	14	0	0	3	4	6	2	0	7	51	1	4	15	83.15	0	2	0	0	3	0	0
Alan Combe	284	3	3	3	0	0	1	1	0	1	0	1	10	0	1	3	81.25	0	0	0	0	2	0	0
Lee Robinson	87	1	0	0	1	0	0	0	0	0	0	0	6	0	0	1	85.71	1	0	0	0	0	0	0

CLYDESDALE BANK PREMIER LEAGUE OUTFIELD PLAYER STATS

Player	Minutes on pitch	Appearances	Match starts	Completed matches	Substitute appearances	Subbed off	Goals scored	Assists	Shots on target	Shots off target	Crosses	Corners taken	Defensive clearances	Defensive blocks	Fouls committed	Free-kicks won	Caught offside	Yellow cards	Red cards
Jamie Adams	12	1	0	0	1	0	0	0	0	0	0	0	0	0	1	0	0	0	0
Craig Bryson	3014	33	33	30	0	3	4	2	13	10	22	68	16	1	32	54	2	4	0
Mark Burchill	760	15	9	1	6	8	1	1	6	2	2	0	0	0	14	1	4	1	0
Tim Clancy	1720	20	19	15	1	4	0	0	2	5	25	0	18	4	19	20	0	5	0
David Fernandez	758	13	9	3	4	6	0	1	3	5	8	7	1	0	20	18	11	0	0
Iain Flannigan	325	7	3	1	4	2	0	0	0	0	11	8	1	0	0	6	0	0	0
Simon Ford	1986	23	22	20	1	2	1	0	3	2	0	0	27	6	12	6	0	0	0
James Fowler	2029	28	19	16	9	3	0	1	3	6	9	1	18	2	25	16	0	4	0
Jamie Hamill	3078	35	31	27	4	4	2	2	10	13	54	5	11	7	45	23	6	10	0
Garry Hay	2544	28	27	24	1	3	1	4	8	3	87	18	14	3	16	32	0	2	0
Danny Invincibile	1489	25	16	8	9	8	2	0	10	8	12	0	5	1	22	11	6	3	0
Liam Kelly	1279	15	13	11	2	2	1	0	4	3	4	0	7	2	15	17	0	3	0
Robert Kiernan	197	4	2	0	2	2	0	0	1	0	0	0	2	0	1	1	0	0	0
Kevin Kyle	2781	32	29	27	3	2	8	3	35	34	7	0	30	1	82	54	43	7	0
Christopher Maguire	1117	14	12	9	2	3	4	2	10	9	24	6	1	0	14	28	6	2	0
Ryan O'Leary	962	11	10	10	1	0	0	0	0	0	0	0	10	4	10	11	1	0	0
Steven Old	680	10	8	4	2	4	0	0	1	1	6	0	10	0	8	4	0	1	0
Graeme Owens	162	6	1	0	5	1	0	0	0	0	0	7	8	0	0	2	4	0	0
Manuel Pascali	1794	22	20	15	2	4	1	0	6	7	7	0	31	5	26	13	2	3	1
Allan Russell	628	14	6	1	8	5	1	1	5	4	3	1	3	1	12	8	4	2	0
Connor Sammon	1416	23	14	8	9	6	1	2	17	11	7	0	6	1	22	16	10	3	0
Scott Severin	1182	14	13	11	1	2	0	0	2	4	8	0	20	3	10	8	0	0	0
Gavin Skelton	1394	20	16	10	4	6	0	0	3	0	15	19	4	3	16	14	1	2	0
Mehdi Taouil	1968	27	21	15	6	6	0	2	9	11	42	30	1	0	18	42	0	4	0
Frazer Wright	2452	27	27	26	0	1	1	0	6	7	1	0	36	7	30	23	1	7	0

actim🔲

Clydesdale Bank PREMIER LEAGUE

SEASON TOTALS

Goals scored	29
Goals conceded	51
Clean sheets	10
Shots on target	157
Shots off target	151
Shots per goal	10.62
Pens awarded	1
Pens scored	
Pens conceded	5
Offsides	97
Corners	171
Crosses	362
Players used	29
Fouls committed	471
Free-kicks won	439

LEAGUE POSITION AT THE END OF EACH MONTH

AUG	SEP	OCT	NOV	DEC	JAN	FEB	MAR	APR	MAY
8	8	9	11	11	11	9	11	11	11

SEASON INFORMATION

Highest position: 2
Lowest position: 12
Average goals scored per game: 0.76
Average goals conceded per game: 1.34

CARDS RECEIVED

63 1

SEQUENCES

Wins	3
(02/02/10–13/02/10)	
Losses	5
(27/02/10–27/03/10)	
Draws	3
(19/09/09–03/10/09)	
Undefeated	6
(26/01/10–20/02/10)	
Without win	8
(12/12/09–30/01/10)	
Undefeated home	4
(30/01/10–20/02/10)	
Undefeated away	2
(on two occasions)	
Without scoring	5
(26/12/09–26/01/10)	
Without conceding	2
(on two occasions)	
Scoring	5
(30/01/10–20/02/10)	
Conceding	7
(on two occasions)	

MATCH RECORDS

Goals scored per match

		W	D	L	Pts
Failed to score	19	0	5	14	5
Scored 1 goal	13	3	3	7	12
Scored 2 goals	3	3	0	0	9
Scored 3 goals	2	2	0	0	6
Scored 4+ goals	1	0	1	0	1

Goals conceded per match

		W	D	L	Pts
Clean sheet	10	5	5	0	20
Conceded 1 goal	13	2	3	8	9
Conceded 2 goals	8	1	0	7	3
Conceded 3 goals	6	0	0	6	0
Conceded 4+ goals	1	0	1	0	1

GOALS SCORED/CONCEDED
PER FIVE-MINUTE INTERVALS

MINS	5	10	15	20	25	30	35	40	45	50	55	60	65	70	75	80	85	90
FOR	1	1	1	1	1	0	2	1	2	0	5	1	3	2	3	3	0	2
AGN	1	1	2	1	3	3	5	2	2	2	3	2	7	3	5	4	2

EARLIEST STRIKE

CONNOR SAMMON
(v St Mirren) 3:41

LATEST STRIKE

CRAIG BRYSON
(v Hearts) 89:16

Danny Invincibile

GOAL DETAILS

How the goals were struck

SCORED		CONCEDED
15	Right foot	28
5	Left foot	14
9	Header	9
0	Other	0

How the goals were struck

SCORED		CONCEDED
19	Open play	32
5	Cross	4
3	Corner	4
0	Penalty	4
0	Direct from free-kick	1
1	Free-kick	5
1	Own goal	1

Distance from goal

SCORED		CONCEDED
14	6YDS	20
11	18YDS	26
4	18+YDS	5

MOTHERWELL

CLUB SUMMARY

FORMED	1886
MANAGER	Craig Brown
GROUND	Fir Park
CAPACITY	13,677
NICKNAME	The Steelmen
WEBSITE	www.motherwellfc.co.uk

The New Football Pools PLAYER OF THE SEASON — John Ruddy

OVERALL

P	W	D	L	F	A	GD
47	16	14	17	67	70	-3

CLYDESDALE BANK PREMIER LEAGUE

Pos	P	W	D	L	F	A	GD	Pts
5	38	13	14	11	52	54	-2	53

HOME

Pos	P	W	D	L	F	A	GD	Pts
5	18	8	5	5	29	25	4	29

AWAY

Pos	P	W	D	L	F	A	GD	Pts
4	20	5	9	6	23	29	-6	24

CUP PROGRESS DETAILS

Competition	Round reached	Knocked out by
Europa League	Q3	Steaua Bucharest
Scottish Cup	R4	Inverness CT
Co-op Insurance Cup	QF	St Mirren

BIGGEST WIN (ALL COMPS)

23/07/09 8–1 v Flamurtari

BIGGEST DEFEAT (ALL COMPS)

19/12/09 1–6 v Rangers

THE PLAYER WITH THE MOST

GOALS SCORED Lukas Jutkiewicz, John Sutton	**12**
SHOTS ON TARGET Lukas Jutkiewicz	**38**
SHOTS OFF TARGET Lukas Jutkiewicz	**28**
SHOTS WITHOUT SCORING Stephen Craigan	**11**
ASSISTS Tom Hateley	**9**
OFFSIDES Lukas Jutkiewicz	**20**
FOULS John Sutton	**50**
FOULS WITHOUT A CARD Lukas Jutkiewicz	**33**
FREE-KICKS WON Jim O'Brien	**94**
DEFENSIVE CLEARANCES Mark Reynolds	**30**

ATTENDANCE RECORD

HIGH	AVERAGE	LOW
9,355	5,307	3,544
v Rangers (12/09/2009)		v Dundee Utd (18/04/2010)

Craig Brown's arrival spurred Motherwell towards yet another European qualification

MOTHERWELL qualified for Europe for a third consecutive year following what seemed a long and eventful season.

The club's campaign started on 2nd July with a Europa League clash against Llanelli, just a few days after Jim Gannon had been appointed as manager.

Asked to rebuild a squad that had been weakened by the departure of several key men, Gannon brought in a host of promising young English players such as Giles Coke, Steve Jennings and Chris Humphrey.

The new manager also promoted from within the club's ranks. Ross Forbes, Steven Saunders and Shaun Hutchinson were all utilised during a Europa League run in which Motherwell beat Albanians Flamurtari 8–1 in Airdrie but then came up short against mighty Steaua Bucharest.

Arguably Gannon's best piece of business was a deal with Everton to take John Ruddy and Lukas Jutkiewicz on loan. Goalkeeper Ruddy kept 15 clean sheets in the Clydesdale Bank Premier League, more than any other goalkeeper, while Jutkiewicz netted 12 goals, despite missing a few games through injury.

Motherwell made a solid start to the season, losing just once in their first 14 SPL games, although many of those matches

Craig Brown proved a major success after taking over at Fir Park

were draws. They then suffered four consecutive defeats in December before Gannon lost his job, with the club in the bottom half of the table.

Former Scotland manager Craig Brown was brought in alongside another veteran, Archie Knox. The pair made an immediate impact, with Brown recalling experienced players Stephen Craigan and Keith Lasley as Motherwell went on a 12-match unbeaten run in the SPL.

However, defeat against 10-man Dundee United in March prevented them from moving into third place, and they then went on to lose the next three games.

Victory over Hibernian in the penultimate game of the season would have secured a guaranteed European place. In a thrilling encounter, the Steelmen found themselves 6–2 down with a quarter of the match to go. However, they embarked on a dramatic comeback to draw 6–6. On the final day of the season, they came back from 3–1 down with seconds to go at Rangers to claim another unlikely point, but Hibs also won to leapfrog them into fourth place.

Motherwell's season went into extra-time as they waited for the result of the Active Nation Scottish Cup final to decide their European fate, with already-qualified Dundee United's triumph ultimately putting Brown's men into the Europa League again.

John Sutton celebrates scoring in the thrilling 6–6 draw against Hibernian

RESULTS 2009/10

2nd	● Llanelli	H	L 0–1	**Att:** 4,307	**Ref:** T Nieminen	
9th	● Llanelli	A	W 0–3	**Att:** 3,025	**Ref:** M Mazic	**Scorers:** Murphy, Sutton2. Agg: 1–3.
16th	● Flamurtari	A	L 1–0	**Att:** 4,012	**Ref:** F Stuchlik	**Booked:** Forbes, Hammell.
23rd	● Flamurtari	H	W 8–1	**Att:** 4,641	**Ref:** M Lerjeus	**Scorers:** Forbes2, Hutchinson, McHugh, Murphy3, Slane. Agg: 8–2.
30th	● Steaua Bucharest	A	L 3–0	**Att:** 25,000	**Ref:** C Cakir	**Booked:** Hutchinson, Saunders.

AUGUST

6th	● Steaua Bucharest	H	L 1–3	**Att:** 4,975	**Ref:** C Clos Gomez	**Scorers:** Forbes. **Booked:** Forbes. Agg: 1–6.
15th	● St Johnstone	A	D 2–2	**Att:** 5,220	**Ref:** D McDonald	**Scorers:** Forbes, Hutchinson. **Booked:** Hutchinson, Murphy, Hammell, Coke.
22nd	● Kilmarnock	H	W 3–1	**Att:** 5,093	**Ref:** C Allan	**Scorers:** Forbes, Hutchinson, Sutton. **Booked:** Hateley.
29th	● Aberdeen	A	D 0–0	**Att:** 11,320	**Ref:** C Boyle	

SEPTEMBER

12th	● Rangers	H	D 0–0	**Att:** 9,355	**Ref:** D McDonald	
19th	● Dundee Utd	A	W 0–1	**Att:** 7,196	**Ref:** D Somers	**Scorers:** Forbes. **Booked:** Jennings, Hammell.
22nd	● Inverness	H	W 3–2	**Att:** 3,905	**Ref:** A Muir	**Scorers:** Forbes, McHugh, Bulvitis OG. **Booked:** Hateley. AET – Score after 90 mins 1–1.
26th	● Hibernian	H	L 1–3	**Att:** 5,221	**Ref:** S Conroy	**Scorers:** Reynolds. **Booked:** O'Brien.

OCTOBER

3rd	● Falkirk	H	W 1–0	**Att:** 4,337	**Ref:** E Norris	**Scorers:** Jutkiewicz.
17th	● Celtic	A	D 0–0	**Att:** 58,000	**Ref:** C Boyle	**Booked:** Coke.
24th	● St Mirren	A	D 3–3	**Att:** 4,327	**Ref:** S O'Reilly	**Scorers:** Forbes, Jutkiewicz2.
27th	● St Mirren	A	L 3–0	**Att:** 4,325	**Ref:** W Collum	
31st	● Hearts	H	W 1–0	**Att:** 4,830	**Ref:** D Somers	**Scorers:** Forbes. **Booked:** Sutton.

NOVEMBER

7th	● Hamilton	A	D 2–2	**Att:** 3,583	**Ref:** C Thomson	**Scorers:** Jutkiewicz, Murphy. **Booked:** Jennings.
21st	● Aberdeen	H	D 1–1	**Att:** 4,668	**Ref:** C Allan	**Scorers:** Jutkiewicz. **Booked:** Coke, Saunders.
28th	● Dundee Utd	H	D 2–2	**Att:** 4,593	**Ref:** A Muir	**Scorers:** Jutkiewicz, Sutton. **Booked:** O'Brien.

DECEMBER

5th	● Hibernian	A	L 2–0	**Att:** 11,240	**Ref:** I Brines	**Booked:** Hammell, Murphy, Hateley.
12th	● Celtic	H	L 2–3	**Att:** 7,807	**Ref:** C Richmond	**Scorers:** Jutkiewicz, Reynolds. **Booked:** Pollock.
19th	● Rangers	A	L 6–1	**Att:** 44,291	**Ref:** C Thomson	**Scorers:** Hutchinson. **Booked:** Hateley.
26th	● St Johnstone	H	L 1–3	**Att:** 4,140	**Ref:** S Conroy	**Scorers:** Jennings.
30th	● Hearts	A	L 1–0	**Att:** 14,411	**Ref:** C Allan	**Booked:** Jennings.

JANUARY

16th	● Kilmarnock	A	W 0–3	**Att:** 5,354	**Ref:** C Thomson	**Scorers:** Jutkiewicz, O'Brien2. **Booked:** O'Brien.
18th	● Inverness	A	L 2–0	**Att:** 1,450	**Ref:** I Brines	**Booked:** O'Brien, Hateley.
23rd	● St Mirren	H	W 2–0	**Att:** 3,621	**Ref:** D McDonald	**Scorers:** Murphy, Sutton. **Booked:** Lasley.
27th	● Falkirk	A	D 0–0	**Att:** 4,321	**Ref:** C Richmond	**Dismissed:** Coke.
30th	● Aberdeen	A	W 0–3	**Att:** 9,555	**Ref:** S Conroy	**Scorers:** Jutkiewicz, Sutton2. **Booked:** Lasley.

FEBRUARY

6th	● Hamilton	H	W 1–0	**Att:** 4,777	**Ref:** M Tumilty	**Scorers:** Jutkiewicz. **Booked:** Hammell.
10th	● Rangers	H	D 1–1	**Att:** 9,352	**Ref:** C Murray	**Scorers:** Hateley. **Booked:** Hateley.
13th	● Hamilton	A	D 0–0	**Att:** 3,133	**Ref:** C Richmond	**Booked:** Jennings, Hateley.
20th	● Hibernian	H	W 1–0	**Att:** 5,055	**Ref:** E Norris	**Scorers:** Murphy. **Booked:** O'Brien.
27th	● Kilmarnock	H	W 1–0	**Att:** 4,178	**Ref:** I Brines	**Scorers:** Murphy. **Booked:** Murphy.

MARCH

6th	● St Johnstone	A	W 1–2	**Att:** 3,669	**Ref:** C Thomson	**Scorers:** Murphy, Sutton. **Booked:** Forbes.
9th	● St Mirren	A	D 0–0	**Att:** 3,154	**Ref:** D McDonald	
13th	● Hearts	H	W 3–1	**Att:** 4,448	**Ref:** S Finnie	**Scorers:** O'Brien, Reynolds, Sutton. **Booked:** Jennings.
27th	● Dundee Utd	A	L 3–0	**Att:** 7,609	**Ref:** W Collum	

APRIL

3rd	● Falkirk	H	L 0–1	**Att:** 4,268	**Ref:** C Thomson	
13th	● Celtic	A	L 2–1	**Att:** 27,750	**Ref:** I Brines	**Scorers:** Reynolds. **Booked:** O'Brien, Coke.
18th	● Dundee Utd	H	L 2–3	**Att:** 3,544	**Ref:** C Murray	**Scorers:** Sutton2. **Booked:** Jennings.
24th	● Hearts	A	W 0–2	**Att:** 13,447	**Ref:** B Winter	**Scorers:** Saunders, Sutton.

MAY

1st	● Celtic	A	L 4–0	**Att:** 24,000	**Ref:** A Muir	**Booked:** Craigan.
5th	● Hibernian	H	D 6–6	**Att:** 6,241	**Ref:** W Collum	**Scorers:** Coke2, Hateley, Jutkiewicz, Sutton2.
9th	● Rangers	A	D 3–3	**Att:** 50,321	**Ref:** B Winter	**Scorers:** Jennings, Jutkiewicz, Murphy. **Booked:** Craigan.

● Clydesdale Bank Premier League ● Scottish Cup ● Co-op Insurance Cup ● UEFA Champions League ● Europa League

CLYDESDALE BANK PREMIER LEAGUE GOALKEEPER STATS

Player	Minutes on pitch	Appearances	Match starts	Completed matches	Sub appearances	Subbed off	Saved with feet	Punched	Parried	Tipped over	Fumbled	Tipped round	Caught	Blocked	Clean sheets	Goals conceded	Save %	Saved	Resulting in goals	Opposition miss	Fouls committed	Free-kicks won	Yellow cards	Red cards
Michael Fraser	425	5	4	4	1	0	0	1	1	1	0	0	13	2	1	8	69.23	0	0	0	0	0	0	0
John Ruddy	3154	34	34	33	0	1	2	6	34	4	0	11	116	3	15	46	79.28	1	0	0	6	0	0

CLYDESDALE BANK PREMIER LEAGUE OUTFIELD PLAYER STATS

Player	Minutes on pitch	Appearances	Match starts	Completed matches	Substitute appearances	Subbed off	Goals scored	Assists	Shots on target	Shots off target	Crosses	Corners taken	Defensive clearances	Defensive blocks	Fouls committed	Free-kicks won	Caught offside	Yellow cards	Red cards
Giles Coke	2352	32	25	17	7	7	2	3	14	13	3	8	3	38	45	2	4	1
Stephen Craigan	2435	28	28	24	0	4	0	1	3	8	4	0	29	15	16	35	0	2	0
Marc Fitzpatrick	107	3	1	0	2	2	0	0	0	0	0	0	1	0	0	1	0	0	0
Ross Forbes	1752	28	22	9	6	13	5	2	15	17	35	61	3	1	19	25	3	1	0
Jordan Halsman	20	1	0	0	1	0	0	0	0	0	0	0	1	0	0	1	0	0	0
Stevie Hammell	3015	33	33	31	0	2	0	0	0	1	40	34	17	5	28	16	1	4	0
Tom Hateley	3502	38	38	34	0	4	2	9	10	15	75	58	14	4	25	44	1	5	0
Chris Humphrey	1069	28	6	3	22	3	0	2	2	5	31	16	0	1	9	10	1	0	0
Shaun Hutchinson	419	5	4	4	1	0	3	0	5	2	0	0	7	3	4	2	0	1	0
Steve Jennings	2056	29	21	17	8	4	2	0	8	6	1	1	9	3	23	12	0	6	0
Lukas Jutkiewicz	2369	33	27	12	6	15	12	3	38	28	5	0	6	1	33	63	20	0	0
Keith Lasley	1344	20	15	10	5	5	0	2	7	4	3	0	6	0	25	17	1	2	0
Steve McGarry	17	1	0	0	1	0	0	0	1	0	0	0	0	0	1	1	0	0	0
Michael McGlinchey	173	8	1	0	7	1	0	1	1	4	1	0	0	1	3	0	0	0	0
Robert McHugh	297	10	2	0	8	2	0	1	0	2	5	1	0	0	1	4	0	0	0
Steven Meechan	123	2	1	1	1	0	0	0	0	0	0	0	0	0	0	2	0	0	0
Yassin Moutaouakil	1215	13	13	12	0	1	0	2	0	2	17	1	5	1	23	15	0	0	0
Jamie Murphy	2276	35	24	11	11	13	6	2	27	13	13	4	1	0	10	40	17	3	0
Jim O'Brien	2660	35	29	13	6	16	3	6	20	17	37	36	9	1	21	94	7	5	0
Jamie Pollock	27	1	0	0	1	0	0	0	0	0	0	0	0	0	2	0	1	1	0
Mark Reynolds	3486	37	37	37	0	0	4	0	5	8	1	0	30	14	23	24	2	0	0
Steven Saunders	2071	25	22	19	3	3	1	0	6	7	14	1	18	6	17	14	1	1	0
Paul Slane	44	2	0	0	2	0	0	0	0	0	0	0	0	0	0	0	0	0	0
John Sutton	2839	35	31	24	4	7	12	3	33	23	0	0	7	2	50	44	11	1	0

actim

Clydesdale Bank PREMIER LEAGUE

SEASON TOTALS	
Goals scored	52
Goals conceded	54
Clean sheets	16
Shots on target	195
Shots off target	175
Shots per goal	7.12
Pens awarded	7
Pens scored	4
Pens conceded	1
Offsides	69
Corners	213
Crosses	285
Players used	26
Fouls committed	369
Free-kicks won	517

	AUG	SEP	OCT	NOV	DEC	JAN	FEB	MAR	APR	MAY
LEAGUE POSITION AT THE END OF EACH MONTH	5	6	4	5	6	5	5	5	4	5

SEASON INFORMATION
Highest position: 3
Lowest position: 8
Average goals scored per game: 1.37
Average goals conceded per game: 1.42

CARDS RECEIVED

36 **1**

SEQUENCES

Wins	3	
(20/02/10–06/03/10)		
Losses	5	
(05/12/09–30/12/09)		
Draws	3	
(07/11/09–28/11/09)		
Undefeated	12	
(16/01/10–13/03/10)		
Without win	8	
(07/11/09–30/12/09)		
Undefeated home	6	
(23/01/10–13/03/10)		
Undefeated away	6	
(on two occasions)		
Without scoring	2	
(on two occasions)		
Without conceding	5	
(16/01/10–06/02/10)		
Scoring	5	
(24/10/09–28/11/09)		
Conceding	8	
(07/11/09–30/12/09)		

MATCH RECORDS

Goals scored per match

		W	D	L	Pts
Failed to score	11	0	6	5	6
Scored 1 goal	12	6	2	4	20
Scored 2 goals	8	3	3	2	12
Scored 3 goals	6	4	2	0	14
Scored 4+ goals	1	0	1	0	1

Goals conceded per match

		W	D	L	Pts
Clean sheet	16	10	6	0	36
Conceded 1 goal	7	3	2	2	11
Conceded 2 goals	5	0	3	2	3
Conceded 3 goals	7	0	2	5	2
Conceded 4+ goals	3	0	1	2	1

GOALS SCORED/CONCEDED
PER FIVE-MINUTE INTERVALS

MINS	5	10	15	20	25	30	35	40	45	50	55	60	65	70	75	80	85	90
FOR	1	0	4	3	0	5	1	2	4	3	4	2	0	9	2	4	3	5
AGN	2	1	3	2	0	3	1	3	5	3	5	5	3	4	3	4	3	4

EARLIEST STRIKE

MARK REYNOLDS
(v Hearts) 1:26

LATEST STRIKE

LUKAS JUTKIEWICZ
(v Hibernian) 92:13

Tom Hateley

GOAL DETAILS

How the goals were struck

SCORED		CONCEDED
21	Right foot	33
16	Left foot	15
15	Header	6
0	Other	0

How the goals were struck

SCORED		CONCEDED
27	Open play	43
3	Cross	3
10	Corner	7
4	Penalty	0
2	Direct from free-kick	1
6	Free-kick	0
0	Own goal	0

Distance from goal

SCORED		CONCEDED
22	6YDS	20
24	18YDS	29
6	18+YDS	5

RANGERS

CLUB SUMMARY

FORMED	1873
MANAGER	Walter Smith
GROUND	Ibrox Stadium
CAPACITY	51,076
NICKNAME	The Gers
WEBSITE	www.rangers.co.uk

The New Football Pools PLAYER OF THE SEASON — Steven Davis

OVERALL

P	W	D	L	F	A	GD
54	32	14	8	103	50	53

CLYDESDALE BANK PREMIER LEAGUE

Pos	P	W	D	L	F	A	GD	Pts
1	38	26	9	3	82	28	54	87

HOME

Pos	P	W	D	L	F	A	GD	Pts
1	19	15	4	0	52	13	39	49

AWAY

Pos	P	W	D	L	F	A	GD	Pts
1	19	11	5	3	30	15	15	38

CUP PROGRESS DETAILS

Competition	Round reached	Knocked out by
Champions League	Group G	–
Scottish Cup	QF	Dundee Utd
Co-op Insurance Cup	WON	

BIGGEST WIN (ALL COMPS)

30/12/09 7–1 v Dundee Utd

BIGGEST DEFEAT (ALL COMPS)

1–4 on 3 occasions

THE PLAYER WITH THE MOST

GOALS SCORED Kris Boyd	**23**
SHOTS ON TARGET Kris Boyd	**50**
SHOTS OFF TARGET Kenny Miller	**34**
SHOTS WITHOUT SCORING David Weir	**24**
ASSISTS Steven Davis	**14**
OFFSIDES Kris Boyd	**37**
FOULS Lee McCulloch	**53**
FOULS WITHOUT A CARD Maurice Edu	**19**
FREE-KICKS WON Lee McCulloch	**54**
DEFENSIVE CLEARANCES David Weir	**71**

ATTENDANCE RECORD

HIGH	AVERAGE	LOW
50,321	47,564	44,291
v Motherwell (09/05/2010)		v Motherwell (19/12/2009)

Walter Smith took Rangers to the title, while Steven Davis was a key figure

RANGERS once again defied the odds to claim a domestic double – including the Clydesdale Bank Premier League title for a second successive year.

Manager Walter Smith was no stranger to winning honours during a successful first spell at Ibrox in the 1990s, but financial restrictions meant that his task was much more difficult during 2009/10.

The Gers started the campaign well with a 4–1 win over Falkirk, which was to set the tone for a run in the SPL that saw the defending champions lose just three games all season, against Aberdeen, St Johnstone and Celtic.

The club also enjoyed success in the Co-operative Insurance Cup, as Smith's men overcame Queen of the South, Dundee and St Johnstone en route to the final. They faced their biggest test at Hampden against a St Mirren side who were superior for periods of the game and had a numerical advantage when Rangers were reduced to nine men, following the dismissal of both Kevin Thomson and Danny Wilson. But the Ibrox side's resilience shone through and a late goal from Kenny Miller proved to be decisive as they claimed their first silverware of the season.

Hopes of a domestic treble were dashed by a quarter-final defeat to Dundee United in the Active Nation Scottish Cup, following a gruelling campaign in which the holders had been forced to replays against Hamilton and St Mirren, as well as United.

European football also proved to be a disappointment for Rangers. Their Champions League campaign began with a

Walter Smith worked wonders as Rangers completed a League and CIS Cup double

creditable 1–1 draw away from home against Stuttgart but it was then derailed by successive 4–1 home defeats against Sevilla and Unirea Urziceni.

Domestic events proved to be far more satisfying as Rangers opened up a commanding lead at the summit of the SPL table. The title was secured with a 1–0 win over Hibernian with three games to spare.

Plaudits followed for Smith, who was widely praised for having completed an impressive job under difficult circumstances. Financial restrictions at the club meant that he had been unable to purchase a new player since August 2008, while several key personnel also departed during that time.

The club's fans will now turn their attentions to developments off the pitch as they await news on a potential takeover. However, Smith – who worked without a contract from January – will lead the defence of the SPL title having signed a new one-year deal in May.

Clydesdale Bank PREMIER LEAGUE

RESULTS 2009/10

AUGUST
15th	● Falkirk	H	W 4–1	Att: 50,239	Ref: M Tumilty	Scorers: McCulloch, Miller2, Naismith. **Booked:** McCulloch, Miller, Whittaker.
23rd	● Hearts	A	W 1–2	Att: 16,284	Ref: C Thomson	Scorers: Boyd, McCulloch. **Booked:** Miller, McCulloch. **Dismissed:** Thomson.
29th	● Hamilton	H	W 4–1	Att: 47,633	Ref: S O'Reilly	Scorers: Boyd2, Whittaker2.

SEPTEMBER
12th	● Motherwell	A	D 0–0	Att: 9,355	Ref: D McDonald	**Booked:** Weir, Papac, Bougherra. **Dismissed:** Bougherra.
16th	● VfB Stuttgart	A	D 1–1	Att: 51,000	Ref: M Busacca	Scorers: Bougherra. **Booked:** Papac.
19th	● Kilmarnock	A	D 0–0	Att: 10,310	Ref: S Conroy	**Booked:** Mendes, Boyd, Weir, Rothen. **Dismissed:** Mendes.
23rd	● Queen of South	A	W 1–2	Att: 6,120	Ref: W Collum	Scorers: Naismith, Novo. **Booked:** Boyd.
26th	● Aberdeen	H	D 0–0	Att: 47,968	Ref: I Brines	**Booked:** McCulloch, Naismith.
29th	● Sevilla	H	L 1–4	Att: 40,572	Ref: J Eriksson	Scorers: Novo. **Booked:** Naismith.

OCTOBER
4th	● Celtic	H	W 2–1	Att: 50,276	Ref: C Thomson	Scorers: Miller2. **Booked:** Mendes, Novo.
17th	● St Johnstone	A	W 1–2	Att: 7,807	Ref: W Collum	Scorers: Boyd, Papac. **Booked:** McCulloch.
20th	● Unirea Urziceni	H	L 1–4	Att: 37,500	Ref: E Braamhaar	Scorers: Gomes OG. **Booked:** Naismith.
24th	● Hibernian	H	D 1–1	Att: 46,892	Ref: C Richmond	Scorers: Boyd. **Booked:** Smith, Naismith, Boyd.
27th	● Dundee	A	W 1–3	Att: 10,654	Ref: D McDonald	Scorers: Fleck, Whittaker, MacKenzie OG. **Booked:** Whittaker, Fleck.

NOVEMBER
4th	● Unirea Urziceni	A	D 1–1	Att: 15,000	Ref: C Bo Larsen	Scorers: McCulloch. **Booked:** Lafferty, Wilson.
7th	● St Mirren	H	W 2–1	Att: 45,750	Ref: I Brines	Scorers: Boyd2. **Booked:** Papac, Weir.
21st	● Kilmarnock	H	W 3–0	Att: 45,358	Ref: A Muir	Scorers: Boyd, Miller, Whittaker.
24th	● VfB Stuttgart	H	L 0–2	Att: 41,468	Ref: R Rosetti	**Booked:** Boyd, Thomson, McCulloch.
28th	● Aberdeen	A	L 1–0	Att: 16,153	Ref: C Thomson	**Booked:** Papac, Boyd, Fleck.

DECEMBER
5th	● Falkirk	A	W 1–3	Att: 6,903	Ref: W Collum	Scorers: Boyd2, Miller. **Booked:** Boyd, Whittaker.
9th	● Sevilla	A	L 1–0	Att: 38,000	Ref: B Layec	**Booked:** Papac, Lafferty, Bougherra.
12th	● St Johnstone	H	W 3–0	Att: 44,662	Ref: D McDonald	Scorers: Boyd2, Novo.
15th	● Dundee Utd	A	W 0–3	Att: 10,037	Ref: M Tumilty	Scorers: Beasley, Miller2. **Booked:** McCulloch, Papac.
19th	● Motherwell	H	W 6–1	Att: 44,291	Ref: C Thomson	Scorers: Beasley, Boyd, Lafferty2, Miller2.
27th	● Hibernian	A	W 1–4	Att: 16,894	Ref: I Brines	Scorers: Boyd, Miller2, Novo.
30th	● Dundee Utd	H	W 7–1	Att: 48,721	Ref: W Collum	Scorers: Bougherra, Boyd5, Whittaker. **Booked:** McCulloch, Little. **Dismissed:** Miller.

JANUARY
3rd	● Celtic	A	D 1–1	Att: 58,300	Ref: S Conroy	Scorers: McCulloch. **Booked:** Lafferty, Boyd, Whittaker, Weir.
10th	● Hamilton	A	D 3–3	Att: 3,940	Ref: C Richmond	Scorers: Miller2, Whittaker. **Booked:** Broadfoot, Weir.
16th	● Hamilton	A	W 0–1	Att: 5,343	Ref: M Tumilty	Scorers: Novo.
19th	● Hamilton	H	W 2–0	Att: 21,856	Ref: C Richmond	Scorers: Whittaker2. **Booked:** Whittaker, Weir, McCulloch. AET – Score after 90 mins 0–0.
23rd	● Hearts	H	D 1–1	Att: 47,031	Ref: C Murray	Scorers: Little. **Booked:** McCulloch.
27th	● St Mirren	A	W 0–2	Att: 5,260	Ref: C Thomson	Scorers: Davis, Novo. **Booked:** Lafferty.
30th	● Falkirk	H	W 3–0	Att: 45,907	Ref: C Allan	Scorers: Davis, Fleck, Whittaker.

FEBRUARY
3rd	● St Johnstone	N	W 2–0	Att: 17,371	Ref: D McDonald	Scorers: Davis, McCulloch. **Booked:** Thomson.
6th	● St Mirren	A	D 0–0	Att: 4,909	Ref: I Brines	
10th	● Motherwell	A	D 1–1	Att: 9,352	Ref: C Murray	Scorers: Boyd. **Booked:** McCulloch, Papac.
14th	● Hibernian	H	W 3–0	Att: 48,161	Ref: S Conroy	Scorers: Boyd, Miller, Whittaker. **Booked:** Thomson, Boyd, Whittaker.
17th	● St Mirren	H	W 1–0	Att: 31,086	Ref: I Brines	Scorers: Boyd.
28th	● Celtic	H	W 1–0	Att: 50,320	Ref: D McDonald	Scorers: Edu. **Booked:** Bougherra, Miller.

MARCH
6th	● St Mirren	H	W 3–1	Att: 47,474	Ref: C Richmond	Scorers: McCulloch2, Novo. **Booked:** McCulloch.
9th	● Kilmarnock	A	W 0–2	Att: 8,906	Ref: A Muir	Scorers: Miller, Whittaker. **Booked:** Papac.
14th	● Dundee Utd	H	D 3–3	Att: 24,096	Ref: D McDonald	Scorers: Boyd2, Novo. **Booked:** McCulloch.
21st	● St Mirren	N	W 0–1	Att: 44,538	Ref: C Thomson	Scorers: Miller. **Booked:** Whittaker, McCulloch, Miller. **Dismissed:** Thomson, Wilson.
24th	● Dundee Utd	A	L 1–0	Att: 11,898	Ref: D McDonald	**Booked:** Naismith.
27th	● Hearts	A	W 1–4	Att: 16,832	Ref: C Murray	Scorers: Miller, Naismith2, Wilson. **Booked:** McCulloch.
30th	● St Johnstone	A	L 4–1	Att: 6,189	Ref: M Tumilty	Scorers: Papac. **Booked:** Naismith.

APRIL
3rd	● Hamilton	H	W 1–0	Att: 48,068	Ref: S O'Reilly	Scorers: Edu.
7th	● Aberdeen	H	W 3–1	Att: 47,061	Ref: W Collum	Scorers: Davis, Lafferty, Miller.
14th	● Dundee Utd	A	D 0–0	Att: 11,100	Ref: B Winter	**Booked:** Papac, Lafferty, Davis.
18th	● Hearts	H	W 2–0	Att: 47,590	Ref: I Brines	Scorers: Lafferty, Miller.
25th	● Hibernian	A	W 0–1	Att: 10,573	Ref: W Collum	Scorers: Lafferty. **Booked:** Thomson, Papac.

MAY
1st	● Dundee Utd	A	W 1–2	Att: 10,003	Ref: S O'Reilly	Scorers: Boyd, Novo. **Booked:** Broadfoot.
4th	● Celtic	A	L 2–1	Att: 58,000	Ref: C Murray	Scorers: Miller. **Booked:** Thomson, McCulloch, Naismith, Miller. **Dismissed:** McCulloch.
9th	● Motherwell	H	D 3–3	Att: 50,321	Ref: B Winter	Scorers: Boyd, Lafferty2.

● Clydesdale Bank Premier League ● Scottish Cup ● Co-op Insurance Cup ● UEFA Champions League ● Europa League

RANGERS

CLYDESDALE BANK PREMIER LEAGUE GOALKEEPER STATS

Player	Minutes on pitch	Appearances	Match starts	Completed matches	Sub appearances	Subbed off	Saved with feet	Punched	Parried	Tipped over	Fumbled	Tipped round	Caught	Blocked	Clean sheets	Goals conceded	Save %	Saved	Resulting in goals	Opposition miss	Fouls committed	Free-kicks won	Yellow cards	Red cards
Neil Alexander	466	5	4	4	1	0	0	4	3	0	0	1	12	0	2	6	76.92	0	1	0	1	1	0	0
Allan McGregor	3095	34	34	33	0	1	5	14	26	2	2	2	105	3	14	22	87.71	1	1	0	0	12	0	0

CLYDESDALE BANK PREMIER LEAGUE OUTFIELD PLAYER STATS

Player	Minutes on pitch	Appearances	Match starts	Completed matches	Substitute appearances	Subbed off	Goals scored	Assists	Shots on target	Shots off target	Crosses	Corners taken	Defensive clearances	Defensive blocks	Fouls committed	Free-kicks won	Caught offside	Yellow cards	Red cards
DaMarcus Beasley	596	9	6	2	3	4	2	4	8	6	19	16	0	0	4	12	0	0	0
Madjid Bougherra	1511	17	16	15	1	0	1	3	7	6	27	0	34	4	18	15	0	2	1
Kris Boyd	2367	31	28	14	3	14	23	5	50	29	11	0	11	2	52	32	37	6	0
Kirk Broadfoot	1037	12	12	9	0	3	0	1	3	3	17	0	7	7	9	8	1	1	0
Steven Davis	3358	36	36	35	0	1	3	14	22	17	109	68	15	5	26	24	6	1	0
Maurice Edu	1030	15	8	6	7	2	2	2	4	10	4	1	4	1	19	17	0	0	0
John Fleck	837	15	8	6	7	2	1	2	11	6	24	29	0	1	11	12	2	1	0
Kyle Lafferty	1672	28	17	7	11	10	7	4	33	22	21	2	14	0	41	26	10	3	0
Andrew Little	149	6	2	1	4	1	1	0	2	0	2	0	3	0	2	0	0	1	0
Lee McCulloch	2918	34	32	27	2	4	5	2	18	25	1	0	43	6	53	54	0	11	1
Pedro Mendes	323	4	4	3	0	0	0	0	3	2	6	12	1	0	5	4	0	2	1
Kenny Miller	2512	33	29	12	4	16	18	9	43	34	42	0	6	1	21	37	24	4	1
Steven Naismith	1879	28	20	14	8	6	3	6	16	7	23	1	8	5	23	49	5	4	0
Nacho Novo	1597	35	14	6	21	8	6	4	23	16	35	39	2	0	14	30	10	1	0
Sasa Papac	3106	34	34	32	0	2	2	2	11	11	48	1	40	16	41	17	2	8	0
Jerome Rothen	252	4	3	1	1	2	0	0	4	2	12	18	0	0	2	7	1	1	0
Steven Smith	751	12	7	4	5	3	0	1	5	0	18	6	5	2	6	7	1	1	0
Kevin Thomson	1625	25	20	13	5	6	0	4	5	5	30	26	0	5	22	13	0	3	1
David Weir	3562	38	38	38	0	0	0	0	9	15	6	0	71	11	23	22	0	4	0
Steven Whittaker	2988	35	32	30	3	2	2	7	18	11	64	2	20	11	40	32	2	4	0
Danny Wilson	1285	14	14	13	0	1	1	1	4	2	6	0	19	10	5	7	0	0	0
Gregg Wylde	19	2	0	0	2	0	0	0	0	0	0	2	0	0	0	0	0	0	0

actim ☷

Clydesdale Bank PREMIER LEAGUE

SEASON TOTALS

Goals scored	82
Goals conceded	28
Clean sheets	16
Shots on target	304
Shots off target	230
Shots per goal	6.44
Pens awarded	6
Pens scored	6
Pens conceded	3
Offsides	107
Corners	227
Crosses	535
Players used	24
Fouls committed	449
Free-kicks won	447

CARDS RECEIVED

58 **5**

SEQUENCES

Wins	6
(05/12/09–30/12/09)	
Losses	–
(–)	
Draws	3
(12/09/09–26/09/09)	
Undefeated	17
(05/12/09–27/03/10)	
Without win	3
(12/09/09–26/09/09)	
Undefeated home	19
(15/08/09–09/05/10)	
Undefeated away	9
(05/12/09–27/03/10)	
Without scoring	3
(12/09/09–26/09/09)	
Without conceding	3
(on two occasions)	
Scoring	20
(05/12/09–07/04/10)	
Conceding	4
(on two occasions)	

LEAGUE POSITION AT THE END OF EACH MONTH

AUG	SEP	OCT	NOV	DEC	JAN	FEB	MAR	APR	MAY
1	2	3	2	1	1	1	1	1	1

SEASON INFORMATION
Highest position: 1
Lowest position: 5
Average goals scored per game: 2.16
Average goals conceded per game: 0.74

MATCH RECORDS

Goals scored per match

		W	D	L	Pts
Failed to score	5	0	4	1	4
Scored 1 goal	10	4	4	2	16
Scored 2 goals	8	8	0	0	24
Scored 3 goals	9	8	1	0	25
Scored 4+ goals	6	6	0	0	18

Goals conceded per match

		W	D	L	Pts
Clean sheet	16	12	4	0	40
Conceded 1 goal	19	14	4	1	46
Conceded 2 goals	1	0	0	1	0
Conceded 3 goals	1	0	1	0	1
Conceded 4+ goals	1	0	0	1	0

EARLIEST STRIKE
KRIS BOYD
(v St Johnstone) 0:40

LATEST STRIKE
MAURICE EDU
(v Celtic) 92:21

Madjid Bougherra

GOAL DETAILS

How the goals were struck

SCORED		CONCEDED
48	Right foot	14
23	Left foot	7
11	Header	7
0	Other	0

How the goals were struck

SCORED		CONCEDED
56	Open play	13
10	Cross	4
4	Corner	4
6	Penalty	2
1	Direct from free-kick	3
5	Free-kick	1
0	Own goal	1

Distance from goal

SCORED		CONCEDED
27	6YDS	14
47	18YDS	9
8	18+YDS	5

GOALS SCORED/CONCEDED
PER FIVE-MINUTE INTERVALS

MINS	5	10	15	20	25	30	35	40	45	50	55	60	65	70	75	80	85	90
FOR	6	3	2	8	4	4	4	4	2	3	5	4	5	4	6	6	6	6
AGN	1	2	1	3	2	2	1	1	2	1	1	0	1	2	1	3	0	4

ST JOHNSTONE

CLUB SUMMARY

FORMED	1884
MANAGER	Derek McInnes
GROUND	McDiarmid Park
CAPACITY	10,673
NICKNAME	The Saints
WEBSITE	www.perthsaints.co.uk

The New Football Pools PLAYER OF THE SEASON

Dave Mackay

OVERALL

P	W	D	L	F	A	GD
45	17	11	17	76	66	10

CLYDESDALE BANK PREMIER LEAGUE

Pos	P	W	D	L	F	A	GD	Pts
8	38	12	11	15	57	61	-4	47

HOME

Pos	P	W	D	L	F	A	GD	Pts
8	19	6	6	7	31	28	3	24

AWAY

Pos	P	W	D	L	F	A	GD	Pts
7	19	6	5	8	26	33	-7	23

CUP PROGRESS DETAILS

Competition	Round reached	Knocked out by
Scottish Cup	R5	Dundee Utd
Co-op Insurance Cup	SF	Rangers

BIGGEST WIN (ALL COMPS)

26/08/09 6–0 v Arbroath

BIGGEST DEFEAT (ALL COMPS)

22/08/09 2–5 v Celtic

THE PLAYER WITH THE MOST

GOALS SCORED Liam Craig	**8**	
SHOTS ON TARGET Kenny Deuchar	**28**	
SHOTS OFF TARGET Liam Craig	**25**	
SHOTS WITHOUT SCORING Kevin Rutkiewicz	**11**	
ASSISTS Chris Millar	**5**	
OFFSIDES Kenny Deuchar	**11**	
FOULS Kenny Deuchar	**47**	
FOULS WITHOUT A CARD Peter MacDonald	**13**	
FREE-KICKS WON Kenny Deuchar	**52**	
DEFENSIVE CLEARANCES Michael Duberry	**46**	

ATTENDANCE RECORD

HIGH	AVERAGE	LOW
7,807	4,717	2,993
v Rangers (17/10/2009)		v St Mirren (19/12/2009)

ST JOHNSTONE were one of the success stories of the Clydesdale Bank Premier League season as they secured an eighth-place finish.

After coming up from the Irn-Bru First Division as champions, many tipped the Perth side to go straight back down again. However, beginning with the 2–2 home draw against Motherwell, Derek McInnes' men showed that they could live with their top-flight opponents.

The Saints boss had worked diligently to recruit the right type of player, such as Kenny Deuchar, Graeme Smith and Danny Grainger. Former Chelsea midfielder Jody Morris was at the fulcrum of much of St Johnstone's good work, helped by the able Murray Davidson.

The McDiarmid Park men captured the scalps of Hibernian and Dundee United in the Co-operative Insurance Cup before losing to Rangers. The Active Nation Scottish Cup was a greater source of disappointment as they went out to Tayside rivals Dundee United, although the Perth club proved themselves in the SPL.

McInnes had to battle against injuries, which at times wrecked his plans, but it became clear as the season moved beyond the midway point that they were going to avoid the drop with something to spare, with the introduction of defender Michael Duberry in January a major factor.

This was not a team hanging on for every point, this was a team playing with confidence and cohesion and it all came together in March with the 4–1 win against Rangers at McDiarmid Park. It was

Astute signings helped Saints impress during their first SPL season in seven years

St Johnstone's biggest ever victory over the Ibrox men and proved to be the highlight of the season.

Unfortunately, they just missed out on making the top six on the last day before the SPL split. However, the ever-demanding McInnes kept his Saints players motivated for the closing weeks of the season, during which time they continued to pick up points.

In some ways, the coming season may be more difficult for St Johnstone who, like many other teams, are having to keep a keen eye on finances.

McInnes will have to work his magic again to keep the Saints out of the relegation battle and the former Rangers and Dundee United midfielder will use his many contacts north and south of the border to replenish his squad during the summer.

One thing is certain, if St Johnstone play in the same manner in the coming season, the loyal McDiarmid Park supporters are in for plenty more excitement.

Murray Davidson (centre) is mobbed after his goal in the 4–1 win against Rangers

RESULTS 2009/10

AUGUST

1st	● Stenhousemuir	A	W 0–5	Att: 1,049	Ref: D Somers	Scorers: Deuchar[2], Milne, Samuel[2]. Booked: Davidson.
15th	● Motherwell	H	D 2–2	Att: 5,220	Ref: D McDonald	Scorers: Davidson, Gartland. Booked: Craig, Gartland, McCaffrey, Samuel.
22nd	● Celtic	A	L 5–2	Att: 58,500	Ref: W Collum	Scorers: Morris, Samuel. Booked: Gartland.
26th	● Arbroath	A	W 0–6	Att: 1,038	Ref: S Conroy	Scorers: Deuchar[2], Milne[2], Morais, Samuel.
30th	● Hearts	H	D 2–2	Att: 5,825	Ref: M Tumilty	Scorers: Davidson, Hardie. Booked: Mackay, Gartland, Deuchar.

SEPTEMBER

12th	● St Mirren	A	D 1–1	Att: 4,543	Ref: S Nicholls	Scorers: Morris. Booked: Mackay, Sheerin, Davidson, Samuel, Grainger, Gartland.
19th	● Hibernian	A	L 3–0	Att: 10,817	Ref: E Norris	Booked: McCaffrey, Gartland.
22nd	● Hibernian	A	W 1–3	Att: 7,078	Ref: C Richmond	Scorers: Millar, Morris, Swankie. Booked: Grainger, Anderson, Morris, Mackay.
26th	● Dundee Utd	H	L 2–3	Att: 7,225	Ref: D McDonald	Scorers: Hardie, Dods OG.

OCTOBER

3rd	● Hamilton	A	W 0–2	Att: 2,199	Ref: C Richmond	Scorers: Anderson, Grainger. Booked: Gartland.
17th	● Rangers	H	L 1–2	Att: 7,807	Ref: W Collum	Scorers: Samuel. Booked: Millar.
24th	● Kilmarnock	A	L 2–1	Att: 4,643	Ref: A Muir	Scorers: Wright OG. Booked: Davidson, Anderson.
27th	● Dundee Utd	H	W 2–1	Att: 5,146	Ref: S Conroy	Scorers: Anderson, Dods OG. Booked: Smith.
31st	● Falkirk	H	W 3–1	Att: 4,423	Ref: D McDonald	Scorers: Davidson, Millar, Samuel.

NOVEMBER

7th	● Aberdeen	A	L 2–1	Att: 10,894	Ref: E Norris	Scorers: Craig. Booked: Grainger.
21st	● Hearts	A	W 1–2	Att: 13,416	Ref: S O'Reilly	Scorers: Johansson, Samuel. Booked: Moon.
28th	● Hamilton	H	D 1–1	Att: 3,426	Ref: W Collum	Scorers: Morais.

DECEMBER

5th	● Kilmarnock	H	L 0–1	Att: 3,518	Ref: C Murray	Booked: Morris.
12th	● Rangers	A	L 3–0	Att: 44,662	Ref: D McDonald	
19th	● St Mirren	H	W 1–0	Att: 2,993	Ref: M Tumilty	Scorers: Millar. Booked: Grainger, Irvine.
26th	● Motherwell	A	W 1–3	Att: 4,140	Ref: S Conroy	Scorers: MacDonald[3]. Booked: Davidson.

JANUARY

18th	● Forfar	A	W 0–3	Att: 1,449	Ref: C Murray	Scorers: Craig[2], Deuchar.
24th	● Celtic	H	L 1–4	Att: 7,743	Ref: W Collum	Scorers: Craig. Booked: Gartland. Dismissed: Gartland.
27th	● Dundee Utd	A	D 3–3	Att: 6,600	Ref: S O'Reilly	Scorers: Craig, MacDonald, Moon. Booked: Craig, Grainger, Morris, Deuchar.
30th	● Hearts	H	W 1–0	Att: 4,752	Ref: E Norris	Scorers: Deuchar. Booked: Davidson, Gartland, Millar.

FEBRUARY

3rd	● Rangers	N	L 2–0	Att: 17,371	Ref: D McDonald	Booked: Irvine.
6th	● Dundee Utd	H	L 0–1	Att: 5,636	Ref: C Thomson	Booked: Irvine, Grainger, Mackay.
10th	● St Mirren	A	D 1–1	Att: 3,009	Ref: M Tumilty	Scorers: Mackay. Booked: Duberry, Milne.
13th	● Kilmarnock	A	L 3–2	Att: 4,605	Ref: S Finnie	Scorers: Gartland, MacDonald. Booked: Morris, Duberry.
17th	● Hibernian	H	W 5–1	Att: 4,100	Ref: B Winter	Scorers: Craig[2], Deuchar, Sheridan[2]. Booked: Anderson.
27th	● Hibernian	A	D 1–1	Att: 12,174	Ref: A Muir	Scorers: Craig. Booked: Smith, Moon, Davidson, Millar.

MARCH

6th	● Motherwell	H	L 1–2	Att: 3,669	Ref: C Thomson	Scorers: Milne.
13th	● Falkirk	A	W 1–2	Att: 5,895	Ref: S O'Reilly	Scorers: Craig, Deuchar. Booked: Smith.
16th	● Aberdeen	H	W 1–0	Att: 3,826	Ref: C Richmond	Scorers: Sheridan. Booked: Duberry.
20th	● Celtic	A	L 3–0	Att: 30,000	Ref: C Murray	Booked: Swankie, Davidson, Grainger.
23rd	● Falkirk	H	D 1–1	Att: 3,107	Ref: E Norris	Scorers: Morais. Booked: Grainger, Duberry.
27th	● Hamilton	A	L 1–0	Att: 2,245	Ref: C Allan	Booked: Connolly, Duberry, Grainger, Morris, Craig.
30th	● Rangers	H	W 4–1	Att: 6,189	Ref: M Tumilty	Scorers: Davidson, Millar, Sheridan, McCulloch OG. Booked: Anderson, Morris.

APRIL

5th	● Dundee Utd	H	L 0–1	Att: 5,769	Ref: S Conroy	Booked: Duberry, Craig, Deuchar.
11th	● Aberdeen	A	W 1–3	Att: 7,568	Ref: C Murray	Scorers: Deuchar, Sheridan[2]. Booked: Duberry, Sheridan, Craig.
17th	● St Mirren	H	D 2–2	Att: 3,557	Ref: C Richmond	Scorers: Duberry, Sheerin. Booked: Morais.
24th	● Aberdeen	H	D 1–1	Att: 3,295	Ref: D McDonald	Scorers: Nelson OG.

MAY

1st	● Kilmarnock	A	W 1–2	Att: 4,679	Ref: I Brines	Scorers: Deuchar, Samuel. Booked: Duberry, Craig, Davidson.
5th	● Falkirk	A	D 0–0	Att: 5,502	Ref: C Thomson	Booked: Deuchar, Morris, Anderson.
8th	● Hamilton	H	L 2–3	Att: 3,188	Ref: W Collum	Scorers: Craig, Davidson. Booked: Davidson.

● Clydesdale Bank Premier League ● Scottish Cup ● Co-op Insurance Cup ● UEFA Champions League ● Europa League

ST JOHNSTONE

CLYDESDALE BANK PREMIER LEAGUE GOALKEEPER STATS

Player	Minutes on pitch	Appearances	Match starts	Completed matches	Sub appearances	Subbed off	Saved with feet	Punched	Parried	Tipped over	Fumbled	Tipped round	Caught	Blocked	Clean sheets	Goals conceded	Save %	Saved	Resulting in goals	Opposition miss	Fouls committed	Free-kicks won	Yellow cards	Red cards
Alan Main	845	9	9	9	0	0	0	1	2	1	1	0	24	0	1	20	58.33	0	2	0	0	0	0	0
Graeme Smith	2725	29	29	29	0	0	5	13	13	4	1	7	87	2	4	41	76.16	0	4	0	4	5	2	0

CLYDESDALE BANK PREMIER LEAGUE OUTFIELD PLAYER STATS

Player	Minutes on pitch	Appearances	Match starts	Completed matches	Substitute appearances	Subbed off	Goals scored	Assists	Shots on target	Shots off target	Crosses	Corners taken	Defensive clearances	Defensive blocks	Fouls committed	Free-kicks won	Caught offside	Yellow cards	Red cards
Steven Anderson	1420	17	14	13	3	1	1	0	2	0	2	0	21	8	20	11	0	4	0
Mark Connolly	45	1	1	0	0	1	0	0	0	0	0	0	1	0	1	1	0	1	0
Liam Craig	2099	31	22	14	9	8	8	2	25	25	85	62	13	0	14	21	1	6	0
Murray Davidson	2695	33	30	17	3	13	5	3	13	23	9	1	19	4	41	42	2	8	0
Kenny Deuchar	2376	35	25	14	10	11	5	4	28	21	9	0	10	2	47	52	11	4	0
Michael Duberry	1597	17	17	17	0	0	1	1	5	4	4	0	46	11	32	21	0	8	0
Josh Falkingham	66	1	0	0	1	0	0	0	0	0	0	0	0	0	2	1	0	0	0
Graham Gartland	1700	21	20	16	1	3	2	0	4	7	0	0	16	4	28	21	1	8	1
Danny Grainger	3325	36	35	33	1	2	1	3	13	5	69	50	26	14	42	34	1	7	0
Martin Hardie	461	10	4	2	6	2	2	2	6	5	1	0	2	0	10	8	2	0	0
Gary Irvine	1257	17	13	12	4	1	0	0	0	0	37	1	5	9	16	12	1	1	0
Andrew Jackson	28	2	0	0	2	0	0	1	2	1	0	0	0	0	0	2	0	0	0
Jonatan Johansson	177	6	2	0	4	2	1	0	4	1	0	0	0	1	2	1	2	0	0
Peter MacDonald	400	7	5	2	2	3	5	1	8	3	5	0	1	0	13	6	0	0	0
David Mackay	3340	36	36	35	0	1	1	1	10	8	33	7	40	12	13	31	1	2	0
Stuart McCaffrey	859	10	9	9	1	0	0	0	1	0	4	0	6	3	14	5	0	2	0
Chris Millar	3093	36	33	27	3	6	3	5	17	11	48	0	9	4	31	38	3	3	0
Steven Milne	971	16	10	5	6	5	1	0	8	11	9	0	3	0	8	10	5	1	0
Kevin Moon	917	14	10	6	4	4	1	2	4	4	5	1	0	0	13	10	0	2	0
Filipe Morais	1736	30	20	7	10	13	2	1	20	18	66	50	2	1	14	19	2	1	0
Jody Morris	3128	34	33	33	1	0	2	2	7	12	12	7	7	3	26	32	1	6	0
Stephen Reynolds	109	4	0	0	4	0	0	0	0	0	0	0	0	0	0	0	0	0	0
Kevin Rutkiewicz	646	7	7	6	0	1	0	0	6	5	0	0	6	2	5	5	0	0	0
Collin Samuel	1531	27	16	5	11	11	5	0	18	15	19	0	2	0	17	35	9	2	0
Paul Sheerin	310	11	3	0	8	3	1	0	1	2	4	1	1	0	3	1	0	1	0
Cillian Sheridan	951	16	12	0	4	12	6	2	13	13	14	0	7	0	14	7	6	1	0
Gavin Swankie	343	10	3	1	7	2	0	0	2	1	12	2	0	0	2	1	1	1	0

actim

SEASON TOTALS

Goals scored	57
Goals conceded	61
Clean sheets	5
Shots on target	217
Shots off target	195
Shots per goal	7.23
Pens awarded	7
Pens scored	5
Pens conceded	6
Offsides	49
Corners	182
Crosses	447
Players used	29
Fouls committed	432
Free-kicks won	436

CARDS RECEIVED

71   **1**

SEQUENCES

Wins	2
(on two occasions)	
Losses	2
(on three occasions)	
Draws	2
(on two occasions)	
Undefeated	5
(11/04/10–05/05/10)	
Without win	6
(15/08/09–26/09/09)	
Undefeated home	3
(16/03/10–30/03/10)	
Undefeated away	3
(on two occasions)	
Without scoring	2
(05/12/09–12/12/09)	
Without conceding	–
(–)	
Scoring	12
(19/12/09–16/03/10)	
Conceding	9
(20/03/10–01/05/10)	

LEAGUE POSITION AT THE END OF EACH MONTH

AUG	SEP	OCT	NOV	DEC	JAN	FEB	MAR	APR	MAY
9	12	10	8	7	8	8	7	7	8

SEASON INFORMATION
Highest position: 6
Lowest position: 12
Average goals scored per game: 1.50
Average goals conceded per game: 1.61

MATCH RECORDS

Goals scored per match

		W	D	L	Pts
Failed to score	7	0	1	6	1
Scored 1 goal	14	3	6	5	15
Scored 2 goals	11	4	3	4	15
Scored 3 goals	4	3	1	0	10
Scored 4+ goals	2	2	0	0	6

Goals conceded per match

		W	D	L	Pts
Clean sheet	5	4	1	0	13
Conceded 1 goal	17	8	6	3	30
Conceded 2 goals	7	0	3	4	3
Conceded 3 goals	7	0	1	6	1
Conceded 4+ goals	2	0	0	2	0

GOALS SCORED/CONCEDED
PER FIVE-MINUTE INTERVALS

MINS	5	10	15	20	25	30	35	40	45	50	55	60	65	70	75	80	85	90
FOR	2	3	2	2	4	3	2	6	3	1	3	2	4	3	3	6	3	5
AGN	2	1	4	5	3	3	4	4	2	3	5	2	3	4	3	4	5	4

EARLIEST STRIKE
COLLIN SAMUEL
(v Falkirk) 1:23

LATEST STRIKE
PAUL SHEERIN
(v St Mirren) 93:47

Danny Grainger

GOAL DETAILS

How the goals were struck

SCORED		CONCEDED
24	Right foot	40
17	Left foot	8
14	Header	13
2	Other	0

How the goals were struck

SCORED		CONCEDED
30	Open play	37
7	Cross	8
4	Corner	3
5	Penalty	6
2	Direct from free-kick	2
5	Free-kick	4
4	Own goal	1

Distance from goal

SCORED		CONCEDED
23	6YDS	22
26	18YDS	29
8	18+YDS	10

OFFICIAL FOOTBALL YEARBOOK OF THE ENGLISH & SCOTTISH LEAGUES 2010-2011   **417**

ST MIRREN

CLUB SUMMARY

FORMED	1877
MANAGER	Danny Lennon
GROUND	St Mirren Park
CAPACITY	8,029
NICKNAME	The Buddies
WEBSITE	www.saintmirren.net

The New **Football Pools** PLAYER OF THE SEASON — **John Potter**

OVERALL

P	W	D	L	F	A	GD
47	13	14	20	53	56	-3

CLYDESDALE BANK PREMIER LEAGUE

Pos	P	W	D	L	F	A	GD	Pts
10	38	7	13	18	36	49	-13	34

HOME

Pos	P	W	D	L	F	A	GD	Pts
9	19	5	9	5	18	18	0	24

AWAY

Pos	P	W	D	L	F	A	GD	Pts
12	19	2	4	13	18	31	-13	10

CUP PROGRESS DETAILS

Competition	Round reached	Knocked out by
Scottish Cup	R5	Rangers
Co-op Insurance Cup	R-UP	Rangers

BIGGEST WIN (ALL COMPS)
24/03/10 4–0 v Celtic

BIGGEST DEFEAT (ALL COMPS)
1–3 on 2 occasions

THE PLAYER WITH THE MOST

GOALS SCORED Andy Dorman	**6**
SHOTS ON TARGET Andy Dorman	**26**
SHOTS OFF TARGET Billy Mehmet	**29**
SHOTS WITHOUT SCORING David Barron	**11**
ASSISTS Billy Mehmet, Andy Dorman	**4**
OFFSIDES Billy Mehmet	**37**
FOULS Hugh Murray	**68**
FOULS WITHOUT A CARD Tom Brighton	**5**
FREE-KICKS WON Hugh Murray	**60**
DEFENSIVE CLEARANCES Jack Ross	**55**

ATTENDANCE RECORD

HIGH	AVERAGE	LOW
6,164	4,414	3,009
v Celtic (26/09/2009)		v St Johnstone (10/02/2010)

A thrilling Co-operative Insurance Cup run provided the basis of a memorable season

ST MIRREN achieved their main target for the season, that of Clydesdale Bank Premier League survival, but 2009/10 will be remembered fondly by all at the Paisley club for the run to the Co-operative Insurance Cup final.

The first game of the campaign – a 6–3 win over East Stirlingshire in the CIS Cup – provided Saints with some early momentum, and that was a sign of what was to come in that particular competition as they came so close to collecting their first piece of major silverware for 23 years.

Victory over Ayr in the next round was followed up by wins against Clydesdale Bank Premier League opposition in the shape of Kilmarnock, Motherwell and Hearts to earn Saints a place in the final against their near-neighbours, Rangers. Walter Smith's men were well below par at Hampden, and Saints also had the luxury of a numerical advantage when Gers pair Kevin Thomson and Danny Wilson were both sent off.

However, Gus MacPherson's side could not capitalise, despite playing against only nine men, with Kenny Miller scoring the decisive goal for the Gers with just six minutes to go.

In the SPL, Saints enjoyed mixed fortunes. A nine-month wait for a home

Steven Robb and Andy Dorman celebrate during the 4–0 win over Celtic

victory in the League at their new St Mirren Park stadium finally came to an end when they defeated Hearts 2–1 in October, and some decent results briefly led to a run towards the top half of the table. However, the Buddies' home form continued to be a problem as they ultimately found themselves battling against relegation once again.

The club put any lingering disappointment from that defeat in the final of the CIS Cup to one side to produce one of the most memorable results of the season – a 4–0 win over Celtic in March, which ultimately cost Tony Mowbray his job at Celtic Park.

A 1–1 draw with bottom side Falkirk a few weeks later all but ensured their status in the top flight for another season, although they were ultimately forced to settle for a bottom-three finish for a fourth successive year.

There was one final twist at the end of the season when the club parted company with boss MacPherson after almost seven years at the helm. Chairman Stewart Gilmour insisted it was time for them to take a fresh approach, saying: 'It was not an easy decision.'

The club appointed Danny Lennon in June, following the 40-year-old's impressive spell at Cowdenbeath.

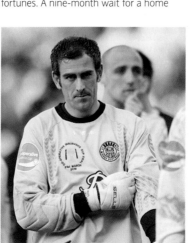

Paul Gallacher is left dejected after the Co-operative Insurance Cup final defeat

RESULTS 2009/10

AUGUST

2nd	● East Stirling	A	W 3–6	Att: 1,024	Ref: S O'Reilly	Scorers: Mehmet5, O'Donnell. Booked: Brady.
15th	● Hibernian	A	L 2–1	Att: 12,313	Ref: A Muir	Scorers: McGinn. Booked: Higdon, Ross. Dismissed: Thomson.
22nd	● Dundee Utd	H	D 0–0	Att: 4,775	Ref: D McDonald	Booked: Higdon.
26th	● Ayr	A	W 0–2	Att: 1,652	Ref: C Richmond	Scorers: Higdon, Mehmet. Booked: McGinn, Barron.
29th	● Kilmarnock	A	W 1–2	Att: 5,645	Ref: E Norris	Scorers: McGinn2. Booked: Potter.

SEPTEMBER

12th	● St Johnstone	H	D 1–1	Att: 4,543	Ref: S Nicholls	Scorers: Mehmet. Booked: Dargo.
19th	● Aberdeen	A	L 1–0	Att: 10,103	Ref: C Thomson	Booked: Barron, Mair. Dismissed: Mair.
22nd	● Kilmarnock	A	W 1–2	Att: 3,561	Ref: D McDonald	Scorers: Dorman, McGinn. Booked: Barron.
26th	● Celtic	H	L 0–2	Att: 6,164	Ref: C Richmond	Booked: Thomson, Potter, Innes.

OCTOBER

3rd	● Hearts	H	W 2–1	Att: 4,652	Ref: B Winter	Scorers: Dargo, Thomson.
17th	● Falkirk	A	W 1–3	Att: 5,084	Ref: C Allan	Scorers: Brighton, Dargo, Mehmet. Booked: Murray.
24th	● Motherwell	H	D 3–3	Att: 4,327	Ref: S O'Reilly	Scorers: Dorman, Murray2. Booked: Mair, Dorman.
27th	● Motherwell	H	W 3–0	Att: 4,325	Ref: W Collum	Scorers: Higdon, Ross, Craigan OG. Booked: Ross.
31st	● Hamilton	H	L 0–2	Att: 4,022	Ref: S Finnie	Booked: Murray, Dorman. Dismissed: Mair.

NOVEMBER

7th	● Rangers	A	L 2–1	Att: 45,750	Ref: I Brines	Scorers: O'Donnell. Booked: Brady.
21st	● Hibernian	H	D 1–1	Att: 4,681	Ref: W Collum	Scorers: Innes. Booked: Barron.
28th	● Celtic	A	L 3–1	Att: 41,000	Ref: S Conroy	Scorers: Higdon. Booked: Mair, Innes.

DECEMBER

5th	● Dundee Utd	A	L 3–2	Att: 6,259	Ref: B Winter	Scorers: O'Donnell, Dods OG. Booked: McGinn, Barron, Innes, O'Donnell.
12th	● Falkirk	H	D 1–1	Att: 4,033	Ref: C Thomson	Scorers: Higdon.
19th	● St Johnstone	A	L 1–0	Att: 2,993	Ref: M Tumilty	Booked: Higdon. Dismissed: Higdon.

JANUARY

2nd	● Kilmarnock	H	W 1–0	Att: 4,917	Ref: A Muir	Scorers: Innes. Booked: Murray, Mehmet, Dargo.
9th	● Alloa	H	W 3–1	Att: 2,587	Ref: S Finnie	Scorers: Mehmet2, Crawford OG.
12th	● Aberdeen	H	W 1–0	Att: 3,867	Ref: W Collum	Scorers: Innes. Booked: Potter.
16th	● Hearts	A	L 1–0	Att: 12,821	Ref: S O'Reilly	Booked: Innes, Murray, Mehmet, Higdon.
23rd	● Motherwell	A	L 2–0	Att: 3,621	Ref: D McDonald	Booked: Robb, O'Donnell.
27th	● Rangers	H	L 0–2	Att: 5,260	Ref: C Thomson	Booked: Thomson.
30th	● Hibernian	A	L 2–1	Att: 11,476	Ref: W Collum	Scorers: Bamba OG.

FEBRUARY

2nd	● Hearts	N	W 0–1	Att: 9,170	Ref: C Richmond	Scorers: Mehmet. Booked: Mehmet.
6th	● Rangers	H	D 0–0	Att: 4,909	Ref: I Brines	Booked: Murray.
10th	● St Johnstone	H	D 1–1	Att: 3,009	Ref: M Tumilty	Scorers: MacKay OG. Booked: Mehmet, Dorman.
13th	● Dundee Utd	H	L 1–2	Att: 3,944	Ref: E Norris	Scorers: Higdon.
17th	● Rangers	A	L 1–0	Att: 31,086	Ref: I Brines	
20th	● Kilmarnock	A	D 1–1	Att: 5,501	Ref: A Muir	Scorers: Mehmet. Booked: Murray, Innes.
27th	● Hamilton	H	D 0–0	Att: 3,628	Ref: C Allan	Booked: Dargo, Mehmet.

MARCH

6th	● Rangers	A	L 3–1	Att: 47,474	Ref: C Richmond	Scorers: Carey. Booked: Thomson.
9th	● Motherwell	H	D 0–0	Att: 3,154	Ref: D McDonald	
13th	● Hamilton	A	L 1–0	Att: 2,179	Ref: E Norris	Booked: Ross, Barron, Mehmet, Mair, Murray.
21st	● Rangers	N	L 0–1	Att: 44,538	Ref: C Thomson	Booked: Murray, Mair, Brady.
24th	● Celtic	H	W 4–0	Att: 5,018	Ref: C Richmond	Scorers: Dorman2, Thomson2.
27th	● Aberdeen	A	L 2–1	Att: 8,764	Ref: B Winter	Scorers: Robb. Booked: Carey.

APRIL

3rd	● Hearts	H	D 1–1	Att: 4,204	Ref: I Brines	Scorers: Carey.
10th	● Falkirk	A	L 2–1	Att: 5,671	Ref: D McDonald	Scorers: Dorman. Booked: Murray, Mehmet.
17th	● St Johnstone	A	D 2–2	Att: 3,557	Ref: C Richmond	Scorers: Carey, Dorman. Booked: Mair, O'Donnell.
24th	● Kilmarnock	H	W 1–0	Att: 5,639	Ref: C Thomson	Scorers: Dorman. Booked: Thomson, Brady, Gallacher.

MAY

1st	● Falkirk	A	D 1–1	Att: 5,919	Ref: W Collum	Scorers: O'Donnell. Booked: Potter, O'Donnell. Dismissed: Innes.
5th	● Hamilton	A	D 0–0	Att: 3,102	Ref: I Brines	Booked: Higdon, Robb.
8th	● Aberdeen	H	L 0–1	Att: 4,022	Ref: S O'Reilly	

● Clydesdale Bank Premier League ● Scottish Cup ● Co-op Insurance Cup ● UEFA Champions League ● Europa League

CLYDESDALE BANK PREMIER LEAGUE GOALKEEPER STATS

Player	Minutes on pitch	Appearances	Match starts	Completed matches	Sub appearances	Subbed off	Saved with feet	Punched	Parried	Tipped over	Fumbled	Tipped round	Caught	Blocked	Clean sheets	Goals conceded	Save %	Saved	Resulting in goals	Opposition miss	Fouls committed	Free-kicks won	Yellow cards	Red cards
Paul Gallacher	3410	36	36	36	0	0	0	12	29	2	1	10	136	0	7	48	79.75	1	4	0	0	4	1	0
Mark Howard	184	2	2	2	0	0	0	0	2	0	0	1	9	0	1	1	92.31	0	0	0	0	1	0	0

CLYDESDALE BANK PREMIER LEAGUE OUTFIELD PLAYER STATS

Player	Minutes on pitch	Appearances	Match starts	Completed matches	Substitute appearances	Subbed off	Goals scored	Assists	Shots on target	Shots off target	Crosses	Corners taken	Defensive clearances	Defensive blocks	Fouls committed	Free-kicks won	Caught offside	Yellow cards	Red cards
David Barron	3162	34	34	31	0	3	0	0	4	7	40	7	20	4	30	33	1	4	0
Garry Brady	1664	22	19	10	3	9	0	0	7	3	9	18	2	2	12	9	1	2	0
Tom Brighton	177	8	1	0	7	1	1	2	2	1	1	0	0	0	5	2	0	0	0
Graham Carey	1069	15	10	9	5	1	3	1	15	10	47	52	6	4	7	24	0	1	0
Craig Dargo	1503	29	13	8	16	5	2	1	15	5	11	0	0	0	18	24	31	3	0
Andy Dorman	2667	34	29	16	5	13	6	4	26	18	53	73	9	2	25	31	4	3	0
Michael Higdon	2157	33	22	12	11	9	3	3	21	16	5	0	18	1	54	36	15	5	1
Chris Innes	1655	21	18	15	3	2	3	0	5	6	2	0	33	5	30	21	0	5	1
Allan Johnston	299	10	1	0	9	1	0	0	0	1	1	0	1	0	3	3	0	0	0
Rory Loy	143	8	0	0	8	0	0	0	5	1	2	1	1	0	1	5	1	0	0
Lee Mair	2740	31	30	25	1	3	0	0	0	2	1	0	47	10	32	33	1	5	2
Stephen McGinn	1576	18	18	13	0	5	3	0	7	10	10	3	10	1	13	24	0	1	0
Billy Mehmet	3321	37	35	29	2	6	3	4	22	29	27	1	7	0	48	58	37	6	0
Hugh Murray	2960	35	35	20	0	15	2	0	3	9	18	0	25	8	68	60	1	7	0
Stephen O'Donnell	951	22	10	3	12	7	3	1	7	8	27	7	6	0	18	11	4	4	0
John Potter	3246	35	35	33	0	2	0	0	2	1	5	1	54	11	38	30	0	4	0
Conor Ramsay	49	5	0	0	5	0	0	0	0	0	1	0	0	0	1	0	0	0	0
Steven Robb	1115	20	12	7	8	5	1	0	2	1	26	5	3	2	12	12	1	2	0
Jack Ross	2589	28	28	25	0	3	0	2	3	6	84	1	55	5	17	25	0	2	0
Steven Thomson	2665	30	30	24	0	5	3	2	9	11	11	0	4	0	41	25	3	4	1

IRN-BRU SECOND DIVISION RESULTS

	Alloa	Arbroath	Brechin	Clyde	Cowdenbeath	Dumbarton	East Fife	Peterhead	Stenhousemr	Stirling
Alloa	–	0–1, 1–0	2–1, 2–3	2–0, 2–2	2–1, 3–1	1–3, 1–2	0–0, 2–0	1–0, 2–1	1–4, 2–1	1–0, 2–1
Arbroath	2–2, 0–0	–	1–4, 1–0	0–3, 2–0	0–1, 1–1	3–1, 3–1	0–1, 2–2	0–1, 1–4	0–3, 1–1	3–4, 2–4
Brechin	2–1, 1–1	0–0, 0–2	–	2–2, 3–1	3–1, 3–3	3–1, 0–1	3–2, 1–0	3–0, 1–2	1–0, 2–2	1–0, 1–1
Clyde	0–1, 0–2	1–0, 0–2	1–0, 0–3	–	0–1, 1–2	0–2, 4–2	1–3, 2–1	1–3, 3–1	2–1, 0–2	0–1, 1–2
Cowdenbeath	1–1, 1–1	1–2, 2–1	0–0, 4–0	1–0, 3–1	–	2–1, 0–0	2–1, 6–2	5–0, 1–3	2–1, 1–0	1–2, 3–3
Dumbarton	1–3, 3–1	1–0, 0–2	0–0, 0–1	3–3, 3–3	0–3, 2–1	–	0–3, 0–1	1–0, 1–3	0–0, 2–1	2–3, 2–4
East Fife	0–2, 0–1	1–1, 3–1	2–0, 2–0	1–0, 1–1	1–1, 2–2	0–1, 2–3	–	1–2, 3–0	2–1, 1–1	1–2, 0–3
Peterhead	0–0, 2–0	1–2, 3–0	1–0, 0–3	2–0, 0–0	0–2, 1–0	1–2, 2–1	1–1, 3–1	–	2–2, 0–1	3–2, 1–1
Stenhousemr	1–0, 0–2	3–0, 1–1	1–1, 1–2	1–0, 0–3	0–2, 0–0	0–3, 1–0	1–1, 1–1	2–0, 1–1	–	1–2, 1–3
Stirling	0–1, 0–3	2–2, 2–2	1–0, 6–2	1–1, 1–0	2–2, 1–0	2–2, 1–2	3–0, 3–3	2–1, 2–0	0–0, 1–1	–

FINAL IRN-BRU SECOND DIVISION TABLE

Pos	Team	P	W	D	L	F	A	W	D	L	F	A	GD	Pts
			HOME					AWAY						
1	Stirling	36	7	8	3	30	22	11	3	4	38	26	20	65
2	Alloa	36	11	2	5	27	21	8	6	4	22	14	14	65
3	Cowdenbeath	36	10	5	3	36	19	6	6	6	24	22	19	59
4	Brechin	36	9	6	3	30	20	6	3	9	20	25	5	54
5	Peterhead	36	8	5	5	23	18	7	1	10	22	31	-4	51
6	Dumbarton	36	5	4	9	21	32	9	2	7	28	26	-9	48
7	East Fife	36	6	5	7	23	22	4	6	8	23	31	-7	41
8	Stenhousemuir	36	5	6	7	16	22	4	7	7	22	20	-4	40
9	Arbroath	36	4	5	9	22	33	6	5	7	19	22	-14	40
10	Clyde	36	6	0	12	17	29	2	7	9	20	28	-20	31

LEADING SCORERS

PLAYER	TEAM	GLS
Rory McAllister	Brechin	21
Gareth Wardlaw	Cowdenbeath	16
Paul McManus	East Fife	15
Paul McQuade	Cowdenbeath	12
Charlie King	Brechin	11
Martin Bavidge	Peterhead	11

PLAYER OF THE SEASON
Rory McAllister (Brechin)
MANAGER OF THE SEASON
Allan Moore (Stirling)

IRN-BRU THIRD DIVISION RESULTS

	Albion	Annan Ath	Berwick	East Stirling	Elgin	Forfar	Livingston	Montrose	Queen's Park	Stranraer
Albion	–	0–0, 1–0	2–1, 4–1	3–0, 2–1	1–1, 1–2	1–1, 0–1	1–0, 0–2	0–0, 1–0	0–1, 1–0	3–1, 0–0
Annan	0–0, 1–2	–	1–1, 0–1	0–1, 1–0	0–2, 3–3	1–0, 1–1	0–0, 2–0	2–0, 0–0	3–1, 0–2	1–0, 3–2
Berwick	2–0, 1–2	2–1, 0–2	–	0–1, 2–2	2–0, 2–1	0–1, 0–4	1–0, 1–1	2–0, 0–2	1–0, 1–1	1–0, 1–0
East Stirling	2–0, 3–1	1–3, 3–1	1–0, 3–2	–	1–1, 2–0	2–1, 4–0	3–1, 0–2	1–0, 2–3	1–0, 0–3	1–1, 2–0
Elgin	0–2, 3–1	1–1, 1–0	3–3, 1–5	1–2, 0–1	–	0–2, 0–2	1–6, 0–1	0–1, 5–2	0–1, 0–1	1–2, 2–3
Forfar	2–2, 1–1	2–1, 1–5	3–0, 2–0	5–1, 4–1	3–3, 1–0	–	0–1, 2–2	2–2, 2–0	0–1, 1–1	1–0, 2–0
Livingston	2–0, 2–0	2–0, 3–2	1–1, 0–0	2–0, 1–0	3–2, 1–0	1–2, 2–3	–	2–0, 1–0	2–1, 2–0	3–0, 2–1
Montrose	0–0, 0–0	0–0, 1–2	1–3, 1–1	0–3, 0–1	1–1, 0–4	1–2, 4–0	0–3, 0–5	–	1–2, 1–2	1–1, 4–5
Queen's Park	0–1, 1–0	0–0, 3–2	2–0, 2–3	1–0, 2–0	0–3, 0–1	2–2, 1–3	1–2, 0–1	3–2, 3–0	–	1–2, 2–5
Stranraer	1–1, 2–1	2–0, 3–2	2–4, 3–1	1–2, 2–2	0–2, 2–1	1–0, 2–0	1–0, 0–0	0–3, 1–1	2–0, 0–2	–

FINAL IRN-BRU THIRD DIVISION TABLE

Pos	Team	P	W	D	L	F	A	W	D	L	F	A	GD	Pts
			HOME					AWAY						
1	Livingston	36	14	2	2	32	12	10	4	4	31	13	38	78
2	Forfar	36	9	6	3	34	21	9	3	6	25	23	15	63
3	East Stirling	36	12	2	4	32	19	7	2	9	18	27	4	61
4	Queen's Park	36	7	2	9	24	27	8	4	6	18	15	0	51
5	Albion	36	9	5	4	21	12	4	6	8	14	23	0	50
6	Berwick	36	9	3	6	19	18	5	5	8	27	32	-4	50
7	Stranraer	36	8	5	5	25	23	5	3	10	23	31	-6	47
8	Annan	36	7	6	5	19	16	4	4	10	22	26	-1	43
9	Elgin	36	3	2	13	19	36	6	5	7	27	23	-13	34
10	Montrose	36	1	6	11	16	35	4	3	11	14	28	-33	24

LEADING SCORERS

PLAYER	TEAM	GLS
Craig Gunn	Elgin	18
Ross Campbell	Forfar	16
Andrew Halliday	Livingston	14
Simon Lynch	East Stirling	13
Damon Gray	Berwick	11
Ian Harty	Forfar	11

PLAYER OF THE SEASON
Robbie Winters (Livingston)
MANAGER OF THE SEASON
Gary Bollan (Livingston)

AIRDRIE UNITED

AIRDRIE were unable to capitalise on their Irn-Bru First Division reprieve as they finished second bottom of the table and were then demoted after losing their play-off semi-final against Brechin.

The Diamonds had been officially relegated at the end of 2008/09 only to be reinstated following Livingston's demotion to the Third Division. However, Kenny Black's men struggled from the outset, falling at the first hurdle in their defence of the ALBA Challenge Cup and also in the Co-operative Insurance Cup in a 14-match winless start.

But they did enjoy a 4–0 victory over Queen of the South in the Active Nation Scottish Cup third round as well as a surprise League double over Dundee.

Airdrie appeared likely to finish bottom until an eight-game unbeaten run spanning March and April lifted them above Ayr and took the battle to avoid the drop right up until the final day of the regular season.

CLUB SUMMARY

FORMED	2002
MANAGER	Kenny Black
GROUND	Excelsior Stadium
CAPACITY	10,171
NICKNAME	The Diamonds
WEBSITE	www.airdrieunited.com

The New Football Pools PLAYER OF THE SEASON

Paul Lovering

OVERALL
P	W	D	L	F	A	GD
43	9	11	23	48	64	-16

IRN-BRU FIRST DIVISION
Pos	P	W	D	L	F	A	GD	Pts
9	36	8	9	19	41	56	-15	33

HOME
Pos	P	W	D	L	F	A	GD	Pts
9	18	5	6	7	25	22	3	21

AWAY
Pos	P	W	D	L	F	A	GD	Pts
9	18	3	3	12	16	34	-18	12

CUP PROGRESS DETAILS
Competition	Round reached	Knocked out by
Scottish Cup	R4	Raith
Co-op Insurance Cup	R1	Alloa
Challenge Cup	R1	Partick

BIGGEST WIN (ALL COMPS)
28/11/09 4–0 v Queen of South

BIGGEST DEFEAT (ALL COMPS)
23/03/10 0–4 v Inverness

ATTENDANCE RECORD
HIGH	AVERAGE	Low
1,864	1,081	703
v Dunfermline (01/05/2010)		v Dunfermline (09/03/2010)

RESULTS 2009/10

JULY
25th	Partick	H	L 0–1	Att: 1,325	Booked: Lagana.

AUGUST
1st	Alloa	H	D 0–0	Att: 756	Booked: Nixon, Smith. **Dismissed:** Lovering.
					AET – Score after 90 mins 0–0. Alloa win 4–3 on penalties.
8th	Ross County	A	L 2–1	Att: 1,781	Scorers: Baird. Booked: Lagana, Smith, Gemmill. **Dismissed:** Lagana.
15th	Queen of South	H	D 1–1	Att: 1,079	Scorers: Donnelly. Booked: McDonald, Donnelly.
22nd	Dunfermline	A	L 2–0	Att: 2,885	Booked: McDonald, Lovering.
29th	Dundee	H	D 1–1	Att: 1,516	Scorers: Lauchlan OG. Booked: McDonald, Parratt.

SEPTEMBER
12th	Ayr	A	D 1–1	Att: 1,745	Scorers: Gemmill. Booked: Lovering, Parratt, Smyth.
19th	Inverness	H	D 1–1	Att: 951	Scorers: Baird.
26th	Morton	A	L 1–0	Att: 2,104	Booked: Lovering, Robertson.

OCTOBER
3rd	Partick	A	L 2–0	Att: 2,839	Booked: Lagana, Parratt, McDonald. **Dismissed:** McLaughlin.
10th	Raith	H	L 1–2	Att: 1,186	Scorers: O'Carroll. Booked: Donnelly. **Dismissed:** Donnelly.
17th	Ross County	H	L 0–1	Att: 756	Booked: O'Carroll.
24th	Queen of South	A	L 3–0	Att: 2,094	Booked: Trouten.
31st	Ayr	H	W 3–1	Att: 1,184	Scorers: O'Carroll, Trouten2. Booked: Nixon, Trouten, Storey.

NOVEMBER
7th	Dundee	A	L 2–1	Att: 4,121	Scorers: Baird. Booked: Trouten.
14th	Inverness	A	L 2–0	Att: 2,780	
21st	Morton	H	L 2–4	Att: 1,164	Scorers: Baird, Nixon. Booked: Donnelly.
28th	Queen of South	H	W 4–0	Att: 1,141	Scorers: Baird, O'Carroll, Trouten2.

DECEMBER
12th	Partick	H	L 2–5	Att: 1,321	Scorers: Baird2. Booked: Baird.
15th	Raith	A	D 1–1	Att: 1,247	Scorers: Gemmill. Booked: Baird.
19th	Ross County	A	L 5–3	Att: 1,823	Scorers: McDonald, O'Carroll, Waddell. Booked: Trouten, McDonald, Lagana. **Dismissed:** Trouten.

JANUARY
3rd	Dundee	A	W 0–1	Att: 4,319	Scorers: McDonald. Booked: Smyth, Donnelly. **Dismissed:** Donnelly.
23rd	Inverness	H	L 0–1	Att: 839	Booked: McCann.
25th	Raith	A	D 1–1	Att: 1,599	Scorers: Baird. Booked: Parratt, Trouten.
27th	Raith	H	L 1–3	Att: 852	Scorers: Donnelly. Booked: Smyth, Robertson, Smith. **Dismissed:** Robertson.

FEBRUARY
13th	Partick	A	L 2–0	Att: 2,404	Booked: Lagana, Gemmill, Trouten, Parratt. **Dismissed:** Trouten.

MARCH
6th	Dunfermline	A	L 2–0	Att: 2,252	Booked: Robertson, Smyth, O'Carroll.
9th	Dunfermline	H	D 1–1	Att: 703	Scorers: Waddell. Booked: Parratt, Waddell, Donnelly, Lagana.
13th	Ayr	H	D 1–1	Att: 1,122	Scorers: Keegan. Booked: Storey, McDonald. **Dismissed:** Baird.
17th	Morton	A	L 2–1	Att: 1,266	Scorers: O'Carroll. Booked: Trouten, Robertson.
20th	Dundee	H	W 3–0	Att: 1,172	Scorers: Gemmill, McLaughlin, O'Carroll. Booked: Lovering.
23rd	Inverness	A	L 4–0	Att: 2,008	
27th	Morton	H	W 3–0	Att: 1,017	Scorers: Lovering2, McGuffie OG.

APRIL
3rd	Partick	H	W 2–0	Att: 1,142	Scorers: Lovering, McLaughlin. Booked: Storey, Lovering.
12th	Queen of South	H	L 0–1	Att: 825	Booked: Lovering, Smyth.
14th	Raith	H	W 3–0	Att: 815	Scorers: Baird2, Waddell. Booked: Smyth, O'Carroll, Storey.
17th	Ross County	H	D 1–1	Att: 798	Scorers: McDonald. Booked: Waddell, Lovering, McDonald.
21st	Ayr	A	W 1–4	Att: 1,781	Scorers: Baird3, Gemmill. Booked: Lovering, Baird.
24th	Queen of South	A	D 2–2	Att: 2,541	Scorers: Gemmill, Waddell.
26th	Raith	A	W 0–1	Att: 1,539	Scorers: McLaughlin. Booked: O'Carroll.

MAY
1st	Dunfermline	H	L 0–1	Att: 1,864	Booked: Parratt.
5th	Brechin	A	L 2–1	Att: 583	Scorers: Gemmill.
8th	Brechin	H	L 0–1	Att: 1,156	Booked: Keegan. Agg: 1–3.

● Irn-Bru First Division/Play-offs ● Scottish Cup ● Co-op Insurance Cup ● Challenge Cup

FIRST DIVISION GOALKEEPER STATS

Player	Appearances	Match starts	Completed matches	Sub appearances	Subbed off	Clean sheets	Yellow cards	Red cards
Lee Hollis	3	2	2	1	0	1	0	0
Stephen Robertson	34	34	33	0	1	5	3	0

FIRST DIVISION OUTFIELD PLAYER STATS

Player	Appearances	Match starts	Completed matches	Substitute appearances	Subbed off	Goals scored	Yellow cards	Red cards
Jamie Bain	1	1	1	0	0	0	0	0
John Baird	31	26	20	5	5	11	3	1
Robert Donnelly	30	28	23	2	3	1	5	2
Scott Gemmill	24	16	10	8	6	5	2	0
Fraser Keast	1	0	0	1	0	0	0	0
Paul Keegan	28	4	2	24	2	1	0	0
Frankie Lagana	19	14	3	5	10	0	5	1
Paul Lovering	24	21	12	3	9	3	8	0
Ryan McCann	29	28	22	1	6	0	1	0
Kevin McDonald	30	21	14	9	7	3	7	0
Scott McLaughlin	33	33	29	0	3	3	0	1
David Nixon	6	6	2	0	4	1	1	0
Diarmuid O'Carroll	30	29	19	1	10	5	4	0
Tom Parratt	11	10	6	1	4	0	6	0
Darren Smith	17	11	9	6	2	0	1	0
Marc Smyth	24	24	24	0	0	0	5	0
Simon Storey	31	31	29	0	2	0	4	0
Alan Trouten	26	23	9	3	12	2	6	2
Richard Waddell	29	27	22	2	5	4	2	0
Kevin Watt	19	2	1	17	1	0	0	0
Anthony Watt	1	0	0	1	0	0	0	0

| AUG | SEP | OCT | NOV | DEC | JAN | FEB | MAR | APR | MAY |

SEASON INFORMATION
Highest position: 3
Lowest position: 10
Average goals scored per game: 1.14
Average goals conceded per game: 1.56

| 9 | 10 | 9 | 10 | 10 | 10 | 10 | 10 | 9 | 9 |

LEAGUE POSITION AT THE END OF EACH MONTH

LONGEST SEQUENCES

Wins	2	Undefeated home	5
(27/03/10–03/04/10)		(09/03/10–03/04/10)	
Losses	5	Undefeated away	3
(26/09/09–24/10/09)		(21/04/10–26/04/10)	
Draws	3	Without scoring	3
(29/08/09–19/09/09)		(23/01/10–06/03/10)	
Undefeated	5	Without conceding	2
(14/04/10–26/04/10)		(27/03/10–03/04/10)	
Without win	11	Scoring	5
(08/08/09–24/10/09)		(on two occasions)	

CARDS RECEIVED

63 **7**

EARLIEST STRIKE
JOHN BAIRD
(v Partick) 1:00

LATEST STRIKE
PAUL KEEGAN
(v Ayr) 94:28

GOALS SCORED/CONCEDED
PER FIVE-MINUTE INTERVALS

MINS	5	10	15	20	25	30	35	40	45	50	55	60	65	70	75	80	85	90
FOR	4	1	0	0	4	1	3	0	3	2	2	3	4	1	4	1	4	4
AGN	2	1	0	3	1	5	4	2	8	5	4	1	2	7	0	3	3	5

AYR UNITED

AYR suffered an immediate relegation back to the Irn-Bru Second Division.

The Somerset Park side were a feature of Scotland's second tier courtesy of a 3–2 aggregate win over Airdrie in the play-offs last year, but they made a poor start to 2009/10 and failed to win any of their opening seven League games.

Their form on the road was the key to their demise, with their only away wins all season coming at Dunfermline in February and at Partick Thistle in April.

Heavy 4–1 and 7–0 losses to relegation rivals Airdrie and eventual champions Inverness respectively proved crucial during the run-in, although their fate was not sealed until they lost to fellow strugglers Morton on the final day of the regular campaign.

One positive for United was the emergence of young striker Daniel McKay. The 19-year-old came into the side in March and scored four goals in only a handful of starts.

CLUB SUMMARY

FORMED	1910
MANAGER	Brian Reid
GROUND	Somerset Park
CAPACITY	10,185
NICKNAME	The Honest Men
WEBSITE	www.ayrunitedfc.c.uk

The New Football Pools PLAYER OF THE SEASON — Craig Samson

OVERALL
P	W	D	L	F	A	GD
42	10	10	22	34	67	-33

IRN-BRU FIRST DIVISION
Pos	P	W	D	L	F	A	GD	Pts
10	36	7	10	19	29	60	-31	31

HOME
Pos	P	W	D	L	F	A	GD	Pts
10	18	5	5	8	17	30	-13	20

AWAY
Pos	P	W	D	L	F	A	GD	Pts
10	18	2	5	11	12	30	-18	11

CUP PROGRESS DETAILS
Competition	Round reached	Knocked out by
Scottish Cup	R5	Dundee
Co-op Insurance Cup	R2	St Mirren
Challenge Cup	R1	Albion

BIGGEST WIN (ALL COMPS)
20/03/10 3–0 v Queen of South

BIGGEST DEFEAT (ALL COMPS)
24/04/10 0–7 v Inverness

ATTENDANCE RECORD
HIGH	AVERAGE	LOW
3,043	1,777	1,032
v Partick (08/08/2009)		v Ross County (28/04/2010)

RESULTS 2009/10

JULY
25th	● Albion	H	L 0–2	Att: 964	

AUGUST
1st	● Stirling	A	W 1–2	Att: 802	Scorers: A Aitken, Easton. Booked: N McGowan.
					AET – Score after 90 mins 1–1.
8th	● Partick	H	D 1–1	Att: 3,043	Scorers: Roberts. Booked: James.
15th	● Inverness	A	D 0–0	Att: 3,297	
22nd	● Morton	H	L 0–2	Att: 2,266	Booked: Keenan, James.
26th	● St Mirren	H	L 0–2	Att: 1,652	Dismissed: Keenan.
29th	● Queen of South	A	L 2–0	Att: 3,034	Booked: Roberts, Gibson.

SEPTEMBER
12th	● Airdrie	H	D 1–1	Att: 1,745	Scorers: Roberts. Booked: James, Gibson, Borris.
19th	● Ross County	A	L 2–1	Att: 1,885	Scorers: Roberts. Booked: Easton, N McGowan, Roberts.
					Dismissed: N McGowan.
26th	● Raith	H	W 1–0	Att: 1,766	Scorers: K Connolly. Booked: Keenan.

OCTOBER
10th	● Dunfermline	A	L 3–1	Att: 2,470	Scorers: C Aitken. Booked: Keenan, Easton.
14th	● Dundee	H	D 2–2	Att: 1,710	Scorers: R McGowan, Stevenson. Booked: Keenan, Gibson.
17th	● Partick	A	L 2–0	Att: 3,055	Booked: Campbell, Easton.
24th	● Inverness	H	L 1–5	Att: 1,600	Scorers: Roberts. Booked: Easton, Borris, Gormley, Gibson.
31st	● Airdrie	A	L 3–1	Att: 1,184	Scorers: McCann OG. Booked: Samson, R McGowan, Campbell, Roberts.

NOVEMBER
7th	● Queen of South	H	L 0–1	Att: 2,406	Booked: Gormley, Stevenson, C Aitken.
14th	● Ross County	H	D 1–1	Att: 1,213	Scorers: Roberts. Booked: Borris, R McGowan, Gibson.
					Dismissed: Stevenson.
21st	● Raith	A	D 0–0	Att: 1,416	
28th	● Deveronvale	A	W 0–1	Att: 192	Scorers: Stevenson. Booked: Keenan, Stevenson, N McGowan, Samson.

DECEMBER
| 5th | ● Dunfermline | H | W 1–0 | Att: 1,652 | Scorers: Stevenson. Booked: A Aitken. |
| 12th | ● Dundee | A | L 3–1 | Att: 4,323 | Scorers: Reynolds. Booked: R McGowan, Easton, Gibson. |

JANUARY
| 18th | ● Brechin | H | W 1–0 | Att: 1,139 | Scorers: Roberts. |
| 23rd | ● Ross County | A | L 1–0 | Att: 1,935 | Booked: Mendes, Campbell. |

FEBRUARY
6th	● Dundee	A	L 2–1	Att: 2,852	Scorers: McManus.
16th	● Queen of South	A	L 3–0	Att: 1,721	Booked: Roberts, Bowey. Dismissed: Samson.
20th	● Dunfermline	A	W 0–1	Att: 2,429	Scorers: McManus. Booked: Keenan, R McGowan, McKay.
27th	● Inverness	H	D 3–3	Att: 2,843	Scorers: A Aitken, McManus, Roberts. Booked: R McGowan, Bowey.

MARCH
6th	● Morton	H	W 2–0	Att: 2,145	Scorers: McManus, Roberts. Booked: Bowey, McManus, R McGowan.
10th	● Partick	H	W 1–0	Att: 1,505	Scorers: Bowey.
13th	● Airdrie	A	D 1–1	Att: 1,122	Scorers: McKay. Booked: A Aitken, Bowey, Keenan, Mitchell, Campbell.
17th	● Dundee	H	D 1–1	Att: 1,375	Scorers: Lafferty. Booked: McManus, Mitchell, Keenan.
20th	● Queen of South	H	W 3–0	Att: 2,139	Scorers: McKay, McManus, Roberts. Booked: Keenan, Lafferty, K Connolly.
27th	● Raith	A	D 1–1	Att: 1,872	Scorers: Mitchell. Booked: Gibson.
30th	● Morton	A	L 1–0	Att: 1,289	Booked: Woodburn.

APRIL
3rd	● Dundee	A	L 3–0	Att: 4,270	Booked: Bowey, Keenan, McManus, Mitchell.
7th	● Raith	H	L 0–2	Att: 1,433	Booked: Mitchell.
10th	● Dunfermline	H	L 1–2	Att: 1,367	Scorers: McManus. Booked: Lafferty, K Connolly.
17th	● Partick	A	W 0–1	Att: 1,877	Scorers: McKay.
21st	● Airdrie	H	L 1–4	Att: 1,781	Scorers: Keenan. Booked: Keenan, Roberts, McKay.
24th	● Inverness	H	L 0–7	Att: 1,804	Booked: Lafferty, Keenan, K Connolly, Gibson.
28th	● Ross County	H	L 1,032		Booked: Bowey.

MAY
| 1st | ● Morton | A | L 2–1 | Att: 3,771 | Scorers: McKay. Booked: Gibson, A Connolly, Lafferty, Roberts. |

● Irn-Bru First Division ● Scottish Cup ○ Co-op Insurance Cup ● Challenge Cup

FIRST DIVISION GOALKEEPER STATS

Player	Appearances	Match starts	Completed matches	Sub appearances	Subbed off	Clean sheets	Yellow cards	Red cards
Stephen Grindlay	5	4	4	1	0	1	0	0
Craig Samson	32	32	31	0	0	8	1	1

FIRST DIVISION OUTFIELD PLAYER STATS

Player	Appearances	Match starts	Completed matches	Substitute appearances	Subbed off	Goals scored	Yellow cards	Red cards
Christopher Aitken	14	12	8	2	4	1	1	0
Andrew Aitken	22	22	16	0	6	1	2	0
Ryan Borris	28	21	11	7	10	0	3	0
Steve Bowey	18	17	15	1	2	1	6	0
Martin Campbell	24	24	20	0	4	0	4	0
Kevin Cawley	11	3	0	8	3	0	0	0
Kenneth Connolly	32	18	11	14	7	1	3	0
Aaron Connolly	3	0	0	3	0	0	1	0
William Easton	22	19	9	3	10	0	5	0
William Gibson	25	19	17	6	2	0	9	0
David Gormley	9	1	0	8	1	0	2	0
Kevin James	14	13	12	1	1	0	3	0
Dean Keenan	34	31	24	3	7	1	11	0
Daniel Lafferty	14	12	11	2	1	1	4	0
Neil McGowan	13	10	5	3	4	0	1	1
Ryan McGowan	28	28	26	0	2	1	6	0
Daniel McKay	13	5	4	8	1	4	2	0
Tom McManus	17	17	9	0	8	5	3	0
Junior Mendes	21	8	3	13	5	0	1	0
Chris Mitchell	14	14	12	0	2	1	4	0
Bryan Prunty	10	6	3	4	3	0	0	0
Stephen Reynolds	4	2	2	2	0	1	0	0
Mark Roberts	33	31	23	2	8	8	6	0
Ryan Stevenson	17	17	15	0	1	2	1	1
Rocky Visconte	3	2	1	1	1	0	0	0
Alastair Woodburn	15	7	1	8	6	0	1	0

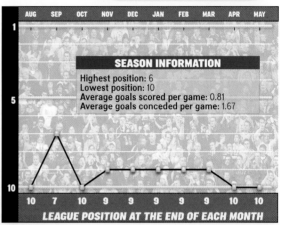

SEASON INFORMATION
Highest position: 6
Lowest position: 10
Average goals scored per game: 0.81
Average goals conceded per game: 1.67

LEAGUE POSITION AT THE END OF EACH MONTH

LONGEST SEQUENCES

Wins	2		Undefeated home		6
(06/03/10–10/03/10)			(14/11/09–20/03/10)		
Losses	4		Undefeated away		4
(on three occasions)			(20/02/10–27/03/10)		
Draws	2		Without scoring		3
(on three occasions)			(on two occasions)		
Undefeated	8		Without conceding		2
(20/02/10–27/03/10)			(on two occasions)		
Without win	8		Scoring		8
(10/10/09–21/11/09)			(20/02/10–27/03/10)		

CARDS RECEIVED

80   3

EARLIEST STRIKE
STEPHEN REYNOLDS
(v Dundee) 3:00

LATEST STRIKE
DANIEL MCKAY
(v Airdrie Utd) 91:00

GOALS SCORED/CONCEDED
PER FIVE-MINUTE INTERVALS

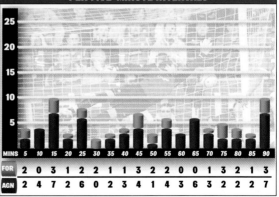

MINS	5	10	15	20	25	30	35	40	45	50	55	60	65	70	75	80	85	90
FOR	2	0	3	1	2	2	1	1	3	2	2	0	0	1	3	2	1	3
AGN	2	4	7	2	6	0	2	3	4	1	4	3	6	3	2	2	2	7

DUNDEE

BIG-SPENDING Dundee may view their season as a disappointment, despite finishing second in the race for promotion to the Clydesdale Bank Premier League and winning the ALBA Challenge Cup.

Jocky Scott was dismissed as the club's manager in March, despite having lost just four Irn-Bru First Division games up to that point. Gordon Chisholm replaced Scott, but back-to-back draws against Queen of the South and Ross County meant that the Dark Blues surrendered the lead they had held at the top of the table for much of the season.

It was an advantage that they struggled to ever recover and a failure to beat Raith in their third-last game handed promotion – and the title – to Inverness, the side they had overcome 3–2 in the ALBA Cup final in November.

The club released a host of players at the end of the campaign, but they will hope to keep hold of Leigh Griffiths and Gary Harkins as they look for a promotion push in the coming season.

CLUB SUMMARY

FORMED	1893
MANAGER	Gordon Chisholm
GROUND	Dens Park
CAPACITY	11,800
NICKNAME	Dark Blues
WEBSITE	www.dundeefc.co.uk

The New **Football Pools** PLAYER OF THE SEASON — *Jim Lauchlan*

OVERALL

P	W	D	L	F	A	GD
47	25	13	9	76	47	29

IRN-BRU FIRST DIVISION

Pos	P	W	D	L	F	A	GD	Pts
2	36	16	13	7	48	34	14	61

HOME

Pos	P	W	D	L	F	A	GD	Pts
1	18	12	4	2	30	13	17	40

AWAY

Pos	P	W	D	L	F	A	GD	Pts
5	18	4	9	5	18	21	-3	21

CUP PROGRESS DETAILS

Competition	Round reached	Knocked out by
Scottish Cup	QF	Raith
Co-op Insurance Cup	QF	Rangers
Challenge Cup	WON	

BIGGEST WIN (ALL COMPS)
01/08/09 5–0 v Stranraer

BIGGEST DEFEAT (ALL COMPS)
20/03/10 0–3 v Airdrie

ATTENDANCE RECORD

HIGH	AVERAGE	Low
5,507	4,760	3,187
v Inverness (22/08/2009)		v Raith (24/04/2010)

RESULTS 2009/10

AUGUST
1st	Stranraer	H	W 5-0	Att: 2,345	Scorers: Cameron, Griffiths, Harkins, Higgins, McMenamin.
8th	Morton	H	W 1-0	Att: 5,449	Scorers: Higgins. Booked: MacKenzie, Lauchlan, Higgins.
15th	Raith	A	D 2-2	Att: 4,744	Scorers: Harkins, McMenamin. Booked: MacKenzie, Malone.
18th	Cowdenbeath	A	W 0-3	Att: 457	Scorers: Antoine-Curier, Griffiths, Harkins.
22nd	Inverness	H	D 2-2	Att: 5,507	Scorers: Harkins². Booked: Harkins, McMenamin, Malone, Lauchlan.
25th	Forfar	A	W 2-4	Att: 1,929	Scorers: Antoine-Curier², Griffiths, Tod OG.
29th	Airdrie	A	D 1-1	Att: 1,516	Scorers: McMenamin.

SEPTEMBER
6th	Stirling	A	W 1-2	Att: 1,277	Scorers: Griffiths². Booked: MacKenzie.
12th	Dunfermline	H	W 1-0	Att: 5,326	Scorers: Harkins.
19th	Queen of South	A	L 2-0	Att: 2,857	Booked: Klimpl, Griffiths, Higgins. Dismissed: Bullock.
22nd	Aberdeen	H	W 3-2	Att: 6,131	Scorers: Forsyth, Griffiths, Malone. Booked: Klimpl. AET – Score after 90 mins 2-2.
26th	Ross County	H	W 2-0	Att: 4,682	Scorers: Griffiths².

OCTOBER
4th	Annan	H	W 3-0	Att: 2,321	Scorers: Clarke, Forsyth, Higgins.
10th	Partick	H	W 2-0	Att: 5,364	Scorers: Griffiths, Harkins. Booked: MacKenzie.
14th	Ayr	A	D 2-2	Att: 1,710	Scorers: Forsyth, Griffiths. Booked: Klimpl, Griffiths.
17th	Morton	A	W 0-1	Att: 2,217	Scorers: Griffiths. Booked: Griffiths, Malone, Clarke.
24th	Raith	H	W 2-1	Att: 5,154	Scorers: MacKenzie, McMenamin. Booked: Forsyth.
27th	Rangers	H	L 1-3	Att: 10,654	Scorers: Griffiths. Booked: Malone.
31st	Dunfermline	A	D 1-1	Att: 3,998	Scorers: Harkins. Booked: Forsyth, Griffiths.

NOVEMBER
7th	Airdrie	H	W 2-1	Att: 4,121	Scorers: Higgins².
14th	Queen of South	H	D 0-0	Att: 4,901	Booked: McHale.
22nd	Inverness	N	W 3-2	Att: 8,031	Scorers: Forsyth, Harkins, Bulvitis OG. Booked: Lauchlan, Kerr.

DECEMBER
1st	Ross County	A	W 0-1	Att: 2,005	Scorers: Harkins. Booked: Griffiths, Lauchlan, Hart.
5th	Partick	A	W 0-2	Att: 4,453	Scorers: Harkins, McMenamin. Booked: Cameron.
12th	Ayr	H	W 3-1	Att: 4,323	Scorers: Forsyth, Griffiths, Harkins. Booked: MacKenzie.
19th	Morton	H	W 3-1	Att: 4,259	Scorers: Griffiths, Harkins, Malone. Booked: Hart, Malone.
26th	Inverness	H	D 1-1	Att: 3,660	Scorers: Griffiths. Booked: Douglas, Harkins. Dismissed: Harkins.

JANUARY
3rd	Airdrie	H	L 0-1	Att: 4,319	Booked: Lauchlan. Dismissed: MacKenzie.
17th	Dunfermline	H	W 3-2	Att: 5,201	Scorers: Griffiths², McMenamin. Booked: Benedictis.
20th	Livingston	A	W 0-1	Att: 1,176	Scorers: Harkins.
23rd	Queen of South	A	D 1-1	Att: 3,415	Scorers: Griffiths. Booked: Benedictis.
30th	Ross County	H	L 0-1	Att: 4,912	Booked: Lauchlan, Young, Benedictis.

FEBRUARY
6th	Ayr	H	W 2-1	Att: 2,852	Scorers: Griffiths, Hutchinson.
20th	Partick	H	W 1-0	Att: 5,216	Scorers: Paton. Booked: Malone.

MARCH
6th	Inverness	H	D 2-2	Att: 4,974	Scorers: Harkins, Kerr. Booked: MacKenzie.
13th	Raith	H	L 1-2	Att: 7,306	Scorers: Forsyth. Booked: Griffiths, MacKenzie.
17th	Ayr	A	D 1-1	Att: 1,375	Scorers: Harkins. Booked: Klimpl, Paton, Kerr, Malcolm. Dismissed: Paton.
20th	Airdrie	A	L 3-0	Att: 1,172	Booked: Malcolm.
23rd	Queen of South	A	D 1-1	Att: 4,508	Scorers: Griffiths. Booked: Griffiths, Malcolm.
27th	Ross County	A	D 1-1	Att: 3,295	Scorers: Hutchinson. Booked: Paton.
30th	Dunfermline	A	L 2-1	Att: 2,134	Scorers: Harkins. Booked: Hutchinson, Paton, Hart, O'Leary.

APRIL
3rd	Ayr	H	W 3-0	Att: 4,270	Scorers: Higgins, McMenamin².
10th	Partick	A	W 0-1	Att: 2,545	Scorers: Clarke. Booked: McMenamin, Malone, Hart.
17th	Morton	A	D 2-2	Att: 1,998	Scorers: Griffiths, Harkins. Booked: McKeown, Lauchlan, Paton.
21st	Raith	A	L 1-0	Att: 1,544	Booked: Clarke, McMenamin.
24th	Raith	H	W 2-0	Att: 3,187	Scorers: Harkins, Higgins. Booked: Kerr, O'Leary, Lauchlan.

MAY
1st	Inverness	A	L 1-0	Att: 6,031	

● Irn-Bru First Division ● Scottish Cup ○ Co-op Insurance Cup ● Challenge Cup

FIRST DIVISION GOALKEEPER STATS

Player	Appearances	Match starts	Completed matches	Sub appearances	Subbed off	Clean sheets	Yellow cards	Red cards
Anthony Bullock	19	19	17	0	1	7	0	1
Robert Douglas	16	15	15	1	0	4	1	0
Robert Geddes	1	0	0	1	0	0	0	0
Derek Soutar	2	2	2	0	0	1	0	0

FIRST DIVISION OUTFIELD PLAYER STATS

Player	Appearances	Match starts	Completed matches	Substitute appearances	Subbed off	Goals scored	Yellow cards	Red cards
Kyle Benedictis	5	4	3	1	1	0	3	0
Colin Cameron	14	5	2	9	3	0	1	0
Christopher Casement	1	0	0	1	0	0	0	0
Patrick Clarke	17	4	1	13	3	1	2	0
David Cowan	6	5	5	1	0	0	0	0
Craig Forsyth	24	21	20	3	1	2	2	0
Leigh Griffiths	29	24	12	5	12	13	6	0
Gary Harkins	34	32	25	2	6	15	2	1
Richard Hart	26	20	10	6	10	0	4	0
Sean Higgins	26	15	3	11	12	5	2	0
Ben Hutchinson	9	5	0	4	5	1	1	0
Brian Kerr	33	29	26	4	3	1	2	0
Maros Klimpl	18	16	11	2	5	0	3	0
Jim Lauchlan	25	25	24	0	1	0	7	0
Gary MacKenzie	25	25	21	0	3	1	5	1
Robert Malcolm	3	2	2	1	0	0	3	0
Edward Malone	33	33	32	0	1	1	6	0
Paul McHale	14	11	8	3	3	0	1	0
Craig McKeown	11	9	9	2	0	0	1	0
Colin McMenamin	31	24	18	7	6	7	3	0
Ryan O'Leary	8	8	8	0	0	0	2	0
Eric Paton	32	32	30	0	1	1	4	1
Andrew Shinnie	12	9	4	3	5	0	0	0
Darren Young	5	2	1	3	1	0	1	0

SEASON INFORMATION

Highest position: 1
Lowest position: 6
Average goals scored per game: 1.33
Average goals conceded per game: 0.94

	AUG	SEP	OCT	NOV	DEC	JAN	FEB	MAR	APR	MAY
LEAGUE POSITION AT THE END OF EACH MONTH	4	5	2	2	1	1	1	2	2	2

LONGEST SEQUENCES

Wins	4		Undefeated home	10
(01/12/09–19/12/09)			(08/08/09–19/12/09)	
Losses	–		Undefeated away	8
(–)			(14/10/09–17/03/10)	
Draws	3		Without scoring	–
(15/08/09–29/08/09)			(–)	
Undefeated	13		Without conceding	3
(26/09/09–26/12/09)			(14/11/09–05/12/09)	
Without win	6		Scoring	7
(06/03/10–30/03/10)			(26/09/09–07/11/09)	

CARDS RECEIVED

62   4

EARLIEST STRIKE

LEIGH GRIFFITHS
(v Dunfermline) 2:00

LATEST STRIKE

GARY HARKINS
(v Ayr) 90:00

GOALS SCORED/CONCEDED
PER FIVE-MINUTE INTERVALS

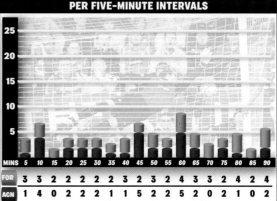

MINS	5	10	15	20	25	30	35	40	45	50	55	60	65	70	75	80	85	90
FOR	3	3	2	2	2	2	3	2	3	2	4	3	3	2	4	2	4
AGN	1	4	0	2	2	2	1	1	5	2	2	5	2	0	2	1	0	2

DUNFERMLINE ATHLETIC

DUNFERMLINE ultimately fell short in their hopes of promotion and now face a fourth consecutive season outside of the Clydesdale Bank Premier League.

The Pars made a poor start to the Irn-Bru First Division season, losing five of their first seven games, but they showed their resilience towards the end of the campaign to make a late surge towards the top of the table. However, solid wins in March over high-flyers Dundee and local rivals Raith were not enough to close the gap at the top after a run of just one win in seven over the turn of the year.

The Pars had mixed fortunes in the Co-operative Insurance Cup and Active Nation Scottish Cup, losing out to SPL sides Hearts and Celtic respectively. However, to face the latter they had to win an appeal against expulsion from the competition after fielding an ineligible player in their 7–1 fourth-round victory over Stenhousemuir. The fourth-round tie was replayed and the Pars won again.

CLUB SUMMARY

FORMED	1885
MANAGER	Jim McIntyre
GROUND	East End Park
CAPACITY	11,780
NICKNAME	The Pars
WEBSITE	www.dafc.co.uk

The New Football Pools PLAYER OF THE SEASON — Steven Bell

OVERALL

P	W	D	L	F	A	GD
44	22	7	15	77	56	21

IRN-BRU FIRST DIVISION

Pos	P	W	D	L	F	A	GD	Pts
3	36	17	7	12	54	44	10	58

HOME

Pos	P	W	D	L	F	A	GD	Pts
5	18	9	3	6	31	23	8	30

AWAY

Pos	P	W	D	L	F	A	GD	Pts
2	18	8	4	6	23	21	2	28

CUP PROGRESS DETAILS

Competition	Round reached	Knocked out by
Scottish Cup	R5	Celtic
Co-op Insurance Cup	R3	Hearts
Challenge Cup	R2	Queen of South

BIGGEST WIN (ALL COMPS)
01/08/09 5–0 v Dumbarton

BIGGEST DEFEAT (ALL COMPS)
26/09/09 1–4 v Queen of South

ATTENDANCE RECORD

High	Average	Low
6,296	2,934	2,134
v Raith (29/08/2009)		v Dundee (30/03/2010)

RESULTS 2009/10

JULY
25th	● Arbroath	H	W 2–1	Att: 1,239	Scorers: Bell, Kirk. Booked: Gibson.

AUGUST
1st	● Dumbarton	A	W 0–5	Att: 953	Scorers: Bell, Burke, Graham, Kirk^2. Booked: McGregor, Bell.
8th	● Inverness	H	L 0–1	Att: 3,258	Booked: Glass, Graham.
15th	● Morton	A	W 0–2	Att: 2,661	Scorers: Cardle, Kirk. Booked: Higgins.
18th	● Queen of South	H	L 1–2	Att: 941	Scorers: Cardle.
22nd	● Airdrie	H	W 2–0	Att: 2,885	Scorers: Bayne, Nolan OG.
26th	● Raith	H	W 3–1	Att: 4,163	Scorers: Kirk^2, Campbell OG. Booked: Bell, McGregor.
29th	● Raith	A	L 0–2	Att: 6,296	Booked: Bayne, Woods. Dismissed: Gibson.

SEPTEMBER
12th	● Dundee	A	L 1–0	Att: 5,326	Booked: Cardle, Dowie.
19th	● Partick	A	L 2–0	Att: 3,163	Booked: Woods, Dowie.
23rd	● Hearts	A	L 2–1	Att: 6,126	Scorers: Bayne. Booked: Gibson.
26th	● Queen of South	H	L 1–4	Att: 2,620	Scorers: Phinn. Booked: Cardle, Gibson, Bayne, Burke.

OCTOBER
10th	● Ayr	H	W 3–1	Att: 2,470	Scorers: Gibson^2, Kirk. Booked: Bayne.
13th	● Ross County	A	D 0–0	Att: 1,757	
17th	● Inverness	A	D 1–1	Att: 3,083	Scorers: Kirk.
24th	● Morton	H	W 3–1	Att: 2,411	Scorers: Bell, Cardle, Graham. Booked: Ross, Bell.
31st	● Dundee	H	D 1–1	Att: 3,998	Scorers: Bayne.

NOVEMBER
7th	● Raith	A	W 1–2	Att: 6,200	Scorers: Bayne, Wilson OG. Booked: Ross, Graham.
14th	● Partick	H	W 3–1	Att: 3,109	Scorers: Gibson^2, McDougall. Booked: McGregor, Ross.

DECEMBER
1st	● Queen of South	A	W 1–2	Att: 1,651	Scorers: Gibson, McGregor. Booked: McDougall, Bell.
5th	● Ayr	A	L 1–0	Att: 1,652	Booked: Bell, McCann.
12th	● Ross County	H	D 3–3	Att: 2,379	Scorers: Gibson, Kirk^2.
19th	● Inverness	H	D 0–0	Att: 2,280	

JANUARY
9th	● Stenhousemuir (VOID) H		W 7–1	Att: 1,832	Scorers: Cardle, Gibson, Graham, Kirk^2, McDougall, Phinn.
17th	● Dundee	A	L 3–2	Att: 5,201	Scorers: Graham, Kirk. Booked: McGregor.
23rd	● Partick	A	W 1–4	Att: 1,549	Scorers: Cardle^3, Woods.
26th	● Stenhousemuir	A	W 1–2	Att: 1,810	Scorers: Cardle, Kirk. Booked: Cardle. AET – Score after 90 mins 1–1.

FEBRUARY
7th	● Celtic	H	L 2–4	Att: 8,933	Scorers: Graham, Kirk. Booked: Graham, Woods, McCann.
13th	● Ross County	A	D 2–2	Att: 2,213	Scorers: Phinn^2. Booked: Cardle, Ross. Dismissed: Holmes.
20th	● Ayr	A	L 0–1	Att: 2,429	Booked: Cardle.
27th	● Morton	A	W 1–2	Att: 1,776	Scorers: Kirk, Mason. Booked: Mason, Gibson.

MARCH
6th	● Airdrie	H	W 2–0	Att: 2,252	Scorers: Bell, Kirk. Booked: Graham, Mason.
9th	● Airdrie	A	D 1–1	Att: 703	Scorers: Gibson. Booked: Gibson, Dowie, Bell, Graham.
13th	● Queen of South	H	W 3–1	Att: 2,163	Scorers: Bell, McDougall, Woods. Booked: Higgins. Dismissed: Woods.
16th	● Raith	H	W 2–1	Att: 4,549	Scorers: Gibson, McDougall. Booked: Dowie. Dismissed: Bell.
20th	● Raith	A	W 1–2	Att: 4,098	Scorers: Graham, Mason. Booked: Fleming, McCann.
23rd	● Partick	H	L 1–2	Att: 2,401	Scorers: McDougall. Booked: Woods.
27th	● Queen of South	A	L 2–0	Att: 2,298	Booked: McCann, Cardle, Gibson. Dismissed: Cardle.
30th	● Dundee	H	W 2–0	Att: 2,134	Scorers: Bell, Gibson.

APRIL
3rd	● Ross County	H	L 1–2	Att: 2,641	Scorers: Bell. Booked: McCann.
10th	● Ayr	A	W 1–2	Att: 1,367	Scorers: Campbell, McDougall. Booked: Bell, Woods, Gibson.
17th	● Inverness	A	L 2–0	Att: 3,728	Booked: Phinn, McCann.
24th	● Morton	H	W 4–1	Att: 2,532	Scorers: Bell^3, Phinn. Booked: Woods, Bell, Dowie.

MAY
1st	● Airdrie	A	W 0–1	Att: 1,864	Scorers: Phinn.

● Irn-Bru First Division ● Scottish Cup ○ Co-op Insurance Cup ● Challenge Cup

FIRST DIVISION GOALKEEPER STATS

Player	Appearances	Match starts	Completed matches	Sub appearances	Subbed off	Clean sheets	Yellow cards	Red cards
Greg Fleming	26	25	25	1	0	4	1	0
Greg Paterson	3	3	2	0	1	1	0	0
Chris Smith	8	8	8	0	0	1	0	0

FIRST DIVISION OUTFIELD PLAYER STATS

Player	Appearances	Match starts	Completed matches	Substitute appearances	Subbed off	Goals scored	Yellow cards	Red cards
Graham Bayne	16	15	12	1	3	3	3	0
Steven Bell	31	29	25	2	3	8	6	1
Alex Burke	27	25	16	2	9	0	1	0
Ross Campbell	13	3	1	10	2	1	0	0
Joe Cardle	25	16	6	9	9	5	5	1
Andy Dowie	32	32	31	0	1	0	5	0
Willie Gibson	34	30	18	4	11	9	5	1
Stephen Glass	1	1	1	0	0	0	1	0
David Graham	29	28	23	1	5	3	4	0
Chris Higgins	17	13	13	4	0	0	2	0
Graeme Holmes	17	6	0	11	5	0	0	1
Andy Kirk	21	17	12	4	5	8	0	0
Gary Mason	13	11	9	2	2	2	2	0
Austin McCann	30	28	27	2	1	0	5	0
Steven McDougall	22	17	5	5	12	5	1	0
Neil McGregor	24	24	21	0	3	1	2	0
Jim McIntyre	2	0	0	2	0	0	0	0
Scott Muirhead	7	2	1	5	1	0	0	0
Nick Phinn	33	16	7	17	9	5	1	0
Greg Ross	24	22	16	2	6	0	4	0
Paul Willis	2	0	0	2	0	0	0	0
Calum Woods	29	25	22	4	2	2	5	1

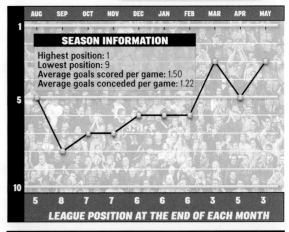

SEASON INFORMATION
Highest position: 1
Lowest position: 9
Average goals scored per game: 1.50
Average goals conceded per game: 1.22

AUG	SEP	OCT	NOV	DEC	JAN	FEB	MAR	APR	MAY
5	8	7	7	6	6	6	3	5	3

LEAGUE POSITION AT THE END OF EACH MONTH

LONGEST SEQUENCES

Wins	3	Undefeated home	6
(on two occasions)		(10/10/09–19/12/09)	
Losses	4	Undefeated away	5
(29/08/09–26/09/09)		(23/01/10–20/03/10)	
Draws	2	Without scoring	3
(on two occasions)		(29/08/09–19/09/09)	
Undefeated	8	Without conceding	2
(10/10/09–01/12/09)		(15/08/09–22/08/09)	
Without win	4	Scoring	7
(on two occasions)		(27/02/10–23/03/10)	

CARDS RECEIVED

53 5

EARLIEST STRIKE
STEVEN MCDOUGALL
(v Partick) 4:00

LATEST STRIKE
STEVEN BELL
(v Morton) 90:41

GOALS SCORED/CONCEDED
PER FIVE-MINUTE INTERVALS

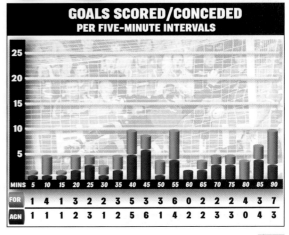

MINS	5	10	15	20	25	30	35	40	45	50	55	60	65	70	75	80	85	90
FOR	1	4	1	3	2	2	3	5	3	3	6	0	2	2	2	4	3	7
AGN	1	1	1	2	3	1	2	5	6	1	4	2	2	3	3	0	4	3

GREENOCK MORTON

MORTON completed a final-day escape act to ensure that they avoided a relegation play-off.

A six-match winless run dragged the Greenock side into the dogfight at the foot of the table, but they beat rock-bottom Ayr on the last day of the regular season to secure their status. The result was not enough for manager James Grady to keep his job, though, with the club replacing him with former Stirling boss Allan Moore in May.

It was a short spell in charge for Grady as he was the replacement for Davie Irons, who was sacked in September after Morton took just three points from their first six League games.

Grady earned what proved to be a crucial win over Airdrie in his first match in charge but he was unable to instill any sense of consistency during his time at the helm. However, he did come close to masterminding a shock Active Nation Scottish Cup result against Celtic in January, with the 'Ton eventually going down 1–0 at the fourth-round stage.

CLUB SUMMARY

FORMED	1874
MANAGER	Allan Moore
GROUND	Cappielow Park
CAPACITY	11,612
NICKNAME	The 'Ton
WEBSITE	www.gmfc.net

The New **Football Pools** PLAYER OF THE SEASON

Colin Stewart

OVERALL
P	W	D	L	F	A	GD
43	14	5	24	47	72	-25

IRN-BRU FIRST DIVISION
Pos	P	W	D	L	F	A	GD	Pts
8	36	11	4	21	40	65	-25	37

HOME
Pos	P	W	D	L	F	A	GD	Pts
8	18	6	4	8	21	24	-3	22

AWAY
Pos	P	W	D	L	F	A	GD	Pts
8	18	5	0	13	19	41	-22	15

CUP PROGRESS DETAILS
Competition	Round reached	Knocked out by
Scottish Cup	R4	Celtic
Co-op Insurance Cup	R2	Kilmarnock
Challenge Cup	R2	Ross County

BIGGEST WIN (ALL COMPS)
14/11/09 5–0 v Raith

BIGGEST DEFEAT (ALL COMPS)
29/08/09 0–5 v Partick

ATTENDANCE RECORD
HIGH	AVERAGE	Low
3,771	1,970	1,219
v Ayr (01/05/2010)		v Ross County (13/04/2010)

RESULTS 2009/10

JULY
26th	● Dumbarton	A	W 0–1	Att: 1,120	Scorers: Jenkins. Booked: Greacen, Masterton, MacFarlane.

AUGUST
1st	● Cowdenbeath	A	W 1–3	Att: 486	Scorers: MacFarlane, Weatherson[2]. Booked: Jenkins.
8th	● Dundee	A	L 1–0	Att: 5,449	Booked: Finlayson, Masterton, Graham.
15th	● Dunfermline	H	L 0–2	Att: 2,661	Booked: Greacen.
18th	● Ross County	A	L 2–1	Att: 588	Scorers: Masterton. Booked: Masterton.
22nd	● Ayr	A	W 0–2	Att: 2,266	Scorers: Weatherson[2]. Booked: Graham.
25th	● Kilmarnock	A	L 3–1	Att: 3,645	Scorers: McGuffie. Booked: Finlayson, Jenkins.
29th	● Partick	A	L 5–0	Att: 2,986	Booked: MacFarlane. Dismissed: Greacen.

SEPTEMBER
12th	● Inverness	H	L 0–3	Att: 1,956	Booked: McAlister.
19th	● Raith	A	L 3–0	Att: 2,040	Booked: Walker, MacFarlane, Greacen.
26th	● Airdrie	H	W 1–0	Att: 2,104	Scorers: Graham. Booked: Graham, MacGregor.

OCTOBER
3rd	● Queen of South	A	W 2–3	Att: 2,630	Scorers: Graham, Jenkins, Weatherson.
10th	● Ross County	H	L 0–1	Att: 2,154	Booked: MacFarlane, Weatherson.
17th	● Dundee	H	L 0–1	Att: 2,217	Booked: McManus.
24th	● Dunfermline	A	L 3–1	Att: 2,411	Scorers: McGuffie. Booked: Paartalu.
31st	● Inverness	A	L 4–1	Att: 3,021	Scorers: Paartalu. Booked: Paartalu.

NOVEMBER
7th	● Partick	H	L 0–2	Att: 2,738	
14th	● Raith	H	W 5–0	Att: 1,716	Scorers: Paartalu, Wake[2], Weatherson[2]. Booked: van Zanten.
21st	● Airdrie	A	W 2–4	Att: 1,164	Scorers: McGuffie, Wake[2], van Zanten. Booked: Paartalu.
28th	● Dumbarton	H	D 0–0	Att: 1,882	Booked: Reid.

DECEMBER
5th	● Dumbarton	A	W 0–1	Att: 1,495	Scorers: Graham. Booked: Paartalu, Graham.
8th	● Ross County	A	L 3–1	Att: 1,752	Scorers: Paartalu. Booked: Monti. Dismissed: Reid.
12th	● Queen of South	H	L 1–2	Att: 1,814	Scorers: Weatherson.
19th	● Dundee	A	L 3–1	Att: 4,259	Scorers: Weatherson. Booked: Monti.

JANUARY
4th	● Partick	A	L 1–0	Att: 2,190	
19th	● Celtic	H	L 0–1	Att: 10,191	Booked: Greacen, MacFarlane.
23rd	● Raith	A	W 1–2	Att: 1,702	Scorers: Weatherson[2]. Booked: Tidser, McGuffie.

FEBRUARY
13th	● Queen of South	A	W 1–2	Att: 2,611	Scorers: Masterton[2]. Booked: Masterton, Finlayson, Graham. Dismissed: Finlayson.
27th	● Dunfermline	H	L 1–2	Att: 1,776	Scorers: McGuffie. Booked: Greacen.

MARCH
6th	● Ayr	A	L 2–0	Att: 2,145	Booked: Shimmin, Greacen. Dismissed: Greacen.
13th	● Inverness	A	L 1–0	Att: 2,788	Booked: Masterton.
17th	● Airdrie	H	W 2–1	Att: 1,266	Scorers: MacGregor, Weatherson. Booked: Weatherson, Tidser, Simmons.
20th	● Partick	H	W 1–0	Att: 2,163	Scorers: McAlister. Booked: Masterton, Weatherson.
23rd	● Raith	H	D 1–1	Att: 1,415	Scorers: Simmons. Booked: McKinlay, Weatherson.
27th	● Airdrie	A	L 3–0	Att: 1,017	Booked: McKinlay. Dismissed: Cuthbert.
30th	● Ayr	A	W 1–0	Att: 1,289	Scorers: Masterton. Booked: Tidser, McAlister.

APRIL
3rd	● Queen of South	H	D 3–3	Att: 1,926	Scorers: Witteveen[3]. Booked: Witteveen.
6th	● Inverness	H	L 0–2	Att: 1,277	
13th	● Ross County	H	D 1–1	Att: 1,219	Scorers: Monti. Booked: Monti, Greacen, Graham.
17th	● Dundee	H	D 2–2	Att: 1,998	Scorers: Monti, Witteveen. Booked: Greacen.
24th	● Dunfermline	A	L 4–1	Att: 2,532	Scorers: Monti. Booked: Shimmin.
26th	● Ross County	A	L 2–1	Att: 1,830	Scorers: Witteveen. Booked: Witteveen, McGuffie, Simmons.

MAY
1st	● Ayr	H	W 2–1	Att: 3,771	Scorers: Greacen, Monti. Booked: Greacen, Monti.

● Irn-Bru First Division ● Scottish Cup ● Co-op Insurance Cup ● Challenge Cup

FIRST DIVISION GOALKEEPER STATS

Player	Appearances	Match starts	Completed matches	Sub appearances	Subbed off	Clean sheets	Yellow cards	Red cards
Kevin Cuthbert	5	5	4	0	0	1	0	1
Bryn Halliwell	1	1	1	0	0	0	0	0
Ryan McWilliams	3	3	3	0	0	1	0	0
Colin Stewart	28	27	27	1	0	3	0	0

FIRST DIVISION OUTFIELD PLAYER STATS

Player	Appearances	Match starts	Completed matches	Substitute appearances	Subbed off	Goals scored	Yellow cards	Red cards
Kevin Finlayson	31	27	24	4	2	0	2	1
James Grady	5	1	0	4	1	0	0	0
Brian Graham	22	10	3	12	7	2	5	0
Stewart Greacen	30	30	28	0	0	1	7	2
Ryan Harding	2	2	1	0	1	0	0	0
Allan Jenkins	24	18	13	6	5	1	0	0
Ryan Kane	4	0	0	4	0	0	0	0
Neil MacFarlane	16	16	8	0	8	0	3	0
David MacGregor	26	21	21	5	0	1	1	0
Steven Masterton	16	11	6	5	5	3	4	0
James McAlister	30	30	30	0	0	1	2	0
Ryan McGuffie	32	30	28	2	2	3	2	0
Kevin McKinlay	8	7	6	1	1	0	2	0
Allan McManus	12	12	12	0	0	0	0	0
Carlo Monti	20	16	11	4	5	4	4	0
Erik Paartalu	26	16	14	10	2	3	4	0
Alan Reid	13	13	10	0	2	0	0	1
Iain Russell	5	4	0	1	4	0	0	0
Dominic Shimmin	17	17	17	0	0	0	2	0
Donovan Simmons	14	7	6	7	1	1	2	0
Michael Tidser	13	13	8	0	5	0	3	0
Brian Wake	12	6	1	6	5	4	0	0
Alexander Walker	3	3	1	0	2	0	1	0
Peter Weatherson	33	31	17	2	14	10	4	0
David Witteveen	9	9	7	0	2	5	2	0
David van Zanten	6	6	6	0	0	1	1	0

AUG	SEP	OCT	NOV	DEC	JAN	FEB	MAR	APR	MAY

SEASON INFORMATION

Highest position: 5
Lowest position: 10
Average goals scored per game: 1.11
Average goals conceded per game: 1.81

LEAGUE POSITION AT THE END OF EACH MONTH

8 9 8 8 8 8 8 8 8 8

LONGEST SEQUENCES

Wins	2	Undefeated home	5
(on four occasions)		(17/03/10–03/04/10)	
Losses	5	Undefeated away	2
(10/10/09–07/11/09)		(23/01/10–13/02/10)	
Draws	2	Without scoring	3
(13/04/10–17/04/10)		(29/08/09–19/09/09)	
Undefeated	3	Without conceding	–
(17/03/10–23/03/10)		(–)	
Without win	6	Scoring	5
(03/04/10–26/04/10)		(14/11/09–19/12/09)	

CARDS RECEIVED

52   5

EARLIEST STRIKE

CARLO MONTI
(v Ross County) 5:40

LATEST STRIKE

DAVID WITTEVEEN
(v Queen of South) 91:54

GOALS SCORED/CONCEDED
PER FIVE-MINUTE INTERVALS

MINS	5	10	15	20	25	30	35	40	45	50	55	60	65	70	75	80	85	90
FOR	0	2	3	1	3	1	3	2	3	0	5	3	2	2	1	3	2	4
AGN	2	3	0	3	1	4	4	2	3	3	4	5	6	5	4	5	3	8

INVERNESS CALEDONIAN THISTLE

INVERNESS secured an immediate return to the Clydesdale Bank Premier League following their relegation at the end of 2008/09.

Terry Butcher's team ended the campaign on a 21-game unbeaten run in the League – including nine straight wins – to overhaul long-time favourites Dundee and secure the Irn-Bru First Division title with two matches to spare.

Key to Caley Thistle's success was their form away from the Caledonian Stadium, with only Ross County and Partick Thistle getting the better of them on the road in the League.

Former Stoke City striker Adam Rooney netted 24 times to fire his team to the top of the table and secure his position as the division's leading scorer in the process.

It was nearly a League and Cup double for Inverness, but they lost out 3–2 to Dundee in the final of the ALBA Challenge Cup, while they were eliminated in the Co-operative Insurance Cup and Active Nation Scottish Cup by Motherwell and Kilmarnock respectively.

CLUB SUMMARY

FORMED	1994
MANAGER	Terry Butcher
GROUND	Caledonian Stadium
CAPACITY	7,753
NICKNAME	Caley Thistle
WEBSITE	www.lctfc.co.uk

The New Football Pools PLAYER OF THE SEASON — Adam Rooney

OVERALL
P	W	D	L	F	A	GD
46	26	12	8	92	43	49

IRN-BRU FIRST DIVISION
Pos	P	W	D	L	F	A	GD	Pts
1	36	21	10	5	72	32	40	73

HOME
Pos	P	W	D	L	F	A	GD	Pts
2	18	11	4	3	36	20	16	37

AWAY
Pos	P	W	D	L	F	A	GD	Pts
1	18	10	6	2	36	12	24	36

CUP PROGRESS DETAILS
Competition	Round reached	Knocked out by
Scottish Cup	R5	Kilmarnock
Co-op Insurance Cup	R3	Motherwell
Challenge Cup	R-UP	Dundee

BIGGEST WIN (ALL COMPS)
24/04/10 7–0 v Ayr

BIGGEST DEFEAT (ALL COMPS)
06/02/10 0–3 v Kilmarnock

ATTENDANCE RECORD
HIGH	AVERAGE	LOW
6,031	3,501	2,008
v Dundee (01/05/2010)		v Airdrie (23/03/2010)

RESULTS 2009/10

JULY
25th	● Montrose	H	D 1-1	Att: 1,122	Scorers: McBain. Booked: Tokely. Inverness CT win 5-3 on penalties.

AUGUST
1st	● Annan	H	W 4-0	Att: 1,095	Scorers: Eagle, Imrie, Rooney, Sanchez. Booked: Imrie, Sanchez.
8th	● Dunfermline	A	W 0-1	Att: 3,258	Scorers: Cox. Bru.
15th	● Ayr	H	D 0-0	Att: 3,297	Booked: Bulvitis.
18th	● Stranraer	H	W 3-0	Att: 1,750	Scorers: Foran², Sanchez.
22nd	● Dundee	A	D 2-2	Att: 5,507	Scorers: Cox, Sanchez. Booked: Hayes.
25th	● Albion	H	W 4-0	Att: 681	Scorers: Bulvitis, Eagle, Munro, Rooney. Booked: Bulvitis, Tokely.
29th	● Ross County	H	L 1-3	Att: 5,474	Scorers: Hayes. Booked: Foran.

SEPTEMBER
6th	● Partick	A	D 1-1	Att: 1,746	Scorers: Sanchez. Booked: Tokely, Foran. AET – Score after 90 mins 1-1. Inverness win 4-3 on penalties.
12th	● Morton	A	W 0-3	Att: 1,956	Scorers: Foran, Proctor, Sanchez.
19th	● Airdrie	A	D 1-1	Att: 951	Scorers: Hayes.
22nd	● Motherwell	A	L 3-2	Att: 3,905	Scorers: Barrowman, Munro. Booked: Proctor, Golabek, Foran. Dismissed: Proctor. AET – Score after 90 mins 1-1.
26th	● Partick	H	L 2-3	Att: 3,218	Scorers: Foran, Rooney. Booked: Bulvitis, Munro.

OCTOBER
4th	● Ross County	H	W 1-0	Att: 2,275	Scorers: Eagle. Booked: Cox, Golabek.
10th	● Queen of South	H	L 1-3	Att: 3,011	Scorers: Hayes. Booked: Foran, Bulvitis, Cox.
13th	● Raith	A	W 0-1	Att: 2,014	Scorers: Proctor. Booked: Imrie.
17th	● Dunfermline	H	D 1-1	Att: 3,083	Scorers: Proctor. Booked: Tokely, Imrie.
24th	● Ayr	A	W 1-5	Att: 1,600	Scorers: Foran³, Imrie, Rooney. Booked: Tokely, Golabek.
31st	● Morton	H	W 4-1	Att: 3,021	Scorers: Bulvitis, Rooney³. Booked: Foran, Duncan.

NOVEMBER
7th	● Ross County	A	L 2-1	Att: 5,506	Scorers: Rooney. Booked: Duncan.
14th	● Airdrie	H	W 2-0	Att: 2,780	Scorers: Odhiambo, Sanchez. Booked: Munro.
22nd	● Dundee	N	L 3-2	Att: 8,031	Scorers: Bulvitis, Rooney. Booked: Bulvitis, Hayes. Dismissed: Imrie.
28th	● Partick	A	L 2-1	Att: 2,352	Scorers: Tokely. Booked: Munro.

DECEMBER
5th	● Queen of South	A	D 1-1	Att: 2,196	Scorers: Hayes. Booked: Odhiambo, Foran. Dismissed: Foran, Duncan.
12th	● Raith	H	W 1-0	Att: 2,994	Scorers: Rooney.
19th	● Dunfermline	A	D 0-0	Att: 2,280	
26th	● Dundee	H	D 1-1	Att: 3,660	Scorers: Rooney. Booked: Cox, Djebi-Zadi.

JANUARY
18th	● Motherwell	H	W 2-0	Att: 1,450	Scorers: Bulvitis, Imrie. Booked: Bulvitis.
23rd	● Airdrie	A	W 0-1	Att: 839	Scorers: Rooney. Booked: Cox.
30th	● Partick	H	W 2-1	Att: 3,107	Scorers: Hayes, Rooney. Booked: Hayes, Munro.

FEBRUARY
6th	● Kilmarnock	A	L 3-0	Att: 4,473	Booked: Cox.
13th	● Raith	A	W 0-4	Att: 1,568	Scorers: Bulvitis, Hayes, Rooney, Stratford. Booked: Golabek.
27th	● Ayr	H	D 3-3	Att: 2,843	Scorers: Foran, Hayes, Rooney. Booked: Proctor, Foran.

MARCH
6th	● Dundee	A	D 2-2	Att: 4,974	Scorers: Foran, Odhiambo. Booked: Cox, Munro.
9th	● Queen of South	H	W 3-1	Att: 3,003	Scorers: Rooney³. Booked: Golabek, Munro.
13th	● Morton	H	W 1-0	Att: 2,788	Scorers: Ross.
20th	● Ross County	A	D 0-0	Att: 5,928	Booked: Duncan, Tokely, Golabek.
23rd	● Airdrie	H	W 4-0	Att: 2,008	Scorers: Foran, Hayes, Munro, Rooney.
27th	● Partick	A	W 0-1	Att: 2,380	Scorers: Rooney. Booked: Bulvitis.
30th	● Ross County	H	W 3-0	Att: 5,411	Scorers: Foran, Hayes, Odhiambo. Booked: Hayes, Rooney.

APRIL
3rd	● Raith	H	W 4-3	Att: 3,562	Scorers: Foran², Odhiambo, Rooney. Booked: Cox, Munro.
6th	● Morton	A	W 0-2	Att: 1,277	Scorers: Foran, Rooney. Booked: Golabek, Duncan.
10th	● Queen of South	A	W 1-3	Att: 2,093	Scorers: Munro, Rooney².
17th	● Dunfermline	H	W 2-0	Att: 3,728	Scorers: Foran, Rooney.
24th	● Ayr	A	W 0-7	Att: 1,804	Scorers: Eagle, Foran, Hayes, Morrison, Odhiambo, Rooney, Sanchez. Booked: Eagle, Morrison.

MAY
1st	● Dundee	H	W 1-0	Att: 6,031	Scorers: Rooney. Booked: Bulvitis.

● Irn-Bru First Division ● Scottish Cup ● Co-op Insurance Cup ● Challenge Cup

FIRST DIVISION GOALKEEPER STATS

Player	Appearances	Match starts	Completed matches	Sub appearances	Subbed off	Clean sheets	Yellow cards	Red cards
Ryan Esson	36	36	36	0	0	18	0	0

FIRST DIVISION OUTFIELD PLAYER STATS

Player	Appearances	Match starts	Completed matches	Substitute appearances	Subbed off	Goals scored	Yellow cards	Red cards
Andrew Barrowman	5	1	0	4	1	0	0	0
Nauris Bulvitis	32	27	24	5	3	2	5	0
Lee Cox	33	27	25	6	2	2	5	0
Lionel Djebi-Zadi	11	10	9	1	1	0	1	0
Stuart Duff	3	3	3	0	0	0	0	0
Russell Duncan	26	23	20	3	2	0	4	1
Robert Eagle	19	7	1	12	6	1	1	0
Richie Foran	31	31	15	0	15	14	5	1
Stuart Golabek	24	24	24	0	0	0	5	0
Jonathan Hayes	35	29	19	6	10	10	3	0
Douglas Imrie	13	8	2	5	6	1	2	0
Roy McBain	7	2	1	5	1	0	0	0
Gavin Morrison	3	1	1	2	0	1	1	0
Grant Munro	35	35	35	0	0	2	7	0
Eric Odhiambo	23	16	0	7	16	5	1	0
David Proctor	34	31	27	3	4	3	1	0
Adam Rooney	35	27	22	8	5	24	1	0
Nicholas Ross	6	3	1	3	2	1	0	0
Danni Sanchez	32	19	5	13	14	4	0	0
Graeme Shinnie	1	1	0	0	1	0	0	0
Daniel Stratford	14	8	7	6	1	1	0	0
Ross Tokely	27	27	27	0	0	1	3	0

SEASON INFORMATION
Highest position: 1
Lowest position: 7
Average goals scored per game: 2.00
Average goals conceded per game: 0.89

LEAGUE POSITION AT THE END OF EACH MONTH

LONGEST SEQUENCES

Wins	9	Undefeated home	14
(23/03/10–01/05/10)		(17/10/09–01/05/10)	
Losses	2	Undefeated away	10
(26/09/09–10/10/09)		(05/12/09–24/04/10)	
Draws	2	Without scoring	–
(on three occasions)		(–)	
Undefeated	21	Without conceding	5
(05/12/09–01/05/10)		(13/03/10–30/03/10)	
Without win	3	Scoring	15
(on two occasions)		(22/08/09–12/12/09)	

CARDS RECEIVED
45 2

EARLIEST STRIKE
JONATHAN HAYES
(v Ayr) 1:51

LATEST STRIKE
ADAM ROONEY
(v Ayr) 94:00

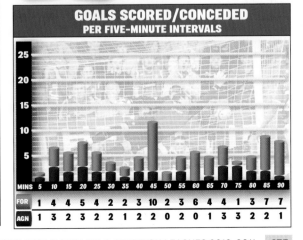

GOALS SCORED/CONCEDED PER FIVE-MINUTE INTERVALS

MINS	5	10	15	20	25	30	35	40	45	50	55	60	65	70	75	80	85	90
FOR	1	4	4	5	4	2	3	10	2	3	6	4	4	1	3	7	7
AGN	1	3	2	3	2	2	1	2	2	0	2	0	1	3	3	2	2	1

PARTICK THISTLE

PARTICK were unable to match their achievements of the previous season as they ended 2009/10 in the bottom half of the table. The Jags had finished second in the Irn-Bru First Division 12 months earlier, but they failed to find any consistency this time around.

They managed to fight off the advances of Dundee for manager Ian McCall in March, but they did miss the power of midfielder Gary Harkins, who left for Dens Park in June 2009.

However, it was still a memorable season for Partick fans, who celebrated their 100th year at Firhill with several impressive home wins, including a 5–0 victory over Morton and a 2–1 success against eventual champions Inverness.

Their form suffered a slump in the second half of the season, as an Active Nation Scottish Cup third-round defeat to Dundee kick-started a run of 11 defeats in 15 games, but they did beat Ross County and Queen of the South in their final two matches to at least end the campaign on a high.

CLUB SUMMARY

FORMED	1876
MANAGER	Ian McCall
GROUND	Firhill Stadium
CAPACITY	10,887
NICKNAME	The Jags
WEBSITE	www.ptfc.co.uk

The New **Football Pools** PLAYER OF THE SEASON — **Jonny Tuffey**

OVERALL
P	W	D	L	F	A	GD
42	17	7	18	57	47	10

IRN-BRU FIRST DIVISION
Pos	P	W	D	L	F	A	GD	Pts
6	36	14	6	16	43	40	3	48

HOME
Pos	P	W	D	L	F	A	GD	Pts
6	18	9	3	6	23	15	8	30

AWAY
Pos	P	W	D	L	F	A	GD	Pts
6	18	5	3	10	20	25	-5	18

CUP PROGRESS DETAILS
Competition	Round reached	Knocked out by
Scottish Cup	R4	Dundee Utd
Co-op Insurance Cup	R2	Queen of South
Challenge Cup	QF	Inverness

BIGGEST WIN (ALL COMPS)
18/08/09 6–1 v Forfar

BIGGEST DEFEAT (ALL COMPS)
23/01/10 1–4 v Dunfermline

ATTENDANCE RECORD
HIGH	AVERAGE	LOW
4,453	2,572	1,151
v Dundee (05/12/2009)		v Raith (19/04/2010)

RESULTS 2009/10

JULY
25th	● Airdrie	A	W 0-1	Att: 1,325	Scorers: Buchanan.

AUGUST
1st	● Berwick	H	W 5-1	Att: 1,472	Scorers: Buchanan2, Erskine2, Hodge. Booked: Paton.
8th	● Ayr	A	D 1-1	Att: 3,043	Scorers: Donnelly. Booked: Maxwell.
15th	● Ross County	H	D 0-0	Att: 2,391	Booked: Cairney, Paton, Hamilton. Dismissed: McKeown.
18th	● Forfar	A	W 1-6	Att: 532	Scorers: Cairney, Donnelly, Doolan, Hamilton2, Rowson. Booked: Cairney.
22nd	● Queen of South	A	L 1-0	Att: 2,915	Booked: Paton, Archibald.
25th	● Queen of South	H	L 1-2	Att: 1,527	Scorers: Donnelly.
29th	● Morton	H	W 5-0	Att: 2,986	Scorers: Buchanan2, Cairney, Corcoran2. Booked: Archibald.

SEPTEMBER
6th	● Inverness	H	D 1-1	Att: 1,746	Scorers: Buchanan. Booked: Archibald, Cairney, Buchanan. AET - Score after 90 mins 1-1. Inverness win 4-3 on penalties.
12th	● Raith	A	D 1-1	Att: 2,370	Scorers: Doolan. Booked: Hamilton. Dismissed: Buchanan.
19th	● Dunfermline	H	W 2-0	Att: 3,163	Scorers: Cairney, Donnelly.
26th	● Inverness	A	W 2-3	Att: 3,218	Scorers: Archibald, Buchanan2. Booked: Paton, Kinniburgh.

OCTOBER
3rd	● Airdrie	H	W 2-0	Att: 2,839	Scorers: Donnelly, Hodge. Booked: Paton.
10th	● Dundee	A	L 2-0	Att: 5,364	Booked: Maxwell.
17th	● Ayr	H	W 2-0	Att: 3,055	Scorers: Buchanan, Corcoran. Booked: Buchanan.
24th	● Ross County	A	D 2-2	Att: 2,369	Scorers: Buchanan, Erskine. Booked: Robertson, Paton.
31st	● Raith	H	L 1-2	Att: 3,084	Scorers: Donnelly.

NOVEMBER
7th	● Morton	A	W 0-2	Att: 2,738	Scorers: Buchanan, Donnelly.
14th	● Dunfermline	A	L 3-1	Att: 3,109	Scorers: Cairney. Booked: Adams, Rowson, Maxwell.
28th	● Inverness	H	W 2-1	Att: 2,352	Scorers: Adams, Lovell. Booked: Cairney.

DECEMBER
5th	● Dundee	H	L 0-2	Att: 4,453	Booked: Donnelly, Archibald.
12th	● Airdrie	A	W 2-5	Att: 1,321	Scorers: Cairney, Donnelly, Lovell2, McKeown. Booked: Lovell.
26th	● Queen of South	H	D 2-2	Att: 2,766	Scorers: Adams, Paton. Booked: Donnelly, Lovell.

JANUARY
4th	● Morton	H	W 1-0	Att: 2,190	Scorers: Cairney.
9th	● Dundee Utd	H	L 0-2	Att: 4,002	Booked: Paton, Cairney, Erskine.
16th	● Raith	A	L 1-0	Att: 1,951	Booked: Shields, Cairney, Paton.
23rd	● Dunfermline	H	L 1-4	Att: 1,549	Scorers: Buchanan. Booked: Shields, Archibald.
30th	● Inverness	A	L 2-1	Att: 3,107	Scorers: Corcoran. Booked: Corrigan. Dismissed: Maxwell.

FEBRUARY
13th	● Airdrie	H	W 2-0	Att: 2,404	Scorers: Cairney2. Booked: Hodge, Rowson. Dismissed: Rowson.
20th	● Dundee	A	L 1-0	Att: 5,216	Booked: Archibald.
27th	● Ross County	H	W 2-1	Att: 2,192	Scorers: Buchanan, Hodge.

MARCH
6th	● Queen of South	A	L 1-0	Att: 2,674	Booked: Corrigan, Hodge.
10th	● Ayr	A	L 1-0	Att: 1,505	Booked: Archibald.
20th	● Morton	A	L 1-0	Att: 2,163	Booked: Cairney.
23rd	● Dunfermline	H	W 1-2	Att: 2,401	Scorers: Buchanan, Donnelly. Booked: Paton.
27th	● Inverness	A	L 0-1	Att: 2,380	

APRIL
3rd	● Airdrie	A	L 2-0	Att: 1,142	
10th	● Dundee	H	L 0-1	Att: 2,545	Booked: Boyle.
17th	● Ayr	H	L 0-1	Att: 1,877	Booked: Paton.
19th	● Raith	H	D 0-0	Att: 1,151	
24th	● Ross County	A	W 1-2	Att: 2,175	Scorers: Donnelly, Grehan. Booked: Donnelly, Halliwell.

MAY
1st	● Queen of South	H	W 1-0	Att: 2,912	Scorers: Doolan.

● Irn-Bru First Division ● Scottish Cup ● Co-op Insurance Cup ● Challenge Cup

FIRST DIVISION GOALKEEPER STATS

Player	Appearances	Match starts	Completed matches	Sub appearances	Subbed off	Clean sheets	Yellow cards	Red cards
David McGurn	35	35	35	0	0	10	2	0
Gary O'Connor	1	1	1	0	0	0	0	0

FIRST DIVISION OUTFIELD PLAYER STATS

Player	Appearances	Match starts	Completed matches	Substitute appearances	Subbed off	Goals scored	Yellow cards	Red cards
Javier Amaya	5	1	0	4	1	0	1	0
David Armstrong	8	7	4	1	2	1	2	1
Kevin Brown	1	1	1	0	0	0	0	0
Lee Bryce	8	0	0	8	0	0	0	0
Greg Cameron	2	2	1	0	1	0	0	0
Mark Campbell	16	15	13	1	0	1	4	2
Damian Casalinuovo	3	3	1	0	2	2	1	0
Javier Corredera	1	1	0	0	1	1	0	0
Iain Davidson	20	18	13	2	5	1	6	0
Laurie Ellis	29	29	26	0	3	1	1	0
Mark Ferry	27	11	10	16	1	1	2	0
Theirry Gathuessi	13	9	6	4	3	0	4	0
Douglas Hill	29	26	18	3	7	2	8	1
Jamie Mackie	3	0	0	3	0	0	0	0
Jamie Mole	8	6	1	2	5	1	0	0
Grant Murray	34	34	33	0	0	3	8	1
Johnny Russell	23	18	8	5	10	4	3	0
Mark Serry	1	0	0	1	0	0	0	0
Dene Shields	9	3	0	6	3	0	0	0
Stephen Simmons	19	17	11	2	4	1	6	2
Robert Sloan	27	10	4	17	6	1	2	0
Darren Smith	27	17	6	10	11	1	3	0
Kevin Smith	5	4	2	1	2	2	0	0
Gregory Tade	32	31	23	1	7	5	6	1
Allan Walker	35	34	31	1	3	3	1	0
Bryan Wallas	4	3	0	1	3	1	0	0
Craig Wedderburn	4	0	0	4	0	0	0	0
Graham Weir	23	13	3	10	10	0	4	0
Iain Williamson	27	25	12	2	13	4	2	0
Craig Wilson	21	21	19	0	2	0	4	0

SEASON INFORMATION

Highest position: 1
Lowest position: 9
Average goals scored per game: 1.00
Average goals conceded per game: 1.31

	AUG	SEP	OCT	NOV	DEC	JAN	FEB	MAR	APR	MAY
	1	4	3	6	7	7	7	7	7	7

LEAGUE POSITION AT THE END OF EACH MONTH

LONGEST SEQUENCES

Wins	2	Undefeated home	3	
(22/08/09–29/08/09)		(on two occasions)		
Losses	3	Undefeated away	3	
(23/01/10–06/03/10)		(08/08/09–29/08/09)		
Draws	2	Without scoring	3	
(on two occasions)		(on three occasions)		
Undefeated	6	Without conceding	2	
(08/08/09–19/09/09)		(on two occasions)		
Without win	5	Scoring	7	
(on two occasions)		(09/03/10–07/04/10)		

CARDS RECEIVED

70   8

EARLIEST STRIKE

GRANT MURRAY
(v Ayr) 3:17

LATEST STRIKE

STEPHEN SIMMONS
(v Ayr) 90:32

GOALS SCORED/CONCEDED
PER FIVE-MINUTE INTERVALS

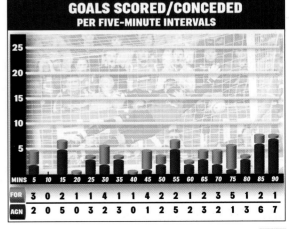

MINS	5	10	15	20	25	30	35	40	45	50	55	60	65	70	75	80	85	90
FOR	3	0	2	1	1	4	1	1	4	2	2	1	2	3	5	1	2	1
AGN	2	0	5	0	3	2	3	0	1	2	5	2	3	2	1	3	6	7

ROSS COUNTY

ROSS COUNTY enjoyed arguably the greatest season in their history as they reached the Active Nation Scottish Cup final.

Derek Adams' men stunned Hibernian and Celtic to set up their first ever trip to the final, but the fairytale ended with a 3–0 defeat to Dundee United at Hampden. That took nothing away from the Highland club, who only joined the Scottish Football League 16 years ago.

County were also in the race for promotion to the Clydesdale Bank Premier League until the last month of the season, when fixture congestion caused by their Scottish Cup run and the worst winter in decades finally caught up with them.

Fifth place still represented their highest League finish, while they also claimed the scalp of top-tier side Hamilton in the Co-operative Insurance Cup. They almost reached a second straight ALBA Challenge Cup final, but lost in the semi-final to eventual First Division champions Inverness.

CLUB SUMMARY

FORMED	1929
MANAGER	Derek Adams
GROUND	Victoria Park
CAPACITY	6,310
NICKNAME	The Staggies
WEBSITE	www.rosscountyfootballclub.co.uk

The New **Football Pools** PLAYER OF THE SEASON

Richard Brittain

OVERALL
P	W	D	L	F	A	GD
50	25	12	13	84	58	26

IRN-BRU FIRST DIVISION
Pos	P	W	D	L	F	A	GD	Pts
5	36	15	11	10	46	44	2	56

HOME
Pos	P	W	D	L	F	A	GD	Pts
4	18	9	6	3	28	20	8	33

AWAY
Pos	P	W	D	L	F	A	GD	Pts
3	18	6	5	7	18	24	-6	23

CUP PROGRESS DETAILS
Competition	Round reached	Knocked out by
Scottish Cup	R-UP	Dundee Utd
Co-op Insurance Cup	R3	Dundee Utd
Challenge Cup	SF	Inverness

BIGGEST WIN (ALL COMPS)
06/02/10 9–0 v Stirling

BIGGEST DEFEAT (ALL COMPS)
01/05/10 1–4 v Raith

ATTENDANCE RECORD
HIGH	AVERAGE	Low
5,928	2,465	1,752
v Inverness (20/03/2010)		v Morton (08/12/2009)

RESULTS 2009/10

JULY
25th ● Alloa ... H ... W 3–2 ... Att: 748 ... Scorers: Gardyne3. Booked: Girvan, Vigurs.

AUGUST
1st ● Montrose ... H ... W 5–0 ... Att: 768 ... Scorers: Craig, Gardyne2, Morrison, Stewart. Booked: Keddie.
8th ● Airdrie ... H ... W 2–1 ... Att: 1,781 ... Scorers: Di Giacomo, Wood. Booked: Lawson, Keddie.
15th ● Partick ... A ... D 0–0 ... Att: 2,391 ... Booked: Keddie, Brittain, Wood, Watt, Morrison. Dismissed: Miller.
18th ● Morton ... H ... W 2–1 ... Att: 588 ... Scorers: Lawson, Wood.
22nd ● Raith ... L 0–1 ... Att: 2,088 ... Booked: Watt, Vigurs, Boyd, Brittain, Kettlewell, Wood.
25th ● Hamilton ... H ... W 2–1 ... Att: 764 ... Scorers: Brittain, Di Giacomo.
29th ● Inverness ... A ... W 1–3 ... Att: 5,474 ... Scorers: Brittain, Di Giacomo, Vigurs.

SEPTEMBER
6th ● Queen of South ... H ... W 2–0 ... Att: 964 ... Scorers: Craig, Di Giacomo. Booked: Kettlewell.
12th ● Queen of South ... H ... W 3–2 ... Att: 1,992 ... Scorers: Brittain, Craig, Gardyne. Booked: Watt, Keddie.
19th ● Ayr ... H ... W 2–1 ... Att: 1,885 ... Scorers: Brittain, Craig. Booked: Keddie, McGovern. Dismissed: Keddie.
22nd ● Dundee Utd ... H ... L 0–2 ... Att: 1,986 ... Dismissed: Scott.
26th ● Dundee ... A ... L 2–0 ... Att: 4,682

OCTOBER
4th ● Inverness ... A ... L 1–0 ... Att: 2,275 ... Booked: Kettlewell, Watt.
10th ● Morton ... A ... W 0–1 ... Att: 2,154 ... Scorers: Wood. Booked: Wood, Brittain.
13th ● Dunfermline ... H ... D 0–0 ... Att: 1,757
17th ● Airdrie ... A ... W 0–1 ... Att: 756 ... Scorers: Wood. Booked: Morrison, Wood, Moore.
24th ● Partick ... H ... D 2–2 ... Att: 2,369 ... Scorers: Gardyne, Lawson. Booked: Scott, Watt. Dismissed: Scott.
31st ● Queen of South ... A ... L 2–0 ... Att: 2,245 ... Booked: Brittain.

NOVEMBER
7th ● Inverness ... H ... W 2–1 ... Att: 5,506 ... Scorers: Boyd, Gardyne. Booked: McGovern, Vigurs.
14th ● Ayr ... A ... D 1–1 ... Att: 1,213 ... Scorers: Boyd. Booked: Miller, Morrison, Gardyne.
28th ● Berwick ... H ... W 5–1 ... Att: 819 ... Scorers: Craig, Di Giacomo2, Lawson, Wood. Booked: Kettlewell, Gardyne.

DECEMBER
1st ● Dundee ... H ... L 0–1 ... Att: 2,005 ... Booked: Brittain, Lawson, Craig.
8th ● Morton ... H ... W 3–1 ... Att: 1,752 ... Scorers: Brittain, Scott, Wood. Booked: Miller.
12th ● Dunfermline ... A ... D 3–3 ... Att: 2,379 ... Scorers: Brittain, Lawson, Vigurs.
19th ● Airdrie ... H ... W 5–3 ... Att: 1,823 ... Scorers: Brittain2, Craig, Gardyne, Scott. Booked: Craig, Kettlewell, Boyd, Keddie.

JANUARY
18th ● Inverurie Loco Works ... H ... W 4–0 ... Att: 835 ... Scorers: Craig2, Miller, Morrison.
23rd ● Ayr ... H ... W 1–0 ... Att: 1,935 ... Scorers: Boyd. Booked: Keddie.
30th ● Dundee ... A ... W 0–1 ... Att: 4,912 ... Scorers: Lawson. Booked: Wood, Gardyne, Lawson.

FEBRUARY
6th ● Stirling ... H ... W 9–0 ... Att: 1,365 ... Scorers: Brittain, Gardyne2, Keddie, Kettlewell, Morrison, Wood3. Booked: Kettlewell.
13th ● Dunfermline ... H ... D 2–2 ... Att: 2,213 ... Scorers: Lawson, Watt. Booked: Miller, Morrison, Lawson, Watt.
27th ● Partick ... A ... L 2–1 ... Att: 2,192 ... Booked: Barrowman.

MARCH
6th ● Raith ... H ... W 1–0 ... Att: 2,033 ... Scorers: Brittain. Booked: Vigurs.
9th ● Raith ... A ... L 2–1 ... Att: 1,186 ... Scorers: Barrowman. Booked: Scott, Boyd.
13th ● Hibernian ... A ... D 2–2 ... Att: 9,857 ... Scorers: Gardyne, Murray OG. Booked: Brittain, Lawson.
20th ● Inverness ... H ... D 0–0 ... Att: 5,928 ... Booked: Morrison.
23rd ● Hibernian ... H ... W 2–1 ... Att: 5,607 ... Scorers: Boyd, Wood.
27th ● Dundee ... H ... D 1–1 ... Att: 3,295 ... Scorers: Craig. Booked: Miller, Keddie, Kettlewell.
30th ● Inverness ... A ... L 3–0 ... Att: 5,411 ... Booked: Craig. Dismissed: Keddie.

APRIL
3rd ● Dunfermline ... A ... W 1–2 ... Att: 2,641 ... Scorers: Barrowman, Vigurs. Booked: Vigurs, Gardyne, Scott.
6th ● Queen of South ... H ... D 1–1 ... Att: 2,004 ... Scorers: Boyd. Booked: Keddie.
10th ● Celtic ... A ... W 0–2 ... Att: 24,535 ... Scorers: Craig, Scott. Booked: Miller.
13th ● Morton ... A ... D 1–1 ... Att: 1,219 ... Scorers: Gardyne. Booked: Keddie, Vigurs, Brittain.
17th ● Airdrie ... A ... D 1–1 ... Att: 798 ... Scorers: Craig. Booked: Keddie.
20th ● Queen of South ... A ... L 1–0 ... Att: 1,183 ... Booked: Kettlewell, Barrowman.
24th ● Partick ... A ... L 1–2 ... Att: 2,175 ... Scorers: Di Giacomo. Booked: Brittain.
26th ● Morton ... H ... W 2–1 ... Att: 1,830 ... Scorers: Barrowman, Brittain. Booked: Kettlewell.
28th ● Ayr ... A ... W 0–1 ... Att: 1,032 ... Scorers: Barrowman. Booked: Kettlewell, Lawson.

MAY
1st ● Raith ... A ... L 4–1 ... Att: 1,935 ... Scorers: Morrison. Booked: Watt.
15th ● Dundee Utd ... N ... L 3–0 ... Att: 47,122 ... Booked: Miller, Wood.

● Irn-Bru First Division ● Scottish Cup ● Co-op Insurance Cup ● Challenge Cup

actim

FIRST DIVISION GOALKEEPER STATS

Player	Appearances	Match starts	Completed matches	Sub appearances	Subbed off	Clean sheets	Yellow cards	Red cards
Joseph Malin	1	1	1	0	0	0	0	0
Michael McGovern	35	35	35	0	0	9	2	0

FIRST DIVISION OUTFIELD PLAYER STATS

Player	Appearances	Match starts	Completed matches	Substitute appearances	Subbed off	Goals scored	Yellow cards	Red cards
Andrew Barrowman	14	12	7	2	5	5	1	0
Scott Boyd	31	29	29	2	0	4	3	0
Richard Brittain	34	34	31	0	3	9	7	0
Steven Craig	24	12	5	12	7	5	3	0
Paul Di Giacomo	31	20	7	11	13	3	0	0
Michael Gardyne	34	30	17	4	13	5	3	0
Graham Girvan	4	3	2	1	1	0	0	0
Ross Grant	1	0	0	1	0	0	0	0
Alexander Keddie	30	30	28	0	0	0	10	2
Stuart Kettlewell	31	22	9	9	13	0	6	0
Paul Lawson	28	25	20	3	5	4	5	0
Gary Miller	32	31	26	1	4	0	4	1
Daniel Moore	3	0	0	3	0	0	1	0
Scott Morrison	35	35	33	0	2	1	5	0
Martin Scott	30	20	16	10	3	2	3	1
Grant Smith	4	1	1	3	0	0	0	0
Robbie Stephen	1	1	1	0	0	0	0	0
John Stewart	2	0	0	2	0	0	0	0
Iain Vigurs	35	25	12	10	13	3	5	0
Steven Watt	19	16	13	3	3	1	6	0
Garry Wood	30	14	6	16	8	4	5	0

	AUG	SEP	OCT	NOV	DEC	JAN	FEB	MAR	APR	MAY

LEAGUE POSITION AT THE END OF EACH MONTH
3 2 4 4 3 2 2 4 4 5

SEASON INFORMATION
Highest position: 1
Lowest position: 10
Average goals scored per game: 1.28
Average goals conceded per game: 1.22

LONGEST SEQUENCES

Wins	3	Undefeated home	8
(on two occasions)		(08/12/09–06/04/10)	
Losses	2	Undefeated away	3
(20/04/10–24/04/10)		(on two occasions)	
Draws	3	Without scoring	2
(06/04/10–17/04/10)		(15/08/09–22/08/09)	
Undefeated	6	Without conceding	3
(08/12/09–13/02/10)		(10/10/09–17/10/09)	
Without win	5	Scoring	9
(06/04/10–24/04/10)		(08/12/09–09/03/10)	

CARDS RECEIVED
69 4

EARLIEST STRIKE
STEVEN CRAIG
(v Airdrie) 1:00

LATEST STRIKE
ANDREW BARROWMAN
(v Morton) 91:37

GOALS SCORED/CONCEDED
PER FIVE-MINUTE INTERVALS

MINS	5	10	15	20	25	30	35	40	45	50	55	60	65	70	75	80	85	90
FOR	1	2	3	3	1	2	4	2	2	5	3	1	2	3	1	5	2	4
AGN	2	2	1	1	1	5	4	3	2	1	6	3	2	1	3	3	3	1

ALLOA ATHLETIC

ALLOA missed out on the Irn-Bru Second Division title on goal difference before losing in the semi-final of the play-offs.

Although they won all four meetings with champions Stirling during the regular season, they were not able to finish above their rivals. Allan Maitland's side then claimed an encouraging 1–1 draw in the first leg of their play-off semi-final at Cowdenbeath, but they were beaten 2–0 in the second leg.

Despite that disappointment, a second-place finish represented a big improvement on the previous campaign, when the Wasps had finished eighth. They made a good start this time around, recording the first of their four wins over Stirling in September courtesy of an Andy Scott goal.

Alloa were top of the table at the start of April, but successive defeats to Brechin, Dumbarton and Peterhead when it mattered most cost them dear as they narrowly missed out on promotion.

CLUB SUMMARY

FORMED	1878
MANAGER	Allan Maitland
GROUND	Recreation Park
CAPACITY	3,100
NICKNAME	The Wasps
WEBSITE	www.alloaathletic.co.uk

The New **Football Pools** PLAYER OF THE SEASON

David Crawford

OVERALL
P	W	D	L	F	A	GD
42	20	10	12	53	43	10

IRN-BRU SECOND DIVISION
Pos	P	W	D	L	F	A	GD	Pts
2	36	19	8	9	49	35	14	65

HOME
Pos	P	W	D	L	F	A	GD	Pts
2	18	11	2	5	27	21	6	35

AWAY
Pos	P	W	D	L	F	A	GD	Pts
2	18	8	6	4	22	14	8	30

CUP PROGRESS DETAILS
Competition	Round reached	Knocked out by
Scottish Cup	R4	St Mirren
Co-op Insurance Cup	R2	Dundee Utd
Challenge Cup	R1	Ross County

BIGGEST WIN (ALL COMPS)
13/03/10 3–0 v Stirling

BIGGEST DEFEAT (ALL COMPS)
14/11/09 1–4 v Stenhousemuir

ATTENDANCE RECORD
High	Average	Low
1,201	658	394
v Stirling (12/09/2009)		v Brechin (12/12/2009)

RESULTS 2009/10

JULY
25th	Ross County	A	L 3–2	Att: 748	Scorers: Spence, Watt OG. Booked: Grant, Agnew, McClune, Walker, Scott. Dismissed: Carroll.

AUGUST
1st	Airdrie	A	D 0–0	Att: 756	Booked: Walker. Dismissed: Anderson. AET – Score after 90 mins 0–0. Alloa win 4–3 on penalties.
8th	Dumbarton	A	W 1–3	Att: 864	Scorers: Carrigan, Grant, Noble. Booked: McClune, Noble, Carroll, Grant.
15th	Peterhead	H	W 1–0	Att: 446	Scorers: Noble.
22nd	Cowdenbeath	A	D 1–1	Att: 369	Scorers: Scott. Booked: Brown.
25th	Dundee Utd	H	L 0–2	Att: 1,000	Booked: Kerr.
29th	Clyde	A	W 0–1	Att: 801	Scorers: Carrigan.

SEPTEMBER
12th	Stirling	H	W 1–0	Att: 1,201	Scorers: Scott. Booked: Brown, Gilhaney.
19th	Stenhousemuir	A	L 1–0	Att: 727	Booked: Walker, Russell, Buist.
26th	Arbroath	H	L 0–1	Att: 469	Booked: Carroll, Buist. Dismissed: Grant.

OCTOBER
3rd	East Fife	H	D 0–0	Att: 580	Booked: Gilhaney.
10th	Brechin	A	L 2–1	Att: 417	Scorers: Grant.
17th	Dumbarton	H	L 1–3	Att: 575	Scorers: Gilhaney. Booked: Grant, Townsley.
24th	Peterhead	A	D 0–0	Att: 485	Booked: McCafferty.
31st	Clyde	H	W 2–0	Att: 649	Scorers: Carrigan, Noble.

NOVEMBER
7th	Stirling	A	W 0–1	Att: 986	Scorers: Scott. Booked: Brown, McCafferty, Carroll.
14th	Stenhousemuir	H	L 1–4	Att: 544	Scorers: Buist. Booked: Brown, Scott.
28th	Cowdenbeath	A	D 0–0	Att: 377	Booked: Townsley, Noble.

DECEMBER
2nd	Arbroath	A	D 2–2	Att: 328	Scorers: Ferguson, Russell. Booked: McClune, Walker.
5th	East Fife	A	W 0–2	Att: 509	Scorers: Carroll, Russell. Booked: Russell, Carroll.
8th	Cowdenbeath	H	W 1–0	Att: 423	Scorers: Gilhaney. Booked: Grant, Walker.
12th	Brechin	H	W 2–1	Att: 394	Scorers: Agnew, Carrigan. Booked: Brown, Scott.

JANUARY
9th	St Mirren	A	L 3–1	Att: 2,587	
23rd	Stenhousemuir	A	W 0–2	Att: 554	Scorers: Ferguson, Prunty. Booked: Scott.
30th	Arbroath	H	W 1–0	Att: 535	Scorers: Prunty. Booked: Grant, Scott.

FEBRUARY
6th	Brechin	A	D 1–1	Att: 434	Scorers: Noble. Booked: Grant, Bloom.
9th	Cowdenbeath	H	W 2–1	Att: 638	Scorers: Noble, Prunty. Booked: Walker, Noble.
13th	East Fife	H	W 2–0	Att: 670	Scorers: Noble[2].
27th	Peterhead	H	W 2–1	Att: 448	Scorers: Noble, MacDonald OG.

MARCH
6th	Clyde	H	D 2–2	Att: 628	Scorers: McClune, Scott.
9th	Dumbarton	A	L 3–1	Att: 552	Scorers: Smith OG. Booked: Walker, Townsley. Dismissed: Walker.
13th	Stirling	A	W 0–3	Att: 1,036	Scorers: Gormley, Prunty[2]. Booked: Hay, Carroll, Grant.
16th	Cowdenbeath	A	D 1–1	Att: 413	Scorers: Ferguson. Booked: Walker, Brown, Grant, Stevenson, Carroll. Dismissed: Scott.
20th	Stenhousemuir	H	W 2–1	Att: 550	Scorers: Gormley, Prunty.
23rd	Stirling	H	W 2–1	Att: 1,147	Scorers: Carroll, Walker. Booked: Brown, Walker.
27th	Arbroath	A	D 0–0	Att: 604	Booked: Brown, McClune.

APRIL
3rd	East Fife	A	W 0–1	Att: 637	Scorers: McAvoy. Booked: Buist, McAvoy.
7th	Clyde	A	W 0–2	Att: 465	Scorers: Noble, Prunty.
10th	Brechin	H	L 2–3	Att: 626	Scorers: Noble, Walker. Booked: Grant.
17th	Dumbarton	H	L 1–2	Att: 622	Scorers: Scott. Booked: McClune, McAvoy. Dismissed: McClune.
24th	Peterhead	A	L 2–0	Att: 561	Booked: Gormley, Gilhaney.

MAY
1st	Cowdenbeath	H	W 3–1	Att: 1,125	Scorers: Prunty, Scott[2].
5th	Cowdenbeath	A	D 1–1	Att: 578	Scorers: Gormley. Booked: Carroll, Hay.
8th	Cowdenbeath	H	L 0–2	Att: 1,234	Booked: Gormley, Grant, McCafferty. Agg: 1–3.

● Irn-Bru Second Division/Play-offs ● Scottish Cup ● Co-op Insurance Cup ● Challenge Cup

IRN BRU
SCOTTISH FOOTBALL LEAGUE

SECOND DIVISION GOALKEEPER STATS

Player	Appearances	Match starts	Completed matches	Sub appearances	Subbed off	Clean sheets	Yellow cards	Red cards
David Crawford	36	36	36	0	0	16	0	0

SECOND DIVISION OUTFIELD PLAYER STATS

Player	Appearances	Match starts	Completed matches	Substitute appearances	Subbed off	Goals scored	Yellow cards	Red cards
Scott Agnew	15	11	9	4	2	1	0	0
James Bloom	5	5	4	0	1	0	1	0
Mark Brown	15	14	13	1	1	0	8	0
Scott Buist	24	23	19	1	4	1	3	0
Brian Carrigan	13	11	4	2	7	4	0	0
Gary Carroll	29	19	10	10	9	2	6	0
Christopher Craig	4	1	0	3	1	0	0	0
Brown Ferguson	27	25	21	2	4	3	0	0
Mark Gilhaney	18	15	7	3	8	1	3	0
David Gormley	17	7	2	10	5	2	1	0
John Grant	31	29	25	2	3	2	7	1
Jamie Hay	6	0	0	6	0	0	1	0
Hugh Kerr	13	2	0	11	3	0	0	0
Danny Main	2	1	1	1	0	0	0	0
Declan McAvoy	8	7	5	1	2	1	2	0
Marc McCafferty	18	16	13	2	3	0	2	0
David McClune	26	26	23	0	2	1	4	1
Stuart Noble	29	24	16	5	8	10	2	0
Ross Philp	5	0	0	5	0	0	0	0
Bryan Prunty	18	18	12	0	6	8	0	0
Iain Russell	6	4	3	2	1	2	2	0
Andrew Scott	33	27	14	6	12	7	4	1
Greig Spence	1	0	0	1	0	0	0	0
Anthony Stevenson	6	5	4	1	1	0	1	0
Jason Thomson	3	0	0	3	0	0	0	0
Chris Townsley	21	18	17	3	1	0	2	0
Scott Walker	31	31	29	0	1	2	6	1
Kevin Welsh	3	3	2	0	1	0	0	0
Douglas Wilson	4	0	0	4	0	0	0	0

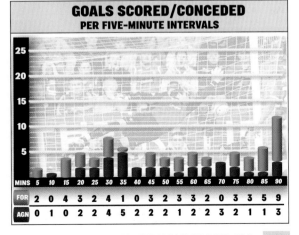

AUG	SEP	OCT	NOV	DEC	JAN	FEB	MAR	APR	MAY

SEASON INFORMATION

Highest position: 1
Lowest position: 5
Average goals scored per game: 1.36
Average goals conceded per game: 0.97

1	2	4	4	3	2	1	1	2	2

LEAGUE POSITION AT THE END OF EACH MONTH

LONGEST SEQUENCES

Wins	4	Undefeated home	8
(05/12/09–30/01/10)		(12/12/09–23/03/10)	
Losses	3	Undefeated away	6
(10/04/10–24/04/10)		(24/10/09–06/02/10)	
Draws	–	Without scoring	3
(–)		(19/09/09–03/10/09)	
Undefeated	10	Without conceding	3
(02/12/09–06/03/10)		(on two occasions)	
Without win	6	Scoring	18
(19/09/09–24/10/09)		(31/10/09–23/03/10)	

CARDS RECEIVED

55 4

EARLIEST STRIKE

JOHN GRANT
(v Brechin) 4:00

LATEST STRIKE

BRYAN PRUNTY
(v Arbroath) 96:05

GOALS SCORED/CONCEDED
PER FIVE-MINUTE INTERVALS

MINS	5	10	15	20	25	30	35	40	45	50	55	60	65	70	75	80	85	90
FOR	2	0	4	3	2	4	1	0	3	2	3	3	2	0	3	3	5	9
AGN	0	1	0	2	2	4	5	2	2	2	1	2	2	3	2	1	1	3

ARBROATH

ARBROATH'S two-year stay in the third tier came to an end as they lost in the final of the play-offs.

The Red Lichties had managed to avoid the drop in their first season back in the third tier but they were beaten by Forfar this time around and returned to the Irn-Bru Third Division. Manager Jim Weir quit at the end of the season, with former St Johnstone player Paul Sheerin taking over in May.

Arbroath won their opening two matches in the League but only one victory in the next 11 games saw them sink to eighth place.

Manager John McGlashan resigned in October and was replaced by former Montrose boss Weir. However, the club's poor run continued and they were knocked out of the Active Nation Scottish Cup by Junior side Irvine Meadow. They also fell at the first hurdle in the ALBA Challenge Cup, although they did manage a victory in the Co-operative Insurance Cup before losing to St Johnstone.

CLUB SUMMARY

FORMED	1878
MANAGER	Paul Sheerin
GROUND	Gayfield Park
CAPACITY	4,415
NICKNAME	The Red Lichties
WEBSITE	www.arbroathfc.co.uk

The New **Football Pools** PLAYER OF THE SEASON

Darren Hill

OVERALL
P	W	D	L	F	A	GD
44	12	12	20	51	68	-17

IRN-BRU SECOND DIVISION
Pos	P	W	D	L	F	A	GD	Pts
9	36	10	10	16	41	55	-14	40

HOME
Pos	P	W	D	L	F	A	GD	Pts
10	18	4	5	9	22	33	-11	17

AWAY
Pos	P	W	D	L	F	A	GD	Pts
5	18	6	5	7	19	22	-3	23

CUP PROGRESS DETAILS
Competition	Round reached	Knocked out by
Scottish Cup	R3	Irvine Meadow
Co-op Insurance Cup	R2	St Johnstone
Challenge Cup	R1	Dunfermline

BIGGEST WIN (ALL COMPS)
05/05/10 4–0 v Queens Park

BIGGEST DEFEAT (ALL COMPS)
26/08/09 0–6 v St Johnstone

ATTENDANCE RECORD
High	Average	Low
649	491	328
v Brechin (12/09/2009)		v Alloa (02/12/2009)

RESULTS 2009/10

JULY
25th	● Dunfermline	A	L 2–1	Att: 1,239	Scorers: Redman. Booked: Rattray. Dismissed: Dobbins.

AUGUST
1st	● Peterhead	A	W 0–3	Att: 499	Scorers: Bishop, Raeside, Sellars. Booked: Rennie.
8th	● Cowdenbeath	A	W 1–2	Att: 303	Scorers: Scott, Sellars. Booked: McCulloch.
15th	● Dumbarton	H	W 3–1	Att: 605	Scorers: Hislop, Ross, Sellars.
22nd	● East Fife	A	D 1–1	Att: 770	Scorers: Ross. Booked: Raeside. Dismissed: Ross.
26th	● St Johnstone	H	L 0–6	Att: 1,038	
29th	● Stenhousemuir	A	L 3–0	Att: 543	Booked: Rattray, Lunan, Scott.

SEPTEMBER
12th	● Brechin	H	L 1–4	Att: 649	Scorers: Raeside. Dismissed: Redman.
19th	● Peterhead	H	L 0–1	Att: 476	Booked: Scott.
26th	● Alloa	A	W 0–1	Att: 469	Scorers: Scott. Booked: Lunan, Bishop, McCulloch, McCaffrey, Hislop.

OCTOBER
10th	● Stirling	A	D 2–2	Att: 689	Scorers: Scott^2. Booked: Watson.
14th	● Clyde	H	L 0–3	Att: 554	
17th	● Cowdenbeath	H	L 0–1	Att: 479	Booked: McCulloch.
24th	● Dumbarton	A	L 1–0	Att: 698	
31st	● Stenhousemuir	H	L 0–3	Att: 402	Booked: Dobbins.

NOVEMBER
7th	● Brechin	A	D 0–0	Att: 617	Booked: McCulloch.
14th	● Peterhead	A	W 1–2	Att: 500	Scorers: Doris, Sellars.
28th	● Irvine Meadow	A	L 1–0	Att: 1,150	Booked: McCulloch.

DECEMBER
2nd	● Alloa	H	D 2–2	Att: 328	Scorers: Hislop^2. Booked: Doris, McCulloch.
5th	● Clyde	A	L 1–0	Att: 551	
12th	● Stirling	H	L 3–4	Att: 491	Scorers: Hislop^2, Scott. Booked: McMullan, Gibson.

JANUARY
16th	● Stenhousemuir	A	D 1–1	Att: 443	Scorers: Hislop. Booked: Gibson, Rattray, Doris.
23rd	● Peterhead	H	L 1–4	Att: 465	Scorers: Winters. Booked: Gibson, McMullan.
27th	● East Fife	H	L 0–1	Att: 376	Booked: McCulloch.
30th	● Alloa	A	L 1–0	Att: 535	Booked: Mclaughlin, Hill, Rattray. Dismissed: Hislop.

FEBRUARY
13th	● Clyde	H	W 2–0	Att: 524	Scorers: Doris, Ross. Booked: Mclaughlin, Jackson.
27th	● Dumbarton	H	W 3–1	Att: 521	Scorers: Booth, Doris, Redman.

MARCH
6th	● Stenhousemuir	H	D 1–1	Att: 458	Scorers: Redman. Booked: Booth, Moyes.
9th	● Cowdenbeath	A	L 2–1	Att: 246	Scorers: Lunan. Booked: Doris, Rattray, McMullan.
13th	● Brechin	A	W 0–2	Att: 637	Scorers: Hislop, Ross. Booked: Moyes.
16th	● East Fife	A	L 3–1	Att: 480	Scorers: Hislop. Booked: Gibson, Redman.
20th	● Peterhead	A	L 3–0	Att: 483	Booked: Gibson, Mclaughlin.
24th	● Brechin	H	W 1–0	Att: 386	Scorers: Rattray. Booked: Doris, Scott, Mclaughlin.
27th	● Alloa	H	D 0–0	Att: 604	

APRIL
3rd	● Clyde	A	W 0–2	Att: 635	Scorers: Megginson, Scott. Booked: McCulloch.
10th	● Stirling	H	L 2–4	Att: 525	Scorers: McLean, Megginson. Booked: Redman, McGuire.
12th	● Stirling	A	D 2–2	Att: 365	Scorers: Doris^2. Booked: McGuire, Ross, Booth, Gibson.
17th	● Cowdenbeath	A	D 1–1	Att: 488	Scorers: Gibson. Booked: Rattray.
24th	● Dumbarton	A	W 0–2	Att: 836	Scorers: Megginson, Redman. Booked: Redman, Mclaughlin.

MAY
1st	● East Fife	H	D 2–2	Att: 512	Scorers: Doris, Redman. Booked: Moyes, Doris.
5th	● Queens Park	A	W 0–4	Att: 651	Scorers: Moyes, Nimmo, Redman, Ross.
8th	● Queens Park	H	D 2–2	Att: 588	Scorers: McCulloch, Megginson. Agg: 6–2.
12th	● Forfar	H	D 0–0	Att: 1,027	Booked: Nimmo, Scott.
16th	● Forfar	A	L 2–0	Att: 2,207	Booked: Rattray. Agg: 2–0.

● Irn-Bru Second Division/Play-offs ● Scottish Cup ● Co-op Insurance Cup ● Challenge Cup

actim

SECOND DIVISION GOALKEEPER STATS

Player	Appearances	Match starts	Completed matches	Sub appearances	Subbed off	Clean sheets	Yellow cards	Red cards
Darren Hill	36	36	36	0	0	8	1	0

SECOND DIVISION OUTFIELD PLAYER STATS

Player	Appearances	Match starts	Completed matches	Substitute appearances	Subbed off	Goals scored	Yellow cards	Red cards
James Bishop	13	12	11	1	1	0	1	0
Callum Booth	15	15	15	0	0	1	2	0
Ian Dobbins	11	11	11	0	0	0	1	0
Steven Doris	30	27	21	3	6	6	5	0
Kyle Faulds	3	3	1	0	2	0	0	0
Scott Gates	2	0	0	2	0	0	0	0
Keith Gibson	32	29	22	3	7	1	6	0
Steven Hislop	29	24	13	5	10	8	1	1
Andrew Jackson	8	6	2	2	4	0	1	0
Paul Lunan	26	19	12	7	7	1	2	0
Dermot McCaffrey	6	6	5	0	1	0	1	0
Marc McCulloch	28	27	25	1	2	0	7	0
Philip McGuire	7	7	6	0	1	0	2	0
Michael McIlravey	3	0	0	3	0	0	0	0
Daniel McKay	1	1	0	0	1	0	0	0
Kenneth McLean	20	15	8	5	7	1	0	0
Kevin McMullan	19	12	9	7	3	0	3	0
Jerry Mclaughlin	11	11	11	0	0	0	5	0
Mitchel Megginson	5	5	2	0	3	3	0	0
Kevin Milne	10	0	0	10	0	0	0	0
Kevin Moffat	1	0	0	1	0	0	0	0
Ewan Moyes	16	16	16	0	0	0	3	0
Ian Nimmo	9	4	0	5	4	0	0	0
Robbie Raeside	7	6	5	1	1	1	1	0
Alan Rattray	30	30	26	0	4	1	5	0
James Redman	24	20	19	4	0	4	3	1
Steven Rennie	22	17	14	5	3	0	0	0
Robert Ross	25	9	0	16	8	4	1	1
Bryan Scott	20	11	3	9	8	6	3	0
Barry Sellars	12	12	5	0	7	3	0	0
Paul Watson	4	3	2	1	1	0	1	0
David Winters	2	2	0	0	2	1	0	0

SEASON INFORMATION

Highest position: 1
Lowest position: 10
Average goals scored per game: 1.14
Average goals conceded per game: 1.53

LEAGUE POSITION AT THE END OF EACH MONTH

AUG SEP OCT NOV DEC JAN FEB MAR APR MAY
3 6 10 9 9 9 9 9 9 9

LONGEST SEQUENCES

Wins	2	Undefeated home	5
(on two occasions)		(13/02/10–27/03/10)	
Losses	4	Undefeated away	3
(14/10/09–31/10/09)		(03/04/10–24/04/10)	
Draws	2	Without scoring	5
(12/04/10–17/04/10)		(14/10/09–07/11/09)	
Undefeated	4	Without conceding	3
(12/04/10–01/05/10)		(24/03/10–03/04/10)	
Without win	7	Scoring	6
(02/12/09–30/01/10)		(13/02/10–16/03/10)	

CARDS RECEIVED

55 | 3

EARLIEST STRIKE

STEVEN HISLOP
(v Brechin) 0:37

LATEST STRIKE

STEVEN DORIS
(v Clyde) 90:55

GOALS SCORED/CONCEDED
PER FIVE-MINUTE INTERVALS

MINS	5	10	15	20	25	30	35	40	45	50	55	60	65	70	75	80	85	90
FOR	1	4	3	3	0	1	2	1	3	2	2	2	0	2	5	4	2	4
AGN	1	2	3	2	3	2	2	2	4	5	4	5	3	1	4	4	3	5

BRECHIN CITY

BRECHIN suffered play-off heartache for the third time in four years, once again missing out on promotion to the Irn-Bru First Division.

Unlike the previous two occasions, this time City reached the final after avenging their 2007 semi-final defeat to Airdrie. They looked to have taken the initiative in the final after drawing at Cowdenbeath in the first leg, but they went down 3–0 at home in the return match to consign themselves to another season in Scotland's third tier.

Jim Duffy kept them in the play-off picture – if not the race for automatic promotion – throughout his first full campaign in charge, but chose to resign at the end of the season. The former Dundee and Hibernian boss was replaced by Jim Weir, who left his role at Arbroath to move to Glebe Park.

While they missed out in the League, their Cup runs were short-lived as they lost in the second round of the Co-operative Insurance Cup and the fourth round of the Scottish Cup.

CLUB SUMMARY

FORMED	1906
MANAGER	Jim Weir
GROUND	Glebe Park
CAPACITY	3,960
NICKNAME	The Hedgemen
WEBSITE	www.brechincity.com

Rory McAllister

The New Football Pools
PLAYER OF THE SEASON

OVERALL

P	W	D	L	F	A	GD
42	17	10	15	63	58	5

IRN-BRU SECOND DIVISION

Pos	P	W	D	L	F	A	GD	Pts
4	36	15	9	12	50	45	5	54

HOME

Pos	P	W	D	L	F	A	GD	Pts
3	18	9	6	3	30	20	10	33

AWAY

Pos	P	W	D	L	F	A	GD	Pts
7	18	6	3	9	20	25	-5	21

CUP PROGRESS DETAILS

Competition	Round reached	Knocked out by
Scottish Cup	R4	Ayr
Co-op Insurance Cup	R2	Hibernian
Challenge Cup	R1	Elgin

BIGGEST WIN (ALL COMPS)
01/08/09 4–0 v Elgin

BIGGEST DEFEAT (ALL COMPS)
14/04/10 2–6 v Stirling

ATTENDANCE RECORD

HIGH	AVERAGE	Low
1,102	487	304
v Stirling (01/05/2010)		v Cowdenbeath (20/04/2010)

RESULTS 2009/10

JULY
25th	● Elgin	A	L 3–1	Att: 378	Scorers: McAllister. Booked: McLean.

AUGUST
1st	● Elgin	H	W 4–0	Att: 406	Scorers: Byers, McAllister2, McKenna. Booked: Fusco.
8th	● East Fife	A	L 2–0	Att: 584	
15th	● Cowdenbeath	H	W 3–1	Att: 375	Scorers: Canning, Harty, McAllister. Booked: Fusco, King.
22nd	● Stirling	A	L 1–0	Att: 608	Booked: Docherty, McAllister.
26th	● Hibernian	A	L 3–0	Att: 7,047	
29th	● Dumbarton	H	W 3–1	Att: 420	Scorers: Docherty, King, McAllister.

SEPTEMBER
12th	● Arbroath	A	W 1–4	Att: 649	Scorers: Janczyk, King, McAllister2.
19th	● Clyde	A	L 1–0	Att: 722	Booked: Janczyk, Fusco.
26th	● Stenhousemuir	H	W 1–0	Att: 421	Scorers: King. Booked: Docherty, McAllister.

OCTOBER
10th	● Alloa	H	W 2–1	Att: 417	Scorers: King, McAllister. Booked: Janczyk, R Walker, McAllister.
13th	● Peterhead	A	L 1–0	Att: 429	Booked: Cowan, Cowan, McLean.
17th	● East Fife	H	W 3–2	Att: 519	Scorers: King2, McLean.
24th	● Cowdenbeath	A	D 0–0	Att: 339	
31st	● Dumbarton	A	D 0–0	Att: 651	

NOVEMBER
7th	● Arbroath	H	D 0–0	Att: 617	Booked: Smith, Seeley.
14th	● Clyde	H	D 2–2	Att: 459	Scorers: King, McAllister. Booked: Smith, McAllister, Renton.
21st	● Stenhousemuir	A	D 1–1	Att: 551	Scorers: McAllister. Booked: Dyer, Barr.
28th	● Wick Academy	A	D 4–4	Att: 177	Scorers: Byers, King2, McAllister. Booked: Nelson.

DECEMBER
8th	● Wick Academy	H	W 4–2	Att: 402	Scorers: Docherty, Fusco, McAllister2.
12th	● Alloa	A	L 2–1	Att: 394	Scorers: McAllister. Booked: Fusco, Dyer, Barr.
15th	● Peterhead	H	W 3–0	Att: 417	Scorers: McAllister2, McLean. Booked: McLean.

JANUARY
18th	● Ayr	A	L 1–0	Att: 1,139	
23rd	● Clyde	A	W 0–3	Att: 623	Scorers: Docherty, Fusco, McAllister. Booked: Janczyk, McLean, Harty.
30th	● Stenhousemuir	H	D 2–2	Att: 413	Scorers: Docherty, McAllister.

FEBRUARY
6th	● Alloa	H	D 1–1	Att: 434	Scorers: McAllister. Booked: McAllister.
13th	● Peterhead	A	W 0–3	Att: 553	Scorers: Byers, King, McAllister. Booked: Smith, R Walker.

MARCH
6th	● Dumbarton	A	W 0–1	Att: 751	Scorers: Byers.
9th	● Stirling	H	W 1–0	Att: 453	Scorers: Docherty. Booked: Janczyk, King, Docherty.
13th	● Arbroath	A	L 0–2	Att: 637	Booked: Smith, Canning.
20th	● Clyde	H	W 3–1	Att: 417	Scorers: King, McAllister2.
24th	● Arbroath	A	L 1–0	Att: 386	Booked: Smith.
27th	● Stenhousemuir	A	W 1–2	Att: 481	Scorers: Archdeacon, McAllister. Booked: McLean, Masson.
30th	● East Fife	A	L 2–0	Att: 213	

APRIL
3rd	● Peterhead	H	L 1–2	Att: 463	Scorers: Archdeacon. Booked: McLean, Janczyk.
6th	● Dumbarton	H	L 0–1	Att: 403	Booked: Janczyk.
10th	● Alloa	A	W 2–3	Att: 626	Scorers: Archdeacon, King, McLean. Booked: Archdeacon.
14th	● Stirling	H	L 6–2	Att: 357	Scorers: McAllister2. Booked: Vallers, McAllister.
17th	● East Fife	H	W 1–0	Att: 492	Scorers: Byers. Booked: McAllister, McLean.
20th	● Cowdenbeath	H	D 3–3	Att: 304	Scorers: McAllister2, Vallers.
24th	● Cowdenbeath	A	L 4–0	Att: 391	Booked: Fusco, Docherty.

MAY
1st	● Stirling	H	D 1–1	Att: 1,102	Scorers: King. Booked: R Walker.
5th	● Airdrie Utd	H	W 2–1	Att: 583	Scorers: King, McAllister. Booked: Archdeacon.
8th	● Airdrie Utd	A	W 0–1	Att: 1,156	Scorers: McAllister. Agg: 1–3.
12th	● Cowdenbeath	A	D 0–0	Att: 1,119	Booked: Fusco, Vallers, McAllister.
16th	● Cowdenbeath	H	L 0–3	Att: 1,627	Booked: Masson, McLean. Agg: 0–3.

● Irn-Bru Second Division/Play-offs ● Scottish Cup ● Co-op Insurance Cup ● Challenge Cup

actim

SECOND DIVISION GOALKEEPER STATS

Player	Appearances	Match starts	Completed matches	Sub appearances	Subbed off	Clean sheets	Yellow cards	Red cards
Craig Nelson	36	36	35	0	1	10	0	0
David Scott	1	0	0	1	0	0	0	0

SECOND DIVISION OUTFIELD PLAYER STATS

Player	Appearances	Match starts	Completed matches	Substitute appearances	Subbed off	Goals scored	Yellow cards	Red cards
Mark Archdeacon	9	8	2	1	6	3	1	0
Bobby Barr	4	4	4	0	0	0	2	0
Kevin Byers	27	19	11	8	8	3	0	0
Stevie Canning	22	8	3	14	5	1	1	0
Mark Cowan	17	2	0	15	2	0	2	0
Mark Docherty	35	30	21	5	9	4	4	0
William Dyer	25	25	23	0	2	0	2	0
Gary Fusco	36	36	31	0	5	1	4	0
Ian Harty	7	4	1	3	3	1	1	0
Neil Janczyk	28	27	20	1	7	1	6	0
Charlie King	36	34	21	2	13	11	2	0
Anton Kurakins	2	2	1	0	1	0	0	0
Terry Masson	7	1	1	6	0	0	1	0
Rory McAllister	34	34	24	0	10	21	7	0
Chris McGroarty	2	0	0	2	0	0	0	0
Sean McKenna	4	0	0	4	0	0	0	0
Paul McLean	33	33	33	0	0	3	6	0
David Murie	1	1	1	0	0	0	0	0
Ian Nimmo	6	1	1	5	0	0	0	0
Kris Renton	11	2	0	9	2	0	3	0
Jonathon Seeley	15	13	12	2	1	0	1	0
Barry Smith	31	31	29	0	0	5	0	0
Barry Tulloch	2	0	0	2	0	0	0	0
Krisjanis Vallers	7	7	5	0	2	1	1	0
Richard Walker	35	35	35	0	0	0	3	0
Alexander Walker	3	3	2	0	1	0	0	0

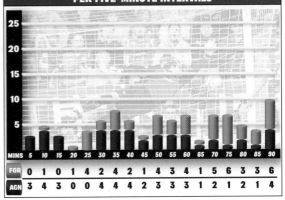

SEASON INFORMATION
Highest position: 2
Lowest position: 10
Average goals scored per game: 1.39
Average goals conceded per game: 1.25

LEAGUE POSITION AT THE END OF EACH MONTH
6 3 3 3 4 4 4 4 4

LONGEST SEQUENCES

Wins (13/02/10–09/03/10)	3	Undefeated home (15/08/09–09/03/10)	11
Losses (30/03/10–06/04/10)	3	Undefeated away (on two occasions)	3
Draws (24/10/09–21/11/09)	5	Without scoring (24/10/09–07/11/09)	3
Undefeated (15/12/09–09/03/10)	7	Without conceding (on two occasions)	3
Without win (24/10/09–12/12/09)	6	Scoring (14/11/09–09/03/10)	10

CARDS RECEIVED 50 0

EARLIEST STRIKE
RORY MCALLISTER
(v Stenhousemuir) 6:59

LATEST STRIKE
RORY MCALLISTER
(v Alloa) 90:00

GOALS SCORED/CONCEDED
PER FIVE-MINUTE INTERVALS

MINS	5	10	15	20	25	30	35	40	45	50	55	60	65	70	75	80	85	90
FOR	0	1	0	1	4	2	4	2	1	4	3	4	1	5	6	3	3	6
AGN	3	4	3	0	0	4	4	4	2	3	3	3	1	2	1	2	1	4

CLYDE

CLYDE slipped into the fourth tier of Scottish football for the first time in their history following a second successive relegation.

Financial concerns resulted in the Bully Wee releasing their entire first-team squad in the summer of last year, and manager John Brown also left following a 3–1 home defeat to East Fife in November.

John McCormack then took charge but he could not change the club's fortunes, with the former Morton manager only leading the team to two victories.

He was eventually relieved of his duties – with Stuart Miller taking over the reins – following the 2–0 defeat to Arbroath in April, which all but confirmed Clyde's drop into the Irn-Bru Third Division.

Although it was a disappointing season, cutbacks on and off the field meant that the club managed to significantly reduce its debts by almost £200,000, while the board has asserted that it will be debt-free by March 2015.

CLUB SUMMARY

FORMED	1877
MANAGER	Stuart Miller
GROUND	Broadwood Stadium
CAPACITY	8,006
NICKNAME	The Bully Wee
WEBSITE	www.clydefc.co.uk

The New **Football Pools** PLAYER OF THE SEASON

Alan Lithgow

OVERALL
P	W	D	L	F	A	GD
40	8	8	24	40	70	-30

IRN-BRU SECOND DIVISION
Pos	P	W	D	L	F	A	GD	Pts
10	36	8	7	21	37	57	-20	31

HOME
Pos	P	W	D	L	F	A	GD	Pts
9	18	6	0	12	17	29	-12	18

AWAY
Pos	P	W	D	L	F	A	GD	Pts
10	18	2	7	9	20	28	-8	13

CUP PROGRESS DETAILS
Competition	Round reached	Knocked out by
Scottish Cup	R3	Livingston
Co-op Insurance Cup	R1	Forfar
Challenge Cup	R1	Stenhousemuir

BIGGEST WIN (ALL COMPS)
3–0 on 2 occasions

BIGGEST DEFEAT (ALL COMPS)
14/12/09 1–7 v Livingston

ATTENDANCE RECORD
HIGH	AVERAGE	LOW
813	636	465
v Stirling (15/08/2009)		v Alloa (07/04/2010)

RESULTS 2009/10

JULY
25th	● Stenhousemuir	A	L 2–0	Att: 603	

AUGUST
1st	● Forfar	H	L 1–3	Att: 784	Scorers: Tod OG. Booked: P Stewart.
8th	● Peterhead	A	L 2–0	Att: 525	Booked: Casey, Gair.
15th	● Stirling	H	L 0–1	Att: 813	Booked: Gair, Lithgow.
22nd	● Dumbarton	A	D 3–3	Att: 944	Scorers: Lithgow², McLachlan. Booked: Lithgow, McKay, Gair. Dismissed: Reidford.
29th	● Alloa	H	L 0–1	Att: 801	Booked: Casey, McKay, Halliday.

SEPTEMBER
12th	● Cowdenbeath	A	L 1–0	Att: 551	Booked: Lang, Casey.
19th	● Brechin	H	W 1–0	Att: 722	Scorers: McLeod. Booked: Halliday.
26th	● East Fife	A	L 1–0	Att: 697	Booked: Lithgow, McLachlan.

OCTOBER
10th	● Stenhousemuir	H	W 2–1	Att: 755	Scorers: Howarth, Sawyers. Booked: Wilson, Halliday, McLachlan, Lang. Dismissed: Halliday.
14th	● Arbroath	A	W 0–3	Att: 554	Scorers: Park, Sawyers².
17th	● Peterhead	H	L 1–3	Att: 673	Scorers: McLeod. Booked: Park. Dismissed: Wilson.
24th	● Stirling	A	D 1–1	Att: 764	Scorers: Sawyers. Booked: Sawyers, Park.
31st	● Alloa	A	L 2–0	Att: 649	Booked: P Stewart.

NOVEMBER
7th	● Cowdenbeath	H	L 0–1	Att: 691	Booked: Halliday, Lithgow.
14th	● Brechin	A	D 2–2	Att: 459	Scorers: McLeod, Sawyers. Booked: Sawyers.
21st	● East Fife	H	L 1–3	Att: 619	Scorers: Sawyers. Booked: Sawyers, McKay.

DECEMBER
5th	● Arbroath	H	W 1–0	Att: 551	Scorers: McLachlan.
9th	● Livingston	H	D 1–1	Att: 538	Scorers: Lithgow. Booked: Higgins.
12th	● Stenhousemuir	A	L 1–0	Att: 532	Booked: P Stewart.
14th	● Livingston	A	L 7–1	Att: 690	Scorers: Lithgow. Booked: Lithgow, McLachlan.

JANUARY
| 23rd | ● Brechin | H | L 0–3 | Att: 623 | Booked: J Stewart. Dismissed: Reidford. |

FEBRUARY
| 6th | ● Stenhousemuir | H | L 0–2 | Att: 650 | |
| 13th | ● Arbroath | A | L 2–0 | Att: 524 | Booked: Strachan, Wilson. |

MARCH
6th	● Alloa	A	D 2–2	Att: 628	Scorers: J Stewart, White. Booked: Kinniburgh, Reidford, Sawyers, P Boyle.
9th	● East Fife	A	D 1–1	Att: 463	Scorers: Park. Booked: Kinniburgh, P Boyle.
13th	● Cowdenbeath	H	L 1–2	Att: 649	Scorers: Borisovs. Booked: P Boyle.
16th	● Dumbarton	H	L 0–2	Att: 531	Booked: Kinniburgh.
20th	● Brechin	A	L 3–1	Att: 417	Scorers: Gramovics. Booked: Lithgow. Dismissed: McGowan.
23rd	● Cowdenbeath	A	L 3–1	Att: 303	Scorers: White. Booked: P Boyle.
27th	● East Fife	H	W 2–1	Att: 495	Scorers: Sawyers, White.
30th	● Peterhead	A	D 0–0	Att: 303	Booked: Lithgow.

APRIL
3rd	● Arbroath	H	L 0–2	Att: 635	Booked: McGowan, Park.
7th	● Alloa	H	L 0–2	Att: 465	
10th	● Stenhousemuir	A	W 0–3	Att: 482	Scorers: Lithgow, Strachan, White. Booked: Gramovics, White.
13th	● Dumbarton	A	D 3–3	Att: 601	Scorers: McGowan, Strachan². Booked: McCulloch, Gramovics.
17th	● Peterhead	H	W 3–1	Att: 515	Scorers: Lithgow, Sawyers, J Stewart.
20th	● Stirling	H	L 1–2	Att: 635	Scorers: Sawyers. Booked: Gramovics.
24th	● Stirling	A	L 1–0	Att: 796	

MAY
| 1st | ● Dumbarton | H | W 4–2 | Att: 631 | Scorers: Sawyers, J Stewart², Strachan. Booked: Gramovics. Dismissed: Gramovics. |

● Irn-Bru Second Division ● Scottish Cup ● Co-op Insurance Cup ● Challenge Cup

SECOND DIVISION GOALKEEPER STATS

Player	Appearances	Match starts	Completed matches	Sub appearances	Subbed off	Clean sheets	Yellow cards	Red cards
Jordan Allan	3	2	2	1	0	0	0	0
Scott Findlay	2	1	1	1	0	0	0	0
Andrew McNeil	1	1	1	0	0	0	0	0
Callum Reidford	32	32	30	0	0	5	1	2

SECOND DIVISION OUTFIELD PLAYER STATS

Player	Appearances	Match starts	Completed matches	Substitute appearances	Subbed off	Goals scored	Yellow cards	Red cards
Alistair Bark	2	2	2	0	0	0	0	0
Dmitrijs Borisovs	10	3	0	7	3	1	0	0
Patrick Boyle	8	8	8	0	0	0	4	0
Connell Boyle	1	0	0	1	0	0	0	0
Mark Casey	17	16	14	1	2	0	3	0
Connor Cassidy	11	9	7	2	2	0	0	0
Adam Coakley	5	2	0	3	2	0	0	0
Robert Davidson	1	1	0	0	1	0	0	0
Kris Doolan	9	9	7	0	2	0	0	0
James Doyle	4	4	1	0	3	0	0	0
Scott Gair	4	3	2	1	1	0	3	0
Lee Graham	6	4	4	2	0	0	0	0
Aleksandrs Gramovics	17	14	9	3	4	1	4	1
Robert Halliday	12	10	7	2	2	0	4	1
Kevin Higgins	9	4	1	5	3	0	0	0
Steven Howarth	11	5	1	6	4	1	0	0
William Kinniburgh	14	14	13	0	1	0	3	0
Jay Lang	8	4	3	4	0	0	2	0
Alan Lithgow	32	32	31	0	1	4	6	0
William McCulloch	6	6	6	0	0	0	1	0
Alan McFadden	9	2	0	7	2	0	0	0
Neil McGowan	17	17	15	0	1	1	1	1
David McKay	7	4	3	3	1	0	3	0
William McLachlan	26	24	24	2	0	2	2	0
Paul McLeod	15	10	7	5	3	3	0	0
Gary Muir	7	4	1	3	3	0	0	0
Steven Odunewu	6	1	0	5	2	0	0	0
Alistair Park	31	31	28	0	3	2	3	0
Willie Sawyers	32	24	13	8	11	10	4	0
Connor Stevenson	21	15	11	6	4	0	0	0
John Stewart	15	10	1	5	9	4	1	0
Paul Stewart	16	14	12	2	2	0	2	0
Adam Strachan	18	18	16	0	2	0	0	0
Darren Walker	3	1	0	2	1	0	0	0
Jordan White	20	17	11	3	6	4	1	0
Marvyn Wilson	14	13	6	1	6	0	2	1

LEAGUE POSITION AT THE END OF EACH MONTH

AUG SEP OCT NOV DEC JAN FEB MAR APR MAY

9 10 9 10 10 10 10 10 10 10

SEASON INFORMATION

Highest position: 4
Lowest position: 10
Average goals scored per game: 1.03
Average goals conceded per game: 1.58

LONGEST SEQUENCES

Wins (10/10/09–14/10/09)	2	Undefeated home (19/09/09–10/10/09)	2
Losses (on two occasions)	4	Undefeated away (30/03/10–13/04/10)	3
Draws (06/03/10–09/03/10)	2	Without scoring (12/12/09–13/02/10)	4
Undefeated (10/04/10–17/04/10)	3	Without conceding (–)	–
Without win (12/12/09–23/03/10)	10	Scoring (on two occasions)	4

CARDS RECEIVED

51 6

EARLIEST STRIKE

WILLIE SAWYERS
(v Peterhead) 0:08

LATEST STRIKE

PAUL MCLEOD
(v Peterhead) 88:00

GOALS SCORED/CONCEDED
PER FIVE-MINUTE INTERVALS

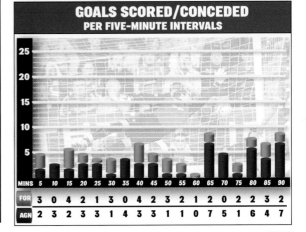

MINS	5	10	15	20	25	30	35	40	45	50	55	60	65	70	75	80	85	90
FOR	3	0	4	2	1	3	0	4	2	3	2	1	2	0	2	2	3	2
AGN	2	3	2	3	3	1	4	3	3	1	1	0	7	5	1	6	4	7

COWDENBEATH

COWDENBEATH took full advantage of their elevation to the Irn-Bru Second Division by sealing promotion to the First Division via the play-offs.

The final saw the Blue Brazil beat Brechin 3–0 away from home after a goalless first leg. They also defeated Alloa away in the semi-final after being held to a 1–1 draw at home.

That result avenged their defeat in the Active Nation Scottish Cup third round, as well as a loss on the final day of the regular season as Cowdenbeath's hopes of winning the Second Division evaporated in the final month.

They had led the table in February, but had to settle for third place as Stirling claimed the title. It was a remarkable transformation in fortunes for Danny Lennon's men, who would have started the season in the Third Division after losing last season's play-off final had Livingston not been demoted.

Lennon's success led to him being recruited by St Mirren in June.

CLUB SUMMARY

FORMED	1881
MANAGER	TBC
GROUND	Central Park
CAPACITY	4,370
NICKNAME	The Blue Brazil
WEBSITE	www.cowdenbeathfc.com

The New **Football Pools** PLAYER OF THE SEASON — Joseph Mbu

OVERALL
P	W	D	L	F	A	GD
41	17	12	12	63	49	14

IRN-BRU SECOND DIVISION
Pos	P	W	D	L	F	A	GD	Pts
3	36	16	11	9	60	41	19	59

HOME
Pos	P	W	D	L	F	A	GD	Pts
1	18	10	5	3	36	19	17	35

AWAY
Pos	P	W	D	L	F	A	GD	Pts
4	18	6	6	6	24	22	2	24

CUP PROGRESS DETAILS
Competition	Round reached	Knocked out by
Scottish Cup	R3	Alloa
Co-op Insurance Cup	R1	Morton
Challenge Cup	R2	Dundee

BIGGEST WIN (ALL COMPS)
10/10/09 5–0 v Peterhead

BIGGEST DEFEAT (ALL COMPS)
18/08/09 0–3 v Dundee

ATTENDANCE RECORD
HIGH	AVERAGE	LOW
1,084	437	246
v Stirling (27/04/2010)		v Arbroath (09/03/2010)

RESULTS 2009/10

JULY
25th	● Peterhead	A	W 1–2	Att: 361	Scorers: McBride, McQuade.

AUGUST
1st	● Morton	H	L 1–3	Att: 486	Scorers: McQuade. Booked: Baxter.
8th	● Arbroath	H	L 1–2	Att: 303	Scorers: McBride. Booked: Droudge. Dismissed: Adamson, Droudge.
15th	● Brechin	A	L 3–1	Att: 375	Scorers: Dempster. Dismissed: Hay.
18th	● Dundee	H	L 0–3	Att: 457	
22nd	● Alloa	H	D 1–1	Att: 369	Scorers: Wardlaw. Booked: Stein.
29th	● East Fife	A	D 1–1	Att: 803	Scorers: Stein. Booked: McQuade, Fairbairn.

SEPTEMBER
12th	● Clyde	H	W 1–0	Att: 551	Scorers: Stein.
19th	● Dumbarton	A	W 0–3	Att: 667	Scorers: McBride[2], Wardlaw.
26th	● Stirling	H	L 1–2	Att: 451	Scorers: McBride. Booked: Wardlaw, Stein.

OCTOBER
3rd	● Stenhousemuir	A	W 0–2	Att: 443	Scorers: McBride, Robertson. Booked: Robertson, Droudge.
10th	● Peterhead	H	W 5–0	Att: 271	Scorers: McQuade[2], Robertson, Wardlaw[2]. Booked: Armstrong.
17th	● Arbroath	A	W 0–1	Att: 479	Scorers: Linton. Booked: Robertson.
24th	● Brechin	H	D 0–0	Att: 339	
31st	● East Fife	A	W 2–1	Att: 739	Scorers: Fairbairn, Robertson. Booked: McQuade.

NOVEMBER
7th	● Clyde	A	W 0–1	Att: 691	Scorers: McBride. Booked: Armstrong.
14th	● Dumbarton	H	W 2–1	Att: 389	Scorers: McQuade[2]. Booked: Winter, Wardlaw.
21st	● Stirling	A	D 2–2	Att: 682	Scorers: Ferguson, Wardlaw. Booked: Adamson, Robertson.
28th	● Alloa	H	D 0–0	Att: 377	Booked: Adamson.

DECEMBER
8th	● Alloa	A	L 1–0	Att: 423	
12th	● Peterhead	A	W 0–2	Att: 440	Scorers: Mbu, Robertson. Booked: Fairbairn, Fairbairn.
15th	● Stenhousemuir	H	W 2–1	Att: 264	Scorers: Fairbairn, McQuade. Dismissed: Adamson.

JANUARY
16th	● East Fife	A	D 2–2	Att: 864	Scorers: Wardlaw[2]. Booked: Winter.
23rd	● Dumbarton	A	L 2–1	Att: 659	Scorers: Baxter.

FEBRUARY
6th	● Peterhead	H	L 1–3	Att: 298	Scorers: Stein. Booked: Adamson.
9th	● Alloa	A	L 2–1	Att: 638	Scorers: McQuade. Booked: Baxter, Wardlaw, Armstrong.
13th	● Stenhousemuir	A	D 0–0	Att: 443	Booked: Wardlaw, Fairbairn, Winter. Dismissed: Adamson.

MARCH
6th	● East Fife	H	W 6–2	Att: 667	Scorers: McGregor, McQuade, Ramsay, Stein[2], Wardlaw. Booked: Wardlaw.
9th	● Arbroath	H	W 2–1	Att: 246	Scorers: McGregor, McQuade. Booked: Wardlaw, Winter.
13th	● Clyde	A	W 1–2	Att: 649	Scorers: Dempster, Wardlaw. Booked: Armstrong.
16th	● Alloa	H	D 1–1	Att: 413	Scorers: Dempster.
20th	● Dumbarton	H	D 0–0	Att: 349	
23rd	● Clyde	H	W 3–1	Att: 303	Scorers: McQuade[2], Robertson.
27th	● Stirling	A	L 1–0	Att: 575	Booked: Wardlaw.

APRIL
3rd	● Stenhousemuir	H	W 1–0	Att: 438	Scorers: Wardlaw. Booked: McBride, McGregor.
10th	● Peterhead	A	L 1–0	Att: 435	Booked: Wardlaw.
17th	● Arbroath	A	D 1–1	Att: 488	Scorers: Wardlaw. Booked: Winter.
20th	● Brechin	A	D 3–3	Att: 304	Scorers: McGregor, Wardlaw[2].
24th	● Brechin	H	W 4–0	Att: 391	Scorers: McGregor, McQuade[2], Wardlaw.
27th	● Stirling	H	D 3–3	Att: 1,084	Scorers: McGregor, Wardlaw[2]. Booked: Baxter, Wardlaw.

MAY
1st	● Alloa	A	L 3–1	Att: 1,125	Scorers: Dempster. Booked: Adamson, McGregor. Dismissed: Armstrong.
5th	● Alloa	H	D 1–1	Att: 578	Scorers: Dempster. Booked: Mbu, Wardlaw.
8th	● Alloa	A	W 0–2	Att: 1,234	Scorers: McQuade, Wardlaw. Agg: 1–3.
12th	● Brechin	H	D 0–0	Att: 1,119	Booked: Winter, Adamson.
16th	● Brechin	A	W 0–3	Att: 1,627	Scorers: Mbu, Wardlaw[2]. Agg: 0–3.

● Irn-Bru Second Division/Play-offs ● Scottish Cup ● Co-op Insurance Cup ● Challenge Cup

SECOND DIVISION GOALKEEPER STATS

Player	Appearances	Match starts	Completed matches	Sub appearances	Subbed off	Clean sheets	Yellow cards	Red cards
Chris Bower	1	0	0	1	0	0	0	0
David Hay	34	34	32	0	1	10	0	1
Cameron McKay	1	1	1	0	1	1	0	0
Artur Veiculis	1	1	1	0	0	0	0	0

SECOND DIVISION OUTFIELD PLAYER STATS

Player	Appearances	Match starts	Completed matches	Substitute appearances	Subbed off	Goals scored	Yellow cards	Red cards
Kenneth Adamson	25	20	12	5	5	0	3	3
John Armstrong	26	26	24	0	1	0	4	1
Mark Baxter	23	14	14	9	0	1	2	0
Peter Bradley	1	1	1	0	0	0	0	0
Dean Brett	1	1	1	0	0	0	0	0
John Dempster	17	5	2	12	3	4	0	0
Dene Droudge	26	25	19	1	5	0	2	1
Brian Fairbairn	31	24	7	7	17	2	4	0
John Ferguson	8	0	0	8	0	1	0	0
Scott Linton	26	24	24	2	0	1	0	0
Daniel Mackay	2	0	0	2	0	0	0	0
Joseph Mbu	32	32	30	0	2	1	0	0
Scott McBride	25	16	7	9	9	6	1	0
Neil McCabe	4	0	0	4	0	0	0	0
Darren McGregor	17	16	16	1	0	5	2	0
Paul McQuade	31	27	13	4	14	12	2	0
Mark Ramsay	31	18	11	13	7	1	0	0
Jon Robertson	31	29	28	2	1	5	3	0
Martyn Robinson	1	1	1	0	0	0	0	0
Jay Shields	3	3	1	0	2	0	0	0
Jay Stein	32	19	13	13	6	5	2	0
Marek Tomana	1	0	0	1	0	0	0	0
Derek Wallace	1	0	0	1	0	0	0	0
Gareth Wardlaw	31	31	20	0	11	16	9	0
Craig Winter	29	26	12	3	14	0	5	0

SEASON INFORMATION

Highest position: 1
Lowest position: 9
Average goals scored per game: 1.67
Average goals conceded per game: 1.14

AUG	SEP	OCT	NOV	DEC	JAN	FEB	MAR	APR	MAY
8	7	2	1	1	1	3	2	3	3

LEAGUE POSITION AT THE END OF EACH MONTH

LONGEST SEQUENCES

Wins	3	Undefeated home	8
(on three occasions)		(06/03/10–27/04/10)	
Losses	3	Undefeated away	8
(23/01/10–09/02/10)		(29/08/09–16/01/10)	
Draws	2	Without scoring	–
(on three occasions)		(–)	
Undefeated	11	Without conceding	4
(03/10/09–16/01/10)		(03/10/09–24/10/09)	
Without win	5	Scoring	10
(16/01/10–13/02/10)		(on two occasions)	

CARDS RECEIVED

39 **6**

EARLIEST STRIKE

GARETH WARDLAW
(v Brechin) 1:52

LATEST STRIKE

SCOTT MCBRIDE
(v Arbroath) 90:00

GOALS SCORED/CONCEDED
PER FIVE-MINUTE INTERVALS

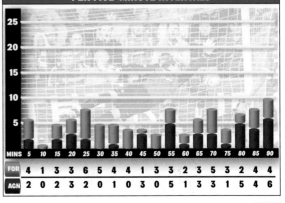

MINS	5	10	15	20	25	30	35	40	45	50	55	60	65	70	75	80	85	90
FOR	4	1	3	3	6	5	4	4	1	3	3	2	3	5	3	2	4	4
AGN	2	0	2	3	2	0	1	0	3	0	5	1	3	3	1	5	4	6

DUMBARTON

ALTHOUGH Dumbarton managed to cement their place in the Irn-Bru Second Division, their season was overshadowed by the death of captain Gordon Lennon.

The 26-year-old was killed in a car crash just weeks after leading the Sons to the 2008/09 Third Division title and, amid that tragedy, events on the pitch were put firmly into perspective.

Failure to win any of their first six League games resulted in suggestions that Dumbarton would struggle to adapt to life in the Second Division. However, Derek Carcary's 90th-minute winner against Peterhead at the end of September led to a turnaround in the club's fortunes and they only lost once in their next six games.

Twenty-five-year-old defender Ben Gordon was a stalwart at the back and only missed a few games throughout the whole campaign to become the club's player of the season as Jim Chapman's side secured a sixth-place finish in the table.

CLUB SUMMARY

FORMED	1872
MANAGER	Jim Chapman
GROUND	Strathclyde Homes Stadium
CAPACITY	2,025
NICKNAME	The Sons
WEBSITE	www.dumbartonfootballclub.com

The New **Football Pools**
PLAYER OF THE SEASON

Ben Gordon

OVERALL
P	W	D	L	F	A	GD
40	14	7	19	49	65	-16

IRN-BRU SECOND DIVISION
Pos	P	W	D	L	F	A	GD	Pts
6	36	14	6	16	49	58	-9	48

HOME
Pos	P	W	D	L	F	A	GD	Pts
8	18	5	4	9	21	32	-11	19

AWAY
Pos	P	W	D	L	F	A	GD	Pts
3	18	9	2	7	28	26	2	29

CUP PROGRESS DETAILS
Competition	Round reached	Knocked out by
Scottish Cup	R3	Morton
Co-op Insurance Cup	R1	Dunfermline
Challenge Cup	R1	Morton

BIGGEST WIN (ALL COMPS)
07/11/09 3–0 v Stenhousemuir

BIGGEST DEFEAT (ALL COMPS)
01/08/09 0–5 v Dunfermline

ATTENDANCE RECORD
HIGH	AVERAGE	LOW
944	678	397
v Clyde (22/08/2009)		v Peterhead (08/12/2009)

RESULTS 2009/10

JULY
26th	● Morton	H	L 0–1	Att: 1,120	Booked: Murray.

AUGUST
1st	● Dunfermline	H	L 0–5	Att: 953	Booked: Chisholm, Gordon, Dunlop. **Dismissed:** Chisholm.
8th	● Alloa	H	L 1–3	Att: 864	Scorers: Grant OG. **Dismissed:** McLaughlin.
15th	● Arbroath	A	L 3–1	Att: 605	Scorers: Hunter. Booked: Smith, Craig.
22nd	● Clyde	H	D 3–3	Att: 944	Scorers: Chisholm, Dunlop, Hunter.
29th	● Brechin	A	L 3–1	Att: 420	Scorers: Dunlop. Booked: Gordon.

SEPTEMBER
12th	● Stenhousemuir	H	D 0–0	Att: 681	Booked: Harvey, McStay. **Dismissed:** Vonacek.
19th	● Cowdenbeath	H	L 0–3	Att: 667	Booked: Geggan, Smith.
26th	● Peterhead	A	W 1–2	Att: 571	Scorers: Carcary, Murray. Booked: Gordon, Dunlop.

OCTOBER
3rd	● Stirling	H	L 2–3	Att: 808	Scorers: Chaplain, Cook. Booked: Smith. **Dismissed:** McNiff.
10th	● East Fife	A	W 0–1	Att: 620	Scorers: McLaughlin. Booked: Geggan, Chaplain, Gordon.
17th	● Alloa	A	W 1–3	Att: 575	Scorers: Chaplain, Cook, Geggan. Booked: McStay, Dunlop.
24th	● Arbroath	H	W 1–0	Att: 698	Scorers: Chaplain. Booked: Chaplain.
31st	● Brechin	H	D 0–0	Att: 651	

NOVEMBER
7th	● Stenhousemuir	A	W 0–3	Att: 568	Scorers: Chaplain, Hunter, O'Donoghue. Booked: Chisholm, McStay.
14th	● Cowdenbeath	A	L 2–1	Att: 389	Scorers: Geggan. Booked: O'Donoghue.
28th	● Morton	A	D 0–0	Att: 1,882	

DECEMBER
5th	● Morton	H	L 0–1	Att: 1,495	Booked: Dunlop, Chaplain. **Dismissed:** Chaplain.
8th	● Peterhead	H	W 1–0	Att: 397	Scorers: Chaplain. Booked: McStay, Geggan.
12th	● East Fife	H	L 0–3	Att: 628	
15th	● Stirling	A	D 2–2	Att: 462	Scorers: Carcary, Craig. Booked: Gordon.

JANUARY
23rd	● Cowdenbeath	H	W 2–1	Att: 659	Scorers: Clark, Hunter.

FEBRUARY
6th	● East Fife	A	W 2–3	Att: 581	Scorers: Carcary, Chaplain, Gordon. Booked: Brannan.
16th	● Stirling	H	L 2–4	Att: 595	Scorers: Gordon, Hunter. Booked: Dunlop, Smith.
27th	● Arbroath	A	L 3–1	Att: 521	Scorers: Winters.

MARCH
2nd	● Peterhead	A	L 2–1	Att: 327	Scorers: Wyness. Booked: Chisholm, McStay.
6th	● Brechin	H	L 0–1	Att: 751	Booked: Dunlop.
9th	● Alloa	H	W 3–1	Att: 552	Scorers: Clark, Cook, Gordon. Booked: Carcary, Gordon.
13th	● Stenhousemuir	A	L 1–0	Att: 469	
16th	● Clyde	A	W 0–2	Att: 531	Scorers: Winters[2]. Booked: Smith.
20th	● Cowdenbeath	A	D 0–0	Att: 349	Booked: Geggan.
23rd	● Stenhousemuir	H	W 2–1	Att: 486	Scorers: Chaplain[2]. Booked: Murray.
27th	● Peterhead	H	L 1–3	Att: 663	Scorers: Chaplain. Booked: Winters.

APRIL
3rd	● Stirling	A	W 1–2	Att: 568	Scorers: Wyness[2]. Booked: Brannan, Clark, Dunlop.
6th	● Brechin	A	W 0–1	Att: 403	Scorers: Chaplain. Booked: Gordon.
10th	● East Fife	H	L 0–1	Att: 728	
13th	● Clyde	H	D 3–3	Att: 601	Scorers: Carcary[2], Winters.
17th	● Alloa	A	W 1–2	Att: 622	Scorers: Winters, Wyness. Booked: Smith.
24th	● Arbroath	H	L 0–2	Att: 836	Booked: Dunlop, Geggan.

MAY
1st	● Clyde	A	L 4–2	Att: 631	Scorers: McStay, Wyness.

● Irn-Bru Second Division ● Scottish Cup ● Co-op Insurance Cup ● Challenge Cup

SECOND DIVISION GOALKEEPER STATS

Player	Appearances	Match starts	Completed matches	Sub appearances	Subbed off	Clean sheets	Yellow cards	Red cards
David McEwan	2	2	1	0	1	0	0	0
Mark McGeown	1	1	1	0	0	0	0	0
Jan Vonacek	24	24	23	0	0	7	0	1
Michael White	11	9	9	2	0	1	0	0

SECOND DIVISION OUTFIELD PLAYER STATS

Player	Appearances	Match starts	Completed matches	Substitute appearances	Subbed off	Goals scored	Yellow cards	Red cards
Kieran Brannan	13	5	0	8	5	0	2	0
Derek Carcary	31	9	7	22	2	5	1	0
Scott Chaplain	34	29	21	5	8	10	2	0
Iain Chisholm	31	27	26	4	1	1	2	0
Ross Clark	22	14	7	8	7	2	1	0
Alan Cook	10	10	5	0	5	3	0	0
Christopher Craig	17	16	2	1	14	1	1	0
Michael Dunlop	34	34	34	0	0	2	6	0
Andrew Geggan	27	27	21	0	6	2	5	0
Ben Gordon	34	34	33	0	1	3	6	0
Ross Harvey	1	1	1	0	0	0	1	0
Roddy Hunter	20	14	7	6	7	5	0	0
Denis McLaughlin	14	10	5	4	4	1	0	1
Martin McNiff	15	13	7	2	5	0	0	1
Ryan McStay	23	19	14	4	5	1	5	0
Stephen Murray	32	17	11	15	6	1	1	0
Ross O'Donoghue	19	15	12	4	3	1	1	0
Chris Smith	34	34	34	0	0	0	6	0
Adam Strachan	2	0	0	2	1	0	0	0
David Winters	15	15	6	0	9	5	1	0
Dennis Wyness	17	16	16	1	0	5	0	0

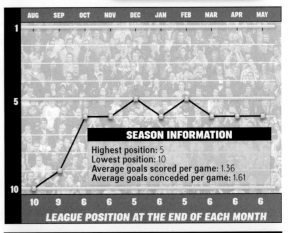

SEASON INFORMATION
Highest position: 5
Lowest position: 10
Average goals scored per game: 1.36
Average goals conceded per game: 1.61

LEAGUE POSITION AT THE END OF EACH MONTH

LONGEST SEQUENCES

Wins	3		Undefeated home		3
(10/10/09–24/10/09)			(24/10/09–08/12/09)		
Losses	4		Undefeated away		5
(16/02/10–06/03/10)			(16/03/10–17/04/10)		
Draws	–		Without scoring		2
(–)			(12/09/09–19/09/09)		
Undefeated	5		Without conceding		3
(10/10/09–07/11/09)			(24/10/09–07/11/09)		
Without win	6		Scoring		6
(08/08/09–19/09/09)			(15/12/09–02/03/10)		

CARDS RECEIVED

41   **3**

EARLIEST STRIKE
BEN GORDON
(v Stirling) 3:10

LATEST STRIKE
DEREK CARCARY
(v Peterhead) 90:00

GOALS SCORED/CONCEDED
PER FIVE-MINUTE INTERVALS

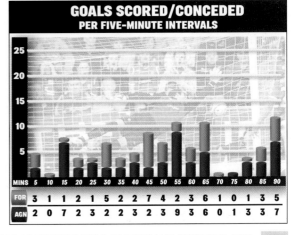

MINS	5	10	15	20	25	30	35	40	45	50	55	60	65	70	75	80	85	90
FOR	3	1	1	2	1	5	2	2	7	4	2	3	6	1	0	1	3	5
AGN	2	0	7	2	3	2	2	3	2	3	9	3	6	0	1	3	3	7

EAST FIFE

STEVIE CRAWFORD helped East Fife avoid relegation in his first full season as manager.

The former Scotland striker was appointed to the role full time in April 2009 following a spell as caretaker boss at the end of last term and his side got off to a good start in the new campaign, with a 2–0 opening-day win over Brechin sparking a five-match unbeaten run.

November brought a downturn in the club's fortunes as they struggled to pick up points in the League and crashed out of the Active Nation Scottish Cup to Montrose, but a 3–0 win at Dumbarton sparked a mini-revival.

The Fifers' ability to respond to poor results was crucial to their survival hopes and they reacted to a 6–2 defeat against Cowdenbeath by picking up seven points from the next available nine.

They remained in the relegation play-off equation until the final day of the regular season, though, when they drew 2–2 at rivals Arbroath to ensure survival.

CLUB SUMMARY

FORMED	1903
MANAGER	Stevie Crawford
GROUND	Bayview Stadium
CAPACITY	1,992
NICKNAME	The Fifers
WEBSITE	www.eastfife.org

The New Football Pools
PLAYER OF THE SEASON

David Muir

OVERALL
P	W	D	L	F	A	GD
39	10	11	18	49	60	-11

IRN-BRU SECOND DIVISION
Pos	P	W	D	L	F	A	GD	Pts
7	36	10	11	15	46	53	-7	41

HOME
Pos	P	W	D	L	F	A	GD	Pts
6	18	6	5	7	23	22	1	23

AWAY
Pos	P	W	D	L	F	A	GD	Pts
9	18	4	6	8	23	31	-8	18

CUP PROGRESS DETAILS
Competition	Round reached	Knocked out by
Scottish Cup	R3	Montrose
Co-op Insurance Cup	R1	Raith
Challenge Cup	R1	Forfar

BIGGEST WIN (ALL COMPS)
3–0 on 2 occasions

BIGGEST DEFEAT (ALL COMPS)
06/03/10 2–6 v Cowdenbeath

ATTENDANCE RECORD
High	Average	Low
864	599	213
v Cowdenbeath (16/01/2010)		v Brechin (30/03/2010)

RESULTS 2009/10

JULY
25th ● Forfar H L 0–2 Att: 446 Booked: Ovenstone.

AUGUST
1st ● Raith H L 2–3 Att: 1,390 Scorers: Linn, Muir. Booked: McManus, Fagan.
8th ● Brechin H W 2–0 Att: 584 Scorers: McManus, S Thomson.
15th ● Stenhousemuir A D 1–1 Att: 645 Scorers: Muir. Booked: Fagan.
22nd ● Arbroath H D 1–1 Att: 770 Scorers: Crawford. Booked: R Campbell, Smart.
29th ● Cowdenbeath H D 1–1 Att: 803 Scorers: McManus. Booked: Fagan, Smart, Ovenstone, Cargill, Linn.

SEPTEMBER
12th ● Peterhead A D 1–1 Att: 551 Scorers: McManus. Booked: Smart.
19th ● Stirling A L 3–0 Att: 678 Booked: Muir, Young, Crawford. Dismissed: Nugent.
26th ● Clyde H W 1–0 Att: 697 Scorers: Kerr. Booked: R Campbell.

OCTOBER
3rd ● Alloa A D 0–0 Att: 580
10th ● Dumbarton H L 0–1 Att: 620 Booked: Cargill.
17th ● Brechin A L 3–2 Att: 519 Scorers: McManus, Muir. Booked: Kerr.
24th ● Stenhousemuir H W 2–1 Att: 509 Scorers: Conway, McManus. Booked: Smart. Dismissed: Fagan.
31st ● Cowdenbeath A L 2–1 Att: 739 Scorers: Crawford. Booked: Smart, Ovenstone.

NOVEMBER
7th ● Peterhead H L 1–2 Att: 574 Scorers: McManus. Booked: Crawford, Ridgers, Ovenstone. Dismissed: Smart.
14th ● Stirling H L 1–2 Att: 633 Scorers: McManus. Booked: McManus.
21st ● Clyde A W 1–3 Att: 619 Scorers: Linn, McManus[2].
28th ● Montrose A L 2–1 Att: 509 Scorers: McManus. Booked: Gourlay.

DECEMBER
5th ● Alloa H L 0–2 Att: 509 Booked: Sludden, Kerr.
12th ● Dumbarton A W 0–3 Att: 628 Scorers: McManus, Muir, Smart.

JANUARY
16th ● Cowdenbeath H D 2–2 Att: 864 Scorers: Linn, Young.
23rd ● Stirling A D 3–3 Att: 665 Scorers: McManus[2], Young. Booked: Fagan.
27th ● Arbroath A W 0–1 Att: 376 Scorers: Linn. Booked: Ovenstone, Conway.

FEBRUARY
6th ● Dumbarton H L 2–3 Att: 581 Scorers: Crawford[2]. Booked: Ovenstone, Smart.
13th ● Alloa A L 2–0 Att: 670 Booked: McManus, Brown, Nugent, Ovenstone.
27th ● Stenhousemuir A D 1–1 Att: 476 Scorers: Young. Booked: Murdoch.

MARCH
6th ● Cowdenbeath A L 6–2 Att: 667 Scorers: Crawford, McManus.
9th ● Clyde H D 1–1 Att: 463 Scorers: Cargill. Booked: Crawford. Dismissed: McManus, Smart.
13th ● Peterhead H W 3–0 Att: 453 Scorers: Crawford, Linn, Young. Booked: Ovenstone.
16th ● Arbroath H W 3–1 Att: 480 Scorers: McCunnie[2], Murdoch. Booked: Murdoch, Linn.
20th ● Stirling A L 0–3 Att: 709 Booked: Muir.
23rd ● Peterhead A L 3–1 Att: 374 Scorers: Muir.
27th ● Clyde A L 2–1 Att: 495 Scorers: McManus. Booked: Crawford.
30th ● Brechin H W 2–0 Att: 213 Scorers: McManus, Ovenstone. Booked: Muir, Ovenstone.

APRIL
3rd ● Alloa H L 0–1 Att: 637 Booked: Young, Ovenstone.
10th ● Dumbarton A W 0–1 Att: 728 Scorers: Linn. Booked: Muir, Murdoch.
17th ● Brechin A L 1–0 Att: 492
24th ● Stenhousemuir H D 1–1 Att: 678 Scorers: Cook.

MAY
1st ● Arbroath A D 2–2 Att: 512 Scorers: Linn, Muir. Booked: Ovenstone, Cook, McCunnie.

● Irn-Bru Second Division ● Scottish Cup ● Co-op Insurance Cup ● Challenge Cup

actim

SECOND DIVISION GOALKEEPER STATS

Player	Appearances	Match starts	Completed matches	Sub appearances	Subbed off	Clean sheets	Yellow cards	Red cards
Stewart Baillie	7	6	6	1	0	2	0	0
Michael Brown	26	26	25	0	1	5	1	0
Mark Ridgers	4	4	4	0	0	0	1	0

SECOND DIVISION OUTFIELD PLAYER STATS

Player	Appearances	Match starts	Completed matches	Substitute appearances	Subbed off	Goals scored	Yellow cards	Red cards
Steven Campbell	5	5	1	0	4	0	0	0
Robert Campbell	18	10	6	8	4	0	2	0
Stuart Cargill	22	7	0	15	7	1	2	0
Aaron Conway	25	10	4	15	6	1	1	0
Andrew Cook	9	6	3	3	3	1	1	0
Stephen Crawford	34	28	15	6	13	6	4	0
Shaun Fagan	15	9	3	6	5	0	3	1
Darren Gourlay	8	4	2	4	2	0	0	0
Guy Kerr	11	7	7	4	0	1	2	0
Robert Linn	33	23	11	10	12	6	2	0
Alan Lowing	7	7	5	0	2	0	0	0
Jamie McCunnie	28	28	26	0	2	2	1	0
Paul McManus	32	28	19	4	8	15	2	1
Johnny McRae	1	1	0	0	1	0	0	0
David Muir	36	36	32	0	4	5	4	0
Stewart Murdoch	14	13	13	1	0	1	3	0
Paul Nugent	23	23	21	0	1	0	1	1
John Ovenstone	33	33	30	0	3	1	10	0
Jordyn Sheerin	9	4	0	5	4	0	0	0
Paul Sludden	5	4	3	1	1	0	1	0
Jonathan Smart	28	27	22	1	3	1	6	2
Mark Staunton	11	5	4	6	1	0	0	0
Scott Thomson	3	3	2	0	1	0	0	0
Darren Thomson	1	0	0	1	0	0	0	0
Keith Watson	6	6	6	0	0	0	0	0
Lloyd Young	35	33	27	2	6	4	2	0

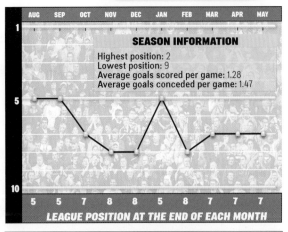

SEASON INFORMATION
Highest position: 2
Lowest position: 9
Average goals scored per game: 1.28
Average goals conceded per game: 1.47

AUG	SEP	OCT	NOV	DEC	JAN	FEB	MAR	APR	MAY

LEAGUE POSITION AT THE END OF EACH MONTH

5	5	7	8	8	5	8	7	7	7

LONGEST SEQUENCES

Wins	2	Undefeated home	4	
(13/03/10–16/03/10)		(08/08/09–26/09/09)		
Losses	3	Undefeated away	4	
(on two occasions)		(21/11/09–27/01/10)		
Draws	4	Without scoring	2	
(15/08/09–12/09/09)		(03/10/09–10/10/09)		
Undefeated	5	Without conceding	2	
(08/08/09–12/09/09)		(26/09/09–03/10/09)		
Without win	5	Scoring	6	
(on two occasions)		(17/10/09–21/11/09)		

CARDS RECEIVED

49 **5**

EARLIEST STRIKE
PAUL MCMANUS
(v Peterhead) 4:00

LATEST STRIKE
ROBERT LINN
(v Arbroath) 91:12

GOALS SCORED/CONCEDED
PER FIVE-MINUTE INTERVALS

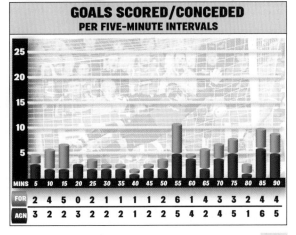

MINS	5	10	15	20	25	30	35	40	45	50	55	60	65	70	75	80	85	90
FOR	2	4	5	0	2	1	1	1	1	2	6	1	4	3	3	2	4	4
AGN	3	2	2	3	2	2	2	1	2	2	5	4	2	4	5	1	6	5

PETERHEAD narrowly missed out on a second successive season in the play-offs.

Neale Cooper's side, who had been beaten by Airdrie in the 2008/09 semi-finals, started the 2009/10 campaign well with a 2–0 League win over Clyde. The Blue Toon were dogged by inconsistency for the remainder of the year, but they managed to regroup after the weather forced the postponement of some of their fixtures in January, and they subsequently achieved resounding victories over Arbroath and Cowdenbeath.

Veteran midfielder Barry Wilson joined in January from Queen of the South and he scored key goals in the away wins over Dumbarton and Brechin. However, the Highland club's failure to beat Stenhousemuir at home in April proved a decisive blow to their play-off hopes.

They ended the season in good form thanks to a 1–0 win over Alloa in their last home game of 2009/10 and a 1–1 draw at Stenhousemuir on the final day.

CLUB SUMMARY

FORMED	1890
MANAGER	Neale Cooper
GROUND	Balmoor Stadium
CAPACITY	4,000
NICKNAME	The Blue Toon
WEBSITE	www.peterheadfc.org

The New Football Pools PLAYER OF THE SEASON — Paul Jarvie

OVERALL

P	W	D	L	F	A	GD
40	15	7	18	47	58	-11

IRN-BRU SECOND DIVISION

Pos	P	W	D	L	F	A	GD	Pts
5	36	15	6	15	45	49	-4	51

HOME

Pos	P	W	D	L	F	A	GD	Pts
5	18	8	5	5	23	18	5	29

AWAY

Pos	P	W	D	L	F	A	GD	Pts
6	18	7	1	10	22	31	-9	22

CUP PROGRESS DETAILS

Competition	Round reached	Knocked out by
Scottish Cup	R3	Raith
Co-op Insurance Cup	R1	Arbroath
Challenge Cup	R1	Cowdenbeath

BIGGEST WIN (ALL COMPS)
23/01/10 4-1 v Arbroath

BIGGEST DEFEAT (ALL COMPS)
10/10/09 0-5 v Cowdenbeath

ATTENDANCE RECORD

HIGH	AVERAGE	LOW
571	470	303
v Dumbarton (26/09/2009)		v Clyde (30/03/2010)

RESULTS 2009/10

JULY
25th	● Cowdenbeath	H	L 1-2	Att: 361	Scorers: Bavidge.

AUGUST
1st	● Arbroath	H	L 0-3	Att: 499	Booked: Cameron.
8th	● Clyde	H	W 2-0	Att: 525	Scorers: Ross². Booked: Strachan, MacDonald, Michie.
15th	● Alloa	A	L 1-0	Att: 446	Booked: Mann.
22nd	● Stenhousemuir	H	D 2-2	Att: 519	Scorers: Bavidge, McVitie. Booked: McVitie, Sharp, Bruce. Dismissed: Sharp.
29th	● Stirling	A	L 2-1	Att: 537	Scorers: Cameron. Booked: Bavidge. Dismissed: Mann.

SEPTEMBER
12th	● East Fife	H	D 1-1	Att: 551	Scorers: Michie. Booked: Cameron.
19th	● Arbroath	A	W 0-1	Att: 476	Scorers: Ross. Booked: Cameron, McVitie.
26th	● Dumbarton	H	L 1-2	Att: 571	Scorers: Bruce.

OCTOBER
10th	● Cowdenbeath	A	L 5-0	Att: 271	
13th	● Brechin	H	W 1-0	Att: 429	Scorers: Stewart. Booked: Mann, Bruce, Stewart.
17th	● Clyde	A	W 1-3	Att: 673	Scorers: Ross², Stewart. Booked: Stewart.
24th	● Alloa	H	D 0-0	Att: 485	Booked: S Smith, Stewart.
31st	● Stirling	H	W 3-2	Att: 546	Scorers: Clark, MacDonald, Stewart.

NOVEMBER
7th	● East Fife	A	W 1-2	Att: 574	Scorers: Mann, Stewart. Booked: Mann, Bavidge.
14th	● Arbroath	H	L 1-2	Att: 500	Scorers: Bavidge. Booked: Donald, Mann.
28th	● Raith	A	D 0-0	Att: 1,418	

DECEMBER
1st	● Raith	H	L 1-4	Att: 537	Scorers: Stewart. Booked: McVitie, Cameron.
8th	● Dumbarton	A	L 1-0	Att: 397	Booked: McVitie, Jarvie, S Smith, Bruce, Stewart.
12th	● Cowdenbeath	H	L 0-2	Att: 440	Booked: Donald.
15th	● Brechin	A	L 3-0	Att: 417	Booked: MacDonald.

JANUARY
23rd	● Arbroath	A	W 1-4	Att: 465	Scorers: Bavidge, Clark, Ross, Wilson. Booked: Clark.

FEBRUARY
6th	● Cowdenbeath	A	W 1-3	Att: 298	Scorers: Bavidge², Wilson. Booked: Jarvie, Mann.
13th	● Brechin	H	L 0-3	Att: 553	Booked: McVitie.
27th	● Alloa	A	L 2-1	Att: 448	Scorers: Clark. Booked: Crawford, Mann, Strachan. Dismissed: Emslie.

MARCH
2nd	● Dumbarton	H	W 2-1	Att: 327	Scorers: Sharp². Booked: Bavidge. Dismissed: Crawford.
6th	● Stirling	H	D 1-1	Att: 497	Scorers: Clark. Booked: McVitie.
9th	● Stenhousemuir	A	L 2-0	Att: 207	
13th	● East Fife	A	L 3-0	Att: 453	Booked: McVitie, Clark, MacDonald.
16th	● Stirling	A	L 2-0	Att: 297	
20th	● Arbroath	H	W 3-0	Att: 483	Scorers: Bavidge², Bruce. Booked: Mann, Emslie.
23rd	● East Fife	H	W 3-1	Att: 374	Scorers: Bavidge, Ross, Wilson. Booked: Emslie.
27th	● Dumbarton	A	W 1-3	Att: 663	Scorers: Bavidge, Mann, Wilson. Booked: Crawford.
30th	● Clyde	H	D 0-0	Att: 303	

APRIL
3rd	● Brechin	A	W 1-2	Att: 463	Scorers: Bavidge, Wilson. Booked: Sharp, Strachan. Dismissed: Mann.
6th	● Stenhousemuir	H	L 0-1	Att: 364	Booked: Moore.
10th	● Cowdenbeath	H	W 1-0	Att: 435	Scorers: Bavidge. Booked: Wilson, Emslie.
17th	● Clyde	A	L 3-1	Att: 515	Scorers: Gethans. Booked: Emslie, S Smith.
24th	● Alloa	H	W 2-0	Att: 561	Scorers: Emslie, Gethans. Booked: Strachan.

MAY
1st	● Stenhousemuir	A	D 1-1	Att: 612	Scorers: Emslie. Booked: Moore.

● Irn-Bru Second Division ● Scottish Cup ● Co-op Insurance Cup ● Challenge Cup

actim

SECOND DIVISION GOALKEEPER STATS

Player	Appearances	Match starts	Completed matches	Sub appearances	Subbed off	Clean sheets	Yellow cards	Red cards
John Bateman	18	17	16	1	1	6	0	0
Paul Jarvie	20	19	18	1	1	2	2	0

SECOND DIVISION OUTFIELD PLAYER STATS

Player	Appearances	Match starts	Completed matches	Substitute appearances	Subbed off	Goals scored	Yellow cards	Red cards
Martin Bavidge	31	31	24	0	7	11	3	0
Cameron Bowden	2	0	0	2	0	0	0	0
Peter Bruce	27	8	2	19	6	2	3	0
Douglas Cameron	14	10	8	4	2	1	2	0
Nicky Clark	23	18	14	5	4	4	2	0
Jonathan Crawford	14	14	13	0	0	0	2	1
David Donald	27	27	24	0	3	0	2	0
Paul Emslie	15	12	10	3	1	2	4	1
Connor Gethans	13	4	3	9	1	2	0	0
Callum MacDonald	22	21	19	1	2	1	3	0
Robert Mann	27	27	24	0	1	2	7	2
Neil McVitie	29	27	24	2	3	1	6	0
Scott Michie	4	2	0	2	2	1	1	0
Daniel Moore	10	10	10	0	0	0	2	0
David Ross	34	33	19	1	14	7	0	0
Graeme Sharp	29	24	17	5	6	2	2	1
Jonathan Smith	9	0	0	9	0	0	0	0
Stuart Smith	36	36	36	0	0	0	3	0
John Stewart	7	6	2	1	4	4	4	0
Ryan Strachan	34	30	23	4	7	0	4	0
Alexander Sutherland	1	1	0	0	1	0	0	0
Barry Wilson	16	15	10	1	5	5	1	0
Paul Young	2	0	0	2	0	0	0	0

| AUG | SEP | OCT | NOV | DEC | JAN | FEB | MAR | APR | MAY |

SEASON INFORMATION
Highest position: 3
Lowest position: 8
Average goals scored per game: 1.25
Average goals conceded per game: 1.36

LEAGUE POSITION AT THE END OF EACH MONTH

| 7 | 8 | 5 | 5 | 6 | 7 | 7 | 5 | 5 | 5 |

LONGEST SEQUENCES

Wins	3		Undefeated home	5	
(20/03/10–27/03/10)			(02/03/10–30/03/10)		
Losses	4		Undefeated away	2	
(14/11/09–15/12/09)			(on three occasions)		
Draws	–		Without scoring	3	
(–)			(on two occasions)		
Undefeated	5		Without conceding	–	
(on two occasions)			(–)		
Without win	4		Scoring	5	
(on three occasions)			(22/08/09–26/09/09)		

CARDS RECEIVED

53   **5**

EARLIEST STRIKE
DAVID ROSS
(v Clyde) 6:00

LATEST STRIKE
BARRY WILSON
(v Cowdenbeath) 88:43

GOALS SCORED/CONCEDED
PER FIVE-MINUTE INTERVALS

MINS	5	10	15	20	25	30	35	40	45	50	55	60	65	70	75	80	85	90
FOR	0	1	4	2	4	2	2	1	1	1	3	4	3	5	2	6	1	3
AGN	3	2	4	0	3	3	2	2	1	4	1	0	2	0	6	5	5	6

STENHOUSEMUIR

STENHOUSEMUIR survived their first season back in the third tier for six years as they avoided a relegation play-off on goal difference.

The Warriors had won a penalty shoot-out against Cowdenbeath in May 2009 to achieve promotion via the play-offs and they made a decent start to this campaign going unbeaten in their first six League games, although they did exit the Co-operative Insurance Cup with a 5–0 defeat to St Johnstone.

Their solid form eventually faltered and they soon found themselves at the bottom end of the table but, despite taking only two points from their final four games of the campaign, a draw with Peterhead was good enough to keep them above Arbroath.

Stenny's season was also significant for their Active Nation Scottish Cup fourth-round tie with Dunfermline, which was eventually replayed after the Pars fielded an ineligible player in a 7–1 win, although Arthur Bell's side also lost the rearranged tie.

CLUB SUMMARY

FORMED	*1884*
MANAGER	*Arthur Bell*
GROUND	*Ochilview Park*
CAPACITY	*3,776*
NICKNAME	*The Warriors*
WEBSITE	*www.stenhousemuir.com*

The New **Football Pools**
PLAYER OF THE SEASON

Chris McCluskey

OVERALL
P	W	D	L	F	A	GD
42	11	13	18	48	59	-11

IRN-BRU SECOND DIVISION
Pos	P	W	D	L	F	A	GD	Pts
8	36	9	13	14	38	42	-4	40

HOME
Pos	P	W	D	L	F	A	GD	Pts
7	18	5	6	7	16	22	-6	21

AWAY
Pos	P	W	D	L	F	A	GD	Pts
8	18	4	7	7	22	20	2	19

CUP PROGRESS DETAILS
Competition	Round reached	Knocked out by
Scottish Cup	R4	Dunfermline
Co-op Insurance Cup	R1	St Johnstone
Challenge Cup	R2	Stirling

BIGGEST WIN (ALL COMPS)
05/12/09 5–0 v Cove Rangers

BIGGEST DEFEAT (ALL COMPS)
09/01/10 1–7 v Dunfermline

ATTENDANCE RECORD
HIGH	AVERAGE	LOW
801	542	207
v Stirling (17/10/2009)		v Peterhead (09/03/2010)

RESULTS 2009/10

JULY
25th	● Clyde	H	W 2–0	**Att:** 603	**Scorers:** Dalziel, O'Reilly. **Booked:** S Thomson.

AUGUST
1st	● St Johnstone	H	L 0–5	**Att:** 1,049	**Booked:** Dalziel.
8th	● Stirling	A	D 0–0	**Att:** 696	
15th	● East Fife	H	D 1–1	**Att:** 645	**Scorers:** Scullion. **Booked:** Scullion, Lyle.
18th	● Stirling	A	L 3–1	**Att:** 275	**Scorers:** Dalziel. **Booked:** Stirling. **Dismissed:** Stirling.
22nd	● Peterhead	A	D 2–2	**Att:** 519	**Scorers:** Diack, Thom. **Booked:** Lyle, Molloy.
29th	● Arbroath	H	W 3–0	**Att:** 543	**Scorers:** Diack, J Smith, I Thomson. **Booked:** Thom, Motion, Lyle, Dalziel, Bradley, Diack.

SEPTEMBER
12th	● Dumbarton	A	D 0–0	**Att:** 681	**Booked:** Scullion, Lyle.
19th	● Alloa	H	W 1–0	**Att:** 727	**Scorers:** Motion. **Booked:** Scullion, J Smith, I Thomson.
26th	● Brechin	A	L 1–0	**Att:** 421	

OCTOBER
3rd	● Cowdenbeath	H	L 0–2	**Att:** 443	**Booked:** McCluskey, Bradley, Diack, Thom.
10th	● Clyde	A	L 2–1	**Att:** 755	**Scorers:** Molloy. **Booked:** Diack, Motion, I Thomson. **Dismissed:** S Thomson.
17th	● Stirling	H	L 1–2	**Att:** 801	**Scorers:** Motion. **Booked:** Lyle, Motion, Love, Diack.
24th	● East Fife	A	L 2–1	**Att:** 509	**Scorers:** Molloy. **Booked:** Thom.
31st	● Arbroath	A	W 0–3	**Att:** 402	**Scorers:** Love2, Motion. **Booked:** Dalziel.

NOVEMBER
7th	● Dumbarton	H	L 0–3	**Att:** 568	**Booked:** Dalziel.
14th	● Alloa	A	W 1–4	**Att:** 544	**Scorers:** Dalziel, Molloy, Motion, Scullion. **Booked:** Lyle.
21st	● Brechin	H	D 1–1	**Att:** 551	**Scorers:** Motion.

DECEMBER
5th	● Cove Rangers	H	W 5–0	**Att:** 409	**Scorers:** Bradley, Molloy, Motion2, I Thomson.
12th	● Clyde	H	W 1–0	**Att:** 532	**Scorers:** Molloy. **Booked:** Bradley.
15th	● Cowdenbeath	H	L 2–1	**Att:** 264	**Scorers:** Dalziel.

JANUARY
9th	● Dunfermline	A	L 7–1	**Att:** 1,832	**Scorers:** Bradley.
16th	● Arbroath	H	D 1–1	**Att:** 443	**Scorers:** Love. **Booked:** Stirling, Currie, Molloy.
23rd	● Alloa	H	L 0–2	**Att:** 554	**Booked:** Lyle.
26th	● Dunfermline	H	L 1–2	**Att:** 1,810	**Scorers:** Bradley. **Booked:** Molloy, Lyle. AET – Score after 90 mins 1–1.
30th	● Brechin	A	D 2–2	**Att:** 413	**Scorers:** Dalziel, Scullion. **Booked:** S Thomson, Gair.

FEBRUARY
6th	● Clyde	A	W 0–2	**Att:** 650	**Scorers:** Motion, J Smith. **Booked:** S Thomson, Love.
13th	● Cowdenbeath	H	D 0–0	**Att:** 443	**Booked:** Scullion, I Thomson. **Dismissed:** Scullion.
27th	● East Fife	H	D 1–1	**Att:** 476	**Scorers:** McLeod. **Booked:** Motion.

MARCH
2nd	● Stirling	A	D 1–1	**Att:** 473	**Scorers:** Thom. **Booked:** McLeod.
6th	● Arbroath	A	D 1–1	**Att:** 458	**Scorers:** Motion. **Booked:** I Thomson, McLeod, S Thomson. **Dismissed:** I Thomson, Lyle.
9th	● Peterhead	H	W 2–0	**Att:** 207	**Scorers:** Dalziel, Gibb.
13th	● Dumbarton	H	W 1–0	**Att:** 469	**Scorers:** Quinn.
20th	● Alloa	A	L 2–1	**Att:** 550	**Scorers:** Dalziel. **Dismissed:** I Thomson.
23rd	● Dumbarton	A	L 2–1	**Att:** 486	**Scorers:** Lyle. **Booked:** Molloy. **Dismissed:** Thom.
27th	● Brechin	H	L 1–2	**Att:** 481	**Scorers:** Diack. **Booked:** Stirling.

APRIL
3rd	● Cowdenbeath	A	L 1–0	**Att:** 438	**Booked:** McLeod.
6th	● Peterhead	A	W 0–1	**Att:** 364	**Scorers:** Love. **Booked:** Dalziel.
10th	● Clyde	H	L 0–3	**Att:** 482	
17th	● Stirling	H	L 1–3	**Att:** 783	**Scorers:** Diack. **Booked:** Gibb, Scullion.
24th	● East Fife	A	D 1–1	**Att:** 678	**Scorers:** Quinn. **Booked:** I Thomson, Molloy.

MAY
1st	● Peterhead	H	D 1–1	**Att:** 612	**Scorers:** Dalziel. **Booked:** Molloy.

● Irn-Bru Second Division ● Scottish Cup ● Co-op Insurance Cup ● Challenge Cup

SECOND DIVISION GOALKEEPER STATS

Player	Appearances	Match starts	Completed matches	Sub appearances	Subbed off	Clean sheets	Yellow cards	Red cards
Scott Bennett	2	2	2	0	0	0	0	0
Chris McCluskey	34	34	34	0	0	11	1	0

SECOND DIVISION OUTFIELD PLAYER STATS

Player	Appearances	Match starts	Completed matches	Substitute appearances	Subbed off	Goals scored	Yellow cards	Red cards
Grant Anderson	1	0	0	1	0	0	0	0
Kevin Bradley	20	10	5	10	5	0	3	0
Andrew Brand	10	5	2	5	3	0	0	0
Lee Currie	2	2	2	0	0	0	1	0
Scott Dalziel	35	31	20	4	11	6	4	0
Iain Diack	26	17	7	9	10	4	4	0
Sean Dickson	2	0	0	2	0	0	0	0
Scott Gair	2	2	1	0	1	0	1	0
Scott Gibb	13	12	11	1	1	1	1	0
Michael Hunter	2	1	1	1	0	0	0	0
Alan Lawson	1	0	0	1	0	0	0	0
Robert Love	23	13	5	10	8	4	2	0
William Lyle	26	24	19	2	4	1	7	1
Christopher McLeod	30	29	27	1	2	1	3	0
Craig Molloy	29	26	24	3	2	4	5	0
Kevin Motion	33	32	27	1	5	7	4	0
Craig O'Reilly	11	4	1	7	3	0	0	0
Paul Quinn	12	2	1	10	1	2	0	0
Alan Reid	2	2	2	0	0	0	0	0
Pat Scullion	29	27	15	2	11	3	5	1
Darren Smith	2	2	1	0	1	0	0	0
Jordan Smith	30	30	29	0	1	2	1	0
Andrew Stirling	15	5	0	10	5	0	2	0
Gary Thom	28	28	26	0	1	2	3	1
Stephen Thomson	27	27	20	0	6	0	3	1
Iain Thomson	30	27	23	3	2	1	5	2
Sean Welsh	2	2	2	0	0	0	0	0

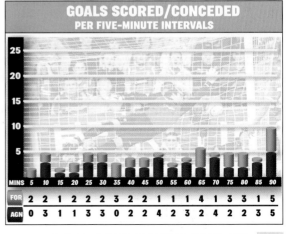

SEASON INFORMATION

Highest position: 2
Lowest position: 10
Average goals scored per game: 1.06
Average goals conceded per game: 1.17

LEAGUE POSITION AT THE END OF EACH MONTH

AUG SEP OCT NOV DEC JAN FEB MAR APR MAY
4 4 8 7 7 8 6 8 8 8

LONGEST SEQUENCES

Wins	2		Undefeated home	4
(09/03/10–13/03/10)			(13/02/10–13/03/10)	
Losses	5		Undefeated away	4
(26/09/09–24/10/09)			(30/01/10–06/03/10)	
Draws	4		Without scoring	2
(13/02/10–06/03/10)			(26/09/09–03/10/09)	
Undefeated	8		Without conceding	3
(30/01/10–13/03/10)			(29/08/09–19/09/09)	
Without win	5		Scoring	8
(26/09/09–24/10/09)			(27/02/10–27/03/10)	

CARDS RECEIVED
55 6

EARLIEST STRIKE
ROBERT LOVE
(v Peterhead) 2:54

LATEST STRIKE
CRAIG MOLLOY
(v East Fife) 90:00

GOALS SCORED/CONCEDED
PER FIVE-MINUTE INTERVALS

MINS	5	10	15	20	25	30	35	40	45	50	55	60	65	70	75	80	85	90
FOR	2	2	1	2	2	3	2	2	1	1	1	4	1	3	3	1	5	
AGN	0	3	1	1	3	3	0	2	2	4	2	3	2	4	2	2	3	5

STIRLING ALBION sealed a dramatic return to the Irn-Bru First Division two years after their relegation.

The Binos clinched the Second Division title on goal difference from Alloa after surviving the sending-off of Brian Allison in their 1–1 draw at Brechin on the final day of the season.

They overcame financial difficulties and fears over their future to launch a prolonged charge for promotion and were top of the table for much of the campaign.

A poor winter – which included a shock 9–0 defeat to Ross County in the Active Nation Scottish Cup – resulted in Albion losing four games out of their next five, but manager Allan Moore got them back on track with just two defeats in their last 13 games to complete one of the most successful campaigns of his eight years in charge.

However, Moore decided to leave for Morton at the end of May, with John O'Neill replacing him at Forthbank.

CLUB SUMMARY

FORMED	1945
MANAGER	John O'Neill
GROUND	Forthbank Stadium
CAPACITY	3,808
NICKNAME	The Binos
WEBSITE	www.stirlingalbion.co.uk

The New
Football Pools
PLAYER OF THE SEASON

Andrew Graham

OVERALL
P	W	D	L	F	A	GD
44	22	12	10	80	65	15

IRN-BRU SECOND DIVISION
Pos	P	W	D	L	F	A	GD	Pts
1	36	18	11	7	68	48	20	65

HOME
Pos	P	W	D	L	F	A	GD	Pts
4	18	7	8	3	30	22	8	29

AWAY
Pos	P	W	D	L	F	A	GD	Pts
1	18	11	3	4	38	26	12	36

CUP PROGRESS DETAILS
Competition	Round reached	Knocked out by
Scottish Cup	R5	Ross County
Co-op Insurance Cup	R1	Ayr
Challenge Cup	QF	Dundee

BIGGEST WIN (ALL COMPS)
14/04/10 6–2 v Brechin

BIGGEST DEFEAT (ALL COMPS)
06/02/10 0–9 v Ross County

ATTENDANCE RECORD
HIGH	AVERAGE	LOW
1,036	624	297
v Alloa (13/03/2010)		v Peterhead (16/03/2010)

RESULTS 2009/10

JULY
25th	● Raith	H	W 2–1	Att: 713	Scorers: Graham, McKenna. Booked: Graham, Roycroft, McCord.

AUGUST
1st	● Ayr	H	L 1–2	Att: 802	Scorers: Devine. Booked: Robertson, Forsyth, Graham. Dismissed: Graham, Forsyth. AET – Score after 90 mins 1–1.
8th	● Stenhousemuir	H	D 0–0	Att: 696	
15th	● Clyde	A	W 0–1	Att: 813	Scorers: Grehan. Booked: Devine, Grehan.
18th	● Stenhousemuir	H	W 3–1	Att: 275	Scorers: McKenna, Mullen, Robertson. Booked: Devine.
22nd	● Brechin	H	W 1–0	Att: 608	Scorers: Grehan. Booked: O'Neill.
29th	● Peterhead	A	W 2–1	Att: 537	Scorers: McKenna[2]. Booked: Roycroft.

SEPTEMBER
6th	● Dundee	H	L 1–2	Att: 1,277	Scorers: Devine. Booked: Grehan, O'Neill, Forsyth.
12th	● Alloa	A	L 1–0	Att: 1,201	Booked: Forsyth, Devine, Roycroft.
19th	● East Fife	H	W 3–0	Att: 678	Scorers: Graham, Grehan, McCord.
26th	● Cowdenbeath	A	W 1–2	Att: 451	Scorers: Grehan, McKenna.

OCTOBER
3rd	● Dumbarton	A	W 2–3	Att: 808	Scorers: Devine, McKenna, Robertson. Booked: Taggart.
10th	● Arbroath	H	D 2–2	Att: 689	Scorers: McKenna, Robertson. Booked: Feaks.
17th	● Stenhousemuir	A	W 1–2	Att: 801	Scorers: Grehan, O'Brien. Booked: Murphy, McKenna, Graham.
24th	● Clyde	H	D 1–1	Att: 764	Scorers: Corr.
31st	● Peterhead	A	L 3–2	Att: 546	Scorers: Devine, Grehan. Booked: Forsyth, Graham. Dismissed: Forsyth.

NOVEMBER
7th	● Alloa	H	L 0–1	Att: 986	Booked: O'Neill.
14th	● East Fife	A	W 1–2	Att: 633	Scorers: Grehan, O'Brien. Booked: Forsyth, Robertson.
21st	● Cowdenbeath	H	D 2–2	Att: 682	Scorers: Forsyth, McKenna. Booked: Grehan, Robertson, O'Brien. Dismissed: Grehan.
28th	● Auchinleck Talbot	H	W 2–1	Att: 1,185	Scorers: Corr, Forsyth. Booked: Christie.

DECEMBER
12th	● Arbroath	A	W 3–4	Att: 491	Scorers: Mullen, Murphy, O'Brien[2].
15th	● Dumbarton	H	D 2–2	Att: 462	Scorers: Devine, Murphy. Booked: Roycroft.

JANUARY
18th	● Albion	A	D 0–0	Att: 395	Booked: Robertson.
20th	● Albion	H	W 3–1	Att: 355	Scorers: Mullen[2], Murphy. Booked: Devine.
23rd	● East Fife	A	D 3–3	Att: 665	Scorers: Forsyth, O'Brien, Smart OG.

FEBRUARY
6th	● Ross County	A	L 9–0	Att: 1,365	Booked: Forsyth, Graham.
16th	● Dumbarton	A	W 2–4	Att: 595	Scorers: Aitken[2], Robertson[2]. Booked: Robertson.

MARCH
2nd	● Stenhousemuir	H	D 1–1	Att: 473	Scorers: Aitken. Booked: O'Brien. Dismissed: Murphy.
6th	● Peterhead	H	D 1–1	Att: 497	Scorers: O'Brien. Booked: Byrne.
9th	● Brechin	A	L 1–0	Att: 453	Booked: Robertson.
13th	● Alloa	H	L 0–3	Att: 1,036	Booked: Aitken, Forsyth, Robertson.
16th	● Peterhead	H	W 2–0	Att: 297	Scorers: McKenna, Bowden OG.
20th	● East Fife	A	W 0–3	Att: 709	Scorers: Elliott, Page[2]. Booked: Page.
23rd	● Alloa	A	L 2–1	Att: 1,147	Scorers: Graham. Booked: Allison.
27th	● Cowdenbeath	H	W 1–0	Att: 575	Scorers: Mullen. Booked: Christie, Aitken, Forsyth, Russell.

APRIL
3rd	● Dumbarton	H	L 1–2	Att: 568	Scorers: Taggart. Booked: Robertson, Aitken.
10th	● Arbroath	A	W 2–4	Att: 525	Scorers: Aitken, Gibson, Graham, Russell. Booked: Page, Robertson, Russell.
12th	● Arbroath	H	D 2–2	Att: 365	Scorers: Graham, Russell. Booked: Russell.
14th	● Brechin	H	W 6–2	Att: 357	Scorers: Aitken, Colquhoun, Mullen[3], Russell.
17th	● Stenhousemuir	H	W 1–3	Att: 783	Scorers: Forsyth, Graham, Russell. Booked: Forsyth.
20th	● Clyde	A	W 1–2	Att: 635	Scorers: Robertson, Russell. Booked: Robertson, Forsyth.
24th	● Clyde	H	W 1–0	Att: 796	Scorers: Robertson. Booked: Aitken.
27th	● Cowdenbeath	A	D 3–3	Att: 1,084	Scorers: Graham, Russell[2]. Booked: Graham.

MAY
1st	● Brechin	A	D 1–1	Att: 1,102	Scorers: Mullen. Booked: Allison, Russell, Forsyth. Dismissed: Allison.

● Irn-Bru Second Division ● Scottish Cup ● Co-op Insurance Cup ● Challenge Cup

SECOND DIVISION GOALKEEPER STATS

Player	Appearances	Match starts	Completed matches	Sub appearances	Subbed off	Clean sheets	Yellow cards	Red cards
Scott Christie	26	26	26	0	0	7	1	0
Myles Hogarth	10	10	10	0	0	1	0	0

SECOND DIVISION OUTFIELD PLAYER STATS

Player	Appearances	Match starts	Completed matches	Substitute appearances	Subbed off	Goals scored	Yellow cards	Red cards
Christoper Aitken	19	18	14	1	4	5	4	0
Brian Allison	17	16	15	1	0	0	2	1
Kurtis Byrne	3	2	1	1	1	0	1	0
Derek Colquhoun	8	4	1	4	3	1	0	0
Liam Corr	11	1	0	10	1	1	0	0
Stewart Devine	15	12	9	3	3	3	2	0
Stuart Elliott	7	5	2	2	3	1	0	0
Kenny Feaks	10	9	7	1	2	0	1	0
Ross Forsyth	32	32	31	0	0	3	8	1
Andy Gibson	35	30	23	5	7	1	0	0
Andrew Graham	36	36	36	0	0	6	3	0
Martin Grehan	16	14	11	2	2	7	2	1
Ross McCord	11	4	1	7	3	1	0	0
David McKenna	34	19	10	15	9	7	1	0
Craig McKeown	2	2	2	0	0	0	0	0
Michael Mullen	28	14	2	14	12	6	0	0
Paul Murphy	28	18	6	10	11	2	1	1
David O'Brien	36	34	29	2	5	6	2	0
John O'Neill	16	10	4	6	6	0	2	0
Jonathan Page	16	16	15	0	1	2	2	0
Bryan Prunty	3	3	0	0	3	0	0	0
Scott Robertson	33	27	17	6	10	6	8	0
Sean Roycroft	10	10	9	0	1	0	3	0
Iain Russell	10	10	6	0	4	7	4	0
Nathan Taggart	21	11	3	10	8	1	1	0
Craig Young	5	3	0	2	3	0	0	0

AUG	SEP	OCT	NOV	DEC	JAN	FEB	MAR	APR	MAY
2	1	1	2	2	3	2	3	1	1

LEAGUE POSITION AT THE END OF EACH MONTH

SEASON INFORMATION
Highest position: 1
Lowest position: 4
Average goals scored per game: 1.89
Average goals conceded per game: 1.33

LONGEST SEQUENCES

Wins	4	Undefeated home	6
(14/04/10–24/04/10)		(08/08/09–24/10/09)	
Losses	2	Undefeated away	5
(on two occasions)		(10/04/10–01/05/10)	
Draws	2	Without scoring	2
(on three occasions)		(09/03/10–13/03/10)	
Undefeated	8	Without conceding	3
(on two occasions)		(08/08/09–22/08/09)	
Without win	4	Scoring	8
(02/03/10–13/03/10)		(14/11/09–06/03/10)	

CARDS RECEIVED
48   4

EARLIEST STRIKE
SCOTT ROBERTSON
(v Dumbarton) 0:58

LATEST STRIKE
ANDREW GRAHAM
(v Cowdenbeath) 94:23

GOALS SCORED/CONCEDED
PER FIVE-MINUTE INTERVALS

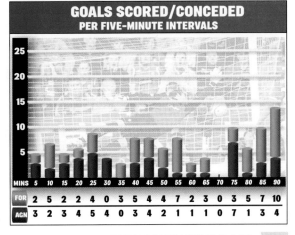

MINS	5	10	15	20	25	30	35	40	45	50	55	60	65	70	75	80	85	90
FOR	2	5	2	2	4	0	3	5	4	4	7	2	3	0	3	5	7	10
AGN	3	2	3	4	5	4	0	3	4	2	1	1	1	0	7	1	3	4

ALBION ROVERS

ALBION ROVERS missed out on the play-offs for promotion to the Irn-Bru Second Division by just a point following a solid campaign.

On the back of last season's eighth-place finish, the Wee Rovers began this term well, putting together an unbeaten run of nine League games until losing to Queen's Park on 17th October.

That failed to derail their challenge, but the New Year sparked a downturn in their fortunes as they suffered consecutive losses at the hands of Stirling, Forfar, Elgin and Livingston.

Inconsistency in the latter part of the campaign cost Albion dearly, but they still went into the final day of the regular season in play-off contention. However, they were held to a goalless draw by Stranraer, allowing Queen's Park to hold on to fourth spot.

Goals were sparce for Albion fans as Paul Martin's side only found the net 35 times – a record worsened only by Montrose – but only League champions Inverness conceded fewer.

CLUB SUMMARY

FORMED	1882
MANAGER	Paul Martin
GROUND	Cliftonhill
CAPACITY	2,496
NICKNAME	The Wee Rovers
WEBSITE	www.albionrovers.co.uk

The New Football Pools PLAYER OF THE SEASON

Marc McCusker

OVERALL
P	W	D	L	F	A	GD
44	17	12	15	44	45	-1

IRN-BRU THIRD DIVISION
Pos	P	W	D	L	F	A	GD	Pts
5	36	13	11	12	35	35	0	50

HOME
Pos	P	W	D	L	F	A	GD	Pts
4	18	9	5	4	21	12	9	32

AWAY
Pos	P	W	D	L	F	A	GD	Pts
8	18	4	6	8	14	23	-9	18

CUP PROGRESS DETAILS
Competition	Round reached	Knocked out by
Scottish Cup	R4	Stirling
Co-op Insurance Cup	R2	Inverness
Challenge Cup	R2	Elgin

BIGGEST WIN (ALL COMPS)
09/03/10 4-1 v Berwick

BIGGEST DEFEAT (ALL COMPS)
25/08/09 0-4 v Inverness CT

ATTENDANCE RECORD
HIGH	AVERAGE	Low
613	359	217
v Queen's Park (17/10/2009)		v Montrose (13/03/2010)

RESULTS 2009/10

JULY
25th	● Ayr	A	W 0–2	Att: 964	Scorers: Barr, McFarlane. Booked: Reid.

AUGUST
1st	● Livingston	H	W 3–0	Att: 602	Scorers: Barr, McCusker, McKenzie OG. Booked: O'Byrne.
8th	● Stranraer	A	D 1–1	Att: 296	Scorers: Tyrrell. Booked: O'Byrne.
15th	● Berwick	H	W 2–1	Att: 322	Scorers: Barr, Walker.
18th	● Elgin	A	L 3–0	Att: 245	Booked: McKeown, McGowan. Dismissed: Canning.
25th	● Inverness	A	L 4–0	Att: 681	Booked: Reid, Walker.
29th	● Livingston	H	W 1–0	Att: 489	Scorers: Moyes OG. Booked: Tyrrell, McFarlane.

SEPTEMBER
12th	● Montrose	A	D 0–0	Att: 323	Booked: Canning, Benton.
19th	● Forfar	H	D 1–1	Att: 279	Scorers: O'Byrne. Booked: Barr.
26th	● Annan	A	D 0–0	Att: 510	Booked: Benton, Barr.
29th	● Queen's Park	A	W 0–1	Att: 376	Scorers: Pollock.

OCTOBER
3rd	● East Stirling	H	W 3–0	Att: 413	Scorers: McFarlane[2], Pollock.
10th	● Elgin	A	W 0–2	Att: 526	Scorers: Canning, McFarlane.
17th	● Queen's Park	H	L 0–1	Att: 613	Booked: Canning.
24th	● Lossiemouth	A	W 0–2	Att: 235	Scorers: Barr, Walker. Booked: McGowan.
31st	● Berwick	A	L 2–0	Att: 471	Booked: McGowan, Benton, O'Byrne, McCusker.

NOVEMBER
7th	● Montrose	H	D 0–0	Att: 257	Booked: Donnelly, Benton, O'Byrne.
21st	● Annan	H	D 0–0	Att: 375	
24th	● Livingston	A	L 2–0	Att: 726	
28th	● Elgin	H	W 1–0	Att: 275	Scorers: Pollock. Booked: McGowan, Boyle.

DECEMBER
5th	● Forfar	A	D 2–2	Att: 434	Scorers: Donnelly, Walker. Booked: O'Byrne, McGowan, Strachaen, McCusker.
12th	● Elgin	H	D 1–1	Att: 225	Scorers: MacAulay OG. Booked: O'Byrne.

JANUARY
18th	● Stirling	H	D 0–0	Att: 395	Booked: O'Byrne.
20th	● Stirling	A	L 3–1	Att: 355	Scorers: Walker. Booked: McCusker, Benton.
23rd	● Forfar	H	L 0–1	Att: 227	Booked: McCusker, O'Byrne, Benton, Donnelly. Dismissed: O'Byrne.

FEBRUARY
6th	● Elgin	A	L 3–1	Att: 326	Scorers: McCusker. Booked: McFarlane.
9th	● Livingston	H	L 0–2	Att: 587	Booked: Tyrrell. Dismissed: McGrath.
17th	● Annan	A	W 1–2	Att: 317	Scorers: Boyle, McLeod. Booked: Canning, Lumsden, Donnelly.

MARCH
2nd	● Montrose	A	D 0–0	Att: 249	Booked: Benton.
9th	● Berwick	H	W 4–1	Att: 227	Scorers: McCusker[2], McLeod, Thomson. Booked: McCusker, Gilmartin.
13th	● Montrose	H	W 1–0	Att: 217	Scorers: McKeown. Booked: Ewings.
17th	● East Stirling	A	L 2–0	Att: 340	Booked: O'Byrne, Boyle, Ewings.
20th	● Forfar	A	D 1–1	Att: 344	Scorers: Boyle. Booked: Reid, McCusker.
23rd	● East Stirling	H	W 2–1	Att: 340	Scorers: McLeod, Walker. Booked: Donnelly.
27th	● Annan	H	W 1–0	Att: 314	Scorers: McCusker. Booked: Donnelly, Tyrrell.

APRIL
3rd	● East Stirling	A	L 3–1	Att: 325	Scorers: McCusker. Booked: McLeod, Reid, McCusker, Gilmartin.
10th	● Elgin	H	L 1–2	Att: 347	Scorers: McCusker.
12th	● Stranraer	H	W 3–1	Att: 252	Scorers: Ferry, McKeown, McLeod. Booked: Canning, O'Byrne.
14th	● Stranraer	A	L 2–1	Att: 214	Scorers: McLeod.
17th	● Queen's Park	H	W 1–0	Att: 410	Scorers: Donnelly. Booked: Thomson, McGowan.
20th	● Queen's Park	A	L 1–0	Att: 522	Booked: O'Byrne, McGowan.
24th	● Berwick	A	W 1–2	Att: 460	Scorers: Boyle, O'Byrne.
27th	● Livingston	A	L 2–0	Att: 628	

MAY
1st	● Stranraer	H	D 0–0	Att: 575	Booked: McLeod, Canning.

● Irn-Bru Third Division ● Scottish Cup ● Co-op Insurance Cup ● Challenge Cup

THIRD DIVISION GOALKEEPER STATS

Player	Appearances	Match starts	Completed matches	Sub appearances	Subbed off	Clean sheets	Yellow cards	Red cards
Jamie Ewings	16	15	15	1	0	4	2	0
Derek Gaston	21	21	20	0	1	8	0	0

THIRD DIVISION OUTFIELD PLAYER STATS

Player	Appearances	Match starts	Completed matches	Substitute appearances	Subbed off	Goals scored	Yellow cards	Red cards
Lee Bannantyne	1	1	0	0	1	0	1	0
Bobby Barr	11	11	6	0	5	1	2	0
Alan Benton	32	31	31	1	0	0	6	0
Christopher Boyle	22	21	5	1	16	3	1	0
Mark Canning	22	20	15	2	5	1	5	0
Brendan Crozier	2	0	0	2	0	0	0	0
Ciaran Donnelly	25	23	23	2	0	2	5	0
Daniel Ferry	10	5	4	5	1	1	0	0
James Gilmartin	9	2	1	7	1	0	2	0
David Gormley	4	4	0	0	4	0	0	0
Lee Hoolickin	4	2	0	2	2	0	0	0
Todd Lumsden	8	8	8	0	0	0	1	0
Marc McCusker	22	12	1	10	11	6	6	0
David McFarlane	24	18	6	6	12	3	2	0
Michael McGowan	36	36	36	0	0	0	4	0
Phillip McGrath	1	1	0	0	0	0	0	1
Steven McKeown	25	17	14	8	3	2	0	0
Dennis McLauchlin	14	7	2	7	5	0	0	0
Paul McLeod	17	9	3	8	6	5	2	0
Jamie O'Boyle	3	1	1	2	0	0	0	0
Michael O'Byrne	30	30	29	0	0	2	9	1
Marc Pollock	13	10	3	3	7	2	0	0
Alan Reid	33	33	31	0	2	0	2	0
Paul Stewart	9	2	0	7	2	0	0	0
Adam Strachaen	4	4	4	0	0	0	1	0
Ryan Thomson	15	11	8	4	3	1	1	0
Paul Tyrrell	26	26	25	0	1	1	3	0
Patrick Walker	31	15	9	16	6	3	0	0

AUG SEP OCT NOV DEC JAN FEB MAR APR MAY

SEASON INFORMATION
Highest position: 1
Lowest position: 7
Average goals scored per game: 0.97
Average goals conceded per game: 0.97

4 3 4 5 5 6 7 6 5 5

LEAGUE POSITION AT THE END OF EACH MONTH

LONGEST SEQUENCES

Wins	3	Undefeated home	4
(29/09/09–10/10/09)		(on two occasions)	
Losses	3	Undefeated away	5
(23/01/10–09/02/10)		(08/08/09–10/10/09)	
Draws	3	Without scoring	5
(12/09/09–26/09/09)		(17/10/09–24/11/09)	
Undefeated	9	Without conceding	4
(08/08/09–10/10/09)		(26/09/09–10/10/09)	
Without win	10	Scoring	8
(17/10/09–09/02/10)		(20/03/10–17/04/10)	

CARDS RECEIVED

55 **2**

EARLIEST STRIKE
CHRISTOPHER BOYLE
(v Berwick) 6:32

LATEST STRIKE
PATRICK WALKER
(v Forfar) 90:00

GOALS SCORED/CONCEDED
PER FIVE-MINUTE INTERVALS

MINS	5	10	15	20	25	30	35	40	45	50	55	60	65	70	75	80	85	90
FOR	0	5	2	0	1	3	3	0	3	1	5	3	3	1	1	3	0	1
AGN	1	1	2	2	2	0	0	4	3	2	1	2	2	3	2	1	2	5

ANNAN ATHLETIC

ANNAN once again justified their invitation to join the Scottish Football League by comfortably finishing eighth.

In only their second season in the Scottish Football League, the Black and Golds started slowly, going on a run of four games without a win, but a 1–0 victory over Forfar kick-started a spell of form that saw them lose only one of their next six matches and included wins over Montrose and Stranraer.

Their success was built on a strong defence, with Harry Cairney's side having the third-best defensive record in the League. Bryan Gilfillan was one of their standout performers over the course of the campaign, also weighing in with five goals to aid his team's cause.

Annan reached the ALBA Challenge Cup semi-finals, but were knocked out of both the Co-operative Insurance Cup and Active Nation Scottish Cup at the early stages by Inverness Caledonian Thistle and Cove Rangers – of the Highland Football League – respectively.

CLUB SUMMARY

FORMED	1942
MANAGER	Harry Cairney
GROUND	Galabank Stadium
CAPACITY	3,500
NICKNAME	The Black and Golds
WEBSITE	www.annanathletic.com

The New Football Pools PLAYER OF THE SEASON — Graeme Bell

OVERALL
P	W	D	L	F	A	GD
42	14	10	18	49	53	-4

IRN-BRU THIRD DIVISION
Pos	P	W	D	L	F	A	GD	Pts
8	36	11	10	15	41	42	-1	43

HOME
Pos	P	W	D	L	F	A	GD	Pts
7	18	7	6	5	19	16	3	27

AWAY
Pos	P	W	D	L	F	A	GD	Pts
9	18	4	4	10	22	26	-4	16

CUP PROGRESS DETAILS
Competition	Round reached	Knocked out by
Scottish Cup	R2	Cove Rangers
Co-op Insurance Cup	R1	Inverness
Challenge Cup	SF	Dundee

BIGGEST WIN (ALL COMPS)
13/03/10 5–1 v Forfar

BIGGEST DEFEAT (ALL COMPS)
01/08/09 0–4 v Inverness CT

ATTENDANCE RECORD
HIGH	AVERAGE	LOW
831	492	278
v Livingston (03/04/2010)		v Montrose (15/04/2010)

RESULTS 2009/10

JULY
25th	● Queen's Park	H	W 2–0	Att: 466	Scorers: Jack². Booked: Gilfillan.

AUGUST
1st	● Inverness	A	L 4–0	Att: 1,095	
8th	● Berwick	A	L 2–1	Att: 438	Scorers: Gilfillan. Booked: Cox.
15th	● East Stirling	H	L 0–1	Att: 525	Booked: Cox.
18th	● East Stirling	H	W 1–0	Att: 357	Scorers: Watson.
22nd	● Stranraer	A	L 2–0	Att: 347	Booked: Neilson.
29th	● Elgin	A	D 1–1	Att: 457	Scorers: Gilfillan. Booked: S Sloan, Muirhead.

SEPTEMBER
6th	● Elgin	H	W 4–2	Att: 534	Scorers: Bell, Gilfillan, Inglis, Storey. Booked: Gilfillan, Neilson, Storey.
12th	● Forfar	H	W 1–0	Att: 525	Scorers: Steele. Booked: Jack, Gilfillan.
19th	● Queen's Park	A	D 0–0	Att: 581	
26th	● Albion	H	D 0–0	Att: 510	Booked: Steele, Storey.

OCTOBER
4th	● Dundee	A	L 3–0	Att: 2,321	Booked: Watson.
10th	● Montrose	H	W 2–0	Att: 504	Scorers: MacBeth, L Sloan. Booked: Neilson, Cox, Storey.
13th	● Livingston	A	L 2–0	Att: 773	Booked: Neilson.
17th	● Stranraer	H	W 1–0	Att: 647	Scorers: Gilfillan. Booked: Inglis.
24th	● Cove Rangers	A	L 2–1	Att: 278	Scorers: Watson.
31st	● East Stirling	A	W 1–3	Att: 359	Scorers: Cox², Watson. Booked: L Sloan, Jardine.

NOVEMBER
7th	● Forfar	A	L 2–1	Att: 477	Scorers: Cox. Booked: Bell, Cox.
14th	● Elgin	H	L 0–2	Att: 416	Booked: Watson. Dismissed: Watson.
21st	● Albion	A	D 0–0	Att: 375	Booked: Gilfillan.

DECEMBER
5th	● Queen's Park	H	W 3–1	Att: 433	Scorers: Gilfillan, Jack².
12th	● Montrose	A	D 0–0	Att: 250	Booked: Gilfillan, Jardine.

JANUARY
23rd	● Queen's Park	A	L 3–2	Att: 484	Scorers: Anson, MacBeth. Booked: MacBeth.

FEBRUARY
9th	● Berwick	H	D 1–1	Att: 382	Scorers: Bell. Booked: MacBeth.
13th	● Livingston	A	L 3–2	Att: 1,085	Scorers: Cox, Neilson. Booked: Jardine, Neilson, Townsley, Cox.
17th	● Albion	A	L 1–2	Att: 317	Scorers: Watson. Booked: Cox, Neilson, Gilfillan.
20th	● Berwick	A	W 0–2	Att: 385	Scorers: Bell, Jardine.
27th	● East Stirling	H	W 1–0	Att: 613	Scorers: Bell. Booked: Neilson.

MARCH
2nd	● Forfar	H	D 1–1	Att: 373	Scorers: Bell.
6th	● Elgin	H	D 3–3	Att: 364	Scorers: Bell², L Sloan. Booked: Watson.
13th	● Forfar	A	W 1–5	Att: 424	Scorers: Anson², Bell, O'Connor, L Sloan. Booked: Jardine.
16th	● Livingston	H	D 0–0	Att: 604	
20th	● Queen's Park	H	L 0–2	Att: 581	Booked: Muirhead.
24th	● Stranraer	A	L 3–2	Att: 259	Scorers: Anson, Storey. Booked: Watson, Summersgill, L Sloan, Steele, Gilfillan.
27th	● Albion	A	L 1–0	Att: 314	

APRIL
3rd	● Livingston	H	W 2–0	Att: 831	Scorers: Bell, S Sloan.
6th	● Elgin	A	L 1–0	Att: 235	Booked: Jardine.
10th	● Montrose	A	W 1–2	Att: 294	Scorers: Cox, Jardine.
13th	● Montrose	H	D 0–0	Att: 278	Booked: Gilfillan, L Sloan.
17th	● Stranraer	H	W 3–2	Att: 392	Scorers: Bell, Gilfillan, L Sloan. Booked: Watson, Storey.
24th	● East Stirling	A	L 3–1	Att: 335	Scorers: Jack. Booked: L Sloan.

MAY
1st	● Berwick	H	L 0–1	Att: 561	Booked: L Sloan.

● Irn-Bru Third Division ● Scottish Cup ● Co-op Insurance Cup ● Challenge Cup

THIRD DIVISION GOALKEEPER STATS

Player	Appearances	Match starts	Completed matches	Sub appearances	Subbed off	Clean sheets	Yellow cards	Red cards
Jonny Jamieson	2	1	1	1	0	0	0	0
Greg Kelly	15	15	15	0	0	6	0	0
Craig Summersgill	20	20	19	0	1	6	1	0

THIRD DIVISION OUTFIELD PLAYER STATS

Player	Appearances	Match starts	Completed matches	Substitute appearances	Subbed off	Goals scored	Yellow cards	Red cards
Scott Anson	19	7	1	12	6	4	0	0
Graeme Bell	33	29	13	4	16	9	1	0
Tom Clarke	1	0	0	1	0	0	0	0
David Cox	30	29	20	1	9	5	6	0
Bryan Gilfillan	33	33	33	0	0	5	6	0
Lee Hoolickin	1	0	0	1	0	0	0	0
Alan Inglis	6	3	3	3	0	0	1	0
Mike Jack	26	20	10	6	10	3	1	0
Chris Jardine	31	31	24	0	7	2	5	0
John MacBeth	34	30	28	4	2	2	2	0
Nathan Muir	2	2	2	0	0	0	0	0
Aaron Muirhead	23	22	21	1	1	0	2	0
Kevin Neilson	31	30	30	1	0	1	6	0
Sean O'Connor	2	2	0	0	2	1	0	0
Jamie Phillips	1	0	0	1	0	0	0	0
Gary Redpath	4	0	0	4	0	0	0	0
Steven Sloan	28	16	12	12	4	1	1	0
Lewis Sloan	31	27	17	4	10	4	5	0
Jack Steele	31	27	20	4	7	1	2	0
Phil Storey	34	11	6	23	5	1	3	0
Derek Townsley	9	9	7	0	2	0	1	0
Peter Watson	33	32	29	1	2	2	4	1

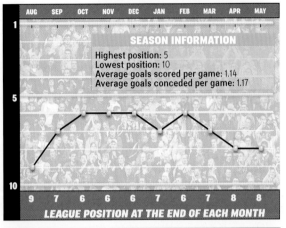

SEASON INFORMATION

Highest position: 5
Lowest position: 10
Average goals scored per game: 1.14
Average goals conceded per game: 1.17

LEAGUE POSITION AT THE END OF EACH MONTH

9 7 6 6 6 7 6 7 8 8

LONGEST SEQUENCES

Wins	2	Undefeated home	4	
(on two occasions)		(on two occasions)		
Losses	3	Undefeated away	2	
(on two occasions)		(on three occasions)		
Draws	2	Without scoring	2	
(on two occasions)		(on four occasions)		
Undefeated	6	Without conceding	4	
(20/02/10–16/03/10)		(12/09/09–10/10/09)		
Without win	5	Scoring	9	
(12/12/09–17/02/10)		(23/01/10–13/03/10)		

CARDS RECEIVED

47   1

EARLIEST STRIKE

GRAEME BELL
(v Livingston) 3:23

LATEST STRIKE

PHIL STOREY
(v Stranraer) 88:49

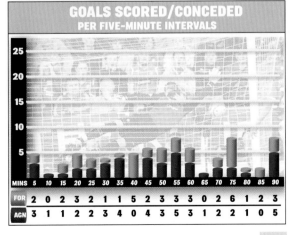

GOALS SCORED/CONCEDED PER FIVE-MINUTE INTERVALS

MINS	5	10	15	20	25	30	35	40	45	50	55	60	65	70	75	80	85	90
FOR	2	0	2	3	2	1	1	5	2	3	3	0	2	6	1	2	3	
AGN	3	1	1	2	2	3	4	0	4	3	5	3	1	2	2	1	0	5

BERWICK RANGERS

BERWICK'S first full season under fan ownership saw them achieve a much-improved sixth position in the Irn-Bru Third Division.

Jimmy Crease's side, who finished second from bottom last term, started well with a 2–1 win over Annan. Three 1–0 home victories against Livingston, Queen's Park and Stranraer put the Borderers amongst the early-season title contenders and they only lost two games at home in the first half of the campaign.

However, inconsistent form after the New Year – which included a five-match winless run – meant their automatic promotion hopes disappeared, while their play-off push was ended by a 2–1 defeat to Albion Rovers at Shielfield Park on the penultimate weekend of the season.

Youngster Damon Gray, who was signed from Hibernian during the summer, was their most consistent performer as the Newcastle-born striker reached double figures in the goal charts in his first season at the club.

CLUB SUMMARY

FORMED	1881
MANAGER	Jimmy Crease
GROUND	Shielfield Park
CAPACITY	4,131
NICKNAME	The Borderers
WEBSITE	www.berwickrangers.net

The New Football Pools
PLAYER OF THE SEASON

Mark Peat

OVERALL
P	W	D	L	F	A	GD
40	15	8	17	52	65	-13

IRN-BRU THIRD DIVISION
Pos	P	W	D	L	F	A	GD	Pts
6	36	14	8	14	46	50	-4	50

HOME
Pos	P	W	D	L	F	A	GD	Pts
5	18	9	3	6	19	18	1	30

AWAY
Pos	P	W	D	L	F	A	GD	Pts
6	18	5	5	8	27	32	-5	20

CUP PROGRESS DETAILS
Competition	Round reached	Knocked out by
Scottish Cup	R3	Ross County
Co-op Insurance Cup	R1	Partick
Challenge Cup	R1	Stranraer

BIGGEST WIN (ALL COMPS)
23/01/10 5–1 v Elgin

BIGGEST DEFEAT (ALL COMPS)
1–5 on 2 occasions

ATTENDANCE RECORD
HIGH	AVERAGE	LOW
608	434	289
v Livingston (22/08/2009)		v Stranraer (06/04/2010)

RESULTS 2009/10

JULY
25th	○ Stranraer	A	L 4–2	Att: 219	Scorers: Ewart, Little. **Booked:** Notman. **Dismissed:** Ewart.

AUGUST
1st	● Partick	A	L 5–1	Att: 1,472	Scorers: Little. **Booked:** Smith.
8th	● Annan	H	W 2–1	Att: 438	Scorers: Currie, Guy. **Booked:** Currie, Smith, Guy, McLean, Callaghan.
15th	● Albion	A	L 2–1	Att: 322	Scorers: Brazil. **Booked:** Smith, Little. **Dismissed:** Callaghan.
22nd	● Livingston	H	W 1–0	Att: 608	Scorers: Brazil. **Booked:** McLean, Currie.
29th	● Queen's Park	H	W 1–0	Att: 519	Scorers: McLaren. **Booked:** Callaghan.

SEPTEMBER
19th	● Elgin	A	D 3–3	Att: 478	Scorers: Brazil, Currie, Little. **Booked:** Callaghan, McLaren.
22nd	● Stranraer	H	W 1–0	Att: 366	Scorers: Greenhill. **Booked:** Smith, Ewart.
26th	● Montrose	H	W 2–0	Att: 436	Scorers: Brazil, McLaren.

OCTOBER
3rd	● Forfar	H	L 0–1	Att: 436	
10th	● East Stirling	A	L 1–0	Att: 433	**Booked:** Smith.
17th	● Livingston	A	D 1–1	Att: 815	Scorers: MacDonald OG. **Booked:** Brazil.
24th	● Civil Service Strollers	A	W 1–2	Att: 387	Scorers: McLaren[2]. **Booked:** Greenhill.
31st	● Albion	H	W 2–0	Att: 471	Scorers: Currie, Gray. **Booked:** Callaghan, McLean, Gray.

NOVEMBER
7th	● Stranraer	A	W 2–4	Att: 250	Scorers: Ewart, Gray[2], Mitchell OG. **Booked:** Russell.
14th	● Queen's Park	H	D 1–1	Att: 487	Scorers: McLean. **Booked:** Horn, Brazil, Smith, Little.
28th	● Ross County	A	L 5–1	Att: 819	Scorers: Brazil.

DECEMBER
1st	● Montrose	A	W 1–3	Att: 265	Scorers: Brazil, McLaren[2]. **Booked:** Ewart, Smith.
5th	● Elgin	H	W 2–0	Att: 368	Scorers: Little, McLean. **Booked:** Callaghan, Smith, Notman.
12th	● East Stirling	H	L 0–1	Att: 428	**Booked:** Ewart.

JANUARY
16th	● Queen's Park	A	L 2–0	Att: 517	**Booked:** Notman.
23rd	● Elgin	A	W 1–5	Att: 307	Scorers: Currie, Greenhill, Little, Radzynski[2]. **Booked:** McLean, Russell.
30th	● Montrose	H	L 0–2	Att: 392	**Booked:** Ewart.

FEBRUARY
6th	● East Stirling	A	L 3–2	Att: 347	Scorers: Gray[2]. **Booked:** Currie.
9th	● Annan	H	D 1–1	Att: 382	Scorers: Currie. **Booked:** Ewart, Smith, Guy.
13th	● Forfar	H	L 0–4	Att: 386	**Dismissed:** Currie.
20th	● Annan	H	L 0–2	Att: 385	

MARCH
6th	● Queen's Park	A	W 2–3	Att: 538	Scorers: Gray[2], Greenhill. **Booked:** McLaren, Shields.
9th	● Albion	A	L 4–1	Att: 227	Scorers: McLean. **Booked:** Shields. **Dismissed:** McLean.
13th	● Stranraer	A	L 3–1	Att: 231	Scorers: Russell. **Booked:** Smith.
20th	● Elgin	H	W 2–1	Att: 317	Scorers: Callaghan, Gray. **Booked:** Callaghan, Notman, Russell.
23rd	● Forfar	A	L 3–0	Att: 310	
27th	● Montrose	A	D 1–1	Att: 376	Scorers: Greenhill. **Booked:** Notman, Smith, Callaghan.

APRIL
3rd	● Forfar	A	L 2–0	Att: 406	**Booked:** Notman, Currie, Smith. **Dismissed:** McLean.
6th	● Stranraer	H	W 1–0	Att: 289	Scorers: McLaren. **Booked:** Callaghan, Notman, Ewart.
10th	● East Stirling	H	D 2–2	Att: 429	Scorers: Callaghan, McMullan. **Booked:** McLaren.
13th	● Livingston	H	D 1–1	Att: 604	Scorers: Gray. **Booked:** Notman, Currie.
17th	● Livingston	A	D 0–0	Att: 1,621	**Booked:** Shields, Smith.
24th	● Albion	H	L 1–2	Att: 460	Scorers: Gray. **Booked:** Currie.

MAY
1st	● Annan	A	W 0–1	Att: 561	Scorers: Gray. **Booked:** Notman, Shields. **Dismissed:** Shields.

● Irn-Bru Third Division ● Scottish Cup ○ Co-op Insurance Cup ● Challenge Cup

actim

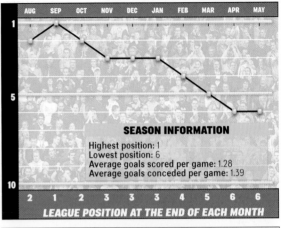

THIRD DIVISION GOALKEEPER STATS

Player	Appearances	Match starts	Completed matches	Sub appearances	Subbed off	Clean sheets	Yellow cards	Red cards
Ian McCaldon	2	2	2	0	0	1	0	0
Mark Peat	34	34	34	0	0	8	0	0

THIRD DIVISION OUTFIELD PLAYER STATS

Player	Appearances	Match starts	Completed matches	Substitute appearances	Subbed off	Goals scored	Yellow cards	Red cards
Alan Brazil	27	26	21	1	5	5	2	0
Stuart Callaghan	32	30	28	2	1	2	8	1
Jordan Cropley	2	0	0	2	0	0	0	0
Paul Currie	31	29	26	2	2	5	6	1
Jamie Ewart	26	25	24	1	1	1	6	0
Scott Gair	5	5	4	0	1	0	0	0
Damon Gray	31	22	13	9	9	11	1	0
David Greenhill	33	25	12	8	13	4	0	0
Graham Guy	18	13	13	5	0	1	2	0
Robert Horn	3	2	2	1	0	0	1	0
Guy Kerr	10	10	10	0	0	0	0	0
Ian Little	31	22	6	9	16	3	2	0
Harry McGregor	3	1	1	2	0	0	0	0
Fraser McLaren	26	25	17	1	8	5	4	0
Andrew McLean	24	21	17	3	2	3	3	2
Chris McMenamin	5	1	1	4	0	0	0	0
Paul McMullan	22	15	11	7	4	1	0	0
Steven Notman	29	29	26	0	3	0	8	0
Steven Radzynski	14	6	3	8	3	2	0	0
Oliver Russell	17	11	5	6	6	1	3	0
Joe Savage	2	0	0	2	0	0	0	0
Jay Shields	13	10	7	3	2	0	4	1
Elliot Smith	33	32	31	1	1	0	12	0

SEASON INFORMATION

Highest position: 1
Lowest position: 6
Average goals scored per game: 1.28
Average goals conceded per game: 1.39

LEAGUE POSITION AT THE END OF EACH MONTH

LONGEST SEQUENCES

Wins (on four occasions)	2	Undefeated home (08/08/09–26/09/09)	5
Losses (on five occasions)	2	Undefeated away (17/10/09–01/12/09)	3
Draws (10/04/10–17/04/10)	3	Without scoring (on three occasions)	2
Undefeated (17/10/09–05/12/09)	6	Without conceding (on two occasions)	2
Without win (30/01/10–20/02/10)	5	Scoring (08/08/09–26/09/09)	7

CARDS RECEIVED

62 **5**

EARLIEST STRIKE

PAUL CURRIE
(v Annan) 3:00

LATEST STRIKE

OLIVER RUSSELL
(v Stranraer) 91:04

GOALS SCORED/CONCEDED
PER FIVE-MINUTE INTERVALS

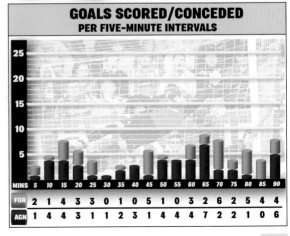

MINS	5	10	15	20	25	30	35	40	45	50	55	60	65	70	75	80	85	90
FOR	2	1	4	3	3	0	1	0	5	1	0	3	2	6	2	5	4	4
AGN	1	4	4	3	1	1	2	3	1	4	4	4	7	2	2	1	0	6

EAST STIRLINGSHIRE

EAST STIRLINGSHIRE suffered a second successive season of play-off disappointment following a near-identical campaign to last term.

Once again, the Shire finished in third place in the Irn-Bru Third Division and again they collected 61 points from their 36 League games. But, just as they did last season, they were beaten in the play-off semi-finals, this time losing 3–2 on aggregate to Forfar.

Livingston's domination of the division meant that Jim McInally's men were never likely to challenge for the Third Division title, but they pushed Forfar all the way for the runners-up spot.

The two clubs had some memorable meetings, with two League wins apiece and plenty of goals scored, including a Simon Lynch hat-trick in the Shire's 4–0 win in March.

Lynch netted 13 times in total, but there was also a big contribution from former Mallorca youngster Jamie Stevenson, who finished the season with nine goals from midfield.

CLUB SUMMARY

FORMED	1881
MANAGER	Jim McInally
GROUND	Ochilview Park
CAPACITY	3,776
NICKNAME	The Shire
WEBSITE	www.eaststirlinghire.co.uk

The New Football Pools PLAYER OF THE SEASON — Jamie Stevenson

OVERALL

P	W	D	L	F	A	GD
39	19	4	16	55	57	-2

IRN-BRU THIRD DIVISION

Pos	P	W	D	L	F	A	GD	Pts
3	36	19	4	13	50	46	4	61

HOME

Pos	P	W	D	L	F	A	GD	Pts
2	18	12	2	4	32	19	13	38

AWAY

Pos	P	W	D	L	F	A	GD	Pts
5	18	7	2	9	18	27	-9	23

CUP PROGRESS DETAILS

Competition	Round reached	Knocked out by
Scottish Cup	R2	Forfar
Co-op Insurance Cup	R1	St Mirren
Challenge Cup	R2	Annan

BIGGEST WIN (ALL COMPS)
06/03/10 4–0 v Forfar

BIGGEST DEFEAT (ALL COMPS)
29/08/09 1–5 v Forfar

ATTENDANCE RECORD

HIGH	AVERAGE	Low
1,062	408	297
v Livingston (20/02/2010)		v Queen's Park (02/03/2010)

RESULTS 2009/10

AUGUST
2nd	St Mirren	H	L 3–6	Att: 1,024	Scorers: Maguire, Rodgers[2]. **Booked:** King.
15th	Annan	A	W 0–1	Att: 525	Scorers: Maguire. **Booked:** Dunn, Hay, Donaldson, King. **Dismissed:** Dunn.
18th	Annan	A	L 1–0	Att: 357	**Booked:** Maguire, Weaver.
22nd	Elgin	H	D 1–1	Att: 373	Scorers: Stevenson. **Booked:** Weaver.
29th	Forfar	A	L 5–1	Att: 425	Scorers: Rodgers.

SEPTEMBER
12th	Queen's Park	H	W 1–0	Att: 393	Scorers: Lynch. **Booked:** Hay, Stevenson.
19th	Montrose	A	W 0–3	Att: 410	Scorers: Bolochoweckyj, Lynch, Rodgers. **Booked:** Bolochoweckyj.
26th	Stranraer	H	D 1–1	Att: 367	Scorers: Tully. **Booked:** Weaver.
30th	Livingston	H	W 3–1	Att: 567	Scorers: Lynch, Maguire[2]. **Booked:** Rodgers, Hay, Stevenson.

OCTOBER
3rd	Albion	A	L 3–0	Att: 413	
10th	Berwick	H	W 1–0	Att: 433	Scorers: Rodgers. **Booked:** Tully, Rodgers, Bolochoweckyj.
17th	Elgin	A	W 1–2	Att: 449	Scorers: Richardson, Rodgers. **Booked:** Stevenson, Tully.
24th	Forfar	A	L 4–2	Att: 396	Scorers: Dunn, Rodgers. **Booked:** Hay, Rodgers, Stevenson. **Dismissed:** Bolochoweckyj.
31st	Annan	H	L 1–3	Att: 359	Scorers: Maguire. **Booked:** Tully, Rodgers.

NOVEMBER
7th	Queen's Park	A	L 1–0	Att: 529	
14th	Forfar	H	W 2–1	Att: 365	Scorers: Lynch, Rodgers. **Booked:** Forrest.
21st	Stranraer	A	W 1–2	Att: 205	Scorers: Rodgers, Stevenson. **Booked:** Weaver.

DECEMBER
6th	Montrose	H	W 1–0	Att: 345	Scorers: Weaver.
12th	Berwick	A	W 0–1	Att: 428	Scorers: Lynch. **Booked:** Donaldson.

JANUARY
23rd	Montrose	A	W 0–1	Att: 310	Scorers: Bolochoweckyj. **Booked:** Forrest.
30th	Stranraer	H	W 2–0	Att: 348	Scorers: Lynch, Rodgers.

FEBRUARY
6th	Berwick	H	W 3–2	Att: 347	Scorers: Maguire[2], Stevenson.
10th	Elgin	H	W 2–0	Att: 349	Scorers: Lynch, Stevenson. **Booked:** Barclay, Stevenson.
20th	Livingston	H	L 0–2	Att: 1,062	**Booked:** Bolochoweckyj, Hay, Harding, Weaver, Richardson. **Dismissed:** Bolochoweckyj.
27th	Annan	A	L 1–0	Att: 613	**Booked:** Richardson, Forrest. **Dismissed:** Dunn.

MARCH
2nd	Queen's Park	H	L 0–3	Att: 297	**Booked:** Rodgers, Forrest, Stevenson.
6th	Forfar	H	W 4–0	Att: 436	Scorers: Lynch[3], Rodgers.
9th	Livingston	A	L 2–0	Att: 864	**Booked:** Lynch, Ure, Richardson, Maguire.
13th	Queen's Park	A	L 2–0	Att: 457	
17th	Albion	H	W 2–0	Att: 340	Scorers: Bolochoweckyj, Richardson. **Booked:** Ure.
20th	Montrose	H	L 2–3	Att: 306	Scorers: Stevenson[2].
23rd	Albion	A	L 2–1	Att: 340	Scorers: Stevenson. **Booked:** Donaldson, Stevenson.
27th	Stranraer	A	D 2–2	Att: 320	Scorers: Maguire, Rodgers. **Booked:** Harding, Ure.
30th	Forfar	A	L 4–1	Att: 286	Scorers: Stevenson.

APRIL
3rd	Albion	H	W 3–1	Att: 325	Scorers: Lynch[2], Stevenson. **Booked:** Harding, Donaldson, Bolochoweckyj.
10th	Berwick	A	D 2–2	Att: 429	Scorers: Donaldson, Dunn. **Booked:** Weaver, Donaldson.
17th	Elgin	A	W 0–1	Att: 398	Scorers: Maguire. **Booked:** McKenzie.
24th	Annan	H	W 3–1	Att: 335	Scorers: Dunn, Lynch, Ure. **Booked:** Rodgers, Maguire.

MAY
1st	Livingston	A	L 1–0	Att: 1,480	**Booked:** Hay, Harding, Brady.
5th	Forfar	H	L 0–1	Att: 487	**Booked:** Barclay, Forrest, Rodgers.
8th	Forfar	A	D 2–2	Att: 745	Scorers: Rodgers[2]. **Booked:** Bolochoweckyj, Forrest, McKenzie. **Dismissed:** Forrest. Agg: 3–2.

● Irn-Bru Third Division/Play-offs ● Scottish Cup ● Co-op Insurance Cup ● Challenge Cup

THIRD DIVISION GOALKEEPER STATS

Player	Appearances	Match starts	Completed matches	Sub appearances	Subbed off	Clean sheets	Yellow cards	Red cards
Jamie Barclay	33	33	33	0	0	12	1	0
Gavin Sorley	3	3	3	0	0	0	0	0

THIRD DIVISION OUTFIELD PLAYER STATS

Player	Appearances	Match starts	Completed matches	Substitute appearances	Subbed off	Goals scored	Yellow cards	Red cards
Michael Bolochoweckyj	30	29	24	1	4	3	4	1
Callum Brady	4	0	0	4	0	0	1	0
Craig Donaldson	26	24	21	2	3	1	5	0
David Dunn	26	14	6	12	6	2	1	2
Jason Elliott	3	0	0	3	0	0	0	0
Edward Forrest	24	24	22	0	2	0	4	0
Ryan Harding	22	20	18	2	2	0	4	0
Paul Hay	32	28	19	4	9	0	5	0
Scott Johnston	13	2	1	11	1	0	0	0
David King	12	12	9	0	3	0	1	0
Simon Lynch	32	31	20	1	11	13	1	0
Stephen Maguire	36	23	10	13	13	8	2	0
Marc McKenzie	29	2	2	27	0	0	1	0
Dean Richardson	33	31	26	2	5	2	3	0
Andrew Rodgers	33	29	7	4	22	9	5	0
Jamie Stevenson	32	32	22	0	10	9	6	0
Craig Tully	17	15	14	2	1	1	3	0
Derek Ure	28	17	12	11	5	1	3	0
Paul Weaver	28	27	23	1	4	1	5	0

AUG	SEP	OCT	NOV	DEC	JAN	FEB	MAR	APR	MAY

LEAGUE POSITION AT THE END OF EACH MONTH

6	2	3	2	2	2	2	2	3	3

SEASON INFORMATION

Highest position: 1
Lowest position: 8
Average goals scored per game: 1.39
Average goals conceded per game: 1.28

LONGEST SEQUENCES

Wins	8	Undefeated home	5
(14/11/09–10/02/10)		(on two occasions)	
Losses	3	Undefeated away	3
(20/02/10–02/03/10)		(21/11/09–23/01/10)	
Draws	–	Without scoring	3
(–)		(20/02/10–02/03/10)	
Undefeated	8	Without conceding	4
(14/11/09–10/02/10)		(06/12/09–30/01/10)	
Without win	,4	Scoring	9
(20/03/10–30/03/10)		(17/03/10–24/04/10)	

CARDS RECEIVED

55 **3**

EARLIEST STRIKE

STEPHEN MAGUIRE
(v Annan) 3:00

LATEST STRIKE

ANDREW RODGERS
(v Stranraer) 91:15

GOALS SCORED/CONCEDED
PER FIVE-MINUTE INTERVALS

MINS	5	10	15	20	25	30	35	40	45	50	55	60	65	70	75	80	85	90
FOR	4	2	3	4	1	3	2	4	2	2	4	1	5	1	2	2	5	3
AGN	0	2	4	1	3	3	2	2	3	2	5	3	3	4	4	3	0	2

ELGIN CITY

ELGIN managed to avoid a second successive rock-bottom finish in the Scottish Football League, but they were unable to push much further up the table.

A run of seven straight defeats spanning March and April cost Ross Jack's side dear and resulted in them sinking to the foot of the division as the season's end approached.

However, a Shane Sutherland goal earned the Black and Whites a vital 1–0 win over Annan during the final month of the campaign, not only ending their losing run but also moving them off the bottom of the Irn-Bru Third Division table.

Further wins over Albion Rovers, Queen's Park and a final-day 5–2 triumph over rivals Montrose ensured that Elgin finished above the latter in ninth position.

The signing of Sutherland from Inverness was undoubtedly a coup for Jack. The midfielder contributed five goals and finished behind only striker Craig Gunn in the club's scoring charts.

CLUB SUMMARY

FORMED	1893
MANAGER	Ross Jack
GROUND	Borough Briggs
CAPACITY	3,927
NICKNAME	The Black and Whites
WEBSITE	www.elgincity.com

The New Football Pools PLAYER OF THE SEASON — **David W Craig**

OVERALL

P	W	D	L	F	A	GD
42	12	7	23	58	71	-13

IRN-BRU THIRD DIVISION

Pos	P	W	D	L	F	A	GD	Pts
9	36	9	7	20	46	59	-13	34

HOME

Pos	P	W	D	L	F	A	GD	Pts
9	18	3	2	13	19	36	-17	11

AWAY

Pos	P	W	D	L	F	A	GD	Pts
4	18	6	5	7	27	23	4	23

CUP PROGRESS DETAILS

Competition	Round reached	Knocked out by
Scottish Cup	R3	Albion
Co-op Insurance Cup	R1	Brechin
Challenge Cup	QF	Annan

BIGGEST WIN (ALL COMPS)
20/02/10 4–0 v Montrose

BIGGEST DEFEAT (ALL COMPS)
07/11/09 1–6 v Livingston

ATTENDANCE RECORD

HIGH	AVERAGE	Low
615	403	203
v Livingston (07/11/2009)		v Queen's Park (30/03/2010)

RESULTS 2009/10

JULY
25th	● Brechin	H	W 3–1	Att: 378	Scorers: Crooks, Edwards, Frizzel.

AUGUST
1st	● Brechin	A	L 4–0	Att: 406	Booked: Mcdonald, Nicolson, David A Craig, Edwards.
8th	● Montrose	A	D 1–1	Att: 361	Scorers: Frizzel. Booked: Dempsie, Edwards.
15th	● Queen's Park	H	L 0–1	Att: 570	Booked: Mcdonald, Kaczan, Edwards, David A Craig, Nicolson.
18th	● Albion	H	W 3–0	Att: 245	Scorers: Crooks, Gunn². Booked: Mcdonald, Nicolson. Dismissed: Mcdonald.
22nd	● East Stirling	A	D 1–1	Att: 373	Scorers: Gunn. Dismissed: David A Craig.
29th	● Annan	H	D 1–1	Att: 457	Scorers: Gunn. Booked: Frizzel.

SEPTEMBER
6th	● Annan	A	L 4–2	Att: 534	Scorers: Cameron, MacBeth OG. Booked: Gibson.
12th	● Livingston	A	L 3–2	Att: 757	Scorers: Crooks, MacAulay. Booked: Frizzel, Niven, Nicolson, Calder, Dempsie. Dismissed: Dempsie.
19th	● Berwick	H	D 3–3	Att: 478	Scorers: Gunn², Nicolson. Booked: Calder, MacDonald.
26th	● Forfar	A	D 3–3	Att: 444	Scorers: Gunn, Nicolson². Booked: Edwards.

OCTOBER
3rd	● Stranraer	A	W 0–2	Att: 229	Scorers: Crooks, Gunn. Booked: M Dunn.
10th	● Albion	H	L 0–2	Att: 526	Booked: Kaczan, Niven.
17th	● East Stirling	H	L 1–2	Att: 449	Scorers: Gunn. Booked: David A Craig, Nicolson.
24th	● Nairn County	A	W 2–4	Att: 600	Scorers: Crooks, Frizzel³. Booked: Niven, Frizzel, Gunn.
31st	● Queen's Park	A	W 0–3	Att: 538	Scorers: Frizzel, Gunn, Tatters. Booked: Gunn, Frizzel.

NOVEMBER
7th	● Livingston	H	L 1–6	Att: 615	Scorers: Gunn. Booked: MacAulay.
14th	● Annan	A	W 0–2	Att: 416	Scorers: MacAulay, Niven. Booked: MacDonald, Gunn.
21st	● Forfar	H	L 0–2	Att: 519	Booked: MacDonald, Niven, Nicolson.
28th	● Albion	A	L 1–0	Att: 275	

DECEMBER
5th	● Berwick	A	L 2–0	Att: 368	Booked: Niven. Dismissed: Kaczan.
12th	● Albion	A	D 1–1	Att: 225	Scorers: MacAulay.

JANUARY
23rd	● Berwick	H	L 1–5	Att: 307	Scorers: Nicolson. Booked: MacDonald. Dismissed: Nicolson.
26th	● Livingston	A	L 1–0	Att: 503	Booked: Niven, Tatters.

FEBRUARY
6th	● Albion	H	W 3–1	Att: 326	Scorers: Cameron, Gunn². Booked: David W Craig, Kaczan.
10th	● East Stirling	A	L 2–0	Att: 349	Booked: Frizzel, Kaczan, Edwards.
16th	● Forfar	A	L 1–0	Att: 402	Booked: MacDonald. Dismissed: MacDonald.
20th	● Montrose	A	W 0–4	Att: 280	Scorers: Gunn², Morrison, Sutherland. Booked: Niven, Kaczan.

MARCH
6th	● Annan	A	D 3–3	Att: 364	Scorers: Smith, Sutherland².
13th	● Livingston	H	L 0–1	Att: 433	Booked: Morrison.
16th	● Stranraer	A	L 2–1	Att: 145	Scorers: Frizzel.
20th	● Berwick	A	L 2–1	Att: 317	Scorers: Greenhill OG. Booked: Niven.
23rd	● Montrose	H	L 0–1	Att: 295	Booked: Frizzel, Niven.
27th	● Forfar	H	L 0–2	Att: 329	Booked: Niven.
30th	● Queen's Park	H	L 0–1	Att: 203	Booked: Morrison, Niven, MacDonald.

APRIL
3rd	● Stranraer	H	L 1–2	Att: 375	Scorers: Crooks. Booked: Morrison, Nicolson.
6th	● Annan	H	W 1–0	Att: 235	Scorers: Sutherland. Booked: Crooks.
10th	● Albion	A	W 1–2	Att: 347	Scorers: Gunn, Morrison. Booked: MacDonald.
17th	● East Stirling	A	L 0–1	Att: 398	
24th	● Queen's Park	A	W 0–1	Att: 644	Scorers: Sutherland. Booked: Gunn.
27th	● Stranraer	H	L 2–3	Att: 232	Scorers: Gunn, Jack. Booked: Kaczan, David W Craig, Nicolson.

MAY
1st	● Montrose	H	W 5–2	Att: 504	Scorers: Gunn³, MacAulay, Smith. Booked: MacDonald, M Dunn. Dismissed: M Dunn.

● Irn-Bru Third Division ● Scottish Cup ● Co-op Insurance Cup ● Challenge Cup

THIRD DIVISION GOALKEEPER STATS

Player	Appearances	Match starts	Completed matches	Sub appearances	Subbed off	Clean sheets	Yellow cards	Red cards
John Gibson	36	36	36	0	0	6	0	0

THIRD DIVISION OUTFIELD PLAYER STATS

Player	Appearances	Match starts	Completed matches	Substitute appearances	Subbed off	Goals scored	Yellow cards	Red cards
David Calder	12	1	0	11	1	0	2	0
Brian Cameron	24	9	3	15	6	1	0	0
David W Craig	27	27	25	0	2	0	2	0
David A Craig	22	15	8	7	6	0	2	1
Jason Crooks	27	15	8	12	7	3	1	0
Allan Dempsie	20	20	13	0	6	0	2	1
Michael Dunn	4	4	3	0	0	0	2	1
Steven Edwards	27	19	12	8	7	0	4	0
Steven Fraser	1	0	0	1	0	0	0	0
Craig Frizzel	34	33	21	1	12	3	5	0
Craig Gunn	36	31	23	5	8	18	3	0
John Inglis	11	6	4	5	2	0	0	0
Jake Inglis	3	3	1	0	2	0	0	0
Alexander Jack	3	1	0	2	1	1	0	0
Paul Kaczan	28	28	25	0	2	0	6	1
Kyle MacAulay	34	27	22	7	5	4	1	0
Neil MacDonald	21	19	6	2	12	0	8	1
Daniel MacLeod	3	0	0	3	0	0	0	0
Murray McConachie	1	0	0	1	0	0	0	0
Neil Mcdonald	2	2	2	0	0	0	1	0
Gavin Morrison	15	15	13	0	2	2	3	0
Mark Nicolson	32	32	30	0	1	4	6	1
David Niven	25	25	23	0	2	1	10	0
David Smith	12	2	0	10	2	2	0	0
Shane Sutherland	17	17	14	0	3	5	0	0
Graham Tatters	6	6	5	0	1	1	1	0
Graham Trappers	3	3	3	0	0	0	0	0

SEASON INFORMATION
Highest position: 6
Lowest position: 10
Average goals scored per game: 1.28
Average goals conceded per game: 1.64

LEAGUE POSITION AT THE END OF EACH MONTH

	AUG	SEP	OCT	NOV	DEC	JAN	FEB	MAR	APR	MAY
	8	8	8	9	9	9	9	10	9	9

LONGEST SEQUENCES

Wins	2	Undefeated home	2
(06/04/10–10/04/10)		(29/08/09–19/09/09)	
Losses	7	Undefeated away	4
(13/03/10–03/04/10)		(26/09/09–14/11/09)	
Draws	2	Without scoring	3
(on two occasions)		(23/03/10–30/03/10)	
Undefeated	3	Without conceding	–
(19/09/09–03/10/09)		(–)	
Without win	8	Scoring	6
(06/03/10–03/04/10)		(22/08/09–03/10/09)	

CARDS RECEIVED
59 6

EARLIEST STRIKE
CRAIG GUNN
(v Stranraer) 5:00

LATEST STRIKE
BRIAN CAMERON
(v Albion) 92:26

GOALS SCORED/CONCEDED
PER FIVE-MINUTE INTERVALS

MINS	5	10	15	20	25	30	35	40	45	50	55	60	65	70	75	80	85	90
FOR	2	0	1	0	1	4	1	3	5	5	4	2	3	1	3	1	3	7
AGN	2	2	4	3	2	3	2	4	3	3	6	1	3	4	3	3	5	6

FORFAR ATHLETIC

THE DICK CAMPBELL revolution at Forfar continued as the Loons sealed promotion via the play-offs.

The club had just finished bottom of the Scottish Football League when former Dunfermline and Partick Thistle boss Campbell took charge two years ago. And, following last season's sixth-place finish, they continued to improve in clinching second spot this time around. They might even have been champions but for Livingston, who ran away with the title following their demotion from the Irn-Bru First Division.

In the play-offs, Forfar edged past East Stirlingshire 3–2 on aggregate to set up a final against Second Division Arbroath. Despite being underdogs, the Loons drew 0–0 away and won 2–0 at home, surviving the sending-off of Stephen Tulloch in the second leg.

During the regular season, in what proved to be a tight division below Livingston, Forfar won only half their games, but that was still enough.

CLUB SUMMARY

FORMED	1885
MANAGER	Dick Campbell
GROUND	Station Park
CAPACITY	5,177
NICKNAME	The Loons
WEBSITE	www.forfarathletic.co.uk

The New **Football Pools**
PLAYER OF THE SEASON

Stephen Tulloch

OVERALL
P	W	D	L	F	A	GD
43	22	9	12	72	60	12

IRN-BRU THIRD DIVISION
Pos	P	W	D	L	F	A	GD	Pts
2	36	18	9	9	59	44	15	63

HOME
Pos	P	W	D	L	F	A	GD	Pts
3	18	9	6	3	34	21	13	33

AWAY
Pos	P	W	D	L	F	A	GD	Pts
2	18	9	3	6	25	23	2	30

CUP PROGRESS DETAILS
Competition	Round reached	Knocked out by
Scottish Cup	R4	St Johnstone
Co-op Insurance Cup	R2	Dundee
Challenge Cup	R2	Partick

BIGGEST WIN (ALL COMPS)
29/08/09 5–1 v East Stirling

BIGGEST DEFEAT (ALL COMPS)
18/08/09 1–6 v Partick

ATTENDANCE RECORD
High	Average	Low
613	438	286
v Livingston (10/10/2009)		v East Stirling (30/03/2010)

RESULTS 2009/10

JULY
25th	East Fife	A	W 0–2	Att: 446	Scorers: M Fotheringham, K Fotheringham. Booked: M Fotheringham, R Campbell, Malcolm.

AUGUST
1st	Clyde	A	W 1–3	Att: 784	Scorers: R Campbell, Deasley, M Fotheringham. Booked: Tod.
8th	Queen's Park	A	D 2–2	Att: 596	Scorers: I Campbell, M Fotheringham.
15th	Stranraer	H	W 1–0	Att: 410	Scorers: R Campbell. Booked: Brady, Malcolm.
18th	Partick	H	L 1–6	Att: 532	Scorers: Templeman. Booked: Templeman, Brady, R Campbell.
22nd	Montrose	A	W 1–2	Att: 548	Scorers: M Fotheringham, K Fotheringham. Booked: K Fotheringham, Malcolm, Tod. Dismissed: Tod.
25th	Dundee	H	L 2–4	Att: 1,929	Scorers: R Campbell, Tulloch. Booked: I Campbell, R Campbell, K Fotheringham.
29th	East Stirling	H	W 5–1	Att: 425	Scorers: R Campbell[3], K Fotheringham, Templeman.

SEPTEMBER
12th	Annan	A	L 1–0	Att: 525	
19th	Albion	A	D 1–1	Att: 279	Scorers: Templeman. Booked: Templeman, McCulloch.
26th	Elgin	H	D 3–3	Att: 444	Scorers: R Campbell[2], Mowat. Booked: McCulloch.

OCTOBER
3rd	Berwick	A	W 0–1	Att: 436	Scorers: R Campbell. Booked: I Campbell.
10th	Livingston	H	L 0–1	Att: 613	Booked: I Campbell, M Fotheringham, Templeman.
17th	Montrose	H	D 2–2	Att: 556	Scorers: R Campbell[2]. Booked: McNally, Templeman.
24th	East Stirling	H	W 4–2	Att: 396	Scorers: R Campbell[2], Harty, Tod. Booked: Andreoni.
31st	Stranraer	A	L 1–0	Att: 210	Booked: Mowat.

NOVEMBER
7th	Annan	H	W 2–1	Att: 477	Scorers: R Campbell, Harty. Booked: Tulloch.
14th	East Stirling	A	L 2–1	Att: 365	Scorers: Gordon. Booked: Templeman, R Campbell, M Fotheringham.
21st	Elgin	A	W 0–2	Att: 519	Scorers: M Fotheringham, Templeman. Booked: Mowat, Tulloch.
28th	Spartans	A	W 0–1	Att: 600	Scorers: Templeman. Booked: M Fotheringham.

DECEMBER
5th	Albion	H	D 2–2	Att: 434	Scorers: Harty[2]. Booked: M Fotheringham, Tod, Templeman, Gibson.
12th	Livingston	A	W 1–2	Att: 1,591	Scorers: Gibson, Tulloch. Booked: I Campbell.

JANUARY
18th	St Johnstone	H	L 0–3	Att: 1,449	
23rd	Albion	A	W 0–1	Att: 227	Scorers: Watson. Booked: Bishop, Templeman.

FEBRUARY
6th	Livingston	H	D 2–2	Att: 510	Scorers: R Campbell, Tulloch. Booked: Templeman, K Fotheringham, Tulloch, I Campbell. Dismissed: K Fotheringham.
13th	Berwick	A	W 0–4	Att: 386	Scorers: R Campbell, Templeman, Tulloch, Watson.
16th	Elgin	H	W 1–0	Att: 402	Scorers: Harty. Booked: Watson, R Campbell, Bishop, Mowat. Dismissed: Tulloch.
20th	Queen's Park	A	W 1–3	Att: 603	Scorers: Harty, Sellars, Watson. Booked: Tod, R Campbell, I Campbell.

MARCH
2nd	Annan	A	D 1–1	Att: 373	Scorers: Harty. Booked: I Campbell, Bishop.
6th	East Stirling	A	L 4–0	Att: 436	Booked: K Fotheringham.
9th	Queen's Park	H	L 0–1	Att: 413	
13th	Annan	H	L 1–5	Att: 424	Scorers: Harty. Booked: I Campbell, Bishop.
16th	Montrose	A	L 4–0	Att: 360	Booked: N Smith.
20th	Albion	H	D 1–1	Att: 344	Scorers: R Campbell. Booked: N Smith.
23rd	Berwick	H	W 3–0	Att: 310	Scorers: R Campbell, K Fotheringham, Watson.
27th	Elgin	A	W 0–2	Att: 329	Scorers: R Campbell, Gibson. Booked: Tulloch, Tod, McCulloch.
30th	East Stirling	H	W 4–1	Att: 286	Scorers: Harty, Sellars[3].

APRIL
3rd	Berwick	H	W 2–0	Att: 406	Scorers: R Campbell, Sellars. Booked: Sellars.
10th	Livingston	A	W 2–3	Att: 1,500	Scorers: I Campbell, Harty[2]. Booked: I Campbell.
17th	Montrose	H	W 2–0	Att: 466	Scorers: M Fotheringham, Templeman. Booked: Tod.
20th	Stranraer	H	W 2–0	Att: 422	Scorers: Deasley[2]. Booked: C Smith.
24th	Stranraer	A	L 2–0	Att: 337	

MAY
1st	Queen's Park	H	D 1–1	Att: 549	Scorers: Bishop. Booked: Bishop, R Campbell. Dismissed: I Campbell.
5th	East Stirling	A	W 0–1	Att: 487	Scorers: R Campbell. Booked: Tod.
8th	East Stirling	H	D 2–2	Att: 745	Scorers: Bishop, Tulloch. Booked: K Fotheringham. Agg: 3–2.
12th	Arbroath	A	D 0–0	Att: 1,027	Booked: Sellars, Watson, McCulloch, Templeman.
16th	Arbroath	H	W 2–0	Att: 2,207	Scorers: Deasley, M Fotheringham. Booked: Tulloch. Dismissed: Tulloch. Agg: 2–0.

● Irn-Bru Third Division/Play-offs ● Scottish Cup ● Co-op Insurance Cup ● Challenge Cup

actim

THIRD DIVISION GOALKEEPER STATS

Player	Appearances	Match starts	Completed matches	Sub appearances	Subbed off	Clean sheets	Yellow cards	Red cards
Alistair Brown	28	28	28	0	0	8	0	0
Connor Grant	2	2	2	0	0	0	0	0
Euan McLean	6	6	6	0	0	3	0	0

THIRD DIVISION OUTFIELD PLAYER STATS

Player	Appearances	Match starts	Completed matches	Substitute appearances	Subbed off	Goals scored	Yellow cards	Red cards
Marco Andreoni	1	1	0	0	1	0	0	0
James Bishop	18	17	17	1	0	1	5	0
Darren Brady	5	4	1	1	3	0	1	0
Iain Campbell	32	32	30	0	1	2	8	1
Ross Campbell	35	29	18	6	11	16	4	0
Bryan Deasley	22	9	3	13	6	2	0	0
Alastair Divine	4	3	1	1	2	0	0	0
Kevin Fotheringham	29	26	18	3	7	3	3	1
Martyn Fotheringham	27	19	12	8	7	4	3	0
Scott Fusco	1	0	0	1	0	0	0	0
Graham Gibson	26	9	1	17	8	2	1	0
Kevin Gordon	18	8	2	10	6	1	0	0
Ian Harty	26	21	12	5	9	10	0	0
Stuart Malcolm	5	5	3	0	2	0	2	0
Mark McCulloch	23	23	23	0	0	0	3	0
Chris McGroarty	1	1	0	0	1	0	0	0
Stephen McNally	5	0	0	5	0	0	1	0
David Mowat	32	31	28	1	3	1	3	0
Barry Sellars	18	15	9	3	6	5	1	0
Nicky Smith	6	3	0	3	3	0	2	0
Calum Smith	13	3	0	10	3	0	1	0
Christopher Templeman	32	25	13	7	12	5	7	0
Andrew Tod	33	33	30	0	2	0	5	1
Stephen Tulloch	31	30	27	1	2	3	4	1
Paul Watson	17	12	5	5	7	4	1	0
Craig Winter	1	0	0	1	0	0	0	0

SEASON INFORMATION
Highest position: 1
Lowest position: 6
Average goals scored per game: 1.64
Average goals conceded per game: 1.22

LEAGUE POSITION AT THE END OF EACH MONTH: 1 4 5 4 4 4 3 3 2 2

LONGEST SEQUENCES

Wins	7	Undefeated home	7	
(23/03/10–20/04/10)		(20/03/10–01/05/10)		
Losses	4	Undefeated away	6	
(06/03/10–16/03/10)		(21/11/09–02/03/10)		
Draws	2	Without scoring	2	
(19/09/09–26/09/09)		(06/03/10–09/03/10)		
Undefeated	9	Without conceding	2	
(21/11/09–02/03/10)		(on three occasions)		
Without win	6	Scoring	11	
(02/03/10–20/03/10)		(07/11/09–02/03/10)		

CARDS RECEIVED
55 4

EARLIEST STRIKE
MARTYN FOTHERINGHAM
(v Queen's Park) 2:00

LATEST STRIKE
STEPHEN TULLOCH
(v Livingston) 94:27

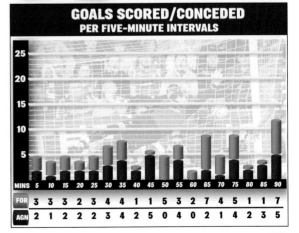

GOALS SCORED/CONCEDED PER FIVE-MINUTE INTERVALS

MINS	5	10	15	20	25	30	35	40	45	50	55	60	65	70	75	80	85	90
FOR	3	3	3	2	3	4	4	1	1	5	3	2	7	4	5	1	1	7
AGN	2	1	2	2	2	3	4	2	5	0	4	0	2	1	4	2	3	5

LIVINGSTON

LIVINGSTON put the disappointment of their demotion from the Irn-Bru First Division behind them by securing the Third Division title with three games to spare.

A 0–0 draw against Berwick Rangers was enough to seal promotion, while manager Gary Bollan believes that his side are good enough to repeat the achievement next season and get back into the First Division at the earliest possible opportunity.

Veteran Robbie Winters and Italian Raffaele De Vita formed an excellent strike partnership, which returned 20 goals for the club, while Andrew Halliday was another key player for the Livi Lions as the midfielder chipped in with vital efforts in key games, including wins over East Stirlingshire and Queen's Park.

The Almondvale side supplemented their good League form with a decent run in the Active Nation Scottish Cup, reaching the third round after a 7–1 win over Clyde before losing to Dundee.

CLUB SUMMARY

FORMED	1943
MANAGER	Gary Bollan
GROUND	Almondvale Stadium
CAPACITY	10,016
NICKNAME	The Livi Lions
WEBSITE	www.livingstonfc.co.uk

The New **Football Pools** PLAYER OF THE SEASON — *Robbie Winters*

OVERALL
P	W	D	L	F	A	GD
42	26	7	9	74	33	41

IRN-BRU THIRD DIVISION
Pos	P	W	D	L	F	A	GD	Pts
1	36	24	6	6	63	25	38	78

HOME
Pos	P	W	D	L	F	A	GD	Pts
1	18	14	2	2	32	12	20	44

AWAY
Pos	P	W	D	L	F	A	GD	Pts
1	18	10	4	4	31	13	18	34

CUP PROGRESS DETAILS
Competition	Round reached	Knocked out by
Scottish Cup	R4	Dundee
Co-op Insurance Cup	R1	Albion
Challenge Cup	R1	Queen of South

BIGGEST WIN (ALL COMPS)
14/12/09 7–1 v Clyde

BIGGEST DEFEAT (ALL COMPS)
01/08/09 0–3 v Albion

ATTENDANCE RECORD
HIGH	AVERAGE	Low
1,621	987	503
v Berwick (17/04/2010)		v Elgin (26/01/2010)

RESULTS 2009/10

JULY
25th	● Queen of South	A	L 1–0	Att: 1,558	Booked: Innes.

AUGUST
1st	● Albion	A	L 3–0	Att: 602	Booked: Hamill.
15th	● Montrose	H	W 2–0	Att: 632	Scorers: Halliday2. Booked: Talbot.
22nd	● Berwick	A	L 1–0	Att: 608	Booked: MacDonald, Hamill, One.
29th	● Albion	A	L 1–0	Att: 489	Booked: Brown.

SEPTEMBER
12th	● Elgin	H	W 3–2	Att: 757	Scorers: De Vita, Fox2. Booked: Moyes.
19th	● Stranraer	A	W 0–3	Att: 313	Scorers: De Vita2, Halliday.
26th	● Queen's Park	H	W 2–1	Att: 961	Scorers: Fox, R Winters. Booked: Moyes, De Vita, Talbot, Halliday. Dismissed: MacDonald.
30th	● East Stirling	A	L 3–1	Att: 567	Scorers: R Winters.

OCTOBER
10th	● Forfar	A	W 0–1	Att: 613	Scorers: R Winters. Booked: R Winters, De Vita, Hamill.
13th	● Annan	H	W 2–0	Att: 773	Scorers: D Winters, R Winters. Booked: Griffin, Keaghan Jacobs.
17th	● Berwick	H	D 1–1	Att: 815	Scorers: Griffin. Booked: Talbot.
24th	● Queen's Park	A	W 1–3	Att: 678	Scorers: De Vita2, Fox.
31st	● Montrose	A	W 0–3	Att: 433	Scorers: De Vita, Halliday, McNulty. Booked: De Vita. Dismissed: Brown.

NOVEMBER
7th	● Elgin	A	W 1–6	Att: 615	Scorers: Halliday, Keaghan Jacobs2, Talbot, D Winters, Nicolson OG. Booked: Fox, MacDonald.
21st	● Queen's Park	A	W 1–2	Att: 620	Scorers: Keaghan Jacobs, Moyes. Booked: Fox, Talbot.
24th	● Albion	H	W 2–0	Att: 726	Scorers: Keaghan Jacobs, Talbot. Booked: Brown.

DECEMBER
5th	● Stranraer	H	W 3–0	Att: 1,267	Scorers: Halliday, R Winters, Mitchell OG. Booked: Brown.
9th	● Clyde	A	D 1–1	Att: 538	Scorers: Hamill. Booked: Moyes, Talbot, MacDonald. Dismissed: Moyes.
12th	● Forfar	H	L 1–2	Att: 1,591	Scorers: Halliday. Booked: R Winters.
14th	● Clyde	H	W 7–1	Att: 690	Scorers: Fox2, Halliday, Keaghan Jacobs, R Winters2, Reidford OG.

JANUARY
20th	● Dundee	H	L 0–1	Att: 1,176	Booked: Brown, MacDonald.
23rd	● Stranraer	A	D 1–1	Att: 323	Scorers: Fox. Booked: Halliday.
26th	● Elgin	H	W 1–0	Att: 503	Scorers: Brown. Booked: Keaghan Jacobs.

FEBRUARY
2nd	● Queen's Park	H	W 2–0	Att: 680	Scorers: Fox, Halliday. Booked: Talbot.
6th	● Forfar	A	D 2–2	Att: 510	Scorers: Hamilton, R Winters. Booked: Tosh.
9th	● Albion	A	W 0–2	Att: 587	Scorers: Hamilton, Tosh. Booked: MacDonald.
13th	● Annan	H	W 3–2	Att: 1,085	Scorers: De Vita, Halliday, R Winters. Booked: Talbot, Fox, Sinclair.
20th	● East Stirling	A	W 0–2	Att: 1,062	Scorers: Halliday, R Winters.

MARCH
9th	● East Stirling	H	W 2–0	Att: 864	Scorers: Halliday, R Winters. Booked: Malone.
13th	● Elgin	A	W 0–1	Att: 433	Scorers: De Vita. Booked: De Vita, Watson.
16th	● Annan	A	D 0–0	Att: 604	
20th	● Stranraer	H	W 2–1	Att: 1,136	Scorers: Fox, R Winters.
27th	● Queen's Park	A	W 0–1	Att: 714	Scorers: De Vita. Booked: Hamilton, Fox.

APRIL
3rd	● Annan	A	L 2–0	Att: 831	Booked: De Vita, MacDonald, Fox. Dismissed: MacDonald.
6th	● Montrose	H	W 1–0	Att: 748	Scorers: Halliday. Booked: Brown.
10th	● Forfar	H	L 2–3	Att: 1,500	Scorers: De Vita, R Winters. Booked: Brown.
13th	● Berwick	A	D 1–1	Att: 604	Scorers: Tosh.
17th	● Berwick	H	D 0–0	Att: 1,621	Booked: Keaghan Jacobs, McNulty.
24th	● Montrose	A	W 0–5	Att: 510	Scorers: De Vita, Halliday2, Keaghan Jacobs, Watson.
27th	● Albion	H	W 2–0	Att: 628	Scorers: Sinclair, McGowan OG.

MAY
1st	● East Stirling	H	W 1–0	Att: 1,480	Scorers: Keaghan Jacobs.

● Irn-Bru Third Division ● Scottish Cup ● Co-op Insurance Cup ● Challenge Cup

actim

THIRD DIVISION GOALKEEPER STATS

Player	Appearances	Match starts	Completed matches	Sub appearances	Subbed off	Clean sheets	Yellow cards	Red cards
Darren Jamieson	1	1	1	0	0	1	0	0
Craig McDowall	2	2	2	0	0	2	0	0
Roderick McKenzie	32	32	32	0	0	17	0	0
Andrew McNeil	1	1	1	0	0	0	0	0

THIRD DIVISION OUTFIELD PLAYER STATS

Player	Appearances	Match starts	Completed matches	Substitute appearances	Subbed off	Goals scored	Yellow cards	Red cards
Bobby Barr	20	13	10	7	3	0	0	0
Jonathan Brown	16	16	14	0	1	1	5	1
Raffaele De Vita	29	23	14	6	9	9	5	0
Liam Fox	31	30	25	1	5	6	5	0
Daniel Griffin	25	23	20	2	3	1	1	0
Andrew Halliday	32	23	15	9	8	14	2	0
Joseph Hamill	10	7	4	3	3	0	2	0
James Hamilton	11	6	1	5	5	2	1	0
Neil Hastings	1	1	1	0	0	0	0	0
Stephen Husband	7	4	2	3	2	0	0	0
Keaghan Jacobs	34	28	20	6	8	6	3	0
Sheldon Jacobs	1	0	0	1	0	0	0	0
Kyle Jacobs	14	6	5	8	1	0	0	0
Devon Jacobs	5	5	5	0	0	0	0	0
Cameron MacDonald	26	24	21	2	1	0	4	2
Chris Malone	9	6	5	3	1	0	1	0
Joe McKee	1	0	0	1	0	0	0	0
Marc McNulty	9	2	1	7	1	1	1	0
Anthony McParland	4	3	0	1	3	0	0	0
Ewan Moyes	7	6	5	1	1	1	2	0
Armand One	2	1	0	1	1	0	1	0
David Sinclair	30	20	16	10	4	1	1	0
Jason Talbot	32	32	29	0	3	2	6	0
Steven Tosh	15	12	6	3	6	2	1	0
Paul Watson	20	20	19	0	1	1	1	0
David Winters	15	10	8	5	2	2	0	0
Robbie Winters	34	33	18	1	15	11	2	0

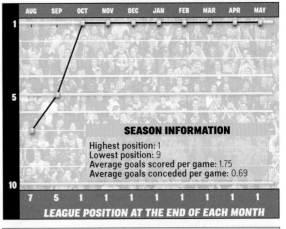

SEASON INFORMATION
Highest position: 1
Lowest position: 9
Average goals scored per game: 1.75
Average goals conceded per game: 0.69

LEAGUE POSITION AT THE END OF EACH MONTH

LONGEST SEQUENCES

Wins	5	Undefeated home	7
(on two occasions)		(15/08/09–05/12/09)	
Losses	2	Undefeated away	11
(22/08/09–29/08/09)		(10/10/09–27/03/10)	
Draws	2	Without scoring	2
(13/04/10–17/04/10)		(22/08/09–29/08/09)	
Undefeated	12	Without conceding	4
(23/01/10–27/03/10)		(20/02/10–16/03/10)	
Without win	3	Scoring	22
(10/04/10–17/04/10)		(12/09/09–13/03/10)	

CARDS RECEIVED

44   3

EARLIEST STRIKE
RAFFAELE DE VITA
(v Forfar) 0:49

LATEST STRIKE
LIAM FOX
(v Stranraer) 93:45

GOALS SCORED/CONCEDED
PER FIVE-MINUTE INTERVALS

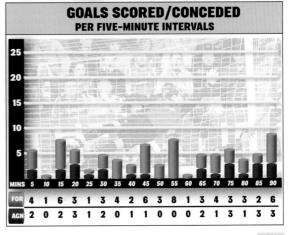

MINS	5	10	15	20	25	30	35	40	45	50	55	60	65	70	75	80	85	90
FOR	4	1	6	3	1	3	4	2	6	3	8	1	3	4	3	3	2	6
AGN	2	0	2	3	1	2	0	1	1	0	0	0	2	1	3	1	3	3

MONTROSE

MONTROSE will be hoping for a better season in 2010/11 having finished bottom of the Scottish Football League this time around.

The club failed to win an Irn-Bru Third Division match until the end of January, when they overcame Berwick 2–0 away from home.

Their 4–0 win over Forfar in March was their only home League victory of the season, and was one of few highlights for fans of the Gable Endies.

Steven Tweed joined from East Fife to become player/manager, replacing Jim Weir in the dugout, and he rallied his troops for a run of only one loss in seven to earn the Irn-Bru Phenomenal Manager of the Month award for March.

The Links Park club fared better in the Active Nation Scottish Cup with victories over Banks O'Dee, East Fife and Edinburgh City. They eventually went out in the fifth round, losing 5–1 to Clydesdale Bank Premier League opponents Hibernian at Easter Road.

CLUB SUMMARY

FORMED	1879
MANAGER	Steven Tweed
GROUND	Links Park
CAPACITY	3,292
NICKNAME	The Gable Endies
WEBSITE	www.montrosefc.co.uk

The New Football Pools PLAYER OF THE SEASON — Steven Tweed

OVERALL
P	W	D	L	F	A	GD
42	8	10	24	40	76	-36

IRN-BRU THIRD DIVISION
Pos	P	W	D	L	F	A	GD	Pts
10	36	5	9	22	30	63	-33	24

HOME
Pos	P	W	D	L	F	A	GD	Pts
10	18	1	6	11	16	35	-19	9

AWAY
Pos	P	W	D	L	F	A	GD	Pts
10	18	4	3	11	14	28	-14	15

CUP PROGRESS DETAILS
Competition	Round reached	Knocked out by
Scottish Cup	R5	Hibernian
Co-op Insurance Cup	R1	Ross County
Challenge Cup	R1	Inverness

BIGGEST WIN (ALL COMPS)
16/03/10 4–0 v Forfar

BIGGEST DEFEAT (ALL COMPS)
0–5 on 2 occasions

ATTENDANCE RECORD
HIGH	AVERAGE	Low
548	340	200
v Forfar (22/08/2009)		v Stranraer (16/01/2010)

RESULTS 2009/10

JULY
25th	● Inverness	A	D 1–1	Att: 1,122	Scorers: Leyden. Booked: Nicol. Inverness CT win 5–3 on penalties.

AUGUST
1st	● Ross County	A	L 5–0	Att: 768	
8th	● Elgin	H	D 1–1	Att: 361	Scorers: Hegarty. Booked: Pope, Nicol.
15th	● Livingston	A	L 2–0	Att: 632	Booked: Tweed. Dismissed: Crighton.
22nd	● Forfar	H	L 1–2	Att: 548	Scorers: Gemmell. Booked: Gemmell, Hegarty.
29th	● Stranraer	A	L 2–0	Att: 271	Booked: Tweed, Davidson, S Anderson, Sinclair, Crighton.

SEPTEMBER
12th	● Albion	H	D 0–0	Att: 323	Booked: Gemmell, Davidson.
19th	● East Stirling	A	L 0–3	Att: 410	Booked: Hegarty.
26th	● Berwick	A	L 2–0	Att: 436	

OCTOBER
10th	● Annan	A	L 2–0	Att: 504	Booked: Hegarty, Crighton, Davidson, Gray, Milligan, Nicol. Dismissed: Hegarty.
13th	● Queen's Park	H	L 1–2	Att: 370	Scorers: Tomana. Booked: Cambell, Crighton.
17th	● Forfar	A	D 2–2	Att: 556	Scorers: S Anderson, Hegarty. Booked: Cambell, Nicol, Hegarty.
24th	● Banks O'Dee	A	W 0–3	Att: 400	Scorers: Cambell, Sinclair, Watson.
31st	● Livingston	H	L 0–3	Att: 433	Booked: Hegarty, Gemmell. Dismissed: S Anderson.

NOVEMBER
7th	● Albion	A	D 0–0	Att: 257	Booked: Gemmell, Watson.
14th	● Stranraer	H	D 1–1	Att: 258	Scorers: S Anderson. Booked: Watson.
28th	● East Fife	H	W 2–1	Att: 509	Scorers: Gemmell, Watson. Booked: Hegarty, Nicol, Davidson.

DECEMBER
1st	● Berwick	H	L 1–3	Att: 265	Scorers: Watson. Booked: Davidson, Watson.
6th	● East Stirling	A	L 1–0	Att: 345	Booked: Watson, Crighton, Hegarty.
12th	● Annan	H	D 0–0	Att: 250	Booked: Davidson, Watson, Hegarty.
19th	● Queen's Park	A	L 3–2	Att: 397	Scorers: Nicol, Tosh.

JANUARY
16th	● Stranraer	H	L 4–5	Att: 200	Scorers: Cambell, Maitland, Tosh[2]. Booked: Hegarty.
18th	● Edinburgh City	A	W 1–3	Att: 1,027	Scorers: Maitland, Nicholas, Nicol. Booked: Fleming, Tweed, Hegarty.
23rd	● East Stirling	H	L 0–1	Att: 310	
30th	● Berwick	A	W 0–2	Att: 392	Scorers: Tosh, Notman OG.

FEBRUARY
6th	● Hibernian	A	L 5–1	Att: 9,068	Scorers: Hegarty. Booked: Fleming, Hegarty, Crighton.
13th	● Queen's Park	H	L 1–2	Att: 325	Scorers: Tosh. Booked: Tosh, Gemmell.
20th	● Elgin	H	L 0–4	Att: 280	Booked: Hegarty, McNalley, Nicol. Dismissed: Hegarty.

MARCH
2nd	● Albion	H	D 0–0	Att: 249	Booked: Nicol. Dismissed: Nicol.
6th	● Stranraer	A	W 0–2	Att: 225	Scorers: Tosh, Tweed. Booked: Sinclair, Hegarty, McNalley.
13th	● Albion	A	L 1–0	Att: 217	Booked: Hegarty.
16th	● Forfar	H	W 4–0	Att: 360	Scorers: Gemmell[2], Milligan, Sinclair. Booked: Tweed, Hegarty, Davidson. Dismissed: Hegarty.
20th	● East Stirling	A	W 2–3	Att: 306	Scorers: Gemmell, Nicol, Sinclair. Booked: Gemmell.
23rd	● Elgin	A	W 0–1	Att: 295	Scorers: Tosh.
27th	● Berwick	H	D 1–1	Att: 376	Scorers: Nicol. Booked: McNalley. Dismissed: Gemmell, Tosh.

APRIL
3rd	● Queen's Park	A	L 3–0	Att: 487	Booked: Milligan.
6th	● Livingston	A	L 1–0	Att: 748	Booked: Milligan.
10th	● Annan	H	L 1–2	Att: 294	Scorers: McNalley. Booked: Tomana.
13th	● Forfar	A	D 0–0	Att: 278	Booked: Davidson. Dismissed: Gemmell.
17th	● Forfar	A	L 2–0	Att: 466	Booked: Davidson.
24th	● Livingston	H	L 0–5	Att: 510	

MAY
1st	● Elgin	A	L 5–2	Att: 504	Scorers: Tosh[2]. Booked: Hegarty, Nicol.

● Irn-Bru Third Division ● Scottish Cup ● Co-op Insurance Cup ● Challenge Cup

actim

THIRD DIVISION GOALKEEPER STATS

Player	Appearances	Match starts	Completed matches	Sub appearances	Subbed off	Clean sheets	Yellow cards	Red cards
Steven Coutts	8	7	6	1	1	0	0	0
Stuart Hall	1	0	0	1	0	0	0	0
Andrew McNeil	29	29	28	0	1	8	0	0

THIRD DIVISION OUTFIELD PLAYER STATS

Player	Appearances	Match starts	Completed matches	Substitute appearances	Subbed off	Goals scored	Yellow cards	Red cards
Kieran Adams	1	1	1	0	0	0	0	0
Andrew Anderson	1	0	0	1	0	0	0	0
Sean Anderson	13	12	8	1	3	2	1	1
Martin Boyle	5	1	0	4	1	0	0	0
Alan Cambell	29	29	28	0	1	1	2	0
James Collier	4	2	1	2	1	0	0	0
Sean Crighton	29	29	27	0	1	0	4	1
Hugh Davidson	32	31	31	1	0	0	8	0
Sean Fleming	10	7	2	3	5	0	0	0
John Gemmell	22	19	13	3	4	4	6	2
Nicholas Gray	6	0	0	6	0	0	1	0
Christopher Hegarty	28	28	25	0	0	2	13	3
Jordan Leyden	6	0	0	6	0	0	0	0
John Maitland	22	15	8	7	7	1	0	0
David McGowan	3	2	2	1	0	0	0	0
Steven McNalley	19	19	18	0	1	1	3	0
Fraser Milligan	28	25	13	3	12	1	3	0
Steven Nicholas	14	13	8	1	5	0	0	0
Daryl Nicol	33	15	8	18	6	3	6	1
Gordon Pope	4	2	1	2	1	0	1	0
Jack Presly	2	0	0	2	0	0	0	0
Mark Russell	1	0	0	1	0	0	0	0
Aaron Sinclair	30	29	22	1	7	2	2	0
Ryan Stewart	8	4	2	4	2	0	0	0
Marek Tomana	20	15	5	5	10	1	1	0
Paul Tosh	18	18	17	0	0	9	1	1
Steven Tweed	31	31	30	0	1	1	3	0
Jon Voigt	3	3	1	0	2	0	0	0
Paul Watson	7	7	6	0	1	1	5	0

AUG	SEP	OCT	NOV	DEC	JAN	FEB	MAR	APR	MAY

SEASON INFORMATION

Highest position: 3
Lowest position: 10
Average goals scored per game: 0.83
Average goals conceded per game: 1.75

LEAGUE POSITION AT THE END OF EACH MONTH

LONGEST SEQUENCES

Wins	3	Undefeated home	3	
(16/03/10–23/03/10)		(02/03/10–27/03/10)		
Losses	4	Undefeated away	2	
(19/09/09–13/10/09)		(on three occasions)		
Draws	2	Without scoring	5	
(07/11/09–14/11/09)		(29/08/09–10/10/09)		
Undefeated	4	Without conceding	2	
(16/03/10–27/03/10)		(02/03/10–06/03/10)		
Without win	19	Scoring	4	
(08/08/09–23/01/10)		(16/03/10–27/03/10)		

CARDS RECEIVED

60 **9**

EARLIEST STRIKE

PAUL TOSH
(v Elgin) 12:00

LATEST STRIKE

CHRISTOPHER HEGARTY
(v Forfar) 90:00

GOALS SCORED/CONCEDED
PER FIVE-MINUTE INTERVALS

MINS	5	10	15	20	25	30	35	40	45	50	55	60	65	70	75	80	85	90
FOR	0	0	1	2	2	1	2	0	4	1	3	0	1	0	3	4	0	1	5
AGN	3	3	3	4	2	4	2	1	2	6	5	2	2	4	4	3	6	7

QUEEN'S PARK

QUEEN'S PARK suffered play-off heartbreak for the second successive season as they failed to bounce straight back from relegation to the fourth tier.

The Spiders had dropped into Scottish football's bottom division after losing to Stenhousemuir in last term's semi-finals and the same fate befell them again, with Arbroath beating them on this occasion.

Their 4–0 first-leg defeat summed up the poor home form that cost them dearly, with Gardner Spiers' men losing half of their 18 League games at Hampden.

Their away performances were more assured, especially towards the end of the season, and kept them in play-off contention. One point from their final two matches almost cost them fourth spot, but Albion Rovers were unable to take advantage.

The club were unable to repeat last season's Active Nation Scottish Cup run as they fell at the first hurdle in all the Cup competitions.

CLUB SUMMARY

FORMED	1867
MANAGER	Gardner Spiers
GROUND	Hampden Park
CAPACITY	52,500
NICKNAME	The Spiders
WEBSITE	www.queenspark.co.uk

The New **Football Pools** PLAYER OF THE SEASON

Tony Quinn

OVERALL
P	W	D	L	F	A	GD
39	15	6	18	44	51	-7

IRN-BRU THIRD DIVISION
Pos	P	W	D	L	F	A	GD	Pts
4	36	15	6	15	42	42	0	51

HOME
Pos	P	W	D	L	F	A	GD	Pts
8	18	7	2	9	24	27	-3	23

AWAY
Pos	P	W	D	L	F	A	GD	Pts
3	18	8	4	6	18	15	3	28

CUP PROGRESS DETAILS
Competition	Round reached	Knocked out by
Scottish Cup	R2	Livingston
Co-op Insurance Cup	R1	Queen of South
Challenge Cup	R1	Annan

BIGGEST WIN (ALL COMPS)
3–0 on 2 occasions

BIGGEST DEFEAT (ALL COMPS)
06/02/10 2–5 v Stranraer

ATTENDANCE RECORD
HIGH	AVERAGE	LOW
714	542	376
v Livingston (27/03/2010)		v Albion (29/09/2009)

RESULTS 2009/10

JULY
25th	● Annan	A	L 2-0	Att: 466	Dismissed: Reilly.

AUGUST
1st	● Queen of South	H	L 1-4	Att: 886	Scorers: Douglas. Booked: Tiernan, Capuano.
8th	● Forfar	H	D 2-2	Att: 596	Scorers: Capuano, Watt. Booked: Brough. Dismissed: Brough.
15th	● Elgin	A	W 0-1	Att: 570	Scorers: Douglas. Booked: Douglas, McBride.
29th	● Berwick	A	L 1-0	Att: 519	Booked: Watt, McBride.

SEPTEMBER
12th	● East Stirling	A	L 1-0	Att: 393	Booked: Douglas.
19th	● Annan	H	D 0-0	Att: 581	
26th	● Livingston	A	L 2-1	Att: 961	Scorers: Douglas. Booked: Walker, Capuano.
29th	● Albion	H	L 0-1	Att: 376	

OCTOBER
10th	● Stranraer	H	L 1-2	Att: 598	Scorers: Douglas. Booked: Capuano, Douglas. Dismissed: Sinclair.
13th	● Montrose	A	W 1-2	Att: 370	Scorers: O'Hara, P Quinn. Booked: Douglas, Capuano, A Quinn.
17th	● Albion	A	W 0-1	Att: 613	Scorers: C Hamilton. Booked: C Hamilton.
24th	● Livingston	H	L 1-3	Att: 678	Scorers: A Quinn.
31st	● Elgin	H	L 0-3	Att: 538	Booked: A Quinn, P Quinn, Reilly, Douglas. Dismissed: A Quinn.

NOVEMBER
7th	● East Stirling	H	W 1-0	Att: 529	Scorers: Carroll. Booked: Capuano, Brough, McBride.
14th	● Berwick	A	D 1-1	Att: 487	Scorers: Guy OG. Booked: Capuano, Little.
21st	● Livingston	H	L 1-2	Att: 620	Scorers: P Quinn. Booked: Little, C Hamilton.

DECEMBER
5th	● Annan	A	L 3-1	Att: 433	Scorers: Holms. Booked: Walker, Douglas, P Hamilton.
12th	● Stranraer	A	D 1-1	Att: 258	Scorers: McBride. Booked: Douglas, A Quinn.
19th	● Montrose	H	W 3-2	Att: 397	Scorers: McBride². Murray. Booked: Sinclair.

JANUARY
16th	● Berwick	H	W 2-0	Att: 517	Scorers: Douglas, Murray.
23rd	● Annan	H	W 3-2	Att: 484	Scorers: Carroll, Douglas, McBride. Booked: Walker.

FEBRUARY
2nd	● Livingston	A	L 2-0	Att: 680	Booked: McBride, Walker.
6th	● Stranraer	H	L 2-5	Att: 553	Scorers: Daly, McBride. Booked: Capuano, A Quinn.
13th	● Montrose	A	W 1-2	Att: 325	Scorers: Murray, A Quinn. Booked: Walker.
20th	● Forfar	H	L 1-3	Att: 603	Scorers: Douglas. Booked: Gallagher. Dismissed: Little.

MARCH
2nd	● East Stirling	A	W 0-3	Att: 297	Scorers: Daly², Murray.
6th	● Berwick	H	L 2-3	Att: 538	Scorers: Henry, Watt. Booked: Henry, Gallagher, McGinn, Murray. Dismissed: McGinn.
9th	● Forfar	A	W 0-1	Att: 413	Scorers: Watson OG.
13th	● East Stirling	H	W 2-0	Att: 457	Scorers: C Hamilton, Stewart. Booked: A Quinn, Douglas.
20th	● Annan	A	W 0-2	Att: 581	Scorers: Daly, Henry. Booked: Daly, A Quinn, Gallagher.
27th	● Livingston	H	L 0-1	Att: 714	Booked: Brough, Gallagher.
30th	● Elgin	A	W 0-1	Att: 203	Scorers: Stewart. Booked: Douglas, McGinn, Stewart, McBride.

APRIL
3rd	● Montrose	H	W 3-0	Att: 487	Scorers: Douglas, McBride, Murray.
10th	● Stranraer	A	D 0-0	Att: 365	Booked: A Quinn.
17th	● Albion	A	L 1-0	Att: 410	Booked: Douglas.
20th	● Albion	H	W 1-0	Att: 522	Scorers: Douglas. Booked: Little.
24th	● Elgin	H	L 0-1	Att: 644	Booked: Brough.

MAY
1st	● Forfar	A	D 1-1	Att: 549	Scorers: Daly. Booked: Capuano, A Quinn, Henry.
5th	● Arbroath	H	L 0-4	Att: 651	Booked: Brough.
8th	● Arbroath	A	D 2-2	Att: 588	Scorers: Daly, Rattray OG. Booked: Stewart, Little. Agg: 6-2.

● Irn-Bru Third Division/Play-offs ● Scottish Cup ● Co-op Insurance Cup ● Challenge Cup

THIRD DIVISION GOALKEEPER STATS

Player	Appearances	Match starts	Completed matches	Sub appearances	Subbed off	Clean sheets	Yellow cards	Red cards
Scott Black	11	11	11	0	0	3	0	0
Peter Hamilton	11	10	10	1	0	2	1	0
Mark McGeown	15	15	14	0	1	7	0	0

THIRD DIVISION OUTFIELD PLAYER STATS

Player	Appearances	Match starts	Completed matches	Substitute appearances	Subbed off	Goals scored	Yellow cards	Red cards
James Brough	30	29	27	1	1	0	4	1
Paul Burns	1	1	1	0	0	0	0	0
Giuseppe Capuano	33	32	27	1	5	1	7	0
Frank Carroll	15	9	4	6	5	2	0	0
Michael Daly	27	22	15	5	7	5	1	0
Barry Douglas	35	35	35	0	0	8	10	0
Ross Dunlop	11	7	4	4	3	0	0	0
Paul Gallagher	14	13	13	1	0	0	4	0
David Green	1	0	0	1	0	0	0	0
Chris Hamilton	29	16	8	13	8	2	2	0
Paul Harkins	1	1	0	0	1	0	0	0
Jack Henry	12	6	2	6	4	2	2	0
Ryan Holms	22	14	6	8	8	1	0	0
Gavin Lauchlan	4	4	2	0	2	0	0	0
Richard Little	24	24	23	0	0	0	3	1
Ryan Martin	1	0	0	1	0	0	0	0
Martin McBride	34	33	29	1	4	6	5	0
Paul McGinn	6	4	3	2	0	0	2	1
David Murray	23	15	6	8	9	5	1	0
Michael O'Hara	8	5	0	3	5	1	0	0
Paul Quinn	9	9	8	0	1	2	1	0
Tony Quinn	27	24	22	3	1	1	8	1
Steven Reilly	3	3	3	0	0	0	0	0
Richard Sinclair	9	9	6	0	2	0	1	1
Paul Stewart	15	15	9	0	6	2	1	0
Fergus Tiernan	1	0	0	1	0	0	0	0
Martin Ure	8	7	6	1	1	0	0	0
Robert Walker	17	17	15	0	2	0	5	0
Ian Watt	19	6	2	4	4	2	1	0

AUG | SEP | OCT | NOV | DEC | JAN | FEB | MAR | APR | MAY

SEASON INFORMATION

Highest position: 2
Lowest position: 9
Average goals scored per game: 1.17
Average goals conceded per game: 1.17

LEAGUE POSITION AT THE END OF EACH MONTH

5 | 9 | 9 | 8 | 7 | 5 | 5 | 4 | 4 | 4

LONGEST SEQUENCES

Wins	3	Undefeated home	3
(on two occasions)		(19/12/09–23/01/10)	
Losses	3	Undefeated away	6
(26/09/09–10/10/09)		(13/02/10–10/04/10)	
Draws	–	Without scoring	3
(–)		(29/08/09–19/09/09)	
Undefeated	4	Without conceding	3
(12/12/09–23/01/10)		(on two occasions)	
Without win	6	Scoring	8
(29/08/09–10/10/09)		(on two occasions)	

CARDS RECEIVED

60 **5**

EARLIEST STRIKE

MARTIN MCBRIDE
(v Montrose) 10:00

LATEST STRIKE

CHRIS HAMILTON
(v East Stirling) 92:15

GOALS SCORED/CONCEDED
PER FIVE-MINUTE INTERVALS

MINS	5	10	15	20	25	30	35	40	45	50	55	60	65	70	75	80	85	90
FOR	0	2	4	1	4	3	0	2	2	2	2	1	3	3	3	2	3	5
AGN	2	3	2	0	1	0	1	2	3	2	1	5	3	2	4	3	2	6

STRANRAER

STRANRAER were unable to bounce straight back from relegation as they finished down in seventh place.

The Stair Park side failed to win more than two games consecutively all campaign and they went out of the ALBA Challenge Cup, Co-operative Insurance Cup and Active Nation Scottish Cup in the early rounds.

The arrival of French striker Armand One from Gateshead in January boosted the club's chances of making a late surge for the play-offs.

The well-travelled 27-year-old Parisian scored eight goals in 19 games for the Blues and was among the scorers in January's thrilling 5–4 victory over Montrose. But Stranraer's inconsistent form continued as they managed only one win in their next four outings.

Losses in April to Albion Rovers, Annan, Berwick and Forfar proved costly and eventually ended their hopes of reaching the play-offs and making an immediate return to the Second Division.

CLUB SUMMARY

FORMED	1870
MANAGER	Keith Knox
GROUND	Stair Park
CAPACITY	5,600
NICKNAME	The Blues
WEBSITE	www.stranraerfc.org

The New **Football Pools**
PLAYER OF THE SEASON

David Mitchell

OVERALL
P	W	D	L	F	A	GD
40	14	8	18	53	66	-13

IRN-BRU THIRD DIVISION
Pos	P	W	D	L	F	A	GD	Pts
7	36	13	8	15	48	54	-6	47

HOME
Pos	P	W	D	L	F	A	GD	Pts
6	18	8	5	5	25	23	2	29

AWAY
Pos	P	W	D	L	F	A	GD	Pts
7	18	5	3	10	23	31	-8	18

CUP PROGRESS DETAILS
Competition	Round reached	Knocked out by
Scottish Cup	R2	Inverurie Loco Works
Co-op Insurance Cup	R1	Dundee
Challenge Cup	R2	Inverness CT

BIGGEST WIN (ALL COMPS)
06/02/10 5–2 v Queen's Park

BIGGEST DEFEAT (ALL COMPS)
01/08/09 0–5 v Dundee

ATTENDANCE RECORD
High	Average	Low
365	267	145
v Queen's Park (10/04/2010)		v Elgin (16/03/2010)

RESULTS 2009/10

JULY
25th	● Berwick	H	W 4–2	Att: 219	Scorers: Jack, Daniel Mitchell[2], Montgomerie. Booked: Wright, Noble, Montgomerie. Dismissed: Noble.

AUGUST
1st	● Dundee	A	L 5–0	Att: 2,345	Booked: Nicoll. Dismissed: David Mitchell.
8th	● Albion	H	D 1–1	Att: 296	Scorers: McInnes. Booked: Moore, Nicoll, Henderson.
15th	● Forfar	A	L 1–0	Att: 410	Booked: Agostini, Henderson, McMahon, Nicoll.
18th	● Inverness	A	L 3–0	Att: 1,750	Booked: Henderson, Wright, McInnes.
22nd	● Annan	H	W 2–0	Att: 347	Scorers: McColm, Moore. Booked: Agostini.
29th	● Montrose	H	W 2–0	Att: 271	Scorers: Daniel Mitchell, Montgomerie. Booked: McInnes, Nicoll.

SEPTEMBER
19th	● Livingston	H	L 0–3	Att: 313	Booked: Noble.
22nd	● Berwick	A	L 1–0	Att: 366	Booked: David Mitchell, Henderson.
26th	● East Stirling	A	D 1–1	Att: 367	Scorers: Daniel Mitchell. Booked: Moore.

OCTOBER
3rd	● Elgin	H	L 0–2	Att: 229	Booked: Montgomerie, Henderson, Moore.
10th	● Queen's Park	A	W 1–2	Att: 598	Scorers: Jack, Moore. Booked: Moore, McGeouch.
17th	● Annan	A	L 1–0	Att: 647	Booked: Sharp, G Mitchell, Nicoll, Moore, Henderson, Henderson.
24th	● Inverurie Loco Works	A	L 2–1	Att: 410	Scorers: Moore. Dismissed: Henderson.
31st	● Forfar	H	W 1–0	Att: 210	Scorers: Moore. Booked: C McManus.

NOVEMBER
7th	● Berwick	H	L 2–4	Att: 250	Scorers: McColm, McGeouch. Booked: Sharp. Dismissed: Henderson.
14th	● Montrose	A	D 1–1	Att: 258	Scorers: Moore. Booked: Moore, McGeouch.
21st	● East Stirling	H	L 1–2	Att: 205	Scorers: McInnes. Booked: McInnes.

DECEMBER
5th	● Livingston	A	L 3–0	Att: 1,267	
12th	● Queen's Park	H	D 1–1	Att: 258	Scorers: Nicoll.

JANUARY
16th	● Montrose	A	W 4–5	Att: 200	Scorers: Agnew, Bouadji, Moore, One[2]. Booked: Bouadji, One, Daniel Mitchell.
23rd	● Livingston	H	D 1–1	Att: 323	Scorers: Nicoll. Booked: Wright, Henderson.
30th	● East Stirling	A	L 2–0	Att: 348	

FEBRUARY
6th	● Queen's Park	A	W 2–5	Att: 553	Scorers: Agnew[2], McColm, Daniel Mitchell, One. Booked: Henderson, Nicoll.

MARCH
6th	● Montrose	H	L 0–2	Att: 225	
13th	● Berwick	H	W 3–1	Att: 231	Scorers: McColm[3]. Booked: Moore.
16th	● Elgin	H	W 2–1	Att: 145	Scorers: Bouadji, Montgomerie.
20th	● Livingston	A	L 2–1	Att: 1,136	Scorers: Moore.
24th	● Annan	H	W 3–2	Att: 259	Scorers: Agnew, Moore, One. Booked: Henderson. Dismissed: Nicoll.
27th	● East Stirling	H	D 2–2	Att: 320	Scorers: Noble, One. Booked: Henderson.

APRIL
3rd	● Elgin	A	W 1–2	Att: 375	Scorers: One[2]. Booked: Henderson, Cawley.
6th	● Berwick	A	L 1–0	Att: 289	Booked: Cawley, Daniel Mitchell, C McManus.
10th	● Queen's Park	H	D 0–0	Att: 365	Booked: Noble, Agnew.
12th	● Albion	A	L 3–1	Att: 252	Scorers: Montgomerie. Booked: One.
14th	● Albion	H	W 2–1	Att: 214	Scorers: Agnew, Noble. Booked: Noble, Montgomerie.
17th	● Annan	A	L 3–2	Att: 392	Scorers: Moore, One. Booked: Henderson.
20th	● Forfar	A	L 2–0	Att: 422	Booked: Henderson.
24th	● Forfar	H	W 2–0	Att: 337	Scorers: Agnew, Henderson. Booked: Moore.
27th	● Elgin	A	W 2–3	Att: 232	Scorers: Cawley[2], Daniel Mitchell. Booked: Daniel Mitchell, Agostini, McInnes. Dismissed: Agostini.

MAY
1st	● Albion	A	D 0–0	Att: 575	

● Irn-Bru Third Division ● Scottish Cup ● Co-op Insurance Cup ● Challenge Cup

actim

THIRD DIVISION GOALKEEPER STATS

Player	Appearances	Match starts	Completed matches	Sub appearances	Subbed off	Clean sheets	Yellow cards	Red cards
Ryan Marshall	1	1	1	0	0	0	0	0
Robert McKillop	1	0	0	1	0	0	0	0
David Mitchell	35	35	34	0	1	6	1	0

THIRD DIVISION OUTFIELD PLAYER STATS

Player	Appearances	Match starts	Completed matches	Substitute appearances	Subbed off	Goals scored	Yellow cards	Red cards
Scott Agnew	20	20	17	0	3	6	1	0
Damiano Agostini	23	21	16	2	4	0	3	1
Stephen Aitken	8	3	1	5	2	0	0	0
Ronald Bouadji	21	21	14	0	7	2	1	0
Andrew Carnaghan	1	0	0	1	0	0	0	0
Kevin Cawley	15	14	7	1	7	2	2	0
Barry Donald	1	0	0	1	0	0	0	0
Murray Henderson	29	26	23	3	2	1	13	1
Martin Jack	16	8	1	8	7	1	0	0
Richard Jones	6	2	0	4	2	0	0	0
Stuart McColm	20	15	5	5	10	6	0	0
Darren McGeouch	18	13	8	5	5	1	2	0
Philip McGrath	2	0	0	2	0	0	0	0
Paul McInnes	16	12	5	4	7	2	3	0
Darren McMahon	1	0	0	1	0	0	1	0
Scott McManus	4	1	0	3	0	0	0	0
Craig McManus	7	4	0	3	4	0	2	0
Glen Mitchell	26	24	22	2	2	0	1	0
Daniel Mitchell	34	34	33	0	1	4	3	0
Ray Montgomerie	32	13	9	19	4	3	2	0
Michael Moore	31	25	16	6	9	8	8	0
Kevin Nicoll	27	26	24	1	1	2	5	1
Steven Noble	34	34	33	0	1	2	3	0
Armand One	19	15	10	4	5	8	2	0
Lee Sharp	25	25	25	0	0	0	2	0
Kyle Wright	7	4	2	3	2	0	1	0

SEASON INFORMATION
Highest position: 3
Lowest position: 9
Average goals scored per game: 1.33
Average goals conceded per game: 1.50

LEAGUE POSITION AT THE END OF EACH MONTH

AUG SEP OCT NOV DEC JAN FEB MAR APR MAY
3 6 7 7 8 8 8 8 7 7

LONGEST SEQUENCES

Wins	2	Undefeated home	7
(on three occasions)		(13/03/10–24/04/10)	
Losses	2	Undefeated away	2
(on three occasions)		(on two occasions)	
Draws	–	Without scoring	2
(–)		(on two occasions)	
Undefeated	3	Without conceding	2
(on three occasions)		(22/08/09–29/08/09)	
Without win	5	Scoring	6
(07/11/09–12/12/09)		(13/03/10–03/04/10)	

CARDS RECEIVED
56   3

EARLIEST STRIKE
MURRAY HENDERSON
(v Forfar) 3:11

LATEST STRIKE
SCOTT AGNEW
(v Albion) 94:23

GOALS SCORED/CONCEDED
PER FIVE-MINUTE INTERVALS

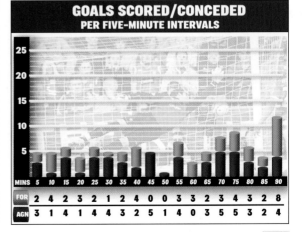

MINS	5	10	15	20	25	30	35	40	45	50	55	60	65	70	75	80	85	90
FOR	2	4	2	3	2	1	2	4	0	0	3	3	2	3	4	3	2	8
AGN	3	1	4	1	4	4	3	2	5	1	4	0	3	5	5	3	2	4

BRAVE FULHAM LEAD THE BRITISH CHARGE IN EUROPE

FROM TOP: Arsenal's Theo Walcott pursues Barcelona's Gabriel Milito; Manchester United's Nani rides a challenge from Bayern Munich's Arjen Robben; Celtic's Georgios Samaras scores against Hapoel Tel-Aviv

IT WAS a disappointing season for British clubs in the UEFA Champions League as the run of success for Barclays Premier League sides came to an end, but European football still provided plenty of highlights in 2009/10 – most notably for battling Fulham.

England had supplied three of the four Champions League semi-finalists in the previous three seasons, and at least one representative in the final for the last five years. However, that record was brought to an end as Arsenal, Chelsea, Liverpool and Manchester United all failed to match their previous feats, leaving Inter Milan and Bayern Munich to contest a thrilling showpiece in Madrid in which the Italians triumphed.

Champions League victory marked another success for Inter boss José Mourinho, who achieved his target of restoring the Italian club to the pinnacle of European football, and put one over on his former employers Chelsea along the way.

From a British perspective, though, Roy Hodgson was very much the man of the moment. His Fulham side may not have emerged victorious in the Europa League final in Hamburg – as Diego Forlan delivered the killer blow in extra-time for Atlético Madrid – but for steering the Cottagers to the first European final in their history, the 62-year-old thoroughly deserved his manager of the year award from the League Managers' Association.

Hodgson freely admitted that he never thought that Fulham would end up where they did when their European journey began in Lithuania on 30th July, as the Cottagers recorded a 3–0 win over FK Vetra. On the back of that, their passage to the group stage was easy enough, unlike Aston Villa, who were knocked out in the final qualifying round thanks to a late away goal for Rapid Vienna. Aberdeen, Motherwell, Hearts and Falkirk also exited in the qualifiers, as the Clydesdale Bank Premier League representatives' challenge ended early.

Fulham's campaign also appeared to be wavering when Roma scored in injury time at Craven Cottage to snatch a draw and then netted twice in the second half at the Stadio Olimpico after Diomansy Kamara had put Hodgson's side ahead. That left the

The Cottagers stunned the continent in what was a modest season for some of Britain's giants

Cottagers' hopes of emerging from the group stage apparently hanging by a thread but, from that position, they began to show the fortitude that took them so close to a magical prize.

Their journey to Hamburg will never be forgotten by the club's fans. CSKA Sofia and Basle were beaten to seal a place in the last 32 before holders Shakhtar Donetsk, narrowly edged out on home soil, were then held off in the return leg. Meanwhile, Everton fell to Sporting Lisbon.

Then came mighty Juventus, one of the most famous clubs on the planet. The Italians appeared to have wrapped things up as they established a 3–1 lead from the first leg and then eased further clear when David Trezeguet netted with barely two minutes gone in the return encounter. There should have been no way back – yet football never loses its capacity to amaze. Bobby Zamora breathed life into the tie before Fabio Cannavaro was sent off for a professional foul. Then Zoltan Gera scored twice to drag the Barclays Premier League side level, and Craven Cottage went wild when Clint Dempsey's elegant late chip settled it.

Stunning comeback

German champions Wolfsburg were the next side to be beaten, at the last-eight stage, which left Fulham facing a semi-final against Hamburg, who felt that destiny was on their side with the final to be held at their home ground. Fulham achieved a goalless draw in the first leg in Germany, and then mounted another stunning comeback at Craven Cottage. After going a goal down, Davies and Gera struck to confirm a first European final in the club's history and a place in the record books for Hodgson.

Liverpool, who reached the semi-finals before being beaten in extra-time by Atlético, had been consigned to the Europa League

CLOCKWISE FROM ABOVE: Fulham's players embrace after beating Wolfsburg in the Europa League; Zoltan Gera celebrates his goal in the semi-final win against SV Hamburg; Danny Murphy is left deflated by Fulham's Europa League final defeat

'Statistics show that the Red Devils were behind for just 20 minutes out of the 180 played in their quarter-final against Bayern Munich'

courtesy of their failure to reach the last 16 of the Champions League. Unirea Urziceni, Lille and Benfica were accounted for in their run in the second-tier competition before former Manchester United forward Forlan ended their hopes, as he would Fulham's.

Such an outcome to Liverpool's European exploits did not look likely when Ryan Babel gave them a lead against Lyon in the fifth round of group games in the Champions League. The Reds' performances up to that point had been unconvincing, but a vital away win in France would probably have steered them into the later stages of the competition. Instead, Lisandro Lopez broke their hearts in the final minute.

The remaining home contingent continued on, but not for long. Celtic had already fallen,

beaten by Arsenal, and they failed to make it out of their Europa League group as well. Old Firm rivals Rangers did not even have the consolation of the second-tier competition to fall back on after finishing bottom of Champions League Group G.

In the knockout phase, Chelsea were paired with Inter and former boss Mourinho, whose side capitalised on the good fortune of a controversial home win at the San Siro by completely outplaying Carlo Ancelotti's men at Stamford Bridge.

Meanwhile, David Beckham's old club were beating his new one, as a 4–0 win for Manchester United at Old Trafford accounted for AC Milan.

Arsenal beat Porto, only to be swept aside by Barcelona. A late loss of concentration

from the Spanish giants allowed the Gunners to snatch a draw in the first leg, but Barca eased through in the return.

For United, it was a story of what might have been – or indeed what should have been. Statistics show that the Red Devils were behind for just 20 minutes out of the 180 played in their quarter-final against Bayern Munich. Ivica Olic scored Bayern's injury-time winner in the first leg and, after Darron Gibson had put Sir Alex Ferguson's men in front on away goals in the decider at Old Trafford, Arjen Robben won the tie.

Having watched Barcelona take Arsenal apart, Mourinho came up with the game plan to thwart them in the semi-finals – and it worked to perfection. Inter scored three times at the San Siro and not even the first-half dismissal of Thiago Motta could shake them in the return leg.

By comparison, beating Bayern in the final was simple, as Diego Milito scored a double to ensure that Mourinho ended the campaign as a Champions League winner for the second time in his glittering career.

CHAMPIONS LEAGUE

GROUP A

	P	W	D	L	F	A	GD	PTS
Bordeaux	6	5	1	0	9	2	7	16
B Munich	6	3	1	2	9	5	4	10
Juventus	6	2	2	2	4	7	-3	8
Maccabi Haifa	6	0	0	6	0	8	-8	0

RESULTS: Sep 15: Juventus 1 Bordeaux 1, Maccabi Haifa 0 Bayern Munich 3. Sep 30: Bayern Munich 0 Juventus 0, Bordeaux 1 Maccabi Haifa 0. Oct 21: Bordeaux 2 Bayern Munich 1, Juventus 1 Maccabi Haifa 0. Nov 3: Bayern Munich 0 Bordeaux 2, Maccabi Haifa 0 Juventus 1. Nov 25: Bayern Munich 1 Maccabi Haifa 0, Bordeaux 2 Juventus 0. Dec 8: Juventus 1 Bayern Munich 4, Maccabi Haifa 0 Bordeaux 1.

GROUP B

	P	W	D	L	F	A	GD	PTS
Man Utd	6	4	1	1	10	6	4	13
CSKA Moscow	6	3	1	2	10	10	0	10
Wolfsburg	6	2	1	3	9	8	1	7
Besiktas	6	1	1	4	3	8	-5	4

RESULTS: Sep 15: Besiktas 0 Man Utd 1, Wolfsburg 3 CSKA Moscow 1. Sep 30: Man Utd 2 Wolfsburg 1, CSKA Moscow 2 Besiktas 1. Oct 21: CSKA Moscow 0 Man Utd 1, Wolfsburg 0 Besiktas 0. Nov 3: Besiktas 0 Wolfsburg 3, Man Utd 3 CSKA Moscow 3. Nov 25: CSKA Moscow 2 Wolfsburg 1, Man Utd 0 Besiktas 1. Dec 8: Besiktas 1 CSKA Moscow 2, Wolfsburg 1 Man Utd 3.

GROUP C

	P	W	D	L	F	A	GD	PTS
Real Madrid	6	4	1	1	15	7	8	13
AC Milan	6	2	3	1	8	7	1	9
Marseille	6	2	1	3	10	10	0	7
FC Zurich	6	1	1	4	5	14	-9	4

RESULTS: Sep 15: FC Zurich 2 Real Madrid 5, Marseille 1 AC Milan 2. Sep 30: AC Milan 0 FC Zurich 1, Real Madrid 3 Marseille 0. Oct 21: FC Zurich 0 Marseille 1, Real Madrid 2 AC Milan 3. Nov 3: AC Milan 1 Real Madrid 1, Marseille 6 FC Zurich 1. Nov 25: FC Zurich 1 AC Milan 1, Real Madrid 1 FC Zurich 0. Dec 8: FC Zurich 1 AC Milan 1, Marseille 1 Real Madrid 3.

GROUP D

	P	W	D	L	F	A	GD	PTS
Chelsea	6	4	2	0	11	4	7	14
FC Porto	6	4	0	2	8	3	5	12
Atlético Madrid	6	0	3	3	12	-9	3	
Apoel Nicosia	6	0	3	3	4	7	-3	3

RESULTS: Sep 15: Atlético Madrid 0 Apoel Nicosia 0, Chelsea 1 FC Porto 0. Sep 30: Apoel Nicosia 0 Chelsea 1, FC Porto 2 Atlético Madrid 0. Oct 21: Chelsea 4 Atlético Madrid 0, FC Porto 2 Apoel Nicosia 0. Nov 3: Apoel Nicosia 0 FC Porto 1, Atlético Madrid 2 Chelsea 2. Nov 25: Apoel Nicosia 1 Atlético Madrid 1, FC Porto 0 Chelsea 1. Dec 8: Atlético Madrid 0 FC Porto 3, Chelsea 2 Apoel Nicosia 2.

GROUP E

	P	W	D	L	F	A	GD	PTS
Fiorentina	6	5	0	1	14	7	7	15
Lyon	6	4	1	1	12	3	9	13
Liverpool	6	2	1	3	5	7	-2	7
Debrecen	6	0	0	6	5	19	-14	0

RESULTS: Sep 16: Liverpool 1 Debrecen 0, Lyon 1 Fiorentina 0. Sep 29: Fiorentina 2 Liverpool 0, Debrecen 0 Lyon 4. Oct 20: Debrecen 3 Fiorentina 4, Liverpool 1 Lyon 2. Nov 4: Fiorentina 5 Debrecen 2, Lyon 1 Liverpool 1. Nov 24: Debrecen 0 Liverpool 1, Fiorentina 1 Lyon 0. Dec 9: Liverpool 1 Fiorentina 2, Lyon 4 Debrecen 0.

GROUP F

	P	W	D	L	F	A	GD	PTS
Barcelona	6	3	2	1	7	3	4	11
Inter Milan	6	2	3	1	7	6	1	9
Rubin Kazan	6	1	3	2	4	7	-3	6
Dyn Kiev	6	1	2	3	7	9	-2	5

RESULTS: Sep 16: Dynamo Kiev 3 Rubin Kazan 1, Inter Milan 0 Barcelona 0. Sep 29: Rubin Kazan 1 Inter Milan 1, Barcelona 2 Dynamo Kiev 0. Oct 20: Barcelona 1 Rubin Kazan 2, Inter Milan 2 Dynamo Kiev 2. Nov 4: Dynamo Kiev 1 Inter Milan 2, Rubin Kazan 0 Barcelona 0. Nov 24: Barcelona 2 Inter Milan 0, Rubin Kazan 0 Dynamo Kiev 0. Dec 9: Dynamo Kiev 1 Barcelona 2, Inter Milan 2 Rubin Kazan 0.

GROUP G

	P	W	D	L	F	A	GD	PTS
Sevilla	6	4	1	1	11	4	7	13
VfB Stuttgart	6	2	3	1	9	7	2	9
Unirea Urziceni	6	2	2	2	8	8	0	8
Rangers	6	0	2	4	3	13	-9	2

RESULTS: Sep 16: Sevilla 2 Unirea Urziceni 0, VfB Stuttgart 1 Rangers 1. Sep 29: Unirea Urziceni 1 VfB Stuttgart 1, Rangers 1 Sevilla 4. Oct 20: Rangers 1 Unirea Urziceni 4, VfB Stuttgart 1 Sevilla 3. Nov 4: Sevilla 1 VfB Stuttgart 1, Unirea Urziceni 1 Rangers 1. Nov 24: Rangers 0 VfB Stuttgart 2, Unirea Urziceni 1 Sevilla 0. Dec 9: Sevilla 1 Rangers 0, VfB Stuttgart 3 Unirea Urziceni 1.

GROUP H

	P	W	D	L	F	A	GD	PTS
Arsenal	6	4	1	1	12	5	7	13
Olympiacos	6	3	1	2	4	5	-1	10
Standard Liège	6	1	2	3	7	9	-2	5
AZ	6	0	4	2	4	8	-4	4

RESULTS: Sep 16: Olympiacos 1 AZ 0, Standard Liège 2 Arsenal 3. Sep 29: Arsenal 2 Olympiacos 0, AZ 1 Standard Liège 1. Oct 20: AZ 1 Arsenal 1, Olympiacos 2 Standard Liège 1. Nov 4: Arsenal 4 AZ 1, Standard Liège 2 Olympiacos 0. Nov 24: AZ 0 Olympiacos 0, Arsenal 2 Standard Liège 0. Dec 9: Olympiacos 1 Arsenal 0, Standard Liège 1 AZ 1.

ROUND OF 16 FIRST LEG

16/02/2010

AC Milan (1) .... 2 Man Utd (1) 3
Ronaldinho 3 | Scholes 36
Seedorf 85 | Rooney 66, 74
Att 80,000

Lyon (0) .... 1 Real Madrid (0) 0
Makoun 47
Att 40,500

17/02/2010

Bayern Munich (1) .... 2 Fiorentina (0) 1
Robben 45 (pen) | Kroldrup 50
Klose 89 | Att 64,500

FC Porto (1) .... 2 Arsenal (1) 1
Fabianski 11 (og) | Campbell 18
Falcao 52
Att 45,600

23/02/2010

Olympiacos (0) .... 0 Bordeaux (1) 1
| Ciani 45
Att 30,000

VfB Stuttgart (1) .... 1 Barcelona (0) 1
Cacau 25 | Ibrahimovic 52
Att 40,000

24/02/2010

CSKA Moscow (0) .... 1 Sevilla (1) 1
Gonzalez 66 | Negredo 25
Att 20,000

Inter Milan (1) .... 2 Chelsea (0) 1
Milito 3 | Kalou 51
Cambiasso 55
Att 84,638

ROUND OF 16 SECOND LEG

09/03/2010

Arsenal (2) .... 5 FC Porto (0) 0
Bendtner 10, 25, 90 (pen) | Att 59,661
Nasri 63
Eboue 66
Aggregate: 6–2

Fiorentina (1) .... 3 Bayern Munich (0) 2
Vargas 28 | Van Bommel 60
Jovetic 54, 64 | Robben 65
Att 40,000
Aggregate: 4–4, Bayern win on away goals

10/03/2010

Man Utd (1) .... 4 AC Milan (0) 0
Rooney 13, 46 | Att 74,595
Park 59
Fletcher 87
Aggregate: 7–2

Real Madrid (1) .... 1 Lyon (0) 1
Ronaldo 6 | Pjanic 75
Att 80,354
Aggregate: 1–2

16/03/2010

Chelsea (0) .... 0 Inter Milan (0) 1
Att 38,107 | Eto'o 79
Aggregate: 1–3

Sevilla (1) .... 1 CSKA Moscow (1) 2
Perotti 41 | Necid 39
Att 40,000 | Honda 55
Aggregate: 2–3

17/03/2010

Barcelona (2) .... 4 VfB Stuttgart (0) 0
Messi 13, 60
Pedro 22
Bojan 89
Att 75,000
Aggregate: 5–1

Bordeaux (1) .... 2 Olympiacos (0) 1
Gourcuff 5 | Mitroglou 64
Chamakh 88 | Att 32,367
Aggregate: 3–1

QUARTER-FINALS FIRST LEG

30/03/2010

Bayern Munich (0) .... 2 Man Utd (1) 1
Ribery 77 | Rooney 2
Olic 90 | Att 66,000
Bayern Munich: Butt, Lahm, Van Buyten, Demichelis, Badstuber, Altintop (Klose 86), Van Bommel, Pranjic (Tymoschuk 89), Ribery, Muller (Gomez 73), Olic. **Subs not used:** Rensing, Gorlitz, Contento, Alaba. **Booked:** Olic, Badstuber.
Man Utd: Van der Sar, Neville, Ferdinand, Vidic, Evra, Fletcher, Carrick (Valencia 70), Scholes, Nani (Giggs 82), Park (Berbatov 70), Rooney. **Subs not used:** Kuszczak, R Da Silva, J Evans, Gibson. **Booked:** Scholes, Rooney, Neville.

Lyon (2) .... 3 Bordeaux (1) 1
Lopez 10, 77 (pen) | Chamakh 14
Michel Bastos 32
Att 40,000
Lyon: Lloris, Reveillere, Cris, Bodmer, Cissokho, Makoun, Toulalan, Delgado (Gonalons 86), Pjanic (Govou 65), Michel Bastos (Kallstrom 66), Lopez. **Subs not used:** Vercoutre, Boumsong, Ederson, Gomis. **Booked:** Lopez, Govou.
Bordeaux: Carrasso, Chalme (Henrique 82), Sane, Ciani, Tremoulinas, Gouffran (Bellion 84), Plasil, Menegazzo, Wendell (Jussie 71), Gourcuff, Chamakh. **Subs not used:** Rame, Jurietti, Cavenaghi, Placente.

CHAMPIONS LEAGUE

31/03/2010

Arsenal (0) 2   Barcelona (0) 2
Walcott 69   *Ibrahimovic 46, 59*
Fabregas 85 (pen)
Att 59,572
Arsenal: Almunia, Sagna (Walcott 66), Gallas (Denilson 44), Vermaelen, Clichy, Fabregas, Song, Diaby, Nasri, Bendtner, Arshavin (Eboue 27). **Subs not used:** Fabianski, Rosicky, Eduardo, Campbell. **Booked:** Diaby, Arshavin, Fabregas, Eboue, Song.
Barcelona: Valdes, Dani Alves, Pique, Puyol, Maxwell, Messi (Milito 86), Keita, Busquets, Xavi, Pedro, Ibrahimovic (Henry 77). **Subs not used:** Pinto, Marquez, Bojan, Toure Yaya, Jeffren. **Booked:** Pique. **Dismissed:** Puyol.

Inter Milan (0) 1   CSKA Moscow (0) 0
Milito 65
Att 64,500
Inter Milan: Julio Cesar, Maicon, Materazzi, Samuel, Zanetti, Stankovic, Cambiasso, Eto'o, Sneijder, Pandev (Mariga 90), Milito. **Subs not used:** Toldo, Cordoba, Quaresma, Muntari, Chivu, Arnautovic. **Booked:** Materazzi.
CSKA Moscow: Akinfeev, Berezutsky, Berezutsky, Ignashevich, Shchennikov, Krasic, Aldonin (Rahimic 75), Semberas, Mamaev (Gonzalez 73), Honda (Dzagoev 69), Necid. **Subs not used:** Chepchugov, Nababkin, Odiah, Guilherme. **Booked:** Krasic, Aldonin.

QUARTER-FINALS SECOND LEG
06/04/2010

Barcelona (3) 4   Arsenal (1) 1
Messi 21, 37, 42, 88   *Bendtner 19*
Att 95,000
Aggregate: 6–3
Barcelona: Valdes, Dani Alves, Marquez, Milito, Abidal (Maxwell 53), Busquets, Xavi, Keita, Pedro (Iniesta 86), Bojan (Toure Yaya 55), Messi. **Subs not used:** Pinto, Henry, Fontas, Jeffren.
Arsenal: Almunia, Sagna, Vermaelen, Silvestre (Eboue 63), Clichy, Denilson, Diaby, Walcott, Nasri, Rosicky (Eduardo 73), Bendtner. **Subs not used:** Fabianski, Traore, Campbell, Merida, Eastmond. **Booked:** Denilson, Eboue, Rosicky.

CSKA Moscow (0) 0   Inter Milan (1) 1
                                    Sneijder 6
                                    Att 50,000
Aggregate: 0–2
CSKA Moscow: Akinfeev, Berezutsky, Berezutsky (Odiah 14), Ignashevich, Shchennikov, Honda (Rahimic 77), Semberas, Mamaev, Dzagoev, Gonzalez, Necid (Guilherme 71). **Subs not used:** Chepchugov, Nababkin, Piliev, Oliseh. **Booked:** Mamaev, Odiah. **Dismissed:** Odiah.
Inter Milan: Julio Cesar, Maicon, Samuel, Lucio, Zanetti, Cambiasso, Sneijder (Muntari 86), Stankovic, Eto'o, Milito (Balotelli 74), Pandev (Chivu 63). **Subs not used:** Orlandoni, Cordoba, Quaresma, Materazzi. **Booked:** Stankovic.

07/04/2010

Bordeaux (1) 1   Lyon (0) 0
Chamakh 45
Att 33,897
Aggregate: 2–3
Bordeaux: Carrasso, Sane, Ciani, Planus (Cavenaghi 84), Tremoulinas, Plasil, Diarra (Chalme 70), Jussie (Gouffran 77), Gourcuff, Wendell, Chamakh. **Subs not used:** Rame, Henrique, Bellion, Traore.
Lyon: Lloris, Reveillere, Cris, Boumsong (Bodmer 77), Cissokho, Toulalan, Gonalons, Kallstrom, Michel Bastos (Ederson 88), Gomis (Pjanic 66), Delgado. **Subs not used:** Vercoutre, Tafer, Gassama, Belfodil. **Booked:** Gonalons, Kallstrom, Toulalan, Cissokho, Delgado.

Man Utd (3) 3   Bayern Munich (1) 2
Gibson 3   *Olic 43*
Nani 7, 41   *Robben 74*
Att 74,482
Aggregate: 4–4, Bayern win on away goals
Man Utd: Van der Sar, R Da Silva, Ferdinand, Vidic, Evra, Fletcher, Carrick (Berbatov 80), Gibson (Giggs 80), Valencia, Rooney (O'Shea 55), Nani. **Subs not used:** Kuszczak, Scholes, J Evans, Macheda. **Booked:** R Da Silva. **Dismissed:** R Da Silva.
Bayern Munich: Butt, Lahm, Van Buyten, Demichelis, Badstuber, Robben (Altintop 76), Van Bommel, Schweinsteiger, Ribery, Olic (Pranjic 84), Muller (Gomez 46). **Subs not used:** Rensing, Klose, Contento, Tymoschuk. **Booked:** Van Bommel, Badstuber.

SEMI-FINALS FIRST LEG
20/04/2010

Inter Milan (1) 3   Barcelona (1) 1
Sneijder 30   *Pedro 19*
Maicon 48
Milito 61
Att 83,000
Inter Milan: Julio Cesar, Maicon (Chivu 74), Lucio, Samuel, Zanetti, Motta, Cambiasso, Pandev (Stankovic 56), Milito (Balotelli 75), Sneijder, Eto'o. **Subs not used:** Orlandoni, Cordoba, Muntari, Materazzi. **Booked:** Eto'o, Stankovic.
Barcelona: Valdes, Dani Alves, Pique, Puyol, Maxwell, Xavi, Busquets, Keita, Ibrahimovic (Abidal 62), Messi, Pedro. **Subs not used:** Pinto, Marquez, Bojan, Henry, Milito, Toure Yaya. **Booked:** Pique, Busquets, Puyol, Keita, Dani Alves.

21/04/2010

Bayern Munich (0) 1   Lyon (0) 0
Robben 69
Att 68,000
Bayern Munich: Butt, Lahm, Van Buyten, Demichelis, Contento, Robben (Altintop 85), Schweinsteiger, Pranjic (Gomez 63), Ribery, Muller, Olic (Tymoschuk 46). **Subs not used:** Rensing, Gorlitz, Klose, Alaba. **Booked:** Pranjic. **Dismissed:** Ribery.
Lyon: Lloris, Reveillere, Cris, Toulalan, Cissokho, Gonalons, Kallstrom, Ederson (Michel Bastos 71), Pjanic (Makoun 55), Delgado (Govou 79), Lopez. **Subs not used:** Vercoutre, Gomis, Anderson, Gassama. **Booked:** Toulalan, Michel Bastos. **Dismissed:** Toulalan.

SEMI-FINALS SECOND LEG
27/04/2010

Lyon (0) 0   Bayern Munich (1) 3
Att 40,000   *Olic 26, 67, 77*
Aggregate: 0–4
Lyon: Lloris, Reveillere, Cris, Boumsong, Cissokho (Gomis 46), Gonalons, Makoun, Govou, Delgado (Pjanic 69), Michel Bastos, Lopez (Ederson 79). **Subs not used:** Vercoutre, Kallstrom, Anderson, Gassama. **Booked:** Cris, Gonalons. **Dismissed:** Cris.
Bayern Munich: Butt, Lahm, Van Buyten (Demichelis 46), Badstuber, Contento, Robben (Klose 76), Schweinsteiger (Alaba 78), Van Bommel, Altintop, Muller, Olic. **Subs not used:** Rensing, Gorlitz, Gomez. **Booked:** Altintop.

28/04/2010

Barcelona (0) 1   Inter Milan (0) 0
Pique 84
Att 95,000
Aggregate: 2–3
Barcelona: Valdes, Dani Alves, Pique, Milito (Maxwell 46), Keita, Xavi, Toure Yaya, Busquets (Jeffren 63), Pedro, Ibrahimovic (Bojan 63), Messi. **Subs not used:** Pinto, Marquez, Henry, Thiago. **Booked:** Pedro.
Inter Milan: Julio Cesar, Maicon, Lucio, Samuel, Zanetti, Cambiasso, Motta, Eto'o (Mariga 86), Chivu, Sneijder (Muntari 66), Milito (Cordoba 81). **Subs not used:** Toldo, Materazzi, Balotelli, Arnautovic. **Booked:** Lucio, Motta, Muntari, Julio Cesar, Chivu. **Dismissed:** Motta.

FINAL
22/05/2010 (MADRID)

Bayern Munich (0) 0   Inter Milan (1) 2
Att 80,100   *Milito 34, 70*
Bayern Munich: Butt, Lahm, Van Buyten, Demichelis, Badstuber, Robben, Van Bommel, Schweinsteiger, Altintop (Klose 63), Muller, Olic (Gomez 74). **Subs not used:** Rensing, Gorlitz, Pranjic, Contento, Tymoschuk. **Booked:** Van Bommel, Demichelis.
Inter Milan: Julio Cesar, Maicon, Lucio, Samuel, Chivu (Stankovic 68), Zanetti, Cambiasso, Eto'o, Sneijder, Pandev (Muntari 79), Milito (Materazzi 90). **Subs not used:** Toldo, Cordoba, Mariga, Balotelli. **Booked:** Chivu.

Inter Milan's players lift the Champions League trophy following their final win against Bayern Munich in Madrid

LEADING SCORERS

PLAYER	TEAM	GLS
Lionel Messi	Barcelona	8
Ivica Olic	Bayern Munich	7
Cristiano Ronaldo	Real Madrid	7
Diego Milito	Inter Milan	6
Nicklas Bendtner	Arsenal	5
Marouane Chamakh	Bordeaux	5
Wayne Rooney	Man Utd	5
Edin Dzeko	Wolfsburg	4
Francesc Fabregas	Arsenal	4
Radamel Falcao	FC Porto	4
Zlatan Ibrahimovic	Barcelona	4
Stevan Jovetic	Fiorentina	4
Milos Krasic	CSKA Moscow	4
Michael Owen	Man Utd	4
Rodriguez Pedro	Barcelona	4
Miralem Pjanic	Lyon	4
Arjen Robben	Bayern Munich	4

OFFICIAL FOOTBALL YEARBOOK OF THE ENGLISH & SCOTTISH LEAGUES 2010-2011   **487**

EUROPA LEAGUE

GROUP A

	P	W	D	L	F	A	GD	PTS
Anderlecht	6	3	2	1	9	4	5	11
Ajax	6	3	1	2	8	6	2	10
Dinamo Zagreb	6	2	0	4	6	8	-2	6
FC Timisoara	6	1	2	3	4	9	-5	5

RESULTS: Sep 17: Ajax 0 FC Timisoara 0, Dinamo Zagreb 0 Anderlecht 2. **Oct 1:** Anderlecht 1 Ajax 1, FC Timisoara 0 Dinamo Zagreb 3. **Oct 22:** Ajax 2 Dinamo Zagreb 1 Anderlecht 0 FC Timisoara 0 Anderlecht 0. **Nov 5:** Anderlecht 3 FC Timisoara 1, Dinamo Zagreb 0 Ajax 2. **Dec 2:** Anderlecht 0 Dinamo Zagreb 1, FC Timisoara 1 Ajax 2. **Dec 17:** Ajax 1 Anderlecht 3, Dinamo Zagreb 1 FC Timisoara 2.

GROUP B

	P	W	D	L	F	A	GD	PTS
Valencia	6	3	3	0	12	8	4	12
Lille	6	3	1	2	15	9	6	10
Genoa	6	2	1	3	8	10	-2	7
Slavia Prague	6	0	3	3	5	13	-8	3

RESULTS: Sep 17: Genoa 2 Slavia Prague 0, Lille 1 Valencia 1. **Oct 1:** Slavia Prague 1 Lille 5, Valencia 3 Genoa 2. **Oct 22:** Lille 3 Genoa 0, Valencia 1 Slavia Prague 1. **Nov 5:** Genoa 3 Lille 2, Slavia Prague 2 Valencia 2. **Dec 2:** Slavia Prague 0 Genoa 0, Valencia 3 Lille 1. **Dec 17:** Genoa 1 Valencia 2, Lille 3 Slavia Prague 1.

GROUP C

	P	W	D	L	F	A	GD	PTS
Hapoel Tel-Aviv	6	4	0	2	13	8	5	12
Hamburg	6	3	1	2	7	6	1	10
Celtic	6	1	3	2	7	7	0	6
Rapid Vienna	6	1	2	3	8	14	-6	5

RESULTS: Sep 17: Hapoel Tel-Aviv 2 Celtic 1, Rapid Vienna 3 Hamburg 0. **Oct 1:** Celtic 1 Rapid Vienna 1, Hamburg 4 Hapoel Tel-Aviv 2. **Oct 22:** Celtic 0 Hamburg 1, Hapoel Tel-Aviv 5 Rapid Vienna 1. **Nov 5:** Hamburg 0 Celtic 0, Rapid Vienna 0 Hapoel Tel-Aviv 3. **Dec 2:** Celtic 2 Hapoel Tel-Aviv 0, Hamburg 2 Rapid Vienna 0. **Dec 17:** Hapoel Tel-Aviv 1 Hamburg 0, Rapid Vienna 3 Celtic 3.

GROUP D

	P	W	D	L	F	A	GD	PTS
Sporting	6	3	2	1	8	6	2	11
Hertha Berlin	6	3	1	2	6	5	1	10
Heerenveen	6	2	2	2	11	7	4	8
FK Ventspils	6	0	3	3	3	10	-7	3

RESULTS: Sep 17: Heerenveen 2 Sporting 3, Hertha Berlin 1 FK Ventspils 1. **Oct 1:** Sporting 1 Hertha Berlin 0, FK Ventspils 0 Heerenveen 0. **Oct 22:** Sporting 1 Sporting 2, Hertha Berlin 2 Heerenveen 1. **Nov 5:** Heerenveen 2 Hertha Berlin 3, Sporting 1 FK Ventspils 1. **Dec 3:** FK Ventspils 0 Hertha Berlin 1, Sporting 1 Heerenveen 1. **Dec 16:** Heerenveen 5 FK Ventspils 0, Hertha Berlin 1 Sporting 0.

GROUP E

	P	W	D	L	F	A	GD	PTS
Roma	6	4	1	1	10	5	5	13
Fulham	6	3	2	1	8	6	2	11
Basle	6	3	0	3	10	7	3	9
CSKA Sofia	6	0	1	5	2	12	-10	1

RESULTS: Sep 17: Basle 2 Roma 0, CSKA Sofia 1 Fulham 1. **Oct 1:** Roma 2 CSKA Sofia 0, Fulham 1 Basle 0. **Oct 22:** CSKA Sofia 0 Basle 2, Fulham 1 Roma 1. **Nov 5:** Basle 3 CSKA Sofia 1, Roma 2 Fulham 1. **Dec 3:** Fulham 1 CSKA Sofia 0, Roma 2 Basle 1. **Dec 16:** Basle 2 Fulham 3, CSKA Sofia 0 Roma 3.

GROUP F

	P	W	D	L	F	A	GD	PTS
Galatasaray	6	4	1	1	12	4	8	13
Panathnks	6	2	0	2	7	4	3	12
Dinamo Bucharest	6	2	0	4	4	12	-8	6
Sturm Graz	6	1	1	4	3	6	-3	4

RESULTS: Sep 17: Panathinaikos 1 Galatasaray 3, SK Sturm Graz 0 Dinamo Bucharest 1. **Oct 1:** Dinamo Bucharest 0 Panathinaikos 1, Galatasaray 1 SK Sturm Graz 0. **Oct 22:** Galatasaray 4 Dinamo Bucharest 1, Panathinaikos 1 SK Sturm Graz 0. **Nov 5:** Dinamo Bucharest 0 Galatasaray 3, SK Sturm Graz 0 Panathinaikos 1. **Dec 3:** Dinamo Bucharest 2 SK Sturm Graz 1, Galatasaray 1 Panathinaikos 0. **Dec 16:** Panathinaikos 3 Dinamo Bucharest 0, SK Sturm Graz 1 Galatasaray 0.

GROUP G

	P	W	D	L	F	A	GD	PTS
SV RB Salzburg	6	6	0	0	9	2	7	18
Villarreal	6	3	0	3	8	6	2	9
Lazio	6	2	0	4	9	10	-1	6
Levski Sofia	6	1	0	5	1	9	-8	3

RESULTS: Sep 17: Lazio 1 SV Red Bull Salzburg 2, Villarreal 1 Levski Sofia 0. **Oct 1:** Levski Sofia 0 Lazio 4, SV Red Bull Salzburg 2 Villarreal 0. **Oct 22:** Lazio 2 Villarreal 1, SV Red Bull Salzburg 1 Levski Sofia 0. **Nov 5:** Levski Sofia 0 SV Red Bull Salzburg 1, Villarreal 4 Lazio 1. **Dec 2:** Levski Sofia 0 Villarreal 2, SV Red Bull Salzburg 2 Lazio 1. **Dec 17:** Lazio 0 Levski Sofia 1, Villarreal 0 SV Red Bull Salzburg 1.

GROUP H

	P	W	D	L	F	A	GD	PTS
Fenerbahce	6	5	0	1	8	3	5	15
FC Twente	6	2	2	2	5	6	-1	8
FC Sheriff	6	1	2	3	4	5	-1	5
Steaua Bucharest	6	1	0	4	2	6	-3	4

RESULTS: Sep 17: Fenerbahce 1 FC Twente 2, Steaua Bucharest 0 FC Sheriff 0. **Oct 1:** FC Twente 0 Steaua Bucharest 0, FC Sheriff 0 Fenerbahce 1. **Oct 22:** FC Sheriff 2 FC Twente 0, Steaua Bucharest 0 Fenerbahce 1. **Nov 5:** FC Twente 2 FC Sheriff 1, Fenerbahce 3 Steaua Bucharest 1. **Dec 2:** FC Sheriff 1 Steaua Bucharest 1, FC Twente 0 Fenerbahce 1. **Dec 17:** Fenerbahce 1 FC Sheriff 0, Steaua Bucharest 1 FC Twente 1.

GROUP I

	P	W	D	L	F	A	GD	PTS
Benfica	6	5	0	1	13	3	10	15
Everton	6	3	0	3	7	9	-2	9
BATE	6	2	1	3	7	9	-2	7
AEK Athens	6	1	1	4	5	11	-6	4

RESULTS: Sep 17: Benfica 2 BATE 0, Everton 4 AEK Athens 0. **Oct 1:** AEK Athens 1 Benfica 0, BATE 1 Everton 2. **Oct 22:** BATE 2 AEK Athens 1, Benfica 5 Everton 0. **Nov 5:** AEK Athens 2 BATE 2, Everton 0 Benfica 2. **Dec 2:** Everton 1, BATE 1 Benfica 2. **Dec 17:** Benfica 2 AEK Athens 1, Everton 0 BATE 1.

GROUP J

	P	W	D	L	F	A	GD	PTS
Sh Donetsk	6	4	1	1	14	3	11	13
Club Brugge	6	3	2	1	10	8	2	11
Toulouse	6	2	1	3	6	11	-5	7
Partizan Belgrade	6	1	0	5	6	14	-8	3

RESULTS: Sep 17: Club Brugge 1 Shakhtar Donetsk 4, Partizan Belgrade 2 Toulouse 3. **Oct 1:** Toulouse 2 Club Brugge 2, Shakhtar Donetsk 3 Partizan Belgrade 1. **Oct 22:** Club Brugge 2 Partizan Belgrade 0, Shakhtar Donetsk 4 Toulouse 0. **Nov 5:** Partizan Belgrade 2 Club Brugge 4, Toulouse 0 Shakhtar Donetsk 2. **Dec 3:** Shakhtar Donetsk 0 Club Brugge 0, Toulouse 1 Partizan Belgrade 0. **Dec 16:** Club Brugge 1 Toulouse 0, Partizan Belgrade 1 Shakhtar Donetsk 0.

GROUP K

	P	W	D	L	F	A	GD	PTS
PSV	6	4	2	0	8	3	5	14
FC Copenhagen	6	3	1	2	7	4	3	10
Sp Prague	6	2	1	3	7	9	-2	7
CFR Cluj-Napoca	6	1	0	5	4	10	-6	3

RESULTS: Sep 17: CFR Cluj-Napoca 2 FC Copenhagen 0, Sparta Prague 2 PSV 2. **Oct 1:** FC Copenhagen 1 Sparta Prague 0, PSV 1 CFR Cluj-Napoca 0. **Oct 22:** PSV 1 FC Copenhagen 0, Sparta Prague 2 CFR Cluj-Napoca 0. **Nov 5:** CFR Cluj-Napoca 2 Sparta Prague 3, FC Copenhagen 1 PSV 1. **Dec 3:** FC Copenhagen 2 CFR Cluj-Napoca 0, PSV 1 Sparta Prague 0. **Dec 16:** CFR Cluj-Napoca 0 PSV 2, Sparta Prague 0 FC Copenhagen 3.

GROUP L

	P	W	D	L	F	A	GD	PTS
W Bremen	6	5	1	0	17	6	11	16
Athletic Bilbao	6	3	1	2	10	8	2	10
Nacional	6	1	2	3	11	12	-1	5
FK Austria Vienna	6	0	2	4	4	16	-12	2

RESULTS: Sep 17: Athletic Bilbao 3 FK Austria Vienna 0, Nacional 2 Werder Bremen 3. **Oct 1:** Werder Bremen 3 Athletic Bilbao 1, FK Austria Vienna 1 Nacional 1. **Oct 22:** Athletic Bilbao 3 Nacional 1, FK Austria Vienna 2 Werder Bremen 2. **Nov 5:** Nacional 1 Athletic Bilbao 1, Werder Bremen 2 FK Austria Vienna 0. **Dec 3:** FK Austria Vienna 0 Athletic Bilbao 3, Werder Bremen 4 Nacional 1. **Dec 16:** Athletic Bilbao 0 Werder Bremen 3, Nacional 5 FK Austria Vienna 1.

(GROUP J continued) Brugge 4, Toulouse 0 Shakhtar Donetsk 2. **Dec 3:** Shakhtar Donetsk 0 Club Brugge 0, Toulouse 1 Partizan Belgrade 0. **Dec 16:** Club Brugge 1 Toulouse 0, Partizan Belgrade 1 Shakhtar Donetsk 0.

ROUND OF 32 FIRST LEG

16/02/2010

Everton (1) 2   **Sporting (0)** 1
Pienaar 35   Veloso 87 (pen)
Distin 49   Att 28,131

18/02/2010

Ajax (1) 1   **Juventus (1)** 2
Sulejmani 16   Amauri 31, 58
Att 51,000

Athletic Bilbao (0) 1   **Anderlecht (1)** 1
San Jose 58   Biglia 35
Att 39,000

Atlético Madrid (1) 1   **Galatasaray (0)** 1
Reyes 23   Keita 77
Att 30,000

Club Brugge (0) 1   **Valencia (0)** 0
Kouemaha 56   Att 21,657

FC Copenhagen (0) 1   **Marseille (0)** 3
Gronkjaer 80 (pen)   Niang 72
Att 26,000   Ben Arfa 84
   Kabore 90

FC Twente (1) 1   **Werder Bremen (0)** 0
Janssen 39   Att 24,000

Fulham (1) 2   **Shakhtar Donetsk (1)** 1
Gera 3   Luiz Adriano 32
Zamora 63   Att 21,832

Hamburg (1) 1   **PSV (0)** 0
Jansen 27 (pen)   Att 35,672

Hertha Berlin (1) 1   **Benfica (1)** 1
Javi Garcia 33 (og)   Di Maria 4
Att 13,684

Lille (1) 2   **Fenerbahce (1)** 1
Balmont 2   Wederson 5
Frau 52   Att 16,783

Liverpool (0) ....1 Unirea Urziceni (0) 0
Ngog 81
Att 40,450

Panathinaikos (0) ....3 Roma (1) 2
Salpingidis 66   Vucinic 29
Christodoulopoulos 84   Pizarro 81 (pen)
Cisse 89   Att 54,274

Rubin Kazan (2) ....3 Hapoel Tel-Aviv (0) 0
Bukharov 14, 24
Semak 69   Att 7,000

Standard Liège (0).......3 SV RB Salzburg (2) 2
Witsel 67 (pen), 82   Janko 4, 45
De Camargo 80   Att 21,000

Villarreal (1) ....2 Wolfsburg (0)................2
Senna 43   Grafite 65, 84 (pen)
Gullon 85   Att 22,000

ROUND OF 32 SECOND LEG
23/02/2010

Benfica (1) ....4 Hertha Berlin (0) 0
Aimar 25, Cardozo 48, 62
Javi Garcia 59   Att 30,402
            Aggregate: 5–1

25/02/2010

Anderlecht (2)...............4 Athletic Bilbao (0).......0
Lukaku 4, San Jose 27 (og)
Boussoufa 50, Legear 68   Att 24,000
            Aggregate: 5–1

Fenerbahce (1) ....1 Lille (0) 1
Belozoglu 34   Rami 86
Att 48,000
            Aggregate: 2–3

Galatasaray (0) ....1 Atlético Madrid (0).......2
Keita 66   Simao 63
Att 22,000   Forlan 90
            Aggregate: 2–3

Hapoel Tel-Aviv (0).......0 Rubin Kazan (0)............0
Att 12,000
            Aggregate: 0–3

Juventus (0)..................0 Ajax (0)..........................0
Att 16,441
            Aggregate: 2–1

Marseille (1)..................3 FC Copenhagen (0) 1
Ben Arfa 43   Almeida 86
Kone 61, 77   Att 15,000
            Aggregate: 6–2

PSV (2).........................3 Hamburg (0)..................2
Toivonen 2   Petric 46
Dzsudzsak 43   Trochowski 79 (pen)
Koevermans 90   Att 30,500
    Aggregate: 3–3, Hamburg win on away goals

Roma (1) ....2 Panathinaikos (3) 3
Riise 11, De Rossi 67   Cisse 40 (pen), 45
Att 50,000   Ninis 43
            Aggregate: 4–6

SV RB Salzburg (0)......0 Standard Liège (0) 0
Att 26,500
            Aggregate: 2–3

Shakhtar Donetsk (0)...1 Fulham (0) 1
Jadson 69   Hangeland 33
Att 47,509
            Aggregate: 2–3

Sporting (0)...................3 Everton (0)....................0
Veloso 64, Mendes 77
Fernandez 90   Att 17,609
            Aggregate: 4–2

Unirea Urziceni (1) ....1 Liverpool (2) 3
Bruno Fernandes 18   Mascherano 29
Att 25,000   Babel 40, Gerrard 57
            Aggregate: 1–4

Valencia (1) ....3 Club Brugge (0)............0
Mata 1
Pablo 97, 117   Att 45,000
    Aggregate: 3–1, Valencia win after extra-time

Werder Bremen (3)........4 FC Twente (1) 1
Pizarro 15, 20, 58   de Jong 33
Naldo 27   Att 20,963
            Aggregate: 4–2

Wolfsburg (3)................4 Villarreal (1)..................1
Dzeko 9, Angel 14 (og)   Capdevila 30
Gentner 41, Grafite 64   Att 17,000
            Aggregate: 6–3

ROUND OF 16 FIRST LEG
11/03/2010

Atlético Madrid (0).......0 Sporting (0)...................0
Att 42,000

Benfica (0) ....1 Marseille (0)..................1
Maxi Pereira 77   Ben Arfa 90
Att 46,635

Hamburg (2) ....3 Anderlecht (1)...............1
Mathijsen 23   Legear 45
van Nistelrooy 40
Jarolim 76   Att 34,921

Juventus (3)..................3 Fulham (1) 1
Legrottaglie 9   Etuhu 36
Zebina 25, Trezeguet 45   Att 11,406

Lille (0) ....1 Liverpool (0)..................0
Hazard 85   Att 18,000

Panathinaikos (0) ....1 Standard Liège (2).........3
Vyntra 48   Witsel 8
Att 55,000   Jovanovic 16
                                           De Camargo 74

Rubin Kazan (1)............1 Wolfsburg (0)................1
Noboa 29   Misimovic 67
Att 12,000

Valencia (0) ....1 Werder Bremen (1)........1
Mata 57   Frings 25 (pen)
Att 35,000

ROUND OF 16 SECOND LEG
18/03/2010

Anderlecht (2)...............4 Hamburg (1)..................3
Lukaku 44   Boateng 42
Suarez 45 (pen)   Jansen 54
Biglia 59   Petric 75
Boussoufa 66   Att 21,000
            Aggregate: 5–6

Fulham (2).....................4 Juventus (1)..................1
Zamora 9   Trezeguet 2
Gera 39, 49 (pen)
Dempsey 82   Att 23,458
            Aggregate: 5–4

Liverpool (1) ....3 Lille (0) 0
Gerrard 9 (pen)
Torres 49, 90   Att 38,139
            Aggregate: 3–1

Marseille (0)..................1 Benfica (0)....................2
Niang 70   Maxi Pereira 75
Att 40,000   Alan Kardec 90
            Aggregate: 2–3

Sporting (2)...................2 Atlético Madrid (2)........2
Liedson 19   Aguero 3, 33
Anderson Polga 45   Att 45,000
    Aggregate: 2–2 Atletico win on away goals

Standard Liège (1)........1 Panathinaikos (0)..........0
Mbokani 45   Att 29,000
            Aggregate: 4–1

Werder Bremen (1).......4 Valencia (3) 4
Hugo Almeida 26   Villa 2, 45, 65
Frings 57 (pen)   Mata 15
Marin 62, Pizarro 84   Att 24,200
    Aggregate: 5–5, Valencia win on away goals

Wolfsburg (0)................2 Rubin Kazan (1)............1
Martins 58   Kasaev 21
Gentner 119   Att 15,412
    Aggregate: 3–2, Wolfsburg win after extra-time

QUARTER-FINALS FIRST LEG
01/04/2010

Benfica (0) ....2 Liverpool (1)..................1
Cardozo 59 (pen), 79 (pen)   Agger 9
Att 62,629

Fulham (0) ....2 Wolfsburg (0)................1
Zamora 59   Madlung 89
Duff 63   Att 22,307

Hamburg (2) ....2 Standard Liège (1).........1
Petric 43 (pen)   Mbokani 30
van Nistelrooy 45   Att 50,000

Valencia (0) ....2 Atlético Madrid (0)........2
Fernandes 67   Forlan 59
Villa 82   Antonio Lopez 72
Att 50,000

QUARTER-FINALS SECOND LEG
08/04/2010

Atlético Madrid (0).......0 Valencia (0)..................0
Att 50,000
    Aggregate: 2–2, Atletico win on away goals

Liverpool (2).................4 Benfica (0)....................1
Kuyt 28   Cardozo 70
Lucas 34
Torres 59, 82
Att 42,377
            Aggregate: 5–3

Standard Liège (1)........1 Hamburg (2)..................3
De Camargo 32   Petric 20, 35
Att 27,000   Guerrero 90
            Aggregate: 2–5

Wolfsburg (0)................0 Fulham (1) 1
Att 24,843   Zamora 1
            Aggregate: 1–3

SEMI-FINALS FIRST LEG
22/04/2010

Atlético Madrid (1).........1 Liverpool (0)..................0
Forlan 9   Att 50,000

Hamburg (0)..................0 Fulham (0) 0
Att 49,000

SEMI-FINALS SECOND LEG
29/04/2010

Fulham (0) ....2 Hamburg (1)..................1
Davies 69   Petric 22
Gera 76
Att 25,700
            Aggregate: 2–1

Liverpool (1) ....2 Atlético Madrid (0).........1
Aquilani 44   Forlan 102
Benayoun 95
Att 42,040
            After extra-time
    Aggregate: 2–2, Atletico win on away goals

FINAL
12/05/2010 (HAMBURG)

Atlético Madrid (1)........2 Fulham (1) 1
Forlan 32, 116   Davies 37
Att 49,000
            After extra-time

Atletico Madrid: De Gea, Ujfalusi, Perea, Dominguez, Antonio Lopez, Reyes (Salvio 78), Paulo Assuncao, Raul Garcia, Simao (Jurado 68), Forlan, Aguero (Valera 119). **Subs not used:** Joel, Camacho, Juanito, Cabrera. **Booked:** Raul Garcia, Forlan.
Fulham: Schwarzer, Baird, Hughes, Hangeland, Konchesky, Duff (Nevland 84), Etuhu, Murphy (Greening 118), Davies, Gera, Zamora (Dempsey 55). **Subs not used:** Zuberbuhler, Pantsil, Riise, Dikgacoi. **Booked:** Hangeland.

CLOCKWISE FROM ABOVE: John Terry lifts the FA Cup trophy after Chelsea's final victory against Portsmouth. In an exciting game, Didier Drogba scored the only goal with a superb free-kick, *below*

Chelsea defended their trophy with a final victory over Portsmouth

DIDIER DROGBA scored the only goal of the 129th FA Cup final as Chelsea retained the trophy and completed the first English League and Cup double in their history with a 1–0 win against Portsmouth at Wembley.

The Blues hit the woodwork five times in the first half and had 29 shots to Portsmouth's seven, but they would have gone behind in the second half had Kevin-Prince Boateng's penalty not been saved by the legs of goalkeeper Petr Cech. Frank Lampard also missed a spot-kick for Chelsea, whose triumph gave Ashley Cole a record sixth FA Cup winner's medal.

It was a Cup competition marked in the early stages by two shocks, with Manchester United and Liverpool both knocked out by lower-league clubs in the third round.

United's demise evoked memories of great past duels as they hosted Leeds at Old Trafford. The Coca-Cola League 1 side more than matched their Barclays Premier League rivals and scored the game's only goal when Jonathan Howson's long pass released Jermaine Beckford. The striker, who was working as an RAC repair man three years ago, slotted home a goal that will be replayed a thousand times, but never too often for the 9,000 Leeds fans who had travelled more in hope than expectation.

Lost opportunity

Shane Long's extra-time header for Reading is also guaranteed the odd action replay in the years to come as it capped a stunning comeback from the Championship side, which saw them beat Liverpool 2–1 in a replay at Anfield.

Leeds almost did it again in the next round, drawing 2–2 with UEFA Champions League hopefuls Tottenham at White Hart Lane before their run caught up with them in the replay at Elland Road.

But if Leeds provided the biggest shock then we should not forget Notts County, who also took a Barclays Premier League scalp in the fourth round, drawing 2–2 at Wigan before winning the replay.

Crystal Palace also supplied their fair share of drama. In administration, with their

CLOCKWISE FROM ABOVE: Frederic Piquionne scores in Portsmouth's semi-final win against Spurs; David James and his Pompey team-mates react to final defeat; Leeds created the shock of the competition by winning at Manchester United

Championship status in jeopardy and players and manager Neil Warnock not knowing whether they were going to be paid, the Eagles conjured up a superb 2–2 draw at Barclays Premier League side Wolves in the fourth round before winning the replay.

They almost repeated the heroics in the fifth round, and Palace would have been in the quarter-finals if an assistant referee had not controversially awarded Aston Villa a corner from which they scored a late equaliser in the 2–2 draw at Selhurst Park. Instead, the Eagles were defeated in the replay at Villa Park and Warnock rued another lost opportunity, although his fine work was rewarded with a move from the Eagles to QPR.

The quarter-finals saw Fulham and Tottenham play out a goalless draw at Craven Cottage, with Spurs eventually

running out 3–1 winners in the replay at White Hart Lane.

All the odds said Harry Redknapp's Spurs were bound for the final when they drew his former club Portsmouth in the semi-final, but the FA Cup has never been that predictable. Somehow, Avram Grant's men, hurtling from one financial uncertainty to another in a turbulent season that ended in relegation, came up with the performance of their lives to emerge victorious from a match at White Hart Lane in which Frederic Piquionne and Boateng each grabbed a goal in extra-time.

The other semi-final saw Aston Villa brushed aside 3–0 by Chelsea to set up the final act as Drogba's clinical strike settled the showpiece against Portsmouth when he curled in a decisive free-kick off the post in the second half.

FA CUP

06/11/2009

Bristol Rovers (0) 2   **Southampton (0)** 3
Duffy 73   Connolly 63, 68
Hughes 90 (pen)   Antonio 70
Att 6,446

Huddersfield (4) 6   **Dag & Red (0)** 1
Williams 9   Benson 74
Roberts 21, 72
Novak 24, 56
Rhodes 44
Att 5,858

Notts County (1) 2   **Bradford (0)** 1
Hawley 45   Boulding 81
Jackson 46
Att 4,213

07/11/2009

AFC Telford (0) 1   **Lincoln City (1)** 3
Blakeman 49   Torres 14
Att 2,809   Clarke 65
   Brown 76

Accrington Stanley (2) 2   **Salisbury (0)** 1
Ryan 19   Tubbs 66
Symes 33
Att 1,379

Aldershot (2) 2   **Bury (0)** 0
Soares 13
Donnelly 33
Att 2,519

Barnet (1) 3   **Darlington (0)** 1
O'Flynn 18, 66   Diop 73
Hyde 47
Att 1,654

Barrow (1) 2   **Eastleigh (0)** 1
Cook 36   Forbes 85
Walker 90
Att 1,655

Bromley (0) 0   **Colchester (2)** 4
Att 4,242   Hackney 32
   Odejayi 35
   Platt 71
   Gillespie 89

Cambridge Utd (1) 4   **Ilkeston Town (0)** 0
Holroyd 5
Reason 64
Pitt 71
Marriott 86
Att 2,395

Carlisle (1) 2   **Morecambe (0)** 2
Harte 21   Jevons 70
Pericard 55   Duffy 85
Att 4,181

Chesterfield (1) 1   **Bournemouth (2)** 3
Lester 4   Igoe 8
Att 3,277   Connell 28, 76

Forest Green (1) 1   **Mansfield (0)** 1
Hodgkiss 28   Garner 87
Att 1,149

Gateshead (0) 2   **Brentford (0)** 2
Price 57 (og)   Cort 61
Winn 90   O'Connor 70
Att 1,150

Gillingham (2) 3   **Southend (0)** 0
Weston 25
Brandy 28
Bentley 62
Att 4,605

Grimsby (0) 0   **Bath City (1)** 2
Att 2,103   Holland 32
   Edwards 52

Notts County celebrate their home victory over Bradford

Hartlepool (0) 0   **Kettering (1)** 1
Att 2,645   Ashikodi 15

Hereford (1) 2   **Sutton Utd (0)** 0
Manset 6
Valentine 86 (pen)
Att 1,713

Luton (3) 3   **Rochdale (0)** 3
Basham 4, 29   Dawson 58
Newton 21   Thompson 87, 89
Att 3,167

Milton Keynes Dons (1) .1   **Macclesfield (0)** 0
Gobern 25
Att 4,868

Northampton (1) 2   **Fleetwood Town (1)** 1
Guttridge 29, 61   Clancy 41
Att 3,077

Nuneaton (0) 0   **Exeter (4)** 4
Att 2,452   Taylor 4, 44
   Corr 31
   Hadland 38 (og)

Oldham (0) 0   **Leeds (1)** 2
Att 5,552   Howson 36
   Grella 90

Oxford Utd (0) 1   **Yeovil (0)** 0
Midson 55
Att 6,144

Paulton (0) 0   **Norwich (3)** 7
Att 2,070   Holt 15, 43
   Martin 24, 77, 83, 85
   Hoolahan 74

Port Vale (1) 1   **Stevenage (0)** 1
Yates 42   Griffin 90
Att 3,999

Rushden & D'monds (1)3   **Hinckley Utd (0)** 1
O'Connor 31, 66   Webster 64
Byrne 82
Att 1,540

Shrewsbury (0) 0   **Staines Town (1)** 1
Att 3,539   Chaaban 21

Stockport (3) 5   **Tooting & Mitcham (0)** . 0
Thompson 13
Poole 20
Baker 38 (pen)
Turnbull 67, 72   Att 3,076

Stourbridge (0) 0   **Walsall (1)** 1
Att 2,014   Jones 34

Swindon (1) 1   **Woking (0)** 0
Paynter 36   Att 4,805

Torquay (2) 3   **Cheltenham (1)** 1
Wroe 10 (pen), 19 (pen), 70   Lewis 8
Att 2,370

Tranmere (0) 1   **Leyton Orient (1)** 1
Shuker 51   Ashworth 7
Att 3,180

Wrexham (0) 1   **Lowestoft Town (0)** 0
Taylor 89   Att 2,402

Wycombe (2) 4   **Brighton (2)** 4
Harrold 18 (pen), 70   Bennett 3
S Davies 38   Forster 45 (pen)
Pittman 61   Murray 51, 83 (pen)
Att 2,749

York (1) 3   **Crewe (2)** 2
Brodie 39, 88   Grant 33
Pacquette 86   Zola 41
Att 3,070

08/11/2009

Burton Albion (2) 3   **Oxford City (1)** 2
Harrad 15 (pen)   Alexis 6
Maghoma 45   Brooks 55
Austin 90
Att 2,207

Northwich (0) 1   **Charlton (0)** 0
Riley 81   Att 2,153

Wealdstone (0) 2   **Rotherham (2)** 3
Ashe 63, 90   Le Fondre 33
Att 1,638   Ellison 44
   Broughton 82

09/11/2009

Millwall (0) 4   **AFC Wimbledon (0)** 1
Harris 49   Taylor 81
Price 72, 89
Schofield 86
Att 9,453

REPLAYS
11/11/2009

Rochdale (0) 0   **Luton (0)** 2
Att 1,982   Gallen 60, 74

17/11/2009

Brentford (2) 5   **Gateshead (0)** 2
Strevens 42   Armstrong 58, 81
MacDonald 45, 60
Weston 67, 73
Att 1,960

Leyton Orient (0) 0   **Tranmere (0)** 1
Att 1,518   Taylor 83

Mansfield (0) 1   **Forest Green (1)** 2
Perry 71   Platt 40, 90
Att 2,496

Morecambe (0) 0   **Carlisle (1)** 1
Att 3,307   Anyinsah 5

Stevenage (0) 0   **Port Vale (1)** 1
Att 2,914   Dodds 24

18/11/2009

Brighton (1) 2   **Wycombe (0)** 0
Crofts 36
Bennett 61
Att 3,383

The FA CUP e-on

SECOND ROUND

28/11/2009

Accrington Stanley (1) 2	Barnet (0) 2
Grant 29	Yakubu 47
Symes 50	O'Flynn 90 (pen)
Att 1,501	

Bath City (1) 1	Forest Green (1) 2
Hogg 43	Smith 24
Att 3,325	Preece 48

Bournemouth (1) 1	Notts County (0) 2
Pitman 38	Hughes 49
Att 6,082	Westcarr 58

Brentford (1) 1	Walsall (0) 0
Legge 13	
Att 2,611	

Brighton (2) 3	Rushden & D'monds (2) 2
Dickinson 3, 86	Tomlin 14
Forster 22 (pen)	O'Connor 40
Att 3,638	

Cambridge Utd (0) 1	York (2) 2
Tonkin 84	Rankine 37
Att 3,505	Brodie 40 (pen)

Carlisle (1) 3	Norwich (1) 1
Pericard 12	Holt 26
Hurst 46	
Keogh 72	Att 3,946

Gillingham (0) 1	Burton Albion (0) 0
Weston 69	
Att 4,996	

Hereford (0) 0	Colchester (0) 1
	O'Toole 90
	Att 2,225

Milton Keynes Dons (1) 4	Exeter (0) 3
Baldock 35, 70	Corr 50, 54
Devaney 75	Stansfield 67
Easter 86	Att 4,867

Northampton (0) 2	Southampton (2) 3
Hammond 68 (og)	Papa Waigo 41
Gilligan 90 (pen)	Lallana 43
Att 4,858	Hammond 59

Northwich (0) 1	Lincoln City (1) 3
Bailey 47	Fagan 18
Att 3,544	Clarke 49, 64

Oxford Utd (1) 1	Barrow (1) 1
Cook 9	Bond 43 (pen)
Att 6,082	

Port Vale (0) 0	Huddersfield (1) 1
Att 5,311	Clarke 12

Rotherham (1) 2	Luton (1) 2
Le Fondre 45	Craddock 21 (pen)
Brogan 62	Nwokeji 74
Att 3,210	

Staines Town (0) 1	Millwall (0) 1
Chaaban 79 (pen)	Robinson 69
Att 2,753	

Tranmere (0) 0	Aldershot (0) 0
Att 3,742	

Wrexham (0) 0	Swindon (0) 1
Att 3,011	Greer 80

29/11/2009

Kettering (0) 1	Leeds (0) 1
Roper 63	Beckford 78
Att 4,837	

15/12/2009

Stockport (0) 0	Torquay (3) 4
Att 1,690	Benyon 2, 33, 79
	Rendell 28

REPLAYS

08/12/2009

Aldershot (0) 1	Tranmere (1) 2
Bozanic 90	Thomas-Moore 43
	Gornell 49
	Att 4,060

Barnet (0) 0	Accrington Stanley (1) 1
Att 1,288	Grant 16

Barrow (1) 3	Oxford Utd (0) 1
Bolland 38	Constable 90
Logan 49	
Goodfellow 66	
Att 2,754	

Leeds (1) 5	Kettering (0) 1
Becchio 20	Elding 62
Grella 108, 116	
Kandol 109	
Beckford 119	Att 10,670

After extra-time

Luton (2) 3	Rotherham (0) 0
Newton 7, White 19	
Gnakpa 68	Att 2,518

09/12/2009

Millwall (1) 4	Staines Town (0) 0
Morison 40	
Smith 50	
Dunne 79	
Schofield 90	Att 3,452

Non-League outfit Kettering took a shock lead against Leeds, thanks to Ian Roper's goal. However, the League 1 giants equalised and comfortably won the Elland Road replay

FA CUP

02/01/2010

Aston Villa (2) .... 3 Blackburn (0) 1
Delfouneso 12   Kalinic 55
Cuellar 37
Carew 90 (pen)   Att 25,453

Blackpool (0) .... 1 Ipswich (1) 2
Ormerod 51   Colback 3
Att 7,332   Garvan 77

Bolton (0) .... 4 Lincoln City (0) 0
Swaibu 49 (og)
Lee 51
Cahill 83
Davies 90   Att 11,193

Everton (1) .... 3 Carlisle (1) 1
Vaughan 12   Hurst 18
Cahill 82
Baines 90 (pen)   Att 31,196

Fulham (1) .... 1 Swindon (0) 0
Zamora 16
Att 19,623

Huddersfield (0) .... 0 West Brom (0) 2
Att 13,472   Dorrans 77
                              Wood 82

Leicester (1) .... 2 Swansea (1) 1
King 39   Cotterill 10
N'Guessan 89   Att 12,307

Middlesbrough (0) .... 0 Man City (1) 1
Att 12,474   Mwaruwari 45

Millwall (0) .... 1 Derby (0) 2
Grabban 49   Commons 52
Att 10,531

Milton Keynes Dons (0) 1 Burnley (2) 2
Morgan 89   Alexander 23 (pen)
Att 11,816   Fletcher 35

Nottm Forest (0) .... 0 Birmingham (0) 0
Att 20,975

Plymouth (0) .... 0 Newcastle (0) 0
Att 16,451

Portsmouth (1) .... 1 Coventry (1) 1
Boateng 45   Bell 30
Att 11,214

Preston (2) .... 7 Colchester (0) 0
Brown 13
Sedgwick 27
Parkin 48, 50, 72 (pen)
Williams 52 (og)
Carter 64
Att 7,621

Reading (1) .... 1 Liverpool (1) 1
Church 24   Gerrard 36
Att 23,656

Scunthorpe (0) .... 1 Barnsley (0) 0
Hayes 68
Att 5,447

Sheff Wed (1) .... 1 Crystal Palace (1) 2
Hill 44 (og)   Danns 19
Att 8,690   Andrew 68

Southampton (1) .... 1 Luton (0) 0
Lambert 36
Att 18,786

Stoke (2) .... 3 York (1) 1
Parslow 24 (og)   Barrett 22
Fuller 25
Etherington 58
Att 15,586

Sunderland (1) .... 3 Barrow (0) 0
Malbranque 17
Campbell 52, 58
Att 25,190

Torquay (0) .... 0 Brighton (0) 1
Att 4,028   Crofts 77

Tottenham (1) .... 4 Peterborough (0) 0
Kranjcar 35, 57
Defoe 70
Keane 90 (pen)   Att 35,862

Wigan (0) .... 4 Hull (1) 1
N'Zogbia 47, 66   Geovanni 35
McCarthy 63
Sinclair 90   Att 5,335

03/01/2010

Chelsea (3) .... 5 Watford (0) 0
Sturridge 5, 68
Eustace 15 (og)
Malouda 22
Lampard 64
Att 40,912

Man Utd (0) .... 0 Leeds (1) 1
Att 74,526   Beckford 19

Sheff Utd (1) .... 1 QPR (1) 1
Cresswell 45   Simpson 39
Att 11,461

Tranmere (0) .... 0 Wolverhampton (0) 1
Att 7,476   Jarvis 77

West Ham (1) .... 1 Arsenal (0) 2
Diamanti 45   Ramsey 78
Att 25,549   Eduardo 83

12/01/2010

Bristol City (0) .... 1 Cardiff (0) 1
G Williams 90   Chopra 76
Att 7,289

19/01/2010

Accrington Stanley (0) 1 Gillingham (0) 0
Miles 81
Att 1,322

Brentford (0) .... 0 Doncaster (0) 1
Att 2,883   O'Connor 87

Notts County (0) .... 2 Forest Green (0) 1
Hunt 50   Rankin 63
Hughes 64
Att 4,389

REPLAYS
12/01/2010

Birmingham (0) .... 1 Nottm Forest (0) 0
Ferguson 62
Att 9,399

Coventry (1) .... 1 Portsmouth (0) 2
Best 22   Wright 90 (og)
Att 7,097   Mokoena 120
                 After extra-time

Derby (0) .... 1 Millwall (0) 1
Davies 114   Morison 108
Att 7,183
     After extra-time, Derby win 5-3 on penalties

QPR (0) .... 2 Sheff Utd (1) 3
Buzsaky 71 (pen)   Williamson 19
Stewart 88   Ward 68
Att 5,780   Cresswell 70

13/01/2010

Liverpool (1) .... 1 Reading (0) 2
Bertrand 45 (og)   Sigurdsson 90 (pen)
Att 31,063   Long 100
                 After extra-time

Newcastle (2) .... 3 Plymouth (0) 0
Lovenkrands 10, 40, 72   Att 15,805

19/01/2010

Cardiff (0) .... 1 Bristol City (0) 0
Orr 74 (og)   Att 6,731

23/01/2010

Accrington Stanley (1) 1 Fulham (1) 3
Symes 25   Nevland 21
Att 3,712   Duff 59, Gera 80

Aston Villa (1) .... 3 Brighton (1) 1
Delfouneso 5   Elphick 41
Young 48   Forster 90
Delph 63   Att 39,725

Bolton (0) .... 2 Sheff Utd (0) 0
Steinsson 48
Elmander 84   Att 14,572

Cardiff (1) .... 4 Leicester (2) 2
Bothroyd 17   Morrison 34
Whittingham 71   N'Guessan 39
Burke 90
McCormack 90   Att 10,961

Derby (0) .... 1 Doncaster (0) 0
McEveley 88   Att 11,316

Everton (0) .... 1 Birmingham (2) 2
Osman 56   Benitez 7
Att 30,875   Ferguson 40

Notts County (2) .... 2 Wigan (0) 2
Hughes 26   Scotland 52
Davies 41   Watson 83
Att 9,073

Portsmouth (1) .... 2 Sunderland (1) 1
Utaka 42, 57   Bent 15
Att 10,315

Preston (0) .... 0 Chelsea (1) 2
Att 23,119   Anelka 37
                              Sturridge 47

Reading (0) .... 1 Burnley (0) 0
Sigurdsson 87   Att 12,910

Southampton (1) .... 2 Ipswich (0) 1
Thomas 31   Counago 90
Antonio 74   Att 20,446

Tottenham (1) .... 2 Leeds (0) 2
Crouch 42   Beckford 52, 90 (pen)
Pavlyuchenko 75   Att 35,750

West Brom (2) .... 4 Newcastle (0) 0
Olsson 17
Dorrans 31 (pen), 72 (pen)
Thomas 76   Att 16,102

Wolverhampton (1) ...... 2 Crystal Palace (1) 2
Jones 37   Lee 3
Zubar 84   Ambrose 49
Att 14,449

24/01/2010

Scunthorpe (1) .... 2 Man City (2) 4
Hayes 29   Petrov 3
Boyata 69 (og)   Onuoha 45
Att 8,861   Sylvinho 57
                              Robinho 84

Stoke (1) .... 3 Arsenal (1) 1
Fuller 2, 78   Denilson 42
Whitehead 86   Att 19,735

REPLAYS
02/02/2010

Crystal Palace (0) .... 3 Wolverhampton (0) 1
Butterfield 62, 65, 68   Henry 90
Att 10,282

Wigan (0) .... 0 Notts County (0) 2
Att 5,519   Hunt 75
                              Caldwell 78 (og)

03/02/2010

Leeds (1) .... 1 Tottenham (1) 3
Becchio 45   Defoe 37, 73, 90
Att 37,704

FIFTH ROUND

13/02/2010

Chelsea (1)...................4 Cardiff (1) 1
Drogba 2, Ballack 51   Chopra 34
Sturridge 69
Kalou 86   Att 40,827

Derby (0).......................1 Birmingham (0)............2
McEveley 55   Dann 73
Att 21,043   Ridgewell 90

Man City (1)...................1 Stoke (0) 1
Wright-Phillips 11   Fuller 57
Att 28,019

Reading (1)....................2 West Brom (1)................2
Kebe 1, Church 73   Koren 18
Att 18,008   Mattock 87

Southampton (0)..........1 Portsmouth (0)..............4
Lambert 70   Owusu-Abeyie 66
Att 31,385   Dindane 75
                                   Belhadj 82, O'Hara 85

14/02/2010

Bolton (1).......................1 Tottenham (0)................1
K Davies 34   Defoe 61
Att 13,596

Crystal Palace (1)..........2 Aston Villa (1)................2
Ertl 24   Collins 35
Ambrose 70   Petrov 87
Att 20,486

Darren Ambrose puts Crystal Palace ahead against Aston Villa

Fulham (2)...................4 Notts County (0)............0
Davies 22, Zamora 41
Duff 73, Okaka 79   Att 16,132

REPLAYS
24/02/2010

Aston Villa (1) ....3 Crystal Palace (0) 1
Agbonlahor 42   Ambrose 73 (pen)
Carew 81 (pen), 89 (pen)
Att 31,874

Stoke (0).......................3 Man City (0)...................1
Kitson 79   Bellamy 81
Shawcross 95
Sanli 99   Att 21,813
After extra-time

Tottenham (2) ....4 Bolton (0)........................0
Pavlyuchenko 23, 87
Jaaskelainen 35 (og)
O'Brien 47 (og)   Att 31,436

West Brom (1)...............2 Reading (1)......................3
Koren 6, 47   Kebe 9, Howard 90
Att 13,985   Sigurdsson 95
After extra-time

QUARTER-FINALS

06/03/2010

Fulham (0) ....0 Tottenham (0)...............0
Att 24,533
Fulham: Schwarzer, Baird, Hughes, Hangeland, Shorey, Duff, Greening, Etuhu, Davies (Elm 73), Gera, Zamora. **Subs not used:** Zuberbuhler, Kelly, Konchesky, Okaka, Riise, Smalling. **Booked:** Etuhu.
Tottenham: Gomes, Corluka, Dawson, Bassong, Assou-Ekotto, Modric, Palacios, Kranjcar, Bale, Crouch, Pavlyuchenko (Defoe 81). **Subs not used:** Alnwick, Gudjohnsen, Rose, Livermore, Dervite, Townsend.

Portsmouth (0) ....2 Birmingham (0)............0
Piquionne 67, 70
Att 20,456
Portsmouth: James, Finnan, Ben-Haim, Hreidarsson, Belhadj, Brown, Wilson, O'Hara, Webber (Diop 85), Piquionne, Utaka. **Subs not used:** Ashdown, Mullins, Owusu-Abeyie, Dindane, Kanu, Basinas. **Booked:** Webber, Brown.
Birmingham: Hart, Carr, R Johnson, Dann, Ridgewell, Larsson (Gardner 84), Bowyer, Ferguson, Fahey (Phillips 72), McFadden (Benitez 75), Jerome. **Subs not used:** M Taylor, Murphy, Michel, Parnaby. **Booked:** Ferguson.

John Carew celebrates his hat-trick in Aston Villa's defeat of Reading

07/03/2010

Chelsea (1)....................2 Stoke (0) 0
Lampard 35
Terry 67
Att 41,322
Chelsea: Hilario, Ivanovic, Alex, Terry, Ferreira, Malouda, Mikel, Lampard, Anelka, Drogba, Kalou. **Subs not used:** Turnbull, J Cole, Deco, Sturridge, Matic, Kakuta, Van Aanholt. **Booked:** Terry.
Stoke: Sorensen, Wilkinson, A Faye, Huth, Collins, Whitehead, Whelan (Pugh 45), Delap, Sanli (Lawrence 60), Sidibe (Kitson 61), Fuller. **Subs not used:** Simonsen, A Faye, Davies, Moult.

Reading (2) ....2 Aston Villa (0)...............4
Long 27, 42   Young 47
                                   Carew 51, 57, 90 (pen)
                                             Att 23,175
Reading: Federici, Griffin, Mills, Ingimarsson, Bertrand, Kebe, Tabb, Howard (Gunnarsson 59), Sigurdsson, Long, Church (Rasiak 71). **Subs not used:** Hamer, Matejovsky, Henry, Robson-Kanu, Pearce. **Booked:** Sigurdsson, Tabb.
Aston Villa: Friedel, Cuellar, Dunne, Collins, Warnock, Downing (Sidwell 90), Milner, Petrov, A Young, Carew, Heskey. **Subs not used:** Guzan, L Young, Albrighton, Delfouneso, Delph, Beye. **Booked:** Collins, Carew, Dunne, A Young, Milner.

REPLAY
24/03/2010

Tottenham (0)..............3 Fulham (1).......................1
Bentley 47   Zamora 17
Pavlyuchenko 60
Gudjohnsen 66
Att 35,432
Tottenham: Gomes, Corluka (Pavlyuchenko 53), Bassong, Dawson, Assou-Ekotto (Huddleston 46), Kranjcar (Bentley 46), Palacios, Modric, Bale, Gudjohnsen, Crouch. **Subs not used:** Alnwick, Rose, Livermore, Townsend. **Booked:** Bassong.
Fulham: Schwarzer, Kelly (Dempsey 69), Hangeland, Hughes, Konchesky, Duff, Etuhu, Murphy, Davies, Gera, Zamora (Okaka 77). **Subs not used:** Zuberbuhler, Baird, Riise, Smalling, Greening. **Booked:** Zamora, Kelly.

SEMI-FINALS

10/04/2010 (WEMBLEY STADIUM)

Aston Villa (0)..............0 Chelsea (0)......................3
Att 85,472   Drogba 68
                                             Malouda 89
                                             Lampard 90
Aston Villa: Friedel, Cuellar, Dunne, Collins, Warnock, A Young, Milner, Petrov, Downing, Agbonlahor, Carew (Heskey 82). **Subs not used:** Guzan, L Young, Sidwell, Delfouneso, Delph, Beye.
Chelsea: Cech, Ferreira, Terry, Alex, Zhirkov, Deco (Ballack 76), Mikel, Lampard, J Cole (Kalou 65), Drogba (Anelka 80), Malouda. **Subs not used:** Hilario, Ivanovic, Sturridge, Belletti. **Booked:** Mikel, Terry, Deco.

11/04/2010 (WEMBLEY STADIUM)

Tottenham (0)..............0 Portsmouth (0)..............2
Att 84,602   Piquionne 99
                                             Boateng 117 (pen)
After extra-time
Tottenham: Gomes, Corluka, Dawson, Bassong, Bale, Bentley (Kranjcar 79), Huddlestone (Gudjohnsen 102), Palacios, Modric, Crouch, Defoe (Pavlyuchenko 59). **Subs not used:** Alnwick, Rose, Livermore, Assou-Ekotto. **Booked:** Palacios, Bassong, Huddlestone.
Portsmouth: James, Finnan, Rocha, Mokoena, Mullins (Hughes 119), Brown, Wilson, Yebda (Utaka 87), Dindane, Piquionne (Diop 112), Boateng. **Subs not used:** Ashdown, Smith, Kanu, Basinas. **Booked:** Boateng, Dindane.

FINAL

15/05/2010 (WEMBLEY STADIUM)

Chelsea (0)....................1 Portsmouth (0)..............0
Drogba 59
Att 88,335
Chelsea: Cech, Ivanovic, Alex, Terry, A Cole, Lampard, Ballack (Belletti 44), Malouda, Anelka (Sturridge 90), Drogba, Kalou (J Cole 71). **Subs not used:** Hilario, Zhirkov, Ferreira, Matic.
Portsmouth: James, Finnan, Rocha, Mokoena, Mullins (Belhadj 81), Brown, Diop (Kanu 81), Boateng (Utaka 73), O'Hara, Piquionne, Dindane. **Subs not used:** Ashdown, Vanden Borre, Hughes, Ben-Haim. **Booked:** Rocha, Boateng, O'Hara.

CLOCKWISE FROM BELOW: Nemanja Vidic brings down Gabriel Agbonlahor for a penalty in the opening minutes of the Carling Cup final; Michael Owen enjoys his equaliser; Patrice Evra lifts the trophy

Owen and Rooney helped Manchester United overcome Villa at Wembley

THE 2010 Carling Cup final saw Wayne Rooney become a Wembley matchwinner for the first time as his looping second-half header helped Manchester United to come from behind and beat Aston Villa 2–1.

Villa had gone ahead through James Milner's early penalty after Gabriel Agbonlahor was brought down in the box by Nemanja Vidic, who escaped further punishment from referee Phil Dowd. Dimitar Berbatov then robbed Richard Dunne of possession and set up Michael Owen for the equaliser, and Rooney continued a run of headed goals when he converted Antonio Valencia's cross from the right to take the trophy back to Old Trafford.

The road to Wembley had started back in August when the first round produced several upsets, the most noteworthy being Port Vale's 2–1 win at Sheffield United and Hartlepool's success at Coventry thanks to a solitary goal from Adam Boyd in extra-time.

In the second round, Manchester City boss Mark Hughes made a clear statement of intent by sending out a team worth in excess of £200million to face Crystal Palace at Selhurst Park. This was a competition that City wanted to win and Shaun Wright-Phillips and Carlos Tevez eased the Blues' passage to the next stage, beginning a run that so nearly ended at Wembley.

With that victory, City ensured they progressed further than Wigan, who were comprehensively beaten 4–1 at Blackpool. West Ham knocked out London rivals Millwall 3–1 in a derby game that was marred by crowd violence and Port Vale were again the scourge of Sheffield with a 2–0 victory over Wednesday.

Young talent

The teams involved in European competition entered in the third round but for Fulham, beaten at Manchester City, it was a short-lived journey. Elsewhere at the same stage, Wolves failed to overcome a Manchester United side that had to play with 10 men for an hour following a red card for defender Fabio Da Silva, while Tottenham and Everton flexed their muscles with comprehensive

CLOCKWISE FROM ABOVE: Carlos Tevez heads a goal in Manchester City's semi-final against United; Richard Dunne scores for Villa in their 10-goal semi-final second leg against Blackburn; Tottenham's Peter Crouch celebrates his hat-trick at Preston

away wins at Preston and Hull respectively. The two Barclays Premier League sides were then paired at the last-16 stage, with Spurs eventually victorious. Tom Huddlestone and Robbie Keane were on target, with the Irishman scoring his last goal in the competition before heading north to join Celtic. Liverpool fell at Arsenal as both clubs showcased their young talent and Villa needed penalties to see off Sunderland.

In the quarter-finals, Arsenal boss Arsène Wenger continued his policy of fielding his youngsters and Manchester City took advantage to claim a 3–0 win. Chelsea looked to have salvaged their hopes with an equaliser in the last minute of extra-time in a thrilling 3–3 draw at Blackburn, only for Gael Kakuta to miss the crucial spot-kick as Rovers won a penalty shoot-out.

Tottenham were beaten 2–0 by Manchester United at Old Trafford in a repeat of the previous season's final, and

that win sent the Red Devils forward to a semi-final meeting with neighbours City.

Both semis were delayed by snow, but Villa grabbed the upper hand in their tie with a first-leg win at Blackburn. Martin O'Neill's side then fell behind on aggregate on home soil, but Christopher Samba's dismissal turned the course of a 10-goal thriller, Villa eventually winning 6–4 on the night and 7–4 overall.

For drama though, Manchester was the place to be. After Ryan Giggs' opening goal, Tevez scored twice against his former club to put City in sight of their first final since 1981. The striker scored again at Old Trafford to apparently set up extra-time after Paul Scholes and Michael Carrick had put United on the road to victory but, with the seconds ticking away, Rooney broke City's hearts.

He would repeat those heroics again in the final, as United claimed the first major silverware of the English season.

CARLING CUP

FIRST ROUND

10/08/2009

Darlington (0)..............0 Leeds (0)......................1
Att 4,487
Showunmi 54

11/08/2009

Accrington Stanley (0) 2 Walsall (1) 1
Grant 53 Nicholls 9
Mullin 90 Att 1,041

Barnet (0) ....0 Watford (0)...................2
Att 3,139 Williamson 105
Severin 120

Brentford (0) ....0 Bristol City (0).............1
Att 3,024 Maynard 58

Bristol Rovers (1) ....2 Aldershot (0).................1
Duffy 37 (pen),58 Morgan 60 (pen)
Att 3,644

Bury (0) ....0 West Brom (2)...............2
Att 3,077 Dorrans 5, Jones 25 (og)

Cardiff (2) ....3 Dag & Red (0) 1
Rae 20, Bothroyd 26 (pen) Scott 81
Whittingham 90 Att 5,545

Carlisle (0) ....1 Oldham (0) 0
Dobie 89 Att 2,509

Cheltenham (1)..........1 Southend (0) 2
Hammond 45 Barnard 77, 88
Att 1,918

Colchester (0) ....1 Leyton Orient (1)...........2
Hackney 90 Patulea 2
Att 3,308 Melligan 63

Crewe (0) ....1 Blackpool (0)................2
Zola 73 Nowland 52
Att 2,991 Nardiello 79

Crystal Palace (0)......2 Torquay (0)..................1
Ambrose 65, 78 (pen) Sills 74
Att 3,140

Exeter (0)....................0 QPR (0).........................5
Att 4,614 Routledge 53, 61, 66 (pen)
Pellicori 85, Ephraim 89

Gillingham (2)............2 Plymouth (0)................1
Jackson 42 Summerfield 49
Barcham 45 Att 3,306

Hereford (0)...............1 Charlton (0)..................0
Godsmark 98 Att 2,017

Huddersfield (1).........3 Stockport (0)................1
Rhodes 45, 48 Griffin 88
Robinson 74 Att 5,120

Lincoln City (0)..........0 Barnsley (0)..................1
Att 3,635 Bogdanovic 72

Millwall (2)................4 Bournemouth (0) 0
Alexander 31
Harris 40,69,74 Att 3,552

Milton Keynes Dons (0) 1 Swindon (1).................4
Easter 53 (pen) McGovern 41, Paynter 56, 72
Att 4,812 McCracken 74 (og)

Notts County (0)..........0 Doncaster (0)................1
Att 4,893 Coppinger 54

Preston (2) ....5 Morecambe (0)..............1
Brown 33, Elliott 45 Twiss 90
Nicholson 57, Trotman 69
Mellor 90 Att 5,407

Reading (4)................5 Burton Albion (0)..........1
Mooney 6,77 Phillips 59
Bignall 7, 9, Sigurdsson 27 Att 5,893

Rotherham (1)............2 Derby (1)......................1
Warne 44 Teale 11
Ellison 65 Att 4,345

Scunthorpe (1)...........2 Chesterfield (0)............1
Sparrow 12 Currie 72 (pen)
Hayes 54 Att 2,501

Sheff Utd (1)..............1 Port Vale (1) 2
Sharp 33 Richards 20,61
Att 7,627

Sheff Wed (2).............3 Rochdale (0)..................0
Esajas 19, Johnson 21,50 Att 6,696

Shrewsbury (2)...........3 Ipswich (2)...................3
Robinson 18, Hibbert 24 Wickham 11, 59
Cansdell-Sherriff 74 Quinn 32
Att 4,184
Ipswich win 4–2 on penalties

Southampton (1) ....2 Northampton (0) 0
Lambert 29, Lallana 68 Att 10,921

Swansea (1) ....3 Brighton (0)..................0
Monk 17, Dobbie 60, 90 Att 6,400

Tranmere (3)..............4 Grimsby (0) 0
McLaren 32
Thomas-Moore 37 (pen)
Curran 40, Edds 71 Att 3,527

Wycombe (0)..............0 Peterborough (2)...........4
Att 2,078 Mclean 24, Rowe 33
Boyd 59
Frecklington 68

Yeovil (0)...................0 Norwich (0)..................4
Att 3,860 Hoolahan 55 (pen)
Holt 64, 82, 90

12/08/2009

Coventry (0) ....0 Hartlepool (0)...............1
Att 6,055 Boyd 105

Macclesfield (0).........0 Leicester (0).................2
Att 2,197 N'Guessan 58
Fryatt 71

Nottm Forest (0) ....3 Bradford (0)..................0
Anderson 46, Blackstock 60
McGugan 82 Att 4,639

SECOND ROUND

24/08/2009

Norwich (0) ....1 Sunderland (3)..............4
Hoolahan 63 Tainio 26, Reid 30, 36
Att 12,345 Tudur Jones 67 (og)

25/08/2009

Gillingham (0)...........1 Blackburn (1)................3
Jackson 70 (pen) Dunn 5
Att 7,293 Hoilett 47, Pedersen 74

Hartlepool (1)............1 Burnley (0)...................2
Boyd 39 Fletcher 84, 108
Att 3,501
After extra-time

Hull (2)......................3 Southend (1).................1
Cairney 7 Moussa 45
Altidore 42, Geovanni 75 Att 7,994

Leeds (1) ....2 Watford (0)...................1
Snodgrass 38, 98 Sordell 87
Att 14,681
After extra-time

Nottm Forest (0) ....2 Middlesbrough (1) 1
Chambers 60 Johnson 43
Majewski 103 Att 8,838
After extra-time

Peterborough (1)........2 Ipswich (1)...................1
Frecklington 32 Priskin 14
Boyd 64 Att 5,451

Port Vale (0) ....2 Sheff Wed (0)...............0
K Taylor 63
R Taylor 65 Att 6,667

Portsmouth (3)...........4 Hereford (0)..................1
Piquionne 20, Utaka 23 Plummer 62 (pen)
Kranjcar 43 Att 6,645
Hughes 56

Preston (1).................2 Leicester (1).................1
Brown 14,65 Adams 6
Att 6,977

QPR (0) ....2 Accrington Stanley (0) .1
Ephraim 68 Symes 90
Routledge 90 Att 5,203

Reading (0)................1 Barnsley (0)..................2
Kozluk 90 (og) Bogdanovic 56, 90 (pen)
Att 5,576

Southampton (0).........1 Birmingham (0) 2
Lallana 51 Bowyer 77
Att 11,753 Carsley 80

Swansea (0) ....1 Scunthorpe (1) 2
Dobbie 79 Canavan 13
Att 7,321 Hooper 111 (pen)
After extra-time

Tranmere (0) ....0 Bolton (1).....................1
Att 5,381 Davies 41

West Ham (0) ....3 Millwall (1) 1
Stanislas 87, 98 (pen) Harris 26
Hines 100 Att 24,492
After extra-time

Wolves (0).................0 Swindon (0)..................0
Att 11,416
Wolves win 6–5 on penalties

26/08/2009

Blackpool (3)............4 Wigan (0).....................1
Demontagnac 3, Burgess 19 Amaya 90
Adam 33, Taylor-Fletcher 67 Att 8,089

Bristol City (0)...........0 Carlisle (0)....................2
Att 6,359 Dobie 61, Madine 77

Cardiff (1)..................3 Bristol Rovers (0)..........1
Chopra 33 Elliott 75
Whittingham 66
Magennis 86 Att 9,767

Doncaster (0) ....1 Tottenham (3)...............5
Woods 61 (pen) Huddlestone 9
Att 12,923 O'Hara 11, Crouch 37
Bentley 52
Pavlyuchenko 69

Leyton Orient (0) ....0 Stoke (0).......................1
Att 2,742 Kitson 94

Newcastle (1).............4 Huddersfield (2)............3
Guthrie 36, Geremi 48 Robinson 37, 39 (pen)
Ameobi 64 (pen) Rhodes 47
Nolan 84 Att 23,815

West Brom (1)............4 Rotherham (1)..............3
Beattie 10, 101 Cummins 29
Dorrans 51 Pope 52, 98
Cox 116 Att 10,659

27/08/2009

Crystal Palace (0)......0 Man City (0).................2
Att 14,725 Wright-Phillips 50
Tevez 71

THIRD ROUND

22/09/2009

Arsenal (0) .... 2 West Brom (0) 0
Watt 68
Vela 76   Att 56,592
Arsenal: Szczesny, Gilbert, Senderos, Silvestre, Traore
(Barazite 69), Wilshere, Coquelin (Randall 58), Ramsey,
Gibbs, Sunu (Vela 58), Watt. **Subs not used:** Shea,
Bartley, Eastmond, Frimpong. **Booked:** Ramsey,
Senderos.
West Brom: Kiely, Zuiverloon, Olsson (Meite 80),
Barnett, Jara, Thomas, Koren, Dorrans, Teixeira, Moore
(Wood 74), Cox (Mulumbu 61). **Subs not used:** Carson,
Bednar, Reid, Martis. **Booked:** Cox. **Dismissed:** Thomas.

Barnsley (2) .... 3 Burnley (1) 2
Macken 22   Fletcher 21
De Silva 45   Eagles 52
Colace 75
Att 6,270
Barnsley: Preece, Kozluk, Moore (Thompson 46), Foster,
Gray, De Silva, Colace, Butterfield, Hammill, Macken,
Hume. **Subs not used:** Rusling, Bogdanovic, Devaney,
Sodje , El Haimour, Heslop. **Booked:** Foster.
Burnley: Jensen (Penny 34), Eckersley (Duff 46),
Carlisle, Bikey, Kalvenes, Eagles, McDonald, Gudjonsson,
Guerrero, Fletcher, Paterson (Rodriguez 15). **Subs not
used:** Elliott, Edgar, Blake, Easton. **Booked:** Duff,
Eckersley.

Bolton (0) .... 3 West Ham (0) 1
Davies 86, Cahill 96   Ilunga 59
Elmander 119
Att 8,050
After extra-time
Bolton: Jaaskelainen, Ricketts, Cahill, Knight, Samuel,
Taylor, Muamba, McCann (Cohen 82), Gardner (Lee 69),
Davies, Klasnic (Elmander 77). **Subs not used:** Al Habsi,
Steinsson, Davies, O'Brien.
West Ham: Green, Spector, Kovac, Tomkins, Ilunga,
Dyer (Cole 75), Parker, Noble, Da Costa (N'Gala 63),
Diamanti, Hines (Faubert 88). **Subs not used:** Kurucz,
Nouble, Payne, Edgar. **Booked:** Parker.

Carlisle (1) ....1 Portsmouth (2) 3
Harte 3 (pen)   Dindane 26, Webber 33
Att 7,042   Vanden Borre 63
Carlisle: Pidgeley, Raven, Livesey (Keogh 73), Murphy
(Bridge-Wilkinson 73), Harte, Hurst, Thirlwell, Taiwo
(Dobie 77), Robson, Offiong, Anyinsah. **Subs not used:**
Collin, Horwood, Rothery, Madine.
Portsmouth: Begovic, Vanden Borre, Kaboul, Mokoena,
Belhadj, Basinas, Mullins, Yebda (Brown 77), Utaka,
Webber (Piquionne 87), Dindane (Kanu 68). **Subs not
used:** Ashdown, Mahoto, Sowah.

Leeds (0) .... 0 Liverpool (0) 1
Att 38,168   Ngog 66
Leeds: Higgs, Crowe, Kisnorbo, Michalik, Hughes
(Kilkenny 78), Howson, Doyle (Showunmi 88), Johnson,
Snodgrass, Beckford, Becchio (Grella 81). **Subs not
used:** Ankergren, Naylor, Prutton, Robinson. **Booked:**
Crowe.
Liverpool: Cavalieri, Degen (Johnson 71), Kyrgiakos,
Carragher, Dossena, Aurelio, Mascherano, Spearing, Riera,
Babel (Skrtel 90), Ngog (Gerrard 78). **Subs not used:**
Reina, Torres, Voronin, Plessis. **Booked:** Kyrgiakos.

Nottm Forest (0) .... 0 Blackburn (1) 1
Att 11,553   McCarthy 37
Nottm Forest: Smith, Gunter, Morgan, Wilson, Lynch,
Cohen, Garner (Anderson 82), McKenna (McGugan 82),
Tyson, Earnshaw, Blackstock (Adebola 74). **Subs not
used:** Camp, Chambers, McGoldrick, Moussi.
Blackburn: Brown, Salgado (Jacobsen 61), Nelsen,
Jones, Olsson, Emerton, Nzonzi, Reid (Andrews 75),
Hoilett, McCarthy (Chimbonda 90), Kalinic. **Subs not
used:** Fielding, Doran, Van Heerden, Gunning. **Booked:**
Salgado.

Steven Fletcher feels the pain of Burnley's defeat to Barnsley

Peterborough (2) .... 2 Newcastle (0) 0
Mackail-Smith 20
Williams 31
Att 10,298
Peterborough: Lewis, Martin, Morgan, Zakuani,
Williams, Frecklington (Keates 46), Coutts (Batt 75),
Diagouraga, Boyd, Mclean, Mackail-Smith (Whelpdale
86). **Subs not used:** McKeown, Rowe, Pearce, Day.
Booked: Diagouraga, Boyd.
Newcastle: Krul, Tavernier, Taylor, Tozer, Taylor, LuaLua
(Smith 59), Guthrie, Donaldson (Geremi 60),
Lovenkrands, Ranger, Vuckic (Nolan 60). **Subs not
used:** Soderberg, Ngo Baheng, Ferguson, Inman.
Booked: Taylor, Guthrie, Krul, Taylor. **Dismissed:**
Guthrie.

Scunthorpe (0) .... 2 Port Vale (0) 0
Hayes 92
McCann 95   Att 3,383
Scunthorpe: Murphy (Slocombe 25), Spence, Mirfin,
Canavan, Williams, Sparrow, O'Connor (Togwell 118),
Wright, McCann, Hayes (Woolford 108), Forte. **Subs not
used:** Wright, Byrne, Morris, Boyes.
Port Vale: Martin, Owen, McCombe, Collins, Stockley
(Yates 90), Taylor, Loft (Richman 78), Fraser, Griffith,
Haldane (Taylor 81), Richards. **Subs not used:** Lloyd-
Weston, Howland, McCrory, Dodds. **Booked:** Fraser,
Stockley, Owen, Griffith, Haldane.

Stoke (0) .... 4 Blackpool (1) 3
Higginbotham 75   Vaughan 40
Etherington 78   Clarke 47, Burgess 81
Fuller 80, Griffin 90   Att 13,957
Stoke: Simonsen, Wilkinson, Cort, Higginbotham,
Griffin, Lawrence, Arismendi (Tonge 46), Pugh, Soares
(Etherington 64), Sanli, Beattie (Fuller 64). **Subs not
used:** Sorensen, Kitson, Shotton, Dickinson. **Booked:**
Griffin.
Blackpool: Gilks, Baptiste, Edwards, Eastham (Eardley
83), Martin, Clarke, Bangura, Adam, Emmanuel-Thomas
(Bouazza 90), Vaughan, Burgess. **Subs not used:**
Halstead, Crainey, Southern, Ormerod, Euell. **Booked:**
Adam.

Sunderland (2) .... 2 Birmingham (0) 0
Henderson 4
Campbell 23   Att 20,576
Sunderland: Gordon, Mensah, Da Silva, Turner,
Richardson, Malbranque (Healy 74), Cana (Nosworthy
86), Reid, Henderson, Campbell, Jones (Murphy 80).
Subs not used: Carson, Ferdinand, Bardsley, Bent.
Booked: Richardson.
Birmingham: Taylor, Espinoza, Ridgewell, Dann,
Parnaby (Preston 79), O'Connor, Sammons, Ferguson
(Fahey 63), McSheffrey, O'Shea (Bowyer 63), Phillips.
Subs not used: Doyle, Benitez, Johnson. **Booked:**
Preston, Espinoza.

THIRD ROUND

23/09/2009

Aston Villa (1) ....1 **Cardiff (0)** 0
Agbonlahor 3
Att 22,527
Aston Villa: Guzan, Beye, Cuellar, Collins, Shorey, Milner, Delph, Petrov, Gardner (Albrighton 79), Agbonlahor, Carew. **Subs not used:** Friedel, Sidwell, Dunne, Delfouneso, Warnock, Clark. **Booked:** Beye, Delph.
Cardiff: Enckelman, Matthews, Gyepes, Gerrard, Capaldi, Burke, Ledley, Scimeca (Chopra 60), Rae (Wildig 90), Whittingham, Bothroyd. **Subs not used:** Marshall, Hudson, Quinn, Comminges, Magennis. **Booked:** Gyepes.

Chelsea (0) ....1 **QPR (0)** 0
Kalou 52
Att 37,781
Chelsea: Hilario, Ivanovic, Ferreira, Hutchinson (Terry 77), Belletti, Malouda (Lampard 46), Zhirkov (A Cole 69), Mikel, J Cole, Borini, Kalou. **Subs not used:** Turnbull, Essien, Matic, Bruma.
QPR: Heaton, Borrowdale, Stewart, Leigertwood, Gorkss, Routledge, Rowlands (Ephraim 73), Faurlin, Buzsaky, Vine (Taarabt 66), Simpson (Pellicori 73). **Subs not used:** Cerny, Ramage, Mahon, Agyemang.

Hull (0) ....0 **Everton (3)** 4
Att 13,558
Yakubu 11, Jo 20
Gosling 24, Osman 57
Hull: Duke, Mendy, Zayatte, Cooper, Halmosi, Barmby (Kilbane 65), Boateng (Marney 46), Featherstone (McShane 46), Cairney, Ghilas, Vennegoor of Hesselink. **Subs not used:** Warner, Fagan, Geovanni, Cousin. **Booked:** Kilbane, Zayatte, Cairney.
Everton: Howard, Hibbert, Heitinga, Distin, Baines (Neill 62), Osman, Gosling, Rodwell, Bilyaletdinov (Agard 84), Jo, Yakubu (Fellaini 46). **Subs not used:** Nash, Saha, Cahill, Duffy.

Man City (0) ....2 **Fulham (1)** 1
Barry 52
Gera 34
Toure 111
Att 24,507
After extra-time
Man City: Given, Zabaleta, Toure, Lescott, Bridge, Wright-Phillips, De Jong (Weiss 91), Barry, Ireland (Petrov 75), Tevez, Bellamy. **Subs not used:** Taylor, Garrido, Sylvinho, Vidal, Ball.
Fulham: Stockdale, Stoor, Baird, Smalling, Kelly, Davies (Dikgacoi 71), Greening, Riise, Gera (Anderson 120), Seol, Johnson (Elm 91). **Subs not used:** Zuberbuhler, Watts, Saunders, Smith. **Booked:** Dikgacoi, Kelly.

Man Utd (0) ....1 **Wolverhampton (0)** 0
Welbeck 66
Att 51,160
Man Utd: Kuszczak, Neville, Brown, Evans, F Da Silva, Welbeck (King 81), Carrick, Gibson, Nani, Owen (Valencia 69), Macheda (De Laet 31). **Subs not used:** Amos, Ferdinand, Tosic, Eikrem. **Dismissed:** F Da Silva.
Wolverhampton: Hahnemann, Foley, Berra, Craddock, Elokobi, Kightly (Keogh 77), Castillo (Milijas 46), Henry, Jones, Ebanks-Blake (Doyle 66), Maierhofer. **Subs not used:** Ikeme, Halford, Zubar, Hill.

Preston (0) ....1 **Tottenham (2)** 5
Brown 83
Crouch 14, 77, 90
Att 16,533
Defoe 37
Keane 87
Preston: Lonergan, Hart (Chaplow 51), Mawene, Chilvers, Nolan, Jones, Shumulikoski, Carter, Wallace, Parkin (Brown 78), Elliott (Mellor 78). **Subs not used:** Henderson, Smyth, McLaughlin, Proctor. **Booked:** Nolan.
Tottenham: Gomes, Hutton, Huddlestone, Dawson (Corluka 80), Bale, Bentley, Jenas, Palacios, Giovani (Lennon 16), Crouch, Defoe (Keane 70). **Subs not used:** Walker, Naughton, Rose, Dervite. **Booked:** Hutton.

FOURTH ROUND

27/10/2009

Barnsley (0) ....0 **Man Utd (1)** 2
Att 20,019
Welbeck 6, Owen 59
Barnsley: Steele, Kozluk, Moore, Foster, Gray, De Silva (Campbell-Ryce 71), Colace (Butterfield 77), Hallfredsson, Hammill, Macken (Hume 65), Bogdanovic. **Subs not used:** Preece, Hassell, Thompson, Devaney. **Booked:** Colace, Bogdanovic, De Silva.
Man Utd: Foster, Neville, Brown, Evans, R Da Silva, Obertan, F Da Silva, Anderson, Welbeck (Tosic 53), Macheda (De Laet 65). **Subs not used:** Amos, O'Shea, Evans, King, James. **Booked:** F Da Silva, Tosic. **Dismissed:** Neville.

Blackburn (2) ....5 **Peterborough (1)** 2
Pedersen 4, Reid 45 (pen)
Whelpdale 17
Salgado 57, McCarthy 72
Boyd 50
Kalinic 74 (pen)
Att 8,419
Blackburn: Brown, Salgado, Jones, Givet (Nelsen 59), Olsson, Hoilett, Reid (Dunn 70), Emerton (Andrews 77), Pedersen, McCarthy, Kalinic. **Subs not used:** Robinson, Jacobsen, Roberts, Van Heerden. **Booked:** Givet.
Peterborough: Lewis, Lee (Martin 35), Morgan, Pearce, Rowe (Day 77), Whelpdale, Frecklington, Diagouraga, Boyd, Mclean, Batt (McKeown 43). **Subs not used:** Coutts, Keates, Green, Koranteng. **Dismissed:** Lewis.

Portsmouth (1) ....4 **Stoke (0)** 0
Piquionne 17,59
Webber 55, Kanu 81
Att 11,251
Portsmouth: Ashdown, Vanden Borre, Kaboul, Wilson, Belhadj, Dindane (Hughes 77), Brown, Mullins, Yebda (Mokoena 63), Piquionne, Webber (Kanu 68). **Subs not used:** Niemi, Ben-Haim, Basinas, Nlundulu. **Booked:** Wilson.
Stoke: Simonsen, Griffin, Higginbotham, Cort, Pugh, Lawrence (Soares 75), Arismendi, Whelan, Tonge, Sanli (Moult 82), Kitson (Sidibe 55). **Subs not used:** Parton, Lund, Wedderburn, Connor. **Booked:** Griffin, Tonge.

Sunderland (0) ....0 **Aston Villa (0)** 0
Att 27,666
Aston Villa win 3–1 on penalties
Sunderland: Gordon, Da Silva, Turner, Nosworthy, McCartney (Ferdinand 78), Henderson, Cana, Richardson, Murphy (Reid 73), Jones, Campbell (Malbranque 95). **Subs not used:** Fulop, Healy, Meyler, Reed. **Booked:** Henderson, Ferdinand.

Fran Merida scores for Arsenal against Liverpool

Aston Villa: Guzan, Cuellar, Dunne, Collins, Warnock, Milner, Reo-Coker (Delph 91), Petrov (Sidwell 115), Young, Agbonlahor, Heskey (Carew 77). **Subs not used:** Friedel, Young, Shorey, Beye. **Booked:** Collins, Petrov, Warnock.

Tottenham (1) ....2 **Everton (0)** 0
Huddlestone 31
Keane 57
Att 35,843
Tottenham: Gomes, Hutton, Bassong, Dawson, Assou-Ekotto, Bentley, Huddlestone, Palacios, Bale, Keane, Pavlyuchenko. **Subs not used:** Button, Jenas, Naughton, Corluka, Dervite, Parrett, Kane.
Everton: Howard, Hibbert, Heitinga, Distin, Neill, Cahill, Gosling, Rodwell, Fellaini, Saha (Jo 46), Yakubu. **Subs not used:** Nash, Coleman, Duffy, Agard, Baxter, Wallace. **Booked:** Cahill, Heitinga, Hibbert.

28/10/2009

Arsenal (1) ....2 **Liverpool (1)** 1
Merida 19
Insua 26
Bendtner 50
Att 60,004
Arsenal: Fabianski, Gilbert, Senderos, Silvestre, Gibbs, Eastmond (Randall 75), Bendtner (Watt 76), Nasri, Ramsey, Merida (Coquelin 87), Eduardo. **Subs not used:** Szczesny, Bartley, Frimpong, Sunu.
Liverpool: Cavalieri, Degen (Eccleston 88), Skrtel, Kyrgiakos, Insua, Kuyt, Spearing, Plessis (Aquilani 76), Babel, Voronin, Ngog (Benayoun 74). **Subs not used:** Reina, Darby, Dossena, Ayala.

Chelsea (2) ....4 **Bolton (0)** 0
Kalou 15
Malouda 26
Deco 67, Drogba 89
Att 41,538
Chelsea: Hilario (Turnbull 23), Belletti, Ivanovic, Alex, Ferreira, Deco, Ballack, Malouda, J Cole, Kalou (Essien 46), Sturridge (Drogba 62). **Subs not used:** Lampard, Matic, Bruma, Borini.
Bolton: Al Habsi, Ricketts, Knight, Cahill, Samuel, Muamba, Steinsson (Elmander 46), Davies, Gardner, Taylor (Basham 64), Klasnic. **Subs not used:** Jaaskelainen, Robinson, Cohen, Lee, O'Brien.

Man City (2) ....5 **Scunthorpe (1)** 1
Ireland 3
Forte 26
Santa Cruz 38
Lescott 56
Tevez 71
Johnson 77
Att 36,358
Man City: Given, Zabaleta, Kompany, Lescott, Sylvinho, Wright-Phillips, De Jong, Barry (Johnson 72), Ireland (Weiss 59), Tevez (Mwaruwari 79), Santa Cruz. **Subs not used:** Taylor, Richards, Bridge, Bellamy. **Booked:** De Jong, Zabaleta.
Scunthorpe: Murphy, Byrne, Jones (Canavan 46), Mirfin, Williams, Wright, McCann (Togwell 77), O'Connor (Hooper 68), Woolford, Forte, Hayes. **Subs not used:** Lillis, Wright, Sparrow, Spence.

QUARTER-FINALS

01/12/2009

Man Utd (2) .... 2 **Tottenham (0)** 0
Gibson 16,38
Att 57,212
Man Utd: Kuszczak, Neville, Brown, Vidic, De Laet, Park, Gibson, Anderson (Tosic 82), Obertan (Carrick 62), Welbeck, Berbatov (Macheda 62). **Subs not used:** Amos, Owen, Giggs, Fletcher. **Booked:** De Laet, Gibson.
Tottenham: Gomes, Hutton, Bassong, Dawson, Bale, Lennon, Jenas, Palacios (Huddlestone 46), Bentley, Defoe, Keane (Crouch 66). **Subs not used:** Walker, Pavlyuchenko, Naughton, Corluka, Rose. **Booked:** Hutton.

Portsmouth (1) .... 2 **Aston Villa (2)** 4
Petrov 10 (og)   *Heskey 12*
Kanu 87   *Milner 27*
                                    Downing 74
Att 17,034   *Young 89*
Portsmouth: Begovic, Vanden Borre, Kaboul, Ben-Haim, Hreidarsson, Yebda, Brown, Hughes (Wilson 85), Belhadj, Webber (Kanu 65), Utaka (Piquionne 76). **Subs not used:** Ashdown, Mullins, Dindane, Basinas. **Booked:** Vanden Borre, Kaboul, Brown.
Aston Villa: Guzan, Young, Dunne, Cuellar, Warnock, Milner, Petrov, Downing, Agbonlahor, Heskey (Delfouneso 90), Young. **Subs not used:** Friedel, Delph, Reo-Coker, Beye, Gardner, Clark. **Booked:** Agbonlahor, Milner.

Blackburn celebrate their penalty shoot-out win against Chelsea

02/12/2009

Blackburn (1) .... 3 **Chelsea (0)** 3
Kalinic 9, Emerton 64   *Drogba 48, Kalou 52*
McCarthy 93 (pen)   *Ferreira 120*
Att 18,136
Blackburn win 4–3 on penalties
Blackburn: Robinson, Salgado, Samba, Nelsen, Chimbonda, Emerton, Nzonzi (Van Heerden 91), Pedersen (Grella 62), McCarthy, Roberts (Hoilett 70), Kalinic. **Subs not used:** Brown, Givet, Diouf, Jones. **Booked:** Grella.
Chelsea: Hilario, Belletti (Bruma 46), Ivanovic, Ferreira, Zhirkov, Mikel, Ballack, Deco (Drogba 46), J Cole (Kakuta 46), Kalou, Malouda. **Subs not used:** Turnbull, Matic, Hutchinson, Borini. **Booked:** Bruma.

Man City (0) .... 3 **Arsenal (0)** 0
Tevez 50, Wright-Phillips 69
Weiss 89   *Att 46,015*
Man City: Given, Richards, Toure, Lescott, Bridge, Wright-Phillips (Weiss 77), Ireland, Barry, Bellamy, Tevez (Kompany 74), Adebayor. **Subs not used:** Taylor, Onuoha, Johnson, Robinho, Santa Cruz. **Booked:** Bellamy, Kompany.
Arsenal: Fabianski, Eboue, Song Billong, Silvestre, Traore, Eastmond (Watt 68), Merida, Ramsey, Rosicky, Wilshere, Vela. **Subs not used:** Mannone, Bartley, Coquelin, Frimpong, Gilbert, Randall. **Booked:** Ramsey, Silvestre, Wilshere, Eastmond, Traore, Song Billong.

SEMI-FINALS

14/01/2010

Blackburn (0) .... 0 **Aston Villa (1)** 1
Att 18,595   *Milner 23*
Blackburn: Robinson, Jacobsen (Olsson 46), Samba, Nelsen, Chimbonda, Salgado (Reid 71), Emerton, Nzonzi, Pedersen (McCarthy 75), Dunn, Kalinic. **Subs not used:** Brown, Hoilett, Di Santo, Jones. **Booked:** McCarthy.
Aston Villa: Guzan, Cuellar, Collins, Dunne, Warnock, Young, Milner, Petrov, Downing, Heskey (Sidwell 71), Agbonlahor. **Subs not used:** Friedel, Young, Carew, Delph, Reo-Coker, Beye. **Booked:** Agbonlahor.

19/01/2010

Man City (1) .... 2 **Man Utd (1)** 1
Tevez 42 (pen), 65   *Giggs 17*
Att 46,067
Man City: Given, Zabaleta, Richards, Boyata (Onuoha 69), Garrido, De Jong, Kompany, Barry, Wright-Phillips (Sylvinho 84), Tevez (Mwaruwari 79), Bellamy. **Subs not used:** Taylor, Ireland, Robinho, Petrov. **Booked:** De Jong, Zabaleta.
Man Utd: Van der Sar, R Da Silva (Diouf 90), Brown, Evans, Evra, Anderson (Owen 72), Carrick, Fletcher, Valencia (Scholes 88), Rooney, Giggs. **Subs not used:** Kuszczak, Neville, Park, Da Silva. **Booked:** Van der Sar, Da Silva.

20/01/2010

Aston Villa (2) .... 6 **Blackburn (2)** 4
Warnock 30   *Kalinic 10, 26*
Milner 40 (pen)   *Olsson 63*
Nzonzi 53 (og)   *Emerton 84*
Agbonlahor 58
Heskey 62
Young 90   *Att 40,406*
Aston Villa: Guzan, Cuellar, Dunne, Collins, Warnock, Petrov, Milner, Downing (Sidwell 86), Young, Agbonlahor, Heskey. **Subs not used:** Friedel, Young, Albrighton, Delfouneso, Delph, Beye. **Booked:** Heskey, Milner.
Blackburn: Robinson, Chimbonda, Samba, Nelsen, Givet, Emerton, Nzonzi (Reid 61), Pedersen, Olsson, Dunn (McCarthy 56), Kalinic (Di Santo 72). **Subs not used:** Brown, Andrews, Hoilett, Salgado. **Booked:** Nzonzi, Givet. **Dismissed:** Samba.

27/01/2010

Man Utd (0) .... 3 **Man City (0)** 1
Scholes 52   *Tevez 76*
Carrick 71
Rooney 90   *Att 74,576*
Man Utd: Van der Sar, R Da Silva (Brown 74), Ferdinand, Evans, Evra, Fletcher, Scholes, Carrick, Nani (Valencia 90), Rooney, Giggs. **Subs not used:** Kuszczak, Owen, Berbatov, Park, Vidic. **Booked:** Scholes, Nani.
Man City: Given, Richards, Kompany, Boyata, Garrido (Ireland 64), De Jong, Barry, Zabaleta, Wright-Phillips (Adebayor 72), Tevez, Bellamy. **Subs not used:** Taylor, Onuoha, Sylvinho, Petrov, Ibrahim. **Booked:** Tevez.

FINAL

28/02/2010 (WEMBLEY STADIUM)

Aston Villa (1) .... 1 **Man Utd (1)** 2
Milner 5 (pen)   *Owen 12*
Att 88,596   *Rooney 74*
Aston Villa: Friedel, Cuellar (Carew 80), Collins, Dunne, Warnock, Young, Milner, Petrov, Downing, Heskey, Agbonlahor. **Subs not used:** Guzan, Young, Sidwell, Delfouneso, Delph, Beye. **Booked:** Collins, Downing.
Man Utd: Kuszczak, R Da Silva (Neville 66), Vidic, Evans, Evra, Valencia, Fletcher, Carrick, Park (Gibson 85), Owen (Rooney 42), Berbatov. **Subs not used:** Foster, Brown, Scholes, Diouf. **Booked:** Vidic, Evra.

Wayne Rooney grabs Manchester United's late winner against Manchester City

Southampton celebrate victory in the Johnstone's Paint Trophy final at Wembley

FROM TOP: Adam Lallana celebrates his goal in the final; Carlisle are thrilled after beating Leeds in a penalty shoot-out; Shane Lowry is inconsolable after his spot-kick miss in the semi-final

SOUTHAMPTON made a triumphant return to the big stage with a 4–1 victory over Carlisle at Wembley to lift the Johnstone's Paint Trophy.

Rickie Lambert, Adam Lallana, Papa Waigo and Michail Antonio grabbed the goals as the Saints claimed their first silverware in 34 years.

Alan Pardew's team, backed by 44,000 supporters, took the lead in the 15th minute when Peter Murphy was penalised for handball and Lambert scored from the penalty spot. They doubled their advantage two minutes before half-time when Lambert flicked on Antonio's long throw and Lallana was left with the simple task of nodding the ball past Adam Collin.

Any hopes of a Cumbrian comeback were ended five minutes into the second half when Evan Horwood failed to clear Lambert's cross. Collin managed to keep out Antonio's shot but Waigo was on hand to head the rebound into an empty net.

Antonio fired home the fourth on the hour mark from the edge of the area before substitute Gary Madine gave the Carlisle fans something to cheer with a late header.

First-round surprises

Carlisle and Southampton had reached the final after battling through arguably the toughest field in the competition's history – the Saints being one of four recent Barclays Premier League clubs involved alongside Leeds, Charlton and Norwich.

The first round witnessed a shock as Barnet knocked out Millwall with a 2–0 home win. Burton were beaten 5–1 by Chesterfield on their competition debut, while Carlisle required penalties to see off Morecambe.

Having received a bye in the first round, Southampton began their journey to Wembley by edging past Torquay through a penalty shoot-out having hit back from 2–0 down to level at 2–2 after 90 minutes. There was another upset when Grimsby knocked out Hartlepool, while Scott Dobie scored twice to give Carlisle a 4–2 home win over Macclesfield.

The glamour tie of the area quarter-finals saw Southampton drawn against another one of the favourites in Charlton, and the Saints ran out 2–1 winners at St Mary's. Leeds enjoyed a comfortable 3–1 win over Grimsby at Elland Road and Carlisle beat Chesterfield by the same scoreline.

Southampton's route to the final did not get any easier with the visit of Norwich in the Southern semi-finals. After a 2–2 draw in normal time, Saints held their nerve once again to triumph 6–5 on penalty kicks.

In the other Southern semi-final, MK Dons brought Hereford's run in the competition to an end with a 4–1 victory. Leeds swept past Accrington 2–0, while Carlisle secured their place in the Northern Area final with a 3–0 win over Bradford.

Joe Anyinsah's late strike gave Carlisle a 2–1 win at Elland Road in the first leg of the area decider. Leeds won the return 3–2 in normal time to level the tie but Shane Lowry's miss in the penalty shoot-out meant Carlisle triumphed.

Paul Ince had led MK Dons to victory in the competition in 2007/08 but he was unable to mastermind another return to Wembley as Southampton won both legs of their area final. Pardew's side took the first leg 3–1 at St Mary's before also winning 1–0 at stadium:mk.

FIRST ROUND
SOUTHERN SECTION
01/09/2009

Barnet (1) ....2 Millwall (0) 0
Hyde 2, Yakubu 65   Att 1,623

Bournemouth (1) ....2 Yeovil (0) 1
Pitman 45   Obika 87
Connell 66   Att 2,655

Cheltenham (0) ....1 Torquay (3) 3
Low 55   Stevens 6, 45
Att 1,397   Benyon 31

Gillingham (0) ....1 Colchester (0) 1
Jackson 77 (pen)   Platt 84
Att 1,725

Gillingham win 4–3 on penalties

Hereford (0) ....0 Bristol Rovers (0) 0
Att 970

Hereford win 4–2 on penalties

Milton Keynes Dons (0)3 Dag & Red (0) 1
Lewington 55   Scott 90
Easter 58, 67   Att 4,413

Norwich (1) ....1 Brentford (0) 0
Martin 30   Att 12,540

Wycombe (0) ....2 Northampton (1) 1
Pittman 62 (pen), 90   Gilligan 40 (pen)
Att 1,035   Guinan 86

Northampton win 3–0 on penalties

NORTHERN SECTION
01/09/2009

Burton Albion (0) ....1 Chesterfield (2) 5
McGrath 46   Small 17, 62
Att 1,493   Talbot 38, 90, Lowry 87

Crewe (0) ....1 Stockport (3) 4
Zola 90   Baker 8, 33, 90
Att 2,331   Bignall 40

Darlington (1) ....1 Lincoln City (0) 0
Thorpe 27   Att 828

Morecambe (1) ....2 Carlisle (0) 2
Hunter 3   Kavanagh 48, 90
Curtis 56   Att 2,016

Carlisle win 4–2 on penalties

Oldham (1) ....1 Accrington Stanley (0) 2
Whitaker 10   Gregan 60 (og)
Att 1,619   Edwards 67

Rochdale (0) ....1 Bradford (0) 2
Dawson 59   Flynn 74
Att 1,800   Neilson 79

Rotherham (1) ....1 Huddersfield (2) 2
Le Fondre 35   Clarke 4
Att 2,246   Simpson 7

Walsall (0) ....0 Bury (0) 0
Att 2,314

Bury win 5–4 on penalties

SECOND ROUND
SOUTHERN SECTION
06/10/2009

Charlton (2) ....4 Barnet (1) 1
McLeod 15, Tuna 40   O'Flynn 11
Bailey 75, Wagstaff 87   Att 4,522

Exeter (0) ....1 Swindon (1) 1
Fleetwood 90   McNamee 17
Att 2,006

Swindon win 4–3 on penalties

Gillingham (0) ....0 Norwich (0) 1
Att 2,814   McDonald 66

Hereford (1) ....2 Aldershot (1) 2
Walker 42   Hudson 15, Soares 90
Manset 89   Att 897

Hereford win 4–3 on penalties

Leyton Orient (0) ....1 Brighton (0) 0
Patulea 89   Att 1,457

Milton Keynes Dons (2)2 Southend (0) 0
Doran 18, Carrington 45   Att 4,792

Northampton (0) ....0 Bournemouth (1) 1
Guinan 66   Hollands 33
Gilligan 90 (pen)   Att 1,718

Southampton (0) ....2 Torquay (2) 2
Papa Waigo 59, 69   Sills 21
Att 9,319   Wroe 42 (pen)

Southampton win 5–3 on penalties

NORTHERN SECTION
06/10/2009

Bradford (1) ....2 Notts County (1) 2
M Boulding 20   Westcarr 10, Facey 85
Brandon 90   Att 3,701

Bradford win 3–2 on penalties

Bury (0) ....2 Tranmere (1) 1
Worrall 54   Curran 4
Jones 81   Att 1,903

Carlisle (0) ....4 Macclesfield (1) 2
Robson 64   Brisley 45
Dobie 68, 80   Rooney 45
Bridge-Wilkinson 78   Att 1,753

Chesterfield (0) ....3 Huddersfield (0) 3
Talbot 57, 74   Pilkington 65, 90
Bowery 90   N Clarke 90
Att 3,003

Chesterfield win 4–2 on penalties

Hartlepool (0) ....0 Grimsby (2) 2
Att 1,675   Sweeney 6
                                       Proudlock 34

Leeds (2) ....2 Darlington (1) 1
Robinson 25   Convery 45
Kandol 28   Att 8,429

Port Vale (3) ....3 Stockport (1) 1
Haldane 4   Bridcutt 22
Dodds 7, Richards 13   Att 3,154

20/10/2009

Accrington Stanley (0) 2 Shrewsbury (0) 0
King 47, Winnard 52   Att 819

QUARTER-FINALS
SOUTHERN SECTION
10/11/2009

Leyton Orient (0) ....1 Hereford (1) 1
Demetriou 90   Constantine 25
Att 1,282

Hereford win 3–2 on penalties

Milton Keynes Dons (3)3 Northampton (0) 1
Wilbraham 6   Guinan 51
Baldock 16, 27 (pen)   Att 8,886

Swindon (0) ....0 Norwich (0) 0
Att 4,978

Norwich win 5–3 on penalties

11/11/2009

Southampton (1) ....2 Charlton (0) 1
Thomas 34   McKenzie 90
Lambert 63   Att 13,906

NORTHERN SECTION
10/11/2009

Accrington Stanley (2) 3 Bury (1) 2
Symes 2, 40   Racchi 41, Jones 48
Grant 82   Att 1,637

Bradford (0) ....2 Port Vale (1) 2
Flynn 49   McCombe 27
Hanson 70   R Taylor 75
Att 5,096

Bradford win 5–4 on penalties

Chesterfield (1) ....1 Carlisle (0) 3
Currie 45 (pen)   Robson 62
Att 2,878   Murphy 69, Clayton 78

Leeds (2) ....3 Grimsby (0) 1
Lancashire 40 (og)   Sweeney 57
Kilkenny 45, Beckford 55   Att 10,430

SEMI-FINALS
SOUTHERN SECTION
15/12/2009

Hereford (0) ....1 Milton Keynes Dons (1). 4
Constantine 63   Baldock 6, Puncheon 69
Att 1,367   Wilbraham 78, Easter 83

Southampton (1) ....2 Norwich (1) 2
Papa Waigo 14, 90   Doherty 33
Att 15,453   Martin 55

Southampton win 6–5 on penalties

NORTHERN SECTION
15/12/2009

Carlisle (1) ....3 Bradford (0) 0
Keogh 44, Dobie 68
Robson 74   Att 3,176

Leeds (1) ....2 Accrington Stanley (0) 0
Ephraim 9, Kilkenny 50   Att 12,696

NORTHERN AREA FINAL 1ST LEG
19/01/2010

Leeds (0) ....1 Carlisle (1) 2
Crowe 56   Kavanagh 21
Att 13,011   Anyinsah 84

SOUTHERN AREA FINAL 1ST LEG
20/01/2010

Milton Keynes Dons (0)0 Southampton (1) 1
Att 7,918   Antonio 26

NORTHERN AREA FINAL 2ND LEG
09/02/2010

Carlisle (1) ....2 Leeds (0) 3
Clayton 33, Hurst 72   Snodgrass 46, Crowe 80
Att 9,430   Grella 86

Carlisle win 6–5 on penalties

SOUTHERN AREA FINAL 2ND LEG
09/02/2010

Southampton (2) ....3 Milton Keynes Dons (1)..1
Lambert 15   Randall 44
Woodards 30 (og)
Lallana 87
Att 29,901

FINAL
28/03/2010

Carlisle (0) ....1 Southampton (2) 4
Madine 84   Lambert 15 (pen)
Att 73,476   Lallana 44
                                       Papa Waigo 50
                                       Antonio 60

Carlisle: Collin, Horwood, Harte, Murphy, Keogh, Thirlwell (Taiwo 79), Kavanagh (Madine 73), Clayton, Bridge-Wilkinson (Anyinsah 61), Dobie, Robson. **Subs not used:** Pidgeley, Kane. **Booked:** Keogh, Murphy. **Southampton:** Davis, Harding, Fonte, Jaidi (Perry 90), Mills, Wotton (Connolly 85), Hammond, Lallana, Papa Waigo (Gillett 76), Lambert, Antonio. **Subs not used:** Bialkowski, James.

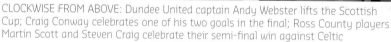

CLOCKWISE FROM ABOVE: Dundee United captain Andy Webster lifts the Scottish Cup; Craig Conway celebrates one of his two goals in the final; Ross County players Martin Scott and Steven Craig celebrate their semi-final win against Celtic

DUNDEE UNITED won the 2010 Active Nation Scottish Cup with a 3–0 victory over Ross County at Hampden.

The dreams that Irn-Bru First Division County had of taking the trophy to Dingwall for the first time in the club's 81-year history were dashed by a Craig Conway double, which followed David Goodwillie's opener.

The Cup was heading for Tannadice for the first time since 1994, and that sparked wild celebrations among the 27,000 United fans who had made the trip to the national stadium, as well as those back on Tayside.

The early rounds of the Cup once again featured the names of minnows, such as Civil Service Strollers, Forres Mechanics and Inverurie Locos, the latter beating Stranraer 2–1 in the second round.

A couple of famous clubs from Junior football also showed their strength, with Ayrshire's Auchinleck Talbot beating Highland League side Huntly in the second round.

In the third round, Irvine Meadow, following earlier wins over Brora Rangers and Selkirk, edged past Arbroath. Ross County began their long journey to the Hampden final by beating Berwick Rangers 5–1, as

goals – and lots of them – became a feature of the Staggies' thrilling Cup run.

Big names

The big names joined the competition at the fourth-round stage. Rangers beat fellow Clydesdale Bank Premier League side Hamilton after a replay and Celtic narrowly edged out Morton at Cappielow.

Ross County beat Inverurie 4–0 at the same stage, while Dundee United began their glorious run with a 2–0 win over Partick Thistle.

Hibernian beat tiny Irvine Meadow at Easter Road, Edinburgh rivals Hearts were dumped out by Aberdeen, and Motherwell suffered a shock, losing 2–0 to Irn-Bru First Division side Inverness.

In the fifth round, Ross County continued on the goal trail, thrashing Stirling Albion 9–0, while Dundee United overcame St Johnstone 1–0 at McDiarmid Park.

It took another replay for Rangers to get past St Mirren, while Celtic beat Dunfermline 4–2 at East End Park.

There were a couple of suprises in the quarter-finals as Ross County battled to a

2–2 draw at Hibs and then beat the Leith side 2–1 in the replay. Dundee United grabbed a late equaliser to draw 3–3 at Rangers and then won 1–0 in the replay thanks to a late David Robertson goal.

Celtic overcame Kilmarnock 3–0 at Rugby Park while Raith Rovers, who had knocked out Aberdeen in the fifth round following a replay, beat fellow First Division side Dundee 2–1 at Dens Park.

The biggest shock of the competition came in the semi-finals at Hampden when Ross County dramatically and deservedly beat Celtic 2–0. Goals from Steven Craig – son of former Hoops striker Joe Craig – and Martin Scott put the Dingwall outfit into their first major final. The following day at the national stadium, Dundee United forced their way past Raith with goals from Goodwillie and on-loan Rangers defender Andy Webster to set up a clash with the Staggies.

Goodwillie broke the deadlock against County in the showpiece with a wonderful lobbed effort from 30 yards before Conway grabbed the headlines with a brace, as the Cup returned to Tannadice.

FIRST ROUND
26/09/2009

Auchinleck Talbot	7	Fort William	0
Brora	0	Irvine Meadow	2
Buckie Thistle	0	Forres Mechanics	0
Civil Service Strollers	1	Gala Fairydean	0
Clachnacuddin	2	Wick Academy	2
Coldstream	1	Edinburgh City	5
Dalbeattie Star	2	Keith	4
Edinburgh Univ	0	Vale Of Leithen	3
Fraserburgh	1	Bonnyrigg Rose	1
Glasgow Univ	1	Girvan	4
Hawick Royal Albert	0	Huntly	7
Inverurie Loco Works	5	St Cuthbert Wndrs	0
Lossiemouth	4	Newton Stewart	1
Nairn County	5	Golspie Sutherland	2
Rothes	1	Banks O'Dee	5
Selkirk	3	Preston Ath	0
Whitehill Welfare	1	Wigtown & Bladnoch	1

REPLAYS
03/10/2009

Bonnyrigg Rose	1	Fraserburgh	2
Forres Mechanics	0	Buckie Thistle	0
Wick Academy	2	Clachnacuddin	1
Wigtown & Bladnoch	0	Whitehill Welfare	3

SECOND ROUND
24/10/2009

Banks O'Dee (0) ...... 0 **Montrose (0)** 3
Watson 57
Sinclair 78
Cambell 89
Att 400

Civil Service Strollers (1) .1 **Berwick (0)** 2
Burgess 32 McLaren 59, 69
Att 387

Cove Rangers (0) ...... 2 **Annan Athletic (1)** 1
Stephen 64 Watson 28
Henderson 82
Att 278

Deveronvale (1) ...... 2 **Buckie Thistle (2)** 2
Smith 35, 82 Stewart 6
MacMillan 16
Att 1,025

Edinburgh City (3) ...... 5 **Burntisland Shipyard (1)** 1
Denholm 10 O'Hanlon 38 (pen)
McFarland 23
Clee 36, 80
Ross 87
Att 123

Forfar (2) ...... 4 **East Stirling (0)** 2
Campbell 25, 73 Rodgers 46
Tod 34 Dunn 63
Harty 90 (pen)
Att 396

Fraserburgh (0) ...... 1 **Spartans (2)** 4
Main 49 Sidwright 11
Main 19 (og)
King 57
Att 389 Henretty 72

Girvan (1) ...... 1 **Wick Academy (0)** 4
Murphy 14 Mackay 53
Att 180 MacAdie 61 (pen)
Allan 65
Shearer 68

Huntly (0) ...... 1 **Auchinleck Talbot (1)** ...1
Lombardi 90 Flavin 38
Att 488

Inverurie Loco Works (1) 2 **Stranraer (1)** 1
Singer 17 Moore 10
Gauld 65
Att 410

Lossiemouth (0) ...... 0 **Albion (1)** 2
Barr 5
Walker 88
Att 235

Nairn County (0) ...... 2 **Elgin (2)** 4
Barron 64 Frizzel 4, 32, 51 (pen)
Campbell 70 Crooks 71 (pen)
Att 600

Queen's Park (0) ...... 1 **Livingston (1)** 3
Quinn 78 De Vita 32, 83
Fox 62 (pen)
Att 678

Selkirk (0) ...... 0 **Irvine Meadow (1)** 3
Wingate 14
Barr 66, 83
Att 238

Vale Of Leithen (1) ...... 1 **Keith (1)** 3
Somerville 26 MacKay 5, 63
Harris 81
Att 73

Whitehill Welfare (0) .... 1 **Threave Rovers (0)** 1
Haynes 74 Kerr 46
Att 215

REPLAYS
31/10/2009

Auchinleck Talbot (3) ..4 **Huntly (0)** 3
Slavin 4 Ewen 57
Boyle 29 Fraser 83
White 39 Soane 90
McKelvie 86
Att 125

Buckie Thistle (0) ......1 **Deveronvale (1)** 3
Bruce 80 McKenzie 16
McGowan 115
Smith 120
Att 1,100

After extra-time

Threave Rovers (0) ......1 **Whitehill Welfare (0)** 0
Warren 60
Att 269

THIRD ROUND
28/11/2009

Airdrie (3) ...... 4 **Queen of South (0)** 0
Trouten 11, 39
Baird 23
O'Carroll 65
Att 1,141

Albion (0) ...... 1 **Elgin (0)** 0
Pollock 62
Att 275

Cowdenbeath (0) ...... 0 **Alloa (0)** 0
Att 377

Deveronvale (0) ...... 0 **Ayr (0)** 1
Stevenson 71

Edinburgh City (2) ...... 3 **Keith (0)** 1
Nicol 19 (og) Harris 90
Gair 24, 70
Att 177

Irvine Meadow (1) ......1 **Arbroath (0)** 0
Barr 36
Att 1,150

Montrose (0) ...... 2 **East Fife (0)** 1
Watson 57 McManus 61
Gemmell 88 Att 509

Morton (0) ...... 0 **Dumbarton (0)** 0
Att 1,882

Raith (0) ...... 0 **Peterhead (0)** 0
Att 1,418

Ross County (3) ...... 5 **Berwick (0)** 1
Di Giacomo 38, 40 Brazil 77
Lawson 42
Craig 82
Wood 87
Att 819

Spartans (0) ...... 0 **Forfar (0)** 1
Templeman 55
Att 600

Stirling (1) ...... 2 **Auchinleck Talbot (1)** 1
Corr 10 McIlroy 35 (pen)
Forsyth 64
Att 1,185

Threave Rovers (0) ....1 **Inverurie Loco Works (1)** . 2
Struthers 89 Park 6
Morrison 71
Att 520

Wick Academy (3) ....4 **Brechin (2)** 4
Allan 8, 45 King 12, 85
Mackay 32, 60 (pen) Byers 17
McAllister 75
Att 177

05/12/2009

Stenhousemuir (5) ....5 **Cove Rangers (0)** 0
Motion 1, 34
Molloy 2
Bradley 13
Thomson 30
Att 409

09/12/2009

Clyde (0) ...... 1 **Livingston (0)** 1
Lithgow 63 Hamill 48
Att 538

REPLAYS
01/12/2009

Peterhead (0) ...... 1 **Raith (0)** 4
Stewart 87 D Smith 46, 73
K Smith 59
Simmons 90
Att 537

05/12/2009

Dumbarton (0) ...... 0 **Morton (0)** 1
Graham 74
Att 1,495

08/12/2009

Alloa (0) ...... 1 **Cowdenbeath (0)** 0
Gilhaney 88
Att 423

Brechin (2) ...... 4 **Wick Academy (1)** 2
Fusco 17 Mackay 39 (pen)
Docherty 42 MacAdie 82
McAllister 57, 72
Att 402

14/12/2009

Livingston (1) ...... 7 **Clyde (1)** 1
Jacobs 5 Lithgow 11
Fox 49, 80
Winters 50, 67
Halliday 51
Reidford 65 (og)
Att 690

FOURTH ROUND
09/01/2010

Aberdeen (0) 2   Hearts (0) 0
Mackie 60
Miller 76
Att 8,226

Dunfermline (4) 7   Stenhousemuir (0) 1
Gibson 15   *Bradley 90*
Kirk 17, 83 (pen)
Phinn 21
Graham 35
McDougall 63
Cardle 69
Att 1,832

Hibernian (2) 3   Irvine Meadow (0) 0
Riordan 32
Zemmama 42
Hanlon 59
Att 10,197

Partick (0) 0   Dundee Utd (1) 2
                                        Casalinuovo 26
                                        Goodwillie 90
                                        Att 4,002

St Mirren (2) 3   Alloa (1) 1
Crawford 27 (og)
Mehmet 45, 87
Att 2,587

10/01/2010

Hamilton (3) 3   Rangers (2) 3
Mensing 39 (pen)   *Whittaker 4*
Paixao 45   *Miller 30, 63 (pen)*
Antoine-Curier 45
Att 3,940

18/01/2010

Albion (0) 0   Stirling (0) 0
Att 395

Ayr (1) 1   Brechin (0) 0
Roberts 3
Att 1,139

Edinburgh City (1) 1   Montrose (1) 3
Gair 37   *Nicholas 20*
                                        Maitland 71
                                        Nicol 84
                                        Att 1,027

Forfar (0) 0   St Johnstone (2) 3
                                        Deuchar 23
                                        Craig 43, 58
                                        Att 1,449

Inverness (1) 2   Motherwell (0) 0
Bulvitis 43
Imrie 62
Att 1,450

Kilmarnock (0) 1   Falkirk (0) 0
Pascali 83
Att 3,378

Ross County (1) 4   Inverurie Loco Works (0) 0
Craig 37, 56
Morrison 53
Miller 73
Att 835

19/01/2010

Morton (0) 0   Celtic (1) 1
                                        McGinn 35
                                        Att 10,191

20/01/2010

Livingston (0) 0   Dundee (1) 1
                                        Harkins 33
                                        Att 1,176

25/01/2010

Raith (0) 1   Airdrie (1) 1
Smyth 56 (og)   *Baird 5*
Att 1,599

REPLAYS
19/01/2010

Rangers (0) 2   Hamilton (0) 0
Whittaker 98, 99
Att 21,856

After extra-time
20/01/2010

Stirling (3) 3   Albion (1) 1
Mullen 9, 33   *Walker 18*
Murphy 43
Att 355

26/01/2010

Stenhousemuir (0) 1   Dunfermline (1) 2
Bradley 67 (pen)   *Cardle 35*
                                        Kirk 112
                                        Att 1,810

After extra-time
27/01/2010

Airdrie (1) 1   Raith (2) 3
Donnelly 39   *Smith 24*
                                        Tade 45
                                        Russell 90 (pen)
                                        Att 852

FIFTH ROUND
06/02/2010

Dundee (1) 2   Ayr (1) 1
Hutchinson 41   *McManus 11*
Griffiths 70
Att 2,852

Hibernian (2) 5   Montrose (0) 1
Nish 5, 25   *Hegarty 74*
Riordan 70
Benjelloun 78
Gow 89
Att 9,068

Kilmarnock (2) 3   Inverness (0) 0
Sammon 28
Kelly 36, 59
Att 4,473

Raith (1) 1   Aberdeen (0) 1
Williamson 31   *McDonald 90*
Att 7,045

Ross County (3) 9   Stirling (0) 0
Keddie 3
Gardyne 15, 20
Wood 55, 59, 90
Brittain 66 (pen)
Kettlewell 83
Morrison 84
Att 1,365

St Johnstone (0) 0   Dundee Utd (1) 1
                                        Goodwillie 45
                                        Att 5,636

St Mirren (0) 0   Rangers (0) 0
Att 4,909

07/02/2010

Dunfermline (2) 2   Celtic (2) 4
Graham 21   *Kamara 20*
Kirk 28 (pen)   *Rasmussen 43*
                                        Woods 59 (og)
                                        Keane 68 (pen)
                                        Att 8,933

REPLAYS
16/02/2010

Aberdeen (0) 0   Raith (0) 1
                                        Tade 58
                                        Att 8,153

17/02/2010

Rangers (0) 1   St Mirren (0) 0
Boyd 86
Att 31,086

QUARTER-FINALS
13/03/2010

Dundee (0) 1   Raith (2) 2
Forsyth 73   *Simmons 3*
                                        Ellis 10
                                        Att 7,306

Hibernian (2) 2   Ross County (1) 2
Nish 7   *Murray 16 (og)*
Riordan 19   *Gardyne 79*
Att 9,857

Kilmarnock (0) 0   Celtic (0) 3
                                        Keane 64, 81, 82
                                        Att 7,351

14/03/2010

Rangers (2) 3   Dundee Utd (1) 3
Boyd 34 (pen), 43 (pen)   *Shala 24*
Novo 48   *Whittaker 63 (og)*
                                        Kovacevic 80
                                        Att 24,096

REPLAYS
23/03/2010

Ross County (0) 2   Hibernian (0) 1
Wood 70   *Stokes 46*
Boyd 90
Att 5,607

24/03/2010

Dundee Utd (0) 1   Rangers (0) 0
Robertson 90
Att 11,898

SEMI-FINALS
10/04/2010 (HAMPDEN PARK)

Celtic (0) 0   Ross County (0) 2
                                        Craig 55
                                        Scott 88
                                        Att 24,535

Celtic: Zaluska, Hinkel (Rasmussen 84), Thompson, O'Dea, Naylor, McGeady, Brown, N'Guemo (Crosas 42), Keane, Fortune (McCourt 67), Samaras. **Subs not used:** Cervi, Wilson. **Booked:** O'Dea.
Ross County: McGovern, Miller, Boyd, Keddie, Morrison, Gardyne (Lawson 90), Brittain, Scott, Vigurs, Barrowman, Craig. **Subs not used:** Malin, Di Giacomo, Kettlewell, Wood. **Booked:** Miller.

11/04/2010 (HAMPDEN PARK)

Dundee Utd (1) 2   Raith (0) 0
Goodwillie 28
Webster 59
Att 17,671

Dundee Utd: Pernis, Dillon, Webster, Dods, Dixon (Watson 16), Conway, Buaben, Gomis, Swanson (Myrie-Williams 77), Daly, Goodwillie (Cadamarteri 83). **Subs not used:** Banks, Sandaza.
Raith: McGurn, Gathuessi, Murray, Hill (Ferry 89), Ellis, Walker, Davidson, Simmons, Williamson (Weir 60), Mole (D Smith 78), Tade. **Subs not used:** O'Connor, Sloan. **Booked:** Weir.

FINAL
15/05/2010 (HAMPDEN PARK)

Dundee Utd (0) 3   Ross County (0) 0
Goodwillie 61
Conway 75, 86
Att 47,122

Dundee Utd: Pernis, Kovacevic (Watson 83), Webster, Kenneth, Dillon, Swanson (S Robertson 74), Buaben, Gomis, Conway, Daly, Goodwillie (D Robertson 78). **Subs not used:** Banks, Cadamarteri. **Booked:** Gomis, Goodwillie.
Ross County: McGovern, Miller, Boyd, Scott (Wood 79), Morrison, Craig (Lawson 52), Vigurs, Keddie, Brittain, Gardyne (Di Giacomo 77), Barrowman. **Subs not used:** Malin, Kettlewell. **Booked:** Wood, Miller.

MG ALBA

DUNDEE won the first silverware of the Scottish football season when they staged a second-half comeback to beat Inverness Caledonian Thistle 3–2 in a dramatic ALBA Challenge Cup final at McDiarmid Park.

Adam Rooney and Nauris Bulvitis had put Caley Thistle 2–0 ahead by the 33rd minute but then Bulvitis scored an own goal shortly after half-time and Gary Harkins equalised in the 53rd minute. Craig Forsyth scored the winning goal seven minutes from the end and then Dougie Imrie was sent off in injury time, only a few moments after coming on as a substitute for Inverness.

Dundee, who had not lifted the Challenge Cup since winning the inaugural competition in 1990, began the 2009 competition with a first-round bye in the North and East Region.

East Stirlingshire enjoyed the same luxury in the South and West Region, where last season's winners, Airdrie, saw their campaign ended as they were beaten at home by Partick Thistle, with Liam Buchanan grabbing the only goal as they took revenge for the previous season's semi-final defeat.

Inverness were given a scare by Montrose and needed a penalty shoot-out to beat the

Irn-Bru Third Division side, with Ryan Esson making the crucial save from Chris Hegarty's spot-kick.

Annan's fighting spirit took them all the way to the semi-finals as Peter Watson scored with the last kick of the game to beat Stirling. The Galabankies then came from two goals down at half-time to edge out Elgin 4–2, although their run was ended by a 3–0 defeat to Dundee.

Esson was again the Inverness hero during another penalty shoot-out against Partick and that set up a semi-final against Highland rivals Ross County, with Robert Eagle's goal enough to take them to the final.

However, while Caley's season would ultimately end with the joy of promotion back to the top flight, they had to settle for second best in the ALBA Cup.

Dundee's players celebrate their ALBA Cup final victory over Inverness, while (far left) the Dark Blues' Gary Harkins beats Inverness' Nauris Bulvitis in the second leg

FIRST ROUND
25/07/2009

Airdrie (0)..........0   Partick (0)..................1
Att 1,325   Buchanan 51

Annan (1)..........2   Queen's Park (0)..........0
Jack 27 (pen), 90
Att 466

Ayr (0)..........0   Albion (0)..................2
Att 964   Barr 79, McFarlane 85

Dunfermline (0)..........2   Arbroath (0)..................1
Kirk 49   Redman 73
Bell 68   Att 1,239

East Fife (0)..........0   Forfar (1)..................2
Att 446   M Fotheringham 38
    K Fotheringham 77

Elgin (1)..........3   Brechin (0)..................1
Crooks 1   McAllister 46
Frizzel 61, Edwards 74   Att 378

Inverness (1)..........1   Montrose (0)..................1
McBain 44   Leyden 87
Att 1,122
Inverness win 5–3 on penalties

Peterhead (1)..........1   Cowdenbeath (0)..........2
Bavidge 12   McBride 52
Att 361   McQuade 61

Queen of South (1)..........1   Livingston (0)..................0
Wilson 9   Att 1,558

Ross County (0)..........3   Alloa (1)..................2
Gardyne 58, 106, 118   Watt 4 (og)
Att 748   Spence 99
After extra-time

Stenhousemuir (0)..........2   Clyde (0)..................0
O'Reilly 75, Dalziel 90   Att 603

Stirling (1)..........2   Raith (0)..................1
Graham 45   Walker 90
McKenna 54   Att 713

Stranraer (2)..........4   Berwick (1)..................2
Jack 9, Mitchell 18 (pen), 59   Ewart 33, Little 86
Montgomerie 87   Att 219

26/07/2009

Dumbarton (0)..........0   Morton (1)..................1
Att 1,120   Jenkins 25

SECOND ROUND
18/08/2009

Annan (0)..........1   East Stirling (0)..........0
Watson 90   Att 357

Cowdenbeath (0)..........0   Dundee (1)..................3
Att 457   Griffiths 20, Harkins 82
    Antoine-Curier 88

Dunfermline (0)..........1   Queen of South (1)..........2
Cardle 53   Kean 12
Att 941   Tosh 90

Elgin (0)..........3   Albion (0)..................0
Crooks 64 (pen), Gunn 80, 90   Att 245

Forfar (0)..........1   Partick (1)..................6
Templeman 59   Doolan 10, Hamilton 51, 52
Att 532   Rowson 61, Donnelly 74
    Cairney 80

Inverness (3)..........3   Stranraer (0)..................0
Foran 12, 32, Sanchez 29   Att 1,076

Ross County (0)..........2   Morton (0)..................1
Lawson 68   Masterton 63
Wood 70   Att 588

Stirling (1)..........3   Stenhousemuir (0)..........1
Mullen 33, Robertson 47   Dalziel 49
McKenna 80   Att 275

QUARTER-FINALS
06/09/2009

Annan (0)..........4   Elgin (2)..................2
Gilfillan 56, Bell 75   Cameron 6, MacBeth 43 (og)
Inglis 78, Storey 88   Att 534

Partick (0)..........1   Inverness (1)..................1
Buchanan 77   Sanchez 6
Att 1,746
Inverness win 4–3 on penalties

Ross County (1)..........2   Queen of South (0)..........0
Di Giacomo 26, Craig 90   Att 964

Stirling (0)..........1   Dundee (2)..................2
Devine 90 (pen)   Griffiths 9, 26
Att 1,277

SEMI-FINALS
04/10/2009

Dundee (1)..........3   Annan (0)..................0
Higgins 37, Clarke 63
Forsyth 71   Att 2,321

Inverness (1)..........1   Ross County (0)..........0
Eagle 44   Att 2,275

FINAL
22/11/2009

Dundee (0)..........3   Inverness (2)..................2
Bulvitis 48 (og)   Rooney 20, Bulvitis 33
Harkins 53, Forsyth 83   Att 8,031

CO-OPERATIVE INSURANCE CUP

CLOCKWISE FROM ABOVE: Rangers celebrate after winning the trophy, but it's agony for beaten finalists, St Mirren; Hearts enjoy their quarter-final victory over Celtic

RANGERS won a dramatic Co-operative Insurance Cup final as they overcame the dismissal of two players to stun St Mirren at Hampden Park.

Kevin Thomson and Danny Wilson were both sent off in the second half for the Ibrox club, but the nine men rallied and won 1–0 courtesy of Kenny Miller's 84th-minute header. Securing the trophy was Rangers' 26th League Cup success, extending their own record of victories in the tournament.

The 2009/10 competition began on 1st August and the involvement of six Scottish teams in Europe meant a slight change to the format. Rather than entering at the second-round stage, two Clydesdale Bank Premier League clubs were entered into the first round.

St Johnstone were 5–0 winners at Irn-Bru Second Division Stenhousemuir, while St Mirren recorded a 6–3 victory at East Stirlingshire 24 hours later. The Irn-Bru Third Division side recovered from an early Billy Mehmet hat-trick to draw level at Ochilview, but Mehmet scored twice more to become the first Saints player to net five goals in a game for 36 years.

Four more SPL clubs entered the competition in the second round, and there was soon a major shock as Hamilton were beaten 2–1 at Irn-Bru First Division side Ross County, who were to become Cup specialists during 2009/10. Elsewhere, Hibernian beat Brechin City 3–0, Dundee United won 2–0 at Alloa, St Johnstone were 6–0 winners at Arbroath and St Mirren recorded a 2–0 victory at Ayr United.

Ross County's reward was a third-round match with Dundee United, but they were unable to produce another upset, losing 2–0 at Victoria Park. The remaining six SPL sides joined the competition in round three, which produced a shock when Dundee survived an Aberdeen fightback to win 3–2 after extra-time at Dens Park. Inverness also went close to knocking out Motherwell at Fir Park, the home side eventually winning 3–2 courtesy of Ross Forbes' 119th-minute goal.

Another surprise result was St Johnstone's 3–1 win at Hibernian, the visitors having recovered from conceding a first-minute goal. Elsewhere, Rangers avoided a Queen of the South fightback to win 2–1 at Palmerston Park and Andy Dorman scored a

last-gasp winner for St Mirren at Kilmarnock. Hearts came from behind to beat Dunfermline 2–1 at Tynecastle, while Paddy McCourt inspired a 4–0 victory for Celtic at Falkirk.

The Old Firm were kept apart in the quarter-finals, although that did not help Tony Mowbray's Celtic, who suffered a shock 1–0 home defeat to Hearts. Michael Stewart scored the winner from the penalty spot and the Bhoys then had captain Stephen McManus sent off in front of the Parkhead faithful.

Rangers survived a brief scare at Dundee to win 3–1, with the match turning in their favour after Gary MacKenzie had scored an own goal. St Johnstone won a tense Tayside derby against Dundee United 2–1, while St Mirren were comfortable 3–0 winners over Motherwell.

The first semi-final was held at Fir Park, where St Mirren edged out Hearts 1–0 thanks to a 20-yard strike from Mehmet. Rangers beat St Johnstone 2–0 to join Saints in the final, with Steven Davis and Lee McCulloch scoring the goals as their march towards silverware continued.

FIRST ROUND

01/08/2009

Airdrie (0) 0   **Alloa (0)** 0
Att 756
Alloa win 4–3 on penalties

Albion (1) 3   **Livingston (0)** 0
McKenzie 9 (og)
Barr 48, McCusker 89   Att 602

Brechin (1) 4   **Elgin (0)** 0
McAllister 13, 63
Byers 77
McKenna 84   Att 406

Clyde (1) 1   **Forfar (0)** 3
Tod 28 (og)   Campbell 51
Att 784   Fotheringham 58
  Deasley 65

Cowdenbeath (1) 1   **Morton (2)** 3
McQuade 31 (pen)   Weatherson 7, 51
Att 486   MacFarlane 12

Dumbarton (0) 0   **Dunfermline (3)** 5
Att 953   Graham 2, Kirk 9, 56
  Burke 45, Bell 65

Dundee (3) 5   **Stranraer (0)** 0
Higgins 23, Harkins 29
Cameron 37
McMenamin 47
Griffiths 67   Att 2,345

East Fife (2) 2   **Raith (0)** 3
Linn 5   Walker 57
Muir 19   Tade 75
Att 1,390   Williamson 90

Inverness (1) 4   **Annan (0)** 0
Rooney 21, Eagle 52
Imrie 72, Sanchez 88   Att 1,095

Partick (1) 5   **Berwick (0)** 1
Hodge 29   Little 71
Buchanan 49, 81 (pen)
Erskine 53, 87   Att 1,472

Peterhead (0) 0   **Arbroath (1)** 3
Att 499   Sellars 6
  Bishop 48, Raeside 54

Queen's Park (0) 1   **Queen of the South (3)** 4
Douglas 82   Quinn 1
Att 886   Wilson 10, 14
  Burns 70

Ross County (1) 5   **Montrose (0)** 0
Craig 43, Gardyne 56, 75
Morrison 72, Stewart 79   Att 768

Stenhousemuir (0) 0   **St Johnstone (2)** 5
Att 1,049   Milne 27
  Deuchar 37, 69
  Samuel 67, 74

Stirling (1) 1   **Ayr (0)** 2
Devine 16   Easton 61
Att 802   Aitken 114
After extra-time

02/08/2009

East Stirling (3) 3   **St Mirren (4)** 6
Maguire 23   Mehmet 6, 13, 17, 44, 67
Rodgers 27, 36   O'Donnell 73
Att 1,024

SECOND ROUND

25/08/2009

Alloa (0) 0   **Dundee Utd (2)** 2
Att 1,000   Shala 23
  Goodwillie 39

Forfar (0) 2   **Dundee (3)** 4
Tulloch 55   Griffiths 11
Campbell 72   Antoine-Curier 15, 31
Att 1,929   Tod 67 (og)

Inverness (3) 4   **Albion (0)** 0
Eagle 8, Rooney 16
Bulvitis 41, Munro 57   Att 681

Kilmarnock (1) 3   **Morton (1)** 1
Sammon 24 (pen), 64   McGuffie 44 (pen)
Kyle 90   Att 3,645

Partick (1) 1   **Queen of the South (0)** 2
Donnelly 30   Weatherston 64,90
Att 1,527

Ross County (1) 2   **Hamilton (0)** 1
Di Giacomo 32   Mensing 90
Brittain 53   Att 764

26/08/2009

Arbroath (0) 0   **St Johnstone (4)** 6
Att 1,038   Milne 24, 45, Morais 27
  Deuchar 42, 67
  Samuel 71

Ayr (0) 0   **St Mirren (1)** 2
Att 1,652   Higdon 25, Mehmet 90

Dunfermline (1) 3   **Raith (1)** 1
Kirk 38, 68   Williamson 50 (pen)
Campbell 52 (og)   Att 4,163

Hibernian (2) 3   **Brechin (0)** 0
Riordan 10, Nimmo 16 (og)
Hanlon 55   Att 7,047

THIRD ROUND

22/09/2009

Dundee (1) 3   **Aberdeen (0)** 2
Malone 39   Paton 63,88
Forsyth 55
Griffiths 105   Att 6,131
After extra-time

Hibernian (1) 1   **St Johnstone (1)** 3
Stokes 1   Swankie 7
Att 7,078   Millar 76, Morris 82

Kilmarnock (0) 1   **St Mirren (1)** 2
Kyle 87   McGinn 64
Att 3,561   Dorman 90

Motherwell (1) 3   **Inverness (0)** 2
McHugh 33   Barrowman 70
Bulvitis 94 (og)   Munro 111
Forbes 119   Att 3,905
After extra-time

Ross County (0) 0   **Dundee Utd (1)** 2
Att 1,986   Wilkie 36
  Russell 77

23/09/2009

Falkirk (0) 0   **Celtic (1)** 4
Att 5,669   McDonald 28, 53
  McCourt 64, Killen 73

Hearts (0) 2   **Dunfermline (1)** 1
Glen 15   Bayne 51
Stewart 73 (pen)   Att 6,126

Queen of the South (0) 1   **Rangers (1)** 2
Harris 90   Naismith 16
Att 6,120   Novo 79

QUARTER-FINALS

27/10/2009

Dundee (1) 1   **Rangers (1)** 3
Griffiths 29   Whittaker 15
Att 10,654   MacKenzie 57 (og)
  Fleck 85
Dundee: Bullock, Paton, Malone, Forsyth, MacKenzie, Lauchlan, McHale, Kerr (Hart 79), Griffiths (McMenamin 72), Higgins (Clarke 70), Harkins. **Subs not used:** Casement, Soutar. **Booked:** Malone.
Rangers: Alexander, Beasley (Naismith 75), Whittaker, McMillan, Papac, Wilson, Smith, Thomson, Lafferty, Novo, Fleck. **Subs not used:** Davis, Boyd, Miller, McGregor. **Booked:** Fleck, Whittaker.

St Johnstone (0) 2   **Dundee Utd (0)** 1
Anderson 72   Buaben 82
Dods 76 (og)
Att 5,146
St Johnstone: Smith, MacKay, Grainger, Rutkiewicz (Anderson 62), Gartland, Millar, Davidson, Craig, Sheerin (Morais 67), Johansson (Moon 87), Deuchar. **Subs not used:** MacDonald, Main. **Booked:** Smith.
Dundee Utd: Banks, Dillon, Webster (Dods 46), Kenneth, Kovacevic, Buaben, Gomis, Swanson (Conway 78), Fotheringham (Casaliuovo 76), Cadamarteri, Goodwillie. **Subs not used:** Cameron, Weaver.

St Mirren (1) 3   **Motherwell (0)** 0
Higdon 23
Ross 61
Craigan 81 (og)
Att 4,325
St Mirren: Gallacher, Ross, Barron, McGinn, Mair, Potter, Murray, Dorman, Mehmet, Johnston (O'Donnell 76), Higdon (Brady 87). **Subs not used:** Innes, Ramsay, Howard. **Booked:** Ross.
Motherwell: Ruddy, Moutaouakil (Humphrey 46), Saunders, Reynolds, Craigan, Coke, O'Brien (Forbes 79), Hutchinson, Jutkiewicz, Murphy (McHugh 46), Hateley. **Subs not used:** Jennings, Kosiorowski.

28/10/2009

Celtic (0) 0   **Hearts (0)** 1
Att 18,675   Stewart 58 (pen)
Celtic: Zaluska, Hinkel, McManus, Caldwell, N'Guemo, Fox, Maloney (McCourt 46), Crosas, Zhi (Samaras 58), Killen (McDonald 58), McGeady. **Subs not used:** Wilson, Cervi. **Booked:** Fox. **Dismissed:** McManus.
Hearts: Balogh, Wallace, Goncalves, Palazuelos, Black (Jonsson 46), Driver, Obua, Nade (Witteveen 76), Bouzid, Stewart, Thomson. **Subs not used:** Kucharski, Glen, Kello. **Booked:** Bouzid, Goncalves, Jonsson.

SEMI-FINALS

02/02/2010

Hearts (0) 0   **St Mirren (0)** 1
Att 9,170   Mehmet 51
Hearts: Kello, Thomson, Zaliukas, Bouzid (Kucharski 24), Wallace, Jonsson, Smith (Glen 83), Black (Santana 55), Stewart, Driver, Nade. **Subs not used:** Ridgers, Mulrooney. **Booked:** Wallace, Nade, Black.
St Mirren: Gallacher, Ross, Innes, Mair, Barron, Potter, Murray, Dorman (O'Donnell 88), Thomson, Mehmet, Higdon (Dargo 75). **Subs not used:** Howard, Brady, Robb. **Booked:** Mehmet.

03/02/2010

Rangers (2) 2   **St Johnstone (0)** 0
Davis 26
McCulloch 37   Att 17,371
Rangers: Alexander, Whittaker, Weir, Wilson, Smith, Davis, McCulloch, Thomson, Fleck, Novo (Naismith 62), Lafferty (Little 61). **Subs not used:** McGregor, Broadfoot, Wylde. **Booked:** Thomson.
St Johnstone: Smith, Irvine, MacKay, Gartland, Grainger, Millar, Morris, Davidson, Morais (Milne 46), Sheridan (MacDonald 67), Craig (Moon 75). **Subs not used:** Main, Anderson. **Booked:** Irvine.

FINAL

21/03/2010

St Mirren (0) 0   **Rangers (0)** 1
Att 44,538   Miller 84
St Mirren: Gallacher, Ross, Potter, Mair, Barron, Brady (O'Donnell 85), Murray (Dorman 60), Thomson, Carey, Mehmet (Dargo 70), Higdon. **Subs not used:** Howard, Robb.
Rangers: Alexander, Whittaker, Weir, Wilson, Papac, Davis (Edu 45), McCulloch, Thomson, Novo (Smith 89), Boyd (Naismith 79), Miller. **Subs not used:** McGregor, Beasley. **Booked:** Miller, McCulloch, Whittaker. **Dismissed:** Wilson, Thomson.

ROONEY LEADS THE WAY IN A YEAR OF DAZZLING DISPLAYS

MANCHESTER UNITED striker Wayne Rooney's stunning form throughout the 2009/10 campaign was recognised when he was named Barclays Player of the Season. Rooney scored 26 goals in 32 Barclays Premier League appearances, easily surpassing his previous best tally of 16, to help sustain United's title challenge until the final day of the campaign. The award was further recognition for the 24-year-old's outstanding performances after he was also rewarded by his fellow professionals and football writers.

The England forward thrived in his new role following the departure of Cristiano Ronaldo to Real Madrid last summer, and netted his 100th Premier League career goal in a 3–1 victory over Arsenal in February. Scoring all four goals in a win against Hull was another memorable performance.

The award was some consolation after Rooney narrowly missed out on the Barclays Golden Boot, which went to Didier Drogba in one of a trio of prizes for Chelsea. Drogba claimed the Barclays Golden Boot for the second time in his career following a personal-best haul of 29 goals in 32 outings. One of those was the winner at Old Trafford in April which proved decisive in the title race. Drogba's exploits in front of goal helped

FROM TOP: Wayne Rooney with his Barclays Player of the Season award; Barclays Manager of the Season, Harry Redknapp of Tottenham Hotspur; Rangers duo David Weir and Walter Smith, who took the top awards in the Clydesdale Bank Premier League

The end of a thrilling 2009/10 season saw recognition for the stand-out performers

Chelsea become the first team to score 100 goals in a Barclays Premier League season, and that achievement was recognised with the Barclays Merit Award. Carlo Ancelotti's men scored seven goals on three separate occasions and sealed the title in style with an 8–0 victory at home to Wigan.

Highlighting their all-round efficiency, Petr Cech claimed the Barclays Golden Glove prize, keeping 17 clean sheets and conceding only 26 goals as the Czech returned to his reliable best. Liverpool's Spanish goalkeeper Jose Reina managed the same number of shut-outs, but narrowly missed out on the award having played more games.

Harry Redknapp was named Barclays Manager of the Season for leading Tottenham to a top-four finish and a place in the UEFA Champions League.

Played every minute

Rangers scooped a double at the Clydesdale Bank Premier League awards when Walter Smith and David Weir won the main prizes. Smith was named as Manager of the Season after his side retained their title, finishing six points clear of Celtic, while 39-year-old Weir was voted top player, having played every minute of his side's Clydesdale Bank Premier League campaign.

Dundee United striker David Goodwillie was the Clydesdale Bank Premier League Young Player of the Season.

Kevin Nolan played a key role in helping Newcastle return to the Barclays Premier League at the first time of asking and he was named the Coca-Cola Championship Player of the Season. The midfielder contributed 17 goals, five of those coming during six games in April, as the Magpies cruised to the title under Chris Hughton.

The prize in Coca-Cola League 1 went to Leeds striker Jermaine Beckford. He produced the two most memorable moments of the

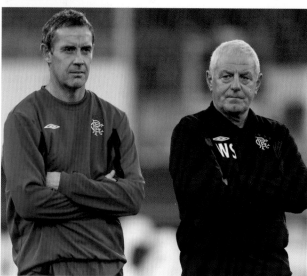

'Rangers scooped a double at the Clydesdale Bank Premier League awards when Walter Smith and David Weir won the main prizes'

campaign for United fans when he scored to knock archrivals Manchester United out of the FA Cup and then netted a winner against Bristol Rovers on the final day of the season to send Simon Grayson's men back up to the second tier.

That took his goal tally in the League to 25, and Grayson was quick to pay tribute, saying: 'He's contributed in so many ways this season and what he's achieved has not been a fluke because he's done it before and I'm sure he'll do it again.'

Rochdale defender Craig Dawson was the winner in Coca-Cola League 2 after making a smooth step up from non-League football. The 19-year-old had spent the previous season playing for Radcliffe Borough but was snapped up by his local club in the summer of 2009 and played his part in Rochdale's long-awaited promotion campaign.

In the Scottish Football League, Inverness Caledonian Thistle duo Terry Butcher and Adam Rooney scooped the prizes for top manager and player respectively in the Irn-

Bru First Division, but the awards for Achievement of the Season and Team of the Season went to Derek Adams and his Ross County side following their glorious run to the final of the Active Nation Scottish Cup. Dundee's Leigh Griffiths, who helped his team to the ALBA Challenge Cup, was named as the best young player in the SFL.

Stirling Albion's title success in the Irn-Bru Second Division resulted in Allan Moore collecting the manager's prize, with Brechin City striker Rory McAllister also rewarded for leading the goalscoring charts with 21 League strikes during 2009/10.

Runaway champions Livingston dominated in the Irn-Bru Third Division prizes, with awards for boss Gary Bollan and striker Robbie Winters.